D0860573

THE CRB COMMODITY YEARBOOK
2007

 Commodity Research Bureau

RECEIVED
JUL 1 2 2007
MINNESOTA STATE UNIVERSITY LIBRARY
MANKATO, MN 56002-8419

BICENTENNIAL
1807
WILEY
2007
BICENTENNIAL

John Wiley & Sons, Inc.

Ref.
HF
1041
.C56
2007

Copyright © 2007 by Commodity Research Bureau. All rights reserved.

Published by John Wiley & Sons, Inc., Hoboken, New Jersey
Published simultaneously in Canada.

Wiley Bicentennial Logo: Richard J. Pacifico

No part of this publication may be reproduced, stored in a retrieval system, or transmitted in any form or by any means, electronic, mechanical, photocopying, recording, scanning, or otherwise, except as permitted under Section 107 or 108 of the 1976 United States Copyright Act, without either the prior written permission of the Publisher, or authorization through payment of the appropriate per-copy fee to the Copyright Clearance Center, Inc., 222 Rosewood Drive, Danvers, MA 01923, (978) 750-8400, fax (978) 646-8600, or on the web at www.copyright.com. Requests to the Publisher for permission should be addressed to the Permissions Department, John Wiley & Sons, Inc., 111 River Street, Hoboken, NJ 07030, (201) 748-6011, fax (201) 748-6008, or online at http://www.wiley.com/go/permissions.

Limit of Liability/Disclaimer of Warranty: While the publisher and author have used their best efforts in preparing this book, they make no representations or warranties with respect to the accuracy or completeness of the contents of this book and specifically disclaim any implied warranties of merchantability or fitness for a particular purpose. No warranty may be created or extended by sales representatives or written sales materials. The advice and strategies contained herein may not be suitable for your situation. You should consult with a professional where appropriate. Neither the publisher nor author shall be liable for any loss of profit or any other commercial damages, including but not limited to special, incidental, consequential, or other damages.

For general information on our other products and services or for technical support, please contact our Customer Care Department within the United States at (800) 762-2974, outside the United States at (317) 572-3993 or fax (317) 572-4002.

Wiley also publishes its books in a variety of electronic formats. Some content that appears in print may not be available in electronic books. For more information about Wiley products, visit our web site at www.wiley.com.

ISBN 978-0-470-08015-3

Printed in the United States of America

10 9 8 7 6 5 4 3 2 1

CRB believes that the information and opinions contained herein are reliable, but CRB does not make any warranties whatsoever, expressed or implied, and CRB assumes no liability for reliance on or use of information and opinion contained herein.

Commodity Research Bureau Editorial Board

Editor in Chief
Christopher J. Lown

Associate Editor
Amy L. Kelley

Contributing Author
Richard W. Asplund

Commodity Research Bureau
330 South Wells Street, Suite 612
Chicago, Illinois 60606-7110 USA
800.621.5271 or +1.312.554.8456
Fax: +1.312.939.4135
Website: www.crbtrader.com
Email: info@crbtrader.com

TABLE OF CONTENTS

Commodity Research Bureau Product Overview

commodity research bureau

Commodity Research Bureau is the oldest and most respected information provider in the industry. CRB was founded in 1934 and is widely recognized in the industry for its accurate and professional products.

CRB's products are tailored for individual traders and brokerage firms. All of our products are available to brokerage firms on a bulk and private-label basis.

Product samples and pricing are located on our web site at www.crbtrader.com.

Please contact us for a free consultation about how our products can help your trading or your business.

Call +1.312.554.8456, or e-mail us at info@crbtrader.com

Commodity Research Bureau

330 South Wells Street, Suite 612

Chicago, Illinois 60606-7110

Phone: +1.312.554.8456

or 800.621.5271

Fax: +1.312.939.4135

Email: info@crbtrader.com

Website: www.crbtrader.com

Price Data	
CRB DataCenter	End-of-day daily price files on futures, Commitments of Traders, options on futures, options volatility (implied/historic), equities and mutual funds. Available in various formats for direct upload to your chart/analysis software.
CRB InfoTech CD	The most comprehensive collection of commodity market information available anywhere, with decades of prices on over 600 cash, futures, foreign exchange, index markets, and option volatilities (implied/historic).
Custom Historical Data	Order a one-time package of price information according to your needs.

Charts	
CRB PriceCharts	Weekly 104-page magazine of charts on over 70 futures markets. Available in print and PDF formats.
PriceCharts.com	Over 400 pages of charts and technical studies covering the 77 major US, Europe, and Asia futures markets. Available in PDF format.
Wall Charts	Large poster-size charts on 35 futures markets with volume/open interest and Commitment of Traders data. Published annually each fall or on demand with your company logo.
Historical Desk Sets	Spiral-bound set of 86 charts on 48 markets with volume/open interest and Commitment of Traders data. Published each spring and fall.

Fundamental and Technical Research and Trading Systems	
Futures Market Service	Weekly 8-page newsletter on futures market fundamentals available in print or PDF formats.
Trends In Futures	Bi-weekly 4-page newsletter on futures market technicals. Available in print and PDF format.
Electronic Futures Trend Analyzer	Computerized daily trading system started in 1963 with specific entry and exit points for over 60 Futures Markets.

Books	
CRB Commodity Yearbook	Annual publication of fundamental data, including supply/demand and production/consumption and price data, on over 100 commodity markets. Concise introductory articles that describe the salient features of each commodity. Available as a hardcover book with CD.
CRB Encyclopedia of Commodity and Financial Prices	Concise introductory articles on the fundamental market factors moving commodity and financial prices, providing a valuable complement to understanding price behavior on the long-term historical price charts. Available as a hardcover book with CD.

For more information and current specials, visit www.crbtrader.com or call +1.312.554.8456 or 800.621.5271

ACKNOWLEDGEMENTS

The editors wish to thank the following for source material:

Agricultural Marketing Service (AMS)

Agricultural Research Service (ARS)

American Bureau of Metal Statistics, Inc. (ABMS)

American Forest & Paper Association (AF & PA)

The American Gas Association (AGA)

American Iron and Steel Institute (AISI)

American Metal Market (AMM)

Bureau of the Census

Bureau of Economic Analysis (BEA)

Bureau of Labor Statistics (BLS)

Chicago Board of Trade (CBT)

Chicago Mercantile Exchange (CME / IMM / IOM)

Coffee, Sugar & Cocoa Exchange (CSCE)

Commodity Credit Corporation (CCC)

Commodity Futures Trading Commision (CFTC)

The Conference Board

Economic Research Service (ERS)

Edison Electric Institute (EEI)

E D & F Man Cocoa Ltd

Farm Service Agency (FSA)

Federal Reserve Bank of St. Louis

Fiber Economics Bureau, Inc.

Florida Department of Citrus

Food and Agriculture Organization of the United Nations (FAO)

Foreign Agricultural Service (FAS)

Futures Industry Association (FIA)

International Cotton Advisory Committee (ICAC)

International Rubber Study Group (IRSG)

Johnson Matthey

Kansas City Board of Trade (KCBT)

Leather Industries of America

MidAmerica Commodity Exchange (MidAm)

Minneapolis Grain Exchange (MGE)

National Agricultural Statistics Service (NASS)

National Coffee Association of U.S.A., Inc. (NCA)

New York Cotton Exchange (NYCE / NYFE / FINEX)

New York Mercantile Exchange (NYMEX) Commodity Exchange, Inc. (COMEX)

Oil World

The Organisation for Economic Co-Operation and Development (OECD)

Random Lengths

The Silver Institute

The Society of the Plastics Industry, Inc. (SPI)

United Nations (UN)

United States Department of Agriculture (USDA)

United States Geological Survey (USGS)

Wall Street Journal (WSJ)

Winnipeg Commodity Exchange (WCE)

THE COMMODITY PRICE TREND

The Reuters-CRB Continuous Commodity Index (CCI) in 2006 extended the rally that began in 2001 and posted a new record high of 409.65 in December 2006. During the 2001-06 bull market, the Reuters/CRB CCI index rallied by a total of 124.1% through December 2006. The Reuters/CRB CCI index closed 2006 up +13.5%, marking the fifth consecutive annual increase (2002 +23.0%, 2003 +8.9%, 2004 11.2%, 2005 +22.5%, 2006 +13.5%).

Four of the six Reuters/CRB Sub-indexes posted gains in 2006: Grains +44.0%, Metals +28.0%, Industrials +21.9%, Softs +13.2%. Two of the sub-indexes showed declines: Energy (-16.1%) and Meats (-1.9%).

The Reuters /CRB CCI index was driven higher in 2006 by continued strong physical demand in most commodity markets, a continued influx of cash into commodity index funds early in the year, and the generally weak dollar seen during 2006. The dollar index fell by −8.2% in 2006, which was an underlying bullish factor for commodity prices in 2006. Commodity prices in 2006 received continued support from very strong GDP growth in China (Q4-2006 10.4%) and India (Q4-2006 +8.6%) and a significant pickup in GDP growth in Japan (Q4-2006 +4.8%) and Europe (Q4-2006 +3.3% yr/yr). US GDP growth eased during 2006 but still showed real GDP growth of +3.3% in 2006 which was slightly higher than +3.2% in 2005.

Energy

The Reuters /CRB Energy Sub-index, which is comprised of Crude Oil, Heating Oil, and Natural Gas, accounts for 18% of the overall Reuters-CRB CCI Index. The Energy Sub-index in 2006 closed −16.1%, falling back after showing double-digit percentage gains for four consecutive years (2005 +54.4%, 2004 +27.5%, 2003 +11.9%, 2002 +56.5%). Crude oil in 2006 on a nearest-futures basis closed virtually unchanged on the year at $61.05 (vs $61.04 in 2005), but gasoline prices fell −6.3% and heating oil prices fell −7.5%. Natural gas plunged 43.9% during the year. Petroleum prices showed strength early in 2006 on a buildup of inventories ahead of the expected active hurricane season and a continuation of speculative buying, but then fell sharply during autumn when there were no hurricane threats and petroleum inventories were excessive.

Grains

The Reuters /CRB Grains and Oilseeds Sub-index, which is comprised of Corn, Soybeans, and Wheat, accounts for 18% of the overall Index. The Grains and Oilseeds Sub-index in 2006 closed +44.0% yr/yr. The corn and soybean crops in 2006 were relatively large due to favorable weather, but corn prices rallied by 80% starting in September 2006 as the extent of strong demand for corn from ethanol producers became clear. The rally in corn prices boosted soybean and wheat prices as well since high corn prices will encourage US farmers to plant more corn in spring 2007, and less soybeans and wheat.

Industrials

The Reuters /CRB Industrials Sub-index, which is comprised of Copper and Cotton, accounts for 12% of the overall Index. The Industrials Sub-index showed a +21.9% gain in 2006, adding to the +30.3% gain in 2005. Copper soared by another 32% in 2006 for its fifth consecutive yearly gain (2002 +6.7%, 2003 +49.6%, 2004 +42.6%, 2005 +45.4%, 2006 +32.0%). Copper prices rallied in early 2006 on continued strong demand, but then fell back due to the weak US housing and auto sectors (which are big copper users) and stepped-up copper mining production. Cotton prices rose only +3.7% in 2006 despite a poor US cotton crop because China avoided US cotton and purchased most of its cotton imports from India.

Livestock

The Reuters /CRB Livestock Sub-index, which is comprised of Live Cattle and Lean Hogs, accounts for 12% of the overall Index. The Livestock Sub-index closed −1.9% in 2006, remaining weak after falling −1.1% in 2005. Live cattle futures prices closed −4.0% in 2006 and lean hog futures prices closed −5.5%. Livestock prices were undercut early in 2006 by price competition from chicken (due to the backup of US poultry exports tied to bird flu in Asia) and later in the year from high corn and feed prices.

Precious Metals

The Reuters /CRB Precious Metals Sub-index, which is comprised of Gold, Platinum, and Silver, accounts for 17% of the overall Index. The Precious Metals Sub-index rallied by +28.0% in 2006, which was the fifth consecutive yearly gain (2002 +17.1%, 2003 +25.9%, 2004 +8.9%, 2005 +20.5%, 2006 +28.0%). Bullish factors included lagging mining output, strong investment and jewelry demand, and the weak dollar in 2006.

Softs

The Reuters /CRB Softs Sub-index, which is comprised of Cocoa, Coffee, Orange Juice, and Sugar #11, accounts for 23% of the overall Index. The Softs Sub-index in 2005 closed +13.2%, which the third consecutive yearly gain (2004 +37.2%, 2005 +22.4%, 2006 +13.2%). Sugar in 2006 showed a sharp decline of −20.0% due to higher sugar production and a washout of long speculators. However, coffee prices rose +17.8% and cocoa prices rose +8.7%. Orange juice rose sharply by +60.7% on the third consecutive year of a poor Florida orange crop due to lasting damage from hurricanes in 2004 and 2005.

Reuters/Jefferies-CRB Index (weekly close) as of December 29, 2006

Monthly Reuters-CRB Futures Index   High, Low and Close (1967=100)

Year		Jan.	Feb.	Mar.	Apr.	May	June	July	Aug.	Sept.	Oct.	Nov.	Dec.	Range
1997	High	244.30	243.91	248.01	249.00	254.79	249.98	243.38	245.30	244.50	247.62	243.52	238.39	254.79
	Low	238.93	236.14	241.64	237.64	245.54	238.52	232.01	236.69	240.03	238.34	235.27	228.84	228.84
	Close	238.99	242.41	245.17	248.29	250.96	239.42	242.75	241.98	243.06	240.04	235.92	229.14	----
1998	High	235.36	236.08	231.74	229.09	226.67	216.75	216.75	207.48	205.03	206.57	206.73	197.29	236.08
	Low	221.56	223.97	223.04	223.42	214.03	208.42	205.99	195.18	196.31	201.34	195.18	187.89	187.89
	Close	234.28	227.65	228.88	223.99	215.90	214.63	206.00	195.68	203.30	203.28	195.42	191.22	----
1999	High	198.96	191.45	193.28	192.89	193.99	193.43	192.91	199.59	209.41	209.91	207.54	206.20	209.91
	Low	187.18	182.76	183.38	187.14	185.05	185.07	182.67	190.14	199.03	199.66	202.23	200.74	182.67
	Close	189.74	182.95	191.83	192.39	186.72	191.54	190.36	199.35	205.19	201.52	204.07	205.14	----
2000	High	213.70	215.29	217.88	214.15	226.12	227.29	225.69	228.02	232.20	234.38	231.46	233.37	234.38
	Low	201.43	206.74	209.61	207.61	211.86	222.23	217.42	217.76	224.74	218.38	220.93	225.46	201.43
	Close	210.46	208.78	214.37	211.03	222.27	223.93	218.61	227.41	226.57	219.28	229.79	227.83	----
2001	High	232.58	228.34	225.75	216.39	219.29	212.39	209.27	202.90	202.34	191.09	192.74	193.94	232.58
	Low	223.02	219.68	210.24	208.87	208.43	203.86	201.84	197.02	188.24	182.83	181.83	187.73	181.83
	Close	224.12	221.78	210.26	214.50	209.00	205.56	202.70	199.63	190.49	185.66	192.66	190.61	----
2002	High	195.97	193.53	205.45	208.39	205.33	209.33	215.10	219.24	229.62	231.67	231.83	238.39	238.39
	Low	186.38	187.19	192.26	195.21	197.42	199.56	207.24	208.46	217.60	223.82	223.29	230.17	186.38
	Close	187.29	192.33	204.92	201.16	204.20	209.29	210.97	219.20	226.53	228.91	230.64	234.52	----
2003	High	248.92	251.59	247.23	236.62	242.16	238.25	237.20	243.74	246.07	250.67	257.54	263.60	263.60
	Low	234.58	245.39	228.10	228.77	231.26	231.39	230.36	233.96	236.79	241.68	244.79	249.60	228.10
	Close	248.45	247.25	232.15	232.53	235.55	233.78	234.21	243.70	243.66	247.58	248.44	255.29	----
2004	High	271.08	275.02	285.28	284.42	277.94	282.03	275.38	278.10	285.37	289.29	292.49	291.02	292.49
	Low	257.49	258.94	270.52	268.53	266.80	264.34	265.50	265.20	269.12	280.53	280.20	276.15	257.49
	Close	262.57	274.73	283.77	272.54	277.25	265.94	267.78	276.50	284.98	283.70	290.94	283.90	----
2005	High	288.38	305.00	323.33	313.23	304.25	315.79	316.46	321.60	333.58	338.19	332.58	349.20	349.20
	Low	277.07	280.19	304.22	297.47	292.06	300.76	302.71	309.21	317.05	326.36	326.09	332.62	277.07
	Close	284.75	305.00	313.57	303.74	300.83	306.91	315.24	318.99	333.33	326.68	332.49	347.89	----
2006	High	363.70	364.28	365.66	382.46	399.66	387.52	396.16	399.90	393.51	389.24	408.91	409.65	409.65
	Low	348.57	345.49	346.56	360.85	376.35	363.63	375.73	380.15	359.07	361.19	385.23	391.77	345.49
	Close	363.30	353.27	361.91	379.53	379.80	385.63	391.49	390.95	370.10	383.92	408.79	394.89	----

Source: Reuters

Reuters/Jefferies-CRB Index
(monthly close) through December 2006

Index Value

Reuters-CRB Index (CCI), CRB Spot Index, and CPI
(monthly close) through December 2006

Index Value

Reuters-CRB Index (CCI) vs. 30-year T-Bond Yield - 12-month Rate of Change
(monthly close) through December 2006

Reuters-CRB Index (CCI) vs. CPI - 12-month Rate of Change
(monthly close) through December 2006

CRB INDEXES

Reuters/Jefferies-CRB Total Return Index (monthly close) through December 2006 — Index Value

Reuters/Jefferies-CRB Total Return Index (monthly close) through December 2006 — Index Value

CRB Livestock Sub-Index (1967=100) (monthly close) through December 2006 — Index Value

CRB Livestock Sub-Index (1967=100) (weekly close) as of December 29, 2006 — Index Value

CRB Grains and Oilseeds Sub-Index (1967=100) (monthly close) through December 2006

CRB Grains and Oilseeds Sub-Index (1967=100) (weekly close) as of December 29, 2006

CRB Softs Sub-Index (1967=100) (monthly close) through December 2006

CRB Softs Sub-Index (1967=100) (weekly close) as of December 29 2006

CRB INDEXES

CRB Precious Metals Sub-Index (1967=100) (monthly close) through December 2006

CRB Precious Metals Sub-Index (1967=100) (weekly close) as of December 29, 2006

CRB Industrials Sub-Index (1967=100) (monthly close) through December 2006

CRB Industrials Sub-Index (1967=100) (weekly close) as of December 29, 2006

CRB Energy Sub-Index (1967=100) (monthly close) through December 2006

CRB Energy Sub-Index (1967=100) (weekly close) as of December 29, 2006

CRB Currencies Index (1977=100) (monthly close) through December 2006

CRB Currencies Index (1977=100) (weekly close) as of December 29, 2006

CRB INDEXES

CRB Metals Sub-Index (1967=100) (monthly close) through December 2006

CRB Metals Sub-Index (1967=100) (weekly close) as of December 29, 2006

CRB Textiles Sub-Index (1967=100) (monthly close) through December 2006

CRB Textiles Sub-Index (1967=100) (weekly close) as of December 29, 2006

14T

CRB INDEXES

CRB Fats & Oils Sub-Index (1967=100) (monthly close) through December 2006

CRB Fats & Oils Sub-Index (1967=100) (weekly close) as of December 29, 2006

CRB Livestock Sub-Index (1967=100) (monthly close) through December 2006

CRB Livestock Sub-Index (1967=100) (weekly close) as of December 29, 2006

CRB Spot Index (monthly close) through December 2006

CRB Spot Index (weekly close) as of December 29, 2006

Reuters-CRB Index (CCI) and Goldman Sachs Commodity Index (GSCI™/SM) (weekly close) as of December 29, 2006

Reuters-CRB Index (CCI) and CRB Spot Index (weekly close) as of December 29, 2006

CRB INDEXES

Reuters-CRB Index (CCI)   (1967=100)

Year	Jan.	Feb.	Mar.	Apr.	May	June	July	Aug.	Sept.	Oct.	Nov.	Dec.	Average
1997	241.57	239.75	245.29	244.60	250.45	243.78	236.30	240.99	242.24	243.67	240.06	234.27	241.91
1998	228.96	230.59	227.27	225.62	221.19	213.19	209.86	202.06	202.19	203.75	201.76	191.76	213.18
1999	192.49	187.21	188.50	189.83	190.04	191.16	187.16	196.72	202.20	203.88	203.90	204.10	194.77
2000	207.65	211.28	213.87	211.29	220.42	224.73	220.51	220.84	228.23	226.36	226.56	228.98	220.06
2001	228.30	223.42	218.06	213.43	214.69	208.37	204.98	200.18	195.34	186.20	188.42	190.42	205.98
2002	191.44	190.91	201.86	200.74	201.69	203.92	211.42	214.01	226.00	227.52	228.54	234.62	211.06
2003	242.04	247.89	237.81	231.73	237.38	235.11	234.05	238.13	241.44	246.15	250.66	258.44	241.74
2004	266.65	264.93	278.19	276.48	272.78	270.78	270.41	271.18	276.47	285.36	286.02	283.28	275.21
2005	282.96	289.01	312.70	305.26	298.11	308.07	311.47	315.00	324.05	333.46	330.39	343.83	312.86
2006	354.56	354.30	353.74	371.33	385.81	374.50	386.50	389.11	372.98	376.70	395.21	397.28	376.00

Average.   *Source: Reuters*

Reuters/Jefferies CRB Futures Index[1]   (1967=100)

Year	Jan.	Feb.	Mar.	Apr.	May	June	July	Aug.	Sept.	Oct.	Nov.	Dec.	Average
1997	241.57	239.75	245.29	244.60	250.45	243.78	236.30	240.99	242.24	243.67	240.06	234.27	241.91
1998	228.96	230.59	227.27	225.62	221.19	213.19	209.86	202.06	202.19	203.75	201.76	191.76	213.18
1999	192.49	187.21	188.50	189.83	190.04	191.16	187.16	196.72	202.20	203.88	203.90	204.10	194.77
2000	207.65	211.28	213.87	211.29	220.42	224.73	220.51	220.84	228.23	226.36	226.56	228.98	220.06
2001	228.30	223.42	218.06	213.43	214.69	208.37	204.98	200.18	195.34	186.20	188.42	190.42	205.98
2002	191.44	190.91	201.86	200.74	201.69	203.92	211.42	214.01	226.00	227.52	228.54	234.62	211.06
2003	242.04	247.89	237.81	231.73	237.38	235.11	234.05	238.13	241.44	246.15	250.66	258.44	241.74
2004	266.65	264.93	278.19	276.48	272.78	270.78	270.41	271.18	276.47	285.36	286.02	283.28	275.21
2005	282.96	289.01	312.70	305.26	298.11	306.97	308.04	318.76	326.19	326.44	315.27	327.58	309.77
2006	340.95	331.30	325.98	345.84	351.22	339.21	346.86	340.18	310.28	304.36	310.84	311.60	329.89

Average.   [1] New calculation begins June 20, 2005.   *Source: Reuters*

Reuters/Jefferies CRB Total Return Index[1]   (01/02/1982 = 100)

Year	Jan.	Feb.	Mar.	Apr.	May	June	July	Aug.	Sept.	Oct.	Nov.	Dec.	Average
1997	128.76	126.39	129.10	127.38	133.37	128.81	127.50	132.36	133.15	137.39	134.51	127.64	130.53
1998	121.37	119.89	116.14	116.50	112.73	106.99	104.52	99.52	102.17	101.37	98.24	90.11	107.46
1999	90.91	87.70	92.84	98.19	99.21	100.32	103.26	109.02	114.04	114.00	116.31	118.58	103.70
2000	122.59	128.50	132.60	128.43	139.10	144.80	143.12	147.23	155.89	155.00	157.45	158.74	142.79
2001	159.32	160.43	154.34	153.31	154.96	148.13	143.62	143.81	137.50	127.30	124.39	123.48	144.22
2002	123.82	124.53	135.70	138.03	138.93	138.66	143.23	145.91	153.53	153.91	151.63	161.51	142.45
2003	171.83	182.79	178.17	171.17	175.28	178.21	178.96	184.60	182.27	191.06	194.53	204.73	182.80
2004	213.15	215.30	226.72	227.21	234.19	230.03	232.57	236.76	238.75	254.24	248.91	241.10	233.24
2005	244.84	250.48	273.57	267.03	254.14	267.60	271.16	281.23	288.68	289.74	280.70	292.65	271.82
2006	305.70	298.05	294.39	313.52	319.76	310.00	318.32	313.52	287.18	282.84	290.08	291.98	302.11

Average.   [1] Theoretical data prior to June 20, 2005.   *Source: Reuters*

Reuters-CRB Livestock Sub-Index   (1967=100)

Year	Jan.	Feb.	Mar.	Apr.	May	June	July	Aug.	Sept.	Oct.	Nov.	Dec.	Average
1997	266.08	264.82	262.53	279.54	282.22	268.15	271.58	265.42	257.26	245.92	244.43	242.39	262.53
1998	239.60	234.03	226.72	235.29	235.76	229.99	207.42	197.30	189.93	199.85	186.52	180.88	213.61
1999	206.47	220.47	218.75	222.97	226.14	219.14	198.18	206.89	209.31	221.68	227.97	239.13	218.09
2000	247.36	249.80	257.10	262.53	256.37	251.37	243.94	229.65	228.34	233.64	239.69	251.99	245.98
2001	254.81	254.62	262.97	259.27	252.40	257.32	257.15	248.31	240.83	230.82	227.86	237.26	248.64
2002	249.43	251.46	243.59	216.16	209.26	199.59	206.70	196.98	197.76	217.97	234.73	247.80	222.62
2003	252.70	242.32	240.06	237.27	251.07	248.86	245.33	244.63	261.29	264.33	264.96	255.07	250.66
2004	248.90	250.53	266.53	274.15	291.60	294.91	292.29	285.44	287.72	287.29	296.26	297.60	281.10
2005	305.39	294.73	302.88	295.95	293.97	269.99	266.35	269.80	280.26	288.27	292.59	297.62	288.15
2006	292.31	280.30	271.42	260.24	267.26	281.87	279.30	286.07	286.33	283.14	287.19	290.82	280.52

Average.   *Source: Reuters*

Reuters-CRB Grains and Oilseeds Sub-Index   (1967=100)

Year	Jan.	Feb.	Mar.	Apr.	May	June	July	Aug.	Sept.	Oct.	Nov.	Dec.	Average
1997	215.98	221.87	237.07	238.69	230.18	215.02	205.02	212.19	216.58	224.63	226.06	218.68	221.83
1998	214.52	214.79	213.25	199.56	196.08	190.83	182.58	166.56	169.78	179.47	184.47	177.89	190.82
1999	174.76	165.92	170.54	166.69	163.22	163.11	152.45	166.33	170.88	161.96	158.72	155.35	164.16
2000	167.48	170.65	174.94	174.44	180.96	169.12	152.62	150.32	160.91	162.60	167.06	171.37	166.87
2001	171.45	163.23	164.33	158.41	155.93	156.71	170.42	168.74	167.95	161.37	163.22	162.14	163.66
2002	164.09	160.38	163.97	160.53	162.97	171.11	188.10	199.34	213.65	204.33	200.95	193.39	181.90
2003	187.57	189.29	183.12	185.98	194.62	193.35	181.84	192.82	201.68	209.28	222.27	226.46	197.36
2004	237.68	243.83	261.79	267.95	247.24	234.25	203.40	188.28	186.93	176.69	176.41	175.24	216.64
2005	173.61	175.50	198.55	189.30	190.57	203.73	209.28	193.48	187.59	186.48	181.90	186.72	189.73
2006	192.42	200.30	201.42	201.28	213.15	209.41	215.23	203.24	211.18	245.19	269.05	271.79	219.47

Average.   *Source: Reuters*

Reuters-CRB Softs Sub-Index   (1967=100)

Year	Jan.	Feb.	Mar.	Apr.	May	June	July	Aug.	Sept.	Oct.	Nov.	Dec.	Average
1997	327.64	350.54	372.52	382.78	413.76	401.03	394.65	398.59	399.18	389.98	401.19	419.17	387.59
1998	415.43	413.98	404.35	387.22	393.07	365.64	367.69	372.51	348.36	351.86	365.91	353.12	378.26
1999	337.91	307.51	285.94	267.35	264.74	281.81	263.21	272.47	277.53	276.51	285.29	284.51	283.73
2000	268.52	254.77	259.39	260.26	267.91	280.26	285.20	273.72	270.43	270.05	257.94	255.68	267.01
2001	269.11	274.59	265.27	254.72	268.62	255.68	251.01	244.01	238.45	231.91	254.36	254.63	255.20
2002	256.23	246.71	259.73	256.73	254.63	252.54	270.15	278.25	307.15	311.84	311.53	311.73	276.44
2003	320.55	326.00	302.23	302.05	293.41	272.95	275.12	273.77	271.84	257.57	258.78	263.99	284.86
2004	265.93	259.29	265.98	259.39	256.91	266.95	285.81	289.61	304.70	309.01	318.42	339.23	285.10
2005	336.40	355.04	382.92	360.12	352.93	356.99	354.86	348.25	351.72	372.25	385.16	407.59	363.69
2006	443.78	452.96	448.44	458.99	460.75	447.03	460.34	451.85	433.83	433.57	461.09	476.10	452.39

Average.   *Source: Reuters*

Reuters-CRB Precious Metals Sub-Index   (1967=100)

Year	Jan.	Feb.	Mar.	Apr.	May	June	July	Aug.	Sept.	Oct.	Nov.	Dec.	Average
1997	247.53	253.11	258.96	247.44	250.59	253.42	239.26	246.69	250.85	255.18	245.16	246.46	249.55
1998	248.47	264.43	260.37	268.39	249.46	237.82	245.86	236.52	233.80	231.20	231.77	229.92	244.83
1999	234.41	242.14	236.84	232.19	232.87	225.71	224.55	225.82	232.58	253.20	246.60	246.81	236.14
2000	247.16	266.43	256.51	253.53	255.44	268.03	267.08	266.97	269.50	263.47	261.97	266.96	261.92
2001	265.48	259.23	253.04	252.17	261.28	254.87	243.70	232.22	239.24	232.66	227.06	237.71	246.56
2002	241.90	245.33	254.47	261.61	266.59	276.27	268.03	264.27	269.19	267.88	272.29	281.24	264.09
2003	295.57	298.35	290.78	279.76	295.52	294.54	302.39	310.85	321.35	321.26	333.13	355.31	308.23
2004	377.11	375.30	400.41	390.82	351.29	354.67	366.98	380.85	377.08	394.42	408.67	402.12	381.64
2005	388.68	397.96	405.72	400.86	396.71	408.05	398.70	407.77	420.18	435.92	446.08	474.28	415.08
2006	505.52	514.07	530.47	595.40	651.48	572.29	599.67	619.15	587.59	567.40	618.12	613.96	581.26

Average.   *Source: Reuters*

Reuters-CRB Industrials Sub-Index   (1967=100)

Year	Jan.	Feb.	Mar.	Apr.	May	June	July	Aug.	Sept.	Oct.	Nov.	Dec.	Average
1997	270.41	270.19	270.85	263.10	268.38	267.49	258.50	251.84	243.77	238.57	230.50	215.60	254.10
1998	210.53	207.84	217.25	210.75	212.15	217.89	215.99	211.93	216.96	206.76	200.15	188.18	209.70
1999	182.97	178.44	180.15	184.41	184.94	176.40	182.58	184.71	191.68	190.18	187.34	187.10	184.24
2000	201.37	202.67	204.59	194.18	207.18	200.83	207.37	217.64	224.10	217.16	217.11	219.27	209.46
2001	206.86	199.04	186.19	174.20	173.72	162.54	158.63	153.43	145.27	131.33	140.85	146.56	164.89
2002	150.49	151.21	156.49	152.31	152.59	167.27	172.54	164.08	161.79	162.28	176.79	178.53	162.20
2003	185.33	190.29	193.39	188.69	186.75	190.80	201.85	198.23	212.04	236.48	243.08	244.56	205.96
2004	262.68	269.43	273.02	256.62	249.14	234.34	224.38	226.27	233.50	227.52	223.80	223.54	242.02
2005	232.07	236.01	253.38	258.44	249.39	252.99	261.77	263.66	267.00	285.21	285.66	298.25	261.99
2006	314.02	326.07	322.13	358.06	398.97	383.23	401.59	408.38	394.84	380.43	372.50	373.90	369.51

Average.   *Source: Reuters*

CRB INDEXES

Reuters-CRB Energy Sub-Index   (1967=100)

Year	Jan.	Feb.	Mar.	Apr.	May	June	July	Aug.	Sept.	Oct.	Nov.	Dec.	Average
1997	220.04	202.43	197.71	191.95	200.26	190.52	192.73	205.97	212.80	225.03	211.70	188.21	203.28
1998	172.94	174.02	167.87	175.68	167.64	160.86	159.57	150.85	166.17	163.45	153.67	133.38	162.18
1999	134.58	129.41	146.56	169.80	174.02	180.31	196.88	219.08	228.80	225.66	225.76	223.94	187.90
2000	231.38	245.97	254.09	244.62	278.91	308.81	301.39	328.52	366.18	356.34	366.76	361.93	303.74
2001	345.00	328.00	312.27	319.96	308.23	292.65	267.20	269.05	253.17	232.68	214.70	206.92	279.15
2002	195.20	202.12	243.96	262.72	269.34	258.24	260.08	274.04	301.33	301.49	278.41	311.52	263.20
2003	337.33	375.64	346.99	313.78	328.18	342.51	332.71	343.58	317.98	338.95	331.81	361.52	339.25
2004	371.45	355.20	376.02	384.99	426.01	419.28	438.34	459.75	475.69	574.75	535.62	475.97	441.09
2005	478.71	491.25	563.52	567.69	526.48	595.62	628.00	716.27	803.00	797.33	716.36	733.16	634.78
2006	693.34	636.54	634.70	692.42	674.95	682.24	710.09	754.36	651.32	633.84	643.38	626.34	669.46

Average.   Source: Reuters

Reuters-CRB Currencies Index   (1977=100)

Year	Jan.	Feb.	Mar.	Apr.	May	June	July	Aug.	Sept.	Oct.	Nov.	Dec.	Average
1997	134.61	130.30	129.56	128.71	130.83	131.75	130.14	126.84	128.02	129.07	129.58	126.93	129.70
1998	125.06	126.10	125.65	124.96	124.33	122.86	121.89	120.65	126.18	130.98	128.86	130.69	125.68
1999	130.97	128.48	126.37	125.74	125.32	124.63	124.08	126.89	128.89	130.66	128.24	127.71	127.33
2000	127.65	124.37	124.01	123.43	119.42	122.54	121.59	119.04	117.11	115.99	114.89	117.55	120.63
2001	118.42	116.58	114.25	113.01	112.24	110.92	111.29	114.02	115.21	114.04	112.69	112.01	113.72
2002	110.20	109.38	110.40	111.33	114.54	117.39	121.30	119.68	119.54	119.02	120.77	121.97	116.29
2003	125.37	126.36	126.61	126.42	132.07	133.04	130.30	128.77	130.93	135.96	136.23	140.44	131.04
2004	143.44	143.23	140.68	139.36	137.62	140.48	141.81	140.92	141.25	144.04	149.66	152.54	142.92
2005	150.16	148.99	150.81	148.53	146.39	143.52	141.21	143.74	144.42	141.94	139.32	140.48	144.96
2006	142.95	140.86	141.45	143.36	149.49	147.98	147.20	148.24	147.65	146.19	147.72	149.64	146.06

Average.   Source: Reuters

Reuters-CRB Interest Rates Index   (1977=100)

Year	Jan.	Feb.	Mar.	Apr.	May	June	July	Aug.	Sept.	Oct.	Nov.	Dec.	Average
1997	111.73	112.69	110.78	109.74	111.02	112.12	113.61	113.14	113.73	114.68	115.77	116.46	112.96
1998	117.89	117.38	116.89	116.99	116.87	118.00	118.13	119.09	121.67	122.67	121.23	122.33	119.10
1999	121.32	119.62	118.11	118.56	116.57	112.78	112.32	110.71	108.79	106.42	107.46	104.56	113.10
2000	100.05	101.51	102.61	103.99	101.80	103.65	104.12	105.21	105.10	105.57	105.94	108.44	104.00
2001	108.79	108.94	109.86	108.61	107.69	107.90	108.24	109.63	110.74	112.26	112.29	108.97	109.49
2002	109.51	110.34	107.65	108.31	109.04	110.08	111.45	114.14	116.24	115.54	115.44	115.27	111.92
2003	115.27	116.68	116.88	116.13	119.22	120.42	116.27	113.02	113.86	NA	NA	NA	116.42
2004	NA	NA	123.94	118.47	115.30	114.52	117.46	119.91	121.02	121.71	121.25	120.64	119.42
2005	121.38	122.44	118.91	120.81	123.07	124.63	123.04	122.40	122.52	120.07	119.11	119.85	121.52
2006	120.69	119.33	117.83	115.44	114.45	114.57	115.02	116.87	118.33	118.28	119.64	119.86	117.53

Average.   Index not calculated for September 16, 2003 to March 17, 2004 due the non-trading status of the 90-day T-Bill futures .   Source: Reuters

Reuters-CRB Energy Index   (1977=100)

Year	Jan.	Feb.	Mar.	Apr.	May	June	July	Aug.	Sept.	Oct.	Nov.	Dec.	Average
1997	206.58	190.96	186.85	179.95	186.96	177.03	179.48	183.81	181.21	189.93	184.01	172.65	184.95
1998	161.58	157.72	151.69	154.94	153.95	146.54	140.94	133.79	143.89	140.22	131.31	118.14	144.56
1999	121.00	116.39	136.44	152.20	153.53	157.52	176.40	185.48	196.52	192.71	202.36	207.81	166.53
2000	220.53	237.09	241.29	221.42	247.72	263.67	255.40	268.97	292.15	287.36	286.70	249.86	256.01
2001	251.05	256.70	246.06	258.47	264.15	248.51	231.56	238.47	231.53	201.64	180.55	180.49	232.43
2002	185.01	190.86	224.68	234.25	233.13	226.56	234.70	240.27	256.04	250.75	228.78	258.02	230.25
2003	279.06	307.09	282.73	243.10	243.92	256.78	264.31	275.82	248.55	265.44	271.25	284.02	268.51
2004	300.37	298.35	314.50	322.72	359.33	342.21	367.52	389.41	402.57	460.54	430.64	389.95	364.84
2005	415.65	428.72	493.69	497.67	461.97	515.29	537.91	593.73	624.18	584.79	538.28	548.87	520.06
2006	593.19	554.80	578.71	649.56	651.96	652.57	680.35	659.03	564.39	534.32	541.08	555.93	601.32

Average.   Source: Reuters

CRB Metals Sub-Index   (1967=100)

Year	Jan.	Feb.	Mar.	Apr.	May	June	July	Aug.	Sept.	Oct.	Nov.	Dec.	Average
1997	301.63	314.62	313.30	307.82	314.72	316.61	316.07	319.28	310.95	296.58	290.01	271.76	306.11
1998	268.29	264.16	267.94	272.68	270.55	265.39	261.89	255.45	243.16	232.73	224.78	218.73	253.81
1999	213.74	221.29	220.66	222.50	227.01	223.50	234.41	237.06	243.65	242.77	247.19	253.77	232.30
2000	261.71	248.29	240.26	237.57	241.56	239.24	232.04	226.20	228.82	225.15	216.25	215.36	234.37
2001	212.47	212.90	210.59	204.94	205.14	205.60	197.04	188.09	181.32	179.50	172.96	173.80	195.36
2002	174.76	176.41	181.22	186.31	189.12	189.38	192.66	184.51	184.03	185.61	183.21	186.27	184.46
2003	199.71	204.17	206.72	202.78	205.57	207.77	212.24	214.09	220.24	240.20	248.49	266.70	219.06
2004	287.40	306.07	320.96	321.90	314.73	308.28	312.29	318.21	333.97	350.45	359.77	361.92	324.66
2005	355.95	364.50	371.99	371.31	365.83	369.32	361.39	363.75	364.70	369.68	370.47	425.84	371.23
2006	458.64	485.21	504.91	571.37	623.28	616.35	621.31	619.41	628.12	668.55	726.02	745.75	605.74

Average.   *Source: Commodity Research Bureau*

CRB Textiles Sub-Index   (1967=100)

Year	Jan.	Feb.	Mar.	Apr.	May	June	July	Aug.	Sept.	Oct.	Nov.	Dec.	Average
1997	269.52	271.25	274.25	271.49	270.16	270.89	271.97	273.21	272.06	270.64	269.23	262.34	270.58
1998	257.45	253.08	259.10	254.41	249.87	250.57	249.00	246.35	244.38	243.39	242.46	240.31	249.20
1999	237.40	233.67	235.09	234.94	234.45	229.24	225.02	226.43	222.21	223.51	227.73	222.63	229.36
2000	226.56	227.69	234.87	234.25	242.70	243.76	241.28	243.73	244.33	244.90	248.17	248.57	240.07
2001	244.74	241.84	233.40	225.97	224.47	222.12	222.44	218.55	214.74	207.79	215.86	218.99	224.24
2002	218.08	216.84	218.40	214.72	211.21	220.16	222.95	221.74	219.02	220.10	225.85	227.76	219.74
2003	231.25	235.31	235.04	234.64	231.66	235.24	240.88	237.50	244.30	256.99	257.59	254.25	241.22
2004	257.58	253.15	252.37	247.97	249.74	242.65	233.48	233.58	237.31	235.03	235.88	236.39	242.93
2005	239.93	240.36	247.12	247.73	246.60	244.69	247.21	243.08	246.64	251.24	248.96	250.83	246.20
2006	255.02	255.52	251.74	248.26	244.26	244.16	242.03	243.89	245.78	244.89	246.37	251.15	247.76

Average.   *Source: Commodity Research Bureau*

CRB Raw Industrials Sub-Index   (1967=100)

Year	Jan.	Feb.	Mar.	Apr.	May	June	July	Aug.	Sept.	Oct.	Nov.	Dec.	Average
1997	339.39	344.54	340.99	333.63	336.84	337.30	334.89	340.47	337.33	334.47	327.64	310.56	334.84
1998	299.61	296.85	302.89	301.25	305.40	299.72	295.56	290.17	280.98	275.73	268.88	265.94	290.25
1999	262.81	259.65	255.03	251.75	250.07	248.91	253.43	255.96	262.56	266.37	270.39	267.30	258.69
2000	267.85	260.91	260.39	258.23	265.37	261.78	255.19	255.69	258.81	257.29	252.58	256.00	259.17
2001	254.54	248.53	246.35	244.03	244.29	245.92	244.22	238.10	228.30	220.52	218.94	221.57	237.94
2002	219.05	222.33	231.03	230.38	231.81	243.72	245.38	240.53	240.77	240.68	243.04	248.21	236.41
2003	255.85	258.59	260.97	258.79	257.65	260.47	263.77	263.99	273.24	291.18	295.88	302.30	270.22
2004	312.24	309.54	316.77	318.52	312.98	308.40	308.84	307.54	315.25	315.13	320.52	322.65	314.03
2005	320.94	324.57	333.31	336.68	331.99	331.88	325.29	324.52	329.36	332.79	332.83	349.53	331.14
2006	363.04	371.00	372.08	385.69	400.62	399.97	403.50	404.29	404.45	417.79	437.08	446.55	400.51

Average.   *Source: Commodity Research Bureau*

CRB Foodstuffs Sub-Index   (1967=100)

Year	Jan.	Feb.	Mar.	Apr.	May	June	July	Aug.	Sept.	Oct.	Nov.	Dec.	Average
1997	235.11	237.80	244.45	240.91	238.45	241.03	237.75	239.92	239.66	247.60	251.08	238.97	241.06
1998	227.01	224.06	227.68	229.62	239.15	238.54	229.77	223.56	221.42	224.02	209.87	193.10	223.98
1999	206.75	196.53	189.81	187.94	191.60	195.96	182.09	191.60	192.12	190.13	183.46	178.24	190.52
2000	180.37	175.68	183.76	189.88	194.32	190.42	176.52	171.63	175.02	183.53	186.75	186.58	182.87
2001	189.68	192.93	200.48	203.57	210.24	213.09	222.61	232.42	224.06	199.51	200.24	203.40	207.69
2002	203.33	202.39	204.04	197.88	195.85	207.11	218.25	222.32	226.98	230.63	230.76	237.99	214.79
2003	238.60	237.01	234.16	234.55	239.15	239.53	232.81	234.30	244.69	251.04	255.36	257.99	241.60
2004	263.90	275.85	287.49	287.41	285.33	278.05	273.83	270.42	272.10	257.76	268.47	261.77	273.53
2005	252.84	246.44	253.58	252.19	254.21	255.43	251.31	247.65	249.22	253.37	252.74	242.54	250.96
2006	243.31	241.95	239.60	243.17	250.70	253.86	261.17	267.04	269.14	267.52	271.19	273.16	256.82

Average.   *Source: Commodity Research Bureau*

CRB INDEXES

CRB Fats and Oils Sub-Index   (1967=100)

Year	Jan.	Feb.	Mar.	Apr.	May	June	July	Aug.	Sept.	Oct.	Nov.	Dec.	Average
1997	251.33	258.86	251.94	227.72	232.31	248.87	248.32	249.72	252.10	283.11	288.95	269.92	255.26
1998	243.27	234.23	243.63	242.61	268.84	271.10	265.68	272.81	280.06	277.37	249.93	231.77	256.78
1999	230.99	194.96	172.59	174.97	176.78	187.84	178.61	191.19	209.68	209.53	194.38	177.98	191.63
2000	171.15	154.77	161.97	165.37	177.74	171.57	152.26	153.11	157.52	160.41	165.44	167.35	163.22
2001	170.49	158.27	165.77	177.63	177.95	196.02	232.89	259.60	237.33	177.05	174.66	184.78	192.70
2002	169.64	165.91	177.34	167.61	164.38	193.38	193.29	192.85	193.20	193.90	211.97	230.05	187.79
2003	222.39	209.89	215.72	216.91	219.56	229.01	225.83	223.36	251.40	285.47	288.08	292.22	239.99
2004	305.30	300.47	318.53	330.54	302.31	295.32	304.60	290.52	302.51	267.12	279.42	271.36	297.33
2005	248.45	238.13	252.70	263.98	262.93	266.01	245.81	243.51	259.50	268.43	269.77	231.17	254.20
2006	231.10	221.46	217.14	214.75	222.03	221.97	247.09	271.97	267.18	257.29	264.75	270.94	242.31

Average.   *Source: Commodity Research Bureau*

CRB Livestock Sub-Index   (1967=100)

Year	Jan.	Feb.	Mar.	Apr.	May	June	July	Aug.	Sept.	Oct.	Nov.	Dec.	Average
1997	361.37	356.89	343.71	333.09	338.67	338.44	343.09	342.90	338.44	344.87	340.87	323.03	342.11
1998	286.77	265.73	279.13	280.03	309.09	301.80	281.81	281.60	258.47	256.56	232.29	217.99	270.94
1999	249.71	231.27	216.59	231.92	236.71	241.07	235.92	254.64	274.60	294.16	279.97	272.14	251.56
2000	261.83	245.67	252.65	258.44	268.41	260.53	241.72	238.62	245.35	252.78	240.45	259.65	252.18
2001	267.57	250.14	261.05	273.14	288.88	306.84	329.73	341.78	313.84	260.77	252.97	264.23	284.25
2002	251.61	260.32	274.95	257.32	256.33	289.40	288.22	279.03	274.13	276.94	288.86	313.14	275.85
2003	316.67	308.65	310.49	311.25	320.03	333.29	324.58	327.63	361.30	386.60	385.63	372.48	338.22
2004	372.16	353.19	362.41	369.65	369.31	374.28	395.48	392.33	395.40	365.68	373.69	370.63	374.52
2005	359.25	341.74	353.05	373.63	377.41	361.10	330.39	331.75	349.24	358.04	369.98	337.97	353.63
2006	331.93	328.72	320.09	314.72	327.28	340.29	359.18	388.13	384.78	366.35	364.05	372.08	349.80

Average.   *Source: Commodity Research Bureau*

CRB Spot Index   (1967=100)

Year	Jan.	Feb.	Mar.	Apr.	May	June	July	Aug.	Sept.	Oct.	Nov.	Dec.	Average
1997	292.16	296.14	297.68	292.11	292.54	294.07	291.18	295.14	293.41	295.82	294.16	279.06	292.79
1998	267.54	264.66	269.59	269.67	276.42	273.07	266.71	260.89	254.96	253.34	242.99	233.36	261.10
1999	238.31	231.76	226.07	223.61	224.55	225.83	221.44	227.35	231.10	232.12	230.78	226.54	228.29
2000	227.91	222.00	225.85	227.78	233.68	229.89	219.54	217.28	220.60	224.15	223.29	224.99	224.75
2001	225.75	224.13	226.51	226.66	229.81	231.98	235.20	235.83	226.62	211.72	211.15	214.01	224.95
2002	212.55	214.02	219.65	216.54	216.43	228.09	233.96	232.98	235.10	236.59	238.01	244.06	227.33
2003	248.72	249.60	249.73	248.66	250.00	251.77	250.71	251.49	261.25	274.11	278.66	283.38	258.17
2004	291.55	295.38	304.54	305.49	301.44	295.70	294.10	291.86	296.90	290.35	298.19	296.26	296.81
2005	291.19	290.08	298.13	299.24	297.73	298.26	292.80	290.63	293.94	297.75	297.48	301.05	295.69
2006	308.31	311.58	310.86	319.47	330.81	332.19	337.82	341.30	342.48	348.24	359.66	365.33	334.00

Average.   *Source: Commodity Research Bureau*

Goldman Sachs Commodity Index (GSCI)   (12/31/1969=100)

Year	Jan.	Feb.	Mar.	Apr.	May	June	July	Aug.	Sept.	Oct.	Nov.	Dec.	Average
1997	214.62	194.88	192.88	191.24	198.60	186.50	185.35	194.25	197.20	205.75	199.35	181.94	195.21
1998	170.94	168.98	164.28	165.89	161.48	154.50	149.22	141.12	148.40	149.57	144.64	131.72	154.23
1999	135.29	132.37	143.86	155.40	156.81	158.22	165.21	177.60	187.64	184.89	191.84	194.62	165.31
2000	200.14	211.15	214.19	200.42	219.11	230.07	222.13	230.88	247.73	243.67	251.82	244.79	226.34
2001	239.18	231.54	220.13	222.86	222.32	213.26	202.89	203.76	197.04	178.07	169.63	167.74	205.70
2002	168.97	172.75	193.58	199.87	200.65	197.07	203.12	208.76	223.69	222.70	212.18	230.03	202.78
2003	241.74	264.19	246.70	221.68	228.18	235.01	233.18	241.35	228.54	242.22	246.24	261.23	240.86
2004	269.18	266.23	280.10	284.06	303.19	292.63	298.97	308.01	315.29	356.70	341.12	314.25	302.48
2005	324.47	332.80	374.05	371.68	350.65	382.96	396.64	431.85	455.28	444.90	418.56	435.45	393.27
2006	442.12	422.49	427.47	469.73	477.93	471.65	490.32	485.65	434.56	431.13	442.05	444.62	453.31

Average.   *Source: Goldman Sachs*

CRB InfoTech CD

Historical Price Data on CD

Instant Access to Decades of Historical Price Data

CRB InfoTech CD provides the widest variety of financial and commodity data available in one electronic source. Nowhere else can you access data on over 600 cash futures, indices and FOREX markets along with options volatility. It's the only source available for many underlying cash markets offering prices extending back to the 50s, 40s, and even earlier. Compiled from major worldwide exchanges, trade associations and government agencies.

InfoTech helps you Perform Analysis, Back-Testing, Modeling, Presentations

InfoTech includes DataXtract, which enables you to download entire trading histories from your CD-ROM in a variety of formats for your own independent analysis. You can create nearby contracts, continuation contracts and synthetic contracts, along with years of cash prices and volatility studies.

Includes PowerSignals Lite - Advanced Technical Charting

Features include 10 chart styles, 7 Line tools, more than 30 built-in studies and Design Studio. One of the **most powerful features** built into PowerSignals is the Technical Study Design Studio. With it, you can create studies that manipulate your price data in almost any way you want. You can take the results of your studies and display them as lines on an existing chart, on a brand new chart with its own scales, or as tabular displays of the raw data. All of the Technical Studies that are included in the PowerSignals software have been created in the Design Studio, exposing properties such as line colors, numbers of periods in calculations and even the underlying formulas to you. If you would prefer some study to be calculated differently than the built-in formula, you can modify the study as desired and save it for future use. If you want to make a brand new study, you can use the existing studies as models for your study.

Update Your Database with Final Markets

InfoTech can be updated with a subscription to Final Markets, our end-of-day data from the CRB DataCenter. You'll receive futures/cash and option volatility data from over 50 major worldwide exchanges.

For more information, visit www.crbtrader.com, or call 800-621-5271

Commodity Research Bureau • 330 South Wells Street, Suite 612 • Chicago IL, 60606 USA
Phone: 312.554.8456 or 800.621.5271 • Fax: 312.939.4135 • info@crbtrader.com • www.crbtrader.com

The Reuters-CRB Continuous Commodity Index (CCI) in 2006 extended the rally that began in 2001 and posted a new record high of 409.65 in December 2006. Over the course of the 2001-06 bull market, the RJ/CRB index rallied by a total of +124.1% through December 2006.

The 2001-06 commodity bull market of +124.1% is the second largest commodity bull market in post-war history, moderately behind the 1971-74 rally which totaled +146.7%. However, the current commodity rally is by far the longest-running rally at 63 months and counting. The 1971-74 rally was comparatively short at 28 months.

The Reuters-CRB Continuous Commodity Index (CCI) fared much better in 2006 than did the Reuters/Jefferies
RJ/CRB index, as seen in the nearby chart. The RJ/CRB index was reformulated in June 2005 with a much heavier weighting on petroleum products of 33% versus the 12% weighting in the old CCI index.

The new, revised RJ/CRB index rallied in early 2006 and posted a record high in March 2006, but then plunged in the latter half of 2006, mainly because of the sharp sell-off in crude oil prices. In fact, the RJ/CRB index through January 2007 fell by a total of -17.6% from its record high of 365.45 posted in March 2006 and showed a year-on-year decline in 2006 of -7.4%.

The Reuters-CRB CCI index, by contrast, showed a renewed rally in late 2006 that pushed the index to a new record high in December and produced a year-on-year gain in 2006 of +8.6%. The rally in late 2006 was driven by strength in corn, soybeans, precious metals, natural gas, coffee, cocoa and orange juice. Strength in those commodities was more than enough to offset the weakness in petroleum prices and copper that pushed the new RJ/CRB index lower in the second half of 2006.

The current 2001-06 commodity bull market has been driven by a progression of factors, which helps explain the longevity of the rally. In the first 3 full years of the rally (2002-04), the commodity rally was driven mainly by the -33% plunge in the dollar, which resulted from the Fed's extraordinarily easy monetary policy during that time frame. The Fed during 2002-04 targeted the federal funds rate in the extraordinarily low range of 1-2% to help the US get through the tough times caused by the post-2000 technology and stock market bust and the 9/11 attack in 2001. Commodities, as real assets, typically rise in price when the currency in which they are quoted depreciates in value. The nearby chart shows how commodity prices rallied sharply during 2002-04 when the dollar plunged. In fact, the weekly correlation of the RJ/CRB index and the dollar index over the 2002-04 period was remarkably strong with a negative correlation of -0.95, illustrating the close connection between the weak dollar and strong commodity prices.

Commodity Bull Markets Ranked by Percentage Gain (1960-2006)

	--------- Low ---------		--------- High ---------		Percent Rally	Rally Duration (months)	Avg CPI (yr-yr%)
1971-74	October 1971	96.40	February 1974	237.80	146.7%	28	4.9%
2001-06	October 2001	182.83	December 2006	409.65	124.1%	63	2.6%
1977-80	August 1977	184.70	November 1980	337.60	82.8%	39	10.2%
1986-88	July 1986	196.16	June 1988	272.19	38.8%	23	3.2%
1992-96	August 1992	198.17	April 1996	263.79	33.1%	44	2.8%

Source: Commodity Research Bureau

However, the Fed started tightening its monetary policy in June 2004 due to the improved economic outlook and concerns that a bubble was emerging in the housing market from extremely low mortgage rates. The Fed's tighter monetary policy provided eventual support for the dollar and halted the dollar's decline, thus removing a linchpin of the commodity rally.

However, during 2004 and particularly in 2005, strong commodity demand from China took over from the dollar as the major factor driving commodity prices higher. China's fast-growing demand for energy, industrial metals, and construction commodities was the key factor driving these sectors higher. In addition to strong demand, production supply in those sectors could not keep up with the new demand because of years of underinvestment in new production, refining, and extraction facilities. That led to a squeeze in energy, industrial metals and construction commodity prices from 2004 through early 2006.

Chinese demand has had less impact in boosting the agricultural markets. China is a large agricultural and meat producer in its own right and China's need to import agricultural products is therefore much less than for energy, industrial, and construction products. Moreover, producers in the agricultural markets can respond more quickly with higher production when prices are high, meaning that prices can more quickly revert to the mean in agricultural markets.

After peaking in early 2006, the commodity indexes then generally fell during late summer when petroleum prices plunged. Oil prices fell in the latter half of 2006 due to plentiful petroleum inventories in the US, adequate production by OPEC, and the lack of any hurricane disruptions to oil production in the Gulf of Mexico for the first time in two years. Weakness in the commodity indexes in the latter half of 2006 was also caused by lower copper prices which stemmed from (1) the fact that mining production finally caught up with demand, and (2) heavy long liquidation pressure by speculators.

The 2001-06 bull market in commodity prices has been a phenomenon caused by a weak dollar and strong commodity demand, not by an outbreak of inflation. The current commodity bull market is therefore very different from the commodity rallies in the 1970s which were driven mostly by double-digit inflation rates. The nearby chart shows how inflation has remained historically low all during the 2001-06 commodity bull market, with an average CPI of only +2.6%.

Looking ahead, there is little reason to suspect that the secular bull market in commodity prices is over. Production has caught up to demand in some markets and that has caused downward corrections in those markets. In addition, commodity prices could see a prolonged downward correction due to global economic risks and a further shake-out of speculative longs. Nevertheless, the long-term secular bull trend in commodity prices will likely remain in place due to (1) the prospects for continued strong global demand in coming years (particularly from hyper-growth countries such as China and India), (2) lagging supply, and (3) the ongoing vulnerability of the dollar.

The US economy came into 2006 in relatively strong shape. Hurricane Katrina had hit the US on August 29, 2005 and had caused US GDP in Q4-2006 to fall to +1.8% from the strong +3.6% average seen in the first three quarters of 2005. However, US GDP then bounced back to +5.6% in Q1-2006. US GDP during 2006 eventually showed a strong annual growth rate of +3.4%.

The US Federal Reserve in early 2006 continued the process of raising interest rates, a process that began in mid-2004. The Fed started raising interest rates in mid-2004 when the US economy appeared to be in a sustained expansion and when the Fed needed to prevent an asset bubble from emerging. The Fed in 2001-03 had driven the federal funds rate target as low as 1% in an attempt to prevent deflation and allow the US economy to recover after the stock market bubble burst in 2000 and after the 9/11 attack on September 11, 2001. The Fed's extraordinarily easy monetary policy in 2001-03 succeeded in supporting the US economy but it also produced a bubble in the housing market stemming from extremely low mortgage rates and easy mortgage credit.

By mid-2006, the Federal Reserve finally decided to halt its interest rate hike regime with the funds rate target at 5.25%. The Fed's 2-year tightening process left the funds rate target up by a total of 4.25 percentage points from the 1% level seen in mid-2004.

The Fed halted its rate hike regime, despite the fact that it still saw upside inflation risks at the time, because the Fed was more worried about the US housing market bubble, the spike in oil prices to over $70 per barrel in spring

2006, and the lagged effect of monetary policy tightening that was already in the pipeline. Federal Reserve members were well-aware of the Fed's historical tendency to overdo its tightening moves and cause recessions. Instead, the Fed wanted to be forward looking and stop tightening before a recession became inevitable.

In fact, the Fed's decision to stop tightening in mid-2006 turned out to be the right decision. The US economy in the last three quarters of 2006 slowed to the low-2% area, but never came close to turning into a recession. When the Fed stopped tightening monetary policy in mid-2006, the 10-year T-note yield fell sharply by 85 bp from 5.25% in June 2006 to 4.40% by December 2006. The decline in long-term interest rates provided some stimulus for the US economy in late 2006 and supported US consumer spending and business investment.

The halt in the Fed's tightening process in mid-2006 also allowed the 30-year mortgage rate to fall sharply by 70 bp from 6.80% in July 2006 to 6.10% by early-December 2006. The decline in mortgage rates allowed the air to come out of the US housing bubble relatively slowly, thus limiting the collateral damage for the rest of the US economy.

The Fed also received some help in the latter half of 2006 from crude oil prices, which fell sharply by $26 from the record level of $78.40 in July 2006 to $50 by January 2007. The fortuitous decline in crude oil prices was mainly due to the lack of any disruptive hurricanes in 2006, which meant that US petroleum inventories remained plentiful in the latter half of 2006 and into early 2007, thus pushing crude oil and petroleum product prices lower.

S&P 500

10-year T-Note Yield

The Fed in the latter half of 2006 adopted post-meeting statement language that noted the upside inflation risks and said that the Fed might still have to tighten monetary policy again to address inflation. However, the marketplace in the latter half of 2006 remained convinced that the Fed's next move would be towards easing sometime in 2007.

The core CPI inflation rate rose steadily in early-2006 and reached an 11-year high of +2.9% in September 2006, where it was far above the generally-accepted 2.0% ceiling for inflation. The core PCE deflator, which is the Fed's preferred inflation measure, was better behaved than the core CPI and only rose as high as +2.4% in Aug-Sep 2006, but that was still an 11-year high for the series and was also above the generally-accepted 2.0% ceiling for inflation. However, the Fed did not reinitiate a tightening move in late 2006 in response to the rise in core inflation because (1) US GDP eased to the 2% area, (2) the Fed was worried about the US housing sector, and (3) the Fed believed that there was a strong chance that core inflation would moderate going into 2007. In the fourth quarter of 2006, core inflation did ease a bit from the peak seen in September 2006, thus validating the Fed's decision to take a wait-and-see approach on inflation.

The US economy came into 2007 in relatively solid shape, although GDP growth had eased to the low 2% level and the market was only expecting moderate GDP growth of 2.5-3.0% through 2007. Expectations for the US economy in 2007 were relatively subdued due to concerns about the US housing and auto sectors and historically high petroleum prices. The overall US economy as of early 2007 had not seen any significant spillover weakness from the housing

sector, but the news from the housing market became worse in February and March 2007 on a raft of bankruptcies among sub-prime mortgage lenders. In addition, the supply of new and existing homes available for sale remained very high in early 2007, meaning that a recovery for US homebuilders would be delayed until at least 2008. In addition, home prices remained soft through early 2007, meaning homeowners had less ability to use their homes as an ATM machine to extract cash via home equity loans.

The global stock markets in early March 2007 fell sharply by about 6%, causing fresh concerns about a possible US recession by late 2007. In fact, former Fed Chairman Alan Greenspan in early March 2007 predicted a one-third chance for a US recession by year-end. A recession could result from a spill-over of weakness from the housing and auto sectors, tighter mortgage credit, and reduced consumer and business confidence stemming from the March 2007 global stock market correction.

Despite those threats, most forecasters as of March 2007 were still predicting that the US economy would remain in an expansion mode with GDP growth in the mid-2% area through the end of 2007. Positive factors for the US economy as of March 2007 included strong overseas economic growth, continued firm US consumer spending, and historically low interest rates. Crude oil prices in early 2007 rose by about $10 per barrel to the $60 per barrel area, but that was substantially below the record high seen in mid-2006. Thus as of March 2007, it once again appeared that the US economy would be able to muddle through its various difficulties and remain in an expansion mode through 2007.

US Dollar Index

Crude Oil (WTI, $/barrrel)

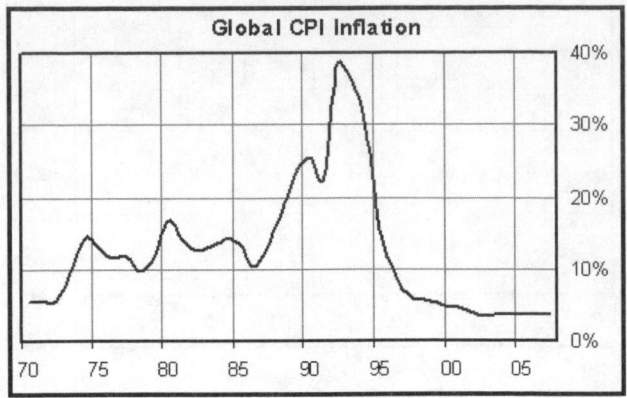

World GDP growth in 2006 was stronger than expected at +5.1% and will continue near that pace at +4.9% in 2007, according to IMF forecasts. The global economy is growing at the highest rates seen in the past several decades.

The main engine of world growth continues to be China with its third straight year of GDP growth near 10% in 2006. Japanese GDP growth was supported by growth in nearby China and Japan's GDP growth reached +4.8% by Q4-2006 (qtr-qtr annualized). India showed very strong growth in 2006 near 8% and was also an important source of world GDP growth. Europe in 2006 even got into the game with its GDP growth improving from the +1.5% area in 2004-05 to +3.3% by Q4-2006. US GDP growth flagged a bit in 2006 but the US economy by then had succeeded in helping to prime world growth over the previous several years.

Global central bank rates generally rose in 2006 as most countries responded to inflation pressures. The Bank of Japan raised its overnight rate from zero to 0.50% by February 2007. The European Central Bank raised its refinancing rate by 175 basis points from 2.00% in late-2005 to 3.75% by early-2007. The Chinese central bank raised interest rates during 2006 and also tightened bank lending by raising the reserve requirements for banks. Yet despite the higher interest rates seen in 2006, the world economy continued to strengthen during the year.

As of early 2007, the outlook still remained generally favorable for the global economy. Global stock markets took a tumble in early 2007, but the fallout for the real economy seemed to be limited. Global interest rates remained generally low and world confidence remained generally strong, supporting the view for continued stable global GDP growth through 2007.

The stable inflation situation should allow world bond yields to remain subdued in 2007. The MSCI World Developed 10-year Government Bond yield was stable near 4.50% in 2006 and is likely to remain near that level in 2007 as global central banks address inflation risks and reassure bond investors that inflation will be kept low. Low world long-term interest rates are helping to offset negative factors such as slower GDP growth in the US and continued elevated energy prices.

While the outlook for the global economy is generally favorable, there are several sources of risk. First, there is the possibility of a stumble in China due to its myriad of imbalances and its inflated stock market. The Chinese government during 2006 clamped down a bit on credit and investment and there is always the possibility they will go too far. Second, the global stock market correction that began in March 2007 could worsen, thus causing negative spillover effects for the real global economy and possibly causing defaults or bankruptcies by some hedge funds or financial institutions. Third, crude oil prices could see a renewed surge if there are any new supply disruptions in 2007 such as hurricanes or terrorist attacks on Middle East oil facilities.

CRUDE OIL PRICES REMAIN STRONG IN 2005

West Texas Intermediate Crude Oil Prices (monthly close, US$/barrel)

Crude oil futures prices in early 2006 extended the rally that began in November 2001 and posted a record high of $78.40 in July 2006. Crude oil prices were driven higher by speculative buying and by predictions for another active hurricane season in the second half of 2006. The US petroleum market was very nervous about another bad hurricane year in 2006 after being hit hard by Hurricane Hugo in 2004 and by Hurricanes Katrina and Rita in 2005. Those hurricanes produced major shut-downs of oil drilling rigs in the Gulf of Mexico and long-term damage to underwater pipes and infrastructure.

Oil prices in early 2006 were also pushed higher by (1) strong global economic growth (world 2006 GDP +4.3%) which produced strong petroleum demand, and (2) lagging production from OPEC and non-OPEC producers. Strong demand and lagging supply were in fact the main bullish factors that drove the 2001-06 bull market, which saw oil prices increase by more than four-fold from the $16.70 per barrel level seen when the bull market began in November 2001 to the record high of $78.40 seen in July 2006.

When crude oil prices hit a record high in nominal terms in July 2006, oil prices in real (inflation-adjusted) terms were still about 25% below the record high posted back in 1982, as seen in the nearby chart. The upward spike in oil prices to about $100 per barrel on an inflation-

Real WTI Crude Oil Prices (current US$)

adjusted basis in 1982 was due to the Iranian revolution and the Iran-Iraq war. Thus while oil prices in 2006 reached a record high in nominal terms, businesses and consumers are not being hit as hard in inflation-adjusted terms as they were back in the early 1980s.

After the strength seen in crude oil prices in the first half of 2006, crude oil prices in August and September 2006 then started falling sharply when no hurricanes approached the Gulf of Mexico and threatened US oil rigs. Hurricanes did come across the Atlantic in late summer and autumn 2006 but virtually all of them turned north before reaching the US mainland. As a result, the Gulf of Mexico in 2006 saw no disruptions in operations from hurricanes.

World Crude Oil Demand (mln bpd)

China Crude Oil Imports (Prev. 12-mo, mln tons)

OPEC Oil Production (mln barrels/day)

Non-OPEC Crude Oil Production (mln bpd)

Crude oil prices fell sharply on the lack of any hurricanes and when it became clear that US petroleum inventories were too high. Petroleum producers and distributors had built up preventative inventories going into autumn 2006 due to predictions of an active hurricane season, but were then left trying to slash inventories in autumn 2006 when no hurricanes arrived. Crude oil prices fell as low of $55 by November, which represented a decline of about $20 per barrel (-27%) from the record high of $74.80 posted in July 2006.

After the sharp sell-off seen in July-October 2006, crude oil prices then showed a moderate upward rebound of about $8 per barrel when OPEC announced on October 20, 2006 that it would cut production by 1.2 million barrels per day starting November 1. OPEC's goal was to reduce excess global petroleum inventories to normal levels. However, OPEC in November and December ended up implementing only about one-half of the promised production cut. That caused oil prices to show a renewed decline in December and January to a 1-1/2 year low near $50 per barrel in January 2007.

OPEC responded to the weak prices in late December and January by announcing a further 500,000 barrel per day production cut effective February 1, 2007. OPEC's Feb 1 production cut, combined with very cold weather in the US in late January and early February, succeeded in pushing crude oil prices higher by about $12 per barrel to the $62 per barrel area by March 2007. Aside from the drawdown in heating oil inventories from cold weather, product inventories were also drawn down in early 2007 by a variety of US refinery snafus which kept the US refinery operating rate below its 10-year average.

Oil prices also received support in Jan-Feb 2007 from President Bush's plan announced in mid-January to start buying 100,000 barrels per day of crude oil in spring 2007 to double the size of the Strategic Petroleum Reserve to 1.5 bln barrels over the next 20 years.

As of March 2007, the US inventory situation remained comfortable, which meant that OPEC remained under pressure to minimize production to support prices. US crude oil inventories in early March 2007 were 9.2% above their 5-year seasonal average. Product inventories were less plentiful than crude oil inventories but were still comfortable. Gasoline inventories were 2.3% above the 5-year seasonal average and distillates inventories (diesel fuel and heating oil) were 5.4% above the 5-year seasonal average.

OPEC in late 2006 and early 2007 was successful in cutting production by enough to boost crude oil prices and protect an apparent floor of $50 per barrel. At the same time, it appears that Saudi Arabia did not want crude oil prices to rally much above $65 per barrel. Saudi Arabia, if not OPEC as a whole, appears to be targeting West-Texas Intermediate crude oil prices in the range of $50-65 per barrel.

While oil prices saw downward pressure in the second half of 2006 and early 2007, bullish factors could emerge later in 2007. Going into spring and summer 2007, the markets will take account of summer gasoline demand and the possibility for hurricane disruptions. Moreover, in the bigger picture, the age of cheap oil appears to be over due to strong long-term global demand for petroleum combined with lagging investment in finding new reserves and increasing production capacity. There is also the perennial threat of supply disruptions from terrorist strikes, weather, or politically-inspired export cutoffs (e.g., from Iran). Crude oil prices in any case are likely to remain volatile in 2007 and will continue to play a key role in influencing the global economy.

Crude Oil Inventories (mln bbls)

The US dollar index in 2006 trended lower during the year and closed −8.2% on the year, reversing about two-thirds of the moderate +12.8% gain seen in 2005. The dollar index as of March 2007 remains near the lower end of the sharp 33% sell-off seen in 2002-04.

The weaker dollar seen in 2006 was a mildly supportive factor for commodity prices, though certainly not to the extent seen in 2002-04 when the 33% plunge in the dollar produced the beginning stages of the 2002-07 commodity bull market.

The dollar fell sharply in April 2006 once it became apparent that the Fed was near the end of its tightening regime. In 2005, by contrast, the dollar was able to show a modest upward rebound mainly because of the Fed's rate hike regime, whereby the Fed raised the federal funds rate from 1% in mid-2004 to 5.25% by mid-2006. The Fed's rate hike regime steadily pushed US dollar interest rate differentials higher against European and Japanese rates, which remained low as the central banks in those countries tried to deal with weak economic growth. Higher US short-term interest rates encouraged foreign investors to put their cash into the US money markets to earn a higher yield than they could earn in Europe or Japan. The Fed's tighter monetary policy also meant that the Fed was pumping fewer dollar reserves into the nation's banking system, making dollars a bit less plentiful.

The 3-month US Libor rate differential rose sharply by 380 bp (to +2.30% from -1.50%) against the 3-month European Euribor rate over the course of the Fed's tightening move from mid-2004 to mid-2006. The 3-month US Libor rate rose by 400 bp against the Japanese 3-month rate over that time frame.

However, by mid-2006 the Fed was done tightening while the European Central Bank and the Bank of Japan were in the midst of starting to raise interest rates. The Bank of Japan raised its overnight rate by 25 bp from zero to 0.25% in July 2006, and then raised its overnight rate by another 25 bp to 0.50% in February 2007. Meanwhile, the European Central Bank from late-2005 through early 2007 raised its 2-week refinancing rate steadily by 25 bp increments for an overall rate hike of 175 bp from the 2.00% level (seen from mid-2003 to late-2005) to 3.75% by March 2007.

The combination of sideways US interest rates and higher European and Japanese interest rates produced a mild deterioration in US interest rate differentials during 2006, thus putting some downward pressure on the dollar. The US-European 3-month interest rate differential fell by 80 bp during 2006 and early 2007 from 2.30% to 1.50%. The US-Japanese 3-month interest rate differential during the latter half of 2006 fell by about 50 bp to 4.60%.

The dollar continued to see underlying support from the fact that US interest rates (5.25% funds rate) were still well above European (3.75%) and Japanese (0.50%) rates. However, the deterioration in the US interest rate advantage against Europe and Japan was still a negative factor for the dollar in the latter half of 2006.

US Export & Import Growth (yoy%)

— Export Growth — Import Growth

US Imports & Exports with China (US$ blns)

US Imports from China

US Exports to China

The dollar during 2006 also continued to see downward pressure from the massive US trade deficit. The US trade deficit in 2006 rose to a new record high of $763.6 billion from $716.7 billion in 2005. Meanwhile, the US current account balance, which is the broadest measure of US trade with the rest of the world and includes goods, services, and transfer payments, hit a record high of $225.6 billion in Q3-2006. As a percentage of US GDP, the US current account deficit was about 6.7% of GDP in 2006, just below the quarterly record of 7.0% seen in Q4-2005.

The US trade deficit did show a moderate improvement in the latter half of 2006, mainly because lower crude oil prices reduced the value of US oil imports and because strong growth overseas boosted US exports. However, there remained little likelihood for any long-term, fundamental improvement in the US trade deficit because of the intractable problems behind the US trade deficit such as (1) the huge US demand for oil imports, (2) the improved comparative advantage of nations such as China and India which have cheap labor and the resources to employ that labor into export powerhouses, and (3) the poor US household savings rate and high Asian savings rate which results in capital flows to the US (which boosts the US capital account surplus and is the flip side of the US current account deficit).

The yen showed a strong 6-yen rally against the dollar and a 9-yen rally against the euro in March 2007 when the global stock markets went into a sharp downward correction. The sell-off sparked a big outflow from yen carry trades, whereby investors and hedge funds in the past few years have built up a huge overall position in speculative global assets by borrowing yen at near-zero rates and then selling those yen to obtain other currencies to invest at higher yields. The yen rallied sharply as investors reversed yen carry trades and needed to convert their foreign currencies back into yen to repay their loans.

Looking ahead, there is little reason to expect a major move either way in the dollar. The dollar has proven that it can survive the massive US trade deficit since US interest rate differentials remain favorable and since foreign investors still want to invest in dollar-denominated assets. US interest rate differentials are not likely to fall much more since the European Central Bank will probably only tighten by another 25-50 bp and the Bank of Japan will drag out its normalization of interest rates over a period of years. Still, there are risks for the dollar stemming from the massive US trade deficit and from China, which has now built up more than $1 trillion in dollar reserves. The dollar could take a severe hit at some point if China and other Asian export powerhouses decide to more aggressively diversify their dollar reserves.

US - Europe 3-mo Rate Diff. vs. Dollar Index

Dollar Index (left scale)

US - Euro 3-mo rate (right scale)

US - Japan 3-mo Rate Diff. vs. Dollar Index

Dollar Index (left scale)

US - Japan 3-mo rate (right scale)

The US housing market kicked into high gear starting in 2002-03 after the Federal Reserve in 2001-03 slashed its federal funds rate target by 5.50 percentage points from 6.5% in late 2000 to 1% by mid-2003. The Fed's easing caused the 30-year mortgage rate to plunge from 8% in late-2000 to the 5.5-6.5% range during 2003-05. Moreover, the extremely low level of short-term rates allowed mortgage lenders to offer initial rates on variable rates that were well below fixed rates of 5.5-6.5%. Mortgage lenders also developed a host of more lenient loans, including zero interest loans, 100% and 120% financing loans, and loans for sub-prime borrowers.

Cheap and easy mortgage credit, combined with speculative fever, produced a gold rush in the US housing market. The gold rush was not only in primary homes but also in vacation condos and homes. Strong demand for homes produced record levels of home sales and housing starts and also pushed housing prices sharply higher.

The good times for the US housing market finally came to an end when the Fed's tighter credit in 2004-06 pushed variable rate mortgages higher and also pushed the 30-year mortgage rate from 5.50% in mid-2005 to as high as 6.80% in mid-2006. That 130 bp rise in the 30-year mortgage rate, combined with extremely high home prices, finally caused buyers to drop out of the market. New and existing home sales peaked in late 2005 and moved sharply lower through 2006. Builders didn't give up on new building until early 2006 when they finally

faced a reckoning and were forced to slash new housing starts activity because of high unsold home inventories.

By mid-2006 it was clear that the US housing bubble had burst. The plunging housing market was one of the reasons why the Fed halted its tightening process in mid-2006 with the funds rate at 5.25%. The halt in the Fed's tightening process allowed the 30-year mortgage rate to fall to 6.11% in December 2006 from the 4-1/2 year high of 6.80% seen in July 2006. Lower mortgage rates helped to prevent an even faster melt-down of the US housing sector.

Home sales picked up a bit in late 2006, which helped to soften the decline in the US housing market. However, the supply of new and existing homes available for sale was near 10-year highs in late-2006 and early-2007. This overhang of homes available for sale kept downward pressure on home prices and also forced US homebuilders to further slash their building plans in an attempt to offload their big inventories of unsold homes. In addition, many sub-prime lenders ran into trouble in late-2006 and early-2007 with high default rates, causing concerns about mortgage lender bankruptcies and a cut-back in credit to the housing sector. Based on high unsold home inventories and tighter mortgage credit, it seems likely that a true recovery in the US housing sector will not occur until 2008 or even 2009. In the meantime, the US housing sector will continue to present spillover risks for the overall US economy.

Corn prices exploded starting in September 2006 when the extent of corn demand from ethanol producers became clear. Corn prices in the space of 5 months rallied by 94% from the $2.25 per bushel level in August 2006 to a 10-year high of $4.37 in February 2007. Corn prices could easily rally further through 2007, depending on whether US farmers plant enough new acres of corn in spring 2007 and whether the weather cooperates during summer 2007.

US ethanol producers use corn almost exclusively as the feedstock for producing ethanol. That contrasts with Brazilian ethanol producers, who use sugar almost exclusively as their feedstock. Brazil is currently the world's second largest world producer of ethanol, just behind the US. Sugar prices saw strength in late-2005 and early-2006, mainly because of strong demand for sugar from Brazilian ethanol producers. Brazilian ethanol producers now use about one-half of Brazil's sugar crop for ethanol. Sugar prices fell back through 2006, however, because sugar production caught up with demand, thus causing a small surplus in the 2006-07 marketing year (Oct-Sep) after three straight years of deficits. Brazil and other countries have plenty of land available to produce more sugar, meaning sugar producers can keep up with increasing demand from ethanol producers.

In the US, ethanol production has been growing very rapidly in the past several years. The US in late 2006 had 106 ethanol plants in production and there were 48 ethanol facilities under construction, according to the Renewable Fuels Association. US ethanol production in December 2006 reached a record high of 11.023 million barrels per month, according to the US Energy Information Administration, which is equivalent to 5.56 billion gallons per year. US ethanol production in December 2006 was up sharply by +27% year-on-year. Meanwhile, US ethanol imports in December 2006 totaled 985,000 barrels per month, which is equivalent to about 500 million gallons per year. The total ethanol supply

(US production plus imports) in December was therefore about 6 billion gallons per year, which accounts for about 4% of US transportation fuel usage.

US ethanol production in December (of an annualized 5.56 billion gallons) used an annualized 1.32 billion bushels of corn (5.56 billion gallons divided by the ethanol yield of 2.8 gallons/bushel of corn, less one-third to account for the fact that about one-third of corn used in ethanol production can be reused as DDG-distillers dried grain feed for livestock feed). US ethanol usage in December therefore took the equivalent of 12.5% of total US corn production (i.e., 1.32 billion bushels divided by the 2006-07 crop of 10.535 billion bushels). In terms of land, the corn used by US ethanol producers in December 2006 (annualized) required the use of 8.82 million acres of land, which is 12.5% of US planted corn acres (79.366 million in 2006-07) and 4.3% of the total US land planted with corn, soybeans or wheat (203.88 million acres).

Corn usage during the 2006/07 marketing year (Sep-Aug) was so strong that the USDA forecasted that corn consumers would use not only all of the corn that US farmers grew during the summer of 2006, but also 62% of the corn held in inventories. Thus, the USDA as of March 2007 was forecasting that the US 2006-07 carry-over would fall by 62% to 752 million bushels, which was the third lowest US carry-over in the past 3 decades.

In order to prevent a further drop in US corn carry-over in the next marketing year, US farmers in spring 2007 needed to plant 10-12 million acres more of corn. The surge in corn prices pushed the profit margin on corn sharply higher and many farmers were eager to plant more corn in spring 2007. However, as of March 2007, the jury remained out on whether those new planted acres of corn would materialize. Moreover, even if US farmers did plant 10-12 million more acres of corn and even if the weather turns out to be favorable during summer 2007, the corn supply situation will tighten even further going into the next marketing year of 2007-08 when ethanol production will be even higher.

President Bush in his State of the Union Address in January 2007 announced a very ambitious plan for the US to use 35 billion gallons of alternative fuels by 2017. That is about 6 times current usage and 5 times the current Renewable Fuel Standard of 7.5 billion gallons per year by 2012. However, the US corn-based ethanol industry simply cannot produce 35 billion gallons per year of ethanol , because (1) there isn't enough farm land in the US, (2) there would not be enough corn left over for human food consumption and livestock feed (about 55% of US corn goes for livestock feed), and (3) corn prices would soar beyond economical levels for ethanol producers. The practical limit for corn-based ethanol is probably about 15 billion gallons per year, which is about three times current production and about 10% of the US fuel supply. Even on that scale, corn-based ethanol producers would need about 3.6 billion bushels of corn (15 bln gallons divided by the yield of 2.8 gallons/bushel less 1/3 for DDG), which would represent one-third of the US 2006-07 corn crop and would require the use of 12% of all US corn/soybean/wheat farmland.

The only way for the 35 billion gallon goal to be met is if the US ethanol industry can produce at least 20 billion gallons of ethanol with cellulosic-based ethanol by 2017. At present, there are no commercial ethanol plants that use cellulosic feedstocks (such as switch grass, corn stalks, wood chips, etc.) because more research needs to be done to work out economical ways to process that cellulosic material into ethanol. The industry consensus is that it will take another 5 years before cellulosic-based ethanol can be produced economically on a large scale.

US ethanol producers are currently receiving strong support from the federal government, which has helped the industry to get on its feet. The federal government gives fuel blenders a 51 cent excise tax credit for blending ethanol into gasoline (the credit lasts until 2010). In addition, the federal government protects US ethanol producers with a 54 cent import tariff on imported ethanol, which is enough to make large-scale ethanol imports from Brazil uneconomical. The 54 cent tariff is currently set to expire at the end of 2008.

Ethanol prices closely follow gasoline prices because ethanol and gasoline have essentially the same characteristics in being able to provide fuel for internal combustion engines. However, ethanol prices trade at a premium of 43 cents on average to wholesale gasoline prices. The premium stems from the 51 cent subsidy for ethanol, the fact that ethanol produces 20% lower mileage than gasoline, and other factors.

The prospects for ethanol in the US are bright, particularly when cellulosic ethanol becomes commercially viable. Ethanol currently accounts for only about 4% of the US fuel supply, meaning there is plenty of room on the upside. Increased ethanol production helps support US farmers, reduces pollution (since ethanol burns cleaner than gasoline), and increases America's energy independence. However, there are downsides to corn-based ethanol in the form of higher food prices and competition with more environmentally-attractive solutions such as vehicles powered by electricity or fuel cells. Still, the ethanol industry is a fast-growing force that will have a major impact on the US agriculture sector for at least the next two decades.

Volume U.S.

U.S. Futures Volume Highlights
2006 in Comparison with 2005

2006 Rank	Top 50 Contracts Traded in 2006	2006 Contracts	%	2005 Contracts	%	2005 Rank
1	Eurodollars (3-month), CME	502,077,391	25.32%	410,355,384	25.63%	1
2	E-Mini S&P 500 Index, CME	257,926,673	13.01%	207,095,732	12.94%	3
3	T-Notes (10-year), CBT	255,571,869	12.89%	215,124,076	13.44%	2
4	T-Notes (5-year), CBT	124,870,313	6.30%	121,908,830	7.62%	4
5	T-Bonds (30-year), CBT	93,754,894	4.73%	86,926,569	5.43%	5
6	E-Mini NASDAQ 100, CME	79,940,222	4.03%	72,453,141	4.53%	6
7	Crude Oil, NYMEX	71,053,203	3.58%	59,650,468	3.73%	7
8	Corn, CBT	47,239,893	2.38%	27,965,057	1.75%	11
9	E-Mini Russell 2000 Index, CME	41,748,538	2.11%	28,902,033	1.81%	10
10	Euro FX, CME	40,790,379	2.06%	34,530,730	2.16%	9
11	T-Notes (2-year), CBT	37,966,797	1.91%	21,205,359	1.32%	13
12	Mini ($5) Dow Jones Industrial Index, CBT	26,792,373	1.35%	24,892,328	1.55%	12
13	Rogers International TRAKRS, CME	26,486,999	1.34%	36,081,429	2.25%	8
14	TRAKRS PIMCO, CME	24,471,474	1.23%			
15	Henry Hub Swap, NYMEX	24,157,726	1.22%	10,406,462	0.65%	23
16	Natural Gas, NYMEX	23,029,988	1.16%	19,142,549	1.20%	15
17	Soybeans, CBT	22,647,784	1.14%	20,216,137	1.26%	14
18	Japanese Yen, CME	19,677,365	0.99%	12,471,672	0.78%	21
19	Federal Funds (30-day), CBT	17,833,331	0.90%	11,602,282	0.72%	22
20	Wheat, CBT	16,224,871	0.82%	10,114,098	0.63%	24
21	British Pound, CME	16,099,540	0.81%	8,769,751	0.55%	25
22	Gold (100 oz.), COMEX Div. of NYMEX	15,917,584	0.80%	15,890,617	0.99%	16
23	Sugar #11, NYBOT	15,100,721	0.76%	13,007,072	0.81%	20
24	S&P 500 Index, CME	14,844,858	0.75%	15,377,489	0.96%	17
25	Heating Oil #2, NYMEX	13,990,589	0.71%	13,135,581	0.82%	19
26	Swiss Franc, CME	11,470,031	0.58%	7,784,498	0.49%	28
27	Canadian Dollar, CME	10,279,576	0.52%	7,930,156	0.50%	27
28	Soybean Oil, CBT	9,488,524	0.48%	7,676,130	0.48%	29
29	Soybean Meal, CBT	9,350,043	0.47%	8,324,616	0.52%	26
30	E-Mini Crude Oil, NYMEX	9,323,467	0.47%	5,682,214	0.35%	31
31	Gasoline, Unleaded, NYMEX	8,620,908	0.43%	13,166,417	0.82%	18
32	Gold, CBT	8,452,484	0.43%			
33	Live Cattle, CME	8,209,698	0.41%	5,833,556	0.36%	30
34	Natural Gas Penultimate Swap, NYMEX	7,973,290	0.40%	2,751,455	0.17%	41
35	Australian Dollar, CME	6,567,650	0.33%	4,749,093	0.30%	34
36	Lean Hogs, CME	6,481,001	0.33%	4,153,543	0.26%	35
37	E-mini S&P SmallCap 600 Index, CME	5,528,263	0.28%	4,885,430	0.31%	33
38	Silver (5,000 oz), COMEX Div. of NYMEX	5,433,063	0.27%	5,536,351	0.35%	32
39	TRAKRS Select 50, CME	5,280,652	0.27%			
40	Crude Oil, E-mini, NYMEX	4,806,526	0.24%			
41	Wheat, KCBT	4,763,168	0.24%	3,682,919	0.23%	39
42	Cotton #2, NYBOT	4,490,407	0.23%	3,848,990	0.24%	38
43	Coffee C, NYBOT	4,407,512	0.22%	3,987,778	0.25%	36
44	Gasoline, RBOB, NYMEX	3,883,261	0.20%			
45	High Grade Copper, COMEX Div. of NYMEX	3,795,538	0.19%	3,950,842	0.25%	37
46	Mexican Peso, CME	3,281,312	0.17%	3,674,886	0.23%	40
47	Cocoa, NYBOT	3,169,302	0.16%	2,582,927	0.16%	43
48	Nikkei 225 Index, CME	2,809,839	0.14%	1,886,270	0.12%	45
49	TRAKRS PIMCO SPTR, CME	2,349,055	0.12%			
50	Socal Basis Swap, NTMEX	2,311,008	0.12%	1,580,162	0.10%	48
	Top 50 Contracts	1,982,740,953	97.01%	1,600,893,079	96.86%	
	Contracts Below the Top 50	61,156,265	2.99%	51,978,280	3.14%	
	TOTAL	**2,043,897,218**	**100.00%**	**1,652,871,359**	**100.00%**	

* For 2005 Top 50 contracts totaled 1,612,086,304 including 6 contracts that are not among 2006's Top 50.

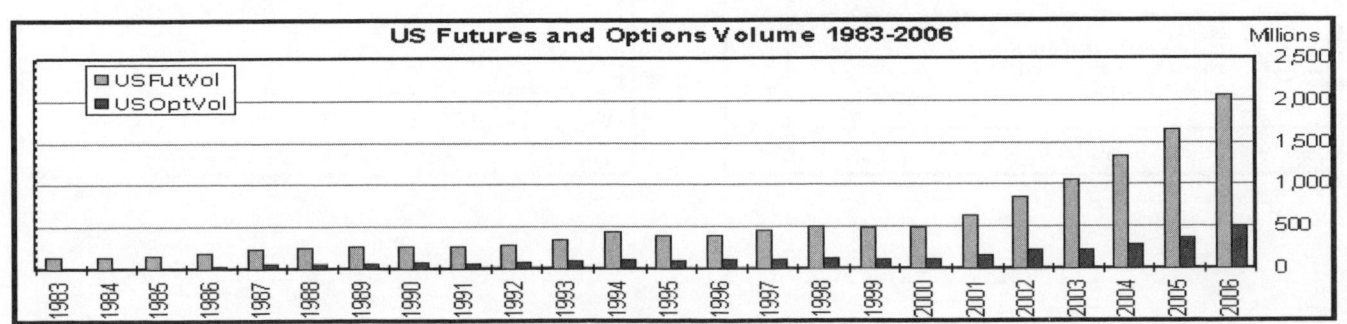

US Futures and Options Volume 1983-2006

U.S. Futures Volume Highlights
2006 in Comparison with 2005

2006 RANK	EXCHANGE	2006 CONTRACTS	%	2005 CONTRACTS	%	2005 RANK
1	Chicago Mercantile Exchange (CME)	1,101,712,533	53.90%	883,118,526	53.43%	1
2	Chicago Board of Trade (CBT)	678,262,052	33.18%	561,145,938	33.95%	2
3	New York Mercantile Exchange (NYMEX)**	216,252,995	10.58%	166,608,642	10.08%	3
4	New York Board of Trade (NYBOT)*	32,746,692	1.60%	29,013,416	1.76%	4
5	OneChicago	7,922,465	0.39%	5,528,046	0.33%	5
6	Kansas City Board of Trade (KCBT)	4,771,711	0.23%	3,690,025	0.22%	6
7	Minneapolis Grain Exchange (MGE)	1,614,543	0.08%	1,389,922	0.08%	8
8	CBOE Futures Exchange (CFE)	478,424	0.02%	177,632	0.01%	9
9	EUREX US	135,803	0.01%	2,200,384	0.13%	7
10	NASDAQ LIFFE Markets (NQLX)			257,000	0.02%	9
	TOTAL	**2,043,897,218**	**100.00%**	**1,652,872,531**	**100.00%**	

* Includes the New York Futures Exchange, New York Cotton Exchange and Coffee, Sugar and Cocoa Exchange.

** Includes Comex Division.

Chicago Board of Trade (CBT)

FUTURE	CONTRACT UNIT	2006	2005	2004	2003	2002
Wheat	5,000 bu	16,224,871	10,114,098	7,955,155	6,967,416	6,872,891
Mini Wheat	1,000 bu	67,637	32,295	31,044	22,288	
Corn	5,000 bu	47,239,893	27,965,057	24,038,233	19,118,715	18,132,447
Mini Corn	1,000 bu	162,545	102,292	86,771	53,404	
Oats	5,000 bu	427,315	351,539	416,448	318,898	415,140
Soybeans	5,000 bu	22,647,784	20,216,137	18,846,021	17,545,714	14,475,100
Mini Soybeans	1,000 bu	581,047	495,313	362,829	250,447	
South American Soybeans	5,000 bu	226	12,088			
Soybean Oil	60,000 lbs	9,488,524	7,676,130	7,593,314	7,417,340	6,816,483
Soybean Meal	100 tons	9,350,043	8,324,616	8,569,243	8,158,445	7,174,507
Rice	200,000 lbs	321,330	228,502	168,165	265,234	193,723
Mini Silver	1,000 oz	547,182	163,395	204,255	34,804	7,723
Mini Gold	33.2 troy oz	1,994,920	389,737	420,604	145,173	9,024
Silver	5,000 oz	1,208,471	86,218	12,398		72
Gold	100 oz	8,452,484	626,901	89,539		55
T-Bonds (30-year)	100,000 USD	93,754,895	86,926,569	72,949,053	63,521,507	56,082,284
T-Notes (10-year)	100,000 USD	255,571,869	215,124,076	196,119,150	146,745,281	95,786,299
T-Notes (5-year)	100,000 USD	124,870,313	121,908,830	105,469,410	73,746,445	50,512,085
T-Notes (2-year)	200,000 USD	37,966,797	21,205,359	9,454,774	4,415,906	3,203,855
Interest Rate Swap (10-year)	100,000 USD	520,090	655,711	856,968	1,038,777	661,527
Interest Rate Swap (5-year)	100,000 USD	272,749	202,737	243,353	110,275	53,030
Municipal Note Index (10-year)	100,000 USD	505	33,502	65,026	94,541	8,678
30-Day Federal Funds	5,000,000 USD	17,833,331	11,602,282	11,940,120	8,271,726	6,285,789
Ethanol	29,000 US Gallons	5,564	2,676			
OTC Ethanol Forward Swap	14,500 US Gallons	42				
OTC Ethanol Previous Swap	14,500 US Gallons	60				
Dow Jones Industrial Index ($25)	25 USD x Index	18,686				
Dow Jones Industrial Index	10 USD x Index	1,919,847	1,787,405	2,577,138	4,416,302	6,485,501
Mini ($5) Dow Jones Industrial Index	5 USD x Index	26,792,373	24,892,328	20,695,848	10,859,690	2,224,757
Dow Jones AIGCI Index	100 x Index	14,669	11,337	40,882	43,321	14,782
Dow Jones AIGER Index	100 x Index	5,990				
Total Futures		**678,262,052**	**561,145,938**	**489,230,144**	**373,669,290**	**276,316,119**

Kansas City Board of Trade (KCBT)

FUTURE	CONTRACT UNIT	2006	2005	2004	2003	2002
Wheat	5,000 bu	4,763,168	3,682,919	2,833,370	2,632,033	2,738,536
Value Line Index	100 USD x Index	8,543	7,106	1,429	2,391	17,370
Total Futures		**4,771,711**	**3,690,025**	**2,834,799**	**2,634,424**	**2,755,949**

Minneapolis Grain Exchange (MGE)

FUTURE	CONTRACT UNIT	2006	2005	2004	2003	2002
Spring Wheat	5,000 bu	1,613,239	1,384,750	1,378,694	1,066,489	1,199,149
Hard Red Spring Wheat Index	5,000 bu	7	647	56		
Hard Red Winter Wheat Index	5,000 bu	18	427	2,521	16,535	
National Corn Index	5,000 bu	1,279	3,848	116	3,996	2,253
Total Futures		**1,614,543**	**1,389,922**	**1,381,456**	**1,087,020**	**1,201,543**

Chicago Mercantile Exchange (CME)

Future	Contract Unit	2006	2005	2004	2003	2002
Lean Hogs	40,000 lbs	6,481,001	4,153,543	3,204,186	2,164,155	1,931,260
Pork Bellies, Frozen	40,000 lbs	107,564	124,418	151,949	161,329	152,054
Butter	40,000 lbs	3,800	7,708	6,167	8,544	5,897
Cash Butter	20,000 lbs	18,673	2,337			
Nonfat Dry Milk	44,000 lbs	954	217	114	230	12
Class III Milk	200,000 lbs	225,137	182,509	345,973	191,351	103,375
Class IV Milk	200,000 lbs	113	138	690	137	4,714
Live Cattle	40,000 lbs	8,209,698	5,833,556	4,510,128	4,436,089	3,851,736
Feeder Cattle	50,000 lbs	1,286,395	1,017,348	741,265	704,852	585,517
Random Lumber	100,000 bd ft	271,024	236,241	242,873	223,891	164,423
Diamonium Phosphate	100 tons	6	38	62		
Urea Ammonium Nitrate	100 tons	79	55	218		
Urea	100 tons	47	208	300		
Eurodollar (3-month)	1,000,000 USD	502,077,391	410,355,384	297,284,038	208,771,164	202,080,832
Euroyen	1,000,000,000 JPY	662,653	200,958	224,821	179,573	231,723
E-Mini Eurodollar (5-year)		4,237				
2-Year SWAP		31,260	30,485	26,240	6,640	5,671
5-Year SWAP		56,320	35,315	56,438	43,616	13,301
10-Year SWAP		44,510	35,170	65,281	40,030	7,234
Consumer Price Index	2,500 USD x CPI	40	41	5,264		
Eurozone Harmonized CPI Index	10,000 EUR x Index	1,369	835			
One Month LIBOR	3,000,000 USD	852,119	1,048,468	2,886,987	1,138,358	1,110,934
Australian Dollar	100,000	6,567,650	4,749,093	2,672,733	1,609,289	1,049,220
British Pound	62,500	16,099,540	8,769,751	4,676,512	2,595,155	2,166,469
Brazilian Real	100,000	94,514	23,144	2,911	277	4
Canadian Dollar	100,000	10,279,576	7,930,156	5,611,328	4,219,618	3,134,963
Czech Koruna		461	118	31		
Euro FX	125,000	40,790,379	34,530,730	20,456,672	11,193,922	6,986,600
E-Mini Euro FX	62,500	386,850	642,857	190,554	16,860	7,252
Hungarian Forint	30,000,000	620	77	10		
Israeli Shekel	1,000,000	113				
Japanese Yen	12,500,000	19,677,365	12,471,672	7,395,322	6,085,209	4,394,982
E-Mini Japanese Yen	6,250,000	9,203	4,887	5,466	2,740	2,557
Korean Won	125,000,000	5,867				
Mexican Peso	500,000	3,795,538	3,674,886	3,247,222	2,123,623	1,354,256
New Zealand Dollar	100,000	529,782	187,437	162,370	120,235	54,148
Norwegian Krone	227,000	6,461	3,966	2,122	388	303
Polish Zloty	500,000	23,899	15,046	4,461		
Russian Ruble	2500000	125,762	45,835	30,620	4,420	
South African Rand	500,000	70,491	63,379	65,749	73,542	55,275
Swedish Krona	193,600	4,618	1,884	812	4	1
Swiss Franc	125,000	11,470,031	7,784,498	4,067,767	3,596,658	2,830,738
Australian Dollar / Canadian Dollar	200,000 AUD	6,708	1,797	676	220	16
Australian Dollar / Japanese Yen	200,000 AUD	19	836	1,066	94	16
Australian Dollar / New Zealand Dollar	200,000 AUD	39	1,990	639		
British Pound / Japanese Yen	125,000 GBP	173	830	651	894	519
British Pound / Swiss Franc	125,000 GBP	6,151	3,209	689	103	263
Canadian Dollar / Japanese Yen	200,000 CAD	24	452	344	102	
Chinese Renimibi / U.S. Dollar	1,000,000 CHR	5,407				
Swiss Franc / Japanese Yen	250,000 CHF	55	338	110	247	54
Euro / Australian Dollar	125,000 EUR	205	823	769	554	306
Euro / Canadian Dollar	125,000 EUR	109	1,032	901	247	5
Euro / Hungarian Forint	30,000,000 EUR	1,050	10			
Euro / Norwegian Krone	125,000 EUR	328	522	98		
Euro / Polish Zloty	500,000	15,194	18,548	3,859		
Euro / British Pound	125,000 EUR	42,053	39,069	43,635	65,696	7,166
Euro / Japanese Yen	125,000 EUR	272,182	123,805	118,614	161,600	58,768
Euro / Swedish Krona	125,000 EUR	151	394	318		
Euro / Swiss Franc	125,000 EUR	49,475	12,264	7,290	1,794	949
Nikkei 225 Index (USD)	5 USD x Index	2,809,839	1,886,270	1,239,010	765,463	571,241
Nikkei 225 Index (JPY)	5 USD x Index	2,126,654	952,618	260,128		
S&P 500 Index	500 USD x Index	14,844,858	15,377,489	16,175,584	20,175,462	23,699,667
E-Mini S&P 500 Index	50 USD x Index	257,926,673	207,095,732	167,202,962	161,176,639	115,741,691
Mini S&P Asia 50 Index	25 USD x Index	960				
S&P 500 Barra Growth Index	500 USD x Index	94	2,533	2,754	5,119	7,756
S&P 500 Barra Value Index	500 USD x Index	18	8,049	8,852	14,131	17,238
S&P Technology-Telecomm Sector Index	125 USD x Index	4	68	197	60	1,410
S&P MidCap 400 Index	500 USD x Index	153,268	205,058	260,764	302,817	387,800
S&P SmallCap 600 Index	200 USD x Index	130	1,882	2,354	1,635	191
S&P Citigroup Growth	250 USD x Index	5,473				

Chicago Mercantile Exchange (CME) (Continued)

Future	Contract Unit	2006	2005	2004	2003	2002
S&P Citigroup Value	250 USD x Index	7,289				
E-mini S&P SmallCap 600 Index	100 USD x Index	5,528,263	4,885,430	3,282,347	1,417,513	343,087
E-Mini MSCI EAFE	50 USD x Index	17,461				
NASDAQ 100 Index	500 USD x Index	2,269,870	2,682,058	4,011,983	4,421,221	4,903,287
E-Mini NASDAQ 100 Index	20 USD x Index	79,940,222	72,453,141	77,168,513	67,888,938	54,491,180
Russell 2000 Index	500 USD x Index	619,286	571,055	614,040	655,778	843,479
E-Mini Russell 2000 Index	100 USD x Index	41,748,538	28,902,033	17,121,233	3,878,935	859,885
Russell 1000 Index	100 USD x Index	38,304	530,665	51,437	14,941	
Long-Short TRAKRS Index II	1 USD x Index	980,098	1,172,321	5,693,223		
Rogers International TRAKRS	1 USD x Index	26,486,999	36,081,429			
TRAKRS BXY	1 USD x Index	304,172				
TRAKRS PIMCO	1 USD x Index	24,471,474				
TRAKRS PIMCO SPTR	1 USD x Index	2,349,055				
TRAKRS Select 50 Index	1 USD x Index	5,280,652				
TRAKRS Commodity	1 USD x Index	746,723	2,250,341	4,138,262	7,424,763	
TRAKRS Euro Currency	1 USD x Index	277,792	397,642	1,248,272	1,196,525	
TRAKRS Gold	1 USD x Index	1,257,549	1,827,018	4,868,842	6,065,013	
HDD Weather	20 USD x Index	115,763	75,266	16,404	6,058	2,334
HDD Seasonal Weather	20 USD x Index	2,875	9,610	2,080	225	
HDD Seasonal Weather Strips	20 USD x Index	13,675	50			
CDD Weather	20 USD x Index	65,258	107,475	23,656	8,176	1,831
CDD Seasonal Weather Strips	20 USD x Index	8,450				
Euro HDD Weather	20 GBP x Index	3,435	7,302	2,015	375	
Euro CAT Weather	20 GBP x Index	950	3,332	535		
Euro Seasonal HDD Weather	20 GBP x Index	1,225				
CSI Housing Index	250 USD x Index	3,632				
Goldman Sachs Commodity Index	250 USD x Index	615,260	498,424	450,036	371,473	518,323
GSCI Excess Return Index	100 USD x Index	13,141				
S&P 500 ETF	100 shares	2,009	4,522			
Russell 2000 ETF	200 shares	785	47			
E-Mini Nasdaq Bio-Tech Index	250 USD x Index	75	3			
Nasdaq 100 ETF	200 shares	1,849	3,817			
Total Futures		**1,101,712,533**	**883,118,526**	**664,584,607**	**530,989,007**	**444,537,987**

New York Board of Trade (NYBOT) (Continued)

FUTURE	CONTRACT UNIT	2006	2005	2004	2003	2002
Euro / US Dollar, Small	100,000 EUR	116,029	110,186	12,409	5,365	2,560
Euro / Australian Dollar	100,000 EUR	58,144	59,644	44,000	30,466	14,635
Euro / Canadian Dollar	100,000 EUR	26,477	12,179	52,496	49,890	17,731
Euro / Czech Koruna	100,000 EUR	17,533	21,525	28,093	2,774	
Euro / Hungarian Forint	100,000 EUR	11,615	12,905	17,640	24	
Euro / Japanese Yen	100,000 EUR	586,129	448,372	363,069	346,751	337,756
Euro / Swedish Krona	100,000 EUR	54,571	129,028	64,334	49,977	45,757
Euro / British Pound	100,000 EUR	304,382	253,818	226,404	117,989	124,485
Euro / Norwegian	100,000 EUR	44,635	55,945	29,536	29,815	17,670
Euro / South African Rand	100,000 EUR	163				
Euro / Swiss Franc	100,000 EUR	183,446	261,897	143,274	133,218	69,057
British Pound / Australian Dollar	125,000 GBP	10				
British Pound / Canadian Dollar	125,000 GBP	2				
British Pound / New Zealand Dollar	125,000 GBP	2				
British Pound / Norwegian Krone	125,000 GBP	2				
British Pound / South Africa Rand	125,000 GBP	2				
British Pound / Swedish Krona	125,000 GBP	2				
Small Australian Dollar / US Dollar	100,000 AUD	27				
Small British Pound / US Dollar	62,500 GBP	17,437	21,762	6,006		
Small New Zealand Dollar / US Dollar	100,000 NZD	80				
Small US Dollar / Canadian Dollar	100,000 USD	18,910	15,624	247		
Small US Dollar / Japanese Yen	100,000 USD	142,751	39,715	5,664		
Small US Dollar / Swiss Franc	100,000 USD	64,417	28,262	41		
US Dollar Index	1,000 USD x Index	1,168,486	1,159,938	748,204	563,032	411,571
Revised NYSE Composite Index	50 USD x Index	3,213	14,047	14,678	7,143	
Russell 1000 Index	500 USD x Index	837,065	885,881	961,771	677,626	646,455
Russell 1000 Growth Index	500 USD x Index	2,730	2,905	2,442	836	
Russell 1000 Value Index	500 USD x Index	2,031	2,391	2,392	415	
Russell 2000 Index	500 USD x Index	1,038	298	424	10	
Reuters-CRB Futures Index (CCI)	500 USD x Index	14,312	9,144	19,230	23,156	14,283
RJ/CRB Futures Index	200 USD x Index	150	7,424			
Total Futures*		**32,746,692**	**29,013,416**	**23,955,212**	**18,822,048**	**16,272,144**

VOLUME U.S.

New York Board of Trade (NYBOT)**

Option	Contract Unit	2006	2005	2004	2003	2002
Coffee 'C'	37,500 lbs	2,785,053	2,370,161	1,970,068	1,328,081	1,063,090
Sugar #11	112,000 lbs	6,250,162	3,631,939	2,854,683	1,690,190	1,380,300
Sugar #11 Options on Futures Spreads		54,880	14,861			
Cocoa	10 metric tons	377,905	512,259	429,769	497,188	743,237
Cotton #2	50,000 lbs	1,820,259	1,709,345	1,725,982	2,157,441	1,171,843
Cotton #2 Options on Futures Spreads		10	534			
Pulp	20 Airdry Metric Tons	1,710	6,478			
Orange Juice Frozen Concentrate	15,000 lbs	426,967	433,288	554,432	195,541	175,794
US Dollar Index	500 USD x Index	39,299	35,356	57,189	29,532	28,694
Euro	200,000 EUR	130	242	352	578	69
Euro / Canadian Dollar	100,000 EUR	525	6			
Euro / Swedish Krona	100,000 EUR	33	122			
Euro / British Pound	100,000 EUR	84	88	67	253	14
Euro / Swiss Franc	100,000 EUR	14				
Euro / Japanese Yen	100,000 EUR	4,021	116	40	776	104
British Pound / Japanese Yen	125,000 GBP	62	14	17	209	156
US Dollar / Japanese Yen	12,500,000 JPY	140				
US Dollar / British Pound	125,000 GBP	14	10	25	31	
Revised NYSE Composite Index	50 USD x Index	42,794	37,872	26,952	18,912	
Russell 1000 Index	500 USD x Index	81,274	142,299	103,944	61,264	1,449
Russell 2000 Index	500 USD x Index	28,639	32,362	36,305	734	
Russell 3000 Index	500 USD x Index	182	1,568	4,647		
Reuters-CRB Futures Index (CCI)	500 USD x Index	6,320	1,539			
Total Options**		**8,932,169**	**7,774,379**	**6,010,110**	**4,656,335**	**3,857,721**

New York Mercantile Exchange (NYMEX)

COMEX Division

FUTURE	CONTRACT UNIT	2006	2005	2004	2003	2002
Gold	100 oz	15,917,584	15,890,617	14,959,617	12,235,689	9,018,183
Silver	5,000 oz	5,433,063	5,536,351	5,006,125	4,111,190	3,135,564
High Grade Copper	25,000 lbs	3,281,312	3,950,842	3,190,625	3,089,270	2,807,286
Aluminum	44,000 lbs	9,149	28,491	72,169	107,490	74,000
Total Futures		**24,641,108**	**25,406,301**	**23,228,536**	**19,543,639**	**15,035,033**

NYMEX Division

FUTURE	CONTRACT UNIT	2006	2005	2004	2003	2002
Palladium	100 oz	378,116	321,923	267,552	95,613	41,053
Platinum	50 oz	373,119	376,179	295,695	268,305	219,771
No. 2 Heating Oil, NY	42,000 gal	13,990,589	13,135,581	12,884,511	11,581,670	10,695,202
E-Mini Heating Oil, NY	42,000 gal	126,191				
Unleaded Gasoline, NY	42,000 gal	8,620,908	13,166,417	12,777,442	11,172,050	10,979,736
E-Mini Unleaded Gasoline, NY	42,000 gal	59,106				
Crude Oil	1,000 bbl	71,053,203	59,650,468	52,883,200	45,436,931	45,679,468
E-Mini Crude Oil	400 bbl	4,806,526	5,682,214	720,421	277,411	210,228
NY Harbor RBOB Gasoline	42,000 gal	3,883,261	1,964			
Brent Crude Oil	1,000 bbl	12,042	986,534	135,385	30	1,516
E-Mini Brent Crude Oil	1,000 bbl	3				
Propane	42,000 gal	1,127	4,010	14,764	14,710	12,826
Natural Gas	10,000 MMBTU	23,029,988	19,142,549	17,441,942	19,037,118	24,357,792
E-Mini Natural Gas	4,000 MMBTU	1,328,409	522,439	136,123	115,502	67,981
Coal	1,500 tons	52,305	28,058	7,490	5,235	4,124
Henry Hub Swap		24,157,726	10,406,462	5,353,792	2,356,600	
Natural Gas Penultimate Swap		7,973,290	2,751,455	294,011		
AECO-C/NIT Basis Swap		1,317,291	1,247,570	488,699		
CIG Rockies		245,305	181,241	69,555	7,026	
San Juan Basis Swap		181,765	160,530	62,048		
Sumas Basis		205,978	429,597	320,144	172,313	5,890
Northwest Rockies Basis Swap		1,408,279	1,261,653	652,511		
Socal Basis Swap		2,311,008	1,580,162	569,540		
WAHA Basis		611,795	338,241	184,909	134,632	
PG&E Malin Basis		533,176	682,135	334,230	241,769	11,564

New York Mercantile Exchange (NYMEX)   (Continued)
NYMEX Division

FUTURE	CONTRACT UNIT	2006	2005	2004	2003	2002
PG&E Citygate Basis		356,769	642,845	209,906	110,812	186
Permian Basis		520,763	306,329	128,814	211,397	1,340
Transco Zone 6 Basis Swap		313,674	529,577	480,197		
Texas Eastern Zone M-3 Basis		642,301	716,299	278,235	178,591	7,702
Dominion Transmission - Appalachian Basis		433,304	459,360	247,191	95,595	1,898
Centerpoint Basis Swap		68,895				
TCO Basis		333,867	316,053	244,049	103,343	3,610
Transco Zone 3 Basis Swap		58,349	92,944	56,993	2,750	
Florida Gas Zone 3 Basis Swap		13,785	972			
Columbia Gulf Onshore Basis		68,181	27,332	24,272	3,526	
Henry Hub Basis Swap		467,158	337,152	98,408		
Chicago Basis Swap		555,309	324,560	174,498		
ANR - Louisiana Basis Swap		24,476	6,869			
ANR - Oklahoma Basis		47,516	57,584	52,967	8,235	856
Michigan Basis		484,925	158,667	94,137	81,074	856
Houston Ship Channel Basis Swap		1,696,435	778,513	429,266		
NGPL Mid-Continent		279,960	160,828	69,854	32,580	1,666
Tennessee 500 Leg Basis Swap		19,071	8,600			
Tennessee Zone 0 Basis Swap		81,632	56,197			
Trunkline, LA Basis Swap		7,001	3,972			
NGPL Louisiana Basis		2,798	11,619	3,724	2,260	
NGPL TEX/OK Basis		1,119,784	401,241	60,266	13,418	2,072
Northern Natural Gas Demarcation Basis		162,381	73,501	17,651	35,901	4,950
Northern Natural Gas Ventura Basis		306,787	207,843	21,771	65,843	5,525
Panhandle Basis Swap		1,404,498	870,855	224,329		
Sonat Basis Swap		18,722	8,966			
Texas Gas Zone SL Basis Swap		49,163	10,640			
TETCO ELA Basis		11,811	8,196	24,755	4,872	
Transco Zone 4 Basis Swap		13,652	1,394			
TETCO STX Basis		69,669	36,481	19,790	13,132	
Socal Index		53,086	23,512			
Dominion Transmission - Appalachian Basis Index		10,120	8,186			
Demarc Natural Gas Index Swap		2,218				
Ventura Natural Gas Index Swap		2,508				
Centerpoint East Index		1,378				
El Paso, San Juan Index Swap		3,702	924			
PG&E Citygate Index		14,331	14,878			
El Paso, Permian Index Swap		16,710	11,740	2,250		
Henry Hub Index Swap		332,129	271,791	65,860		
Houston Ship Channel Index Swap		131,702	148,249	12,791		
Rockies Kern Opal - NW Index		29,994	8,562			
Chicago Index Swap		5,114	6,605	1,581		
Transco Zone 6 Index		11,199	8,796			
Sumas Index		14,976	13,088			
Panhandle Index Swap		9,444	6,171	1,798		
NGPL Midcontinental Index		1,615				
Tetco M-3 Index		44,685	19,601			
WAHA Index Swap		26,784	26,923	4,549		
NGPL TEXOK Index		3,537				
Demarc Natural Gas Swing Swap		1,073				
NGPL TEXOK Swing Swap		472				
NGPL Midcontinental Swing Swap		202				
Socal Swing Swap		19,888	11,528			
Dominion Transmission - Appalachian Swing Swap		3,344	3,832			
San Juan Swing Index		852	248			
PG&E Citygate Swing Swap		2,960	4,147			
El Paso Permian Swing		5,092	2,606			
Houston Ship Channel Swing		10,247	6,384	1,078		
Henry Hub Swing		37,243	85,830	40,102		
Kern River Opal Plant Swing Swap		8,495	3,380			
Chicago Swing		572	991	102		
Transco Zone 6 Swing Swap		1,515	914			
Sumas Swing Swap Future		2,546	1,434			
Panhandle Swing		3,634	2,780	599		
Texas Eastern Zone M-3 Swing		2,394	498			
WAHA Swing		7,918	5,252	1,310		
Ventura Natural Gas Swing Swap		434				
Centerpoint East Swing Swap		58				
PJM Daily		3,530	217,349	190,591	30,221	

VOLUME U.S.

New York Mercantile Exchange (NYMEX) (Continued)
NYMEX Division

FUTURE	CONTRACT UNIT	2006	2005	2004	2003	2002
PJM Monthly		171,655	652,077	234,207	142,859	
PJM Weekly		1,900	36,900	18,725	3,963	
Northern Illinois Hub Daily		1,080	700			
Northern Illinois Hub Monthly		38,220	21,038			
AER-Dayton Hub Daily		590	13,860			
AER-Dayton Hub Monthly		8,026	18,020			
PJM Off-Peak LMP Swap		83,734	85,922			
Northern Illinois Off-Peak Monthly		88,724	59,640			
AER-Dayton Off-Peak Monthly		12,710	13,500			
Dow Jones NP15		100	900	3,770		
Dow Jones Mid-Columbia		120	5,830	3,310		
Dow Jones SP15		290	1,740	6,594		
NYISO A		61,394	118,351	91,067	88,826	1,268
NYISO G		50,385	62,913	26,018	52,996	4,848
NYISO J		26,492	40,495	13,214	10,245	758
NYISO A Off-Peak		18,054	15,580			
NYISO G Off-Peak		13,568	8,060			
NYISO J Off-Peak		9,380	3,160			
NYISO Zone A LBMP Daily Peak Swap		26,630				
NYISO Zone G LBMP Daily Peak Swap		10,666				
NYISO Zone J LBMP Daily Peak Swap		920				
MISO-Cinergy Hub LMP Swap-Peak		13,728	5,840			
MISO-Michigan Hub LMP Swap-Peak		1,040				
MISO-Illinois Hub LMP Swap-Peak		880				
Cinergy Hub Off-Peak LMP Swap		24,076	9,780			
Michigan Hub Off-Peak Calendar Swap		280	240			
Cinergy Hub Daily Peak Swap		440				
ISO New England Internal Hub Peak LMP		44,965	119,569	4,030		
ISO New England Internal Hub LMP Swap Off-Peak		25,445	41,573			
ISO New England Internal Hub Daily Peak Swap		59,270				
ERCOT Sellers Choice Peak Swap		860				
WTI Crude Oil Calendar Swap		377,086	41,931	152,680	33,785	
Dubai Crude Oil Calendar Swap		88,601				
Euro Gasoil 50 CIF vs ICE		70				
European ULSD (ppm) CIF Med Swap		6				
Euro ULSD 50ppm CIF Calendar Swap		16				
Gasoil Calendar Swap		419				
Argus Gasoline Crack Spread SW		9,052				
RBOB vs Heating Oil Swap		2,175				
RBOB Calendar Swap		13,562				
RBOB Bullet Swap		480				
RBOB Up-Down Calendar Swap		6,169				
NYMEX Brent Calendar Swap		1,557	126			
NYMEX WTI-Brent Calendar Swap		495	1,200			
Dated Brent Crude Oil Calendar Swap		1,425				
WTI Bullet Swap		34,373				
Gulf Coast Jet Fuel Calendar Swap		3,052	615			
Gulf Coast Heating Oil Calendar Swap		3,269	861			
Gulf Coast Gasoline Calendar Swap		21,921	3,352			
Gulf Coast No 6 Fuel Oil 3.0% Swap		27,673	21,515	200		
NY Harbor Residual Fuel 1.0% Sulfur Swap		38,366	15,163	625	375	
NY Harbor Heating Oil Calendar Swap		44,436	24,760	51,347	2,355	
NYMEX Gasoline Calendar Swap		3,738	21,697	20,279		
NY Harbor Conv Gasoline vs RBOB		600				
Singapore Jet Kerosene Swap		4,898				
Singapore 380CST Fuel Oil Swap		461	118			
Singapore Gasoil Swap		13,484	305			
Singapore Naptha Swap		2,750	150			
Europe SINPO Fuel 180CST CALS		20,213	6,629			
NW Europe Gasoline Swap-Argus Price		5,133	603			
Brent Bullet Swap		5,341				
Brent (ICE) Calendar Swap		38,305				
Mediterranean Premium Unleaded Gasoline (50ppm) Swap		26				
European Gasoil 0.2 NEW Calendar Swap		2				
Europe 1% Fuel Oil NWE CALS		3,047	1,382			
Europe 1% Fuel Oil RDAM CALS		681	707			
Europe 3.5% Fuel Oil NWE CALS		105	20			
Europe Naptha Calendar Swap		811	140			

New York Mercantile Exchange (NYMEX) (Continued)

NYMEX Division

FUTURE	CONTRACT UNIT	2006	2005	2004	2003	2002
European ULSD Rotterdam Calendar Swap		45				
Europe Gasoil 0.2 Med Calendar Swap		10	128			
Europe 3.5 Fuel Oil RDAM CALS		14,699	8,639			
NY Harbor No 2 Crack Spread Calendar Swap		48,323	37,792	120,780		
Gulf Coast Gas vs Heating Oil Spread Swap		3,378	1,800	3,650		
Gulf Coast Jet vs NYMEX HO Spread Swap		2,427	6,137	1,750		
Gulf Coast No 6 Fuel Oil Crack Swap		360	1,875			
NYH Conv Gas vs NY Unleaded Gas Spread Swap		200				
NY Harbor Residual Fuel Oil Crack Swap		4,877	4,700			
Los Angeles Jet Fuel vs NYH #2 Heating Oil Spread Swap		5,550				
Gasoline vs. Heating Oil Swap		1,646	12,307	20,795	150	
US Gulf Coast No 2 Crack Spread Calendar		1,203	704	1,375		
US Gulf Coast Unleaded 87 Crack Spread Calendar		19,933	5,876	45,775		
NY Harbor Unleaded Crack Spread Calendar		3,775	32,542	45,336		
No 2 Up-Down Spread Calendar Swap		4,193	1,848	2,352		
Unleaded 87 Up-Down Calendar Swap		12,010	2,525	6,675		
Singapore Jet Kerosene vs Gasoil Spread Swap		3,075				
RBOB Crack Spread		13,254				
Singapore Fuel Oil Spread Swap		913	95			
WTI-Brent (ICE) Calendar Swap		35,343				
WTI-Brent (ICE) Bullet Swap		200				
Brent-Dubai Swap		15,455				
European Gasoil 0.2 CIF NEW vs Gasoil Swap		30				
European Gasoil 0.2 FOB MED vs Gasoil Swap		75				
European Gasoil 0.2 Rotterdam Barges vs Gasoil Swap		15				
European Naptha Crack Spread		2,332				
European Gasoil (10ppm) Rotterdam Barges vs Gasoil		27				
East/West Fuel Oil Spread Swap		2,069	668			
European ULSD (50ppm) CIF NEW vs Gasoil		148				
European 3.5% Fueal Oil Spread		5				
1% Fuel Oil New Crack Spread Swap		95				
3.5% Fuel Oil Rotterdam Crack Swap		152				
High-Low Sulfur Fuel Oil Spread Swap		1,701	592			
Dated-to-Frontline Brent Swap		21,394				
Singapore Gasoil vs Rotterdam Gasoil Swap		5,610				
European Gasoil Crack Spread Swap		14,040				
TD5 West Africa to US Atlantic Coast Freight		65	810			
TD7 North Sea to Europe Freight		30				
TD3 Middle Eastern Gulf to Japan Freight		30	125			
European Jet CIF NEW vs Gasoil Swap		480				
European Jet Rotterdam Barges vs Gasoil Swap		5				
TC2 Rotterdam to US Atlantic Coast		630	460			
Nitrogen Oxide (NOX) Emissions		5	131			
Sulfur Dioxide (SO2) Emissions		4,105				
Sugar #11		10				
Total Futures		**178,934,185**	**141,201,756**	**110,054,812**	**92,246,019**	**92,324,686**

GLOBEX Futures Traded on NYMEX

FUTURE	CONTRACT UNIT	2006	2005	2004	2003	2002
Crude Oil miNY		9,323,467				
Brent Crude Oil		1,442				
Brent Crude Oil miNY		11				
Gasoil Rotterdam Physical		13				
Heating Oil miNY		422,248				
RBOB Gasoline miNY		872				
Natural Gas miNY		2,035,824				
Palladium miNY		3				
Brent Bullet Swap		20,432				
RBOB Financial		3,020				
WTI Financial		820,579				
Henry Hub Financial Last Day		28,495				
Henry Hub Full Penultimate		6,540				
Heating Oil Financial		19,231				
Gold miNY		313				
Silver miNY		40				
Copper miNY		77				
Asian Gold		39				
London Copper		56				
Total Futures		**12,682,702**				
Total Futures**		**216,257,995**	**166,608,057**	**133,283,348**	**111,789,658**	**107,359,719**

VOLUME U.S.

US Futures Exchange (USFE)

FUTURE	CONTRACT UNIT	2006	2005	2004	2003	2002
Russell 1000 Index	100 USD x Index	688	251,293			
Russell 2000 Index	100 USD x Index	19,618	738,156			
CAD / USD	250,000	49	1,831			
CHF / EUR	250,000	18,984	60,801			
CHF / USD	250,000	122	841			
GBP / EUR	250,000	7,895	38,518			
JPY / USD	250,000	194	2,826			
USD / AUD	250,000	195	532			
USD / EUR	250,000	1,875	19,758			
USD / GBP	250,000	628	1,330			
Jumbo 2-Year Treasury Note	1,000,000 USD	525	1,760			
T-Notes (5-year)	200,000 USD	14,000	431,742	2,332,942		
T-Notes (10-year)	200,000 USD	66,630	365,369	2,818,977		
T-Bonds	200,000 USD	4,400	282,469	980,426		
Total Futures		**135,803**	**2,200,384**	**6,186,008**		

ONECHICAGO

FUTURE	CONTRACT UNIT	2006	2005	2004	2003	2002
Single Stock Futures		7,777,241	5,474,663	1,890,097	1,488,573	151,878
Exchange Traded Funds		9,124	14,162	29,585	127,424	32,203
Narrow-Based Equity Index		136,100	39,000			
Total Futures		**7,922,465**	**5,528,046**	**1,922,726**	**1,619,194**	**184,081**

Total US Futures Volume

	2006	2005	2004	2003	2002
TOTAL FUTURES	2,043,902,218	1,652,871,946	1,323,726,632	1,042,968,664	851,310,459
PERCENT CHANGE	23.66%	24.87%	26.92%	22.51%	35.30%

* Includes the New York Futures Exchange, New York Cotton Exchange and Coffee, Sugar and Cocoa Exchange.

** Includes Commodity Exchange, Inc.

Options Traded on U.S. Securities Exchanges Volume Highlights

2006 in Comparison with 2005

2006 RANK	EXCHANGE	2006 CONTRACTS	%	2005 CONTRACTS	%	2005 RANK
1	Chicago Board of Options Exchange	674,735,348	33.27%	468,249,301	31.13%	1
2	International Securities Exchange	591,961,518	29.19%	448,695,669	29.83%	2
3	Philadelphia Stock Exchange	273,093,003	13.47%	162,618,812	10.81%	4
4	American Stock Exchange	197,045,745	9.72%	201,631,832	13.40%	3
5	Pacific Stock Exchange	196,586,356	9.69%	144,780,498	9.63%	5
6	Boston Options Exchange	94,390,602	4.65%	78,202,185	5.20%	6
	Total Options	**2,027,812,572**	**100.00%**	**1,504,178,297**	**100.00%**	

Options Traded on U.S. Futures Exchanges Volume Highlights

2006 in Comparison with 2005

2006 RANK	EXCHANGE	2006 CONTRACTS	%	2005 CONTRACTS	%	2005 RANK
1	Chicago Mercantile Exchange (CME)	301,551,501	60.12%	207,233,185	56.32%	1
2	Chicago Board of Trade (CBT)	127,622,361	25.45%	113,505,455	30.85%	2
3	New York Mercantile Exchange (NYMEX)**	59,899,331	11.94%	38,002,895	10.33%	3
4	New York Board of Trade (NYBOT)*	11,920,477	2.38%	8,932,169	2.43%	4
5	Kansas City Board of Trade (KCBT)	515,479	0.10%	263,511	0.07%	5
6	Minneapolis Grain Exchange (MGE)	40,491	0.01%	32,464	0.01%	6
7	EUREX US	0	0.00%	800	0.00%	7
	Total Options	**501,549,640**	**100.00%**	**367,969,679**	**100.00%**	

* Includes the New York Futures Exchange, New York Cotton Exchange and Coffee, Sugar and Cocoa Exchange.

** Includes Commodity Exchange, Inc.

Options Volume on U.S. Futures Exchange 2002-2006

Chicago Board of Trade (CBT)

Option	Contract Unit	2006	2005	2004	2003	2002
Wheat	5,000 bu	2,597,975	1,870,541	1,465,760	1,788,500	1,773,559
Corn	5,000 bu	11,317,388	6,257,027	7,593,355	4,515,240	5,397,748
Oats	5,000 bu	25,738	22,320	36,498	36,163	90,780
Soybeans	5,000 bu	6,042,797	6,817,588	6,045,952	4,885,399	4,227,445
Soybean Crush	50,000 bu	6,828				
Soybean Oil	60,000 lbs	902,096	682,825	947,383	665,532	659,302
Soybean Meal	100 tons	746,185	685,830	971,335	546,267	404,351
Rice	200,000 lbs	26,868	17,834	22,064	34,978	35,272
Silver (5,000 oz)	5,000 oz	1,521				
Gold (100 oz)	100 oz	193,944				
T-Bonds	100,000 USD	20,731,673	15,661,021	13,788,908	15,180,025	15,324,548
T-Notes (10-year)	100,000 USD	61,888,144	55,648,782	56,878,013	41,165,629	31,741,521
T-Notes (5-year)	100,000 USD	11,585,131	17,691,564	17,215,903	9,697,455	7,533,556
T-Notes (2-year)	200,000 USD	804,975	23,251	10,206	11,874	32,468
30-Day Federal Funds	5,000,000 USD	9,424,628	6,534,587	4,707,103	1,614,319	
Binary		47,237				
Flexible US T-Bonds		392,648	600,641	193,663	57,442	38,456
Flexible T-Notes (10-year)		311,295	259,295	96,192	56,920	60,577
Flexible T-Notes (5-year)		24,100	4,000	29,900	200	4,225
Dow Jones Industrial Index	10 USD x Index	100,589	114,353	190,708	263,629	234,219
Mini ($5) Dow Jones Industrial Index	5 USD x Index	450,601	613,996	571,299		
Total Options		**127,622,361**	**113,505,455**	**110,764,242**	**80,521,459**	**67,566,482**

Chicago Mercantile Exchange (CME)

Option	Contract Unit	2006	2005	2004	2003	2002
Lean Hogs	40,000 lbs	225,013	198,274	179,093	129,227	156,699
Pork Bellies, Frozen	40,000 lbs	1,198	3,228	4,010	7,991	5,595
Butter	40,000 lbs	241	203	401	800	259
Nonfat Dry Milk	44,000 lbs	116				
Mini BFP Milk	100,000 lbs	549	796	1,654	1,269	2,107
Class III Milk	200,000 lbs	85,713	71,431	122,014	79,901	23,852
Live Cattle	40,000 lbs	930,169	502,021	500,927	664,291	476,467
Feeder Cattle	50,000 lbs	156,292	142,253	142,638	179,347	121,226
Random Lumber	100,000 bd ft	20,909	25,171	20,056	18,139	14,665
Euroyen	100,000,000 JPY	87	48	437	53	318
Eurodollar (3-month)	1,000,000 USD	268,957,052	188,001,048	130,598,377	100,823,779	105,580,961
British Pound	62,500	158,473	146,893	166,360	156,569	121,443
Canadian Dollar	100,000	375,257	231,329	190,976	206,862	153,329
Japanese Yen	12,500,000	544,716	419,232	465,261	489,123	849,646
Mexican Peso	500,000	371	1,284	3,664	5,050	5,688
Russian Ruble	2,500,000	433				
Swiss Franc	125,000	47,984	50,107	55,596	53,766	82,285
Australian Dollar	100,000	36,562	109,970	60,593	42,495	18,098
Euro FX	125,000 EUR	1,849,119	2,100,595	1,492,887	1,187,819	929,518
Euro FX European	125,000 EUR	190,610	72,119			
British Pound European	62,500	18,191				
Canadian Dollar European	100,000	7,256				
Japanese Yen European	12,500,000 EUR	53,753	50,996			
Swiss Franc European	125,000	6,773				
Nikkei 225	5 USD x Index	59,200	44,458	8,774	8,564	4,197
S&P 500 Index	500 USD x Index	15,785,802	9,810,489	5,834,225	4,986,456	5,235,388
E-Mini S&P 500 Index	50 USD x S&P Index	9,893,979	4,289,038	477,712	112,864	46,355
EOM S&P 500 Index	250 USD x Index	80,424				
EOM E-Mini S&P 500 Index	EOM x Index	147,471				
S&P MidCap 400 Index	500 USD x Index	435	670	375	780	2,573
NASDAQ 100 Index	100 USD x Index	71,499	35,306	37,612	50,439	71,991
E-Mini NASDAQ 100 Index	20 USD x Index	317,765	110,093	10,015		
Russell 2000 Index	500 USD x Index	5,812	4,779	6,205	4,048	4,602
E-Mini Russell 2000 Index	100 USD x Index	933,224	175,226			
CDD Weather	20 USD x Index	18,050	28,725	3,475	230	32
HDD Weather	20 USD x Index	75,277	16,400	11,527	501	281
HDD Seasonal Weather	20 USD x Index	114,000	310,925	39,650	3,390	
CDD Seasonal Weather	20 USD x Index	27,100	225,550	5,650	150	
HDD Seasonal Weather Strip	20 USD x Index	209,300	13,674			
CDD Seasonal Weather Strip	20 USD x Index	97,200				
Euro CAT Weather	20 GBP x Index	500	900	450		
Euro HDD Seasonal Weather	20 GBP x Index	2,000	33,625	13,950		
Euro CAT Seasonal Weather	20 GBP x Index	33,100	5,400			
Euro CDD Seasonal Strip Weather	20 GBP x Index	9,350				
Goldman Sachs Commodity Index	250 USD x Index	377	729	1,392	1,492	1,318
CSI Housing Index	250 USD x Index	2,799				
Total Options		**301,551,501**	**207,233,185**	**140,457,074**	**109,220,627**	**113,909,833**

Kansas City Board of Trade (KCBT)

Option	Contract Unit	2006	2005	2004	2003	2002
Wheat	5,000 bu	515,479	263,511	254,304	465,381	570,823
Total Options		515,479	263,511	254,304	465,381	570,887

Minneapolis Grain Exchange (MGEX)

Option	Contract Unit	2006	2005	2004	2003	2002
American Spring Wheat	5,000 bu	40,468	27,245	34,260	39,764	61,086
National Corn Index	5,000 bu	23	2,697			
Total Options		32,464	34,826	46,711	61,226	29,830

New York Board of Trade (NYBOT)** (Continued)

Option	Contract Unit	2005	2004	2003	2002	2001
Australian Dollar / Japanese Yen	200,000 AUD	2				
Australian Dollar / New Zealand Dollar	200,000 AUD	1				
Euro / Australian Dollar	100,000 EUR	1				
Euro / Canadian Dollar	100,000 EUR	6				
Euro / Swedish Krona	100,000 EUR	122				
Euro / British Pound	100,000 EUR	88	67	253	14	936
Euro / Japanese Yen	100,000 EUR	116	40	776	104	685
British Pound / Japanese Yen	125,000 GBP	14	17	209	156	16
Canadian Dollar / Japanese Yen	200,000 CAN	1				
New Zealand Dollar / US Dollar	200,000 NZD	2				
US Dollar / Canadian Dollar	200,000 USD	3	45	60	140	
US Dollar / British Pound	125,000 GBP	10	25	31		
Revised NYSE Composite Index	50 USD x Index	37,872	26,952	18,912		
Russell 1000 Index	500 USD x Index	142,299	103,944	61,264	1,449	9,905
Russell 2000 Index	500 USD x Index	32,362	36,305	734		
Russell 3000 Index	500 USD x Index	1,568	4,647			
Reuters-CRB Futures Index (CCI)	500 USD x Index	1,694	3,515	1,913	974	891
RJ/CRB Futures Index	200 USD x Index	1,539				
Total Options**		8,932,169	7,774,379	6,010,110	4,656,335	3,857,721

New York Mercantile Exchange (NYMEX)*

COMEX Division

Option	Contract Unit	2006	2005	2004	2003	2002
Gold	100 oz	3,708,573	2,889,803	4,667,523	4,310,318	1,948,564
Silver	5,000 oz	1,646,959	1,131,812	1,022,348	560,018	530,831
High Grade Copper	25,000 lbs	75,403	143,609	216,350	47,326	37,315
Total Options		5,430,935	4,165,224	5,906,221	4,920,341	2,516,710

NYMEX Division

Option	Contract Unit	2006	2005	2004	2003	2002
Platinum	50 oz	321	404	637	633	456
Heating Oil	42,000 gal	595,427	983,388	800,277	668,859	602,170
Heating Oil 1-month CSO		10,185	12,868	1,880	2,430	747
Heating Oil 6-month CSO		500				
Heating Oil APO		18,868	8,302	1,134		
Unleaded Gasoline	1,000 bbl	583,342	973,849	904,466	616,245	721,932
Unleaded Gasoline 1-month CSO		3,210	2,700	3,175	3,465	1,087
Unleaded Gasoline APO		2,227	5,841	300		
Crude Oil	1,000 bbl	21,016,562	14,726,263	11,512,918	10,237,121	11,460,857
Crude Oil 1-month CSO		1,209,952	440,234	357,156	164,928	92,603
Crude Oil 2-month CSO		100	510			
Crude Oil 6-month CSO		400				
Crude Oil 12-month CSO		24,750	12,267	9,600	825	2,905
Crude Oil One Day		21,416				
Crude Oil APO		838,985	45,250	23,622	131	
RBOB Gasoline		82,176				
RBOB Crack Spread		220				
RBOB 2-month CSO		25				
RBOB Average Price		142				
RBOB European Expiration		995				
Natural Gas	10,000 MMBTU	9,581,663	9,168,354	8,071,967	8,742,277	10,966,023
Natural Gas 1-month CSO		246,472	103,058	47,328	13,557	4,636
Natural Gas 2-month CSO		1,150	1,525			
Natural Gas 3-month CSO		24,556	3,175	500		200

New York Mercantile Exchange (NYMEX)*

NYMEX Division

Option	Contract Unit	2005	2004	2003	2002	2001
Natural Gas 5-month CSO		5,500				
Natural Gas One Day		795				
Gas-Crude Oil Spread	1,000 bbl	21,440	56,142	79,664	35,797	6,521
Heating Oil-Crude Oil Spread	1,000 bbl	29,862	82,505	98,503	28,747	6,364
PJM Monthly		247,040	73,640	3,985		
European Style Natural Gas		19,515,968	6,968,569	2,012,703		
European Style Crude Oil		379,250	119,218	17,080		
European Style Heating Oil		1,525	24,339	8,023		
European Style Unleaded Gasoline		3,372	25,270	12,270		
Total Options		54,468,396	33,837,671	23,967,338	20,515,440	23,868,006
Total Options*		59,899,331	38,002,895	29,873,559	25,435,781	26,384,716

Total US Options Volume

	2006	2005	2004	2003	2002
TOTAL OPTIONS	501,549,640	367,969,679	289,158,384	221,700,069	213,149,576
PERCENT CHANGE	36.30%	27.26%	30.43%	4.01%	26.88%

* Includes the New York Futures Exchange, New York Cotton Exchange and Coffee, Sugar and Cocoa Exchange.

** Includes Commodity Exchange, Inc.

Volume Worldwide

Australian Stock Exchange (ASX), Australia

	2006	2005	2004	2003	2002
S&P/ASX Index	110,769	106,237	66,256	67,769	
All Futures on Individual Equities	693,683	490,238	460,501	267,630	
Total Futures	**804,452**	**596,475**	**526,757**	**335,399**	
S&P / ASX Index	1,170,793	1,163,213	794,121	578,066	
All Options on Individual Equities	20,477,083	21,828,002	19,164,851	15,988,740	
Total Options	**21,647,876**	**22,991,215**	**19,958,972**	**16,566,806**	

BOVESPA, Brazil

	2006	2005	2004	2003	2002
Ibovespa Index	1,818,764	2,257,756	1,586,762	1,600,261	1,144,628
All Options on Individual Equities	285,699,806	266,362,631	233,759,713	175,622,679	89,740,269
Total Options	**287,518,570**	**268,620,460**	**235,349,514**	**177,223,140**	**90,884,897**

Bolsa de Mercadorias & Futuros (BM&F), Brazil

	2006	2005	2004	2003	2002
Arabica Coffee	528,462	485,902	620,997	478,544	446,115
Arabica Coffee, Mini	13				
Live Cattle	392,012	311,459	225,200	113,473	152,939
Live Cattle, Mini	61,935	24,984			
Feeder Cattle	296	3,031	1,024	9,475	1,295
Sugar Crystal	69,351	63,385	47,347	40,257	48,326
Cotton	2,920	3,338	60	172	75
Corn	135,188	97,795	52,600	43,902	16,616
Soybean Futures	98,112	47,360	7,225	2,917	624
Gold Forward	308	668	15	483	4,425
Gold	3,180	2,640	2,742		
Gold Spot	24,369	42,336	57,609	98,386	65,892
Anhydrous Fuel Alcohol	26,426	25,466	40,453	49,158	62,896
Bovespa Stock Index Futures	13,232,399	6,065,361	7,063,923	6,630,407	5,231,780
INrX-50	5,118	6,362	6,265	85	
IPAC	965	5,220			
Bovespa Mini Index	3,702,409	606,582	2,892,016	1,158,155	592,342
Interest Rate	161,654,736	121,249,186	100,290,263	57,641,625	48,568,401
Interest Rate Swap	192,356	260,404	1,005,212	888,957	474,713
Interest Rate x Exchange Rate Swap	398,757	382,326	1,189,805	3,520,170	3,185,443
Interest Rate x Reference Rate Swap	189,796	18,536	9,762	5,052	1,628
Interest Rate x Price Index Swap (formerly Inflation)	2,760,520	829,982	775,591	666,988	183,647
Interest Rate x Ibovespa Index Swap	1,813	1,760	1,175	435	224
Exchange Rate Swap	26,443	21,035	27,069	9,778	1
Price Index x Exchange Rate Swap	5,885	42			
Price Index	200	5,401	14,255	13,200	
Interest Rate x IBrX-50	7,448	776			
ID x US Dollar Spread Futures	1,016,176	926,171	536,358	731,544	586,143
FRA on ID x US Dollar Spread	14,396,347	20,642,962	33,326,518	22,823,905	18,571,494
ID x US Dollar Spread Swap	145,943	232,609	126,525	234,958	981,454
Mini ID x US Dollar Swap with reset	207,107	37,330			
ID x IPCA Spread	58,840				
Global 2010	820				
Global 2014	60	460			
Global 2015	702				
Global 2019	273	760			
Global 2027	449				
Global 2034	4,321				
Global 2037	270				
Global 2040	57,590	232,883	79,645	160	
US T-Note	630				
A-Bond 2018	2,186	396			
US Dollar	52,350,517	33,466,104	23,943,757	16,784,939	16,132,798
Mini US Dollar	5,053,580	827,427	608,772	625,382	182,673
US Dollar forward points	1,648,807	908,062	365,914	227,097	116,199
Euro	70				
Total Futures	**258,466,105**	**187,850,634**	**173,533,508**	**113,895,061**	**95,912,579**
Gold on Actuals	119,378	149,932	236,058	173,142	213,130
Gold Exercise	19,492	28,540	62,378	82,728	102,904
US $ Denominated Arabica Coffee	30,602	22,341	50,148	37,423	34,689
US $ Denominated Arabica Coffee Exercise	2,370	1,662	3,206	1,143	2,720
Corn	3,119				
Corn, Exercise	175				
Soybeans	1,345				

Bolsa de Mercadorias & Futuros (BM&F), Brazil   (Continued)

	2006	2005	2004	2003	2002
Live Cattle	987	71	550	764	
Live Cattle, Exercise	251		2	42	
Bovespa Stock	26,625	6,344	21,730		
Bovespa Stock Exercise	2,072	9,380	11,350		
Interest Rate	945,250	268,819	1,253,545	182,183	
Interest Rate (IDI)	9,279,101	2,058,806	2,224,832	1,772,583	2,539,353
Interest Rate (IDI) Exercise	18,080	147,840	154,100	155,263	15,910
Interest Rate (volatility)	933,445	539,825	879,575	9,810	
IDI Index (exercise)	105,410	237,895	131,099		
IDI Index (volatility)	1,848,810	351,575	143,180	1,185	
Fexible Bovespa Stock Index	199,557	85,279	687,412	1,216,418	578,467
US Dollar on Actuals	9,766,867	6,251,235	2,708,961	2,148,440	947,759
US Dollar Exercise	552,837	391,221	147,645	130,187	152,174
US Dollar Volatility	1,042,235	793,665	255,150	30,030	
Flexible Currency	206,128	207,585	866,474	949,200	1,098,543
Total Options	**25,104,136**	**11,595,830**	**9,894,430**	**6,890,541**	**5,703,209**

Budapest Stock Exchange (BSE), Hungary

(BCE merged with BSE in 2005)	2006	2005	2004	2003	2002
Feed Corn	5,050	6,431	9,617	12,513	9,450
Feed Wheat	840	755	1,351	711	1,316
Wheat	521	928	4,246	6,883	9,271
Euro Wheat	126				
Extra Wheat	124				
Feed Barley	238	41	366	354	118
Sunflower Seed	1,235	1,499	1,909	1,031	392
Rapeseed	471	148	270	24	
Soybeans	9				
Ammonium Nitrate	4	1	1	3	2
Gold	130				
Budapest Stock Index (BUX)	1,879,034	529,512	376,679	400,003	292,128
Budapest Stock Mid & SmallCap Index (BUMIX)	30	51	51		
5-Year Government Bond	2,500	500			
JPY/HUF	29,267	18,000	41,350	67,390	3,761
CHF/HUF	100,200	31,208	71,800	326,090	75,150
CZK/HUF	48,180	61,120	26,410	3,770	
EUR/HUF	2,688,100	682,116	583,060	514,451	
GBP/HUF	82,415	54,850	28,000	1,000	1,600
PLN/HUF	33,600	21,550	42,092	1,800	
TRY/HUF	66,500	41,500			
USD/HUF	814,635	494,057	227,235	36,586	125,689
AUD/USD	46,400	950			
CAD/JPY	19,000	34,900			
CHF/JPY	19,050	46,000			
GBP/USD	631,500	1,137,635	197,560	72,350	3,100
GBP/CHF	388,770	395,540	100,630	33,000	
GBP/JPY	361,450	368,703	311,030	4,800	
GBP/SEK	242,950	100,600	33,800	23,300	
EURO/CHF	86,350	67,850	38,700	43,575	
EURO/CSD	2,900				
EURO/CZK	35,600	58,620	2,200		
EURO/GBP	227,500	106,800	17,500	25,100	
EURO/HRK	13,000				
EURO/NOK	93,200	38,050	18,600	23,900	
EURO/JPY	198,151	465,122	46,200	8,200	
EURO/PLN	110,070	95,300	28,300	24,200	
EURO/RON	16,400	29,100			
EURO/RUB	19,600				
EURO/SEK	81,630	153,200	51,200	2,039,000	
EURO/TRY	379,473	105,740	1,500		
EURO/USD	1,117,803	1,112,158	501,448	249,750	41,800
DAUD/USD	4,300	31,800			
DCAD/JPY	150	1,950			
DEUR/CHF	1,300	2,300			
DEUR/CZK	1,300	6,000			
DEUR/GBP	1,600	4,800			
DEUR/JPY	13,400	43,100			
DEUR/PLN	300	7,200			
DEUR/USD	77,850	151,100			

Budapest Stock Exchange (BSE), Hungary (Continued)

(BCE merged with BSE in 2005)	2006	2005	2004	2003	2002
DGBP/CHF	26,000	12,400			
DGBP/JPY	39,500	52,600			
DGBP/USD	23,200	81,140			
DUSD/CAD	6,100	138,600			
DUSD/CHF	600	6,200			
DUSD/CZK	500	200			
DUSD/JPY	2,400	6,800			
DUSD/PLN	700	3,900			
USD/BRL	6,700				
USD/CAD	345,405	17,750			
USD/CHF	258,422	249,547	117,700	16,440	
USD/CZK	6,700	11,400			
USD/JPY	239,572	573,360	666,030	146,525	1,700
USD/MXN	3,400				
USD/NOK	2,200				
USD/PLN	8,600	57,500	5,400		
USD/RUB	22,810				
USD/TRY	305,634	253,532	3,800		
USD/SEK	5,100				
USD/UAH	10,000				
EUR (1 week)	910,300	12,300			
GBP (1 week)	2,100				
USD (1 week)	24,000	12,500			
DAUD/USD (1 week)	9,100				
DEUR/CZK (1 week)	18,000	750			
DEUR/GBP (1 week)	2,000				
DEUR/JPY (1 week)	26,450	4,500			
DEUR/PLN (1 week)	24,500	20,000			
DEUR/USD (1 week)	92,800	34,250			
DGBP/CHF (1 week)	28,400				
DGBP/JPY (1 week)	39,000	25,700	249,750	41,800	
DGBP/USD (1 week)	41,400	63,900			
DUSD/CAD (1 week)	22,650	400			
DUSD/JPY (1 week)	7,500	1,200			
AUD/USD (1 week)	500				
EUR/JPY (1 week)	22,350				
EUR/PLN (1 week)	4,000				
EUR/USD (1 week)	100,690				
GBP/CHF (1 week)	13,200				
GBP/JPY (1 week)	25,700				
GBP/USD (1 week)	34,350				
USD/CAD (1 week)	22,100				
USD/CHF (1 week)	4,900				
USD/JPY (1 week)	3,000				
All Futures on Individual Equities	919,426	737,069	707,875	694,553	452,638
Total Futures	13,656,165	9,322,332	5,440,102	8,176,981	2,411,412
Corn	527	365	432	888	305
Wheat	125	150	90	242	150
Sunflower Seed	180	55			
BUX	3,125				
MOL	300				
OTP	50				
US Dollar	2,000	11,000			
EUR	205,000	92,200	113,970	414,095	260,850
CAD/JPY (HUF settlement)	80,000				
EUR/CZK (Foreign currency settlement)	2,300	500			
EUR/CZK (HUF settlement)	2,200				
EUR/GBP	25,000				
EUR/JPY (Foreign currency settlement)	41,000	4,015			
EUR/JPY (HUF settlement)	500				
EUR/PLN	36,756	35,830	225		
EUR/PLN (HUF settlement)	1,200				
EUR/USD (Foreign currency settlement)	6,000	4,269	44	15	
EUR/USD (HUF settlement)	514,901				
GBP/CHF (Foreign currency settlement)	38,600	3,959			
GBP/CHF (HUF settlement)	500				
GBP/JPY (Foreign currency settlement)	25,200	4,829	10		
GBP/JPY (HUF settlement)	6,600				
GBP/USD (Foreign currency settlement)	500	515			
GBP/USD (HUF settlement)	800				
USD/CHF (Foreign currency settlement)	1,000				
USD/CHF (HUF settlement)	500				
USD/JPY (Foreign currency settlement)	30,500				
USD/JPY (HUF settlement)	1,400				
Total Options	1,026,764	160,617	115,219	436,890	285,955

Dalian Commodity Exchange (DCE), China

	2006	2005	2004	2003	2002
Corn	64,976,076	21,859,732	5,828,045		
No 1 Soybeans	8,897,061	40,035,707	57,340,803	60,000,808	12,689,935
No 2 Soybeans	1,925,226	541,093	114,347		
Soybean Oil	10,333,006				
Soybean Meal	31,549,669	36,738,182	24,750,958	14,953,398	4,404,134
Total Futures	**117,681,038**	**99,174,714**	**88,034,153**	**74,973,493**	**48,407,404**

EUREX, Frankfurt, Germany

(formerly DTB and SOFFEX)	2006	2005	2004	2003	2002
DAX	40,425,513	32,722,572	29,229,847	27,181,218	19,996,503
HEX 25	33,860	41,761	24,934	32,589	44,524
MDAX	395,550	72,351			
TecDAX	515,891	269,354	456,346	181,954	
DJ Global Titans 50	6,481	2,038	333	2,017	965
DJ Global Italy Titans 50	4,361	27,079	70,403		
DJ Euro STOXX 50	213,514,918	139,983,083	121,661,944	116,035,326	86,354,731
DJ Euro STOXX Automobiles	83,868	82,203	99,776	152,714	83,677
DJ Euro STOXX Banks	225,960	233,955	243,541	483,451	560,757
DJ Euro STOXX Basic Resources	21,200	31,221	18,018	10,185	
DJ Euro STOXX Chemicals	12,464	9,464	5,254	54	
DJ Euro STOXX Construction	7,492	2,343	573	481	
DJ Euro STOXX Financial Services	15,804	5,111	1,050	995	110
DJ Euro STOXX Food and Beverage	9,161	22,700	16,382	8,538	
DJ Euro STOXX Healthcare	12,982	9,694	4,288	3,281	9,037
DJ Euro STOXX Industry Goods and Services	17,537	11,220	844	230	
DJ Euro STOXX Insurance	192,065	169,198	236,325	323,207	151,250
DJ Euro STOXX Media	30,860	26,035	8,863	8,339	698
DJ Euro STOXX Energy	101,586	118,601	118,457	105,614	77,762
DJ Euro STOXX Non-Cyclical Goods and Services	8,326	5,910	2,035	444	
DJ Euro STOXX Media	2,441	9,568	1,983	42	
DJ Euro STOXX Technology	210,081	218,982	160,160	281,967	303,315
DJ Euro STOXX Telecom	246,288	177,863	182,949	192,907	279,535
DJ Euro STOXX Cyclical Goods and Services	17,618	12,963	5,358	40	
DJ Euro STOXX Utilities	107,036	75,356	12,705	16,927	1,304
DJ STOXX 50	1,064,167	807,761	798,106	970,107	690,719
DJ STOXX Mid 200	36,901	3,554			
DJ STOXX 600	21,783	895			
DJ STOXX 600 Automobiles & Parts	43,692	30,368			
DJ STOXX 600 Banks	185,682	84,118	32,222	8,595	25,376
DJ STOXX 600 Basic Resources	90,361	30,441	647		
DJ STOXX 600 Chemicals	18,340	3,861			
DJ STOXX 600 Construction & Materials	11,482	4,103			
DJ STOXX 600 Financial Services	14,349	9,695	166		
DJ STOXX 600 Food & Beverage	91,537	24,807	347		
DJ STOXX 600 Healthcare	171,262	117,720	70,931	41,394	100,674
DJ STOXX 600 Industrial G&S	81,265	21,844	1,527		
DJ STOXX 600 Insurance	120,278	65,660	18,803	170	
DJ STOXX 600 Media	25,242	14,955	305		
DJ STOXX 600 Oil & Gas	146,585	35,459	3,261		
DJ STOXX 600 Personal & Household Goods	21,262	7,187			
DJ STOXX 600 Retail	32,829	6,161			
DJ STOXX 600 Technology	89,405	55,280	15,887	8,331	13,306
DJ STOXX 600 Telecom	164,519	112,686	19,596	20,537	20,403
DJ STOXX 600 Tracel & Leisure	25,622	9,706			
DJ STOXX 600 Utilities	59,958	63,814	29,622	9,651	
Swiss Market Index (SMI)	11,369,444	8,639,822	8,098,575	8,969,235	7,019,626
Swiss Market Index Mid-Cap (SMIM)	29,643	4,638			
Volatility Index on Dax-New (VDAX)	1,419	166			
Volatility Index on SMI (VSMI)	211				
DJ Euro STOXX 50 (VSTOXX)	1,406	109			
Swiss Government Bond (CONF)	334,314	372,385	308,206	284,809	275,392
Euro-BUND	319,889,369	299,287,916	239,787,517	244,414,274	191,263,413
Euro-BOBL	167,312,119	158,262,122	159,166,394	150,087,139	114,678,996
Euro-BUXL	1,265,079	470,831		666	12,668
3-Month Euribor	767,458	688,831	585,142	503,951	527,815
Euro-SCHATZ	165,318,779	141,228,207	122,928,076	117,370,528	108,760,955
Exchange Traded Funds	17,569	13,425	78,393	187,996	56,126
All Futures on Individual Equities	35,589,089	77,802			
Total Futures	**960,631,763**	**784,896,954**	**684,630,502**	**668,650,028**	**536,013,920**

VOLUME WORLDWIDE

EUREX, Frankfurt, Germany (Continued)
(formerly DTB and SOFFEX)

	2006	2005	2004	2003	2002
DAX	61,411,659	53,633,130	42,184,611	41,521,920	44,027,830
DAX 1st Friday Weekly	148,881				
DAX 2nd Friday Weekly	100,406				
DAX 3rd Friday Weekly	122,774				
DAX 4th Friday Weekly	49,821				
DAX 5th Friday Weekly	10,543				
HEX 25	1,075	1,201	1,050	7,128	14
TecDAX	33,025	23,923	27,370	13,477	
DJ Global Titans 50 Index	10	15	29	48	40
DJ Euro STOXX 50 Index	150,049,918	90,808,086	71,406,377	61,794,673	39,477,430
DJ Euro STOXX 50 Index - 1st Friday	90,475				
DJ Euro STOXX 50 Index - 2nd Friday	79,783				
DJ Euro STOXX 50 Index - 4th Friday	76,568				
DJ Euro STOXX 50 Index - 5th Friday	48,623				
DJ Euro STOXX Automobile	40,516	35,719	24,536	50,673	35,303
DJ Euro STOXX Banks	105,512	119,125	150,913	413,834	898,989
DJ Euro STOXX Basic Resources	50				
DJ Euro STOXX Chemicals	1,540	458	2	2	
DJ Euro STOXX Construction & Materials	6,520				
DJ Euro STOXX Financial Services	2,000	250	160	307	146
DJ Euro STOXX Food and Beverage	2,000	17,910	300		
DJ Euro STOXX Healthcare	2,460	5,250	600	19	2,456
DJ Euro STOXX Industrial Goods & Services	3,150	1,050			
DJ Euro STOXX Insurance	36,561	46,600	91,371	269,736	114,021
DJ Euro STOXX Media	7,300	22,492	799		
DJ Euro STOXX Oil & Gas	108,053	90,726	46,243	63,427	64,012
DJ Euro STOXX Personal & Household Goods	906				
DJ Euro STOXX Retail	1,300	2,500			
DJ Euro STOXX Technology	68,125	58,830	28,102	86,830	382,141
DJ Euro STOXX Telecom	49,856	113,758	39,396	110,664	314,976
DJ Euro STOXX Travel & Leisure	15,552	18,700			
DJ Euro STOXX Utilities	87,546	33,230			
DJ STOXX 50 Index	63,064	29,052	14,952	55,417	39,594
DJ STOXX 600 Index	4,208				
DJ STOXX 600 Automobiles & Parts	3,100				
DJ STOXX 600 Banks	30,701	10,887	1,865		
DJ STOXX 600 Basic Resources	94,486	13,966	3,850		
DJ STOXX 600 Chemicals	1,610				
DJ STOXX 600 Construction & Materials	305				
DJ STOXX 600 Financial Services	3,600				
DJ STOXX 600 Food & Beverage	568				
DJ STOXX 600 Healthcare	18,971	32,984	20,017	11,270	45,040
DJ STOXX 600 Industrial Goods & Services	41,602	1,360			
DJ STOXX 600 Insurance	11,604	8,399			
DJ STOXX 600 Media	5,206	310			
DJ STOXX 600 Oil & Gas	55,822	29,824			
DJ STOXX 600 Retail	320				
DJ STOXX 600 Technology	4,081	600	1,000	4	
DJ STOXX 600 Telecom	52,023	27,723	3,405	2	
DJ STOXX 600 Travel & Leisure	18,761	486			
DJ STOXX 600 Utilities	23,308	13,679	1,000	1,633	
DJ STOXX Mid 200 Index	52,899	1,584			
Swiss Market Index (SMI)	3,948,593	4,134,470	3,645,596	3,983,918	4,230,082
Swiss Market Index (SMI) - 1st Friday	4,810				
Swiss Market Index (SMI) - 2nd Friday	7,342				
Swiss Market Index (SMI) - 4th Friday	4,424				
Swiss Market Index (SMI) - 5th Friday	4,017				
Swiss Market Index Mid-Cap (SMIM)	14,616				
Euro-BUND	41,764,550	39,014,844	30,896,920	27,316,536	18,125,981
Euro-SCHATZ	17,344,245	11,546,405	9,782,863	11,723,090	8,954,263
Euro-BOBL	17,220,011	7,990,587	10,829,250	10,498,534	4,529,387
All Options on Individual SMI Component Equities	57,323,550	58,463,793	47,714,268	46,302,221	34,496,338
All Options on Nordic Equities	16,396,662	16,109,249	17,836,215	13,265,471	20,601,113
All Options on Dutch Equities	10,420,237	12,834,633	8,364,977	6,862,703	2,708,256
All Options on Exchange Traded Funds	15,732	42,278	85,478	70,350	6,069
All Options on French Equities	6,667,994	4,867,961	2,743,950	1,487,428	246,562
All Options on German Equities	180,695,967	162,437,728	134,857,678	120,211,761	85,111,674
All Options on Italian Equities	1,006,419	785,918	187,948	80,041	16,675
All Options on Spanish Equities	22,988				
All Options on US Equities	9,235	419,511	15,207	30,198	123,966
Total Options	**566,120,139**	**463,851,198**	**381,008,508**	**346,282,284**	**265,186,953**

EURONEXT, Amsterdam

(Formerly EOE, AFM and AEX, Netherlands)	2006	2005	2004	2003	2002
Potatoes (FAP)	14,517	27,867	11,876		
AEX Stock Index (FTI)	11,165,258	7,397,665	5,651,747	5,215,465	4,231,053
Light AEX Stock Index (FTIL)	1,599	14,704	5,827	6,639	12,401
Euro/US Dollar (FED)	7,474	5,640	2,026	1,405	568
US Dollar/Euro (FDE)	1,333	1,795	1,959	1,088	1,077
Total Futures	**11,190,181**	**7,447,671**	**5,701,122**	**5,298,861**	**4,328,952**
Potato (OPA)	2,639	7,104	2,426		
Euro / US Dollar (EDX)	651,810	290,839	139,758	74,279	21,692
US Dollar / Euro	81,229	113,118	99,322	64,045	40,677
EOE Stock Index	23,694,580	19,753,393	17,093,573	14,120,099	9,133,875
AEX Index Weekly (AX1)	627,717				
AEX Index Weekly (AX2)	598,614				
AEX Index Weekly (AX4)	619,673				
AEX Index Weekly (AX5)	233,221				
Light AEX Stock Index (AEXL)	18,148	23,934	34,539	131,209	86,403
All Options on Individual Equities	89,115,941	71,297,264	60,196,898	59,754,703	64,076,106
Total Options	**115,643,572**	**91,485,652**	**77,566,516**	**74,145,895**	**73,368,051**

EURONEXT, Brussels

(Formerly BELFOX)	2006	2005	2004	2003	2002
Bel 20 Index (BXF)	654,520	603,069	759,710	328,673	507,229
Total Futures	**654,520**	**603,069**	**759,710**	**328,673**	**2,653,399**
Bel 20 Index	127,000	117,795	271,717	320,540	747,161
All Options on Individual Equities	518,489	392,377	326,844	319,850	450,734
Total Options	**645,489**	**510,172**	**598,561**	**640,390**	**1,197,895**

EURONEXT, United Kingdom

(LCE merged with LIFFE in 1996)	2006	2005	2004	2003	2002
3 Month Short Sterling	83,003,622	68,029,052	51,324,125	42,323,094	34,307,727
3-Month Euroswiss	10,743,902	8,286,258	7,296,932	5,009,460	4,976,206
3-Month Euroyen Tibor	99,543	22	736		
1-Month Eonia	5	2,640	35,152	58,341	
3-Month Euribor	202,091,612	166,682,115	157,746,684	137,692,190	105,756,584
3-Month Eurodollar	69,760	5,662,806	4,666,508		
Long Gilt	22,009,284	17,760,359	14,045,404	10,150,267	7,789,011
2-Year Swapnote EUR	274,459	322,212	458,492	580,516	977,127
5-Year Swapnote EUR	401,365	387,005	688,952	1,022,358	1,437,955
10-Year Swapnote EUR	405,011	434,759	653,046	1,031,016	1,613,672
10-Year Swapnote USD	14,898	63,566	2,968	28,595	50,102
Japanese Government Bond	140,487	101,127	80,569	44,613	37,723
FTSE 100 Index	25,120,880	21,522,583	20,772,878	20,252,114	17,238,726
FTSE Eurotop 100 Index	32,694	74,667	88,475	109,846	129,414
FTSE Eurotop 300 Index	789,255	539,802	814,030	344,100	
FTSEurofirst 80 Index	48,598	68,036	277,661	210,171	
MSCI Euro Index	18,036	21,114	60,414	107,207	114,576
MSCI Pan-Euro Index	701,066	521,591	474,949	563,944	552,460
FTSE Mid 250 Index	62,304	39,238	32,896	5,422	804
Other Bclear	19,033				
Cocoa #7	3,095,346	2,690,105	2,643,199	2,328,609	1,802,142
Robusta Coffee	3,550,938	3,263,253	3,054,386	2,320,831	1,905,319
Wheat	76,239	65,324	75,455	91,387	80,784
White Sugar	1,668,674	1,497,150	1,251,233	1,062,494	1,044,806
All Futures on Individual Equities	28,930,769	11,744,778	12,929,406	6,349,198	3,935,121
Total Futures	**383,367,780**	**309,779,562**	**279,474,981**	**231,708,154**	**184,026,644**
3-Month Short Sterling	34,231,229	25,096,889	16,139,006	14,162,149	7,364,057
3-Month Sterling Mid-curve	3,212,817	3,173,334	1,461,723	967,384	346,001
3-Month Euroswiss	9,897	44,103	49,251	65,925	81,467
3-Month Euribor	48,176,163	44,138,922	52,245,463	57,733,239	33,481,758
3-Month Euribor Mid Curve	7,355,609	7,017,840	6,433,100	4,907,879	1,419,271
FTSE 100 Index (ESX)	15,717,186	14,473,441	17,866,310	14,619,893	13,263,116
FTSEurofirst 80 Index	20	485	521	1,841	
FTSE 100 Index FLEX	1,979,620	1,189,652	1,178,067	1,066,997	595,486
Other Bclear	16,700				
Cocoa	102,819	95,814	170,079	188,822	194,682
US Dollar Coffee	467,706	237,544	248,990	143,148	139,394
Wheat	2,320	3,070	2,387	3,262	8,092
White Sugar	81,647	81,598	94,705	66,561	43,900
All Options on Individual Equities	20,757,421	9,085,505	11,578,961	10,108,068	12,889,422
Total Options	**132,111,154**	**104,649,117**	**107,484,253**	**104,117,793**	**69,954,984**

VOLUME WORLDWIDE

EURONEXT, Paris

(Formerly MATIF and MONEP, France)	2006	2005	2004	2003	2002
Wheat #2	407,843	217,171	160,200	114,758	107,602
Corn	72,044	81,965	71,124	90,973	98,654
Rapeseed	238,594	211,281	191,644	174,538	165,462
CAC 40 Stock Index 10 Euro	33,405,804	25,011,372	24,058,528	29,319,624	26,411,321
FTSEurofirst 80	26,412				
FTSEurofirst 100	990				
Total Futures	34,151,687	25,521,789	24,481,496	29,711,816	26,991,450
Rapeseed	26,843	8,192	8,075	7,003	9,834
Wheat	41,398	9,810	7,109	7,643	1,679
Corn	1,818	1,622			
CAC 40 Index, 1 EUR	1,376	31,069,890	63,152,339	73,668,131	84,342,670
CAC 40 Index, 10 EUR	6,633,635	2,802,039			
All Options on Individual Equities*	45,160,159	183,560,708	230,863,609	174,487,319	246,165,884
Total Options	**51,865,229**	**217,452,261**	**294,031,132**	**248,170,096**	**330,520,413**

Intercontinental Exchange (ICE), United Kingdom

	2006	2005	2004	2003	2002
Crude Oil, Brent	44,345,927	30,412,027	25,458,259	24,012,969	21,493,486
Crude Oil, Brent - Quarters	150				
Gas Oil	18,289,877	10,971,719	9,355,767	8,429,981	8,156,358
Gas Oil - Quarters	300				
Natural Gas - Seasons	42,660	11,520	15,090	600	450
Natural Gas - Quarters	16,080	9,045	24,045	1,590	4,155
Natural Gas Daily (NBP)	15	50	90	74,180	180
Natural Gas Monthly (NBP)	543,550	423,565	609,350	737,610	578,925
ECX European Emissions - Monthly	452,359	94,348			
WTI Crude - Monthly	28,672,639				
WTI Crude - Quarters	15				
Gasoline - Monthly	9,692				
Heating Oil - Monthly	199,187				
Rotterdam Coal - Monthly	45				
Rotterdam Coal - Quarters	630				
Rotterdam Coal - Seasons	30				
Rotterdam Coal - Calendar	120				
Richards Bay Coal - Monthly	60				
Richards Bay Coal - Quarters	15				
Electricity Baseload - Monthly	3,155	2,500	1,070		
Electricity Baseload - Quarters	930	1,380	900		
Electricity Baseload - Seasons	3,870	8,190	2,280		
Electricity Peak - Monthly	490	420			
Electricity Peak - Quarters	345	30			
Electricity Peak - Seasons	780	1,680			
Total Futures	**92,582,921**	**41,936,609**	**35,466,941**	**33,258,385**	**30,233,664**
Crude Oil	33,249	44,421	28,688	49,520	146,809
ECX CFI	560				
Gasoil	104,320	74,055	45,154	33,339	61,001
Total Options	**138,129**	**118,476**	**73,842**	**82,859**	**207,810**

Korea Futures Exchange (KFE), Korea

* Transferred from KSE	2006	2005	2004	2003	2002
Korea Treasury Bonds	10,343,605	11,223,244	7,352,307	10,285,042	12,777,991
5-Year Treasury Bond	1,807	567	61	171,538	
CD	101				
Monetary Stabilization Bond	414	2,757	2,621	207,209	1,688
*KOPSI 200	46,611,008	43,848,706	55,608,856	62,204,783	42,868,164
STAR Index	107,538	103,619			
US Dollar	3,104,641	2,667,005	2,090,291	1,506,123	1,434,591
Total Futures	**60,169,114**	**57,883,098**	**65,261,326**	**75,159,690**	**57,465,025**
*KOPSI 200 Index	2,414,422,952	2,535,201,692	2,521,557,274	2,837,724,953	1,889,823,786
*All Options on Individual Equities	1,195	3,655	1	8,159	57,918
Total Options	**2,414,424,147**	**2,535,205,347**	**2,521,557,276**	**2,837,734,344**	**1,889,908,138**

Italian Derivatives Market of the Italian Stock Exchange, Italy

	2006	2005	2004	2003	2002
MIB 30 Index	4,037,973	3,580,695	3,331,843	4,263,886	4,877,464
Mini FIB 30 Index	1,659,649	1,294,606	1,485,112	2,570,238	2,132,937
All Futures on Individual Equities	7,031,974	5,957,674	1,734,256	468,083	59,853
Total Futures	**12,729,596**	**10,832,975**	**6,551,211**	**7,302,565**	**7,071,028**
MIB 30 Index	2,819,916	2,597,830	2,220,807	2,505,351	2,588,402
All Options on Individual Equities	16,056,751	12,439,716	9,500,498	7,924,078	7,587,199
Total Options	**18,876,667**	**15,037,546**	**11,721,305**	**10,429,429**	**10,175,601**

London Metal Exchange (LME), United Kingdom

	2006	2005	2004	2003	2002
High Grade Primary Aluminium	36,418,131	30,426,465	29,232,921	26,953,102	22,330,491
Aluminium Alloy	444,738	501,960	429,459	703,356	895,726
North American Special Aluminium Alloy	1,031,411	1,001,412	1,192,100	833,022	173,127
Copper - Grade A	18,864,246	19,231,371	18,171,204	19,437,740	16,579,090
Standard Lead	4,568,140	4,061,819	3,786,375	4,504,246	3,411,156
Primary Nickel	4,177,557	3,482,593	3,177,206	4,220,434	3,187,275
Special High Grade Zinc	11,706,008	10,620,618	10,211,096	10,470,171	8,100,114
Tin	1,283,897	1,095,031	971,612	1,448,083	1,625,470
LMEX	1,496				
LMEmini Copper Grade A	1,411				
LMEmini Primary Aluminium	1,987				
LMEmini Special High Grade Zinc	283				
Polypropylene	13,303	15,770			
Linear Low	15,231	7,626			
Total Futures	**78,527,839**	**70,444,665**	**67,171,973**	**68,570,154**	**56,303,779**
High Grade Primary Aluminium	4,690,867	4,107,102	2,217,021	1,618,895	877,429
Aluminium Alloy	315	369,068	288	541	379
North American Special Aluminium Alloy	4,420	10,069	2,385	50	22
Copper - Grade A	1,850,993	2,091,198	1,721,914	1,239,523	888,068
Standard Lead	164,410	128,283	76,342	95,967	50,413
Primary Nickel	158,496	189,903	119,942	144,489	67,781
Special High Grade Zinc	1,335,184	1,011,429	471,097	386,652	300,347
Tin	17,315	14,012	3,227	8,070	14,671
Primary Aluminium TAPOS	93,540	129,657	55,539	137,598	74,943
Aluminium Alloy TAPOS	2,141				
Copper Grade A TAPOS	45,346	55,907	37,438	90,381	32,939
Lead TAPOS	3,335	8,116	10,653	1,551	1,697
Nickel TAPOS	14,502	12,610	4,014	4,950	6,642
Tin TAPOS	850	2,014	475		
NASAA TAPOS	1,170	33,194	1,632	768	
Special High Grade Zinc TAPOS	29,466	21,625	12,571	8,738	14,884
Total Options	**8,412,350**	**8,184,187**	**4,734,928**	**3,738,173**	**2,330,225**

Mexican Derivatives Exchange (MEXDER), Mexico

	2006	2005	2004	2003	2002
US Dollar	6,026,940	2,934,658	1,289,386	81,395	52,108
Euro FX	50,469	125			
IPC Stock Index	620,557	410,565	327,942	220,731	49,243
CETE 91	3,290,100	4,509,002	2,418,381	11,398,544	3,568,951
TIIE 28	264,160,131	99,830,916	206,027,203	162,077,312	80,595,463
M3 Bond	28,600				
M10 Bond	471,879	284,460	278,644	38,279	
All Futures on Individual Equities	3,000	19,400	13,455		
Total Futures	**274,651,676**	**107,989,126**	**210,355,031**	**173,820,944**	**84,274,979**
MXN / USD	2,343				
IPC Stock Index	115,531	38,329	35,943		
All Options on Individual Equities	448,120	149,091	4,290		
Total Options	**565,994**	**188,150**	**40,233**		

Montreal Exchange (ME), Canada

	2006	2005	2004	2003	2002
3-Month Bankers Acceptance (BAX)	16,702,302	11,157,298	7,765,060	6,578,451	4,789,319
2-Year Canadian Gov't Bond (CGZ)	85,301	132,637	218,069		
10-Year Canadian Gov't Bond (CGB)	7,691,797	4,692,287	3,005,359	2,397,119	1,803,420
S&P Canada 60 Index (SXF)	3,064,695	2,234,406	1,906,038	1,681,994	1,450,860
Gold Index (SXA)	23,645	9,898	774	1,454	739
Banking Index (SXB)	140	266	186	110	187
Information Technology Index (SXH)	22	172	726	6,890	7,071
Energy Index (SXY)	10,157	13,662	2,524	452	85
Total Futures	**27,578,059**	**18,240,633**	**12,900,821**	**10,676,279**	**8,058,498**
3-Month Bankers Acceptance (OBX)	605,806	377,370	265,937	341,245	57,950
Canadian Government Bond (OGB)	2,275				
US Dollar (USX)	31,262	7,264			
S&P Canada 60 Index (SXO)	57,974	27,897	38,892	38,221	47,749
i60 Index (XIU)	317,637	176,498	120,502	130,508	237,325
CDN S&P/TSX Capped Gold Index Fund (XGD)	144,695	111,502	54,561	18,199	
CDN S&P/TSX Capped Financials Index Fund (XFN)	130,730	99,079	73,006	101,914	
CDN S&P/TSX Capped IT Index Fund (XIT)	10,018	7,942	11,800	9,721	
CDN S&P/TSX Capped Materials Index Fund (XMA)	11,012				
CDN S&P/TSX Capped Energy Index Fund (XEG)	234,611	227,268	37,783	10,917	
All Options on Individual Equities	11,416,758	9,409,938	8,311,818	6,355,251	6,086,675
Total Options	**12,962,778**	**10,444,758**	**8,914,307**	**7,006,720**	**6,433,473**

New Zealand Futures Exchange (NZFOE), New Zealand

	2006	2005	2004	2003	2002
10-Year Government Stock	594	891	788	735	2,000
90-Day Bank Bill	1,801,132	982,302	491,706	484,263	607,453
Total Futures	**1,801,726**	**983,223**	**492,666**	**486,120**	**614,831**
90-Day Bank Bill	24,190	2,850	4,515	7,130	8,909
All Options on Individual Equities	111				1,428
Total Options	**24,301**	**2,850**	**4,515**	**7,130**	**12,187**

OMX Exchanges (OMX), Sweden

(formerly Copenhagen (FUTOP), FOME, Helsinki, Stockholm)	2006	2005	2004	2003	2002
Interest Rate	12,205,955	8,223,372	6,546,035	6,674,408	5,586,173
OMX Index	24,374,765	20,259,029	16,460,920	14,567,900	13,331,795
All Futures on Individual Equities	8,459,165	5,659,824	4,257,168	1,424,890	1,290,181
Total Futures	**45,039,885**	**34,142,225**	**27,819,175**	**24,926,194**	**22,799,941**
OMX Index	13,613,210	12,229,146	8,946,939	6,371,381	4,916,726
All Options on Individual Equities	64,514,641	57,138,565	58,171,571	43,098,768	35,795,942
Total Options	**78,127,851**	**69,367,711**	**67,267,464**	**49,941,546**	**41,302,030**

Shanghai Metal Exchange, China

	2006	2005	2004	2003	2002
Copper	5,393,419	12,352,026	21,248,370	11,166,288	5,796,300
Aluminum	13,931,476	2,125,020	6,829,499	2,155,498	2,355,796
Rubber	26,047,061	9,503,158	9,680,649	26,757,964	4,020,987
Fuel Oil	12,734,045	9,809,550	2,818,855		
Total Futures	**58,106,001**	**33,789,754**	**40,577,373**	**40,079,750**	**12,173,083**

Singapore Exchange (SGX), Singapore

	2006	2005	2004	2003	2002
Eurodollar	26,569	88,393	8,241,545	18,802,104	19,504,044
Singapore Dollar Interest Rate	5,978	18,680	42,486	58,353	128,034
Nikkei 225 Index	18,017,221	11,916,557	7,769,675	7,098,920	4,857,565
USD 'Nikkei 225 Index	871				
Straits Times Index	4	546	1,830	6,601	7,329
FTSE/China A50 Index	8,932				
S&P CNX Nifty Index	134,445	9,910	38		
MSCI Singapore Index	2,214,521	1,707,865	1,658,600	1,046,326	711,687
MSCI Taiwan Index	10,824,249	8,100,202	6,998,626	5,455,812	4,628,247
Euroyen TIBOR	3,538,237	2,774,916	2,490,390	2,015,211	1,812,175
Euroyen LIBOR	2,881	8,740	34,547	110,529	255,256
10-Year Japanese Gov't Bond	4	236	86	92	360
Mini Japanese Gov't Bond	1,427,458	1,241,616	931,110	745,091	630,761
Total Futures	**36,201,370**	**25,867,661**	**28,169,379**	**35,356,776**	**32,623,190**
EuroYen Tibor	8,700				
MSCI Taiwan Index	29,642	1,293	41,971	40,274	47,897
Nikkei 225 Index	358,031	156,449	205,417	249,087	201,206
Total Options	**396,373**	**158,467**	**249,378**	**291,448**	**264,205**

Taiwan Futures Exchange, Taiwan

	2006	2005	2004	2003	2002
TAIEX	9,914,999	6,917,375	8,861,278	6,514,691	4,132,040
Mini TAIEX	1,760,583	1,088,523	1,943,269	1,316,712	1,044,058
Taiwan Stock Exchange Electronic Sector Index	1,459,821	1,179,643	1,568,391	990,752	834,920
Taiwan Stock Exchange Bank & Insurance Sector Index	786,477	909,621	2,255,478	1,126,895	366,790
Taiwan 50 Index	332	9,483	6,157	4,068	
MSCI Taiwan Index (MSF)	9,894				
10-Year Government Bond	40,675	2,887	67,705		
30-Day Commercial Paper Interest Rate	1,022	217	209,561		
Gold (GDF)	32,484				
Total Futures	**14,006,287**	**10,107,749**	**14,911,839**	**9,953,118**	**6,377,808**
TAIEX	96,929,940	80,096,506	43,824,511	21,720,083	15,664,464
TSE Electronic Sector Index	773,353	680,026			
TSE Financial Sector Index	937,044	756,570			
MSCI Taiwan Index (MSO)	867,597				
All Options on Individual Equities	1,089,158	1,018,917	6,237,079	201,733	
Total Options	**100,597,092**	**82,552,019**	**50,061,590**	**21,921,816**	**15,664,464**

Sydney Futures Exchange (SFE), Australia

	2006	2005	2004	2003	2002
SPI 200	6,516,247	5,597,066	4,622,139	4,288,848	3,761,904
Listed Property Index	25,385	10,300			
Australian Dollar	1,361	3,446	41,862	25,566	29,076
30-Day Interbank Cash Rate	2,009,291	1,399,499	659,926	53,141	
90-Day Bank Bills	19,501,781	16,119,237	14,213,188	11,435,471	8,486,560
3-Year Treasury Bonds	31,017,644	22,862,363	22,805,279	19,246,934	16,459,043
10-Year Treasury Bonds	15,051,399	11,021,452	8,557,437	6,705,904	5,200,290
d-cypha NSW Base Load Electricity	10,707	5,692	3,700	2,730	160
d-cypha VIC Base Load Electricity	13,581	2,341	2,693	2,766	100
d-cypha QLD Base Load Electricity	9,532	2,956	1,378	1,335	80
d-cypha SA Base Load Electricity	2,127	1,322	1,630	1,420	
d-cypha NSW Peak Period Electricity	1,926	1,254	1,142	1,927	310
d-cypha VIC Peak Period Electricity	5,038	4,104	1,466	1,762	160
d-cypha QLD Peak Period Electricity	1,981	793	994	660	230
d-cypha SA Peak Period Electricity	110	161	358	235	45
d-cypha NSW Base $300 CAP	1,276	52			
d-cypha SA Base $300 CAP	62				
d-cypha QLD Base $300 CAP	986	595			
d-cypha VIC Base $300 CAP	1,590	308	10		
Fine Wool	2,686	2,207	2,013	2,467	1,755
Broad Wool	53	409	826	2,003	2,756
Greasy Wool	16,869	15,767	9,520	9,095	14,180
MLA/SFE Cattle	1,860	1,167	1,354	1,175	175
All Futures on Individual Equities	10,843	38,156	29,986	47,822	29,286
Total Futures	**74,204,335**	**57,091,807**	**50,968,901**	**41,831,862**	**33,987,967**
SPI 200	636,033	673,899	518,511	585,620	414,598
SPI 200 Intra Day Cash Settled	10,594	6,404	4,917		
90-Day Bank Bills	182,663	244,940	175,286	250,876	227,208
3-Year Treasury Bond	856,723	477,764	369,708	220,382	237,509
Overnight 3-Year Treasury Bond	1,522,000	1,212,700	1,262,942	1,151,097	1,048,753
3-Year Bonds Intra-Day	576,935	508,754	534,302	583,719	277,905
10-Year Treasury Bonds	52,623	40,041	60,619	38,972	24,037
10-Year Bonds Intra-Day	1,266	10,700	1,845	6,307	1,880
Overnight 10-Year Treasury Bond	76,909	57,700	71,140	86,313	22,629
d-cypha VIC Peak Period Electricity	5		65	5	
Greasy Wool	20	197	1,159	177	1,038
Total Options	**3,915,771**	**3,233,159**	**3,000,544**	**2,923,478**	**2,255,557**

Winnipeg Commodity Exchange (WCE), Canada

	2006	2005	2004	2003	2002
Wheat	66,555	87,634	87,758	59,194	89,136
Canola (Rapeseed)	2,607,354	1,822,985	1,737,972	1,547,283	1,828,122
Western Barley	195,024	136,564	204,635	200,701	212,019
Total Futures	**2,868,933**	**2,047,183**	**2,030,455**	**1,811,616**	**2,155,796**
Western Barley	1,080	876	3,273	2,778	1,819
Canola	26,523	27,111	20,568	28,368	35,470
Total Options	**27,603**	**29,447**	**23,841**	**31,160**	**37,487**

Hong Kong Futures Exchange (HKFE), Hong Kong

	2006	2005	2004	2003	2002
Hang Seng Index	12,718,380	9,910,565	8,601,559	6,800,360	4,802,422
Mini Hang Seng Index	2,140,242	1,501,342	1,457,681	1,248,295	1,107,964
H-Shares Index	4,880,470	1,978,673	1,743,700	47,941	
FTSE/Xinhua China 25 Index	8,154	2,882			
1-Month HIBOR	155	246	733	310	970
3-Month HIBOR	13,888	24,935	58,307	47,799	280,257
All Futures on Individual Equities	102,010	13,069	17,274	18,654	21,056
Total Futures	**19,863,299**	**13,433,386**	**11,884,152**	**8,174,652**	**6,228,037**
Hang Seng Index	4,095,679	3,071,822	2,029,068	2,118,792	1,070,431
Mini Hang Seng Index	53,456	30,595	26,882	32,131	6,176
FTSE/Xinhua China 25 Index	7,881	7,386			
H-Shares Index	758,247	257,425	77,758		
All Options on Individual Equities	18,127,353	8,722,393	5,611,832	4,220,638	3,724,760
Total Options	**23,042,616**	**12,089,621**	**7,745,540**	**6,371,561**	**4,801,367**

Zhengzhou Commodity Exchange (ZCE), China

	2006	2005	2004	2003	2002
Cotton #1	2,084,541	10,870,825	2,994,046		
White Sugar	29,342,066				
PTA	167,220				
Strong Gluten Wheat	14,676,238	16,620,096	11,587,269		
Hard White Winter Wheat	28,052	981,649	9,655,959		
Total Futures	**46,298,117**	**28,472,570**	**24,237,274**		

VOLUME WORLDWIDE

Kansai Commodities Exchange (KCE), Japan

(Formerly KANEX, FFE, OGE, OSE, and KGE)	2006	2005	2004	2003	2002
Red Beans	8,491	13,760	21,148	52,755	88,436
Imported Soybeans	1,497	10,264	31,310	28,938	30,108
Non-GMO Soybeans	19,460	98,435	585,339	1,121,863	1,591,835
Corn	121,135	765,921	2,406,808	1,881,771	1,331,933
Refined Sugar	4,225	4,290	4,287	4,263	4,296
Broiler	5,786	16,873	92,022	44,376	754,626
Raw Sugar	7,671	8,181	36,822	18,956	42,736
Soybean Meal	8,425	29,516	187,926	242,676	185,608
Raw Silk	1,446	6,346	6,665	8,009	69,609
Frozen Shrimp	66,651	511,944	1,385,143	1,144,264	1,937,842
Corn 75 Index	11,087	91,007	350,029	317,561	499,912
Coffee Index	59,627	269,269	726,741	1,274,190	961,715
Total Futures	**315,501**	**1,825,806**	**5,840,545**	**6,180,748**	**7,659,900**
Raw Sugar	2,982	2,944	2,928	2,931	3,040
Total Options	**2,982**	**2,944**	**2,928**	**2,931**	**3,040**

Central Japan Commodity Exchange (CJCE), Japan

(Formerly CCE, NGSE, NTE, and TDCE)	2006	2005	2004	2003	2002
Hen Egg	12,275	65,142	798,308	399,167	338,291
Gasoline	4,953,168	11,972,407	15,869,951	16,705,638	15,212,512
Gas Oil	8,882	37,087	1,056,257		
Kerosene	4,027,192	9,790,465	15,454,906	13,984,740	14,338,356
Ferrous Scrap	17,899	84,465			
Total Futures	**9,019,416**	**21,949,566**	**33,193,259**	**31,538,530**	**30,011,863**

Osaka Securities Exchange(OSE), Japan

	2006	2005	2004	2003	2002
Nikkei 225 Index	24,823,682	17,909,404	14,415,884	13,058,425	10,841,300
Nikkei 225 Index, Mini	6,215,507				
Nikkei 300 Index	124,913	141,534	167,399	172,862	293,438
Russell/Nomura Prime Index	6,252	19,414			
Total Futures	**31,170,354**	**18,070,352**	**14,583,283**	**13,231,287**	**11,134,754**
Nikkei 225 Index	28,456,731	24,894,389	16,560,874	14,958,100	9,428,235
Nikkei 300 Index	510	536	491	234	568
All Options on Individual Equities	759,780	1,206,987	1,481,415	45,412	21,415
Total Options	**29,217,021**	**26,101,912**	**18,042,780**	**15,003,746**	**9,450,218**

Osaka Mercantile Exchange (OME), Japan

(formerly KRE and OTE)	2006	2005	2004	2003	2002
Rubber (RSS3)	314,914	581,293	756,411	1,550,423	1,300,492
Rubber (TSR20)	34,031	212,805	826,045	1,985,225	587,641
Rubber Index	180,654	320,871	814,328	1,423,491	1,885,262
Aluminum	75,659	459,244	1,101,198	963,464	1,285,419
Nickel	11,014	28,044	344,571	220,618	69,133
Total Futures	**616,272**	**1,602,257**	**3,842,553**	**6,162,589**	**5,207,652**

Tokyo Commodity Exchange (TOCOM), Japan

	2006	2005	2004	2003	2002
Gold	22,228,198	17,958,240	17,385,766	26,637,897	20,506,652
Silver	858,153	817,624	1,473,370	1,160,565	930,886
Platinum	11,018,069	8,573,313	13,890,300	14,211,824	14,436,155
Palladium	361,478	323,347	438,934	275,322	87,883
Aluminum	157,781	219,694	321,131	329,565	513,892
Gasoline	12,932,848	17,448,561	23,648,587	25,677,079	20,866,237
Kerosene	4,492,904	7,295,741	13,036,277	13,208,350	10,482,433
Crude Oil	1,961,190	1,981,389	2,284,572	1,809,711	2,037,215
Gas Oil	2	6,312	235,844	372,977	
Rubber	9,661,388	7,156,225	1,732,645	3,568,929	5,551,837
Total Futures	**63,672,011**	**61,780,446**	**74,447,426**	**87,252,219**	**75,413,190**
Gold	14,690	33,843	64,308		
Total Options	**14,690**	**33,843**	**64,308**		

Tokyo International Financial Futures Exchange (TIFFE), Japan

	2006	2005	2004	2003	2002
3-Month Euroyen TIBOR	31,495,084	10,977,591	7,259,779	4,155,800	4,470,763
5-Year Yen Swapnote	8,430	42,500	245,049	205,092	
10-Year Yen Swapnote	5,250	36,443	147,482	408,025	
Total Futures	**31,508,764**	**11,057,134**	**7,655,510**	**4,771,917**	**4,470,763**

VOLUME WORLDWIDE

Tokyo Grain Exchange (TGE), Japan

(Formerly YCE, TGE and TSE)	2006	2005	2004	2003	2002
American Soybeans	1,259,515	2,050,803	2,125,458	1,745,697	1,001,747
Non-GMO Soybeans	9,885,557	10,964,812	9,971,499	6,735,421	3,416,660
Soybean Meal	5,677	9,503	43,553	52,039	210,829
Arabic Coffee	1,669,181	5,591,946	4,293,422	5,019,572	4,844,715
Red Beans	478,379	659,002	363,328	555,190	593,087
Corn	4,656,352	5,165,693	8,122,448	5,984,743	7,431,128
Raw Silk	9,430				
Refined Sugar	2,896	2,860	2,854	2,842	2,864
Robusta Coffee	206,546	662,994	427,466	617,327	460,507
Raw Sugar	928,316	465,625	355,659	371,896	709,394
Japan Raw Silk	4,740	113,938	239,446	919,049	698,321
Potato	336	95,392	869,589	894,160	738,569
Vegetables	9,823	173,098	47,215		
Total Futures	**19,116,748**	**25,957,307**	**26,870,498**	**22,936,885**	**20,178,141**
American Soybean	15,260	16,678	17,758	17,548	21,515
Corn	9,806	7,467	16,072	12,214	16,511
Raw Sugar	2,196	2,956	5,405	5,979	19,309
Total Options	**27,262**	**27,101**	**39,235**	**35,741**	**57,335**

Tokyo Stock Exchange (TSE), Japan

	2006	2005	2004	2003	2002
10-Year Government Yen Bond	12,049,979	9,844,617	8,025,268	6,465,073	6,356,612
TOPIX Stock Index	14,907,723	12,785,962	10,305,318	9,359,047	7,131,178
Total Futures	**26,957,702**	**22,630,719**	**18,331,928**	**15,965,175**	**13,630,046**
TOPIX	18,354	20,004	17,643	98,137	93,249
10-Year Government Yen Bond	2,060,624	1,699,037	1,262,994	972,518	1,036,395
All Options on Individual Equities	190,876				
Total Options	**2,269,854**	**1,719,041**	**1,280,637**	**1,070,655**	**1,129,644**

Total Worldwide Volume

	2006	2005	2004	2003	2002
Total Futures	**3,235,742,882**	**2,378,883,321**	**2,167,519,755**	**1,927,572,094**	**1,473,598,607**
Percent Change	**36.02%**	**9.75%**	**12.45%**	**30.81%**	**25.62%**
Total Options	**4,050,264,365**	**4,066,769,167**	**3,907,845,226**	**4,012,631,132**	**2,912,881,726**
Percent Change	**-0.41%**	**4.07%**	**-2.61%**	**37.75%**	**78.68%**
Total Futures and Options	**7,286,007,247**	**6,445,652,488**	**6,075,364,981**	**5,940,203,226**	**4,386,480,333**
Percent Change	**13.04%**	**6.09%**	**2.28%**	**35.42%**	**56.48%**

Non-US Futures and Options Volume 1989-2006

Conversion Factors

Commonly Used Agricultural Weights and Measurements

Bushel Weights:
wheat and soybeans = 60 lbs.
corn, sorghum and rye = 56 lbs.
barley grain = 48 lbs.
barley malt = 34 lbs.
oats = 32 lbs.

Bushels to tonnes:
wheat and soybeans = bushels X 0.027216
barley grain = bushels X 0.021772
corn, sorghum and rye = bushels X 0.0254
oats = bushels X 0.014515

1 tonne (metric ton) equals:
2204.622 lbs.
1,000 kilograms
22.046 hundredweight
10 quintals

1 tonne (metric ton) equals:
36.7437 bushels of wheat or soybeans
39.3679 bushels of corn, sorghum or rye
45.9296 bushels of barley grain
68.8944 bushels of oats
4.5929 cotton bales (the statistical bale used by the USDA and ICAC contains a net weight of 480 pounds of lint)

Area Measurements:
1 acre = 43,560 square feet = 0.040694 hectare
1 hectare = 2.4710 acres = 10,000 square meters
640 acres = 1 square mile = 259 hectares

Yields:
wheat: bushels per acre X 0.6725 = quintals per hectare
rye, corn: bushels per acre X 0.6277 = quintals per hectare
barley grain: bushels per acre X 0.538 = quintals per hectare
oats: bushels per acre X 0.3587 = quintals per hectare

Commonly Used Weights

The troy, avoirdupois and apothecaries' grains are identical in U.S. and British weight systems, equal to 0.0648 gram in the metric system. One avoirdupois ounce equals 437.5 grains. The troy and apothecaries' ounces equal 480 grains, and their pounds contain 12 ounces.

Troy weights and conversions: 100 kilograms = 1 quintal
24 grains = 1 pennyweight
20 pennyweights = 1 ounce
12 ounces = 1 pound
1 troy ounce = 31.103 grams
1 troy ounce = 0.0311033 kilogram
1 troy pound = 0.37224 kilogram
1 kilogram = 32.1507 troy ounces
1 tonne = 32,151 troy ounces

Avoirdupois weights and conversions:
27 11/32 grains = 1 dram
16 drams = 1 ounce
16 ounces = 1 lb.
1 lb. = 7,000 grains
14 lbs. = 1 stone (British)
100 lbs. = 1 hundredweight (U.S.)
112 lbs. = 8 stone = 1 hundredweight (British)
2,000 lbs. = 1 short ton (U.S. ton)
2,240 lbs. = 1 long ton (British ton)
160 stone = 1 long ton
20 hundredweight = 1 ton
1 lb. = 0.4536 kilogram
1 hundredweight (cwt.) = 45.359 kilograms
1 short ton = 907.18 kilograms
1 long ton = 1,016.05 kilograms

Metric weights and conversions:
1,000 grams = 1 kilogram

1 tonne = 1,000 kilograms = 10 quintals
1 kilogram = 2.204622 lbs.
1 quintal = 220.462 lbs.
1 tonne = 2204.6 lbs.
1 tonne = 1.102 short tons
1 tonne = 0.9842 long ton

U.S. dry volumes and conversions:
1 pint = 33.6 cubic inches = 0.5506 liter
2 pints = 1 quart = 1.1012 liters
8 quarts = 1 peck = 8.8098 liters
4 pecks = 1 bushel = 35.2391 liters
1 cubic foot = 28.3169 liters

U.S. liquid volumes and conversions:
1 ounce = 1.8047 cubic inches = 29.6 milliliters
1 cup = 8 ounces = 0.24 liter = 237 milliliters
1 pint = 16 ounces = 0.48 liter = 473 milliliters
1 quart = 2 pints = 0.946 liter = 946 milliliters
1 gallon = 4 quarts = 231 cubic inches = 3.785 liters
1 milliliter = 0.033815 fluid ounce
1 liter = 1.0567 quarts = 1,000 milliliters
1 liter = 33.815 fluid ounces
1 imperial gallon = 277.42 cubic inches = 1.2 U.S. gallons = 4.546 liters

ENERGY CONVERSION FACTORS

U.S. Crude Oil (average gravity)
1 U.S. barrel = 42 U.S. gallons
1 short ton = 6.65 barrels
1 tonne = 7.33 barrels

Barrels per tonne for various origins

Abu Dhabi	7.624
Algeria	7.661
Angola	7.206
Australia	7.775
Bahrain	7.335
Brunei	7.334
Canada	7.428
Dubai	7.295
Ecuador	7.58
Gabon	7.245
Indonesia	7.348
Iran	7.37
Iraq	7.453
Kuwait	7.261
Libya	7.615
Mexico	7.104
Neutral Zone	6.825
Nigeria	7.41
Norway	7.444
Oman	7.39
Qatar	7.573
Romania	7.453
Saudi Arabia	7.338
Trinidad	6.989
Tunisia	7.709
United Arab Emirates	7.522
United Kingdom	7.279
United States	7.418
Former Soviet Union	7.35
Venezuela	7.005
Zaire	7.206

Barrels per tonne of refined products:

aviation gasoline	8.9
motor gasoline	8.5
kerosene	7.75
jet fuel	8
distillate, including diesel	7.46
(continued above)	

residual fuel oil	6.45
lubricating oil	7
grease	6.3
white spirits	8.5
paraffin oil	7.14
paraffin wax	7.87
petrolatum	7.87
asphalt and road oil	6.06
petroleum coke	5.5
bitumen	6.06
LPG	11.6

Approximate heat content of refined products:
(Million Btu per barrel, 1 British thermal unit is the amount of heat required to raise the temperature of 1 pound of water 1 degree F.)

Petroleum Product	Heat Content
asphalt	6.636
aviation gasoline	5.048
butane	4.326
distillate fuel oil	5.825
ethane	3.082
isobutane	3.974
jet fuel, kerosene	5.67
jet fuel, naptha	5.355
kerosene	5.67
lubricants	6.065
motor gasoline	5.253
natural gasoline	4.62
pentanes plus	4.62

Petrochemical feedstocks:

naptha less than 401*F	5.248
other oils equal to or greater than 401*F	5.825
still gas	6
petroleum coke	6.024
plant condensate	5.418
propane	3.836
residual fuel oil	6.287
special napthas	5.248
unfinished oils	5.825
unfractionated steam	5.418
waxes	5.537

Source: U.S. Department of Energy

Natural Gas Conversions

Although there are approximately 1,031 Btu in a cubic foot of gas, for most applications, the following conversions are sufficient:

Cubic Feet			MMBtu		
1,000	(one thousand cubic feet)	=	1 Mcf	=	1
1,000,000	(one million cubic feet)	=	1 MMcf	=	1,000
10,000,000	(ten million cubic feet)	=	10 MMcf	=	10,000
1,000,000,000	(one billion cubic feet)	=	1 Bcf	=	1,000,000
1,000,000,000,000	(one trillion cubic feet)	=	1 Tcf	=	1,000,000,000

CRB Futures Market Service

CRB's *"Futures Market Service"* is a weekly publication designed to make you a more powerful trader through an understanding of the fundamental factors moving the commodity and financial futures markets.

The CRB *Futures Market Service* has stood the test of time with its status as the industry's oldest and most respected fundamental newsletter. The first edition was published on February 3, 1934.

Most traders make their trading decisions based on technical analysis and technical trading systems. However, combining both fundamentals and technicals gives you an even more powerful trading approach to the markets. Understanding the fundamentals helps you to gauge market direction, how far the market may move, and when the market may move.

We help you to understand these factors through our fundamental commentary and our weekly commodity and financial calendars. We analyze factors such as Fed policy, inflation, interest rates, stock market earnings and valuation, the dollar, metal and petroleum fundamentals, crop reports and global crop conditions, and livestock and softs fundamentals. We also use the Commitment of Traders to analyze how the big funds are impacting the markets.

Also included in the service is a weekly version of CRB's *Electronic Futures Trend Analyzer*, which is an automated trading system providing specific trade recommendations with exact market entry and exit points.

For more information, visit www.crbtrader.com, or call 800.621.5271

Commodity Research Bureau • 330 South Wells Street, Suite 612 • Chicago IL, 60606 USA
Phone: 312.554.8456 or 800.621.5271 • Fax: 312.939.4135 • info@crbtrader.com • www.crbtrader.com

Aluminum

Aluminum (symbol Al) is a silvery, lightweight metal that is the most abundant metallic element in the earth's crust. Aluminum was first isolated in 1825 by a Danish chemist, Hans Christian Oersted, using a chemical process involving a potassium amalgam. A German chemist, Friedrich Woehler, improved Oersted's process by using metallic potassium in 1827. He was the first to show aluminum's lightness. In France, Henri Sainte-Claire Deville isolated the metal by reducing aluminum chloride with sodium and established a large-scale experimental plant in 1854. He displayed pure aluminum at the Paris Exposition of 1855. In 1886, Charles Martin Hall in the US and Paul L.T. Heroult in France simultaneously discovered the first practical method for producing aluminum through electrolytic reduction, which is still the primary method of aluminum production today.

By volume, aluminum weighs less than a third as much as steel. This high strength-to-weight ratio makes aluminum a good choice for construction of aircraft, railroad cars, and automobiles. Aluminum is used in cooking utensils and the pistons of internal-combustion engines because of its high heat conductivity. Aluminum foil, siding, and storm windows make excellent insulators. Because it absorbs relatively few neutrons, aluminum is used in low-temperature nuclear reactors. Aluminum is also useful in boat hulls and various marine devices due to its resistance to corrosion in salt water.

Aluminum futures and options are traded on the New York Mercantile Exchange (NYMEX) and the London Metal Exchange. Aluminum futures are traded on the Tokyo Commodity Exchange (TOCOM), the Osaka Mercantile Exchange (OME), and the Shanghai Futures Exchange (SHFE). The NYMEX aluminum futures contract calls for the delivery of 44,000 pounds of aluminum and the contract is priced in terms of cents per pound.

Prices – NYMEX aluminum futures prices showed modest overall strength in 2006. Aluminum opened the year at about 120 cents per pound, rallied to 146 cents per pound in May, and then settled into a range of 110-130 cents per pound for the rest of the year. Aluminum at the end of 2006 was about 128 cents per pound.

Supply – World production of aluminum rose +6.7% yr/yr in 2005, the latest reporting year, to a record high of 31.900 million metric tons. The world's largest producers of aluminum are China with 25% of world production in 2005, Russia (11%), Canada (9%), US (8%), and Australia (6%). US production of primary aluminum in 2006 (through November, annualized) fell –1.0% yr/yr to 2.228 million metric tons, which was only about one-half of the record high of 4.654 million metric tons produced in 1980. US production of aluminum from secondary sources in 2005 fell –1.0% yr/yr to 3.000 million metric tons.

Demand – World consumption of aluminum in 2001, the latest reporting year for the series, fell -4.8% yr/yr to 23.613 million metric tons, which was moderately below the record high of 24.811 million metric tons consumed in 2000. US consumption of aluminum in 2005 rose +3.2% yr/yr to 6.800 million metric tons, up from 2003's 12-year low of 6.130 metric tons.

Trade – US exports in 2005 (the latest reporting year for the series) rose +30.2% yr/yr to a new record high of 2.370 million metric tons. US imports of aluminum in 2005 rose +12.9% yr/yr to a record high of 5.330 million metric tons. The US relied on imports for 44% of its consumption in 2006.

World Production of Primary Aluminum In Thousands of Metric Tons

Year	Australia	Brazil	Canada	China	France	Germany	Norway	Russia	Spain	United Kingdom	United States	Vene-zuela	World Total
1997	1,495	1,200	2,327	1,960	399	572	919	2,906	360	248	3,603	634	21,700
1998	1,627	1,208	2,374	2,340	424	612	996	3,005	362	258	3,713	585	22,600
1999	1,718	1,250	2,390	2,530	455	634	1,020	3,146	364	272	3,779	570	23,600
2000	1,769	1,277	2,373	2,800	441	644	1,026	3,245	366	305	3,668	571	24,300
2001	1,797	1,140	2,583	3,250	462	652	1,068	3,300	376	341	2,637	571	24,300
2002	1,836	1,318	2,709	4,300	463	653	1,096	3,347	380	344	2,707	605	26,100
2003	1,857	1,381	2,792	5,450	443	661	1,192	3,478	389	343	2,703	601	28,000
2004[1]	1,894	1,457	2,592	6,670	451	668	1,322	3,592	398	360	2,516	624	29,900
2005[2]	1,903	1,499	2,894	7,800	442	668	1,372	3,647	395	360	2,481	610	31,900

[1] Preliminary. [2] Estimate. Source: U.S. Geological Survey (USGS)

Production of Primary Aluminum (Domestic and Foreign Ores) in the U.S. In Thousands of Metric Tons

Year	Jan.	Feb.	Mar.	Apr.	May	June	July	Aug.	Sept.	Oct.	Nov.	Dec.	Total
1997	305	277	307	295	304	296	305	304	294	307	298	310	3,603
1998	309	280	312	305	316	307	319	318	309	315	307	317	3,713
1999	315	287	320	309	319	310	319	324	310	323	316	328	3,779
2000	329	308	327	316	327	299	296	296	291	300	289	291	3,668
2001	256	220	232	225	229	215	214	212	206	214	208	205	2,637
2002	210	197	220	216	228	225	238	237	227	235	232	241	2,707
2003	242	220	238	225	228	221	226	225	217	224	215	221	2,702
2004	216	202	217	209	217	204	209	210	203	211	207	211	2,516
2005	209	191	214	211	214	206	210	208	199	207	204	208	2,481
2006[1]	197	179	198	190	197	189	192	185	183	190	188		2,278

[1] Preliminary. Source: U.S. Geological Survey (USGS)

ALUMINUM

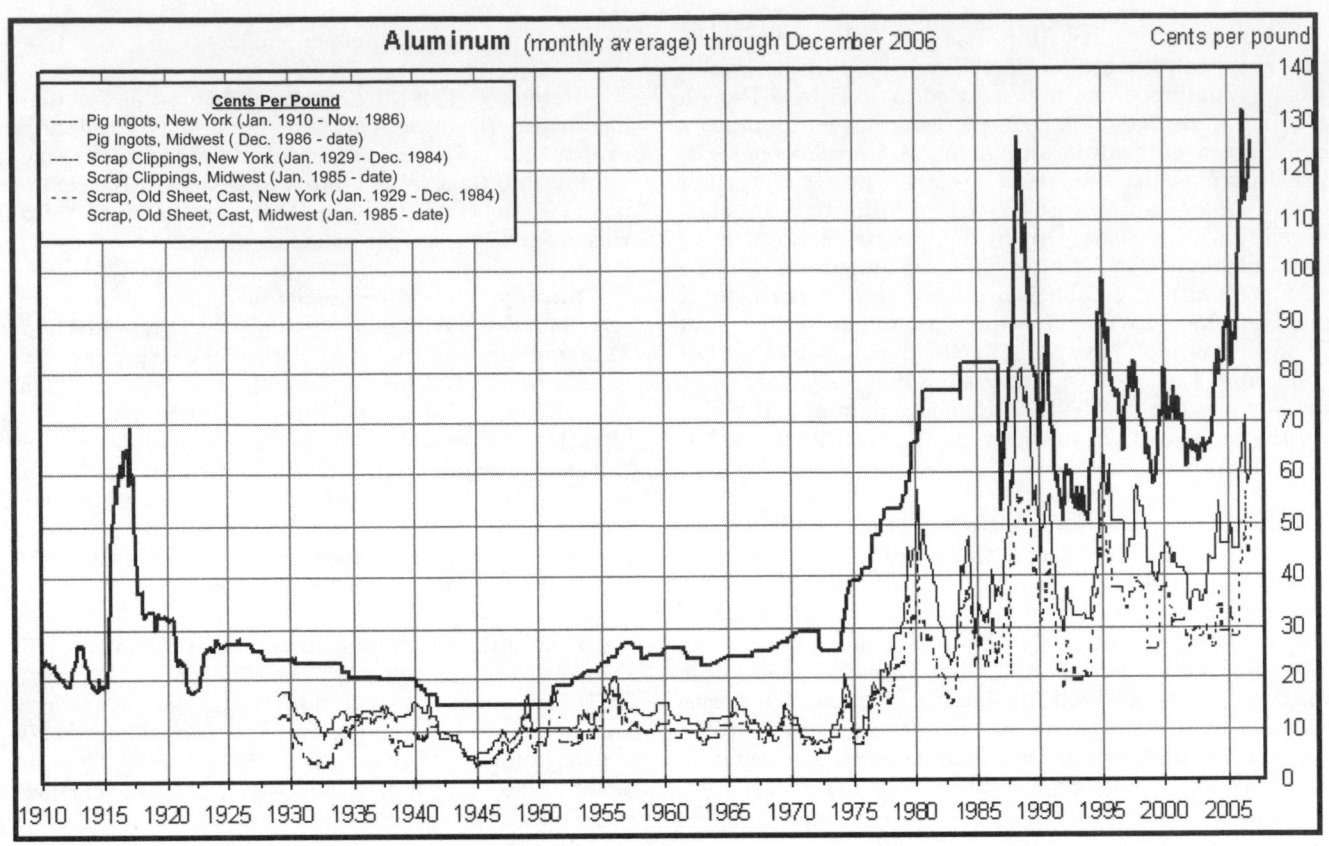

Aluminum (monthly average) through December 2006 — Cents per pound

Cents Per Pound
- Pig Ingots, New York (Jan. 1910 - Nov. 1986)
  Pig Ingots, Midwest (Dec. 1986 - date)
- Scrap Clippings, New York (Jan. 1929 - Dec. 1984)
  Scrap Clippings, Midwest (Jan. 1985 - date)
- Scrap, Old Sheet, Cast, New York (Jan. 1929 - Dec. 1984)
  Scrap, Old Sheet, Cast, Midwest (Jan. 1985 - date)

Salient Statistics of Aluminum in the United States — In Thousands of Metric Tons

	Net Import Reliance as a % of Apparent	--- Production ---		Primary Ship-	Recovery from Scrap		Apparent Con-	Plate, Sheet,	Rolled Structural	Ex-truded		Perma-nent				Total All Net Ship-
Year	Consumption	Primary	Second-ary	ments	OLd	New	sumption	Foil	Shapes[3]	Shapes[4]	All	Mold	Die	Sand	All	ments
1996	22	3,577	3,310	8,330	1,570	1,730	6,610	4,430	350	1,540	6,480	473	612	180	1,390	7,860
1997	23	3,603	3,550	8,880	1,530	2,020	6,720	4,710	315	1,610	6,800	468	670	153	1,410	8,210
1998	25	3,713	3,440	9,260	1,500	1,950	7,090	4,760	551	1,560	7,040	511	584	134	1,350	8,390
1999	30	3,779	3,700	9,840	1,570	2,120	7,770	5,000	549	1,640	7,360	484	1,020	158	1,790	9,150
2000	33	3,668	3,450	9,830	1,370	2,080	7,530	4,840	592	1,640	7,240	549	991	152	1,850	9,080
2001	35	2,637	2,970	9,310	1,210	1,760	6,230	4,370	512	1,550	6,580	484	873	251	1,760	8,340
2002	39	2,707	2,930	9,640	1,170	1,750	6,320	4,450	559	1,550	6,710	693	1,280	279	2,450	9,160
2003	41	2,703	2,820	9,760	1,070	1,750	6,130	4,370	531	1,670	6,580	719	1,210	285	2,400	8,970
2004	41	2,516	3,030	10,400	1,160	1,870	6,590	4,750	579	1,810	7,140	735	1,250	221	2,370	9,510
2005[1]	47	2,481	3,000	10,600	1,940	1,060	6,800	4,680	590	1,900	7,160	780	1,100	287	2,280	9,440

Net Shipments[5] by Producers — Wrought Products — Castings

[1] Preliminary. [2] To domestic industry. [3] Also rod, bar & wire. [4] Also rod, bar, tube, blooms & tubing. [5] Consists of total shipments less shipments to other mills for further fabrication. NA = Not available. E = Net exporter. *Source: U.S. Geological Survey (USGS)*

Supply and Distribution of Aluminum in the United States — In Thousands of Metric Tons

	Apparent Consump-	---- Production ----				Inventories -- December 31 --			Apparent Consump-	---- Production ----				Inventories -- December 31 --	
Year	tion	Primary	From Old Scrap	Imports	Exports	Private	Govern-ment[2]	Year	tion	Primary	From Old Scrap	Imports	Exports	Private	Govern-ment[2]
1994	6,879	3,299	1,503	3,382	1,365	2,149	57	2000	7,530	3,668	1,370	3,910	1,760	1,550	----
1995	6,295	3,375	1,505	2,975	1,610	2,099	57	2001	6,230	2,637	1,210	3,740	1,590	1,300	----
1996	6,610	3,577	1,570	2,810	1,500	1,860	57	2002	6,320	2,707	1,170	4,060	1,590	1,320	----
1997	6,720	3,603	1,530	3,080	1,570	1,860	[4]	2003	6,130	2,703	1,070	4,130	1,540	1,400	----
1998	7,090	3,713	1,500	3,550	1,590	1,930	----	2004[1]	6,590	2,516	1,160	4,720	1,820	1,470	----
1999	7,770	3,779	1,570	4,000	1,650	1,870	----	2005[2]	6,800	2,481	1,940	5,330	2,370	1,430	----

[1] Preliminary. [2] Estimate. [3] National Defense Stockpile. [4] Less than 1/2 unit. Source: U.S. Geological Survey (USGS)

Aluminum Products Distribution of End-Use Shipments in the United States   In Thousands of Metric Tons

Year	Building & Construction	Consumer Durables	Containers & Packaging	Electrical	Exports	Machinery & Equipment	Trans-portaion	Other	Total
1996	1,330	655	2,180	671	1,290	569	2,640	291	9,610
1997	1,320	694	2,220	708	1,360	626	2,990	318	10,200
1998	1,390	725	2,270	714	1,260	629	3,250	273	10,500
1999	1,470	760	2,320	739	1,330	661	3,600	293	11,200
2000	1,450	767	2,260	771	1,280	679	3,600	293	11,100
2001	1,500	681	2,250	686	902	641	3,190	367	10,200
2002	1,560	722	2,260	677	1,070	616	3,410	390	10,700
2003	1,560	689	2,240	653	905	659	3,540	415	10,700
2004	1,680	713	2,310	720	930	730	3,860	416	11,400
2005[1]	1,680	708	2,320	752	484	755	3,940	424	11,100

[1] Preliminary.   Source: U.S. Geological Survey (USGS)

World Consumption of Primary Aluminum   In Thousands of Metric Tons

Year	Brazil	Canada	China	France	Germany	India	Italy	Japan	Rep. of Korea	Russia	United Kingdom	United States	World Total
1992	377.1	420.4	1,253.8	730.5	1,457.1	414.3	660.0	2,271.6	397.0	1,242.0	550.0	4,616.9	18,529.5
1993	378.9	492.5	1,339.9	667.2	1,150.7	475.3	554.0	2,138.3	524.8	657.0	540.0	4,877.1	18,122.6
1994	414.1	559.0	1,500.1	736.3	1,370.3	475.0	660.0	2,344.8	603.9	470.0	570.0	5,407.1	19,670.8
1995	500.6	611.9	1,941.6	743.8	1,491.3	581.0	665.4	2,335.6	675.4	476.0	620.0	5,054.8	20,480.9
1996	497.0	619.9	2,135.3	671.7	1,355.4	584.8	585.1	2,392.6	674.3	443.8	571.0	5,348.0	20,596.4
1997	478.6	628.2	2,260.3	724.2	1,558.4	553.4	671.0	2,434.3	666.3	469.2	583.0	5,390.0	21,721.8
1998	521.4	720.6	2,425.4	733.8	1,519.0	566.5	675.4	2,082.0	505.7	489.2	579.0	5,813.6	21,797.2
1999	463.1	777.2	2,925.9	774.2	1,438.6	569.5	735.3	2,112.3	814.0	562.8	496.8	6,203.3	23,323.0
2000	513.8	798.7	3,499.1	780.4	1,490.3	602.4	780.3	2,224.9	822.6	748.4	575.5	6,079.5	24,811.4
2001[1]	550.8	759.6	3,545.4	772.9	1,590.9	558.0	770.4	2,014.0	849.6	786.2	433.3	5,117.0	23,612.8

[1] Preliminary.   Source: American Metal Market (AMM)

Salient Statistics of Recycling Aluminum in the United States

Year	Percent Recycled	New Scrap[1]	Old Scrap[2]	Recycled Metal[3]	Apparent Supply	New Scrap[1]	Old Scrap[2]	Recycled Metal[3]	Apparent Supply
		In Thousands of Metric Tons				Value in Millions of Dollars			
1996	40	1,730	1,570	3,310	8,340	2,730	2,480	5,200	13,100
1997	41	2,020	1,530	3,550	8,740	3,430	2,590	6,020	14,800
1998	38	1,950	1,500	3,440	9,040	2,810	2,160	4,970	13,100
1999	37	2,120	1,570	3,700	9,890	3,070	2,280	5,350	14,300
2000	36	2,080	1,370	3,450	9,610	3,420	2,260	5,670	15,800
2001	37	1,760	1,210	2,970	7,990	2,670	1,830	4,500	12,100
2002	36	1,750	1,170	2,930	8,070	2,510	1,680	4,190	11,500
2003	36	1,750	1,070	2,820	7,880	2,620	1,610	4,230	11,800
2004	36	1,870	1,160	3,030	8,460	3,640	2,140	5,600	15,700
2005	36	1,930	1,060	2,990	8,390	3,870	2,140	6,000	16,800

[1] Scrap that results from the manufacturing process.   [2] Scrap that results from consumer products.   [3] Metal recovered from new plus old scrap.
Source: U.S. Geological Survey (USGS)

Producer Prices for Aluminum Used Beverage Can Scrap   In Cents Per Pound

Year	Jan.	Feb.	Mar.	Apr.	May	June	July	Aug.	Sept.	Oct.	Nov.	Dec.	Average
1997	56.98	59.00	59.00	58.27	58.05	58.05	58.32	59.60	59.50	59.13	59.00	57.12	58.50
1998	54.53	57.00	57.00	52.95	49.85	47.09	45.50	44.50	46.21	44.50	44.50	46.14	49.15
1999	44.50	44.50	44.20	45.68	47.45	46.50	48.40	49.00	49.00	53.79	55.50	57.64	48.84
2000	58.58	62.90	61.50	56.85	54.50	54.50	56.50	57.00	57.00	56.20	53.50	53.50	56.88
2001	54.26	55.50	55.45	54.50	54.23	50.79	46.93	45.50	45.50	44.63	44.50	44.50	49.71
2002	44.50	44.66	47.21	49.41	48.68	48.50	46.89	45.06	46.36	47.07	49.76	50.29	47.37
2003	50.50	52.30	52.45	49.43	50.17	49.75	49.22	49.83	47.43	50.17	52.00	53.73	50.58
2004	57.44	61.64	61.65	63.00	57.85	60.00	62.23	60.57	59.48	62.07	61.45	63.81	60.93
2005	64.80	65.79	71.91	71.40	64.75	62.23	60.05	62.96	60.40	61.76	65.25	72.90	65.35
2006	81.03	85.76	85.13	91.08	99.41	83.50	83.40	82.74	80.70	79.66	83.90	85.00	85.11

Source: American Metal Market (AMM)

ALUMINUM

Average Price of Cast Aluminum Scrap (Crank Cases) in Chicago   In Cents Per Pound

Year	Jan.	Feb.	Mar.	Apr.	May	June	July	Aug.	Sept.	Oct.	Nov.	Dec.	Average
1997	36.09	36.50	36.50	36.50	36.50	36.50	36.50	39.36	38.60	38.50	38.50	38.07	37.34
1998	37.50	37.50	37.50	35.95	35.50	31.59	25.50	25.50	25.50	25.50	25.50	25.50	30.71
1999	25.50	25.50	25.50	25.50	26.45	29.23	36.83	37.50	37.50	37.50	37.50	37.50	31.87
2000	37.50	37.50	37.50	35.55	31.09	30.32	30.30	32.00	32.00	31.09	31.00	31.00	33.04
2001	31.00	31.00	31.00	31.00	31.00	31.00	28.29	28.00	28.00	28.00	26.40	26.00	29.25
2002	26.00	27.47	28.95	30.00	30.00	30.00	30.00	29.64	28.00	28.00	28.00	28.00	28.67
2003	28.10	30.00	30.00	29.00	29.00	27.90	26.68	26.00	26.00	26.00	26.00	26.00	27.56
2004	30.00	31.26	36.00	36.00	33.00	29.00	29.00	29.00	29.00	29.00	29.00	29.00	30.77
2005	29.00	29.00	31.61	33.00	31.33	28.00	28.00	28.00	28.00	28.00	28.00	39.71	30.14
2006	42.50	42.50	43.80	47.50	47.50	55.91	46.48	45.46	44.50	46.45	51.15	51.10	47.07

Source: American Metal Market (AMM)

Aluminum Exports of Crude Metal and Alloys from the United States   In Thousands of Metric Tons

Year	Jan.	Feb.	Mar.	Apr.	May	June	July	Aug.	Sept.	Oct.	Nov.	Dec.	Total
1997	31.0	25.5	22.5	33.0	24.1	34.9	23.9	33.2	34.4	26.5	33.0	30.0	352.0
1998	21.2	21.4	21.8	17.4	22.6	21.8	20.9	21.5	28.0	23.9	20.4	24.7	265.6
1999	18.6	26.7	23.9	22.7	25.2	27.7	23.7	27.5	26.1	31.4	30.3	34.8	318.6
2000	18.7	27.2	30.2	21.9	24.4	22.4	20.5	24.2	20.5	20.7	20.7	21.6	273.0
2001	19.6	16.1	18.9	14.7	16.8	15.6	12.4	14.5	12.6	18.9	16.7	15.1	191.9
2002	17.1	15.2	15.6	16.4	19.4	18.3	15.0	15.5	17.5	19.8	19.4	16.4	205.6
2003	14.3	14.8	14.5	16.9	17.0	17.8	16.5	20.4	18.7	22.9	20.4	19.7	213.9
2004	18.2	20.8	24.3	25.2	25.1	27.6	23.7	23.0	28.3	26.9	28.0	27.4	298.5
2005	26.5	23.4	24.3	27.0	28.9	29.6	25.9	33.1	27.2	29.5	29.6	23.9	328.9
2006[1]	40.0	26.0	30.5	29.4	38.8	25.3	23.7	32.0	26.1	25.8			357.1

[1] Preliminary.   *Source: U.S. Geological Survey (USGS)*

Aluminum General Imports of Crude Metal and Alloys into the United States   In Thousands of Metric Tons

Year	Jan.	Feb.	Mar.	Apr.	May	June	July	Aug.	Sept.	Oct.	Nov.	Dec.	Total
1997	145.0	147.0	209.0	196.0	198.0	167.0	157.0	152.0	150.0	175.0	146.0	222.0	2,060.0
1998	220.0	204.0	202.0	200.0	189.0	243.0	170.0	204.0	198.0	198.0	189.0	177.0	2,394.0
1999	191.0	200.0	240.0	311.0	281.0	258.0	213.0	219.0	178.0	202.0	178.0	180.0	2,651.0
2000	246.0	213.0	206.0	211.0	233.0	234.0	250.0	206.0	189.0	186.0	181.0	137.0	2,490.0
2001	193.0	200.0	237.0	197.0	209.0	179.0	201.0	198.0	252.0	220.0	248.0	227.0	2,561.0
2002	272.0	205.0	223.0	221.0	221.0	263.0	228.0	279.0	235.0	196.0	264.0	186.0	2,793.0
2003	215.0	246.0	350.0	202.0	265.0	261.0	233.0	194.0	215.0	210.0	233.0	243.0	2,867.0
2004	211.0	288.0	248.0	254.0	282.0	309.0	297.0	225.0	279.0	286.0	272.0	294.0	3,245.0
2005	334.0	289.0	262.0	372.0	372.0	324.0	324.0	264.0	282.0	298.0	240.0	299.0	3,660.0
2006[1]	348.0	247.0	289.0	353.0	315.0	298.0	249.0	315.0	289.0	259.0			3,554.4

[1] Preliminary.   *Source: U.S. Geological Survey (USGS)*

Average Open Interest of Aluminum Futures in New York   In Contracts

Year	Jan.	Feb.	Mar.	Apr.	May	June	July	Aug.	Sept.	Oct.	Nov.	Dec.
1999	----	----	----	----	1,032	1,461	1,875	1,984	1,767	1,244	625	615
2000	794	580	254	326	965	2,035	3,938	4,803	4,580	4,598	3,587	2,046
2001	2,446	3,173	3,450	3,529	3,269	3,724	3,891	3,459	2,753	3,728	3,644	3,276
2002	3,277	2,744	2,738	2,250	2,397	2,902	3,903	4,618	4,643	5,139	8,057	10,479
2003	9,573	9,163	6,960	7,190	7,686	8,529	8,402	8,445	7,655	7,283	8,434	9,427
2004	8,815	7,384	9,666	10,575	10,363	10,370	9,626	10,287	10,292	10,035	9,706	8,879
2005	8,183	8,487	7,464	6,612	5,654	5,061	4,359	3,223	3,225	2,676	2,232	1,670
2006	1,066	708	482	1,110	948	816	1,068	1,125	1,116	865	994	950

Source: New York Mercantile Exchange (NYMEX), COMEX Division

Volume of Trading of Aluminum Futures in New York   In Contracts

Year	Jan.	Feb.	Mar.	Apr.	May	June	July	Aug.	Sept.	Oct.	Nov.	Dec.	Total
1999	----	----	----	----	6,179	5,875	5,275	3,373	3,114	2,801	639	722	27,978
2000	1,224	2,394	1,664	1,901	3,859	3,566	6,295	3,767	5,993	6,365	5,055	4,016	46,099
2001	7,361	1,694	4,410	2,822	2,853	4,634	4,404	3,794	1,428	2,887	4,251	2,551	43,089
2002	2,774	4,635	4,924	2,593	5,388	5,389	8,953	4,194	2,571	7,328	16,185	9,066	74,000
2003	12,565	9,625	8,163	5,440	10,567	8,463	11,797	9,451	5,119	6,222	8,536	11,542	107,490
2004	9,425	9,621	9,548	9,770	5,438	5,453	5,280	2,063	5,533	4,822	2,525	2,691	72,169
2005	5,294	2,829	3,244	2,627	2,613	1,832	1,247	902	1,625	623	3,135	2,520	28,491
2006	633	245	1,343	1,558	210	471	1,046	1,546	662	323	842	270	9,149

Source: New York Mercantile Exchange (NYMEX), COMEX Division

Antimony

Antimony (symbol Sb) is a lustrous, extremely brittle and hard crystalline semi-metal that is silvery white in its most common allotropic form. Antimony is a poor conductor of heat and electricity. In nature, antimony has a strong affinity for sulfur and for such metals as lead, silver, and copper. Antimony is primarily a byproduct of the mining, smelting and refining of lead, silver, and copper ores. There is no longer any mine production of antimony in the US.

The most common use of antimony is in antimony trioxide, a chemical that is used as a flame retardant in textiles, plastics, adhesives and building materials. Antimony trioxide is also used in battery components, ceramics, bearings, chemicals, glass, and ammunition.

Prices – Antimony prices in 2006 rallied very sharply by 49.7% to a record high average of 233.30 cents per pound. Antimony prices in 2006 were more than three and a half times the 33-year low of 66.05 cents posted as recently as 1999. Bullish factors included stronger US and global economic growth, the weak dollar, and tight supplies.

Supply – World mine production of antimony in 2005 (the latest year available) rose by +7.8% to 139,000 metric tons. China accounted for 86% of world antimony production in 2005, down from 91% in 2002. After China, the only significant producers were South Africa (3.6% of world production) and Bolivia (2.2%). China's production level rose +9.1% in 2005 to offset all of the decreases in South Africa and Bolivia. Estimated US secondary production of antimony in 2005 rose by +0.5% yr/yr to 3,670 metric tons from 3,650 metric tons in 2004.

Demand – US industrial consumption of antimony in 2005 fell –21.8% to 8,910 metric tons from 11,400 metric tons in 2004. Of the consumption in the US in 2005, 40% was used for flame-retardants, 33% was used for metal products, and 27% was used for non-metal products.

Trade – US imports of antimony ore in 2005 fell more than 88% from 2004, which had been the highest year since 2000. (Gross weight fell 89% to 207 metric tons and antimony content fell 88% to 204 metric tons). Imports of antimony oxide in 2005 fell by –3.5% to 27,300 metric tons from 28,300 metric tons in 2004. US exports of antimony oxide fell by –56.8% to 1,400 metric tons from 3,240 metric tons in 2003.

World Mine Production of Antimony (Content of Ore)   In Metric Tons

Year	Australia	Bolivia	Canada	China[2]	Guat-emala	Kyrgy-zstan	Mexico[3]	Peru[4]	Russia	South Africa	Thai-land	Turkey	World Total
2002	1,200	2,336	173	100,000		150		356	1,000	5,746	1	250	114,000
2003	1,300	2,911	153	100,000	20	40		356	2,000	5,291	38	650	115,000
2004[1]	1,800	3,118	112	110,000	2,686	20		356	3,000	4,967	52	900	129,000
2005[2]	1,900	3,100	120	120,000	2,700	10		360	3,000	5,000	50	900	139,000

[1] Preliminary.   [2] Estimate.   [3] Includes antimony content of miscellaneous smelter products.   [4] Recoverable.
Source: U.S. Geological Survey (USGS)

Salient Statistics of Antimony in the United States   In Metric Tons

	Avg. Price cents/lb. CIF	Production[3]			Imports for Consumption				Industry Stocks, December 31[3]				
		Primary[2]		Secondary	Ore		Oxide						
Year	U.S. Ports	Mine	Smelter	(Alloys)[2]	Gross Weight	Antimony Content	(Gross Weight)	Exports (Oxide)	Metallic	Oxide	Sulfide	Other	Total[4]
2002	88.4	----	W	5,350	1,320	1,310	27,900	3,260	729	4,080	W	254	5,060
2003	107.5	----	W	5,600	428	412	26,000	2,910	578	3,540	W	2,200	6,320
2004[1]	130.3	----	W	3,650	1,820	1,750	28,300	3,240	483	2,330	W	16	2,830
2005[2]	160.5	----	W	3,670	207	204	27,300	1,400	425	1,690	W	17	2,130

[1] Preliminary.   [2] Estimate.   [3] Antimony content.   [4] Including primary antimony residues & slag.   W = Withheld proprietary data.
Source: U.S. Geological Survey (USGS)

Industrial Consumption of Primary Antimony in the United States   In Metric Tons (Antimony Content)

	Metal Products						Non-Metal Products					
	Ammu-nition	Antimonial Lead	Sheet & Pipe	Bearing Metal & Bearings	Solder	Total All Metal Products	Flame Retardants		Ceramics & Glass	Pigments	Plastics	Total	Grand Total
Year							Plastics	Total					
2002	W	887	W	42	89	2,760	4,930	6,310	505	565	837	2,460	11,500
2003	W	910	W	43	85	2,410	3,680	4,720	487	597	532	2,100	9,230
2004	W	1,200	W	51	85	3,020	4,680	5,910	535	536	W	2,480	11,400
2005[1]	W	W	W	33	81	2,940	2,650	3,600	421	535	W	2,360	8,910

[1] Preliminary.   [2] Estimated coverage based on 77% of the industry.   W=Withheld proprietary data.   *Source: U.S. Geological Survey (USGS)*

Average Price of Antimony[1] in the United States   In Cents Per Pound

Year	Jan.	Feb.	Mar.	Apr.	May	June	July	Aug.	Sept.	Oct.	Nov.	Dec.	Average
2003	121.53	109.15	118.48	119.49	119.77	119.07	107.86	105.01	105.01	105.01	102.76	97.52	110.89
2004	110.10	122.47	132.83	133.81	133.81	126.23	125.87	133.81	138.35	138.35	138.35	138.35	131.03
2005	138.35	138.35	146.63	147.42	147.42	148.66	156.49	157.48	168.96	174.63	174.63	170.72	155.81
2006	172.99	183.14	212.50	242.22	244.94	238.86	241.81	252.39	255.15	250.30	252.47	252.88	233.30

[1] Prices are for antimony metal (99.65%) merchants, minimum 18-ton containers, c.i.f. U.S. Ports.   *Source: American Metal Market (AMM)*

Apples

The apple tree is the common name of trees from the rose family, Rosaceae, and the fruit that comes from them. The apple tree is a deciduous plant and grows mainly in the temperate areas of the world. The apple tree is believed to have originated in the Caspian and Black Sea area. Apples were the favorite fruit of the ancient Greeks and Romans. The early settlers brought apple seeds with them and introduced them to America. John Champman, also known as Johnny Appleseed, was responsible for extensive planting of apple trees in the Midwestern United States.

Prices – The average monthly price of apples received by growers in the US rose by +35.0% yr/yr to 29.6 cents per pound in 2006.

Supply – World apple production in the 2005-6 marketing year fell –8.8% yr/yr to 41.837 million metric tons, which was a 10-year low. The world's largest apple producers in 2005-06 were the US (with 11% of world production), Turkey (6%), Italy (5%), and Germany (3%). US apple production in 2005-06 fell –5.5% yr/yr to 4.474 million metric tons, but remained above the 2-decade low of 3.866 million metric tons posted in 2002-03.

Demand – The utilization breakdown of the 2005 apple crop showed that 63% of apples were for fresh consumption, 18% for juice and cider, 12% for canning, 3% for frozen apples, and 2% for dried apples. US per capita apple consumption in 2005 was 16.9 pounds.

World Production of Apples, Fresh (Dessert & Cooking)   In Thousands of Metric Tons

Year	Argen- tina	Canada	France	Germany	Hungary	Italy	Japan	Nether- lands	South Africa	Spain	Turkey	United States	World Total
2001-02	900	467	2,055	1,522	605	2,220	931	500	591	962	2,450	4,274	45,440
2002-03	1,000	402	2,060	1,563	540	2,206	926	370	682	651	2,200	3,866	43,629
2003-04	900	379	2,080	1,518	500	1,878	842	385	769	888	2,600	3,988	45,079
2004-05	1,200	381		1,945	680	2,058	755		659	603	2,100	4,735	45,885
2005-06[1]	1,040	394		1,405	466	2,097	819		720	770	2,570	4,474	41,837
2006-07[2]		360		1,905	550	1,974	860			716	2,000	4,464	42,343

[1] Preliminary.   [2] Estimate.   *Source: Foreign Agricultural Service, U.S. Department of Agriculture (FAS-USDA)*

Salient Statistics of Apples[2] in the United States

	-- Production --		- Growers Prices -		--------------- Utilization of Quantities Sold ---------------							------ Foreign Trade[4] ------			Fresh Per Capita Con- sump- tion
					Fresh	--------------------- Processed[5] ---------------------					Avg. Farm Price cents	Farm Value Million	---- Domestic ----			
Year	Total	Utilized	Fresh cents/lb.	Pro- cessing $/ton	Fresh	Canned	Dried	Frozen	Juice & Cider	Other[3]	/lb.	$	Exports Fresh	Imports Fresh Dried[5] & Dried[5]		Lbs.
	-------------------------------------- Millions of Pounds --------------------------------------												------ Metric Tons ------			
2000	10,581	10,320	17.8	101.0	6,266	1,184	248	196	2,334	93	12.8	1,320.8	743.6	33.3	180.6	17.5
2001	9,423	9,209	22.9	108.0	5,468	1,257	221	249	1,945	71	15.8	1,453.1	593.0	21.2	193.9	15.6
2002	8,524	8,374	25.8	130.0	5,366	1,079	208	192	1,479	51	18.9	1,572.2	522.5	26.3	231.5	16.0
2003	8,793	8,703	29.4	131.0	5,462	1,236	182	283	1,435	106	20.9	1,817.2	528.3	33.0	186.6	16.9
2004	10,441	10,361	21.8	107.0	6,638	1,258	201	256	1,876	79	13.5	1,403.0	474.5	32.4	207.4	18.8
2005[1]	9,865	9,763	27.6	105.0	6,183	1,202	201	244	1,782	79	17.5	1,680.7	679.1		122.8	16.9

[1] Preliminary.   [2] Commercial crop.   [3] Mostly crushed for vinegar, jam, etc.   [4] Year beginning July.   [5] Fresh weight basis.
Source: Economic Research Service, U.S. Department of Agriculture (ERS-USDA)

Price of Apples Received by Growers (for Fresh Use) in the United States   In Cents Per Pound

Year	Jan.	Feb.	Mar.	Apr.	May	June	July	Aug.	Sept.	Oct.	Nov.	Dec.	Average
2001	15.8	15.2	14.6	15.7	15.2	14.9	15.2	17.3	21.2	24.8	23.5	23.1	18.0
2002	22.1	21.6	22.0	21.8	21.5	22.0	20.6	24.5	30.0	30.1	26.8	26.3	24.1
2003	25.8	24.6	22.6	23.4	21.8	22.4	20.8	34.6	27.1	27.9	29.7	27.9	25.7
2004	30.4	30.0	30.4	29.8	29.6	30.1	30.0	26.8	26.8	26.1	24.5	22.2	28.1
2005	21.6	20.3	18.4	17.3	17.4	16.2	15.7	21.1	30.9	28.8	29.4	25.8	21.9
2006[1]	21.7	20.6	25.6	24.7	23.8	27.7	33.6	39.9	39.9	37.3	34.1	26.1	29.6

[1] Preliminary.   Source: Economic Research Service, U.S. Department of Agriculture (ERS-USDA)

Arsenic

Arsenic (symbol As) is a silver-gray, extremely poisonous, semi-metallic element. Arsenic, which is odorless and flavorless, has been known since ancient times, but it wasn't until the Middle Ages that its poisonous characteristics first became known. Metallic arsenic was first produced in the 17th century by heating arsenic with potash and soap. Arsenic is rarely found in nature in its elemental form and is generally recovered as a by-product of ore processing. Recently, small doses of arsenic have been found to put some forms of cancer into remission. It can also help thin blood. Homoeopathists have successfully used undetectable amounts of arsenic to cure stomach cramps.

The US does not produce any arsenic and instead imports all its consumption needs for arsenic metals and compounds. More than 95 percent of the arsenic consumed in the US is in compound form, mostly as arsenic trioxide, which in turn is converted into arsenic acid. Production of chromated copper arsenate, a wood preservative, accounts for about 90% of the domestic consumption of arsenic trioxide. Three companies in the US manufacture chromate copper arsenate. Another company used arsenic acid to produce an arsenical herbicide. Arsenic metal is used to produce nonferrous alloys, primarily for lead-acid batteries.

One area where there is increased consumption of arsenic is in the semiconductor industry. Very high-purity arsenic is used in the production of gallium arsenide. High speed and high frequency integrated circuits that use gallium arsenide have better signal reception and lower power consumption. An estimated 30 metric tons per year of high-purity arsenic is used in the production of semiconductor materials.

Since roughly 75% of US arsenic production used to be used for wood preservative treatments, the demand for arsenic was closely tied to new home construction, home renovation, and deck construction. However, future demand for arsenic is questionable given its toxicity and the possibility of tighter environmental regulations in the future. In fact, in 2005 the percent of arsenic used for wood preservative treatments was down to 65%.

Supply – World production of white arsenic (arsenic trioxide) in 2005 fell by –0.4% to 52,500 metric tons from last year's level of 52,700 metric tons. The world's largest producer is China with about 57% of world production, followed by Chile with 22% of world production, Peru with 7%, Mexico with 3%, and Russia with 3%. China's production of arsenic was fairly constant at about 40,000 metric tons per year but that has dropped to about 30,000 in the last two years. The US supply of arsenic in 2005 rose by 32.2% to 9,142 metric tons from last year's 30-year low of 7,022 metric tons.

Demand – US demand for arsenic in 2004 fell by –68% to a record low of 6,800 metric tons from last year's level of 21,600 metric tons. Of that demand, 65% was for wood preservatives, 13% was for non-ferrous alloys and electric usage, 11% was for agricultural use, 8% was for glass, and 3% was for other uses.

Trade – US imports of trioxide arsenic in 2005 rose by 36% to 11,000 metric tons from 8,090 metric tons in 2004. US exports of trioxide arsenic were low at 327 metric tons, but still up +49% from the 220 metric tons in 2004.

World Production of White Arsenic (Arsenic Trioxide)   In Metric Tons

Year	Belgium	Bolivia	Canada[4]	Chile	China	France	Germany	Mexico	Namibia[3]	Peru	Phillippines	Russia[5]	World Total
1996	2,000	255	250	8,000	15,000	3,000	250	2,942	1,559	111	----	1,500	42,900
1997	2,000	282	250	8,350	15,000	2,500	250	2,999	1,297	637	----	1,500	42,000
1998	1,500	284	250	8,400	15,500	2,000	200	2,573	175	624	----	1,500	40,300
1999	1,500	437	250	8,000	16,000	1,000	200	2,419	----	1,611	----	1,500	41,800
2000	1,500	318	250	8,000	40,000	1,000	200	2,522	----	2,495	----	1,500	62,800
2001	1,000	846	250	11,500	39,500	1,000	200	2,381	----	2,800	----	1,500	63,000
2002	1,000	237	250	11,400	40,000	1,000	200	1,946	----	2,970	----	1,500	62,500
2003	1,000	276	250	11,600	40,000	1,000	200	1,729	----	3,000	----	1,500	62,400
2004[1]	1,000	168	250	11,600	30,000	1,000	200	1,829	----	3,500	----	1,500	52,700
2005[2]	1,000	150	250	11,500	30,000	1,000	200	1,650	----	3,600	----	1,500	52,500

[1] Preliminary.　[2] Estimate.　[3] Output of Tsumeb Corp. Ltd. only.　[4] Includes low-grade dusts that were exported to the U.S. for further refining.　[5] Formerly part of the U.S.S.R.; not reported separately until 1992.　*Source: U.S. Geological Survey (USGS)*

Salient Statistics of Arsenic in the United States   In Metric Tons (Arsenic Content)

	---------- Supply ----------				-- Distribution --		---------- Estimated Demand Pattern ----------						-- Average Price --			
	---- Imports ----		Industry			Industry	Agricul-			Wood	Non-Ferrous				Trioxide Mexican	Metal Chinese		
Year	Metal	Compounds	Stocks Jan. 1	Total	Apparent Demand	Stocks Dec.31	tural Chemicals	Glass	Preservatives	Alloys & Electric	Other	Total	-- Cents/Pound --			Imports Trioxide[3]	Exports
1996	252	21,200	----	21,400	21,400	----	950	700	19,200	250	300	21,400	33	40	28,000	36
1997	909	22,800	----	23,700	23,700	----	1,400	700	20,000	900	300	23,700	31	32	30,000	61
1998	997	29,300	----	30,300	30,100	----	1,500	900	26,500	1,200	300	30,100	30	40	38,600	177
1999	1,300	22,100	----	23,400	22,000	----	1,100	600	19,500	850	200	22,000	----	----	29,100	1,350
2000	830	23,600	----	24,430	24,400	----	----	700	21,800	700	250	24,400	----	----	31,100	41
2001	1,030	23,900	----	24,930	24,900	----	----	750	21,900	1,000	250	24,900	----	----	31,500	57
2002	879	18,800	----	19,679	19,600	----	----	700	17,300	650	200	19,600	----	----	24,700	100
2003	990	20,800	----	21,790	21,600	----	----	660	19,200	660	200	21,600	----	----	27,300	173
2004[1]	872	6,150	----	7,022	6,800	----	----	650	4,450	650	200	6,800	----	----	8,090	220
2005[2]	812	8,330	----	9,142	8,820	----	----	700	5,760	1,100	250	8,810	----	----	11,000	327

[1] Preliminary.　[2] Estimate.　[3] For Consumption.　Source: U.S. Geological Survey (USGS)

Barley

Barley is the common name for the genus of cereal grass and is native to Asia and Ethiopia. Barley is an ancient crop and was grown by the Egyptians, Greek, Romans and Chinese. Barley is now the world's fourth largest grain crop, after wheat, rice, and corn. Barley is planted in the spring in most of Europe, Canada and the United States. The U.S. barley crop year begins June 1. It is planted in the autumn in parts of California, Arizona and along the Mediterranean Sea. Barley is hardy and drought resistant and can be grown on marginal cropland. Salt-resistant strains are being developed for use in coastal regions. Barley grain, along with hay, straw, and several by-products are used for animal feed. Barley is used for malt beverages and in cooking. Barley, like other cereals, contains a large proportion of carbohydrate (67%) and protein (12.8%). Barley futures are traded on the Winnipeg Commodity Exchange (WCE), the London International Financial Futures and Options Exchange (LIFFE) and the Budapest Commodity Exchange.

Prices – The monthly average price for all barley received by US farmers in the 2006-07 marketing year (through February 2007) rose by +14.6% yr/yr to $2.83 per bushel.

Supply – World barley production in the 2006-07 marketing year rose +0.4%yr/yr to 138.678 million metric tons. The world's largest barley crop of 179.038 million metric tons occurred in 1990-91. The world's largest barley producers are the European Union with 39.6% of world production in 2006-07, Russia (13.3%), Ukraine (8.5%), Canada (7.2%), Turkey (5.2%), Australia (3.0%), and the US (2.8%).

US barley production in the 2006-07 marketing year fell by –15.0% yr/yr to 180.051 million bushels. That was only about 30% of the record US barley crop of 608.532 million bushels seen in 1986-87. US farmers harvested 2.951 million acres of barley in 2006-07, which was the lowest acreage since the late 1800s (specifically, 1894-95). Furthermore, the barley yield in 2006-07 fell to 61.0 bushels per acre from the 2004-05 record high of 69.6. Ending stocks for the 2006-07 marketing year fell to 73 million bushels which was 43.2% below the 12-year high of 128.4 million bushels in 2004-05.

Demand – U.S. total barley disappearance in 2006-07 fell –3.2% yr/yr to 230.0 million bushels, which is down from 2004-05 4-year high of 284 million bushels. About 65% of barley is used for food and alcoholic beverages, 22% for animal feed, and 3% for seed.

Trade – World exports of barley in 2006-07 fell by –11.5% yr/yr to 15.755 million metric tons, but was still better than the 7-year low of 15.311 million metric tons seen in 2003-04. The largest world exporters of barley in 2006-07 were Australia with 17% of world exports, the European Union with 22%, Canada with 9%, and the US with only 3%. The single largest importer of barley is Saudi Arabia with 6.000 million metric tons of imports in 2006-07.

World Barley Supply and Demand   In Thousands of Metric Tons

	---------------------------------- Exports ----------------------------------					------------- Imports -------------			------------- Utilization -------------		-------- Ending Stocks --------		
Year	Aus-tralia	Can-ada	EC-15	Total Non-US	U.S.	Total Exports	Saudi Arabia	Unac-ounted	Total Imports	Russia	U.S.	Total Util-ization	Canada	U.S.	Total Stocks
1997-98	2,838	1,897	2,990	11,750	1,076	12,826	4,026	483	12,826	16,494	6,879	145,266	2,459	2,596	32,137
1998-99	4,241	1,185	8,894	17,234	551	17,785	5,814	809	17,785	12,900	7,195	139,032	2,737	3,084	28,870
1999-00	2,870	1,806	10,738	17,927	853	18,780	5,900	110	18,780	11,441	6,571	132,196	2,838	2,424	24,047
2000-01	3,924	1,956	6,275	15,847	1,068	16,915	5,100	537	16,544	12,700	6,407	133,730	2,516	2,314	22,752
2001-02	4,590	1,126	3,236	17,083	517	17,600	6,000	489	17,159	14,250	5,661	135,654	2,047	2,006	28,738
2002-03	2,159	304	6,307	16,212	552	16,764	7,502	225	16,539	15,500	5,179	136,810	1,475	1,510	27,202
2003-04	6,104	1,937	984	14,446	384	14,830	5,508	226	14,604	18,600	4,990	146,185	2,102	2,619	22,561
2004-05	4,481	1,476	3,881	16,544	771	17,315	6,420	451	16,864	16,500	5,672	144,368	3,435	2,796	33,300
2005-06[1]	5,231	1,876	2,500	17,450	357	17,807	7,000	566	17,241	15,500	4,571	141,275	3,289	2,350	29,127
2006-07[2]	2,300	1,500	3,500	15,255	500	15,755	6,000	275	15,530	16,100	4,246	145,724	1,639	1,807	21,939

[1] Preliminary.   [2] Estimate.   *Source: Foreign Agricultural Service, U.S. Department of Agriculture (FAS-USDA)*

World Production of Barley   In Thousands of Metric Tons

Year	Aus-tralia	Belarus	Canada	China	European Union	India	Iran	Kazak-stan	Russia	Turkey	Ukraine	United States	World Total
1997-98	6,482	2,359	13,527	4,000	52,608	1,462	2,500	2,670	20,800	7,300	7,407	7,835	154,315
1998-99	5,987	1,623	12,709	2,656	51,907	1,680	2,300	1,100	9,800	7,500	5,870	7,655	135,659
1999-00	5,032	1,181	13,196	2,970	57,538	1,470	1,600	2,250	10,600	6,600	6,425	5,922	127,490
2000-01	6,743	1,378	13,172	2,646	58,816	1,447	1,400	1,675	14,100	7,400	6,872	6,919	132,785
2001-02	8,280	1,700	10,846	2,893	56,962	1,432	2,423	2,200	19,500	6,900	10,186	5,407	142,327
2002-03	3,865	1,681	7,489	3,322	56,509	1,500	3,085	2,200	18,700	7,200	10,364	4,940	134,847
2003-04	10,387	1,800	12,328	2,717	54,826	1,410	2,900	2,100	18,000	6,900	6,850	6,059	142,906
2004-05	7,708	2,000	13,186	3,222	61,753	1,310	2,900	1,500	17,200	7,400	11,100	6,091	154,220
2005-06[1]	9,869	1,800	12,481	3,400	52,917	1,080	2,900	1,500	15,800	7,600	9,000	4,613	138,140
2006-07[2]	4,200	1,350	10,000	3,500	54,863	1,400	2,900	1,500	18,500	7,200	11,800	3,920	138,678

[1] Preliminary.   [2] Estimate.   *Source: Foreign Agricultural Service, U.S. Department of Agriculture (FAS-USDA)*

Barley Acreage and Prices in the United States

Year Begin-ning June 1	Acreage ----- 1,000 Acres ----- Planted	Harvested for Grain	Yield Per Harvested Acre -- Bushels --	Seasonal Prices — Received by Farmers[3] — All	Feed[4]	Malting[4]	Portland No. 2 Western	National Average Loan Rate	Target Price	Put Under Support (mil. Bu.)	% of Pro-duction
1999-00	5,194	4,734	59.2	2.13	1.65	2.50	2.11	1.59	NA	13.6	4.9
2000-01	5,864	5,213	61.1	2.11	1.74	2.36	2.25	1.62	NA	16.0	5.0
2001-02	4,967	4,289	58.2	2.18	1.74	2.58	2.31	1.65	NA	10.6	4.2
2002-03	5,008	4,123	55.0	2.68	2.16	2.96	2.71	1.88	2.21	10.4	4.6
2003-04	5,348	4,727	58.9	2.81	2.27	3.07	2.74	1.88	2.21	17.9	6.4
2004-05	4,527	4,021	69.6	2.46	1.76	2.79	2.39	1.85	2.24	8.3	3.0
2005-06[1]	3,875	3,269	64.8	2.55	1.89	2.81	2.44	1.85	2.24		
2006-07[2]	3,452	2,951	61.0	2.83	2.56	2.96					

[1] Preliminary.   [2] Estimate.   [3] Excludes support payments.   [4] Duluth through May 1998.   *Source: Economic Research Service, U.S. Department of Agriculture (ERS-USDA)*

Salient Statistics of Barley in the United States   In Millions of Bushels

Year Begin-ning June 1	Supply — Beginning Stocks	Produc-tion	Imports	Total Supply	Disappearance — Domestic Use — Food & Acohol Beverages	Seed	Feed & Residual	Total	Exports	Total Disap-pearance	Ending Stocks — Gov't Owned[3]	Privately Owned[4]	Total Stocks
1999-00	141.7	280.3	25.0	448.5	162.5	9.5	136.0	308.0	30.0	338.0	0	111.0	111.0
2000-01	111.0	318.7	29.0	459.0	164.0	8.0	122.0	294.0	58.0	353.0	0	106.0	106.0
2001-02	106.3	248.3	23.9	378.5	147.3	8.3	104.3	260.0	26.4	286.4	0	92.1	92.1
2002-03	92.1	226.9	18.5	337.5	145.7	8.7	83.6	237.9	30.3	268.2	0	69.3	69.3
2003-04	69.3	278.3	20.6	368.3	147.5	7.4	74.3	229.2	18.8	247.9	0	120.3	120.3
2004-05	120.3	279.7	12.1	412.2	150.8	6.4	103.3	260.5	23.3	283.8	0	128.4	128.4
2005-06[1]	128.4	211.9	5.4	345.7	152.2	5.8	52.0	210.8	28.0	237.7	0	108.0	108.0
2006-07[2]	108.0	180.1	15.0	303.0	148.4	6.6	50.0	195.0	25.0	230.0	0	73.0	73.0

[1] Preliminary.   [2] Estimate.   [3] Uncommitted inventory.   [4] Includes quantity under loan & farmer-owned reserve.   *Source: Economic Research Service, U.S. Department of Agriculture (ERS-USDA)*

Barley (monthly average) through December 2006 — Cents per pound

Cents Per Bushel
----- Malting, Top Quality, Mpls. (Jan. 1972 - date)
----- No. 2 Mpls. (Jan. 1909 - June 1925)
No. 3 Mpls. (July 1925 - June 1976)
No. 2 Feed, Mpls. (July 1976 - Dec. 1986)
No. 2 Feed, Duluth (Mar. 1987 - Dec. 1990)
- - - No. 1 Western Feed, Lethbridge (Aug. 1991 - date)

BARLEY

Average Price Received by Farmers for All Barley in the United States   In Dollars Per Bushel

Year	June	July	Aug.	Sept.	Oct.	Nov.	Dec.	Jan.	Feb.	Mar.	Apr.	May	Average
1999-00	1.70	2.04	2.37	2.03	1.96	2.14	2.25	2.04	2.13	2.23	2.09	2.19	2.10
2000-01	2.04	2.70	2.23	1.81	1.97	2.15	2.22	2.00	2.10	2.07	2.05	2.12	2.12
2001-02	1.98	2.00	2.41	2.24	2.29	2.30	2.21	2.09	2.17	2.17	2.09	2.24	2.18
2002-03	2.09	2.14	2.68	2.64	2.64	2.79	2.91	2.85	2.87	2.83	2.85	2.91	2.68
2003-04	2.99	2.74	2.91	2.88	2.74	2.83	2.93	2.69	2.73	2.77	2.78	2.78	2.81
2004-05	2.63	2.54	2.77	2.43	2.29	2.45	2.49	2.41	2.31	2.49	2.26	2.46	2.46
2005-06	2.54	2.37	2.50	2.36	2.41	2.58	2.48	2.42	2.55	2.71	2.67	2.97	2.55
2006-07[1]	2.78	2.70	2.70	2.56	2.76	2.92	2.95	3.03	3.10				2.83

[1] Preliminary.   *Source: Economic Research Service, U.S. Department of Agriculture (ERS-USDA)*

Average Price Received by Farmers for Feed Barley in the United States   In Dollars Per Bushel

Year	June	July	Aug.	Sept.	Oct.	Nov.	Dec.	Jan.	Feb.	Mar.	Apr.	May	Average
1999-00	1.55	1.48	1.50	1.64	1.61	1.66	1.64	1.63	1.68	1.78	1.68	1.94	1.65
2000-01	1.73	1.71	1.50	1.54	1.71	1.87	1.90	1.80	1.77	1.76	1.73	1.91	1.74
2001-02	1.77	1.63	1.54	1.71	1.86	1.79	1.77	1.67	1.69	1.75	1.79	1.89	1.74
2002-03	1.83	1.88	2.05	2.23	2.26	2.32	2.14	2.17	2.20	2.30	2.20	2.33	2.16
2003-04	2.33	2.22	2.39	2.27	2.24	2.43	2.26	2.15	2.16	2.19	2.17	2.39	2.27
2004-05	2.20	2.21	1.83	1.64	1.58	1.78	1.66	1.65	1.60	1.67	1.56	1.71	1.76
2005-06	1.91	1.88	1.77	1.84	1.81	1.91	1.76	1.94	1.83	1.80	1.83	2.45	1.89
2006-07[1]	2.08	2.04	2.06	2.33	2.67	2.85	2.79	3.12	3.13				2.56

[1] Preliminary.   *Source: National Agricultural Statistical Service, U.S. Department of Agriculture (NASS-USDA)*

Average Open Interest of Western Feed Barley Futures in Winnipeg   In Contracts

Year	Jan.	Feb.	Mar.	Apr.	May	June	July	Aug.	Sept.	Oct.	Nov.	Dec.
1999	8,231	10,635	10,579	9,713	8,333	8,993	10,348	11,959	13,206	15,014	15,662	15,031
2000	16,709	20,500	21,100	22,501	20,299	17,402	15,128	15,095	15,885	14,921	17,192	19,605
2001	19,453	20,515	19,163	19,458	16,020	15,778	16,475	17,202	16,926	13,577	11,407	10,480
2002	9,771	10,653	11,255	11,113	11,141	11,068	11,271	13,046	13,845	12,172	9,000	8,027
2003	8,559	8,203	8,546	9,028	9,631	10,290	10,676	9,580	8,409	7,154	7,524	5,346
2004	6,731	6,881	6,262	9,779	10,497	9,930	9,992	9,743	11,140	11,956	12,786	10,916
2005	9,321	8,164	9,144	9,476	9,475	9,140	6,481	6,880	6,046	5,839	6,538	7,281
2006	8,179	10,505	10,719	12,131	12,543	12,762	12,948	13,680	14,938	16,026	13,803	14,620

Source: Winnipeg Commodity Exchange (WCE)

Volume of Trading of Western Barley Futures in Winnipeg   In Contracts

Year	Jan.	Feb.	Mar.	Apr.	May	June	July	Aug.	Sept.	Oct.	Nov.	Dec.	Total
1999	15,463	17,539	13,853	17,179	8,911	16,294	17,936	15,837	29,141	16,662	26,445	16,117	211,377
2000	23,371	22,598	21,563	23,631	19,816	24,298	15,230	11,981	23,105	23,447	42,529	14,508	266,077
2001	26,836	18,732	16,962	24,993	26,361	20,465	20,849	20,137	19,735	21,276	14,926	6,302	237,574
2002	14,268	16,370	15,924	17,663	21,440	18,349	19,860	23,436	22,431	14,471	17,035	10,772	212,019
2003	10,555	18,933	13,069	18,879	13,900	15,153	13,293	29,799	19,438	18,937	17,768	10,977	200,701
2004	11,405	16,265	12,784	23,806	13,179	27,081	15,326	14,933	23,072	15,790	22,516	8,478	204,635
2005	15,452	12,171	19,849	9,325	16,469	14,741	4,100	11,815	7,573	12,665	8,452	3,952	136,564
2006	16,241	9,238	23,987	9,361	26,466	8,083	4,294	25,858	14,903	37,489	12,620	6,484	195,024

Source: Winnipeg Commodity Exchange (WCE)

Bauxite

Bauxite is a naturally occurring, heterogeneous material comprised of one or more aluminum hydroxide minerals plus various mixtures of silica, iron oxide, titanium, alumina-silicates, and other impurities in trace amounts. Bauxite is an important ore of aluminum and forms by the rapid weathering of granite rocks in warm, humid climates. It is easily purified and can be converted directly into either alum or metallic aluminum. It is a soft mineral with hardness varying from 1 to 3, and specific gravity from 2 to 2.55. Bauxite is dull in appearance and may vary in color from white to brown. It usually occurs in aggregates in pea-sized lumps.

Bauxite is the only raw material used in the production of alumina on a commercial scale in the United States. Bauxite is classified according to the intended commercial application, such as abrasive, cement, chemical, metallurgical, and refractory. Of all the bauxite mined, about 95 percent is converted to alumina for the production of aluminum metal with some smaller amounts going to nonmetal uses as various forms of specialty alumina. Small amounts are used in non-metallurgical bauxite applications. Bauxite is also used to produce aluminum chemicals and is used in the steel industry.

Supply – World production of bauxite rose 5.6% yr/yr in 2005 to a new record high 169 million metric tons. The world's largest producer of bauxite is Australia with 35.5% of world production in 2005, followed by Brazil (11.7%), China (10.7%), Guinea (8.9%), Jamaica (8.4%), and India (7.1%). Chinese production of bauxite has quadrupled in the past 10 years. India's bauxite production has also risen rapidly and is more than triple the amount seen 15 years ago.

Demand – US consumption of bauxite in 2005 fell by – 2.9% yr/yr to 13.200 million metric tons from 13.600 million metric tons in 2004, which was still well below the record high of 15.962 million metric tons seen in 1980. The alumina industry took 92% of bauxite production in 2005, or 12.200 million metric tons. The refractory industry took only 1.4% of the US bauxite supply in 2005 (187,000 metric tons), the abrasive industry took 0.2% (26,000 metric tons), and the chemical industry took the remainder.

Trade – The US relies on imports for almost 100% of its consumption needs. Domestic ore, which provides less than 1 percent of the US requirement for bauxite, was mined by one company from surface mines in the states of Alabama and Georgia. US imports of bauxite fell –1.5% yr/yr to 9,850 million metric tons in 2005, which was well below the record of 14.976 million metric tons seen in 1974. US exports of bauxite in 2005 were negligible at 34,000 metric tons.

World Production of Bauxite   In Thousands of Metric Tons

Year	Australia	Brazil	China	Greece	Guinea	Guyana[2]	Hungary	India	Jama-ica[3]	Russia[3]	Sierra Leone	Suri-name	World Total
1996	43,063	10,998	6,200	2,452	15,600	2,475	1,044	5,757	11,863	3,300	----	3,695	117,000
1997	44,465	11,671	8,000	1,877	16,359	2,467	743	6,019	11,987	3,350	----	3,877	122,000
1998	44,553	11,961	8,200	1,823	15,570	2,267	1,138	6,102	12,646	3,450	----	3,931	123,000
1999	48,416	14,372	8,500	1,883	15,590	2,359	935	6,712	11,688	3,750	----	3,715	129,000
2000	53,802	13,866	9,000	1,991	15,700	2,471	1,047	7,562	11,127	4,200	----	3,610	136,000
2001	53,799	13,032	9,800	2,052	15,100	1,950	1,000	7,864	12,370	4,000	----	4,394	137,000
2002	54,135	13,260	12,000	2,492	15,300	1,690	720	9,647	13,120	4,500	----	4,002	144,000
2003	55,602	17,363	13,000	2,418	15,000	1,701	666	10,414	13,444	5,500	----	4,215	153,000
2004[1]	56,593	19,700	15,000	2,444	15,000	1,466	647	11,285	13,296	6,000	----	4,052	160,000
2005[2]	59,959	19,800	18,000	2,450	15,000	1,500	511	11,957	14,118	6,400	----	4,584	169,000

[1] Preliminary.   [2] Estimate.   [3] Dry Bauxite equivalent of ore processed.   *Source: U.S. Geological Survey (USGS)*

Salient Statistics of Bauxite in the United States   In Thousands of Metric Tons

Year	Net Import Reliance as a % of Apparent Consumption	Average Price FOB Mine $ per Ton	Total	Alumina	Abrasive	Chemical	Refractory	Imports[3] (for Consumption)	Exports[3]	Consumption	Producers & Consumers	Government	Total
1996	100	15-18	11,000	10,300	117	W	380	10,552	132	11,000	1,930	15,700	17,600
1997	100	15-18	11,500	10,700	98	W	466	11,069	85	11,500	2,260	14,300	16,500
1998	100	25	12,700	12,000	135	W	332	11,393	99	12,700	1,860	11,000	12,800
1999	100	23	11,700	11,100	113	W	251	10,189	149	11,700	1,440	6,800	8,250
2000	100	23	10,800	10,100	111	W	160	8,550	133	10,800	1,300	5,710	7,000
2001	100	23	9,770	9,010	61	W	175	8,300	67	9,770	1,740	2,070	3,810
2002	100	20	9,980	9,290	52	W	115	7,340	27	9,980	1,280	1,770	3,050
2003	100	19	11,300	10,600	53	W	150	8,390	55	11,300	3,830	66	3,900
2004[1]	100	22	13,600	12,500	53	W	260	10,000	42	13,600	3,120	----	3,120
2005[2]	100	25	13,200	12,200	26	W	187	9,850	34	13,200	2,730	----	2,730

Column group headers: Consumption by Industry (Total, Alumina, Abrasive, Chemical, Refractory); Dry Equivalent (Imports, Exports); Stocks, December 31 (Consumption, Producers & Consumers, Government, Total)

[1] Preliminary.   [2] Estimate.   [3] Including concentrates.   W = Withheld to avoid disclosing company proprietary data.
Source: U.S. Geological Survey (USGS)

Bismuth

Bismuth (symbol Bi) is a rare metallic element with a pinkish tinge. Bismuth has been known since ancient times, but it was confused with lead, tin, and zinc until the middle of the 18ᵗʰ century. Among the elements in the earth's crust, bismuth is ranked about 73ʳᵈ in natural abundance. This makes bismuth about as rare as silver. Most industrial bismuth is obtained as a by-product of ore extraction.

Bismuth is useful for castings because of the unusual way that it expands after solidifying. Some of bismuth's alloys have unusually low melting points. Bismuth is one of the most difficult of all substances to magnetize. It tends to turn at right angles to a magnetic field. Because of this property, it is used in instruments for measuring the strength of magnetic fields.

Bismuth finds a wide variety of uses such as pharmaceutical compounds, ceramic glazes, crystal ware, and chemicals and pigments. Bismuth is found in household pharmaceuticals and is used to treat stomach ulcers. Bismuth is opaque to X-rays and can be used in fluoroscopy. Bismuth has also found new use as a nontoxic substitute for lead in various applications such as brass plumbing fixtures, crystal ware, lubricating greases, pigments, and solders. There has been environmental interest in the use of bismuth as a replacement for lead used in shot for waterfowl hunting and in fishing sinkers. Another use has been for galvanizing to improve drainage characteristics of galvanizing alloys. Zinc-bismuth alloys have the same drainage properties as zinc-lead without being as hazardous.

Prices – The average price of bismuth (99.99% pure) in the US in 2005 (the latest data available) rose 19.7% to $3.57 per pound from $2.98 per pound in 2004. The increase is due primarily to the strengthening global economy over the past few years.

Supply – World mine production of bismuth in 2005 fell –1.8% to 5,500 metric tons from last year's record of 5,600 metric tons. The world's largest producer in 2005 was China with 55% of world production, followed by Mexico with 18%, Peru with 18%, and Canada with 3%. Regarding production of the refined metal, China had 71% of production, Mexico had 8%, Belgium had 7%, and Peru had 5% in 2004. The US does not have any significant domestic refinery production of bismuth.

Demand – US consumption of bismuth in 2005 fell –3.3% to 2,340 metric tons, down from the record high of 2,420 metric tons in 2003. Of that consumption, 49% went for metallurgical additives, 29% for fusible alloys, 21% for chemicals, and 1% for other uses.

Trade – US imports of bismuth rose 27.8% to 2,530 metric tons which was a 7-year high. Of US imports, 42% came from Belgium and 19% came from Mexico. US exports of bismuth and alloys were negligible in 2005 at 142 metric tons, but up 30% from the 109 metric tons in 2004.

World Production of Bismuth   In Metric Tons (Mine Output=Metal Content)

| | Mine Output, Metal Content | | | | | | Refined Metal | | | | | | |
Year	Canada	China	Japan	Mexico	Peru	Total	Belgium	China	Kazak-hastan	Japan	Mexico	Peru	Total
1998	186	240	24	1,204	1,000	3,980	700	820	50	479	1,030	832	4,330
1999	311	2,680	24	548	1,000	4,860	700	860	55	481	412	705	3,570
2000	243	1,120	26	1,112	1,000	3,800	700	770	55	520	1,083	744	4,200
2001	258	2,000	28	1,390	1,000	5,100	700	2,000	130	551	1,390	640	5,800
2002	189	2,000	24	1,126	1,000	4,700	1,000	3,000	130	474	1,126	568	6,700
2003	145	2,500	26	1,064	1,000	5,100	1,000	5,000	130	513	1,064	600	8,700
2004¹	145	3,000	23	1,064	1,000	5,600	800	7,000	130	522	1,064	600	10,000
2005²	190	3,000	27	970	1,000	5,500	800	8,500	120	530	970	600	12,000

¹ Preliminary.   ² Estimate.   *Source U.S. Geological Survey (USGS)*

Salient Statistics of Bismuth in the United States   In Metric Tons

| | Bismuth Consumed, By Uses | | | | | | | Imports from | | | | Dealer Price $ Per Pound |
Year	Metal-lurgical Additives	Other Alloys & Uses	Fusible Alloys	Chem-icals³	Total Con-sumption	Consumer Stocks Dec. 31	Exports of Metal & Alloys	Belgium	Mexico	Peru	Total	
1998	335	32	741	884	1,990	175	245	739.0	807.0	68.8	2,720	3.60
1999	340	31	823	855	2,050	130	257	742.0	277.0	6.8	2,110	3.85
2000	346	34	889	861	2,130	118	491	832.0	516.0	20.4	2,410	3.70
2001	369	45	981	805	2,200	95	541	728.0	605.0	----	2,220	3.74
2002	388	50	1,070	813	2,320	111	131	724.0	518.0	19.5	1,930	3.14
2003	833	25	646	616	2,120	279	108	778.0	532.0	0.1	2,320	2.87
2004¹	1,110	22	703	584	2,420	134	109	793.0	495.0	39.8	1,980	3.35
2005²	1,150	14	685	498	2,340	136	142	1,050.0	480.0	----	2,530	3.91

¹ Preliminary.   ² Estimate.   ³ Includes pharmaceuticals.   *Source: U.S. Geological Survey (USGS)*

Average Price of Bismuth (99.99%) in the United States   In Dollars Per Pound

Year	Jan.	Feb.	Mar.	Apr.	May	June	July	Aug.	Sept.	Oct.	Nov.	Dec.	Average
2003	2.90	2.90	2.90	2.92	2.98	2.98	2.98	2.98	2.98	2.98	2.98	2.98	2.96
2004	2.98	2.98	2.98	2.98	2.98	2.98	2.98	2.98	2.98	2.98	2.98	2.98	2.98
2005	2.98	2.98	2.98	2.98	2.98	2.98	3.20	4.10	4.17	4.30	4.54	4.63	3.57
2006	4.63	4.63	4.63	4.63									4.63

Source: American Metal Market (AMM)

Broilers

Broiler chickens are raised for meat rather than for eggs. The broiler industry was started in the late 1950's when chickens were selectively bred for meat production. Broiler chickens are housed in massive flocks mainly between 20,000 and 50,000 birds, with some flocks reaching over 100,000 birds. Broiler chicken farmers usually rear five or six batches of chickens per year.

After just six or seven weeks, broiler chickens are slaughtered (a chicken's natural lifespan is around seven years). Chickens marketed as pouissons, or spring chickens, are slaughtered after four weeks. A few are kept longer than seven weeks to be sold as the larger roasting chickens.

Prices – The average monthly price received by farmers for broilers (live weight) fell in 2006 by –10.8% yr/yr to 38.7 cents per pound from the 2004 record high of 45.2. The average monthly price for wholesale broilers (ready-to-cook) in 2006 fell –9.2% to 64.34 cents per pound, from the 2004 record high of 74.12.

Supply – Total production of broilers in 2006 rose by +2.3% yr/yr to 36.100 billion pounds, which was a new record high. The number of broilers raised for commercial production in 2006 fell by –0.1% yr/yr to 8.834 billion from 2005's record high of 8.842 billion birds. The average weight per bird rose by 1.8% to 5.47 pounds, which was a new record high and was nearly 50% heavier than the average bird weight of 3.62 pounds seen in 1970, attesting to the increased efficiency of the industry.

Demand – US per capita consumption of broilers in 2006 rose to a new record high of 87.2 pounds (ready-to-cook) per person per year. US consumption of chicken has nearly doubled in the past two decades, up from 47.0 pounds in 1980, as consumers have increased their consumption of chicken because of the focus on low-carb diets and because chicken is a leaner and healthier meat than either beef or pork.

Broiler Supply and Prices in the United States

Year & Quarters	Number (Millions)	Average Weight (Pounds)	Liveweight Pounds (Mil. Lbs.)	Certified RTC Weight (Mil. Lbs.)	Total Production RTC[3] (Mil. Lbs.)	Per Capita Consumption RTC Basis (Mil. Lbs.)	Farm	Geogia Dock[4]
							Cents per Pound	
2001	8,387	5.04	42,337	31,257	31,266	76.6	39.58	62.08
2002	8,511	5.12	43,529	32,190	32,240	80.5	30.42	61.65
2003	8,522	5.19	44,247	32,700	32,749	81.6	35.33	64.80
2004	8,762	5.26	46,097	34,064	34,063	84.3	45.17	74.69
2005[1]	8,842	5.37	47,475	35,238	35,293	85.6	43.33	72.83
2006[2]	8,835	5.47	48,309	35,730	36,100	87.2	38.67	68.25
I	2,201	5.46	12,023	8,937	8,825	21.7	37.67	68.09
II	2,245	5.47	12,269	9,129	9,125	22.2	35.67	66.87
III	2,222	5.42	12,038	8,883	9,100	21.9	41.33	69.52
IV	2,167	5.52	11,978	8,780	9,050	21.3	40.00	68.50

[1] Preliminary. [2] Estimate. [3] Total production equals federal inspected slaughter plus other slaughter minus cut-up & further processing condemnation. [4] Ready-to-cook basis. Source: Economic Research Service, U.S. Department of Agriculture (ERS-USDA)

Salient Statistics of Broilers in the United States

	Commercial Production		Average			Production			Storage Stocks		Broiler	Consumption	
Year	Number (Mil. Lbs.)	Liveweight (Mil. Lbs.)	Liveweight Per Bird (Pounds)	Average Price (Cents/Lb.)	Value of Production (Mil. $)	Federally Inspected	Other Chickens	Total	January 1	Exports	Feed Ratio (Pounds)	Total (Mil. Lbs.)	Per Capita[4] (Pounds)
						In Millions of Pounds							
2000	8,284	41,626	5.03	33.6	13,989	30,209	531	31,740	804	5,138	6.7	25,606	77.40
2001	8,390	42,452	5.06	39.3	16,696	30,938	515	31,453	807	5,737	7.8	25,819	76.60
2002	8,591	44,059	5.13	30.5	13,437	31,895	547	32,442	720	4,941	5.5	27,467	80.50
2003	8,493	43,958	5.18	34.6	15,215	32,399	502	32,901	768	4,920	5.4	32,749	81.60
2004	8,741	45,796	5.24	44.6	20,446	33,699	504	34,203	611	4,768	5.9	34,063	84.30
2005[1]	8,854	47,579	5.37	43.6	20,902	34,816	515	35,331	716	5,211	7.0	35,293	85.60
2006[2]	8,835	48,309	5.47			35,936	525	35,461	926	5,405	6.2	36,325	87.90

[1] Preliminary. [2] Estimate. [3] Ready-to-cook. [4] Retail weight basis. Source: Economic Research Service, U.S. Department of Agriculture (ERS-USDA)

Average Wholesale Broiler[1] Prices RTC (Ready-to-Cook) (In Cents Per Pound)

Year	Jan.	Feb.	Mar.	Apr.	May	June	July	Aug.	Sept.	Oct.	Nov.	Dec.	Average
2000	55.43	53.84	54.48	55.39	55.71	56.01	56.61	55.47	58.35	57.22	58.22	57.23	56.16
2001	56.87	57.47	58.95	58.46	59.40	59.88	60.43	60.90	61.93	60.17	58.89	55.98	59.11
2002	56.86	55.91	55.17	53.47	56.42	58.44	57.47	55.72	55.88	52.97	53.42	54.74	55.54
2003	60.46	60.49	60.02	57.78	59.44	61.56	62.80	63.20	64.08	63.59	64.45	65.71	61.97
2004	68.66	74.96	75.94	76.40	79.54	82.00	81.59	75.44	70.07	68.79	68.08	68.01	74.12
2005	71.40	71.43	72.81	73.21	72.54	72.19	72.47	71.45	72.51	69.02	66.95	63.98	70.83
2006[2]	63.13	63.19	61.77	58.91	59.57	64.44	67.10	68.26	68.18	65.16	65.93	66.48	64.34

[1] 12-city composite wholesale price. [2] Preliminary. Source: Economic Research Service, U.S. Department of Agriculture (ERS-USDA)

Butter

Butter is a dairy product produced by churning the fat from milk, usually cow's milk, until it solidifies. In some parts of the world, butter is also made from the milk of goats, sheep, and even horses. Butter has been in use since at least 2,000 BC. Today butter is used principally as a food item, but in ancient times it was used more as an ointment, medicine, or illuminating oil. Butter was first churned in skin pouches thrown back and forth over the backs of trotting horses.

It takes about 10 quarts of milk to produce 1 pound of butter. The manufacture of butter is the third largest use of milk in the US. California is generally the largest producing state, followed closely by Wisconsin, with Washington as a distant third. Commercially finished butter is comprised of milk fat (80% to 85%), water (12% to 16%), and salt (about 2%). Although the price of butter is highly correlated with the price of milk, it also has its own supply and demand dynamics.

The consumption of butter has dropped in recent decades because pure butter has a high level of animal fat and cholesterol that have been linked to obesity and heart disease. The primary substitute for butter is margarine, which is produced from vegetable oil rather than milk fat. US per capita consumption of margarine has risen from 2.6 pounds in 1930 to recent levels near 8.3 pounds, much higher than US butter consumption.

Futures on butter are traded at the Chicago Mercantile Exchange (CME). The CME's butter futures contract calls for the delivery of 40,000 pounds of Grade AA butter and is priced in cents per pound.

Prices – The average monthly price of butter at the Chicago Mercantile Exchange in 2006 fell by -20.2% to 123.64 cents/pound, down from the 2004 record high of 181.66. That was, however, still higher than the 8-year low of 110.59 cents posted in 2002.

Supply – World production of butter in 2006 rose +4.4% yr/yr to 7.036 million metric tons, which is the highest production level since the record high of 7.217 million metric tons in 1986. The world's largest producers of butter are India with 46% of the world production in 2006, the European Union with 28%, the United States with 9%, New Zealand with 5%, and Russia with 4%. Production of creamery butter by US factories in 2006 rose +7.2% to1.444 billion pounds. That was the highest level since 1954.

Demand – US usage of butter in 2005 (the latest data available) rose by +0.7% yr/yr to 1.335 billion pounds. That was only about two thirds of the usage levels of over 2 billion pounds seen back in the 1930s and 1940s, illustrating the downtrend in US butter consumption. Per capita consumption of butter in the US in 2004, the latest reporting year for the series, was 4.6 pounds per person per year, little changed from 1980 but sharply lower than the 7.5 pounds in 1960 and the 17.3 pounds back in the 1930's.

Trade – US imports of butter in 2005 (the latest data available) fell sharply by –37.9% yr/yr to 31.42 million pounds. US butter exports in 2004 (latest data available) rose +201% to a 6-year high of 26 million pounds.

Supply and Distribution of Butter in the United States In Millions of Pounds

Year	Supply — Production	Supply — Cold Storage Stocks[3] Jan. 1[5]	Supply — Imports	Supply — Total Supply	Distribution — Domestic Disappearance — Total	Distribution — Domestic Disappearance — Per Capita (Pounds)	Distribution — Exports	Distribution — Dept of Agriculture — Jan. 1 Stocks[4]	Distribution — Dept of Agriculture — Dec. 31 Stocks[4]	Distribution — Dept of Agriculture — Removed by USDA Programs	Total Use	93 Score AA Wholesale Price California $ per Pound	93 Score AA Wholesale Price Chicago $ per Pound
1997	1,151	14	24.154	1,177	1,115	4.1	46	0	0	38.4	1,156	----	1.1625
1998	1,082	21	70.369	1,243	1,220	4.4	33	0	0	12.6	1,229	----	1.7685
1999	1,167	26	39.813	1,337	1,307	4.7	20	0	0	3.7	1,314	----	1.2396
2000	1,274	25	32.400	1,331	1,329	4.5	7	0	0	8.9	1,289	----	1.1768
2001	1,237	24	75.000	1,336	1,268	4.4	18	0	0		1,275	----	1.6630
2002	1,355	56	34.800	1,446	1,293	4.4	8	0	1		1,288	----	1.1059
2003	1,242	158	32.200	1,432	1,307	4.5	9	1	6	29.1	1,332	----	1.1450
2004[1]	1,250	100	50.600	1,400	1,326	4.6	26	6	0	-6.6	1,356	----	1.8166
2005[2]	1,347	45	31.418	1,424	1,335			0				----	1.5484

[1] Preliminary. [2] Estimates. [3] Includes butter-equivalent. [4] Includes butteroil. [5] Includes stocks held by USDA.
Source: Economic Research Service, U.S. Department of Agriculture (ERS-USDA)

Commercial Disappearance of Creamery Butter in the United States In Millions of Pounds

Year	First Quarter	Second Quarter	Third Quarter	Fourth Quarter	Total	Year	First Quarter	Second Quarter	Third Quarter	Fourth Quarter	Total
1995	335.7	269.0	261.2	304.9	1,186.0	2001	290.9	278.4	316.1	397.0	1,282.4
1996	325.6	301.8	237.5	310.3	1,180.0	2002	313.5	263.5	317.4	393.4	1,287.8
1997	302.7	250.7	265.8	287.6	1,109.0	2003	304.2	275.4	317.2	411.8	1,308.6
1998	289.0	276.3	255.3	308.6	1,137.0	2004	286.3	303.2	340.8	421.1	1,351.4
1999	299.3	316.4	318.3	374.8	1,308.8	2005	287.1	276.7	349.6	423.1	1,336.5
2000	300.8	286.9	332.3	380.6	1,300.6	2006[1]	320.2	322.6	333.2	397.4	1,373.4

[1] Preliminary. *Source: Economic Research Service, U.S. Department of Agriculture (ERS-USDA)*

World (Total) Butter[3] Production — In Thousands of Metric Tons

Year	Aus- tralia	France	Ger many	India	Ireland	Nether- lands	New Zealand	Poland	Russia	Ukraine	United Kingdom	United States	World Total
2000	180	72	77	10	1,995	1,950	88	70	344	265	135	570	5,814
2001	160	78	84	12	2,021	2,250	80	70	352	270	156	559	6,145
2002	164	70	77	12	2,226	2,400	83	70	380	280	131	615	6,565
2003	163	72	84	13	2,226	2,450	80	77	405	280	148	563	6,612
2004	132	75	84	12	2,154	2,600	80	88	418	270	138	566	6,626
2005	131	77	84	12	2,155	2,749	84	93	341	275	118	611	6,741
2006[1]	129	78	81	10	2,065	3,050	84	92	390	290	105	650	7,036
2007[2]	124	79	82	10	2,050	3,425	85	93	395	300	110	655	7,420

[1] Preliminary. [2] Forecast. [3] Factory (including creameries and dairies) & farm. *Source: Foreign Agricultural Service, U.S. Department of Agriculture (FAS-USDA)*

Production of Creamery Butter in Factories in the United States — In Millions of Pounds

Year	Jan.	Feb.	Mar.	Apr.	May	June	July	Aug.	Sept.	Oct.	Nov.	Dec.	Total
1999	123.3	111.5	113.7	106.4	104.7	86.0	75.8	66.1	78.8	93.0	90.4	117.2	1,166.8
2000	139.9	128.2	121.0	111.7	108.9	89.1	85.4	83.7	89.9	103.9	100.4	111.6	1,273.6
2001	127.4	111.8	111.4	109.0	111.0	86.8	84.2	75.6	86.7	109.9	100.1	123.0	1,236.8
2002	140.1	124.2	127.7	131.6	125.5	95.8	94.4	88.9	92.8	102.6	103.9	127.6	1,355.1
2003	141.9	128.1	126.4	122.8	114.9	84.2	80.1	70.9	73.3	96.8	88.4	114.6	1,242.4
2004	129.3	108.6	100.4	100.3	110.1	99.2	92.6	90.3	94.2	104.4	101.4	118.8	1,249.7
2005	128.0	116.9	122.4	117.1	120.7	106.6	95.9	93.2	100.6	108.9	110.9	126.0	1,347.2
2006[1]	147.3	137.0	142.0	128.5	128.1	100.8	94.6	88.3	103.8	118.6	117.6	137.9	1,444.3

[1] Preliminary. *Source: Economic Research Service, U.S. Department of Agriculture (ERS-USDA)*

Cold Storage Holdings of Creamery Butter on First of Month in the United States — In Millions of Pounds

Year	Jan.	Feb.	Mar.	Apr.	May	June	July	Aug.	Sept.	Oct.	Nov.	Dec.
1999	25.9	60.8	95.0	108.4	125.5	136.6	120.6	123.6	90.7	71.5	64.2	30.2
2000	25.1	82.4	107.8	114.0	126.9	138.2	145.8	136.9	101.3	85.0	58.3	27.3
2001	24.1	68.4	86.1	96.2	112.3	138.0	153.5	151.1	118.0	110.9	100.8	57.9
2002	55.9	99.2	130.1	145.2	196.6	226.8	243.0	245.3	229.5	209.1	164.6	135.6
2003	157.8	204.8	239.9	249.0	263.7	298.0	301.4	283.9	253.9	207.2	170.2	122.5
2004	99.6	152.4	159.1	158.1	155.7	178.7	189.2	193.5	161.0	133.0	107.2	57.2
2005	45.0	77.2	110.9	132.4	164.5	178.0	179.6	176.7	148.9	124.1	98.1	60.4
2006[1]	58.6	125.3	148.5	170.3	200.2	229.9	230.4	228.4	188.8	167.5	137.8	94.3

[1] Preliminary. *Source: Agricultural Statistics Board, U.S. Department of Agriculture (ASB-USDA)*

Average Price of Butter at Chicago Mercantile Exchange[1] — In Cents Per Pound

Year	Jan.	Feb.	Mar.	Apr.	May	June	July	Aug.	Sept.	Oct.	Nov.	Dec.	Average
1999	144.4	133.1	130.3	103.9	111.0	147.7	134.7	141.4	135.8	113.8	109.6	94.2	125.0
2000	91.6	92.9	99.7	108.7	122.2	128.6	120.3	120.3	119.1	116.9	151.7	150.0	118.5
2001	122.3	138.1	154.9	174.7	190.4	197.4	192.4	204.5	219.7	151.9	135.2	130.2	167.6
2002	134.5	124.3	124.7	117.1	105.9	104.3	103.0	97.5	96.4	103.2	104.3	112.0	110.6
2003	108.2	104.1	109.2	109.1	109.2	111.4	119.9	117.1	117.3	118.5	120.6	129.7	114.5
2004	143.2	171.3	213.5	222.0	203.6	193.0	174.6	154.1	176.6	164.8	192.4	170.8	181.7
2005	157.8	161.5	155.3	149.3	140.4	153.1	162.1	168.6	169.9	162.0	142.6	135.5	154.8
2006	133.7	119.3	116.6	116.3	117.6	116.4	116.5	130.4	131.7	132.1	129.2	124.1	123.6

[1] Data through December 2001 are for Wholesale Price of 92 Score Creamery (Grade A) Butter, Central States;
Source: Economic Research Service, U.S. Department of Agriculture (ERS-USDA)

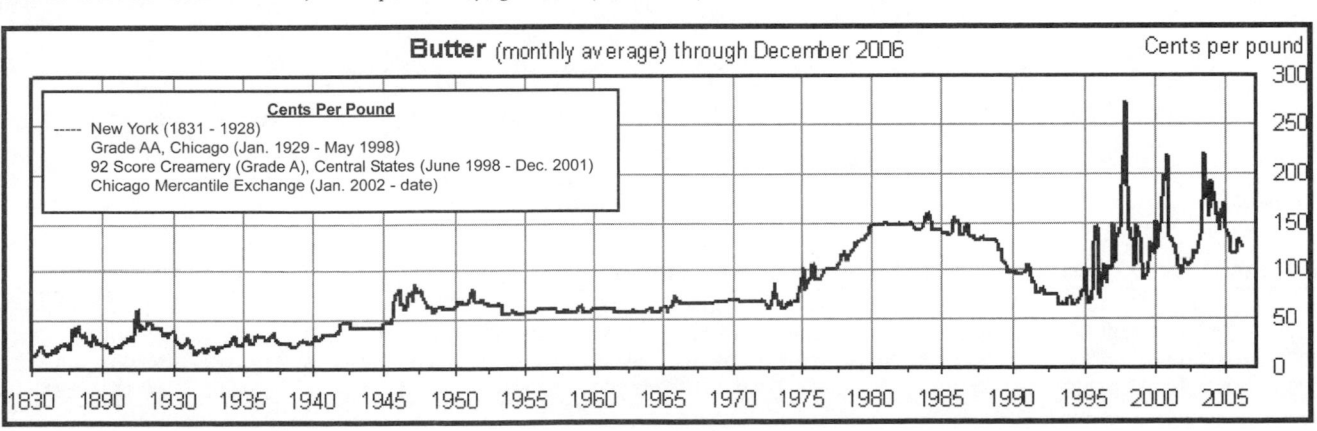

Butter (monthly average) through December 2006 — Cents per pound

Cents Per Pound
----- New York (1831 - 1928)
Grade AA, Chicago (Jan. 1929 - May 1998)
92 Score Creamery (Grade A), Central States (June 1998 - Dec. 2001)
Chicago Mercantile Exchange (Jan. 2002 - date)

Cadmium

Cadmium (symbol Cd) is a soft, bluish-white, metallic element that can easily be shaped and cut with a knife. Cadmium melts at 321 degrees Celsius and boils at 765 degrees Celsius. Cadmium burns brightly in air when heated, forming the oxide CdO. In 1871, the German chemist Friedrich Stromeyer discovered cadmium in incrustations in zinc furnaces.

Rare greenockite is the only mineral bearing cadmium. Cadmium occurs most often in small quantities associated with zinc ores, such as sphalerite. Electrolysis or fractional distillation is used to separate the cadmium and zinc. About 80% of world cadmium output is a by-product from zinc refining. The remaining 20% comes from secondary sources and recycling of cadmium products. Cadmium recycling is practical only from nickel-cadmium batteries and from some alloys and dust from electric-arc furnaces.

Cadmium is used primarily for metal plating and coating operations in transportation equipment, machinery, baking enamels, photography, and television phosphors. It is also used in pigments and lasers, and in nickel-cadmium and solar batteries.

Prices – Cadmium prices in the past 8 years have been at severely depressed levels, reflecting the decreased demand for the substance. However, in 2005 cadmium prices rose very sharply by +172.7% to $1.50 cents per pound from 55 cents per pound in 2004. That was far above the record low of 14 cents in 1999 and only a little below the 20-year average of $1.59 per pound. The record high of $6.91 per pound was posted in 1988.

Supply – World cadmium production in 2005 rose +3.7% yr/yr to 19,400 metric tons, up from the 22-year low of 18,000 metric tons in 2002. The largest producer was China with 16% of total world production followed by Japan with 12%. US production of both primary and secondary cadmium in 2005 rose +5.9% yr/yr to 1,070 metric tons, up from the 22-year low of 1,010 metric tones posted in 2004. The US in 2005 accounted for 5.5% of world cadmium production.

Demand – Consumption of cadmium has been declining fairly steeply in the last few years due to environmental concerns. US cadmium consumption fell by −43.9% yr/yr in 2005 to 656 metric tons, only slightly above the 7-decade low of 637 metric tons in 2003. Of the total apparent consumption, about 75% is used for batteries, 12% for pigments, 8% for coatings and plating, 4% for nonferrous alloys, and 1% for other uses.

Trade – The US in 2006 relied on imports for 29% of its cadmium usage, down from 38% as recently as 1996. US imports of cadmium have plunged in the past 10 years but imports in 2005 rose +9.5% to 288 metric tons, up from only 81metric tons in 2003, but down sharply from levels above 1,000 metric tons seen as recently as 1994. US exports of cadmium in 2005 rose very sharply by +350.0% to 686 metric tons.

World Refinery Production of Cadmium   In Metric Tons

Year	Australia	Belgium	Canada	China	Finland	Germany	Italy	Japan	Kazakhstan	Mexico	United Kingdom	United States[3]	World Total
1998	585	1,318	2,090	2,130	520	1,020	328	2,337	1,622	1,218	440	1,240	20,200
1999	462	1,235	1,911	2,150	700	1,145	360	2,567	1,246	1,275	547	1,190	20,000
2000	552	1,148	1,941	2,370	683	458	284	2,472	1,250	1,268	503	1,890	20,300
2001	378	1,236	1,493	2,510	604	539	312	2,460	1,250	1,421	485	1,450	20,000
2002	350	117	1,706	2,440	4	422	391	2,444	1,300	1,382	422	1,430	18,000
2003	350	----	1,759	2,710	----	640	22	2,497	1,351	1,590	529	1,420	18,500
2004[1]	350	----	1,880	2,800	----	640	----	2,233	1,900	1,594	532	1,010	18,700
2005[2]	374	----	1,703	3,000	----	640	----	2,297	2,000	1,600	481	1,070	19,400

[1] Preliminary.   [2] Estimate.   [3] Primary and secondary metal.   *Source: U.S. Geological Survey (USGS)*

Salient Statistics of Cadmium in the United States   In Metric Tons of Contained Cadmium

Year	Net Import Reliance as a % of Apparent Consumption	Production (Metal)	Producer Shipments	Cadmium Sulfide Production	Production Other Compounds	Imports of Cadmium Metal[3]	Exports[4]	Apparent Consumption	Industry Stocks Dec. 31[5]	New York Dealer Price $ per Pound
1998	38	1,240	1,570	125	638	514	180	2,100	729	.28
1999	9	1,190	1,020	64	604	294	20	1,850	893	.14
2000	6	1,890	1,580	42	417	425	314	2,010	1,200	.16
2001	3	680	954	31	----	107	272	659	1,090	.23
2002	0	700	776	33	----	25	194	561	1,750	.29
2003	0	1,420	995	----	----	112	615	637	1,460	.59
2004[1]	0	1,010	1,060	----	----	263	154	1,170	1,420	.55
2005[2]	0	1,070	1,050	----	----	288	686	656		1.50

[1] Preliminary.   [2] Estimate.   [3] For consumption.   [4] Cadmium metal, alloys, dross, flue dust.   [5] Metallic, Compounds, Distributors.
[6] Sticks & Balls in 1 to 5 short ton lots.   E = Net exporter.   *Source: U.S. Geological Survey (USGS)*

Average Price of Cadmium (99.95%) in the United States   In Dollars Per Pound

Year	Jan.	Feb.	Mar.	Apr.	May	June	July	Aug.	Sept.	Oct.	Nov.	Dec.	Average
2004	57.50	62.24	62.50	62.50	62.50	62.50	62.50	62.50	62.50	62.50	62.50	62.50	62.06
2005	62.50	62.50	79.46	92.50	92.50	110.80	159.50	200.76	205.00	194.76	195.00	195.00	137.52
2006	162.75	140.00	140.00	140.00	144.55	171.36	175.00	169.78	155.00	136.36	145.00	167.75	153.96

Source: American Metal Market (AMM)

Canola (Rapeseed)

Canola is a genetic variation of rapeseed that was developed by Canadian plant breeders specifically for its nutritional qualities and its low level of saturated fat. The term *Canola* is a contraction of "Canadian oil." The history of canola oil begins with the rapeseed plant, a member of the mustard family. The rape plant is grown both as feed for livestock and birdfeed. For 4,000 years, the oil from the rapeseed was used in China and India for cooking and as lamp oil. During World War II, rapeseed oil was used as a marine and industrial lubricant. After the war, the market for rapeseed oil plummeted. Rapeseed growers needed other uses for their crop, and that stimulated the research that led to the development of canola. In 1974, Canadian plant breeders from the University of Manitoba produced canola by genetically altering rapeseed. Each canola plant produces yellow flowers, which then produce pods. The tiny round seeds within each pod are crushed to produce canola oil. Each canola seed contains approximately 40% oil. Canola oil is the world's third largest source of vegetable oil accounting for 13% of world vegetable oils, following soybean oil at 32%, and palm oil at 28%. The rest of the seed is processed into canola meal, which is used as high protein livestock feed.

The climate in Canada is especially suitable for canola plant growth. Today, over 13 million acres of Canadian soil are dedicated to canola production. Canola oil is Canada's leading vegetable oil. Due to strong demand from the US for canola oil, approximately 70% of Canada's canola oil is exported to the US. Canola oil is used as a salad oil, cooking oil, and for margarine as well as in the manufacture of inks, biodegradable greases, pharmaceuticals, fuel, soap, and cosmetics.

Canola futures and options are traded at the Winnipeg Exchange. The futures contract calls for the delivery of 20 metric tons of canola and 5 contracts are together called a "1 board lot." The futures contract is priced in Canadian dollars per metric ton.

Prices – Canola prices on the Winnipeg nearest-futures chart started 2006 at about CD\$240 per metric ton and then rallied almost the entire year to end the year at about CD\$380 per metric ton.

The average monthly wholesale price of canola oil in the Midwest in 2005 fell –7.5% yr/yr to 30.73 cents per pound, down from last year's 7-year high of 33.21. The average monthly wholesale price of canola meal (delivery Pacific Northwest) in the 2005/06-crop year rose by 0.6% to \$140.52 per short ton, up slightly from the 5-year low of \$139.75 per short ton in the 2004-05-crop year. By early in 2007, however, the price was up into the \$150 to \$170 range so that for the first four months of the 2006/07-crop year the average price was up to an average monthly price of \$163.26 per short ton.

Supply – World canola production in the 2006/07 marketing year fell by –4.0% yr/yr to 46.612, down from the 2005/06 record high of 48.549 million metric tons. The world's largest canola producers were the European Union with 34% of world production in 2006/07, China (27%), Canada (20%), and India (13%). US production of canola in 2006/07 fell –11.8% yr/yr to 633,000 metric tons.

Regarding canola products, world production of canola oil in 2006/07 rose +4.9% to 18.018 million metric tons, which was a record high. US production of canola oil in 2006/07 rose +12.2% to 461,000 metric tons, which was a record high. World production of canola meal in 2006/07 rose +4.1% to a record high of 27.255 million metric tons.

Demand – World crush demand for canola in 2006/07 rose +4.4% yr/yr to 46.082 million metric tons, which was a record high. World consumption of canola oil in 2006/07 rose +5.3% yr/yr to a new record high of 17.826 million metric tons. World consumption of canola meal in 2006/07 rose +4.6% to a record high of 27.412 million metric tons.

Trade – World canola exports in 2006/07 rose +6.5% to 7.454 million metric tons, world canola oil exports rose +11.8% to 1.917 million metric tons, and world canola meal exports rose +3.0% yr/yr to 2.646 million metric tons. World canola imports in 2006/07 rose +11.4% to 7.471 million metric tons, world canola oil imports rose +9.1% to 1.605 million metric tons, and world canola meal imports rose 1.4% to 2.54 million metric tons. Regarding US canola trade, US canola imports in 2006/07 rose +44.8% to 750,000 metric tons and US exports were unchanged at 155,000 metric tons.

World Production of Canola (Rapeseed)   In Thousands of Metric Tons

Year	Australia	Canada	China	Bangla-desh	Belarus	EU-25	India	Pakistan	Romania	Russia	Ukraine	United States	World Total
1995-96	557	6,436	9,777	239	25	8,271	6,000	255	1	125	17	250	34,435
1996-97	624	5,062	9,200	246	19	7,330	6,942	255	2	110	13	219	31,489
1997-98	856	6,392	9,578	249	21	8,636	4,935	286	12	71	44	355	33,161
1998-99	1,690	7,643	8,300	254	52	9,517	4,900	292	29	125	67	710	35,812
1999-00	2,460	8,798	10,132	254	57	14,253	5,110	279	108	135	148	621	42,483
2000-01	1,775	7,205	11,381	249	73	11,288	3,725	297	76	148	132	909	37,413
2001-02	1,756	5,017	11,331	238	95	11,483	4,500	231	102	140	135	908	36,033
2002-03	871	4,178	10,552	233	60	11,652	4,050	221	100	115	61	697	32,908
2003-04	1,703	6,771	11,420	218	55	11,174	6,800	235	20	192	51	686	39,434
2004-05[1]	1,496	7,728	13,182	230	143	15,336	6,500	241	101	276	149	613	46,143
2005-06[2]	1,441	9,660	13,050	248	120	15,396	6,800	260	90	303	285	718	48,549
2006-07[3]	450	9,100	12,500	255	60	15,696	6,200	260	110	500	600	633	46,612

[1] Preliminary.   [2] Estimate.   [3] Forecast.   *Source: Economic Research Service, U.S. Department of Agriculture (ERS-USDA); The Oil World*

CANOLA

Canola Futures - Winnipeg Comodity Exchange
(weekly close) as of December 29, 2006

CAD per metric ton

Volume of Trading of Canola Futures in Winnipeg   In Contracts

Year	Jan.	Feb.	Mar.	Apr.	May	June	July	Aug.	Sept.	Oct.	Nov.	Dec.	Total
1997	121,433	133,056	131,473	148,647	117,219	116,117	80,867	72,602	93,967	150,065	97,984	124,245	1,387,675
1998	100,926	144,309	110,708	140,789	130,551	121,829	107,816	89,457	121,573	181,002	127,120	181,278	1,557,358
1999	129,758	59,772	132,732	143,282	102,838	134,179	94,256	113,913	130,505	184,973	157,428	179,798	1,563,434
2000	137,528	182,744	163,038	169,807	168,164	152,358	79,071	91,762	146,890	208,639	154,727	204,045	1,858,773
2001	196,137	292,226	286,463	247,744	205,798	188,175	163,901	155,531	143,220	205,016	174,910	165,852	2,424,973
2002	164,945	179,753	166,889	159,981	133,202	139,256	132,524	174,527	131,034	170,873	105,661	169,477	1,828,122
2003	129,903	152,738	108,991	153,528	120,178	152,979	90,909	66,768	109,760	217,310	90,950	153,269	1,547,283
2004	145,339	204,567	178,516	192,429	120,218	128,843	73,417	97,483	113,368	175,776	110,922	196,094	1,736,972
2005	116,678	207,198	141,717	124,636	102,424	178,001	87,724	121,749	138,701	200,004	145,231	258,922	1,822,985
2006	195,189	240,070	237,537	229,470	211,688	238,967	129,433	145,133	212,164	284,033	191,676	291,994	2,607,354

Source: Winnipeg Commodity Exchange (WCE)

Average Open Interest of Canola Futures in Winnipeg   In Contracts

Year	Jan.	Feb.	Mar.	Apr.	May	June	July	Aug.	Sept.	Oct.	Nov.	Dec.
1997	48,681	48,281	50,815	50,025	49,212	43,941	35,496	30,039	25,255	36,674	38,702	42,510
1998	35,864	46,678	49,161	48,683	56,163	60,285	57,627	51,462	53,919	56,651	51,426	60,663
1999	57,958	64,014	57,851	57,351	51,808	53,039	49,273	41,819	53,425	67,244	63,780	64,286
2000	59,057	65,545	65,296	66,253	65,855	59,673	46,813	51,367	59,342	72,618	64,862	65,170
2001	57,537	73,539	88,111	78,143	77,425	84,315	72,430	70,137	67,275	71,651	65,580	66,884
2002	57,821	56,443	53,321	56,830	50,924	38,901	48,329	54,286	53,630	50,379	56,896	57,983
2003	52,818	54,749	55,369	53,480	50,549	49,930	47,479	45,314	44,510	49,008	45,423	48,655
2004	54,524	57,944	71,624	77,357	69,783	59,012	50,669	51,009	49,659	53,855	65,215	68,719
2005	64,147	75,090	65,205	63,514	54,341	53,390	57,706	56,305	65,700	68,186	66,117	87,246
2006	82,651	88,576	84,828	88,970	84,710	81,561	81,243	77,356	81,597	80,800	90,694	102,651

Source: Winnipeg Commodity Exchange (WCE)

World Supply and Distribution of Canola and Products   In Thousands of Metric Tons

	Canola					Canola Meal					Canola Oil				
Year	Pro- duction	Exports	Imports	Crush	Ending Stocks	Pro- duction	Exports	Imports	Con- sumption	Ending Stocks	Pro- duction	Exports	Imports	Con- sumption	Ending Stocks
1999-00	42,483	8,207	8,170	37,138	4,204	22,090	2,315	2,260	21,988	384	13,940	1,738	1,739	13,839	550
2000-01	37,413	7,205	7,018	35,427	2,689	21,134	1,834	1,919	21,314	289	13,284	1,158	1,232	13,332	576
2001-02	36,033	4,927	4,978	33,486	2,776	19,946	1,486	1,535	19,981	303	13,046	1,006	1,108	13,225	499
2002-03	32,908	4,134	4,039	31,592	1,809	18,801	1,606	1,726	18,945	279	12,238	907	909	12,242	497
2003-04	39,434	5,484	5,147	36,424	1,835	21,756	2,474	2,430	21,355	636	14,135	1,149	1,351	14,432	402
2004-05[1]	46,143	4,900	5,049	40,653	4,466	24,162	2,229	2,282	24,258	593	15,741	1,149	1,171	15,670	495
2005-06[2]	48,549	6,998	6,709	44,140	5,395	26,178	2,570	2,505	26,154	552	17,175	1,715	1,471	16,922	504
2006-07[3]	46,612	7,454	7,471	46,082	3,011	27,255	2,646	2,540	27,412	289	18,018	1,917	1,605	17,826	384

[1] Preliminary.   [2] Estimate.   [3] Forecast.   *Source: Economic Research Service, U.S. Department of Agriculture (ERS-USDA); The Oil World*

Salient Statistics of Canola and Canola Oil in the United States   In Thousands of Metric Tons

	Canola							Canola Oil						
	Supply				Disappearance			Supply				Disappearance		
Year	Stocks June 1	Pro- duction	Imports	Total	Crush	Exports	Total[3]	Stocks June 1	Pro- duction	Imports	Total	Domestic	Exports	Total
1999-00	77	621	242	940	722	136	858	79	281	534	894	669	129	798
2000-01	50	909	217	1,176	773	220	993	96	292	545	933	797	85	882
2001-02	39	908	125	1,072	757	218	975	51	265	503	819	679	116	795
2002-03	68	697	197	962	575	287	862	24	226	445	695	587	73	660
2003-04	72	686	244	1,002	630	305	935	35	274	555	864	697	126	823
2004-05	40	613	467	1,120	901	139	1,040	41	363	514	918	738	122	860
2005-06[1]	60	718	518	1,296	1,032	155	1,187	58	411	728	1,197	864	214	1,078
2006-07[2]	87	633	750	1,470	1,205	155	1,360	119	461	730	1,310	980	275	1,255

[1] Preliminary.   [2] Forecast.   [3] Includes planting seed and residual.   *Source: Economic Research Service, U.S. Department of Agriculture*

Wholesale Price of Canola Oil in Midwest   In Cents Per Pound

Year	Jan.	Feb.	Mar.	Apr.	May	June	July	Aug.	Sept.	Oct.	Nov.	Dec.	Average
1998	28.00	29.00	30.30	30.58	31.13	28.45	28.44	26.85	29.75	28.20	27.19	26.10	28.67
1999	25.31	21.44	20.69	21.50	20.38	20.58	19.33	19.75	19.25	18.44	18.19	17.95	20.23
2000	17.31	16.50	17.25	18.69	17.75	16.45	15.50	15.69	15.60	15.00	15.31	15.50	16.38
2001	14.81	15.19	16.69	16.69	18.00	19.25	22.50	21.80	19.94	19.00	20.56	21.88	18.86
2002	20.81	21.31	27.44	21.94	21.95	23.19	25.06	28.45	29.81	30.75	34.19	41.19	27.17
2003	24.30	28.88	27.63	27.44	28.13	27.13	26.56	26.30	28.44	31.88	32.67	33.92	28.61
2004	33.44	37.19	38.19	36.81	35.60	32.88	31.63	29.50	31.38	28.35	31.75	31.75	33.21
2005[1]	29.80	28.88	31.38	31.00	31.25	33.00	31.95	29.75	30.50	31.50	30.88	28.81	30.73

[1] Preliminary.   *Source: Economic Research Service, U.S. Department of Agriculture (ERS-USDA)*

Average Price of Canola in Vancouver   In Canadian Dollars Per Metric Ton

Year	Jan.	Feb.	Mar.	Apr.	May	June	July	Aug.	Sept.	Oct.	Nov.	Dec.	Average
1999	402.74	368.17	363.24	362.16	353.21	356.53	317.36	305.73	302.93	302.68	297.76	287.62	335.01
2000	286.09	277.92	280.97	287.34	284.59	274.12	265.32	262.24	269.17	265.32	267.75	278.59	274.95
2001	279.07	285.05	302.04	299.59	310.00	320.79	356.98	368.33	351.01	332.16	328.99	334.53	322.38
2002	329.23	328.38	329.39	316.74	318.67	330.21	369.42	401.78	408.43	413.64	436.25	418.74	366.74
2003	396.78	380.81	351.97	362.89	344.59	333.48	322.64	319.37	324.07	338.93	343.65	338.57	346.48
2004	345.51	370.53	402.02	395.92	384.09	378.62	360.93	349.57	341.29	288.64	275.37	265.15	346.47
2005	261.56	250.02	270.29	273.13	275.58	286.78	279.45	259.58	240.30	235.00	233.21	226.39	257.61
2006	230.48	231.43	241.57	248.63	267.11	263.66	277.90	265.70	265.20	295.90	335.39	348.60	272.63

Source: Winnipeg Commodity Exchange (WCE)

Average Wholesale Price of Canola Meal, 36% Pacific Northwest   In Dollars Per Short Ton

Crop Year	Oct.	Nov.	Dec.	Jan.	Feb.	Mar.	Apr.	May	June	July	Aug.	Sept.	Average
1999-00	----	----	----	----	----	----	----	----	----	----	----	----	117.07
2000-01	122.58	132.30	142.34	140.53	132.90	132.01	140.25	144.00	149.30	154.29	142.60	137.27	139.20
2001-02	142.85	142.44	129.48	135.34	137.33	150.15	146.60	141.90	142.10	153.40	149.10	149.30	143.33
2002-03	131.50	134.70	142.17	154.10	155.80	147.55	145.60	148.50	146.95	137.10	135.50	149.20	144.06
2003-04	169.65	187.19	181.35	201.07	205.50	228.65	214.40	200.03	189.00	192.09	146.99	145.55	188.46
2004-05	133.39	138.81	135.13	129.21	139.55	146.08	140.85	139.25	153.98	150.48	138.12	132.10	139.75
2005-06	130.13	139.55	158.06	150.05	143.94	134.74	136.04	136.59	139.63	137.83	143.28	136.38	140.52
2006-07[1]	149.77	166.80	163.17	173.30									163.26

[1] Preliminary.   *Source: Economic Research Service, U.S. Department of Agriculture (ERS-USDA)*

Cassava

Cassava is a perennial woody shrub with an edible root. Cassava, which is also called manioc, mandioca, or yucca, grows in tropical and subtropical areas of the world. Cassava has been known since the 1500s and originates in Latin America. The cassava's starchy roots are a major source of dietary energy for more than 500 million people. Cassava is the highest producer of carbohydrates among staple crops, and it ranks fourth in food crops in developing countries. The leaves of the cassava plant are also edible and are relatively rich in protein and vitamins A and B.

Cassava is drought-tolerant and needs less soil preparation and weeding than other crops. Because cassava can be stored in the ground for up to 3 years, it also serves as a reserve food when other crops fail. The cassava is propagated by cuttings of the woody stem, thereby resulting in a low multiplication rate compared to crops propagated by true seeds.

One problem with cassava is the poisonous cyanides, which need to be destroyed before consumption. The cyanide content differs with each variety of cassava, but higher cyanide is usually correlated to high yields. The cyanide content can be destroyed through heat and various processing methods such as grating, sun drying, and fermenting.

Cassava is the primary source of tapioca. Cassava is also eaten raw or boiled, and is processed into livestock feed, starch and glucose, flour, and pharmaceuticals. One species of cassava has been successfully grown for its rubber.

Prices – The price of tapioca (hard pellets, FOB Rotterdam) rose by 16% in the first four months of 2005 to a 9-year high of $149 per metric ton. The 2005 price was 82% higher than the record low of $82 in 2001.

Supply – World production of cassava in 2002, the latest full reporting year for that series, rose by +0.9% to 184.853 million metric tons from 183.289 million in 2001. The world's largest producers of cassava in 2002 were Nigeria (with 18.7% of world production), Brazil (12.5%), Thailand (9.1%), and Indonesia (9.0%).

Trade – World exports of tapioca in 2005 fell –29.6% to 3.954 million metric tons from 5.616 million in 2004. Thailand accounted for 77% of world exports in 2005, followed by Vietnam with 16% of world exports and Indonesia with 6%. The world's two main importers of tapioca in 2005 were China with 82% of world imports and the European Union with 9% of world imports.

World Cassava Production   In Thousands of Metric Tons

Year	Brazil	China	Ghana	India	Indo-nesia	Mozam-bique	Nigeria	Para-guay	Tan-zania	Thailand	Uganda	Dem. Rep. Congo[2]	World Total
1995	25,423	3,501	6,612	5,929	15,442	4,178	31,404	3,054	5,969	17,388	2,224	17,500	165,436
1996	24,584	3,601	7,111	5,443	17,002	4,734	31,418	2,648	5,992	17,388	2,245	18,000	164,711
1997	24,305	3,651	7,000	5,868	15,134	5,337	30,409	3,155	5,700	18,084	2,291	16,973	164,373
1998	19,503	3,701	7,227	6,000	14,696	5,639	32,695	3,300	6,128	15,591	3,204	17,060	162,856
1999	20,864	3,751	7,845	6,700	16,438	5,353	32,697	3,694	7,182	16,507	4,875	16,500	171,918
2000	23,336	3,801	8,107	6,800	16,089	5,362	32,010	2,719	7,120	19,064	4,966	15,959	178,567
2001	22,479	3,851	8,966	6,900	17,055	5,400	32,586	3,568	6,884	18,396	5,265	15,436	183,289
2002[1]	23,108	3,851	9,731	6,900	16,723	5,400	34,476	4,142	6,888	16,870	5,300	14,929	184,853

[1] Estimate.   [2] Formerly Zaire.   *Source: Food and Agriculture Organization of the United Nations (FAO-UN)*

Prices of Tapioca, Hard Pellets, F.O.B. Rotterdam   U.S. Dollars Per Tonne

Year	Jan.	Feb.	Mar.	Apr.	May	June	July	Aug.	Sept.	Oct.	Nov.	Dec.	Average
1997	133	118	112	108	114	110	100	97	100	102	102	100	108
1998	96	100	98	104	106	104	105	106	112	122	124	109	107
1999	104	102	101	102	108	104	99	102	100	99	100	97	102
2000	94	90	88	92	85	88	88	81	78	74	76	79	84
2001	83	80	77	78	80	82	84	84	87	83	84	84	82
2002	86	82	82	84	87	91	96	97	95	93	93	89	90
2003	91	92	95	96	101	101	103	108	114	134	138	143	110
2004	138	132	121	118	117	118	120	122	128	134	139	148	128
2005	147	149	153	145									149

Source: The Oil World

World Trade in Tapioca   In Thousands of Metric Tons

| | ----------------------- Exports ----------------------- | | | | --- Imports --- | | | | | | |
Year	China	Indonesia	Thailand	Viet Nam	Total World Exports	China	EC-12[2]	Japan	Rep. of Korea	United States	Former USSR	Total World Imports
1998	5	221	3,199	87	3,555	250	2,620	19	463	11	18	3,536
1999	7	340	4,341	117	4,857	381	3,781	18	212	1	18	4,501
2000	7	151	3,915	215	4,334	170	3,765	19	292	12	20	4,543
2001	9	177	4,494	409	5,140	1,950	2,154	20	445	17	19	4,714
2002	12	130	3,067	308	3,556	1,760	1,560	14	157	10	19	3,588
2003	14	42	3,994	681	4,785	2,368	1,869	21	247	6	19	4,626
2004	17	234	4,579	730	5,616	3,442	2,075	30	460	12	19	6,133
2005[1]	18	230	3,028	620	3,954	3,335	362	23	265	ÑÑ	21	4,062

[1] Estimate.   [2] Intra-EU trade is excluded.   *Source: The Oil World*

Castor Beans

Castor bean plants are native to the Ethiopian region of tropical east Africa. The seeds of the castor bean are used to produce castor oil. The average castor bean seed contains 35% to 55% oil. The oil is removed from the bean seeds by either pressing or solvent extraction. Castor oil is used in many products. In the US, the paint and varnish industry is the single largest market for castor oil. Castor oil is also used for coating fabrics, insulation, cosmetics, skin emollients, hair oils, inks, nylon plastics, greases, and hydraulic fluids.

Ricin is found in all parts of the castor bean plant, but the most concentrated amounts are found in the cake by-product after oil extraction. Ricin is one of the most deadly, naturally occurring poisons known. Ricin received attention when it was used in a subway attack in Japan in 1995 and again when it was sent to a Congressional office in an envelope in February 2004. One non-deadly use for ricin is for medical research where it is being studied for use as a potential treatment for cancer.

Supply – World production of castor-seed beans in the 2005-06 marketing year rose by +5.7% to a record high of 1.425 million metric tons. The world's largest producer of castor-seed beans by far is India with 64% of world production in 2005-06 at 910,000 metric tons. The second and third largest producers are China with 18% of world production (250,000 metric tons) and Brazil with 12% of world production (162,000 metric tons).

Demand – US consumption of castor oil in 2005-06 fell by –10.5% to 19.227 million pounds. In 2006-07, however, it is forecasted to rise +9.2% to 21.004 million pounds.

World Production of Castorseed Beans   In Thousands of Metric Tons

Crop Year	Brazil	China	Ecuador	India	Mexico	Paraguay	Pakistan	Philip-pines	Sudan	Tanzania	Thailand	Former U.S.S.R.	World Total
1999-00	33	250	4	910	1	8	3	4	1	3	7	2	1,261
2000-01	116	300	4	867	1	11	1	4	1	3	9	2	1,353
2001-02	100	260	4	610	1	13	2	4	1	3	9	2	1,043
2002-03	72	265	4	640	1	7	1	4	1	3	9	2	1,043
2003-04[1]	78	258	4	700	1	11	9	4	1	3	9	2	1,133
2004-05[2]	129	250	4	870	1	11	5	4	1	3	9	2	1,348
2005-06[3]	162	250	4	910	1	10	8	4	1	3	9	2	1,425

[1] Preliminary.   [2] Estimate.   [3] Forecast.   Sources: Foreign Agricultural Service, U.S.Department of Agriculture (FAS-USDA); The Oil World

Castor Oil Consumption[2] in the United States   In Thousands of Pounds

Year	Oct.	Nov.	Dec.	Jan.	Feb.	Mar.	Apr.	May	June	July	Aug.	Sept.	Total
2000-01	2,694	4,601	2,386	3,975	2,896	3,209	3,159	3,840	3,112	3,050	4,686	2,257	39,865
2001-02	4,127	2,346	1,650	3,012	3,703	3,129	3,062	3,096	1,243	2,992	2,872	2,867	34,099
2002-03	3,281	1,887	1,528	1,641	1,642	1,629	1,123	1,315	1,518	1,839	1,449	2,119	20,971
2003-04	2,072	1,836	1,779	1,526	1,251	2,241	2,396	2,250	1,905	1,542	2,382	2,366	23,546
2004-05	2,155	1,391	1,581	1,365	1,915	1,992	2,175	2,211	1,827	1,689	2,021	1,162	21,484
2005-06	1,389	1,761	1,654	1,602	1,610	1,426	1,457	1,766	1,899	1,516	1,768	1,379	19,227
2006-07[1]	1,583	2,026	1,642										21,004

[1] Preliminary.   [2] In inedible products (Resins, Plastics, etc.).   Source: Bureau of the Census, U.S. Department of Commerce

Castor Oil Stocks in the United States, on First of Month   In Thousands of Pounds

Year	Oct.	Nov.	Dec.	Jan.	Feb.	Mar.	Apr.	May	June	July	Aug.	Sept.
2000-01	32,585	35,858	30,058	24,728	32,566	35,186	24,808	51,808	57,910	48,415	40,279	59,461
2001-02	53,083	45,933	23,973	38,459	31,058	36,743	39,591	39,528	43,227	50,814	49,283	53,075
2002-03	41,322	37,282	33,195	32,983	25,926	20,551	22,460	15,337	23,212	24,138	32,110	27,827
2003-04	26,463	17,753	16,630	18,582	14,097	13,985	7,507	22,751	W	25,593	18,381	14,922
2004-05	34,525	31,608	24,287	19,476	32,641	25,318	27,876	19,098	31,493	22,919	15,963	35,604
2005-06	38,357	45,720	37,111	29,428	21,047	25,076	15,756	25,543	25,070	22,165	21,329	14,389
2006-07[1]	39,635	24,055	18,780	44,560								

[1] Preliminary.   Source: Bureau of the Census, U.S. Department of Commerce

Average Wholesale Price of Castor Oil No. 1, Brazilian Tanks in New York   In Cents Per Pound

Year	Jan.	Feb.	Mar.	Apr.	May	June	July	Aug.	Sept.	Oct.	Nov.	Dec.	Average
1999	48.00	48.00	48.00	48.00	48.00	48.00	48.00	48.00	48.00	48.00	48.00	48.00	48.00
2000	47.00	47.00	47.00	47.00	47.00	47.00	47.00	48.00	48.00	48.00	48.00	18.00	47.42
2001	48.00	48.00	48.00	48.00	48.00	48.00	48.00	48.00	48.00	48.00	47.50	47.50	47.92
2002	47.50	47.50	47.50	47.50	47.50	47.50	47.00	47.00	47.00	47.00	47.00	47.00	47.25
2003	47.00	47.00	47.00	47.00	47.00	47.00	47.00	47.00	47.00	47.00	47.00	47.00	47.00
2004	47.00	47.00	47.00	47.00	47.00	47.00	47.00	47.00	47.00	47.00	47.00	48.00	47.08
2005	50.00	50.00	50.00	50.00	50.00	50.00	50.00	49.00	49.00	47.00	45.50	45.00	48.79

Source: Foreign Agricultural Service, U.S. Department of Agriculture (FAS-USDA)

Cattle and Calves

The beef cycle begins with the cow-calf operation, which breeds the new calves. Most ranchers breed their herds of cows in summer, thus producing the new crop of calves in spring (the gestation period is about nine months). This allows the calves to be born during the milder weather of spring and provides the calves with ample forage through the summer and early autumn. The calves are weaned from the mother after 6-8 months and most are then moved into the "stocker" operation. The calves usually spend 6-10 months in the stocker operation, growing to near full-sized by foraging for summer grass or winter wheat. When the cattle reach 600-800 pounds, they are typically sent to a feedlot and become "feeder cattle." In the feedlot, the cattle are fed a special food mix to encourage rapid weight gain. The mix includes grain (corn, milo, or wheat), a protein supplement (soybean, cottonseed, or linseed meal), and roughage (alfalfa, silage, prairie hay, or an agricultural by-product such as sugar beet pulp). The animal is considered "finished" when it reaches full weight and is ready for slaughter, typically at around 1,200 pounds, which produces a dressed carcass of around 745 pounds. After reaching full weight, the cattle are sold for slaughter to a meat packing plant. Futures and options on live cattle and feeder cattle are traded at the Chicago Mercantile Exchange. Both the live and feeder cattle futures contracts trade in terms of cents per pound.

Prices – Live cattle futures prices in the first half of the year 2006 extended the decline seen in late 2005 but then rebounded in the latter half of the year, finally closing 2006 at 133.93 cents per pound, down −2.5% versus 2005. Cattle prices fell in early 2006 as US beef exports remained weak and as beef supplies were plentiful. Even though key countries dropped their bans on US beef in late 2005 and early 2006, US beef exports had difficulty getting restarted because of hyper-sensitive testing requirements and because Australia had taken over much of the premium beef market previously held by the US. Japan dropped its ban in December 2005 but then quickly reinstituted its ban in January 2006 when some bone fragments were found in a US beef shipment. Japan in July 2006 finally dropped its ban on US beef exports after an extended inspection process for US beef packing houses. Cattle prices rallied in the latter half of 2006 on continued firm US domestic demand and on higher corn prices starting in September 2006, which increased feed costs and raised the breakeven price for cattle prices.

Supply – The world cattle and buffalo figures showed a small +0.7% increase in 2006 (as of Jan 1) to 995 million head, which is just slightly above the 3-decade low of 935 million head seen in 1995. As of January 1, 2006 there were 97.102 million cattle and calves on US farms, up +1.7% y/yr and slightly above 94.888 million in 2004, which was the lowest level since 1959. World production of beef and veal in 2006 rose +2.2% to 53.511 million metric tons (carcass weight equivalent) and USDA is forecasting a further rise of +2.2% to 54.717 million metric tons in 2007. US commercial production of beef in 2006 rose +5.6% to 26.075 billion pounds and the USDA is forecasting a further rise of +2.4% to 26.700 billion pounds in 2007.

Demand – World consumption of beef and veal in 2006 rose +14.6% to 52.509 million metric tons and the USDA is forecasting a further rise of +2.1% in 2007 to 52.580 million metric tons. US consumption of beef and veal in 2006 rose by +1.0% to 12.800 million metric tons and the USDA is forecasting a further rise of +1.75% in 2007 to 13.024 million metric tons.

Trade – US imports of live cattle in 2006 rose by +14.2% to 2.072 million head, recovering from the low levels seen when mad cow disease caused the US to close the Canadian border to live cattle in 2003. US exports of live cattle in 2006 rose by +107.7% yr/yr to 43,948 head, up sharply from the multi-decade low of 21,155 in 2005 caused by to cattle trading bans by key US trading partners.

By weight, US imports of beef in 2006 fell −14.6% to 3.073 billion pounds but the USDA is forecasting an increase of +6.7% to 3.280 billion pounds in 2007. US exports of beef in 2006 rose steeply by +66.9% to 1.150 billion pounds and the USDA is forecasting a further rise of +25.2% to 1.440 billion pounds in 2007. That, however, remains far below the levels of about 2.5 billion pounds seen before mad cow disease hit in December 2003 and largely shut down US beef exports.

World Cattle and Buffalo Numbers as of January 1   In Thousands of Head

Year	Argentina	Australia	Brazil	Canada	China	European Union	India	Mexico	Russia	South Africa	Ukraine	United States	World Total (Mil. Head)
1998	49,238	26,710	144,670	13,360	121,757	83,271	288,799	29,051	31,500	13,667	12,579	99,744	1,031.6
1999	49,437	26,688	143,893	13,211	124,354	94,570	286,569	29,246	28,600	13,772	11,722	99,115	934.6
2000	49,832	27,588	146,272	13,201	126,983	93,772	285,220	28,313	27,000	13,580	10,627	98,199	1,026.6
2001	50,167	27,720	150,382	13,608	128,663	91,419	284,822	28,449	25,500	13,460	9,424	97,298	1,020.0
2002	50,369	27,870	156,314	13,762	128,242	90,339	285,124	28,481	24,510	13,505	9,433	96,723	1,026.0
2003	50,869	27,870	161,463	13,488	130,848	88,719	286,079	29,224	23,500	13,635	9,108	96,100	989.7
2004	50,768	26,640	165,492	14,653	134,672	87,478	283,103	28,437	22,285	13,540	7,712	94,888	986.9
2005	50,167	27,270	169,567	15,063	137,818	86,412	282,500	27,572	21,100	13,510	6,992	95,438	988.0
2006[1]	50,166	27,782	173,816	14,830	141,575	85,806	282,300	26,949	19,850	13,790	6,704	97,102	994.7
2007[2]	50,766	28,600	180,103	14,400	145,349	85,150	282,000	26,644	18,695	14,200	6,570	98,400	1,004.2

[1] Preliminary.   [2] Forecast.   *Source: Foreign Agricultural Service, U.S. Department of Agriculture (FAS-USDA)*

Cattle Supply and Distribution in the United States   In Thousands of Head

	Cattle & Calves on Farms January 1	Imports	Calves Born	Total Supply	Federally Inspected	Other[3]	All Commercial	Farm	Total Slaughter	Deaths on Farms	Exports	Total Disap-pearance
Year												
1997	101,656	2,046	38,961	142,663	37,101	792	37,893	218	38,111	4,676	282	43,069
1998	99,744	2,034	38,812	140,590	36,209	714	36,923	215	37,138	4,210	285	41,633
1999	99,115	1,945	38,796	139,856	36,738	695	37,432	210	37,642	4,114	329	42,085
2000	98,198	2,187	38,631	139,016	36,720	658	37,378	210	37,588	4,097	481	42,166
2001	97,277	2,437	38,280	137,994	35,751	625	36,377	200	36,577	4,209	678	41,464
2002	96,704	2,503	38,224	137,431	36,139	641	36,780	190	36,970	4,076	243	41,289
2003	96,100	1,752	37,903	135,754	35,883	611	36,494	192	36,686	4,030	100	40,816
2004	94,888	1,374	37,505	133,767	32,979	592	33,571	189	33,760	4,003	31	37,794
2005[1]	95,438	1,815	37,575	134,828	32,549	573	33,122	184	33,306	4,052	21	37,379
2006[2]	96,702	2,073	37,567	136,341	33,843	555	34,396				44	

The header spans: Livestock Slaughter - Cattle and Calves; Commercial (Federally Inspected, Other[3], All Commercial).

[1] Preliminary.   [2] Estimate.   [3] Wholesale and retail.   Source: Economic Research Service, U.S. Department of Agriculture (ERS-USDA)

Beef Supply and Utilization in the United States

Year/ Quarter	Beginning Stocks	Production Commercial	Total	Imports	Total Supply	Exports	Ending Stocks	Total Disap-pearance	Per Capita Disappearance Carcass Weight	Retail Weight
				Million Pounds					Pounds	
2003		26,238	26,238	3,006	29,244	2,518				64.9
I		6,282	6,282	810	7,092	582				16.2
II		6,902	6,902	741	7,643	678				16.9
III		7,081	7,081	619	7,700	680				16.9
IV		5,973	5,973	836	6,809	578				15.0
2004		24,548	24,548	3,679	28,227	461				66.1
I		5,838	5,838	873	6,711	36				16.0
II		6,253	6,253	929	7,182	120				16.9
III		6,360	6,360	940	7,300	138				16.9
IV		6,097	6,097	937	7,034	167				16.3
2005		24,683	24,683	3,599	28,282	689				65.5
I		5,725	5,725	831	6,556	130				15.6
II		6,189	6,189	1,065	7,254	189				16.8
III		6,560	6,560	906	7,466	150				17.0
IV		6,209	6,209	797	7,006	220				16.0
2006[1]		26,075	26,075	3,073	29,148	1,150				65.6
I		6,078	6,078	843	6,921	223				15.8
II		6,699	6,699	789	7,488	315				16.8
III		6,808	6,808	731	7,539	307				16.8
IV		6,490	6,490	710	7,200	305				16.2
2007[2]		26,700	26,700	3,280	29,980	1,440				66.4
I		6,375	6,375	760	7,135	325				16.0
II		6,800	6,800	880	7,680	350				17.1
III		7,000	7,000	830	7,830	380				17.3
IV		6,525	6,525	810	7,335	385				16.0

[1] Preliminary.   [2] Forecast.   Source: Economic Research Service, U.S. Department of Agriculture (ERS-USDA)

United States Cattle on Feed in 13 States   In Thousands of Head

Year/ Quarter	Number on Feed[3]	Placed on Feed	Marketings	Other Disappearance	Year/ Quarter	Number on Feed[3]	Placed on Feed	Marketings	Other Disappearance
2003	10,658	24,930	23,467	868	2005[1]	11,299	23,556	22,172	879
I	10,658	5,771	5,508	208	I	11,299	5,161	5,369	218
II	10,713	5,849	6,450	189	II	10,873	5,652	5,881	250
III	9,923	6,855	6,377	183	III	10,394	6,026	5,767	171
IV	10,218	6,455	5,132	288	IV	10,482	6,717	5,155	240
2004	11,253	23,267	22,849	917	2006[2]	11,804	23,640	22,532	948
I	11,253	5,176	5,436	230	I	11,804	5,634	5,380	246
II	10,763	5,617	6,002	246	II	11,812	5,488	6,163	265
III	10,132	6,196	6,196	175	III	10,872	6,490	5,792	185
IV	10,502	6,278	5,215	266	IV	11,385	6,028	5,197	252

[1] Preliminary.   [2] Estimate.   [3] Beginning of period.   Source: Economic Research Service, U.S. Department of Agriculture (ERS-USDA)

CATTLE AND CALVES

Live Cattle (monthly average) through December 2006   Cents per pound

Cents Per Pound
----- All Grades, Chicago (Jan. 1909 - Dec. 1947)
Good, Chicago (Jan. 1948 - Dec. 1964)
Choice, Chicago (Jan. 1965 - July 1971)
Choice, Average, Omaha (Aug. 1971 - Aug. 1987)
Average, Texas-Oklahoma (Sept. 1987 - date)

United States Cattle on Feed, 1000+ Capacity Feedlots[2], on First of Month   In Thousands of Head

Year	Jan.	Feb.	Mar.	Apr.	May	June	July	Aug.	Sept.	Oct.	Nov.	Dec.
1997	8,943	8,813	8,769	8,904	8,484	8,231	7,679	7,536	7,850	8,558	9,390	9,718
1998	9,455	9,180	8,835	8,607	8,295	8,289	7,825	7,706	7,750	8,376	9,190	9,404
1999	9,021	8,917	8,878	8,899	8,583	8,547	8,183	7,889	8,185	8,793	9,789	10,020
2000	9,752	9,885	9,695	9,593	9,391	9,411	8,959	8,812	8,972	9,502	10,192	10,213
2001	11,798	11,941	11,695	11,523	11,170	11,245	11,011	10,891	10,855	11,125	11,863	11,891
2002	11,565	11,572	11,518	11,587	10,971	10,990	10,507	10,109	10,159	10,452	10,785	10,946
2003	10,658	10,700	10,546	10,713	10,535	10,539	9,923	9,590	9,839	10,218	11,043	11,335
2004	11,253	11,138	10,987	10,763	10,375	10,640	10,132	9,868	9,988	10,502	11,334	11,334
2005	11,299	11,342	11,154	10,873	10,641	10,771	10,394	10,093	10,000	10,482	11,473	11,726
2006[1]	11,804	12,110	12,023	11,812	11,559	11,187	10,872	10,822	10,986	11,385	11,969	11,973

[1] Preliminary.   [2] 7 States through 2000.   *Source: Economic Research Service, U.S. Department of Agriculture (ERS-USDA)*

United States Cattle Placed on Feed, 1000+ Capacity Feedlots[2]   In Thousands of Head

Year	Jan.	Feb.	Mar.	Apr.	May	June	July	Aug.	Sept.	Oct.	Nov.	Dec.	Total
1997	1,663	1,552	1,694	1,296	1,612	1,224	1,751	2,111	2,278	2,454	1,826	1,304	20,765
1998	1,492	1,290	1,421	1,358	1,740	1,314	1,677	1,773	2,254	2,396	1,732	1,250	19,697
1999	1,681	1,563	1,741	1,443	1,733	1,515	1,565	2,085	2,345	2,629	1,823	1,408	21,531
2000	1,931	1,606	1,736	1,470	1,998	1,413	1,674	2,091	2,286	2,387	1,678	1,440	21,710
2001	2,263	1,580	1,842	1,551	2,372	1,965	1,986	2,204	2,141	2,702	1,908	1,578	24,092
2002	2,179	1,810	1,963	1,463	2,267	1,644	1,840	2,228	2,194	2,396	1,982	1,610	23,576
2003	2,089	1,650	2,032	1,870	2,307	1,672	1,997	2,384	2,474	2,781	1,926	1,748	24,930
2004	1,754	1,612	1,810	1,600	2,370	1,647	1,719	2,102	2,375	2,701	1,743	1,834	23,267
2005	1,888	1,523	1,750	1,660	2,223	1,769	1,678	1,993	2,355	2,788	2,045	1,884	23,556
2006[1]	2,199	1,598	1,837	1,629	1,913	1,946	1,963	2,300	2,227	2,425	1,889	1,714	23,640

[1] Preliminary.   [2] 7 States through 2000.   *Source: Economic Research Service, U.S. Department of Agriculture (ERS-USDA)*

United States Cattle Marketings, 1000+ Capacity Feedlots[2]   In Thousands of Head

Year	Jan.	Feb.	Mar.	Apr.	May	June	July	Aug.	Sept.	Oct.	Nov.	Dec.	Total
1997	1,728	1,554	1,497	1,648	1,785	1,732	1,852	1,755	1,528	1,545	1,429	1,499	19,552
1998	1,689	1,579	1,580	1,609	1,681	1,727	1,755	1,687	1,577	1,537	1,455	1,564	19,440
1999	1,738	1,560	1,668	1,681	1,696	1,835	1,816	1,747	1,682	1,570	1,530	1,601	20,124
2000	1,747	1,749	1,764	1,601	1,863	1,828	1,784	1,895	1,708	1,647	1,568	1,500	20,654
2001	2,042	1,745	1,916	1,815	2,196	2,122	2,047	2,186	1,825	1,896	1,800	1,811	23,401
2002	2,083	1,801	1,825	1,996	2,171	2,076	2,193	2,135	1,848	1,979	1,731	1,799	23,637
2003	1,972	1,733	1,803	1,985	2,238	2,227	2,270	2,075	2,032	1,855	1,537	1,740	23,467
2004	1,775	1,694	1,967	1,891	2,026	2,085	1,925	1,926	1,800	1,803	1,635	1,777	22,304
2005	1,772	1,634	1,963	1,801	1,997	2,083	1,918	2,033	1,816	1,739	1,701	1,715	22,172
2006[1]	1,810	1,612	1,958	1,795	2,170	2,198	1,955	2,077	1,760	1,770	1,802	1,625	22,532

[1] Preliminary.   [2] 7 States through 2000.   *Source: Economic Research Service, U.S. Department of Agriculture (ERS-USDA)*

Quarterly Trade of Live Cattle in the United States   In Head

| | Imports | | | | | Exports | | | | |
| | First Quarter | Second Quarter | Third Quarter | Fourth Quarter | | First Quarter | Second Quarter | Third Quarter | Fourth Quarter | |
Year					Annual					Annual
1997	494,637	500,052	423,838	627,825	2,046,352	63,217	58,153	81,095	79,879	282,344
1998	538,018	503,547	373,451	618,993	2,034,009	69,824	63,459	53,145	98,781	285,209
1999	549,847	424,182	313,211	657,836	1,945,076	51,830	59,195	47,049	171,245	329,319
2000	580,174	537,009	346,087	724,016	2,187,286	117,889	67,895	72,028	223,430	481,242
2001	700,239	612,645	444,637	679,194	2,436,715	111,549	75,152	297,069	194,683	678,453
2002	785,559	398,072	474,128	845,214	2,502,973	73,401	62,140	49,930	57,472	242,943
2003	630,303	408,833	142,780	569,669	1,751,585	38,246	34,145	10,953	16,926	100,270
2004	309,712	315,800	281,020	467,236	1,373,768	4,091	20,955	2,216	3,652	30,914
2005	335,687	348,897	341,834	788,270	1,814,688	5,128	6,446	5,977	3,604	21,155
2006[1]	708,579	470,073	375,744		2,072,528	8,721	12,465	11,775		43,948

[1] Preliminary.   *Source: Economic Research Service, U.S. Department of Agriculture (ERS-USDA)*

CATTLE AND CALVES

Average Slaughter Steer Price, Choice 2-4, Texas, 1100-1300 Lb.   In Dollars Per 100 Pounds

Year	Jan.	Feb.	Mar.	Apr.	May	June	July	Aug.	Sept.	Oct.	Nov.	Dec.	Average
2000	69.07	68.88	71.74	73.13	71.28	69.41	67.22	65.02	65.43	68.51	72.19	76.41	69.86
2001	78.79	79.40	79.44	76.50	74.93	72.64	70.71	69.07	68.75	66.30	63.60	63.62	71.98
2002	67.25	70.72	72.59	67.79	65.32	63.64	62.49	62.96	64.43	64.93	70.12	72.24	67.04
2003	77.18	78.77	77.52	79.24	79.50	76.73	76.89	81.74	90.59	105.50	101.88	90.75	84.69
2004	80.36	79.15	86.96	87.04	88.22	89.19	84.27	84.15	82.33	84.03	84.64	86.60	84.75
2005	87.77	87.73	91.78	91.98	88.83	83.06	79.37	80.80	85.19	87.40	90.32	93.08	87.28
2006	92.90	89.09	85.73	81.30	79.02	80.85	81.14	85.87	89.18	87.43	86.56	85.83	85.41

Source: Economic Research Service, U.S. Department of Agriculture (ERS-USDA)

Average Price of Feeder Steers in Oklahoma City   In Dollars Per 100 Pounds

Year	Jan.	Feb.	Mar.	Apr.	May	June	July	Aug.	Sept.	Oct.	Nov.	Dec.	Average
2000	96.49	97.21	101.16	99.01	95.88	97.01	102.11	99.05	93.41	90.84	96.19	97.40	97.15
2001	93.08	86.63	94.17	105.06	99.71	102.16	100.39	96.74	98.31	91.06	90.83	94.51	96.05
2002	92.43	93.66	94.06	91.76	90.78	85.68	83.29	85.19	84.71	84.23	85.69	89.43	88.41
2003	87.76	88.84	91.31	92.94	93.58	96.04	99.28	99.15	102.68	102.63	106.87	98.09	96.60
2004	79.35	80.18	107.35	109.99	115.40	121.10	124.63	124.65	116.97	116.96	117.13	113.01	110.56
2005	112.40	116.87	120.48	126.77	127.13	126.91	122.73	119.96	119.61	120.29	122.84	122.75	121.56
2006	125.49	123.56	121.41	122.29	119.35	122.29	124.55	120.35	123.90	114.85	100.78	99.80	118.22

Source: Economic Research Service, U.S. Department of Agriculture (ERS-USDA)

Federally Inspected Slaughter of Cattle in the United States   In Thousands of Head

Year	Jan.	Feb.	Mar.	Apr.	May	June	July	Aug.	Sept.	Oct.	Nov.	Dec.	Total
2000	2,878	2,883	3,078	2,735	3,128	3,191	2,918	3,211	2,984	3,082	2,879	2,665	35,631
2001	2,947	2,533	2,867	2,667	3,152	3,075	2,898	3,193	2,758	3,103	2,854	2,726	34,771
2002	2,999	2,564	2,688	2,899	3,098	3,017	3,141	3,163	2,816	3,205	2,812	2,719	35,120
2003	2,950	2,519	2,725	2,918	3,201	3,208	3,245	3,094	3,082	2,953	2,387	2,626	34,907
2004	2,527	2,381	2,818	2,654	2,792	2,949	2,745	2,775	2,689	2,693	2,492	2,642	32,156
2005	2,477	2,297	2,675	2,517	2,751	2,894	2,677	2,948	2,729	2,625	2,623	2,619	31,831
2006[1]	2,591	2,301	2,806	2,566	2,994	3,116	2,795	3,089	2,721	2,803	2,797	2,566	33,145

[1] Preliminary.   *Source: National Agricultural Statistics Board, U.S. Department of Agriculture (NASS-USDA)*

Feeder Cattle Futures - Chicago Mercantile Exchange
(weekly close) as of December 29, 2006 — Cents per Pound

Average Open Interest of Live Cattle Futures in Chicago   In Contracts

Year	Jan.	Feb.	Mar.	Apr.	May	June	July	Aug.	Sept.	Oct.	Nov.	Dec.
1997	97,014	103,437	108,157	98,354	99,640	96,279	99,042	98,590	94,137	93,579	100,368	102,741
1998	105,559	102,036	101,264	88,257	88,167	87,493	86,776	86,874	95,013	102,636	108,263	106,156
1999	115,254	115,283	115,410	104,482	103,290	101,078	96,843	101,858	121,305	123,466	126,040	120,204
2000	128,918	123,980	123,925	122,596	117,834	106,196	116,266	120,526	123,945	123,517	131,773	132,239
2001	132,298	132,866	131,312	123,075	112,180	114,970	116,162	105,252	114,214	109,677	108,574	95,182
2002	93,589	91,566	98,176	98,343	98,846	91,129	93,541	92,966	109,651	111,338	121,671	116,588
2003	111,874	105,882	98,943	96,875	107,193	111,397	113,324	115,417	130,836	124,525	113,224	106,522
2004	98,752	99,491	112,449	124,930	128,727	126,481	114,656	109,588	104,928	109,832	112,709	123,483
2005	142,333	140,869	146,062	141,610	145,235	133,768	135,971	134,329	148,094	167,175	174,496	197,090
2006	225,313	220,947	220,042	240,567	261,496	235,783	231,914	213,918	214,583	205,776	211,814	224,501

Source: Chicago Mercantile Exchange (CME)

Volume of Trading of Live Cattle Futures Chicago   In Thousands of Contracts

Year	Jan.	Feb.	Mar.	Apr.	May	June	July	Aug.	Sept.	Oct.	Nov.	Dec.	Total
1997	361,620	352,173	312,113	331,948	285,885	303,369	387,526	324,943	316,822	374,632	238,003	330,608	3,919,642
1998	355,728	400,210	327,169	400,584	296,651	321,370	334,424	369,604	370,282	373,207	318,152	349,125	4,216,506
1999	298,814	342,572	338,076	320,457	296,512	342,854	287,557	266,544	371,735	345,269	375,960	253,198	3,839,548
2000	347,290	323,524	356,258	236,494	302,001	244,755	248,377	293,450	277,913	293,972	397,879	359,599	3,681,512
2001	511,050	357,474	385,581	302,829	348,294	289,093	318,564	324,614	340,969	403,101	403,009	294,695	4,279,273
2002	331,026	275,699	387,115	448,508	304,900	247,940	286,248	288,525	314,927	352,487	315,658	298,703	3,851,736
2003	378,862	343,931	334,007	306,713	391,477	311,239	449,966	319,677	473,218	469,405	324,732	332,862	4,436,089
2004	362,295	265,370	442,636	353,886	419,888	345,611	381,151	340,973	382,536	344,517	511,516	359,749	4,510,128
2005	519,794	395,847	598,171	377,494	503,753	405,687	506,253	406,010	569,040	438,631	627,585	485,291	5,833,556
2006	783,018	498,779	849,546	570,015	817,491	709,706	718,772	670,410	698,285	631,911	757,795	503,970	8,209,698

Source: Chicago Mercantile Exchange (CME)

CATTLE AND CALVES

Beef Steer-Corn Price Ratio in the United States

Year	Jan.	Feb.	Mar.	Apr.	May	June	July	Aug.	Sept.	Oct.	Nov.	Dec.	Average
1999	30.2	31.0	31.8	32.4	32.8	33.9	37.5	37.8	38.3	41.5	41.7	38.9	35.7
2000	37.5	35.9	36.2	37.0	34.7	37.4	42.9	44.7	42.6	40.5	39.7	39.0	39.0
2001	40.1	40.2	41.1	42.1	42.5	43.6	40.1	38.7	37.7	38.1	36.6	34.6	39.6
2002	36.1	38.1	38.2	37.0	35.3	34.0	31.2	28.3	27.4	29.3	31.5	32.3	33.2
2003	33.4	33.4	32.9	33.7	33.4	33.6	36.4	38.6	40.6	46.1	45.4	41.4	37.4
2004	35.7	31.5	32.0	30.8	32.3	33.6	36.4	38.9	40.7	42.6	44.0	45.0	37.0
2005	44.5	47.7	47.1	49.1	48.5	45.3	41.8	45.0	48.5	52.8	54.9	51.9	48.1
2006[2]	51.0	48.3	45.1	42.3	39.9	41.4	42.2	44.0	43.5	37.0	31.4	29.7	41.3

[1] Bushels of corn equal in value to 100 pounds of steers and heifers.   [2] Preliminary.   *Source: Economic Research Service, U.S. Department of Agriculture*

Farm Value, Income and Wholesale Prices of Cattle and Calves in the United States

	January 1		Gross Income From C & C[2]	At Ohama				Feeder Heifers at Oklahoma City[5]	Cows, Boning Utility Sioux Falls[6]	Cows, Com- mercial Sioux Falls	Wholesale Prices, Central U.S.		
				Steers[3]		Heifers[4]					Choice 700-850 lb.	Select 700-850 lb.	Cow[6], Canner[7]
Year	Per Head Dollars	Total Million $	Million $	Choice	Select	Select	Choice						
								Dollars per 100 Pounds					
2000	683	67,099	41,078	69.52			69.55	82.23	41.71	44.45	117.45	108.83	72.57
2001	725	70,495	40,903	67.68			67.81	84.19	44.39	52.20	122.17	114.42	55.32
2002	747	72,284	38,429	66.39			67.39	76.70	40.47	39.63	113.59	107.66	NA
2003	728	69,949	45,465	82.37			82.06	85.88	49.74	46.62	143.20	130.07	NA
2004	818	77,595	47,935	84.78			84.40	100.09	55.20	52.35	141.33	132.65	NA
2005	916	87,386	49,668	86.54			87.35	106.87	55.52	54.36	145.78	136.36	NA
2006[1]	1,008	97,873						102.08	50.50	47.56	146.82	133.09	NA

[1] Preliminary.   [2] Excludes interfarm sales & Gov't. payments. Cash receipts from farm marketings + value of farm home consumption.   [3] 1,000 to 1,100 lb.   [4] 1,000 to 1,200 lb.   [5] 1992 to date are 700 to 750 lb., 1987 thru 1991 are 600 to 700 lb.   [6] All weights.   [7] & Cutter.
Source: Economic Research Service, U.S. Department of Agriculture (NASS-USDA)

Average Price Received by Farmers for Beef Cattle in the United States   In Dollars Per 100 Pounds

Year	Jan.	Feb.	Mar.	Apr.	May	June	July	Aug.	Sept.	Oct.	Nov.	Dec.	Average
1999	59.00	60.60	62.40	62.70	62.10	63.70	62.60	63.50	63.80	66.20	66.20	66.60	63.28
2000	67.80	67.60	69.80	71.30	69.40	68.50	67.50	65.50	65.30	66.70	69.10	71.90	68.37
2001	74.80	74.70	76.00	75.40	73.60	73.60	71.80	70.60	69.00	66.50	64.00	64.80	71.23
2002	67.10	70.00	70.60	67.30	65.10	64.00	63.70	64.40	64.50	64.60	67.30	70.40	66.58
2003	73.20	73.90	72.60	74.50	75.50	74.90	75.80	79.30	84.90	91.50	93.40	90.40	79.99
2004	80.90	78.50	83.70	85.00	88.50	89.80	88.10	87.70	85.90	86.50	85.40	86.80	85.57
2005	89.40	88.80	91.00	93.70	92.10	88.00	85.00	84.40	88.00	90.40	90.80	93.30	89.58
2006[1]	95.10	92.40	88.10	84.80	82.20	84.20	86.10	87.70	90.80	88.50	84.70	83.60	87.35

[1] Preliminary.   *Source: National Agricultural Statistics Service, U.S. Department of Agriculture (NASS-USDA)*

Average Price Received by Farmers for Calves in the United States   In Dollars Per 100 Pounds

Year	Jan.	Feb.	Mar.	Apr.	May	June	July	Aug.	Sept.	Oct.	Nov.	Dec.	Average
1999	83.20	86.90	87.30	88.20	87.60	89.00	89.20	89.60	90.90	91.90	93.00	98.60	89.62
2000	103.00	105.00	109.00	111.00	107.00	104.00	106.00	106.00	103.00	102.00	106.00	106.00	105.67
2001	108.00	109.00	112.00	112.00	111.00	110.00	108.00	106.00	107.00	99.70	96.70	101.00	106.70
2002	102.00	105.00	105.00	101.00	99.50	96.50	92.40	94.90	92.40	92.00	91.90	95.30	97.33
2003	96.80	97.20	96.70	98.90	100.00	101.00	102.00	106.00	109.00	112.00	111.00	112.00	103.55
2004	110.00	111.00	115.00	117.00	121.00	125.00	130.00	131.00	128.00	126.00	123.00	122.00	121.58
2005	125.00	129.00	136.00	141.00	143.00	140.00	133.00	133.00	135.00	135.00	137.00	137.00	135.33
2006[1]	141.00	143.00	138.00	135.00	132.00	133.00	136.00	134.00	135.00	127.00	118.00	115.00	132.25

[1] Preliminary.   *Source: National Agricultural Statistics Board, U.S. Department of Agriculture (NASS-USDA)*

Federally Inspected Slaughter of Calves and Vealers in the United States   In Thousands of Head

Year	Jan.	Feb.	Mar.	Apr.	May	June	July	Aug.	Sept.	Oct.	Nov.	Dec.	Total
1999	103	98	115	95	87	102	109	115	117	102	100	110	1,252
2000	91	92	97	75	86	91	92	98	91	95	91	90	1,088
2001	89	77	82	72	77	75	81	92	77	91	85	82	981
2002	86	71	76	80	76	74	94	94	87	98	88	96	1,019
2003	92	81	83	77	74	72	83	78	80	85	76	95	976
2004	77	70	75	69	63	65	67	71	66	61	66	73	823
2005	66	61	67	60	57	58	57	64	60	54	55	59	718
2006[1]	54	52	58	46	56	58	57	66	57	62	66	67	699

[1] Preliminary.   *Source: Crop Reporting Board, U.S. Department of Agriculture (CRB-USDA)*

Cement

Cement is made in a wide variety of compositions and is used in many different ways. The best-known cement is *Portland cement*, which is bound with sand and gravel to create concrete. Concrete is used to unite the surfaces of various materials and to coat surfaces to protect them from various chemicals. Portland cement is almost universally used for structural concrete. It is manufactured from lime-bearing materials, usually limestone, together with clays, blast-furnace slag containing alumina and silica or shale. The combination is usually approximately 60 percent lime, 19 percent silica, 8 percent alumina, 5 percent iron, 5 percent magnesia, and 3 percent sulfur trioxide. To slow the hardening process, gypsum is often added. In 1924, the name "Portland cement" was coined by Joseph Aspdin, a British cement maker, because of the resemblance between concrete made from his cement and Portland stone. The United States did not start producing Portland cement in any great quantity until the 20th century. Hydraulic cements are those that set and harden in water. Clinker cement is an intermediate product in cement manufacture. The production and consumption of cement is directly related to the level of activity in the construction industry.

Prices – The average value (F.O.B. mill) of Portland cement in 2005 rose +14.5% yr/yr to $91.00 per ton, which was a new record.

Supply – World production of hydraulic cement in 2005 rose +5.5% yr/yr to a new record high of 2.310 billion metric tons. The world's largest hydraulic cement producers are China with 45% of world production in 2004, India (6%), US (4%), and Japan (3%). US production of Portland cement in 2005 rose +1.6% yr/yr to a new record high of 93.904 million tons. US shipments of finished Portland cement from mills in the US in 2006 (through November, annualized) rose +0.7% to 98.744 million metric tons, which was a new record high.

Demand – US consumption of cement in 2005 rose +5.2% to 128.280 million tons, which was a new record high.

Trade – The US relied on imports for 24% of its cement consumption in 2006. The two main suppliers of cement to the US are Canada and Mexico. US exports of cement in 2005 rose 2.3% yr/yr to 766,000 tons.

World Production of Hydraulic Cement   In Thousands of Short Tons

Year	Brazil	China	France	Germany	India	Italy	Japan	Rep. of Korea	Russia	Spain	Turkey	United States	World Total
1998	39,942	536,000	19,500	36,610	85,000	35,512	81,328	46,091	26,000	33,080	38,200	85,522	1,540,000
1999	40,270	573,000	20,219	35,912	90,000	37,299	80,120	48,157	28,400	35,782	34,258	87,777	1,600,000
2000	39,208	597,000	20,137	35,414	95,000	38,925	81,097	51,255	32,400	38,154	35,825	89,510	1,660,000
2001	38,927	661,040	19,839	32,118	105,000	39,804	76,550	52,046	35,300	40,512	30,125	90,450	1,740,000
2002	38,027	725,000	19,437	31,009	115,000	41,416	71,828	55,514	37,700	42,417	32,577	91,266	1,850,000
2003	34,010	862,080	19,655	32,749	123,000	43,433	68,766	59,194	41,000	44,747	35,077	94,329	2,030,000
2004[1]	34,413	970,000	20,962	31,854	130,000	46,045	67,376	54,330	45,700	46,593	38,796	99,015	2,190,000
2005[2]	36,673	1,038,300	21,277	30,629	145,000	46,404	69,629	51,391	48,700	50,347	42,787	100,903	2,310,000

[1] Preliminary.   [2] Estimate.   *Source: U.S. Geological Survey (USGS)*

Salient Statistics of Cement in the United States

Year	Net Import Reliance as a % of Apparent Consumption	Production Portland	Production Others[3]	Production Total	Capacity Used at (Portland Mills) %	Shipments From Mills Total Mil. MT	Shipments From Mills Value[4] Mil. $	Average Value (F.O.B. Mill) $ per MT	Stocks at Mills Dec. 31	Exports	Apparent Consumption	Imports for Consumption[5] by Country Canada	Japan	Mexico	Spain	Total
		1,000 Metric Tons							**1,000 Metric Tons**			**1,000 Metric Tons**				
1998	19	79,942	3,989	83,931	84.9	96,857	7,404	76.45	5,393	743	103,460	5,957		1,280	2,204	24,086
1999	23	81,577	4,375	85,952	83.6	103,271	8,083	78.27	6,367	694	108,862	5,511		1,286	1,900	29,351
2000	20	83,514	4,332	87,846	80.7	105,557	8,293	78.56	7,566	738	110,470	4,948		1,409	1,177	28,683
2001	21	84,450	4,450	88,900	79.1	113,136	8,600	76.50	6,600	746	112,810	5,110		1,645	651	25,861
2002	19	85,283	4,449	89,732	78.7	108,778	8,250	76.00	7,680	834	110,020	5,181		1,228	327	24,169
2003	20	88,106	4,737	92,843	78.5	111,000	8,340	75.00	6,610	837	114,090	6,319		891	355	23,959
2004[1]	23	92,434	5,000	97,434	81.6	120,000	9,520	79.50	6,710	749	121,980	5,753	2	1,429	408	27,305
2005[2]	25	93,904	5,415	99,319	82.3	127,000	11,600	91.00	7,390	766	128,280	5,404	4	2,173	236	33,652

[1] Preliminary.   [2] Estimate.   [3] Masonry, natural & pozzolan (slag-line).   [4] Value received F.O.B. mill, excluding cost of containers.   [5] Hydraulic & clinker cement for consumption.   [6] Less than 1/2 unit.   *Source: U.S. Geological Survey (USGS)*

Shipments of Finished Portland Cement from Mills in the United States   In Thousands of Metric Tons

Year	Jan.	Feb.	Mar.	Apr.	May	June	July	Aug.	Sept.	Oct.	Nov.	Dec.	Total
2000	4,765.5	5,343.1	7,196.9	6,930.2	8,448.2	8,391.5	7,843.8	8,982.3	7,860.8	8,474.2	6,587.0	4,865.5	84,980.3
2001	5,107.6	5,088.8	6,684.5	7,799.4	8,507.9	8,385.8	8,333.2	8,851.2	7,512.2	8,953.3	7,353.3	5,548.0	88,124.9
2002	5,554.3	5,369.3	6,133.9	7,859.7	8,291.4	8,135.6	8,466.9	8,676.2	7,909.7	8,326.1	6,956.3	5,293.4	86,972.9
2003	5,485.6	4,559.9	6,482.6	8,008.5	8,288.4	8,492.2	9,063.8	8,829.1	8,755.3	9,780.8	6,987.5	6,348.3	91,081.9
2004	5,240.7	5,145.5	8,059.2	8,837.4	8,623.8	9,103.2	9,134.3	9,325.6	8,883.4	8,608.9	7,417.2	6,528.4	94,907.6
2005	5,337.1	5,731.9	7,497.9	8,316.4	9,101.7	9,595.5	8,305.1	9,603.6	8,847.0	8,869.7	8,064.8	6,316.9	95,587.6
2006[1]	6,560.5	6,116.4	7,747.2	7,801.7	8,916.3	9,276.9	7,951.7	9,185.7	8,057.2	8,582.5	7,569.3		95,743.9

[1] Preliminary.   *Source: U.S. Geological Survey (USGS)*

Cheese

Since prehistoric times, humans have been making and eating cheese. Dating back as far as 6,000 BC, archaeologists have discovered that cheese had been made from cow and goat milk and stored in tall jars. The Romans turned cheese making into a culinary art, mixing sheep and goat milk and adding herbs and spices for flavoring. By 300 AD, cheese was being exported regularly to countries along the Mediterranean coast.

Cheese is made from the milk of cows and other mammals such as sheep, goats, buffalo, reindeer, camels, yaks, and mares. More than 400 varieties of cheese exist. There are three basic steps common to all cheese making. First, proteins in milk are transformed into curds, or solid lumps. Second, the curds are separated from the milky liquid (or whey) and shaped or pressed into molds. Finally, the shaped curds are ripened according to a variety of aging and curing techniques. Cheeses are usually grouped according to their moisture content into fresh, soft, semi-soft, hard, and very hard. Many classifications overlap due to texture changes with aging.

Cheese is a multi-billion-dollar a year industry in the US. Cheddar cheese is the most common natural cheese produced in the US, accounting for 35% of US production. Cheeses originating in America include Colby, cream cheese, and Monterey Jack. Varieties other than American cheeses, mostly Italian, now have had a combined level of production that easily exceeds American cheeses.

Prices – Average monthly cheese prices at the Chicago Mercantile Exchange in 2006 (through December) fell by – 14.9% yr/yr to 123.85 cents per pound, down from 2004's 24-year high of 164.92 cents per pound. The all time record monthly average high of 168.40 cents per pound was posted in 1982.

Supply – World production of cheese in 2006 rose +2.0% yr/yr to 14.128 million metric tons, which was a new record high. The European Union is the world's largest producer of cheese with 47% of the total world production. The US production was the next largest in 2006 with 30% of the total. US production of cheese in 2006 rose +3.6% to 9.459 billion pounds, which was a new record high.

Demand – US consumption of cheese in 2005 fell – 2.2% to 8.741 billion pounds. US per capita cheese consumption in 2002, the latest reporting year for this series, rose to 30.60 pounds per person per year to a new record high.

Trade – US imports of cheese in 2005 fell –52.6% to 225 million pounds. US exports of cheese in 2005 fell – 10.3% to 115 million pounds, down from 2004's record high of 128 million pounds.

World Production of Cheese   In Thousands of Metric Tons

Year	Argentina	Australia	Brazil	Canada	Egypt	European Union	Japan	Mexico	Zealand	Russia	Ukraine	United States	World Total
1997	415	285	405	329	370	5,047	34	112	240	165	45	3,325	11,100
1998	407	305	421	330	380	5,291	35	127	266	170	52	3,398	11,518
1999	446	320	434	329	382	5,711	35	126	245	185	53	3,581	12,016
2000	445	373	445	328	380	5,861	34	134	297	220	67	3,746	12,499
2001	440	374	460	329	395	5,865	34	140	281	260	105	3,747	12,602
2002	370	413	470	350	410	5,993	36	145	312	340	129	3,877	13,019
2003	325	368	460	342	450	6,100	35	126	301	335	169	3,881	13,013
2004	370	389	470	305	455	6,430	35	134	308	350	224	4,026	13,561
2005[1]	400	376	480	307	460	6,515	37	136	300	355	270	4,145	13,847
2006[2]	425	395	495	308	462	6,580	38	138	295	360	290	4,275	14,128

[1] Preliminary.   [2] Estimate.   Source: Foreign Agricultural Service, U.S. Department of Agriculture (FAS-USDA)

Supply and Distribution of All Cheese in the United States   In Millions of Pounds

Year	Supply — Production Whole Milk[2]	Supply — Production All Cheese[3]	Supply — January 1 Commercial Stocks	Supply — Imports[4]	Supply — Total Supply	Cheese 40-lb. Blocks Wisconsin Assembly Points cents/lb.	Distribution — Exports & Shipments[5]	Distribution — Gov't - Dec. 31 Stocks	Distribution — American Cheese Removed by USDA Programs	Distribution — Total Disappearance	Distribution — Domestic Disappearance American Cheese Donated	Distribution — Domestic Disappearance Total	Distribution — Domestic Disappearance Per Capita
1996	3,281	7,218	412	338	7,968	146.80	72	.3	4.6	7,478	0	7,365	27.30
1997	3,286	7,330	487	312	8,130	132.40	83	.5	11.3	7,646	0	7,510	27.50
1998	3,315	7,492	481	371	8,344	158.10	81	.6	8.2	7,797	0	7,664	27.70
1999	3,533	7,894	518	436	8,847	142.28	85	1.0	4.6	8,219	0	8,086	29.00
2000	3,642	8,258	621	416	9,295	116.14	105	2.3	28.0	8,580		8,406	29.80
2001	3,544	8,261	706	445	9,412	144.93	115	4.0	3.9	8,744		8,586	30.00
2002	3,691	8,547	659	475	9,681	118.22	119	2.7	15.8	9,001		8,819	30.60
2003	3,622	8,557	730	476	9,763	131.24	115	27.4	41.3	9,007			
2004	3,739	8,873	715	474	10,062	164.92	128	9.0	5.9	8,933			
2005[1]	3,813	9,127	701	225	10,053	145.53	115			8,741			

[1] Preliminary.   [2] Whole milk American cheddar.   [3] All types of cheese except cottage, pot and baker's cheese.   [4] Imports for consumption.
[5] Commercial.   Source: Economic Research Service, U.S. Department of Agriculture (ERS-USDA)

Production of Cheese in the United States   In Millions of Pounds

Year	American — Whole Milk	American — Part Skim	American — Total	Swiss, Including Block	Munster	Brick	Lim- burger	Cream & Neufchatel Cheese	Italian Varieties	Blue Mond	All Other Varieties	Total of All Cheese[2]	Cottage Cheese — Lowfat	Cottage Cheese — Curd[3]	Cottage Cheese — Creamed[4]
1996	3,281	NA	3,281	219.0	106.8	10.6	.7	574.7	2,812.4	38.3	106.7	7,218	329.9	448.3	360.4
1997	3,286	NA	3,286	207.6	100.2	8.5	.7	614.9	2,881.4	42.8	119.8	7,330	346.7	458.5	359.5
1998	3,315	NA	3,315	206.4	94.6	7.6	.9	621.3	3,004.7	5	166.0	7,492	361.2	465.8	366.8
1999	3,533	NA	3,533	221.0	80.3	8.1	.7	639.3	3,144.7	5	181.0	7,894	359.3	464.8	360.6
2000	3,642	NA	3,642	229.3	85.5	8.6	.6	687.4	3,288.9	5	219.7	8,258	363.7	461.0	371.5
2001	3,544	NA	3,544	245.5	82.2	8.7	.7	645.1	3,425.9	5	199.6	8,261	370.2	453.2	371.6
2002	3,691	NA	3,691	254.1	81.1	10.0	.7	686.2	3,470.0	5	229.8	8,547	374.3	436.6	374.2
2003	3,622	NA	3,622	264.7	79.4	9.8	.7	676.7	3,524.0	5	246.7	8,557	384.4	448.0	385.2
2004	3,739	NA	3,739	281.3	72.8	8.1	.9	699.1	3,661.6	5	268.1	8,873	396.4	464.0	382.4
2005[1]	3,813	NA	3,813	294.0	77.9	8.9	.8	692.4	3,804.7	5	268.1	9,127	396.1	457.4	368.2

[1] Preliminary.   [2] Excludes full-skim cheddar and cottage cheese.   [3] Includes cottage, pot, and baker's cheese with a butterfat content of less than 4%.
[4] Includes cheese with a butterfat content of 4 to 19 %.   [5] Included in All Other Varieties.   Source: Economic Research Service, U.S. Department of Agriculture ERS-USDA)

Average Price of Cheese, 40-lb. Blocks, Chicago Mercantile Exchange[2]   In Cents Per Pound

Year	Jan.	Feb.	Mar.	Apr.	May	June	July	Aug.	Sept.	Oct.	Nov.	Dec.	Average
1997	127.9	132.3	134.0	125.6	116.5	117.9	123.3	137.6	141.4	142.4	143.8	146.1	132.4
1998	144.5	144.7	138.8	129.7	123.0	151.3	162.6	166.9	171.0	183.5	188.7	192.5	158.1
1999	162.4	131.5	134.0	133.6	124.8	138.1	159.7	189.0	167.3	134.0	117.3	115.7	142.3
2000	114.6	111.6	112.2	110.7	110.6	120.0	125.2	125.5	133.4	109.4	107.5	113.0	116.1
2001	110.3	120.0	131.9	140.5	160.3	166.8	168.5	171.8	173.9	139.7	126.4	129.1	144.9
2002	132.4	120.8	121.3	124.5	120.1	113.0	108.9	115.8	120.4	119.5	108.9	113.1	118.2
2003	109.3	109.2	108.2	112.3	114.2	118.6	151.2	160.0	160.0	158.8	139.3	133.8	131.2
2004	130.6	139.6	182.0	216.9	199.3	171.1	144.9	157.3	157.0	151.7	169.6	159.2	164.9
2005	162.7	149.3	153.2	154.1	147.7	150.7	105.4	142.5	156.4	144.7	137.6	142.2	145.5
2006[1]	133.4	119.9	116.4	116.5	118.6	119.2	116.3	123.5	129.3	123.5	137.5	132.2	123.8

[1] Preliminary.   [2] Data through December 2001 are for Wholesale Price of Cheese, 40-lb. Blocks, Wisconsin Assembly Points.
Source: Economic Research Service, U.S. Department of Agriculture (ERS-USDA)

Production[2] of Cheese in the United States   In Millions of Pounds

Year	Jan.	Feb.	Mar.	Apr.	May	June	July	Aug.	Sept.	Oct.	Nov.	Dec.	Total
1997	598.1	577.1	638.0	598.5	642.0	623.4	613.2	596.5	604.3	615.5	594.5	627.9	7,329
1998	617.2	574.3	646.7	636.9	650.4	639.9	607.9	596.4	583.8	633.2	637.8	667.4	7,492
1999	631.6	591.7	698.2	663.8	668.9	664.4	641.3	642.6	637.6	666.5	683.4	704.2	7,894
2000	692.9	649.5	714.8	694.0	730.4	695.7	687.6	683.8	653.8	688.5	675.0	688.4	8,255
2001	680.3	625.3	713.7	670.2	706.8	678.5	676.0	660.0	641.8	682.1	691.2	703.1	8,129
2002	717.5	667.9	742.8	719.2	748.3	708.3	692.2	714.3	683.9	732.2	725.4	747.2	8,599
2003	714.8	648.6	730.3	718.8	737.0	712.3	718.3	700.1	708.7	740.0	710.0	758.9	8,598
2004	738.0	705.5	785.6	761.0	752.1	715.3	708.7	719.5	714.4	748.0	754.3	773.9	8,876
2005	754.0	704.6	797.5	754.8	783.9	764.5	739.5	757.4	745.5	760.4	766.1	798.9	9,127
2006[1]	772.3	721.0	812.6	786.5	811.6	793.9	767.4	788.9	784.3	800.3	791.1	829.0	9,459

[1] Preliminary.   [2] Excludes cottage cheese.   Source: National Agricultural Statistics Service, U.S. Department of Agriculture (NASS-USDA)

Cold Storage Holdings of All Varieties of Cheese in the United States, on First of Month Millions of Pounds

Year	Jan.	Feb.	Mar.	Apr.	May	June	July	Aug.	Sept.	Oct.	Nov.	Dec.
1997	487.0	501.5	494.6	517.0	555.4	584.3	604.8	604.9	582.3	543.7	505.0	474.4
1998	480.4	509.3	521.5	533.1	557.6	568.5	583.7	595.8	576.8	553.0	522.7	494.5
1999	517.2	622.4	635.9	645.1	688.7	741.3	728.4	748.7	694.7	651.3	622.0	591.7
2000	621.3	728.1	757.2	765.1	794.0	811.4	828.1	870.3	839.9	780.9	732.0	696.0
2001	707.8	709.9	723.9	711.6	711.8	712.1	739.2	752.6	721.2	708.7	672.2	631.3
2002	660.0	693.6	720.3	731.7	765.6	789.0	797.6	833.6	801.5	753.9	720.4	697.1
2003	730.1	761.2	770.0	771.3	781.1	791.0	800.1	809.0	794.2	762.2	722.4	695.5
2004	724.4	756.9	766.1	759.5	767.6	804.5	842.0	870.0	811.5	790.7	756.1	704.3
2005	705.8	713.8	723.7	749.2	780.8	815.6	823.4	837.2	812.9	769.0	755.9	720.8
2006[1]	758.2	765.0	771.0	799.2	820.0	846.3	863.5	892.6	862.0	831.3	794.9	764.5

Quantities are given in net weight.   [1] Preliminary.   Source: National Agricultural Statistics Service, U.S. Department of Agriculture (NASS-USDA)

Chromium

Chromium (symbol Cr) is a steel-gray, hard, and brittle, metallic element that can take on a high polish. Chromium and its compounds are toxic. Discovered in 1797 by Louis Vauquelin, chromium is named after the Greek word for color, khroma. Vauquelin also discovered that an emerald's green color is due to the presence of chromium. Many precious stones owe their color to the presence of chromium compounds.

Chromium is primarily found in chromite ore. The primary use of chromium is to form alloys with iron, nickel, or cobalt. Chromium improves hardness and resistance to corrosion and oxidation in iron, steel, and nonferrous alloys. It is a critical alloying ingredient in the production of stainless steel, making up 10% or more of the final composition. More than half of the chromium consumed is used in metallic products, and about one-third is used in refractories. Chromium is also used as a lustrous decorative plating agent, in pigments, leather processing, plating of metals, and catalysts.

Supply – World production of chromium in 2005 rose +9.0% yr/yr to 19.300 million metric tons, which was up sharply from the 9-year low of 12.100 million metric tons in 2001. The world's largest producers of chromium in 2005 were South Africa with 39% of world production, Kazakhstan with 19%, India with 17%, and with Turkey and Zimbabwe far behind with 4% each. India has emerged as a major producer of chromium in the past two decades. India's 2005 production level of 3.255 million metric tons was more than 8 times the level of 360,000 metric tons seen 20 years earlier. South Africa's production in 2005 fell slightly to 7.502 million metric tons from last year's record 7.635 million metric tons, but that is still more than double the levels seen as recently as the early-1990s. Kazakhstan's production in 2005 of 3.579 million was a 13-year high. Zimbabwe's chromium production in 2005 was a record high of 819.9 metric tons. US Government stocks of chromium as of Dec 31, 2005 fell –46% yr/yr to a record low of 73.4 metric tons.

Demand – Based on the most recently available data, the metallurgical and chemical industry accounts for 94% of chromium usage in the US, with the remaining 6% used by the refractory industry.

Trade – The US relied on imports for 75% of its chromium consumption in 2006, up from the record low of 63% seen in 2002. That is well below the record high of 91% posted back in the 1970s. US chromium imports in 2005 rose +8.3% yr/yr to 353,300 metric tons. US exports of chromium in 2005 rose a sharp +64.9% yr/yr to 64.9 metric tons.

World Mine Production of Chromite   In Thousands of Metric Tons (Gross Weight)

Year	Albania	Brazil	Cuba	Finland	India	Iran	Kazakh-stan	Mada-gascar	Philip-pines	South Africa	Turkey	Zim-babwe	World Total
1996	144	408	37	582	1,363	130	1,190	137	107	5,078	1,279	697	11,600
1997	106	301	44	589	1,363	169	1,796	140	88	6,162	1,703	640	13,600
1998	102	537	46	498	1,311	212	1,603	104	54	6,480	1,404	605	13,700
1999	71	458	52	597	1,473	255	2,406	----	20	6,817	770	653	14,200
2000	120	550	56	628	1,947	153	2,607	131	26	6,622	546	668	14,700
2001	130	409	50	575	1,678	145	2,046	24	27	5,502	390	780	12,200
2002	73	284	20	566	2,699	513	2,369	11	24	6,436	314	749	14,600
2003	98	404	33	549	2,210	97	2,928	45	13	7,405	229	637	15,400
2004[1]	54	593	40	580	2,949	139	3,267	77	70	7,677	506	668	17,700
2005[2]	66	677	40	598	3,255	224	3,579	141	60	7,503	859	820	19,300

[1] Preliminary.   [2] Estimate.   *Source: U.S. Geological Survey (USGS)*

Salient Statistics of Chromite in the United States   In Thousands of Metric Tons (Gross Weight)

Year	Net Import Reliance as a % of Apparent Con-sumption	Production of Ferro-chromium	Exports	Imports for Con-sumption	Reexports	Consumption by - Primary Conumer Groups - Total	Metal-lurgical & Chemical	Refractory	Government[5] Stocks, Dec. 31-- Metal-lurgical & Chemical	Refractory	Total Stocks	$ per Metric Ton - South Africa[3]	Turkish[4]
1996	79	37	47	361		W	W	W	165	8	173	80	230
1997	75	61	27	349		W	W	W	167	8	175	75	150
1998	80	W	55	383		W	W	W	W	W	159	68	145
1999	80	W	53	475		W	W	W	W	W	130	63	145
2000	78	W	86	453		W	W	W	396	241	637	60-65	140-150
2001	78	W	43	239		W	W	W	396	241	637	NA	NA
2002	63	W	29	263		W	W	W	78	126	204	NA	NA
2003	74	W	46	317		W	W	W	79	156	235	NA	NA
2004[1]	72	W	35	326		W	W	W	46	88	135	NA	NA
2005[2]	69	W	57	353		W	W	W	4	70	73	NA	NA

[1] Preliminary.   [2] Estimate.   [3] Cr_2O_3, 44% (Transvaal).   [4] 48% Cr_2O_3.   [5] Data through 1999 are for Consumer.   W = Withheld.
Source: U.S. Geological Survey (USGS)

Coal

Coal is a sedimentary rock composed primarily of carbon, hydrogen, and oxygen. Coal is a fossil fuel formed from ancient plants buried deep in the Earth's crust over 300 million years ago. Historians believe coal was first used commercially in China for smelting copper and for casting coins around 1,000 BC. Almost 92% of all coal consumed in the US is burned by electric power plants, and coal accounts for about 55% of total electricity output. Coal is also used in the manufacture of steel. The steel industry first converts coal into coke, then combines the coke with iron ore and limestone, and finally heats the mixture to produce iron. Other industries use coal to make fertilizers, solvents, medicine, pesticides, and synthetic fuels.

There are four types of mined coal: anthracite (used in high-grade steel production), bituminous (used for electricity generation and for making coke), sub-bituminous, and lignite (both used primarily for electricity generation).

Coal futures trade at the New York Mercantile Exchange (NYMEX). The contract trades in units of 1,550 tons and is priced in terms of dollars and cents per ton.

Supply – US production of bituminous coal in 2006 (annualized through Dec) rose by +3.6% yr/yr to a record high of 1.172 billion short tons.

Demand – US consumption of coal in 2005, the latest reporting year for the series, rose by +1.19% to 1.128 billion tons, which was a new record high.

Trade – US exports of coal in 2005 fell –3.9% yr/yr to 47.998 million tons, and imports rose +11.7% yr/yr to 30.460 million tons. The major exporting destinations for the US are Canada and Europe.

World Production[3] of Coal (Monthly Average) In Thousands of Metric Tons

Year	Australia	Canada	China	Czech-Rep.	Germany	India	Indonesia	Kazakhstan	Poland	Russia	Ukraine	United Kingdom	United States
1997	17,235	3,435	114,402	1,339	4,267	24,764	4,340	6,268	11,427	13,317	6,293	4,041	82,398
1998	18,424	3,190	94,806	1,343	3,776	24,356	5,027	5,672	9,644	12,779	6,431	3,431	84,484
1999	18,643	3,043	80,200	1,193	3,657	25,004	5,892	4,644	9,301	13,799	6,804	3,090	66,796
2000	19,958	2,817	70,782	1,238	3,111	25,802	6,402	5,960	8,598	14,292	6,749	2,600	65,220
2001	22,018	2,845	80,040	1,261	2,406	26,563	7,554	6,810	8,658	15,507	6,908	2,677	68,666
2002	23,123	5,573	92,339	1,206	2,197	27,938	8,588	6,493	8,676	15,198	5,163	2,499	66,565
2003	30,000	5,177	109,602	1,137	2,396	29,036	9,551	7,060	8,529	16,329	5,354	2,353	81,023
2004	31,250	5,499	130,434	1,109	2,429	31,438	11,021	6,795	8,414	17,495	4,965	2,089	92,953
2005[1]	32,750	5,445	150,891	1,104	2,335	33,129	11,510	6,855	8,154	18,472	4,999	1,668	94,439
2006[2]	32,334	5,232	166,190	1,118	1,926	34,443	11,546	6,428	8,041	19,121	5,114	1,713	97,286

[1] Preliminary.   [2] Estimate.   [3] All grades of anthracite and bituminous coal, but excludes recovered slurries, lignite and brown coal..
NA = Not avaliable.   *Source: United Nations*

Production of Bituminous & Lignite Coal in the United States   In Thousands of Short Tons

Year	Alabama	Colorado	Illinois	Indiana	Kentucky	Montana	Ohio	Pennsylvania	Texas	Virginia	West Virginia	Wyoming	Total
1997	24,468	27,449	41,159	35,497	155,853	41,005	29,154	76,198	53,328	35,837	173,743	281,881	1,089,932
1998	23,224	30,825	38,182	36,297	145,609	42,092	28,600	76,519	53,578	34,059	175,794	313,983	1,109,768
1999	19,504	29,989	40,417	34,004	139,626	41,102	22,480	76,368	53,071	32,181	157,919	337,119	1,095,474
2000	19,324	29,137	33,444	27,965	130,688	38,352	22,269	74,619	49,498	32,834	158,257	338,900	1,073,612
2001	19,513	33,372	33,783	36,738	134,298	39,143	25,400	74,784	45,042	33,060	162,631	368,749	1,125,749
2002	19,062	35,103	33,358	35,513	124,388	37,386	21,157	67,104	45,247	30,126	150,222	373,161	1,092,916
2003	20,207	35,831	31,760	35,512	113,126	36,994	22,009	63,792	47,517	31,771	139,755	376,270	1,071,753
2004	22,329	39,870	31,912	35,206	114,743	39,989	23,222	66,023	45,863	31,647	148,017	396,493	1,110,393
2005[1]	21,453	38,510	32,014	34,457	120,029	40,354	24,718	65,852	45,939	27,964	153,655	404,319	1,129,794
2006[2]	20,065	36,846	32,343	35,244	119,683	40,778	23,111	63,534	45,770	31,731	151,191	446,152	1,158,435

[1] Preliminary.   [2] Estimate.   *Source: Energy Information Administration, U.S. Department of Energy (EIA-DOE)*

Production[2] of Bituminous Coal in the United States   In Thousands of Short Tons

Year	Jan.	Feb.	Mar.	Apr.	May	June	July	Aug.	Sept.	Oct.	Nov.	Dec.	Total
1997	92,425	88,028	92,265	87,909	94,296	86,382	88,666	89,319	92,298	94,562	83,344	94,913	1,085,254
1998	97,012	86,167	95,091	91,735	90,397	92,099	90,497	91,212	95,442	96,723	90,544	94,567	1,106,128
1999	90,928	92,015	98,672	88,630	84,436	89,734	87,759	92,600	92,248	89,146	90,885	92,450	1,089,503
2000	87,222	86,846	99,045	81,793	88,715	90,583	84,442	96,361	88,848	92,542	94,035	87,272	1,077,704
2001	96,721	86,802	99,176	89,954	94,840	92,657	89,037	99,048	88,985	99,529	93,736	88,234	1,118,719
2002	101,939	90,208	90,108	90,039	91,673	85,555	86,190	92,054	92,212	94,033	87,836	91,058	1,092,905
2003	92,649	82,130	88,976	89,202	90,435	88,348	88,301	89,355	90,344	93,928	84,155	94,154	1,071,977
2004	93,182	86,306	94,876	91,739	87,210	94,835	92,260	95,209	93,525	92,618	92,268	95,478	1,109,506
2005	92,804	89,039	102,178	93,296	90,168	95,374	91,930	97,907	95,493	93,532	94,842	92,774	1,129,337
2006[1]	98,385	89,720	102,415	97,694	102,427	99,436	96,014	102,017	95,177	97,988	95,725	95,148	1,172,146

[1] Preliminary.   [2] Includes small amount of lignite.   *Source: Energy Information Administration, U.S. Department of Energy (EIA-DOE)*

COAL

Production[2] of Pennsylvania Anthracite Coal — In Thousands of Short Tons

Year	Jan.	Feb.	Mar.	Apr.	May	June	July	Aug.	Sept.	Oct.	Nov.	Dec.	Total
1997	351	366	492	374	351	390	407	423	415	448	384	415	4,678
1998	306	305	309	405	384	388	525	454	452	533	167	167	4,612
1999	355	369	389	354	459	402	343	436	479	414	407	406	4,808
2000	271	283	382	342	375	383	366	430	412	417	402	366	4,432
2001	302	275	323	283	300	297	328	358	318	375	349	173	3,681
2002	131	117	116	121	122	240	116	126	119	130	120	126	1,584
2003	108	98	98	115	114	107	97	95	101	130	111	116	1,290
2004	197	183	147	111	101	214	141	145	150	145	151	127	1,812
2005	131	127	149	137	135	157	125	140	135	156	179	127	1,698
2006[1]	142	163	197	179	195	192	173	195	160	100	94	93	1,883

[1] Preliminary.   [2] Represents production in Pennsylvania only.   Source: Energy Information Administration, U.S. Department of Energy (EIA-DOE)

Salient Statistics of Coal in the United States — In Thousands of Short Tons

Year	Production	Imports	Consumption	Exports Brazil	Exports Canada	Exports Europe	Exports Asia	Exports Total	Total Ending Stocks[2]	Losses & Unaccounted For[3]
1996	1,063,856	7,126	1,005,573	6,540	12,029	47,193	17,980	90,473	151,627	-7,366
1997	1,089,932	7,487	1,030,453	7,455	14,975	41,331	14,498	83,545	140,374	-4,418
1998	1,117,535	8,724	1,038,972	6,475	19,901	33,773	12,311	77,295	164,602	-13,118
1999	1,100,431	9,089	1,038,648	4,442	19,826	22,508	9,157	58,476	188,590	-11,592
2000	1,073,612	12,513	1,084,094	4,536	18,769	24,969	6,702	58,489	140,282	-8,150
2001	1,127,689	19,787	1,060,146	4,574	17,633	20,821	3,246	48,666	181,912	-2,966
2002	1,094,283	16,875	1,066,355	3,538	16,686	15,574	1,735	39,601	192,127	-5,012
2003	1,071,753	25,044	1,094,861	3,514	20,760	15,148	266	43,014	165,468	-14,419
2004	1,112,099	27,280	1,107,255	4,199	19,466	18,825	5,082	49,942	154,006	-4,412
2005[1]	1,133,253	30,460	1,128,299	4,361	17,760	15,211	7,475	47,998	143,999	-4,520

[1] Preliminary.   [2] Producer & distributor and consumer stocks, excludes stocks held by retail dealers for consumption by the residential and commercial sector.   [3] Equals production plus imports minus the change in producer & distributor and consumer stocks minus consumption minus exports.
Source: Energy Information Administraion, U.S. Department of Energy (EIA-DOE)

Consumption and Stocks of Coal in the United States — In Thousands of Short Tons

Year	Consumption Electric Utilities Anthracite	Electric Utilities Bituminous	Electric Utilities Lignite	Electric Utilities Total	Industrial Coke Plants	Industrial Other Industrial[2]	Residential and Commercial	Total	Stocks, Dec. 31[3] Consumer Electric Utilities	Consumer Coke Plants	Consumer Other Industrials	Producers and Distributors
1996	1,009	795,252	78,421	896,921	31,706	71,689	6,006	1,006,321	114,623	2,667	5,688	28,648
1997	1,014	821,823	77,524	921,364	30,203	71,515	6,463	1,029,544	98,826	1,978	5,597	33,973
1998	867	832,094	77,906	936,619	28,189	67,439	4,856	1,037,103	120,501	2,026	5,545	36,530
1999	686	815,909	77,525	940,922	28,108	64,738	4,878	1,038,647	141,604	1,943	5,569	39,475
2000	NA	781,821	75,794	985,821	28,939	65,208	4,127	1,084,095	102,296	1,494	4,587	31,905
2001	NA	NA	NA	964,433	26,075	65,268	4,369	1,060,146	138,496	1,510	6,006	35,900
2002	NA	NA	NA	977,507	23,656	60,747	4,445	1,066,355	141,714	1,364	5,792	43,257
2003	NA	NA	NA	1,005,116	24,248	61,261	4,236	1,094,861	121,567	905	4,718	38,277
2004	NA	NA	NA	1,016,268	23,670	62,195	5,122	1,107,255	106,669	1,344	4,842	41,151
2005[1]	NA	NA	NA	1,038,962	23,434	60,781	5,121	1,128,299	101,237	2,615	5,582	34,565

[1] Preliminary.   [2] Including transportation.   [3] Excludes stocks held at retail dealers for consumption by the residential and commercial sector.
Source: Energy Information Administration, U.S. Department of Energy (EIA-DOE)

Average Prices of Coal in the United States — In Dollars Per Short Ton

Year	End-Use-Sector Electric Utilities	Coke Plants	Other Industrial[2]	Imports[3]	Exports Steam	Exports Metallurgical	Total Average[3]	Year	End-Use-Sector Electric Utilities	Coke Plants	Other Industrial[2]	Imports[3]	Exports Steam	Exports Metallurgical	Total Average[3]
1996	26.45	47.33	32.32	33.78	34.09	45.49	40.76	2001	24.68	46.42	32.26	34.00	31.88	41.63	36.97
1997	26.16	47.36	32.41	34.32	32.45	45.47	40.55	2002	24.74	50.67	35.49	35.51	34.51	45.41	40.44
1998	25.64	46.06	32.30	32.18	30.27	44.53	38.89	2003	25.29	50.63	34.70	31.45	26.94	44.55	35.98
1999	24.72	45.85	31.59	30.77	29.91	41.91	36.50	2004	NA	61.50	39.30	37.52	42.03	63.63	54.11
2000	24.28	44.38	31.46	30.10	29.67	38.99	34.89	2005[1]	NA	83.79	47.63	46.71	47.64	81.56	67.10

[1] Preliminary.   [2] Manufacturing plants only.   [3] Based on the free alongside ship (F.A.S.) value.
Source: Energy Information Administration, U.S. Department of Energy (EIA-DOE)

Trends in Bituminous Coal, Lignite and Pennsylvania Anthracite in the U.S.   In Thousands of Short Tons

	Bituminous Coal and Lignite				Labor Productivity			Pennsylvania Anthracite					All Mines
	Production				Under-ground	Surface	Average	Under-ground			Miners[1]	Labor Product. Short Tons	Labor Product. Short Tons
Year	Under-gound	Surface	Total	Miners[1] Employed	Short Tons Per Miner Per Hour			ground	Surface	Total	Employed	Miner/Hr.	Miner/Hr.
1996	409,849	654,007	1,063,856	83,462	3.57	9.05	5.69	391	4,360	4,751	1,171	1.92	5.69
1997	420,657	669,274	1,089,932	81,516	3.83	9.46	6.04	419	4,259	4,678	1,287	1.76	6.04
1998	417,728	699,807	1,117,535	85,418	3.90	9.58	6.20	408	4,823	5,231	1,281	2.04	6.20
1999	391,790	708,642	1,100,431	78,723	3.99	10.39	6.61	377	4,376	4,753	1,326	1.76	6.61
2000	373,659	699,953	1,073,612	72,748	4.15	11.01	6.99	301	4,271	4,572	1,272	1.89	6.99
2001	380,627	745,308	1,127,689	77,088	4.02	10.60	6.82	341	1,143	1,484	955	.81	6.82
2002	357,385	735,910	1,094,283	75,466	3.98	10.38	6.80	305	998	1,303	872	.78	6.80
2003	352,785	717,870	1,071,753	71,023	4.04	10.76	6.95	282	961	1,243	814	.82	6.95
2004	367,557	743,552	1,112,099	73,912	3.96	10.57	6.80	271	1,408	1,679	890	.97	6.80
2005	368,612	762,190	1,131,498	79,283	3.62	10.04	6.36	264	1,296	1,560	891	.95	6.36

[1] Excludes miners employed at mines producing less than 10,000 tons.   Source: Energy Information Administration, U.S. Department of Energy (EIA-DOE)

Average Mine Prices of Coal in the United States   In Dollars Per Short Ton

	Average Mine Price by Method			Average Mine Prices by Rank				Bituminous & Lignite	Anthracite	All Coal CIF[3]
Year	Under-ground	Surface	Total	Lignite	Sub-bituminous	Bituminous	Anthracite[1]	FOB Mines[2]	FOB Mines[2]	Electric Utility Plants
1996	25.96	13.82	18.50	10.92	7.87	25.17	36.78	25.17	36.78	26.45
1997	25.68	13.39	18.14	10.91	7.42	24.64	35.12	24.64	35.12	26.16
1998	25.64	12.92	17.67	10.80	6.96	24.87	42.91	24.87	42.91	25.64
1999	24.33	12.37	16.63	11.04	6.87	23.92	35.13	23.92	35.13	24.72
2000	23.84	12.26	16.44	11.41	7.12	24.15	40.90	24.15	40.90	24.28
2001	25.37	13.18	17.38	11.52	6.67	25.36	47.67	25.36	47.67	24.68
2002	26.68	13.65	17.98	11.07	7.34	26.57	47.78	26.57	47.78	24.74
2003	26.71	13.42	17.85	11.20	7.73	26.73	49.55	26.73	49.55	25.29
2004	30.36	14.75	19.93	12.27	8.12	30.56	39.77	30.56	39.77	27.30
2005	36.42	17.37	23.59	13.49	8.68	36.80	41.00	36.80	41.00	31.22

[1] Produced in Pennsylvania.   [2] FOB = free on board.   [3] CIF = cost, insurance and freight.   W = Withheld data.

Source: Energy Information Adminstration, U.S. Department of Energy (EIA-DOE)

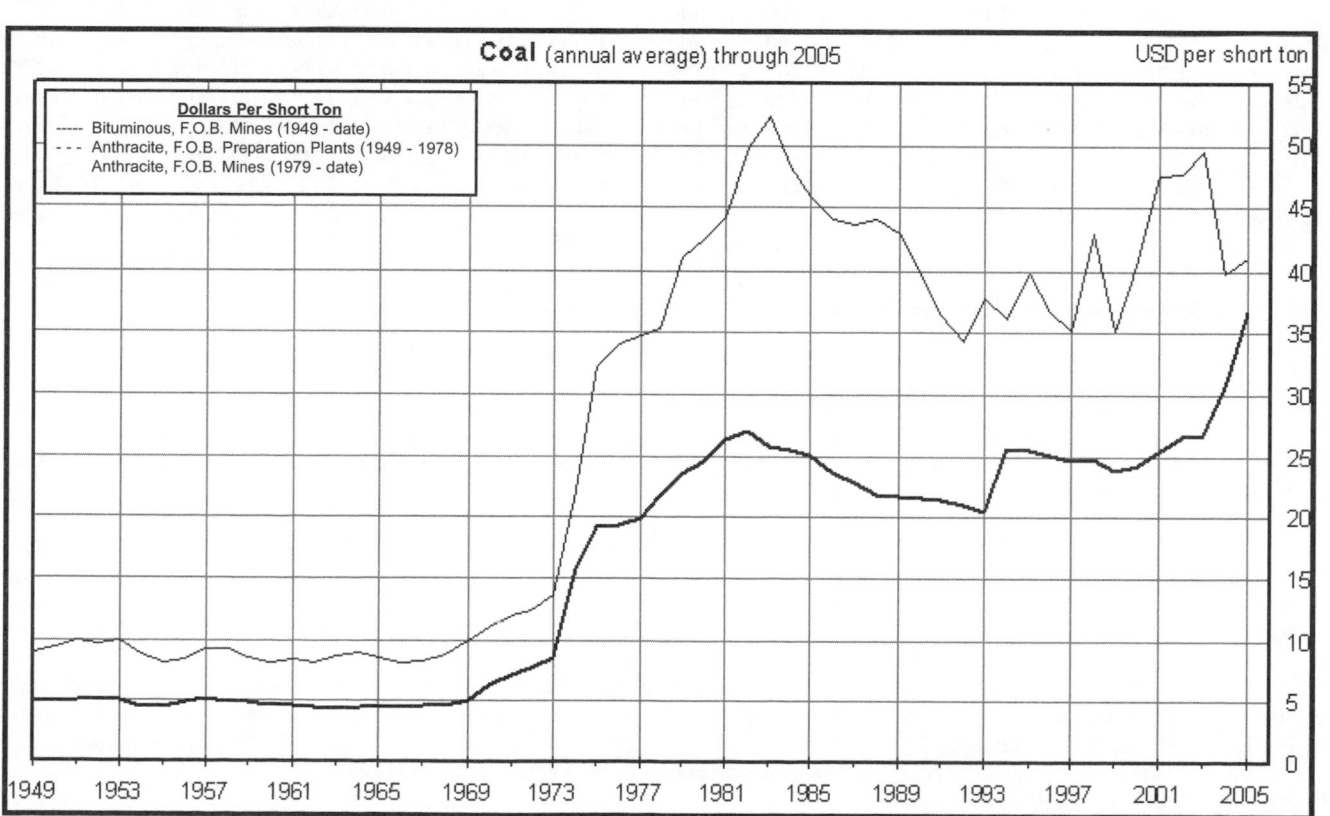

Coal (annual average) through 2005

Dollars Per Short Ton
----- Bituminous, F.O.B. Mines (1949 - date)
--- Anthracite, F.O.B. Preparation Plants (1949 - 1978)
Anthracite, F.O.B. Mines (1979 - date)

Cobalt

Cobalt (symbol Co) is a lustrous, silvery-white, magnetic, metallic element used chiefly for making alloys. Cobalt was known in ancient times and used by the Persians in 2250 BC to color glass. The name cobalt comes from the German word kobalt or kobold, meaning evil spirit. Miners gave cobalt its name because it was poisonous and troublesome since it polluted and degraded other mined elements, like nickel. In the 1730s, George Brandt first isolated metallic cobalt and was able to show that cobalt was the source of the blue color in glasses. In 1780, it was recognized as an element. Cobalt is generally not found in nature as a free metal and is instead found in ores. Cobalt is generally produced as a by-product of nickel and copper mining.

Cobalt is used in a variety of applications: high temperature steel alloys; fasteners in gas turbine engines; magnets and magnetic recording media; drying agents for paints and pigments; and steel-belted radial tires. Cobalt-60, an important radioactive tracer and cancer-treatment agent, is an artificially produced radioactive isotope of cobalt.

Prices – The price of cobalt fell sharply by –33.3% in 2005 to $15.96 per pound. That is still more than double the 18-year low of $6.91 per pound in 2002 but well below the record high of $29.21 per pound posted in 1995.

Supply – World production of cobalt in 2005 rose by +1.4% to a record high of 57,900 metric tons. The world's largest cobalt mine producers are the Congo with 38% of world production in 2005, Zambia (16%), Australia (10%), and Canada (10%).

The US does not specifically mine or refine cobalt although some cobalt is produced as a by-product of mining operations. Imports, stock releases, and secondary materials comprise the US cobalt supply. Secondary production includes extraction from super-alloy scrap, cemented carbide scrap, and spent catalysts. In the US, there are two domestic producers of extra-fine cobalt powder. One company produces the powder from imported primary metal and the other from recycled materials. There are seven companies that produce cobalt compounds. US secondary production of cobalt in 2005 fell –11.7% yr/yr to 2,030 metric tons and is still well below the record high of 3,080 metric tons seen in 1998.

Demand – US consumption of cobalt in 2005 rose by +20.0% yr/yr to 11,900 metric tons, which was a new record high. The largest use of cobalt by far was for super-alloys with 4,140 metric tons of consumption in 2005. Other smaller-scaled applications for cobalt include cutting and wear-resistant materials (763 metric tons), welding materials (227 metric tons), and magnetic alloys (337 metric tons).

Trade – US imports of cobalt in 2005 rose by +27.3% to 11,100 metric tons, which was not far below the record high of 11,481 metric tons seen in 1984. In 2005 the US relied on imports for 81% of its cobalt consumption, which is down from the 99% level seen in the early 1970s.

World Mine Production of Cobalt   In Metric Tons (Cobalt Content)

Year	Australia	Bots-wana	Canada	Cuba	Finland (Refinery)	France (Refinery)	Japan (Refinery)	New Caledonia	Norway (Refinery)	Russia	Congo[3]	Zambia	World Total
1996	2,800	408	5,714	2,011	4,160	174	258	1,100	3,098	3,300	2,000	6,959	26,200
1997	3,000	334	5,709	2,358	5,000	159	264	1,000	3,417	3,300	3,500	6,037	27,400
1998	3,300	335	5,861	2,665	10,600	300	480	1,000	4,500	3,600	5,000	11,900	35,300
1999	4,100	331	5,323	2,537	10,000	300	480	1,100	4,500	3,900	7,000	5,640	32,700
2000	5,600	308	5,298	2,852	7,700	204	311	1,200	3,433	4,000	11,000	4,600	37,900
2001	6,300	325	5,326	3,425	8,100	199	350	1,400	3,314	4,600	12,000	8,000	44,800
2002	6,700	269	5,148	3,442	8,200	176	354	1,400	3,994	4,600	14,500	10,000	50,600
2003	6,900	294	4,327	3,274	7,990	181	379	1,400	4,556	4,800	14,500	11,300	50,800
2004[1]	6,700	223	5,060	3,554	7,893	199	429	1,400	4,670	4,700	20,500	10,000	57,100
2005[2]	6,000	200	5,533	3,600				1,200		5,000	22,000	9,300	57,900

[1] Preliminary.   [2] Estimate.   [3] Formerly Zaire.   *Source: U.S. Geological Survey (USGS)*

Salient Statistics of Cobalt in the United States   In Metric Tons (Cobalt Content)

Year	Net Import Reliance as a % of Apparent Consumption	Cobalt Secondary Production	Processors and Consumer Stocks Dec. 31	Imports for Consumption	Consumption by End Uses — Ground Coat Frit	Stainless & Heat Resisting	Catalysts	Super-alloys	Tool Steel	Magnetic Alloys	Pigments	Drier in Paints, etc.[3]	Cutting & Wear-Resistant Material	Welding Materials	Total Apparent Uses	Price $ Per Pound[4]
1996	76	2,280	770	6,710	391	38	652	3,360	95	719	191	733	722	347	9,380	25.50
1997	76	2,750	763	8,430	490	38	734	4,170	112	879	201	556	789	342	11,200	23.34
1998	73	3,080	750	7,670	W	38	W	4,060	96	771	W	W	844	421	11,500	21.43
1999	73	2,720	738	8,150	W	W	W	3,830	W	794	W	W	755	291	10,700	17.02
2000	74	2,550	820	8,770	W	W	W	4,070	W	625	W	W	760	867	11,600	15.16
2001	78	2,780	852	9,410	W	W	W	4,850	W	472	W	W	720	661	11,800	10.55
2002	75	2,800	917	8,450	W	W	W	3,700	W	416	W	W	618	634	9,830	6.91
2003	78	2,130	649	8,080	W	W	W	3,400	W	282	W	W	662	632	10,000	10.60
2004[1]	76	2,300	719	8,720	W	W	W	3,650	W	396	W	W	765	627	9,920	23.93
2005[2]	78	2,030	664	11,100	W	W	W	4,140	W	337	W	W	763	227	11,900	15.96

[1] Preliminary.   [2] Estimate.   [3] Or related usage.   [4] Annual spot for cathodes.   W = Withheld proprietary data.
Source: U.S. Geological Survey (USGS)

Cocoa

Cocoa is the common name for a powder derived from the fruit seeds of the cacao tree. The Spanish called cocoa "the food of the gods" when they found it in South America 500 years ago. Today, it remains a valued commodity. Dating back to the time of the Aztecs, cocoa was mainly used as a beverage. The processing of the cacao seeds, also known as cocoa beans, begins when the harvested fruit is fermented or cured into a pulpy state for three to nine days. The cocoa beans are then dried in the sun and cleaned in special machines before they are roasted to bring out the chocolate flavor. After roasting, they are put into a crushing machine and ground into cocoa powder. Cocoa has a high food value because it contains as much as 20 percent protein, 40 percent carbohydrate, and 40 percent fat. It is also mildly stimulating because of the presence of theobromine, an alkaloid that is closely related to caffeine. Roughly two-thirds of cocoa bean production is used to make chocolate and one-third to make cocoa powder.

Four major West African cocoa producers, the Ivory Coast, Ghana, Nigeria and Cameroon, together account for about two-thirds of world cocoa production. Outside of West Africa, the major producers of cocoa are Indonesia, Brazil, Malaysia, Ecuador, and the Dominican Republic. Cocoa producers like Ghana and Indonesia have been making efforts to increase cocoa production while producers like Malaysia have been switching to other crops. Ghana has had an ongoing problem with black pod disease and with smuggling of the crop into neighboring Ivory Coast. Brazil was once one of the largest producers of cocoa but has had problems with witches' broom disease. In West Africa, the main crop harvest starts in the September-October period and can be extended into the January-March period. Cocoa trees reach maturity in 5-6 years but can live to be 50 years old or more. During the course of a growing season, the cocoa tree will produce thousands of flowers but only a few will develop into cocoa pods.

Cocoa futures and options are traded at the CSCE Division of the New York Board of Trade (NYBOT) and on the London International Financial Futures and Options Exchange (LIFFE). The futures contracts call for the delivery of 10 metric tons of cocoa and the contract is priced in US dollars per metric ton.

Prices – Cocoa prices on the CSCE nearest-futures chart in 2006 remained within the 2004-05 consolidation range that developed near the middle of the range established by the sharp rally from the 3-decade low near

$674 per metric ton posted in December 2000 to the 2-decade high of $2,420 posted in early 2003. Cocoa futures closed 2006 at $1,635 per metric ton, up +8.7% from the close of $1504 in 2005. Bullish factors for cocoa in 2006 included (1) a 2% decline in the size of the 2005-06 cocoa crop, which added to the 6% decline seen in 2004-05, (2) relatively strong world cocoa demand which produced a net deficit for the 2005-06 marketing year, and (3) generally strong commodity prices stemming from the weak dollar. There were minimal disruptions of cocoa production in the Ivory Coast as the conflict settled down between the government and rebels in the north. The Ivory Coast is the world's largest cocoa producer with 40% of world production.

Supply – The world net cocoa crop in 2005-06 fell –2.8% yr/yr to 3.190 million metric tons from the record high of 3.492 million metric tons seen in 2003-04. The drop in production caused closing stocks in 2005-06 to fall –15.3% yr/yr to 1.227 million metric tons, and the stocks/consumption ratio to fall to a low level of 36%. World grindings in 2005-06 rose by +2.7% yr/yr to 3.411 million metric tons, which was a new record high. The world's largest cocoa producer by far is the Ivory Coast where production in 2005-06 fell –6.1% yr/yr to 1.195 million metric tons from the record high of 1.386 million metric tons in 2003-04. The Ivory Coast accounted for 37% of world cocoa production in 2005-06. Other major cocoa producers included Ghana with 20% of world production, Indonesia with 14%, Cameroon with 5%, Brazil with 5%, and Nigeria with 5.0%.

Demand – World consumption of cocoa in 2004-05 (latest data available) rose +2.8% yr/yr to a new record high of 3.321 million metric tons. The world's largest cocoa consumers are the European Union with 40% of world consumption in 2004-05, followed by the US with 12% of world consumption. US consumption of cocoa in 2004-05 rose by +2.0% to 409,000 metric tons. There were large consumption increases in 2004-05 in Malaysia (+14%), in Russia (+8%), and in the European Union (+6%). There were large consumption decreases in Turkey (–18%), in Canada (–10%) and in Japan (–7%).

Trade – US imports of cocoa and cocoa products in 2005 rose sharply by +11.5% yr/yr to 1.306 million metric tons, which was a new record high. US imports of cocoa have soared in the past 15 years and are roughly 6 times the average of 225,000 metric tons of cocoa seen in the 1980s.

World Supply and Demand Cocoa   In Thousands of Metric Tons

Crop Year Beginning October	Stocks Oct. 1	Net World Production[4]	Total Availability	Seasonal Grindings	Closing Stocks	Stock Change	Stock/ Consumption Ratio %
1996-97	1,602	2,690	4,292	2,730	1,562	-40	57.2
1997-98	1,562	2,605	4,167	2,773	1,394	-168	50.3
1998-99	1,394	2,786	4,180	2,757	1,423	29	51.6
1999-00	1,423	3,030	4,453	2,975	1,478	55	49.7
2000-01	1,478	2,766	4,244	3,072	1,172	-306	38.2
2001-02	1,172	2,793	3,965	2,843	1,123	-49	39.5
2002-03	1,123	3,115	4,238	3,014	1,224	101	40.6
2003-04[1]	1,224	3,492	4,716	3,230	1,486	262	46.0
2004-05[2]	1,486	3,283	4,769	3,321	1,448	-38	43.6
2005-06[3]	1,448	3,190	4,638	3,411	1,227	-221	36.0

[1] Preliminary.   [2] Estimate.   [3] Forecast.   [4] Obtained by adjusting the gross world crop for a one percent loss in weight.
Source: ED&F Man Cocoa Ltd.

COCOA

World Production of Cocoa Beans   In Thousands of Metric Tons

Crop Year Beginning October	Brazil	Cameroon	Colombia	Dominican Republic	Ecuador	Ghana	Indonesia	Ivory Coast	Malaysia	Mexico	Nigeria	Papua New Guinea	World Total
1996-97	183	121	39	47	101	323	327	1,130	102	35	160	28	2,712
1997-98	173	114	38	60	28	409	322	1,090	57	30	165	26	2,626
1998-99	138	123	39	22	72	398	396	1,175	79	25	200	35	2,808
1999-00	124	115	37	28	92	435	428	1,404	37	31	180	46	3,054
2000-01	163	133	36	37	81	395	381	1,185	29	33	180	39	2,788
2001-02	124	131	34	45	72	340	459	1,240	10	29	195	38	2,816
2002-03	163	155	36	45	81	497	418	1,360	10	35	180	43	3,140
2003-04[1]	163	165	37	46	111	737	464	1,386	10	27	190	39	3,520
2004-05[2]	171	185	37	33	110	583	471	1,273	10	36	180	40	3,309
2005-06[3]	165	170	37	44	120	630	450	1,195	10	28	150	40	3,216

[1] Preliminary.   [2] Estimate.   [3] Forecast.   *Source: ED&F Man Cocoa Ltd*

World Consumption of Cocoa[4]   In Thousands of Metric Tons

Year	Canada	Brazil	European Union	Ghana	Indonesia	Cote d'Ivoire	Japan	Malaysia	Singapore	Turkey	United States	Russia	World Total
1995-96	39	183	1,225	60	60	130	49	96	63	16	345	75	2,655
1996-97	35	180	1,203	68	72	145	53	103	61	16	394	74	2,730
1997-98	53	188	1,228	67	74	195	43	94	68	22	399	50	2,773
1998-99	42	191	1,186	65	83	210	47	109	63	22	406	48	2,757
1999-00	56	202	1,235	75	88	230	48	117	60	25	439	62	2,975
2000-01	58	195	1,263	80	91	285	49	121	59	39	445	67	3,072
2001-02	56	173	1,159	80	108	265	50	93	62	39	393	69	2,843
2002-03[1]	57	196	1,190	69	115	290	64	129	71	50	400	60	3,014
2003-04[2]	72	207	1,256	78	122	321	57	200	59	71	401	63	3,230
2004-05[3]	65	209	1,328	76	111	320	53	228	57	58	409	68	3,321

[1] Preliminary.   [2] Estimate.   [3] Forecast.   [4] Figures represent the grindings of cocoa beans in each country.   NA = Not available.
Source: ED&F Man Cocoa Ltd

Imports of Cocoa Butter in Selected Countries   In Metric Tons

Year	Australia	Austria	Belgium	Canada	France	Germany	Italy	Japan	Netherlands	Sweden	Switzerland	United Kingdom	United States
1995	12,150	7,425	26,185	11,146	40,245	69,928	12,027	12,898	38,300	7,078	17,835	30,654	57,210
1996	14,316	7,124	23,771	12,166	47,349	69,298	11,178	16,096	39,193	5,698	18,690	32,781	68,761
1997	14,896	6,922	34,222	16,782	46,516	71,094	9,706	16,609	29,023	6,937	19,058	37,021	87,687
1998	16,305	5,984	25,722	16,941	43,610	76,057	8,957	15,363	28,523	7,403	19,857	32,951	65,306
1999	22,573	5,363	42,278	17,323	49,722	70,323	8,281	17,824	35,602	6,884	21,278	39,648	80,475
2000	20,591	4,425	52,917	22,005	48,033	71,985	11,106	21,696	27,253	5,986	19,923	36,360	94,649
2001	20,634	3,814	51,576	23,307	51,029	80,839	11,764	21,663	36,643	6,350	18,901	40,668	80,808
2002	20,800	3,638	49,467	24,397	58,949	82,313	12,101	20,212	37,569	6,401	20,187	39,117	54,788
2003	22,307	3,963	58,076	26,314	58,651	77,880	13,343	22,579	55,820	6,564	21,455	38,799	78,315
2004[1]	23,516	4,467	55,840	27,632	61,613	84,269	13,966	22,164	50,097	6,667	22,960	47,979	94,891

[1] Preliminary.   NA = Not available.   *Source: ED&F Man Cocoa Ltd*

Imports of Cocoa Liquor and Cocoa Powder in Selected Countries   In Metric Tons

	Cocoa Liqour						Cocoa Powder						
Year	France	Germany	Japan	Netherlands	United Kingdom	United States	Denmark	France	Germany	Italy	Japan	Netherlands	United States
1995	46,570	5,083	6,822	1,832	5,030	19,192	3,229	17,081	32,247	15,265	6,310	10,048	66,075
1996	62,938	7,437	9,926	2,133	5,069	15,357	3,711	18,398	36,211	15,006	13,069	6,678	68,658
1997	61,148	10,299	8,401	1,393	5,860	17,850	4,189	19,555	35,069	15,872	8,941	4,424	71,024
1998	70,883	9,121	12,534	1,144	3,813	21,894	3,865	19,533	32,479	17,122	8,779	3,746	84,211
1999	74,721	13,833	1,421	25,639	4,396	12,823	3,676	19,342	33,404	16,464	9,779	8,405	84,975
2000	67,812	14,295	1,618	33,815	8,529	10,902	3,348	21,932	34,601	18,261	11,245	22,492	86,908
2001	67,500	17,548	1,553	41,913	10,289	17,940	4,014	25,736	32,621	20,164	11,949	30,149	113,593
2002	64,820	28,100	1,193	46,369	14,038	22,215	NA	24,445	36,583	19,201	10,299	26,021	95,499
2003	71,337	31,391	1,764	35,089	20,154	20,018	NA	31,933	32,805	18,573	12,895	35,275	99,977
2004[1]	72,057	42,975	2,773	40,847	17,753	20,758	NA	33,148	42,732	19,637	14,393	35,263	104,880

[1] Preliminary.   NA = Not available.   *Source: ED&F Man Cocoa Ltd*

Imports of Cocoa and Products in the United States   In Thousands of Metric Tons

Year	Jan.	Feb.	Mar.	Apr.	May	June	July	Aug.	Sept.	Oct.	Nov.	Dec.	Total
1996	90	87	90	80	55	49	62	53	53	60	60	86	821
1997	80	47	77	71	64	54	59	47	64	61	56	88	768
1998	86	105	90	71	55	65	65	62	72	63	54	77	865
1999	100	79	81	93	51	60	77	62	68	67	82	102	922
2000	111	128	101	91	70	67	70	70	86	76	59	69	999
2001	108	97	77	47	68	61	80	78	76	86	92	118	989
2002	87	74	73	61	76	72	87	98	61	66	90	72	916
2003	115	74	92	71	68	74	95	82	79	95	85	116	1,046
2004	110	82	130	100	101	103	94	94	100	90	80	89	1,171
2005[1]	129	109	156	108	104	93	91	103	86	87	112	129	1,308

[1] Preliminary.   Source: Foreign Agricultural Service, U.S. Department of Agriculture (FAS-USDA)

Visible Stocks of Cocoa in Port of Hampton Road Warehouses[1], at End of Month   In Thousands of Bags

Year	Jan.	Feb.	Mar.	Apr.	May	June	July	Aug.	Sept.	Oct.	Nov.	Dec.
1996	1,439.8	1,492.8	1,458.0	1,549.6	1,561.7	1,493.9	1,412.3	1,315.4	1,239.6	1,338.9	1,108.1	1,116.2
1997	1,128.3	1,132.1	1,133.0	1,094.0	1,010.5	970.2	872.4	840.1	727.3	763.9	695.7	704.8
1998	726.5	693.4	841.9	842.5	811.6	764.7	714.3	712.3	795.4	801.9	705.9	673.0
1999	661.6	693.2	642.5	579.7	536.9	500.7	489.0	472.7	473.4	451.8	438.9	421.2
2000	469.7	448.4	571.7	583.4	711.1	672.4	720.3	925.2	921.4	839.7	762.9	816.0
2001	741.9	657.4	632.0	607.7	577.3	518.8	498.2	487.5	475.2	506.8	509.0	511.4
2002	504.7	462.8	436.7	424.0	383.8	353.4	327.4	273.3	255.4	194.8	181.5	169.9
2003	149.9	121.7	103.1	102.3	80.5	71.9	69.2	67.7	56.9	53.0	49.6	49.3
2004	48.6	47.8	47.5	47.5	44.3	43.9	41.2	40.4	40.1	38.0	38.0	36.8
2005	31.1	30.9	28.6	28.0	28.0	27.4	27.4	27.4	27.4	27.4	27.4	27.4

[1] Licensed and unlicensed warehouses approved by the CSCE.   Source: New York Board of Trade (NYBOT)

Visible Stocks of Cocoa in Philadelphia (Del. River) Warehouses[1], at End of Month   In Thousands of Bags

Year	Jan.	Feb.	Mar.	Apr.	May	June	July	Aug.	Sept.	Oct.	Nov.	Dec.
1996	960.2	1,005.2	1,205.6	1,658.8	1,871.3	1,851.7	1,969.1	1,816.2	1,851.1	1,705.1	1,671.7	1,696.5
1997	1,753.0	1,634.4	1,579.6	1,641.0	1,578.7	1,625.9	1,696.2	1,637.6	1,530.9	1,491.8	1,414.2	1,394.0
1998	1,420.3	1,435.7	1,592.6	1,555.3	1,398.5	1,287.8	1,279.8	1,376.9	1,373.7	1,260.6	1,406.7	1,637.1
1999	1,763.0	1,832.8	1,982.7	2,217.8	2,019.4	1,999.6	2,084.6	2,133.4	2,144.1	2,015.5	1,774.4	1,608.5
2000	1,619.0	1,801.7	2,466.4	2,582.0	2,581.6	2,363.7	2,168.3	2,101.6	2,105.1	2,039.1	1,697.4	1,589.4
2001	1,844.0	2,082.3	2,173.3	1,960.0	1,785.9	1,610.4	1,391.6	1,543.0	1,391.3	1,131.4	1,303.2	1,682.1
2002	1,701.5	1,876.7	1,849.3	1,708.0	1,746.4	1,689.5	1,793.1	1,832.7	1,750.9	1,334.5	1,162.7	1,250.6
2003	1,347.2	1,422.0	1,327.9	1,326.5	1,217.2	1,202.3	1,229.2	1,123.7	930.6	798.9	723.7	806.0
2004	1,294.9	1,061.5	1,259.1	1,187.1	1,238.8	1,342.0	1,432.6	1,529.3	1,366.4	1,569.4	1,312.8	1,335.7
2005	1,588.9	1,809.8	2,066.3	2,264.5	2,439.3	2,258.3	2,465.0	2,481.0	2,470.5	2,373.5	2,635.5	2,712.8

[1] Licensed and unlicensed warehouses approved by the CSCE.   Source: New York Board of Trade (NYBOT)

Visible Stocks of Cocoa in New York Warehouses[1], at End of Month   In Thousands of Bags

Year	Jan.	Feb.	Mar.	Apr.	May	June	July	Aug.	Sept.	Oct.	Nov.	Dec.
1996	667.6	646.1	632.7	627.2	656.1	633.5	1,191.7	1,154.2	1,121.4	973.2	950.1	919.0
1997	984.7	981.3	945.0	1,250.0	1,574.4	1,524.7	1,512.8	1,348.0	1,217.3	1,073.7	1,020.0	980.4
1998	973.9	1,342.7	1,271.3	1,675.7	1,552.3	1,516.7	1,404.6	1,293.1	1,300.1	1,126.4	989.2	1,031.6
1999	1,085.0	1,089.3	1,083.1	1,134.1	1,139.4	1,114.3	1,093.5	974.5	941.9	821.7	847.5	1,573.1
2000	1,633.7	1,689.5	1,926.9	2,049.8	1,926.7	1,789.6	1,632.2	1,383.7	1,323.7	1,234.8	1,100.0	1,019.4
2001	1,005.6	1,173.8	1,119.6	1,024.9	967.5	906.6	776.2	758.5	657.6	687.4	750.8	1,196.2
2002	1,088.9	870.8	892.0	816.1	739.1	736.0	640.9	553.6	670.1	525.7	473.1	554.8
2003	614.6	625.4	593.7	612.9	515.1	476.1	423.6	388.2	483.4	301.9	391.3	342.9
2004	229.9	415.2	616.1	579.9	712.7	680.1	676.3	596.1	486.3	334.5	272.0	209.6
2005	201.2	446.3	495.9	677.7	806.6	916.5	805.2	625.2	457.2	430.3	388.3	599.2

[1] Licensed and unlicensed warehouses approved by the CSCE.   Source: New York Board of Trade (NYBOT)

Cocoa (monthly average) through December 2006 — USD per metric ton

USD Per Metruc Ton
----- Ivory Coast (Oct. 1980 - date)
----- Caracas, Philadelphia (1825 - 1854)
Guayaquil, Philadelphia (1855 - 1897)
Guayaquil, London (1898 - 1906)
Bahia, New York (1907- 1912)
Accra, New York (1913 - 1925)
Exchange Standard, New York (Dec. 1926 - Dec. 1947)
Accra, New York (Jan. 1948 - Dec. 1984)

Average Cash Price of Cocoa, Ivory Coast in New York   In Dollars Per Metric Ton

Year	Jan.	Feb.	Mar.	Apr.	May	June	July	Aug.	Sept.	Oct.	Nov.	Dec.	Average
1996	1,455	1,476	1,421	1,536	1,558	1,577	1,556	1,563	1,559	1,578	1,546	1,560	1,532
1997	1,517	1,452	1,591	1,628	1,624	1,748	1,736	1,743	1,864	1,832	1,770	1,819	1,694
1998	1,750	1,721	1,812	1,835	1,902	1,812	1,792	1,761	1,767	1,750	1,694	1,630	1,769
1999	1,565	1,498	1,415	1,276	1,144	1,263	1,209	1,154	1,156	1,133	1,037	1,027	1,240
2000	1,027	962	1,025	993	998	1,033	1,034	980	988	991	905	911	987
2001	1,093	1,299	1,290	1,244	1,281	1,146	1,152	1,200	1,183	1,288	1,439	1,543	1,263
2002	1,586	1,674	1,794	1,800	1,814	1,836	2,081	2,191	2,391	2,471	2,123	2,322	2,007
2003	2,483	2,506	2,258	2,232	1,996	1,818	1,803	1,843	1,877	1,713	1,737	1,832	2,008
2004	1,840	1,763	1,695	1,610	1,588	1,571	1,733	1,889	1,698	1,654	1,867	1,848	1,730
2005	1,740	1,827	1,950	1,744	1,656	1,687	1,625	1,626	1,640	1,598	1,585	1,670	1,696

Source: Economic Research Service, U.S. Department of Agriculture (ERS-USDA)

Cocoa Futures - New York Board of Trade
(weekly close) as of December 29, 2006

USD per metric ton

Average Open Interest of Cocoa Futures in New York   In Contracts

Year	Jan.	Feb.	Mar.	Apr.	May	June	July	Aug.	Sept.	Oct.	Nov.	Dec.
1996	90,478	93,533	98,049	95,390	96,346	88,232	80,873	77,134	77,942	79,572	77,139	78,592
1997	86,960	90,589	96,771	96,956	94,651	97,385	101,815	101,138	106,487	108,263	99,544	97,009
1998	90,574	82,205	78,022	73,237	79,294	74,347	74,295	73,975	71,978	74,139	74,127	73,480
1999	77,067	72,324	69,221	65,856	71,990	75,195	70,787	69,939	74,572	79,770	89,035	92,609
2000	100,540	110,316	106,056	102,382	113,239	111,948	112,864	117,260	123,463	138,523	139,141	138,266
2001	132,711	119,459	114,036	102,275	107,008	111,224	104,473	99,280	92,235	96,204	93,088	92,326
2002	97,563	98,169	96,336	98,851	103,746	100,701	107,080	102,441	107,294	107,880	82,236	82,844
2003	96,375	91,944	83,625	83,230	95,307	96,813	89,846	78,197	76,468	86,392	99,038	94,010
2004	88,879	84,078	99,918	100,429	108,150	99,476	103,350	111,318	101,998	119,033	117,876	118,769
2005	117,091	115,007	144,055	124,417	124,925	128,203	126,388	129,562	118,468	132,629	131,733	123,302

Source: New York Board of Trade (NYBOT)

Volume of Trading of Cocoa Futures in New York   In Contracts

Year	Jan.	Feb.	Mar.	Apr.	May	June	July	Aug.	Sept.	Oct.	Nov.	Dec.	Total
1996	177,720	226,701	213,189	242,988	164,749	183,544	159,070	164,719	107,634	167,227	185,226	128,809	2,121,576
1997	180,669	172,510	219,896	235,020	130,041	251,471	186,280	200,707	168,981	204,394	180,805	143,735	2,274,509
1998	175,844	145,311	171,333	192,120	143,602	183,719	131,642	156,737	115,066	125,320	155,280	114,606	1,810,580
1999	136,109	155,090	141,090	180,837	130,019	230,925	125,360	144,290	147,124	143,335	209,608	124,249	1,868,036
2000	156,812	231,562	232,803	186,837	147,072	267,470	124,906	191,849	111,740	174,216	186,515	98,266	2,110,048
2001	311,900	168,587	164,131	136,021	154,397	201,299	108,189	207,569	118,428	124,884	202,847	107,565	2,005,817
2002	155,699	187,550	129,833	217,590	160,364	220,289	176,450	209,249	138,394	207,310	162,982	114,270	2,079,980
2003	172,845	215,240	136,564	179,956	176,969	207,255	143,888	206,428	146,113	197,316	209,775	135,857	2,128,206
2004	174,684	180,693	181,667	244,946	174,452	238,201	219,018	260,025	146,090	150,443	290,227	128,604	2,389,050
2005	185,624	239,511	231,917	249,209	134,330	288,809	151,339	252,868	222,122	182,337	283,663	191,198	2,612,927

Source: New York Board of Trade (NYBOT)

Coconut Oil and Copra

Coconut oil and copra come from the fruit of the coconut palm tree, which originated in Southeast Asia. Coconut oil has been used for thousands of years as cooking oil, and is still a staple in the diets of many people living in tropical areas. Until shortages of imported oil developed during WWII, Americans also used coconut oil for cooking.

Copra is the meaty inner lining of the coconut. It is an oil-rich pulp with a light, slightly sweet, nutty flavor. Copra is used mainly as a source of coconut oil and is also used shredded for baking. High-quality copra contains about 65% to 72% oil, and oil made from the copra is called crude coconut oil. Crude coconut oil is processed from copra by expeller press and solvent extraction. It is not considered fit for human consumption until it has been refined, which consists of neutralizing, bleaching and deodorizing it at high heat with a vacuum. The remaining oil cake obtained as a by-product is used for livestock feed.

Premium grade coconut oil, also called virgin coconut oil, is oil made from the first pressing without the addition of any chemicals. Premium grade coconut oil is more expensive than refined or crude oil because the producers use only selected raw materials and there is a lower production yield due to only one pressing.

Coconut oil accounts for approximately 20% of all vegetable oils used worldwide. Coconut oil is used in margarines, vegetable shortening, salad oils, confections, and in sports drinks to boost energy and enhance athletic performance. It is also used in the manufacture of soaps, detergents, shampoos, cosmetics, candles, glycerin and synthetic rubber. Coconut oil is very healthy, unless it is hydrogenated, and is easily digested.

Prices – The average monthly price of coconut oil (crude) in 2005 fell –14.7% to 32.44 cents per pound, up from the 15-year low of 21.94 cents posted in 2002. The record high of 60.21 cents per pound was posted in 1984.

Supply – World production of copra in 2006 rose slightly by +0.5% yr/yr to 5.245 million metric tons but that was still well below the record high of 5.662 million metric tons posted in 2001. The world's largest producers of copra are the Philippines with 41% of world production, Indonesia with 27%, India with 13%, and Mexico with 4%. World production of coconut oil in the 2005-06 marketing year rose +3.8% yr/yr to 3.283 million metric tons.

Demand – Virtually all of world production of copra in 2005-06 went for crushing into coconut meal and oil (over 99%). World consumption of coconut oil in 2005-06 rose +5.4% yr/yr to 3.263 million metric tons, not far below the record of 3.349 million metric tons in 2000-01.

Trade – Copra is generally crushed in the country of origin, meaning that less than 4% of copra itself is exported; the rest is exported in the form of coconut oil. World exports of coconut oil in 2005-06 rose by +3.0% yr/yr to a record high of 2.615 million metric tons.

World Production of Copra   In Thousands of Metric Tons

Year	India	Indonesia	Ivory Coast	Malaysia	Mexico	Mozam-bique	New Guinea	Philip-pines	Sri Lanka	Thailand	Vanuatu	Vietnam	World Total
1997	720	1,300	45	60	217	76	159	2,210	67	61	34	96	5,363
1998	735	965	43	50	237	76	143	2,270	71	61	43	68	5,077
1999	718	860	36	48	199	73	146	1,250	68	65	30	72	3,874
2000	700	1,330	45	49	202	75	152	2,140	98	69	27	45	5,248
2001	690	1,185	45	47	198	75	95	2,790	113	60	30	41	5,662
2002	713	1,290	45	50	203	75	71	2,065	70	61	16	46	5,004
2003	690	1,260	45	51	183	72	85	2,390	75	65	29	49	5,297
2004[1]	700	1,300	45	51	182	75	90	1,980	85	70	39	49	4,972
2005[2]	660	1,470	45	48	184	75	112	2,100	67	65	30	50	5,218
2006[3]	670	1,430	45	48	185	75	115	2,150	68	65	30	51	5,245

[1] Preliminary.   [2] Estimate.   [3] Forecast.   *Source: The Oil World*

World Supply and Distribution of Coconut Oil   In Thousands of Metric Tons

Year	India	Indo-nesia	Mal-aysia	Philip-pines	Total	Exports	Imports	European Union	India	Indo-nesia	Philip-pines	United States	Total	Philip-pines	United States	Total
		Production							Consumption						Ending Stocks	
1996-97	424	756	35	1,257	3,150	1,726	1,658	688	432	213	339	504	3,067	92	68	384
1997-98	442	652	39	1,628	3,411	2,125	2,111	771	440	211	302	540	3,184	32	178	598
1998-99	431	458	51	783	2,370	1,040	1,142	578	446	110	295	461	2,750	58	69	319
1999-00	421	787	54	1,198	3,084	1,788	1,718	770	435	110	299	420	2,921	112	62	411
2000-01	419	700	48	1,731	3,496	2,159	2,173	751	439	277	348	437	3,349	60	118	572
2001-02	421	773	45	1,441	3,242	1,850	1,884	706	448	278	370	516	3,341	62	103	507
2002-03	417	758	41	1,428	3,209	1,966	1,983	781	454	273	356	372	3,315	53	98	418
2003-04[1]	419	731	41	1,379	3,135	1,856	1,854	708	434	246	311	412	3,181	58	60	370
2004-05[2]	402	881	42	1,257	3,162	2,102	2,066	809	425	173	247	358	3,095	73	110	401
2005-06[3]	401	844	42	1,410	3,283	2,165	2,171	830	432	191	258	434	3,263	75	100	427

[1] Preliminary.   [2] Estimate.   [3] Forecast.   *Source: The Oil World*

Supply and Distribution of Coconut Oil in the United States   In Millions of Pounds

Year	Rotterdam — Copra Tonne $ U.S.	Rotterdam — Coconut Oil, CIF $ U.S.	Imports For Consumption	Stocks Oct. 1	Total Supply	Exports	Disappearance — Total Domestic	Disappearance — Edible Products	Disappearance — Inedible Products	Production of Coconut Oil (Refined) — Total	Production — Oct.-Dec.	Production — Jan.-Mar.	Production — April-June	Production — July-Sept.
1996-97	452	693	1,188	83	1,271	11	1,111	120	471	324.2	77.0	61.5	101.5	84.2
1997-98	391	625	1,440	149	1,589	7	1,190	141	472	397.8	113.4	103.6	100.4	80.4
1998-99	468	748	791	392	1,183	11	1,021	144	380	363.2	89.6	82.9	99.3	91.4
1999-00	357	539	926	152	1,078	14	927	221	371	442.3	69.1	117.0	129.6	126.7
2000-01	208	323	1,100	136	1,236	8	968	237	297	534.9	135.7	128.3	146.9	124.0
2001-02	245	388	1,150	260	1,410	11	1,100	294	302	501.8	139.5	126.1	115.4	120.8
2002-03	286	450	838	226	1,065	29	1,205	305	310	546.7	128.8	137.0	155.6	125.2
2003-04	424	630	840	219	1,058	17	1,312	330	274	594.9	160.7	132.8	162.8	138.6
2004-05[1]	431	636	929	131	1,061	29	1,374	341	280	623.3	153.7	157.5	160.8	151.3
2005-06[2]	382	577	970	163	1,133	35	1,323	366	270	599.9	141.9	156.2	160.5	141.4

[1] Preliminary.   [2] Estimate.   *Source: Bureau of Census, U.S. Department of Commerce*

Consumption of Coconut Oil in End Products (Edible and Inedible) in the U.S.   In Millions of Pounds

Year	Jan.	Feb.	Mar.	Apr.	May	June	July	Aug.	Sept.	Oct.	Nov.	Dec.	Total
1997	44.1	44.8	52.8	46.1	41.9	49.4	49.9	48.3	66.9	53.4	43.9	48.0	589.5
1998	51.5	48.1	59.4	54.3	54.5	47.0	49.3	50.3	53.7	49.4	50.0	42.1	609.6
1999	39.9	44.7	50.8	43.0	41.4	45.4	36.9	33.3	46.2	41.5	43.6	38.8	505.5
2000	49.4	44.0	52.7	54.6	51.4	56.5	49.1	56.2	54.7	44.1	44.3	43.0	600.0
2001	49.3	40.6	45.5	42.5	48.3	43.3	46.5	45.6	48.4	50.3	44.4	45.5	550.2
2002	55.4	41.3	50.8	59.3	53.9	46.4	50.7	51.8	45.9	54.3	56.1	49.4	615.4
2003	51.2	49.3	56.8	50.6	52.3	46.7	48.9	49.6	50.3	47.8	41.8	38.5	583.7
2004	50.0	51.7	58.5	54.6	48.5	55.6	52.9	55.1	48.9	48.2	64.3	51.7	640.0
2005	46.7	52.0	47.9	48.8	51.4	55.5	47.2	58.1	49.2	52.8	53.4	58.1	621.1
2006[1]	70.4	62.7	50.4	47.5	50.7	51.6	43.1	51.6	43.8	49.6	44.4	40.9	606.6

[1] Preliminary.   *Source: Bureau of Census, U.S. Department of Commerce*

Stocks of Coconut Oil (Crude and Refined) in the U.S., on First of Month   In Millions of Pounds

Year	Jan.	Feb.	Mar.	Apr.	May	June	July	Aug.	Sept.	Oct.	Nov.	Dec.
1997	125.9	147.4	141.1	204.5	174.5	161.3	143.8	143.4	154.3	149.6	162.1	194.2
1998	274.2	332.4	344.5	337.4	318.8	300.6	366.3	424.6	434.4	392.6	431.8	447.3
1999	401.7	446.5	387.5	366.3	309.8	240.5	134.7	197.5	191.8	152.0	106.4	142.2
2000	93.6	123.6	100.1	99.6	102.3	104.0	137.7	163.6	161.4	136.4	178.1	161.6
2001	245.4	280.3	357.8	276.5	286.9	194.3	254.4	260.9	246.4	259.7	234.1	231.3
2002	245.9	238.8	249.6	251.3	233.5	231.6	303.3	301.6	245.8	226.5	273.8	264.1
2003	195.2	194.0	214.3	224.9	223.7	187.8	162.2	202.9	195.6	218.9	184.6	186.1
2004	167.2	160.3	192.6	181.7	131.4	108.7	90.6	132.8	149.2	131.3	147.7	182.5
2005	225.9	163.7	188.4	191.0	170.6	187.7	263.5	250.4	253.7	242.1	252.3	273.3
2006[1]	268.3	236.9	224.5	227.3	260.2	229.1	213.8	214.4	204.7	224.5	179.2	180.2

[1] Preliminary.   NA = Not available.   *Source: Bureau of Census, U.S. Department of Commerce*

Average Price of Coconut Oil (Crude) Tank Cars in New York   In Cents Per Pound

Year	Jan.	Feb.	Mar.	Apr.	May	June	July	Aug.	Sept.	Oct.	Nov.	Dec.	Average
1996	35.80	36.63	36.75	38.75	39.50	42.25	41.80	42.80	47.20	48.00	49.50	50.00	42.42
1997	44.20	44.00	42.88	42.50	42.50	35.00	36.50	36.50	37.00	37.25	37.25	37.25	39.40
1998	37.25	37.25	37.25	37.25	37.25	37.00	36.50	35.50	36.50	39.00	37.50	38.50	37.23
1999	35.38	35.00	34.00	34.06	38.25	42.13	39.83	36.08	46.00	46.00	46.00	46.00	39.89
2000	40.88	32.94	28.81	26.63	24.25	21.90	19.63	18.58	16.40	16.81	17.50	15.70	23.34
2001	26.00	24.00	22.75	22.50	21.00	21.00	24.00	26.50	26.50	26.50	24.50	24.50	24.15
2002	16.38	17.38	17.25	18.75	20.05	21.13	21.06	21.35	28.50	28.25	27.13	26.00	21.94
2003	26.00	26.00	24.60	24.50	24.50	25.00	25.00	25.00	25.00	25.00	28.75	31.00	25.86
2004	32.00	33.38	34.56	39.20	45.00	46.00	46.00	46.00	39.25	32.65	31.25	31.25	38.05
2005[1]	31.05	31.00	32.67	35.00	34.67	34.00	33.00	33.00	33.00	35.00	29.13	27.75	32.44

[1] Preliminary.   *Source: Economic Research Service, U.S. Department of Agriculture (ERS-USDA)*

Coffee

Coffee is one of the world's most important cash commodities. Coffee is the common name for any type of tree in the genus madder family. It is actually a tropical evergreen shrub that has the potential to grow 100 feet tall. The coffee tree grows in tropical regions between the Tropics of Cancer and Capricorn in areas with abundant rainfall, year-round warm temperatures averaging about 70 degrees Fahrenheit, and no frost. In the US, the only areas that produce any significant amount of coffee are Puerto Rico and Hawaii. The coffee plant will produce its first full crop of beans at about 5 years old and then be productive for about 15 years. The average coffee tree produces enough beans to make about 1 to 1 ½ pounds of roasted coffee per year. It takes approximately 4,000 handpicked green coffee beans to make a pound of coffee. Wine was actually the first drink made from the coffee tree using the coffee cherries, honey, and water. In the 17th century, the first coffee house, also known as a "penny university" because of the price per cup, opened in London. The London Stock Exchange grew from one of these first coffee houses.

Coffee is generally classified into two types of beans: arabica and robusta. The most widely produced coffee is arabica, which makes up about 70 percent of total production. It grows mostly at high altitudes of 600 to 2,000 meters, with Brazil and Colombia being the largest producers. Arabic coffee is traded on the New York Board of Trade. The stronger of the two types is robusta. It is grown at lower altitudes with the largest producers being Indonesia, West Africa, Brazil, and Vietnam. Robusta coffee is traded on the LIFFE exchange.

Ninety percent of the world coffee trade is in green (unroasted) coffee beans. Seasonal factors have a significant influence on the price of coffee. There is no extreme peak in world production at any one time of the year, although coffee consumption declines by 12 percent or more below the year's average in the warm summer months. Therefore, coffee imports and roasts both tend to decline in spring and summer and pick up again in fall and winter.

The very low prices for coffee in 2000-03 created serious problems for coffee producers. When prices fall below the costs of production, there is little or no economic incentive to produce coffee. The result is that coffee trees are neglected or completely abandoned. When prices are low, producers cannot afford to hire the labor needed to maintain the trees and pick the crop at harvest. The result is that trees yield less due to reduced use of fertilizer and fewer employed coffee workers. One effect is a decline in the quality of the coffee that is produced. Higher quality Arabica coffee is often produced at higher altitudes, which entails higher costs. It is this coffee that is often abandoned. Although the pressure on producers can be severe, the market eventually comes back into balance as supply declines in response to low prices.

Coffee prices are subject to upward spikes in June, July and August due to possible freeze scares in Brazil during the winter months in the Southern Hemisphere. The Brazilian coffee crop is harvested starting in May and extending for several weeks into what are the winter months in Brazil. A major freeze in Brazil occurs roughly every five years on average.

Coffee futures are traded on the Bolsa de Mercadorias & Futuros (BM&F), the Tokyo Grain Exchange (TGE), the London International Financial Futures and Options Exchange (LIFFE), and the CSCE Division of the New York Board of Trade (NYBOT). Options are traded on the BM&F, the LIFFE and the CSCE.

Prices – Nybot Arabica coffee futures prices in 2006 traded near the top of the rally seen in 2002-05 and closed 2006 at 126.20 cents per pound, up +18% from the 2005 close of 107.10 cents per pound. Coffee prices were supported in the latter half of 2006 by a dry flowering season in Brazil which, along with the biennial cycle, will likely cut the Brazilian 2007-08 coffee crop by 26% to 31.5 mln bags from 42.5 mln bags in 2006-07. Lower Brazilian production is expected to help push the world 2007-08 (Oct-Sep) coffee crop lower by –9% to 109-112 million bags from 122 million bags in 2006-07, according to the International Coffee Organization. The world coffee market in 2007-08 is likely to see a production deficit relative to demand after a small surplus in 2006-07, thus providing support for coffee prices. World coffee ending stocks remained tight in 2006-07 at 23.0 mln bags, just slightly above the recent record low of 19.8 mln seen in 2005-06, according to the USDA. Coffee prices in 2006 were supported by the El Nino conditions, which caused dry conditions in some key coffee producing countries.

Supply – World coffee production in the 2006-07 marketing year (July-June) rose +13.1% yr/yr to 128.561 million bags (1 bag equals 60 kilograms or 132.3 pounds). The 2006-07 production level of 128.561 million bags was a new record high. The increase in production caused the 2006-07 ending stocks to rise +16.2% to 22.961 million bags.

Brazil is the world's largest coffee producer by far with 46.5 million bags of production in 2006-07, accounting for 36% of total world production. Other key producers include Vietnam with 13% of the world's production and Columbia with 10%. Brazil's coffee production in 2006-07, however, rose by +28.8% to 46.500 million bags. Vietnam in recent years has become a major coffee producer, boosting its production to 16.5 million bags in 2006-07 from less than a million bags in 1990.

Demand – US coffee consumption rose slightly by +3.9% to 22.649 million bags in 2006, mildly below the 4-decade high of 22.8 million bags seen in 2000.

Trade – World coffee exports in 2006-07 rose +9.8% yr/yr to 95.986 million bags, which was a record high. The world's largest exporters of coffee are Brazil with 28% of world exports in 2005-06, Vietnam with 15%, and Columbia with 12%.

US coffee imports in 2006 rose +3.9% to 22.649 million bags, which was a 4-decade high. The all-time high of 24.549 million bags was posted in 1962. The key countries from which the US imported coffee in 2006 were Brazil (which accounted for 28% of US imports), Columbia (12%), Mexico (4%), and Guatemala (4%).

World Supply and Distribution of Coffee   In Thousands of 60 Kilogram Bags (132.276 Lbs. Per Bag)

Crop Year	Beginning Stocks	Pro- duction	Imports	Supply	Total Exports	Bean Exports	Rst/Grn Exports	Soluble Exports	Domestic Use	Ending Stocks
1997-98	29,095	97,687	1,220	128,002	77,939	73,249	193	4,497	25,180	24,883
1998-99	24,883	108,953	1,435	135,271	85,133	80,855	269	4,009	25,738	24,400
1999-00	24,400	113,553	1,303	139,256	92,733	87,572	288	4,873	25,648	20,875
2000-01	20,875	117,521	1,478	139,874	90,492	84,408	289	5,795	26,319	23,063
2001-02	23,063	111,507	1,652	136,222	87,811	81,256	339	6,216	27,780	20,631
2002-03	20,631	126,450	1,550	148,631	91,721	85,028	292	6,401	27,398	29,512
2003-04	29,512	109,048	1,765	140,325	91,099	83,658	314	7,127	28,396	20,830
2004-05[1]	20,830	120,178	2,527	143,535	91,456	83,597	278	7,581	30,223	21,856
2005-06[2]	21,856	113,661	2,807	138,324	87,451	79,589	345	7,517	31,115	19,758
2006-07[3]	19,758	128,561	2,713	151,032	95,986	88,243	356	7,387	32,085	22,961

[1] Preliminary.   [2] Estimate.   [3] Forecast.   *Source: Foreign Agricultural Service, U.S. Department of Agriculture (FAS-USDA)*

World Production of Green Coffee   In Thousands of 60 Kilogram Bags (132.276 Lbs. Per Bag)

Crop Year	Brazil	Colombia	Costa Rica	El Salvador	Ethiopia	Guate- mala	India	Indo- nesia	Ivory Coast	Mexico	Uganda	Vietnam	World Total
1997-98	23,500	12,043	2,455	2,040	3,833	4,200	3,805	7,000	4,080	4,950	3,032	7,000	97,687
1998-99	35,600	10,868	2,459	1,860	3,867	4,300	4,415	6,950	2,217	5,010	3,640	7,500	108,953
1999-00	30,800	9,512	2,688	2,612	3,505	4,364	4,870	6,660	5,700	6,193	3,097	11,010	113,553
2000-01	34,100	10,500	2,502	1,624	2,768	4,564	5,020	6,495	5,100	4,800	3,401	15,333	117,521
2001-02	35,100	11,950	2,338	1,610	3,756	3,530	5,010	6,160	3,568	4,200	3,158	12,833	111,507
2002-03	53,600	11,712	2,207	1,351	3,693	3,802	4,588	6,140	2,119	4,350	2,890	11,167	126,450
2003-04	33,200	11,053	2,106	1,343	3,874	3,671	4,500	6,000	1,610	4,428	2,598	15,000	109,048
2004-05[1]	43,600	11,532	1,907	1,329	5,000	3,817	4,590	6,600	1,750	3,900	2,593	14,500	120,178
2005-06[2]	36,100	11,953	1,776	1,359	5,500	3,589	4,400	6,750	2,500	4,000	2,366	13,500	113,661
2006-07[3]	46,500	12,200	1,950	1,400	5,500	3,817	4,665	7,080	2,200	4,200	2,300	16,500	128,561

[1] Preliminary.   [2] Estimate.   [3] Forecast.   *Source: Foreign Agricultural Service, U.S. Department of Agriculture (FAS-USDA)*

World Exportable[4] Production of Green Coffee   In Thousands of 60 Kilogram Bags (132.276 Lbs. Per Bag)

Crop Year	Brazil	Colombia	Costa Rica	El Salvador	Ethiopia	Guate- mala	Indonesia	Ivory Coast	Kenya	Mexico	Uganda	Vietnam	World Total
1997-98	14,850	10,863	2,083	3,940	2,554	3,400	5,040	5,055	4,072	1,630	3,032	6,500	77,939
1998-99	22,908	10,304	1,750	4,141	2,255	3,450	6,038	2,540	4,170	1,820	3,648	6,667	85,133
1999-00	20,164	9,060	2,005	4,234	2,825	4,250	5,657	5,797	5,138	2,380	2,917	11,433	92,733
2000-01	19,676	9,460	1,418	4,414	2,470	3,702	5,536	4,045	3,822	2,664	3,075	14,667	90,492
2001-02	24,795	10,665	1,939	3,330	2,617	3,442	4,729	3,058	3,200	2,360	3,153	12,000	87,811
2002-03	29,396	10,478	2,277	3,500	2,438	3,553	4,801	2,522	3,400	2,575	2,810	11,176	91,721
2003-04	24,920	10,154	2,374	3,314	2,794	3,822	4,408	2,604	3,550	2,685	2,523	14,500	91,099
2004-05[1]	27,920	11,032	2,620	3,451	2,397	3,305	4,600	1,958	2,107	3,306	2,489	13,992	91,456
2005-06[2]	24,538	10,840	2,675	3,350	2,930	3,455	5,070	2,084	2,600	2,225	2,002	12,975	87,451
2006-07[3]	27,000	11,200	3,650	3,400	2,500	3,455	5,115	2,100	3,500	3,290	2,200	15,334	95,986

[1] Preliminary.   [2] Estimate.   [3] Forecast.   [4] Marketing year begins in October in some countries and April or July in others. Exportable production represents total harvested production minus estimated domestic consumption.   *Source: Foreign Agricultural Service, U.S. Department of Agriculture*

Coffee Imports in the United States   In Thousands of 60 Kilogram Bags (132.276 Lbs. Per Bag)

Year	Brazil	Colombia	Costa Rica	Dominican Republic	Ecuador	El Salvador	Ethiopia	Guate- mala	Indonesia	Mexico	Peru	Vene- zuela	Grand Total
1997	2,446	3,260	609	155	442	501	308	1,922	1,328	3,039	652	65	19,673
1998	2,804	3,510	776	165	377	501	184	1,565	1,274	2,589	774	146	20,101
1999	4,847	3,418	783	80	461	550	77	2,149	724	3,276	766	372	21,787
2000	2,747	3,191	780	73	177	1,209	91	2,380	693	3,725	868	32	22,840
2001	3,007	3,272	915	50	230	507	80	2,040	887	2,057	692	4	20,490
2002	5,060	3,596	987	51	145	470	74	1,626	759	2,034	842	170	20,631
2003	5,321	3,883	914	80	133	569	101	2,023	966	1,510	807	180	21,694
2004	4,475	3,714	957	2	157	524	121	1,624	1,636	1,477	788	103	22,046
2005	4,464	4,090	920	2	74	406	177	1,752	1,599	1,285	587	0	21,791
2006[1]	4,792	3,903	751	60	147	435	250	1,654	1,676	1,529	850	2	22,649

[1] Preliminary.   *Source: Bureau of Census, U.S. Department of Commerce*

COFFEE

Monthly Coffee Imports in the United States   In Thousands of 60 Kilogram Bags[2]

Year	Jan.	Feb.	Mar.	Apr.	May	June	July	Aug.	Sept.	Oct.	Nov.	Dec.	Total
1997	1,582	1,837	1,966	1,792	1,738	1,583	1,783	1,391	1,147	1,215	1,184	1,629	18,848
1998	1,747	1,893	1,827	1,587	1,540	1,412	1,386	1,478	1,369	1,499	1,423	1,837	18,998
1999	1,742	1,866	2,243	1,787	1,602	1,691	1,488	1,639	1,491	1,470	1,639	1,903	20,561
2000	2,189	2,092	2,416	2,003	2,199	1,960	1,912	1,815	1,598	1,583	1,546	1,527	22,840
2001	1,747	1,690	1,906	1,825	1,823	1,685	1,863	1,605	1,430	1,502	1,581	1,833	20,490
2002	1,652	1,364	1,613	1,697	1,672	1,547	1,802	1,794	1,850	1,877	1,807	1,958	20,631
2003	1,994	1,755	2,007	1,916	1,715	1,710	2,015	1,732	1,712	1,750	1,525	1,863	21,694
2004	1,813	1,635	1,967	1,862	2,049	2,034	1,784	1,766	1,708	1,684	1,798	1,947	22,047
2005	1,939	1,942	2,072	1,965	1,893	1,891	1,781	1,606	1,481	1,718	1,699	1,803	21,791
2006[1]	1,850	1,649	2,042	1,671	2,006	1,913	1,786	2,083	2,098	1,892	1,833	1,826	22,649

[1] Preliminary.   [2] 132.276 pounds per bag.   *Source: Bureau of the Census, U.S. Department of Commerce*

Average Price of Brazilian[1] Coffee in New York   In Cents Per Pound

Year	Jan.	Feb.	Mar.	Apr.	May	June	July	Aug.	Sept.	Oct.	Nov.	Dec.	Average
1997	127.28	160.21	179.75	183.73	209.62	184.21	158.52	158.25	167.77	152.12	149.07	171.12	166.80
1998	179.83	177.78	154.84	141.11	124.89	104.09	96.04	101.92	92.76	91.32	96.67	100.28	121.81
1999	99.43	91.72	88.90	86.14	96.29	91.69	78.13	76.67	70.43	78.74	98.41	109.47	88.84
2000	97.68	91.51	89.93	86.46	87.23	78.32	79.89	70.57	71.14	72.28	68.95	64.39	79.86
2001	62.38	62.50	60.35	55.11	57.19	51.86	46.43	46.49	42.42	38.63	42.28	41.60	50.60
2002	42.56	42.79	48.79	49.90	45.19	42.96	43.58	40.55	44.46	45.28	48.37	46.70	45.09
2003	49.14	48.54	43.77	48.71	51.06	47.11	49.64	52.88	55.19	53.51	54.15	56.92	50.89
2004	64.32	66.08	65.79	62.89	64.31	67.62	59.39	60.25	69.46	68.63	80.20	89.17	68.18
2005	94.00	108.05	117.03	112.82	111.89	105.08	94.66	95.66	87.02	94.54	99.35	96.23	101.36
2006	115.89	109.51	103.52	105.89	99.00	91.26	91.01	98.90	97.36	97.39	109.34	115.60	102.89

[1] And other Arabicas.   *Source: Coffee Publications, Inc.*

Coffee (monthly average) through December 2006

Cents Per Pound
- - - - - Spot, New York (1826 - 1900)
Santos No. 4 (Jan. 1901 - July 1975)
Brazilian, New York (Aug. 1975 - date)
- - - Colombian Maniz, New York (Jan. 1948 - July 1953)
Colombian Medellin, New York (Aug. 1953 - Dec. 1977)
Colombian, New York (Jan. 1978 - date)

Exchange Closed
Sep. 1941 - Sep. 1946

Average Monthly Retail [1] Price of Coffee in the United States   In Cents Per Pound

Year	Jan.	Feb.	Mar.	Apr.	May	June	July	Aug.	Sept.	Oct.	Nov.	Dec.	Average
1999	343.5	342.8	347.6	346.6	349.5	342.1	342.0	342.8	339.3	348.2	333.7	334.7	342.7
2000	365.4	367.7	363.3	358.4	353.1	343.1	344.6	344.4	333.9	331.7	324.3	321.2	345.9
2001	322.4	321.7	320.5	312.8	309.7	315.6	309.7	304.6	302.5	301.5	298.8	291.3	309.3
2002	293.6	294.6	285.9	297.6	301.1	293.8	297.7	292.9	292.1	287.2	288.2	283.8	292.4
2003	299.9	292.4	293.3	300.8	293.7	293.1	294.4	292.1	291.9	282.5	277.9	287.5	291.6
2004	289.2	285.6	293.2	290.8	283.1	275.0	287.8	287.8	287.4	284.0	277.8	277.6	284.9
2005	304.9	294.0	300.9	324.0	332.9	341.6	333.4	342.8	337.6	344.7	329.3	323.5	325.8
2006	323.2	317.4	330.1	329.2	334.9	315.8	315.4	319.6	317.3	313.8	315.8		321.1

[1] Roasted in 13.1 to 20 ounce cans.   *Source: Coffee Publications, Inc.*

Average Price of Colombian Mild Arabicas[1] in the United States   In Cents Per Pound

Year	Jan.	Feb.	Mar.	Apr.	May	June	July	Aug.	Sept.	Oct.	Nov.	Dec.	Average
1999	123.07	116.92	117.05	114.02	123.95	121.45	107.05	105.28	97.77	103.69	126.76	140.35	116.45
2000	130.13	124.73	119.51	112.67	110.31	100.30	101.67	91.87	89.98	90.25	84.01	75.81	102.60
2001	75.33	76.70	76.94	78.25	80.92	74.38	69.70	73.50	68.80	62.88	65.72	62.57	72.14
2002	63.46	65.64	71.16	70.17	63.44	60.86	59.60	58.98	62.49	66.54	72.83	67.92	65.26
2003	69.68	69.60	61.82	66.12	67.56	65.01	67.84	68.65	68.37	66.59	67.04	69.38	67.31
2004	76.61	79.34	80.12	77.08	80.61	85.62	78.27	78.85	85.71	85.52	95.63	106.48	84.15
2005	110.03	124.34	137.10	129.80	128.36	122.47	112.48	111.21	101.31	108.77	111.66	106.54	117.01
2006	129.64	123.17	117.00	119.87	113.03	106.84	109.45	116.22	112.26	113.73	126.23	132.85	118.36

[1] ICO monthly and composite indicator prices on the New York Market, 1979 ICA Agreement basis.   *Source: Coffee Publications, Inc.*

Average Price of Other Mild Arabicas[1] in the United States   In Cents Per Pound

Year	Jan.	Feb.	Mar.	Apr.	May	June	July	Aug.	Sept.	Oct.	Nov.	Dec.	Average
1999	110.99	103.24	103.23	99.69	109.10	104.21	90.85	87.64	81.06	92.22	112.74	123.56	101.54
2000	109.17	101.17	98.26	92.76	91.76	84.10	85.20	74.52	73.83	75.43	70.47	64.81	85.12
2001	64.98	67.00	65.88	65.68	68.94	63.79	58.47	59.68	57.71	56.23	58.96	55.63	61.91
2002	57.34	60.51	66.38	65.78	58.45	55.12	53.07	52.02	57.58	64.05	70.15	64.75	60.43
2003	65.22	67.60	61.66	65.35	66.47	61.34	62.32	63.60	65.50	62.58	62.36	65.01	64.08
2004	74.25	77.51	77.29	74.24	76.40	82.24	73.64	72.99	81.22	79.90	89.88	102.19	80.15
2005	107.07	122.20	134.81	128.80	126.21	119.87	108.45	108.43	98.17	106.09	108.81	102.68	114.30
2006	124.26	118.46	112.20	114.65	107.96	101.21	102.77	112.13	109.36	110.91	123.57	129.93	113.95

[1] ICO monthly and composite indicator prices on the New York Market, 1979 ICA Agreement basis.   *Source: Coffee Publications, Inc.*

Average Price of Robustas 1976[1] in the United States   In Cents Per Pound

Year	Jan.	Feb.	Mar.	Apr.	May	June	July	Aug.	Sept.	Oct.	Nov.	Dec.	Average
1999	81.65	77.68	72.70	68.89	68.28	66.20	62.28	63.80	60.44	59.25	64.10	66.40	67.64
2000	53.62	49.41	47.26	45.21	45.19	43.72	41.93	38.94	39.47	36.55	33.34	30.78	42.12
2001	31.00	31.96	30.96	28.59	29.71	29.33	27.59	25.86	23.79	21.26	22.03	23.57	27.14
2002	22.88	24.46	29.77	30.35	29.43	29.26	29.31	28.74	33.31	34.44	39.38	38.68	30.83
2003	42.75	42.35	38.26	38.68	38.90	35.33	36.71	37.92	38.76	37.32	36.05	37.59	38.39
2004	41.32	39.10	38.61	38.02	38.04	41.09	36.44	34.81	35.10	31.77	34.07	38.98	37.28
2005	39.63	44.61	50.70	53.32	58.66	62.96	60.57	55.60	50.07	50.84	54.72	58.79	53.37
2006	66.46	65.50	62.92	64.45	63.97	64.14	68.66	75.73	77.88	76.26	79.67	77.71	70.28

[1] ICO monthly and composite indicator prices on the New York Market, 1979 ICA Agreement basis.   *Source: Coffee Publications, Inc.*

Average Price of Composite 1979[1] in the United States   In Cents Per Pound

Year	Jan.	Feb.	Mar.	Apr.	May	June	July	Aug.	Sept.	Oct.	Nov.	Dec.	Average
1999	97.63	92.36	89.41	85.72	89.51	85.41	78.21	77.22	71.94	76.36	88.22	95.63	85.64
2000	82.15	76.15	73.49	69.53	69.23	64.56	64.09	57.59	57.31	56.40	52.18	48.27	64.25
2001	49.19	49.39	48.52	47.31	49.38	46.54	43.07	42.77	41.17	42.21	44.24	43.36	45.60
2002	43.46	44.30	49.49	50.19	47.30	45.56	44.70	42.79	47.96	50.79	54.69	51.68	47.74
2003	54.04	54.07	49.61	51.87	53.19	48.90	50.89	52.22	54.10	51.72	49.81	52.44	51.91
2004	58.69	59.87	60.80	58.80	59.91	64.28	58.46	56.98	61.47	61.10	67.74	77.72	62.15
2005	79.35	89.40	101.44	98.20	99.78	96.29	88.48	85.31	78.79	82.55	85.93	86.85	89.36
2006	101.20	97.39	92.76	94.20	90.00	86.04	101.20	95.78	95.98	95.53	103.48	108.01	96.80

[1] ICO monthly and composite indicator prices on the New York Market, 1979 ICA Agreement basis.   *Source: Coffee Publications, Inc.*

COFFEE

Average Open Interest of Coffee 'C' Futures in New York   In Contracts

Year	Jan.	Feb.	Mar.	Apr.	May	June	July	Aug.	Sept.	Oct.	Nov.	Dec.
1997	38,516	42,888	39,092	32,644	30,324	22,552	21,497	19,818	22,788	25,109	23,636	28,577
1998	30,042	30,539	30,211	32,617	36,345	36,651	37,531	30,074	30,429	32,940	31,677	32,816
1999	36,194	36,693	41,294	43,846	45,947	45,675	45,411	46,725	46,255	47,956	46,271	46,764
2000	47,829	50,620	50,565	53,662	49,692	50,293	45,513	40,177	40,133	42,906	43,187	45,086
2001	48,914	53,050	58,111	57,722	53,481	58,311	57,888	57,243	55,674	58,345	55,317	53,953
2002	57,897	66,825	66,798	66,207	66,289	68,994	69,197	69,635	70,079	73,753	73,431	69,343
2003	69,508	71,682	76,934	77,954	72,716	72,155	72,110	68,259	73,809	79,038	81,253	76,670
2004	92,388	103,966	102,281	98,430	96,738	102,276	89,446	88,021	83,001	78,047	83,360	107,832
2005	102,163	107,715	117,419	105,245	96,063	94,139	93,303	89,662	85,518	86,489	81,525	81,234
2006	102,195	102,614	99,982	102,882	104,230	120,907	120,007	107,928	105,175	111,392	117,469	123,259

Source: New York Board of Trade (NYBOT)

Volume of Trading of Coffee 'C' Futures in New York   In Contracts

Year	Jan.	Feb.	Mar.	Apr.	May	June	July	Aug.	Sept.	Oct.	Nov.	Dec.	Total
1997	242,719	280,014	267,369	223,330	219,214	186,227	135,664	136,807	142,610	151,171	145,610	163,446	2,294,181
1998	155,774	194,435	186,712	194,732	157,935	189,768	165,868	189,047	156,556	172,956	197,776	133,471	2,095,030
1999	216,810	201,670	252,841	243,630	237,968	243,164	187,019	232,817	151,724	270,013	244,258	177,309	2,659,223
2000	158,962	232,174	166,970	224,266	177,753	218,467	198,975	175,868	119,304	163,399	187,230	111,593	2,134,961
2001	189,977	221,775	167,466	236,757	182,621	220,708	134,809	250,151	100,443	153,739	229,495	111,430	2,199,371
2002	201,327	279,966	229,764	295,701	159,670	225,177	174,567	254,563	232,255	250,483	236,307	178,728	2,718,508
2003	205,420	283,317	169,611	334,188	255,935	270,424	237,210	278,746	332,473	309,930	314,182	219,595	3,211,031
2004	389,864	397,656	301,270	395,552	324,849	467,887	247,439	366,171	305,196	280,733	424,146	292,540	4,193,303
2005	280,912	469,605	356,855	459,018	240,989	428,227	224,531	404,307	259,177	266,697	376,844	220,616	3,987,778
2006	357,994	416,964	326,256	429,249	322,932	476,542	289,027	481,870	238,953	313,459	492,904	261,362	4,407,512

Source: New York Board of Trade (NYBOT)

Coffee 'C' Futures - New York Board of Trade   Cents per pound
(weekly close) as of December 29, 2006

Coke

Coke is the hard and porous residue left after certain types of bituminous coals are heated to high temperatures (up to 2,000 degrees Fahrenheit) for about 17 hours. It is blackish-gray and has a metallic luster. The residue is mostly carbon. Coke is used as a reducing agent in the smelting of pig iron and the production of steel. Petroleum coke is made from the heavy tar-like residue of the petroleum refining process. It is used primarily to generate electricity.

Supply – Petroleum coke production in the US in 2006 (annualized through Oct) rose +2.1% yr/yr to 310.124 million barrels. That was a new 3-decade high but still far below the US production record of 369.305 million barrels posted back in 1957. US stocks at coke plants (Dec 31) in 2005 rose steeply by +123% yr/yr to 784,000 tons.

Trade – US coke exports in 2005 rose by +32.5% to 1.747 million tons, and almost one-half of those exports were to Canada. US coke imports in 2005 fell sharply by –48.7% yr/yr to 3.529 million tons. About 20% of the imports were from Japan.

Salient Statistics of Coke in the United States — In Thousands of Short Tons

| | Coke and Breeze Production at Coke Plants | | | | | | | | Producer and Distributor | Exports | | Imports | |
| | By Census Division | | | | | Coke | Breeze | Consump- | Stocks | | | | |
Year	Middle Atlantic	East North Central	East South Central	Other	Total	Total	Total	tion[2]	Dec. 31	Canada	Total	Japan	Total
2000	6,095	10,835	2,558	2,608	22,096	20,808	1,289	23,242	1,054	795	1,146	1,884	3,781
2001	W	10,272	1,979	7,893	20,144	18,949	1,195	20,202	981	793	1,069	1,508	2,340
2002	W	8,287	1,925	7,712	17,924	16,778	1,146	19,603	606	610	792	1,554	3,242
2003	W	8,642	2,068	7,738	18,448	17,173	1,275	19,436	380	436	722	1,395	2,759
2004	W	8,614	2,104	7,356	18,074	16,909	1,165	22,492	351	596	1,319	943	6,873
2005[1]	W	8,448	W	9,456	17,904	16,719	1,184	18,239	614	764	1,747	699	3,529

[1] Preliminary. [2] Equal to production plus imports minus the change in producer and distributor stocks minus exports.
Source: Energy Information Administration, U.S. Department of Energy (EIA-DOE)

Production of Petroleum Coke in the United States — In Thousands of Barrels

Year	Jan.	Feb.	Mar.	Apr.	May	June	July	Aug.	Sept.	Oct.	Nov.	Dec.	Total
2000	21,502	20,017	21,654	21,161	21,785	22,095	23,321	22,835	22,455	22,121	22,628	24,262	265,836
2001	23,970	21,112	23,299	23,713	42,465	23,345	23,838	23,339	22,321	23,306	23,350	24,203	298,261
2002	24,543	22,849	23,529	23,850	24,713	23,305	24,556	23,939	23,465	22,527	23,497	24,913	285,686
2003	23,420	20,030	23,810	23,768	24,831	24,054	26,080	25,746	24,072	24,588	24,208	26,560	291,167
2004	25,640	22,380	24,025	25,086	26,789	25,874	26,263	26,151	24,259	25,899	25,897	27,599	305,862
2005	25,093	23,806	26,896	25,648	27,209	26,950	26,612	26,410	22,209	22,039	24,372	26,575	303,819
2006[1]	26,180	23,706	25,722	24,987	26,690	26,128	26,372	26,395	26,300	25,957	25,048		309,256

[1] Preliminary. *Source: Energy Information Administration, U.S. Department of Energy (EIA-DOE)*

Coal Receipts and Average Prices at Coke Plants in the United States

| | Coal Receipts at Coke Plants | | | | | Average Price of Coal Receipts at Coke Plants | | | | |
| | By Census Division, In Thousands of Short Tons | | | | | By Census Division, In Dollars per Short Ton | | | | |
Year	Middle Atlantic	East North Central	East South Central	Other	Total	Middle Atlantic	East North Central	East South Central	Other	Total
2000	7,971	14,020	3,209	3,520	28,720	42.89	45.62	44.74	W	44.38
2001	W	13,084	2,678	10,622	26,384	W	47.53	47.69	W	46.42
2002	W	11,184	2,335	10,136	23,655	W	52.80	50.03	W	50.67
2003	W	11,252	2,452	10,019	23,723	W	52.94	48.20	W	50.63
2004	W	11,591	2,710	9,795	24,096	W	63.30	59.16	W	61.50
2005[1]	W	11,523	W	12,778	24,301	W	89.97	W	W	83.79

[1] Preliminary. W = Withheld proprietary data. *Source: Energy Information Administration, U.S. Department of Energy (EIA-DOE)*

Coal Carbonized and Coke and Breeze Stocks at Coke Plants in the U.S. — In Thousands of Short Tons

| | Coal Carbonized at Coke Plants | | | | | Stocks at Coke Plants, Dec. 31 | | | | | | |
| | By Census Division | | | | | By Census Division | | | | | Coke | Breeze |
Year	Middle Atlantic	East North Central	East South Central	Other	Total	Middle Atlantic	East North Central	East South Central	Other	Total	Total	Total
2000	8,129	13,971	3,290	3,549	28,939	148	628	166	255	1,197	1,054	143
2001	W	12,981	2,608	10,486	26,075	W	637	266	607	1,510	981	88
2002	W	11,154	2,319	10,183	23,656	W	424	155	169	748	606	141
2003	W	11,410	2,541	10,297	24,248	W	233	135	144	512	380	132
2004	W	11,322	2,644	9,704	23,670	W	166	154	144	464	351	113
2005[1]	W	11,064	W	12,370	23,434	W	449	W	484	933	784	148

[1] Preliminary. W = Withheld proprietary data. *Source: Energy Information Administration, U.S. Department of Energy (EIA-DOE)*

Copper

The word *copper* comes from name of the Mediterranean island Cyprus that was a primary source of the metal. Dating back more than 10,000 years, copper is the oldest metal used by humans. From the Pyramid of Cheops in Egypt, archeologists recovered a portion of a water plumbing system whose copper tubing was found in serviceable condition after more than 5,000 years.

Copper is one of the most widely used industrial metals because it is an excellent conductor of electricity, has strong corrosion-resistance properties, and is very ductile. It is also used to produce the alloys of brass (a copper-zinc alloy) and bronze (a copper-tin alloy), both of which are far harder and stronger than pure copper. Electrical uses of copper account for about 75% of total copper usage, and building construction is the single largest market (the average US home contains 400 pounds of copper). Copper is biostatic, meaning that bacteria will not grow on its surface, and it is therefore used in air-conditioning systems, food processing surfaces, and doorknobs to prevent the spread of disease.

Copper futures and options are traded on the London Metal Exchange (LME) and the COMEX Division of the New York Mercantile Exchange (Nymex). Copper futures are traded on the Shanghai Futures Exchange. The Nymex copper futures contract calls for the delivery of 25,000 pounds of Grade 1 electrolyte copper and is priced in terms of cents per pound.

Prices – Nymex copper futures prices in 2006 peaked at a record $416 per pound in May 2006 but then fell sharply in the latter half of the year by 43%. Copper in 2006 still closed +13% yr/yr at $2.85 per pound, more than triple the price of 75 cents seen as recently as 2003. Physical and speculative demand for copper was very strong early in 2006, but copper prices then fell back in the latter half of 2006 on long liquidation pressure and on the fact that mining supply caught up with demand. There was a net copper surplus of 84,000 tons in Jan-Aug 2006, according to the International Copper Study Group.

Supply – World production of copper in 2005 (the latest data available) rose by +2.1% yr/yr to 14.900 million metric tons, which was a new record high. US production of refined copper in 2006 (annualized through November) fell –0.8% yr/yr to 1.245 million short tons, which was far below the record US production level of 2.490 million short tons seen in 1998.

Demand – US consumption of copper in 2004 (latest available data) rose +5.2% yr/yr to 2.410 million metric tons. The primary users of copper in the US in 2004 by class of consumer are wire rod mills with 74% of usage, brass mills with 24% of usage, and nominal use of 1% or less by foundries, ingot makers, and chemical plants.

Trade - US exports of copper in 2006 (annualized through October) rose sharply by +156.0% to 104,724 metric tons but remained below the 9-year high of 118,350 metric tons seen in 2004. US imports of copper in 2006 (annualized through October) rose by +17.6% yr/yr to 1.181 million metric tons, recovering from the 8-year low of 807,000 metric tons seen in 2004.

World Mine Production of Copper (Content of Ore)   In Thousands of Metric Tons

Year	Australia	Canada[3]	Chile	China	Indonesia	Mexico	Peru	Poland	Russia[4]	South Africa	United States[3]	Zambia	World Total
1996	547.3	688.4	3,115.8	439	507.5	340.7	484.2	421.9	523	152.6	1,920	334.0	11,000
1997	558.0	659.5	3,392.0	511	529.1	390.5	506.5	414.8	505	153.1	1,940	352.9	11,500
1998	607.0	705.8	3,686.8	504	780.8	384.6	483.3	436.2	500	166.0	1,860	315.0	12,100
1999	739.0	620.1	4,391.2	533	766.0	381.2	536.4	463.2	530	144.3	1,600	280.0	12,800
2000	829.0	633.9	4,602.4	613	1,012.1	364.6	553.9	454.1	570	137.1	1,440	249.1	13,200
2001	871.0	633.5	4,739.0	605	1,081.0	371.1	722.3	474.0	600	141.9	1,340	312.0	13,700
2002	883.0	603.5	4,581.0	593	1,171.7	329.9	843.2	502.8	695	129.6	1,140	330.0	13,700
2003	830.0	557.1	4,904.2	620	1,005.8	355.7	831.2	495.0	675	120.8	1,120	349.0	13,700
2004[1]	854.1	566.5	5,412.5	752	840.3	405.5	1,035.6	531.0	675	120.6	1,160	426.9	14,700
2005[2]	927.0	566.5	5,320.5	755	1,065.0	425.0	1,009.9	523.0	700	103.9	1,140	436.0	15,100

[1] Preliminary.   [2] Estimate.   [3] Recoverable.   [4] Formerly part of the U.S.S.R.; data not reported separately until 1992.
Source: U.S. Geological Survey (USGS)

Commodity Exchange Inc. Warehouse Stocks of Copper, on First of Month   In Thousands of Short Tons

Year	Jan.	Feb.	Mar.	Apr.	May	June	July	Aug.	Sept.	Oct.	Nov.	Dec.
1997	29.5	19.0	24.8	43.6	49.5	43.0	46.3	30.0	46.5	61.5	67.8	79.8
1998	91.5	100.7	112.3	112.6	107.6	84.8	63.5	55.7	56.6	67.7	69.4	74.7
1999	93.9	101.8	112.3	123.1	132.6	131.7	133.7	120.2	108.8	97.5	90.9	90.9
2000	91.6	95.6	95.6	95.9	865.2	75.0	73.6	73.2	62.8	62.3	63.4	64.9
2001	64.7	79.3	90.0	105.1	126.5	150.9	165.1	176.1	186.8	199.6	211.0	236.5
2002	269.2	284.8	304.0	314.1	326.0	337.4	355.7	374.6	375.9	380.3	381.6	382.8
2003	399.3	395.2	373.7	362.7	351.2	336.7	320.5	310.6	303.9	299.0	294.4	288.1
2004	280.9	262.7	241.9	213.3	171.7	130.7	95.1	79.0	62.3	49.2	45.5	42.4
2005	48.2	45.8	46.8	43.3	30.1	22.0	15.3	11.0	9.3	7.2	3.7	3.7
2006	6.8	11.7	30.4	20.7	16.7	9.5	7.9	6.8	12.4	22.3	23.2	31.3

Source: New York Mercantile Exchange (NYMEX), COMEX division

Salient Statistics of Copper in the United States   In Thousands of Metric Tons

| | New Copper Produced | | | | | Imports[5] | | | Exports | | | Stocks, Dec 31 | | | Apparent Consumption | |
| | From Domestic Ores | | | From | | Secon- | | | Ore, | | | | Primary | Blister & | | Refined | Primary |
Year	Mines	Smelters	Refin-eries	Foreign Ores[3]	Total New	dary Re-covered[4]	Unmanu-factured	Refined	Concen-trate[6]	Refined[7]	COMEX	Producers (Refined)	Material in Solution	Copper (Reported)	& Old Copper[8]
1996	1,920	1,300	1,290	147	2,010	428	961	543	195	169	27	146	173	2,610	2,830
1997	1,940	1,440	1,370	113	2,070	498	999	632	127	93	83	314	180	2,790	2,940
1998	1,860	1,490	1,290	238	2,140	466	1,190	683	37	86	85	532	160	2,890	3,030
1999	1,600	1,090	1,110	196	1,890	381	1,280	837	63	25	83	565	138	2,980	3,130
2000	1,450	W	865	163	1,580	358	1,350	1,060	107	94	59	345	122	3,020	3,090
2001	1,340	W	808	192	1,630	316	1,400	991	45	23	244	952	98	2,620	2,500
2002	1,140	W	725	116	1,440	190	1,230	927	23	27	362	1,030	44	2,370	2,610
2003	1,120	539	532	130	1,250	207	1,140	882	10	93	255	657	57	2,290	2,430
2004[1]	1,160	542	531	140	1,260	191	1,060	807	24	118	44	134	51	2,410	2,550
2005[2]	1,140	523	524	130	1,180	182	1,230	1,000	110	40	6	66	44	2,270	2,400

[1] Preliminary.   [2] Estimate.   [3] Also from matte, etc., refinery reports.   [4] From old scrap only.   [5] For consumption.   [6] Blister (copper content).   [7] Ingots, bars, etc.   [8] Old scrap only.   *Source: U.S. Geological Survey (USGS)*

Consumption of Refined Copper[3] in the United States   In Thousands of Metric Tons

| | | By-Products | | | | | By Class of Consumer | | | | | | Total |
Year	Cathodes	Wire Bars	Ingots & Ingot Bars	Cakes & Slabs	Billets	Other[4]	Wire Rod Mills	Brass Mills	Chemical Plants	Ingot Makers	Foundries	Miscel-laneous[5]	Con-sumption
1996	2,320.0	W	26.8	80.8	W	181.0	1,980.0	588.0	1.1	3.6	15.8	28.6	2,610.0
1997	2,490.0	W	29.4	81.1	W	194.0	2,140.0	597.0	1.0	4.2	16.6	29.9	2,790.0
1998	2,600.0	W	30.7	76.2	W	184.0	2,170.0	659.0	1.1	5.4	19.2	31.8	2,890.0
1999	2,710.0	W	24.4	79.3	W	166.0	2,230.0	691.0	1.2	4.5	21.2	29.8	2,980.0
2000	2,730.0	W	23.8	101.0	W	175.0	2,240.0	723.0	1.2	4.6	24.3	32.5	3,030.0
2001	2,360.0	W	24.0	95.9	W	140.0	1,940.0	623.0	1.2	4.6	21.6	28.6	2,620.0
2002	2,140.0	W	22.8	72.6	W	126.0	1,710.0	593.0	1.0	4.6	19.8	35.7	2,370.0
2003	2,070.0	W	22.3	41.8	W	153.0	1,640.0	587.0	1.0	4.6	21.9	36.7	2,290.0
2004[1]	2,160.0	W	21.4	57.0	W	173.0	1,780.0	573.0	1.2	4.6	21.0	35.2	2,410.0
2005[2]	2,040.0	W	28.8	35.3	W	167.0	1,680.0	528.0	1.2	4.5	20.2	39.3	2,270.0

[1] Preliminary.   [2] Estimate.   [3] Primary & secondary.   [4] 1991 to date include Wirebars and Billets.   [5] Includes iron and steel plants, primary smelters producing alloys other than copper, consumers of copper powder and copper shot, and other manufacturers.   W - Withheld proprietary data.
Source: U.S. Geological Survey (USGS)

London Metals Exchange Warehouse Stocks of Copper, at End of Month   In Thousands of Metric Tons

Year	Jan.	Feb.	Mar.	Apr.	May	June	July	Aug.	Sept.	Oct.	Nov.	Dec.
1997	194.2	216.2	177.2	145.8	133.0	128.3	234.9	278.7	332.8	344.6	338.8	337.8
1998	365.7	376.0	339.5	262.3	261.8	249.3	260.9	307.7	414.2	460.6	511.9	590.1
1999	646.9	695.9	722.2	748.2	776.6	754.8	769.6	789.0	774.0	793.8	779.7	790.5
2000	807.3	824.1	755.4	697.8	605.7	553.4	487.8	449.2	401.5	380.9	349.4	357.4
2001	349.9	327.9	400.5	445.2	431.3	464.7	651.9	661.2	729.0	737.2	780.4	799.5
2002	855.5	910.9	950.9	973.8	958.3	892.1	893.6	896.6	870.6	863.2	862.8	855.9
2003	833.8	825.9	813.2	768.2	740.8	665.8	612.6	620.3	580.4	516.5	467.0	430.7
2004	358.2	281.6	187.5	151.3	132.3	101.5	87.7	111.3	91.8	77.9	59.8	48.9
2005	46.4	52.5	45.3	61.0	44.4	28.9	31.6	68.0	79.9	65.1	72.6	92.3
2006[1]	96.0	115.3	120.7	117.6	111.2	93.6	100.6	125.4	116.9	135.2	156.8	92.3

[1] Preliminary.   *Source: American Bureau of Metal Statistics (ABMS)*

Copper Refined from Scrap in the United States   In Thousands of Metric Tons

Year	Jan.	Feb.	Mar.	Apr.	May	June	July	Aug.	Sept.	Oct.	Nov.	Dec.	Total
1997	35.9	30.0	36.4	32.6	35.4	30.8	26.4	28.4	34.3	36.5	24.6	29.3	383.0
1998	25.9	28.6	23.7	31.0	17.8	21.4	24.2	23.9	23.8	31.8	23.2	26.3	336.0
1999	20.1	21.8	23.7	17.6	16.2	17.5	21.2	18.2	21.3	21.0	17.7	20.0	230.0
2000	19.4	18.6	25.8	22.5	22.1	15.4	11.7	19.7	14.1	14.3	19.7	15.6	208.0
2001	15.4	14.2	15.2	13.4	12.8	13.2	13.9	13.5	12.3	10.2	6.4	5.7	154.0
2002	7.1	6.2	7.2	7.6	8.2	7.8	7.0	7.6	7.1	6.3	5.1	3.9	81.1
2003	5.8	3.9	5.7	3.9	4.1	4.9	4.9	3.9	4.2	4.5	4.1	4.1	53.8
2004	4.2	3.9	4.3	4.4	4.2	4.5	4.1	3.9	4.7	4.5	4.2	4.0	50.8
2005	4.4	4.4	4.2	4.2	3.8	3.6	3.9	3.6	3.6	3.8	3.8	3.9	47.1
2006[1]	3.8	3.7	3.8	3.7	3.7	3.7	3.7	3.7	3.8	3.7	3.7		44.7

[1] Preliminary.   *Source: U.S. Geological Survey (USGS)*

COPPER

Copper Futures - New York Mercantile Exchange
(weekly close) as of December 29, 2006

Cents per pound

Average Open Interest of Copper Futures in New York   In Contracts

Year	Jan.	Feb.	Mar.	Apr.	May	June	July	Aug.	Sept.	Oct.	Nov.	Dec.
1997	54,468	56,022	58,205	50,574	56,740	56,774	47,767	44,632	49,612	54,912	67,026	67,502
1998	69,607	72,302	67,154	68,670	65,033	66,002	63,271	61,116	60,520	62,944	67,984	76,846
1999	76,861	73,109	75,318	70,534	76,341	70,842	75,640	70,084	80,188	72,240	69,179	69,819
2000	82,289	73,778	68,026	75,520	69,531	63,786	71,389	79,565	83,546	73,609	74,161	70,349
2001	77,952	76,721	78,034	83,647	72,970	85,495	83,690	88,782	87,004	88,166	85,809	68,981
2002	72,823	79,806	79,156	75,229	74,350	80,981	82,661	102,056	99,225	99,470	89,213	79,218
2003	81,820	81,499	72,484	85,485	77,704	81,509	82,868	94,517	92,768	106,924	103,218	90,208
2004	91,726	88,136	77,158	71,705	65,531	64,879	65,310	71,096	81,162	85,421	81,928	88,822
2005	85,363	96,537	116,004	120,138	98,240	106,218	109,156	109,481	102,652	106,829	110,972	104,062
2006	102,227	93,813	93,069	97,283	83,758	75,841	74,471	72,158	69,004	72,023	72,517	68,402

Source: New York Mercantile Exchange (NYMEX), COMEX division

Volume of Trading of Copper Futures in New York   In Contracts

Year	Jan.	Feb.	Mar.	Apr.	May	June	July	Aug.	Sept.	Oct.	Nov.	Dec.	Total
1997	193,543	221,504	190,000	218,607	164,728	238,918	191,609	198,156	197,746	202,615	203,376	135,368	2,356,170
1998	172,133	223,117	197,652	264,061	175,956	217,316	202,596	213,541	196,355	195,255	250,986	174,642	2,483,610
1999	159,147	288,394	230,716	296,162	224,221	319,157	244,567	267,325	220,958	193,628	231,399	177,288	2,852,962
2000	220,488	276,374	195,668	261,971	232,971	241,854	187,453	283,328	171,080	243,342	266,051	197,544	2,778,124
2001	240,588	246,052	247,722	279,348	260,697	317,001	159,394	298,639	129,622	190,469	337,589	149,520	2,856,641
2002	217,598	233,704	164,747	254,259	218,091	267,201	263,395	303,642	195,637	232,731	276,492	179,789	2,807,286
2003	232,921	269,806	249,306	274,079	221,364	301,709	252,713	324,175	196,481	230,413	363,865	172,438	3,089,270
2004	213,536	385,848	265,312	340,236	203,906	280,882	208,415	310,299	212,082	245,011	317,220	207,878	3,190,625
2005	199,938	391,949	298,181	469,849	288,399	475,756	227,917	435,848	252,733	265,234	458,258	186,780	3,950,842
2006	234,295	401,404	284,478	406,984	260,422	321,626	182,175	310,023	189,405	216,369	320,780	153,351	3,281,312

Source: New York Mercantile Exchange (NYMEX), COMEX division

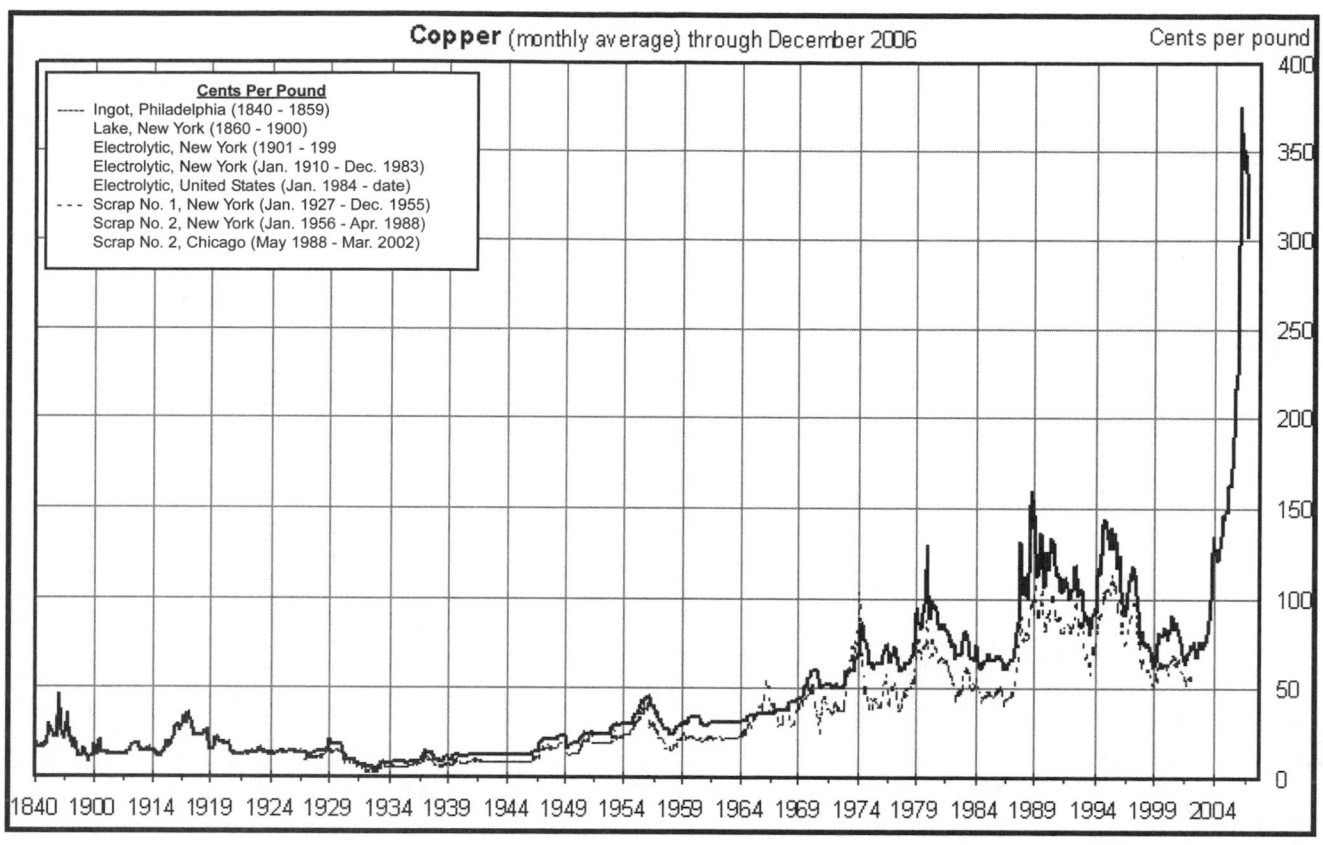

Copper (monthly average) through December 2006 — Cents per pound

Cents Per Pound
- ----- Ingot, Philadelphia (1840 - 1859)
- Lake, New York (1860 - 1900)
- Electrolytic, New York (1901 - 199
- Electrolytic, New York (Jan. 1910 - Dec. 1983)
- Electrolytic, United States (Jan. 1984 - date)
- - - - Scrap No. 1, New York (Jan. 1927 - Dec. 1955)
- Scrap No. 2, New York (Jan. 1956 - Apr. 1988)
- Scrap No. 2, Chicago (May 1988 - Mar. 2002)

Producers' Price of Electrolytic (Wirebar) Copper, Delivered to U.S. Destinations   In Cents Per Pound

Year	Jan.	Feb.	Mar.	Apr.	May	June	July	Aug.	Sept.	Oct.	Nov.	Dec.	Average
1997	120.29	121.02	126.50	121.70	127.25	129.57	121.94	114.11	107.14	105.08	99.53	91.39	115.55
1998	88.88	87.52	91.69	93.54	90.02	86.90	87.37	85.30	87.62	84.26	83.51	78.30	87.09
1999	77.07	75.96	74.50	78.79	81.07	77.23	88.02	87.88	92.89	91.26	91.10	93.35	84.09
2000	96.83	94.41	91.63	89.32	94.80	92.74	95.81	98.67	103.49	99.63	95.25	98.92	95.96
2001	95.70	94.01	92.07	88.27	88.85	84.58	81.44	79.34	77.41	75.21	78.13	79.83	84.57
2002	81.79	84.23	86.60	85.11	85.22	88.23	84.44	79.82	79.71	80.16	84.57	75.56	82.62
2003	78.62	80.21	78.87	75.60	78.56	80.44	81.55	83.51	85.34	91.50	96.47	103.72	84.53
2004	113.93	129.91	139.96	135.82	129.44	129.11	134.34	135.50	138.74	142.01	147.99	151.88	135.72
2005	151.25	152.89	154.68	155.42	154.19	168.31	169.62	178.39	182.00	197.61	208.60	224.25	174.77
2006	225.07	230.74	238.31	302.74	382.65	346.65	368.49	359.91	353.01	345.83	322.45	307.00	315.24

Source: American Metal Market (AMM)

Dealers' Buying Price of No. 2 Heavy Copper Scrap in Chicago   In Cents Per Pound

Year	Jan.	Feb.	Mar.	Apr.	May	June	July	Aug.	Sept.	Oct.	Nov.	Dec.	Average
1997	68.73	71.63	77.50	79.18	77.33	78.19	72.64	70.24	65.67	63.74	61.31	58.43	70.38
1998	53.26	52.58	53.09	54.00	52.60	49.64	48.00	47.71	46.00	44.00	40.00	40.00	48.41
1999	36.32	36.00	36.00	36.00	39.60	41.77	41.00	45.09	46.19	48.00	48.00	48.67	41.90
2000	50.00	50.00	50.00	49.15	49.00	49.00	49.30	52.65	54.60	55.00	52.65	51.00	51.04
2001	51.62	49.16	49.00	49.81	50.00	50.00	49.14	44.00	44.00	43.48	41.45	41.47	46.93
2002	41.00	41.00	41.00	41.00	41.00	41.00	41.00	41.00	41.00	41.00	41.00	41.00	41.00
2003	41.00	41.00	41.00	41.00	41.00	41.00	41.00	41.00	41.00	48.17	56.00	56.00	43.99
2004	56.65	69.00	69.00	69.32	76.00	76.00	76.64	90.00	90.00	90.00	90.00	90.00	78.55
2005	90.00	90.00	90.00	90.00	90.00	94.09	100.00	100.00	100.00	100.00	100.00	129.52	97.80
2006	137.50	137.50	139.46	145.00	145.00	171.36	175.25	185.89	184.10	192.09	192.85	183.30	165.78

Source: American Metal Market (AMM)

COPPER

Imports of Refined Copper into the United States In Thousands of Metric Tons

Year	Jan.	Feb.	Mar.	Apr.	May	June	July	Aug.	Sept.	Oct.	Nov.	Dec.	Total
1997	55.4	48.0	43.6	43.6	61.0	42.0	53.1	73.3	53.8	55.0	53.4	42.0	632.0
1998	62.8	49.6	59.9	64.7	57.6	52.8	45.0	51.7	71.1	52.7	62.0	63.4	683.0
1999	64.7	53.2	68.1	59.9	62.3	63.8	73.0	84.5	90.3	81.0	59.0	77.5	837.0
2000	84.9	67.8	85.5	92.1	83.6	84.5	89.4	83.0	98.6	112.0	100.0	73.7	1,060.0
2001	105.0	91.6	90.1	94.4	70.3	72.7	61.7	66.3	83.5	71.0	110.0	74.4	991.0
2002	82.5	87.8	53.0	92.6	59.9	76.2	80.3	90.5	69.9	79.0	82.0	73.0	927.0
2003	60.7	87.8	69.9	78.5	72.7	62.3	74.0	78.1	81.7	82.0	73.2	61.1	882.0
2004	55.4	48.8	70.7	59.3	70.8	51.3	83.9	78.7	91.7	68.4	77.0	51.1	807.1
2005	85.2	66.5	75.8	63.7	107.0	64.7	75.8	79.4	79.4	99.4	101.0	106.0	1,003.9
2006[1]	138.0	108.0	80.1	69.1	100.0	94.1	91.4	101.0	106.0	96.4			1,180.9

[1] Preliminary. *Source: U.S. Geological Survey (USGS)*

Exports of Refined Copper from the United States In Thousands of Metric Tons

Year	Jan.	Feb.	Mar.	Apr.	May	June	July	Aug.	Sept.	Oct.	Nov.	Dec.	Total
1997	11.1	9.8	6.5	6.5	71.9	8.2	6.9	7.5	6.3	7.4	8.2	8.5	93.3
1998	6.2	12.1	12.2	7.5	7.8	6.4	7.5	6.4	5.8	5.0	3.6	6.2	86.2
1999	2.4	1.1	1.8	1.3	1.6	4.2	1.6	1.5	1.2	1.4	3.7	3.3	25.2
2000	1.6	5.3	22.0	12.2	18.1	12.8	6.7	4.4	2.9	4.3	1.2	2.1	93.6
2001	1.2	.9	.8	1.9	1.0	.8	1.7	2.6	1.2	4.6	5.3	.6	22.5
2002	.4	.7	3.2	.7	.8	6.8	7.7	2.6	1.3	.6	.5	1.5	26.6
2003	2.5	.8	1.5	.6	15.9	23.0	5.1	4.1	4.3	4.6	8.5	22.3	93.2
2004	11.0	18.5	23.9	28.4	3.7	2.7	5.5	9.4	.6	3.9	2.5	8.4	118.4
2005	4.5	3.2	2.8	1.9	7.2	4.3	3.0	2.7	1.8	3.3	3.3	3.0	40.9
2006[1]	5.6	7.3	6.8	9.6	6.3	13.1	6.0	9.6	9.3	13.7			104.7

[1] Preliminary. *Source: U.S. Geological Survey (USGS)*

Stocks of Refined Copper in the United States, on First of Month In Thousands of Short Tons

Year	Jan.	Feb.	Mar.	Apr.	May	June	July	Aug.	Sept.	Oct.	Nov.	Dec.
1997	88.2	98.8	104.4	116.0	117.9	121.7	122.9	148.8	177.1	197.9	227.6	253.3
1998	281.5	282.2	312.7	315.7	304.5	308.6	306.2	319.0	334.1	367.4	407.2	444.6
1999	562.6	593.1	614.6	653.5	676.6	687.8	668.4	657.2	639.7	611.2	626.5	608.2
2000	619.2	620.8	619.5	582.9	537.0	508.8	467.8	418.0	397.7	394.3	379.1	344.2
2001	383.8	408.4	416.2	481.9	552.6	585.7	626.7	733.1	767.4	895.6	916.6	985.7
2002	1,045.1	1,096.2	1,132.4	1,155.3	1,175.0	1,158.8	1,126.7	1,132.2	1,123.0	1,123.7	1,110.5	1,109.0
2003	1,119.8	109.7	1,038.8	1,042.1	998.3	959.8	891.8	848.9	855.6	825.5	761.2	768.0
2004	733.8	646.3	566.7	463.9	367.0	311.8	247.8	218.3	194.5	169.2	158.9	147.4
2005	145.8	151.0	143.4	134.4	129.3	116.2	105.3	98.5	83.0	68.2	56.8	59.4
2006[1]	66.8	76.9	103.3	109.0	88.2	84.5	68.3	76.4	80.1	88.4	103.5	59.4

Recoverable copper content. [1] Preliminary. *Source: American Bureau of Metal Statistics (ABMS)*

Stocks of Refined Copper Outside the United States, on First of Month In Thousands of Short Tons

Year	Jan.	Feb.	Mar.	Apr.	May	June	July	Aug.	Sept.	Oct.	Nov.	Dec.
1997	405.4	469.5	476.3	445.7	413.5	402.4	408.3	489.6	550.9	607.7	574.5	553.3
1998	580.8	512.4	487.3	438.1	371.1	368.0	335.7	324.0	387.2	468.0	506.9	509.0
1999	922.6	944.3	960.3	963.0	990.5	1,008.3	993.3	990.0	1,017.0	996.9	1,001.5	992.0
2000	983.8	1,034.9	1,040.7	1,011.4	988.6	880.9	866.0	857.3	837.0	826.7	784.1	764.8
2001	795.0	999.5	986.4	971.2	995.7	969.4	1,000.8	1,091.0	1,108.7	1,083.3	1,021.0	1,104.5
2002	1,241.3	1,273.5	1,291.5	1,370.4	1,391.1	1,399.4	1,289.0	1,342.6	1,369.1	1,321.1	1,219.7	1,224.5
2003	1,238.8	2,147.6	1,188.0	1,216.3	1,147.4	1,109.8	1,129.2	1,139.9	1,150.9	1,140.2	1,170.8	1,157.1
2004	1,191.5	1,149.9	1,139.5	995.5	968.4	826.0	807.1	812.4	830.2	825.2	778.0	816.8
2005	833.8	802.2	929.8	848.0	758.2	771.3	822.6	786.4	846.9	774.3	803.4	805.0
2006	871.2	956.8	923.2	797.7	816.4	819.2	789.1	812.9	872.4	830.1	877.5	817.9

Recoverable copper content. [1] Preliminary. *Source: American Bureau of Metal Statistics (ABMS)*

Production of Refined Copper in the United States   In Thousands of Short Tons

Year	Jan.	Feb.	Mar.	Apr.	May	June	July	Aug.	Sept.	Oct.	Nov.	Dec.	Total
1997	206.0	192.0	204.0	202.0	198.0	179.0	207.0	203.0	213.0	222.0	205.0	212.0	2,470
1998	214.0	204.0	216.0	209.0	197.0	188.0	197.0	203.0	201.0	217.0	207.0	217.0	2,490
1999	185.0	178.0	220.0	198.0	186.0	175.0	163.0	161.0	172.0	172.0	157.0	162.0	2,130
2000	157.0	149.0	173.0	144.0	161.0	146.0	134.0	149.0	141.0	140.0	147.0	154.0	1,800
2001	155.0	144.0	156.0	145.0	155.0	157.0	146.0	143.0	148.0	149.0	152.0	150.0	1,800
2002	134.0	117.0	124.0	129.0	134.0	128.0	130.0	124.0	120.0	129.0	120.0	119.0	1,508
2003	124.0	110.0	118.0	98.7	98.8	106.0	110.0	110.0	112.0	108.0	101.0	111.0	1,308
2004	104.0	98.9	105.0	111.0	109.0	113.0	104.0	107.0	112.0	111.0	109.0	123.0	1,307
2005	102.0	102.0	104.0	105.0	109.0	101.0	100.0	102.0	103.0	104.0	108.0	115.0	1,255
2006[1]	99.9	101.0	117.0	109.0	113.0	114.0	100.0	101.0	102.0	89.8	94.4		1,245

Recoverable copper content.   [1] Preliminary.   Source: U.S. Geological Survey (USGS)

Stocks of Refined Copper in the United States, on First of Month   In Thousands of Short Tons

Year	Jan.	Feb.	Mar.	Apr.	May	June	July	Aug.	Sept.	Oct.	Nov.	Dec.
1992	75.3	76.3	67.2	69.7	75.9	65.0	62.2	71.2	87.1	99.5	110.3	107.1
1993	135.4	152.7	144.3	132.3	146.0	153.6	137.1	151.0	128.4	117.2	124.6	107.1
1994	103.0	87.7	83.6	72.8	70.7	70.4	73.3	81.1	74.6	66.5	52.7	53.6
1995[2]	55.8	39.6	37.0	22.6	33.1	30.8	27.0	50.0	60.6	71.1	69.4	73.4
1996	120.0	131.4	125.5	123.1	126.3	107.9	102.8	106.2	104.7	68.0	76.0	77.5
1997	88.2	98.8	104.4	116.0	117.9	121.7	122.9	148.8	177.1	197.9	227.6	253.3
1998	281.5	282.2	312.7	315.7	304.5	308.6	306.2	319.0	334.1	367.4	407.2	444.6
1999	562.6	593.1	614.6	653.5	676.6	687.8	668.4	657.2	639.7	611.2	626.5	608.2
2000	619.2	620.8	619.5	582.9	537.0	508.8	467.8	418.0	397.7	394.3	379.1	344.2
2001[1]	383.8	408.4	416.2	481.9	552.6	585.7	626.7	733.1	767.4	895.6		

Recoverable copper content.   [1] Preliminary.   [2] New reporting method beginning January 1995, includes Comex, London Metal Exchange, and Refiners.
Beginning January 1999, includes Consumers.   Source: American Bureau of Metal Statistics (ABMS)

Deliveries of Refined Copper to Fabricators in the United States   In Thousands of Short Tons

Year	Jan.	Feb.	Mar.	Apr.	May	June	July	Aug.	Sept.	Oct.	Nov.	Dec.	Total
1997	246.3	234.5	240.6	247.4	254.9	228.1	241.1	258.2	252.3	259.2	256.0	236.6	2,959
1998	284.5	248.4	288.1	289.2	278.7	258.0	252.4	242.1	260.7	232.0	251.9	220.0	3,106
1999	199.6	202.8	235.0	221.4	206.3	201.9	188.0	186.8	193.7	182.3	182.4	175.2	2,375
2000	166.8	161.3	176.3	157.0	173.7	161.3	145.2	149.7	150.6	154.8	149.8	162.7	1,909
2001	166.1	150.8	167.4	148.4	167.6	165.2	162.7	154.0	151.6	160.7	154.7	147.5	1,897
2002	152.1	126.0	140.7	149.3	148.6	136.2	147.9	141.1	129.5	141.6	124.5	129.7	1,667
2003	136.4	123.4	124.6	106.6	107.7	117.0	127.1	120.6	125.8	127.9	114.4	133.8	1,465
2004	126.4	131.1	137.6	137.7	130.9	143.5	133.3	132.9	136.8	129.3	128.8	137.5	1,606
2005	120.1	120.0	131.2	125.4	125.7	119.2	106.9	112.8	108.0	110.9	112.6	115.9	1,409
2006[1]	124.8	110.3	131.5	121.9	121.8	132.7	117.5	119.9	112.7	95.4	95.6		1,401

Recoverable copper content.   [1] Preliminary.   Source: American Bureau of Metal Statistics (ABMS)

Deliveries of Refined Copper to Fabricators Outside the United States   In Thousands of Short Tons

Year	Jan.	Feb.	Mar.	Apr.	May	June	July	Aug.	Sept.	Oct.	Nov.	Dec.	Total
1990	419.9	466.3	436.7	392.9	408.3	466.7	303.7	373.5	370.8	448.9	469.1	420.7	4,972
1991	405.0	404.4	391.5	361.2	406.3	433.5	368.5	323.4	420.7	499.1	391.4	483.4	4,807
1992	453.7	408.9	441.8	416.4	413.4	432.4	410.4	364.7	432.6	403.5	406.1	461.3	5,045
1993	427.9	392.9	452.3	361.7	422.2	442.6	384.4	347.9	387.5	414.8	463.4	458.5	4,956
1994	399.8	429.5	481.2	466.5	468.9	428.1	387.9	369.2	423.5	448.9	457.1	436.0	5,197
1995[2]	758.5	810.1	892.8	882.2	853.0	867.3	863.7	814.1	803.4	835.1	796.6	726.2	9,903
1996	875.2	859.4	934.3	907.2	816.7	950.7	908.3	817.4	911.5	1,056.0	922.7	918.3	10,878
1997	862.2	889.7	977.9	1,007.1	991.1	982.7	897.8	873.9	886.2	1,009.0	980.4	966.6	11,349
1998	1,091.7	973.8	1,062.0	1,055.5	995.7	1,014.8	986.8	924.8	913.3	987.9	982.1	1,023.0	12,011
1999[1]	314.5	745.5											6,360

Recoverable copper content.   [1] Preliminary.   [2] New reporting method beginning January 1995, includes crude copper deliveries.
Source: American Bureau of Metal Statistics (ABMS)

Corn

Corn is a member of the grass family of plants and is a native grain of the American continents. Fossils of corn pollen that are over 80,000 years old have been found in lake sediment under Mexico City. Archaeological discoveries show that cultivated corn existed in the southwestern US for at least 3,000 years, indicating that the indigenous people of the region cultivated corn as a food crop long before the Europeans reached the New World. Corn is a hardy plant that grows in many different areas of the world. It can grow at altitudes as low as sea level and as high as 12,000 feet in the South American Andes Mountains. Corn can also grow in tropical climates that receive up to 400 inches of rainfall per year, or in areas that receive only 12 inches of rainfall per year. Corn is used primarily as livestock feed in the United States and the rest of the world. Other uses for corn are alcohol additives for gasoline, adhesives, corn oil for cooking and margarine, sweeteners, and as food for humans. Corn is the largest crop in the US, both in terms of the value of the crop and of the acres planted.

The largest futures market for corn is at the Chicago Board of Trade. Corn futures also trade at the Bolsa de Mercadorias & Futuros (BM&F) in Brazil, the Budapest Commodity Exchange, the Marche a Terme International de France (MATIF), the Mercado a Termino de Buenos Aires in Argentina, the Kanmon Commodity Exchange (KCE) in Korea, and the Tokyo Grain Exchange (TGE). The CBOT futures contract calls for the delivery of 5000 bushels of No. 2 yellow corn at par contract price, No. 1 yellow at 1-1/2 cents per bushel over the contract price, or No. 3 yellow at 1-1/2 cents per bushel below the contract price.

Prices – Corn futures prices traded mildly higher in early 2006 but then soared starting in September 2006 to post a 10-year high of $4.37 per bushel by early 2007. Corn prices closed 2006 up +81% at $3.90 per bushel. The US corn crop size in 2006-07 was the third largest ever seen at 10.54 billion bushels, which was only 11% below the record high of 11.81 billion bushels seen in 2004-05. However, the main factor driving corn prices higher in late 2006 was very strong demand from US ethanol producers who were expected to take up to 18% of the corn crop in 2006-07. Strong demand from ethanol producers resulted in a sharp drawdown in 2006-07 US carry-over inventories to only 752 million bushels, which was the third tightest inventory level seen in the past two decades. Corn demand from ethanol producers was expected to strengthen even further in 2007 and 2008, which raised talk of corn rationing among corn consumers. As of March 2007, the market was worried about whether US farmers will boost their corn planting acreage by the 10-12 million acres that are necessary just for corn supply to keep pace with demand and prevent the US corn carry-over from dropping to even more dangerously low levels. The strong demand for corn from ethanol producers affected global carry-over stocks as well, pushing global 2006-07 carry-over of corn/maize down to the 92.7 million metric tons, which was the tightest level of global stocks in two decades. While growing conditions as of early 2007 appeared favorable for the summer growing season, any glitches with hot or dry weather could caused prices to soar to new record highs above the current record high of $5.544 per bushel posted in 1996.

Supply – World production of corn in the 2006-07 marketing year fell by –0.4% to 682.886 million metric tons from the record high of 712.782 million metric tons seen in 2004-05. The world's largest corn producers are the US with 39% of world production, China (21%), and Brazil (6%). Corn production in both China and Brazil has nearly doubled since 1980. Production in the US over that time frame has risen by about 50%. The world area harvested with corn in 2006-07 rose +0.7% yr/yr to 303.5 million hectares, which was only mildly above the post-war record low of 293.0 million hectares seen in 2002-03. World ending stocks of corn and coarse grains in 2006-07 fell –28.3% to 119.3 million metric tons, which is a 3-decade low.

US corn production in the 2006-07 marketing year (Sep-Aug) fell by –5.2% yr/yr to 10.535 billion bushels from the record level of 11.807 billion bushels seen in 2004-05. US farmers harvested 70.648 million acres of corn for grain usage in 2006-07, which was down –5.9% from 2005-06 which was a 26-year high. US Corn yield in 2006-07 rose +0.8% to 149.1 bushels per acre but still below the record high of 160.2 bushels per acre seen in 2004-05. US carry-over stocks on Sep 1, 2006 fell –6.9% to 1.967 million bushels from 2.114 billion bushels in 2005. The largest corn producing states in the US are Iowa with 19.8% of US production in 2006, Illinois (18.1%), Nebraska (11.8%), Minnesota (10.7%), and Indiana (8.4%). The value of the US corn crop in 2005-06 was $21.041 billion.

Demand – World consumption of corn and rough grains in 2006-07 rose by +2.42% yr/yr to 1,014.4 million metric tons, which was a new record high. The US distribution tables for corn show that the largest category of usage, aside from animal feed, is for ethanol production (alcohol fuel) with 2.150 billion bushels of usage in 2006-07, representing 51.2% of total non-feed usage. Corn usage for ethanol has more than tripled in the past 7 years, and that usage category is likely to grow due to the high prices of crude oil and gasoline. After ethanol, the largest non-feed usage categories are for high fructose corn syrup (HFCS) with 14.8% of US usage, corn starch (7.9%), glucose and dextrose sugars (6.8%), cereal and other corn products (5.4%), and alcoholic beverages (3.8%).

Trade – US exports of corn in 2005-06 rose +24.0% yr/yr to 56.134 million metric tons, which remained far below the record high of 61.417 million metric tons posted in 1979-80. The largest destination countries for US corn exports are Japan, which accounted for 29.4% of US corn exports in 2005-06, Mexico (12.0%), South Korea (10.3%), Taiwan (7.9%), Egypt (7.4%), and Canada (3.4%).

World Production of Corn or Maize   In Thousands of Metric Tons

Crop Year	Argentina	Brazil	Canada	China	EU-25	Egypt	India	Mexico	Romania	South Africa	United States	Ukraine	World Total
1997-98	19,360	30,100	7,180	104,309	38,165	6,010	10,852	17,368	12,680	7,693	233,864	5,340	573,800
1998-99	13,500	32,393	8,952	132,954	34,920	5,605	10,680	17,789	8,000	7,946	247,882	2,301	605,725
1999-00	17,200	31,641	9,161	128,086	45,229	5,678	11,470	19,240	10,500	11,455	239,549	1,737	607,462
2000-01	15,400	41,536	6,827	106,000	44,529	5,636	12,068	17,917	4,800	8,040	251,854	3,848	590,488
2001-02	14,700	35,501	8,389	114,088	50,142	6,160	13,510	20,400	7,000	10,050	241,377	3,641	599,722
2002-03	15,500	44,500	8,999	121,300	49,360	6,000	11,100	19,280	7,300	9,675	227,767	4,180	602,974
2003-04	15,000	42,000	9,600	115,830	39,876	5,740	14,720	21,800	7,020	9,700	256,278	6,850	625,690
2004-05[1]	20,500	35,000	8,840	130,290	53,478	5,840	14,180	22,050	12,000	11,716	299,914	8,800	712,782
2005-06[2]	15,800	41,700	9,461	139,365	48,318	5,860	15,090	19,500	10,300	6,935	282,260	7,150	695,225
2006-07[3]	19,000	42,000	9,300	143,000	44,385	5,870	14,500	22,000	8,500	10,000	272,931	6,500	692,886

[1] Preliminary.   [2] Estimate.   [3] Forecast.   *Source: Foreign Agricultural Service, U.S. Department of Agriculture (FAS-USDA)*

World Supply and Demand of Course Grains   In Millions of Metric Tons/Hectares

Crop Year Beginning Oct.1	Area Harvested	Yield	Pro- duction	World Trade	Total Con- sumption	Ending Stocks	Stocks as % of Con- sumption[3]
1997-98	311.2	2.80	881.2	85.8	867.2	215.8	24.9
1998-99	308.5	2.90	890.9	96.7	869.2	237.4	27.3
1999-00	299.7	2.90	877.6	104.8	882.4	232.2	26.3
2000-01	296.7	2.90	862.3	104.4	884.4	210.1	23.8
2001-02	301.4	3.00	893.7	102.7	906.6	197.1	21.7
2002-03	293.0	3.00	875.1	104.6	902.3	169.9	18.8
2003-04	306.9	3.00	915.9	102.7	945.9	139.9	14.8
2004-05	300.4	3.40	1,014.1	102.1	975.9	178.0	18.2
2005-06[1]	301.3	3.20	977.6	109.0	989.2	166.4	16.8
2006-07[2]	303.5	3.20	967.2	106.8	1,014.4	119.3	11.8

[1] Preliminary.   [2] Estimate.   [3] Represents the ratio of marketing year ending stocks to total consumption.   *Source: Foreign Agricultural Service, U.S. Department of Agriculture (FAS-USDA)*

Acreage and Supply of Corn in the United States   In Millions of Bushels

Crop Year Beginning Sept. 1	Planted	Harvested For Grain	Harvested For Silage	Yield Per Harvested Acre Bushels	Carry-over, Sept. 1 On Farms	Carry-over, Sept. 1 Off Farms	Supply Beginning Stocks	Supply Pro- duction	Supply Imports	Total Supply
	In Thousands of Acres									
1997-98	79,537	72,671	6,054	126.7	475.0	408.2	883	9,207	9	10,099
1998-99	80,165	72,589	5,913	134.4	640.0	667.8	1,308	9,759	19	11,088
1999-00	77,386	70,487	6,037	133.8	797.0	990.0	1,787	9,431	15	11,239
2000-01	79,551	72,440	6,082	136.9	793.0	924.5	1,718	9,915	7	11,693
2001-02	75,752	68,808	6,148	138.2	753.2	1,146.0	1,899	9,507	10	11,412
2002-03	78,894	69,330	7,122	129.3	586.8	1,009.6	1,596	8,967	14	10,578
2003-04	78,603	70,944	6,583	142.2	484.9	601.8	1,087	10,089	14	11,190
2004-05	80,930	73,632	6,103	160.4	438.0	520.1	958	11,807	11	12,776
2005-06[1]	81,759	75,107	5,920	147.9	820.5	1,293.5	2,114	11,112	9	13,237
2006-07[2]	78,327	70,648	6,477	149.1	749.5	1,217.7	1,967	10,535	10	12,512

[1] Preliminary.   [2] Estimate.   *Source: Economic Research Service, U.S. Department of Agriculture (ERS-USDA)*

Production of Corn (For Grain) in the United States, by State   In Million of Bushels

Year	Illinois	Indiana	Iowa	Kansas	Mich- igan	Minn- esota	Missouri	Nebraska	Ohio	South Dakota	Texas	Wis- consin	Total
1997	1,425.5	701.5	1,642.2	371.8	255.1	851.4	299.0	1,135.2	475.7	326.4	241.5	402.6	9,206.8
1998	1,473.5	760.4	1,769.0	419.0	227.6	1,032.8	285.0	1,239.8	470.9	429.6	185.0	404.2	9,758.7
1999	1,491.0	748.4	1,758.2	420.2	253.5	990.0	247.4	1,153.7	403.2	367.3	228.3	407.6	9,437.3
2000	1,668.6	815.9	1,740.0	416.0	244.3	957.0	396.1	1,014.3	485.1	431.2	235.6	363.0	9,968.4
2001	1,649.2	884.5	1,664.4	387.4	199.5	806.0	345.8	1,139.3	437.5	370.6	167.6	330.2	9,506.8
2002	1,471.5	631.6	1,931.6	301.6	234.0	1,051.9	283.5	940.8	264.3	308.8	202.3	391.5	8,966.8
2003	1,812.2	786.9	1,868.3	300.0	259.8	970.9	302.4	1,124.2	478.9	427.4	194.7	367.7	10,089.2
2004	2,088.0	929.0	2,244.4	432.0	257.3	1,121.0	466.6	1,319.7	491.4	539.5	233.5	353.6	11,807.2
2005	1,708.9	888.6	2,162.5	465.8	288.9	1,191.9	329.7	1,270.5	464.8	470.1	210.9	429.2	11,112.1
2006[1]	1,906.7	882.8	2,083.2	387.5	289.1	1,128.8	369.2	1,247.8	471.7	378.0	168.2	422.8	10,534.9

[1] Preliminary.   *Source: National Agricultural Statistics Service, U.S. Department of Agriculture (NASS-USDA)*

CORN

Supply and Disappearance of Corn in the United States   In Millions of Bushels

Crop Year Beginning Sept. 1	Supply — Beginning Stocks	Supply — Production	Supply — Imports	Supply — Total Supply	Domestic Use — Food, Alcohol & Industrial	Domestic Use — Seed	Domestic Use — Feed & Residual	Domestic Use — Total	Exports	Total Disappearance	Ending Inventory — Gov't Owned[3]	Ending Inventory — Privately Owned[4]	Ending Inventory — Total
2002-03	1,596	8,967	14.4	10,578	2,320	20.1	5,558	7,899	1,593	9,491			1,087
Sept.-Nov.	1,596	8,967	3.4	10,567	549	0	1,986	2,535	393	2,929			7,638
Dec.-Feb.	7,638	----	4.1	7,642	563	0	1,547	2,110	400	2,510			5,132
Mar.-May	5,132	----	5.2	5,137	598	19.0	1,141	1,759	393	2,152			2,985
June-Aug.	2,985	----	1.8	2,987	610	1.1	884	1,494	406	1,900			1,087
2003-04	1,087	10,114	14.0	11,190	2,537	20.0	5,795	8,352	1,900	10,232			958
Sept.-Nov.	1,087	10,114	2.5	11,178	589	0	2,166	2,755	470	3,225			7,954
Dec.-Feb.	7,954	----	3.0	7,957	609	0	1,571	2,180	506	2,686			5,271
Mar.-May	5,271	----	5.0	5,277	676	0	1,166	1,842	465	2,306			2,970
June-Aug.	2,970	----	3.0	2,973	664	0	892	1,556	459	2,015			958
2004-05	958	11,807	11.0	12,776	2,686	0	6,158	8,844	1,818	10,662			2,114
Sept.-Nov.	958	11,807	2.0	12,767	643	0	2,175	2,818	499	3,316			9,451
Dec.-Feb.	9,451	----	2.0	9,452	637	0	1,620	2,257	439	2,696			6,756
Mar.-May	6,756	----	4.0	6,760	700	0	1,611	2,311	428	2,440			4,321
June-Aug.	4,321	----	3.0	42,324	706	0	1,053	1,759	452	2,210			2,114
2005-06[1]	2,114	11,114	9.0	13,237	2,981	0	6,141	9,122	2,147	11,270			1,967
Sept.-Nov.	2,114	11,114	1.0	13,230	697	0	2,241	2,938	477	3,415			9,815
Dec.-Feb.	9,815	----	4.0	9,816	708	0	1,636	2,344	485	2,829			6,987
Mar.-May	6,987	----	1.0	6,991	774	0	1,291	2,065	565	2,630			4,362
June-Aug.	4,362	----	9.0	4,363	802	0	974	1,776	620	2,396			1,967
2006-07[2]	1,967	10,535	10.0	12,512	3,535	0	5,975	9,510	2,250	11,760			752
Sept.-Nov.	1,967	10,535	1.0	12,503	808	0	2,173	2,981	592	3,573			8,930

[1] Preliminary.   [2] Estimate.   [3] Uncommitted inventory.   [4] Includes quantity under loan and farmer-owned reserve.
Source: Economic Research Service, U.S. Department of Agriculture (ERS-USDA)

Corn Production Estimates and Cash Price in the United States

Year	Corn for Grain Production Estimates (In Thousands of Bushels) — Aug. 1	Sept. 1	Oct. 1	Nov. 1	Final	St. Louis No. 2 Yellow	Omaha No. 2 Yellow	Gulf Ports No. 2 Yellow	Kansas City No. 2 White	Chicago No. 2 Yellow	Average Farm Price[2]	Value of Production (Million Dollars)
1998-99	9,592,089	9,737,949	9,743,399	9,836,069	9,758,685	1.99	1.88	2.35	2.51	2.06	1.94	18,922
1999-00	9,560,919	9,380,947	9,466,977	9,537,137	9,430,612	2.02	1.80	2.23	1.98	1.97	1.82	17,104
2000-01	10,369,369	10,362,374	10,191,817	10,053,942	9,915,051	2.01	1.82	2.26	2.06	1.99	1.85	18,499
2001-02	9,266,397	9,238,356	9,429,543	9,545,513	9,506,840	2.15	1.95	2.35	2.20	2.13	1.98	18,888
2002-03	8,886,009	8,848,529	8,969,836	9,003,364	8,966,787	2.49	2.29	2.71	2.94	2.46	2.32	20,882
2003-04	10,064,452	9,944,418	10,207,141	10,277,932	10,089,222	2.49	2.23	2.94	2.66	2.66	2.50	24,477
2004-05	10,923,099	10,960,710	11,613,226	11,740,920	11,807,217	2.73	2.50	2.48	2.01	2.08	2.05	24,381
2005-06	10,349,841	10,638,661	10,857,440	11,032,105	11,112,072	2.13	1.82	2.69	2.11	2.10	2.01	22,198
2006-07[1]	10,975,740	11,113,766	10,905,194	10,744,806	10,534,860	2.19	1.88	3.86	3.55	3.21	2.83	33,837

[1] Preliminary.   [2] Season-average price based on monthly prices weighted by monthly marketings.   *Source: Economic Research Service, U..S. Department of Agriculture (ERS-USDA)*

Distribution of Corn in the United States   In Millions of Bushels

Crop Year Beginning Sept. 1	Food, Seed and Industrial Use — HFCS	Glucose & Dextrose	Starch	Alcohol — Fuel	Alcohol — Beverage[3]	Seed	Cereal & Other Products	Total	Livestock Feed[4]	Exports (Including Grain Equiv. of Products)	Domestic Disappearance	Total Utilization
1998-99	531	219	240	526	127	19.8	184	1,826	5,468	1,984.2	7,314	9,298
1999-00	540	222	251	566	130	20.3	185	1,893	5,665	1,936.6	7,578	9,515
2000-01	530	218	247	628	130	19.3	185	1,938	5,842	1,941.3	7,799	9,740
2001-02	541	217	246	706	131	20.1	186	2,026	5,864	1,904.8	7,911	9,815
2002-03	532	219	256	996	131	20.1	187	2,320	5,558	1,592.5	7,899	9,491
2003-04	530	228	271	1,168	132	20.5	187	2,537	5,795	1,899.8	8,332	10,232
2004-05	521	222	277	1,323	133	20.8	189	2,666	6,158	1,818.1	8,844	10,662
2005-06[1]	529	229	275	1,603	135	20.2	190	2,961	6,100	2,100.0	9,075	11,175
2006-07[2]	520	240	279	2,150	135	20.0	191	3,515	6,125	2,150.0	9,665	11,815

[1] Preliminary.   [2] Estimate.   [3] Also includes nonfuel industrial alcohol.   [4] Feed and waste (residual, mostly feed).   *Source: Economic Research Service, U.S. Department of Agriculture (ERS-USDA)*

Corn (monthly average) through December 2006 — Cents per bushel

Cents Per Bushel
- - - - - Contract Grade or better, Chicago (1863 - 1900)
No. 3 Yellow, Chicago (Jan. 1901 - Apr. 1947)
No. 2 Yellow, Chicago (May 1947 - Mar. 1982)
No. 2 Yellow, Central, IL (Apr. 1982 - date)

Average Cash Price of Corn, No. 2 Yellow in Central Illinois   In Dollars Per Bushel

Year	Sept.	Oct.	Nov.	Dec.	Jan.	Feb.	Mar.	Apr.	May	June	July	Aug.	Average
1997-98	2.61	2.66	2.70	2.60	2.60	2.58	2.59	2.41	2.37	2.29	2.16	1.86	2.45
1998-99	1.78	1.94	2.09	2.08	2.07	2.05	2.09	2.05	2.03	1.99	1.67	1.84	1.97
1999-00	1.81	1.72	1.82	1.84	1.95	2.03	2.08	2.09	2.15	1.83	1.53	1.49	1.86
2000-01	1.58	1.81	1.96	2.01	1.99	1.95	1.92	1.87	1.78	1.76	1.92	2.00	1.88
2001-02	1.94	1.84	1.90	1.97	1.95	1.92	1.92	1.89	1.96	2.04	2.22	2.50	2.00
2002-03	2.57	2.41	2.36	2.32	2.29	2.33	2.31	2.36	2.40	2.37	2.13	2.26	2.34
2003-04	2.25	2.11	2.26	2.38	2.52	2.73	2.89	3.03	2.90	2.76	2.26	2.17	2.52
2004-05	1.98	1.77	1.79	1.87	1.86	1.86	1.97	1.94	1.93	2.02	2.20	1.98	1.93
2005-06	1.75	1.67	1.75	1.89	1.98	2.07	2.04	2.18	2.22	2.15	2.22	2.07	2.00
2006-07[1]	2.21	2.82	3.43	3.53									3.00

[1] Preliminary.   *Source: Economic Research Service, U.S. Department of Agriculture (ERS-USDA)*

Average Cash Price of Corn, No. 2 Yellow at Gulf Ports[2]   In Dollars Per Bushel

Year	Sept.	Oct.	Nov.	Dec.	Jan.	Feb.	Mar.	Apr.	May	June	July	Aug.	Average
1997-98	2.88	3.05	2.98	2.89	2.90	2.88	2.89	2.71	2.69	2.64	2.55	2.24	2.78
1998-99	2.18	2.43	2.47	2.42	2.48	2.40	2.45	2.39	2.35	2.36	2.12	2.20	2.35
1999-00	2.21	2.17	2.17	2.21	2.36	2.42	2.42	2.43	2.43	2.13	1.91	1.91	2.23
2000-01	2.03	2.15	2.26	2.45	2.40	2.35	2.32	2.22	2.14	2.11	2.30	2.36	2.26
2001-02	2.27	2.19	2.28	2.35	2.34	2.30	2.28	2.21	2.29	2.37	2.53	2.79	2.35
2002-03	2.89	2.79	2.77	2.71	2.69	2.69	2.67	2.67	2.74	2.72	2.72	2.44	2.71
2003-04	2.63	2.65	2.75	2.84	2.95	3.12	3.26	3.39	3.28	3.13	2.65	2.64	2.94
2004-05	2.49	2.37	2.39	2.43	2.44	2.40	2.54	2.45	2.42	2.49	2.69	2.59	2.48
2005-06	2.47	2.58	2.44	2.61	2.61	2.72	2.67	2.74	2.81	2.78	2.90	2.92	2.69
2006-07[1]	3.05	3.82	4.17	4.08	4.19								3.86

[1] Preliminary.   [2] Barge delivered to Louisiana Gulf.   *Source: Economic Research Service, U.S. Department of Agriculture (ERS-USDA)*

CORN

Weekly Outstanding Export Sales and Cumulative Exports of U.S. Corn   In Thousands of Metric Tons

Marketing Year 2004/05 Week Ending	Out-standing Sales	Cumu-lative Exports	Marketing Year 2005/06 Week Ending	Out-standing Sales	Cumu-lative Exports	Marketing Year 2006/07 Week Ending	Out-standing Sales	Cumu-lative Exports
Sep 02, 2004	6,935.9	230.3	Sep 01, 2005	7,863.6	10.3	Sep 07, 2006	11,500.7	1,103.2
Sep 09, 2004	7,430.6	943.3	Sep 08, 2005	7,985.8	436.0	Sep 14, 2006	11,138.2	2,478.4
Sep 16, 2004	7,896.0	1,634.2	Sep 15, 2005	7,817.6	1,350.7	Sep 21, 2006	10,731.6	3,714.7
Sep 23, 2004	7,798.2	2,637.5	Sep 22, 2005	7,564.1	2,307.1	Sep 28, 2006	10,706.6	4,897.9
Sep 30, 2004	7,397.0	3,817.8	Sep 29, 2005	7,735.2	3,088.6	Oct 05, 2006	10,893.3	5,998.0
Oct 07, 2004	7,933.9	4,765.3	Oct 06, 2005	7,645.1	4,111.8	Oct 12, 2006	10,625.6	7,086.0
Oct 14, 2004	8,638.0	5,361.7	Oct 13, 2005	7,379.6	5,343.4	Oct 19, 2006	10,871.5	7,886.0
Oct 21, 2004	8,531.5	6,558.1	Oct 20, 2005	7,149.9	6,291.6	Oct 26, 2006	10,796.9	8,987.8
Oct 28, 2004	9,339.7	7,203.0	Oct 27, 2005	7,353.7	7,303.4	Nov 02, 2006	11,552.1	10,161.8
Nov 04, 2004	9,052.7	8,320.9	Nov 03, 2005	7,315.0	8,220.8	Nov 09, 2006	11,943.8	11,165.7
Nov 11, 2004	8,740.6	9,357.7	Nov 10, 2005	7,748.1	9,284.0	Nov 16, 2006	11,765.1	12,386.6
Nov 18, 2004	9,141.4	10,258.0	Nov 17, 2005	7,813.5	10,251.3	Nov 23, 2006	11,889.0	13,283.9
Nov 25, 2004	8,917.1	11,067.4	Nov 24, 2005	7,759.2	10,917.4	Nov 30, 2006	11,329.3	14,656.3
Dec 02, 2004	8,624.0	12,275.4	Dec 01, 2005	7,432.4	11,938.5	Dec 07, 2006	11,493.0	15,892.9
Dec 09, 2004	8,113.4	13,422.7	Dec 08, 2005	7,334.4	12,955.0	Dec 14, 2006	11,854.8	16,792.6
Dec 16, 2004	7,770.2	14,491.7	Dec 15, 2005	7,037.3	14,137.5	Dec 21, 2006	11,890.1	17,911.0
Dec 23, 2004	7,496.3	15,462.5	Dec 22, 2005	6,618.9	14,916.1	Dec 28, 2006	11,503.1	18,871.5
Dec 30, 2004	6,974.5	16,415.0	Dec 29, 2005	5,991.3	16,013.8	Jan 04, 2007	11,827.1	19,724.4
Jan 06, 2005	6,999.0	17,048.8	Jan 05, 2006	5,905.2	16,713.4	Jan 11, 2007	12,245.8	20,729.5
Jan 13, 2005	7,156.5	17,798.5	Jan 12, 2006	6,184.1	17,656.8	Jan 18, 2007	12,204.2	21,755.3
Jan 20, 2005	6,839.6	18,878.1	Jan 19, 2006	7,115.7	18,582.6	Jan 25, 2007	11,799.6	22,957.2
Jan 27, 2005	6,256.8	19,798.5	Jan 26, 2006	7,858.4	19,502.3	Feb 01, 2007	11,687.2	23,987.0
Feb 03, 2005	6,744.2	20,306.4	Feb 02, 2006	8,455.0	20,517.6	Feb 08, 2007	12,076.9	24,983.6
Feb 10, 2005	6,768.7	21,024.2	Feb 09, 2006	8,829.4	21,340.4	Feb 15, 2007	11,657.4	26,214.1
Feb 17, 2005	6,996.4	21,706.7	Feb 16, 2006	9,280.8	22,379.6	Feb 22, 2007	11,083.8	27,105.8
Feb 24, 2005	6,950.4	22,564.4	Feb 23, 2006	8,934.8	23,328.2	Mar 01, 2007	10,730.9	28,531.5
Mar 03, 2005	6,746.2	23,502.0	Mar 02, 2006	9,246.3	24,379.9	Mar 08, 2007	10,329.7	29,682.2
Mar 10, 2005	7,001.7	24,256.1	Mar 09, 2006	9,442.6	25,213.1	Mar 15, 2007	10,065.6	30,587.2
Mar 17, 2005	7,290.7	24,895.6	Mar 16, 2006	9,141.4	26,425.7	Mar 22, 2007		
Mar 24, 2005	7,635.8	25,711.2	Mar 23, 2006	9,285.0	27,320.9	Mar 29, 2007		
Mar 31, 2005	7,394.9	26,613.5	Mar 30, 2006	8,754.8	28,510.5	Apr 05, 2007		
Apr 07, 2005	7,576.2	27,347.8	Apr 06, 2006	8,687.4	29,392.6	Apr 12, 2007		
Apr 14, 2005	7,394.0	28,200.0	Apr 13, 2006	8,888.4	30,281.8	Apr 19, 2007		
Apr 21, 2005	6,885.1	29,202.2	Apr 20, 2006	8,475.4	31,477.3	Apr 26, 2007		
Apr 28, 2005	6,565.8	30,145.1	Apr 27, 2006	8,702.5	32,532.4	May 03, 2007		
May 05, 2005	7,097.5	30,997.2	May 04, 2006	8,702.9	33,637.1	May 10, 2007		
May 12, 2005	7,135.9	31,812.8	May 11, 2006	9,156.9	34,723.0	May 17, 2007		
May 19, 2005	6,734.0	32,765.2	May 18, 2006	8,815.5	36,200.8	May 24, 2007		
May 26, 2005	6,668.4	33,575.3	May 25, 2006	8,717.4	37,454.9	May 31, 2007		
Jun 02, 2005	6,385.7	34,418.9	Jun 01, 2006	8,420.4	38,619.2	Jun 07, 2007		
Jun 09, 2005	6,208.2	35,230.2	Jun 08, 2006	8,745.9	39,758.4	Jun 14, 2007		
Jun 16, 2005	5,649.6	36,296.9	Jun 15, 2006	9,037.3	41,042.2	Jun 21, 2007		
Jun 23, 2005	5,808.6	37,355.1	Jun 22, 2006	9,213.5	42,219.8	Jun 28, 2007		
Jun 30, 2005	5,977.4	38,129.0	Jun 29, 2006	8,999.8	43,223.2	Jul 05, 2007		
Jul 07, 2005	5,724.8	38,702.4	Jul 06, 2006	8,655.6	44,156.6	Jul 12, 2007		
Jul 14, 2005	5,507.7	39,515.7	Jul 13, 2006	7,794.0	45,358.3	Jul 19, 2007		
Jul 21, 2005	5,159.9	40,502.7	Jul 20, 2006	7,387.1	46,741.0	Jul 26, 2007		
Jul 28, 2005	4,498.1	41,410.8	Jul 27, 2006	7,113.7	47,911.4	Aug 02, 2007		
Aug 04, 2005	4,608.6	42,373.5	Aug 03, 2006	6,961.4	49,226.2	Aug 09, 2007		
Aug 11, 2005	4,329.7	43,117.0	Aug 10, 2006	6,305.9	50,450.2	Aug 16, 2007		
Aug 18, 2005	3,798.7	43,948.2	Aug 17, 2006	5,304.9	51,632.3	Aug 23, 2007		
Aug 25, 2005	2,780.4	44,953.3	Aug 24, 2006	3,470.1	53,120.3	Aug 30, 2007		
			Aug 31, 2006	2,454.2	54,353.6			

Source: Foreign Agricultural Service, U.S. Department of Agriculture (FAS-USDA)

Average Price Received by Farmers for Corn in the United States   In Dollars Per Bushel

Year	Sept.	Oct.	Nov.	Dec.	Jan.	Feb.	Mar.	Apr.	May	June	July	Aug.	Average
1997-98	2.52	2.54	2.51	2.52	2.56	2.55	2.54	2.41	2.34	2.28	2.19	1.89	2.40
1998-99	1.83	1.91	1.93	2.00	2.06	2.05	2.06	2.04	1.99	1.97	1.74	1.75	1.94
1999-00	1.75	1.69	1.70	1.82	1.91	1.98	2.03	2.03	2.11	1.91	1.64	1.52	1.84
2000-01	1.61	1.74	1.86	1.97	1.98	1.96	1.96	1.89	1.82	1.76	1.87	1.90	1.86
2001-02	1.91	1.84	1.85	1.98	1.97	1.93	1.94	1.91	1.93	1.97	2.13	2.38	1.98
2002-03	2.47	2.34	2.28	2.32	2.33	2.34	2.33	2.34	2.38	2.34	2.17	2.15	2.32
2003-04	2.20	2.12	2.20	2.31	2.39	2.61	2.75	2.89	2.87	2.79	2.51	2.34	2.50
2004-05	2.20	2.14	2.05	2.04	2.12	1.95	2.02	2.00	1.98	2.03	2.11	1.95	2.05
2005-06	1.90	1.82	1.77	1.92	2.00	2.02	2.06	2.11	2.17	2.14	2.14	2.09	2.01
2006-07[1]	2.20	2.54	2.87	3.01	3.05	3.32							2.83

[1] Preliminary.   Source: Economic Research Service, U.S. Department of Agriculture (ERS-USDA)

Corn Price Support Data in the United States

Crop Year Beginning Sept. 1	National Average Loan Rate[3] --- Dollars Per Bushel ---	Target Price	Placed Under Loan	% of Pro-duction	Acquired by CCC	Owned by CCC Aug. 31	CCC Owned	Under CCC Loan	Quantity Pledged (Thousands of Bushels)	Face Amount (Thousands of Dollars)
				------- Millions of Bushels -------			CCC Inventory As of Dec. 31			
1995-96	1.89	2.75	970	13.1	0		42	579	677,115	1,232,669
1996-97	1.89	NA	561	6.1	0		30	756	970,590	1,764,291
1997-98	1.89	NA	1,132	12.3	19		2	81	1,129,915	2,062,308
1998-99	1.89	NA	823	8.4	0		15		1,129,915	2,062,308
1999-00	1.89	NA					26		1,420,878	2,590,443
2000-01	1.89	NA					36		1,393,947	2,562,172
2001-02	1.89	NA					24		1,394,561	2,557,874
2002-03	1.98	2.60					18		1,366,513	2,622,823
2003-04[1]	1.98	2.60					16			
2004-05[2]	1.95	2.63								

[1] Preliminary.   [2] Estimate.   [3] Findley or announced loan rate.   Source: National Agricultural Statistics Service, U.S. Department of Agriculture (NASS-USDA)

U.S. Exports[1] of Corn (Including Seed), By Country of Destination   In Thousands of Metric Tons

Year Beginning Oct. 1	Algeria	Canada	Egypt	Irael	Japan	Mexico	Rep. of Korea	Russia	Saudi Arabia	Spain	Taiwan	Vene-zuela	Total
1996-97	862	879	2,364	556	15,425	3,141	5,404	88	1,025	1,080	5,609	730	46,638
1997-98	829	1,404	1,951	141	13,957	4,423	3,364	1	883	141	3,488	645	37,755
1998-99	947	898	2,954	395	15,375	5,576	6,659	405	1,175	92	4,538	1,329	51,949
1999-00	1,099	1,080	3,542	748	14,939	4,910	2,822	491	1,197	16	4,989	1,146	49,378
2000-01	1,180	2,797	4,116	621	14,091	5,928	3,109	26	1,003	0	4,894	1,152	48,192
2001-02	1,343	3,979	4,283	847	14,817	4,025	1,085	86	670	5	4,599	502	47,058
2002-03	1,009	3,811	2,904	313	14,384	5,220	272	0	222	0	4,139	651	40,780
2003-04	1,158	2,014	3,120	1,154	14,968	5,730	3,942	70	402	5	4,757	669	48,724
2004-05	1,036	2,210	3,738	393	15,036	5,935	2,210	13	126	14	4,446	90	45,262
2005-06[2]	1,255	1,908	4,156	725	16,521	6,759	5,802	15	619	8	4,456	133	56,134

[1] Excludes exports of corn by-products.   [2] Preliminary.   Source: Economic Research Service, U.S. Department of Agriculture (ERS-USDA)

Stocks of Corn (Shelled and Ear) in the United States   In Millions of Bushels

Year	On Farms Mar. 1	June 1	Sept. 1	Dec. 1	Off Farms Mar. 1	June 1	Sept. 1	Dec. 1	Total Stocks Mar. 1	June 1	Sept. 1	Dec. 1
1997	2,870.0	1,501.0	475.0	4,822.0	1,624.1	995.6	408.2	2,424.8	4,494.1	2,496.6	883.2	7,246.8
1998	2,975.0	1,830.0	640.0	5,320.0	1,964.9	1,209.8	667.8	2,731.8	4,939.9	3,039.8	1,307.8	8,051.8
1999	3,570.0	2,257.0	797.0	5,195.0	2,128.4	1,359.2	990.0	2,844.4	5,698.4	3,616.2	1,787.0	8,039.4
2000	3,300.0	2,029.8	793.0	5,550.0	2,301.9	1,556.1	924.5	2,972.2	5,601.9	3,585.9	1,717.5	8,522.2
2001	3,600.0	2,230.8	753.2	5,275.0	2,443.0	1,693.2	1,146.0	2,989.7	6,043.0	3,924.0	1,899.1	8,264.7
2002	3,355.0	2,020.6	586.8	4,800.0	2,440.3	1,576.3	1,009.6	2,838.0	5,795.3	3,596.9	1,596.4	7,638.0
2003	2,940.0	1,620.2	484.9	5,286.0	2,191.9	1,364.7	601.8	2,667.8	5,131.9	2,984.9	1,086.7	7,953.8
2004	3,030.0	1,540.0	438.0	6,144.0	2,241.5	1,430.1	520.1	3,308.5	5,271.5	2,970.1	958.1	9,452.5
2005	4,137.0	2,462.3	820.5	6,325.0	2,619.3	1,858.5	1,293.5	3,490.0	6,756.3	4,320.8	2,114.0	9,815.0
2006[1]	4,055.0	2,350.5	749.5	5,627.0	2,932.3	2,011.2	1,217.7	3,302.8	6,987.3	4,361.7	1,967.2	8,929.8

[1] Preliminary.   Source: National Agricultural Statistics Service, U.S. Department of Agriculture (NASS-USDA)

CORN

Corn Futures - Chicago Board of Trade
(weekly close) as of December 29, 2006

Cents per bushel

Volume of Trading of Corn Futures in Chicago   In Thousands of Contracts

Year	Jan.	Feb.	Mar.	Apr.	May	June	July	Aug.	Sept.	Oct.	Nov.	Dec.	Total
1997	1,160.6	1,483.0	1,693.3	1,780.1	1,291.7	1,347.5	1,527.7	1,318.3	1,060.2	1,700.2	1,434.4	1,188.0	16,985.0
1998	1,250.2	1,276.5	1,432.8	1,620.3	1,148.5	1,771.0	1,415.3	1,231.4	1,126.3	1,319.3	1,217.2	986.6	15,795.5
1999	955.1	1,374.2	1,440.1	1,420.6	975.1	1,597.4	1,708.0	1,669.8	1,131.9	1,096.2	1,500.9	855.6	15,724.8
2000	1,502.2	1,580.9	1,713.1	1,386.3	1,789.7	1,830.7	1,178.3	1,291.8	1,057.4	1,256.1	1,612.8	986.1	17,185.4
2001	1,397.2	1,197.4	1,329.5	1,518.7	1,173.2	1,612.1	2,023.5	1,549.0	1,072.3	1,223.3	1,741.2	891.4	16,728.7
2002	996.3	1,449.6	944.7	1,498.0	1,434.5	1,851.5	1,958.4	2,158.7	1,635.4	1,523.3	1,801.4	880.5	18,132.4
2003	1,204.0	1,559.1	1,156.9	1,633.1	1,657.0	1,951.2	1,499.3	1,830.6	1,389.7	2,057.7	1,815.9	1,364.3	19,118.7
2004	2,025.7	2,367.0	2,190.9	2,870.9	1,855.3	2,538.6	1,740.5	1,883.0	1,446.9	1,476.4	2,473.3	1,169.6	24,038.2
2005	1,467.8	2,680.8	2,278.1	2,519.1	2,188.3	3,446.1	2,626.0	2,993.6	1,618.5	1,504.2	2,892.2	1,750.3	27,965.1
2006	2,494.6	3,599.1	3,041.0	3,507.5	3,773.1	4,693.4	3,743.6	4,226.9	3,760.5	5,300.2	6,279.4	2,820.6	47,239.9

Source: Chicago Board of Trade (CBT)

Average Open Interest of Corn Futures in Chicago   In Contracts

Year	Jan.	Feb.	Mar.	Apr.	May	June	July	Aug.	Sept.	Oct.	Nov.	Dec.
1997	305,779	347,392	382,261	351,852	290,649	274,760	267,531	281,194	307,415	378,453	379,045	331,386
1998	328,020	341,444	358,221	366,657	337,703	327,237	297,894	318,162	321,992	332,337	342,868	322,157
1999	357,682	363,153	357,126	343,624	338,467	323,658	329,460	315,858	316,247	410,955	461,037	389,187
2000	445,999	478,892	482,080	487,758	476,891	445,018	391,967	387,289	356,583	397,966	454,920	414,851
2001	454,326	469,027	440,548	455,718	424,386	423,840	389,898	387,710	370,315	419,447	462,930	416,593
2002	459,314	464,368	431,923	430,712	411,346	430,856	458,081	509,069	501,523	485,859	496,998	450,016
2003	455,967	469,611	445,343	411,983	406,987	385,775	384,561	383,590	356,181	420,680	470,165	447,455
2004	543,985	641,380	678,041	704,868	637,417	621,898	566,465	562,172	548,816	606,307	639,531	588,889
2005	629,286	654,066	659,684	673,818	677,308	702,369	713,077	733,578	714,197	794,427	852,459	774,187
2006	875,314	1,048,797	1,065,997	1,175,984	1,288,155	1,327,827	1,360,186	1,347,166	1,302,121	1,312,589	1,405,651	1,381,477

Source: Chicago Board of Trade (CBT)

Corn Oil

Corn oil is a bland, odorless oil produced by refining the crude corn oil that is mechanically extracted from the germ of the plant seed. High-oil corn, the most common type of corn used to make corn oil, typically has an oil content of 7% or higher compared to about 4% for normal corn. Corn oil is widely used as cooking oil, for making margarine and mayonnaise, and for making inedible products such as soap, paints, inks, varnishes, and cosmetics. For humans, studies have shown that no vegetable oil is more effective than corn oil in lowering blood cholesterol levels.

Prices – The average monthly price of corn oil (wet mill price in Chicago) in the 2005-06 marketing year (Oct-Sep) fell –9.6% yr/yr to 25.18 cents per pound, which was well below the record high of 36.50 cents posted in 1973-74. Seasonally, prices tend to be highest around March/April and lowest late in the calendar year.

Supply – US corn oil production in the 2005-06 marketing year rose by +2.4% yr/yr to 2.450 billion pounds, which was a 4 year high. Seasonally, production tends to peak around December and March and reaches a low in July. US stocks in the 2005-06 marketing year (Oct 1) rose +2.0% yr/yr to 156 million pounds.

Demand – US usage (domestic disappearance) in 2005-06 rose +5.0% to 1.731 billion pounds.

Exports – US corn oil exports in 2005-06 rose +1.4% to 800 million pounds. US corn oil imports in 2005-06 rose 22.4% to 60 million pounds.

Supply and Disappearance of Corn Oil in the United States　In Millions of Pounds

Crop Year Beginning Oct. 1	Stocks Oct. 1	Pro- duction	Imports	Total Supply	Baking and Frying Fats	Salad and Cooking Oil	Marg- arine	Total Edible Products	Domestic Disap- pearance	Exports	Total Disap- pearance
1999-00	135	2,501	17.5	2,654	W	800	W	953	1,417	970	2,387
2000-01	267	2,403	27.0	2,698	W	502	56	1,298	1,630	951	2,581
2001-02	117	2,461	61.0	2,639	W	W	W	950	1,363	1,172	2,535
2002-03	104	2,453	66.0	2,623	W	W	W	W	1,615	888	2,503
2003-04	119	2,396	66.0	2,582	W	W	W	1,724	1,662	767	2,429
2004-05[1]	153	2,392	49.0	2,594	W	1,466	W	1,690	1,649	789	2,439
2005-06[2]	156	2,450	60.0	2,666	W	1,367	W	1,607	1,731	800	2,531

[1] Preliminary.　[2] Estimate.　W = Withheld proprietary data.　*Source: Economic Research Service, U.S. Department of Agriculture (ERS-USDA)*

Production[2] of Crude Corn Oil in the United States　In Millions of Pounds

Year	Oct.	Nov.	Dec.	Jan.	Feb.	Mar.	Apr.	May	June	July	Aug.	Sept.	Total
2000-01	208.6	192.7	190.4	198.9	180.5	201.6	200.7	206.2	204.0	205.7	211.1	203.2	2,404
2001-02	196.0	203.3	206.5	200.1	183.8	187.1	189.4	219.8	227.3	220.2	217.0	211.0	2,462
2002-03	218.6	195.0	212.3	206.8	181.7	206.0	199.7	203.6	207.1	216.5	202.5	203.2	2,453
2003-04	209.1	196.5	193.2	201.0	182.9	195.8	200.0	197.7	210.7	204.3	205.2	200.1	2,397
2004-05	208.8	187.1	191.0	205.2	182.5	206.6	217.2	188.2	211.5	206.7	198.5	189.0	2,392
2005-06	207.5	199.9	200.3	209.2	184.8	217.6	191.7	218.7	206.7	215.3	222.0	209.0	2,483
2006-07[1]	228.7	216.0	226.1	228.7									2,699

[1] Preliminary.　[2] Not seasonally adjusted.　*Source: Bureau of the Census, U.S. Department of Commerce*

Consumption Corn Oil, in Refining, in the United States　In Millions of Pounds

Year	Oct.	Nov.	Dec.	Jan.	Feb.	Mar.	Apr.	May	June	July	Aug.	Sept.	Total
2000-01	136.2	112.2	129.3	106.7	122.6	118.7	111.9	140.4	W	W	W	W	1,467
2001-02	W	W	W	W	W	W	W	W	W	W	W	W	W
2002-03	W	W	W	W	W	W	W	W	W	W	W	W	W
2003-04	W	W	W	W	W	W	134.6	W	152.8	W	W	W	1,724
2004-05	W	165.4	131.6	140.3	W	147.3	132.2	124.8	149.0	142.9	142.4	132.1	1,690
2005-06	148.4	140.4	140.3	148.4	123.4	128.0	110.8	145.2	138.9	121.6	131.6	130.0	1,607
2006-07[1]	143.6	146.7	152.9										1,773

[1] Preliminary.　W = Withheld proprietary data.　*Source: Bureau of Census, U.S. Department of Commerce*

Average Corn Oil Price, Wet Mill in Chicago　In Cents Per Pound

Year	Oct.	Nov.	Dec.	Jan.	Feb.	Mar.	Apr.	May	June	July	Aug.	Sept.	Average
2000-01	10.52	10.37	10.54	10.25	11.06	11.91	13.76	14.84	15.94	17.28	18.73	17.30	13.54
2001-02	17.18	18.30	22.45	20.54	18.35	18.37	17.70	17.00	17.60	19.10	21.72	21.40	19.14
2002-03	22.45	26.90	28.25	29.30	28.90	27.20	27.55	29.10	30.15	29.90	30.68	27.71	28.17
2003-04	26.99	27.56	28.73	29.26	30.16	30.56	30.36	30.34	28.36	27.33	25.61	25.07	28.36
2004-05	23.10	24.24	26.67	27.41	27.58	28.08	29.29	30.65	30.73	30.01	28.83	27.75	27.86
2005-06	27.50	27.08	26.08	25.22	23.65	22.61	23.19	25.25	25.70	25.75	25.42	24.71	25.18
2006-07[1]	24.70	26.47	28.05	28.05									26.82

[1] Preliminary.　*Source: Economic Research Service, U.S. Department of Agriculture (ERS-USDA)*

Cotton

Cotton is a natural vegetable fiber that comes from small trees and shrubs of a genus belonging to the mallow family, one of which is the common American Upland cotton plant. Cotton has been used in India for at least the last 5,000 years and probably much longer, and was also used by the ancient Chinese, Egyptians, and North and South Americans. Cotton was one of the earliest crops grown by European settlers in the US.

Cotton requires a long growing season, plenty of sunshine and water during the growing season, and then dry weather for harvesting. In the United States, the Cotton Belt stretches from northern Florida to North Carolina and westward to California. In the US, planting time varies from the beginning of February in Southern Texas to the beginning of June in the northern sections of the Cotton Belt. The flower bud of the plant blossoms and develops into an oval boll that splits open at maturity. At maturity, cotton is most vulnerable to damage from wind and rain. Approximately 95% of the cotton in the US is now harvested mechanically with spindle-type pickers or strippers and then sent off to cotton gins for processing. There it is dried, cleaned, separated, and packed into bales.

Cotton is used in a wide range of products from clothing to home furnishings to medical products. The value of cotton is determined according to the staple, grade, and character of each bale. Staple refers to short, medium, long, or extra-long fiber length, with medium staple accounting for about 70% of all US cotton. Grade refers to the color, brightness, and amount of foreign matter and is established by the US Department of Agriculture. Character refers to the fiber's diameter, strength, body, maturity (ratio of mature to immature fibers), uniformity, and smoothness. Cotton is the fifth leading cash crop in the US and is one of the nation's principal agricultural exports. The weight of cotton is typically measured in terms of a "bale," which is deemed to equal 480 pounds.

Cotton futures and options are traded on the New York Cotton Exchange, a division of the New York Board of Trade. Cotton futures are also traded on the Bolsa de Mercadorias & Futuros (BM&F). Cotton yarn futures are traded on the Central Japan Commodity Exchange (CCOM) and the Osaka Mercantile Exchange (OME). The New York Cotton Exchange's futures contract calls for the delivery of 50,000 pounds net weight (approximately 100 bales) of No. 2 cotton with a quality rating of Strict Low Middling and a staple length of 1-and-2/32 inch. Delivery points include Texas (Galveston and Houston), New Orleans, Memphis, and Greenville/Spartanburg in South Carolina.

Prices – Cotton prices on the New York Board of Trade nearest-futures chart in 2006 remained within the 3-year trading range, trading in a choppy range during the year and closing the year +3.7% at 56.19 cents per pound. Cotton prices were supported during 2006 by a –9.0% decline in the 2006-07 US cotton crop to 21.729 million bales because of hot and dry weather in key cotton growing areas in the US. However, the year-on-year decline must be compared to the record year seen in 2005-06. In fact, the 2006-07 cotton crop was the third largest US cotton crop ever. In

any case, demand for US cotton dropped sharply in the 2006-07, mainly because China went to India for much of its cotton needs in 2006. The result was that the US cotton carry-over in 2006-07 rose sharply by +20.7% yr/yr to 7.30 million bales, thus pressuring prices. Cotton prices were able to rally in late 2006 as the sharp 80% rally in corn prices in 2006 ensured that some US farmers would be planting corn instead of cotton in spring 2007, likely reducing the US cotton crop in 2007-08. Cotton supply and demand on a global basis was in relative balance in 2006-07 with a small decline in the global carry-over of –1.7% yr/yr to 52.920 million bales.

Supply – World cotton production in 2006-07 rose +2.5% yr/yr to 116.750 million bales (480 pounds per bale) but still down from the record high of 120.120 million bales seen in 2004-05. The world's largest cotton producers are China with 27% of world production in 2005-06, the US with 19%, India with 18%, and Pakistan with 8%. World beginning stocks in 2006-07 rose +0.1% yr/yr to 53.947 million bales, recovering further from the 9-year low of 43.031 million bales seen in 2004-05.

The US cotton crop in 2006-07 fell by –9.0% yr/yr to 21.729 million bales, down from the 2005-06 record high of 23.890 million bales. US farmers harvested 12.732 million acres of cotton in 2006-07, down –7.8% yr/yr. The US cotton yield in 2006-07 was 819 pounds per acre, down from the record of 855 pounds per acre in 2004-05 but still a very strong yield. The leading US producing states of Upland cotton are Texas with 27% of US production in 2005, Arkansas (12%), Mississippi (10%), Georgia (10%), and California (7%). US production of cotton cloth has fallen sharply by almost half in the past decade due to the movement of the textile industry out of the US to low-wage foreign countries. Specifically, US production of cotton cloth in 2006 fell –12.1% yr/yr to a record low of 2.312 billion square yards, less than one-fourth of the production level seen in 1950.

Demand – World consumption of cotton in 2006-07 rose by +4.9% yr/yr to 118.796 million bales, which was a new record high. Consumption of cotton continues to move toward countries with low wages, where the raw cotton is utilized to produce textiles and other cotton products. The largest consumers of cotton in 2005-06 were China (40%), India (15%), and Pakistan (10%). US consumption of cotton by mills in 2006-07 fell –11.7% yr/yr to 5.200 million bales, and accounted for 24% of US production. The remaining 76% of US cotton production went for exports.

Trade – World exports of cotton in 2006-07 fell by –13.7% yr/yr to 38.535 million bales, down from the 2005-06 record high. The US is the world's largest cotton exporter by far and accounts for 36% of world cotton exports. Key world cotton importers include Turkey with 8% of total world imports in 2006-07, Indonesia with 6%, Mexico with 4%, and Russia with 4%. US cotton exports in 2005-06 rose by +8.1% yr/yr to 15.603 million bales, which was a new record high. The main destinations for US exports in 2005-06 were China (52%), Mexico (8%), Indonesia (5%), Taiwan (3%), and Thailand (4%).

Supply and Distribution of All Cotton in the United States   In Thousands of 480-Pound Bales

Crop Year Beginning Aug. 1	Acre Planted	Acre Harvested	Yield Lbs./acre	Beginning Stocks[3]	Production[4]	Imports	Total	Mill Use	Exports	Total	Unac- counted	Ending Stocks	Farm Price[5]	"A" Index Price[6]	Value of Pro- duction Million $
	---- 1,000 Acres ----												-- Cents per Lb. --		
1997-98	13,898	13,406	673	3,971	18,793	13	22,777	11,349	7,500	18,849	-41	3,887	66.2	72.11	5,975.6
1998-99	13,393	10,684	625	3,887	13,918	443	18,248	10,401	4,344	14,699	394	3,939	61.7	58.97	4,119.9
1999-00	14,874	13,425	607	3,939	16,968	97	21,004	10,240	6,750	16,944	-145	3,915	46.8	52.85	3,809.6
2000-01	15,517	13,053	632	3,915	17,188	16	21,119	8,862	6,740	15,602	483	6,000	51.6	57.25	4,260.4
2001-02	15,769	13,828	705	6,000	20,303	21	26,324	7,696	11,000	18,696	-180	7,448	32.0	41.88	3,121.8
2002-03	13,958	12,417	665	7,448	17,209	67	24,724	7,273	11,900	19,173	-166	5,385	45.7	55.81	3,777.1
2003-04	13,480	12,003	730	5,385	18,255	45	23,685	6,266	13,758	20,024	-211	3,450	63.0	69.24	5,516.8
2004-05	13,659	13,057	855	3,450	23,251	29	26,730	6,691	14,436	21,127	-108	5,495	43.5	53.53	4,993.6
2005-06[1]	14,245	13,803	831	5,495	23,890	27	29,412	5,888	18,036	23,924	562	6,050	49.0	57.10	5,695.2
2006-07[2]	15,274	12,732	819	6,050	21,729	30	27,379	5,200	16,200	21,400	21	6,000	49.6		5,175.7

[1] Preliminary.   [2] Estimate.   [3] Excludes preseason ginnings (adjusted to 480-lb. bale net weight basis).   [4] Includes preseason ginnings.
[5] Marketing year average price.   [6] Average of 5 cheapest types of SLM 1 3/32 staple length cotton *offered on the European market.*
Source: Economic Research Service, U.S. Department of Agriculture (ERS-USDA)

World Production of All Cotton   In Thousands of 480-Pound Bales

Crop Year Beginning Aug. 1	Argen- tina	Australia	Brazil	Burkina	China	Egypt	Greece	India	Pakistan	Turkey	United States	Uzbek- istan	World Total
1997-98	1,428	3,166	1,890	635	21,100	1,532	1,698	12,337	7,175	3,651	18,793	5,228	92,234
1998-99	918	3,327	2,391	550	20,700	1,050	1,783	12,883	6,300	3,860	13,918	4,600	85,501
1999-00	615	3,458	3,216	505	17,600	1,055	2,021	12,180	8,600	3,634	16,968	5,180	87,719
2000-01	758	3,700	4,312	525	20,300	920	2,035	10,931	8,200	3,600	17,188	4,400	88,849
2001-02	300	3,340	3,519	725	24,400	1,441	2,093	12,300	8,300	3,975	20,303	4,900	98,745
2002-03	290	1,680	3,890	750	22,600	1,310	1,715	10,600	7,800	4,179	17,209	4,600	88,251
2003-04	515	1,700	6,015	965	22,300	920	1,530	14,000	7,750	4,100	18,255	4,100	95,267
2004-05	675	3,000	5,900	1,180	29,000	1,285	1,800	19,000	11,143	4,150	23,251	5,200	120,120
2005-06[1]	625	2,800	4,700	1,350	26,200	925	1,975	19,050	9,850	3,550	23,890	5,550	113,940
2006-07[2]	800	1,100	6,000	1,450	30,900	950	1,400	21,500	9,700	4,000	21,729	5,400	116,750

[1] Preliminary.   [2] Estimate.   *Source: Foreign Agricultural Service, U.S. Department of Agriculture (FAS-USDA)*

World Stocks and Trade of Cotton   In Thousands of 480-Pound Bales

Crop Year Beginning Aug. 1	Beginning Stocks United States	Beginning Stocks Uzbek- istan	Beginning Stocks China	Beginning Stocks World Total	Imports Indo- nesia	Imports Mexico	Imports Russia	Imports Turkey	Imports World Total	Exports United States	Exports Uzbek- istan	Exports China	Exports World Total
1997-98	3,971	822	20,197	44,597	1,910	1,371	1,225	1,450	25,928	7,500	4,570	25	26,722
1998-99	3,887	635	24,547	49,351	2,323	1,422	850	1,139	24,480	4,298	3,812	676	23,524
1999-00	3,939	603	26,928	52,162	2,076	1,813	1,600	2,411	27,976	6,750	4,200	1,692	27,195
2000-01	3,915	738	22,378	50,206	2,650	1,865	1,650	1,758	26,227	6,740	3,450	442	26,258
2001-02	6,000	668	19,766	48,230	2,356	2,065	1,800	2,977	29,304	11,000	3,500	342	29,060
2002-03	7,448	918	18,948	53,702	2,228	2,330	1,650	2,265	30,112	11,900	3,400	751	30,322
2003-04	5,385	1,018	14,999	44,217	2,150	1,858	1,475	2,370	34,013	13,758	3,100	173	33,220
2004-05	3,450	923	14,958	43,031	2,200	1,810	1,450	3,414	33,392	14,436	3,950	30	34,975
2005-06[1]	5,495	1,298	13,063	53,868	2,200	1,744	1,425	3,383	44,002	18,036	4,800	36	44,668
2006-07[2]	6,050	1,248	15,661	53,947	2,200	1,500	1,425	3,100	39,014	14,000	4,650	50	38,535

[1] Preliminary.   [2] Estimate.   *Source: Foreign Agricultural Service, U.S. Department of Agriculture (FAS-USDA)*

World Consumption of All Cottons in Specified Countries   In Thousands of 480-Pound Bales

Year	Bangla- desh	Brazil	China	Egypt	India	Indonesia	Mexico	Pakistan	Russia	Thailand	Turkey	United States	World Total
1997-98	651	3,551	18,450	1,056	12,675	1,900	2,035	7,212	1,200	1,376	5,000	11,390	86,686
1998-99	701	3,674	17,975	973	12,620	2,241	2,235	7,025	920	1,335	4,600	10,007	83,646
1999-00	801	4,111	20,575	823	13,547	2,050	2,425	7,675	1,550	1,606	5,600	10,339	90,456
2000-01	1,001	4,025	22,700	773	13,544	2,500	2,125	8,125	1,600	1,685	5,167	8,379	90,794
2001-02	1,201	3,650	25,325	673	13,275	2,350	2,225	8,525	1,800	1,825	6,150	7,876	93,517
2002-03	1,552	3,500	28,925	913	13,300	2,300	2,125	9,425	1,650	1,975	6,300	7,439	97,526
2003-04	1,727	3,850	31,000	913	13,500	2,200	2,025	9,625	1,500	1,875	6,000	6,477	97,246
2004-05	1,880	4,100	37,250	963	14,800	2,200	2,125	10,775	1,425	2,125	7,100	6,799	107,700
2005-06[1]	2,205	4,050	42,850	1,013	16,500	2,225	2,125	11,775	1,425	2,075	6,900	5,326	113,195
2006-07[2]	2,310	3,950	47,000	1,013	18,300	2,225	2,075	12,125	1,425	2,075	7,000	4,994	118,796

[1] Preliminary.   [2] Estimate.   *Source: Foreign Agricultural Service, U.S. Department of Agriculture (FAS-USDA)*

COTTON

Cotton (monthly average) through December 2006   Cents per pound

Cents Per Pound
----- Spot Average, New York (1791 - 1914)
7/8" Middling, Designated Markets (Aug. 1915 - July 1930)
15/16" Middling, Designated Markets (Aug. 1930 - Feb. 1967)
1 1/16" 7 Market Average (Mar. 1967 - date)

Average Spot Cotton Prices[2], C.I.F. Northern Europe   In U.S. Cents Per Pound

Crop Year Beginning Aug. 1	Argentina "C"[3] 1 1/16"	Australia M 1 3/32"	Cotlook Index A	Cotlook Index B	Egypt Giza[4] 81	Greece M 1 3/32"	Mexico[5] M 1 3/32"	Pakistan Sind/ Punjab[6]	Tanzania AR[7] Type 3	Turkey Izmir[8] 1 3/32"	U.S. Calif. ACALA SJV[9]	U.S. Memphis Terr.[10] M 1 3/32"	U.S. Orleans/ Texas[11] M 1 1/32"
1990-1	77.06	85.58	82.90	77.80	177.43	84.24	84.46	77.19	89.62	81.32	92.84	88.13	80.35
1991-2	55.08	65.97	63.05	58.50	128.10	65.90	68.19	58.14	68.90	74.66	74.47	66.35	63.41
1992-3	64.31	64.01	57.70	53.70	99.24	56.92	----	52.66	62.24	----	68.37	63.08	58.89
1993-4	80.20	72.81	70.60	67.30	88.35	58.81	----	54.42	69.83	59.80	77.55	72.80	69.78
1994-5	101.88	81.05	92.75	92.40	93.70	88.64	82.65	73.75	----	----	106.40	98.67	95.70
1995-6	82.98	93.75	85.61	81.06	----	84.95	94.94	81.86	96.20	90.38	103.49	94.71	90.37
1996-7	79.71	83.24	78.59	74.80	----	75.85	79.60	73.37	79.22	----	89.55	82.81	79.77
1997-8	69.96	77.49	72.19	70.69	----	72.03	81.70	72.93	84.04	----	85.11	78.12	74.74
1998-9	57.19	66.48	58.91	54.26	----	58.66	65.78	----	72.70	----	78.57	73.65	70.95
1999-00[1]	----	61.97	52.80	49.55	----	51.71	56.43	----	55.67	----	68.76	60.22	55.67

[1] Preliminary.   [2] Generally for prompt shipment.   [3] 1 1/32 prior to January 20, 1984; 1 1/16 since.   [4] Dendera until 1969/70; Giza 67 1969/70 until December 1983; Giza 69/75/81 until November 1990; Giza 81 since.   [5] S. Brazil Type 5, 1 1/32 prior to 1968-69; 1 1/16 until 1987/88; Brazilian Type 5/6, 1 1/16 since.   [6] Punjab until 1979/80; Sind SG until June 1984; Sind/Punjab SG until January 1985; Afzal 1 until January 1986; Afzal 1 1/32 since.   [7] No. 1 until 1978/79; No. 1/2 until February 1986; AR' Mwanza No. 3 until January 1992; AR' Type 3 since.   [8] Izmir ST 1 White 1 1/16 RG prior to 1981/82; 1 3/32 from 1981/82 until January 1987; Izmir/Antalya ST 1 White -3/32 RG since.   [9] SM 1 3/32 prior to 1975/76; SM 1 1/8 since.   [10] SM 1 1/16 prior to 1981/82; Middling 1 3/32 since.   [11] Middling 1 prior to 1988/89; Middling 1 1/32 since.   *Source: International Cotton Advisory Committee*

Average Producer Price Index of Gray Cotton Broadwovens   Index 1982 = 100

Year	Jan.	Feb.	Mar.	Apr.	May	June	July	Aug.	Sept.	Oct.	Nov.	Dec.	Average
1997	120.3	120.8	120.7	120.8	121.2	120.6	121.4	121.6	121.4	120.8	121.6	121.2	121.0
1998	122.8	122.0	122.1	121.5	121.8	120.8	120.0	119.1	118.8	118.1	117.3	117.8	120.2
1999	117.1	117.3	118.8	116.5	116.4	116.1	116.5	112.9	112.9	113.1	112.6	108.6	114.9
2000	112.1	111.1	106.9	108.2	108.6	107.7	108.3	108.8	110.1	110.2	112.3	112.3	109.7
2001	112.8	113.1	113.1	112.7	112.8	112.9	113.2	112.9	112.9	112.0	111.2	111.1	112.6
2002	110.7	109.9	110.1	108.1	107.3	108.0	106.9	107.0	106.9	105.9	105.7	106.2	107.7
2003	105.7	105.2	105.0	105.9	106.0	106.7	107.2	109.1	110.1	111.0	110.6	108.9	107.6
2004	109.9	111.2	110.6	111.5	112.3	112.6	113.7	113.2	113.5	113.6	113.3	112.5	112.3
2005	112.6	112.0	111.9	111.8	111.2	111.2	111.1	111.2	111.2	111.3	110.9	111.1	111.5
2006[1]	111.1	110.5	109.9	109.9	110.1	110.1	110.1	110.1	110.1	110.0	110.1	109.9	110.2

[1] Preliminary.   *Source: Bureau of Labor Statistics (0337-01), U.S. Department of Commerce*

Average Price of SLM 1 1/16",Cotton[2] at Designated US Mkts   In Cents Per Pound (Net Weight)

Year	Aug.	Sept.	Oct.	Nov.	Dec.	Jan.	Feb.	Mar.	Apr.	May	June	July	Average
1997-98	71.61	70.75	69.46	68.90	64.57	62.75	63.66	67.04	61.88	65.21	73.50	74.18	67.79
1998-99	71.87	71.75	67.61	64.95	59.88	56.20	55.46	58.17	57.01	55.54	53.74	49.23	60.12
1999-00	49.72	48.39	49.46	48.12	46.65	51.92	54.29	57.67	53.76	58.31	54.97	55.13	52.36
2000-01	59.33	60.62	60.54	62.16	61.04	56.66	54.10	47.22	42.19	40.02	37.38	37.48	51.56
2001-02	36.05	33.22	28.42	31.23	32.21	32.13	31.60	33.23	31.86	31.14	36.36	39.78	33.10
2002-03	39.20	37.91	39.62	44.98	46.38	48.60	51.35	53.82	53.38	48.94	50.92	54.45	47.46
2003-04	51.94	58.02	69.38	68.88	65.09	68.21	63.35	61.78	57.50	60.22	52.35	45.05	60.15
2004-05	44.92	47.48	44.55	42.62	41.68	43.21	42.90	48.19	49.58	48.57	45.92	47.78	45.62
2005-06	45.38	47.43	51.02	48.80	49.53	51.91	52.39	50.04	49.00	47.00	47.90	47.15	48.96
2006-07[1]	48.65	46.80	45.15	46.32	49.85	49.90	48.77						47.92

[1] Preliminary.   [2] Grade 41, leaf 4, staple 34, mike 35-36 and 43-49 , strength 23.5-26.4.   *Source: Agricultural Marketing Service, U.S. Department of Agriculture (AMS-USDA)*

Average Spot Cotton, 1 3/32", Price (SLM) at Designated U.S. Markets   In Cents Per Pound (Net Weight)

Year	Aug.	Sept.	Oct.	Nov.	Dec.	Jan.	Feb.	Mar.	Apr.	May	June	July	Average
1997-98	73.69	72.64	71.13	70.35	66.30	64.55	65.78	69.25	64.31	67.66	76.02	76.63	69.86
1998-99	73.93	73.75	69.90	67.18	62.18	58.56	58.27	61.34	60.33	58.89	56.85	52.61	62.82
1999-00	52.90	51.27	52.43	51.51	49.73	55.02	57.38	61.02	57.52	63.09	59.28	58.80	55.83
2000-01	62.60	63.62	63.13	65.08	64.73	60.18	57.18	50.08	44.94	42.54	39.88	39.96	54.49
2001-02	38.88	36.11	31.55	34.03	34.82	34.55	34.08	36.04	34.84	34.03	39.31	42.86	35.93
2002-03	42.31	41.07	43.08	48.78	50.70	52.87	55.34	57.88	57.54	52.96	55.09	58.46	51.34
2003-04	55.87	61.76	73.27	72.63	68.90	71.96	67.34	66.42	63.11	65.97	57.99	51.11	64.69
2004-05	50.45	52.55	49.45	47.23	46.41	48.16	48.17	53.37	54.67	53.76	51.26	52.97	50.70
2005-06	50.59	52.81	56.01	53.78	54.47	56.69	57.16	55.03	54.07	52.02	52.97	52.35	54.00
2006-07[1]	53.80	51.95	50.20	51.13	54.71	54.75							52.76

[1] Preliminary.   *Source: Agricultural Marketing Service, U.S. Department of Agriculture (AMS-USDA)*

Average Spot Prices of U.S. Cotton[2], Base Quality (SLM) at Designated Markets   In Cents Per Pound

Crop Year Beginning Aug. 1	Dallas (East Tex.-Okl.)	Fresno (San Joaquin Valley)	Greenville (South-east)	Greenwood (South Delta)	Lubbock (West Texas)	Memphis (North Delta)	Phoenix Desert (South-west)	Average
1996-97[1]	70.29	74.47	72.33	72.11	69.89	72.11	69.88	71.58
1997-98	65.93	71.79	68.60	68.36	65.88	68.36	65.63	67.79
1998-99	57.66	63.78	62.06	61.82	57.76	61.82	55.92	60.12
1999-00	50.49	56.67	53.81	53.34	50.12	53.34	48.79	52.36
2000-01	51.03	52.45	52.63	52.32	50.71	52.32	49.47	51.56
2001-02	32.59	34.64	33.02	33.24	32.39	33.24	32.60	33.10
2002-03	46.76	47.52	48.28	48.46	46.51	48.47	46.27	47.46
2003-04	59.95	59.71	60.80	60.85	59.71	60.78	59.23	60.15
2004-05	44.22	47.38	45.91	46.02	44.08	46.02	45.66	45.61
2005-06[1]	47.69	50.06	49.65	49.63	47.78	49.67	48.26	48.96

[1] Preliminary.   [2] Prices are for mixed lots, net weight, uncompressed in warehouse.   *Source: Agricultural Marketing Service, U.S. Department of Agriculture (AMS-USDA)*

Average Price[1] Received by Farmers for Upland Cotton in the United States   In Cents Per Pound

Year	Aug.	Sept.	Oct.	Nov.	Dec.	Jan.	Feb.	Mar.	Apr.	May	June	July	Average
1997-98	67.0	69.6	69.4	67.9	63.8	61.1	62.5	63.9	63.6	63.5	69.7	68.0	65.2
1998-99	66.0	66.2	65.9	64.6	60.6	58.1	55.6	55.1	55.6	55.0	54.6	53.8	60.2
1999-00	52.7	45.3	46.3	44.3	42.8	43.1	46.8	47.7	45.4	47.6	45.1	48.8	45.0
2000-01	51.4	50.6	55.5	58.0	57.8	52.1	48.5	41.1	42.6	40.9	39.2	38.9	49.8
2001-02	37.3	36.5	30.7	27.8	30.8	27.3	28.0	28.4	27.2	26.7	33.7	35.3	29.8
2002-03	33.0	35.2	39.4	43.0	44.3	45.5	46.5	48.6	45.4	45.9	45.5	46.3	43.2
2003-04	46.3	55.7	67.8	63.0	63.3	62.2	61.9	61.6	60.3	59.7	59.9	53.8	59.6
2004-05	53.7	49.3	50.6	43.2	39.3	38.5	38.3	40.3	41.4	39.6	41.9	41.1	43.1
2005-06	42.1	44.3	48.5	48.5	48.0	48.6	48.9	50.4	48.6	46.8	47.7	47.1	47.5
2006-07[2]	45.8	47.3	46.1	47.6	49.3	49.7	48.9						47.8

[1] Weighted average by sales.   [2] Preliminary.   *Source: Agricultural Marketing Service, U.S. Department of Agriculture (AMS-USDA)*

COTTON

Purchases Reported by Exchanges in Designated U.S. Spot Markets[1] In Running Bales

Crop Year Beginning Aug. 1	Aug.	Sept.	Oct.	Nov.	Dec.	Jan.	Feb.	Mar.	Apr.	May	June	July	Market Total
1997-98	48,504	106,503	323,400	367,010	617,470	655,432	482,625	396,946	92,072	210,906	105,139	39,647	3,445,654
1998-99	27,193	52,066	114,998	229,743	498,082	414,832	191,872	236,762	71,993	63,335	62,192	64,092	2,027,160
1999-00	83,564	95,241	195,370	320,434	517,579	744,400	294,843	189,460	89,473	129,879	49,012	33,942	2,743,197
2000-01	63,607	69,083	143,938	323,891	288,242	217,755	215,318	191,667	274,185	193,774	152,905	167,647	2,302,012
2001-02	118,000	94,697	214,785	644,860	225,869	289,778	180,362	278,853	84,259	155,391	143,422	93,489	2,523,765
2002-03	43,047	49,671	194,020	204,564	369,838	481,730	432,055	169,064	170,951	213,679	149,780	86,830	2,565,229
2003-04	125,240	245,295	273,028	167,285	321,083	417,090	267,237	167,357	62,031	70,979	79,061	58,400	2,254,086
2004-05	135,568	46,749	91,390	263,999	369,597	402,504	445,448	424,472	210,285	93,471	95,154	20,398	2,599,035
2005-06	67,318	63,884	138,910	220,961	363,287	434,818	183,744	183,273	62,703	73,726	117,934	60,708	1,971,266
2006-07	87,527	58,849	111,619	112,634	214,384	174,852	140,273						1,543,094

[1] Seven markets.   Source: Agricultural Marketing Service, U.S. Department of Agriculture (AMS-USDA)

Production of Cotton (Upland and American-Pima) in the U.S.   In Thousands of 480-Pound Bales

Year	Alabama	Arizona	Arkansas	California	Georgia	Louisiana	Mississippi	Missouri	North Carolina	South Carolina	Tennessee	Texas	Total American-Pima
1997	550	847	1,683	2,191	1,919	986	1,821	565	930	410	662	5,140	548.0
1998	553	608	1,209	1,146	1,542	641	1,731	472	816	281	595	5,050	442.3
1999	625	716	1,428	1,580	1,567	901	1,731	540	1,429	379	710	3,940	389.1
2000	543	791	1,425	2,210	1,663	911	1,711	540	1,429	379	710	3,940	389.1
2001	920	690	1,833	1,770	2,220	1,034	2,396	695	1,673	423	978	4,260	700.4
2002	570	613	1,669	1,460	1,578	739	1,935	610	806	131	818	5,040	678.3
2003	820	550	1,804	1,495	2,110	1,027	2,120	700	1,037	326	890	4,330	432.3
2004	814	723	2,089	1,790	1,797	885	2,346	830	1,360	390	984	7,740	745.6
2005[1]	848	622	2,202	1,623	2,140	1,098	2,147	864	1,437	410	1,122	8,484	630.5
2006[2]	600	593	2,560	1,430	2,120	1,280	2,150	980	1,350	430	1,310	5,735	729.0

[1] Preliminary.   [2] Forecasted.   Source: Agricultural Statistics Board, U.S. Department of Agriculture (ASB-USDA)

Cotton Production and Yield Estimates

Year	Forecast of Production (1,000 Bales of 480 Lbs.[1])						Actual Crop	Forecasts of Yield (Lbs. Per Harvested Acre)						Actual Crop
	Aug. 1	Sept. 1	Oct. 1	Nov. 1	Dec. 1	Jan. 1		Aug. 1	Sept. 1	Oct. 1	Nov. 1	Dec. 1	Jan. 1	
1997	17,783	18,418	18,410	18,848	18,819	18,977	18,793	637	658	665	673	672	686	673
1998	14,263	13,563	13,288	13,231	13,452	----	13,918	640	614	616	612	621	----	625
1999	18,304	17,535	16,430	16,531	16,875	----	16,968	649	621	588	592	604	----	607
2000	19,159	18,315	17,485	17,510	17,399	----	17,188	648	622	620	622	619	----	632
2001	20,003	19,992	20,072	20,175	20,064	----	20,303	670	679	681	685	691	----	705
2002	18,439	18,134	18,070	17,815	17,375	----	17,209	675	675	674	665	648	----	665
2003	17,104	16,939	17,559	18,215	18,215	----	18,255	667	667	696	722	722	----	730
2004	20,183	20,895	21,545	22,545	22,815	----	23,251	727	758	782	818	828	----	855
2005	21,291	22,282	22,717	23,161	23,703	----	23,890	748	782	797	813	832	----	831
2006	20,431	20,345	20,659	21,299	21,297	----	21,729	765	762	774	798	798	----	819

[1] Net weight bales.   Source: Agricultural Statistics Board, U.S. Department of Agriculture (ASB-USDA)

Supply and Distribution of Upland Cotton in the United States   In Thousands of 480-Pound Bales

Crop Year Beginning Aug. 1	Area		Yield Lbs./Acre	Supply				Disappearance				Farm Price[5] Cents/Lb.
	Planted	Harvested		Beginning Stocks[3]	Production[4]	Imports	Total	Mill Use	Exports	Total	Ending Stocks	
	1,000 Acres											
1997-98	13,648	13,157	666	3,920	18,245	13	22,178	11,234	7,060	18,294	3,822	65.2
1998-99	13,064	10,449	619	3,822	13,476	431	17,729	10,254	4,056	14,264	3,836	60.2
1999-00	14,584	13,138	595	3,836	16,294	53	20,183	10,055	6,303	16,358	3,665	45.0
2000-01	15,347	12,884	626	3,665	16,799	8	20,472	8,738	6,303	15,041	5,879	49.8
2001-02	15,499	13,560	694	5,879	19,603	6	25,488	7,592	10,603	18,195	7,120	29.8
2002-03	13,714	12,174	652	7,120	16,530	10	23,661	7,170	11,266	18,436	5,140	43.2
2003-04	13,301	11,826	723	5,140	17,823	3	22,966	6,159	13,220	19,379	3,428	59.6
2004-05	13,409	12,809	843	3,384	22,505	8	25,897	6,629	13,645	20,274	5,482	43.1
2005-06[1]	13,975	13,534	825	5,482	23,260	9	28,751	5,837	17,437	23,274	5,981	47.5
2006-07[2]	14,948	12,408	811	5,981	20,973	10	26,501	5,150	15,450	20,600	5,912	47.8

[1] Preliminary.   [2] Estimate.   [3] Excludes preseason ginnings (adjusted to 480-lb. bale net weight basis).   [4] Includes preseason ginnings.   [5] Marketing year average price.   Source: Economic Research Service, U.S. Department of Agriculture (ERS-USDA)

Cotton Futures - New York Board of Trade
(weekly close) as of December 29, 2006
Cents per pound

Average Open Interest of #2 Cotton Futures in New York   In Contracts

Year	Jan.	Feb.	Mar.	Apr.	May	June	July	Aug.	Sept.	Oct.	Nov.	Dec.
1997	59,909	65,392	72,130	76,779	73,464	70,296	73,893	79,309	87,134	92,430	89,150	87,120
1998	89,358	86,739	81,236	85,505	84,562	90,178	81,652	78,571	85,378	88,970	88,917	77,873
1999	79,598	75,794	62,857	60,384	61,470	66,789	68,975	65,690	63,976	60,369	63,746	61,474
2000	63,987	67,720	69,788	56,038	54,058	48,024	53,621	63,069	73,735	67,767	65,017	62,931
2001	71,849	73,383	71,389	70,407	66,680	64,032	61,183	65,257	65,496	59,777	56,896	58,156
2002	64,096	64,572	63,451	63,827	67,601	65,848	74,892	72,612	69,554	71,526	82,802	74,685
2003	83,775	89,852	91,336	78,658	73,146	69,137	62,565	62,781	80,348	108,981	97,809	79,627
2004	93,191	81,871	84,600	89,082	81,988	79,310	77,029	75,449	69,514	76,556	86,280	84,409
2005	92,651	94,047	118,183	120,416	103,446	93,818	92,284	99,959	105,874	117,889	103,466	100,660
2006	118,234	129,108	129,728	141,156	165,386	170,190	161,719	166,806	178,539	184,002	170,275	164,797

Source: New York Board of Trade (NYBOT)

Volume of Trading of #2 Cotton Futures in New York   In Contracts

Year	Jan.	Feb.	Mar.	Apr.	May	June	July	Aug.	Sept.	Oct.	Nov.	Dec.	Total
1997	201,610	253,475	302,609	258,851	175,227	314,406	234,718	202,008	212,966	216,771	266,800	197,839	2,837,280
1998	221,308	289,222	310,075	362,688	218,595	407,922	226,138	230,752	195,690	303,849	272,775	161,816	3,200,830
1999	179,049	244,300	209,127	250,622	157,552	260,649	187,631	178,236	175,282	193,552	298,531	120,120	2,454,651
2000	270,792	279,566	248,017	220,222	232,947	272,023	147,878	175,707	154,735	172,875	242,013	180,982	2,597,757
2001	267,930	270,876	237,356	215,903	175,808	214,513	132,065	118,685	98,947	152,702	258,847	116,033	2,259,665
2002	156,834	248,299	162,781	237,861	188,340	234,442	170,893	128,185	145,946	199,779	296,859	157,741	2,327,960
2003	202,615	267,234	217,791	325,627	249,314	271,822	164,027	127,080	283,988	422,132	356,052	148,310	3,035,992
2004	272,948	359,105	300,820	376,669	184,869	357,548	159,924	195,886	196,739	224,431	341,709	185,370	3,156,018
2005	356,817	407,277	317,486	465,210	306,971	456,584	171,139	189,584	271,268	290,650	408,580	207,424	3,848,990
2006	311,926	495,729	375,624	515,709	330,785	601,971	184,482	259,259	268,847	308,584	587,710	249,781	4,490,407

Source: New York Board of Trade (NYBOT)

COTTON

Daily Rate of Upland Cotton Mill Consumption[2] on Cotton-System Spinning Spindles in the U.S.
In Thousands of Running Bales

Crop Year Beginning Aug. 1	Aug.	Sept.	Oct.	Nov.	Dec.	Jan.	Feb.	Mar.	Apr.	May	June	July	Average
1997-98	40.7	42.4	42.0	42.4	43.9	41.8	41.7	41.1	40.5	40.8	40.0	41.5	41.6
1998-99	39.3	38.7	39.9	37.4	37.5	38.6	38.2	37.9	37.8	37.5	37.7	36.8	38.1
1999-00	36.1	36.4	37.3	37.2	37.6	36.8	37.5	37.6	37.5	37.0	38.1	36.5	37.1
2000-01	36.4	35.6	34.5	33.0	34.4	33.5	31.9	31.8	30.6	29.7	27.6	28.6	32.3
2001-02	28.8	28.1	27.5	26.3	27.1	27.1	27.5	27.9	27.4	28.4	29.3	30.6	28.0
2002-03	28.0	28.3	27.9	27.4	27.2	26.5	26.8	26.4	26.0	25.0	24.3	24.7	26.5
2003-04	23.0	22.7	22.6	23.0	22.7	21.8	22.7	22.7	22.2	22.7	23.0	24.2	22.8
2004-05	25.2	24.9	24.9	24.3	25.1	24.8	24.0	24.0	24.2	23.9	25.7	25.0	24.7
2005-06	23.1	22.0	22.5	21.0	20.2	22.9	23.2	22.2	20.8	20.4	20.8	19.9	21.6
2006-07[1]	18.8	19.0	18.5										18.8

[1] Preliminary.   [2] Not seasonally adjusted.   Source: Bureau of the Census: U.S. Department of Commerce

Consumption of American and Foreign Cotton in the United States   In Thousands of Running Bales

Year	Aug.	Sept.	Oct.	Nov.	Dec.	Jan.	Feb.	Mar.	Apr.	May	June	July	Total
1997-98	868	1,100	872	855	951	848	861	1,068	839	854	1,017	770	10,902
1998-99	835	1,013	834	758	796	979	795	983	777	793	970	678	10,210
1999-00	762	949	793	757	801	736	769	966	772	771	990	670	9,735
2000-01	766	929	741	663	749	661	657	837	641	628	727	510	8,510
2001-02	616	751	600	521	563	541	580	759	575	594	754	571	7,425
2002-03	574	733	585	545	598	671	556	708	541	523	616	456	7,106
2003-04	476	599	482	468	504	478	475	609	461	473	582	446	6,053
2004-05	484	604	483	460	500	470	472	601	469	463	581	449	6,035
2005-06	454	574	472	415	438	452	476	593	430	422	531	381	5,637
2006-07[1]	385	492	389	357	370	361							4,706

[1] Preliminary.   Source: Bureau of the Census, U.S. Department of Commerce

Exports of All Cotton[2] from the United States   In Thousands of Running Bales

Year	Aug.	Sept.	Oct.	Nov.	Dec.	Jan.	Feb.	Mar.	Apr.	May	June	July	Total
1997-98	458	299	400	581	774	734	777	888	669	477	574	571	7,202
1998-99	402	280	265	795	1,027	156	182	221	169	256	260	330	4,344
1999-00	254	146	167	455	654	658	736	978	708	659	508	479	6,402
2000-01	430	336	382	435	541	564	614	720	568	692	784	648	6,715
2001-02	612	824	678	649	927	964	1,042	1,225	999	842	1,067	679	10,505
2002-03	472	653	373	626	935	1,206	873	1,597	1,174	1,150	1,273	1,231	11,561
2003-04	810	555	446	758	1,116	1,194	1,238	1,869	1,453	1,117	1,576	1,021	13,154
2004-05	760	374	422	632	1,087	1,179	1,214	1,839	1,461	1,094	1,411	1,828	13,301
2005-06	1,407	742	533	763	1,236	946	1,541	2,195	1,758	1,725	1,906	1,903	16,655
2006-07[1]	688	412	487	599	812	683							7,361

[1] Preliminary.   Source: Foreign Agricultural Service, U.S. Department of Agriculture (FAS-USDA)

U.S. Exports of American Cotton to Countries of Destination   In Thousands of 480-Pound Bales

Crop Year Beginning Aug. 1	Canada	China	Hong Kong	Indonesia	Italy	Japan	Rep. of Korea	Mexico	Philippines	Taiwan	Thailand	United Kingdom	Total
1996-97	253	1,756	129	594	46	630	568	733	84	197	255	66	6,862
1997-98	288	737	151	464	85	637	712	1,447	53	220	376	13	7,202
1998-99	281	71	245	229	29	406	381	1,359	59	82	249	6	4,298
1999-00	245	147	316	573	61	424	307	1,500	71	257	476	4	6,401
2000-01	322	124	287	558	52	355	489	1,760	42	237	367	1	6,740
2001-02	235	306	407	947	58	385	577	1,516	126	693	693	0	10,397
2002-03	303	1,840	364	869	81	380	480	1,777	104	592	556	4	11,607
2003-04	303	4,919	169	889	63	284	469	1,620	100	527	396	20	13,758
2004-05[1]	305	4,085	274	1,138	75	301	643	1,589	110	846	711	60	14,436
2005-06[2]	154	8,085	246	773	31	218	384	1,226	33	449	566	23	15,603

[1] Preliminary.   [2] Estimate.   Source: Foreign Agricultural Service, U.S. Department of Agriculture (FAS-USDA)

Cotton[1] Government Loan Program in the United States

Crop Year Beginning Aug. 1	Support Price -- Cents Per Lb. --	Target Price -- Cents Per Lb. --	Put Under Support Ths Bales	% of Pro-duction	Acquired ----- Ths. Bales -----	Owned July 31 ----- Ths. Bales -----	Crop Year Beginning Aug. 1	Support Price -- Cents Per Lb. --	Target Price -- Cents Per Lb. --	Put Under Support Ths Bales	% of Pro-duction	Acquired ----- Ths. Bales -----	Owned July 31 ----- Ths. Bales -----
1996-97	51.92	NA	3,340	18.1	0	0	2001-02	51.92	NA	13,655	69.7	257	2
1997-98	51.92	NA	4,281	23.5	1	0	2002-03	52.00	74.2	12,740	77.1	44	106
1998-99	51.92	NA	4,724	36.8	31	3	2003-04	52.00	74.2	10,345	58.0	4	0
1999-00	51.92	NA	8,721	54.9	0	1	2004-05	52.00	72.4	17,091	79.1	0	0
2000-01	51.92	NA	8,837	52.6	89	5	2005-06[2]	52.00	74.2				

[1] Upland. [2] Preliminary. [3] Less than 500 bales. NA = Not applicable. *Source: Economic Research Service, U.S. Department of Agriculture (ERS-USDA)*

Production of Cotton Cloth[1] in the United States   In Millions of Square Yards

Year	First Quarter	Second Quarter	Third Quarter	Fourth Quarter	Total Year	Year	First Quarter	Second Quarter	Third Quarter	Fourth Quarter	Total Year
1997	1,211	1,276	1,283	1,309	5,078	2002	893	912	894	825	3,524
1998	1,226	1,167	1,218	1,142	4,753	2003	836	780	662	620	2,898
1999	1,170	1,164	1,078	1,039	4,451	2004	648	644	640	614	2,547
2000	1,075	1,129	1,111	1,079	4,395	2005	672	640	653	664	2,629
2001	1,047	976	873	811	3,706	2006[2]	583	609	542		2,312

[1] Cotton broadwoven goods over 12 inches in width. [2] Preliminary. *Source: Bureau of Census, U.S. Department of Commerce*

Cotton Ginnings[1] in the United States To: In Thousands of Running Bales

Crop Year	Aug. 1	Sept. 1	Sept. 15	Oct. 1	Oct. 15	Nov. 1	Nov. 15	Dec. 1	Dec. 15	Jan. 1	Jan. 15	Feb. 1	Total Crop
1997-98	2	359	683	1,210	3,752	7,930	11,601	14,735	16,662	17,613	18,013	18,170	18,301
1998-99	146	523	739	2,056	4,265	7,359	9,366	11,310	12,558	13,160	13,376	13,458	13,534
1999-00	81	561	1,018	2,690	4,885	8,263	11,006	13,379	14,992	15,965	16,322	16,468	16,528
2000-01	245	842	1,454	3,264	5,930	9,221	11,546	13,657	15,364	16,097	16,518	16,648	16,742
2001-02	99	609	802	2,072	4,616	8,806	12,558	15,564	17,606	18,759	19,268	19,532	19,771
2002-03	56	538	898	1,656	3,520	6,697	9,265	12,368	14,392	15,654	16,285	16,576	16,710
2003-04	29	567	958	2,001	3,819	7,393	10,507	13,466	15,678	16,883	17,409	17,601	17,709
2004-05	48	563	1,157	2,227	4,788	8,758	12,019	14,754	17,072	18,925	20,155	21,249	22,556
2005-06	69	592	976	2,314	4,556	8,691	12,569	15,991	18,401	20,108	21,282	22,255	23,253
2006-07[2]	23	406	996	2,589	5,043	8,742	11,833	15,142	17,711	19,219	20,132	20,590	21,729

[1] Excluding linters. [2] Preliminary. *Source: National Agricultural Statistics Service, U.S. Department of Agriculture (NASS-USDA)*

Fiber Prices in the United States   In Cents Per Pound

Year	Cotton[1] Actual	Cotton[1] Raw[5] Equivalent	Rayon[2] Actual	Rayon[2] Raw[5] Equivalent	Polyester[3] Actual	Polyester[3] Raw[5] Equivalent	Price Ratios[4] in Percent Cotton/ Rayon	Price Ratios[4] in Percent Cotton/ Polyester
1998	74.21	82.45	110.25	114.84	62.50	65.11	.72	1.29
1999	61.45	68.28	98.92	103.04	51.67	53.82	.66	1.27
2000	64.06	71.17	97.58	101.65	57.08	59.46	70.00	119.10
2001	47.08	52.32	98.50	102.61	60.42	62.93	52.0	83.0
2002	45.56	50.63	97.83	101.91	61.17	63.72	50.0	79.0
2003	62.54	69.49	90.25	94.01	60.67	63.20	74.1	111.0
2004	60.42	67.13	99.08	103.21	62.67	65.28	66.5	103.5
2005	54.75	60.00	114.58	119.36	67.75	70.57	51.0	86.2
2006[6]	56.70	63.00	113.00	117.71	69.00	71.86	53.5	88.0
Jan.	59.55	66.17	113.00	117.71	65.00	67.71	56.2	97.7
Feb.	60.94	67.71	113.00	117.71	65.00	67.71	57.5	100.0
Mar.	57.77	64.19	113.00	117.71	65.00	67.71	54.5	94.8
Apr.	56.35	62.61	113.00	117.71	65.00	67.71	53.2	92.5
May	53.69	59.66	113.00	117.71	67.00	69.79	50.7	85.5
June	56.64	62.93	113.00	117.71	67.00	69.79	53.5	90.2
July	55.96	62.18	113.00	117.71	69.00	71.88	52.8	86.5
Aug.	57.45	63.83	113.00	117.71	69.00	71.88	54.2	88.8
Sept.	54.78	60.87	113.00	117.71	74.00	77.08	51.7	79.0
Oct.	53.67	59.63	113.00	117.71	74.00	77.00	50.7	77.4
Nov.	54.82	60.91	113.00	117.71	74.00	77.00	51.7	79.0
Dec.	58.74	65.27	113.00	117.71	74.00	77.00	55.4	84.7

[1] SLM-1 1/16 at group B Mill points, net weight. [2] 1.5 and 3.0 denier, regular rayon staples. [3] Reported average market price for 1.5 denier polyester staple for cotton blending. [4] Raw fiber equivalent. [5] Actual prices converted to estimated raw fiber equivalent as follows: cotton, divided by 0.90, rayon and polyester, divided by 0.96. [6] Preliminary. *Source: Economic Research Service, U.S. Department of Agriculture (ERS-USDA)*

Cottonseed and Products

Cottonseed is crushed to produce both oil and meal. Cottonseed oil is typically used for cooking oil and cottonseed meal is fed to livestock. Before the cottonseed is crushed for oil and meal, it is de-linted of its linters. Linters are used for padding in furniture, absorbent cotton swabs, and for the manufacture of many cellulose products. The sediment left by cottonseed oil refining, called foots, provides fatty acids for industrial products. The value of cottonseeds represents a substantial 18% of a cotton producer's income.

Prices – The monthly average price of cottonseed oil in 2006 fell by –6.0% yr/yr to 28.56 cents per pound. The average monthly price of cottonseed meal in 2006 rose by +9.0% yr/yr to $142.28 per ton, but still well below 2004's 9-year high of $169.45 per ton.

Supply – World production of cottonseed in the 2005-6 marketing year fell –6.2% yr/yr to 42.555 million metric tons, down from the record high of 45.354 million metric tons posted in 2004-05. The world's largest cottonseed producers are China with 24% of world production, India with 19%, the US with 17%, and Pakistan with 10%. US production of cottonseed in the 2006-07 marketing year fell by –6.6% yr/yr to 7.632 million tons. US production of cottonseed oil in 2006-07 fell by –7.5% yr/yr to 880 million pounds, down from the 9-year high of 957 million pounds posted in 2004-05. US annualized production of cottonseed cake and meal in six months of the 2006-07 marketing year (Aug-Jan) fell by -8.8% yr/yr to 1.257 million tons.

Demand – US cottonseed crushed (consumed) in the US annualized for six months of the 2006-07 marketing year fell by –18.7% to 2.480 million tons, far below the levels of over 4 million tons seen in the 1970s.

Trade – US exports of cottonseed in 2006-07 rose +9.9% to 575,000 short tons, while imports were virtually zero.

World Production of Cottonseed   In Thousands of Metric Ton

Crop Year	Argen-tina	Australia	Brazil	China	Egypt	Greece	India	Mexico	Pakistan	Turkey	United States	Former USSR	World Total
1997-98	542	941	763	8,193	564	590	5,150	348	3,124	1,193	6,291	2,692	34,522
1998-99	337	1,012	961	8,012	379	665	5,420	369	2,990	1,282	4,867	2,580	32,868
1999-00	223	1,047	1,310	6,817	385	740	5,300	237	3,824	1,159	5,764	2,832	33,398
2000-01	257	1,062	1,720	7,868	371	726	4,760	128	3,651	1,289	5,838	2,531	33,914
2001-02	102	1,054	1,407	9,476	527	743	5,372	152	3,610	1,320	6,761	2,753	37,360
2002-03	90	470	1,451	8,750	480	718	4,624	68	3,472	1,457	5,610	2,575	33,634
2003-04	159	494	2,390	8,669	330	611	6,018	119	3,416	1,419	6,046	2,439	36,218
2004-05[1]	170	912	2,308	11,250	480	680	8,000	210	4,976	1,450	7,437	2,885	45,354
2005-06[2]	173	819	1,793	10,000	335	720	8,200	225	4,220	1,250	7,414	3,056	42,555

[1] Preliminary. [2] Estimate. *Source: The Oil World*

Salient Statistics of Cottonseed in the United States   In Thousands of Short Tons

	Supply			Disappearance					Products Produced		
Crop Year Beginning Aug. 1	Stocks	Pro-duction	Total Supply	Crush	Exports	Other	Total Disap-pearance	Farm Price $/Ton	Value of Pro-duction Mil. $	Oil Million Lbs.	Meal Thousand Sh. Tons
1998-99	563	5,365	6,135	2,719	68	2,955	5,742	129	687.2	832	1,232
1999-00	393	6,354	7,055	3,079	198	3,505	6,781	89	565.5	939	1,390
2000-01	274	6,436	7,084	2,753	235	3,669	6,657	105	675.7	847	1,338
2001-02	427	7,452	8,206	2,791	274	4,742	7,807	91	667.3	876	1,294
2002-03	400	6,184	6,687	2,495	370	3,477	6,341	101	616.4	725	1,115
2003-04	347	6,665	7,013	2,643	354	3,595	6,592	117	779.0	874	1,244
2004-05	421	8,242	8,664	2,923	379	4,770	8,072	107	872.8	957	1,362
2005-06[1]	592	8,172	8,764	3,011	523	4,629	8,163	96	779.5	951	1,373
2006-07[2]	602	7,632	8,234	2,800	575	4,405	7,780	101-124	842.9	880	1,300

[1] Preliminary. [2] Estimate. *Source: Economic Research Service, U.S. Department of Agriculture (ERS-USDA)*

Average Wholesale Price of Cottonseed Meal (41% Solvent)[2] in Memphis   In Dollars Per Short Ton

Year	Jan.	Feb.	Mar.	Apr.	May	June	July	Aug.	Sept.	Oct.	Nov.	Dec.	Average
1998	153.10	139.10	128.70	116.25	105.00	129.40	146.65	130.30	115.60	106.50	107.90	119.75	124.85
1999	110.60	101.25	106.90	110.90	108.75	114.50	115.00	100.65	111.92	111.83	112.00	124.20	110.71
2000	126.88	130.50	129.38	125.00	123.25	130.63	131.88	130.50	153.12	150.00	141.88	160.83	136.15
2001	184.00	148.75	138.13	140.00	137.50	126.88	129.69	130.63	131.25	131.25	128.13	134.17	138.37
2002	133.13	125.00	131.88	124.30	120.88	137.50	151.50	159.75	156.38	150.10	150.00	156.00	141.37
2003	157.38	143.60	142.40	142.40	131.75	131.50	143.00	151.70	153.20	163.50	182.50	185.00	152.33
2004	188.00	193.00	205.10	219.67	203.00	185.40	177.50	156.20	142.75	126.75	119.00	117.00	169.45
2005	112.50	111.25	110.80	108.00	110.40	138.75	151.00	143.00	140.00	133.13	132.50	175.00	130.53
2006[1]	172.50	152.50	148.75	144.38	131.50	135.00	132.50	134.50	139.00	132.40	131.88	152.50	142.28

[1] Preliminary. *Source: Economic Research Service, U.S. Department of Agriculture (ERS-USDA)*

Cottonseed Meal (monthly average) through December 2006 — USD per short ton

USD Per Ton
----- 36% Protein, Memphis, TN (Aug. 1910 - Sept. 1920)
41% Protein, Memphis, TN (Oct. 1920 - Sept. 1946)
41% Protein (Expeller), Memphis, TN (Oct. 1946 - Dec. 1981)
41% Protein (Solvent), Clarksdale, MS (Jan. 1982 - date)

Supply and Distribution of Cottonseed Oil in the United States   In Millions of Pounds

Crop Year Beginning Oct. 1	Supply				Disappearance			Per Capita Cunsump. of Salad & Cook Oils - In Lbs. -	Utilization Food Uses			Prices	
	Stocks	Pro-duction	Imports	Total Supply	Domestic	Exports	Total		Short-ening	Salad & Cooking Oils	Total	U.S.[3] (Crude) ------ $/Met. Ton ------	Rott[4] (Cif)
2000-01	49	847	0	896	673	131	804	34	188	304	426	352	428
2001-02	93	876	0	969	779	150	930	36	185	203	539	396	441
2002-03	39	725	21.0	786	640	110	750	38	195	302	427	832	920
2003-04	36	874	0	910	690	111	801	38	167	295		688	814
2004-05	109	957	2.0	1,068	935	57	991	37	166	304		617	
2005-06[1]	76	951	1.0	1,029	860	67	928	40	213	390		649	
2006-07[2]	101	880	0	981	841	75	916					658	

[1] Preliminary.   [2] Estimate.   [3] Valley Points FOB; Tank Cars.   [4] Rotterdam; US, PBSY, fob gulf.   W = Withheld proprietary data.
Source: Economic Research Service, U.S. Department of Agriculture (ERS-USDA)

Consumption of Crude Cottonseed Oil in Refining in the United States   In Millions of Pounds

Year	Oct.	Nov.	Dec.	Jan.	Feb.	Mar.	Apr.	May	June	July	Aug.	Sept.	Total
2000-01	56.9	53.7	56.7	67.4	61.6	59.5	38.1	46.0	51.4	42.8	49.6	29.8	613.6
2001-02	48.5	63.9	61.6	65.2	58.3	58.9	56.6	56.9	45.2	37.1	53.0	47.5	652.7
2002-03	48.5	59.5	56.0	66.8	55.8	57.1	59.2	49.7	42.4	31.9	38.7	34.9	600.5
2003-04	60.1	63.5	61.6	64.5	58.6	68.5	55.1	55.2	52.5	43.8	53.6	52.2	689.1
2004-05	60.0	66.4	67.0	73.7	69.2	66.8	72.6	52.9	64.7	57.0	71.8	55.2	777.1
2005-06	72.7	79.0	75.1	70.9	64.0	71.1	58.2	71.6	61.2	52.6	61.4	52.4	790.2
2006-07[1]	65.7	55.7	62.0										733.5

[1] Preliminary.   Source: U.S. Bureau of Census, U.S. Department of Commerce

Exports of Cottonseed Oil (Crude and Refined) from the United States   In Thousands of Pounds

Year	Jan.	Feb.	Mar.	Apr.	May	June	July	Aug.	Sept.	Oct.	Nov.	Dec.	Total
2000	10,627	9,447	13,181	8,258	7,402	7,550	11,546	10,642	16,467	13,263	11,652	8,898	128,934
2001	14,684	6,638	7,237	10,595	12,722	7,525	10,325	20,809	6,439	19,891	5,662	19,831	142,359
2002	12,905	17,550	12,137	8,319	21,013	9,444	7,863	8,727	6,831	12,698	11,105	10,761	139,352
2003	7,017	8,483	10,054	8,234	9,706	8,161	6,593	8,663	8,764	8,640	9,349	8,176	101,839
2004	14,203	8,982	8,321	10,399	9,632	10,720	7,931	9,891	4,617	5,669	7,619	7,507	105,492
2005	3,490	3,161	5,191	3,461	5,873	3,029	3,147	3,763	4,823	3,847	2,926	4,676	47,387
2006[1]	5,084	5,676	5,410	7,738	5,519	6,510	7,587	6,608	5,755	8,827	9,377	14,365	88,456

[1] Preliminary.   Source: Economic Research Service, U.S. Department of Agriculture (ERS-USDA)

COTTONSEED AND PRODUCTS

Cottonseed Crushed (Consumption) in the United States   In Thousands of Short Tons

Year	Aug.	Sept.	Oct.	Nov.	Dec.	Jan.	Feb.	Mar.	Apr.	May	June	July	Total
1998-99	246.0	174.9	272.7	254.3	262.7	282.2	259.5	280.2	205.5	172.0	159.9	149.2	2,719
1999-00	166.8	230.7	281.6	302.5	296.4	300.2	299.4	297.7	263.5	250.3	221.3	153.5	3,064
2000-01	170.8	141.1	265.9	252.3	241.5	295.2	268.7	261.9	186.0	228.3	241.9	199.2	2,753
2001-02	186.8	147.6	267.5	287.0	273.1	281.3	253.2	251.8	243.0	233.3	200.3	166.3	2,791
2002-03	195.1	131.4	207.8	242.5	236.6	274.5	224.5	230.4	241.5	203.6	179.4	127.4	2,495
2003-04	138.7	98.9	251.6	254.8	252.0	265.2	242.3	278.0	217.1	240.2	217.7	182.4	2,639
2004-05	193.8	141.0	247.9	260.3	263.5	283.1	266.3	270.2	287.7	221.0	266.6	221.6	2,923
2005-06	240.7	170.3	272.2	289.4	296.9	291.3	245.0	276.7	235.0	280.3	227.2	203.4	3,028
2006-07[1]	204.8	158.2	252.4	223.3	236.7	164.7							2,480

[1] Preliminary.   *Source: Economic Research Service, U.S. Department of Agriculture* (ERS-USDA)

Production of Cottonseed Cake and Meal in the United States   In Thousands of Short Tons

Year	Aug.	Sept.	Oct.	Nov.	Dec.	Jan.	Feb.	Mar.	Apr.	May	June	July	Total
1998-99	114.7	77.1	118.7	115.9	122.5	130.2	114.8	127.2	90.6	75.6	75.6	71.0	1,234
1999-00	82.1	107.5	132.1	140.8	138.3	135.3	137.7	140.2	120.0	109.4	109.3	79.5	1,432
2000-01	74.1	79.3	134.1	121.4	117.1	136.0	118.9	120.3	83.4	101.0	114.3	89.7	1,290
2001-02	83.9	70.8	118.5	126.5	118.2	129.0	112.5	115.0	109.2	107.9	96.3	73.7	1,261
2002-03	92.4	79.3	95.5	112.6	108.0	123.0	100.3	96.7	108.9	89.8	81.4	63.0	1,151
2003-04	74.9	59.5	112.3	111.0	112.5	113.9	105.1	123.4	94.2	104.7	97.7	91.0	1,200
2004-05	95.3	82.5	105.4	110.4	118.7	125.7	119.3	120.4	124.4	103.6	121.0	106.2	1,333
2005-06	116.4	91.1	109.6	134.6	129.3	128.8	108.2	119.4	104.5	129.3	107.2	99.0	1,377
2006-07[1]	102.0	83.0	118.8	101.8	102.4	120.4							1,257

[1] Preliminary.   *Source: Bureau of Census, U.S. Department of Commerce*

Production of Crude Cottonseed Oil[2] in the United States   In Millions of Pounds

Year	Aug.	Sept.	Oct.	Nov.	Dec.	Jan.	Feb.	Mar.	Apr.	May	June	July	Total
1998-99	77.8	59.6	78.3	80.0	80.6	84.0	80.2	86.7	64.4	53.4	52.4	45.9	843
1999-00	56.1	69.6	88.3	95.4	94.2	93.4	93.2	93.8	82.6	75.7	70.2	49.2	962
2000-01	55.1	52.1	84.3	76.8	73.5	85.9	78.4	76.4	53.9	66.8	66.6	55.7	826
2001-02	57.5	42.2	79.4	86.2	81.7	87.5	78.3	78.2	74.6	74.5	61.8	50.6	853
2002-03	60.2	53.7	62.8	72.1	67.9	80.8	65.6	66.7	71.0	59.9	52.8	39.9	753
2003-04	45.0	40.7	77.5	78.2	79.0	82.4	75.7	87.2	67.0	73.8	66.7	59.7	833
2004-05	68.6	58.1	77.1	82.2	81.4	88.7	83.4	84.3	90.7	71.3	81.6	69.5	937
2005-06	84.3	62.0	86.9	95.7	90.9	92.8	77.2	87.8	70.9	90.4	70.4	68.1	977
2006-07[1]	68.4	59.2	77.1	71.7	73.9	81.9							864

[1] Preliminary.   [2] Not seasonally adjusted.   *Source: Bureau of Census, U.S. Department of Commerce*

Production of Refined Cottonseed Oil in the United States   In Millions of Pounds

Year	Aug.	Sept.	Oct.	Nov.	Dec.	Jan.	Feb.	Mar.	Apr.	May	June	July	Total
1998-99	55.8	29.1	51.1	47.9	48.5	45.4	47.3	49.0	35.2	27.4	27.5	29.7	494
1999-00	44.8	42.4	50.4	55.6	59.5	58.3	56.7	65.8	60.0	51.0	41.9	22.0	608
2000-01	44.4	36.2	55.1	52.2	54.9	65.7	59.8	57.8	36.9	44.8	50.0	41.5	599
2001-02	49.4	29.6	48.2	63.6	61.3	64.9	58.0	58.5	56.2	56.7	45.2	36.8	628
2002-03	52.7	47.1	48.3	59.2	55.7	66.5	55.6	56.8	58.9	49.4	42.4	31.7	624
2003-04	38.5	34.6	59.8	63.5	61.4	64.3	58.4	68.3	55.1	55.1	52.4	43.8	655
2004-05	53.4	52.0	59.7	66.1	66.9	73.4	68.8	66.6	72.3	52.7	64.6	56.6	753
2005-06	71.2	54.7	72.8	78.5	74.7	70.3	63.8	70.8	57.8	71.2	60.8	52.3	799
2006-07[1]	61.0	52.0	65.2	55.3	61.5								708

[1] Preliminary.   *Source: Bureau of the Census, U.S. Department of Commerce*

Stocks of Cottonseed Oil (Crude and Refined) in the U.S., at End of Month   In Millions of Pounds

Year	Aug.	Sept.	Oct.	Nov.	Dec.	Jan.	Feb.	Mar.	Apr.	May	June	July
1998-99	97.3	78.6	89.1	110.0	85.5	109.5	113.3	125.3	126.0	112.0	100.7	83.7
1999-00	107.8	76.0	81.1	88.7	85.1	84.5	79.6	115.2	127.4	127.5	103.0	81.3
2000-01	59.9	49.0	66.5	75.2	95.0	109.5	134.4	139.9	133.5	123.5	126.8	114.0
2001-02	97.7	91.8	113.8	112.9	109.8	124.9	120.3	106.9	110.3	97.3	82.7	61.8
2002-03	46.1	39.7	32.8	40.2	38.0	46.1	58.8	72.2	83.3	84.2	91.4	64.0
2003-04	50.5	36.0	51.9	56.1	68.7	85.9	100.6	117.6	116.8	125.7	121.0	123.0
2004-05	123.3	109.0	106.6	110.6	111.3	116.6	122.0	112.9	121.2	111.5	90.0	86.2
2005-06	90.6	76.4	69.0	76.1	74.0	84.0	99.0	108.5	103.3	110.8	105.895.6	
2006-07[1]	98.9	101.1	93.2	92.3	107.2							

[1] Preliminary.   *Source: Bureau of Census, U.S. Department of Commerce*

Cottonseed Oil (monthly average) through December 2006   Cents per pound

Cents Per Pound
----- Prime Yellow Summer, New York (1875 - 1908)
Crude, FOB Southeast Mills (Aug. 1909 - Dec. 1974)
PBSY, Greenwood, MS (Jan. 1975 - date)

Average Price of Crude Cottonseed Oil, PBSY, Greenwood, MS. in Tank Cars   In Cents Per Pound

Year	Jan.	Feb.	Mar.	Apr.	May	June	July	Aug.	Sept.	Oct.	Nov.	Dec.	Average
1997	25.21	25.44	26.18	25.10	25.19	25.01	26.53	27.11	28.03	28.47	29.11	26.78	26.51
1998	27.69	29.37	30.46	32.47	33.13	30.22	29.40	30.11	33.26	33.99	34.16	33.40	31.47
1999	31.72	28.21	26.27	24.39	24.25	25.19	24.70	21.39	20.22	20.15	19.69	21.25	23.95
2000	21.98	22.65	23.70	24.57	22.97	21.54	21.03	20.17	18.52	18.16	17.83	17.25	20.86
2001	16.24	15.20	15.53	14.03	14.53	13.27	16.78	17.18	15.78	14.44	15.91	16.07	15.41
2002	16.38	15.89	16.77	16.98	17.95	19.48	21.30	22.32	22.32	26.84	36.90	46.89	23.34
2003	49.82	49.90	47.52	44.57	42.33	28.69	24.38	25.51	29.64	32.93	32.24	33.26	36.73
2004	32.76	34.21	34.91	34.47	32.57	30.72	27.83	25.29	23.29	22.74	23.88	23.81	28.87
2005	23.70	24.38	28.19	29.80	30.63	33.13	34.15	30.44	31.25	34.44	34.09	30.50	30.39
2006	29.63	29.50	29.75	27.05	28.06	27.25	29.20	26.69	27.13	27.44	30.25	30.75	28.56

Source: Economic Research Service, U.S. Department of Agriculture (ERS-USDA)

Exports of Cottonseed Oil to Important Countries from the United States   In Thousands of Metric Tons

Year	Canada	Dominican Republic	Egypt	Guate-mala	Japan	Mexico	Nether-lands	El Salvador	South Korea	Turkey	Vene-zuela	Total
1997	28.0	.0		.4	11.3	2.5	4.2	25.3	1.9	2.5		110.6
1998	37.6	.1	0	0	6.0	6.1	0	16.1	2.1	0	.0	86.9
1999	37.5	0	0	0	4.2	5.4	.5	.8	.0	0	0	57.0
2000	40.2	.0	0	0	7.6	7.9	.4	0	.1	0	0	58.5
2001	26.0	.0	0	.5	6.5	8.6	3.1	4.8	2.5	0	0	64.6
2002	36.4	0	3.0	0	5.4	6.9	0	1.8	4.7	.3	0	63.2
2003	33.6	0	0	0	3.5	7.2	0	.0	.7	0	0	46.2
2004	26.5	0	0	0	11.6	8.6	0	0	.0	0	0	47.9
2005	12.7	0	0	0	1.0	6.5	0	0	.1	0	0	21.5
2006[1]	9.9	.0	0	.0	1.3	11.2	0	0	14.1	0	.1	40.1

[1] Preliminary.   *Source: Foreign Agricultural Service, U.S. Department of Agriculture (FAS-USDA)*

Reuters-CRB Index (CCI)

The Reuters Commodity Research Bureau Index (CCI) was first calculated by Commodity Research Bureau, Inc. in 1957 and made its inaugural appearance in the 1958 CRB Commodity Year Book.

The Index originally consisted of two cash markets and 26 futures markets which were traded on exchanges in the U.S. and Canada. It included barley and flaxseed from the Winnipeg exchange; cocoa, coffee "B", copper, cotton, cottonseed oil, grease wool, hides, lead, potatoes, rubber, sugar #4, sugar #6, wool tops and zinc from New York exchanges; and corn, oats, wheat, rye, soybeans, soybean oil, soybean meal, lard, onions, and eggs from Chicago exchanges. In addition to those 26, the Index also included the spot New Orleans cotton and Minneapolis wheat markets.

Like the Bureau of Labor Statistics spot index, the Reuters-CRB Index (CCI) is calculated to produce an unweighted geometric mean of the individual commodity price relatives. In other words, a ratio of the current price to the base year average price. Currently, 1967 is the base year the Index is calculated against (1967=100).

The formula considers all future delivery contracts that expire on or before the end of the sixth calendar month from the current date, using up to a maximum of five contracts per commodity. However, a minimum of two contracts must be used to calculate the current price, even if the second contract is outside the six-month window. Contracts are excluded when in their delivery period.

The 2006 closing value of 408.25 was 13.51 percent higher than the 2005 close of 347.89. 12 of the 17 component commodities finished higher for the year.

Futures Markets

Futures and options on the Reuters-CRB Index (CCI) are traded on the New York Board of Trade (NYBOT).

Reuters-CRB Index (CCI) Component Commodities by Group

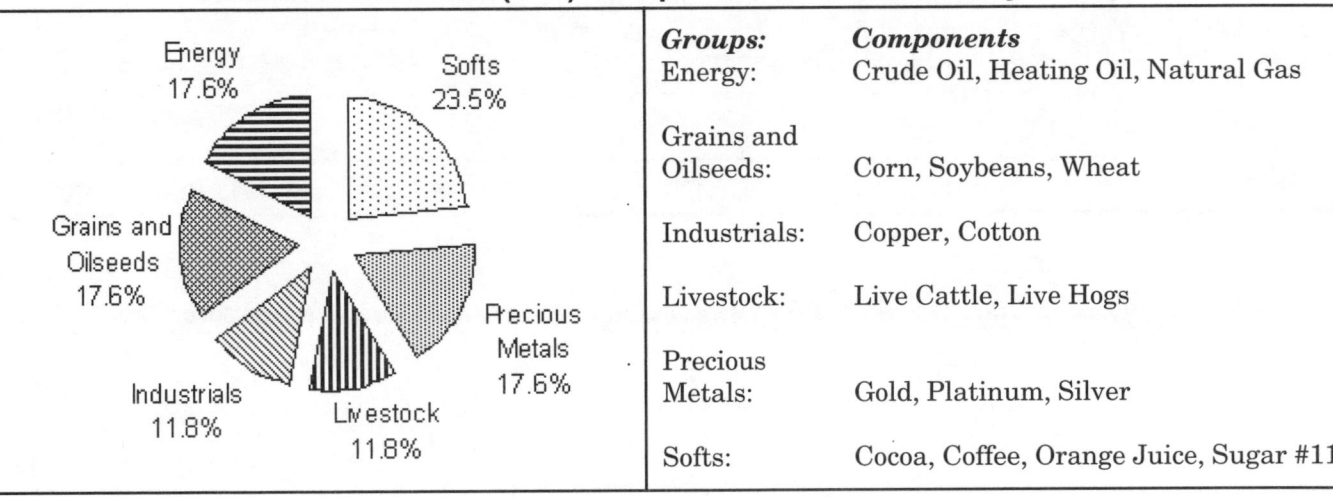

Groups:	Components
Energy:	Crude Oil, Heating Oil, Natural Gas
Grains and Oilseeds:	Corn, Soybeans, Wheat
Industrials:	Copper, Cotton
Livestock:	Live Cattle, Live Hogs
Precious Metals:	Gold, Platinum, Silver
Softs:	Cocoa, Coffee, Orange Juice, Sugar #11

The Reuters-CRB Index (CCI) is computed using a three-step process:

1) Each of the Index's 17 component commodities is arithmetically averaged using the prices for all of the designated contract months which expire on or before the end of the sixth calendar month from the current date, except that: a) no contract shall be included in the calculation while in delivery; b) there shall be a minimum of two contract months for each component commodity (adding contracts beyond the six month window if necessary); c) there shall be a maximum of five contract months for each commodity (dropping the most deferred contracts to remain at five, if necessary). The result is that the Index extends six to seven months into the future depending on where one is in the current month. For example, live cattle's average price on October 30, 1995 would be computed as follows:

$$\text{Cattle Average} = \frac{\text{Dec. '96} + \text{Feb. '97}}{2}$$

2) These 17 component averages are then geometrically averaged by multiplying all of the numbers together and taking the 17th root.

$$\text{Geometric Average} = \sqrt[17]{\text{Crude Avg.} * \text{Heating Oil Avg.} * \text{Sugar Avg.}...}$$

3) The resulting average is divided by 30.7766, the 1967 base-year average for these 17 commodities. That result is then multiplied by an adjustment factor of .8486. This adjustment factor is necessitated by the nine revisions to the Index since its inception in 1957. Finally, that result is multiplied by 100 in order to convert the Index into percentage terms:

$$\text{Reuters-CRB Index (CCI)} = \frac{\text{Current Geometric Average}}{\text{1967 Geometric Avg. (30.7766)}} * .8486 * 100$$

Reuters-CRB Index (CCI) - New York Board of Trade
(weekly close) as of December 29, 2006

Index Value

**Reuters-CRB Futures Index
17 Futures Markets**
Cattle (Live), Cocoa, Coffee, Copper, Corn, Cotton, Crude Oil, Gold (NY), Heating Oil #2, Hogs (Lean), Natural Gas, Orange Juice, Platinum, Silver (NY), Soybeans, Sugar #11 (World), Wheat (Chi.)

Average Open Interest of Reuters-CRB Futures Index in New York   In Contracts

Year	Jan.	Feb.	Mar.	Apr.	May	June	July	Aug.	Sept.	Oct.	Nov.	Dec.
1997	1,944	2,128	2,090	2,245	2,192	1,817	1,957	1,741	1,656	1,843	1,789	1,752
1998	1,679	1,557	1,626	1,509	1,641	1,895	1,832	1,719	1,839	2,162	2,639	2,787
1999	2,863	3,027	3,153	3,041	3,785	3,388	3,300	3,443	4,231	4,851	4,579	4,087
2000	3,487	3,525	3,271	3,117	3,155	2,737	2,104	1,640	1,551	1,632	1,544	1,438
2001	1,280	1,063	1,032	1,036	969	1,006	1,058	1,048	993	559	354	404
2002	422	514	458	384	400	412	489	399	583	646	684	710
2003	748	877	835	849	939	905	858	917	1,078	1,029	1,013	760
2004	838	870	942	704	357	305	413	412	539	600	581	604
2005	540	561	710	663	644	683	861	1,023	1,016	1,024	1,016	1,035
2006	1,045	1,025	998	1,061	1,045	964	939	919	935	948	955	959

Source: New York Board of Trade (NYBOT)

Volume of Trading of Reuters-CRB Futures Index in New York   In Contracts

Year	Jan.	Feb.	Mar.	Apr.	May	June	July	Aug.	Sept.	Oct.	Nov.	Dec.	Total
1997	6,645	4,942	5,245	8,600	8,156	7,776	6,248	7,685	4,537	4,588	3,468	3,592	71,482
1998	7,659	4,623	3,953	3,890	2,933	5,634	3,394	4,578	5,101	4,013	8,814	4,401	58,993
1999	7,606	7,766	7,556	7,808	4,986	8,404	4,378	12,053	6,660	8,063	9,497	3,932	88,709
2000	14,975	6,760	3,941	7,582	7,402	8,924	2,023	3,973	1,333	2,122	3,254	1,205	63,494
2001	2,428	1,823	1,310	2,062	930	1,965	880	2,021	625	1,263	843	728	16,878
2002	1,251	1,231	896	1,472	785	1,191	1,217	915	1,100	1,654	1,430	1,141	14,283
2003	2,289	2,154	1,826	1,634	1,514	2,106	1,632	1,350	1,712	2,123	2,502	2,314	23,156
2004	2,477	1,695	3,169	2,672	1,209	1,618	792	1,341	759	813	1,630	979	19,154
2005	1,154	861	2,023	1,891	1,027	2,105	1,623	1,931	605	707	1,258	882	16,067
2006	2,231	1,114	1,017	1,836	1,563	1,323	927	1,020	892	461	1,220	708	14,312

Source: New York Board of Trade (NYBOT)

Currencies

A currency rate involves the price of the base currency (e.g., the dollar) quoted in terms of another currency (e.g., the yen), or in terms of a basket of currencies (e.g., the dollar index). The world's major currencies have traded in a floating-rate exchange rate regime ever since the Bretton-Woods international payments system broke down in 1971 when President Nixon broke the dollar's peg to gold. The two key factors affecting a currency's value are central bank monetary policy and the trade balance. An easy monetary policy (low interest rates) is bearish for a currency because the central bank is aggressively pumping new currency reserves into the marketplace and because foreign investors are not attracted to the low interest rate returns available in the country. By contrast, a tight monetary policy (high interest rates) is bullish for a currency because of the tight supply of new currency reserves and attractive interest rate returns for foreign investors.

The other key factor driving currency values is the nation's current account balance. A current account *surplus* is bullish for a currency due to the net inflow of the currency, while a current account *deficit* is bearish for a currency due to the net outflow of the currency. Currency values are also affected by economic growth and investment opportunities in the country. A country with a strong economy and lucrative investment opportunities will typically have a strong currency because global companies and investors want to buy into that country's investment opportunities. Futures on major currencies and on cross-currency rates are primarily traded at the Chicago Mercantile Exchange.

Dollar – The dollar index in 2006 showed a moderate sell-off and closed the year –8.2% yr/yr, giving back part of the +15.2% recovery seen in 2005. The dollar index closed 2006 near the bottom of the 33.6% plunge seen in the dollar index in 2002-04 from the 20-year high posted in July 2001 to the 10-year low of 80.39 seen in December 2004.

The dollar faded in 2006 because the US Federal Reserve in July 2006 finally halted its 2-year tightening regime, which took the federal funds rate higher by 425 basis points from 1.00% in mid-2004 to 5.25% in mid-2006. The Fed's switch to a neutral monetary policy caused US interest rate differentials to stop improving, thus taking away the main factor that caused the dollar to show a moderate upside recovery in 2005. US interest rate differentials in 2006 were also hurt by the fact that the European Central Bank raised its benchmark rate five times

in 2006 (by a total of 125 bp) and the Bank of Japan in mid-2006 finally retracted its zero interest rate policy and raised its overnight rate by 25 basis points to 0.25%.

When US interest rate differentials stopped improving, the market refocused its attention on the bearish factor of the massive US trade deficit. The US trade deficit in 2006 rose to a new record high of $763.6 billion from $716.7 billion in 2005. Meanwhile, the US current account balance as a percentage of US GDP was about 6.7% of GDP in 2006, just below the quarterly record of 7.0% seen in Q4-2005.

Looking ahead, the dollar is likely to remain subject to continued weakness due to the massive US trade deficit, expectations for Fed easing by the end of 2007, the possibility of reserve diversification by the Chinese central bank, and the possibility of a further exit from yen carry trades (which is bullish for the yen). However, the dollar should continue to receive underlying support from the fact that US investments remain attractive and that US interest rates are still above those in Europe and Japan.

Euro – The euro in 2006 rallied fairly steadily against the dollar to close the year +11.4% at $1.3199 per euro. Against the yen, the euro extended its 2001-07 bull market and posted a record high of 159.64 yen/euro in February 2007. The euro received strong support from the European Central Bank's steady series of interest rate hikes. The ECB from late-2005 through March-2007 raised its benchmark 2-week refinancing rate by a total of 175 basis points from the 2.00% level that prevailed from mid-2003 to late-2005 to 3.75% by March 2007. In addition, Europe's GDP grew steadily through 2006 and reached +3.3% yr/yr by Q4-2006.

Yen – The yen showed general weakness against both the dollar and the euro in 2006. The yen continued to suffer from the Bank of Japan's extremely easy monetary policy, which made yen plentiful and also encouraged the yen carry trade where global investors borrow in yen, sell the yen, and then invest the proceeds in higher-yielding non-Japanese investments. However, the Bank of Japan in mid-2006 did finally raise its overnight rate by 25 basis points to 0.25% and implemented another 25 basis point rate hike to 0.50% in March 2007 as the Japanese economy showed a sustained recovery and appeared to be throwing off deflationary pressures.

British Pound Futures - International Monetary Market
(weekly close) as of December 29, 2006
USD per GBP

U.S. Dollars per British Pound

Year	Jan.	Feb.	Mar.	Apr.	May	June	July	Aug.	Sept.	Oct.	Nov.	Dec.	Average
1997	1.6590	1.6258	1.6095	1.6285	1.6325	1.6457	1.6717	1.6044	1.6020	1.6331	1.6887	1.6606	1.6385
1998	1.6347	1.6402	1.6615	1.6720	1.6370	1.6509	1.6429	1.6355	1.6814	1.6933	1.6613	1.6713	1.6568
1999	1.6495	1.6269	1.6213	1.6085	1.6147	1.5957	1.5754	1.6051	1.6237	1.6570	1.6206	1.6131	1.6176
2000	1.6395	1.6007	1.5810	1.5807	1.5084	1.5102	1.5082	1.4885	1.4341	1.4509	1.4252	1.4657	1.5161
2001	1.4767	1.4522	1.4438	1.4350	1.4268	1.4025	1.4149	1.4376	1.4646	1.4520	1.4358	1.4422	1.4403
2002	1.4314	1.4233	1.4233	1.4434	1.4601	1.4849	1.5566	1.5375	1.5562	1.5576	1.5718	1.5882	1.5029
2003	1.6184	1.6077	1.5832	1.5751	1.6230	1.6606	1.6242	1.5942	1.6141	1.6778	1.6899	1.7536	1.6352
2004	1.8223	1.8675	1.8273	1.8050	1.7888	1.8292	1.8433	1.8195	1.7932	1.8069	1.8608	1.9298	1.8328
2005	1.8783	1.8883	1.9034	1.8961	1.8538	1.8179	1.7518	1.7947	1.8078	1.7649	1.7355	1.7454	1.8198
2006	1.7665	1.7478	1.7446	1.7690	1.8693	1.8435	1.8451	1.8934	1.8858	1.8766	1.9124	1.9634	1.8431

Average.   Source: FOREX

Volume of Trading of British Pound Futures in Chicago   In Thousands of Contracts

Year	Jan.	Feb.	Mar.	Apr.	May	June	July	Aug.	Sept.	Oct.	Nov.	Dec.	Total
1997	240.3	168.7	289.4	185.3	236.6	279.3	265.1	194.6	234.1	202.1	145.0	286.1	2,726.6
1998	174.3	126.9	231.9	175.7	217.1	323.0	211.7	277.3	291.4	202.0	146.8	255.5	2,633.7
1999	182.4	151.8	350.2	205.3	285.0	332.1	250.3	178.2	275.9	177.9	163.2	181.5	2,734.0
2000	199.6	179.8	270.9	138.9	133.3	225.8	136.2	155.9	245.1	100.7	100.7	152.5	2,039.3
2001	125.6	126.2	198.7	127.0	166.3	248.9	164.2	183.6	197.1	178.9	161.4	187.4	2,065.4
2002	182.0	168.2	230.4	168.2	174.1	239.8	133.3	138.3	185.3	177.5	160.9	198.0	2,155.9
2003	158.3	161.8	217.4	158.1	164.7	288.6	214.9	163.5	284.5	212.6	206.2	364.5	2,595.2
2004	310.3	291.6	470.3	293.1	282.5	427.8	373.4	367.1	471.4	405.4	348.4	635.2	4,676.5
2005	376.7	410.5	628.7	453.3	555.5	763.5	640.2	735.3	1,034.5	887.8	1,080.6	1,203.1	8,769.8
2006	1,013.7	1,012.0	1,479.2	1,207.6	1,465.1	1,262.1	963.1	1,262.2	1,486.2	1,387.1	1,563.9	1,997.4	16,099.5

Source: International Monetary Market (IMM), division of the Chicago Mercantile Exchange (CME)

Average Open Interest of British Pound Futures in Chicago   In Contracts

Year	Jan.	Feb.	Mar.	Apr.	May	June	July	Aug.	Sept.	Oct.	Nov.	Dec.
1997	40,479	38,370	43,742	37,701	40,956	48,890	60,592	50,829	41,801	35,752	56,825	44,667
1998	33,616	31,282	38,712	41,256	47,303	55,511	39,156	49,645	63,756	53,458	54,004	53,578
1999	51,519	59,705	66,913	64,937	58,744	60,414	65,206	54,373	50,949	65,038	49,468	34,191
2000	37,192	45,329	51,645	41,488	51,965	43,009	30,766	36,320	42,781	30,978	34,627	32,913
2001	28,776	30,555	36,532	34,713	39,836	48,310	33,273	40,935	50,083	38,579	40,461	35,424
2002	26,450	31,023	30,474	39,952	46,178	47,355	38,138	31,320	31,513	29,599	40,901	36,671
2003	36,892	33,066	27,042	25,274	36,171	50,118	41,702	46,979	40,183	55,884	66,660	70,197
2004	61,694	68,173	51,968	43,830	45,843	53,615	68,262	71,503	60,274	66,565	87,487	86,572
2005	67,140	70,872	81,799	80,850	88,397	79,278	75,387	73,199	81,479	79,854	84,884	91,497
2006	83,051	97,226	83,641	83,275	106,555	98,417	91,563	129,334	120,737	106,288	145,026	157,837

Source: International Monetary Market (IMM), division of the Chicago Mercantile Exchange (CME)

CURRENCIES

Canadian Dollar Futures - International Monetary Market
(weekly close) as of December 29, 2006
USD per CAD

Canadian Dollars per U.S. Dollar

Year	Jan.	Feb.	Mar.	Apr.	May	June	July	Aug.	Sept.	Oct.	Nov.	Dec.	Average
1997	1.3484	1.3555	1.3727	1.3947	1.3793	1.3844	1.3769	1.3894	1.3865	1.3863	1.4127	1.4272	1.3845
1998	1.4407	1.4335	1.4159	1.4294	1.4449	1.4647	1.4865	1.5344	1.5212	1.5430	1.5400	1.5429	1.4831
1999	1.5189	1.4971	1.5174	1.4868	1.4614	1.4691	1.4877	1.4921	1.4772	1.4767	1.4671	1.4713	1.4852
2000	1.4480	1.4499	1.4600	1.4681	1.4944	1.4762	1.4778	1.4819	1.4841	1.5119	1.5425	1.5219	1.4847
2001	1.5021	1.5227	1.5579	1.5581	1.5403	1.5238	1.5294	1.5384	1.5665	1.5708	1.5934	1.5793	1.5486
2002	1.5996	1.5961	1.5872	1.5814	1.5491	1.5312	1.5447	1.5685	1.5747	1.5783	1.5715	1.5588	1.5701
2003	1.5395	1.5119	1.4752	1.4567	1.3819	1.3520	1.3801	1.3948	1.3638	1.3226	1.3128	1.3121	1.4003
2004	1.2967	1.3292	1.3282	1.3410	1.3774	1.3582	1.3225	1.3127	1.2880	1.2476	1.1958	1.2177	1.3013
2005	1.2248	1.2386	1.2157	1.2368	1.2553	1.2402	1.2239	1.2048	1.1781	1.1777	1.1813	1.1619	1.2116
2006	1.1573	1.1488	1.1571	1.1440	1.1094	1.1139	1.1287	1.1191	1.1161	1.1281	1.1365	1.1531	1.1343

Average.   Source: FOREX

Volume of Trading of Canadian Dollar Futures in Chicago   In Thousands of Contracts

Year	Jan.	Feb.	Mar.	Apr.	May	June	July	Aug.	Sept.	Oct.	Nov.	Dec.	Total
1997	189.9	127.3	295.2	151.1	230.7	276.8	146.9	187.1	262.3	268.4	130.5	322.9	2,589.1
1998	172.0	202.0	277.1	142.6	143.2	291.5	153.4	214.0	288.7	148.7	148.9	210.0	2,392.2
1999	171.0	173.0	279.9	203.4	164.4	309.7	216.1	186.0	263.4	167.7	165.6	277.2	2,577.5
2000	184.2	182.5	280.9	155.0	162.8	295.5	166.0	188.5	241.2	161.6	150.3	265.8	2,434.1
2001	194.7	201.1	317.9	188.2	228.4	351.0	221.6	235.9	265.1	214.1	218.1	287.3	2,923.3
2002	222.9	191.5	338.3	249.6	222.2	358.7	278.8	204.2	279.1	245.3	207.4	324.4	3,122.3
2003	270.8	256.7	475.5	289.2	353.1	494.2	331.3	266.2	393.3	285.7	294.4	509.3	4,219.6
2004	380.7	328.0	516.3	380.3	337.1	504.0	366.5	419.4	640.8	512.0	499.5	726.8	5,611.3
2005	548.6	483.0	678.0	592.9	555.2	761.5	562.2	566.3	914.2	671.3	736.0	861.0	7,930.2
2006	695.1	648.6	1,040.9	654.9	816.6	1,043.4	658.3	811.0	1,073.7	805.8	960.8	1,070.4	10,279.6

Source: International Monetary Market (IMM), division of the Chicago Mercantile Exchange (CME)

Average Open Interest of Canadian Dollar Futures in Chicago   In Contracts

Year	Jan.	Feb.	Mar.	Apr.	May	June	July	Aug.	Sept.	Oct.	Nov.	Dec.
1997	55,949	56,600	72,803	82,732	73,747	57,243	43,937	59,112	56,387	59,265	75,027	74,221
1998	63,300	67,862	61,528	58,938	64,859	74,027	71,313	75,193	60,863	51,967	61,318	50,271
1999	50,061	71,819	63,782	73,773	84,885	71,923	65,877	71,458	61,994	58,749	59,941	51,967
2000	66,374	64,528	58,621	60,389	76,444	69,033	67,198	65,370	65,779	81,995	77,746	65,452
2001	54,369	58,660	72,051	64,550	65,407	62,489	54,742	54,580	73,647	71,610	82,083	67,578
2002	68,927	72,132	70,484	68,120	81,574	86,250	74,347	63,116	63,605	57,031	60,648	71,852
2003	82,870	105,051	107,507	97,515	96,689	85,665	68,741	63,518	70,261	79,754	82,366	74,271
2004	74,577	64,032	61,981	72,750	84,356	68,458	73,164	83,483	97,486	112,648	110,035	81,976
2005	74,703	84,753	93,986	77,680	95,229	79,464	86,451	101,128	120,542	108,095	106,773	122,584
2006	103,427	118,978	103,066	92,541	114,587	107,605	89,443	91,591	112,788	99,209	121,729	146,474

Source: International Monetary Market (IMM), division of the Chicago Mercantile Exchange (CME)

Euro FX Futures - International Monetary Market
(weekly close) as of December 29, 2006
USD per EUR

Euro[1] per U.S. Dollar

Year	Jan.	Feb.	Mar.	Apr.	May	June	July	Aug.	Sept.	Oct.	Nov.	Dec.	Average
1997	1.2088	1.1592	1.1460	1.1396	1.1441	1.1309	1.0999	1.0694	1.0976	1.1190	1.1418	1.1114	1.1306
1998	1.0859	1.0896	1.0854	1.0931	1.1099	1.1015	1.0991	1.1041	1.1566	1.2015	1.1680	1.1746	1.1224
1999	1.1584	1.1202	1.0882	1.0700	1.0622	1.0385	1.0366	1.0603	1.0501	1.0705	1.0327	1.0117	1.0666
2000	1.0135	.9842	.9644	.9450	.9080	.9496	.9394	.9042	.8706	.8533	.8554	.9004	.9240
2001	.9380	.9208	.9085	.8931	.8747	.8536	.8616	.9023	.9123	.9062	.8882	.8913	.8959
2002	.8828	.8706	.8767	.8866	.9179	.9567	.9924	.9781	.9810	.9818	1.0020	1.0210	.9456
2003	1.0636	1.0778	1.0795	1.0875	1.1580	1.1670	1.1374	1.1154	1.1260	1.1701	1.1714	1.2314	1.1321
2004	1.2604	1.2633	1.2263	1.1999	1.2013	1.2147	1.2265	1.2192	1.2226	1.2504	1.3001	1.3415	1.2439
2005	1.3110	1.3020	1.3178	1.2940	1.2685	1.2156	1.2049	1.2299	1.2246	1.2030	1.1796	1.1861	1.2448
2006	1.2121	1.1940	1.2033	1.2282	1.2773	1.2665	1.2693	1.2811	1.2734	1.2623	1.2893	1.3200	1.2564

Average.   [1] Data through December 1998 are theoretical based on DEM * 1.95583.   *Source: FOREX*

Volume of Trading of Euro FX Futures in Chicago   In Thousands of Contracts

Year	Jan.	Feb.	Mar.	Apr.	May	June	July	Aug.	Sept.	Oct.	Nov.	Dec.	Total
1998	----	----	----	----	0.0	0.0	0.0	0.0	0.0	0.0	0.0	0.0	0.0
1999	69.0	96.6	288.4	157.6	183.7	276.4	259.7	258.1	422.8	302.5	303.1	383.0	3,000.8
2000	404.9	335.0	452.4	289.4	318.3	382.2	234.9	303.3	486.3	287.7	297.0	466.7	4,258.2
2001	453.5	373.2	556.4	368.3	407.7	585.3	425.1	494.7	533.9	533.6	545.0	781.1	6,057.8
2002	567.8	582.3	783.3	650.2	611.4	917.7	821.6	525.5	675.3	525.2	426.7	625.4	7,712.3
2003	610.6	749.2	977.9	785.5	902.7	1,103.8	866.2	824.5	1,112.4	1,069.6	958.9	1,232.6	11,193.9
2004	1,487.3	1,469.2	1,837.7	1,326.7	1,328.9	1,682.2	1,491.2	1,518.5	1,798.7	1,786.0	2,138.5	2,591.9	20,456.7
2005	2,646.0	2,266.4	2,772.9	2,992.0	2,771.6	3,656.1	2,732.6	2,765.1	3,206.6	2,613.6	3,164.2	2,943.6	34,530.7
2006	2,956.0	2,563.9	3,411.2	2,984.4	4,496.3	3,765.7	2,789.0	3,229.5	3,364.0	3,123.5	3,790.4	4,316.6	40,790.4

Source: International Monetary Market (IMM), division of the Chicago Mercantile Exchange (CME)

Average Open Interest of Euro FX Futures in Chicago   In Contracts

Year	Jan.	Feb.	Mar.	Apr.	May	June	July	Aug.	Sept.	Oct.	Nov.	Dec.
1998	----	----	----	----	1	1	1	1	1	0	7	7
1999	8,261	30,546	37,837	37,881	46,446	50,615	46,777	55,858	49,352	57,380	58,846	65,346
2000	63,124	68,413	61,180	59,110	67,644	63,361	57,723	69,561	77,617	73,314	79,577	92,730
2001	89,049	91,130	90,127	78,762	89,390	94,160	84,637	104,437	112,797	108,445	108,999	104,323
2002	100,258	108,955	113,075	112,413	136,660	135,364	112,462	101,992	99,365	85,462	103,156	108,602
2003	105,762	106,905	100,759	85,604	108,619	111,651	96,338	98,671	95,553	102,568	113,601	131,560
2004	125,879	133,690	115,712	112,361	138,193	120,281	140,430	160,315	121,180	136,959	202,074	175,374
2005	135,748	152,110	140,879	130,131	154,751	163,584	142,826	148,309	149,184	142,879	171,035	160,065
2006	133,092	150,085	152,674	166,920	196,057	177,700	155,865	173,151	155,567	152,410	182,079	214,241

Source: International Monetary Market (IMM), division of the Chicago Mercantile Exchange (CME)

CURRENCIES

Japanese Yen Futures - International Monetary Market
(weekly close) as of December 29, 2006

USD per JPY

Japanese Yen per U.S. Dollar

Year	Jan.	Feb.	Mar.	Apr.	May	June	July	Aug.	Sept.	Oct.	Nov.	Dec.	Average
1997	117.93	122.90	122.72	125.66	118.93	114.25	115.30	117.90	120.85	121.06	125.35	129.62	121.04
1998	129.39	125.71	129.04	131.79	135.01	140.40	140.75	144.51	134.45	120.49	120.41	117.01	130.75
1999	113.23	116.62	119.49	119.73	121.88	120.69	119.38	113.16	107.00	105.94	104.62	102.64	113.70
2000	105.29	109.49	106.34	105.65	108.19	106.15	108.03	108.06	106.79	108.39	108.94	112.18	107.79
2001	116.83	116.17	121.44	123.64	121.66	122.38	124.45	121.29	118.64	121.35	122.39	127.72	121.50
2002	132.77	133.50	131.11	130.75	126.29	123.25	118.02	119.04	120.88	123.92	121.50	121.83	125.24
2003	118.76	119.39	118.76	119.81	117.37	118.31	118.64	118.61	114.94	109.51	109.17	107.70	115.91
2004	106.38	106.70	108.51	107.61	112.05	109.44	109.46	110.24	110.10	108.81	104.71	103.79	108.15
2005	103.29	104.98	105.35	107.19	106.71	108.75	111.92	110.62	111.19	114.84	118.42	118.39	110.14
2006	115.53	117.92	117.31	116.97	111.77	114.65	115.69	115.95	117.14	118.61	117.28	117.43	116.35

Average.   Source: FOREX

Volume of Trading of Japanese Yen Futures in Chicago   In Thousands of Contracts

Year	Jan.	Feb.	Mar.	Apr.	May	June	July	Aug.	Sept.	Oct.	Nov.	Dec.	Total
1997	411.6	457.2	564.8	402.7	604.6	564.2	424.3	528.2	611.8	529.6	425.8	644.8	6,169.6
1998	557.8	500.9	636.6	480.3	453.4	1,017.0	515.9	590.8	895.8	551.9	386.3	467.2	7,053.8
1999	418.1	524.6	672.7	400.4	473.4	687.1	476.9	422.3	679.1	310.5	390.5	469.1	5,924.8
2000	433.9	299.1	569.7	250.5	265.8	427.4	248.8	285.9	367.1	213.9	222.7	405.2	3,990.0
2001	258.6	223.7	598.4	295.4	351.2	459.4	307.4	369.4	518.6	286.2	350.1	595.9	4,614.1
2002	415.7	417.5	630.8	391.7	318.5	461.7	301.2	234.2	499.2	349.5	255.4	535.8	4,811.1
2003	423.9	388.3	634.4	453.4	495.6	621.0	518.8	427.0	731.0	396.6	353.4	641.8	6,085.2
2004	410.1	484.9	741.8	516.4	415.5	685.8	487.5	490.7	807.6	629.6	650.5	1,074.9	7,395.3
2005	789.9	718.8	1,045.2	915.4	876.2	1,263.0	946.9	1,012.4	1,285.4	963.7	1,001.0	1,653.9	12,471.7
2006	1,221.1	1,128.7	1,950.5	1,385.9	1,890.9	1,905.3	1,317.9	1,395.9	1,965.8	1,525.1	1,852.8	2,137.5	19,677.4

Source: International Monetary Market (IMM), division of the Chicago Mercantile Exchange (CME)

Average Open Interest of Japanese Yen Futures in Chicago   In Contracts

Year	Jan.	Feb.	Mar.	Apr.	May	June	July	Aug.	Sept.	Oct.	Nov.	Dec.
1997	73,391	82,542	78,466	81,117	85,984	73,322	62,488	82,369	96,468	90,080	130,606	121,001
1998	95,338	101,448	97,183	97,389	106,139	132,732	113,084	145,241	108,808	88,991	89,108	79,262
1999	78,767	81,859	96,271	87,829	118,819	120,681	118,329	136,826	115,884	82,657	87,869	87,595
2000	93,785	125,318	95,034	75,631	80,840	68,359	60,966	79,195	64,845	64,648	68,719	100,713
2001	89,680	90,652	109,536	96,244	89,377	82,838	93,430	107,588	102,710	75,096	97,368	137,756
2002	129,917	123,735	95,535	72,358	88,905	88,324	77,168	71,683	79,980	80,104	74,584	99,643
2003	116,574	107,929	101,809	81,168	107,090	102,507	107,450	125,884	149,978	152,368	138,799	147,255
2004	156,929	156,416	120,848	117,483	108,078	105,505	106,280	110,234	93,780	127,644	181,093	172,526
2005	164,708	155,593	132,268	134,802	172,574	164,580	161,763	170,290	159,227	186,631	202,939	191,591
2006	168,309	198,855	203,450	201,459	210,578	197,160	191,480	218,893	239,426	258,509	242,216	265,490

Source: International Monetary Market (IMM), division of the Chicago Mercantile Exchange (CME)

Swiss Francs per U.S. Dollar

Year	Jan.	Feb.	Mar.	Apr.	May	June	July	Aug.	Sept.	Oct.	Nov.	Dec.	Average
1997	1.3925	1.4543	1.4622	1.4614	1.4298	1.4419	1.4810	1.5123	1.4702	1.4507	1.4057	1.4393	1.4501
1998	1.4756	1.4616	1.4896	1.5050	1.4782	1.4951	1.5126	1.4927	1.4002	1.3376	1.3856	1.3600	1.4495
1999	1.3856	1.4273	1.4656	1.4972	1.5078	1.5359	1.5472	1.5092	1.5251	1.4891	1.5541	1.5827	1.5022
2000	1.5888	1.6326	1.6624	1.6638	1.7151	1.6422	1.6503	1.7146	1.7564	1.7727	1.7772	1.6778	1.6878
2001	1.6296	1.6681	1.6903	1.7115	1.7525	1.7842	1.7564	1.6791	1.6338	1.6337	1.6501	1.6569	1.6872
2002	1.6710	1.6972	1.6741	1.6527	1.5868	1.5389	1.4731	1.4968	1.4929	1.4922	1.4647	1.4360	1.5564
2003	1.3748	1.3609	1.3617	1.3770	1.3091	1.3196	1.3597	1.3813	1.3741	1.3234	1.3314	1.2627	1.3446
2004	1.2425	1.2458	1.2773	1.2954	1.2818	1.2501	1.2458	1.2625	1.2624	1.2338	1.1702	1.1455	1.2428
2005	1.1802	1.1906	1.1763	1.1955	1.2183	1.2663	1.2935	1.2626	1.2657	1.2872	1.3100	1.3056	1.2460
2006	1.2781	1.3056	1.3044	1.2822	1.2185	1.2319	1.2362	1.2319	1.2440	1.2597	1.2351	1.2102	1.2532

Average.   Source: FOREX

Volume of Trading of Swiss Franc Futures in Chicago   In Thousands of Contracts

Year	Jan.	Feb.	Mar.	Apr.	May	June	July	Aug.	Sept.	Oct.	Nov.	Dec.	Total
1997	360.5	316.3	436.8	343.6	432.5	389.5	316.1	305.2	394.1	429.7	221.0	344.9	4,290.1
1998	308.0	256.8	448.0	318.5	319.2	367.4	310.7	360.4	438.1	300.7	251.3	290.8	3,970.0
1999	294.6	262.1	417.0	284.0	323.3	384.7	351.1	311.8	482.4	407.6	287.2	304.5	4,110.3
2000	326.2	313.1	385.3	252.1	247.7	301.2	214.6	216.6	344.5	176.2	185.4	267.3	3,230.2
2001	193.5	203.0	280.3	168.7	191.6	326.0	257.6	229.4	261.8	227.5	238.2	297.3	2,874.8
2002	195.3	183.2	281.3	211.5	208.1	297.0	187.2	218.5	323.1	237.6	207.8	271.6	2,822.1
2003	236.1	289.9	412.7	256.9	277.8	384.9	315.0	252.1	349.9	237.2	283.8	300.5	3,596.7
2004	216.1	230.1	359.6	260.0	255.7	370.9	331.4	313.7	404.5	428.3	329.0	568.4	4,067.8
2005	444.3	389.1	575.5	605.0	521.4	753.4	546.4	596.4	888.8	765.9	797.1	901.2	7,784.5
2006	803.5	745.9	1,129.0	837.5	1,011.3	993.3	771.2	1,014.8	1,046.8	919.6	1,078.1	1,118.9	11,470.0

Source: International Monetary Market (IMM), division of the Chicago Mercantile Exchange (CME)

Average Open Interest of Swiss Franc Futures in Chicago   In Contracts

Year	Jan.	Feb.	Mar.	Apr.	May	June	July	Aug.	Sept.	Oct.	Nov.	Dec.
1997	51,652	54,114	51,121	45,725	48,651	42,530	55,279	58,098	49,296	43,585	51,822	48,560
1998	57,740	46,160	67,722	67,303	63,477	77,564	85,984	70,569	81,465	57,413	44,810	43,436
1999	39,434	58,279	66,250	66,530	73,322	75,322	66,603	71,060	60,214	65,020	67,936	64,507
2000	55,660	69,983	57,703	41,732	46,159	41,727	36,894	50,595	57,439	47,313	48,870	55,982
2001	50,121	44,405	46,470	41,641	53,265	60,943	53,687	60,986	61,689	48,962	53,445	46,771
2002	35,116	44,388	45,434	38,248	55,039	54,573	42,060	38,102	37,675	35,796	48,951	50,107
2003	56,268	57,099	50,008	37,451	53,642	49,688	41,489	50,677	52,641	54,259	62,584	60,475
2004	45,259	42,950	41,250	38,563	38,024	48,654	51,116	40,256	33,539	47,200	74,988	70,330
2005	51,858	56,240	50,827	41,322	55,995	78,794	72,596	67,489	66,009	75,088	91,072	98,443
2006	80,904	107,509	101,445	82,280	98,416	89,254	67,127	69,406	83,545	97,034	89,039	74,522

Source: International Monetary Market (IMM), division of the Chicago Mercantile Exchange (CME)

CURRENCIES

United States Merchandise Trade Balance[1] In Millions of Dollars

Year	Jan.	Feb.	Mar.	Apr.	May	June	July	Aug.	Sept.	Oct.	Nov.	Dec.	Total
1997	-18,167	-16,780	-14,896	-16,505	-16,982	-15,610	-15,864	-16,909	-16,524	-16,270	-16,605	-16,962	-196,652
1998	-17,187	-18,331	-20,615	-20,860	-22,236	-20,404	-21,066	-22,291	-21,611	-20,990	-21,539	-21,059	-246,853
1999	-23,409	-25,233	-25,741	-25,851	-27,753	-30,381	-31,227	-30,518	-30,573	-31,576	-32,401	-32,255	-345,434
2000	-34,116	-34,708	-37,215	-36,934	-36,910	-37,827	-38,091	-36,839	-39,682	-40,205	-38,955	-39,360	-452,423
2001	-39,161	-34,648	-38,815	-37,270	-34,690	-35,760	-35,633	-34,458	-35,660	-35,034	-34,095	-31,534	-427,215
2002	-33,407	-31,405	-31,865	-39,875	-39,229	-37,590	-46,642	-44,082	-43,241	-45,583	-44,076	-45,303	-482,298
2003	-43,619	-38,301	-43,538	-46,145	-43,275	-43,882	-51,798	-45,166	-49,478	-51,812	-42,937	-47,345	-547,296
2004	-46,104	-42,621	-50,545	-52,314	-49,848	-60,221	-60,068	-60,752	-57,766	-62,556	-66,320	-56,294	-665,409
2005	-57,625	-54,860	-56,700	-60,386	-61,475	-64,686	-66,999	-70,417	-73,183	-77,869	-72,663	-65,876	-782,7
392006[2]	-70,969	-59,692	-63,453	-65,459	-72,366	-70,980	-78,918	-79,932	-71,740	-73,679	-67,394	-61,495	-836,077

[1] Not seasonally adjusted. [2] Preliminary. *Source: Bureau of Economic Analysis, U.S. Department of Commerce (BEA)*

Index of Real Trade-Weighted Dollar Exchange Rates for Total Agriculture[2] 2000 = 100

Year		Jan.	Feb.	Mar.	Apr.	May	June	July	Aug.	Sept.	Oct.	Nov.	Dec.
1999	U.S. Markets	91.9	93.7	95.4	95.5	95.4	96.0	96.3	94.8	94.5	93.7	94.2	93.9
	U.S. Competitors	75.0	78.4	80.9	82.2	82.3	84.7	85.2	83.7	85.2	83.7	86.5	87.9
2000	U.S. Markets	94.2	96.3	96.8	97.3	99.6	98.4	99.0	99.7	101.2	102.9	103.4	102.3
	U.S. Competitors	87.6	91.0	93.5	95.5	100.5	96.1	97.3	101.1	106.1	109.0	108.9	102.5
2001	U.S. Markets	103.1	104.0	106.0	107.5	107.5	108.6	108.8	106.4	106.5	107.0	107.5	107.7
	U.S. Competitors	99.0	102.1	104.0	106.5	108.5	111.7	110.6	105.1	104.6	105.2	106.5	104.7
2002	U.S. Markets	109.3	110.4	109.8	109.4	107.1	105.5	103.5	104.8	105.5	106.6	105.1	103.8
	U.S. Competitors	106.7	109.8	109.1	108.0	104.3	100.4	97.1	99.4	99.3	99.6	97.1	93.9
2003	U.S. Markets	102.2	103.1	103.1	102.0	98.2	98.4	99.7	100.7	99.3	96.6	96.1	94.3
	U.S. Competitors	89.6	88.6	89.0	87.1	80.6	80.1	82.8	85.0	83.6	79.4	78.7	74.5
2004	U.S. Markets	92.7	93.3	94.6	95.3	97.5	96.4	95.4	95.4	92.3	91.0	88.0	86.1
	U.S. Competitors	72.5	72.7	75.4	77.2	78.3	77.6	76.2	76.6	75.7	73.7	70.1	67.1
2005	U.S. Markets	86.2	86.7	86.4	87.9	91.2	92.7	93.9	93.0	93.9	95.4	95.7	94.4
	U.S. Competitors	68.3	69.2	68.4	70.1	71.7	75.0	76.4	74.8	75.7	77.4	78.2	76.9
2006[1]	U.S. Markets	93.2	93.8	94.0	93.6	91.3	92.9	93.1	92.3	92.0	92.0	90.7	90.7
	U.S. Competitors	76.0	76.8	76.5	75.1	71.9	73.3	73.3	72.3	72.2	72.2	70.0	69.7

[1] Preliminary. [2] Real indexes adjust nominal exchange rates for differences in rates of inflation, to avoid the distortion caused by high-inflation countries. A higher value means the dollar has appreciated. Federal Reserve Board Index of trade-weighted value of the U.S. dollar against 10 major currencies. Weights are based on relative importance in world financial markets. *Source: Economic Research Service, U.S. Department of Agriculture*

United States Balance on Current Account[1] In Millions of Dollars

Year	First Quarter	Second Quarter	Third Quarter	Fourth Quarter	Annual
1997	-25,610	-29,346	-43,871	-41,575	-140,402
1998	-33,568	-51,455	-69,380	-59,125	-213,528
1999	-53,342	-72,162	-90,269	-84,053	-299,826
2000	-86,928	-100,085	-116,923	-111,214	-415,150
2001	-95,822	-98,602	-102,318	-92,217	-388,959
2002	-95,877	-119,655	-130,901	-126,013	-472,446
2003	-124,432	-131,868	-142,863	-128,351	-527,514
2004	-133,037	-167,121	-178,006	-187,122	-665,286
2005	-175,780	-195,103	-197,164	-223,461	-791,508
2006[2]	-197,357	-218,756	-239,962		-874,767

[1] Not seasonally adjusted. [2] Preliminary. *Source: Bureau of Economic Analysis, U.S. Department of Commerce (BEA)*

Merchandise Trade and Current Account Balances In Billions of Dollars

Year	Merchandise Trade Balance					Current Account Balance				
	Canada	Germany	Japan	Switzerland	U.K.	Canada	Germany	Japan	Switzerland	U.K.
1998	12.3	29.8	72.3	13.2	-11.9	-7.7	-17.0	119.9	25.1	-5.3
1999	24.2	18.0	69.4	14.9	-25.0	1.7	-27.8	115.7	29.4	-35.2
2000	41.6	6.9	68.0	14.1	-29.2	19.7	-33.9	118.7	30.9	-37.4
2001	41.2	38.4	26.2	10.9	-38.6	16.3	.5	88.7	20.0	-31.5
2002	32.4	93.4	51.2	17.7	-46.5	12.6	41.4	112.4	23.6	-24.7
2003	32.2	97.4	69.2	21.6	-48.3	10.2	47.9	137.1	43.3	-24.5
2004	41.1	136.3	89.0	26.3	-64.1	21.1	101.1	171.6	48.7	-35.3
2005	43.1	143.9	63.4	24.8	-82.2	26.5	116.6	168.3	54.3	-47.7
2006[1]	29.6	153.9	55.5	24.9	-99.7	13.6	116.8	164.9	57.6	-55.6
2007[2]	17.6	182.4	74.5	26.9	-109.5	1.3	146.3	200.5	65.1	-52.1

[1] Estimate. [2] Projection. *Source: Organization for Economic Cooperation and Development (OECD)*

Euro / Swiss Franc (weekly close) as of December 29, 2006 — EUR per CHF

Euro / British Pound (weekly close) as of December 29, 2006 — EUR per GBP

Japanese Yen / British Pound (weekly close) as of December 29, 2006 — JPY per GBP

Euro / Japanese Yen (weekly close) as of December 29, 2006 — JPY per EUR

Diamonds

The diamond, which is the mineral form of carbon, is the hardest, strongest natural material known on earth. The name diamond is derived from adamas, the ancient Greek term meaning "invincible." Diamonds form deep within the Earth's crust and are typically billions of years old. Diamonds have also have been found in and near meteorites and their craters. Diamonds are considered precious gemstones but lower grade diamonds are used for industrial applications such as drilling, cutting, grinding and polishing.

Supply – World production of natural gem diamonds in 2005 rose by +2.0% yr/yr to a record high of 102.000

million carats (one carat equals 1/5 gram or 200 milligrams). The world's largest producers of natural gem diamonds are Botswana with 23.4% of world production in 2005, Russia a close second with 22.6%, Australia with 20%, Congo with 6%, and South Africa also with 6%. World production of natural industrial diamonds in 2005 fell by –0.2% yr/yr to 81.000 million carats. The main producer of synthetic diamonds is the US with 256.000 million carats of production in 2005, representing 45% of world production.

Trade – The US in 2006 relied on net imports for 82% of its consumption of natural diamonds, which totaled 2.3 million carats in 2005.

World Production of Natural Gem Diamonds   In Thousands of Carats

Year	Angola	Aust-ralia	Bots-wana	Brazil	Central African Republic	China	Congo[3]	Ghana	Namibia	Russia	Sierra Leone	South Africa	World Total
2000	3,880	11,956	18,500	1,000	348	230	3,500	792	1,450	17,500	58	4,320	67,100
2001	4,643	14,397	19,812	700	340	100	3,638	936	1,487	17,500	102	4,465	72,900
2002	4,520	15,136	21,297	500	312	100	4,223	770	1,562	17,400	162	4,351	76,400
2003	5,130	13,981	22,800	400	250	100	5,381	675	1,481	20,000	233	5,144	87,700
2004[1]	5,490	20,602	23,300	300	263	100	6,180	690	2,004	21,400	318	5,780	100,000
2005[2]	5,580	20,000	23,900	300	265	100	6,300	760	1,900	23,000	318	5,780	102,000

[1] Preliminary. [2] Estimate. [3] Formerly Zaire.   Source: U.S. Geological Survey (USGS)

World Production of Natural Industrial Diamonds   In Thousands of Carats

Year	Angola	Aust-ralia	Bots-wana	Brazil	Central African Republic	China	Congo[3]	Ghana	Russia	Sierra Leone	South Africa	Vene-zuela	World Total
2000	431	14,612	6,160	----	116	920	14,200	198	11,700	19	6,470	80	55,400
2001	516	11,779	6,604	600	113	950	14,560	234	11,700	120	6,698	28	54,300
2002	502	18,500	7,100	600	104	955	17,456	193	11,600	190	6,526	61	64,200
2003	570	17,087	7,600	600	83	955	21,600	225	13,000	274	7,540	24	69,900
2004[1]	610	22,709	7,800	600	88	960	24,700	230	14,200	374	8,500	60	81,200
2005[2]	620	20,000	8,000	600	88	960	25,200	253	15,000	374	9,380	69	81,000

[1] Preliminary. [2] Estimate. [3] Formerly Zaire.   Source: U.S. Geological Survey (USGS)

World Production of Synthetic Diamonds   In Thousands of Carats

Year	Belarus	China	Czech Republic	France	Greece	Ireland	Japan	Russia	South Africa	Sweden	Ukraine	United States	World Total
2000	25,000	16,800	----	3,000	750	60,000	33,000	80,000	----	20,000	8,000	182,000	429,000
2001	25,000	17,000	----	3,000	----	60,000	33,000	80,000	60,000	20,000	8,000	202,000	508,000
2002	25,000	17,000	----	3,000	----	60,000	34,000	80,000	60,000	20,000	8,000	222,000	529,000
2003	25,000	17,000	----	3,000	----	60,000	34,000	80,000	60,000	20,000	8,000	236,000	543,000
2004[1]	25,000	17,000	----	3,000	----	60,000	34,000	80,000	60,000	20,000	8,000	252,000	559,000
2005[2]	25,000	17,000	----	3,000	----	60,000	34,000	80,000	60,000	20,000	8,000	256,000	563,000

[1] Preliminary. [2] Estimate.   Source: U.S. Geological Survey (USGS)

Salient Statistics of Industrial Diamonds in the United States   In Millions of Carats

	Bort, Grit & Powder & Dust — Natural and Synthetic								Stones (Natural)						
	Production														Net Import Reliance
Year	Manu-factured Diamond	Secondary	Imports for Con-sumption	Exports & Reexports	In Manu-factured Products	Gov't Sales	Apparent Con-sumption	Price Value of Imports $ Per Carat	Secon-dary Pro-duction	Imports for Con-sumption	Exports & Reexports	Gov't Sales	Apparent Con-sumption	Price Value of Imports $ Per Carat	% of Con-sumption
2000	182.0	10.0	291.0	98.0	----	----	385.0	.39	[3] 2.5	1.6	1.0	2.2	5.31	86
2001	202.0	10.0	281.0	88.0	----	----	405.0	.31	[3] 2.5	1.0	.5	2.2	3.54	91
2002	219.0	5.7	185.0	82.0	----	----	328.0	.34	[3] 2.0	1.1	.4	1.6	5.43	88
2003	236.0	4.7	250.0	74.0	----	----	417.0	.26	[3] 1.8	.3	.4	2.1	3.09	80
2004[1]	252.0	4.6	240.0	86.0	----	----	411.0	.25	[3] 1.8	.5	.4	2.1	7.77	85
2005[2]	252.0	4.6	289.0	95.0	----	----	451.0	.28	[3] 2.3			2.7	12.55	84

[1] Preliminary. [2] Estimate. [3] Less than 1/2 unit.   Source: U.S. Geological Survey (USGS)

Eggs

Eggs are a low-priced protein source and are consumed worldwide. Each commercial chicken lays between 265-280 eggs per year. In the United States, the grade and size of eggs are regulated under the federal Egg Products Inspection Act (1970). The grades of eggs are AA, A, and B, and must have sound, whole shells and must be clean. The difference among the grades of eggs is internal and mostly reflects the freshness of the egg. Table eggs vary in color and can be determined by the color of the chicken's earlobe—white earlobes lay white eggs, reddish-brown earlobes lay brown eggs, etc. In the US, egg size is determined by the weight of a dozen eggs, not individual eggs, and range from Peewee to Jumbo. Store-bought eggs in the shell stay fresh for 3 to 5 weeks in a home refrigerator, according to the USDA.

Eggs are primarily used as a source of food, although eggs are also widely used for medical purposes. Fertile eggs, as a source of purified proteins, are used to produce many vaccines. Flu vaccines are produced by growing single strains of the flu virus in eggs, which are then extracted to make the vaccine. Eggs are also used in biotechnology to create new drugs. The hen's genetic make-up can be altered so the whites of the eggs are rich in tailored proteins that form the basis of medicines to fight cancer and other diseases. The US biotech company Viragen and the Roslin Institute in Edinburgh have produced eggs with 100 mg or more of the easily-extracted proteins used in new drugs to treat various illnesses including ovarian and breast cancers.

Prices – The average monthly price of all eggs received by farmers in the US in 2006 rose by +8.3.4% yr/yr to 58.9 cents per dozen, which was down from the 10-year high of 73.8 cents posted in 2003.

Supply – World egg production in 2001, the latest reporting year, was 795.711 billion eggs. The world's largest egg producers at that time were China with 49% of world production, the US with 11% (85.884 billion eggs), Japan with 5%, Russia with 4%, and Mexico with 4%. US egg production in 2006 rose +0.9% to 90.857 billion eggs, which was a new record high. The average number of hens and pullets on US farms in 2006 rose by +0.7% yr/yr to 346.078 million, which was a new record high.

Demand – US consumption of eggs in 2006 rose +1.8% yr/yr to 6.419 billion eggs. That was a new record high and was up about 23% from 10-years earlier, reflecting sharply higher egg consumption due to the popularity of a low-carbohydrate diet since eggs are high in protein. US per capita egg consumption in 2006 rose +0.4% yr/yr to 256.0 eggs per year per person. Per capita egg consumption was at a high of 277.2 eggs in 1970, fell sharply in the 1990s to a low of 174.9 in 1995, and then began rebounding in 1997 to current levels of over 250 eggs per year.

Trade – US imports of eggs in 2005 fell by –32.3% yr/yr to 8.6 million dozen eggs, falling from the 16-year high of 15.0 million posted in 2002. US exports of eggs in 2005 rose by +22.9% yr/yr to 205.9 million dozen eggs, but that was still well below the record export level of 253.1 million dozen eggs in 1996.

World Production of Eggs   In Millions of Eggs

Year	Brazil	China	France	Germany	Italy	Japan	Mexico	Russia	Spain	Ukraine	United Kingdom	United States	World Total[3]
1993	12,700	235,960	15,355	13,678	11,502	43,252	21,471	40,300	8,454	11,766	10,645	72,072	593,734
1994	13,460	281,010	16,370	13,960	11,599	43,047	25,896	37,400	9,670	10,145	10,620	74,136	643,045
1995	16,065	301,860	16,911	13,838	12,017	42,167	25,760	33,720	9,983	9,404	10,644	74,592	670,211
1996	15,932	253,680	16,500	13,922	11,923	42,786	26,045	31,500	8,952	8,763	10,668	76,536	631,846
1997	12,596	282,350	16,084	14,025	12,298	42,588	28,170	31,900	9,450	8,242	10,752	77,676	666,748
1998	13,636	307,760	16,900	14,164	12,433	42,117	29,898	33,000	9,084	8,269	10,812	79,896	695,281
1999	14,768	365,300	17,550	14,341	12,660	41,975	32,428	33,000	9,216	8,740	10,293	82,944	762,077
2000[1]	15,654	377,420	17,500	14,350	12,400	41,800	33,310	33,500	8,900	8,000	10,000	84,420	778,995
2001[2]	16,435	389,000	17,450	14,350	12,400	42,000	33,640	34,200	9,000	7,700	9,800	85,020	795,711

[1] Preliminary.   [2] Forecast.   [3] Selected countries.   *Source: Foreign Agricultural Service, U.S. Department of Agriculture (FAS-USDA)*

Salient Statistics of Eggs in the United States

| | -- Hens & Pullets -- | | Rate of Lay | --------- Eggs --------- | | | | | ----- Consumption ----- | | | |
| | On Farm Dec. 1[3] | Average Number During Year | Per Layer During Year[4] | Total Produced | Price in Cents Per Dozen | Value of Production[5] Million Dollars | Total Egg Production | Imports[6] | Exports[6] | Used for Hatching | Total | Per Capita Eggs[6] |
Year	----- Thousands -----		(Number)	------- Millions -------				---------------------------- Million Dozen ----------------------------				(Number)
1998	321,718	312,035	255	79,754	66.8	4,439	6,658	5.8	218.8	921.8	5,522	240.2
1999	329,320	322,354	257	82,715	62.2	4,287	6,912	7.4	161.9	941.7	5,817	250.1
2000	332,410	327,985	257	84,386	61.8	4,346	7,034	8.4	171.1	940.2	5,927	252.1
2001	338,628	335,012	256	85,745	62.2	4,446	7,157	8.9	190.0	964.2	6,013	252.7
2002	339,827	339,024	257	87,252	58.9	4,281	7,270	15.0	174.0	961.3	6,149	256.0
2003	340,979	338,393	259	87,473	73.2	5,333	7,297	13.3	146.2	959.4	6,201	255.7
2004	343,922	341,956	261	89,091	71.4	5,299	7,440	12.7	167.5	988.1	6,296	257.2
2005[1]	453,301	343,792	262	90,027	53.9	4,042	7,504	8.6	205.9	999.8	6,308	255.1
2006[2]	453,036	346,078	263	90,877			7,583	8.0	175.4	994.3	6,419	256.0

[1] Preliminary.   [2] Forecast.   [3] All layers of laying age.   [4] Number of eggs produced during the year divided by the average number of all layers of laying age on hand during the year.   [5] Value of sales plus value of eggs consumed in households of producers.   [6] Shell-egg equivalent of eggs and egg products.   *Source: National Agricultural Statistics Service, U.S. Department of Agriculture (NASS-USDA)*

EGGS

Eggs (monthly average) through December 2006   Cents per dozen

Cents Per Dozen
- - - - Fresh, Boston (1856 - 1899)
Fresh, New York (1900 - 1909)
Fresh Firsts, New York (Jan. 1910 - Dec. 1926)
Fresh Firsts, Chicago (Jan. 1927 - June 1943)
US Standards, Chicago (July 1943 - Dec. 1947)
Large, Chicago (Jan. 1948 - date)

Average Price Received by Farmers for All Eggs in the United States   In Cents Per Dozen

Year	Jan.	Feb.	Mar.	Apr.	May	June	July	Aug.	Sept.	Oct.	Nov.	Dec.	Average
1997	76.5	76.1	72.3	66.0	64.2	59.4	65.6	63.1	69.6	65.9	80.8	78.7	69.9
1998	74.3	64.9	69.9	63.7	54.9	59.6	58.2	65.0	63.3	66.3	72.8	75.5	65.7
1999	72.5	66.1	68.6	60.3	54.9	56.2	58.8	59.7	57.5	52.0	64.1	60.3	60.9
2000	57.8	67.8	56.9	64.7	52.0	61.8	56.5	66.4	59.2	66.8	72.0	80.7	63.6
2001	67.2	68.2	69.1	65.0	55.2	55.0	54.0	56.6	55.5	59.9	64.1	59.0	60.7
2002	62.3	55.9	68.5	52.2	50.5	62.1	60.8	66.4	57.1	56.0	70.7	62.8	60.4
2003	63.6	59.3	68.7	68.6	58.7	67.2	68.7	80.8	77.6	83.8	102.0	86.8	73.8
2004	92.6	87.5	110.0	76.7	62.6	77.3	64.0	52.6	53.8	49.4	60.4	65.4	71.0
2005	55.8	55.1	52.6	47.4	45.6	45.2	52.7	47.1	63.6	51.1	65.0	71.9	54.4
2006[1]	61.0	49.5	67.0	51.2	43.9	56.3	45.6	57.4	56.0	56.7	81.7	80.7	58.9

[1] Preliminary.   *Source: Economic Research Service, U.S. Department of Agriculture (NASS-USDA)*

Average Wholesale Price of Shell Eggs (Large) Delivered, Chicago   In Cents Per Dozen

Year	Jan.	Feb.	Mar.	Apr.	May	June	July	Aug.	Sept.	Oct.	Nov.	Dec.	Average
1997	79.77	75.18	77.25	68.55	64.40	61.02	74.66	66.07	74.26	68.39	89.87	82.68	73.51
1998	75.20	64.92	74.68	63.64	51.91	61.86	65.00	68.76	67.76	71.45	75.85	75.27	68.03
1999	72.34	62.13	67.85	52.74	51.35	47.86	58.40	59.30	52.86	48.38	59.26	56.38	57.40
2000	54.97	59.65	52.93	61.71	42.59	55.18	52.80	64.39	58.08	66.45	74.26	84.90	60.66
2001	68.52	64.45	69.00	66.12	50.61	49.81	52.83	55.46	50.21	57.41	62.50	58.05	58.75
2002	60.43	52.00	68.00	47.23	43.73	56.40	53.02	57.16	53.20	54.43	74.00	66.38	57.17
2003	69.57	65.39	71.05	68.83	59.10	68.76	72.39	88.26	86.21	92.07	113.16	101.09	79.66
2004	105.10	103.89	115.00	86.88	67.28	70.00	63.12	59.45	55.81	53.79	60.36	69.83	75.88
2005	54.78	60.26	48.32	42.00	41.57	40.72	51.38	42.78	61.19	48.38	62.41	70.21	52.00
2006[1]	65.40	46.08	65.11	57.11	41.32	56.14	40.30	57.46	54.97	55.64	84.38	87.65	59.30

[1] Preliminary.   *Source: National Agricultural Statistics Service, U.S. Department of Agriculture (NASS-USDA)*

Total Egg Production in the United States   In Millions of Eggs

Year	Jan.	Feb.	Mar.	Apr.	May	June	July	Aug.	Sept.	Oct.	Nov.	Dec.	Total
1997	6,577	5,909	6,625	6,355	6,519	6,292	6,457	6,500	6,366	6,664	6,572	6,841	77,677
1998	6,766	6,109	6,869	6,603	6,665	6,456	6,720	6,694	6,480	6,791	6,723	7,047	79,923
1999	6,979	6,281	7,052	6,784	6,941	6,742	6,903	6,971	6,860	7,131	7,016	7,279	82,939
2000	7,157	6,648	7,234	7,013	7,104	6,801	7,061	7,104	6,854	7,130	7,027	7,287	84,420
2001	7,226	6,524	7,336	7,099	7,240	6,992	7,195	7,221	7,044	7,347	7,191	7,420	85,835
2002	7,264	6,581	7,417	7,105	7,297	7,126	7,347	7,356	7,147	7,412	7,226	7,451	86,729
2003	7,390	6,665	7,424	7,187	7,327	7,105	7,403	7,367	7,112	7,439	7,326	7,554	87,299
2004	7,386	6,901	7,547	7,358	7,513	7,289	7,557	7,538	7,344	7,659	7,482	7,721	89,295
2005	7,626	6,928	7,738	7,407	7,572	7,346	7,563	7,528	7,348	7,665	7,514	7,793	90,028
2006[1]	7,727	6,980	7,843	7,543	7,637	7,401	7,645	7,647	7,430	7,678	7,549	7,777	90,857

[1] Preliminary.   Source: National Agricultural Statistics Service, U.S. Department of Agriculture (NASS-USDA)

Per Capita Disappearance of Eggs in the United States   In Number of Eggs

Year	First Quarter	Second Quarter	Third Quarter	Fourth Quarter	Total	Total Consumption (Million Dozen)	Year	First Quarter	Second Quarter	Third Quarter	Fourth Quarter	Total	Total Consumption (Million Dozen)
1996	44.5	42.1	43.4	45.0	175.0	5,242	2002	62.4	62.6	64.0	64.6	256.0	6,150
1997	59.0	59.3	59.7	62.1	240.1	5,359	2003	62.6	63.0	63.8	65.3	255.7	6,200
1998	60.5	60.5	61.1	63.2	244.9	5,522	2004	63.7	63.9	64.1	65.5	257.2	6,296
1999	62.7	62.8	63.8	66.2	255.7	5,817	2005[1]	63.4	63.0	63.5	65.0	255.1	6,308
2000	64.5	64.0	64.2	65.6	258.2	5,927	2006[2]	63.9	63.5	63.8	64.8	256.0	6,419
2001	64.5	64.2	64.7	66.6	252.7	6,013	2007[3]	63.6	63.8	64.4	65.3	257.1	6,530

[1] Preliminary.   [2] Estimate.   [3] Forecast   Source: Economic Research Service, U.S. Department of Agriculture (ERS-USDA)

Egg-Feed Ratio[1] in the United States

Year	Jan.	Feb.	Mar.	Apr.	May	June	July	Aug.	Sept.	Oct.	Nov.	Dec.	Average
1997	10.1	9.9	8.6	7.4	7.1	6.6	8.2	7.8	9.3	8.7	11.4	11.0	8.8
1998	10.1	8.3	9.4	8.5	6.7	8.0	7.9	10.8	10.7	11.3	12.6	12.8	9.7
1999	11.7	10.6	11.3	9.2	7.8	8.2	9.9	10.1	9.3	8.0	11.9	10.1	9.8
2000	8.9	11.3	8.0	9.9	6.4	9.5	9.2	12.9	10.3	12.2	13.1	15.0	10.6
2001	10.9	11.4	11.6	11.3	8.6	8.5	7.9	8.4	8.5	10.3	11.5	9.3	9.9
2002	10.2	8.4	11.6	7.4	6.7	9.5	7.5	7.9	7.1	6.6	10.5	8.9	8.5
2003	9.0	8.0	9.5	9.3	6.9	8.8	9.8	12.7	11.6	12.6	15.7	12.2	10.5
2004	12.9	10.7	13.2	7.8	6.0	6.6	5.9	5.6	6.5	5.8	8.8	9.8	8.3
2005	7.2	7.4	6.3	5.2	4.6	4.4	5.9	5.1	9.3	6.6	10.3	11.3	7.0
2006[2]	8.5	5.9	9.8	6.2	4.4	7.1	4.8	7.8	7.3	6.7	10.6	10.1	7.4

[1] Pounds of laying feed equivalent in value to one dozen eggs.   [2] Preliminary.   Source: Economic Research Service, U.S. Department of Agriculture (ERS-USDA)

Hens and Pullets of Laying Age (Layers) in the United States, on First of Month   In Thousands

Year	Jan.	Feb.	Mar.	Apr.	May	June	July	Aug.	Sept.	Oct.	Nov.	Dec.
1997	305,011	303,449	304,276	303,997	302,766	300,692	299,007	298,844	300,138	305,664	307,146	312,137
1998	311,593	312,111	314,322	313,833	309,945	309,235	309,049	308,747	309,706	312,807	316,840	321,718
1999	322,137	322,382	323,161	322,162	320,783	320,211	320,672	318,944	321,349	323,365	327,135	329,320
2000	328,307	328,767	330,876	330,807	327,597	325,012	324,843	326,240	325,212	327,219	329,092	332,410
2001	332,107	335,449	336,131	337,472	336,755	333,522	332,274	332,148	333,417	336,573	337,549	338,625
2002	339,423	338,465	337,478	337,376	336,131	335,547	335,236	335,717	336,561	337,923	338,350	339,827
2003	340,752	341,019	340,080	339,645	336,678	335,611	333,925	334,381	334,248	334,103	336,528	339,989
2004	338,272	338,774	340,479	342,879	342,305	343,233	342,392	342,522	343,405	344,794	345,267	344,278
2005	347,273	348,412	349,117	344,759	342,346	341,247	338,424	338,674	339,984	341,803	343,789	347,917
2006[1]	349,763	349,930	350,184	349,958	346,308	343,088	341,219	340,223	341,748	343,436	344,313	348,268

[1] Preliminary.   Source: National Agricultural Statistics Service, U.S. Department of Agriculture (NASS-USDA)

EGGS

Eggs Laid Per Hundred Layers in the United States In Number of Eggs

Year	Jan.	Feb.	Mar.	Apr.	May	June	July	Aug.	Sept.	Oct.	Nov.	Dec.	Average
1997	2,161	1,943	2,176	2,093	2,156	2,093	2,155	2,165	2,096	2,172	2,122	2,193	2,127
1998	2,169	1,950	2,187	2,117	2,153	2,088	2,175	2,165	2,082	2,157	2,109	2,190	2,129
1999	2,165	1,946	2,185	2,110	2,166	2,104	2,158	2,177	2,128	2,192	2,138	2,214	2,140
2000	2,178	2,016	2,186	2,130	2,177	2,093	2,169	2,181	2,101	2,173	2,125	2,193	2,144
2001	2,165	1,943	2,178	2,106	2,160	2,100	2,166	2,170	2,103	2,180	2,130	2,188	2,132
2002	2,143	1,947	2,198	2,110	2,173	2,125	2,190	2,188	2,119	2,192	2,139	2,189	2,143
2003	2,168	1,957	2,184	2,125	2,180	2,122	2,215	2,203	2,128	2,218	2,166	2,223	2,157
2004	2,182	2,032	2,209	2,148	2,192	2,126	2,207	2,198	2,134	2,220	2,170	2,234	2,171
2005	2,192	1,986	2,230	2,156	2,215	2,162	2,234	2,218	2,155	2,236	2,172	2,234	2,183
2006[1]	2,210	1,995	2,239	2,164	2,213	2,161	2,241	2,239	2,166	2,229	2,175	2,234	2,189

[1] Preliminary.   *Source: National Agricultural Statistics Service, U.S. Department of Agriculture (NASS-USDA)*

Egg-Type Chicks Hatched by Commercial Hatcheries in the United States   In Thousands

Year	Jan.	Feb.	Mar.	Apr.	May	June	July	Aug.	Sept.	Oct.	Nov.	Dec.	Total
1997	33,752	35,655	37,347	38,842	39,020	36,796	33,772	33,061	37,118	35,262	28,122	35,796	424,543
1998	37,168	34,597	40,604	39,057	39,206	39,323	35,576	33,398	37,959	34,667	31,217	35,501	438,273
1999	35,242	36,367	41,172	42,285	40,726	41,439	34,275	35,518	39,287	39,044	32,802	33,564	451,721
2000	34,181	34,659	38,877	36,653	41,185	37,268	33,240	34,328	36,325	36,080	32,438	35,178	430,412
2001	36,728	37,836	41,015	42,789	42,655	40,822	38,651	34,987	37,140	35,825	32,355	31,870	452,673
2002	35,655	34,473	36,985	38,096	38,760	35,144	35,581	35,689	35,742	32,157	31,154	32,113	421,549
2003	33,521	30,474	36,775	37,820	37,630	36,602	35,578	33,199	35,763	34,812	30,241	33,588	416,003
2004	35,155	31,923	37,545	37,466	38,347	37,508	34,919	36,854	36,631	34,866	38,758	37,332	437,304
2005	38,291	34,427	41,701	38,049	38,792	35,034	34,897	38,700	33,623	35,461	32,285	35,917	437,177
2006[1]	35,422	33,665	38,918	34,613	40,320	37,700	33,224	34,892	36,845	36,271	31,748	33,430	427,048

[1] Preliminary.   *Source: National Agricultural Statistics Service, U.S. Department of Agriculture (NASS-USDA)*

Cold Storage Holdings of Frozen Eggs in the United States, on First of Month   In Millions of Pounds[2]

Year	Jan.	Feb.	Mar.	Apr.	May	June	July	Aug.	Sept.	Oct.	Nov.	Dec.
1997	10.2	11.0	11.5	8.5	8.5	8.2	8.3	8.9	11.1	10.8	10.9	10.3
1998	9.7	12.0	12.3	10.4	9.2	12.9	10.2	11.8	9.0	8.2	9.0	9.3
1999	11.0	11.0	10.8	9.2	9.4	9.7	11.3	11.1	8.8	9.5	9.0	8.5
2000	10.1	17.6	14.8	14.0	12.8	13.5	14.1	14.4	14.9	14.4	16.6	15.4
2001	15.0	16.9	15.5	14.6	15.9	15.8	14.4	16.7	17.8	17.7	15.5	13.9
2002	13.7	13.1	13.9	11.7	10.2	11.1	12.7	12.9	13.2	13.2	13.1	11.2
2003	13.5	15.3	17.1	17.0	15.7	17.7	18.0	18.6	18.0	16.6	16.9	14.9
2004	18.0	21.3	21.1	19.2	20.9	20.6	18.3	16.7	17.3	18.7	17.9	17.3
2005	19.1	18.6	17.9	18.5	18.9	17.7	19.7	19.6	19.9	18.8	17.6	17.6
2006[1]	21.0	22.5	24.4	20.8	23.3	21.0	22.1	23.6	21.6	19.0	16.3	17.1

[1] Preliminary.   [2] Converted on basis 39.5 pounds frozen eggs equals 1 case.   *Source: National Agricultural Statistics Service, U.S. Department of Agriculture (NASS-USDA)*

Electric Power

The modern electric utility industry began in the 1800s. In 1807, Humphry Davy constructed a practical battery and demonstrated both incandescent and arc light. In 1831, Michael Faraday built the first electric generator proving that rotary mechanical power could be converted into electric power. In 1879, Thomas Edison perfected a practical incandescent light bulb. The electric utility industry evolved from gas and electric carbon-arc commercial and street lighting systems. In 1882, in New York City, Thomas Edison's Pearl Street electricity generating station established the industry by displaying the four key elements of a modern electric utility system: reliable central generation, efficient distribution, successful end use, and a competitive price.

Electricity is measured in units called watts and watt-hours. Electricity must be used shortly after it is generated and cannot be stored to any significant degree. That means the power utilities must match the level of electricity generation to the level of demand in order to avoid wasteful over-production. The power industry has been deregulated to some degree in the past decade and now major utility companies sell power back and forth across major national grids in order to meet supply and demand needs. The quick changes in the supply-demand situation means that the price of electricity can be volatile.

Electricity futures trade at the New York Mercantile Exchange (NYMEX). The futures contract is a financially settled contract, which is priced based on electricity prices in the PJM western hub at 111 delivery points, mainly on the utility transmission systems of Pennsylvania Electric Co. and the Potomac Electric Co. The contract is priced in dollars and cents per megawatt hours.

Supply – US electricity production in 2006 (through October, annualized) rose +0.6% yr/yr to 2.568 trillion kilowatt-hours. That was well below the record high of 3.212 trillion kilowatt-hours in 1998 and indicated that recent electricity production has been reduced by more efficient production and distribution systems, and to some extent by electricity conservation by business and residential consumers. US electricity generation in 2005 (latest data available) required the use of 2.148 trillion cubic feet of natural gas (+18.8% yr/yr), 781 million short tons of coal (+1.1% yr/yr), and 98 million barrels of fuel oil (-5.1% yr/yr).

In terms of kilowatt-hours, coal is the most widely used source of electricity production, accounting for 60% of US electricity production in 2005 (latest data available), followed by nuclear (18%), hydro (11%), natural gas (9%), and fuel oil (3%). Alternative sources of fuel for electricity generation that are gaining favor include biomass, solar, wind, and fuel cells.

Demand – Residential use of electricity accounts for the largest single category of electricity demand with usage of 1.359 trillion kilowatt hours in 2005 (latest data available) accounting for 36% of overall usage. Business users together use more electricity than residential users, but business users are broken into the categories of commercial with 33% of usage and industrial with 27% of usage.

World Electricity Production (Monthly Average)   In Millions of Kilowatt Hours

Year	Australia	Canada	China	Germany	India	Italy	Japan	Rep. of Korea	Russia	South Africa	Ukraine	United Kingdom	United States
1997	15,256	47,929	94,539	45,961	35,146	20,898	86,676	18,704	69,511	16,108	14,834	27,012	291,185
1998	14,974	54,393	97,183	46,367	37,379	21,659	76,763	17,942	68,930	17,119	14,402	27,928	301,489
1999	15,399	55,809	100,345	45,820	40,148	22,136	76,755	19,944	70,611	16,961	14,342	28,095	308,572
2000	15,712	58,337	109,426	46,417	41,725	22,986	78,391	22,200	73,117	17,557	14,287	28,484	316,845
2001	15,548	56,576	118,439	47,107	42,434	23,242	77,742	23,768	74,031	17,508	14,414	29,415	311,387
2002	15,646	57,873	133,513	47,211	44,141	23,638	77,139	25,500	74,078	18,142	14,477	29,220	321,538
2003	15,564	56,294	153,229	49,060	52,773	24,386	76,661	26,856	76,158	17,534	15,030	35,006	307,250
2004	16,095	56,844	176,169	44,439	48,968	24,975	71,574	28,472	77,562	20,238	15,180	34,924	316,000
2005[1]	16,336	49,559	199,785	46,738	50,465		80,267	30,363	79,355	19,575	15,418	34,462	336,499
2006[2]	16,835	48,558	225,575	44,023	53,687		82,024	31,345	79,450	21,536	15,595		344,502

[1] Preliminary.   [2] Estimate.   *Source: United Nations*

Installed Capacity, Capability & Peak Load of the U.S. Electric Utility Industry   In Millions of Kilowatt Hours

Year	Total Electric Utility Industry	Hydro	Gas, Turbine & Steam	Nuclear Power	Internal Combustion	Investor Owned	Cooperative	Subtotal Gov't	Municipal Utilities	Federal	Power Districts, State Projects	Capability at Winter Peak Load	Non-Coincident Winter Peak Load	Capacity Margin Non-Coincident Peak Load (%)	Total Electric Utility Industry Generation	Annual Peak Load Factor (%)
1990	735.1	87.2	531.1	108.0	8.7	568.8	26.3	139.9	40.1	65.4	34.4	696.8	484.0	20.4	2,808.2	60.4
1991	740.0	88.7	534.1	108.4	8.8	573.0	26.5	140.5	40.4	65.6	34.5	703.2	485.4	20.2	2,825.0	60.9
1992	741.7	89.7	534.5	107.9	9.6	572.9	26.0	142.7	41.6	66.1	35.0	707.8	493.0	21.1	2,797.2	61.1
1993	744.7	90.2	536.9	107.8	9.8	575.2	26.1	143.4	41.8	66.1	35.5	712.0	521.7	17.1	2,882.5	61.0
1994	746.0	90.3	537.9	107.9	9.9	574.8	26.4	144.7	42.0	66.3	36.4	715.1	518.3	16.7	2,910.7	61.2
1995	750.5	91.1	541.6	107.9	9.9	578.7	27.1	144.8	42.2	65.9	36.6	727.7	544.7	13.2	2,994.5	59.8
1996	756.5	91.0	546.6	109.0	9.9	582.2	27.2	147.1	43.0	67.2	36.9	740.5	545.1	14.9	3,073.1	61.0
1997	759.9	92.5	549.7	107.6	10.0	582.5	28.0	149.4	43.8	68.9	36.7	743.8	560.2	13.4	3,119.1	61.3
1998	728.3	91.2	522.1	104.8	10.2	531.3	32.5	164.5	50.5	68.7	45.3	835.3	652.4	12.0	3,212.2	62.0
1999[1]	678.0	89.8	476.3	102.3	9.6	483.7	34.6	159.6	50.2	68.7	40.7	848.9	656.3	10.3	3,173.7	61.2

[1] Preliminary.   *Source: Edison Electric Institute (EEI)*

ELECTRIC POWER

Available Electricity and Energy Sales in the United States — In Billions of Kilowatt Hours

	Net Generation — Electric Utility Industry							Sales to Ultimate Customers							
Year	Total[2]	Hydro	Natural Gas	Coal	Fuel Oil	Nu-clear	Other Source[3]	Total	Total Million $	Total	Resi-den-tial	Inter-depart-mental	Com-mercial	Indust-rial	Street & Highway Lighting	Other Public Auth.	Rail ways & Rail-roads
1996	3,077	347.2	262.7	1,737	67.3	674.7	7.2	3,444	212,609	3,101	1,083	2.5	887.4	1,034	18.0	70.3	5.3
1997	3,123	356.5	283.6	1,788	77.8	628.6	7.5	3,492	215,334	3,146	1,076	2.6	928.6	1,037	19.7	75.6	5.3
1998	3,212	323.3	309.2	1,807	110.2	673.7	7.2	3,620	219,848	3,264	1,130	[4]	979.4	1,051	16.3	87.2	[4]
1999	3,174	319.5	296.4	1,768	86.9	725.0	3.7	3,695	219,896	3,312	1,145	[4]	1,002.0	1,058	15.9	107.0	[4]
2000	3,015	275.6	290.7	1,697	72.2	705.4	2.2	3,802	233,163	3,421	1,192	[4]	1,055.2	1,064	[4]	109.5	[4]
2001	2,630	217.0	264.4	1,560	78.9	534.2	2.2	3,737	247,325	3,382	1,201	[4]	1,088.0	985	[4]	108.4	[4]
2002	2,549	264.3	229.6	1,515	59.1	507.4	3.6	3,858	250,189	3,466	1,265	[4]	1,104.7	990	[4]	105.8	[4]
2003	2,462	275.8	187.0	1,500	69.9	458.8	3.9	3,883	259,767	3,662	1,276	[4]	1,198.7	1,012	[4]	NA	[4]
2004	2,505	268.4	199.7	1,514	73.7	475.7	4.1	3,971	270,119	3,716	1,292	[4]	1,230.4	1,018	[4]	NA	[4]
2005[1]	2,554	269.6	238.5	1,534	70.8	465.1	5.3	4,055	298,003	3,816	1,359	[4]	1,275.1	1,019	[4]	NA	[4]

[1] Preliminary. [2] Includes internal combustion. [3] Includes electricity produced from geothermal, wood, waste, wind, solar, etc. [4] Included in Other. NA = Not available. *Source: Edison Electric Institute (EEI)*

Electric Power Production by Electric Utilities in the United States — In Millions of Kilowatt Hours

Year	Jan.	Feb.	Mar.	Apr.	May	June	July	Aug.	Sept.	Oct.	Nov.	Dec.	Total
1997	273,410	233,907	244,659	230,512	243,143	266,588	304,628	294,557	266,649	253,267	243,726	267,477	3,122,523
1998	265,435	235,340	256,575	232,457	265,077	291,029	317,521	312,538	279,198	251,380	239,089	266,532	3,212,171
1999	275,230	239,825	258,678	238,969	255,266	281,233	318,745	307,835	261,347	243,212	235,129	258,205	3,173,674
2000	265,991	237,324	241,397	227,031	253,890	268,128	279,421	286,682	245,137	228,389	226,765	255,229	3,015,383
2001	236,467	199,802	211,942	197,499	215,508	233,622	253,400	258,901	214,236	204,307	192,518	211,742	2,629,946
2002	215,684	187,929	200,833	194,038	208,436	227,940	248,962	241,449	215,408	201,705	194,205	212,868	2,549,457
2003	217,338	189,944	193,305	181,914	200,634	212,297	234,888	234,675	201,966	192,198	189,362	213,758	2,462,281
2004	221,782	198,675	193,763	182,744	207,224	219,767	235,266	227,785	209,507	197,320	191,813	219,585	2,505,231
2005	218,914	191,246	202,430	183,701	203,461	228,298	246,778	246,019	217,938	200,389	194,838	220,039	2,554,051
2006[1]	212,083	198,062	202,443	189,111	209,400	229,154	248,782	247,571	205,328	198,306	195,313		2,547,876

[1] Preliminary. *Source: Energy Information Administration, U.S. Department of Energy (EIA-DOE)*

Use of Fuels for Electric Generation in the United States

Year	Coal (Thousand Short Tons)	Fuel Oil (Thousand Barels)[2]	Gas (Million Cubic Feet)	Total Fuel in Coal Equivalent[3] (Thousand Short Tons)	Net Generation by Fuels[4] (Million Kilowatthour)	Pounds of Coal Per Kilowatthour (Pounds)	Cost of Fossil-fuel at Elec. Util. Cents/MBTU	Average Cost of Fuel Per Kiliowatthour (Cents)	Heat Rate BTU Per kilowatthour	Cost Per Million BTU Consumed (Cents)
1996	874,681	113,274	2,732,107	1,063,755	2,066,666	1.007	151.9	1.55	10,176	151.9
1997	900,361	125,146	2,968,453	1,103,037	2,148,756	1.005	152.2	1.53	10,081	152.2
1998	910,867	178,614	3,258,054	1,147,317	2,226,860	.996	143.8	1.49	10,360	143.8
1999	894,120	143,830	3,113,419	1,113,614	2,150,989	1.012	144.1	1.48	10,301	144.1
2000	859,335	120,129	3,043,094				173.8			
2001	806,269	126,367	2,686,287				173.0			
2002	767,803	88,595	2,259,684				151.5			
2003	757,384	105,319	1,763,764							
2004	772,224	103,785	1,808,836							
2005[1]	781,031	98,458	2,148,035							

[1] Preliminary. [2] 42-gallon barrels. [3] Coal equivalents are calculated on the basis of Btu instead of generation data. [4] Excludes wood & waste fuels.
Source: Edison Electric Institute (EEI)

Ethanol

World Production of Ethanol   In Millions of Gallons

Year	Brazil	China	France	Germany	India	Russia	Saudi Arabia	South Africa	Spain	Thailand	United Kingdom	United States	Total World
2004	3,989	964	219	71	462	198	79	110	79	74	106	3,535	10,770
2005[1]	4,227	1,004	240	114	449	198	32	103	93	79	92	4,264	12,150

[1] Preliminary.   *Source: Renewable Fuels Association*

Salient Statistics of Ethanol in the United States

Year	Ethanol Plants	Ethanol Production Capacity (mgy)	Plants Under Construction	Capacity Under Construction (mgy)	Farmer Owned Plants	Farmer Owned Capacity (mgy)	Percent of Total Capacity Farmer	Farmer Owned UC Plants	Farmers Owned UC Capacity	Percent of UC Capacity	States with Ethanol Plants
1999	50	1,701.7	5	77.0	14	293.3	17	5	77	100	17
2000	54	1,748.7	6	91.5	18	340.3	19	3	60	66	17
2001	56	1,921.9	5	64.7	21	473.0	25	3	60	71	18
2002	61	2,347.3	13	390.7	25	645.6	28	10	335	86	19
2003	68	2,706.8	11	483.0	28	796.6	29	8	318	66	20
2004	72	3,100.8	15	598.0	33	1,041.1	34	12	447	75	19
2005	81	3,643.7	16	754.0	40	1,388.6	38	10	450	60	18
2006[1]	95	4,336.4	31	1,778.0	46	1,677.1	39	4	187	11	20

[1] Preliminary.   *Source: Renewable Fuels Association*

Production of Fuel Ethanol in the United States   In Thousands of Barrels Per Day

Year	Jan.	Feb.	Mar.	Apr.	May	June	July	Aug.	Sept.	Oct.	Nov.	Dec.	Average
1997	80	82	86	77	89	75	77	80	80	87	98	98	84
1998	96	85	86	85	81	83	85	87	98	103	97	100	91
1999	102	99	102	99	93	83	77	93	97	106	100	100	96
2000	110	108	104	110	103	104	103	98	101	111	109	113	106
2001	115	116	113	108	108	110	112	113	116	121	126	124	115
2002	135	122	128	126	129	123	128	136	145	159	166	176	139
2003	177	169	175	179	175	181	178	180	190	188	194	207	183
2004	211	212	214	218	221	222	218	225	226	226	232	232	221
2005	241	245	243	238	237	249	258	260	261	269	275	280	255
2006[1]	288	302	301	289	293	318	316	329	333	333	343		313

[1] Preliminary.   *Source: Energy Information Administration, U.S. Department of Energy (EIA-DOE)*

Production of Fuel Ethanol in the United States   In Thousands of Barrels

Year	Jan.	Feb.	Mar.	Apr.	May	June	July	Aug.	Sept.	Oct.	Nov.	Dec.	Total
1999	3,159	2,782	3,163	2,975	2,894	2,496	2,399	2,884	2,917	3,272	2,998	3,102	35,041
2000	3,329	3,145	3,209	3,143	3,179	3,128	3,208	3,052	3,026	3,438	3,281	3,505	38,643
2001	3,574	3,249	3,500	3,226	3,339	3,310	3,472	3,526	3,470	3,743	3,794	3,836	42,039
2002	3,974	3,429	3,996	3,788	4,007	3,705	3,970	4,203	4,342	4,939	4,965	5,451	50,769
2003	5,497	4,734	5,430	5,384	5,426	5,440	5,529	5,589	5,685	5,829	5,806	6,423	66,772
2004	6,551	6,155	6,648	6,525	6,857	6,648	6,749	6,977	6,766	7,007	6,946	7,180	81,009
2005	7,461	6,847	7,521	7,135	7,357	7,463	8,007	8,050	7,841	8,335	8,259	8,676	92,952
2006[1]	8,942	8,452	9,338	8,656	9,093	9,532	9,804	10,185	9,992	10,308	10,279		114,088

[1] Preliminary.   *Source: Energy Information Administration, U.S. Department of Energy (EIA-DOE)*

Stocks of Fuel Ethanol in the United States   In Thousands of Barrels

Year	Jan.	Feb.	Mar.	Apr.	May	June	July	Aug.	Sept.	Oct.	Nov.	Dec.
1997	2,169	2,139	2,291	2,302	2,681	2,966	2,620	3,036	3,109	2,605	3,005	2,758
1998	2,633	2,519	2,360	2,423	2,732	2,829	2,951	2,991	3,169	3,195	3,300	2,814
1999	2,973	3,240	3,722	4,222	4,624	4,382	4,440	4,640	4,868	4,798	4,362	3,592
2000	3,692	4,097	3,949	4,353	4,202	4,805	4,916	4,553	4,436	4,103	3,647	3,227
2001	2,582	2,525	2,547	2,807	3,029	3,095	3,388	4,226	4,225	3,521	3,785	4,013
2002	4,627	4,613	5,192	5,590	5,728	5,962	5,883	6,029	6,231	6,350	5,871	6,176
2003	6,680	5,841	6,783	6,704	6,695	6,752	6,474	6,218	6,745	6,674	5,848	5,255
2004	5,291	5,200	5,245	4,989	5,170	5,090	5,554	6,072	6,020	6,281	6,095	5,991
2005	6,136	6,199	6,562	6,823	6,762	6,016	5,848	5,246	5,324	5,591	5,720	5,563
2006[1]	6,173	7,376	8,708	9,087	7,848	6,731	7,727	9,160	9,727	9,814	9,212	

[1] Preliminary.   *Source: Energy Information Administration, U.S. Department of Energy (EIA-DOE)*

ETHANOL

Ethanol Futures - Chicago Board of Trade
(weekly close) as of December 29, 2006

Cents per pound

Average Price of Ethanol in the United States   In Dollars Per Gallon

Year	Jan.	Feb.	Mar.	Apr.	May	June	July	Aug.	Sept.	Oct.	Nov.	Dec.	Average
1997	----	----	----	----	----	----	----	----	1.238	1.251	1.260	1.256	1.251
1998	1.242	1.212	1.144	1.083	1.078	1.114	1.130	1.135	1.132	1.113	1.075	1.034	1.124
1999	1.033	1.032	1.044	1.023	1.016	0.992	0.986	0.990	0.991	0.996	1.032	1.170	1.025
2000	1.285	1.275	1.331	1.329	1.314	1.471	1.402	1.405	1.533	1.558	1.687	1.696	1.441
2001	1.783	1.737	1.579	1.571	1.707	1.646	1.457	1.551	1.593	1.375	1.188	1.012	1.517
2002	0.979	0.973	1.125	1.070	0.982	1.046	1.156	1.330	1.335	1.238	1.263	1.210	1.142
2003	1.151	1.278	1.427	1.269	1.131	1.242	1.234	1.262	1.388	1.381	1.645	1.716	1.344
2004	1.423	1.398	1.666	1.791	1.753	1.862	1.762	1.624	1.585	1.878	1.995	1.812	1.712
2005	1.733	1.597	1.365	1.237	1.221	1.405	1.786	2.031	2.695	2.511	2.130	1.916	1.802
2006	1.967	2.428	2.450	2.475	2.903	3.597	3.208	2.668	2.148	1.815	2.045	2.234	2.495

[1] Northeast and Northwest Iowa.   *Source: Agricultural Marketing Service, U.S. Department of Agriculture (AMS-USDA)*

Volume of Trading of Ethanol Futures in Chicago   In Contracts

Year	Jan.	Feb.	Mar.	Apr.	May	June	July	Aug.	Sept.	Oct.	Nov.	Dec.	Total
2005	----	----	350	119	222	61	155	321	227	390	559	272	2,676
2006	443	508	329	421	330	686	1,141	365	779	348	97	117	5,564

Source: Chicago Board of Trade (CBT)

Month-End Open Interest of Ethanol Futures in Chicago   In Contracts

Year	Jan.	Feb.	Mar.	Apr.	May	June	July	Aug.	Sept.	Oct.	Nov.	Dec.
2005	----	----	246	215	88	39	61	208	301	461	759	778
2006	774	856	860	900	745	735	829	599	474	442	396	322

Source: Chicago Board of Trade (CBT)

Fertilizer

Fertilizer is a natural or synthetic chemical substance, or mixture, that enriches soil to promote plant growth. The three primary nutrients that fertilizers provide are nitrogen, potassium, and phosphorus. In ancient times, and still today, many commonly used fertilizers contain one or more of the three primary ingredients: manure (containing nitrogen), bones (containing small amounts of nitrogen and large quantities of phosphorus), and wood ash (containing potassium).

At least fourteen different nutrients have been found essential for crops. These include three organic nutrients (carbon, hydrogen, and oxygen, which are taken directly from air and water), three primary chemical nutrients (nitrogen, phosphorus, and potassium), and three secondary chemical nutrients (magnesium, calcium, and sulfur). The others are micronutrients or trace elements and include iron, manganese, copper, zinc, boron, and molybdenum.

Prices – The average price of ammonia, a key source of ingredients for fertilizers, rose by 14.6% yr/yr in 2005 to a record high of $314 per metric ton. The average price of phosphate rock in the US in 2005 rose by 4.9% yr/yr to a record high of $29.20 per metric ton. The average price of potash in the US in 2005 rose by +15.0% yr/yr to a record high of $230.00 per metric ton.

Supply – World production of nitrogen (as contained in ammonia) in 2005 rose by +3.4% yr/yr to a new record high of 121.000 million metric tons. The world's largest producers of nitrogen in 2005 were China with 31% of world production, India (8.9%), Russia (8.3%), and the US (6.6%). US nitrogen production in 2005 fell –10.6% to 8,040 million metric tons.

World production of phosphate rock, basic slag and guano in 2005 rose +4.3% yr/yr to a 14-year high of 147.000 million metric tons. The world's largest producers of phosphate rock in 2005 were the US with 25% of world production, China (21%), Morocco (17%), and Russia (8%). US production in 2005 rose +1.4% y/y to 36.300 million metric tons.

World production of marketable potash rose by +2.3% yr/yr in 2005 to a 17-year high of 31.100 million metric tons. The world's largest producers of potash in 2005 were Canada with 32% of world production, Russia (18%), Belarus (16%), and Germany (12%). US production of potash in 2005 fell –7.7% yr/yr 1.200 million metric tons.

Demand – US consumption of nitrogen in 2005 fell –5.0% yr/yr to 11.300 million metric tons, down from last year's 4-year high of 11.900. US consumption of phosphate rock in 2005 fell –1.0% to 38.600 million metric tons but remained above the 18-year low of 35.300 million metric tons in 2001. US consumption of potash in 2005 was unchanged from last year's 6.000 million metric tons which is a 6-year high.

Trade – US imports of nitrogen in 2005 rose +10.5% to 6.520 million metric tons and the US relied on imports for 41% of consumption. US imports of phosphate rock in 2005 rose +4.9% yr/yr to 2.630 million metric tons, slightly below the 2002 record high of 2.700 million metric tons. US imports of potash was unchanged from last year's 4.920 million metric tons, and imports accounted for 80% of US consumption.

World Production of Ammonia   In Thousands of Metric Tons of Contained Nitrogen

Year	Canada	China	France	Germany	India	Indo-nesia	Japan	Mexico	Nether-lands	Poland	Russia	United States	World Total
1997	4,081	24,700	1,757	2,471	9,328	3,770	1,509	1,448	2,478	1,824	7,150	13,300	103,000
1998	3,900	25,800	1,570	2,512	10,240	3,600	1,389	1,449	2,350	1,683	6,500	13,800	104,000
1999	4,135	28,300	1,580	2,406	10,376	3,450	1,385	1,003	2,430	1,474	7,633	12,900	107,000
2000	4,130	27,700	1,620	2,473	10,148	3,620	1,410	701	2,540	1,862	8,735	11,800	108,000
2001	3,439	28,200	1,380	2,522	10,081	3,655	1,318	548	1,989	1,735	8,690	9,120	105,000
2002	3,700	30,200	1,172	2,623	9,827	4,200	1,192	437	2,053	1,311	8,600	10,300	109,000
2003	3,662	31,500	1,153	2,803	10,048	4,250	1,061	440	1,750	1,906	9,100	8,450	110,000
2004[1]	4,107	34,800	1,120	2,741	10,718	4,120	1,101	568	1,970	1,976	9,800	8,990	117,000
2005[2]	4,000	37,800	1,150	2,700	10,800	4,400	1,083	440	1,700	2,000	10,000	8,040	121,000

[1] Preliminary. [2] Estimate. *Source: U.S. Geological Survey (USGS)*

Salient Statistics of Nitrogen[3] (Ammonia) in the United States   In Thousands of Metric Tons

Year	Net Import Reliance as a % of Apparent Consumption	Production[3] (Fixed) Fertilizer	Non-fertilizer	Total	Imports[4] (Fixed)	Exports	Nitrogen[5] Compounds Produced	Con-sumption	Stocks, Dec. 31 Ammonia	Fixed Nitrogen Com-pounds	Ammonia Con-sumption (Apparent)	Urea FOB Gulf[6] Coast	Urea FOB Corn Belt	Ammonium Nitrate: FOB Corn Belt	Ammonia FOB Gulf Coast
1998	19	11,800	1,950	13,800	3,460	614	11,712	11,300	1,050	1,270	17,100	82-85	110-125	110-115	121
1999	21	11,400	1,550	12,900	3,890	562	11,303	11,500	996	1,240	16,300	107-110	115-125	110-115	109
2000	21	10,300	1,510	11,800	3,880	662	10,272	12,500	1,120	1,400	14,900	158-161	175-180	140-150	169
2001	31	8,190	929	9,120	4,550	647	7,852	10,600	261	1,340	13,200	104-108	130-135	120-130	183
2002	29	9,300	1,030	10,300	4,670	437	9,937	11,000	286	1,140	14,500	128-132	150-160	120-130	137
2003	39	7,490	961	8,450	5,720	400	9,122	11,000	195	476	13,900	192-195	215-225	190-195	245
2004[1]	38	8,470	524	8,990	5,900	381	9,258	11,900	298	590	14,400	225-230	255-270	195-210	274
2005[2]	41	7,190	842	8,040	6,520	525	8,897	11,300	197	532	14,100	260-267	300-325	265-270	314

[1] Preliminary. [2] Estimate. [3] Anhydrous ammonia, synthetic. [4] For consumption. [5] Major downstream nitrogen compounds. [6] *Granular.*

E = Net exporter. *Source: U.S. Geological Survey (USGS)*

FERTILIZER

World Production of Phosphate Rock, Basic Slag & Guano   In Thousands of Metric Tons (Gross Weight)

Year	Brazil	China	Egypt	Israel	Jordan	Morocco	Russia	Senegal	Syria	Togo	Tunisia	United States	World Total
1996	3,823	21,000	808	3,839	5,355	20,855	8,300	1,340	2,189	2,731	7,167	45,400	135,000
1997	4,276	24,500	1,067	4,047	5,896	23,084	9,800	1,565	2,392	2,631	6,941	45,900	143,000
1998	4,421	25,000	1,076	4,067	5,925	23,587	10,100	1,478	2,496	2,250	7,901	44,200	144,000
1999	4,344	20,000	1,018	4,128	6,014	22,163	11,400	1,814	2,084	1,600	8,006	40,600	134,000
2000	4,725	19,400	1,096	4,110	5,526	21,463	11,100	1,738	2,166	1,370	8,339	38,600	132,000
2001	4,805	21,000	972	3,511	5,843	21,983	10,500	1,708	2,043	1,067	8,144	31,900	126,000
2002	5,084	23,000	1,550	3,476	7,179	23,041	10,700	1,551	2,483	1,271	7,461	36,100	135,000
2003	5,584	25,200	2,183	3,208	6,763	22,877	11,000	1,765	2,414	1,471	7,890	35,000	138,000
2004[1]	6,074	25,500	2,219	2,947	6,223	25,369	11,000	1,754	2,883	1,115	7,954	35,800	141,000
2005[2]	6,100	30,400	2,730	2,900	6,230	25,200	11,000	1,520	3,500	1,215	8,000	36,300	147,000

[1] Preliminary.   [2] Estimate.   Source: U.S. Geological Survey (USGS)

Salient Statistics of Phosphate Rock in the United States   In Thousands of Metric Tons

Year	Mine Production	Marketable Production	Value Million Dollars	Imports For Consumption	Exports	Apparent Consumption	Stocks, Dec. 31 (Producer)	Price - $ Avg. Per Metric Ton (FOB Mine)	Avg. Price of Florida & N. Carolina - $/Tonne - FOB Mine (-60% to +74%) - Domestic	Export	Average
1996	179,000	45,400	1,060	1,800	1,570	43,700	6,390	23.40	22.90	35.82	23.40
1997	166,000	45,900	1,080	1,830	335	43,600	7,910	24.50	24.40	34.80	24.50
1998	170,000	44,200	1,130	1,760	378	45,000	7,920	25.87	25.46	42.70	25.87
1999	161,000	40,600	1,240	2,170	272	43,500	6,920	31.49	30.56	41.96	31.49
2000	163,000	38,600	932	1,930	299	39,000	8,170	24.29	24.14	40.38	24.29
2001	130,000	31,900	856	2,500	9	35,300	7,510	26.82	26.82	W	26.81
2002	154,000	36,100	993	2,700	62	37,400	8,860	27.47	27.69	W	27.69
2003	153,000	35,000	946	2,400	64	38,800	7,540	27.01	26.95	W	26.95
2004[1]	146,000	35,800	995	2,500	----	39,000	7,220	27.79	27.76	W	27.76
2005[2]	159,000	38,300	993	2,630	----	38,600	6,970	2734.00	29.20	W	29.20

[1] Preliminary.   [2] Estimate.   Source: U.S. Geological Survey (USGS)

World Production of Marketable Potash   In Thousands of Metric Tons (K_2O Equivalent)

Year	Belarus	Brazil	Canada	China	France	Germany	Israel	Jordan	Russia	Spain	United Kingdom	United States	World Total
1996	2,716	243	8,120	110	751	3,332	1,500	1,080	2,620	717	618	1,390	23,300
1997	3,247	280	8,989	115	725	3,423	1,488	850	3,400	639	565	1,400	25,200
1998	3,451	326	9,201	120	453	3,582	1,668	916	3,500	597	608	1,300	26,000
1999	4,553	348	8,475	260	345	3,543	1,700	1,080	4,200	656	495	1,200	27,300
2000	3,786	352	9,202	380	320	3,407	1,750	1,160	3,700	653	600	1,300	27,000
2001	3,700	319	8,237	385	244	3,550	1,770	1,180	4,300	471	532	1,200	26,400
2002	3,800	337	8,361	450	130	3,450	1,920	1,170	4,400	407	540	1,200	26,600
2003	4,230	416	9,093	500	----	3,563	1,960	1,230	4,740	510	620	1,100	28,400
2004[1]	4,600	403	10,114	551	----	3,626	2,060	1,230	5,000	500	600	1,300	30,400
2005[2]	4,844	405	10,120	600	----	3,600	2,060	1,230	5,500	500	600	1,200	31,100

[1] Preliminary.   [2] Estimate.   Source: U.S. Geological Survey (USGS)

Salient Statistics of Potash in the United States   In Thousands of Metric Tons (K_2O Equivalent)

Year	Net Import Reliance as a % of Consumption	Production	Sales by Producers	Value Million Dollars	Imports For Consumption	Exports	Apparent Consumption	Producer Stocks Dec. 31	Avg. Value Per Ton of Product ($)	Avg. Value of K_2O Equiv.	Avg. Price[3] $ Per Tonne
1996	77	1,390	1,430	299.0	4,940	481	5,890	265	101.08	208.57	134.07
1997	80	1,400	1,400	320.0	5,490	466	6,500	200	110.00	230.00	138.00
1998	80	1,300	1,300	330.0	4,780	477	5,600	300	115.00	250.00	145.00
1999	80	1,200	1,200	280.0	4,470	459	5,100	300	110.00	230.00	150.00
2000	70	1,300	1,200	290.0	4,600	367	5,600		110.00	230.00	157.50
2001	80	1,200	1,100	260.0	4,540	366	5,300		110.00	230.00	165.00
2002	80	1,200	1,200	280.0	4,620	371	5,300		110.00	230.00	155.00
2003	80	1,100	1,200	280.0	4,720	329	5,400		110.00	230.00	170.00
2004[1]	70	1,300	1,300	340.0	4,920	233	6,000		125.00	270.00	200.00
2005[2]	80	1,200	1,200	410.0	4,920	200	6,000		165.00	350.00	230.00

[1] Preliminary.   [2] Estimate.   [3] Unit of K_2O, standard 60% muriate F.O.B. mine.   Source: U.S. Geological Survey (USGS)

Fish

Fish are the primary source of protein for a large portion of the world's population. The worldwide yearly harvest of all sea fish (including aquaculture) is between 85 and 130 million metric tons. There are approximately 20,000 species of fish, of which 9,000 are regularly caught. Only 22 fish species are harvested in large amounts. Ground-fish, which are fish that live near or on the ocean floor, account for about 10% of the world's fishery harvest, and include cod, haddock, pollock, flounder, halibut and sole. Large pelagic fish such as tuna, swordfish, marlin, and mahi-mahi, account for about 5% of world harvest. The fish eaten most often in the United States is canned tuna.

Rising global demand for fish has increased the pressure to harvest more fish to the point where all 17 of the world's major fishing areas have either reached or exceeded their limits. Atlantic stocks of cod, haddock and blue-fin tuna are all seriously depleted, while in the Pacific, anchovies, salmon and halibut are all over-fished. Aquaculture, or fish farming, reduces pressure on wild stocks and now accounts for nearly 20% of world harvest.

Supply – The US supply of fishery products rose +2.6% to 20.373 billion pounds in 2004 (the latest reporting year)

from 19.850 billion pounds in 2003. The US domestic catch in 2004 rose by +1.4% to 9.643 billion pounds, and that comprised 47% of total US supply. Of the US domestic catch in 2004, 69% of the catch was finfish for human consumption, 20% of the catch was a variety of fish for industrial use, and 11% was shellfish for human consumption. The principal species of US fishery landings in 2004 were Pollock (with 3.362 billion pounds landed), Menhaden (1.498 billion pounds), Pacific Salmon (738 million pounds), Flounder (362 million pounds), and Sea Herring (258 million pounds).

About 30% the fish harvested in the world are processed directly into fishmeal and fish oil. Fishmeal is used primarily in animal feed. Fish oil is used in both animal feed and human food products. World fishmeal production in the 2005-06 marketing year fell by –6.4% to 5.660 million metric tons. World production of fish oil in 2005-06 fell –5.6% to 978.600 metric tons. Peru and Chile are the world's largest producers of fishmeal and fish oil.

Trade – US imports of fishery products in 2004 rose 3.7% yr/yr to a record high of 10.730 billion pounds, comprising 52.7% of total US supply.

Fishery Products -- Supply in the United States   In Millions of Pounds[2]

Year	Grand Total	Finfish	Shellfish[3]	For Industrial Use[4]	Total	% of Grand Total	Finfish	Shellfish[3]	For Industrial Use[4]	Total	% of Grand Total	Finfish	Shellfish[3]	For Industrial Use[4]
		- For Human Food -			---------- Domestic Catch ----------		- For Human Food -				---------- Imports ----------	- For Human Food -		
1998	16,898	10,837	3,338	2,723	9,194	54.4	5,935	1,238	2,021	7,704	45.6	4,901	2,100	702
1999	17,378	10,831	3,630	2,916	9,339	53.7	5,490	1,341	2,507	8,039	46.3	5,341	2,289	409
2000	17,339	11,006	3,734	2,599	9,068	52.3	5,637	1,275	2,157	8,271	47.7	5,369	2,459	442
2001	18,119	11,330	3,977	2,812	9,492	52.4	6,162	1,152	2,178	8,627	47.6	5,168	2,825	634
2002	19,028	11,770	4,237	3,022	9,397	49.4	6,013	1,192	2,193	9,631	50.6	5,757	3,045	829
2003	19,850	12,617	4,570	2,663	9,507	47.9	6,388	1,133	1,986	10,343	52.1	6,229	3,437	677
2004[1]	20,373	12,954	4,668	2,751	9,643	47.3	6,636	1,132	1,875	10,730	52.7	6,318	3,536	876

[1] Preliminary. [2] Live weight, except percent. [3] For univalue and bivalues mollusks (conchs, clams, oysters, scallops, etc.) the weight of meats, excluding the shell is reported. [4] Fish meal and sea herring. *Source: Fisheries Statistics Division, U.S. Department of Commerce*

Fisheries -- Landings of Principal Species in the United States   In Millions of Pounds

Year	Cod, Atlantic	Flounder	Halibut	Herring, Sea	Man-haden	Pollock	Salmon, Pacific	Tuna	Whiting	Clams (Meats)	Crabs	Lobsters (American)	Oysters (Meats)	Scallops (Meats)	Shrimp
1998	25	391	73	272	1,706	2,729	644	85	33	108	553	80	34	13	278
1999	21	331	80	267	1,989	2,336	815	58	31	112	458	87	27	27	304
2000	25	413	75	235	1,760	2,616	629	51	27	118	299	83	41	33	332
2001	33	352	78	300	1,741	3,188	723	52	28	123	272	74	33	47	324
2002	29	373	82	214	1,751	3,349	567	49	18	130	308	82	34	53	317
2003	24	365	80	287	1,599	3,372	674	62	19	128	332	74	37	56	315
2004[1]	16	362	79	256	1,498	3,362	738	57	19	119	314	75	39	65	308

[1] Preliminary. *Source: National Marine Fisheries Service, U.S. Department of Commerce*

U.S. Fisheries: Quantity & Value of Domestic Catch & Consumption & World Fish Oil Production

Year	Fresh & Frozen	Canned	Cured	For Meal, Oil, Etc.	Total	For Human Food	For Industrial Products	Ex-vessel Value[3] - Million $ -	Average Price - Cents/Lb. -	Fish Per Capita Consumption - Pounds -	World[2] Fish Oil Production - 1,000 Tons -
	---------- Disposition ----------										
	---------- Millions of Pounds ----------										
1998	6,870	516	129	1,679	9,194	7,173	2,021	3,128	34.0	NA	886
1999	6,416	712	133	2,078	9,339	6,832	2,507	3,467	37.1	NA	1,413
2000	6,657	530	119	1,763	9,069	6,912	2,157	3,550	39.1	NA	1,428
2001	7,085	536	123	1,748	9,492	7,314	2,178	3,228	34.0	NA	1,132
2002	6,826	652	117	1,802	9,397	7,205	2,192	3,092	32.9	NA	942
2003	7,266	498	119	1,624	9,507	7,521	1,986	3,347	35.2		979
2004[1]	7,448	552	137	1,506	9,643	7,768	1,875	3,652	37.9		

[1] Preliminary. [2] Crop years on a marketing year basis. [3] At the Dock Prices. *Source: Fisheries Statistics Division, U.S. Department of Commerce*

FISH

Imports of Seafood Products into the United States   In Thousands of Pounds

Year	Fresh Atlantic Salmon	Fresh Pacific Salmon[2]	Fresh Shrimp	Fresh & Frozen Trout	Frozen Atlantic Salmon	Frozen Pacific Salmon[2]	Frozen Shrimp	Canned & Prepared Salmon[3]	Fresh & Prepared Shrimp[4]	Oysters[5]	Mussels[6]	Clams[7]	Tilapia[8]
1998	190,131	38,486		5,670	19,092	17,134	599,466	3,430	95,942	18,049	34,099	6,541	61,336
1999	217,948	26,467		5,259	24,222	16,596	617,089	5,627	114,191	18,325	34,969	7,537	82,837
2000	257,218	19,908		7,083	32,089	12,866	621,231	8,893	139,526	20,810	43,141	8,074	89,218
2001	316,837	17,472		7,382	41,176	10,515	714,706	11,298	167,877	18,438	39,973	8,007	124,202
2002	356,164	23,210		9,887	56,883	18,317	730,002	16,378	216,439	19,084	45,695	7,457	148,122
2003	349,474	22,462		9,023	64,999	26,658	878,124	25,177	234,084	22,257	43,236	8,752	198,957
2004	324,358	22,387		8,573	69,894	40,767	871,638	24,418	269,502	23,121	50,855	7,875	248,986
2005[1]	352,778	22,522		7,190	70,000	42,296	871,902	25,421	293,970	22,932	51,669	6,708	297,331

[1] Preliminary.   [2] Also contains salmon with no specific species noted.   [3] Includes smoked and cured salmon.   [4] Shrimp, canned, breaded, or prepared.
[5] Oysters fresh or prepared.   [6] Mussels fresh or prepared.   [7] Clams, fresh or prepared.   [8] Tilapia, frozen whole fish plus fresh and frozen fillets.

Source: Bureau of the Census, U.S. Department of Commerce

Exports of Seafood Products into the United States   In Thousands of Pounds

Year	Fresh Atlantic Salmon	Fresh Pacific Salmon[2]	Fresh Shrimp	Fresh & Frozen Trout	Frozen Atlantic Salmon	Frozen Pacific Salmon[2]	Frozen Shrimp	Canned & Prepared Salmon[3]	Fresh & Prepared Shrimp[4]	Oysters[5]	Mussels[6]	Clams[7]
1998	7,978	34,645		1,453	243	105,869	11,323	77,201	13,882	2,496	1,347	5,375
1999	10,717	40,683		1,697	182	157,278	13,607	113,556	13,153	2,727	1,861	5,240
2000	15,942	38,750		1,816	299	161,515	15,162	81,098	14,229	3,229	1,513	3,413
2001	18,417	20,651		1,077	84	167,933	13,905	109,109	13,640	3,915	1,485	3,939
2002	8,456	29,672		1,163	84	132,646	13,890	95,955	13,148	3,896	1,178	3,861
2003	11,337	38,902		2,592	99	150,766	16,466	94,338	14,307	5,827	1,337	4,003
2004	13,606	33,863		1,118	197	172,476	12,711	117,570	12,719	7,505	911	5,761
2005[1]	10,949	18,537		945	379	260,159	9,106	114,273	10,689	7,797	1,035	4,384

[1] Preliminary.   [2] Also contains salmon with no specific species noted.   [3] Includes smoked and cured salmon.   [4] Shrimp, canned, breaded, or prepared.
[5] Oysters fresh or prepared.   [6] Mussels fresh or prepared.   [7] Clams, fresh or prepared.   *Source: Bureau of the Census, U.S. Department of Commerce*

World Production of Fish Meal   In Thousands of Metric Tons

Year	Chile	Spain	Denmark	EU-25	FSU-12	Iceland	Japan	Norway	Peru	South Africa	Thailand	United States	World Total
1998-99	823.4	86.1	319.1	542.7	147.1	240.6	388.5	352.6	1,597.4	76.2	398.0	389.9	6,341.6
1999-00	890.0	110.8	314.2	582.6	132.3	281.2	390.0	315.0	2,449.4	113.7	392.4	346.8	7,383.5
2000-01	731.0	116.6	311.9	577.7	102.8	283.0	350.0	238.8	2,144.2	97.8	385.9	337.1	6,763.8
2001-02	766.0	95.5	308.2	554.1	72.2	307.9	318.0	222.9	1,688.1	115.7	390.9	349.8	6,193.3
2002-03	818.1	92.7	238.9	482.5	75.3	268.5	326.0	199.2	1,344.6	131.8	398.8	322.4	5,735.1
2003-04[1]	851.8	96.6	255.9	508.8	80.3	214.6	319.0	234.2	1,842.2	126.3	404.3	305.0	6,185.4
2004-05[2]	806.2	95.0	231.2	487.9	85.3	202.1	319.0	155.6	1,949.2	112.0	407.9	282.6	6,045.7
2005-06[3]	810.0	96.0	220.0	480.4	88.3	168.0	320.0	178.0	1,550.0	118.0	411.0	292.0	5,660.0

[1] Preliminary.   [2] Estimate.   [3] Forecast.   *Source: The Oil World*

World Production of Fish Oil   In Thousands of Metric Tons

Year	Canada	Chile	China	Denmark	Iceland	Japan	Norway	Peru	South Africa	FSU-12	United States	World Total	Fish Oil CIF[4]
1998-99	3.3	176.8	28.8	135.2	92.1	72.8	99.2	376.5	6.8	14.5	141.6	1,277.3	408
1999-00	3.7	166.0	20.6	139.7	98.0	69.7	98.3	699.4	8.9	2.9	81.3	1,523.4	268
2000-01	4.1	142.9	17.6	121.3	98.0	65.8	66.4	400.8	4.5	2.7	123.3	1,209.4	375
2001-02	4.3	140.2	19.0	108.7	84.6	64.7	61.2	162.2	5.3	2.9	103.9	916.2	593
2002-03	4.5	134.0	17.1	104.9	122.0	65.6	51.6	208.0	5.4	3.5	89.6	973.5	560
2003-04[1]	4.8	146.0	14.0	112.0	74.2	68.1	40.5	263.5	6.5	3.6	81.9	986.2	648
2004-05[2]	5.2	166.0	12.0	99.0	66.0	67.0	29.7	341.2	6.8	3.7	72.5	1,037.1	716
2005-06[3]	5.0	170.0	12.1	103.0	55.0	68.0	36.0	262.0	7.0	3.8	75.4	978.6	774

[1] Preliminary.   [2] Estimate.   [3] Forecast.   [4] Any origin, N.W. Europe.   NA = Not available.   *Source: The Oil World*

Monthly Production of Catfish--Round Weight Processed, in the US   In Thousands of Pounds (Live Weight)

Year	Jan.	Feb.	Mar.	Apr.	May	June	July	Aug.	Sept.	Oct.	Nov.	Dec.	Total
1999	48,723	48,891	56,310	46,830	47,703	48,445	50,074	50,372	50,414	52,407	48,118	48,341	596,628
2000	50,552	50,942	56,856	48,781	48,424	48,011	49,023	53,204	49,422	51,412	45,535	41,441	593,603
2001	46,999	50,257	57,766	52,478	51,736	47,883	47,829	51,690	49,699	52,264	44,670	43,837	597,108
2002	52,551	52,856	58,340	50,694	52,902	49,450	52,363	54,383	53,366	56,576	50,072	48,048	631,601
2003	55,523	55,461	65,007	57,105	58,424	52,441	54,089	54,153	51,885	57,652	51,246	48,518	661,504
2004	53,849	54,173	60,272	53,896	52,324	50,155	51,055	53,295	51,329	52,396	49,536	48,170	630,450
2005	53,856	51,720	57,117	50,306	51,552	49,626	47,241	50,686	47,151	49,034	46,674	45,707	600,670
2006[1]	50,703	49,145	56,315	43,126	42,865	41,214	45,528	51,736	47,296	50,788	45,680	41,735	566,131

[1] Preliminary.   *Source: Economic Research Service, U.S. Department of Agriculture (ERS-USDA)*

Average Price Paid to Producers for Farm-Raised Catfish in the US   In Cents Per Pound (Live Weight)

Year	Jan.	Feb.	Mar.	Apr.	May	June	July	Aug.	Sept.	Oct.	Nov.	Dec.	Average
1999	70.3	71.4	73.2	75.6	77.7	77.5	76.8	74.3	72.8	71.6	71.3	71.6	73.7
2000	74.4	78.8	78.9	78.9	78.5	78.6	76.0	74.1	72.7	71.0	69.6	68.2	75.0
2001	69.3	69.6	69.7	69.4	68.7	66.9	65.6	62.4	61.0	59.6	56.6	55.4	64.5
2002	54.9	55.5	56.5	56.1	57.4	58.8	59.0	58.2	57.6	56.8	56.0	54.4	56.8
2003	52.9	54.4	58.5	63.0	61.8	58.6	56.4	55.2	56.0	56.7	61.0	62.9	58.1
2004	66.8	70.3	72.3	72.8	72.0	68.9	68.2	68.3	68.3	69.5	68.9	69.0	69.6
2005	72.5	73.1	73.3	72.5	72.2	72.1	72.3	72.4	72.4	72.4	72.4	72.6	72.5
2006[1]	72.7	72.9	74.5	78.5	79.6	80.7	81.2	81.1	83.2	83.6	83.7	83.8	79.6

[1] Preliminary.   Source: Economic Research Service, U.S. Department of Agriculture (ERS-USDA)

Sales of Fresh Catfish in the United States   In Thousands of Pounds

Year	Jan.	Feb.	Mar.	Apr.	May	June	July	Aug.	Sept.	Oct.	Nov.	Dec.	Total
Whole
2001	3,516	3,242	4,260	3,644	3,271	3,166	3,233	3,204	3,174	3,294	2,865	2,803	39,672
2002	3,713	3,656	3,826	3,373	3,644	3,313	3,477	3,733	3,418	3,822	3,031	2,986	41,992
2003	3,833	3,785	4,339	3,643	3,692	3,266	3,553	3,510	3,233	3,231	2,798	2,693	41,576
2004	3,205	3,266	3,808	3,001	2,853	2,707	2,875	3,002	2,861	3,076	2,950	2,704	36,308
2005	3,111	3,177	3,402	2,938	2,679	2,765	2,686	2,673	2,687	2,546	2,615	2,784	34,063
2006[1]	3,195	3,331	4,024	2,940	2,795	2,464	2,716	2,711					36,264
Fillets[2]
2001	4,884	6,112	6,751	5,709	5,587	5,122	5,191	5,313	5,264	5,273	4,463	4,489	64,158
2002	5,684	6,132	6,010	5,236	5,682	5,093	5,327	5,442	5,317	5,420	4,447	4,119	63,909
2003	5,362	5,158	6,715	5,700	6,364	5,737	5,984	6,013	5,308	6,082	5,187	4,710	68,320
2004	5,964	6,455	6,815	5,887	5,688	5,500	5,559	5,483	4,865	4,992	4,336	4,162	65,706
2005	5,274	5,615	5,795	4,979	5,274	4,987	4,714	4,998	4,848	5,072	4,291	4,209	60,056
2006[1]	5,160	5,109	6,090	5,077	4,653	4,446	4,279	4,447					58,892
Other[3]
2001	1,443	1,292	2,156	1,309	1,282	1,298	1,375	1,436	1,449	1,430	1,223	1,252	16,945
2002	1,526	1,446	1,375	1,356	1,732	1,527	1,576	1,569	1,441	1,596	1,165	1,205	17,514
2003	1,668	1,532	1,599	1,458	1,472	1,319	1,425	1,366	1,473	1,361	1,138	1,134	16,945
2004	1,435	1,518	1,567	1,426	1,299	1,248	1,181	1,173	1,228	1,263	1,152	1,095	15,585
2005	1,300	1,295	1,370	1,271	1,204	1,130	1,097	1,128	1,084	1,121	965	900	13,865
2006[1]	1,126	1,024	1,214	987	915	807	863	879					11,723

[1] Preliminary.   [2] Includes regular, shank and strip fillets; excludes breaded products.   [3] Includes steaks, nuggets and all other products not reported.
Source: Economic Research Service, U.S. Department of Agriculture (ERS-USDA)

Prices of Fresh Catfish in the United States   In Dollars per Pound

Year	Jan.	Feb.	Mar.	Apr.	May	June	July	Aug.	Sept.	Oct.	Nov.	Dec.	Average
Whole
2001	1.59	1.68	1.63	1.65	1.65	1.62	1.59	1.55	1.53	1.49	1.42	1.37	1.56
2002	1.36	1.35	1.30	1.34	1.36	1.37	1.35	1.32	1.32	1.28	1.24	1.25	1.32
2003	1.28	1.30	1.35	1.37	1.36	1.39	1.33	1.33	1.34	1.36	1.40	1.43	1.35
2004	1.49	1.53	1.57	1.60	1.60	1.57	1.57	1.58	1.56	1.59	1.51	1.57	1.56
2005	1.64	1.64	1.61	1.61	1.61	1.58	1.58	1.57	1.58	1.63	1.55	1.50	1.59
2006[1]	1.53	1.49	1.54	1.65	1.70	1.74	1.72	1.76					1.64
Fillets[2]
2001	2.80	2.79	2.80	2.80	2.80	2.78	2.77	2.75	2.69	2.63	2.60	2.55	2.73
2002	2.52	2.49	2.49	2.51	2.53	2.55	2.55	2.54	2.54	2.52	2.49	2.47	2.52
2003	2.44	2.45	2.44	2.49	2.51	2.50	2.48	2.48	2.49	2.49	2.50	2.54	2.48
2004	2.59	2.62	2.71	2.73	2.74	2.74	2.73	2.73	2.74	2.76	2.77	2.77	2.72
2005	2.81	2.75	2.85	2.87	2.86	2.85	2.84	2.83	2.83	2.84	2.84	2.84	2.83
2006[1]	2.86	2.87	2.89	2.98	3.08	3.14	3.18	3.20					3.03
Other[3]
2001	1.64	1.68	1.57	1.64	1.69	1.64	1.61	1.57	1.52	1.59	1.59	1.53	1.61
2002	1.53	1.57	1.54	1.51	1.45	1.51	1.51	1.50	1.54	1.48	1.55	1.46	1.51
2003	1.40	1.41	1.51	1.53	1.47	1.54	1.52	1.58	1.50	1.58	1.60	1.64	1.52
2004	1.63	1.70	1.71	1.78	1.78	1.78	1.62	1.76	1.69	1.72	1.70	1.71	1.72
2005	1.67	1.67	1.74	1.71	1.77	1.78	1.72	1.68	1.64	1.65	1.60	1.65	1.69
2006[1]	1.64	1.63	1.65	1.75	1.73	1.86	1.86	1.85					1.75

[1] Preliminary.   [2] Includes regular, shank and strip fillets; excludes breaded products.   [3] Includes steaks, nuggets and all other products not reported.
Source: Economic Research Service, U.S. Department of Agriculture (ERS-USDA)

Flaxseed and Linseed Oil

Flaxseed, also called linseed, is an ancient crop that was cultivated by the Babylonians around 3,000 BC. Flaxseed is used for fiber in textiles and to produce oil. Flaxseeds contain approximately 35% oil, of which 60% is omega-3 fatty acid. Flaxseed or linseed oil is obtained through either the expeller extraction or solvent extraction method. Manufacturers filter the processed oil to remove some impurities and then sell it as unrefined. Unrefined oil retains its full flavor, aroma, color, and naturally occurring nutrients. Flaxseed oil is used for cooking and as a dietary supplement as well as for animal feed. Industrial linseed oil is not for internal consumption due to possible poisonous additives and is used for making putty, sealants, linoleum, wood preservation, varnishes, and oil paints.

Flaxseed futures and options trade at the Winnipeg Commodity Exchange. The futures contract calls for the delivery of 20 metric tons of flaxseed. The contract is now priced in US dollars per metric ton.

Prices – The average monthly price received by US farmers for flaxseed in the 2006-07 marketing year (through February 2007) fell by –7.8% yr/yr to $5.66 per bushel from $6.14 per bushel in the 2005-06 marketing year.

Supply – World production of flaxseed in the 2005-06 marketing year rose sharply by 42.9% yr/yr to a record high of 2.597 million metric tons from the 13-year low of 2.011 million metric tons posted in 2001-02. The world's largest

producer of flaxseed is Canada with 39% of world production in 2005-06, followed by the US (17%), China (16%), and India (8%). US production of flaxseed in 2005-06 rose sharply by +88.1% yr/yr to a new record high of 19.695 million bushels from the 23-year high of 11.863 million bushels posted in 2002-03. North Dakota is by far the largest producing state of flaxseed and accounted for 94.0% of flaxseed production in 2006, followed by South Dakota with 2.1% of production and Minnesota with 1.1% of production

World production of linseed oil in 2005-06 rose by +9.5% yr/yr to 677,500 metric tons. The world's largest producers of linseed oil are China (with 20% of world production in 2005-06), the US (23%), Belgium (13%), and India (10%). US production of linseed oil in 2004-05 (latest data available) fell by –4.2% yr/yr to 203 million pounds.

Demand – US distribution of flaxseed in 2004-05 (latest data available) fell –5.9% yr/yr to 13.996 million bushels. The breakdown was 75% for crushing into meal and oil, 14% for exports, 7% for residual, and 4% for seed. US consumption of linseed oil (inedible products) in the 2006-07 marketing year (through Dec) rose +2.5% yr/yr to 51.802 million pounds.

Trade – US exports of flaxseed in 2004-05 (latest data available) fell by –20.0% yr/yr to 2.013 million bushels. US imports of flaxseed in 2004-05 fell by –22.7% yr/yr to 3.537 million bushels.

World Production of Flaxseed — In Thousands of Metric Tons

Year	Argen-tina	Aust-ralia	Bang-ladesh	Canada	China	Egypt	France	Hungary	India	Rom-ania	United States	Former USSR	World Total
1996-97	72	7	46	851	480	17	29	4	319	5	41	86	2,300
1997-98	75	9	50	1,038	393	19	31	ÑÑ	275	5	62	47	2,370
1998-99	85	10	50	1,210	523	24	29	1	265	3	170	55	2,828
1999-00	47	9	46	1,100	404	30	34	2	289	3	200	42	2,868
2000-01	22	9	48	775	520	30	38	1	240	1	273	74	2,361
2001-02	16	9	50	770	253	26	29	1	240	2	291	82	2,011
2002-03	11	9	50	750	463	15	49	1	200	2	301	60	2,101
2003-04[1]	29	9	50	835	450	22	53	1	230	2	265	82	2,302
2004-05[2]	36	10	50	592	460	31	54	1	200	3	263	97	2,069
2005-06[3]	54	10	50	1,160	475	28	57	1	230	1	500	95	2,957

[1] Preliminary. [2] Estimate. [3] Forecast. *Source: The Oil World*

Supply and Distribution of Flaxseed in the United States — In Thousands of Bushels

Crop Year Beginning June 1	Planted 1,000 Acres	Harvested 1,000 Acres	Yield Per Acre (Bushels)	Beginning Stocks	Pro-duction	Imports	Total Supply	Seed	Crush	Exports	Residual	Total Distribution
1997-98	151	146	16.6	453	2,420	9,636	12,509	272	10,500	174	382	11,328
1998-99	336	329	20.4	1,181	6,708	5,992	13,881	313	10,600	476	333	11,723
1999-00	387	381	20.6	2,158	7,864	6,629	16,651	434	11,500	201	2,735	14,884
2000-01	536	517	20.8	1,767	10,730	2,849	15,346	474	12,000	1,017	572	14,038
2001-02	585	578	19.8	1,308	11,455	1,904	14,667	635	10,000	2,386	753	13,774
2002-03	784	703	16.9	893	11,863	2,901	15,657	482	10,500	3,181	416	14,579
2003-04	595	588	17.9	1,078	10,516	4,573	16,167	509	10,860	2,516	994	14,879
2004-05[1]	523	516	20.3	1,288	10,471	3,537	15,296	529	10,410	2,013	1,041	13,996
2005-06[2]	983	955	20.6		19,695							
2006-07[3]	718	704	14.4									

[1] Preliminary. [2] Estimate. [3] Forecast. *Source: Economic Research Service, U.S. Department of Agriculture*

Production of Flaxseed in the United States, by States   In Thousands of Bushels

Crop Year	Minnesota	North Dakota	South Dakota	Other States	Total	Crop Year	Minnesota	North Dakota	South Dakota	Other States	Total
1997	432	1,997	252	75	2,420	2002	64	11,560	44	195	11,863
1998	300	5,817	294	165	6,708	2003	161	9,990	144	221	10,516
1999	198	6,867	357	340	7,864	2004	51	9,840	135	445	10,471
2000	198	9,975	361	196	10,730	2005	132	18,165	480	918	19,695
2001	52	10,900	323	180	11,455	2006[1]	126	10,368	228	297	11,019

[1] Preliminary.   *Source: National Agricultural Statistics Service, U.S. Department of Agriculture (NASS-USDA)*

Factory Shipments of Paints, Varnish and Lacquer in the United States   In Millions of Dollars

Year	First Quarter	Second Quarter	Third Quarter	Fourth Quarter	Total	Year	First Quarter	Second Quarter	Third Quarter	Fourth Quarter	Total
1998	3,600.7	4,216.4	4,063.9	3,804.4	15,685	2002	3,729.9	4,440.7	4,251.4	3,600.7	16,023
1999	3,926.2	4,452.2	4,216.5	3,925.7	16,521	2003	3,981.5	4,671.8	4,374.7	3,905.8	16,934
2000	4,073.1	4,573.5	4,082.0	3,474.7	16,203	2004	4,306.1	5,000.1	4,843.2	4,104.7	18,254
1999	3,926.2	4,452.2	4,216.5	3,925.7	16,521	2005	4,061.7	5,274.8	4,951.7	4,249.5	18,538
2001	3,625.0	4,345.4	4,094.5	3,652.6	15,718	2006[1]	4,647.7	5,390.4	5,046.8		20,113

[1] Preliminary.   *Source: Bureau of the Census, U.S. Department of Commerce*

Consumption of Linseed Oil (Inedible Products) in the United States   In Millions of Pounds

Year	July	Aug.	Sept.	Oct.	Nov.	Dec.	Jan.	Feb.	Mar.	Apr.	May	June	Total
1999-00	5.4	6.2	5.5	5.2	5.6	4.5	4.2	6.1	5.8	7.0	7.6	6.6	69.8
2000-01	6.5	7.2	7.3	7.5	6.5	5.7	8.0	6.7	7.7	7.6	9.3	9.4	89.3
2001-02	9.6	8.4	9.2	7.4	5.3	5.0	8.2	7.1	6.9	8.0	7.7	8.7	91.3
2002-03	11.7	9.6	10.0	7.0	5.7	7.3	6.8	6.4	8.7	8.5	6.6	6.7	94.9
2003-04	7.9	6.9	6.0	6.8	3.5	5.0	5.6	7.3	6.0	7.7	8.1	8.2	79.1
2004-05	7.3	7.3	6.7	5.6	4.8	5.1	3.7	4.8	4.9	4.0	5.7	4.7	64.6
2005-06	4.8	4.5	4.2	3.7	2.7	2.7	3.9	3.8	4.9	3.3	5.9	6.0	50.5
2006-07[1]	4.4	5.8	5.7	3.5	3.7	2.8							51.8

[1] Preliminary.   *Source: Bureau of the Census, U.S. Department of Commerce*

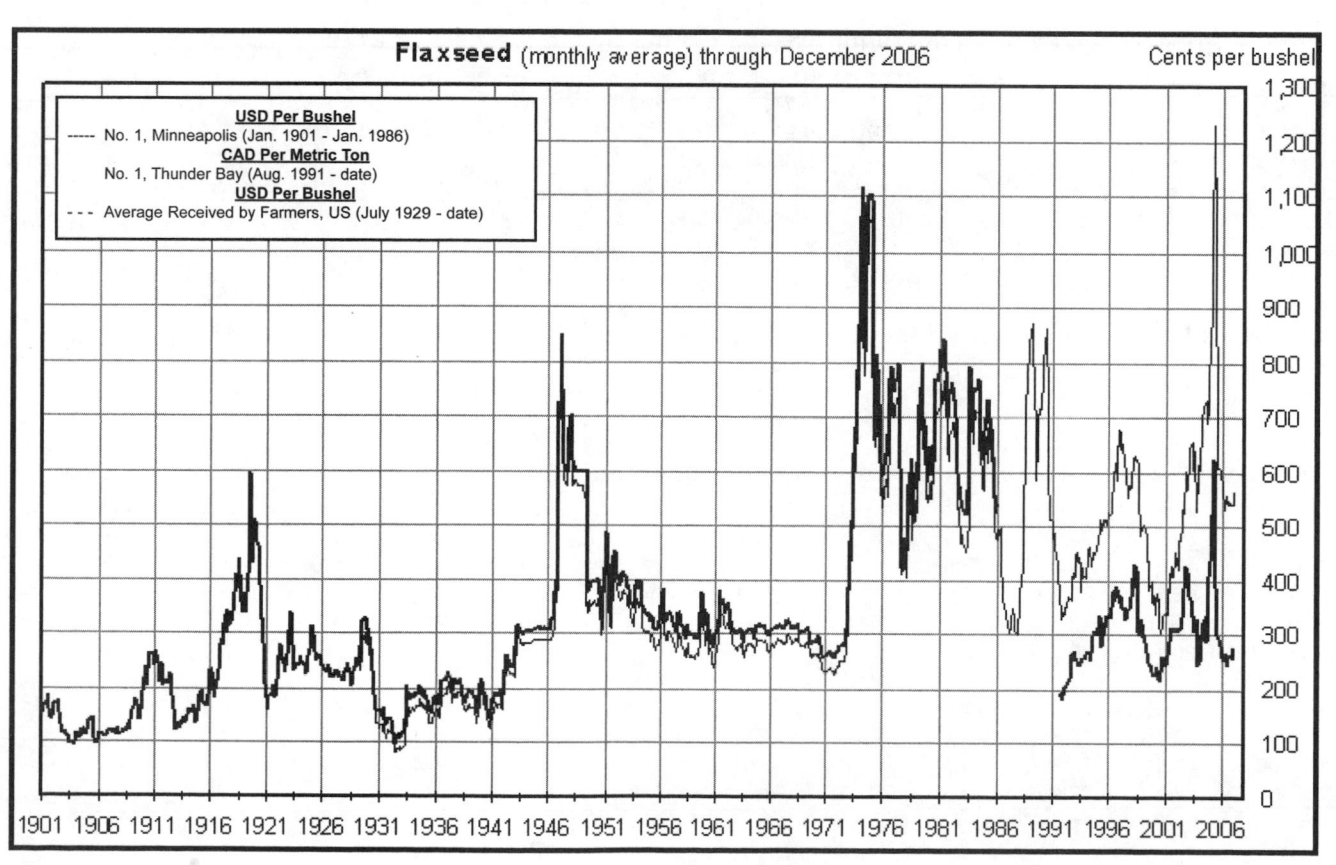

Flaxseed (monthly average) through December 2006   Cents per bushel

USD Per Bushel
----- No. 1, Minneapolis (Jan. 1901 - Jan. 1986)
CAD Per Metric Ton
No. 1, Thunder Bay (Aug. 1991 - date)
USD Per Bushel
- - - Average Received by Farmers, US (July 1929 - date)

FLAXSEED AND LINSEED OIL

Supply and Distribution of Linseed Oil in the United States   In Millions of Pounds

Crop Year Beginning June 1	Stocks June 1	Production	Total	Exports	Domestic	Total Disappearance	Average Price at Minneapolis Cents/Lb.
		Supply			Disappearance		
1995-96	45	180	229	26	153	179	36.5
1996-97	50	200	256	66	155	221	36.0
1997-98	35	205	247	58	147	205	36.3
1998-99	42	207	261	63	150	213	36.4
1999-00	48	224	285	74	162	236	35.8
2000-01	49	234	295	73	179	252	36.0
2001-02	43	195	249	50	153	204	38.1
2002-03	45	205	263	70	148	218	39.9
2003-04[1]	45	212	272	76	151	227	41.8
2004-05[2]	45	203	263	78	140	218	38.5-40.5

[1] Preliminary.   [2] Forecast.   Source: Economic Research Service, U.S. Department of Agriculture (ERS-USDA)

World Production and Price of Linseed Oil   In Thousands of Metric Tons

Year	Argentina	Bangladesh	Belgium	China	Egypt	Germany	India	Japan	United Kingdom	United States	Former USSR	World Total	Rotterdam Ex-Tank $/Tonne
1996-97	17.1	12.5	52.1	142.5	9.6	52.2	90.0	31.0	34.1	97.9	16.5	676.7	560
1997-98	24.1	13.4	54.7	120.0	11.1	66.9	84.3	31.3	35.1	100.7	7.2	678.6	686
1998-99	24.5	13.6	59.2	150.0	15.2	74.1	80.1	26.5	34.3	107.6	10.7	731.1	575
1999-00	13.1	12.6	68.8	118.3	15.0	73.6	85.9	23.8	34.1	124.9	7.9	709.4	413
2000-01	6.2	12.9	75.2	133.0	23.0	63.4	74.7	21.1	17.0	114.7	16.4	669.0	378
2001-02	3.8	13.5	95.0	81.3	16.6	57.3	72.4	18.9	9.9	95.7	18.7	589.1	454
2002-03	2.1	13.6	92.1	124.9	14.8	64.4	63.3	8.6	5.9	105.5	13.0	597.5	679
2003-04	2.3	13.6	119.6	124.0	11.1	66.6	67.7	7.5	6.7	105.5	15.7	636.0	757
2004-05[1]	6.9	13.6	104.3	127.0	14.6	37.9	62.7	6.8	3.5	135.5	15.9	618.7	1,191
2005-06[2]	11.8	13.6	89.6	132.4	17.7	53.0	67.7	7.2	3.5	156.5	14.9	677.5	697

[1] Preliminary.   [2] Forecast.   Source: The Oil World

Average Price Received by Farmers for Flaxseed in the United States   In Dollars Per Bushel

Year	July	Aug.	Sept.	Oct.	Nov.	Dec.	Jan.	Feb.	Mar.	Apr.	May	June	Average
1997-98	6.07	5.53	5.72	5.81	5.71	5.72	5.82	6.27	6.26	6.23	6.33	6.17	5.97
1998-99	6.17	5.45	5.09	4.86	4.97	5.00	5.05	5.05	4.94	4.93	4.89	4.38	5.07
1999-00	4.40	3.86	4.00	3.76	3.66	3.61	3.75	3.43	3.70	3.66	3.77	3.64	3.77
2000-01	3.25	3.05	3.10	3.17	3.39	4.45	3.42	3.43	3.90	3.68	3.91	4.10	3.57
2001-02	4.28	4.09	4.10	4.21	4.33	4.55	4.22	4.75	4.75	4.80	5.02	5.29	4.53
2002-03	5.38	5.27	5.55	5.76	6.04	5.92	5.71	6.25	6.47	6.57	6.05	6.02	5.92
2003-04	6.38	5.30	5.43	5.77	6.02	6.15	6.08	6.39	6.53	7.01	7.10	7.23	6.28
2004-05	7.33	6.90	7.19	7.36	8.62	8.42	8.89	10.90	11.40	12.30	11.60	11.20	9.34
2005-06	10.40	6.28	6.10	6.05	5.94	5.81	5.64	5.59	5.35	5.56	5.58	5.40	6.14
2006-07[1]	5.47	5.50	5.46	5.41	5.40	5.73	6.07	6.25					5.66

[1] Preliminary.   Source: National Agricultural Statistics Service, U.S. Department of Agriculture (NASS-USDA)

Stocks of Linseed Oil (Crude and Refined) at Factories and Warehouses in the US   In Millions of Pounds

Year	July 1	Aug. 1	Sept. 1	Oct. 1	Nov. 1	Dec. 1	Jan. 1	Feb. 1	Mar. 1	Apr. 1	May 1	June 1
1997-98	39.9	35.2	40.3	33.3	38.6	40.3	46.9	60.8	55.8	63.1	54.6	49.4
1998-99	49.6	45.3	38.5	55.4	35.7	44.5	53.2	68.2	54.6	68.2	65.3	76.2
1999-00	68.7	65.5	68.9	74.0	92.4	69.6	72.0	69.5	65.7	53.9	49.1	44.2
2000-01	39.5	42.5	41.3	54.3	58.7	87.0	61.6	50.1	50.5	51.2	39.2	44.8
2001-02	29.1	30.2	22.6	38.4	32.4	29.9	33.4	36.6	26.8	33.4	32.3	31.1
2002-03	27.8	17.7	12.8	21.8	30.5	29.0	31.9	35.9	34.6	36.2	33.7	33.7
2003-04	30.2	27.2	22.3	78.5	42.0	35.0	40.0	43.4	37.6	32.9	24.5	19.9
2004-05	15.1	15.8	8.0	13.0	17.1	26.9	31.3	35.4	35.4	41.0	43.9	47.2
2005-06	38.1	24.8	14.1	33.9	31.1	21.0	29.4	38.4	42.2	32.2	25.5	29.8
2006-07[1]	22.2	27.9	21.6	23.6	28.4	33.5	38.5					

[1] Preliminary.   Source: Bureau of the Census, U.S. Department of Commerce

Flaxseed Futures - Winnipeg Commodity Exchange
(weekly close) as of October 31, 2005
CAD per metric ton

Wholesale Price of Raw Linseed Oil at Minneapolis in Tank Cars   In Cents Per Pound

Year	July	Aug.	Sept.	Oct.	Nov.	Dec.	Jan.	Feb.	Mar.	Apr.	May	June	Average
1995-96	35.00	35.50	37.00	37.00	37.00	37.00	37.00	37.00	37.00	37.00	37.00	37.00	36.71
1996-97	37.00	37.20	37.50	37.00	33.75	32.12	36.00	36.00	36.00	36.00	36.00	36.00	35.88
1997-98	36.00	36.00	36.00	37.00	37.00	37.00	36.00	36.00	36.00	36.00	37.00	37.00	36.42
1998-99	37.00	37.00	37.00	37.00	37.00	37.00	36.00	36.00	36.00	36.00	36.00	36.00	36.50
1999-00	36.00	36.00	36.00	36.00	36.00	36.00	36.00	36.00	36.00	36.00	36.00	36.00	36.00
2000-01	36.00	36.00	36.00	36.00	36.00	36.00	36.00	36.00	36.00	36.00	36.00	32.00	35.67
2001-02	35.50	38.00	39.00	39.00	39.00	39.00	39.00	39.00	39.00	39.00	39.65	40.35	38.79
2002-03	40.00	38.00	41.00	31.75	41.00	41.00	41.00	41.00	41.00	41.00	41.19	41.75	39.97
2003-04	41.75	41.75	42.00	42.75	43.13	43.25	42.60	40.00	40.00	40.00	45.00	45.50	42.31
2004-05[1]	48.50	50.00	55.00	57.20	60.00	58.17							54.81

[1] Preliminary.   Source: Economic Research Service, U.S. Department of Agriculture (ERS-USDA)

Average Open Interest of Flaxseed Futures in Winnipeg   In Contracts

Year	Jan.	Feb.	Mar.	Apr.	May	June	July	Aug.	Sept.	Oct.	Nov.	Dec.
1996	6,059	6,056	4,402	5,192	6,970	4,435	3,102	2,989	3,257	3,438	4,326	5,119
1997	5,420	5,356	5,591	5,151	4,923	4,075	3,891	4,031	7,131	8,284	7,255	7,955
1998	10,059	10,190	9,707	8,540	6,480	6,874	6,030	6,767	7,421	7,221	7,564	5,828
1999	4,372	4,552	4,533	4,238	3,719	2,456	2,149	2,758	3,725	4,236	4,493	4,276
2000	4,365	4,907	5,588	6,218	5,066	3,696	3,152	3,585	3,936	4,666	4,922	4,914
2001	4,101	3,476	4,270	3,043	3,169	3,661	2,745	2,350	2,400	3,158	2,726	3,031
2002	2,225	1,981	1,921	1,787	1,270	935	612	699	776	704	424	249
2003	235	316	477	604	394	489	298	305	253	193	94	49
2004	38	23	15	0	0	0	0	0	179	15	214	578
2005	0	0	0	0	0	0	0	0	0	0	0	0

Source: Winnipeg Commodity Exchange (WCE)

Volume of Trading of Flaxseed Futures in Winnipeg   In Contracts

Year	Jan.	Feb.	Mar.	Apr.	May	June	July	Aug.	Sept.	Oct.	Nov.	Dec.	Total
1996	9,617	8,301	4,110	13,531	10,855	7,997	6,517	4,153	5,430	11,126	7,532	10,720	99,889
1997	7,640	6,486	7,123	10,912	6,256	7,851	7,662	7,081	20,967	23,418	20,049	15,311	140,756
1998	15,713	19,906	8,275	9,060	5,231	7,642	4,468	4,062	7,328	13,085	13,824	6,958	115,552
1999	4,855	8,922	4,383	8,460	5,241	5,891	4,863	2,833	5,852	12,078	7,710	7,345	78,433
2000	9,022	9,340	9,292	12,604	7,372	7,393	2,676	2,525	9,822	11,915	14,436	7,819	100,040
2001	8,232	6,428	6,928	7,117	6,514	6,745	4,344	2,620	5,242	7,291	4,689	6,326	72,476
2002	2,990	2,838	2,519	3,832	3,320	3,018	1,153	810	777	3,030	955	344	25,586
2003	333	724	412	368	452	738	343	96	491	273	183	25	4,438
2004	35	10	15	0	0	0	0	0	15	0	0	15	90
2005	0	0	0	0	0	0	0	0	0	0	0	0	0

Source: Winnipeg Commodity Exchange (WCE)

Fruits

A fruit is any see-bearing structure produced from a flowering plant. A widely used classification system divides fruit into fleshy or dry types. Fleshy fruits are juicy and include peaches, mangos, apples, and blueberries. Dry fruits include tree nuts such as almonds, walnuts, and pecans. Some foods that are commonly called vegetables, such as tomatoes, squash, peppers and eggplant, are technically fruits because they develop from the ovary of a flower.

Worldwide, over 430 million tons of fruit are produced each year and are grown everywhere except the Arctic and the Antarctic. The tropics, because of their abundant moisture and warm temperatures, produce the most diverse and abundant fruits. Mexico and Chile produce more than half of all the fresh and frozen fruit imported into the US. In the US, the top three fruits produced are oranges, grapes, and apples. Virtually all US production of almonds, pistachios, and walnuts occurs in California, which leads the US in tree nut production.

Prices – Fruit prices were fairly strong in 2005 with the fresh fruit Consumer Price Index rising +3.7% to 297.4 and the processed fruit CPI index rising +3.8% to 114.0. Fruit prices were mixed but generally rose in 2005: Red Delicious Apples (–9.0% to 94.9 cents per pound), bananas (–0.6% to 49.2 cents per pound), Anjou pears (+11.8% to $1.114 per pound), Thompson seedless grapes (+0.9% to $2.078 per pound), lemons (+14.2% to $1.411 per pound), grapefruit (+21.9% to 99.8 cents per pound), navel oranges (+15.9% to 99.6 cents per pound), and Valencia oranges (+29.8% to 89.7 cents per pound).

Supply – US commercial production of selected fruits in 2005 fell –10.3% to 29.616 million short tons. By weight, oranges accounted for 31% of that US fruit production figure, followed by grapes at 26%, and apples at 17%. The value of US fruit production in 2005 rose +8.4% yr/yr to $16.226 billion.

Demand – US per capita fresh fruit consumption in 2005 fell –2.4% to 99.91 pounds per year, down from the 2004 record high of 102.4.

The highest per capita consumption categories for noncitrus fruits in 2005 were bananas (25.14 pounds) and apples (16.92 pounds). Per capital consumption of citrus fruits was the highest for oranges (11.40 pounds), lemons (2.94 pounds), and grapefruit (2.65 pounds).

The utilization breakdown for 2005 shows that 39% of total US non-citrus fruit utilization went for fresh fruit, 25% for wine, 12% for dried fruit, 9% for canned fruit, 9% for juice, and 4% for frozen fruit. The value of utilized non-citrus fruit production in 2005 rose +11.1% yr/yr to $9.955 billion.

Commercial Production for Selected Fruits in the United States   In Thousands of Short Tons

Year	Apples	Cherries[2]	Cran-berries	Grapes	Grape-fruit	Lemons	Nect-arines	Oranges	Peaches	Pears	Pine-apples[3]	Prunes & Plums	Straw-berries	Tangelos	Tang-erines	Total All Fruits
1999	5,316	344	318	6,236	2,513	747	274	9,824	1,252	1,044	352	735	916	115	327	30,819
2000	5,291	352	286	7,688	2,763	840	267	12,997	1,276	993	354	902	950	99	458	36,115
2001	4,712	415	267	6,569	2,462	996	275	12,221	1,204	1,027	323	651	826	95	373	32,916
2002	4,262	213	285	7,339	2,424	801	300	12,374	1,268	890	320	736	942	97	420	33,173
2003	4,397	359	310	6,644	2,063	1,026	273	11,545	1,260	934	300	803	1,078	105	382	31,992
2004	5,220	390	309	6,240	2,165	798	269	12,872	1,307	878	220	325	1,107	45	417	33,027
2005[1]	4,933	386	312	7,829	1,018	870	251	9,252	1,185	825	212	454	1,161	70	335	29,616

[1] Preliminary.   [2] Sweet and tart.   [3] Utilized production.   Source: Economic Research Service, U.S. Department of Agriculture (ERS-USDA)

Utilized Production for Selected Fruits in the United States   In Thousands of Short Tons

Year	Utilized Production				Value of Production			
	Citrus[2]	Noncitrus	Tree Nuts[3]	Total	Citrus[2]	Noncitrus	Tree Nuts[3]	Total
	In Thousands of Short Tons				In Thousands of Dollars			
1999	13,633	17,347	1,288	32,267	2,431,179	8,077,404	1,505,926	12,014,509
2000	17,276	18,854	1,086	37,216	2,513,174	7,883,036	1,496,584	11,892,794
2001	16,216	16,740	1,304	34,260	2,319,917	7,918,636	1,513,063	11,751,616
2002	16,194	17,122	1,448	34,764	2,610,559	8,137,640	2,078,670	12,826,869
2003	15,180	16,853	1,458	33,491	2,259,976	8,617,592	2,472,480	13,350,048
2004	16,360	16,837	1,524	34,720	2,485,052	8,959,313	3,527,904	14,972,269
2005[1]	11,574	18,328	1,483	31,385	2,303,425	9,955,176	3,967,114	16,225,715

[1] Preliminary.   [2] Year harvest was completed.   [3] Tree nuts on an in-shell equivalent.
Source: Economic Research Service, U.S. Department of Agriculture (ERS-USDA)

Annual Average Retail Prices for Selected Fruits in the United States   In Dollars Per Pound

Year	Red Delicious Apples	Bananas	Anjou Pears	Thompson Seedless Grapes	Lemons	Grapefruit	Oranges Navel	Oranges Valen-cias
1999	.897	.491	.950	1.841	1.236	.612	.843	.947
2000	.919	.501	.986	1.745	1.289	.610	.613	.610
2001	.868	.507	.966	1.850	1.265	.651	.722	.524
2002	.948	.508	.997	1.887	1.391	.648	.836	.565
2003	.980	.509	NA	1.899	1.317	.723	.838	.575
2004	1.043	.495	NA	2.059	1.235	.819	.859	.691
2005[1]	.949	.492	1.114	2.078	1.411	.998	.996	.897

[1] Estimate.   Source: Economic Research Service, U.S. Department of Agriculture (ERS-USDA)

Utilization of Noncitrus Fruit Production, and Value in the U.S.   1,000 Short Tons (Fresh Equivalent)

Year	Utilized Pro- duction	Fresh	Processed Canned	Processed Dried	Processed Juice	Processed Frozen	Processed Wine	Processed Other	Value of utilized Production $1,000
1996	16,103	6,313	1,873	2,275	1,582	604	3,043	180	7,265,788
1997	18,400	6,642	2,130	2,660	1,666	699	4,035	293	8,189,821
1998	16,552	6,514	1,845	1,911	1,786	711	3,315	198	7,251,032
1999	17,347	6,691	1,986	2,154	1,887	717	3,351	244	8,077,404
2000	18,854	7,015	1,812	3,023	1,712	691	4,130	191	7,883,036
2001	16,740	6,488	1,859	2,290	1,462	665	3,568	169	7,918,636
2002	17,122	6,549	1,727	2,582	1,251	591	3,999	138	8,137,640
2003	16,853	6,676	1,762	2,293	1,295	716	3,582	219	8,617,592
2004	16,837	7,177	1,711	1,425	1,421	685	3,819	290	8,959,313
2005[1]	18,328	7,194	1,594	2,102	1,598	705	4,552	271	9,955,176

[1] Preliminary.   Source: Economic Research Service, U.S. Department of Agriculture (ERS-USDA)

Average Price Indexes for Fruits in the United States

Year	Index of all Fruit and Nut Prices Received by Growers (1990-92=100)	Producer Price Index Fresh Fruit	Producer Price Index Dried Fruit	Producer Price Index Canned Fruits and Juices	Producer Price Index Frozen Fruits and Juices	Consumer Price Index Fresh Fruit	Consumer Price Index Processed Fruit
		1982 = 100				1982-84 = 100	
1996	118	100.8	119.1	137.5	83.6	234.4	83.1
1997	110	99.4	123.3	138.4	148.2	236.3	148.5
1998	111	90.5	121.8	134.3	101.5	246.5	101.9
1999	115	103.6	122.9	137.0	106.1	266.3	105.4
2000	98	91.4	122.4	139.5	108.9	258.3	106.9
2001	109	97.7	120.3	143.3	111.9	265.1	109.0
2002	105	91.5	120.7	141.6	111.2	270.2	111.5
2003	107	84.1	122.1	142.3	115.7	279.1	113.7
2004	124	104.9	NA	142.4	112.1	286.8	114.0
2005[1]	134	102.8	NA	148.0	112.4	297.4	118.4

[1] Estimate.   Source: Economic Research Service, U.S. Department of Agriculture (ERS-USDA)

Fresh Fruit: Per Capita Consumption[1] in the United States   In Pounds

Year	Citrus Fruit Oranges	Tangerines and Tangelos	Lemons	Grapefruit	Total	Noncitrus Fruit Apples	Apricots	Avacados	Bananas	Cherries	Cran- berries
1996	12.58	2.15	2.86	5.85	24.58	18.67	.09	1.58	27.60	.40	.08
1997	13.91	2.52	2.76	6.18	26.52	18.09	.14	1.73	27.16	.60	.07
1998	14.61	2.17	2.46	5.94	26.58	18.98	.12	1.52	28.01	.52	.07
1999	8.38	2.30	2.61	5.75	20.37	18.50	.12	1.92	30.70	.63	.11
2000	11.74	2.86	2.44	5.09	23.51	17.46	.15	2.21	28.44	.60	.14
2001	11.88	2.72	2.95	4.85	23.89	15.60	.08	2.50	26.63	.77	.13
2002	11.73	2.55	3.32	4.63	23.33	15.99	.09	2.33	26.77	.70	.11
2003	11.89	2.72	3.33	4.10	23.95	16.91	.13	2.74	26.15	.92	.10
2004	10.78	2.76	3.12	4.14	22.68	18.83	.13	3.05	25.74	.99	.11
2005[2]	11.40	2.49	2.94	2.65	21.63	16.92	.14	3.27	25.14	.86	.10

[1] All data on calendar-year basis except for citrus fruits; apples, August; grapes and pears, July; grapefruit, September; lemons, August of prior year; all other citrus, November.   [2] Preliminary.   Source: Economic Research Service, U.S. Department of Agriculture (ERS-USDA)

Fresh Fruit: Per Capita Consumption[1] in the United States   In Pounds

Year	Noncitrus Fruit Continued Grapes	Kiwifruit	Mangos	Nectarines & Peaches	Pears	Pine- apples	Papaya	Plums & Prunes	Straw- berries	Total Noncitrus	Total Fruit
1996	6.73	.45	1.34	4.38	3.05	1.90	.54	1.43	4.32	72.83	97.41
1997	7.76	.54	1.44	5.51	3.39	2.34	.47	1.51	4.10	75.14	101.66
1998	7.17	.52	1.49	4.69	3.43	2.75	.47	1.18	3.92	75.16	101.74
1999	7.97	.52	1.62	5.29	3.53	3.03	.62	1.28	4.57	80.72	101.09
2000	7.44	.58	1.75	5.30	3.39	3.22	.68	1.19	4.86	77.67	101.18
2001	7.38	.43	1.79	5.16	3.25	3.16	.78	1.33	4.21	73.54	97.43
2002	8.41	.37	1.97	5.23	3.06	3.82	.79	1.26	4.65	75.94	99.27
2003	7.65	.39	2.06	5.17	3.08	4.39	.87	1.24	5.28	77.46	101.41
2004	7.79	.41	2.01	5.14	2.95	4.42	1.03	1.12	5.47	79.72	102.40
2005[2]	8.58	.45	1.88	4.82	2.92	4.90	.93	1.11	5.82	78.28	99.91

[1] All data on calendar-year basis except for citrus fruits; apples, August; grapes and pears, July; grapefruit, September; lemons, August of prior year; all other citrus, November.   [2] Preliminary.   Source: Economic Research Service, U.S. Department of Agriculture (ERS-USDA)

Gas

Natural gas is a fossil fuel that is colorless, shapeless, and odorless in its pure form. It is a mixture of hydrocarbon gases formed primarily of methane, but it can also include ethane, propane, butane, and pentane. Natural gas is combustible, clean burning, and gives off a great deal of energy. Around 500 BC, the Chinese discovered that the energy in natural gas could be harnessed. They passed it through crude bamboo-shoot pipes and then burned it to boil sea water to create potable fresh water. Around 1785, Britain became the first country to commercially use natural gas produced from coal for streetlights and indoor lights. In 1821, William Hart dug the first well specifically intended to obtain natural gas and he is generally regarded as the "father of natural gas" in America. There is a vast amount of natural gas estimated to still be in the ground in the US. Natural gas as a source of energy is significantly less expensive than electricity per Btu.

Natural gas futures and options are traded on the New York Mercantile Exchange (NYMEX). The NYMEX natural gas futures contract calls for the delivery of natural gas representing 10,000 million British thermal units (mmBtu) at the Henry Hub in Louisiana, which is the nexus of 16 intra-state and inter-state pipelines. The contract is priced in terms of dollars per mmBtu. NYMEX also has basic swap futures contracts available for 30 different natural gas pricing locations versus the benchmark Henry Hub location. Natural gas futures are also listed in London on the International Petroleum Exchange (IPE).

Prices – NYMEX natural gas futures on the nearest-futures chart in 2006 traded in a range of about $4.00-$9.82 per mmBtu. The futures price posted the year's high of $9.82 per mmBtu in late January, moved down to a low of $4.05 in late September, and then rallied to $9.05 in late November of 2006.

Supply – US recovery of natural gas in 2005 fell –2.0% to 23,488 billion cubic feet, which was farther below the record high of 24,501 billion cubic feet recovered in 2001. The top US producing states of natural gas were Texas with 28.0% of US production in 2005, Oklahoma with 8.8%, New Mexico with 8.7%, Wyoming with 8.7%, and Louisiana with 6.8%. In 2006 the world's largest natural gas producers were Russia with 2,101,406 terajoules of production and the US with 1,677,791 terajoules.

Demand – US delivered consumption of natural gas in 2005 fell –0.7% yr/yr to 22,241 billion cubic feet, of which about 30% was delivered to industrial establishments, 26% to electrical utility plants, 22% was delivered to residences, and 14% to commercial establishments.

Trade – US imports of natural gas (consumed) in 2005 rose +1.9% yr/yr to a record high of 4,431 billion cubic feet. US exports of natural gas in 2005 fell –14.7% yr/yr to 728 billion cubic feet from the 2004 record high of 854 billion cubic feet.

World Production of Natural Gas (Monthly Average Marketed Production[3]) (In Terajoule[4])

Year	Australia	Canada	China	Germany	Indonesia	India	Italy	Mexico	Netherlands	Romania	Russia	United Kingdom	United States
1997	99,077	537,295	81,954	61,804	248,585	84,892	61,173	109,568	209,526	41,547	1,771,467	299,503	1,711,134
1998	95,265	538,273	84,033	60,748	274,281	88,195	60,159	182,615	198,554	32,932	1,665,726	314,506	1,722,107
1999	92,440	569,819	79,523	62,651	282,485	91,468	56,616	182,610	186,672	38,952	1,807,313	345,040	1,790,617
2000	92,746	588,447	90,287	59,164	267,707	94,783	54,289	178,861	178,989	38,254	1,898,046	377,565	1,812,716
2001	96,523	550,463	98,431	60,463	258,122	91,063	48,008	171,940	192,180	40,422	1,887,953	370,237	1,848,810
2002	96,841	553,183	106,720	61,147	280,939	92,568	46,190	168,675	186,206	38,004	1,934,011	361,414	1,792,367
2003	99,771	534,434	111,352	61,441	289,371	89,570	42,812	174,733	201,433	38,831	2,016,895	358,798	1,726,221
2004	104,731	537,643	132,281	55,108	282,364	98,773	39,760	177,650	232,485	41,725	2,055,061	333,492	1,564,674
2005[1]	92,780	547,204	163,802	55,089	273,554	101,301	38,167	187,151	218,699	40,959	2,065,477	307,775	1,659,233
2006[2]	94,205	549,058	190,703	54,639	273,907	101,359	35,221	206,358	241,803	33,785	2,101,406	292,706	1,677,791

[1] Preliminary.   [2] Estimate.   [3] Compares all gas collected & utilized as fuel or as a chemical industry raw material, including gas used in oilfields and/or gasfields as a fuel by producers.   [4] Terajoule = 10 to the 12th power Joule = approximately 10 to the 9th power BTU.   NA = Not available.
Source: United Nations

Marketed Production of Natural Gas in the United States, by States   (In Million Cubic Feet)

Year	Alaska	California	Colorado	Kansas	Louisiana	Michigan	Mississippi	New Mexico	Oklahoma	Texas	Wyoming	Total
1996	480,828	286,494	572,071	712,796	5,289,742	245,740	103,263	1,554,087	1,734,887	6,470,620	666,036	19,812,241
1997	468,311	285,690	637,375	687,215	1,505,014	305,950	107,300	1,558,633	1,703,888	5,167,334	738,368	19,866,093
1998	466,648	315,277	696,321	603,586	1,551,979	278,076	108,068	1,501,098	1,669,367	5,227,477	903,836	19,961,348
1999	462,967	382,715	722,738	553,419	1,566,916	277,364	111,021	1,511,671	1,594,002	5,054,486	971,230	19,804,848
2000	458,995	376,580	752,985	525,729	1,455,014	296,556	88,558	1,695,295	1,612,890	5,282,104	1,088,328	20,197,511
2001	471,440	377,824	817,206	480,145	1,502,086	275,036	107,541	1,689,125	1,615,384	5,282,723	1,363,879	20,570,295
2002	463,301	360,205	937,245	454,901	1,361,751	274,476	112,980	1,632,080	1,581,606	5,141,075	1,453,957	19,884,780
2003	489,757	337,216	1,011,285	418,893	1,350,399	236,987	133,901	1,604,015	1,558,155	5,243,567	1,539,318	19,911,802
2004	471,899	319,919	1,079,235	397,121	1,353,249	259,681	63,353	1,632,539	1,655,769	5,067,315	1,592,203	19,517,491
2005[1]	487,282	317,637	1,133,086	377,229	1,296,048	261,112	52,923	1,645,166	1,670,137	5,254,974	1,639,317	18,950,734

[1] Preliminary.   *Source: Energy Information Administration, U.S. Department of Energy (EIA-DOE)*

World Production of Natural Gas Plant Liquids   (Thousand Barrels per Day)

Year	Algeria	Canada	Mexico	Saudi Arabia	Russia	United States	Persian Gulf[2]	OAPEC[3]	OPEC[4]	World
1997	160	636	388	712	195	1,817	1,152	1,384	1,589	5,729
1998	155	651	424	755	220	1,759	1,225	1,449	1,662	5,883
1999	190	653	439	745	231	1,850	1,232	1,491	1,728	6,075
2000	230	699	438	1,008	232	1,911	1,556	1,904	2,101	6,616
2001	250	709	433	1,051	237	1,868	1,721	2,108	2,304	7,016
2002	270	698	408	1,095	246	1,880	1,797	2,226	2,403	7,030
2003	280	724	418	1,220	390	1,719	1,972	2,407	2,548	7,325
2004	292	658	442	1,310	456	1,809	2,100	2,516	2,702	7,631
2005	295	645	426	1,460	457	1,717	2,267	2,640	2,915	7,798
2006[1]	308	687	431	1,479	412	1,736	2,308	2,696	3,007	7,917

[1] Preliminary.   [2] Bahrain, Iran, Iraq, Kuwait, Qatar, Saudi Arabia and the United Arab Emirates.   [3] Organization of Arab Petroleum Exporting Countries.   [4] Organization of Pertroleum Exporting Countries.   *Source: Energy Information Administration, U.S. Department of Energy (EIA-DOE)*

Recoverable Reserves and Deliveries of Natural Gas in the United States   (in Billions of Cubic Feet)

Year	Gross Withdrawals	Recoverable Reserves of Natural Gas Dec. 31[2]	Residential	Commercial	Electric Utility Plants[3]	Industrial	Total Deliveries	Lease & Plant Fuel	Used as Pipeline Fuel	Heating Value BTU per Cubic Foot
1996	24,114	166,474	5,241	3,161	2,732	8,870	20,006	1,250	711	1,027
1997	24,213	167,223	4,984	3,215	4,065	8,511	20,782	1,203	751	1,026
1998	24,108	164,041	4,520	2,999	4,588	8,320	20,438	1,173	635	1,031
1999	23,823	167,406	4,726	3,045	4,820	8,079	20,681	1,079	645	1,027
2000	24,174	177,427	4,996	3,182	5,206	8,142	21,540	1,151	642	1,025
2001	24,501	183,460	4,771	3,023	5,342	7,344	20,495	1,119	624	1,028
2002	23,941	186,946	4,889	3,144	5,672	7,507	23,007	1,113	667	1,027
2003	24,119	189,044	5,079	3,179	5,135	7,150	22,277	1,122	591	1,031
2004	23,970	192,513	4,869	3,129	5,463	7,243	22,389	1,098	566	1,027
2005[1]	23,488	204,385	4,806	3,102	5,797	6,746	22,241	1,112	585	1,029

[1] Preliminary.   [2] Estimated proved recoverable reserves of dry natural gas.   [3] Figures include gas other than natural (impossible to segregate); therefore, shown separately from other consumption.   *Source: Energy Information Administration, U.S. Department of Energy (EIA-DOE)*

Gas Utility Sales in the United States by Types and Class of Service   (In Trillions of BTUs)

Year	Total Utility Sales	Number of Customers (Millions)	Residential	Commercial	Industrial	Electric Generation	Other	Total	Residential	Commercial	industrial	Electric Generation	Other
1994	9,248	57.9	4,845	2,253	1,690	420	159	49,852	30,552	12,276	5,529	1,170	597
1995	9,221	58.7	4,803	2,281	1,591	328	218	46,436	28,742	11,573	4,816	836	549
1996	10,242	60.0	5,333	2,518	1,748	641	3	53,630	32,942	13,250	5,812	1,615	12
1997	9,722	61.0	5,056	2,341	1,593	728	4	54,876	34,187	13,203	5,556	1,912	18
1998	8,781	61.5	4,534	2,063	1,370	810	5	47,084	30,130	11,020	4,189	1,726	20
1999	8,975	60.8	4,622	2,067	1,553	729	5	47,202	30,095	10,731	4,715	1,641	21
2000	9,232	61.3	4,741	2,077	1,698	709	6	59,243	35,828	13,338	7,432	2,612	33
2001[1]	8,667	61.4	4,525	2,053	1,461	620	8	69,150	42,454	16,848	7,513	2,286	49
2002[2]	8,864	62.0	4,589	2,055	1,748	459	13	57,112	35,062	13,512	6,840	1,639	59

[1] Preliminary.   [2] Estimate.   *Source: American Gas Association (AGA)*

Salient Statistics of Natural Gas in the United States

Year	Marketed Production	Extraction Loss	Dry Production	Storage Withdrawals	Imports (Consumed)	Total Supply	Consumption	Exports	Added to Storage	Total Disposition	Wellhead Price	Imports	Exports	Residential	Commercial	Industrial	Electric Utilities
1996	19,812	958	18,854	2,981	2,937	25,635	22,610	153	2,979	24,114	2.17	1.97	2.97	6.34	5.40	3.42	2.69
1997	19,866	964	18,902	2,894	2,994	25,502	22,737	157	2,870	24,213	2.32	2.17	3.02	6.94	5.80	3.59	2.78
1998	24,108	938	19,024	2,432	3,152	25,826	22,246	159	2,961	25,826	1.96	1.97	2.45	6.82	5.48	3.14	2.40
1999	23,823	973	18,832	2,808	3,586	25,699	22,405	163	2,636	25,699	2.19	2.24	2.61	6.69	5.33	3.12	2.62
2000	24,174	1,016	19,182	3,550	3,782	26,815	23,333	244	2,721	26,815	3.68	3.95	4.10	7.76	6.59	4.45	4.38
2001	24,501	954	19,616	2,344	3,977	26,697	22,239	373	3,510	26,697	4.00	4.43	4.19	9.63	8.43	5.24	4.61
2002	23,941	957	18,928	3,180	4,015	26,767	23,007	516	2,713	26,767	2.95	3.14	3.41	7.89	6.63	4.02	3.68
2003	24,119	876	19,099	3,161	3,944	26,963	22,277	680	3,358	26,963	4.88	5.17	5.54	9.63	8.40	5.89	5.57
2004[1]	24,055	927	18,591	3,088	4,259	26,985	22,389	854	3,202	26,985	5.46	5.81	6.09	10.75	9.43	6.53	6.11
2005[2]	23,518	876	18,074	3,048	4,341		22,241	729	2,998		7.33	8.12	7.59	12.84	11.59	8.56	8.48

In Billions of Cubic Feet (Supply/Disposition columns); USD Per Thousand Cubic Feet (Average Price columns)

[1] Preliminary.   [2] Estimate.   *Source: Energy Information Administration, U.S. Department of Energy (EIA-DOE)*

Average Price of Natural Gas at Henry Hub   In Dollars Per MMBtu

Year	Jan.	Feb.	Mar.	Apr.	May	June	July	Aug.	Sept.	Oct.	Nov.	Dec.	Average
1997	3.31	2.22	1.89	2.03	2.24	2.20	2.19	2.48	2.85	3.04	3.02	2.36	2.49
1998	2.10	2.22	2.24	2.43	2.14	2.17	2.17	1.85	2.02	1.89	2.10	1.72	2.09
1999	1.85	1.77	1.79	2.15	2.25	2.30	2.31	2.79	2.54	2.72	2.35	2.36	2.27
2000	2.42	2.65	2.79	3.03	3.58	4.28	3.96	4.41	5.11	5.02	5.54	8.95	4.31
2001	8.18	5.62	5.16	5.16	4.21	3.71	3.11	2.95	2.15	2.45	2.35	2.43	3.96
2002	2.25	2.31	3.03	3.42	3.49	3.22	2.98	3.09	3.55	4.12	4.04	4.75	3.35
2003	5.49	7.41	6.08	5.27	5.81	5.83	5.03	4.97	4.61	4.66	4.47	6.13	5.48
2004	6.17	5.39	5.38	5.71	6.30	6.29	5.93	5.44	5.11	6.39	6.15	6.64	5.91
2005	6.13	6.13	6.91	7.22	6.48	7.15	7.63	9.46	11.87	13.42	10.28	13.05	8.81
2006	8.65	7.54	6.90	7.16	6.23	6.19	6.22	7.14	4.90	5.84	7.36	6.73	6.74

Source: Energy Information Administration, U.S. Department of Energy (EIA-DOE)

Volume of Trading of Natural Gas Futures in New York   In Thousands of Contracts

Year	Jan.	Feb.	Mar.	Apr.	May	June	July	Aug.	Sept.	Oct.	Nov.	Dec.	Total
1997	922.8	693.6	664.7	836.3	945.4	803.7	812.9	1,313.8	1,377.1	1,394.0	1,104.8	1,054.6	11,923.6
1998	1,005.6	1,089.1	1,193.5	1,625.9	1,245.2	1,568.8	1,310.4	1,237.0	1,656.3	1,339.5	1,243.1	1,464.0	15,978.3
1999	1,296.7	1,158.6	1,788.5	1,655.8	1,465.3	1,474.2	1,865.8	1,892.1	1,978.6	1,676.5	1,552.3	1,360.7	19,165.1
2000	1,388.8	1,470.9	1,505.0	1,179.3	1,822.2	1,853.7	1,331.4	1,483.9	1,510.2	1,594.9	1,759.5	975.1	17,875.0
2001	1,044.4	1,044.6	1,131.7	1,144.8	1,632.5	1,536.9	1,350.3	1,510.9	901.1	1,639.7	1,891.7	1,639.6	16,468.4
2002	1,942.5	1,668.6	2,381.1	2,421.7	2,281.4	1,911.7	2,266.1	2,115.6	1,990.0	2,103.4	1,569.2	1,706.4	24,357.8
2003	2,134.4	1,909.1	1,362.4	1,321.3	1,521.7	1,584.8	1,543.7	1,315.3	1,503.7	1,948.9	1,376.6	1,515.2	19,037.1
2004	1,162.1	1,125.1	1,420.3	1,443.1	1,587.5	1,588.5	1,508.8	1,724.1	1,885.6	1,458.3	1,320.0	1,218.6	17,441.9
2005	1,442.2	1,490.4	1,653.3	1,586.0	1,504.1	1,931.9	1,528.4	2,044.4	1,587.6	1,433.1	1,449.5	1,491.7	19,142.5
2006	1,609.9	1,833.9	1,682.2	1,911.6	2,272.5	1,920.6	1,786.2	2,428.7	2,017.7	1,935.1	1,799.6	1,832.0	23,030.0

Source: New York Mercantile Exchange (NYMEX)

Average Open Interest of Natural Gas Futures in New York   In Contracts

Year	Jan.	Feb.	Mar.	Apr.	May	June	July	Aug.	Sept.	Oct.	Nov.	Dec.
1997	156,231	162,567	171,467	181,745	206,685	197,637	199,296	213,640	235,509	242,184	231,556	210,259
1998	192,652	198,853	203,402	251,344	255,837	264,517	255,878	273,350	275,868	252,827	236,292	240,832
1999	244,472	268,649	284,312	315,336	332,398	330,725	316,034	353,767	336,622	316,157	309,130	292,161
2000	262,845	266,826	295,176	313,739	342,455	347,353	330,604	339,025	373,654	369,448	389,363	377,470
2001	364,532	346,343	360,032	380,632	421,145	456,512	473,675	497,972	494,475	488,187	455,766	415,882
2002	458,924	491,215	527,765	559,413	556,277	526,016	494,133	437,285	419,532	413,312	393,953	391,424
2003	415,642	420,329	367,673	354,154	365,838	366,610	357,299	343,622	354,568	352,685	356,622	340,756
2004	322,762	312,475	322,366	338,786	382,160	366,135	373,853	378,787	393,477	392,626	383,712	387,605
2005	401,829	405,692	458,013	479,880	480,318	472,631	498,440	524,235	544,165	551,121	545,270	551,444
2006	545,165	582,231	634,072	700,588	795,375	851,655	883,492	938,024	940,339	931,949	903,355	889,759

Source: New York Mercantile Exchange (NYMEX)

Gasoline

Gasoline is a complex mixture of hundreds of lighter liquid hydrocarbons and is used chiefly as a fuel for internal-combustion engines. Petroleum crude, or crude oil, is still the most economical source of gasoline with refineries turning more than half of every barrel of crude oil into gasoline. The three basic steps to all refining operations are the separation process (separating crude oil into various chemical components), conversion process (breaking the chemicals down into molecules called hydrocarbons), and treatment process (transforming and combining hydrocarbon molecules and other additives). Another process, called *hydro treating,* removes a significant amount of sulfur from finished gasoline as is currently required by the state of California.

Octane is a measure of a gasoline's ability to resist pinging or knocking noise from an engine. Most gasoline stations offer three octane grades of unleaded fuel—regular at 87 (R+M)/2, mid-grade at 89 (R+M)/2, and premium at 93 (R+M)/2. Additional refining steps are needed to increase the octane, which increases the retail price. This does not make the gasoline any cleaner or better, but yields a different blend of hydrocarbons that burn more slowly.

In an attempt to improve air quality and reduce harmful emissions from internal combustion engines, Congress in 1990 amended the Clean Air Act to mandate the addition of ethanol to gasoline. Some 2 billion gallons of ethanol are now added to gasoline each year in the US. The most common blend is E10, which contains 10% ethanol and 90% gasoline. Auto manufacturers have approved that mixture for use in all US vehicles. Ethanol is an alcohol-based fuel produced by fermenting and distilling crops such as corn, barley, wheat and sugar.

Unleaded gasoline futures and options trade at the New York Mercantile Exchange (NYMEX). The NYMEX gasoline futures contract calls for the delivery of 1,000 barrels (42,000 gallons) of unleaded gasoline in the New York harbor and is priced in terms of dollars and cents per gallon.

Price – NYMEX gasoline futures prices fluctuated widely in 2006. They started the year at about $1.81 per gallon, after a slight dip in February prices rose to a high of $2.23 per gallon and then moved lower to finish the year at about $1.54 per gallon. The record high on the nearest-futures chart of $2.92 per gallon was posted on August 31, 2005. The average monthly retail price of regular unleaded gasoline in 2006 (through December) rose +12.8% yr/yr to $2.59 per gallon, which was a record high. The average monthly retail price of unleaded premium motor gasoline in the US in 2006 (through December) rose by +12.8% to $2.81 per gallon, which was a new record high. The average monthly refiner price of finished aviation gasoline to end users in 2006 (through October) rose by +22.8% yr/yr to a new record high of $2.72 per gallon.

Supply – US production of gasoline in 2006 (through December, annualized) rose +0.1% yr/yr to 8.323 million barrels per day. Gasoline stocks in November 2006 were 115.3 million barrels, down from 132.9 million barrels in November 2005.

Demand – US consumption of finished motor gasoline in 2006 (through December, annualized) rose +0.9% yr/yr to 9.238 million barrels per day, which was a new record high.

Production of Finished Motor Gasoline in the United States   In Thousand Barrels per Day

Year	Jan.	Feb.	Mar.	Apr.	May	June	July	Aug.	Sept.	Oct.	Nov.	Dec.	Average
1997	7,308	7,315	7,322	7,822	8,056	8,180	7,947	8,048	8,147	8,039	7,984	8,143	7,870
1998	7,749	7,485	7,591	8,029	8,057	8,372	8,287	8,200	8,029	7,995	8,263	8,395	8,082
1999	7,886	7,607	7,531	8,138	8,207	8,402	8,280	8,183	8,187	8,266	8,142	8,471	8,111
2000	7,798	7,658	8,032	8,130	8,398	8,550	8,320	8,251	8,358	8,031	8,394	8,298	8,186
2001	7,888	7,822	8,011	8,450	8,651	8,637	8,481	8,277	8,381	8,446	8,366	8,301	8,312
2002	8,160	8,117	8,072	8,626	8,729	8,661	8,665	8,666	8,320	8,190	8,738	8,734	8,475
2003	7,870	7,800	7,724	8,161	8,311	8,293	8,320	8,355	8,228	8,253	8,450	8,540	8,194
2004	7,956	7,979	8,102	8,233	8,447	8,336	8,370	8,357	7,993	8,384	8,346	8,659	8,264
2005	8,157	8,194	8,119	8,549	8,475	8,589	8,352	8,326	8,129	7,953	8,468	8,503	8,318
2006[1]	8,185	7,969	7,760	7,946	8,414	8,878	8,566	8,584	8,415	8,214	8,313	8,628	8,323

[1] Preliminary.   *Source: Energy Information Administration, U.S. Department of Energy (EIA-DOE)*

Disposition of Finished Motor Gasoline, Total Product Supplied in the U.S.   In Thousand Barrels per Day

Year	Jan.	Feb.	Mar.	Apr.	May	June	July	Aug.	Sept.	Oct.	Nov.	Dec.	Average
1997	7,312	7,651	7,808	8,067	8,128	8,260	8,471	8,195	8,004	8,166	7,955	8,093	8,017
1998	7,590	7,755	7,956	8,137	8,070	8,437	8,659	8,500	8,308	8,405	8,136	8,401	8,253
1999	7,701	8,031	8,128	8,506	8,420	8,886	8,942	8,579	8,305	8,542	8,240	8,859	8,431
2000	7,653	8,291	8,305	8,375	8,661	8,824	8,642	8,921	8,518	8,417	8,384	8,670	8,472
2001	8,099	8,234	8,532	8,575	8,706	8,690	9,023	8,953	8,557	8,655	8,677	8,585	8,610
2002	8,227	8,607	8,655	8,766	9,078	9,140	9,143	9,313	8,687	8,814	8,829	8,893	8,848
2003	8,414	8,525	8,602	8,838	9,042	9,170	9,192	9,411	8,926	9,108	8,946	9,011	8,935
2004	8,705	8,838	9,024	9,126	9,179	9,322	9,357	9,327	9,015	9,097	9,055	9,206	9,104
2005	8,813	8,861	8,994	9,128	9,278	9,373	9,534	9,537	8,915	9,036	9,115	9,296	9,157
2006[1]	8,727	8,836	9,129	9,140	9,312	9,440	9,583	9,585	9,222	9,286	9,263	9,327	9,238

[1] Preliminary.   *Source: Energy Information Administration, U.S. Department of Energy (EIA-DOE)*

GASOLINE

RBOB Gasoline Futures - New York Mercantile Exchange
(weekly close) as of December 29, 2006

USD per gallon

Average Spot Price of Unleaded Gasoline in New York   In Cents Per Gallon

Year	Jan.	Feb.	Mar.	Apr.	May	June	July	Aug.	Sept.	Oct.	Nov.	Dec.	Average
1997	67.64	62.49	61.28	58.59	62.08	55.17	58.58	70.42	62.17	58.35	55.60	51.75	60.34
1998	47.85	45.14	44.13	46.98	48.26	43.95	42.29	40.14	42.70	43.71	36.78	30.92	42.74
1999	34.24	31.81	42.33	50.11	48.86	48.65	58.35	63.89	69.37	62.63	69.57	70.55	54.20
2000	70.43	81.30	89.11	73.15	89.06	96.18	86.76	86.97	96.04	94.71	93.94	73.66	85.94
2001	83.32	82.56	78.18	94.95	92.37	71.85	68.31	77.18	75.00	59.79	51.34	51.85	73.89
2002	54.30	55.41	69.64	74.66	70.32	71.65	76.62	76.75	78.36	82.34	76.08	80.56	72.22
2003	87.56	99.62	95.51	80.08	76.16	80.65	87.17	100.42	90.41	87.12	87.33	88.37	88.37
2004	99.66	104.63	109.12	112.02	133.98	115.70	122.65	120.89	126.17	137.75	126.96	106.90	118.04
2005	123.85	122.42	143.90	147.06	137.06	151.02	158.89	191.13	214.78	170.87	147.73	159.88	155.72
2006	173.39	149.98	175.87	214.62	204.68	206.50	223.99	203.23	158.42	152.00	158.71	166.70	182.34

Source: Energy Information Administration, U.S. Department of Energy (EIA-DOE)

Volume of Trading of Gasoline, RBOB[1] Futures in New York   In Thousands of Contracts

Year	Jan.	Feb.	Mar.	Apr.	May	June	July	Aug.	Sept.	Oct.	Nov.	Dec.	Total
1997	590.1	563.2	605.1	623.2	618.3	555.5	721.4	795.4	664.9	613.6	509.9	614.6	7,475.1
1998	613.6	612.3	766.4	789.3	681.1	753.1	680.6	592.0	654.2	670.2	577.8	601.7	7,992.3
1999	561.5	619.7	876.4	741.5	721.1	737.7	822.0	800.4	751.3	705.1	748.8	615.7	8,701.2
2000	693.6	721.9	921.6	730.0	927.5	838.5	650.6	677.2	641.2	635.7	612.1	595.1	8,645.2
2001	825.2	701.2	809.2	981.0	1,056.5	895.0	737.3	790.8	581.9	664.9	613.3	567.2	9,223.5
2002	795.0	744.7	942.7	1,019.3	985.2	834.5	967.8	893.6	867.6	1,105.0	865.9	958.4	10,979.7
2003	1,054.1	968.7	1,010.9	909.0	933.7	944.0	987.5	1,021.5	943.0	877.1	760.8	761.6	11,172.1
2004	956.1	998.7	1,169.2	1,169.0	1,203.8	1,194.5	1,027.0	1,177.7	1,052.9	983.7	849.0	995.9	12,777.5
2005	974.6	1,000.9	1,193.5	1,252.5	1,060.2	1,104.7	1,103.2	1,341.3	1,221.3	999.2	928.1	989.0	13,168.4
2006	1,149.6	1,233.0	1,259.1	1,079.6	1,122.7	1,039.8	939.8	1,145.5	891.4	839.6	838.1	966.0	12,504.2

[1] Data thru September 2005 are Unleaded, October 2005 thru December 2006 are Unleaded and RBOB.   *Source: New York Mercantile Exchange*

Average Open Interest of Gasoline, RBOB[1] Futures in New York   In Contracts

Year	Jan.	Feb.	Mar.	Apr.	May	June	July	Aug.	Sept.	Oct.	Nov.	Dec.
1997	68,188	84,693	92,520	97,619	90,407	78,492	83,082	103,538	103,250	94,602	92,852	103,497
1998	106,353	102,656	108,667	117,521	107,235	100,792	89,846	86,902	85,188	81,991	87,306	103,079
1999	105,532	113,683	111,449	110,531	107,644	102,927	113,619	120,468	120,328	111,758	109,428	96,652
2000	89,049	103,586	105,448	105,133	103,831	96,772	80,886	66,598	74,735	80,446	88,509	92,041
2001	117,540	126,762	124,631	124,162	111,576	103,058	101,249	92,156	87,841	102,414	115,699	126,634
2002	136,795	139,191	133,649	129,274	120,224	114,663	106,463	94,648	95,754	100,427	105,175	109,737
2003	117,558	124,288	113,380	98,627	96,405	93,285	95,433	99,394	85,457	90,007	95,002	105,919
2004	125,207	141,837	150,573	146,375	148,782	138,248	140,691	146,532	147,088	150,643	138,280	153,907
2005	162,432	161,603	172,012	166,620	145,587	148,482	156,730	156,282	140,270	134,833	138,659	144,396
2006	157,562	173,978	168,067	165,233	150,913	138,578	146,173	135,367	131,771	124,963	128,906	135,085

[1] Data thru September 2005 are Unleaded, October 2005 thru December 2006 are Unleaded and RBOB.   *Source: New York Mercantile Exchange*

RBOB Gasoline (monthly Average) through December 2006 — USD per gallon

USD Per Gallon
----- Unleaded, New York (Jan. 1976 - date)
- - - Leaded, New York (Oct. 1973 - Apr. 1991)

Stocks of Finished Gasoline[2] on Hand in the United States, at End of Month — In Millions of Barrels

Year	Jan.	Feb.	Mar.	Apr.	May	June	July	Aug.	Sept.	Oct.	Nov.	Dec.
1997	164.9	161.3	153.8	152.0	157.8	163.9	150.6	149.6	158.1	158.0	161.1	166.1
1998	175.3	172.8	166.4	168.3	174.9	177.7	172.5	168.8	164.7	160.0	167.5	172.0
1999	185.2	178.4	167.8	168.9	176.5	172.3	163.6	158.6	159.2	158.8	160.5	151.6
2000	165.3	156.4	157.1	160.6	162.2	164.5	164.6	151.0	154.2	147.4	156.7	153.0
2001	158.7	154.6	144.7	150.3	160.1	169.4	162.3	150.6	158.0	160.2	161.2	161.5
2002	169.7	165.5	159.8	167.0	168.3	167.6	164.8	157.3	157.4	148.2	158.0	161.9
2003	157.2	151.1	144.7	151.4	155.2	153.0	150.1	145.2	146.1	140.4	146.3	146.9
2004	138.7	133.5	132.1	133.1	137.2	140.2	140.5	137.9	135.7	138.4	141.5	143.2
2005	144.8	148.4	137.8	141.6	141.0	141.9	135.1	125.0	128.1	130.0	132.9	135.0
2006[1]	143.3	140.8	124.5	115.8	121.4	119.7	118.3	116.6	120.6	113.1	115.3	135.0

[1] Preliminary.   [2] Includes oxygenated and other finished.   *Source: Energy Information Administration, U.S. Department of Energy (EIA-DOE)*

Average Refiner Price of Finished Motor Gasoline to End Users[1] in the U.S. — In Cents Per Gallon

Year	Jan.	Feb.	Mar.	Apr.	May	June	July	Aug.	Sept.	Oct.	Nov.	Dec.	Average
1997	86.6	86.1	84.3	83.9	84.5	83.3	81.5	86.8	87.2	84.3	81.6	77.8	83.9
1998	73.3	69.0	65.6	67.4	71.0	70.4	69.4	66.7	65.4	66.4	64.0	60.0	67.3
1999	59.2	56.8	65.1	79.0	78.2	75.6	80.6	86.5	88.8	87.1	88.4	90.3	78.1
2000	91.7	98.7	113.1	108.7	110.3	121.3	117.3	110.3	117.5	115.5	113.5	106.3	110.6
2001	106.8	106.7	103.9	117.7	130.1	120.7	103.2	102.5	1,009.2	89.9	76.9	68.5	103.2
2002	70.6	71.8	87.2	100.4	99.9	99.1	100.3	100.1	100.1	104.0	101.2	98.1	94.7
2003	106.0	122.1	130.0	120.1	110.0	109.3	110.6	123.1	126.5	115.0	109.5	106.5	115.7
2004	117.3	125.6	133.8	139.6	156.9	154.4	148.3	145.1	145.0	158.6	155.1	141.3	143.4
2005	139.5	146.8	163.7	180.3	171.4	172.1	185.0	208.0	241.7	226.2	182.4	173.9	182.6
2006[2]	187.3	183.5	198.5	233.4	246.1	243.9	253.0	248.8	207.8	178.4			218.1

[1] Excludes aviation and taxes.   [2] Preliminary.   *Source: Energy Information Administration, U.S. Department of Energy (EIA-DOE)*

GASOLINE

Average Retail Price of Unleaded Premium Motor Gasoline[2] in the United States   In Cents per Gallon

Year	Jan.	Feb.	Mar.	Apr.	May	June	July	Aug.	Sept.	Oct.	Nov.	Dec.	Average
1997	144.1	143.4	141.5	141.3	140.9	141.1	138.8	143.3	145.8	142.6	139.7	136.3	141.6
1998	131.9	127.1	122.9	123.7	127.5	127.9	126.8	124.4	123.0	123.6	122.5	118.7	125.0
1999	117.1	115.5	118.6	136.7	137.0	133.9	137.8	144.1	146.8	146.4	145.4	148.6	135.7
2000	148.6	155.1	172.3	169.8	168.2	178.6	177.3	168.9	176.4	174.4	173.8	167.9	169.3
2001	165.7	167.1	163.8	174.8	193.4	188.1	169.5	163.6	172.6	156.0	142.7	131.2	165.7
2002	132.3	133.0	145.0	162.2	162.5	160.8	160.7	162.0	161.9	164.3	164.3	158.9	157.8
2003	166.6	182.8	192.4	184.6	172.9	170.0	171.0	180.8	191.1	178.9	172.4	168.6	177.7
2004	177.9	185.8	194.9	201.2	218.6	222.5	213.0	209.1	208.2	221.5	220.3	208.0	206.8
2005	201.7	210.5	225.1	246.8	240.3	236.5	250.2	270.1	313.0	300.1	256.0	239.3	249.1
2006[1]	252.1	251.9	260.3	296.7	316.9	313.9	321.9	320.7	281.9	249.3	245.9	255.0	280.5

[1] Preliminary.   [2] Including taxes.   *Source: Energy Information Administration, U.S. Department of Energy (EIA-DOE)*

Average Retail Price of Unleaded Regular Motor Gasoline[2] in the United States   In Cents per Gallon

Year	Jan.	Feb.	Mar.	Apr.	May	June	July	Aug.	Sept.	Oct.	Nov.	Dec.	Average
1997	126.1	125.5	123.5	123.1	122.6	122.9	120.5	125.3	127.7	124.2	121.3	117.7	123.4
1998	113.1	108.2	104.1	105.2	109.2	109.4	107.9	105.2	103.3	104.2	102.8	98.6	105.9
1999	97.2	95.5	99.1	117.7	117.8	114.8	118.9	125.5	128.0	127.4	126.4	129.8	116.5
2000	130.1	136.9	154.1	150.6	149.8	161.7	159.3	151.0	158.2	155.9	155.5	148.9	151.0
2001	147.2	148.4	144.7	156.4	172.9	164.0	148.2	142.7	153.1	136.2	126.3	113.1	146.1
2002	113.9	113.0	124.1	140.7	142.1	140.4	141.2	142.3	142.2	144.9	144.8	139.4	135.8
2003	147.3	164.1	174.8	165.9	154.2	151.4	152.4	162.8	172.8	160.3	153.5	149.4	159.1
2004	159.2	167.2	176.6	183.3	200.9	204.1	193.9	189.8	189.1	202.9	201.0	188.2	188.0
2005	182.3	191.8	206.5	228.3	221.6	217.6	231.6	250.3	292.7	278.5	234.3	218.6	229.5
2006[1]	231.5	231.0	240.1	275.7	294.7	291.7	299.9	298.5	258.9	227.2	224.1	233.4	258.9

[1] Preliminary.   [2] Including taxes.   *Source: Energy Information Administration, U.S. Department of Energy (EIA-DOE)*

Average Retail Price of All-Types[2] Motor Gasoline[3] in the United States   In Cents per Gallon

Year	Jan.	Feb.	Mar.	Apr.	May	June	July	Aug.	Sept.	Oct.	Nov.	Dec.	Average
1997	131.8	131.2	129.3	128.8	128.4	128.6	126.3	131.0	133.4	130.0	127.1	123.6	129.1
1998	118.6	113.7	109.7	110.6	114.6	114.8	113.4	110.8	109.1	109.9	108.6	104.6	111.5
1999	103.1	101.4	104.8	123.2	123.3	120.4	124.4	130.9	133.4	132.9	131.9	135.3	122.1
2000	135.6	142.2	159.4	156.1	155.2	166.6	164.2	155.9	163.5	161.3	160.8	154.4	156.3
2001	152.5	153.8	150.3	161.7	181.2	173.1	156.5	150.9	160.9	144.2	132.4	120.0	153.1
2002	120.9	121.0	132.4	149.3	150.8	148.9	149.6	150.8	150.7	153.5	153.4	147.7	144.1
2003	155.7	168.6	179.1	170.4	158.7	155.8	156.7	167.1	177.1	164.6	157.8	153.8	163.8
2004	163.5	171.5	180.9	187.5	205.0	208.3	198.2	194.1	193.4	207.2	205.3	192.6	192.3
2005	186.6	196.0	210.7	232.5	225.7	221.8	235.7	254.8	296.9	283.0	238.7	223.0	233.8
2006[1]	235.9	235.4	244.4	280.1	299.3	296.3	304.6	303.3	263.7	231.9	228.7	238.0	263.5

[1] Preliminary.   [2] Also includes types of motor oil not shown separately.   [3] Including taxes.   *Source: Energy Information Administration, U.S. Department of Energy (EIA-DOE)*

Average Refiner Price of Finished Aviation Gasoline to End Users[2] in the U.S.   In Cents per Gallon

Year	Jan.	Feb.	Mar.	Apr.	May	June	July	Aug.	Sept.	Oct.	Nov.	Dec.	Average
1997	113.7	114.9	113.8	114.7	115.7	114.6	112.5	114.6	115.6	113.9	113.0	107.7	113.8
1998	104.3	101.1	98.2	98.6	99.9	99.0	98.4	95.9	94.1	95.1	93.2	88.5	97.2
1999	87.1	85.1	90.1	101.4	104.2	104.1	107.9	113.2	115.4	117.6	116.4	119.6	105.9
2000	118.7	119.5	129.1	124.3	126.8	139.8	142.6	NA	138.2	134.9	134.9	126.1	130.6
2001	128.5	129.2	124.5	134.9	150.9	145.1	134.6	136.3	142.4	125.3	119.4	115.8	132.3
2002	111.8	110.6	122.6	129.8	128.9	127.3	139.2	136.9	139.1	143.0	141.8	139.8	128.8
2003	139.7	W	W	W	139.8	145.1	151.9	162.2	158.9	150.8	W	146.6	149.4
2004	W	W	W	177.4	194.4	192.3	185.4	184.9	187.8	195.5	187.0	176.7	186.8
2005	173.8	186.7	201.5	221.7	212.1	211.6	223.0	238.6	280.8	270.8	218.6	219.3	221.5
2006[1]	239.1	232.4	247.3	286.9	301.3	305.7	310.3	305.8	253.2	238.4			272.0

[1] Preliminary.   [2] Excluding taxes.   W = Withheld.   *Source: Energy Information Administration, U.S. Department Energy (EIA-DOE)*

Gold

Gold is a dense, bright yellow metallic element with a high luster. Gold is an inactive substance and is unaffected by air, heat, moisture, and most solvents. Gold has been coveted for centuries for its unique blend of rarity, beauty, and near indestructibility. The Egyptians mined gold before 2,000 BC. The first known, pure gold coin was made on the orders of King Croesus of Lydia in the sixth century BC.

Gold is found in nature in quartz veins and secondary alluvial deposits as a free metal. Gold is produced from mines on every continent with the exception of Antarctica, where mining is forbidden. Because it is virtually indestructible, much of the gold that has ever been mined still exists above ground in one form or another. The largest producer of gold in the US by far is the state of Nevada, with Alaska and California running a distant second and third.

Gold is a vital industrial commodity. Pure gold is one of the most malleable and ductile of all the metals. It is a good conductor of heat and electricity. Gold melts at 1,064 degrees Celsius and boils at about 2,808 degrees Celsius. The prime industrial use of gold is in electronics. Another important sector is dental gold where it has been used for almost 3,000 years. Other applications for gold include decorative gold leaf, reflective glass, and jewelry.

In 1792, the United States first assigned a formal monetary role for gold when Congress put the nation's currency on a bimetallic standard, backing it with gold and silver. Under the gold standard, the US government was willing to exchange its paper currency for a set amount of gold, meaning the paper currency was backed by a physical asset with real value. However, President Nixon in 1971 severed the convertibility between the US dollar and gold, which led to the breakdown of the Bretton Woods international payments system. Since then, the prices of gold and of paper currencies have floated freely. US and other central banks now hold physical gold reserves primarily as a store of wealth.

Gold futures and options are traded at the New York Mercantile Exchange. Gold futures are traded on the Bolsa de Mercadorias e Futuros (BM&F) and on the Tokyo Commodity Exchange (TOCOM), the Chicago Board of Trade (CBOT) and the Korea Futures Exchange (KOFEX). The Nymex gold futures contract calls for the delivery of 100 troy ounces of gold (0.995 fineness), and the contract trades in terms of dollars and cents per troy ounce.

Prices – Nymex gold futures prices in 2006 extended the rally that began in 2001 and posted a new high of $732.00 per ounce in May 2006. Gold prices then fell sharply and consolidated through the remainder of the year on a washout of speculators and reduced fundamental demand due to high prices. The World Gold Council estimated that gold demand in 2006 fell -10% to 3,362 tonnes due to high prices, but that supply fell by even more by -13% to 3,451 tonnes. Gold futures prices finally closed 2006 up +23% yr/yr at $638 per ounce. Gold prices remained generally strong in 2006 due to the weak dollar and tight supplies caused by stagnant mine production.

Supply – World mine production of gold rose +0.8% yr/yr to 2.450 million kilograms in 2005, which was still below the record high of 2.570 million kilograms seen in 1999 and 2000 (1 kilogram = 32.1507 troy ounces). The world's largest producers of gold are South Africa with 12% of world production in 2005, followed by Australia (10%), the US (10%), China (9%), Russia (7%), Indonesia (6%), and Canada (5%).

Gold mine production has been moving lower in most major gold-producing countries such as South Africa, Australia, Canada and the US. South Africa's production of 300,000 kilograms in 2005 was down –12.1% yr/yr and was less than half the production levels above 600,000 kilograms seen in the 1980s and early 1990s. However, China's gold production in 2005 rose +4.7% to a record 225,000 kilograms.

US gold mine production in 2005 rose +0.8% yr/yr to 260,000 kilograms, up slightly from the 258,000 kilograms in 2004, which was the lowest production level since 1988. US refinery production of gold from domestic and foreign ore sources in 2005 rose by +3.6% yr/yr to 230,000 kilograms. US refinery production of gold from secondary scrap sources in 2005 rose by +9.1% yr/yr to 100,000 kilograms.

Demand – US consumption of gold in 2005 rose +5.4% yr/yr to 195,000 kilograms, which was a 7-year high. The most recent data available from the early 1990s showed that 71% of gold demand came from jewelry and the arts, 22% from industrial uses, and 7% from dental uses.

Trade - US exports of gold (excluding coinage) in 2005 rose by +26.1% yr/yr to 324,000 kilograms from the 17-year low of 257,000 kilograms seen in 2004. US imports of gold for consumption in 2005 rose +20.5% yr/yr to 341,000 kilograms, which was a 20-year high.

World Mine Production of Gold   In Kilograms (1 Kilogram = 32.1507 Troy Ounces)

Year	Aust-ralia	Brazil	Canada	Chile	China	Ghana	Indo-nesia	Papua N. Guinea	Russia	South Africa	United States	Uzbek-istan	World Total
1996	289,530	60,011	166,378	53,174	145,000	49,211	83,564	51,119	123,300	496,846	326,000	72,000	2,290,000
1997	314,500	58,488	171,479	49,459	175,000	54,662	86,927	45,418	124,000	491,680	362,000	81,700	2,450,000
1998	310,070	49,567	165,599	44,980	178,000	72,541	124,018	61,641	114,900	465,100	366,000	80,000	2,500,000
1999	301,070	52,634	157,617	48,069	173,000	79,946	127,184	65,747	125,870	451,300	341,000	85,000	2,570,000
2000	296,410	50,393	156,207	54,143	180,000	72,100	124,596	74,540	143,000	430,800	353,000	85,000	2,570,000
2001	280,100	42,884	158,875	42,673	185,000	68,341	166,091	67,043	152,500	394,800	335,000	87,000	2,560,000
2002	266,100	41,662	151,904	38,688	192,000	69,271	142,238	63,200	168,411	398,523	298,000	90,000	2,550,000
2003	282,000	40,416	140,861	38,954	205,000	70,749	141,019	68,100	170,068	373,300	277,000	90,000	2,560,000
2004[1]	259,000	47,596	129,478	39,986	215,000	63,139	92,936	73,500	163,148	340,500	258,000	93,000	2,440,000
2005[2]	262,000	41,154	118,528	40,447	225,000	62,100	140,000	66,700	169,297	294,803	256,000	90,000	2,470,000

[1] Preliminary.   [2] Estimate.   *Source: U.S. Geological Survey (USGS)*

GOLD

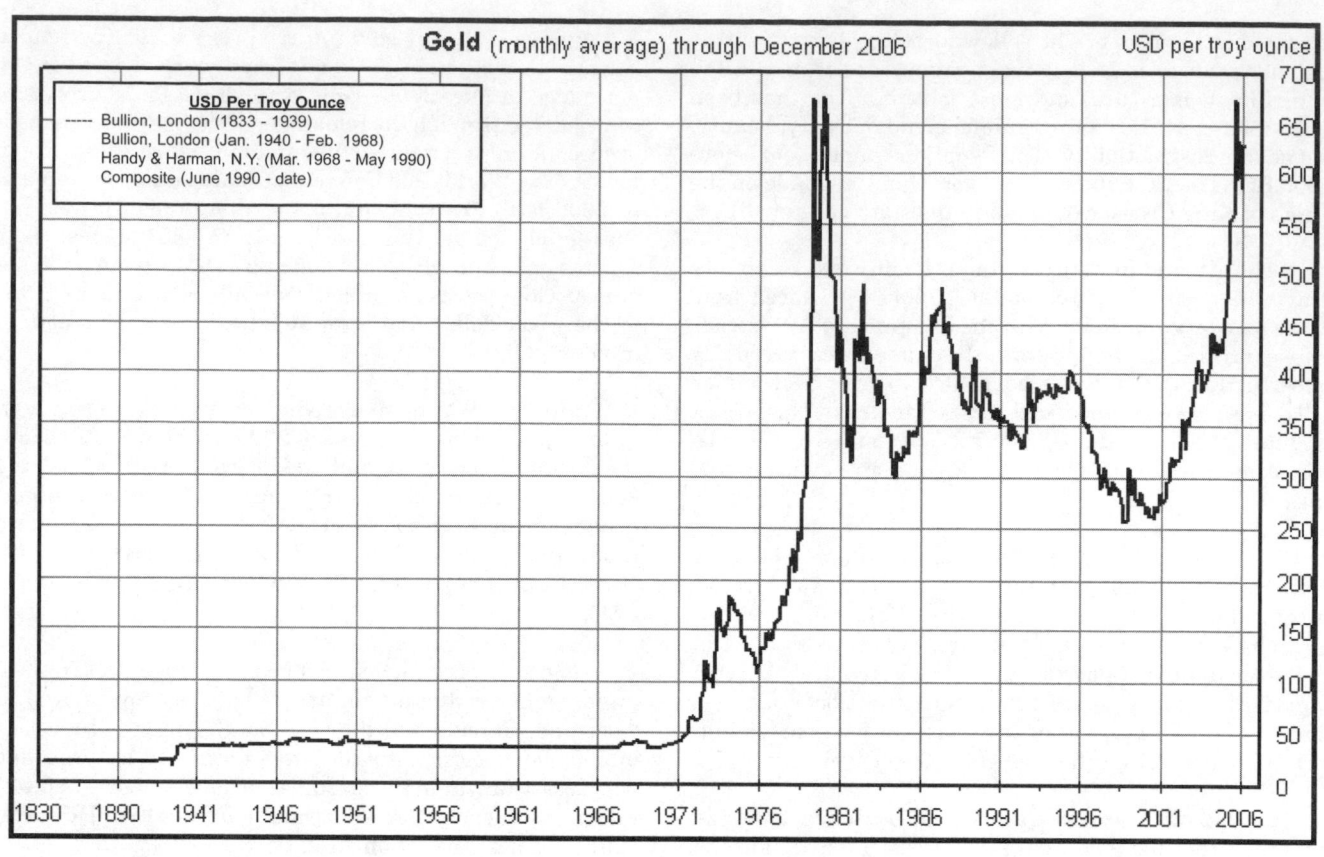

Gold (monthly average) through December 2006 — USD per troy ounce

USD Per Troy Ounce
- Bullion, London (1833 - 1939)
- Bullion, London (Jan. 1940 - Feb. 1968)
- Handy & Harman, N.Y. (Mar. 1968 - May 1990)
- Composite (June 1990 - date)

Salient Statistics of Gold in the United States — In Kilograms (1 Kilogram = 32.1507 Troy Ounces)

			Refinery Production				Stocks, Dec. 31				Consumption			
			Domestic Secondary		Exports	Imports	Treasury			Official				
	Mine	Value	& Foreign	(Old	(Excluding	for Con-	Depar	Futures		World			Jewelry	
Year	Production	Million $	Ores	Scrap)	Coinage)	sumption	tment[3]	Exchange	Industry	Reserves[4]	Dental	Industrial[5]	& Arts	Total
1996	326,000	4,090.0	NA	NA	471,000	159,000	8,140,000	20,700	NA	34,400	NA	NA	NA	NA
1997	362,000	3,870.0	270,000	100,000	476,000	209,000	8,140,000	15,200	17,300	34,000	NA	NA	NA	137,000
1998	366,000	3,480.0	277,000	163,000	522,000	278,000	8,130,000	25,200	16,600	33,600	NA	NA	NA	219,000
1999	341,000	3,070.0	265,000	143,000	523,000	221,000	8,170,000	37,900	14,700	33,500	NA	NA	NA	245,000
2000	353,000	3,180.0	197,000	81,600	547,000	223,000	8,140,000	52,900	9,300	33,000				183,000
2001	335,000	2,940.0	191,000	82,700	489,000	194,000	8,120,000	38,000	3,670	33,000				179,000
2002	298,000	2,980.0	196,000	78,100	257,000	217,000	8,140,000	63,900	3,490	32,200				163,000
2003	277,000	3,250.0	194,000	89,100	352,000	249,000	8,140,000	97,100	3,590	31,800				183,000
2004[1]	258,000	3,400.0	222,000	91,700	257,000	283,000	8,140,000	180,000	1,080	31,400				185,000
2005[2]	256,000	3,670.0	163,000	75,600	324,000	341,000	8,140,000	211,000	2,040	30,800				183,000

[1] Preliminary. [2] Estimate. [3] Includes gold in Exchange Stabilization Fund. [4] Held by market economy country central banks and governments andinternational monetary orgainzations. [5] Including space and defense. NA = Not available. *Source: U.S. Geological Survey (USGS)*

Monthly Average Gold Price (Handy & Harman) in New York — In Dollars Per Troy Ounce

Year	Jan.	Feb.	Mar.	Apr.	May	June	July	Aug.	Sept.	Oct.	Nov.	Dec.	Average
1997	355.10	346.71	351.67	344.47	343.75	340.75	324.08	324.03	322.74	324.87	307.10	288.65	331.16
1998	289.18	297.49	295.90	308.40	299.39	292.31	292.79	283.76	289.01	295.92	293.89	291.29	294.12
1999	287.05	287.22	285.96	282.45	276.94	261.31	255.81	256.56	265.23	310.72	292.74	283.69	278.81
2000	284.26	299.60	286.39	279.75	275.10	285.73	281.01	274.44	273.53	270.00	266.05	271.68	278.96
2001	265.58	261.99	263.03	260.56	272.07	270.23	267.53	272.40	283.78	283.06	276.49	275.98	271.06
2002	281.47	295.40	294.06	302.68	314.08	321.81	313.51	310.18	319.49	316.56	319.14	333.21	310.13
2003	356.91	359.60	340.55	328.25	355.03	356.35	351.01	359.91	379.07	378.92	389.13	407.44	363.51
2004	414.09	404.52	405.99	403.96	383.94	392.73	398.08	400.86	405.45	420.46	438.21	442.20	409.21
2005	424.39	423.15	433.91	429.23	422.53	430.66	424.33	438.03	456.52	469.90	474.87	510.01	444.79
2006[1]	549.27	555.02	557.09	610.41	673.97	596.15	634.89	632.10	596.76	585.78	627.12	629.38	604.00

[1] Preliminary. *Source: U.S. Geological Survey (USGS)*

Gold Futures - New York Mercantile Exchange
(weekly close) as of December 29, 2006

USD per troy ounce

Volume of Trading of Gold Futures in New York (NYMEX)   In Thousands of Contracts

Year	Jan.	Feb.	Mar.	Apr.	May	June	July	Aug.	Sept.	Oct.	Nov.	Dec.	Total
1997	1,102.8	830.2	899.4	508.5	762.1	522.7	1,147.5	667.8	715.8	988.0	808.8	588.1	9,541.9
1998	1,078.2	534.2	877.2	698.1	845.2	718.7	712.4	680.0	851.7	769.6	705.6	519.0	8,990.1
1999	860.8	517.4	1,147.6	561.1	1,069.6	573.6	964.3	709.6	1,067.3	993.8	674.7	436.1	9,575.8
2000	616.4	833.5	767.7	362.2	701.5	625.5	532.5	374.4	403.2	424.9	625.7	349.0	6,643.5
2001	755.2	483.3	766.6	438.1	971.6	481.4	578.3	547.4	341.0	481.4	573.6	367.4	6,785.3
2002	733.6	613.2	717.7	559.8	1,089.6	775.5	998.9	585.8	621.8	669.0	844.8	808.5	9,018.2
2003	1,260.1	1,007.5	987.6	667.8	1,160.3	824.3	1,191.7	837.5	1,034.0	1,091.3	1,397.3	776.3	12,235.5
2004	1,581.3	962.6	1,649.5	1,202.9	1,344.8	960.6	1,405.0	953.0	944.9	1,067.2	1,864.7	1,053.2	14,989.6
2005	1,502.3	944.4	1,599.0	858.1	1,451.7	1,240.0	1,432.4	1,234.4	1,380.2	1,174.0	1,852.7	1,221.5	15,890.6
2006	2,018.8	1,162.7	2,052.7	1,302.9	2,071.0	1,148.6	1,487.2	804.5	884.7	857.1	1,284.7	842.7	15,917.6

Source: New York Mercantile Exchange (NYMEX), COMEX division

Average Open Interest of Gold in New York (NYMEX)   In Thousands of Contracts

Year	Jan.	Feb.	Mar.	Apr.	May	June	July	Aug.	Sept.	Oct.	Nov.	Dec.
1997	199,710	190,524	167,595	157,176	160,512	170,640	207,352	198,099	201,267	188,365	212,757	188,558
1998	180,994	171,507	183,358	180,267	158,157	172,250	169,180	192,623	183,351	186,680	164,304	153,063
1999	179,726	185,345	178,456	198,202	193,978	207,122	205,687	193,023	206,186	216,034	189,433	156,754
2000	149,606	158,026	160,325	155,188	162,516	144,099	133,087	126,893	132,731	132,546	134,630	113,830
2001	134,401	142,673	126,558	120,111	118,426	116,788	114,098	116,687	125,907	125,639	114,238	111,622
2002	124,222	142,763	142,638	159,892	190,845	174,123	166,042	146,596	167,620	162,456	164,581	191,594
2003	221,495	210,247	186,656	176,033	191,459	198,808	199,741	224,694	284,906	258,238	275,346	277,183
2004	283,813	238,816	256,873	274,898	250,963	225,001	239,579	237,940	259,181	306,522	344,665	329,669
2005	277,112	263,191	301,758	283,546	277,469	275,508	268,068	304,000	339,269	356,526	334,562	331,527
2006	348,949	338,851	331,223	350,380	336,735	288,309	316,969	309,186	320,850	330,152	346,141	335,204

Source: New York Mercantile Exchange (NYMEX), COMEX division

GOLD

Commodity Exchange, Inc. (COMEX) Depository Warehouse Stocks of Gold   In Thousands of Troy Ounces

Year	Jan. 1	Feb. 1	Mar. 1	Apr. 1	May 1	June 1	July 1	Aug. 1	Sept. 1	Oct. 1	Nov. 1	Dec. 1
1997	665.8	837.1	582.9	1,000.1	946.0	878.2	850.2	914.0	733.1	894.4	614.7	760.8
1998	488.4	445.9	480.9	719.8	658.5	1,077.3	1,054.7	1,092.3	911.3	958.4	827.1	819.3
1999	809.5	809.1	859.7	1,034.0	895.9	879.3	818.3	936.1	1,198.2	928.0	874.4	1,137.4
2000	1,219.4	1,392.9	1,373.9	1,968.1	1,966.7	1,900.6	1,890.1	2,012.6	1,961.1	1,918.1	1,865.5	1,863.6
2001	1,701.2	1,775.3	1,653.7	1,302.4	858.3	864.2	891.3	901.1	793.6	824.3	1,164.6	1,425.7
2002	1,220.3	1,186.7	1,285.7	1,322.3	1,372.3	1,764.1	1,850.7	1,835.6	1,915.0	1,892.4	1,994.9	2,046.5
2003	2,056.5	2,159.8	2,262.4	2,383.9	2,460.7	2,474.9	2,675.1	2,743.8	2,729.4	2,822.6	2,912.1	3,058.9
2004	3,122.2	3,324.0	3,476.9	3,677.1	4,142.0	4,391.8	4,399.6	4,657.0	4,880.1	5,122.4	5,334.7	5,374.3
2005	5,795.6	5,962.6	5,913.9	5,960.7	6,156.7	6,036.6	5,751.0	5,713.8	6,008.5	6,737.1	6,351.5	6,614.3
2006	6,657.7	7,320.9	7,518.9	7,426.6	7,334.4	7,796.0	8,031.2	8,199.0	7,980.8	7,695.2	7,565.8	7,491.1

Source: New York Mercantile Exchange (NYMEX), COMEX division

Central Gold Bank Reserves   In Millions of Troy Ounces

															Bank for	
		---- Industrial Countries ----										Deve-		Int'l	
				Ger-			Nether-	Switer-	United	United	Industrial	Deve-	loping		Settle-	World
Year	Belgium	Canada	France	many	Italy	Japan	lands	land	Kingdom	States	Total	loping Oil	Non-Oil	IMF[2]	ments	Total
1992	25.0	9.9	81.9	95.2	66.7	24.2	43.9	83.3	18.6	261.8	877.4	42.0	100.3	103.4	6.8	1,129.9
1993	25.0	6.1	81.9	95.2	66.7	24.2	35.1	83.3	18.5	261.8	860.4	42.4	108.1	103.4	8.6	1,123.0
1994	25.0	3.9	81.9	95.2	66.7	24.2	34.8	83.3	18.4	261.7	856.9	42.4	106.6	103.4	7.0	1,116.2
1995	20.5	3.4	81.9	95.2	66.7	24.2	34.8	83.3	18.4	261.7	848.7	41.9	111.9	103.4	7.3	1,113.2
1996	15.3	3.1	81.9	95.2	66.7	24.2	34.8	83.3	18.4	261.7	840.1	42.5	115.5	103.4	6.6	1,108.2
1997	15.3	3.1	81.9	95.2	66.7	24.2	27.1	83.3	18.4	261.6	821.9	42.3	115.8	103.4	6.2	1,089.7
1998	9.5	2.5	102.4	119.0	83.4	24.2	33.8	83.3	23.0	261.6	809.0	41.6	115.7	103.4	6.4	1,076.1
1999	8.3	1.8	97.2	111.5	78.8	24.2	31.6	83.3	20.6	261.7	810.4	41.2	112.9	103.4	6.5	1,074.5
2000	8.3	1.2	97.3	111.5	78.8	24.6	29.3	78.8	16.5	261.6	796.5	41.6	112.0	103.4	6.5	1,060.1
2001[1]	8.0	1.2	97.0	112.0	79.0	24.6	29.0	74.6	13.4	261.6	791.3	42.3	111.3	103.4	6.5	1,054.7

[1] Preliminary.   [2] International Monetary Fund.   *Source: American Metal Market (AMM)*

Mine Production of Recoverable Gold in the United States   In Kilograms

Year	Arizona	California	Idaho	Montana	Nevada	Alaska	Colorado	South Dakota	New Mexico	Utah	Other States	Total
1996	1,740	23,800	7,410	9,110	213,000	5,020	W	W	W	W	57,920	318,000
1997	2,140	24,200	7,490	10,200	243,000	18,400	W	16,400	W	W	40,170	362,000
1998	1,840	18,700	W	8,200	273,000	18,300	W	12,100	W	W	33,860	366,000
1999	786	17,500	W	7,540	9,310	16,200	W	10,300	W	W	279,364	341,000
2000	442	17,200	W	9,310	268,000	15,600	W	8,230	W	W	34,218	353,000
2001	W	13,800	W	W	253,000	16,700	W	W	W	W	51,500	335,000
2002	W	9,180	W	W	240,000	W	W	W	W	W	48,820	298,000
2003	W	4,270	W	W	227,000	W	W	W	W	W	45,730	277,000
2004	W	3,260	W	W	216,000	W	W	W	W	W	38,740	258,000
2005[1]	W	W	W	W	212,000	W	W	W	W	W	44,000	256,000

[1] Preliminary.   W = Withheld proprietary data, included in Other States.   *Source: U.S. Geological Survey (USGS)*

Consumption of Gold, By End-Use in the United States   In Kilograms

| | ---- Jewelry and the Arts ---- | | | | | ---- Industrial ---- | | | | |
| | Gold-Filled | Electro- | Karat | | | Gold-Filled | Electro- | Karat | | | Grand |
Year	& Other	plating	Gold	Total	Dental	& Other	plating	Gold	Total		Total
1987	9,256	3,133	58,635	71,024	6,944	21,010	12,343	1,892	35,245		113,319
1988	7,598	1,469	57,959	67,027	7,576	21,034	15,088	1,104	37,226		111,836
1989	7,364	1,283	60,877	69,524	7,927	15,723	20,684	1,215	37,621		115,078
1990	8,132	429	69,952	78,514	8,700	12,725	17,251	1,020	30,996		118,216
1991	3,848	373	79,875	84,096	8,485	8,102	12,624	1,068	21,793		114,375
1992	3,546	581	79,381	83,508	6,543	8,802	10,476	1,082	20,360		110,410
1993	3,530	373	61,700	65,600	6,170	9,470	9,090	1,100	19,700		91,400
1994[1]	3,650	369	49,700	53,700	5,430	7,450	9,470	96	17,000		76,100
1995[1]	NA	NA	NA	NA	NA	NA	NA	NA	NA		NA
1996[1]	NA	NA	NA	NA	NA	NA	NA	NA	NA		NA

[1] Preliminary.   *Source: U.S. Geological Survey (USGS)*

Gold in British Pound (weekly close) as of December 29, 2006 — GBP per troy ounce

Gold in Euro (weekly close) as of December 29, 2006 — EUR per troy ounce

Gold in Japanese Yen (weekly close) as of December 29, 2006 — JPY per troy ounce

Gold in Swiss Franc (weekly close) as of December 29, 2006 — CHF per troy ounce

Grain Sorghum

Grain sorghums include milo, kafir, durra, feterita, and kaoliang. Grain sorghums are tolerant of drought by going into dormancy during dry and hot conditions and then resuming growth as conditions improve. Grain sorghums are a staple food in China, India, and Africa but in the US they are mainly used as livestock feed. The two key US producing states are Texas and Kansas, each with about one-third of total US production. US sorghum production has become more popular with the breeding of dwarf grain sorghum hybrids which are only about 3 feet tall (versus up to 10 feet tall for wild sorghum) and are easier to harvest with a combine. The U.S. sorghum crop year begins September 1.

Prices – The monthly average price for sorghum grain received by US farmers in the 2005-06 marketing year (Sep 05-Aug 06) rose by +9.5% yr/yr to $3.57 per hundred pounds. Sorghum prices in the first six months of the 2006-07 marketing year (annualized through February 2007) rose another +60.3% to an average of $5.73 per hundred pounds. The value of US grain sorghum production in the 2006-07 marketing year is forecasted to rise +18.3% yr/yr to $871.9 million.

Supply – World production of sorghum in the 2006-07 marketing year if forecasted to fall -3.8% to 56.899 million metric tons, but remain well above the 52.818 million metric

ton crop in 2002-03 that was the smallest crop since 1968-69. US grain sorghum production in 2006-07 is forecasted to fall –29.5% yr/yr to 277.538 million bushels. Sorghum acreage harvested in 2006-07 is forecasted to fall –13.9% to 4.937 million acres, which was the smallest sorghum acreage harvested since the late 1930s. Yield will be about average in 2006-07 at 56.2 bushels per acre, but down from 2004-05's 12-year high of 69.8 bushels per acre.

Demand – World utilization (consumption) of grain sorghum in the 2006-07 marketing year fell –0.4% to 57.798 million metric tons, but that is still up from the 53.538 million metric ton utilization level seen in 2002-03, which was the lowest since 1967-68.

Trade – World exports of sorghum in the 2006-07 marketing year fell –13.0% to 4.720 million metric tons, which is a 4-decade low. US exports in 2006-07 fell by –23.0% yr/yr to 3.810 million metric tons, and accounted for 81% of total world exports. Argentina is the world's other major exporter with 600,000 metric tons of exports in 2006-07, accounting for 13% of world exports. Major world importers are Mexico with 48% of world imports and Japan with 28% of world imports.

World Supply and Demand Grain Sorghum   In Thousands of Metric Tons

	------- Exports -------				------- Imports -------			Total	------- Utilization -------				------ Ending Stocks ------		
Year	Argen-tina	Non-U.S.	U.S.	Total	Japan	Mexico	Unac-counted	Total	Pro-duction	China	Mexico	U.S.	Total	Non-U.S.	U.S.	Total
2001-02	419	980	6,142	7,122	1,776	4,837	202	7,034	58,310	2,700	10,750	6,427	57,185	3,248	1,549	4,797
2002-03	639	1,028	4,681	5,709	1,562	3,384	36	5,511	52,818	2,825	9,900	4,939	53,538	2,786	1,093	3,879
2003-04	192	1,490	5,049	6,539	1,434	3,002	13	6,519	58,969	3,000	9,800	5,638	58,191	3,785	852	4,637
2004-05[1]	351	728	4,675	5,403	1,374	2,931	145	5,306	57,785	2,400	9,300	6,255	58,230	2,649	1,446	4,095
2005-06[2]	200	479	4,945	5,424	1,393	3,029		5,234	59,143	2,500	8,600	4,814	58,015	3,365	1,668	5,033
2006-07[3]	600	910	3,810	4,720	1,350	2,300		4,760	56,899	2,550	8,500	3,938	57,798	3,204	970	4,174

[1] Preliminary.　　[2] Estimate.　　[3] Forecast.　　Source: Foreign Agricultural Service, U.S. Department of Agriculture (FAS-USDA)

Salient Statistics of Grain Sorghum in the United States

	Acreage Planted[4] for All Purposes	Acreage Harvested	Pro-duction	Yield Per Acre	Price in Cents Per Bushel	Value of Pro-duction Million $	Acreage Harvested	Pro-duction	Yield Per Acre	On Farms	Off Farms	On Farms	Off Farms
	----- 1,000 Acres -----												
Year			1,000 Bushels	Bushels			1,000 Acres	1,000 Tons	1,000 Harvested	------------- 1,000 Bushels -------------			
2001-02	2,750	2,021	773	1,200	2,697	750	1,830	8,390	5,900	7,800	4,470	13,057	58,310
2002-03	2,800	1,465	1,900	1,260	3,327	900	1,100	7,060	6,338	7,850	2,930	9,163	52,818
2003-04	2,200	2,009	2,103	1,520	2,865	900	1,700	7,330	7,300	9,000	5,190	10,446	58,969
2004-05[1]	2,900	2,177	2,051	1,400	2,328	900	2,150	7,240	5,890	10,000	2,700	11,523	57,785
2005-06[2]	2,200	2,019	1,850	1,837	2,546	900	2,800	7,790	5,500	10,500	4,380	9,981	59,143
2006-07[3]	3,100	1,900	1,900	1,600	2,580	900	2,900	7,800	6,150	10,500	3,700	7,050	56,899

Column groups: For Grain (Production, Yield Per Acre, Price, Value of Production); For Silage (Acreage Harvested, Production, Yield Per Acre); Sorghum Grain Stocks — Dec. 1 (On Farms, Off Farms), June 1 (On Farms, Off Farms).

[1] Preliminary.　　[2] Estimate.　　[3] Forecast.　　NA = Not available.　　Source: Economic Research Service, U.S. Department of Agriculture (ERS-USDA)

Production of All Sorghum for Grain in the United States, by States   In Thousands of Bushels

Year	Arkansas	Colorado	Illinois	Kansas	Louisiana	Miss-issippi	Missouri	Nebraska	New Mexico	Oklahoma	South Dakota	Texas	Total
2001	14,620	9,460	8,085	232,500	17,850	7,134	20,680	35,700	6,300	15,120	8,850	130,000	514,524
2002	17,710	1,800	6,308	135,000	13,365	6,237	16,150	16,000	2,450	13,500	3,060	122,400	360,713
2003	17,220	4,320	8,610	130,500	14,025	6,132	16,170	31,000	1,674	9,250	6,750	153,900	411,237
2004	4,704	5,400	8,938	220,400	5,200	1,422	15,660	33,615	4,232	14,400	6,300	127,100	453,650
2005	4,960	3,410	7,636	195,000	8,712	----	9,880	21,750	4,365	12,480	4,420	111,000	393,893
2006[1]	5,192	3,360	6,930	132,000	8,448	----	7,885	20,800	2,800	8,050	4,000	816,000	277,538

[1] Preliminary.　　Source: National Agricultural Statistics Service, U.S. Department of Agriculture (NASS-USDA)

Grain Sorghum Quarterly Supply and Disappearance in the United States   In Millions of Bushels

Crop Year Beginning Sept. 1	Supply				Disappearance — Domestic Use						Ending Stocks		
	Beginning Stocks	Pro- duction	Imports	Total Supply	Food Alcohol & Industrial	Seed	Feed & Residual	Total	Export	Total	Gov't Owned[3]	Privately Owned[4]	Total Stocks
2003-04	43.0	411.2	0	454.3	39.9		182.1	420.7	198.8	619.5			33.6
Sept.-Nov.	43.0	411.2	0	454.3	9.0		148.6	218.3	60.8	279.1			235.9
Dec.-Feb.	235.9	----	0	235.9	10.0		11.4	77.3	55.9	133.2			158.7
Mar.-May	158.7	----	0	158.7	10.5		21.1	78.1	46.5	124.6			80.6
June-Aug.	80.6	----	0	80.6	10.4		1.1	47.1	35.6	82.6			33.6
2004-05	33.6	453.7	.0	487.2	54.9		191.3	430.3	184.0	614.3			56.9
Sept.-Nov.	33.6	453.7	0	487.2	13.6		147.5	205.0	44.0	249.0			282.2
Dec.-Feb.	282.2	----	0	282.2	13.4		10.0	78.7	55.3	134.0			203.5
Mar.-May	203.5	----	.0	203.5	14.2		25.0	90.4	51.2	141.6			113.2
June-Aug.	113.2	----	0	113.2	13.8		8.9	56.2	33.6	89.8			56.9
2005-06[1]	56.9	392.9	0	449.9	50.0		139.5	384.2	194.7	578.9			65.7
Sept.-Nov.	56.9	392.9	0	449.9	12.3		107.2	159.5	40.0	199.5			290.4
Dec.-Feb.	290.4	----	0	290.4	15.5		24.0	97.2	57.7	154.9			193.1
Mar.-May	193.1	----	0	193.1	11.8		3.7	78.3	62.8	141.1			114.9
June-Aug.	114.9	----	0	114.9	10.4		4.6	49.2	34.2	83.4			65.7
2006-07[2]	65.7	277.5	0	343.2	45.0		110.0	305.0	150.0	455.0			38.2
Sept.-Nov.	65.7	277.5	0	343.2	13.2		86.9	136.5	36.4	173.0			206.7

[1] Preliminary.   [2] Forecast.   [3] Uncommitted inventory.   [4] Includes quantity under loan & farmer-owned reserve.   *Source: Economic Research Service, U.S. Department of Agriculture (ERS-USDA)*

Average Price of Sorghum Grain, No. 2, Yellow in Kansas City   In Dollars Per Hundred Pounds (Cwt.)

Year	Sept.	Oct.	Nov.	Dec.	Jan.	Feb.	Mar.	Apr.	May	June	July	Aug.	Average
1999-00	2.97	2.71	2.75	2.87	3.20	3.28	3.51	3.53	3.75	3.18	2.71	2.76	3.10
2000-01	2.67	3.14	3.41	3.66	3.64	3.63	3.56	3.45	3.30	3.26	3.59	3.65	3.41
2001-02	3.55	3.38	3.44	3.59	3.61	3.55	3.58	3.47	3.44	3.57	3.97	4.60	3.65
2002-03	4.86	4.70	4.72	4.62	4.52	4.43	4.07	4.24	4.12	4.06	3.71	3.71	4.31
2003-04	4.15	4.18	4.50	4.61	4.71	4.88	5.18	5.37	4.94	4.67	3.92	3.75	4.57
2004-05	3.45	3.21	3.17	3.21	3.13	3.23	3.44	3.30	3.30	3.56	3.90	3.53	3.37
2005-06	3.22	3.08	3.30	3.30	3.46	3.58	3.44	3.79	4.03	3.90	4.15	3.79	3.59
2006-07[1]	3.82	5.07	2.97										3.95

[1] Preliminary.   *Source: Economic Research Service, U.S. Department of Agriculture (ERS-USDA)*

Exports of Grain Sorghum, by Country of Destination from the United States   In Metric Tons

Year Beginning Oct. 1	Canada	Ecuador	Ethiopia	Israel	Japan	Jordan	Mexico	South Africa	Spain	Sudan	Turkey	World Total
1999-00	4,061	0	21,940	167,816	1,045,253	0	4,773,760	12,857	178,829	0	0	6,297,344
2000-01	4,170	0	24,117	82,776	853,211	0	4,864,414	0	0	0	0	5,866,340
2001-02	4,912	0	0	25,082	1,233,799	0	4,695,814	37,272	8,193	0	0	6,014,304
2002-03	5,921	91	48,000	65,725	1,035,634	0	3,150,014	43,918	266,892	5,880	0	4,690,875
2003-04	8,025	210	54,320	105,170	889,054	0	2,814,386	156	267,691	11,430	0	4,626,171
2004-05[1]	5,270	0	53,540	26,654	1,088,171	0	2,883,335	2,000	167,896	116,577	0	4,474,017
2005-06[2]	4,216	0	31,500	16,177	1,201,979	0	3,004,518	30,398	131,995	211,021	0	4,938,629

[1] Preliminary.   [2] Estimate.   *Source: Economic Research Service, U.S. Department of Agriculture (ERS-USDA)*

Grain Sorghum Price Support Program and Market Prices in the United States

Year	Price Support Operations							Effective Base[3] Million Acres	Partici- pation Rate[4] % of Base	No. 2 Yellow ($ Per Cwt.)			
	Price Support Quantity	% of Pro- duction	Aquired by CCC	Owned by CCC at Year End	Basic Loan Rate	Target Price	Findley Loan Rate			Kansas City	Texas High Plains	Los Angeles	Gulf Ports
	Million Cwt.				$ Per Bushel								
1998-99	12.0	4.1	.6	.2	[5]	NA	1.74	13.6	98.8	3.29	3.78	----	3.97
1999-00	9.6	2.9	1.0	----	[5]	NA	1.74	13.7	98.8	3.10	3.36	----	3.79
2000-01	8.6	3.3	.4	----	[5]	NA	1.71	13.6	----	3.41	3.94	----	4.22
2001-02	9.6	3.3	.1	.1	[5]	NA	1.71	13.6	----	3.65	4.05	----	4.34
2002-03	3.7	1.8	0	0	[5]	2.54	1.98	12.1	----	4.34	4.69	----	5.01
2003-04[1]	3.5	1.5	0	0	[5]	2.54	1.98	12.1	----	4.57	5.01	----	5.36
2004-05[2]	5.5	2.1	.1	0	[5]	2.57	1.95		----	3.37	3.95	----	4.44

[1] Preliminary.   [2] Estimate.   [3] National effective crop acreage base as determined by ASCS.   [4] Percentage of effective base acres enrolled in acreage reduction programs.   [5] Beginning with the 1996-7 marketing year, target prices are no longer applicable.   Source: Economic Research Service, U.S. Department of Agriculture (ERS-USDA)

Hay

Hay is a catchall term for forage plants, typically grasses such as timothy and Sudan-grass, and legumes such as alfalfa and clover. Alfalfa and alfalfa mixtures account for nearly half of all hay production. Hay is generally used to make cured feed for livestock. Curing, which is the proper drying of hay, is necessary to prevent spoilage. Hay, when properly cured, contains about 20% moisture. If hay is dried excessively, however, there is a loss of protein, which makes it less effective as livestock feed. Hay is harvested in virtually all of the lower 48 states.

Prices – The average monthly price of hay received by US farmers rose by +10.8% yr/yr to a record high of $109.00 per ton in the first ten months of the 2006-07 marketing year (i.e., May 2006 through February 2007). The farm production value of hay produced in 2006-07 was $13.506 million.

Supply – US hay production in 2006-07 fell –6.2% yr/yr to 141.7 million tons. US farmers harvested 60.807 million acres of hay in 2006-07, down –1.4% yr/yr. The yield in 2006-07 was 2.33 tons per acre, down from the 2004-05 record high of 2.55. US carryover (May 1) in 2006-07 fell –23.1% to 21.3 million tons.

The largest hay producing states in the US for 2006 are California (with 6.4% of US hay production), Texas (6.1%), Missouri (4.9%), Minnesota (4%), Idaho (4.0%), Nebraska (4.0%), South Dakota (3.3%), and Oklahoma (2.5%).

Salient Statistics of All Hay in the United States

Crop Year Beginning May 1	Acres Harvested 1,000 Acres	Yield Per Acre Tons	Pro-duction	Carryover May 1	Disap-pearance	Supply Per Animal Unit	Disap-pearance Per Animal Unit	Animal Units Fed[3] Millions	Farm Price $ Per Ton	Farm Pro-duction Value Million $	Alfalfa (Certified)	Timothy	Red Clover	Sudan-Grass
			Millions of Tons			In Tons					Dollars Per Cwt.			
2001-02	63,521	2.47	156.8	21.1	155.1	2.46	2.15	72.1	96.5	12,597	278.00	105.00	132.00	53.00
2002-03	63,942	2.34	149.5	22.5	149.9	2.39	2.08	72.0	93.7	12,338	280.00	90.00	130.00	56.00
2003-04	63,383	2.49	157.6	22.0	152.7	2.52	2.16	70.7	85.7	12,007	286.00	107.00	144.00	55.30
2004-05	61,916	2.55	158.2	25.9	156.4	2.57	2.19	71.6	92.1	12,212	291.00	110.00	145.00	55.60
2005-06[1]	61,649	2.44	151.0	27.8		2.44		73.0	98.4	12,585	280.00	105.00	174.00	57.40
2006-07[2]	60,807	2.33	141.7	21.3					109.0	13,506				

Header note: Retail Price Paid by Farmers for Seed, April 15

[1] Preliminary. [2] Estimate. [3] Roughage-consuming animal units fed annually. NA = Not available. *Source: Economic Research Service, U.S. Department of Agriculture (ERS-USDA)*

Production of All Hay in the United States, by States   In Thousands of Tons

Year	Cali-fornia	Idaho	Iowa	Minne-sota	Missouri	New York	North Dakota	Ohio	Okla-homa	South Dakota	Texas	Wis-consin	Total
2001	8,915	4,938	5,565	6,195	7,853	7,578	5,065	4,275	4,025	9,150	10,837	4,790	156,764
2002	9,774	5,288	5,645	5,810	8,323	5,750	3,920	3,400	5,985	4,815	13,410	5,340	149,467
2003	9,485	4,950	5,515	5,245	8,122	7,600	4,598	3,974	5,304	7,210	12,388	4,380	157,585
2004	9,220	5,350	6,240	5,895	9,420	6,423	3,666	3,232	5,958	6,870	12,295	4,880	158,247
2005	9,206	5,382	5,860	6,055	6,718	6,945	5,646	3,630	5,084	7,560	9,140	4,470	151,017
2006[1]	9,048	5,720		5,679	6,944	5,675	3,137	3,421	3,598	4,180	8,675	5,404	141,666

[1] Preliminary. *Source: Agricultural Statistics Board, U.S. Department of Agriculture (ASB-USDA)*

Hay Production and Farm Stocks in the United States   In Thousands of Short Tons

Year	Alfalfa & Mixtures	All Others	All Hay	Corn for Silage[1]	Sorghum Silage[1]	Farm Stocks May 1	Farm Stocks Dec. 1
	Production						
2001	80,327	76,437	156,764	102,077	3,728	21,106	110,384
2002	83,014	76,453	149,467	102,293	3,913	22,458	102,978
2003	76,273	81,312	157,585	107,378	3,552	22,013	111,027
2004	75,481	82,766	158,247	107,293	4,776	25,947	114,516
2005	76,149	74,868	151,017	106,486	4,218	27,758	105,205
2006[2]	71,666	70,000	141,666	104,849	4,642	21,345	96,397

[1] Not included in all tame hay. [2] Preliminary. *Source: Agricultural Statistics Board, U.S. Department of Agriculture (ASB-USDA)*

Mid-Month Price Received by Farmers for All Hay (Baled) in the United States   In Dollars Per Ton

Year	May	June	July	Aug.	Sept.	Oct.	Nov.	Dec.	Jan.	Feb.	Mar.	Apr.	Average[2]
2001-02	106.0	95.8	96.3	97.4	99.0	98.0	95.9	95.6	91.7	91.7	92.3	98.3	96.5
2002-03	103.0	95.8	93.6	92.4	93.0	93.8	93.2	91.1	91.4	91.4	92.8	92.9	93.7
2003-04	98.0	94.6	89.0	85.0	84.4	83.7	81.5	80.6	80.1	81.2	81.8	88.9	85.7
2004-05	101.0	95.2	90.4	92.2	91.4	92.8	88.7	86.0	87.8	88.2	92.6	99.4	92.1
2005-06	107.0	102.0	99.7	99.7	99.0	97.7	91.7	92.0	93.1	95.8	97.1	106.0	98.4
2006-07[1]	114.0	109.0	107.0	106.0	107.0	107.0	106.0	108.0	112.0	114.0			109.0

[1] Preliminary. [2] Marketing year average. *Source: Economic Research Service, U.S. Department of Agriculture (ERS-USDA)*

Heating Oil

Heating oil is a heavy fuel oil that is derived from crude oil. Heating oil is also known as No. 2 fuel oil and accounts for about 25% of the yield from a barrel of crude oil. That is the second largest "cut" after gasoline. The price to consumers of home heating oil is generally comprised of 42% for crude oil, 12% for refining costs, and 46% for marketing and distribution costs (Source: EIA's Petroleum Marketing Monthly, 2001). Generally, a $1 increase in the price of crude oil translates into a 2.5-cent per gallon rise in heating oil. Because of this, heating oil prices are highly correlated with crude oil prices, although heating oil prices are also subject to swift supply and demand shifts due to weather changes or refinery shutdowns.

The primary use for heating oil is for residential heating. In the US, approximately 8.1 million households use heating oil as their main heating fuel. Most of the demand for heating oil occurs from October through March. The Northeast region, which includes the New England and the Central Atlantic States, is most reliant on heating oil. This region consumes approximately 70% of US heating oil. However, demand for heating oil has been dropping as households switch to a more convenient heating source like natural gas. In fact, demand for heating oil is down by about 10 billion gallons/year from its peak use in 1976 (Source: American Petroleum Institute).

Refineries produce approximately 85% of US heating oil as part of the "distillate fuel oil" product family, which includes heating oil and diesel fuel. The remainder of US heating oil is imported from Canada, the Virgin Islands, and Venezuela.

Recently, a team of Purdue University researchers developed a way to make home heating oil from a mixture of soybean oil and conventional fuel oil. The oil blend is made by replacing 20% of the fuel oil with soybean oil, potentially saving 1.3 billion gallons of fuel oil per year. This soybean heating oil can be used in conventional furnaces without altering existing equipment. The soybean heating oil is relatively easy to produce and creates no sulfur emissions.

The "crack-spread" is the processing margin earned when refiners buy crude oil and refine it into heating oil and gasoline. The crack-spread ratio commonly used in the industry is the 3-2-1, which involves buying 1 heating oil contract and 2 gasoline futures contracts, and then selling 3 crude oil contracts. As long as the crack spread is positive, it is profitable for refiners to buy crude oil and refine it into products. The NYMEX has a crack-spread calculator on their web site at www.NYMEX.com.

Heating oil futures and options trade at the New York Mercantile Exchange (NYMEX). The heating oil futures contract calls for the delivery of 1,000 barrels of fungible No. 2 heating oil in the New York harbor. In London, gas/oil futures and options are traded on the International Petroleum Exchange (IPE).

Prices – NYMEX heating oil futures prices on the nearest-futures chart started the year 2006 at around $1.80 per gallon, rallied to a high of about $2.04 in August and then drifted lower to close the year at about $1.60 per gallon. Heating oil had posted a record high of $2.21 per gallon in September of 2005.

Supply – US production of distillate fuel oil in 2006 (through December, annualized) rose by +2.6% yr/yr to 4.055 million barrels per day, which was a new record high. Stocks of distillate fuel oil in December 2006 were 140.6 million barrels, up from 133.8 million barrels in December 2005. US production of residual fuel in 2006 (through December, annualized) rose by 0.5% yr/yr to an average of 631,000 barrels per day, which less than half the production levels of well over 1 million barrels per day produced in the 1970s. US stocks of residual fuel oil as of July 2006 rose +15.5% to 43.2 million barrels from 37.4 million barrels a year earlier.

Demand – US usage of distillate fuel oil in 2006 (through December, annualized) rose +1.6% yr/yr to 4.185 million barrels per day, which was a new record high. That figure includes both heating oil and diesel fuel usage.

Trade – US imports of distillate fuel oil in 2005 (through December, annualized) rose 11.9% to an average of a record high 368,000 barrels per day. US exports of distillate fuel oil in 2006 (through December, annualized) rose by +67.3% yr/yr to an average of a 12-year high 224,000 barrels per day. US imports of residual fuel oil in 2006 fell –35.7% yr/yr to 341,000 barrels per day, which was less than a third of the levels of over 1 million barrels per day seen back in the 1970s. US exports of residual fuel oil in 2006 rose +11.6% to 280,000 barrels per day, which was a record high.

Average Price of #2 Heating Oil   In Cents Per Gallon

Year	Jan.	Feb.	Mar.	Apr.	May	June	July	Aug.	Sept.	Oct.	Nov.	Dec.	Average
1997	69.90	61.15	54.83	57.74	56.31	52.32	53.11	54.02	53.19	57.24	56.23	51.09	56.43
1998	46.59	44.26	42.12	42.97	41.07	37.88	36.24	34.48	40.15	38.29	35.59	31.38	39.25
1999	33.41	30.48	38.74	43.07	41.68	43.36	50.02	54.81	60.27	58.34	64.89	67.36	48.87
2000	91.32	94.37	77.29	75.32	75.88	78.32	78.14	89.13	98.87	97.46	102.70	94.08	87.74
2001	84.30	78.55	74.17	78.02	77.11	75.74	69.88	73.41	71.65	62.63	54.37	52.60	71.04
2002	53.52	54.03	63.52	66.60	66.54	64.50	67.79	69.81	77.25	76.55	72.14	81.70	67.83
2003	90.09	112.84	99.70	79.75	74.31	75.95	79.03	81.61	73.54	81.97	83.35	89.04	85.10
2004	97.91	91.19	90.88	91.87	101.65	99.41	109.42	116.86	125.73	148.55	138.16	127.32	111.58
2005	132.01	134.26	155.44	152.35	140.89	161.20	163.71	180.75	196.50	188.75	168.67	170.32	162.07
2006	174.99	163.68	177.70	198.27	197.17	191.76	192.30	198.25	169.17	154.53	165.00	167.85	179.22

Source: Energy Information Administration, U.S. Department of Energy (EIA-DOE)

HEATING OIL

Heating Oil Futures - New York Mercantile Exchange
(weekly close) as of December 29, 2006
USD per gallon

Average Open Interest of #2 Heating Oil Futures in New York   In Contracts

Year	Jan.	Feb.	Mar.	Apr.	May	June	July	Aug.	Sept.	Oct.	Nov.	Dec.
1997	100,333	105,223	122,149	139,981	135,523	141,864	151,403	149,243	151,407	141,008	126,528	145,153
1998	171,177	163,114	177,158	174,587	176,663	196,903	205,071	198,527	188,096	188,019	192,835	184,100
1999	167,686	160,388	166,472	172,127	170,842	168,307	182,383	188,726	192,883	179,040	165,334	146,997
2000	135,431	132,407	108,646	100,389	117,055	129,872	153,914	169,092	177,997	168,388	155,475	142,145
2001	138,980	127,219	120,899	127,395	130,328	141,436	149,577	145,605	145,692	155,540	162,392	153,850
2002	166,824	173,110	160,205	144,936	139,979	136,201	131,742	141,084	147,692	153,739	161,137	156,268
2003	178,932	174,224	134,616	111,706	118,822	124,675	127,273	146,821	150,893	156,142	145,857	145,555
2004	153,794	145,924	161,945	174,618	176,784	167,331	193,291	206,099	197,783	188,843	176,298	163,629
2005	155,528	152,479	174,437	179,923	176,770	185,831	182,710	185,185	174,229	172,772	178,199	178,008
2006	170,094	165,627	168,415	170,955	171,732	169,123	179,773	185,648	208,848	221,942	228,152	216,033

Source: New York Mercantile Exchange (NYMEX)

Volume of Trading of #2 Heating Oil Futures in New York   In Thousand of Contracts

Year	Jan.	Feb.	Mar.	Apr.	May	June	July	Aug.	Sept.	Oct.	Nov.	Dec.	Total
1997	794.4	719.0	588.6	710.1	592.0	679.4	679.6	694.7	828.3	742.7	619.3	722.9	8,371.0
1998	793.6	641.8	776.4	578.4	688.5	904.9	720.2	683.0	748.2	768.2	766.5	793.9	8,863.8
1999	738.9	662.3	973.3	706.3	768.1	802.7	770.4	707.9	720.1	819.6	818.6	712.7	9,200.7
2000	914.0	770.3	645.2	556.1	673.3	705.9	663.0	1,004.4	954.9	878.1	939.0	927.3	9,631.4
2001	914.4	650.7	758.0	728.6	722.8	849.9	712.9	745.8	694.0	853.8	835.5	798.1	9,264.5
2002	998.5	810.8	885.5	844.1	789.8	720.1	798.8	866.0	794.4	1,017.9	1,039.5	1,129.9	10,695.2
2003	1,340.1	1,158.9	965.9	757.7	811.6	802.9	849.9	891.3	1,118.5	1,095.5	817.3	971.8	11,581.7
2004	1,153.8	1,059.7	1,139.9	1,007.8	910.0	1,100.5	920.7	1,105.7	1,060.8	1,148.6	1,112.7	1,164.4	12,884.5
2005	1,090.6	1,046.1	1,204.2	1,062.5	999.7	1,193.5	1,058.5	1,150.4	1,165.1	1,019.5	1,009.5	1,136.0	13,135.6
2006	1,157.5	1,131.2	1,121.7	974.8	1,185.1	1,114.0	1,027.1	1,166.1	1,235.9	1,291.1	1,228.6	1,357.5	13,990.6

Source: New York Mercantile Exchange (NYMEX)

Heating Oil (monthly average) through December 2006

USD per gallon

USD Per Gallon
----- No. 2, New York Harbor

Stocks of Distillate and Residual Fuel in the United States, on First of Month — In Millions of Barrels

Year	Jan.	Feb.	Mar.	Apr.	May	June	July	Aug.	Sept.	Oct.	Nov.	Dec.	Residual Fuel Oil Stocks Jan. 1	July 1
1997	126.7	111.3	105.9	101.8	97.5	108.4	118.2	123.0	132.9	138.9	136.2	140.5	45.9	39.2
1998	139.0	133.1	127.9	124.4	125.7	136.8	139.1	148.8	150.5	152.5	147.5	154.6	40.4	39.8
1999	156.2	147.9	142.3	125.7	125.3	134.8	133.2	138.1	142.0	145.2	137.6	140.6	44.9	42.5
2000	124.1	106.7	105.2	96.0	100.1	105.4	106.4	112.9	111.0	115.3	116.5	121.1	35.8	37.0
2001	118.0	118.2	117.0	105.0	104.9	107.1	113.9	125.2	122.0	127.0	128.9	138.9	36.2	41.7
2002	144.5	137.8	130.0	123.0	122.6	127.4	130.9	133.4	130.6	126.9	121.4	124.4	41.0	32.7
2003	134.1	112.6	97.7	98.6	97.2	106.7	112.2	118.0	126.5	131.3	132.1	136.1	31.3	35.3
2004	136.5	122.8	112.2	104.4	101.5	107.5	114.3	121.9	130.8	123.1	118.3	123.2	37.8	37.5
2005	126.3	121.4	116.4	104.5	104.5	111.0	118.8	132.0	139.4	127.7	124.8	133.8	42.4	37.4
2006[1]	136.0	138.8	134.9	120.1	115.8	123.8	129.9	138.8	144.9	149.3	143.1	140.6	37.4	43.2

[1] Preliminary.   *Source: Energy Information Administration; U.S. Department of Energy (EIA-DOE)*

Production of Distillate Fuel Oil in the United States — In Thousand Barrels per Day

Year	Jan.	Feb.	Mar.	Apr.	May	June	July	Aug.	Sept.	Oct.	Nov.	Dec.	Average
1997	3,119	3,089	3,258	3,291	3,525	3,517	3,362	3,427	3,452	3,488	3,543	3,578	3,389
1998	3,323	3,280	3,397	3,468	3,560	3,520	3,569	3,482	3,399	3,215	3,438	3,431	3,424
1999	3,176	3,253	3,183	3,407	3,458	3,374	3,521	3,419	3,482	3,506	3,608	3,401	3,399
2000	3,123	3,348	3,342	3,533	3,650	3,481	3,520	3,678	3,844	3,774	3,785	3,872	3,580
2001	3,609	3,612	3,483	3,650	3,652	3,702	3,837	3,654	3,625	3,796	3,968	3,744	3,695
2002	3,508	3,498	3,360	3,647	3,709	3,679	3,561	3,538	3,536	3,380	3,768	3,922	3,592
2003	3,403	3,459	3,732	3,796	3,833	3,728	3,673	3,730	3,721	3,750	3,800	3,845	3,707
2004	3,592	3,446	3,550	3,874	3,857	3,956	3,902	3,981	3,625	3,808	4,004	4,159	3,813
2005	3,777	3,797	3,874	4,028	4,179	4,274	4,236	4,108	3,570	3,585	3,966	4,044	3,953
2006[1]	3,833	3,952	3,835	3,833	4,114	4,106	4,067	4,237	4,300	4,083	4,072	4,230	4,055

[1] Preliminary.   *Source: Energy Information Administration, U.S. Department of Energy (EIA-DOE)*

HEATING OIL

Imports of Distillate Fuel Oil in the United States In Thousand Barrels per Day

Year	Jan.	Feb.	Mar.	Apr.	May	June	July	Aug.	Sept.	Oct.	Nov.	Dec.	Average
1999	304	322	248	213	261	238	234	273	249	216	265	188	250
2000	218	510	260	234	316	258	199	234	283	259	332	447	295
2001	789	635	348	288	310	302	209	212	317	253	244	241	344
2002	298	248	234	219	193	204	188	205	196	350	373	496	267
2003	325	503	460	246	287	337	299	375	352	281	241	305	333
2004	370	507	449	267	275	324	283	313	272	243	319	292	326
2005	353	344	257	264	281	236	243	263	275	507	486	435	329
2006[1]	541	385	289	291	434	292	357	366	422	301	280	457	368

[1] Preliminary. *Source: Energy Information Administration, U.S. Department of Energy (EIA-DOE)*

Exports of Distillate Fuel Oil in the United States In Thousand Barrels per Day

Year	Jan.	Feb.	Mar.	Apr.	May	June	July	Aug.	Sept.	Oct.	Nov.	Dec.	Average
1999	117	116	159	191	187	180	123	130	162	192	170	212	162
2000	132	112	211	178	127	149	132	253	194	255	191	135	173
2001	67	77	75	107	146	120	113	140	152	99	132	202	119
2002	109	279	67	68	74	93	44	119	127	96	114	171	112
2003	119	132	161	139	162	101	103	80	43	62	81	100	107
2004	72	86	99	92	100	163	113	120	88	101	102	176	109
2005	49	102	165	192	199	227	189	163	108	109	92	65	138
2006[1]	123	156	120	200	229	187	231	191	456	291	252	258	225

[1] Preliminary. *Source: Energy Information Administration, U.S. Department of Energy (EIA-DOE)*

Disposition of Distillate Fuel Oil, Total Product Supplied in the U.S. In Thousand Barrels per Day

Year	Jan.	Feb.	Mar.	Apr.	May	June	July	Aug.	Sept.	Oct.	Nov.	Dec.	Average
1999	3,788	3,542	3,785	3,415	3,314	3,407	3,479	3,437	3,431	3,749	3,608	3,892	3,572
2000	3,818	3,794	3,693	3,455	3,681	3,549	3,369	3,726	3,786	3,712	3,829	4,250	3,722
2001	4,325	4,212	4,143	3,834	3,746	3,659	3,569	3,829	3,624	3,888	3,746	3,604	3,847
2002	3,940	3,714	3,750	3,821	3,679	3,587	3,683	3,728	3,730	3,808	3,929	3,934	3,776
2003	4,301	4,362	4,001	3,951	3,651	3,781	3,680	3,752	3,871	3,945	3,824	4,037	3,927
2004	4,334	4,232	4,152	4,145	3,840	3,888	3,827	3,887	4,065	4,104	4,058	4,176	4,059
2005	4,223	4,202	4,349	4,101	4,037	4,038	3,854	4,020	4,116	4,079	4,061	4,339	4,118
2006[1]	4,161	4,318	4,481	4,069	4,062	4,007	3,906	4,215	4,118	4,292	4,333	4,252	4,185

[1] Preliminary. *Source: Energy Information Administration, U.S. Department of Energy (EIA-DOE)*

Production of Residual Fuel Oil in the United States In Thousands Barrels per Day

Year	Jan.	Feb.	Mar.	Apr.	May	June	July	Aug.	Sept.	Oct.	Nov.	Dec.	Average
1999	775	726	683	679	725	706	736	701	702	658	596	690	698
2000	640	627	649	620	640	679	741	760	702	747	778	768	696
2001	809	743	750	817	786	783	639	622	653	710	685	655	721
2002	625	613	617	601	582	540	566	583	607	593	648	641	601
2003	658	683	652	632	729	666	632	663	662	640	616	686	660
2004	656	659	635	701	668	648	618	631	617	610	703	723	656
2005	701	691	619	598	645	673	614	594	555	530	642	674	628
2006[1]	659	634	644	643	580	645	658	651	619	597	594	648	631

[1] Preliminary. *Source: Energy Information Administration U.S. Department of Energy (EIA-DOE)*

Supply and Disposition of Residual Fuel Oil in the United States

Year	Supply — Total Production	Imports	Disposition — Stock Change	Exports	Product Supplied	Ending Stocks Million Barrels	Average Sales to End Users[3] Cents per Gallon
	Thousand Barrels Per Day						
1999	698	237	-25	129	830	36	37.4
2000	696	352	1	139	909	36	60.2
2001	721	295	13	191	811	41	53.1
2002	601	249	-27	177	700	31	56.9
2003	660	327	18	197	772	38	69.8
2004	655	426	12	205	865	42	73.9
2005	628	530	-14	251	920	37	104.8
2006[1]	631	341	17	280	675	43	

[1] Preliminary. [2] Less than +500 barrels per day and greater than -500 barrels per day. [3] Refiner price excluding taxes.

Source: Energy Information Administration, U.S. Department of Energy (EIA-DOE)

Hides and Leather

Hides and leather have been used since ancient times for boots, clothing, shields, armor, tents, bottles, buckets, and cups. Leather is produced through the tanning of hides, pelts, and skins of animals. The remains of leather have been found in the Middle East dating back at least 7,000 years.

Today, most leather is made of cowhide but it is also made from the hides of lamb, deer, ostrich, snakes, crocodiles, and even stingray. Cattle hides are the most valuable byproduct of the meat packing industry. US exports of cowhides bring more than $1 billion in foreign trade, and US finished leather production is worth about $4 billion.

Prices – The average monthly price of wholesale cattle hides (packer heavy native steers FOB Chicago) in 2006 rose +7.2% yr/yr to 86.31 cents per pound, but that was still well below the record high of 90.06 cents per pound posted in 1989.

Supply – World production of cattle and buffalo hides in 2005 rose by +1.8% yr/yr to a record high of 8.033 million metric tons. The world's largest producers of cattle and buffalo hides in 2005 were the US with 13% of world production, Brazil with 10%, and Argentina with 5%. US new supply of cattle hides from domestic slaughter in 2003 fell –0.8% yr/yr to 35.454 million hides, which was far below the record high of 43.582 million hides posted in 1976.

US production of leather footwear has been dropping off sharply in recent years due to the movement of production offshore to lower cost producers. US production of leather footwear in 2003 (latest data available) fell –46% yr/yr to 22.3 million pairs and was a mere 4% of the 562.3 million pairs produced in 1970.

Demand – World consumption of cowhides and skins in 2000, the last reporting year for the series, rose +1.4% to 4,774 metric tons, which was a record high for the data series, which goes back to 1984. The world's largest consumers of cowhides and skins in 2000 were the US with 13.0% of world consumption, Italy (10.6%), Brazil (8.9%), Mexico, (6.0%), Argentina (6.0%), and South Korea (5.9%).

Trade – US net exports of cattle hides in 2004 (latest data available) fell –4.3% yr/yr to 17.388 million hides from the 15-year high of 21.750 million hides posted in 2001. The total value of US leather exports in 2004 rose +16.8% yr/yr to $1.344 billion. The largest destinations for US exports in 2006 were South Korea (which took 19% of US exports), Taiwan (10%), Mexico (7%), Italy (3%), and Thailand (2%). World imports of cowhides and skins in 2000 (latest data available) rose +2.8% yr/yr to a record high of 2,058 metric tons. The world's largest importers of cowhides and skins in 2000 were South Korea (with 13% of world imports in 2000), Italy (11%) and Taiwan (7%).

World Production of Cattle and Buffalo Hides   In Thousands of Metric Tons

Year	Argentina	Australia	Brazil	Canada	Colombia	France	Germany	Italy	Mexico	Russia	United Kingdom	United States	World Total
1996	388	206	605	88	84	164	176	150	160	325	67	1,065	6,927
1997	384	219	622	91	81	163	176	148	161	294	64	1,063	7,195
1998	338	233	637	94	81	154	161	142	170	275	65	1,070	7,214
1999	364	241	667	98	86	151	162	145	170	229	64	1,099	7,304
2000	372	238	670	96	82	150	152	143	175	232	68	1,116	7,416
2001	348	254	725	95	76	150	153	130	176	220	61	1,031	7,266
2002	345	243	750	96	72	160	151	132	176	224	65	1,054	7,444
2003	375	248	770	88	72	157	141	130	176	229	63	1,046	7,642
2004[1]	432	243	792	111	80	150	141	132	176	223	66	1,046	7,894
2005[2]	432	255	792	115	80	150	141	132	176	220	66	1,046	8,033

[1] Preliminary.   [2] Forecast.   Source: Food and Agricultural Organization of the United Nations (FAO-UN)

Salient Statistics of Hides and Leather in the United States   In Thousands of Equivalent Hides

	New Supply of Cattle Hides				Wholesale Prices					Wholesale Leather				
	Domestic Slaughter				Cents Per Pound		Production		Value of Leather	Indexes		Footwear	
	Federally Inspected	Unin- spected[4]	Total Production	Net Exports	Heavy Native Cows[2]	Heavy Native Steers[3]	All U.S. Tanning	Cattle- hide	Exports $1,000	Upper Men	Women	Pro- duction[5]	Exports
Year	Thousands of Equivalent Hides						In 1,000 Equiv. Hides			1982 = 100		Million Pairs	
1995	34,879	760	35,639	18,336	93.69	87.6	18,092	17,480	870,247	150.1	129.0	147,550	20,571
1996	36,583	177	36,760	18,626	92.15	86.4	18,769	18,135	950,510	152.4	132.1	127,315	23,726
1997	35,567	751	36,492	17,562	90.99	86.1	19,592	18,930	1,145,664	156.4	132.2	124,444	21,958
1998	34,787	677	35,637	15,937	75.45	69.5	20,297	19,706	1,289,547	158.0	132.4	108,536	19,009
1999	36,150	664	36,320	15,700	73.80	73.1	21,342	20,620	1,137,534	157.0	133.0	78,581	18,176
2000	36,246	615	36,416	19,670	83.41	81.2	17,332	16,746	1,125,957	157.2	133.6	58,870	20,157
2001	34,771	599	35,370	21,750	85.52	89.8	14,212	13,779	1,221,131	158.4	133.8	55,600	19,472
2002	35,120	614	35,734	19,484	85.73	82.3		16,403	1,161,944	158.8	133.5	41,100	21,582
2003	34,907	590	35,493	18,177	88.34	83.8		17,470	1,150,212	161.4	132.1	22,300	21,319
2004[1]	32,156		32,728	17,388		82.2		15,492	1,344,017	161.7	129.2		21,464

[1] Preliminary.   [2] Central U.S., heifers.   [3] F.O.B. Chicago.   [4] Includes farm slaughter; diseased & condemned animals & hides taken off fallen animals.   [5] Other than rubber.   Sources: Leather Industries of America (LIA); Bureau of Labor Statistics, U.S. Department of Commerce (BLS)

HIDES AND LEATHER

Production of All Footwear (Shoes, Sandals, Slippers, Athletic, Etc.) in the U.S.   In Millions of Pairs

Year	First Quarter	Second Quarter	Third Quarter	Fourth Quarter	Total	Year	First Quarter	Second Quarter	Third Quarter	Fourth Quarter	Total
1994	42.5	40.8	40.1	39.5	163.0	1999	26.7	26.1	24.5	21.7	78.6
1995	37.2	38.3	34.8	36.7	147.0	2000	----	----	----	----	68.7
1996	33.2	31.8	29.7	33.2	128.0	2001	----	----	----	----	54.8
1997	31.4	33.1	28.6	30.6	124.4	2002	----	----	----	----	41.1
1998	32.8	31.8	29.3	28.6	108.5	2003[1]	----	----	----	----	22.3

[1] Preliminary.   *Source: Bureau of the Census, U.S. Department of Commerce*

Average Factory Price[2] of Footwear in the United States   In Dollars Per Pair

Year	First Quarter	Second Quarter	Third Quarter	Fourth Quarter	Total	Year	First Quarter	Second Quarter	Third Quarter	Fourth Quarter	Total
1994	25.77	23.60	21.49	22.44	23.22	1999	23.33	22.70	19.90	19.50	21.19
1995	19.61	21.46	25.37	21.26	21.79	2000	----	----	----	----	24.14
1996	23.65	22.78	22.14	20.38	22.07	2001	----	----	----	----	25.66
1997	22.42	21.56	22.21	22.24	22.11	2002	----	----	----	----	24.12
1998	24.39	24.21	20.27	19.78	21.84	2003[1]	----	----	----	----	45.95

[1] Preliminary.   [2] Average value of factory shipments per pair.   *Source: Bureau of the Census, U.S. Department of Commerce*

Imports and Exports of All Cattle Hides in the United States   In Thousands of Hides

	Imports		U.S. Exports - by Country of Destination										
Year	Total	From Canada	Total	Canada	Italy	Japan	Rep. of Korea	Mexico	Portugal	Romania	Spain	Taiwan	Thailand
1997	1,496	1,405	19,195	1,320	469	1,802	7,470	2,501	55	0	148	2,866	323
1998	1,909	1,808	17,867	1,126	1,164	1,407	4,897	2,846	91	0	440	2,701	336
1999	1,906	1,742	17,621	829	738	1,252	6,038	2,723	46	0	262	2,863	343
2000	1,972	1,876	21,658	875	1,163	1,529	7,673	2,196	37	0	189	2,844	562
2001	1,721	1,615	23,471	716	920	1,343	7,602	1,647	54	0	159	2,751	888
2002	1,298	1,227	20,784	837	1,099	584	5,812	1,470	14	0	189	2,145	914
2003	2,934	1,888	19,139	530	779	483	4,784	1,257	6	0	63	1,982	788
2004	7,342	6,165	18,795	346	417	468	4,218	1,419	4	0	16	1,842	684
2005	3,698	2,888	19,231	141	568	334	4,048	1,288	2	0	8	1,730	652
2006[1]	2,186	1,601	10,164	26	324	58	1,930	701	3	0	13	1,007	241

[1] Preliminary.   *Source: Leather Industries of America*

Imports of Bovine Hides and Skins by Selected Countries   In Metric Tons

Year	Brazil	Canada	Hong Kong	Italy	Japan	Mexico	Portugal	Rep. of Korea	Spain	Taiwan	Turkey	United States	World Total
1992	11	17	80	131	188	71	32	385	26	91	28	65	1,266
1993	21	26	81	141	188	71	39	372	35	94	37	57	1,426
1994	16	28	95	243	139	60	56	356	29	112	17	49	1,556
1995	33	35	100	250	152	30	43	342	42	112	43	57	1,715
1996	20	34	79	263	123	71	42	341	33	124	50	60	1,692
1997	13	39	64	254	114	96	37	323	44	140	68	60	1,985
1998	10	42	71	249	96	110	39	229	44	142	45	59	1,876
1999[1]	8	34	91	215	95	115	42	254	29	142	55	57	2,002
2000[2]	8	36	93	220	95	115	43	260	30	142	60	57	2,058

[1] Preliminary.   [2] Forecast.   *Source: Foreign Agricultural Service, U.S. Department of Agriculture (FAS-USDA)*

Exports of Bovine Hides and Skins by Selected Countries   In Metric Tons

Year	Australia	Brazil	Canada	Germany	Hong Kong	Italy	Nether-lands	New Zealand	Poland	Russia	United Kingdom	United States	World Total
1992	144	71	74	38	75	9	66	31	17	28	19	610	1,261
1993	142	76	87	40	76	7	35	21	5	150	25	581	1,374
1994	96	84	79	24	93	10	37	22	2	216	22	455	1,271
1995	85	148	90	34	100	10	47	22	2	195	22	510	1,351
1996	93	174	97	33	72	20	47	28	3	212	24	506	1,423
1997	115	216	97	35	60	16	48	27	3	210	25	473	1,475
1998	111	220	86	31	69	24	32	28	6	202	17	443	1,400
1999[1]	115	230	83	28	90	7	30	30	7	190	15	436	1,389
2000[2]	108	250	85	31	92	8	25	30	7	170	15	427	1,399

[1] Preliminary.   [2] Forecast.   *Source: Foreign Agricultural Service, U.S. Department of Agriculture (FAS-USDA)*

Hides (monthly average) through December 2006 — Cents per pound

Cents Per Pound
----- Heavy Native Steers, Chicago (Jan. 1901 - date)
- - - Light Native Steers, Chicago (Jan. 1901 - Feb. 1966)

Utilization of Bovine Hides and Skins by Selected Countries   In Metric Tons

Year	Argentina	Brazil	Colombia	Germany	Italy	Japan	Mexico	Rep. of Korea	Spain	Taiwan	Turkey	United States	World Total
1991	308	396	98	143	435	253	225	400	119	101	78	491	4,009
1992	298	382	97	129	435	229	231	400	98	91	90	528	3,977
1993	302	510	94	100	435	226	232	385	98	94	95	554	4,322
1994	304	505	96	83	550	200	226	374	94	112	85	536	4,282
1995	300	493	89	79	570	191	200	355	98	112	100	523	4,365
1996	308	461	91	80	615	165	230	353	95	124	110	548	4,332
1997	332	387	89	101	570	150	251	347	106	140	120	572	4,609
1998	285	412	91	100	540	135	275	265	108	142	100	603	4,584
1999[1]	300	415	89	102	500	130	280	280	104	142	110	623	4,707
2000[2]	285	425	89	103	505	130	285	283	108	142	120	623	4,774

[1] Preliminary.   [2] Forecast.   *Source: Foreign Agricultural Service, U.S. Department of Agriculture (FAS-USDA)*

Wholesale Price of Hides (Packer Heavy Native Steers) F.O.B. Chicago   In Cents Per Pound

Year	Jan.	Feb.	Mar.	Apr.	May	June	July	Aug.	Sept.	Oct.	Nov.	Dec.	Average
1997	89.77	93.47	99.44	99.40	89.44	81.45	80.20	83.92	84.86	86.35	89.20	82.61	88.34
1998	66.88	77.33	82.61	83.72	85.05	83.13	81.17	81.11	75.23	67.95	67.53	68.26	76.66
1999	69.42	69.97	70.84	67.36	65.96	66.89	68.17	72.41	77.52	80.43	79.67	78.00	72.22
2000	75.92	76.29	77.86	78.83	79.24	75.18	77.25	81.64	85.60	84.89	84.41	85.31	80.20
2001	85.33	84.12	93.02	102.64	106.19	97.31	87.59	77.28	73.51	70.58	73.30	69.16	85.00
2002	68.23	72.39	80.41	83.21	84.32	86.72	84.43	85.77	85.84	85.75	83.35	85.18	82.13
2003	83.77	85.81	86.04	85.81	79.42	77.64	80.53	84.09	86.78	86.13	85.89	86.05	84.00
2004	85.17	81.79	82.89	79.15	80.16	82.43	85.11	84.54	85.05	82.23	81.42	78.02	82.33
2005	78.14	80.90	79.04	80.45	79.49	83.07	82.70	81.78	80.58	80.44	80.07	79.03	80.47
2006	79.28	81.01	83.86	84.95	87.76	88.07	87.93	87.15	88.29	88.08	88.81	90.50	86.31

Source: National Agricultural Statistics Service, U.S. Department of Agriculture (NASS-USDA)

Hogs

Hogs are generally bred twice a year in a continuous cycle designed to provide a steady flow of production. The gestation period for hogs is 3-1/2 months and the average litter size is 9 pigs. The pigs are weaned at 3-4 weeks of age. The pigs are then fed so as to maximize weight gain. The feed consists primarily of grains such as corn, barley, milo, oats, and wheat. Protein is added from oilseed meals. Hogs typically gain 3.1 pounds per pound of feed. The time from birth to slaughter is typically 6 months. Hogs are ready for slaughter at about 254 pounds, producing a dressed carcass weight of around 190 pounds and an average 88.6 pounds of lean meat. The lean meat consists of 21% ham, 20% loin, 14% belly, 3% spareribs, 7% Boston butt roast and blade steaks, and 10% picnic, with the remaining 25% going into jowl, lean trim, fat, miscellaneous cuts, and trimmings. Futures on lean hogs are traded at the Chicago Mercantile Exchange. The futures contract is settled in cash based on the CME Lean Hog Index price, meaning that no physical delivery of hogs occurs. The CME Lean Hog Index is based on the 2-day average net price of slaughtered hogs at the average lean percentage level.

Prices – Lean hog futures prices on the nearest futures chart in early 2006 initially sustained the weakness that had been seen in late 2005 due to price competition from poultry. US-produced poultry backed up into US supermarkets as bird flu in Asia curbed US poultry exports. However, lean hog prices were then able to rally through summer as poultry producers curbed their inventories and price competition abated. Hog prices then trended lower through the remainder of 2006 on adequate supplies and somewhat lower export demand as US beef export bans were finally rescinded. Lean hog futures prices finally closed 2006 at 61.70 cents per pound, -5.5% yr/yr from the 2005 close of 65.27 cents per pound. Lean hog prices rallied in early 2007 the severe winter weather in the Plains caused lower carcass weights and disrupted hog production. Hog prices were also supported in late 2006 and early 2007 by the 80% rally in corn prices, which made hog production more expensive and required higher prices to keep producers in the black.

Supply – World pork production in 2006 rose +3.7% yr/yr to 98.914 million metric tons. The USDA is forecasting a further +3.6% rise in 2007 to 103.386 million metric tons. The world's largest pork producers are China with 53.000 million metric tons of production in 2006, the European Union with 21.450 million metric tons, and the US with 9.543 million metric tons. US pork production in 2006 rose +1.6% to 9.543 million metric tons, and is forecasted by the USDA to rise another +3.6% to 9.809 million metric tons in 2007. The number of hogs and pigs on US farms in 2006 (Dec 1) rose slightly by +1.1% to a 9-year high of 62.149 million. The federally-inspected hog slaughter in the US in 2006 rose +1.1% to a record high of 103.690 million head.

Demand – World consumption of pork in 2006 rose by +3.9% yr/yr to 99.914 million metric tons. The USDA is forecasting a further +3.5% rise in 2007 to 102.374 million metric tons. US consumption of pork in 2006 was virtually unchanged from last year at 8.657 million metric tons, but the USDA is forecasting a rise of +2.5% in 2007 to 8.874 million metric tons. The US accounted for 8.8% of world consumption in 2005.

Trade – World pork exports in 2006 fell by –0.6% yr/yr to 5.178 million metric tons, but the USDA is forecasting an increase in growth of +2.6% in 2007 to 5.314 million metric tons. The world's largest pork exporters are the European Union with 27% of world exports in 2006, the US with 26%, Canada with 21%, and Brazil with 10%. US pork exports in 2006 rose +11.5% yr/yr to 1.346 million metric tons and the USDA is forecasting a further +4.1% rise in 2007 to 1.402 million metric tons. World pork imports in 2006 fell –2.5% to 4.232 million metric tons, and the USDA is forecasting virtually no change for 2007 at 4.235 million metric tons. The world's largest pork importers are Japan, which accounted for 30% of world imports in 2006, Russia (19%), Mexico (11%), the US (11%), and South Korea (7%).

Salient Statistics of Pigs and Hogs in the United States

	Pig Crop						Value of Hogs on Farms, Dec. 1		Hog Marketings	Quantity Produced (Live Wt.)	Value of Production	Hogs Slaughtered in Thousand Head				
	Spring[3]			Fall[4]								Commercial				
	Sows Farrowed	Pig Crop	Pigs Per Litter	Sows Farrowed	Pig Crop	Pigs Per Litter	$ Per Head	Total Million $	Thousand Head	Mill. Lbs.	Mil. $	Federally Inspected	Other	Total	Farm	Total
Year	--- 1,000 Head ---		Litter	--- 1,000 Head ---		Litter										
1997	5,595	48,393	8.65	5,885	51,190	8.70	82.0	4,986	104,301	23,979	12,552	90,228	1,733	91,960	165	92,125
1998	6,015	52,469	8.73	6,047	52,536	8.69	44.0	2,766	117,240	25,715	8,674	99,285	1,745	101,029	165	101,194
1999	5,877	51,519	8.77	5,764	50,835	8.82	72.0	4,254	121,137	25,791	7,766	99,739	1,806	101,544	150	101,694
2000	5,683	50,087	8.81	5,727	50,660	8.85	77.0	4,542	118,418	25,717	10,791	96,436	1,540	97,976	130	98,106
2001	5,619	49,472	8.81	5,767	51,031	8.85	77.0	4,590	119,262	25,884	11,430	96,528	1,434	97,962	120	98,082
2002	5,776	50,858	8.81	5,716	50,820	8.89	71.0	4,231	124,013	26,274	8,691	98,915	1,348	100,263	115	100,378
2003	5,655	50,029	8.85	5,773	51,462	8.91	67.0	4,025	124,383	26,260	9,663	99,685	1,233	100,931	116	101,047
2004	5,706	50,737	8.89	5,793	52,043	8.98	103.0	6,303	127,563	26,689	13,072	102,361	1,103	103,463	114	103,577
2005[1]	5,716	51,330	8.98	5,818	52,635	9.05	92.0	5,672	129,056	27,489	13,644	102,519	1,063	103,582	109	103,690
2006[2]	5,756	52,141	9.06	5,834	53,282	9.13						103,690	1,048	104,739		

[1] Preliminary.   [2] Estimate.   [3] December-May.   [4] June-November.   Source: Economic Research Service, U.S. Department of Agriculture (ERS-USDA)

World Hog Numbers in Specified Countries as of January 1   In Thousands of Head

Year	Brazil	Canada	China	Denmark	France	Germany	Philip- pines	Poland	Russia	Spain	Ukraine	United States	World Total
1998	31,427	11,985	400,348	118,450	9,904	7,096	10,520	10,210	16,579	7,967	9,479	61,158	741,044
1999	31,427	12,429	422,563	118,918	9,879	6,700	10,860	10,398	16,400	6,539	10,083	62,204	736,967
2000	31,860	12,904	430,198	156,534	9,805	7,000	10,781	10,764	16,100	7,243	10,073	59,335	777,122
2001	32,440	13,576	446,815	152,825	9,788	7,350	10,649	11,715	15,780	7,495	7,652	59,110	805,645
2002	32,710	14,367	457,430	152,473	9,612	7,856	10,569	11,816	16,570	7,165	8,317	59,722	820,881
2003	32,655	14,672	462,915	154,311	9,725	8,110	10,549	12,218	17,000	6,794	9,204	59,554	832,294
2004	32,081	14,623	466,017	152,793	9,724	8,367	10,668	12,518	17,200	6,779	7,321	60,444	834,421
2005	32,323	14,619	481,891	151,143	9,550	8,044	10,303	12,139	16,500	6,819	6,466	60,975	847,590
2006[1]	32,938	14,690	503,348	151,673	9,620	8,098	10,125	13,041	16,550	7,172	7,052	61,449	873,842
2007[2]	33,147	14,250	519,052	152,000	9,600	8,304	10,250	13,693	17,610	7,102	7,970	61,400	893,370

[1] Preliminary.   [2] Forecast.   *Source: Foreign Agricultural Service, U.S. Department of Agriculture (FAS-USDA)*

Hogs and Pigs on Farms in the United States on December 1   In Thousands of Head

Year	Georgia	Illinois	Indiana	Iowa	Kansas	Minne- sota	Missouri	Nebraska	North Carolina	Ohio	South Dakota	Wis- consin	Total
1997	520	4,700	3,950	14,600	1,530	5,700	3,550	3,500	9,600	1,700	1,400	740	61,158
1998	480	4,850	4,050	15,300	1,590	5,700	3,300	3,400	9,700	1,700	1,400	690	62,206
1999	480	4,050	3,250	15,400	1,460	5,500	3,150	3,000	9,500	1,480	1,260	570	59,342
2000	380	4,150	3,350	15,100	1,520	5,800	2,900	3,050	9,300	1,490	1,320	610	59,138
2001	315	4,250	3,200	15,400	1,570	5,800	3,000	2,900	9,800	1,430	1,290	540	59,804
2002	345	4,150	3,250	15,500	1,530	6,100	2,950	3,000	9,700	1,440	1,330	520	59,554
2003	295	4,000	3,100	15,900	1,650	6,500	2,950	2,900	10,000	1,520	1,280	480	60,444
2004	275	4,100	3,200	16,300	1,710	6,500	2,900	2,850	9,900	1,450	1,340	430	60,975
2005	270	4,000	3,250	16,600	1,790	6,600	2,700	2,850	9,800	1,560	1,490	430	61,449
2006[1]	245	4,200	3,300	17,200	1,840	6,800	2,750	3,000	9,500	1,680	1,330	440	62,149

[1] Preliminary.   *Source: National Agricultural Statistics Service, U.S. Department of Agriculture (NASS-USDA)*

Hog-Corn Price Ratio[2] in the United States

Year	Jan.	Feb.	Mar.	Apr.	May	June	July	Aug.	Sept.	Oct.	Nov.	Dec.	Average
1997	20.0	19.9	17.7	19.2	21.6	22.6	24.3	22.1	20.0	18.6	18.0	16.5	20.0
1998	14.1	14.1	13.7	14.8	18.1	18.6	16.8	18.6	16.1	14.6	9.7	7.3	14.7
1999	12.8	13.5	13.6	14.8	18.4	17.3	18.2	20.7	19.4	20.2	19.6	19.6	17.3
2000	19.3	20.2	20.5	23.3	22.9	25.6	29.5	28.8	25.8	23.8	19.8	20.2	23.3
2001	18.8	20.0	23.5	25.3	27.7	29.7	27.6	26.6	23.7	21.8	18.9	16.8	23.4
2002	19.1	19.9	18.6	16.6	17.2	18.2	18.4	13.4	10.7	13.2	12.2	13.1	15.9
2003	14.2	14.7	14.9	14.9	17.4	19.2	19.7	18.4	18.0	17.3	15.8	14.8	16.6
2004	15.4	16.3	17.2	16.4	19.7	20.3	22.7	23.6	24.9	24.4	27.1	25.7	21.1
2005	25.1	26.0	25.3	25.6	27.7	24.4	23.6	26.2	26.0	25.8	24.6	23.1	25.3
2006[1]	20.4	21.1	20.8	19.6	22.2	25.1	23.5	24.7	22.2	18.3	15.6	14.5	20.7

[1] Preliminary.   [2] Bushels of corn equal in value to 100 pounds of hog, live weight.   *Source: Economic Research Service, U.S. Department of Agriculture (ERS-USDA)*

Cold Storage Holdings of Frozen Pork[2] in the United States, on First of Month   In Millions of Pounds

Year	Jan.	Feb.	Mar.	Apr.	May	June	July	Aug.	Sept.	Oct.	Nov.	Dec.
1997	313.8	342.2	383.9	404.7	440.2	413.4	406.2	388.7	371.8	346.6	354.2	334.1
1998	346.4	446.1	464.5	458.8	487.0	477.4	426.8	414.6	392.6	388.9	411.9	443.4
1999	503.5	510.3	540.9	552.8	596.9	572.7	528.6	494.6	432.6	430.6	438.1	422.5
2000	415.4	481.4	523.5	534.7	532.1	537.9	495.5	478.5	455.6	439.5	438.6	445.6
2001	411.5	471.4	468.3	432.3	432.6	421.5	374.1	339.5	332.6	366.9	430.6	432.7
2002	465.0	503.9	510.9	531.5	567.7	548.0	497.8	472.2	464.4	480.2	489.8	463.9
2003	468.5	512.7	519.7	530.5	520.0	499.7	460.0	440.7	430.2	435.2	446.8	438.9
2004	470.7	504.1	477.1	447.3	448.6	412.8	373.0	366.8	382.1	413.8	423.1	436.3
2005	482.9	498.7	541.2	543.8	563.8	512.9	492.5	448.0	414.5	431.6	446.5	437.4
2006[1]	428.5	527.7	525.1	502.6	517.4	473.3	408.4	413.5	404.4	440.7	470.7	462.1

[1] Preliminary.   [2] Excludes lard.   *Source: Economic Research Service, U.S. Department of Agriculture (ERS-USDA)*

HOGS

Average Price of Hogs, National Base 51-52% lean[2] In Dollars Per Hundred Pounds (Cwt.)

Year	Jan.	Feb.	Mar.	Apr.	May	June	July	Aug.	Sept.	Oct.	Nov.	Dec.	Average
1997	52.96	51.36	48.52	54.41	57.84	57.43	58.89	54.17	49.45	46.12	44.86	40.33	51.36
1998	35.60	34.53	37.22	37.22	45.51	45.32	39.85	37.98	32.00	29.60	19.95	16.62	34.28
1999	28.58	29.65	28.25	31.69	38.45	35.39	32.84	38.56	35.71	35.84	35.34	37.70	34.00
2000	38.32	41.58	43.52	49.59	50.21	51.48	50.45	45.35	43.49	43.09	37.84	41.40	44.69
2001	38.61	41.47	48.41	49.28	52.34	54.53	53.75	52.47	46.93	41.27	35.49	35.14	45.81
2002	40.16	40.65	37.47	32.97	34.64	37.32	40.53	34.00	26.98	31.69	29.99	32.35	34.90
2003	34.39	35.64	36.11	36.42	43.62	47.88	44.98	41.90	41.82	38.63	36.02	36.02	39.45
2004	39.02	45.21	48.30	48.34	58.45	57.95	58.21	56.19	55.34	53.68	56.23	53.15	52.51
2005	53.36	51.11	51.30	51.00	55.40	49.86	49.96	51.60	49.98	47.49	37.70	44.81	49.46
2006[1]	41.37	43.17	43.34	41.45	49.00	54.90	51.89	53.32	50.28	47.57	45.97	44.84	47.26

[1] Preliminary. [2] Data Prior to January 1998 are for Sioux City. *Source: Economic Research Service, U.S. Department of Agriculture (ERS-USDA)*

Average Price Received by Farmers for Hogs in the United States   In Cents Per Pound

Year	Jan.	Feb.	Mar.	Apr.	May	June	July	Aug.	Sept.	Oct.	Nov.	Dec.	Average
1997	53.8	52.8	49.4	53.8	58.2	57.8	58.9	55.3	50.4	47.3	45.1	41.6	52.0
1998	36.0	35.9	34.9	35.6	42.4	42.5	36.9	35.2	29.5	27.8	18.9	15.0	32.6
1999	26.5	27.7	28.0	30.1	36.6	34.1	31.6	36.2	33.9	34.2	33.4	35.6	32.3
2000	36.8	39.9	41.7	47.4	48.3	48.9	48.3	43.8	41.6	41.4	36.8	39.8	42.9
2001	37.2	39.2	45.9	47.8	50.4	52.2	51.7	50.8	45.2	40.2	35.0	33.3	44.1
2002	37.7	38.5	36.0	31.7	33.2	35.8	39.2	31.9	26.5	30.8	27.8	30.3	33.3
2003	33.0	34.3	34.7	34.8	41.3	45.0	42.7	39.6	39.7	36.7	34.7	34.2	37.6
2004	36.8	42.6	47.2	47.4	56.6	56.7	57.1	55.3	54.8	52.2	55.6	52.4	51.2
2005	53.2	50.7	51.2	51.1	54.9	49.5	49.8	51.0	49.4	47.0	43.5	44.3	49.6
2006[1]	40.7	42.6	42.8	41.3	48.2	53.8	50.2	51.6	48.9	46.5	44.8	43.5	46.2

[1] Preliminary. *Source: Economic Research Service, U.S. Department of Agriculture (ERS-USDA)*

Quarterly Hogs and Pigs Report in the United States, 10 States   In Thousands of Head

Year[2]	Inventory[3]	Breeding[3]	Market[3]	Farrowings	Pig Crop	Year[2]	Inventory[3]	Breeding[3]	Market[3]	Farrowings	Pig Crop
1997	56,124	6,578	49,546	11,480	99,583	2002	59,804	6,209	53,594	11,492	101,677
I	56,141	6,667	49,474	2,684	23,164	I	59,804	6,209	53,594	2,835	24,857
II	55,049	6,637	48,412	2,911	25,229	II	59,256	6,230	53,026	2,941	26,001
III	57,366	6,789	50,577	2,946	25,696	III	60,391	6,208	54,183	2,883	25,725
IV	60,456	6,858	53,598	2,939	25,494	IV	60,753	6,051	54,702	2,833	25,094
1998	61,158	6,957	54,200	12,062	104,981	2003	59,554	6,058	53,496	11,429	101,491
I	61,158	6,957	54,200	2,929	25,480	I	59,554	6,058	53,496	2,769	24,400
II	60,163	6,942	53,220	3,086	26,989	II	58,183	6,027	52,156	2,886	25,629
III	62,213	6,958	55,254	3,054	26,634	III	59,602	6,026	53,576	2,918	25,974
IV	63,488	6,875	56,612	2,993	25,878	IV	61,009	5,938	55,071	2,856	25,488
1999	62,206	6,682	55,523	11,641	102,354	2004	60,444	6,009	54,434	11,499	102,781
I	62,206	6,682	55,523	2,891	25,247	I	60,444	6,009	54,434	2,836	25,105
II	60,191	6,527	53,663	2,986	26,272	II	59,520	5,961	53,558	2,870	25,633
III	60,896	6,515	54,380	2,920	25,862	III	60,698	5,937	54,760	2,905	26,162
IV	60,776	6,301	54,474	2,844	24,973	IV	61,519	5,962	55,556	2,888	25,881
2000	59,342	6,234	53,109	11,410	100,747	2005	60,975	5,969	55,005	11,535	103,965
I	59,342	6,234	53,109	2,798	24,522	I	60,975	5,969	55,005	2,835	25,343
II	57,782	6,190	51,593	2,885	25,565	II	59,699	5,941	53,757	2,882	25,986
III	59,117	6,234	52,884	2,889	25,548	III	60,732	5,977	54,754	2,918	26,449
IV	59,495	6,246	53,250	2,838	25,112	IV	61,846	5,972	55,873	2,900	26,187
2001	59,138	6,270	52,868	11,385	100,503	2006[1]	61,449	6,011	55,438	11,589	105,423
I	59,138	6,270	52,868	2,748	23,963	I	61,449	6,011	55,438	2,840	25,661
II	57,524	6,232	51,292	2,870	25,509	II	60,176	6,025	54,151	2,916	26,480
III	58,603	6,186	52,417	2,878	25,539	III	61,687	6,060	55,627	2,924	26,731
IV	59,777	6,158	53,619	2,889	25,492	IV	62,814	6,079	56,735	2,909	26,551

[1] Preliminary.   [2] Quarters are Dec. preceding year-Feb.(I), Mar.-May(II), June-Aug.(III) and Sept.-Nov.(IV).   [3] Beginning of period.
Source: National Agricultural Statistics Service, U.S. Department of Agriculture (NASS-USDA)

Federally Inspected Hog Slaughter in the United States   In Thousands of Head

Year	Jan.	Feb.	Mar.	Apr.	May	June	July	Aug.	Sept.	Oct.	Nov.	Dec.	Total
1997	7,610	6,836	7,437	7,590	6,971	6,859	7,169	7,197	7,872	8,625	7,601	8,461	90,228
1998	8,454	7,590	8,335	8,198	7,443	7,596	8,130	8,024	8,443	9,192	8,650	9,231	99,285
1999	8,373	7,746	8,945	8,386	7,303	8,176	7,778	8,256	8,501	8,806	8,750	8,719	99,739
2000	8,010	7,955	8,695	7,108	7,816	7,823	7,235	8,481	7,992	8,746	8,633	7,943	96,436
2001	8,521	7,491	8,207	7,722	7,836	7,368	7,333	8,247	7,687	9,210	8,610	8,298	96,528
2002	8,552	7,400	7,879	8,321	8,215	7,425	7,957	8,425	8,384	9,276	8,548	8,534	98,915
2003	8,680	7,587	8,069	8,238	7,715	7,665	8,008	7,951	8,466	9,547	8,506	9,254	99,685
2004	8,704	7,805	8,942	8,567	7,494	8,415	8,008	8,616	8,897	8,883	8,881	9,150	102,361
2005	8,402	8,031	8,858	8,369	7,939	8,470	7,582	8,888	8,778	9,027	9,038	9,138	102,519
2006[1]	8,834	7,978	9,148	7,882	8,453	8,256	7,806	8,991	8,738	9,541	9,276	8,788	103,690

[1] Preliminary. *Source: National Agricultural Statistics Service, U.S. Department of Agriculture (NASS-USDA)*

Average Live Weight of all Hogs Slaughtered Under Federal Inspection   In Pounds Per Head

Year	Jan.	Feb.	Mar.	Apr.	May	June	July	Aug.	Sept.	Oct.	Nov.	Dec.	Average
1997	257	256	256	256	256	257	253	252	255	257	261	260	256
1998	259	258	257	257	256	255	252	252	253	257	262	261	257
1999	259	259	259	260	260	260	257	254	256	259	262	262	259
2000	262	262	263	263	264	263	260	258	260	263	266	265	262
2001	265	264	264	265	264	264	261	258	262	267	269	268	264
2002	268	267	267	268	267	266	261	259	261	264	268	268	265
2003	268	267	268	268	268	266	263	261	263	268	270	269	267
2004	269	268	268	268	266	265	263	263	266	267	270	270	267
2005	270	270	271	271	270	269	265	263	265	269	272	272	269
2006[1]	273	272	272	273	272	269	265	263	267	270	273	273	270

[1] Preliminary. *Source: Economic Research Service, U.S. Department of Agriculture (ERS-USDA)*

HOGS

Lean Hog Futures - Chicago Mercantile Exchange
(weekly close) as of December 29, 2006

Cents per pound

Data through December 1996 contract are for Live Hogs * .74 Adjusted to correspond to the Lean Hogs contract.

Average Open Interest of Lean Hog[1] Futures in Chicago   In Contracts

Year	Jan.	Feb.	Mar.	Apr.	May	June	July	Aug.	Sept.	Oct.	Nov.	Dec.
1997	33,105	33,953	31,289	34,071	41,978	37,398	36,141	33,712	31,483	36,928	39,363	39,394
1998	45,908	42,241	38,965	33,610	34,257	32,456	32,085	31,199	34,165	34,051	42,224	45,241
1999	46,003	44,211	43,803	48,277	55,951	52,398	54,723	49,915	53,055	54,089	54,432	50,691
2000	49,209	54,094	57,472	68,535	64,938	54,208	45,730	38,233	38,802	38,254	40,075	45,141
2001	41,425	41,892	48,381	45,296	41,910	45,715	51,661	47,760	42,072	36,983	32,821	27,687
2002	28,720	31,662	33,056	33,472	33,161	28,719	29,338	32,030	36,136	35,245	42,852	43,974
2003	40,660	39,862	40,446	37,883	43,672	47,338	39,706	37,700	49,469	46,295	43,552	43,352
2004	46,380	55,058	63,889	77,756	80,271	81,370	79,860	84,840	86,092	86,423	94,336	98,328
2005	102,580	97,550	95,841	94,008	96,662	91,871	97,160	95,841	107,617	113,754	116,005	124,492
2006	133,258	144,506	145,020	144,250	157,259	158,276	157,899	165,781	176,336	174,971	188,965	179,057

Source: Chicago Mercantile Exchange (CME)

Volume of Trading of Lean Hog Futures in Chicago   In Contracts

Year	Jan.	Feb.	Mar.	Apr.	May	June	July	Aug.	Sept.	Oct.	Nov.	Dec.	Total[1]
1997	180,241	159,600	200,118	212,810	222,759	188,615	181,637	146,297	149,950	175,135	152,876	130,871	2,100.9
1998	180,241	182,698	174,752	132,952	155,737	167,767	185,427	157,973	164,964	173,163	218,950	241,767	2,136.3
1999	218,608	171,108	196,825	189,773	214,852	237,240	239,096	167,787	190,238	187,794	205,505	139,270	2,358.1
2000	175,399	186,352	231,532	158,765	218,222	235,036	172,725	145,849	146,240	142,240	153,043	146,404	2,111.8
2001	183,493	159,020	197,004	142,892	165,220	184,421	198,503	164,712	152,178	177,601	163,798	129,497	2,018.3
2002	145,266	120,994	168,929	196,956	163,816	158,074	166,064	140,154	174,797	167,065	165,039	164,106	1,931.3
2003	186,436	137,479	186,511	156,370	209,740	210,901	199,782	124,677	232,705	207,247	164,190	148,117	2,164.2
2004	212,420	170,270	249,205	211,501	295,271	304,279	315,197	215,233	356,295	242,204	376,823	255,488	3,204.2
2005	347,467	237,079	380,658	287,828	412,655	398,201	354,819	315,949	391,121	295,817	421,714	310,235	4,153.5
2006	561,152	319,827	597,852	356,950	658,973	826,312	578,656	478,837	577,375	533,532	649,293	342,242	6,481.0

[1] In thousands of contracts.   *Source: Chicago Mercantile Exchange (CME)*

Honey

Honey is the thick, supersaturated sugar solution produced by bees to feed their larvae. It is composed of fructose, glucose and water in varying proportions and also contains several enzymes and oils. The color of honey varies due to the source of nectar and age of the honey. Light colored honeys are usually of higher quality than darker honeys. The average honeybee colony can produce more than 700 pounds of honey per year but only 10 percent is usually harvested by the beekeeper. The rest of the honey is consumed by the colony during the year. American per capita honey consumption is 1 pound per person per year. Honey is said to be humanity's oldest sweet, and beeswax the first plastic.

Honey is used in many ways, including direct human consumption, baking, and medicine. Honey has several healing properties. Its high sugar content nourishes injured tissues, thus enhancing faster healing time. Honey's phytochemicals create a form of hydrogen peroxide that cleans out the wound, and the thick consistency protects the wound from contact with air Honey has also proven superior to antibiotic ointments for reducing rates of infection in people with burns.

Prices – US average domestic honey prices in 2005 fell by –14.1% to 91.8 cents per pound from 2004's 106.9 cents per pound, but are still far above the 10-year low of 59.7 cents in 2000. The value of US honey production in 2005 fell –18.3% to $160 million to move farther below the 2003 record of $253 million.

Supply – World production of honey in 2002, the latest reporting year for the series, rose +1.2% to a record 1.270 million metric tons from 1.255 million metric tons in 2001. The world's largest producer of honey by far is China with 258,000 metric tons of production in 2002, representing about 20% of total world production, followed by the US with 90,000 metric tons, and Argentina with 85,000 metric tons.

US production of honey in 2005 fell by –4.8% to 174.8 million pounds, and remained well below the 10-year high of 220.3 million pounds posted in 2000. Stocks rose by +2.1% to 62.5 million pounds in 2005 (Jan 1) from the 25-year low of 39.4 million pounds posted in 2002. Yield per colony rose +0.8% to 72.4 pounds per colony in 2005. The number of colonies, however, fell –5.6% to a record low of 2.413 million in 2005.

Trade – The US in 2004 (the latest data available) imported almost as much honey as it produced, with imports of 178.8 million pounds versus US domestic production in that year of 183.6 million pounds. US exports of honey are generally small and in 2004 they totaled only 7.8 million pounds, which was only 4.2% of US production.

World Production of Honey   In Metric Tons

Year	Argentina	Australia	Brazil	Canada	China	Germany	Japan	Mexico	Russia	United States	Total
1996	57,000	26,000	18,000	27,000	189,000	15,000	3,000	49,000	46,000	90,000	1,091,000
1997	70,000	27,000	18,000	31,000	215,000	15,000	3,000	54,000	49,000	89,000	1,148,000
1998	65,000	22,000	18,000	46,000	211,000	16,000	3,000	55,000	50,000	100,000	1,178,000
1999	93,000	19,000	20,000	37,000	236,000	20,000	3,000	55,000	51,000	94,000	1,234,000
2000	93,000	21,000	22,000	32,000	252,000	20,000	3,000	59,000	54,000	100,000	1,246,000
2001	80,000	22,000	22,000	35,000	255,000	26,000	3,000	59,000	53,000	84,000	1,255,000
2002[1]	85,000	22,000	22,000	33,000	258,000	22,000	3,000	55,000	55,000	90,000	1,270,000

[1] Preliminary.   Source: Foreign Agricultural Service, U.S. Department of Agriculture (FAS-USDA)

Salient Statistics of Honey in the United States   In Millions of Pounds

Year	Number of Colonies (1,000)	Yield Per Colony Pounds	Stocks Jan. 1	Total U.S. Production	Imports for Consumption	Domestic Disappearance	Exports	Total Supply	Placed Under Loan	CCC Take Over	Net Gov't Expenditure[3] Mil. $	Domestic Avg. Price All Honey - Cents Per Pound -	National Avg. Price Support - Cents Per Pound -	Per Capita Consumption Pounds
2001	2,506	74.0	64.6	185.5	144.8	----	7.4	----	----	----	----	70.4	----	----
2002	2,574	66.7	39.4	171.7	202.6	----	6.9	----	----	----	----	132.7	----	----
2003	2,599	70.0	40.8	181.7	200.4	----	6.9	----	----	----	----	138.7	----	----
2004	2,556	71.8	61.2	183.6	178.8	----	7.8	----	----	----	----	106.9	----	----
2005[1]	2,413	72.4	62.5	174.8								90.4		
2006[2]	2,392	64.7	60.5	154.8								104.2		

[1] Preliminary.   [2] Forecast.   [3] Fiscal year.   Source: Economic Research Service, U.S. Department of Agriculture (ERS-USDA)

Production and Yield of Honey in the United States

	Production in Thousands of Pounds						Value of Production $1,000	Yield per Colony in Pounds					
Year	California	Florida	Minnesota	North Dakota	South Dakota	Total		California	Florida	Minnesota	North Dakota	South Dakota	Average
2001	27,625	22,000	10,935	26,880	15,275	185,461	132,225	65	100	81	96	65	74.0
2002	23,500	20,460	8,541	24,000	11,475	171,718	228,338	50	93	73	75	51	66.7
2003	32,160	14,910	9,960	29,580	15,050	181,727	253,106	67	71	83	87	70	70.0
2004	17,550	20,090	10,125	30,420	22,575	183,582	196,259	45	98	75	78	105	71.8
2005	30,000	13,760	8,880	33,670	17,380	174,818	160,428	75	86	74	91	79	72.4
2006[1]	19,760	13,770	10,000	25,900	10,575	154,846	161,314	52	81	80	74	47	64.7

[1] Preliminary.   Source: National Agricultural Statistics Service, U.S. Department of Agriculture (NASS-USDA)

Interest Rates, U.S.

US interest rates can be characterized in two main ways, by credit quality and maturity. Credit quality refers to the level of risk associated with a particular borrower. US Treasury securities, for example, carry the lowest risk. Maturity refers to the time at which the security matures and must be repaid. Treasury securities carry the full spectrum of maturities, from short-term cash management bills, to T-bills (4-weeks, 3-months, and 6-months), T-notes (2-year, 3-year, 5-year and 10-year), and 30-year T-bonds. The most active futures markets are the Treasury note and bond futures traded at the Chicago Board of Trade (CBOT) and the Eurodollar futures traded at the Chicago Mercantile Exchange (CME).

Prices – The 10-year US Treasury note yield moved higher from mid-2005 to post a new 4-1/2 year high in mid-2006 of 5.25% as the Fed's persistent tightening monetary policy took its toll and as inflation moved higher through mid-2006 driven in part by rising energy prices. However, the 10-year yield then fell back in the latter half of 2006, finally closing the year at 4.40%, just 7 bp higher than the 2005 close of 4.33%. The 10-year T-note yield moved lower in the second half of 2006 after the Fed halted its tightening regime in July 2006 and as the market grew increasingly concerned about the US housing market bust.

The Federal Reserve in 2006 implemented its last three 25 basis point rate hikes, with the last rate hike to 5.25% coming in June 2006. The Fed in 2004-06 raised its federal funds rate target by a total of 425 basis points from the 1.00% level that prevailed from mid-2003 to mid-2004 to 5.25% by June 2006. The Fed tightened its monetary policy over that time frame to move short-term rates back to normalized levels after the Fed in 2001-03 was forced to slash the funds rate to 1.00% to address the economic problems caused by the bursting of the stock market bubble in 2000 and the 9/11 terrorist attack in 2001.

The Fed finally halted its tightening regime in mid-2006, even though the Fed still saw inflation risks, because the Fed was worried about the bursting US housing bubble and about the impact on the US economy of the surge in crude oil prices above $70 per barrel in May 2006 to a record high of $78.40 by July 2006. The Fed halted its tightening process in time and the US economy in the latter half of 2006 saw a soft-landing with GDP growth in the mid-2% area. The Fed also received some help in the latter half of 2006 by the drop in crude oil prices back to the $60 per barrel area.

The US core CPI rate in mid-2006 rose sharply from the low-2% area in early 2006 to an 11-year high of +2.9% by September 2006. The Fed took that rise in the core CPI in stride because the Fed expected core inflation to moderate in late 2006 and through 2007 as US economic growth slowed and as energy prices fell back. The core CPI fell back to +2.6% by December 2006 but that was still above the generally-accepted 2.00% ceiling for inflation.

As of March 2007, the marketplace was generally looking for US interest rates to move mildly lower through 2007. While core inflation remained elevated at that time, the US economy was showing some weakness stemming from the weak US housing and auto sectors. The market as of March 2007 was expecting the Fed to cut its funds rate target by 50 basis points by Q1-2008 to address below-par US economic growth.

U.S. Producer Price Index[2] for All Commodities   1982 = 100

Year	Jan.	Feb.	Mar.	Apr.	May	June	July	Aug.	Sept.	Oct.	Nov.	Dec.	Average
1997	129.7	128.5	127.3	127.0	127.4	127.2	126.9	127.2	127.5	127.8	127.9	126.8	127.6
1998	125.4	125.0	124.7	124.9	125.1	124.8	124.9	124.2	123.8	124.0	123.6	122.8	124.4
1999	122.9	122.3	122.6	123.6	124.7	125.2	125.7	126.9	128.0	127.7	128.3	127.8	125.5
2000	128.3	129.8	130.8	130.7	131.6	133.8	133.7	132.9	134.7	135.4	135.0	136.2	132.7
2001	140.0	137.4	135.9	136.4	136.8	135.5	133.4	133.4	133.3	130.3	129.8	128.1	134.2
2002	128.5	128.4	129.8	130.8	130.8	130.9	131.2	131.5	132.3	133.2	133.1	132.9	131.1
2003	135.3	137.6	141.2	136.8	136.7	138.0	137.7	138.0	138.5	139.3	138.9	139.5	138.1
2004	141.4	142.1	143.1	144.8	146.8	147.2	147.4	148.0	147.7	150.0	151.4	150.2	146.7
2005	150.9	151.6	153.7	155.0	154.3	154.3	156.3	157.6	162.2	166.2	163.7	163.0	157.4
2006[1]	164.3	161.8	162.2	164.3	165.8	166.1	166.8	167.9	165.4	162.0	165.1	166.0	164.8

[1] Preliminary.   [2] Not seasonally adjusted.   *Source: Bureau of Labor Statistics, U.S. Department of Commerce (BLS)*

U.S. Consumer Price Index[2] for All Urban Consumers   1982-84 = 100

Year	Jan.	Feb.	Mar.	Apr.	May	June	July	Aug.	Sept.	Oct.	Nov.	Dec.	Average
1997	159.1	159.6	160.0	160.2	160.1	160.3	160.5	160.8	161.2	161.6	161.5	161.3	160.5
1998	161.6	161.9	162.2	162.5	162.8	163.0	163.2	163.4	163.6	164.0	164.0	163.9	163.0
1999	164.3	164.5	165.0	166.2	166.2	166.2	166.7	167.1	167.9	168.2	168.3	168.3	166.6
2000	168.8	169.8	171.2	171.3	171.5	172.4	172.8	172.8	173.7	174.0	174.1	174.0	172.2
2001	175.1	175.8	176.2	176.9	177.7	178.0	177.5	177.5	178.3	177.7	177.4	176.7	177.1
2002	177.1	177.8	178.8	179.8	179.8	179.9	180.1	180.7	181.0	181.3	181.3	180.9	179.9
2003	181.7	183.1	184.2	183.8	183.5	183.7	183.9	184.6	185.2	185.0	184.5	184.3	184.0
2004	185.2	186.2	187.4	188.0	189.1	189.7	189.4	189.5	189.9	190.9	191.0	190.3	188.9
2005	190.7	191.8	193.3	194.6	194.4	194.5	195.4	196.4	198.8	199.2	197.6	196.8	195.3
2006[1]	198.3	198.7	199.8	201.5	202.5	202.9	203.5	203.9	202.9	201.8	201.5	201.8	201.6

[1] Preliminary.   [2] Not seasonally adjusted.   *Source: Bureau of Labor Statistics, U.S. Department of Commerce (BLS)*

3-Month Eurodollar Futures - International Monetary Market
(weekly close) as of December 29, 2006

Volume of Trading of 3-month Eurodollar Futures in Chicago   In Thousands of Contracts

Year	Jan.	Feb.	Mar.	Apr.	May	June	July	Aug.	Sept.	Oct.	Nov.	Dec.	Total
1997	7,903	6,918	8,936	9,352	8,447	8,050	7,292	9,295	7,635	12,570	6,314	7,058	99,770
1998	10,908	7,861	8,842	9,488	7,202	8,350	5,452	9,811	13,594	11,757	9,628	6,579	109,473
1999	7,471	7,675	8,719	7,347	8,957	9,650	7,746	8,898	7,629	7,501	6,223	5,604	93,418
2000	8,380	9,723	10,198	10,172	10,261	9,791	7,385	7,010	8,205	9,276	7,561	10,152	108,115
2001	17,515	12,908	15,479	15,192	15,691	14,310	12,673	14,948	16,776	14,139	21,150	13,234	184,015
2002	19,487	14,491	17,987	17,947	18,717	17,932	20,367	17,758	15,310	18,496	13,349	10,240	202,081
2003	13,534	12,315	18,275	15,393	19,403	21,163	18,733	18,724	18,817	20,004	15,432	16,978	208,771
2004	20,809	16,042	22,584	26,674	25,549	28,067	25,114	24,859	32,283	25,737	27,945	21,920	297,584
2005	27,794	28,549	34,472	42,437	36,600	37,997	26,795	32,921	45,483	35,149	34,776	27,382	410,355
2006	35,602	34,218	47,464	37,752	44,155	45,443	36,794	45,127	45,180	46,454	42,701	41,188	502,077

Source: International Monetary Market (IOM), division of the Chicago Mercantile Exchange (CME)

Average Open Interest of 3-month Eurodollar Futures in Chicago   In Thousands of Contracts

Year	Jan.	Feb.	Mar.	Apr.	May	June	July	Aug.	Sept.	Oct.	Nov.	Dec.
1997	2,190.8	2,333.2	2,423.1	2,523.1	2,671.3	2,706.5	2,699.2	2,788.0	2,769.3	2,815.1	2,799.5	2,661.6
1998	2,713.4	2,821.5	2,797.9	2,892.6	3,089.0	3,093.9	3,027.7	3,223.0	3,359.9	3,303.4	3,297.4	3,000.1
1999	2,917.9	3,039.5	2,973.5	2,894.7	3,183.2	3,208.8	3,064.4	3,115.6	2,904.0	2,918.2	2,879.7	2,859.4
2000	2,971.3	3,261.4	3,138.7	3,156.6	3,331.7	3,272.1	3,160.3	3,225.7	3,181.8	3,067.2	3,201.1	3,349.7
2001	3,576.4	3,878.6	4,117.4	4,109.3	4,316.3	4,471.7	4,452.4	4,753.5	4,567.8	4,524.0	4,950.8	4,559.1
2002	4,592.0	4,937.0	4,727.9	4,411.6	4,421.0	4,295.5	4,123.7	4,482.4	4,243.4	4,237.9	4,553.7	4,072.5
2003	4,007.1	4,500.1	4,517.3	4,448.6	5,098.7	5,514.2	5,218.4	5,277.9	5,034.1	4,935.4	5,024.2	4,936.1
2004	5,128.0	5,624.1	5,640.5	5,602.2	6,060.0	6,117.3	6,026.7	6,236.3	5,992.8	5,968.9	6,527.8	6,706.7
2005	7,163.3	7,858.5	8,124.1	8,244.1	8,604.5	8,045.7	7,416.0	8,044.7	8,054.2	8,471.9	9,264.8	9,145.1
2006	8,833.5	9,574.0	9,586.0	9,679.6	10,126.2	9,995.4	9,572.4	10,153.9	9,949.4	9,809.8	10,345.5	10,201.1

Source: International Monetary Market (IOM), division of the Chicago Mercantile Exchange (CME)

2-Year Treasury Note Futures - Chicago Board of Trade
(weekly close) as of December 29, 2006

Nominal Value

Prior to the March 2000 contract, prices are theoretical based on a 6% coupon.

Volume of Trading of 2-Year U.S. Treasury Note Futures in Chicago   In Thousands of Contracts

Year	Jan.	Feb.	Mar.	Apr.	May	June	July	Aug.	Sept.	Oct.	Nov.	Dec.	Total
1997	32.4	93.9	79.0	44.5	100.2	102.7	53.1	138.5	97.0	68.5	107.8	100.6	1,018.3
1998	77.1	104.3	107.1	52.0	140.9	123.3	59.4	177.4	160.1	93.1	140.7	72.9	1,308.4
1999	64.5	132.7	67.0	62.9	132.3	93.6	46.5	139.2	71.3	44.0	124.1	72.3	1,050.1
2000	51.5	159.3	97.9	76.9	160.2	105.2	43.0	181.0	107.4	97.4	287.6	126.5	1,493.8
2001	174.6	299.2	160.9	194.8	274.0	163.3	93.4	316.4	198.1	122.9	303.8	160.6	2,462.0
2002	195.0	332.9	290.4	159.2	377.0	242.9	177.0	377.0	253.0	174.8	387.2	232.3	3,198.7
2003	146.8	392.9	292.5	153.3	513.9	339.2	274.1	514.0	522.8	281.1	496.7	488.5	4,415.9
2004	310.4	829.8	630.0	462.4	872.2	788.8	406.7	1,009.9	1,014.5	678.0	1,393.3	1,058.5	9,454.8
2005	953.7	1,997.5	1,706.1	1,548.3	2,306.3	1,811.4	1,153.0	2,144.2	2,118.0	1,344.1	2,451.5	1,671.3	21,205.4
2006	2,053.3	3,223.3	3,206.5	2,090.0	4,690.9	2,837.1	2,525.1	4,461.0	2,768.3	2,422.9	4,826.4	2,862.0	37,966.8

Source: Chicago Board of Trade (CBT)

Average Open Interest of 2-Year U.S. Treasury Note Futures in Chicago   In Contracts

Year	Jan.	Feb.	Mar.	Apr.	May	June	July	Aug.	Sept.	Oct.	Nov.	Dec.
1997	20,599	23,027	22,750	24,090	29,379	33,225	36,047	47,253	44,003	40,960	37,785	37,701
1998	39,649	40,462	40,840	40,899	46,833	47,241	44,701	48,888	47,030	37,245	38,222	40,303
1999	39,971	40,747	40,339	40,078	34,731	35,959	35,349	37,624	38,693	38,157	38,702	34,135
2000	34,325	43,026	44,512	43,772	49,033	51,216	55,806	53,449	47,912	53,338	60,894	77,860
2001	82,168	79,389	81,688	72,517	66,185	63,601	56,610	72,951	74,353	65,433	72,697	71,270
2002	86,505	103,331	103,568	87,850	102,040	105,931	99,383	107,955	110,434	108,089	115,503	113,618
2003	107,084	114,234	123,909	108,979	120,264	118,776	112,052	149,099	151,922	144,646	149,014	156,506
2004	161,948	195,229	186,836	172,374	198,864	210,667	191,740	207,103	216,394	205,549	221,643	248,517
2005	287,341	345,687	329,608	307,013	341,492	372,896	362,299	371,076	364,420	351,255	357,270	363,186
2006	437,806	489,256	469,014	489,450	607,562	541,129	595,108	701,432	683,556	680,738	698,407	716,023

Source: Chicago Board of Trade (CBT)

5-Year Treasury Note Futures - Chicago Board of Trade
(weekly close) as of December 29, 2006
Nominal Value

Prior to the March 2000 contract, prices are theoretical based on a 6% coupon.

Volume of Trading of 5-Year U.S. Treasury Note Futures in Chicago   In Thousands of Contracts

Year	Jan.	Feb.	Mar.	Apr.	May	June	July	Aug.	Sept.	Oct.	Nov.	Dec.	Total
1997	928	1,157	1,271	984	1,191	1,144	761	1,245	1,244	1,314	1,068	1,183	13,489
1998	1,452	1,482	1,391	1,155	1,281	1,377	944	2,481	1,913	1,583	1,723	1,279	18,060
1999	1,120	1,554	1,337	1,115	1,906	1,544	1,166	2,164	1,034	1,245	1,607	1,193	16,984
2000	1,801	2,874	2,010	1,708	2,548	1,757	1,189	2,253	1,516	1,774	2,260	1,643	23,332
2001	2,423	2,592	2,281	2,063	3,222	2,264	1,702	2,697	2,617	2,526	4,053	2,684	31,122
2002	2,868	3,826	3,848	3,092	4,638	4,096	4,437	5,354	4,859	5,027	5,013	3,453	50,512
2003	4,436	5,178	5,534	4,624	7,268	6,166	6,463	7,090	7,454	6,364	6,885	6,286	73,746
2004	5,857	7,389	7,776	7,793	10,979	9,458	7,110	10,656	10,312	7,686	11,037	9,417	105,469
2005	7,798	11,168	11,849	10,720	12,320	9,164	7,698	12,663	11,000	8,511	11,996	7,021	121,909
2006	9,388	12,142	11,865	7,870	12,972	9,369	8,102	13,348	9,369	8,731	13,424	8,291	124,870

Source: Chicago Board of Trade (CBT)

Average Open Interest of 5-Year U.S. Treasury Note Futures in Chicago   In Thousands of Contracts

Year	Jan.	Feb.	Mar.	Apr.	May	June	July	Aug.	Sept.	Oct.	Nov.	Dec.
1997	176.7	208.9	219.5	235.5	227.9	225.7	226.3	225.8	234.3	233.5	248.4	257.9
1998	257.1	270.0	282.3	277.5	274.1	257.2	264.8	389.1	382.9	383.8	353.4	326.9
1999	290.4	268.6	247.5	246.9	311.1	348.6	325.3	341.5	298.9	328.6	272.6	288.5
2000	387.0	475.5	420.8	417.9	428.2	379.6	402.7	405.1	372.8	373.7	381.4	380.2
2001	377.7	392.0	374.5	376.9	436.3	422.0	461.0	483.3	451.4	463.2	554.6	491.1
2002	507.2	576.2	585.6	632.2	656.4	594.9	554.9	652.8	655.0	662.5	720.7	692.8
2003	685.1	743.2	777.8	835.5	856.3	827.5	781.7	840.4	737.0	819.4	925.6	880.1
2004	874.2	1,008.1	987.2	1,043.0	1,145.4	1,118.5	1,217.3	1,322.5	1,168.1	1,099.4	1,290.7	1,318.7
2005	1,160.2	1,237.0	1,325.0	1,383.0	1,320.9	1,127.9	1,247.7	1,450.3	1,190.2	1,342.0	1,397.6	1,126.8
2006	1,105.1	1,404.8	1,238.0	1,257.2	1,326.0	1,264.7	1,258.3	1,409.8	1,341.3	1,413.8	1,484.4	1,423.8

Source: Chicago Board of Trade (CBT)

INTEREST RATES, U.S.

10-Year Treasury Note Futures - Chicago Board of Trade
(weekly close) as of December 29, 2006
Nominal Value

Prior to the March 2000 contract, prices are theoretical based on a 6% coupon.

Volume of Trading of 10-year U.S. Treasury Note Futures in Chicago   In Thousands of Contracts

Year	Jan.	Feb.	Mar.	Apr.	May	June	July	Aug.	Sept.	Oct.	Nov.	Dec.	Total
1997	1,781	1,940	2,052	1,703	2,026	1,942	1,510	2,536	2,063	2,594	1,826	1,991	23,962
1998	2,394	2,749	2,817	2,342	2,696	2,682	1,704	3,632	3,560	2,883	2,912	2,112	32,483
1999	2,269	3,562	2,994	2,145	3,519	3,153	2,438	3,736	2,509	2,471	3,202	2,048	34,046
2000	3,557	4,975	3,750	3,530	4,712	3,706	2,581	4,460	3,780	3,824	4,514	3,313	46,701
2001	4,633	4,915	4,501	4,299	5,483	4,084	3,493	5,683	4,390	4,145	7,270	4,690	57,586
2002	5,540	6,407	6,521	5,463	8,309	7,548	8,981	10,590	8,529	11,199	9,679	7,020	95,786
2003	9,121	10,746	11,321	9,377	13,817	12,149	15,285	14,249	13,707	13,587	12,475	10,912	146,745
2004	13,608	14,569	16,984	16,478	17,786	15,184	12,954	17,419	18,468	16,622	21,006	15,039	196,119
2005	13,901	19,565	21,133	19,487	22,689	16,779	13,895	20,120	18,348	15,357	20,705	13,144	215,124
2006	17,189	21,263	22,740	17,241	26,175	20,311	16,645	24,797	22,125	20,603	28,414	18,070	255,572

Source: Chicago Board of Trade (CBT)

Average Open Interest of 10-year U.S. Treasury Note Futures in Chicago   In Thousands of Contracts

Year	Jan.	Feb.	Mar.	Apr.	May	June	July	Aug.	Sept.	Oct.	Nov.	Dec.
1997	332.3	343.7	324.0	348.7	350.8	336.9	363.7	407.1	387.3	398.6	405.0	374.4
1998	430.3	508.0	474.9	494.4	533.2	513.4	512.2	604.9	555.3	482.9	508.3	503.5
1999	528.5	549.5	515.4	510.1	541.1	574.5	588.3	623.8	607.3	653.1	582.0	487.9
2000	595.2	653.8	571.9	615.6	621.4	583.9	608.4	602.1	547.6	564.6	555.2	508.9
2001	550.3	541.6	560.0	595.1	628.7	512.1	550.2	627.3	610.4	590.3	662.0	559.9
2002	572.9	643.9	679.6	699.1	806.5	793.0	877.6	958.3	888.7	970.2	938.0	751.6
2003	772.9	896.9	914.9	897.1	968.1	993.6	1,009.5	1,032.5	856.2	985.7	1,140.7	965.0
2004	1,145.9	1,320.6	1,312.9	1,347.7	1,392.4	1,300.3	1,348.2	1,456.6	1,503.6	1,626.9	1,767.4	1,642.0
2005	1,671.3	1,888.6	1,980.2	2,003.5	2,140.8	1,869.0	1,859.3	1,992.8	1,749.4	1,677.7	1,778.6	1,635.6
2006	1,700.0	1,990.4	2,048.7	2,259.7	2,321.0	2,054.2	2,087.1	2,265.3	2,271.5	2,408.2	2,398.2	2,236.0

Source: Chicago Board of Trade (CBT)

Volume of Trading of 30-year U.S. Treasury Bond Futures in Chicago   In Thousands of Contracts

Year	Jan.	Feb.	Mar.	Apr.	May	June	July	Aug.	Sept.	Oct.	Nov.	Dec.	Total
1997	8,104.7	7,522.8	7,493.3	7,519.9	8,339.1	7,400.2	7,679.8	10,228.1	8,356.2	12,467.6	7,735.5	6,980.4	99,827.7
1998	9,595.3	9,368.1	9,763.9	8,516.7	9,054.1	10,208.6	8,070.9	12,024.8	11,159.2	10,698.1	8,155.0	5,609.2	112,224.1
1999	8,075.2	10,031.5	8,667.5	7,196.9	9,555.8	8,072.1	6,415.1	7,995.2	6,559.6	6,301.1	6,909.0	4,263.5	90,042.3
2000	7,966.4	8,157.4	5,378.6	5,282.3	5,972.9	4,458.6	3,080.0	4,709.9	4,529.2	4,460.4	5,072.8	3,682.3	62,750.8
2001	5,123.0	5,545.9	5,196.3	4,584.0	6,022.2	4,233.2	3,347.0	4,965.6	4,331.0	4,598.6	6,746.4	3,886.0	58,579.3
2002	4,132.7	4,721.1	4,504.8	3,932.8	5,191.4	4,722.2	5,157.9	5,666.5	4,534.5	5,190.1	4,722.8	3,605.6	56,082.3
2003	3,625.3	4,840.9	5,106.9	3,795.0	7,188.4	5,896.2	6,352.1	6,198.0	5,738.4	5,121.8	4,823.4	4,835.2	63,521.5
2004	5,025.4	5,762.8	6,687.9	5,983.2	6,463.8	5,556.9	4,540.1	6,343.5	7,638.7	5,658.6	7,374.2	5,914.0	72,949.0
2005	6,134.8	8,973.5	8,573.7	7,293.5	8,558.9	7,407.2	5,367.0	7,771.3	7,193.6	6,450.4	7,928.8	5,274.0	86,926.6
2006	7,044.8	8,511.6	8,980.6	6,969.2	10,354.4	7,564.5	5,854.2	8,736.7	7,553.9	6,375.1	9,461.6	6,348.2	93,754.9

Source: Chicago Board of Trade (CBT)

Average Open Interest of 30-year U.S. Treasury Bond Futures in Chicago   In Contracts

Year	Jan.	Feb.	Mar.	Apr.	May	June	July	Aug.	Sept.	Oct.	Nov.	Dec.
1997	497,539	545,775	509,573	493,511	554,418	480,669	530,011	608,474	624,231	723,321	719,186	737,703
1998	744,894	764,309	766,233	806,559	888,215	1,040,659	1,084,889	1,061,223	837,986	769,932	782,677	662,025
1999	657,180	801,115	664,131	618,453	717,453	674,225	672,983	748,974	647,816	621,816	637,656	561,919
2000	637,023	612,298	530,957	503,412	434,771	390,928	394,075	440,437	402,156	399,880	443,282	445,386
2001	413,244	479,165	519,987	509,558	503,194	455,799	458,613	531,098	525,972	567,177	602,647	478,418
2002	468,455	520,573	479,939	463,100	472,778	458,020	427,896	465,971	496,815	467,440	459,877	440,225
2003	420,797	506,910	487,277	449,286	566,887	596,186	554,632	521,928	423,995	443,177	489,185	471,848
2004	488,484	571,445	557,595	488,921	553,721	512,566	517,893	594,905	584,416	594,353	640,026	634,008
2005	674,170	792,247	749,403	710,061	735,910	665,235	579,724	600,565	595,736	586,653	618,647	574,121
2006	601,094	662,314	622,927	739,601	858,812	760,240	760,749	813,905	763,092	737,070	810,426	803,020

Source: Chicago Board of Trade (CBT)

Municipal Note Futures - Chicago Board of Trade
(weekly close) as of March 22, 2006

Nominal Value

U.S. Federal Funds Rate   In Percent

Year	Jan.	Feb.	Mar.	Apr.	May	June	July	Aug.	Sept.	Oct.	Nov.	Dec.	Average
1997	5.25	5.19	5.39	5.51	5.50	5.56	5.52	5.54	5.54	5.50	5.52	5.50	5.46
1998	5.56	5.51	5.49	5.45	5.49	5.56	5.54	5.55	5.51	5.07	4.83	4.68	5.35
1999	4.63	4.76	4.81	4.74	4.74	4.76	4.99	5.07	5.22	5.20	5.42	5.30	4.97
2000	5.46	5.73	5.85	6.02	6.27	6.53	6.54	6.50	6.52	6.51	6.51	6.40	6.24
2001	5.98	5.49	5.31	4.80	4.21	3.97	3.77	3.65	3.07	2.49	2.09	1.82	3.89
2002	1.73	1.74	1.73	1.75	1.75	1.75	1.73	1.74	1.75	1.75	1.34	1.24	1.67
2003	1.24	1.26	1.25	1.26	1.26	1.22	1.01	1.03	1.01	1.01	1.00	0.98	1.13
2004	1.00	1.01	1.00	1.00	1.00	1.03	1.26	1.43	1.61	1.76	1.93	2.16	1.35
2005	2.28	2.50	2.63	2.79	3.00	3.04	3.26	3.50	3.62	3.78	4.00	4.16	3.21
2006	4.29	4.49	4.59	4.79	4.94	4.99	5.24	5.25	5.25	5.25	5.25	5.24	4.96

Source: Bureau of Economic Analysis, U.S. Department of Commerce (BEA)

U.S. Municipal Bond Yield[1]   In Percent

Year	Jan.	Feb.	Mar.	Apr.	May	June	July	Aug.	Sept.	Oct.	Nov.	Dec.	Average
1997	5.72	5.63	5.76	5.88	5.70	5.53	5.35	5.41	5.39	5.38	5.33	5.19	5.52
1998	5.06	5.10	5.21	5.23	5.20	5.12	5.14	5.10	4.99	4.93	5.03	4.98	5.09
1999	5.02	5.03	5.10	5.08	5.18	5.37	5.36	5.58	5.69	5.92	5.86	5.95	5.43
2000	6.08	6.00	5.83	5.75	6.00	5.80	5.63	5.51	5.56	5.59	5.54	5.22	5.71
2001	5.10	5.18	5.13	5.27	5.29	5.20	5.20	5.03	5.09	5.05	5.04	5.25	5.15
2002	5.16	5.11	5.29	5.22	5.19	5.09	5.02	4.95	4.74	4.88	4.95	4.85	5.04
2003	4.90	4.81	4.76	4.74	4.41	4.33	4.74	5.10	4.92	4.89	4.73	4.65	4.75
2004	4.61	4.55	4.41	4.82	5.07	5.05	4.87	4.70	4.56	4.49	4.52	4.48	4.68
2005	4.41	4.35	4.57	4.46	4.31	4.23	4.31	4.32	4.29	4.48	4.57	4.46	4.40
2006	4.37	4.41	4.44	4.58	4.59	4.60	4.61	4.39	4.27	4.30	4.14		4.43

[1] 20-bond average.   *Source: Bureau of Economic Analysis, U.S. Department of Commerce (BEA)*

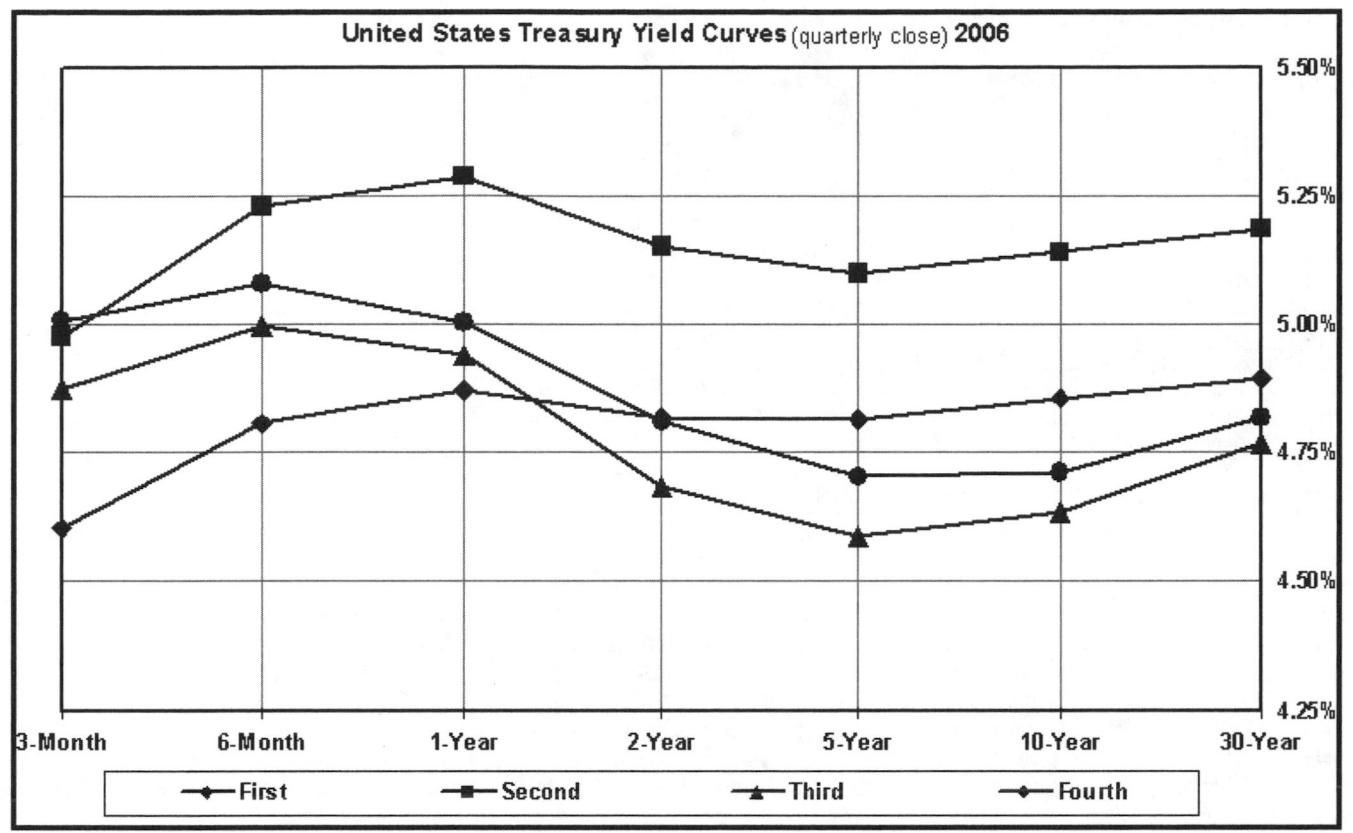

United States Treasury Yield Curves (quarterly close) 2006

U.S. Industrial Production Index[1]   1997 = 100

Year	Jan.	Feb.	Mar.	Apr.	May	June	July	Aug.	Sept.	Oct.	Nov.	Dec.	Average
1997	121.3	122.1	122.5	123.1	123.3	123.5	124.5	125.2	125.6	129.3	129.9	130.3	127.0
1998	130.3	130.2	130.7	131.3	131.9	130.6	130.5	132.4	131.9	134.1	133.8	133.8	132.4
1999	134.1	134.5	135.1	135.5	136.2	136.6	137.4	137.7	138.1	139.1	141.9	142.8	139.2
2000	143.6	144.3	145.2	146.3	147.2	147.9	147.6	148.7	148.8	146.3	145.8	145.1	145.7
2001	143.9	143.5	142.9	142.0	141.6	140.3	140.4	140.0	138.5	137.7	108.8	108.3	111.5
2002	109.0	109.2	109.6	110.1	110.4	110.8	111.6	111.3	111.2	111.0	111.2	110.6	111.0
2003	111.2	111.6	110.8	110.1	110.0	110.0	110.8	110.9	111.5	111.8	112.7	112.9	110.9
2004	113.2	114.4	114.1	114.7	115.5	115.1	115.9	116.0	105.1	105.8	106.0	106.7	104.7
2005	106.9	107.4	107.3	107.2	107.4	108.3	108.3	108.6	107.2	107.1	108.2	109.2	107.7
2006[2]	109.1	109.4	110.0	110.9	110.9	111.9	112.3	112.5	112.2	112.1	112.0		111.2

[1] Total Index of the Federal Reserve Index of Quantity Output, seasonally adjusted.   [2] Preliminary.
Source: Bureau of Economic Analysis, U.S. Department of Commerce (BEA)

U.S. Gross National Product, National Income, and Personal Income   In Billions of Constant Dollars[1]

	Gross Domestic Product					National Income					Personal Income				
Year	First Quarter	Second Quarter	Third Quarter	Fourth Quarter	Annual Average	First Quarter	Second Quarter	Third Quarter	Fourth Quarter	Annual Average	First Quarter	Second Quarter	Third Quarter	Fourth Quarter	Annual Average
1997	8,114	8,250	8,382	8,471	8,304	7,115	7,220	7,361	7,473	7,292	6,773	6,847	6,957	7,084	6,915
1998	8,587	8,658	8,790	8,954	8,747	7,573	7,688	7,823	7,927	7,753	7,247	7,376	7,486	7,583	7,423
1999	9,067	9,174	9,314	9,520	9,268	8,074	8,161	8,255	8,456	8,237	7,658	7,729	7,824	7,999	7,802
2000	9,629	9,823	9,862	9,954	9,817	8,681	8,750	8,858	8,892	8,795	8,266	8,372	8,514	8,566	8,430
2001	10,022	10,129	10,135	10,226	10,128	8,988	9,002	8,890	9,040	8,980	8,689	8,720	8,733	8,755	8,724
2002	10,333	10,427	10,527	10,591	10,470	9,131	9,212	9,248	9,327	9,229	8,815	8,892	8,895	8,926	8,882
2003	10,706	10,832	11,086	11,220	10,961	9,407	9,538	9,699	9,885	9,632	8,998	9,111	9,204	9,341	9,164
2004	11,431	11,649	11,799	11,970	11,712	10,084	10,207	10,244	10,489	10,256	9,498	9,641	9,768	10,019	9,731
2005	12,173	12,346	12,574	12,731	12,456	10,702	10,795	10,643	11,106	10,812	10,049	10,162	10,263	10,484	10,239
2006[2]	13,008	13,197	13,323	13,450	13,245	11,551	11,612	11,734		11,632	10,721	10,807	10,939	11,068	10,884

[1] Seasonally adjusted at annual rates.   [2] Preliminary.   Source: Bureau of Economic Analysis, U.S. Department of Commerce (BEA)

INTEREST RATES, U.S.

U.S. Money Supply M1[2]   In Billions of Dollars

Year	Jan.	Feb.	Mar.	Apr.	May	June	July	Aug.	Sept.	Oct.	Nov.	Dec.	Average
1997	1,080.0	1,077.5	1,071.0	1,062.6	1,062.9	1,065.1	1,065.3	1,073.8	1,066.7	1,065.1	1,069.1	1,072.2	1,069.3
1998	1,073.5	1,077.7	1,076.9	1,076.2	1,077.6	1,076.0	1,074.4	1,074.3	1,078.4	1,084.3	1,093.0	1,094.8	1,079.8
1999	1,096.3	1,096.7	1,097.3	1,101.1	1,102.2	1,098.7	1,097.9	1,097.9	1,095.6	1,101.2	1,110.3	1,122.6	1,101.5
2000	1,121.5	1,108.8	1,107.5	1,113.4	1,105.7	1,103.4	1,103.0	1,100.4	1,099.7	1,098.8	1,092.4	1,087.6	1,103.5
2001	1,096.8	1,100.8	1,108.6	1,115.2	1,119.9	1,126.7	1,139.6	1,150.4	1,205.3	1,166.3	1,171.5	1,182.1	1,140.3
2002	1,190.0	1,189.5	1,191.3	1,185.7	1,190.2	1,192.7	1,199.9	1,186.7	1,195.9	1,204.3	1,209.1	1,219.5	1,196.2
2003	1,226.2	1,237.0	1,237.2	1,248.2	1,269.7	1,281.0	1,288.5	1,295.1	1,298.1	1,297.9	1,297.4	1,305.5	1,273.5
2004	1,305.2	1,319.1	1,328.3	1,332.3	1,333.9	1,343.8	1,342.0	1,354.7	1,363.1	1,361.5	1,375.0	1,375.3	1,344.5
2005	1,365.5	1,368.9	1,371.6	1,358.0	1,367.5	1,380.9	1,368.6	1,378.5	1,379.5	1,374.9	1,375.9	1,373.2	1,371.9
2006[1]	1,378.9	1,375.2	1,383.8	1,380.1	1,387.3	1,375.6	1,371.1	1,371.5	1,363.9	1,369.1	1,370.5	1,365.7	1,374.4

[1] Preliminary.   [2] M1 -- The sum of currency held outside the vaults of depository institutions, Federal Reserve Banks, and the U.S. Treasury; travelers checks; and demand and other checkable deposits issued by financial institutions (except demand deposits due to the Treasury and depository institutions), minus cash items in process of collection and Federal Reserve float. Seasonally adjusted.
Source: Board of Governors of the Federal Reserve System

U.S. Money Supply M2[2]   In Billions of Dollars

Year	Jan.	Feb.	Mar.	Apr.	May	June	July	Aug.	Sept.	Oct.	Nov.	Dec.	Average
1997	3,828.7	3,839.5	3,854.5	3,870.8	3,883.9	3,902.0	3,921.7	3,950.6	3,970.0	3,987.8	4,008.9	4,030.0	3,920.7
1998	4,054.2	4,086.5	4,113.6	4,136.7	4,157.3	4,183.6	4,202.0	4,227.4	4,269.3	4,310.7	4,349.9	4,382.2	4,206.1
1999	4,404.0	4,431.1	4,441.4	4,472.1	4,491.5	4,512.8	4,537.1	4,558.0	4,573.7	4,592.2	4,618.1	4,647.5	4,523.3
2000	4,667.9	4,683.4	4,713.1	4,762.8	4,756.1	4,772.1	4,786.0	4,817.9	4,850.0	4,867.7	4,877.9	4,920.9	4,789.7
2001	4,976.4	5,015.9	5,076.2	5,136.6	5,136.7	5,175.9	5,208.3	5,241.9	5,350.8	5,343.6	5,383.8	5,430.3	5,206.4
2002	5,455.1	5,483.1	5,490.8	5,495.5	5,520.5	5,541.8	5,590.9	5,629.3	5,653.0	5,702.5	5,748.6	5,774.1	5,590.4
2003	5,801.9	5,842.3	5,860.4	5,902.5	5,960.1	5,998.1	6,049.4	6,098.3	6,077.1	6,065.1	6,059.7	6,062.0	5,981.4
2004	6,064.2	6,108.3	6,151.1	6,194.5	6,263.7	6,271.3	6,280.5	6,303.2	6,334.2	6,356.6	6,393.5	6,411.7	6,261.1
2005	6,415.1	6,436.9	6,457.4	6,466.2	6,481.3	6,509.1	6,532.4	6,566.7	6,599.9	6,625.0	6,644.7	6,669.4	6,533.7
2006[1]	6,713.6	6,737.0	6,755.8	6,774.9	6,785.7	6,811.1	6,835.7	6,863.4	6,886.5	6,936.2	6,977.0	7,020.8	6,841.5

[1] Preliminary.   [2] M2 -- M1 plus savings deposits (including money market deposit accounts) and small-denomination (less than $100,000) time deposits issued by financial institutions; and shares in retail money market mutual funds (funds with initial investments of less than $50,000), net of retirement accounts. Seasonally adjusted.   *Source: Board of Governors of the Federal Reserve System*

U.S. Money Supply M3[2]   In Billions of Dollars

Year	Jan.	Feb.	Mar.	Apr.	May	June	July	Aug.	Sept.	Oct.	Nov.	Dec.	Average
1997	5,013.2	5,041.7	5,080.2	5,119.8	5,147.1	5,177.4	5,235.8	5,291.4	5,332.3	5,376.3	5,417.1	5,460.5	5,224.4
1998	5,508.8	5,541.3	5,611.5	5,647.3	5,686.9	5,728.4	5,750.0	5,815.0	5,882.0	5,953.7	6,010.1	6,051.9	5,765.6
1999	6,080.7	6,129.5	6,133.6	6,172.3	6,201.0	6,237.7	6,269.0	6,299.1	6,323.0	6,378.4	6,464.1	6,551.8	6,270.0
2000	6,605.5	6,642.2	6,704.0	6,767.3	6,776.9	6,823.6	6,875.2	6,945.0	7,003.5	7,027.0	7,038.3	7,117.6	6,860.5
2001	7,237.2	7,308.5	7,372.0	7,507.8	7,564.1	7,644.7	7,691.9	7,696.3	7,853.2	7,897.8	7,973.0	8,035.4	7,648.5
2002	8,063.9	8,109.3	8,117.3	8,142.6	8,175.1	8,190.8	8,244.2	8,298.1	8,331.5	8,368.9	8,498.8	8,568.0	8,259.0
2003	8,588.1	8,628.7	8,648.8	8,686.0	8,741.9	8,791.6	8,888.7	8,918.2	8,906.5	8,896.8	8,880.3	8,872.3	8,787.3
2004	8,930.2	9,000.3	9,080.7	9,149.6	9,243.8	9,275.7	9,282.7	9,314.4	9,351.8	9,359.4	9,395.1	9,433.0	9,234.7
2005	9,487.2	9,531.6	9,565.3	9,620.9	9,665.0	9,725.3	9,762.4	9,864.6	9,950.8	10,032.0	10,078.5	10,154.0	9,786.5
2006[1]	10,242.8	10,298.7	Discontinued										10,270.8

[1] Preliminary.   [2] M3 -- M2 plus large-denomination ($100,000 or more) time deposits; repurchase agreements issued by depository institutions; Eurodollar deposits, specifically, dollar-denominated deposits due to nonbank U.S. addresses held at foreign offices of U.S. banks worldwide and all banking offices in Canada and the United Kingdom; and institutional money market mutual funds (funds with initial investments of $50,000 or more). Seasonally adjusted.   *Source: Board of Governors of the Federal Reserve System*

U.S. Money Supply MZM[2]   In Billions of Dollars

Year	Jan.	Feb.	Mar.	Apr.	May	June	July	Aug.	Sept.	Oct.	Nov.	Dec.	Average
1997	3,207.3	3,224.0	3,245.9	3,262.0	3,275.6	3,296.4	3,322.2	3,356.5	3,384.4	3,406.9	3,430.2	3,459.4	3,322.6
1998	3,490.9	3,527.7	3,564.0	3,602.9	3,638.5	3,676.9	3,704.6	3,745.6	3,804.1	3,866.9	3,925.1	3,972.3	3,710.0
1999	4,004.2	4,049.0	4,061.6	4,106.4	4,135.1	4,164.5	4,189.2	4,218.2	4,234.5	4,257.4	4,293.8	4,332.1	4,170.5
2000	4,363.5	4,372.3	4,410.0	4,456.7	4,452.1	4,467.1	4,497.7	4,538.8	4,584.3	4,606.7	4,620.5	4,673.9	4,503.6
2001	4,763.9	4,862.9	4,950.4	5,049.6	5,100.8	5,180.8	5,236.8	5,262.0	5,423.9	5,501.6	5,583.0	5,662.5	5,214.9
2002	5,698.1	5,746.2	5,765.1	5,785.6	5,816.7	5,835.7	5,885.7	5,916.3	5,928.4	5,962.1	6,087.3	6,138.0	5,880.4
2003	6,151.7	6,187.2	6,193.6	6,219.5	6,265.1	6,311.1	6,415.6	6,442.3	6,427.3	6,411.6	6,397.6	6,375.3	6,316.5
2004	6,383.8	6,427.7	6,479.6	6,528.2	6,605.3	6,607.7	6,604.1	6,614.8	6,630.1	6,632.7	6,663.2	6,666.8	6,570.3
2005	6,652.0	6,655.4	6,658.3	6,659.9	6,658.6	6,681.9	6,703.4	6,733.8	6,770.5	6,799.0	6,810.2	6,834.1	6,718.1
2006[1]	6,876.0	6,884.8	6,896.1	6,916.1	6,927.9	6,953.4	6,973.4	7,002.9	7,030.4	7,085.7	7,127.2	7,189.7	6,988.6

[1] Preliminary.   [2] MZM (money, zero maturity) -- M2 minus small-denomination time deposits, plus institutional money market mutual funds (that is, those included in M3 but excluded from M2). The label MZM was coined by William Poole (1991); the aggregate itself was proposed earlier by Motley (1988).   Seasonally adjusted.   *Source: Board of Governors of the Federal Reserve System*

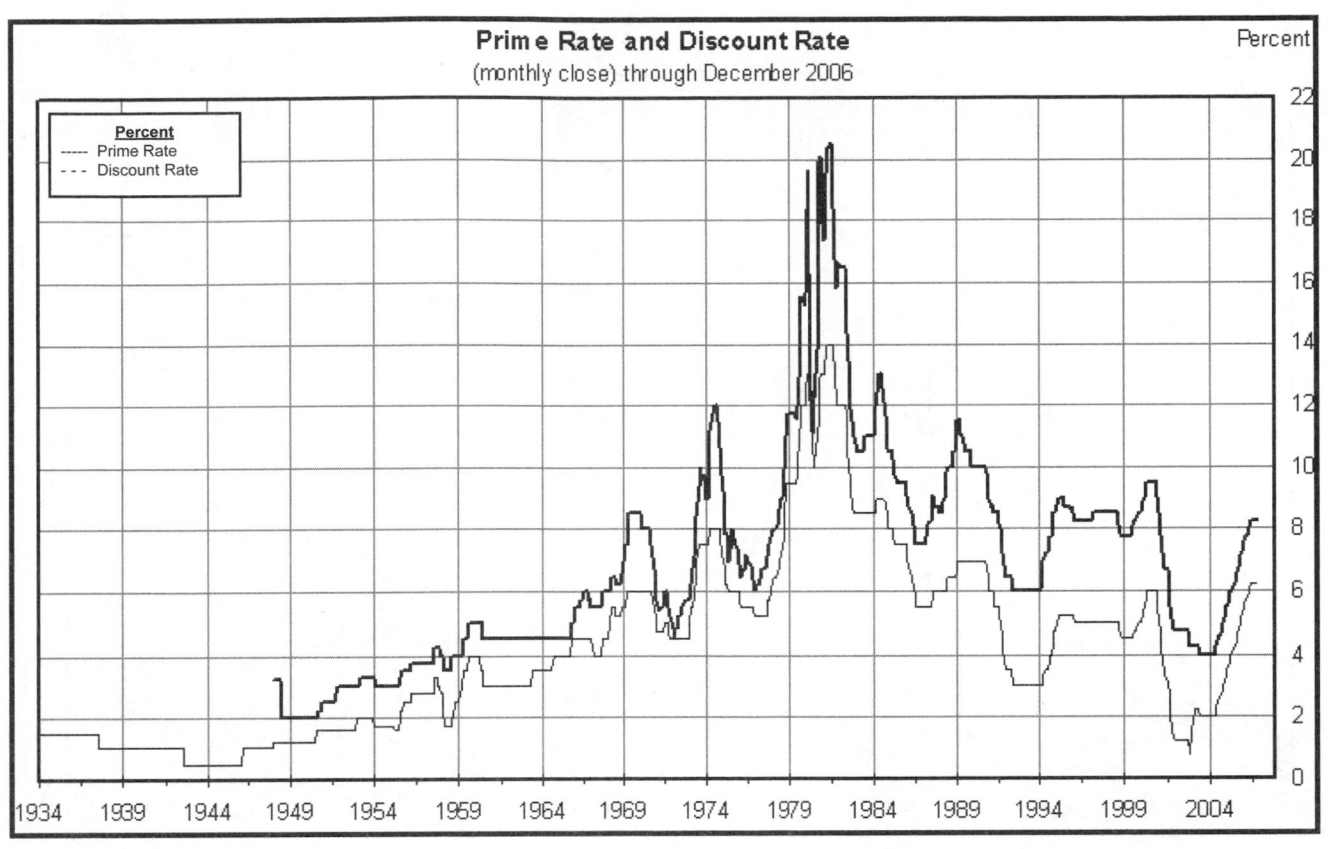

Prime Rate and Discount Rate
(monthly close) through December 2006

Percent

Percent
—— Prime Rate
- - - Discount Rate

Municipal Bonds and Corporate AAA Bond Yields
(monthly average) through December 2006

Percent

Percent
—— Municipal Bonds
- - - Corporate AAA Bonds

Key Interest Rates
(weekly close) as of December 29, 2006

Percent

Legend:
Percent
Prime Rate
30-Year Bond
Discount Rate
3-Month Treasury Bill

5-Year Treasury Note Yield
(monthly average) through December 2006

Percent

Interest Rates, Worldwide

Interest rate futures contracts are widely traded throughout the world. The most popular futures contracts are generally 10-year government bonds and the 3-month interest rate contracts. In Europe, futures on German interest rates are traded at the all-electronic Eurex Exchange in Frankfurt. Futures on UK interest rates are traded at the Liffe Exchange in London. Futures on Canadian interest rates are traded at the Montreal Exchange. Futures on Japanese interest rates are traded at the Singapore Exchange (Simex) and at the Tokyo Stock Exchange. A variety of other interest rate futures contracts are traded throughout the rest of the world (please see the front of this Yearbook for a complete list).

Euro-Zone – The Eurex 10-year Euro Bund futures contract in early 2006 fell sharply and then traded in a choppy sideways range during the remainder of the year, finally closing 2006 at 116.03, down –5.81 points from the 2005 close of 121.84. The German 10-year government bond yield in 2006 rose sharply by 115 bp early in the year from the 3.00% low posted in September 2005 to a 2-year high of 4.15% by July 2006, but then settled back to close 2006 at 3.65%. The 3-month Euribor rate in 2006 moved sharply higher from the low 2% level seen from mid-2003 through late-2005 to close 2006 at 3.72%.

European interest rates generally rose during 2006 as the European Central Bank steadily raised interest rates. The ECB raised its benchmark 2-week refinancing rate by a total of 175 basis points from the 2.00% level that prevailed in mid-2003 through late-2005 to 3.75% by March 2007. The ECB steadily tightened its monetary policy in response to its perception of significant inflation risks. The Eurozone CPI moved within the high range of 2.2-2.6% from mid-2005 through mid-2006, which was above the ECB's ceiling of 2.0%, before dropping to the 1.6-1.9% range in late 2006 in response to lower crude oil prices. The ECB in 2006 was also concerned about very strong M3 money supply growth, which rose sharply in late 2006 to as high as +9.9% by December 2006. The ECB felt that it needed to stay ahead of potential inflation risks and therefore progressively raised interest rates back to more normalized levels above 3%. The ECB in 2006 had some flexibility to raise interest rates since the Eurozone economy in 2006 performed surprisingly well. The Eurozone GDP improved from the sub-2% performance seen in 2002-05 to as high as +3.3% by December 2006. Eurozone GDP was boosted by strong export demand and improved domestic consumption. As of March 2007, the market consensus was for a further 25 bp ECB rate hike by summer 2007.

UK – The Liffe 10-year Gilt futures contract in January 2006 initially extended the 2004-05 rally to post a 3-year high but then fell sharply during the year to close at 108.13, down –6.32 points. The 10-year Gilt yield, after posting a 3-year low of 3.92% in January 2006, rose during the year to close at 4.45, up 38 basis points from 4.07% in 2005. The Gilt yield then rose sharply in early 2007 to post a 1-year high of 5.02% by February 2007. The 3-month UK Libor rate traded near 4.60% in early 2006 but then rose sharply by 95 basis points to post a 5-1/2 year high of 5.55% by early 2007. UK interest rates were driven higher in 2006 by the improving UK economy, above-target inflation, and the Bank of England's rate hikes that started in mid-2006. UK GDP improved from the 2% area in late-2005 to +3.0% by Q4-2006. The BOE raised the base rate by 75 bp from 4.50% in mid-2006 to a 5-1/2 year high of 5.25% by early 2007.

Canada – The Montreal Exchange's Canadian 10-year T-note futures contract in early 2006 fell back from the record high posted in mid-2005, but then regained some ground through the remainder of 2006 to close the year at 113.82, down –0.56 points from 2005. The 10-year Canadian bond yield in 2006 moved mildly higher from the multi-decade low of 3.72% posted in June 2005 but remained subdued in 2006 and closed the year at 3.86%, –5 bp from the 2005 close of 3.91%. The 3-month Canadian Libor rate rose by 70 bp from 2.60% in mid-2005 to 4.30% in the latter half of 2006. Canadian interest rates in 2006 rose mildly but still remained at historically low levels. The Bank of Canada raised its benchmark rate by a total of 175 basis points from 2.50% in late 2005 to 4.25% by May 2006 in response to inflation risks and generally strong GDP growth. However, the Bank of Canada stopped tightening in May 2006 and left interest rates unchanged through the remainder of the 2006 in an effort to counteract the negative impact on the Canadian economy from high crude oil prices and slower growth in the US. Canada's GDP nevertheless faded during 2006 from the +3.1% pace in 2005 to the low-2% area by the end of 2006.

Japan – The SGX 10-year JGB futures contract sold off from mid-2005 through mid-2006, but then recovered somewhat in the latter half of 2006 to close at 133.93, –4.48 points on the year. The 10-year JGB yield in early 2006 continued to move higher from the 3-year low of 1.17% posted in June 2005, but then topped out near 2% and fell back to trade in the 1.60-1.80% range through the remainder of the year. The 3-month Japanese Libor rate, after trading below 0.10% from mid-2001 through early-2006, finally climbed sharply by 60 bp to 0.70% by early 2007 after the BOJ ended its zero interest rate monetary policy and started raising interest rates. The Bank of Japan first raised its overnight benchmark rate by 25 basis points to 0.25% in July 2006, and then implemented a further 25 basis point rate hike to 0.50% in March 2007. The BOJ implemented those rate hikes as the Japanese economy entered a sustainable expansion mode and as inflation finally rose above the zero mark. Japan has been battling deflation since the late 1980s when its property and stock market bubble burst. Japan's core CPI (excluding fresh foods) rose above zero in June 2006, but only rose as far as +0.3% in August 2006 and then started fading again and was back to zero by January 2007. Japan's GDP was relatively strong during 2006 and reached a growth rate of an annualized +4.8% in Q4-2006.

Long Gilt Futures - Euronext-LIFFE
(weekly close) as of December 29, 2006

Nominal Value

9% through March 1998 contract
7% June 1998 contract to December 2003 contract
6% March 2004 contract to date

Jan-97 Jan-98 Dec-98 Dec-99 Dec-00 Dec-01 Dec-02 Dec-03 Dec-04 Dec-05 Dec-06

3-Month Sterling Futures - Euronext-LIFFE
(weekly close) as of December 29, 2006

Points of 100%

Jan-97 Jan-98 Dec-98 Dec-99 Dec-00 Dec-01 Dec-02 Dec-03 Dec-04 Dec-05 Dec-06

10-Year Japanese Government Bond Futures - Tokyo Stock Exch.
(weekly close) as December 29, 2006

Nominal Value

3-Month Euroyen Futures - TIFFE
(weekly close) as of December 29, 2006

Points of 100%

10-Year Canadian Government Bond Futures - Montreal Exch.
(weekly close) as of December 29, 2006

Nominal Value

9% through March 2000 contract
6% June 2000 contract to date

3-Month Canadian Bankers' Acceptance Futures - Montreal Exch.
(weekly close) as of December 29, 2006

Points of 100%

Australia -- Economic Statistics   Percentage Change from Previous Period

Year	Real GDP	Nominal GDP	Real Private Consump-tion	Real Public Consump-tion	Grossed Fixed Invest-ment	Real Total Domestic Demand	Real Exports of Goods & Services	Real Imports of Goods & Services	Consumer Prices[1]	Unem-ployment Rate
1999	4.4	5.0	5.0	3.2	5.9	5.2	5.2	8.8	1.5	6.9
2000	3.4	7.7	3.6	4.3	-1.3	2.0	10.8	7.5	4.5	6.3
2001	2.4	6.2	3.1	1.7	-3.5	1.0	2.3	-4.3	4.4	6.8
2002	3.9	6.9	3.9	3.0	16.6	6.2	.1	11.1	3.0	6.4
2003	3.3	6.4	3.8	3.7	7.8	5.9	-2.3	10.4	2.8	6.0
2004	3.3	6.9	5.9	3.8	7.6	5.4	4.1	15.1	2.3	5.5
2005	2.9	7.7	3.1	3.1	7.1	4.2	2.1	8.2	2.7	5.1
2006[2]	2.6	7.0	2.6	2.6	7.4	3.2	2.7	5.8	3.7	5.0
2007[3]	3.0	6.6	2.4	3.3	6.0	3.3	4.4	6.0	2.8	5.0

[1] National accounts implicit private consumption deflator.   [2] Estimate.   [3] Projection.   *Source: Organization for Economic Co-opertation and Development (OECD)*

Canada -- Economic Statistics   Percentage Change from Previous Period

Year	Real GDP	Nominal GDP	Real Private Consump-tion	Real Public Consump-tion	Grossed Fixed Invest-ment	Real Total Domestic Demand	Real Exports of Goods & Services	Real Imports of Goods & Services	Consumer Prices[1]	Unem-ployment Rate
1999	5.5	7.4	3.8	2.1	7.3	4.2	10.7	7.8	1.7	7.6
2000	5.2	9.6	4.0	3.1	4.7	4.7	8.9	8.1	2.7	6.8
2001	1.8	2.9	2.3	3.9	4.0	1.3	-3.0	-5.1	2.5	7.2
2002	2.9	4.0	3.6	2.5	1.6	3.3	1.2	1.7	2.2	7.6
2003	1.8	5.2	3.0	3.5	6.5	4.6	-2.4	4.5	2.8	7.6
2004	3.3	6.4	3.3	3.0	8.0	4.3	5.2	8.2	1.8	7.2
2005	2.9	6.2	3.9	2.7	7.1	4.8	2.1	7.1	2.2	6.8
2006[2]	2.8	4.7	3.9	3.5	6.3	4.3	1.3	5.8	2.1	6.4
2007[3]	2.7	3.9	3.4	3.3	3.4	3.5	1.7	3.7	1.5	6.6

[1] National accounts implicit private consumption deflator.   [2] Estimate.   [3] Projection.   *Source: Organization for Economic Co-opertation and Development (OECD)*

France -- Economic Statistics   Percentage Change from Previous Period

Year	Real GDP	Nominal GDP	Real Private Consump-tion	Real Public Consump-tion	Grossed Fixed Invest-ment	Real Total Domestic Demand	Real Exports of Goods & Services	Real Imports of Goods & Services	Consumer Prices[1]	Unem-ployment Rate
1999	3.0	3.0	3.3	1.4	7.9	3.5	4.0	5.8	.6	10.8
2000	4.0	5.6	3.5	2.0	7.5	4.5	12.9	15.1	1.8	9.4
2001	1.8	3.8	2.5	1.1	2.3	1.7	2.7	2.2	1.8	8.7
2002	1.1	3.5	2.4	1.9	-1.7	1.2	1.3	1.6	1.9	9.0
2003	1.1	3.0	2.2	2.0	2.3	1.9	-1.1	1.5	2.2	9.8
2004	2.0	3.8	2.5	2.2	2.6	2.8	3.3	6.0	2.3	10.0
2005	1.2	3.1	2.1	1.1	3.7	2.1	3.2	6.4	1.9	9.9
2006[2]	2.1	3.9	2.6	2.2	3.7	2.4	7.7	8.8	2.0	9.1
2007[3]	2.2	3.9	2.5	1.8	3.3	2.6	5.7	6.7	1.4	8.5

[1] National accounts implicit private consumption deflator.   [2] Estimate.   [3] Projection.   *Source: Organization for Economic Co-opertation and Development (OECD)*

Germany -- Economic Statistics   Percentage Change from Previous Period

Year	Real GDP	Nominal GDP	Real Private Consump-tion	Real Public Consump-tion	Grossed Fixed Invest-ment	Real Total Domestic Demand	Real Exports of Goods & Services	Real Imports of Goods & Services	Consumer Prices[1]	Unem-ployment Rate
1999	1.9	2.2	2.9	1.2	4.5	2.6	5.6	8.3	.6	7.5
2000	3.5	2.8	2.5	1.4	3.8	2.4	14.1	10.7	1.4	6.8
2001	1.4	2.6	1.9	.5	-3.5	-.4	6.8	1.5	1.9	6.9
2002	.0	1.4	-.8	1.5	-6.3	-2.0	4.3	-1.4	1.4	7.6
2003	-.2	.8	-.1	.4	-.7	.7	2.3	5.3	1.0	8.7
2004	.8	1.6	-.3	-1.3	-1.4	-.4	8.8	6.2	1.8	9.2
2005	1.1	1.7	.3	.6	1.0	.6	7.1	6.7	1.9	9.1
2006[2]	2.6	3.3	.8	1.2	5.8	2.0	10.4	10.0	1.7	8.0
2007[3]	1.8	3.5	.3	.4	4.3	1.2	6.2	5.3	1.9	7.7

[1] National accounts implicit private consumption deflator.   [2] Estimate.   [3] Projection.
Source: Organization for Economic Co-operation and Development (OECD)

INTEREST RATES, WORLDWIDE

Italy -- Economic Statistics   Percentage Change from Previous Period

Year	Real GDP	Nominal GDP	Real Private Consumption	Real Public Consumption	Grossed Fixed Investment	Real Total Domestic Demand	Real Exports of Goods & Services	Real Imports of Goods & Services	Consumer Prices[1]	Unemployment Rate
1999	1.9	3.2	2.6	1.3	3.5	3.1	-1.8	2.9	1.7	11.1
2000	3.8	5.9	2.4	2.3	6.7	2.9	9.6	6.4	2.6	10.2
2001	1.7	4.8	.7	3.6	2.3	1.6	.3	-.3	2.3	9.2
2002	.3	3.7	.2	2.1	4.0	1.3	-4.0	-.5	2.6	8.7
2003	.1	3.2	1.0	2.0	-1.5	.9	-2.2	1.0	2.8	8.6
2004	.9	3.8	.5	.5	1.9	.7	2.5	1.9	2.3	8.1
2005	.1	2.2	.1	1.2	-.4	.4	.7	1.8	2.2	7.8
2006[2]	1.8	3.9	1.6	.7	3.7	1.2	5.1	3.4	2.2	7.1
2007[3]	1.4	3.3	1.0	.3	3.9	1.4	3.5	3.7	1.9	6.8

[1] National accounts implicit private consumption deflator.   [2] Estimate.   [3] Projection.   *Source: Organization for Economic Co-opertation and Development (OECD)*

Japan -- Economic Statistics   Percentage Change from Previous Period

Year	Real GDP	Nominal GDP	Real Private Consumption	Real Public Consumption	Grossed Fixed Investment	Real Total Domestic Demand	Real Exports of Goods & Services	Real Imports of Goods & Services	Consumer Prices[1]	Unemployment Rate
1999	-.2	-1.5	1.1	4.1	-.7	-.1	1.5	3.7	-.3	4.7
2000	2.9	1.2	1.1	4.3	1.2	2.5	12.2	8.5	-.5	4.7
2001	.4	-.9	1.4	3.0	-.9	1.2	-6.7	.9	-.8	5.0
2002	.1	-1.4	1.1	2.4	-5.0	-.6	7.6	.9	-.9	5.4
2003	1.8	.2	.6	2.3	.3	1.2	9.0	3.9	-.3	5.3
2004	2.3	1.1	1.9	2.0	1.1	1.5	13.9	8.5	.0	4.7
2005	2.7	1.3	2.3	1.7	3.2	2.5	7.0	6.2	-.6	4.4
2006[2]	2.8	1.8	1.3	.6	4.0	2.0	10.4	5.3	.3	4.2
2007[3]	2.0	2.2	1.4	1.1	2.1	1.3	7.2	3.1	.3	3.9

[1] National accounts implicit private consumption deflator.   [2] Estimate.   [3] Projection.   *Source: Organization for Economic Co-opertation and Development (OECD)*

Switzerland -- Economic Statistics   Percentage Change from Previous Period

Year	Real GDP	Nominal GDP	Real Private Consumption	Real Public Consumption	Grossed Fixed Investment	Real Total Domestic Demand	Real Exports of Goods & Services	Real Imports of Goods & Services	Consumer Prices[1]	Unemployment Rate
1999	1.3	2.0	2.3	.3	1.2	.3	6.5	4.3	.8	2.9
2000	3.6	4.4	2.3	2.6	4.3	2.1	12.2	9.6	1.6	2.5
2001	1.0	1.7	2.0	4.2	-3.1	2.3	.2	3.2	1.0	2.5
2002	.3	1.9	.0	1.7	.3	-.5	-.7	-2.6	.6	3.1
2003	-.2	1.0	.8	2.6	-1.4	.4	-.4	1.0	.6	4.1
2004	2.3	2.9	1.5	-.8	4.5	1.5	8.4	7.4	.8	4.2
2005	1.9	1.9	1.3	-1.6	3.2	1.1	6.4	5.3	1.2	4.3
2006[2]	3.0	3.9	1.8	-1.8	5.0	2.8	8.4	8.8	1.0	3.9
2007[3]	2.2	3.2	1.8	.2	3.8	1.9	6.0	6.1	.9	3.6

[1] National accounts implicit private consumption deflator.   [2] Estimate.   [3] Projection.   *Source: Organization for Economic Co-opertation and Development (OECD)*

United Kingdom -- Economic Statistics   Percentage Change from Previous Period

Year	Real GDP	Nominal GDP	Real Private Consumption	Real Public Consumption	Grossed Fixed Investment	Real Total Domestic Demand	Real Exports of Goods & Services	Real Imports of Goods & Services	Consumer Prices[1]	Unemployment Rate
1999	3.0	5.3	4.5	3.7	2.8	4.2	3.8	7.9	1.3	6.0
2000	3.8	5.1	4.6	3.1	2.7	3.9	9.1	9.0	.8	5.5
2001	2.4	4.6	3.0	2.4	2.5	2.9	2.9	4.8	1.2	5.1
2002	2.1	5.2	3.5	3.5	3.7	3.2	1.0	4.8	1.3	5.2
2003	2.7	5.9	2.9	3.5	.4	2.7	1.7	2.0	1.4	5.0
2004	3.3	6.0	3.4	3.2	6.0	3.8	4.9	6.6	1.3	4.7
2005	1.9	4.1	1.4	2.8	2.7	1.8	7.1	6.5	2.0	4.8
2006[2]	2.6	4.9	2.1	2.0	5.4	2.7	12.8	12.1	2.2	5.5
2007[3]	2.6	5.2	2.1	1.3	6.2	2.6	5.6	5.2	2.0	5.7

[1] National accounts implicit private consumption deflator.   [2] Estimate.   [3] Projection.   *Source: Organization for Economic Co-opertation and Development (OECD)*

Iron and Steel

Iron (symbol Fe) is a soft, malleable, and ductile metallic element. Next to aluminum, iron is the most abundant of all metals. Pure iron melts at about 1535 degrees Celsius and boils at 2750 degrees Celsius. Archaeologists in Egypt discovered the earliest iron implements dating back to about 3000 BC, and iron ornaments were used even earlier.

Steel is an alloy of iron and carbon, often with an admixture of other elements. The physical properties of various types of steel and steel alloys depend primarily on the amount of carbon present and how it is distributed in the iron. Steel is marketed in a variety of sizes and shapes, such as rods, pipes, railroad rails, tees, channels, and I-beams. Steel mills roll and form heated ingots into the required shapes. The working of steel improves the quality of the steel by refining its crystalline structure and making the metal tougher. There are five classifications of steel: carbon steels, alloy steels, high-strength low-alloy steels, stainless steel, and tool steels.

Prices – In 2006 the average wholesale price for No. 1 heavy melting steel scrap in Chicago rose by +14.3% to $225.16 per metric ton. This was a new record high. The price was holding firm into 2007.

Supply – World production of iron ore in 2006 rose by +13.4% to 1.522 billion metric tons, which was a new record high. The world's largest producers of iron ore are China (with 24% of world production in 2005), Brazil (with 20%), and Australia (with 18%). The US accounted for only 4.0% of world iron ore production in 2005. World production of raw steel (ingots and castings) in 2005 rose +5.7% to 1,120 million metric tons, with the largest producers being China (with 31% of world production), Japan (with 10%), and the US (with 8%).

US production of steel ingots in 2006 rose by +5.7% to a 7-year high of 106.6 million short tons. US production of pig iron (excluding ferro-alloys) in 2006 rose by +4.4% to 41.780 million short tons from 40.036 million short tons in 2005.

Demand – US consumption of ferrous scrap and pig iron fell –2.1% yr/yr in 2005 to 103.400 million metric tons, but still above the 102.900 million metric tons in 2003, which was the lowest level since 1986. The largest consumers of ferrous scrap and pig iron were the manufacturers of pig iron and steel ingots and castings with 88% of consumption at 91.500 million metric tons in 2005. Iron foundries and miscellaneous users accounted for 10% of consumption, and manufacturers of steel castings (scrap) accounted for 2% of consumption.

Trade – The US imported 13.0 million metric tons of iron ore in 2005, up +10.2%yr/yr from 11.8 million metric tons in 2004. The bulk of US iron ore imports came from Canada (58% with 7.510 million metric tons) and Brazil (32% with 54.180 million metric tons).

World Production of Raw Steel (Ingots and Castings)   In Thousands of Metric Tons

Year	Brazil	Canada	China	France	Germany	Italy	Japan	Rep. of Korea	Russia	Ukraine	United Kingdom	United States	World Total
1996	25,237	14,735	101,237	17,633	39,793	23,910	98,801	38,903	49,253	22,332	17,992	95,535	749,992
1997	26,153	15,554	108,911	19,767	45,007	25,842	104,545	42,554	48,502	25,629	18,489	98,486	798,892
1998	25,800	15,930	115,590	20,126	44,046	25,798	93,548	39,896	43,822	23,461	17,066	98,600	770,000
1999	24,600	16,300	124,260	20,211	42,056	24,964	94,192	41,042	51,524	27,390	16,634	97,400	790,000
2000	27,865	15,900	128,500	21,002	46,376	26,544	106,444	43,107	59,098	31,780	15,022	102,000	850,000
2001	26,718	16,300	151,630	19,431	44,775	26,483	102,866	43,852	59,030	33,110	13,610	90,100	853,000
2002	29,605	16,300	182,370	20,524	44,999	25,930	107,745	45,390	59,777	34,538	11,718	91,600	906,000
2003	31,150	17,000	222,340	19,578	44,809	26,832	110,511	46,310	62,710	36,900	13,128	93,700	972,000
2004[1]	32,918	17,000	272,450	20,770	46,374	28,317	112,718	47,521	65,646	38,740	13,766	99,700	1,060,000
2005[2]	31,631	1,700	349,360	19,481	44,524	29,061	112,471	47,820	66,186	38,636	13,210	93,300	1,120,000

[1] Preliminary.   [2] Estimate.   *Source: U.S. Geological Survey (USGS)*

Average Wholesale Prices of Iron and Steel in the United States

	No. 1 Heavy Melting Steel Scrap		Hot Rolled Sheet	Sheet Bars		Pittsburg Prices					
	Pittsburg	Chicago		Hot Rolled	Cold Finished	Hot Rolled Strip	Carbon Steel Plates	Cold Rolled Strip	Galvan-ized Sheets	Railroad Steel Scrap[2]	Used Steel Cans[3]
Year	---- $ Per Gross Ton ----		---------------------------- Cents Per Pound ----------------------------							------ $ Per Gross Ton ------	
1997	133.38	139.40	18.12	----	25.65	----	32.00	----	28.62	169.00	108.13
1998	110.10	118.76	15.57	----	25.50	----	22.50	----	24.11	164.29	109.44
1999	97.86	102.49	14.74	----	23.50	----	14.00	----	21.20	150.00	68.94
2000	103.73	96.07	15.67	----	23.08	----	15.69	----	21.38	150.00	82.23
2001	79.34	74.17	11.71	----	22.76	----	12.94	----	16.41	----	68.52
2002	101.06	89.92	16.46	----	23.26	----	----	----	22.00	----	66.71
2003	128.32	113.82	14.80	----	25.15	----	----	----	20.08	----	116.21
2004	221.05	220.13	30.84	----	38.67	----	----	----	36.69	----	192.80
2005	199.10	196.75	27.83	----	44.96	----	----	----	33.77	----	172.00
2006[1]	222.39	225.21	29.78	----	44.02	----	----	----	38.09	----	212.63

[1] Preliminary.   [2] Specialties scrap.   [3] Consumer buying prices.   NA = Not available.   *Source: American Metal Market (AMM)*

IRON AND STEEL

Salient Statistics of Steel in the United States   In Thousands of Short Tons

Year	Pig Iron Production	Producer Price Index for Steel Mill Products (1982=100)	Raw Steel Production — By Type of Furnace — Basic Oxygen	Open Hearth	Electric[2]	Stainless	Carbon	Alloy	Total	Net Shipments Steel Mill Products	Total Steel Products — Exports	Imports
1997	54,679	116.4	61,053	----	47,508	2,382	95,933	10,246	108,561	105,858	7,369	34,389
1998	53,164	113.8	59,686	----	49,067	2,214	97,054	9,484	108,752	102,420	5,520	41,520
1999	51,002	105.3	57,722	----	49,673	2,086	98,694	5,421	107,395	106,201	5,426	35,731
2000	52,787	108.4	59,485	----	52,756	2,104	102,141	5,379	111,903	109,050	6,529	37,957
2001	46,424	101.3	52,204	----	47,118	1,836	92,946	4,666	99,322	99,448	6,144	30,080
2002	44,341	104.8	50,114	----	51,564	1,894	92,518	4,779	101,679	99,191	6,009	32,686
2003	43,122	109.5	50,942	----	48,751	1,952	98,772	4,901	99,693	105,625	8,220	23,125
2004	44,731	147.2	50,613	----	58,456	2,073	105,161	4,851	109,069	112,085	7,933	35,808
2005	40,036	159.7	45,231	----	57,599	1,903	96,636	4,935	102,830	103,474	9,393	32,108
2006[1]	41,781	174.3	46,802	----	61,838	2,081	101,572	4,956	108,640	108,609	9,728	45,272

[1] Preliminary.   [2] Includes crucible steels.   *Sources: American Iron & Steel Institute (AISI); U.S. Geological Survey (USGS)*

Production of Steel Ingots, Rate of Capability Utilization[1] in the United States   In Percent

Year	Jan.	Feb.	Mar.	Apr.	May	June	July	Aug.	Sept.	Oct.	Nov.	Dec.	Average
1997	85.3	89.3	89.6	89.2	87.9	87.0	85.1	86.4	91.2	86.9	89.6	86.3	89.4
1998	90.0	95.2	93.1	92.5	89.1	86.1	83.0	86.4	83.0	81.0	74.4	74.8	85.7
1999	77.2	79.5	81.7	81.8	81.7	79.7	79.4	82.8	82.3	88.2	89.1	88.5	82.7
2000	89.7	89.4	91.2	92.0	91.3	89.6	85.3	83.5	82.7	81.0	75.1	72.0	85.2
2001	77.6	82.3	81.8	82.9	81.5	81.6	79.8	80.4	80.5	77.5	73.5	65.9	78.8
2002	84.5	88.4	86.7	90.3	89.4	92.5	86.8	91.0	94.0	90.8	86.8	83.9	88.8
2003	83.1	87.3	85.0	87.8	81.1	86.2	78.9	78.3	80.7	82.8	82.8	81.9	83.0
2004	88.0	90.9	93.8	93.3	92.9	94.4	93.5	95.0	97.3	97.5	94.8	91.5	93.6
2005	90.9	92.9	88.4	89.2	84.2	79.8	77.1	81.3	86.4	89.3	88.1	85.0	86.1
2006[2]	85.6	89.5	92.8	91.4	92.5	92.1	88.7	88.7	91.2	86.2	81.5	75.0	87.9

[1] Based on tonnage capability to produce raw steel for a full order book.   [2] Preliminary.   *Sources: American Iron and Steel Institute (AISI); U.S. Geological Survey (USGS)*

Production of Steel Ingots in the United States   In Thousands of Short Tons

Year	Jan.	Feb.	Mar.	Apr.	May	June	July	Aug.	Sept.	Oct.	Nov.	Dec.	Total
1997	8,735	8,266	9,175	8,882	9,048	8,662	8,692	8,818	9,006	9,128	9,116	9,071	107,488
1998	9,510	9,087	9,839	9,524	9,483	8,863	8,832	9,194	8,548	8,681	7,710	8,013	107,643
1999	8,422	7,837	8,854	8,643	8,914	8,413	8,619	8,993	8,650	9,574	9,357	9,604	105,882
2000	9,838	9,170	10,009	9,843	10,097	9,592	9,411	9,213	8,830	8,978	8,054	7,982	111,015
2001	8,475	8,122	8,932	8,685	8,832	8,550	8,459	8,525	8,263	8,125	7,226	6,695	98,889
2002	8,050	7,609	8,261	8,214	8,401	8,414	8,510	8,918	8,916	9,015	8,340	8,329	100,976
2003	8,617	8,175	8,817	8,692	8,047	8,534	8,163	8,096	8,026	8,514	8,347	8,414	100,442
2004	8,656	8,400	9,268	8,901	9,163	9,006	9,164	9,314	9,234	9,551	8,989	8,660	108,305
2005	9,123	8,419	9,028	8,757	8,543	7,837	7,896	8,330	8,562	9,032	8,629	8,599	102,754
2006[1]	8,918	8,506	9,770	9,382	9,811	9,458	9,324	9,320	9,282	8,922	8,169	7,760	108,621

[1] Preliminary.   *Source: American Iron and Steel Institute (AISI)*

Shipments of Steel Products[1] by Market Classifications in the United States   In Thousands of Short Tons

Year	Appliances Utensils & Cutlery	Automotive	Containers, Packaging & Shipping Materials	Construction Including Maint.	Contractors Products	Electrical Equipment	Export	Machinery, Industrial Equipment & Tools	Oil and Gas	Rail Transportaion	Steel for Converting & Processing[2]	Steel Service Center & Distributors	All Other[3]	Total Shipments
1997	1,635	15,251	4,163	15,885	5	2,434	2,610	2,355	3,811	1,410	11,263	27,800	17,241	105,858
1998	1,729	15,842	3,829	15,289	5	2,255	2,556	2,147	2,649	1,657	9,975	27,751	16,741	102,420
1999	1,712	15,639	3,768	14,685	5	2,260	2,292	1,547	1,544	876	7,599	21,439	32,840	106,201
2000	1,530	14,697	3,684	14,763	5	2,039	2,752	1,513	2,268	994	7,753	22,537	35,093	109,624
2001	1,675	12,767	3,193	16,339	5	1,694	2,281	1,210	2,134	720	7,462	23,887	26,086	99,448
2002	1,734	12,562	3,251	15,729	5	1,336	1,844	1,137	1,658	751	7,201	22,828	29,160	99,191
2003	1,891	11,937	2,949	14,403	5	1,200	2,572	1,108	1,800	799	6,798	24,266	35,905	105,628
2004	1,919	12,527	2,978	15,114	5	1,139	2,426	1,332	2,043	957	7,295	25,385	38,969	112,085
2005	1,895	13,031	2,504	15,858	5	1,088	2,592	1,300	2,056	1,019	7,559	23,213	31,359	103,474
2006[4]	1,781	14,003	2,535	17,544	5	1,228	3,068	1,360	2,459	1,242	8,531	23,706	31,153	108,609

[1] All grades including carbon, alloy and stainless steel.   [2] Net total after deducting shipments to reporting companines for conversion or resale.
[3] Includes agricultural; bolts, nuts rivets & screws; forgings (other than automotive); shipbuilding & marine equipment; aircraft; mining, quarrying & lumbering; other domestic & commercial equipment machinery; ordnance & other direct military; and shipments of non-reporting companies.
[4] Preliminary.   *Source: American Iron and Steel Institute (AISI)*

Net Shipments of Steel Products[2] in the United States   In Thousands of Short Tons

Year	Cold Finished Bars	Rails & Acces- sories	Wire Drawn	Tin Mill Products	Plates (Cut & Coils)	Sheet & Strip Galv. (Hot Dipped)	Hot Rolled Bars	Pipe & Tubing	Structural Shapes & Steel Piling	Rein- forcing Bars	Hot Rolled Sheets	Cold Rolled Sheets	Carbon	Alloy	Stain- less
1997	1,809	875	619	4,057	8,855	12,439	8,153	6,548	6,029	6,188	18,221	13,322	97,509	6,282	2,067
1998	1,780	938	725	3,714	8,864	13,481	8,189	5,409	5,595	5,909	15,715	13,185	94,536	5,847	2,037
1999	1,775	646	611	3,771	8,200	14,870	8,078	4,772	5,995	6,183	17,740	13,874	98,694	5,421	2,086
2000	1,756	783	579	3,742	8,898	14,917	7,901	5,385	7,402	6,893	19,236	14,802	102,141	5,379	2,104
2001	1,369	630	481	3,202	8,349	14,310	7,032	5,377	6,789	6,976	18,866	12,352	92,314	4,789	1,837
2002	1,404	789	733	3,419	8,769	14,944	6,581	4,809	6,729	6,359	19,243	12,673	92,518	4,779	1,894
2003	1,426	739	684	3,513	9,230	15,221	6,486	4,597	7,437	7,970	22,218	13,485	98,772	4,901	1,952
2004	1,520	843	428	3,247	10,740	16,306	7,181	5,328	7,812	8,274	23,106	14,762	105,161	4,851	2,073
2005	1,495	920	560	2,874	10,274	15,249	6,674	5,096	8,070	7,464	20,569	12,793	97,884	5,183	1,903
2006[1]	1,487	1,016	603	2,880	10,827	16,358	7,595	5,426	8,652	7,419	20,862	13,281	101,572	4,956	2,081

[1] Preliminary.   [2] All grades, including carbon, alloy and stainless steel.   *Source: American Iron and Steel Institute (AISI)*

World Production of Pig Iron (Excludes Ferro-Alloys)   In Thousands of Metric Tons

Year	Belgium	Brazil	China	France	Ger- many	India	Italy	Japan	Russia	Ukraine	United Kingdom	United States	World Total
1996	8,628	23,978	107,225	12,108	30,012	19,864	10,347	74,597	36,061	18,143	12,830	49,400	549,000
1997	8,077	25,336	115,110	13,424	30,939	19,898	11,348	78,519	37,327	20,561	13,057	49,600	577,000
1998	8,730	25,111	118,600	13,603	30,162	20,194	10,704	74,981	34,827	20,840	12,574	48,200	572,000
1999	8,472	25,060	125,390	13,854	27,931	20,139	10,509	74,520	40,854	21,937	12,399	46,300	578,000
2000	8,472	27,952	131,010	13,621	30,846	21,321	11,223	81,071	44,618	25,700	10,891	47,900	616,000
2001	7,732	27,623	155,540	12,004	29,184	21,900	10,650	78,836	44,980	26,400	9,861	42,125	624,086
2002	8,053	29,667	170,850	13,217	29,427	24,315	9,736	80,979	46,060	27,560	8,579	40,217	653,256
2003	8,000	32,036	213,660	12,756	29,481	24,000	10,000	82,092	48,368	29,570	8,561	40,636	711,627
2004[1]	8,000	34,579	251,850	13,000	30,018	25,000	10,000	82,974	50,427	31,000	10,200	42,283	760,490
2005[2]	8,000	34,382	330,410	13,000	28,854	25,500	10,000	83,058	48,419	30,747	10,200	37,214	837,926

[1] Preliminary.   [2] Estimate.   *Source: U.S. Geological Survey (USGS)*

Production of Pig Iron (Excludes Ferro-Alloys) in the United States   In Thousands of Short Tons

Year	Jan.	Feb.	Mar.	Apr.	May	June	July	Aug.	Sept.	Oct.	Nov.	Dec.	Total
1997	4,489	4,243	4,713	4,440	4,690	4,452	4,420	4,443	4,605	4,662	4,717	4,861	54,680
1998	4,955	4,433	4,881	4,600	4,731	4,299	4,418	4,502	4,170	4,212	3,837	4,119	53,174
1999	4,140	3,802	4,257	4,157	4,352	4,045	4,204	4,280	4,167	4,572	4,447	4,722	51,145
2000	4,571	4,325	4,793	4,741	4,887	4,577	4,454	4,387	4,262	4,138	3,675	3,781	52,591
2001	3,808	3,691	4,255	4,183	4,278	4,143	4,048	4,121	3,920	3,837	3,202	2,965	46,451
2002	3,493	3,308	3,616	3,480	3,584	3,612	3,854	3,983	4,006	4,018	3,710	3,677	44,341
2003	3,832	3,631	3,906	3,810	3,381	3,569	3,395	3,253	3,289	3,527	3,530	3,733	42,856
2004	3,682	3,524	4,018	3,749	3,670	3,633	3,590	3,839	3,818	3,940	3,668	3,389	44,520
2005	3,773	3,592	4,030	3,397	3,395	2,962	2,895	3,183	3,127	3,237	3,310	3,135	40,036
2006[1]	3,519	3,421	3,765	3,612	3,816	3,667	3,540	3,525	3,544	3,403	3,059	2,909	41,780

[1] Preliminary.   *Source: American Iron and Steel Institute*

Salient Statistics of Ferrous Scrap and Pig Iron in the United States   In Thousands of Metric Tons

	Consumption: Ferrous Scrap & Pig Iron Charged To											Stocks -- Dec. 31		
	Mfg. of Pig Iron & Steel Ingots & Castings			Iron Foundries & Misc. Users			Mfg. of Steel	All Uses			Imports of	Exports of	Ferrous Scrap & Pig Iron at Consumers		
Year	Scrap	Pig Iron	Total	Scrap	Pig Iron	Total	Castings (Scrap)	Ferrous Scrap	Pig Iron	Grand Total	Scrap[2]	Scrap[3]	Scrap	Pig Iron	Total Stocks
1996	56,000	50,000	106,000	13,000	1,100	14,100	2,700	72,000	52,000	124,000	2,600	8,440	5,200	600	5,800
1997	58,000	51,000	109,000	13,000	1,200	14,200	1,800	73,000	52,000	125,000	2,870	8,930	5,500	510	6,010
1998	58,000	49,000	107,000	13,000	1,200	14,200	2,000	73,000	50,000	123,000	3,060	5,570	5,300	570	5,870
1999	56,000	48,000	104,000	13,000	1,100	14,100	1,900	71,000	49,000	120,000	3,360	5,000	5,450	724	6,174
2000	59,000	49,000	108,000	13,000	1,200	14,200	2,200	74,000	50,000	124,000	3,040	5,230	5,300	930	6,230
2001	57,000	47,000	104,000	12,000	1,100	13,100	2,200	71,000	48,000	119,000	2,390	6,750	4,920	787	5,707
2002	56,000	42,000	98,000	11,000	1,500	12,500	1,800	69,000	44,000	113,000	3,130	8,950	4,960	754	5,714
2003	54,800	39,700	94,500	4,460	655	5,115	2,680	61,900	41,000	102,900	3,480	10,800	4,430	381	4,811
2004	57,100	38,000	95,100	8,490	1,020	9,510	1,330	66,500	39,100	105,600	4,660	11,800	5,420	722	6,142
2005[1]	54,600	36,900	91,500	9,010	1,090	10,100	1,810	65,400	38,000	103,400	3,840	13,000	5,130	665	5,795

[1] Preliminary.   [2] Includes tinplate and terneplate.   [3] Excludes used rails for rerolling and other uses and ships, boats, and other vessels for scrapping.
Source: U.S. Geological Survey (USGS)

Steel Scrap (monthly average) through December 2006 — USD per gross ton

USD Per Ton
----- No. 1 Heavy, Chicago (Dec. 1900 - date)
- - - No. 1 Heavy, Pittsburg (Jan. 1907 - date)

Consumption of Pig Iron in the U.S., by Type of Furnace or Equipment   In Thousands of Metric Tons

Year	Open Hearth	Electric	Cupola	Basic Oxygen Process	Air & Other Furnace	Direct Casting	Total
1996	----	2,200	530	49,000	W	42	52,000
1997	----	2,400	400	50,000	W	41	52,000
1998	----	4,000	590	46,000	W	36	50,000
1999	----	3,100	520	45,000	W	36	49,000
2000	----	2,900	530	47,000	W	35	50,000
2001	----	2,700	500	45,000	W	36	48,000
2002	----	3,200	520	40,000	W	36	44,000
2003	----	2,310	792	37,900	W	36	41,000
2004[1]	----	3,030	354	35,700	W	36	39,100
2005[2]	----	3,040	528	34,400	W	36	38,000

[1] Preliminary.   [2] Estimate.   W = Withheld.   *Source: U.S. Geological Survey (USGS)*

Wholesale Price of No. 1 Heavy Melting Steel Scrap in Chicago   In Dollars Per Metric Ton

Year	Jan.	Feb.	Mar.	Apr.	May	June	July	Aug.	Sept.	Oct.	Nov.	Dec.	Average
1997	131.14	143.50	139.70	132.59	136.50	136.50	143.50	146.50	139.60	139.63	142.50	142.50	139.51
1998	144.29	140.39	135.50	133.50	135.30	135.50	131.50	120.88	107.79	85.64	78.71	76.68	118.81
1999	89.66	101.50	90.89	90.50	100.00	104.32	100.98	105.95	106.50	106.50	113.40	120.17	102.49
2000	120.50	111.10	110.50	108.15	101.50	94.59	92.50	92.50	92.50	82.59	72.80	74.20	96.07
2001	83.55	74.50	74.50	74.50	73.23	72.50	75.93	76.50	76.50	72.54	67.50	67.50	74.17
2002	70.21	75.03	75.50	85.05	93.09	97.10	97.50	97.50	100.50	98.85	93.50	93.50	89.78
2003	96.93	101.97	105.07	105.50	101.69	96.88	101.05	116.79	122.02	122.50	138.22	159.74	114.03
2004	187.75	219.92	250.85	224.55	181.90	180.00	222.50	249.32	217.38	237.62	248.00	223.57	220.28
2005	203.00	190.00	190.00	217.14	180.95	124.32	135.50	189.78	241.19	204.29	246.25	242.43	197.07
2006	222.70	237.76	237.07	245.00	249.23	249.23	245.25	204.41	207.25	202.55	197.90	203.55	225.16

Source: American Metal Market (AMM)

World Production of Iron Ore[3]   In Thousands of Metric Tons (Gross Weight)

Year	Australia	Brazil	Canada	China	India	Maur-itania	Russia	South Africa	Sweden	Ukraine	United States	Vene-zuela	World Total
1996	147,100	174,157	34,400	249,550	66,657	11,360	72,100	30,830	21,020	47,600	62,083	18,480	1,018,436
1997	157,766	184,970	37,277	268,000	69,453	11,700	70,900	33,225	21,893	53,000	62,971	18,503	1,070,000
1998	155,731	197,500	37,808	247,000	72,532	11,400	72,343	32,948	20,930	50,758	62,931	16,553	1,050,000
1999	154,268	194,000	33,900	237,000	70,220	10,400	81,311	29,508	18,558	47,769	57,749	14,051	1,016,289
2000	167,935	212,576	35,427	223,000	75,950	11,345	86,630	33,707	20,557	55,883	63,089	17,353	1,078,746
2001	181,553	201,430	27,119	220,000	79,200	10,302	82,500	34,757	19,486	54,650	46,192	16,902	1,042,657
2002	182,704	214,560	30,902	231,000	86,400	9,553	84,236	36,484	20,300	58,900	51,570	16,684	1,093,417
2003	187,219	234,470	33,322	261,000	99,100	10,100	91,760	38,086	21,500	62,498	48,554	17,954	1,187,901
2004[1]	230,955	255,000	28,256	310,000	120,600	10,600	96,980	39,333	22,300	65,550	54,724	21,600	1,341,677
2005[2]	280,000	300,000	30,000	370,000	140,000	11,000	95,000	40,000	23,000	69,000	55,000	22,000	1,522,000

[1] Preliminary.   [2] Estimate.   [3] Iron ore, iron ore concentrates and iron ore agglomerates.   Source: U.S. Geological Survey (USGS)

Salient Statistics of Iron Ore[3] in the United States   In Thousands of Metric Tons

Year	Net Import Reliance as a % of Apparent Con-sumption	Production Total	Lake Superior	Other Regions	Ship-ments	Value Million $ (at Mine)	Average Value $ at Mine Per Ton	Mines	Stocks -- Dec. 31 Con suming Plants	Lake Erie Docks	Imports	Exports	Con-sumption	Value Million $ Imports
1996	14	62,132	61,748	383	62,200	1,750.0	28.07	4,650	18,800	2,260	18,400	6,260	79,600	556.0
1997	14	63,000	62,600	327	62,800	1,860.0	29.60	4,860	20,200	2,890	18,500	6,340	79,500	551.0
1998	17	62,900	62,591	327	63,200	1,970.0	31.14	6,020	20,500	4,080	16,900	6,000	78,200	517.0
1999	17	57,700	57,410	NA	58,500	1,550.0	26.47	5,710	17,900	2,770	14,300	6,120	75,100	399.0
2000	19	63,100	62,983	NA	61,000	1,560.0	25.57	9,150	16,800	2,860	15,700	6,150	76,500	420.0
2001	15	46,200	46,100	NA	50,600	1,210.0	23.87	3,800	12,300	1,960	10,700	5,610	67,300	293.0
2002	11	51,600	51,500	NA	51,500	1,340.0	26.04	4,090	12,400	1,820	12,500	6,750	59,700	313.0
2003	11	48,600	NA	NA	46,100	1,490.0	32.30	4,910	10,900	1,630	12,600	6,770	61,600	328.0
2004[1]	8	54,700	NA	NA	54,900	2,080.0	37.92	3,930	NA	NA	11,800	8,400	64,500	371.0
2005[2]	4	55,000	NA	NA	52,100		44.00		NA	NA	13,000	11,000	62,000	

[1] Preliminary.   [2] Estimate.   [3] Usable iron ore exclusive of ore containing 5% or more manganese and includes byproduct ore.
NA = Not available.   Source: U.S. Geological Survey (USGS)

U.S. Imports (for Consumption) of Iron Ore[2]   In Thousands of Metric Tons

Year	Australia	Brazil	Canada	Chile	Maur-itania	Peru	Sweden	Vene-zuela	Total
1996	511	5,170	9,800	164	275	43	48	2,140	18,400
1997	742	4,970	10,000	228	----	252	149	2,090	18,600
1998	807	5,980	8,520	48	----	126	373	970	16,900
1999	694	5,540	6,860	69	----	63	421	327	14,300
2000	755	6,090	7,990	135	----	40	250	349	15,700
2001	576	4,260	4,530	711	----	71	70	87	10,700
2002	567	5,750	5,540	319	----	86	44	49	12,500
2003	128	4,980	6,970	296	----	77	88	21	12,600
2004	1	5,020	5,830	244	----	56	111	262	11,800
2005[1]	[3]	4,180	7,510	270	----	33	133	148	13,000

[1] Preliminary.   [2] Including agglomerates.   [3] Less than 1/2 unit.   Source: U.S. Geological Survey (USGS)

Iron Ore Stocks[2] in the United States, at End of Month   In Thousands of Metric Tons

Year	Jan.	Feb.	Mar.	Apr.	May	June	July	Aug.	Sept.	Oct.	Nov.	Dec.
1997	25,913	25,262	24,745	24,812	25,001	25,620	26,076	26,971	27,562	28,029	28,053	27,912
1998	27,977	26,317	24,039	25,251	25,576	26,197	27,605	29,037	30,301	30,095	30,199	30,624
1999	29,631	28,463	28,614	28,292	29,151	29,021	28,857	27,840	26,506	25,528	25,290	26,371
2000	24,885	24,810	23,556	23,714	24,032	24,613	24,993	26,278	26,815	27,530	27,987	28,779
2001	27,583	26,076	24,570	23,800	23,600	21,664	21,010	20,440	20,050	19,660	18,690	18,000
2002	16,980	15,970	14,660	14,920	15,680	16,090	16,120	16,080	15,520	15,790	16,740	17,410
2003	17,640	19,790	21,100	18,560	17,690	17,880	17,950	18,360	17,220	17,140	17,440	16,460
2004	4,220	7,260	8,780	8,360	7,660	7,080	5,670	4,500	3,470	3,850	3,700	2,990
2005	4,060	6,770	8,410	7,690	7,730	7,370	7,420	7,240	6,550	5,840	6,250	5,740
2006[1]	6,750	9,620	11,900	11,100	10,800	10,100	9,350	8,760	8,190	8,120		

[1] Preliminary.   [2] Through August 1997 includes mines, plants and loading docks plus furnace yards and receiving/transfer docks; Beginning September 1997 includes mines, plants and loading docks.   Source: U.S. Geological Survey (USGS)

Lard

Lard is the layer of fat found along the back and underneath the skin of a hog. The hog's fat is purified by washing it with water, melting it under constant heat, and straining it several times. Lard is an important byproduct of the meatpacking industry. It is valued highly as cooking oil because there is very little smoke when it is heated. However, demand for lard in cooking is declining because of the trend toward healthier eating. Lard is also used for medicinal purposes such as ointments, plasters, liniments, and occasionally as a laxative for children. Lard production is directly proportional to commercial hog production, meaning the largest producers of hogs are the largest producers of lard.

Prices – The average monthly wholesale price of lard in 2006 rose by 0.2% to 21.17 cents per pound, but remained well below the 2004 22-year high of 26.35 cents per pound. The record price of 29.654 cents was seen in 1975.

Supply - World production of lard in the 2005-06 marketing year rose by +3.0% yr/yr to 7.720 million metric tons, which was a new record high. The world's largest lard producers are China (with 45% of world production), United States (7%), Germany (6%), Brazil (5%), former USSR (4%), Spain (4%), and Poland (3%). US production of lard in 2005-06 rose 7.9% yr/yr to 1.206 billion pounds.

Demand – US consumption of lard in 2005 fell –4.7% to 222.222 million pounds which is a new record low. The current level of consumption is only about 14% of the consumption seen in 1971 of 1.574 billion pounds. The decrease is probably due to concerns about healthy eating.

Exports – US exports of lard in 2005-06 fell sharply by –67.5% to 94.0 million pounds, and accounted for only 8% of US production.

World Production of Lard   In Thousands of Metric Tons

Year	Brazil	Canada	China	France	Germany	Italy	Japan	Poland	Romania	Spain	United States	Former USSR	World Total
1997-98	214.3	91.5	2,624.8	162.3	413.4	194.0	67.9	266.4	96.9	238.5	478.9	339.7	6,406.1
1998-99	234.3	99.7	2,665.5	167.4	444.5	201.3	66.4	270.1	92.9	258.1	501.7	336.6	3,593.0
1999-00	325.7	107.5	2,771.4	164.7	423.5	200.9	65.1	254.7	81.1	262.0	491.6	328.4	6,750.9
2000-01	336.8	112.6	2,832.1	155.7	415.2	195.9	62.3	239.5	72.7	264.9	488.6	314.8	6,748.6
2001-02	361.4	112.1	2,920.9	157.4	422.3	199.3	61.8	252.0	76.9	263.9	508.1	324.6	6,960.8
2002-03	350.2	124.2	3,040.4	156.2	433.7	204.8	59.3	272.5	79.2	280.9	510.0	345.1	7,181.1
2003-04[1]	343.2	128.4	3,154.3	155.5	439.5	208.3	59.3	257.7	81.9	273.4	531.7	340.0	7,320.3
2004-05[2]	349.5	130.6	3,303.2	153.4	456.9	199.2	59.4	243.8	83.6	278.1	532.4	330.8	7,495.6
2005-06[3]	358.9	132.3	3,448.4	153.4	461.7	194.6	60.2	252.8	85.3	281.6	546.8	341.3	7,719.6

[1] Preliminary.   [2] Estimate.   [3] Forecast.   *Source: The Oil World*

Supply and Distribution of Lard in the United States   In Millions of Pounds

Year	---------- Supply ---------- Pro- duction	Stocks Oct. 1	Total Supply	Domestic	Baking & Frying Fats	Mar garine[3]	Exports	Total Disap- pearance	Direct Use	Per Capita (Lbs.)
1997-98	1,064.7	19.9	1,086.7	924.6	285.0	17.0	121.8	1,046.4	623.3	3.4
1998-99	1,106.1	40.4	1,148.4	987.6	250.0	26.0	139.9	1,127.5	654.0	3.6
1999-00	1,091.0	20.8	1,097.8	917.8	234.0	14.0	155.0	1,072.8	675.0	3.5
2000-01	1,058.0	27.0	1,087.0	897.0	W	12.0	174.0	1,071.0	561.0	2.0
2001-02	1,058.0	16.0	1,077.0	960.0	W	7.0	103.0	1,064.0	659.0	2.3
2002-03	1,083.0	14.0	1,105.0	1,010.0	W	16.0	84.0	1,094.0	709.0	2.5
2003-04	1,090.0	11.0	1,108.0	977.0	W	16.0	117.0	1,094.0	708.0	2.4
2004-05[1]	1,117.0	13.0	1,136.0	834.0	W	6.0	289.0	1,122.0	566.0	1.9
2005-06[2]	1,205.5	14.0	1,219.5		W	3.0	94.0		462.0	1.6

[1] Preliminary.   [2] Forecast.   [3] Includes edible tallow.   NA = not avaliable.   *Source: Economic Research Service, U.S. Department of Agriculture (ERS-USDA)*

Consumption of Lard (Edible and Inedible) in the United States   In Millions of Pounds

Year	Jan.	Feb.	Mar.	Apr.	May	June	July	Aug.	Sept.	Oct.	Nov.	Dec.	Total
1998	34.1	29.9	31.1	29.6	28.5	35.9	33.0	33.0	37.1	37.7	38.9	33.9	402.7
1999	34.6	30.2	28.8	31.1	30.5	32.9	28.9	33.0	29.2	31.2	31.3	30.3	372.1
2000	27.3	25.7	29.1	23.3	30.3	27.6	24.4	31.3	31.1	32.6	29.6	31.7	343.9
2001	27.8	22.2	28.3	24.5	22.5	23.3	21.8	27.1	23.2	27.9	26.7	24.4	299.8
2002	26.4	26.1	21.8	26.7	24.8	21.2	22.9	26.4	23.6	26.4	28.1	28.7	303.2
2003	22.6	22.3	23.4	21.4	23.3	24.0	23.0	21.4	22.5	24.3	20.2	21.0	269.5
2004	22.9	25.8	25.9	23.9	23.5	22.0	19.1	19.7	21.3	22.4	21.9	19.9	268.1
2005	19.0	15.4	21.4	18.7	19.9	20.4	18.9	19.5	20.1	19.7	22.2	17.9	233.1
2006[1]	15.7	16.4	20.6	21.4	20.2	16.7	14.9	17.7	17.8	18.9	22.3	19.7	222.2

[1] Preliminary.   *Source: Bureau of the Census, U.S. Department of Commerce*

Lard (monthly average) through December 2006 — Cents per pound

Average Wholesale Price of Lard, Loose, Tank Cars, in Chicago In Cents Per Pound

Year	Jan.	Feb.	Mar.	Apr.	May	June	July	Aug.	Sept.	Oct.	Nov.	Dec.	Average
1997	24.93	25.47	24.69	20.82	20.94	22.68	23.83	23.95	23.14	23.41	23.97	22.85	23.39
1998	19.09	16.03	17.36	17.64	18.66	19.38	17.93	18.65	16.58	17.39	17.60	16.27	17.72
1999	16.89	13.91	11.98	13.12	13.43	12.98	11.87	13.89	17.44	20.55	17.74	16.12	14.99
2000	15.66	12.38	11.99	11.96	12.68	12.64	10.32	10.35	11.14	13.04	12.06	12.14	12.20
2001	13.57	11.92	11.07	12.09	11.84	13.38	18.05	24.11	22.00	13.04	13.18	14.92	14.93
2002	12.69	12.50	13.07	12.42	11.38	14.64	14.60	15.00	15.21	14.39	16.28	18.42	14.22
2003	18.61	17.11	16.85	16.72	17.29	18.90	18.93	20.08	23.98	27.50	26.40	25.18	20.63
2004	26.50	25.83	23.77	22.58	21.31	22.50	27.53	32.06	32.38	27.95	27.26	26.50	26.35
2005	22.10	18.30	17.71	20.72	22.95	21.30	18.08	17.75	20.97	27.38	27.76	18.60	21.14
2006	17.16	16.44	16.82	18.00	17.13	17.63	22.21	29.91	31.86	23.55	20.78	22.58	21.17

Source: Economic Research Service, U.S. Department of Agriculture (ERS-USDA)

United States Cold Storage Holdings of all Lard[1], on First of Month In Millions of Pounds

Year	Jan.	Feb.	Mar.	Apr.	May	June	July	Aug.	Sept.	Oct.	Nov.	Dec.
1997	18.9	16.3	18.5	19.2	18.9	18.7	23.0	23.2	21.5	19.9	21.3	19.7
1998	22.2	30.1	38.3	42.5	41.6	47.6	43.7	44.8	38.8	40.4	34.8	26.3
1999	28.4	30.4	30.6	34.0	27.1	39.9	30.7	25.5	29.4	20.8	19.1	22.8
2000	26.7	27.8	29.2	30.1	20.2	22.5	18.9	19.3	17.3	17.4	16.3	16.8
2001	16.0	14.9	14.9	17.9	13.7	13.1	10.3	12.4	11.8	13.6	13.0	11.7
2002	13.2	18.0	16.4	16.5	20.3	22.4	18.9	18.3	12.0	10.5	14.6	11.3
2003	10.5	14.0	19.6	18.7	16.5	13.5	11.9	9.7	8.4	9.3	10.1	12.4
2004	13.3	19.8	18.6	20.3	20.5	15.0	12.9	10.8	10.3	11.8	11.4	13.2
2005	13.7	14.6	20.6	19.0	17.8	12.3	12.0	12.3	12.5	13.0	12.2	14.7
2006[2]	9.6	11.5	13.7	13.6	9.3	9.9	13.0	12.4	13.0	11.5	16.1	16.0

[1] Stocks in factories and warehouses (except that in hands of retailers). [2] Preliminary. *Source: Bureau of the Census, U.S. Department of Commerce*

Lead

Lead (symbol Pb) is a dense, toxic, bluish-gray metallic element, and is the heaviest stable element. Lead was one of the first known metals. The ancients used lead in face powders, rouges, mascaras, paints, condiments, wine preservatives, and water supply plumbing. The Romans were slowly poisoned from lead because of its diverse daily usage.

Lead is usually found in ore with zinc, silver, and most often copper. The most common lead ore is galena, containing 86.6% lead. Cerussite and angleside are other common varieties of lead. More than half of the lead currently used comes from recycling.

Lead is used in building construction, bullets and shot, tank and pipe lining, storage batteries, and electric cable sheathing. Lead is used extensively as a protective shielding for radioactive material (e.g., X-ray apparatus) because of its high density and nuclear properties. Lead is also part of solder, pewter, and fusible alloys.

Lead futures and options trade at the London Metal Exchange (LME). The LME lead futures contract calls for the delivery of 25 metric tons of at least 99.970% purity lead ingots (pigs). The contract is priced in US dollars per metric ton. Lead first started trading on the LME in 1903.

Prices – During the first quarter of 2006 lead prices held steady at about $1,200 per metric ton, but then fell to about $900 per metric ton by the end of the quarter. From there the price rallied the rest of the year to reach a high of about $1,900 to $2,000 per metric ton by December 2006. In early 2007 the prices fell to about $1,800 per metric ton.

Supply – World smelter production of lead (both primary and secondary) in 2004 (the latest data available)

rose +2.5% yr/yr to 6.950 million metric tons and posted a new record high production level. The world's largest smelter producers of lead (both primary and secondary) are China with 28% of world production in 2005, followed by the US with 18%, Germany with 5%, and the UK with 4%.

US mine production of recoverable lead fell –4.2% yr/yr to 430,000 metric tons in 2004, to post an 8-year low. Missouri was responsible for 95% of US production, with the remainder produced mainly by Idaho and Montana. Lead recovered from scrap in the US (secondary production) rose +4.2% yr/yr in 2006 (through November, annualized) to 1.159 million metric tons, to post a new record high. The amount of lead recovered from scrap is more than twice the amount of lead produced in the US from mines (primary production). The value of US refined lead production in 2004 (latest data available) fell to $143 million, which was a record low, down considerably from the record high of $668 million posted back in 1979.

Demand – US lead consumption in 2006 (through November, annualized) rose + 3.1% to 1.526 million metric tons, continuing to recover from the 9-year low of 1.417 million metric tons seen in 2004. The record level of US lead consumption was 1.680 million metric tons posted in 1999.

Trade – The US relied on imports for 11% of its lead consumption in 2003 (latest data available). US imports of lead pigs and bars in 2004 rose +12.6% yr/yr to 197,000 metric tons. US lead exports in 2004 were comprised by ore concentrate (292,000 metric tons), unwrought lead (58,600 metric tons), scrap (56,300 metric tons), and wrought lead (23,800 metric tons).

World Smelter (Primary and Secondary) Production of Lead   In Thousands of Metric Tons

Year	Australia[3]	Belgium[4]	Canada[3]	China[2]	France	Germany	Italy	Japan	Mexico[3]	Spain	United Kingdom[3]	United States	World Total
1996	228.0	125.0	309.4	706.0	302.8	238.1	209.8	287.4	160.0	86.0	345.6	1,400	5,630
1997	238.0	110.8	271.4	707.0	302.3	329.2	211.6	296.8	178.0	74.9	391.0	1,450	5,880
1998	206.0	91.5	265.5	757.0	318.0	380.2	199.3	302.1	173.0	90.0	348.9	1,450	5,970
1999	272.8	103.2	266.4	918.0	279.0	373.6	215.3	293.4	221.1	96.0	348.1	1,460	6,280
2000	251.8	118.0	284.8	1,100.0	258.0	414.5	235.0	311.7	253.2	120.0	337.2	1,470	6,650
2001	303.0	96.0	230.9	1,200.0	238.0	373.4	203.0	302.4	253.5	98.0	366.0	1,390	6,600
2002	302.0	88.0	251.6	1,330.0	204.0	379.9	205.0	285.8	237.2	116.0	370.0	1,380	6,780
2003	307.0	65.0	223.4	1,580.0	94.0	354.6	214.0	295.3	247.5	102.0	320.0	1,380	6,780
2004[1]	273.0	63.0	241.4	1,930.0	104.0	359.2	210.0	282.9	247.1	105.0	243.0	1,260	6,950
2005[2]	268.0	83.0	244.0	2,390.0	105.0	359.0	206.0	274.6	260.0	106.0	240.0	1,280	7,470

[1] Preliminary.   [2] Estimate.   [3] Refinded & bullion.   [4] Includes scrap.   *Source: U.S. Geological Survey (USGS)*

Consumption of Lead in the United States, by Products   In Metric Tons

Year	Ammunition	Bearing Metals	Pipes, Traps & Bends[2]	Cable Covering	Calking Lead	Casting Metals	Other Metal Products[3]	Total Other Oxides[4]	Sheet Lead	Storage Battery — Solder	Storage Battery — Grids, Post, etc.	Storage Battery — Oxides	Brass and Bronze	Total Consumption
1996	52,100	4,350	1,810	W	767	18,900	5,220	62,100	19,400	9,020	635,000	706,000	5,460	1,540,000
1997	52,400	2,490	1,860	4,930	1,390	34,000	7,570	67,000	19,100	9,580	634,000	761,000	4,410	1,620,000
1998	52,800	2,210	3,130	4,630	1,350	32,600	8,160	53,400	15,500	10,900	685,000	742,000	3,460	1,630,000
1999	58,300	1,570	2,020	2,410	971	34,300	7,130	58,200	15,400	13,100	765,000	707,000	3,940	1,680,000
2000	63,700	1,490	2,010	W	1,140	35,100	25,800	52,400	23,800	11,500	796,000	690,000	3,670	1,720,000
2001	53,600	837	2,370	W	927	31,800	17,100	43,900	22,400	6,120	655,000	694,000	2,590	1,550,000
2002	57,600	406	2,250	W	1,060	34,800	24,200	51,900	25,600	6,450	554,000	641,000	2,730	1,440,000
2003	48,800	13,500	1,550	W	822	31,700	9,730	35,600	24,400	6,310	523,000	642,000	2,810	1,390,000
2004	61,500	1,300	W	W	W	17,900	W	25,700	31,600	7,440	657,000	630,000	2,390	1,480,000
2005[1]	61,300	1,180	1,220	W	W	19,500	500	14,100	29,000	8,370	581,000	705,000	2,100	1,460,000

[1] Preliminary.   [2] Including building.   [3] Including terne metal, type metal, and lead consumerd in foil, collapsible tubes, annealing, plating, galvanizing and fishing weights.   [4] Includes paints, glass and ceramic products, and other pigments and chemicals.   W = Withheld proprietary data.

Source: U.S. Geological Survey (USGS)

Salient Statistics of Lead in the United States   In Thousands of Metric Tons

Year	Net Import Reliance as a % of Apparent Consumption	Production — of Refined Lead From — Domestic Ores[3]	Production — of Refined Lead From — Foreign Ores[3]	Production — of Refined Lead From — Total Primary	Total Value of Refined Million $	Secondary Lead Recovered — As Soft Lead	Secondary Lead Recovered — In Antimonial Lead	Secondary Lead Recovered — In Other Alloys	Total	Total Value of Secondary Million $	Stocks, Dec. 31 - Primary	Stocks, Dec. 31 - Consumer[4]	Average Price - Cents Per Pound - New York	Average Price - Cents Per Pound - London[5]
1996	17	326.0	W	326.0	351.0	625.0	420.0	9.2	1,070.0	1,150.0	8.1	72.1	48.83	31.22
1997	14	343.0	W	343.0	352.0	663.0	411.0	14.2	1,110.0	1,130.0	11.9	89.1	46.54	28.29
1998	21	337.0	W	337.0	336.0	667.0	417.0	16.1	1,120.0	1,110.0	10.9	77.9	45.27	23.96
1999	20	350.0	W	350.0	337.0	635.0	444.0	18.1	1,110.0	1,070.0	12.3	78.7	43.72	22.78
2000	24	341.0	W	341.0	328.0	651.0	428.0	36.8	1,130.0	1,090.0	18.6	106.0	43.57	20.57
2001	20	290.0	W	290.0	279.0	734.0	291.0	75.9	1,100.0	1,060.0	W	100.0	43.64	21.58
2002	18	262.0	W	262.0	252.0	754.0	289.0	72.8	1,120.0	1,070.0	W	111.0	43.56	20.52
2003	11	245.0	W	245.0	236.0	829.0	303.0	4.2	1,140.0	1,110.0	W	84.6	43.76	23.34
2004[1]	0	148.0	W	148.0	143.0	841.0	283.0	3.0	1,130.0	1,370.0	W	59.0	55.14	40.19
2005[2]	0	143.0	W	143.0		869.0	271.0	4.5	1,140.0	1,540.0	W	64.7	61.03	44.23

[1] Preliminary.   [2] Estimate.   [3] And base bullion.   [4] Also at secondary smelters.   [5] LME data in dollars per metric ton beginning July 1993.
W = Withheld Proprietary data.   E = Net exporter.   Source: U.S. Geological Survey (USGS)

United States Foreign Trade of Lead   In Thousands of Metric Tons

Year	Exports — Ore Concentrate	Exports — Unwrought Lead[3]	Exports — Wrought Lead[4]	Exports — Scrap	Exports — Ash & Residues	Imports for Consumption — Ores, Flue Dust or Fume & Mattes	Imports for Consumption — Base Bullion	Imports for Consumption — Pigs & Bars	Imports for Consumption — Reclaimed Scrap, etc.	Imports for Consumption — Value Million $	General Imports From: Ore, Flue Dust & Matte — Australia	General Imports From: Ore, Flue Dust & Matte — Canada	General Imports From: Ore, Flue Dust & Matte — Peru	General Imports From: Pigs & Bars — Canada	General Imports From: Pigs & Bars — Mexico	General Imports From: Pigs & Bars — Peru
1996	59.7	44.0	16.7	85.3	19.4	6.6	0.0	268.0	0.2	217.0	----	4.4	----	192.0	56.9	17.1
1997	42.2	37.4	15.9	88.4	16.8	17.8	0.0	265.0	0.1	200.3	----	0.8	3.4	186.0	70.4	6.4
1998	72.4	24.1	15.4	99.2	9.0	32.7	0.5	267.0	[6]	191.9	2.4	6.5	18.5	181.0	63.6	11.4
1999	93.5	23.4	13.9	117.0	1.4	12.3	0.1	311.0	----	196.5	0.1	1.2	8.8	198.0	27.2	6.9
2000	117.0	21.4	27.2	71.6	11.3	31.2	0.1	356.0	0.0	217.1	----	[6]	10.8	216.0	18.4	1.8
2001	181.0	17.0	17.7	108.0	14.2	2.2	----	271.0	10.2	166.8	----	----	----	167.0	12.4	2.3
2002	241.0	31.4	11.7	106.0	----	0.0	----	210.0	2.6	124.9	----	----	----	172.0	7.5	----
2003	253.0	92.1	30.5	92.8	----	----	----	175.0	4.2	111.9	----	----	----	167.0	8.3	----
2004[1]	292.0	58.6	23.8	56.3	----	----	----	197.0	4.8	235.3	----	----	----	166.0	8.8	7.3
2005[2]	390.0	45.5	19.0	67.3	----	----	----	298.0	3.3	334.8	----	----	----	190.0	15.2	23.9

[1] Preliminary.   [2] Estimate.   [3] And lead alloys.   [4] Blocks, pigs, etc.   [6] Less than 1/2 unit.   Source: U.S. Geological Survey (USGS)

Annual Mine Production of Recoverable Lead in the United States   In Metric Tons

Year	Total	Idaho	Missouri	Montana	Other States	Missouri's % of Total
1996	426,000	W	397,000	7,970	21,200	93%
1997	448,000	W	412,000	9,230	26,600	92%
1998	481,000	W	439,000	7,310	35,100	91%
1999	503,000	W	464,000	7,950	31,200	92%
2000	449,000	W	410,000	W	38,700	91%
2001	454,000	W	423,000	W	30,900	93%
2002	440,000	W	428,000	W	12,300	97%
2003	449,000	W	432,000	W	17,200	96%
2004[1]	430,000	W	407,000	W	23,400	95%
2005[2]	426,000	W	397,000	W	29,500	93%

[1] Preliminary.   [2] Estimate.   W = Withheld, included in Other States.   NA = Not Avaliable.   Source: U.S. Geological Survey (USGS)

Mine Production of Recoverable Lead in the United States   In Thousands of Metric Tons

Year	Jan.	Feb.	Mar.	Apr.	May	June	July	Aug.	Sept.	Oct.	Nov.	Dec.	Total
1997	36.7	36.7	37.2	38.6	38.6	35.1	33.4	33.7	34.4	35.4	31.7	32.8	448.0
1998	37.4	35.4	37.8	37.3	35.7	34.7	34.3	35.6	36.1	40.3	37.8	39.2	449.0
1999	41.2	42.1	44.4	43.1	41.7	42.6	47.2	43.6	41.5	41.2	37.8	38.1	505.0
2000	35.1	36.7	43.0	37.5	37.4	37.8	33.0	36.8	36.8	32.4	38.8	36.9	447.0
2001	42.9	37.8	39.4	33.7	35.0	32.2	38.2	39.6	32.4	39.5	32.1	35.4	450.0
2002	39.5	35.5	41.2	36.1	39.3	36.1	35.0	39.6	33.2	34.8	34.1	34.2	438.6
2003	33.7	34.9	38.5	36.2	38.8	39.2	41.3	38.0	38.3	37.2	34.0	33.9	444.0
2004	33.4	32.8	33.5	35.1	31.2	33.1	33.8	36.9	36.9	36.2	35.0	31.8	409.7
2005	31.1	31.1	34.6	35.2	33.4	41.4	39.5	37.4	38.2	37.9	34.6	37.9	432.3
2006[1]	36.7	33.3	38.1	33.6	33.4	33.9	36.6	36.3	37.0	38.0	35.0		427.5

[1] Preliminary.   Source: U.S. Geological Survey (USGS)

LEAD

Lead (monthly average) through December 2006   Cents per pound

Cents Per Pound
----- Pig, New York (Jan. 1910 - date)
- - - Scrap, Smelters' Heavy, Soft, New York (Dec. 1985 - date)

Average Price of Pig Lead, U.S. Primary Producers (Common Corroding)[1] In Cents Per Pound

Year	Jan.	Feb.	Mar.	Apr.	May	June	July	Aug.	Sept.	Oct.	Nov.	Dec.	Average
1997	50.00	50.00	48.70	48.00	48.00	48.00	48.00	48.00	48.00	48.00	48.00	48.00	48.39
1998	48.00	48.00	48.00	48.00	48.00	48.00	48.00	48.00	48.00	48.00	45.47	45.00	47.54
1999	45.00	45.00	45.00	45.00	45.00	45.00	45.00	45.00	45.00	45.00	45.00	45.00	45.00
2000	45.00	45.00	45.00	45.00	45.00	45.00	45.00	45.00	45.00	45.00	45.00	45.00	45.00
2001	45.00	45.00	45.00	45.00	45.00	45.00	45.00	45.00	45.00	45.00	45.00	45.00	45.00
2002	45.00	45.00	45.00	45.00	45.00	45.00	45.00	45.00	45.00	45.00	45.00	45.00	45.00
2003	23.14	24.65	23.81	23.13	24.56	24.77	26.93	26.05	27.23	30.16	32.09	35.46	26.83
2004	38.48	44.79	45.30	39.93	42.44	45.16	48.20	47.46	48.08	48.01	49.54	49.75	45.60
2005	50.46	52.20	54.00	53.25	53.41	53.26	47.22	47.53	49.76	54.01	54.68	59.63	52.45
2006	66.16	67.16	63.28	61.58	61.16	51.92	56.07	61.48	69.24	77.64	82.09	86.22	67.00

[1] New York Delivery.   Source: American Metal Market (AMM)

Refiners Production[1] of Lead in the United States In Metric Tons

Year	Jan.	Feb.	Mar.	Apr.	May	June	July	Aug.	Sept.	Oct.	Nov.	Dec.	Total
1997	28,800	28,500	31,900	30,400	30,800	28,700	25,900	28,000	21,600	30,500	29,000	28,700	343,000
1998	29,200	25,900	30,000	29,700	29,500	20,300	28,900	NA	NA	NA	NA	NA	337,000
1999	NA	NA	NA	NA	NA	NA	NA	NA	NA	NA	NA	NA	350,000
2000	NA	NA	NA	NA	NA	NA	NA	NA	NA	NA	NA	NA	341,000
2001	NA	NA	NA	NA	NA	NA	NA	NA	NA	NA	NA	NA	290,000
2002	NA	NA	NA	NA	NA	NA	NA	NA	NA	NA	NA	NA	262,000
2003	NA	NA	NA	NA	NA	NA	NA	NA	NA	NA	NA	NA	245,000
2004	NA	NA	NA	NA	NA	NA	NA	NA	NA	NA	NA	NA	NA
2005	NA	NA	NA	NA	NA	NA	NA	NA	NA	NA	NA	NA	NA
2006[2]	NA	NA	NA	NA	NA	NA	NA	NA	NA	NA	NA		

[1] Represents refined lead produced from domestic ores by primary smelters plus small amounts of secondary material passing through these smelters. Includes GSA metal purchased for remelt.   [2] Preliminary.   *Source: U.S. Geological Survey (USGS)*

Total Stocks of Lead[1] in the United States at Refiners, at End of Month   In Metric Tons

Year	Jan.	Feb.	Mar.	Apr.	May	June	July	Aug.	Sept.	Oct.	Nov.	Dec.
1997	8,460	11,800	21,400	19,900	15,000	10,900	6,530	7,790	5,370	7,310	8,710	11,900
1998	13,000	15,900	18,700	20,900	11,400	11,400	13,700	NA	NA	NA	NA	10,900
1999	NA	NA	NA	NA	NA	NA	NA	NA	NA	NA	NA	12,300
2000	NA	NA	NA	NA	NA	NA	NA	NA	NA	NA	NA	18,600
2001	NA	NA	NA	NA	NA	NA	NA	NA	NA	NA	NA	NA
2002	NA	NA	NA	NA	NA	NA	NA	NA	NA	NA	NA	NA
2003	NA	NA	NA	NA	NA	NA	NA	NA	NA	NA	NA	NA
2004	NA	NA	NA	NA	NA	NA	NA	NA	NA	NA	NA	NA
2005	NA	NA	NA	NA	NA	NA	NA	NA	NA	NA	NA	NA
2006[2]	NA	NA	NA	NA	NA	NA	NA	NA	NA	NA	NA	

[1] Primary refineries.   [2] Preliminary.   Source: U.S. Geological Survey (USGS)

Total[1] Lead Consumption in the United States   In Thousands of Metric Tons

Year	Jan.	Feb.	Mar.	Apr.	May	June	July	Aug.	Sept.	Oct.	Nov.	Dec.	Total
1997	139.0	138.0	138.0	140.0	137.0	141.0	116.0	119.0	122.0	123.0	117.0	117.0	1,600
1998	116.0	115.0	119.0	128.0	127.0	129.0	128.0	128.0	129.0	129.0	134.0	125.0	1,550
1999	128.0	129.0	130.0	127.0	128.0	130.0	137.0	136.0	141.0	136.0	140.0	133.0	1,680
2000	139.0	139.0	139.0	139.0	140.0	140.0	135.0	141.0	139.0	139.0	136.0	132.0	1,660
2001	145.0	135.0	133.0	130.0	138.0	136.0	135.0	136.0	142.0	146.0	138.0	138.0	1,652
2002	132.0	131.0	133.0	142.0	142.0	144.0	143.0	145.0	141.0	145.0	142.0	133.0	1,673
2003	134.0	129.0	126.0	120.0	121.0	121.0	121.0	122.0	123.0	127.0	122.0	125.0	1,491
2004	119.0	118.0	119.0	119.0	117.0	119.0	118.0	118.0	117.0	117.0	117.0	119.0	1,417
2005	125.0	117.0	109.0	108.0	134.0	130.0	124.0	129.0	126.0	126.0	126.0	126.0	1,480
2006[2]	124.0	130.0	129.0	128.0	128.0	128.0	125.0	126.0	127.0	128.0	126.0		1,526

[1] Represents total consumption of primary & secondary lead as metal, in chemicals, or in alloys.   [2] Preliminary.   Source: U.S. Geological Survey (USGS)

Lead Recovered from Scrap in the United States   In Thousands of Metric Tons (Lead Content)

Year	Jan.	Feb.	Mar.	Apr.	May	June	July	Aug.	Sept.	Oct.	Nov.	Dec.	Total
1997	88.0	89.8	91.7	86.0	88.2	85.7	86.7	94.7	97.3	96.2	95.2	91.7	1,110.0
1998	95.0	92.0	92.6	94.1	92.5	89.7	89.3	95.7	94.4	95.0	95.1	90.7	1,110.0
1999	89.5	89.1	88.9	91.0	90.2	91.1	81.3	91.9	91.6	93.5	91.4	93.1	1,110.0
2000	91.0	88.0	91.1	91.4	90.5	91.3	88.6	95.1	94.0	96.0	95.4	93.7	1,110.0
2001	90.3	90.4	86.7	92.6	93.7	93.6	90.4	95.1	93.9	96.7	94.6	94.6	1,112.6
2002	89.3	82.3	88.2	93.1	93.9	93.6	88.0	96.1	93.3	97.5	95.0	95.7	1,106.0
2003	95.7	83.6	86.2	85.1	94.0	94.8	95.7	93.9	93.3	102.0	93.7	95.2	1,113.2
2004	94.0	94.2	96.3	97.9	94.4	96.6	97.4	96.3	94.8	96.8	94.9	95.4	1,149.0
2005	94.4	95.1	86.8	86.8	87.1	94.6	94.7	94.8	93.0	95.9	96.4	92.4	1,112.0
2006[1]	90.2	96.7	97.4	98.2	99.5	95.7	94.9	97.0	95.6	98.4	98.4		1,158.5

[1] Preliminary.   Source: U.S. Geological Survey (USGS)

Domestic Shipments[1] of Lead in the United States, by Refiners   In Thousands of Short Tons

Year	Jan.	Feb.	Mar.	Apr.	May	June	July	Aug.	Sept.	Oct.	Nov.	Dec.	Total
1989	29.3	28.5	32.2	35.7	45.1	36.4	32.8	41.5	40.0	44.2	40.2	31.1	437.1
1990	39.3	33.9	39.1	33.5	38.4	32.9	32.6	38.9	36.6	38.9	37.9	31.7	433.7
1991	35.4	33.8	34.3	39.8	33.9	26.0	31.8	37.9	35.1	35.7	28.7	26.7	399.2
1992	31.3	23.9	30.4	26.3	25.6	27.2	27.3	28.7	26.3	28.5	26.3	21.7	323.5
1993	24.6	23.6	32.5	30.0	31.3	35.1	28.9	34.0	35.5	35.5	31.7	33.5	376.2
1994	35.9	32.8	35.2	32.7	34.7	36.7	31.6	33.4	34.8	34.3	34.0	33.3	409.3
1995	36.5	30.3	35.1	31.1	33.7	31.9	28.6	40.3	34.9	40.9	33.2	29.8	406.4
1996	37.2	32.4	29.5	30.2	29.4	26.7	27.7	33.5	30.1	33.5	28.1	27.6	366.0
1997[2]	31.5	27.8	24.7	35.2	39.2	36.1	33.4	29.4	26.4	31.5	30.4	28.1	377.8
	Data No longer Available												

[1] Includes GSA metal.   [2] Preliminary.   Source: American Metal Market (AMM)

Lumber & Plywood

Humans have utilized lumber for construction for thousands of years, but due to the heaviness of timber and the manual methods of harvesting, large-scale lumbering didn't occur until the mechanical advances of the Industrial Revolution. Lumber is produced from both hardwood and softwood. Hardwood lumber comes from deciduous trees that have broad leaves. Most hardwood lumber is used for miscellaneous industrial applications, primarily wood pallets, and includes oak, gum, maple, and ash. Hardwood species with beautiful colors and patterns are used for such high-grade products as furniture, flooring, paneling, and cabinets and include black walnut, black cherry, and red oak. Wood from cone-bearing trees is called softwood, regardless of its actual hardness. Most lumber from the US is softwood. Softwoods, such as southern yellow pine, Douglas fir, ponderosa pine, and true firs, are primarily used as structural lumber such as 2x4s and 2x6s, poles, paper and cardboard.

Plywood consists of several thin layers of veneer bonded together with adhesives. The veneer sheets are layered so that the grain of one sheet is perpendicular to that of the next, which makes plywood exceptionally strong for its weight. Most plywood has from three to nine layers of wood. Plywood manufacturers use both hard and soft woods, although hardwoods serve primarily for appearance and are not as strong as those made from softwoods. Plywood is primarily used in construction, particularly for floors, roofs, walls, and doors. Homebuilding and remodeling account for two-thirds of US lumber consumption. The price of lumber and plywood is highly correlated with the strength of the US home-building market.

The forest and wood products industry is dominated by Weyerhaeuser Company (ticker symbol WY), which has about $20 billion in annual sales. Weyerhaeuser is a forest products conglomerate that engages not only in growing and harvesting timber, but also in the production and distribution of forest products, real estate development, and construction of single-family homes. Forest products include wood products, pulp and paper, and containerboard. The timberland segment of the business manages 7.2 million acres of company-owned land and 800,000 acres of leased commercial forestlands in North America. The company's Canadian division has renewable, long-term licenses on about 35 million acres of forestland in five Canadian provinces. In order to maximize its long-term yield from its acreage, Weyerhaeuser engages in a number of forest management activities such as extensive planting, suppression of non-merchantable species, thinning, fertilization, and operational pruning.

Lumber futures and options are traded on the Chicago Mercantile Exchange (CME). The CME's lumber futures contract calls for the delivery of 111,000 board feet (one 73 foot rail car) of random length 8 to 12 foot 2 x 4s, the type used in construction. The contract is priced in terms of dollars per thousand board feet.

Prices – CME lumber futures prices fell almost steadily throughout 2006 starting the year at about $360.00. The price hit a low of about $236 at the end of October and then rallied a bit into the end of the year to finally close at about $265 at the end of December.

Supply – The US led the world in the production of industrial round wood with an increase of +3.1% yr/yr to 418.131 million cubic meters of production in 2004 (latest data available), followed by Canada with 196.442 million cubic meters (+9.7% yr/yr), and Russia with 139.500 million cubic meters (+3.2% yr/yr). The US also led the world in the production of plywood with 14.833 million cubic meters of production in 2004 (–0.2% yr/yr), followed by Canada with 2.344 million cubic meters (+6.3% yr/yr), and Russia with 2.246 million cubic meters (+3.5% yr/yr). US softwood lumber production in 2006 (through October, annualized) fell –2.0% yr/yr to 39.462 billion board feet, down from the 2005 11-year high of 40.576 billion board feet.

Demand – US consumption of softwood lumber in 2005, the last full reporting year, fell by –1.9% yr/yr to 63.080 billion board feet, down from the 2004 record high of 64.279.

Trade – US total lumber imports in 2005, the last full reporting year, rose +5.1% to 25.737 billion board feet, which was a record high. US imports of hardwood in 2005 rose by +8.1% to 1,075 million board feet. US imports of softwood in 2005 rose by +4.9% to 24.626 billion board feet. The leading softwood import was spruce with 1.769 billion board feet of imports in 2005, followed by cedar at 637 million board feet.

Total US exports of lumber in 2005 rose +5.9% yr/yr to 2.682 billion board feet, which is a 5-year high. The record high was 4.528 billion board feet in 1988. US exports of hardwood in 2005 fell by –1.3% yr/yr to 1.477 billion board feet. US exports of softwood in 2005 rose by 9.2% yr/yr to 897 million board feet. The largest types of US softwood exports were southern pine with 235 million board feet of exports, Ponderosa white pine (112 million board feet), and Douglas Fir (93 million board feet). The world's largest exporter of plywood in 2003 (latest data available) was Russia with 1.202 million cubic meters of exports, followed by Finland with 1.172 million cubic meters, and Canada with 1.017 million cubic meters.

World Production of Industrial Roundwood by Selected Countries   In Thousands of Cubic Meters

Year	Austria	Canada	Czech Repulic	Finland	France	Germany	Poland	Romania	Russia	Spain	Sweden	Turkey	United States
1996	11,812	177,943	11,882	42,178	30,643	34,538	18,824	9,441	73,005	12,433	52,500	10,229	406,625
1997	11,902	183,531	12,881	47,757	32,162	35,488	20,097	9,837	67,508	12,433	56,400	9,773	416,092
1998	10,858	173,901	13,171	49,541	32,718	36,441	21,793	8,629	77,400	13,164	54,700	9,979	422,034
1999	10,988	190,988	13,363	49,593	33,237	35,063	22,842	9,484	94,600	13,160	52,800	10,065	423,298
2000	10,416	197,357	13,501	50,147	43,440	51,088	24,489	10,116	105,800	12,721	57,400	10,429	420,619
2001	10,562	184,689	13,364	47,727	37,471	36,502	23,375	9,806	117,800	13,276	57,300	9,976	403,212
2002	11,810	193,727	13,534	48,529	32,736	37,755	24,995	12,092	118,600	13,850	60,700	11,191	404,958
2003	13,719	187,357	13,960	49,246	30,540	45,415	27,204	12,537	126,600	14,075	61,200	10,729	405,613
2004[1]	12,943	205,617	14,411	49,281	31,289	48,657	29,337	12,794	130,600	14,235	61,400	11,225	418,131
2005[2]	12,786	196,442	14,285	47,116	31,620	50,905	28,531	11,542	139,500	13,352	91,700	11,202	427,971

[1] Preliminary.   [2] Estimate.   NA = Not available.   *Source: Food and Agriculture Organization of the United Nations (FAO-UN)*

Lumber Production and Consumption in the United States   In Millions of Board Feet

Year	Production						Domestic Consumption						
	California Redwood	Inland Region	Southern Pine	West Coast	Other Softwood	Total Softwood	Inland Region	California Redwood	Southern Pine	West Coast	Other Softwood	Softwood Imports	Total Softwood
1998	1,391	7,298	16,151	7,797	2,040	34,677	7,256	1,409	15,788	7,502	1,567	18,686	52,209
1999	1,325	7,580	16,922	8,625	2,153	36,605	7,445	1,358	16,525	8,115	1,641	19,178	54,262
2000	1,320	7,078	16,672	8,782	2,115	35,967	6,926	1,257	16,374	8,300	1,629	19,449	53,934
2001	1,121	6,563	16,094	8,764	2,035	34,577	6,490	1,132	15,937	8,471	1,724	20,075	53,828
2002	1,035	6,759	16,686	9,244	2,106	35,830	6,641	1,056	16,571	8,966	1,832	20,986	56,050
2003	977	6,716	16,841	9,904	2,151	36,591	6,709	976	16,743	9,585	1,750	21,188	56,952
2004	1,049	6,742	18,050	10,934	2,300	39,075	6,600	1,021	17,935	10,705	1,971	23,584	61,819
2005	1,048	21,386	18,986	11,599	2,139	40,458	6,635	1,060	18,829	11,346	1,781	24,626	64,279
I	280	1,789	4,725	2,914	542	10,250	1,712	246	4,615	2,708	455	5,632	15,368
II	265	16,394	4,939	2,928	548	10,374	1,690	283	4,934	2,948	472	6,685	17,014
III	271	1,692	4,731	2,877	535	10,106	1,709	291	4,720	2,844	446	6,297	16,308
IV	232	1,511	4,591	2,880	514	9,728	1,524	240	4,560	2,846	408	6,012	15,589
2006[1] I	243	1,601	4,890	2,925	539	10,198	1,580	190	4,693	2,833	420	6,053	15,770
II													
III													

[1] Preliminary.   NA = Not available.   *Source: American Forest & Paper Association (AFPA)*

U.S. Housing Starts: Seasonally Adjusted Annual Rate   In Thousands of Units

Year	Jan.	Feb.	Mar.	Apr.	May	June	July	Aug.	Sept.	Oct.	Nov.	Dec.	Average
1997	1,355	1,486	1,457	1,492	1,442	1,494	1,437	1,390	1,546	1,520	1,510	1,566	1,475
1998	1,525	1,584	1,567	1,540	1,536	1,641	1,698	1,614	1,582	1,715	1,660	1,792	1,621
1999	1,748	1,670	1,710	1,553	1,611	1,559	1,669	1,648	1,635	1,608	1,648	1,708	1,647
2000	1,636	1,737	1,604	1,626	1,575	1,559	1,463	1,541	1,507	1,549	1,551	1,532	1,573
2001	1,600	1,625	1,590	1,649	1,605	1,636	1,670	1,567	1,562	1,540	1,602	1,568	1,601
2002	1,698	1,829	1,642	1,592	1,764	1,717	1,655	1,633	1,804	1,648	1,753	1,788	1,710
2003	1,853	1,629	1,726	1,643	1,751	1,867	1,897	1,833	1,939	1,967	2,083	2,057	1,854
2004	1,911	1,846	1,998	2,003	1,981	1,828	2,002	2,024	1,905	2,072	1,782	2,042	1,950
2005	2,137	2,213	1,856	2,079	2,034	2,078	2,070	2,075	2,158	2,046	2,131	2,002	2,073
2006[1]	2,265	2,132	1,972	1,832	1,953	1,833	1,760	1,659	1,724	1,478	1,565	1,643	1,818

[1] Preliminary.   Total Privately owned.   Source: American Forest & Paper Association (AF&PA)

Stocks (Gross) of Softwood Lumber in the United States, on First of Month   In Millions of Board Feet

Year	Jan.	Feb.	Mar.	Apr.	May	June	July	Aug.	Sept.	Oct.	Nov.	Dec.
1997	3,973	4,019	4,113	4,067	3,963	4,017	3,915	3,871	3,875	3,927	3,925	3,865
1998	3,884	3,970	4,048	4,062	4,158	4,084	NA	NA	NA	NA	NA	NA
1999	3,519	3,595	3,688	3,726	3,698	3,581	3,512	3,485	3,533	3,491	3,562	3,536
2000	3,639	3,704	3,811	3,887	3,960	2,738	3,902	3,936	3,878	3,848	3,957	3,875
2001	3,919	3,864	4,013	3,951	4,095	3,955	NA	3,961	3,938	4,076	4,100	4,248
2002	4,784	3,735	3,826	3,756	3,273	3,316	3,242	3,230	3,136	3,098	3,173	3,127
2003	3,175	3,177	3,202	3,249	3,308	3,211	3,075	3,085	3,081	3,158	3,076	3,055
2004	2,904	2,904	2,904	2,873	2,966	2,966	2,966	2,966	3,030	3,030	3,031	2,450
2005	2,912	2,994	3,076	3,056	2,866	2,687	2,554	2,641	2,497	2,986	3,059	2,913
2006[1]	3,004	3,100	3,111	2,978	2,952	2,925	2,918	2,917	2,956	2,960	3,059	

[1] Preliminary.   NA = Not available.   *Source: American Forest & Paper Association (AFPA)*

Lumber (Softwood)[2] Production in the United States   In Millions of Board Feet

Year	Jan.	Feb.	Mar.	Apr.	May	June	July	Aug.	Sept.	Oct.	Nov.	Dec.	Total
1997	3,012	2,791	2,866	3,149	2,890	3,027	3,097	2,889	2,905	3,094	2,536	2,487	34,743
1998	2,767	2,760	2,928	3,084	2,647	3,051	3,079	2,930	2,953	3,167	2,667	2,754	34,787
1999	2,783	2,921	3,190	3,227	3,071	3,318	3,115	3,054	2,992	3,096	2,954	2,795	36,516
2000	3,020	3,128	3,474	3,058	3,276	3,249	2,730	2,971	2,839	3,041	2,761	2,342	35,889
2001	2,832	2,457	2,918	2,928	NA	3,032	2,812	3,240	2,743	3,188	2,740	2,372	34,104
2002	3,019	2,761	3,074	3,284	3,126	3,200	3,104	3,128	2,862	3,386	2,599	2,482	36,025
2003	2,971	2,801	2,937	2,994	2,931	3,109	3,088	2,981	3,052	3,335	2,793	2,740	35,732
2004	3,037	2,978	3,380	3,434	3,021	3,329	3,227	3,271	3,147	3,321	3,082	2,931	38,158
2005	3,233	3,169	3,596	3,486	3,339	3,535	3,248	3,490	3,385	3,574	3,180	3,052	40,287
2006[1]	3,511	3,216	3,550	3,294	3,360	3,420	3,195	3,349	2,877	3,113			39,462

[1] Preliminary.   *Source: American Forest & Paper Association (AFPA)*

Lumber and Plywood (monthly average) through December 2006   USD per 1,000 board feet

Lumber: USD Per 1,000 Board Feet
- - - - - White-Fir, 2x4 (Jan. 1959 - Dec. 1970)
Spruce-Hem-Fir, 2x4 (Jan. 1971 - Mar. 1980)
Spruce-Pine-Fir, 2x4 (Apr. 1980 - date)

Plywood: USD Per 1,000 Square Feet
- - - Sheathing, 1/2"-B (Aug. 1975 - date)

Lumber (Softwood)[2] Shipments in the United States   In Millions of Board Feet

Year	Jan.	Feb.	Mar.	Apr.	May	June	July	Aug.	Sept.	Oct.	Nov.	Dec.	Total
1997	2,966	2,697	2,890	3,253	2,834	3,126	3,139	2,885	2,852	3,096	2,598	2,461	34,797
1998	2,685	2,685	2,863	3,019	2,684	3,175	3,132	2,963	2,948	3,205	2,703	2,865	34,927
1999	2,689	2,829	3,177	3,227	3,071	3,383	3,141	3,004	3,037	3,021	2,944	2,691	36,214
2000	2,953	3,039	3,394	2,974	3,292	3,309	2,686	3,027	2,871	2,931	2,752	2,444	35,672
2001	2,859	2,372	2,981	2,974	NA	2,961	2,936	3,279	2,644	3,166	2,732	2,396	34,145
2002	3,032	2,815	3,049	3,212	3,064	3,260	3,234	3,111	2,858	3,299	2,675	2,501	36,110
2003	3,018	2,742	2,843	3,134	2,969	3,173	3,209	3,137	3,030	3,413	2,787	2,722	36,177
2004	3,067	2,840	3,262	3,582	3,061	3,385	3,485	3,372	3,086	3,345	3,135	2,964	38,584
2005	3,264	3,087	3,506	3,506	3,542	3,696	3,389	3,512	3,413	3,542	3,145	3,196	40,798
2006[1]	3,423	3,122	3,536	3,280	3,386	3,447	3,202	3,349	2,838	3,110			39,232

[1] Preliminary.   Source: American Forest & Paper Association (AFPA)

Imports and Exports of Lumber in the United States, by Type   In Millions of Board Feet

								Exports[2]						
	Imports[2]								Softwood					
	Software									Pond-erosa/				
Year	Cedar	Douglas Fir	Hemlock	Pine	Spruce	Total	Total Hardwood	Total Lumber	Douglas Fir	Hemlock	White Pine	Southern Pine	Total Hardwood	Total Lumber
1997	586	264	250	314	1,040	18,014	465	18,506	436	105	122	299	1,820	1,281	3,189
1998	514	417	268	363	849	18,686	589	19,306	252	39	113	279	1,265	1,119	2,601
1999	591	426	259	449	803	19,178	708	19,903	249	54	140	326	1,431	1,242	2,867
2000	694	455	184	450	812	19,449	795	20,268	232	46	116	298	1,355	1,319	2,822
2001	667	471	199	365	838	20,075	645	20,737	168	26	86	232	968	1,222	2,351
2002	648	385	69	445	1,046	20,986	739	21,774	111	19	83	205	848	1,219	2,313
2003	536	356	53	472	854	21,188	794	22,023	96	18	100	132	948	1,236	2,368
2004	630	570	67	580	1,183	23,483	995	24,499	88	19	93	156	821	1,496	2,533
2005	637	494	76	439	1,769	24,626	1,075	25,738	93	19	112	235	897	1,477	2,682
2006[1] I	180	88	31	100	432	6,054	261	6,321	19	3	29	58	246	449	695
II														
III														

[1] Preliminary.   [2] Includes sawed timber, board planks & scantlings, flooring, box shook and railroad ties.

Source: American Forest & Paper Association (AFPA)

Lumber Futures - Chicago Mercantile Exchange
(weekly close) as of December 29, 2006

USD per 1,000 board feet

Average Open Interest of Random Lumber[1] Futures in Chicago — In Contracts

Year	Jan.	Feb.	Mar.	Apr.	May	June	July	Aug.	Sept.	Oct.	Nov.	Dec.
1997	3,745	3,211	3,048	3,337	2,895	3,137	2,767	3,119	3,267	4,006	3,606	4,068
1998	4,249	3,332	3,394	4,102	4,353	4,773	4,048	4,081	3,466	4,295	3,434	3,893
1999	4,864	5,497	4,698	4,456	4,927	6,405	6,263	4,882	3,457	3,704	2,963	2,868
2000	3,004	3,131	2,728	3,175	3,171	3,218	3,064	3,638	3,845	4,277	4,208	4,405
2001	4,605	4,494	3,654	3,644	3,867	3,733	2,612	2,949	2,148	2,102	2,173	2,416
2002	2,106	2,382	2,441	2,011	1,502	2,136	1,879	2,265	2,654	2,974	3,315	3,249
2003	3,238	3,222	2,521	2,804	2,937	3,188	2,370	2,827	3,492	3,033	1,824	1,887
2004	2,884	3,996	3,790	5,414	5,436	5,042	5,123	6,216	4,667	3,826	3,489	3,540
2005	3,759	5,169	5,040	4,705	3,463	3,576	3,401	4,227	3,913	3,883	4,713	5,202
2006	5,893	5,144	4,084	4,959	4,586	5,449	5,317	6,429	5,912	6,351	6,121	7,018

Source: Chicago Mercantile Exchange (CME)

Volume of Trading of Random Lumber[1] Futures in Chicago — In Contracts

Year	Jan.	Feb.	Mar.	Apr.	May	June	July	Aug.	Sept.	Oct.	Nov.	Dec.	Total
1997	28,561	20,946	21,071	24,624	18,248	24,797	20,308	18,503	21,736	24,416	15,131	21,977	260,318
1998	19,556	20,339	20,881	24,673	20,519	24,112	21,763	20,453	19,412	19,578	22,002	16,559	249,847
1999	25,962	22,184	28,151	22,618	23,835	30,410	30,791	25,683	24,177	18,125	20,802	15,118	287,856
2000	19,871	19,486	18,936	16,136	21,003	18,057	16,636	16,563	19,037	17,155	20,706	17,582	221,168
2001	21,567	15,076	24,561	22,458	23,681	18,878	15,210	16,440	12,882	11,608	11,989	12,490	206,840
2002	15,328	13,239	16,401	13,910	12,427	11,950	12,046	10,154	13,518	13,442	15,828	16,180	164,423
2003	24,241	17,533	17,027	11,573	20,132	21,840	21,097	22,418	22,891	19,387	12,480	13,272	223,891
2004	17,921	17,713	22,544	25,743	19,951	17,190	22,672	20,902	24,238	17,111	17,271	19,617	242,873
2005	20,838	20,257	24,595	20,360	17,338	17,115	16,244	19,590	22,895	15,896	23,404	17,709	236,241
2006	26,803	19,152	18,504	21,358	21,619	23,959	21,568	23,800	22,618	24,804	22,385	24,454	271,024

Source: Chicago Mercantile Exchange (CME)

LUMBER & PLYWOOD

Production of Plywood by Selected Countries   In Thousands of Cubic Meters

Year	Austria	Canada	Finland	France	Germany	Italy	Japan	Poland	Romania	Russia	Spain	Sweden	United States
1998	150	2,049	992	541	428	420	3,267	178	76	1,102	382	114	17,468
1999	155	2,228	1,076	546	364	450	3,261	223	65	1,324	382	105	17,551
2000	155	2,244	1,170	558	357	450	3,218	261	72	1,484	380	110	17,271
2001	186	2,026	1,140	509	321	488	2,771	242	79	1,590	380	106	15,417
2002	186	2,176	1,240	459	285	520	2,735	261	90	1,821	360	87	15,307
2003	186	2,206	1,300	415	245	511	3,024	289	94	1,978	370	75	14,870
2004[1]	186	2,344	1,350	435	283	485	3,149	342	117	2,246	375	71	14,833
2005[2]	195	2,323	1,305	430	232	460	3,212	361	126	2,551	365	92	14,537

[1] Preliminary.   [2] Estimate.   NA = Not available.   *Source: Food and Agricultural Organization of the United Nations (FAO-UN)*

Imports of Plywood by Selected Countries   In Thousands of Cubic Meters

Year	Austria	Belgium	Canada	Denmark	France	Germany	Italy	Japan	Nether- lands	Sweden	Switzer- land	United Kingdom	United States
1998	121	313	273	302	359	1,105	378	3,938	528	147	143	969	1,964
1999	136	530	222	222	365	1,021	367	4,888	558	152	150	972	2,494
2000	151	534	230	247	272	965	422	5,033	594	178	153	1,207	2,385
2001	138	526	520	250	358	954	425	5,021	600	157	143	1,300	3,009
2002	156	505	489	254	349	905	558	5,119	541	152	128	1,297	3,890
2003	180	572	509	394	363	1,103	558	4,221	527	161	130	1,253	4,249
2004[1]	144	624	350	413	383	1,214	581	5,122	542	164	140	1,474	5,900
2005[2]	140	521	330	371	401	1,098	532	4,732	526	189	145	1,417	6,181

[1] Preliminary.   [2] Estimate.   *Source: Food and Agricultural Organization of the United Nations (FAO-UN)*

Exports of Plywood by Selected Countries   In Thousands of Cubic Meters

Year	Austria	Baltic States	Belgium	Canada	Finland	France	Germany	Italy	Nether- lands	Poland	Russia	Spain	United States
1997	172	198	101	557	725	201	152	125	68	95	559	77	984
1998	180	224	101	755	832	222	166	139	56	93	736	331	833
1999	192	200	403	956	939	243	160	139	51	95	913	220	712
2000	246	194	380	941	1,006	231	210	146	55	109	974	104	673
2001	286	232	378	1,030	1,009	200	232	125	57	128	1,032	88	530
2002	240	238	371	1,056	1,117	190	167	204	43	138	1,157	82	523
2003	262	245	436	1,017	1,172	187	200	208	32	149	1,201	88	512
2004[2]	265	255	474	1,027	1,234	192	265	201	46	171	1,438	114	525

[1] Preliminary.   [2] Estimate.   NA = Not available.   *Source: Food and Agricultural Organization of the United Nations (FAO-UN)*

Imports of Industrial Roundwood by Selected Countries   In Thousands of Cubic Meters

Year	Austria	Belgium	Canada	Finland	France	Germany	Italy	Norway	Poland	Portugal	Spain	Sweden	United States
1998	5,113	2,823	6,955	9,235	1,980	2,255	5,223	3,494	371	2,122	4,136	9,172	970
1999	7,093	3,393	6,157	10,160	2,154	2,722	4,952	3,037	590	1,432	3,228	10,280	1,855
2000	8,451	3,992	6,507	9,875	2,012	3,549	5,805	3,315	732	1,340	3,771	11,721	2,453
2001	7,493	4,505	7,557	11,869	1,994	3,493	5,211	2,772	882	1,109	4,128	9,505	2,430
2002	7,289	2,653	6,941	12,586	1,993	2,623	4,703	2,561	726	901	3,374	9,705	2,687
2003	7,498	2,667	6,615	12,869	2,250	2,519	4,323	2,722	663	468	3,191	9,021	2,551
2004[1]	8,812	2,879	5,961	12,961	2,175	2,227	4,614	2,866	943	364	2,973	9,398	2,437
2005[2]	8,629	3,187	6,092	16,031	2,310	2,820	4,755	3,143	2,009	362	3,513	8,686	3,569

[1] Preliminary.   [2] Estimate.   *Source: Food and Agricultural Organization of the United Nations (FAO-UN)*

Exports of Industrial Roundwood by Selected Countries   In Thousands of Cubic Meters

Year	Canada	Czech Republic	Estonia	France	Germany	Hungary	Latvia	Lithuania	Russia	Slovakia	Sweden	Switzer- land	United States
1998	2,029	2,497	3,792	2,857	4,871	1,204	2,760	792	19,972	714	1,420	1,006	12,290
1999	2,213	2,626	3,903	3,093	4,552	1,079	2,953	938	27,600	1,193	1,315	1,220	11,739
2000	2,903	1,857	4,257	5,522	5,558	1,282	4,190	1,200	30,835	1,550	1,431	3,754	11,952
2001	3,835	2,276	3,482	5,116	4,906	1,227	3,990	1,314	31,693	1,550	1,303	3,149	11,412
2002	4,471	2,302	3,132	4,244	4,907	1,210	4,225	1,420	36,800	1,187	1,755	1,970	11,067
2003	5,004	2,955	3,029	4,111	4,592	1,366	3,922	1,378	37,518	1,034	1,520	1,748	10,288
2004[1]	3,899	2,858	2,297	3,851	5,589	1,137	4,136	1,178	41,553	1,142	1,522	1,741	10,402
2005[2]	5,197	2,942	1,806	3,761	6,070	871	3,919	1,129	48,000	1,691	3,095	1,734	9,815

[1] Preliminary.   [2] Estimate.   *Source: Food and Agricultural Organization of the United Nations (FAO-UN)*

Magnesium

Magnesium (symbol Mg) is a silvery-white, light, and fairly tough, metallic element and is relatively stable. Magnesium is one of the alkaline earth metals. Magnesium is the eighth most abundant element in the earth's crust and the third most plentiful element found in seawater. Magnesium is ductile and malleable when heated, and with the exception of beryllium, is the lightest metal that remains stable under ordinary conditions. First isolated by the British chemist Sir Humphrey Davy in 1808, magnesium today is obtained mainly by electrolysis of fused magnesium chloride.

Magnesium compounds, primarily magnesium oxide, are used in the refractory material that line the furnaces used to produce iron and steel, nonferrous metals, glass, and cement. Magnesium oxide and other compounds are also used in the chemical, agricultural, and construction industries. Magnesium's principal use is as an alloying addition for aluminum. These aluminum-magnesium alloys are used primarily in beverage cans. Due to their lightness and considerable tensile strength, the alloys are also used in structural components in airplanes and automobiles.

Prices – The price of magnesium in 2005 fell to $1.20 per pound, down –16.6% from $1.44 last year, but still up by 15.4 % from $1.04 in 2003. However, the recent price of magnesium is still well below the record high in the $1.93-2.25 range seen in 1995.

Supply – World primary production of magnesium in 2005 rose +5.2% yr/yr to a new record high of 626,000 metric tons. The current level of magnesium production has more than doubled since the mid-1970s (production was 249,367 metric tons in 1976). The world's largest primary producers of magnesium are China with 470,000 metric tons of production in 2005, Russia with 45,000 metric tons, and Canada with 54,000 metric tons. The US production amount is not available because it is considered proprietary data but is probably less than about 50,000 metric tons. China's production has increased six-fold over the past 5 years from 70,500 metric tons in 1998 to 470,000 metric tons in 2005. Brazil's production has grown by six-fold from the early 1980s. Canada's production has grown by more than seven-fold from the mid-1980s.

Demand – Total US consumption of primary magnesium in 2005 rose +8.7% to 55,304 metric tons. US consumption of magnesium for structural products in 2005 rose +8.7% yr/yr to 55,304 metric tons. Of the structural product consumption category, 98% was for castings and the remaining 2% was for wrought products. US consumption of magnesium for aluminum alloys fell –10.6% yr/yr in 2005 to 30,300 metric tons. The consumption of magnesium for "other uses" fell by –9.8% yr/yr in 2005 to 14,800 metric tons.

Trade – US exports of magnesium in 2005 fell –18.2% yr/yr to a record low of 9,650 metric tons. US imports of magnesium in 2005 fell –14.2% yr/yr to 84,700 metric tons.

World Production of Magnesium (Primary and Secondary)   In Metric Tons

| | Primary Production | | | | | | | | Secondary Production | | | | |
Year	Brazil	Canada	China	France	Norway	Russia	United States	World Total	Japan	United Kingdom	United States	Former USSR	World Total
2000	5,700	80,000	190,000	16,500	41,400	45,000	W	422,000	7,900	500	82,300	NA	92,300
2001	5,500	83,000	200,000	4,000	36,000	48,000	W	428,000	7,800	500	65,800	NA	75,700
2002	6,000	88,000	250,000	----	10,000	50,000	W	452,000	----	----	----	----	----
2003	6,000	54,000	340,000	----	----	43,000	W	485,000	----	----	----	----	----
2004[1]	6,000	54,000	442,000	----	----	45,000	W	595,000	----	----	----	----	----
2005[2]	6,000	54,000	470,000	----	----	45,000	W	626,000	----	----	----	----	----

[1] Preliminary.   [2] Estimate.   W = Withheld proprietary data.   Source: U.S. Geological Survey (USGS)

Salient Statistics of Magnesium in the United States   In Metric Tons

| | Production | | | | | | | | $ Price | Domestic Consumption of Primary Magnesium | | | | | |
| | | Secondary | | | | Imports | | | | Castings | Wrought | Total | | | |
Year	Primary (Ingot)	New Scrap	Old Scrap	Total	Total Exports[3]	for Consumption	Stocks Dec. 31[4]	Per Pound[5]	Structural Products			Aluminum Alloys	Other Uses[6]	Total
2000	W	52,200	30,100	82,300	23,800	91,400	W	1.23-1.30	29,457	2,120	31,577	55,400	17,400	72,800
2001	W	38,600	27,200	65,800	19,600	68,500	W	1.21-1.28	44,712	3,280	47,992	35,000	12,700	47,700
2002	W	47,100	26,400	73,600	25,400	88,000	W	1.10-1.22	46,362	4,350	50,712	34,900	16,000	50,900
2003	W	44,700	25,400	70,100	20,400	83,400	W	1.10-1.17	49,565	3,190	52,755	33,800	16,200	50,000
2004[1]	W	W	20,500	72,000	11,800	98,700	W	1.55-1.60	48,629	2,240	50,869	33,900	16,400	50,300
2005[2]	W	W	19,400	72,800	9,650	84,700	W	1.15-1.30	52,424	2,880	55,304	30,300	14,800	45,100

[1] Preliminary.   [2] Estimate.   [3] Metal & alloys in crude form & scrap.   [4] Estimate of Industry Stocks, metal.   [5] Magnesium ingots (99.8%), f.o.b. Valasco, Texas.   [6] Distributive or sacrificial purposes.   W = Withheld proprietary data.   Source: U.S. Geological Survey (USGS)

Average Price of Magnesium   In Dollars Per Pound

Year	Jan.	Feb.	Mar.	Apr.	May	June	July	Aug.	Sept.	Oct.	Nov.	Dec.	Average
2002	1.08	1.08	1.08	1.08	1.08	1.08	1.08	1.08	1.08	1.08	1.06	1.02	1.07
2003	1.02	1.03	1.03	1.03	1.03	1.03	1.03	1.03	1.04	1.05	1.05	1.05	1.04
2004	1.08	1.11	1.23	1.30	1.42	1.55	1.55	1.55	1.55	1.55	1.60	1.60	1.42
2005	1.60	1.57	1.57	1.57	1.54	1.48	1.40	1.40	1.33	1.32	1.29	1.25	1.44
2006	1.25	1.18	1.18	1.16	1.16	1.16	1.16	1.16	1.20	1.21	1.29	1.33	1.20

Source: American Metal Market (AMM)

Manganese

Manganese (symbol Mn) is a silvery-white, very brittle, metallic element used primarily in making alloys. Manganese was first distinguished as an element and isolated in 1774 by Johan Gottlieb Gahn. Manganese dissolves in acid and corrodes in moist air.

Manganese is found in the earth's crust in the form of ores such as rhodochrosite, franklinite, psilomelane, and manganite. Pyrolusite is the principal ore of manganese. Pure manganese is produced by igniting pyrolusite with aluminum powder or by electrolyzing manganese sulfate.

Manganese is used primarily in the steel industry for creating alloys, the most important ones being ferromanganese and spiegeleisen. In steel, manganese improves forging and rolling qualities, strength, toughness, stiffness, wear resistance, and hardness. Manganese is also used in plant fertilizers, animal feed, pigments, and dry cell batteries.

Prices – The average monthly price of ferromanganese (high carbon, FOB plant) rose +32.7% yr/yr in 2006 to $846.44 per gross ton but still below the record high of $1,355.90 per gross ton posted in 2004. The 2006 price, however, was still far above the 17-year low of $447.44 per gross ton posted as recently as 2001.

Supply – World production of manganese ore in 2005 rose by +5.1% to 29.1 million metric tons, which was a record

high. That was well above the record low of 17.8 million metric tons posted in 1999. The world's largest producers of manganese ore are China with 19% of world production in 2005, South Africa with 16%, Australia with 14%, Brazil with 11%, and the Ukraine with 8%. China's production in 2005 was unchanged from 2004 at 5.5 million metric tons.

Demand – US consumption of manganese ore in 2004 (latest data available) rose +10.8% to 441,000 metric tons, continuing to recover from the record low of 360,000 metric tons in 2002. US consumption of ferromanganese in 2004 rose 27.0% yr/yr to a 7-year high of 315,000 metric tons, but that was still almost a third less than US consumption of 908,000 metric tons in 1970.

Trade – The US still relies on imports for 100% of its manganese consumption, as it has since 1985. US imports of manganese ore for consumption in 2004 (latest data available) rose +30.0% yr/yr to 451,000 metric tons. US imports of ferromanganese for consumption in 2004 rose +80.3% yr/yr to a 15-year high of 429,000 metric tons. US imports of silico-manganese in 2004 rose +58.1% yr/yr to 422,000 metric tons. The primary sources of US imports of manganese ore in 2004 were Gabon with 188,000 metric tons of imports, Australia (27,700 metric tons), and South Africa (13,200 metric tons).

World Production of Manganese Ore   In Thousands of Metric Tons (Gross Weight)

Year	Australia[2] 37-53[4]	Brazil 37[4]	China 20-30[4]	Gabon 45-53[4]	Georgia 29-30[4]	Ghana 32-34[4]	India 10-54[4]	Kazakstan 29-30[4]	Mexico 27-50[4]	South Africa 30-48+[4]	Ukraine 29-30[4]	Other	World Total
1996	2,109	2,506	7,600	1,983	97	448	1,797	430	485	3,240	3,070	632	24,300
1997	2,136	2,124	6,000	1,904	----	437	1,596	400	534	3,121	3,040	608	21,900
1998	1,500	1,940	5,300	2,092	----	537	1,557	634	510	3,044	2,226	522	19,900
1999	1,892	1,656	3,190	1,908	----	639	1,500	980	459	3,122	1,985	458	17,800
2000	1,614	1,925	3,500	1,743	----	896	1,550	1,136	435	3,635	2,741	433	19,600
2001	2,069	1,970	4,300	1,791	----	1,077	1,600	1,387	277	3,266	2,700	490	20,900
2002	2,187	2,529	4,500	1,856	----	1,136	1,700	1,792	233	3,322	2,470	474	22,200
2003	2,555	2,544	4,600	2,000	----	1,509	1,650	2,361	310	3,501	2,591	490	24,100
2004	3,381	3,143	5,500	2,460	----	1,624	1,700	2,318	377	4,207	2,362	651	27,700
2005[1]	4,000	3,150	5,500	2,500	----	1,915	1,750	2,208	470	4,612	2,260	762	29,100

[1] Preliminary.   [2] Metallurgical Ore.   [3] Concentrate.   [4] Ranges of percentage of manganese.   *Source: U.S. Geological Survey (USGS)*

Salient Statistics of Manganese in the United States   In Thousands of Metric Tons (Gross Weight)

Year	Net Import Reliance as a % of Apparent Consumption	Manganese Ore (35% or More Manganese) Imports for Consumption	Exports	Consumption	Stocks, Dec. 31[3]	Ferromanganese Imports for Consumption	Exports	Consumption	Avg. Price Mn. Metallurgical Ore $ Lg. Ton Unit[4]	Silicomanganese Exports	Imports
1996	100	478	32	478	319	374	10	326	2.55	5.3	323.0
1997	100	355	84	510	241	304	12	337	2.44	5.4	306.0
1998	100	332	8	499	163	339	14	290	2.40	6.7	346.0
1999	100	460	4	479	172	312	12	281	2.26	3.7	301.0
2000	100	447	10	486	226	312	8	300	2.39	1.9	378.0
2001	100	358	9	425	138	251	9	266	2.44	3.6	269.0
2002	100	427	15	360	151	275	9	253	2.30	0.5	247.0
2003	100	347	18	398	156	238	11	248	2.41	0.6	267.0
2004[1]	100	451	123	441	159	429	9	315	2.89	0.5	422.0
2005[2]	100	656	13	368	337	255	14	286	4.39	0.9	327.0

[1] Preliminary.   [2] Estimate.   [3] Including bonded warehouses; excludes Gov't stocks; also excludes small tonnages of dealers' stocks.   [4] 46-48% Mn, C.I.F. U.S. Ports.   *Source: U.S. Geological Survey (USGS)*

Ferromanganese (monthly average) through December 2006 — USD per gross ton

USD Per Gross Ton
----- Baltimore, (Jan. 1908 - Dec. 1920)
FOB Plant (Jan. 1921 - date)

No Quotes
Oct. 1984 - Apr. 1987

Imports[3] of Manganese Ore (20% or More Mn) in the United States   In Metric Tons (Mn Content)

Year	Australia	Brazil	Gabon	Mexico	Morocco	South Africa	Total	Customs Value Thous. $
1996	48,900	5,640	140,000	16,100	9	20,800	231,000	42,400
1997	16,400	9,100	99,400	30,100	37	----	156,000	30,800
1998	18,700	12,100	94,900	14,600	----	13,800	160,000	27,800
1999	23,500	1	142,000	9,130	----	39,100	224,000	37,200
2000	18,100	3,250	188,000	3,250	----	----	219,000	32,100
2001	18,000	3,480	158,000	1,720	----	17,400	199,000	28,000
2002	18,400	12,900	140,000	1,100	----	41,800	214,000	29,200
2003	12,900	7	123,000	1,520	----	36,900	175,000	27,000
2004[1]	27,700	23	188,000	1,640	----	13,200	234,000	37,700
2005[2]	21,300	----	252,000	4,320	----	33,100	334,000	58,200

[1] Preliminary.   [2] Estimate.   [3] Imports for consumption.   *Source: U.S. Geological Survey (USGS)*

Average Price of Ferromanganese   In Dollars Per Gross Ton

Year	Jan.	Feb.	Mar.	Apr.	May	June	July	Aug.	Sept.	Oct.	Nov.	Dec.	Average
1997	477.50	467.50	470.00	482.50	490.00	490.00	490.00	492.50	475.00	475.00	475.00	475.00	480.00
1998	175.00	175.00	175.00	190.00	190.00	510.00	510.00	510.00	510.00	510.00	510.00	510.00	497.92
1999	510.00	510.00	510.00	510.00	510.00	498.75	482.50	482.50	482.50	482.50	482.50	482.50	495.21
2000	482.50	482.50	482.50	482.50	482.50	482.50	501.63	505.00	509.00	510.00	510.00	477.50	492.40
2001	473.93	467.89	460.00	454.29	450.00	450.00	446.90	444.57	430.79	430.00	430.00	430.00	447.44
2002	430.00	430.00	437.14	447.73	449.55	456.75	481.82	556.14	597.00	589.67	552.89	518.93	495.64
2003	509.52	510.00	502.38	497.61	492.50	481.79	477.27	470.00	478.57	497.83	516.67	559.76	499.49
2004	610.00	790.00	1,382.61	1,700.00	1,700.00	1,674.43	1,490.34	1,488.64	1,500.00	1,371.43	1,207.50	1,019.52	1,327.87
2005	904.50	818.68	739.46	651.67	586.19	547.39	528.13	512.07	522.14	550.24	597.75	694.05	637.69
2006	707.25	712.50	737.50	759.00	764.55	870.23	987.50	1,025.00	1,021.25	946.25	836.25	790.00	846.44

Domestic standard, high carbon, FOB plant, carloads.   *Source: American Metal Market (AMM)*

Meats

US commercial red meat includes beef, veal, lamb, and pork. Red meat is a good source of iron, vitamin B12, and protein, and eliminating it from the diet can lead to iron and zinc deficiencies. Today, red meat is far leaner than it was 30 years ago due to newer breeds of livestock that carry less fat. The leanest cuts of beef include tenderloin, sirloin, and flank. The leanest cuts of pork include pork tenderloin, loin chops, and rib chops.

The USDA (United States Department of Agriculture) grades various cuts of meat. "Prime" is the highest USDA grade for beef, veal, and lamb. "Choice" is the grade designation below Prime for beef, veal, and lamb. "Commercial" and "Cutter" grades are two of the lower designations for beef, usually sold as ground meat, sausage, and canned meat. "Canner" is the lowest USDA grade designation for beef and is used primarily in canned meats not sold at retail.

Supply – World meat production in 2007 is forecasted to rise +3.1% to a new record high of 158.103 million metric tons. China is forecasted to be the world's largest meat producer in 2007 with 63.710 million metric tons of production (up +5.3% yr/yr), accounting for 40% of world production.

US production of meat in 2007 is forecasted to rise by +3.0% yr/yr to 49.026 billion pounds, which will be a new record high. US production of beef in 2007 is forecasted to rise 33.1% yr/yr to 26.802 billion pounds, which will be just moderately below the record of 27.192 billion pounds in 2002. Beef accounted for 55.0% of all US meat production. US production of pork in 2007 is forecasted to rise +3.7% yr/yr to a new record high of 21.870 billion pounds. Pork accounts for 45.0% of US meat production. Veal accounts for only 0.3% of US meat production, and lamb and mutton account for only 0.4% of US meat production.

Demand – US per capita meat consumption in 2007 is forecasted to rise by 2.6% to 119.0 pounds per person per year, but that is only slightly above the 2006 record low of 116 pounds per person reflecting the trend towards eating more chicken and fish and the availability of meat substitutes. Per-capita beef consumption in 2007 is forecasted to rise to 66.0 pounds per person per year, which was about half the record high of 127.5 pounds seen in 1976. Per capita pork consumption in 2007 is forecasted to rise to 51.0 pounds per person per year from he record low of 49.0 pounds posted in 2006.

Trade – World red meat exports in 2007 is forecasted to rise +4.9% to a new record high of 12.768 million metric tons. The world's largest red meat exporters will be Brazil with 20% of world exports in 2007, the US with 16%, the European Union with 13%, and Australia and Canada each with 12%.

World Total Meat Production[3]   In Thousands of Metric Tons

Year	Argentina	Australia	Brazil	Canada	China[4]	EU-25	India	Mexico	New Zealand	Russia[5]	South Africa	United States	World Total
1999	2,840	2,318	8,105	2,802	45,110	29,941	1,660	2,894	562	3,390	584	20,882	132,243
2000	2,880	2,353	8,530	2,886	45,642	28,941	1,700	2,935	575	3,340	630	20,894	132,130
2001	2,640	2,428	9,125	2,981	47,333	28,511	1,770	2,990	609	3,320	665	20,674	134,586
2002	2,700	2,496	9,805	3,148	49,112	29,083	1,810	3,015	589	3,370	645	21,356	139,252
2003	2,800	2,492	9,945	3,072	51,491	29,211	1,960	3,050	693	3,380	613	21,095	140,583
2004	3,130	2,475	10,575	3,432	53,775	29,199	2,130	3,249	720	3,315	655	20,573	144,128
2005	3,200	2,490	11,392	3,437	57,221	28,872	2,250	3,320	705	3,260	679	20,709	148,601
2006[1]	3,100	2,530	11,595	3,260	60,500	29,330	2,375	3,375	650	3,260	660	21,440	153,287
2007[2]	3,150	2,668	11,995	3,195	63,710	29,380	2,500	3,450	690	3,290	656	21,977	158,103

[1] Preliminary.   [2] Forecast.   [3] Data through 2000, includes beef, veal, pork, sheep and goat meat. Beginning 2001, excludes sheep and goat.
[4] Predominately pork production.   *Source: Foreign Agricultural Service, U.S. Department of Agriculture (FAS-USDA)*

Production and Consumption of Red Meats in The United States

	Beef			Veal			Lamb & Mutton			Pork (Excluding Lard)			All Meats		
	Commercial Production	Consumption		Commercial Production	Consumption		Commercial Production	Consumption		Commercial Production	Consumption		Commercial Production	Consumption	
		Total	Per Capita		Total	Per Capita		Total	Per Capita		Total	Per Capita		Total	Per Capita
Year	-- Million Pounds --		Lbs.	- Million Pounds -		Lbs.	- Million Pounds -		Lbs.	-- Million Pounds --		Lbs.	-- Million Pounds --		Lbs.
1999	26,493	26,936	68.0	235	235	1.0	248	358	1.0	19,308	18,954	53.0	46,284	46,483	122.0
2000	26,888	27,338	68.0	225	225	1.0	234	354	1.0	18,952	18,643	51.0	46,299	46,560	121.0
2001	26,212	27,026	66.0	205	204	1.0	227	368	1.0	19,160	18,492	50.0	45,804	46,089	118.0
2002	27,192	27,877	68.0	205	204	1.0	223	381	1.0	19,685	19,146	52.0	47,305	47,608	121.0
2003	26,339	27,000	65.0	202	204	1.0	203	367	1.0	19,966	19,436	52.0	46,710	47,006	118.0
2004	24,650	27,750	66.0	176	177	1.0	200	372	1.0	20,529	19,437	51.0	45,555	47,735	119.0
2005	24,784	27,751	66.0	165	164	0.5	191	355	1.0	20,706	19,115	50.0	45,846	47,385	117.0
2006[1]	20,137	27,971	65.0	165	166	0.5	192	343	1.0	21,085	19,063	49.0	47,579	47,543	116.0
2007[2]	26,802	28,667	66.0	164	164	0.5	190	362	1.0	21,870	19,790	51.0	49,026	48,983	119.0

[1] Preliminary.   [2] Forecast.   *Source: Economic Research Service, U.S. Department of Agriculture (ERS-USDA)*

Total Red Meat Imports[3] (Carcass Weight Equivalent) of Principal Countries   In Thousands of Metric Tons

Year	Brazil	Canada	EU-25	Egypt	Hong Kong	Japan	Rep. of Korea	Mexico	Philip-pines	Russia[3]	Taiwan	United States	World Total5
1998	108	296	458	158	266	1,766	191	451	91	1,452	104	1,519	7,429
1999	55	319	390	215	284	1,926	398	548	136	1,392	180	1,678	7,956
2000	72	331	387	221	318	2,062	498	696	153	730	137	1,813	7,895
2001	44	391	380	142	331	2,070	369	720	138	1,176	93	1,866	8,173
2002	78	399	478	173	346	1,874	585	814	157	1,553	121	1,945	9,113
2003	63	365	493	123	383	1,984	597	741	151	1,445	152	1,901	9,036
2004	53	216	604	168	413	1,949	438	745	188	1,359	141	2,168	9,063
2005	49	273	620	214	397	2,039	571	745	163	1,758	131	2,096	9,765
2006[1]	30	290	562	225	402	1,943	447	815	167	1,640	131	1,902	9,239
2007[2]	45	305	582	240	410	1,993	450	835	175	1,730	136	1,991	9,600

[1] Preliminary.   [2] Forecast.   [3] Data through 2000, includes beef, veal, pork, sheep and goat meat. Beginning 2001, excludes sheep and goat.
Source: Foreign Agricultural Service, U.S. Department of Agriculture (FAS-USDA)

Total Red Meat Exports[3] (Carcass Weight Equivalent) of Principal Countries   In Thousands of Metric Tons

Year	Argentina	Australia	Brazil	Canada	China	Denmark	France	India	Ireland	Nether-lands	New Zealand	United States	World Total
1998	303	1,285	411	861	294	1,814	245	488	16	125	1,543	218	8,338
1999	359	1,308	573	1,046	200	2,653	224	443	9	156	1,676	189	9,096
2000	357	1,387	654	1,182	198	2,067	349	485	22	167	1,704	236	8,984
2001	169	1,466	1,085	1,301	283	1,637	370	496	20	100	1,736	145	9,050
2002	348	1,444	1,471	1,473	351	1,643	417	486	20	183	1,841	262	10,172
2003	386	1,338	1,778	1,358	440	1,622	439	558	27	222	1,921	325	10,594
2004	623	1,453	2,249	1,529	598	1,821	499	606	29	124	1,198	410	11,357
2005	762	1,466	2,628	1,635	593	1,612	627	589	39	89	1,524	487	12,303
2006[1]	500	1,476	2,485	1,555	590	1,600	750	540	35	11	1,869	510	12,174
2007[2]	600	1,549	2,555	1,560	595	1,600	800	570	35	20	2,082	520	12,768

[1] Preliminary.   [2] Forecast.   [3] Data through 2000, includes beef, veal, pork, sheep and goat meat. Beginning 2001, excludes sheep and goat.
Source: Foreign Agricultural Service, U.S. Department of Agriculture (FAS-USDA)

United States Meat Imports by Type of Product   In Metric Tons

Year	Beef and Veal Fresh	Beef and Veal Frozen	Beef and Veal Other Prepared or Preserved	Lamb, Mutton and Goat, Except Canned	Pork Fresh and Chilled	Pork Frozen	Pork Other Prepared or Preserved	Variety Meats, Fresh, hilled and Frozen	Other Livestock Meats NSE	Total
1996	227,874	412,805	66,719	33,009	125,220	58,336	72,650	32,579	13,744	1,042,934
1997	262,985	469,949	63,181	37,848	126,061	65,000	72,903	44,317	14,215	1,156,457
1998	295,820	527,063	68,884	51,630	146,965	70,227	76,230	47,031	13,058	1,296,907
1999	337,899	542,524	82,669	50,209	188,556	77,638	84,207	51,640	13,625	1,428,966
2000	336,117	608,737	73,750	59,968	229,395	91,446	92,672	57,388	14,281	1,563,753
2001	368,529	618,897	73,713	66,785	240,275	84,687	83,724	62,541	16,723	1,615,873
2002	400,484	586,500	84,640	73,863	276,639	90,423	91,379	55,384	19,401	1,678,713
2003	285,772	612,569	85,439	77,546	293,169	107,749	107,964	47,688	21,367	1,639,263
2004[1]	387,758	717,942	92,123	82,930	266,583	109,915	96,840	33,776	23,797	1,811,664

[1] Preliminary.   NSE = Not specified elsewhere.   *Source: Foreign Agricultural Service, U.S. Department of Agriculture (FAS-USDA)*

United States Meat Exports by Type of Product   In Metric Tons

Year	Beef and Veal Fresh and Chilled	Beef and Veal Frozen	Beef and Veal Prepared and Preserved	Lamb and Mutton, Fresh or Frozen	Pork Fresh and Chilled	Pork Frozen	Pork Prepared and Preserved	Variety Meats, Fresh, Chilled or Frozen	Other Meats	Total
1996	273,276	324,329	14,577	2,478	101,975	166,058	38,481	495,343	434,759	1,851,276
1997	316,534	359,460	15,227	2,545	134,684	151,121	38,301	469,789	435,258	1,922,918
1998	346,403	352,050	17,966	2,528	147,006	209,134	43,789	495,643	423,980	2,038,500
1999	370,184	414,458	19,323	2,219	160,910	225,492	47,898	524,325	455,561	2,220,369
2000	395,588	417,538	21,791	2,184	208,055	185,241	44,836	604,738	503,942	2,380,912
2001	393,105	362,972	23,932	2,770	240,275	83,724	84,687	685,063	513,969	2,390,496
2002	407,599	393,836	27,232	3,042	276,639	91,379	90,423	592,185	619,491	2,501,826
2003	430,071	390,543	37,572	2,909	293,169	107,964	107,749	598,726	567,565	2,536,267
2004[1]	114,966	20,458	9,068	3,671	266,583	96,840	109,915	456,480	189,127	1,267,108

[1] Preliminary.   *Source: Foreign Agricultural Service, U.S. Department of Agriculture (FAS-USDA)*

MEATS

Wholesale Price of Boxed Beef Cut-Out a Central Markets
(monthly average) through December 2006 — Cents per pound

Cents Per Pound
----- Choice, 1-3, 550-700 Pound (Jan. 1975 - date)

Exports and Imports of Meats in the United States (Carcass Weight Equivalent)[3]   In Millions of Pounds

| | Exports | | | | Imports | | | |
Year	Beef and Veal	Lamb and Mutton	Pork[3]	All Meat	Beef and Veal	Lamb and Mutton	Pork[3]	All Meat
1997	2,136	5	1,044	3,185	2,343	83	634	3,061
1998	2,171	6	1,230	3,407	2,643	112	705	3,461
1999	2,412	5	1,277	3,694	2,873	112	827	3,813
2000	2,468	5	1,287	3,760	3,032	130	967	4,128
2001	2,269	7	1,559	3,835	3,163	146	951	4,260
2002	2,448	7	1,612	4,067	3,218	160	1,071	4,448
2003	2,518	7	1,717	4,242	3,006	168	1,185	4,359
2004	460	9	2,181	2,650	3,679	180	1,099	4,959
2005[1]	644	9	2,683	3,336	3,587	179	1,002	4,768
2006[2]	680	8	2,785	3,473	3,560	175	960	4,695

[1] Preliminary.   [2] Estimate.   [3] Includes meat content of minor meats and of mixed products.   Source: Economic Research Service, U.S. Department of Agriculture (FAS-USDA)

Average Wholesale Prices of Meats in the United States   In Cents Per Pound

Year	Composite Retail Price of Beef, Choice, Grade 3	of Pork[3]	Wholesale Value[4] Beef	Pork	Net Farm Value of Pork[5]	Cow Beef Canner & Cutter, Central US	Boxed Beef Cut-out, Choice 1-3, Central US, 550-700 Lbs.	Pork Carcass Cut-out, US No. 2	Lamb Carcass, Choice-Prime, East Coast, 55-65 Lbs.	Pork Loins, Central US, 14-18 Lbs.	Skinned Ham, Central US, 20-26 Lbs.	Pork Bellies, Central US, 12-14 Lbs.
1998	277.12	242.69	153.80	97.30	61.20	61.33	99.86	53.08	156.75	101.63	53.07	52.38
1999	287.76	241.44	171.55	99.00	60.40	66.51	111.06	53.45	170.29	100.38	51.35	57.12
2000	306.42	258.20	182.27	114.50	79.40	72.57	117.51	64.07	177.78	117.13	60.85	77.46
2001	337.73	269.39	192.12	117.80	81.30	79.50	122.61	66.83	148.96	116.97	64.86	78.61
2002	331.53	265.75	180.02	100.70	61.90	NA	114.42	53.49	151.28	97.98	47.52	69.91
2003	374.62	265.82	222.90	107.40	69.60	NA	143.58	58.87	185.21	100.96	45.48	86.42
2004	406.53	279.16	218.90	127.40	92.10	NA	142.15	73.53	189.08	117.14	64.98	99.35
2005[1]	409.22	282.69	226.10	124.90	88.00	NA	145.78	69.84	209.88	113.22	64.07	81.46
2006[2]	397.02	280.72	228.17	121.38	83.27	NA	146.82	67.62	199.10	104.46	64.04	82.81

[1] Preliminary.   [2] Estimate.   [3] Sold as retail cuts (ham, bacon, loin, etc.).   [4] Quantity equivalent to 1 pound of retail cuts.   [5] Portion of gross farm value minus farm by-product allowance.   Source: Economic Research Service, U.S. Department of Agriculture (ERS-USDA)

MEATS

Average Wholesale Price of Boxed Beef Cut-Out[1], Choice, at Central Markets   In Cents Per Pound

Year	Jan.	Feb.	Mar.	Apr.	May	June	July	Aug.	Sept.	Oct.	Nov.	Dec.	Average
1997	101.90	98.98	104.87	104.17	105.97	101.83	102.38	105.14	104.06	103.72	104.63	101.50	103.26
1998	100.26	96.27	95.34	98.32	102.09	100.38	99.96	104.28	99.28	102.08	102.61	97.49	99.86
1999	101.37	99.37	103.62	107.55	110.89	115.39	111.14	114.00	115.13	119.21	117.38	117.71	111.05
2000	114.74	112.59	118.42	123.45	124.88	123.30	115.85	111.20	108.68	112.58	118.05	126.41	117.51
2001	129.78	128.87	129.58	128.93	129.03	126.82	118.93	120.20	119.30	115.93	110.95	113.04	122.61
2002	111.99	111.53	120.54	116.61	115.14	114.06	109.88	110.93	111.83	111.64	116.41	122.45	114.42
2003	128.59	128.77	126.35	133.03	141.44	141.16	130.13	139.91	156.64	176.06	167.15	153.71	143.58
2004	138.60	129.29	141.34	157.53	155.70	148.54	140.27	139.33	137.82	138.45	135.64	143.31	142.15
2005	148.93	143.02	150.66	157.34	156.82	140.02	131.19	132.85	137.97	144.30	148.81	157.49	145.78
2006[2]	155.60	149.71	144.94	141.83	147.45	153.09	147.01	146.22	144.69	144.79	143.64	142.92	146.82

[1] Choice 1-3, 550-700 pounds.   [2] Preliminary.   *Source: Economic Research Service, U.S. Department of Agriculture (ERS-USDA)*

Production (Commercial) of All Red Meats in the United States   In Millions of Pounds (Carcass Weight)

Year	Jan.	Feb.	Mar.	Apr.	May	June	July	Aug.	Sept.	Oct.	Nov.	Dec.	Total
1997	3,735	3,278	3,444	3,592	3,571	3,492	3,657	3,619	3,665	4,005	3,453	3,715	43,226
1998	3,836	3,476	3,726	3,701	3,582	3,732	3,781	3,770	3,827	4,033	3,725	3,945	45,134
1999	3,833	3,535	4,016	3,824	3,604	3,940	3,781	3,913	3,933	4,002	3,895	3,862	46,138
2000	3,784	3,767	4,044	3,460	3,878	3,941	3,644	4,113	3,861	4,096	3,919	3,619	46,126
2001	3,935	3,761	3,761	3,506	3,881	3,758	3,643	4,060	3,664	4,264	3,970	3,813	46,016
2002	4,081	3,501	3,677	3,902	4,018	3,813	4,016	4,141	3,873	4,382	3,908	3,859	47,171
2003	4,075	3,496	3,705	3,845	3,944	3,948	4,046	3,913	4,007	4,155	3,524	3,876	46,534
2004	3,713	3,404	3,944	3,713	3,597	3,928	3,708	3,878	3,905	3,921	3,770	3,931	45,412
2005	3,648	3,423	3,879	3,622	3,714	3,963	3,616	4,100	3,933	3,926	3,942	3,954	45,719
2006[1]	3,890	3,485	4,111	3,614	4,048	4,120	3,782	4,245	3,933	4,182	4,136	3,862	47,408

[1] Preliminary.   *Source: Economic Research Service, U.S. Department of Agriculture (ERS-USDA)*

Cold Storage Holdings of All[2] Meats in the United States, on First of Month   In Millions of Pounds

Year	Jan.	Feb.	Mar.	Apr.	May	June	July	Aug.	Sept.	Oct.	Nov.	Dec.
1997	621.3	655.9	669.9	719.5	752.5	719.7	742.9	726.3	731.5	728.2	739.1	741.0
1998	722.4	802.8	825.8	816.3	849.3	814.3	771.0	747.2	728.2	738.8	794.9	794.1
1999	821.0	833.0	863.1	883.5	936.4	901.2	843.9	810.4	834.9	746.3	780.3	750.5
2000	748.3	853.1	913.9	934.3	951.3	963.5	926.7	896.2	881.0	871.1	868.0	883.0
2001	836.2	907.8	852.6	787.9	771.4	772.5	742.2	717.4	732.6	775.3	849.0	880.9
2002	946.8	982.6	970.7	961.9	996.6	973.0	918.0	912.6	950.7	997.8	1,038.9	997.7
2003	1,011.5	1,015.2	978.2	951.9	926.8	901.5	847.5	825.0	817.3	832.1	836.9	828.1
2004	879.0	953.7	926.9	879.4	883.6	829.3	797.9	807.7	841.9	886.1	889.2	912.6
2005	979.0	966.8	956.2	931.6	909.5	848.6	851.7	855.9	848.9	890.9	905.9	888.2
2006[1]	884.4	1,012.4	973.7	946.0	964.1	926.2	865.1	898.6	893.6	934.8	964.6	989.7

[1] Preliminary.   [2] Includes beef and veal, mutton and lamb, pork and products, rendered pork fat, and miscellaneous meats. Excludes lard.
Source: Economic Research Service, U.S. Department of Agriculture (ERS-USDA)

Cold Storage Holdings of Frozen Beef in the United States, on First of Month   In Millions of Pounds

Year	Jan. 1	Feb. 1	Mar. 1	Apr. 1	May 1	June 1	July 1	Aug. 1	Sept. 1	Oct. 1	Nov. 1	Dec. 1
1997	284.9	290.3	261.7	290.4	285.4	278.7	305.6	302.8	324.6	349.1	351.6	378.2
1998	350.2	331.1	334.9	329.7	335.5	310.2	316.5	303.0	306.7	323.1	358.2	328.2
1999	296.4	301.1	300.1	309.2	316.8	306.7	293.1	292.7	377.9	294.4	322.5	308.9
2000	314.2	350.9	369.0	378.2	396.1	401.1	405.1	391.5	398.8	405.7	404.4	411.8
2001	401.7	410.9	360.2	332.6	315.3	325.1	340.8	351.4	373.2	382.8	395.1	427.6
2002	460.7	455.5	439.0	410.5	405.7	401.8	396.9	416.5	461.8	494.9	525.2	512.6
2003	524.6	482.4	441.9	403.1	389.7	385.1	371.5	368.2	371.0	379.8	375.2	373.8
2004	395.1	434.4	435.0	416.8	421.2	402.8	411.8	427.0	446.0	457.2	452.6	463.3
2005	484.3	453.3	400.2	372.3	329.4	318.2	342.1	385.2	410.6	438.8	439.2	429.9
2006[1]	434.4	465.9	428.3	424.0	428.5	434.6	436.8	466.0	471.7	477.4	475.6	507.9

[1] Preliminary.   *Source: Economic Research Service, U.S. Department of Agriculture (ERS-USDA)*

Mercury

Mercury (symbol Hg) was known to the ancient Hindus and Chinese, and was also found in Egyptian tombs dating back to 1500 BC. The ancient Greeks used mercury in ointments, and the Romans used it in cosmetics. Alchemists thought mercury turned into gold when it hardened.

Mercury, also called quicksilver, is a heavy, silvery, toxic, transitional metal. Mercury is the only common metal that is liquid at room temperatures. When subjected to a pressure of 7,640 atmospheres (7.7 million millibars), mercury becomes a solid. Mercury dissolves in nitric or concentrated sulfuric acid, but is resistant to alkalis. It is a poor conductor of heat. Mercury has superconductivity when cooled to sufficiently low temperatures. It has a freezing point of about –39 degrees Celsius and a boiling point of about 357 degrees Celsius.

Mercury is found in its pure form or combined in small amounts with silvers, but is found most often in the ore cinnabar, a mineral consisting of mercuric sulfide. By heating the cinnabar ore in air until the mercuric sulfide breaks down, pure mercury metal is produced. Mercury forms alloys called amalgams with all common metals except iron and platinum. Most mercury is used for the manufacture of industrial chemicals and for electrical and electronic applications. Other uses for mercury include its use in gold recovery from ores, barometers, diffusion pumps, laboratory instruments, mercury-vapor lamps, pesticides, batteries, and catalysts. A decline in mercury production and usage since the 1970s reflects a trend for using mercury substitutes due to its toxicity.

Prices – The average monthly price of mercury in 2006 fell sharply by –23.2% yr/yr to $594.84 per flask (34.5 kilograms). That is down from last year's price that was a record high of $774.04.

Supply – World mine production of mercury in 2005 fell by –11.1% yr/yr to 1,680 metric tons. The record low of 1,320 metric tons was posted in 1999 and the record high of 10,364 metric tons was posted in 1971.

The world's largest miners of mercury are China with 66% of world production, Kyrgyzstan with 12%, Spain with 15%, and Finland with 4%. China's production rose to 1,100 metric tons in 2005, which is more than five times the record low of 190 metric tons seen in 2001 and almost equal to its record of 1,200 metric tons posted in 1989.

Demand – The breakdown of domestic consumption of mercury by particular categories is no longer available, but the data as of 1997 showed that chlorine and caustic soda accounted for 46% of US mercury consumption, followed by wiring devices and switches (17%), dental equipment (12%), electrical lighting (8%), and measuring control instruments (7%). Substitutes for mercury include lithium and composite ceramic materials.

Trade – US foreign trade in mercury is still relatively small but US imports of mercury in 2005 rose by 130% yr/yr to 212 metric tons and posted a new 9-year high. US imports were mostly from Chile and Peru. US exports of mercury in 2005 rose by 14.7% to a 12-year high of 319 metric tons.

World Mine Production of Mercury   In Metric Tons (1 tonne = 29.008216 flasks)

Year	Algeria	China	Finland	Kyrgyzstan	Mexico	Spain	Tajikistan	Russia	Ukraine	United States	World Total
1997	447	830	63	550	15	389	40	50	25	W	2,410
1998	224	230	54	250	15	675	35	50	20		1,580
1999	240	200	40	300	15	433	35	50			1,320
2000	216	200	76	257	15	500	40	50			1,360
2001	321	190	71	300	15	500	40	50			1,500
2002	307	435	51	300	15	300	20	50			1,490
2003	176	610	25	300	15	150	30	50			1,370
2004[1]	73	1,140	24	300	15	250	30	50			1,890
2005[2]	4	1,100	65	200	15	250	30	50			1,680

[1] Preliminary. [2] Estimate. W = Withheld to avoid disclosing company proprietary data. NA = Not available. *Source: U.S. Geological Survey (USGS)*

Salient Statistics of Mercury in the United States   In Metric Tons

Year	Producing Mines	Secondary Production Industrial	Secondary Production Government[3]	Secondary Production NDS[4] Shipments	Consumer & Dealer Stocks, Dec. 31	Industrial Demand	Exports	Imports
1997	5	389	----	----	203	346	134	164
1998	NA	NA	----	----	NA	NA	63	128
1999	NA	NA	----	----	NA	NA	181	62
2000	NA	NA	----	----	NA	NA	182	103
2001	NA	NA	----	----	NA	NA	108	100
2002	NA	NA	----	----	NA	NA	201	209
2003	NA	NA	----	----	NA	NA	287	46
2004[1]	NA	NA	----	----	NA	NA	278	92
2005[2]	NA	NA	----	----	NA	NA	319	212

[1] Preliminary.   [2] Estimate.   [3] Secondary mercury shipped from the Department of Energy.   [4] National Defense Stockpile.   NA = Not available.
Source: U.S. Geological Survey (USGS)

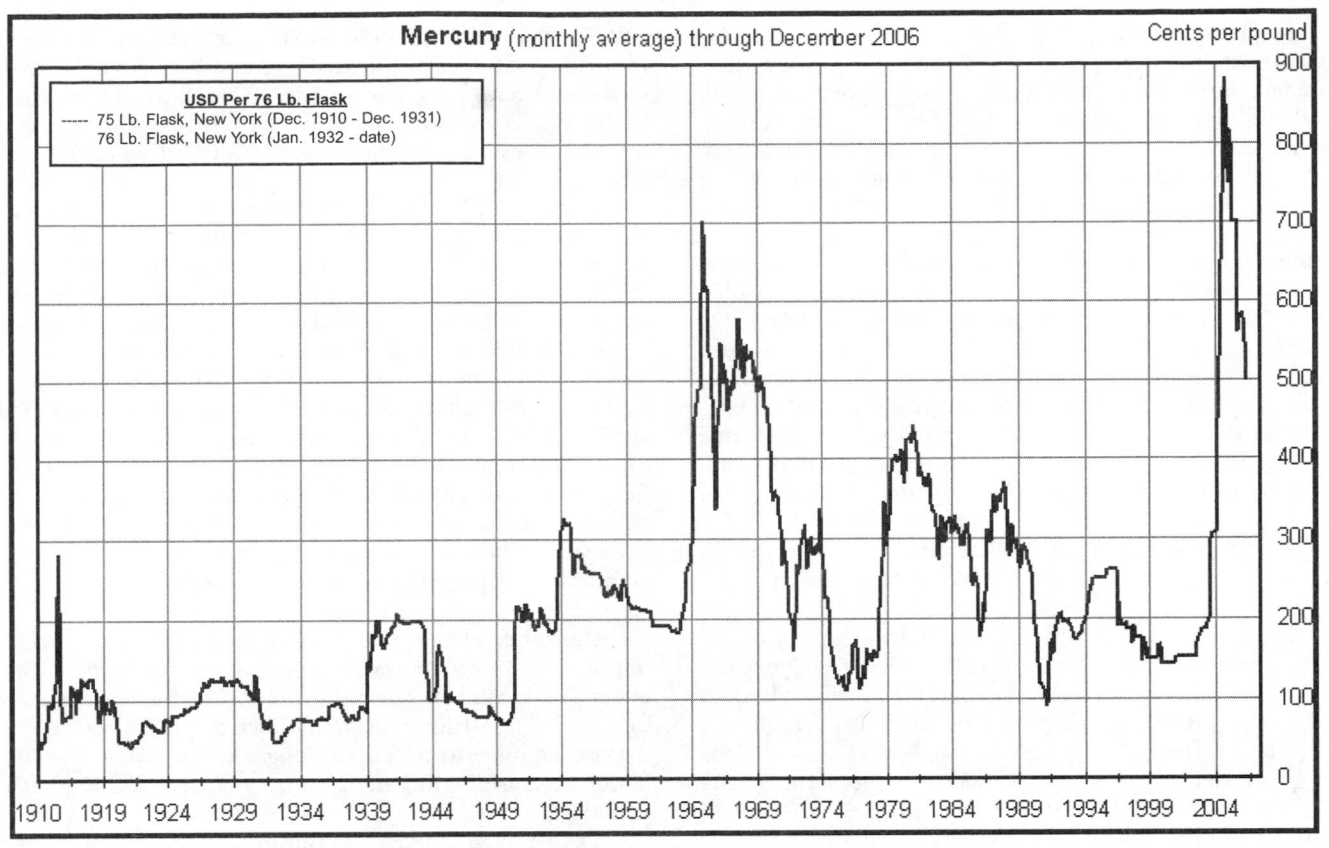

Mercury (monthly average) through December 2006 — Cents per pound

USD Per 76 Lb. Flask
----- 75 Lb. Flask, New York (Dec. 1910 - Dec. 1931)
76 Lb. Flask, New York (Jan. 1932 - date)

Average Price of Mercury in New York   In Dollars Per Flask of 76 Pounds (34.5 Kilograms)

Year	Jan.	Feb.	Mar.	Apr.	May	June	July	Aug.	Sept.	Oct.	Nov.	Dec.	Average
1997	233.98	232.76	228.88	228.64	220.00	199.05	200.00	198.10	190.83	198.83	191.47	187.00	209.13
1998	187.00	187.00	187.00	187.00	187.00	181.55	175.00	175.00	175.00	175.00	175.00	175.00	180.55
1999	175.00	152.63	150.00	150.00	150.00	150.00	150.00	150.00	150.00	150.00	150.00	150.00	152.09
2000	150.00	157.88	167.50	167.50	167.50	158.23	142.00	142.00	142.00	142.00	142.00	142.00	151.90
2001	142.00	142.00	142.00	142.00	142.00	143.71	154.00	154.00	154.00	154.00	154.00	154.00	148.12
2002	154.00	154.00	154.00	154.00	154.00	154.00	154.00	154.00	154.00	154.00	154.00	154.00	154.00
2003	165.43	175.00	175.00	175.00	185.23	187.50	187.50	187.50	187.50	187.50	195.63	200.00	184.07
2004	200.00	256.25	297.61	305.00	305.00	305.00	305.00	305.00	417.05	485.12	649.24	650.00	373.36
2005	678.57	747.50	867.39	873.81	850.00	817.05	759.52	750.00	813.64	730.95	700.00	700.00	774.04
2006	700.00	700.00	691.30	552.50	574.02	582.50	582.50	582.50	582.50	576.59	513.64	500.00	594.84

Source: American Metal Market (AMM)

Mercury Consumed in the United States   In Metric Tons

Year	Batteries[3]	Chlorine & Caustic Soda	Catalysts, Misc.	Dental Equip.	Electrical Lighting[3]	General Lab Use	Measuring Contraol Instrument	Paints	Wiring Devices & Switches[3]	Other Uses	Total
1989	250	379	40	39	31	18	87	192	141	32	1,212
1990	106	247	29	44	33	32	108	14	70	38	720
1991	18	184	26	41	39	30	90	6	71	49	554
1992	13	209	20	42	55	28	80	-----	82	92	621
1993	10	180	18	35	38	26	65	-----	83	103	558
1994	6	135	25	24	27	24	53	-----	79	110	483
1995	-----	154	-----	32	30	-----	43	-----	84	93	436
1996[1]	-----	136	-----	31	29	-----	41	-----	49	86	372
1997[2]	-----	160	-----	40	29	-----	24	-----	57	36	346
	Data No Longer Available										

[1] Preliminary.   [2] Estimate.   W = Withheld proprietary data.   *Source: U.S. Geological Survey (USGS)*

Milk

Evidence of man's use of animal milk as food was discovered in a temple in the Euphrates Valley near Babylon, dating back to 3,000 BC. Humans drink the milk produced from a variety of domesticated mammals, including cows, goats, sheep, camels, reindeer, buffaloes, and llama. In India, half of all milk consumed is from water buffalo. Camels' milk spoils slower than other types of milk in the hot desert, but the vast majority of milk used for commercial production and consumption comes from cows.

Milk directly from a cow in its natural form is called raw milk. Raw milk is processed by spinning it in a centrifuge, homogenizing it to create a consistent texture (i.e., by forcing hot milk under high pressure through small nozzles), and then sterilizing it through pasteurization (i.e., heating to a high temperature for a specified length of time to destroy pathogenic bacteria). Condensed, powdered, and evaporated milk are produced by evaporating some or all of the water content. Whole milk contains 3.5% milk fat. Lower-fat milks include 2% low-fat milk, 1% low- fat milk, and skim milk which has only 1/2 gram of milk fat per serving.

The Chicago Mercantile Exchange has three different milk futures contracts: Milk Class III which is milk used in the manufacturing of cheese, Milk Class IV which is milk used in the production of butter and all dried milk products, and Nonfat Dry Milk which is used in commercial or consumer cooking or to reconstitute nonfat milk by the consumer. The Milk Class III contract has the largest volume and open interest.

Prices – The average monthly price received by farmers for all milk sold to plants in 2006 fell by –14.8% yr/yr to $12.90 per hundred pounds, moving farther below the 2004 record high of $16.04. The average monthly price received by farmers for fluid grade milk in 2006 fell by –14.7% yr/yr to $12.92. The average monthly price received by farmers for manufacturing grade milk in 2006 fell by –15.6% to $12.19.

Supply – The world's largest milk producers are the European Union with 130.500 million metric tons of production in 2006, the US with 83.000 million metric tons of production, and Russia with 32.800 million metric tons of production. US milk production in 2006 rose +2.7% yr/yr to 181.839 billion pounds, which was a new record high. The number of dairy cows on US farms has fallen sharply in the past 3 decades from the 12 million level seen in 1970. In 2005, there were 9.040 million dairy cows on US farms, up slightly from 2004's record low of 9.010 million. Dairy farmers have been able to increase milk production even with fewer cows because of a dramatic increase in milk yield per cow. In 2005, the average cow produced a record 19,577 pounds of milk per year, more than double the 9,751 pounds seen in 1970.

Demand – Per capita consumption of milk in the US fell to a new record low of 206 pounds per year in 2002 (the latest data available), down sharply by 26% from 277 pounds in 1977. The utilization breakdown for 2002 shows the largest manufacturing usage categories are cheese (64.504 billion pounds of milk) and creamery butter (30.250 billion pounds).

Trade – US imports of milk in 2005 fell –12.8% yr/yr to 4.600 billion pounds, moving even farther below the record high of 5.716 billion pounds posted in 2001.

World Fluid Milk Production (Cow's Milk)   In Thousands of Metric Tons

Year	Argentina	Australia	Brazil	China	EU-25	India	Japan	Mexico	New Zealand	Russia	Ukraine	United States	World Total
2000	9,800	11,172	22,134	8,274	129,392	36,250	8,497	9,305	12,235	31,900	12,400	75,929	386,769
2001	9,500	10,864	22,300	10,255	130,069	36,400	8,300	9,501	13,162	33,000	13,169	74,994	391,409
2002	8,500	11,608	22,635	12,998	131,040	36,200	8,385	9,560	13,925	33,500	13,860	77,140	402,266
2003	7,950	10,636	22,860	17,463	131,847	36,500	8,400	9,784	14,346	33,000	13,400	77,290	406,378
2004	9,250	10,377	23,317	22,606	130,620	37,500	8,329	9,874	15,000	32,000	13,787	77,535	412,337
2005	9,500	10,429	24,025	27,534	131,652	37,520	8,285	9,855	14,500	32,000	13,423	80,286	418,184
2006[1]	10,300	10,395	24,745	32,800	130,500	38,750	8,170	9,998	15,200	32,200	12,890	82,508	425,103
2007[2]	10,800	10,000	25,365	38,100	130,600	40,050	8,150	10,100	15,400	32,800	13,100	83,007	434,017

[1] Preliminary.   [2] Forecast.   Source: Foreign Agricultural Service, U.S. Department of Agriculture (FAS-USDA)

Salient Statistics of Milk in the United States   In Millions of Pounds

Year	Number of Milk Cows on Farms[3] (Thousands)	Production Per Cow[4] (Pounds)	Production Total[4]	Beginning Stocks[5]	Imports	Total Supply	Exports[5]	Domestic Fed to Calves	Domestic Humans	Total Use	All Milk, Wholesale	Milk, Eligible for Fluid Market	Milk, Manufacturing Grade	Per Capita Consumption[6] (Fluid Milk in Lbs.)
2000	9,206	18,202	167,559	6,186	4,445	178,190		1,107	166,256	167,363	12.33	12.38	10.54	210
2001	9,114	18,158	165,497	7,010	5,716	178,223		1,036	164,123	165,159	14.98	14.99	14.78	208
2002	9,139	18,608	170,063	7,259	5,103	182,425		959	168,944	169,903	12.10	12.10	10.92	206
2003	9,083	18,761	170,394	9,891	5,040	185,325		964	169,276	170,240	12.52	12.53	11.77	
2004	9,010	18,958	170,805	8,333	5,278	184,416		956	169,699	170,655	16.04	16.04	15.41	
2005[1]	9,040	19,577	176,989	7,154	4,600	188,743					15.14	15.14	14.45	
2006[2]	9,115	19,949	181,839	7,154	4,700	193,693					12.90	12.92	12.19	

[1] Preliminary.   [2] Estimate.   [3] Average number on farms during year including dry cows, excluding heifers not yet fresh.   [4] Excludes milk sucked by calves.   [5] Government and commercial.   [6] Product pounds of commercial sales and on farm consumption.   Source: Economic Research Service, U.S. Department of Agriculture (ERS-USDA)

Utilization of Milk in the United States   In Millions of Pounds (Milk Equivalent)

Year	Butter from Whey Cream	Creamery Butter[2]	Cheese[3]	Cottage Cheese (Creamed)	Canned Milk[4]	Bulk Condensed Whole Milk Unsweet-ened	Bulk Condensed Whole Milk Sweet-ened	Dry Whole Milk Products	Ice Cream[5]	Other Frozen Dairy Products	Other Manu-factured Por-ducts[6]	Used on Farms Farm-Churned Butter	Total
1999	5,392	28,657	60,154	NA	1,037	216	171	868	2,305	14,370	682	219	1,328
2000	5,538	28,059	62,257	NA	965	180	163	815	2,218	14,447	700	196	1,303
2001	5,612	27,557	61,804	NA	991	170	163	303	2,220	14,395	701	170	1,181
2002	5,791	30,250	64,504	NA	593	77	56	47	2,320	14,373	706	160	1,119
2003[1]					595	128	76	39				149	1,105
2004[1]					549	117	76	42				149	1,105

[1] Preliminary.   [2] Excludes whey butter.   [3] American and other.   [4] Includes evaporated and sweetened condensed.   [5] Milk equivalent of butter and condensed milk used in ice cream.   [6] Whole milk equivalent of dry cream, malted milk powder, part-skim milk, dry or concentrated ice cream mix, dehydrated butterfat and other miscellaneous products using milkfat.   *Source: National Agricultural Statistics Service, U.S. Department of Agriculture (NASS-USDA)*

Milk-Feed Price Ratio[1] in the United States   In Pounds

Year	Jan.	Feb.	Mar.	Apr.	May	June	July	Aug.	Sept.	Oct.	Nov.	Dec.	Average
1999	4.09	3.67	3.57	2.97	2.89	3.17	3.61	3.85	4.09	3.96	3.87	3.24	3.58
2000	3.07	2.94	2.91	2.84	2.63	2.96	3.29	3.38	3.34	3.12	3.03	3.04	3.05
2001	3.08	3.03	3.24	3.29	3.41	3.74	3.60	3.62	3.75	3.55	3.29	2.99	3.38
2002	3.03	3.00	2.89	2.81	2.64	2.54	2.34	2.27	2.30	2.46	2.44	2.44	2.60
2003	2.40	2.35	2.27	2.25	2.19	2.21	2.60	2.89	3.16	3.23	3.05	2.89	2.62
2004	2.70	2.60	2.80	3.11	3.15	3.12	2.96	2.93	3.22	3.27	3.57	3.67	3.09
2005	3.45	3.50	3.35	3.18	2.93	2.87	2.93	3.08	3.27	3.42	3.45	3.28	3.23
2006[2]	3.17	2.93	2.70	2.46	2.33	2.35	2.35	2.47	2.58	2.53	2.46	2.41	2.56

[1] Pounds of 16% protein mixed dairy feed equal in value to one pound of whole milk.   [2] Preliminary.   *Source: Economic Research Service, U.S. Department of Agriculture (ERS-USDA)*

Milk Production[1] in the United States   In Millions of Pounds

Year	Jan.	Feb.	Mar.	Apr.	May	June	July	Aug.	Sept.	Oct.	Nov.	Dec.	Total
2000	14,263	13,606	14,761	14,390	14,791	14,008	14,117	13,798	13,246	13,708	13,212	13,758	167,658
2001	13,998	12,894	14,375	14,078	14,646	13,957	13,877	13,564	13,129	13,611	13,305	13,902	165,332
2002	14,304	13,229	14,864	14,580	15,118	14,317	14,196	14,128	13,467	13,866	13,478	14,211	170,063
2003	14,584	13,441	15,044	14,634	15,003	14,328	14,263	14,015	13,468	13,898	13,470	14,164	170,394
2004	14,402	13,595	14,762	14,519	15,012	14,293	14,405	14,215	13,619	14,070	13,610	14,303	170,805
2005	14,614	13,530	15,206	15,047	15,697	15,087	14,978	14,896	14,260	14,611	14,209	14,854	176,989
2006[1]	15,333	14,248	15,972	15,541	16,056	15,311	15,159	15,088	14,492	14,880	14,542	15,217	181,839

[1] Excludes milk sucked by calves.   [2] Preliminary.   *Source: Economic Research Service, U.S. Department of Agriculture (ERS-USDA)*

Average Price Received by U.S. Farmers for All Milk (Sold to Plants)   In Dollars Per Hundred Pounds (Cwt.)

Year	Jan.	Feb.	Mar.	Apr.	May	June	July	Aug.	Sept.	Oct.	Nov.	Dec.	Average
2000	12.00	11.80	11.90	11.90	12.00	12.30	12.60	12.50	12.90	12.50	12.60	13.00	12.33
2001	13.20	13.00	13.90	14.60	15.50	16.20	16.20	16.50	17.10	15.60	14.40	13.50	14.98
2002	13.40	13.10	12.70	12.50	12.10	11.50	11.10	11.30	11.60	12.10	11.90	11.90	12.10
2003	11.70	11.40	11.00	11.00	11.00	11.00	12.10	13.30	14.50	15.00	14.40	13.80	12.52
2004	13.20	13.60	15.40	18.10	19.30	18.20	16.10	14.90	15.50	15.60	16.20	16.40	16.04
2005	15.90	15.50	15.60	15.20	14.70	14.40	14.80	14.80	15.30	15.60	15.10	14.80	15.14
2006[1]	14.50	13.50	12.60	12.10	12.00	11.90	11.80	12.00	12.90	13.50	13.90	14.10	12.90

[1] Preliminary.   *Source: Economic Research Service, U.S. Department of Agriculture (ERS-USDA)*

Average Farm Price of Milk Eligible for Fluid Market   In Dollars Per Hundred Pounds (Cwt.)

Year	Jan.	Feb.	Mar.	Apr.	May	June	July	Aug.	Sept.	Oct.	Nov.	Dec.	Average
2000	12.00	11.90	12.00	11.90	12.10	12.30	12.60	12.50	13.00	12.60	12.60	13.10	12.38
2001	13.20	13.10	13.90	14.60	15.50	16.20	16.20	16.50	17.10	15.60	14.50	13.50	14.99
2002	13.40	13.10	12.70	12.50	12.10	11.50	11.10	11.30	11.60	12.10	11.90	11.90	12.10
2003	11.80	11.40	11.00	11.00	11.00	11.00	12.10	13.30	14.50	15.00	14.40	13.80	12.53
2004	13.20	13.60	15.40	18.10	19.30	18.20	16.10	14.90	15.50	15.60	16.20	16.40	16.04
2005	15.90	15.50	15.60	15.20	14.70	14.40	14.80	14.80	15.30	15.60	15.10	14.80	15.14
2006[1]	14.50	13.50	12.60	12.20	12.00	11.90	11.80	12.10	12.90	13.50	13.90	14.10	12.92

[1] Preliminary.   *Source: Economic Research Service, U.S. Department of Agriculture (ERS-USDA)*

Molybdenum

Molybdenum (symbol Mo) is a silvery-white, hard, malleable, metallic element. Molybdenum melts at about 2610 degrees Celsius and boils at about 4640 degrees Celsius. Swedish chemist Carl Wilhelm Scheele discovered molybdenum in 1778.

Molybdenum occurs in nature in the form of molybdenite and wulfenite. Contributing to the growth of plants, it is an important trace element in soils. Approximately 70% of the world supply of molybdenum is obtained as a by-product of copper mining. Molybdenum is chiefly used as an alloy to strengthen steel and resist corrosion. It is used for structural work, aircraft parts, and forged automobile parts because it withstands high temperatures and pressures and adds strength. Other uses include lubricants, a refractory metal in chemical applications, electron tubing, and as a catalyst.

Prices – The average monthly US merchant price of molybdic oxide in 2006 fell sharply by –23.3% yr/yr to $25.08 per pound. That was down from last year's 2005 record high of $32.70 per pound but still almost 11 times the decade low of $2.37 seen in 2001.

Supply – World production of molybdenum in 2005 rose by +16.4% yr/yr to a record high of 185,000 metric tons, continuing the recovery from the 11-year low of 122,000 metric tons seen in 2002. The world's largest producers of molybdenum are the US with 31% of world production in 2005, Chili with 26%, and China with 22%.

US production of molybdenum concentrate in 2005 rose +39.8% yr/yr to 58,000 metric tons, continuing the recovery from the 20-year low of 32,300 metric tons posted in 2002. US production of molybdenum primary products in 2005 rose +22.6% to 29,800 metric tons, with 28,700 metric tons of that production in molybdic oxide and 1,100 metric tons in molybdenum metal powder.

Demand – US consumption of molybdenum concentrate in 2005 rose by +20.4% yr/yr to 46,600 metric tons, continuing to recover from the 11-year low of 21,200 metric tons posted in 2002. US consumption of molybdenum concentrate has more than doubled over the last 10 years. US consumption of molybdenum primary products rose by +8.6% yr/yr in 2005 to 18,900 metric tons.

Trade – US imports of molybdenum concentrate for consumption in 2005 rose +35.5% yr/yr to 11,900 metric tons, continuing to recover from the 11-year low of 4,710 metric tons posted in 2002.

World Mine Production of Molybdenum   In Metric Tons (Contained Molybdenum)

Year	Armenia	Canada[3]	Chile	China	Iran	Kazak-hstan	Mexico	Mongolia	Peru	Russia	United States	Uzbek-isten	World Total
1999	2,800	6,250	27,309	29,700	1,600	155	7,961	1,910	5,470	2,400	42,400	500	129,000
2000	3,820	7,457	33,639	28,800	1,600	215	6,886	1,335	7,193	2,400	40,900	500	135,000
2001	2,943	8,233	33,492	28,200	2,400	225	5,518	1,514	9,499	2,600	37,600	500	133,000
2002	2,884	8,043	29,466	29,300	2,300	230	3,428	1,590	8,613	2,900	32,300	500	122,000
2003	2,763	9,090	33,374	31,000	2,200	230	3,524	1,793	9,561	2,900	33,500	500	131,000
2004[1]	2,950	9,520	41,883	38,500	1,800	230	3,730	1,141	14,246	2,900	41,500	500	159,000
2005[2]	2,750	7,910	47,748	40,000	2,000	230	4,246	1,188	17,325	3,000	58,000	500	185,000

[1] Preliminary.   [2] Estimate.   [3] Shipments.   Source: U.S. Geological Survey (USGS)

Salient Statistics of Molybdenum in the United States   In Metric Tons (Contained Molybdenum)

| | Concentrate | | | | | | Primary Products[4] | | | | | | |
| | | Shipments | | | | | Net Production | | | Shipments | | | |
Year	Pro-duction	Total (Includes Exports)	Value Million $	For Exports	Con-sumption	Imports For Con-sumption	Stocks, Dec. 31[3]	Grand Total	Molybolic Oxide[5]	Moly-bolic Metal Powder	Price Average Value $ / Kg.[6]	To Domestic Dest-inations	Oxide for Exports (Groos Weight)	Con-sumption	Producer Stocks, Dec. 31
1999	42,400	42,800	251.0	----	34,500	6,390	4,580	19,200	17,400	1,880	5.90	39,000	1,130	18,700	5,340
2000	40,900	40,400	210.0	----	33,800	6,120	4,030	19,700	17,500	2,190	5.64	34,600	1,190	18,300	5,360
2001	37,600	37,000	192.0	----	33,300	6,010	4,210	15,700	14,900	771	5.20	32,600	940	15,800	5,600
2002	32,300	32,300	232.0	----	21,200	4,710	3,870	10,500	10,000	513	8.27	27,500	1,670	15,300	4,300
2003	33,500	33,600	324.0	----	27,500	5,190	2,520	11,800	11,000	760	11.65	30,100	2,580	16,400	2,760
2004[1]	41,500	42,000	1,420.0	----	38,700	8,780	2,610	24,300	23,400	868	29.67	39,300	5,280	17,400	2,840
2005[2]	58,000	57,900	NA	----	46,600	11,900	3,610	29,800	28,700	1,050	72.07	46,700	14,600	18,900	3,770

[1] Preliminary.   [2] Estimate.   [3] At mines & at plants making molybdenum products.   [4] Comprises ferromolybdenum, molybdic oxide, & molybdenum salts & metal.   [5] Includes molybdic oxide briquets, molybdic acid, molybdenum trioxide, all other.   [6] U.S. producer price per kilogram of molybdenum oxide contained in technical-grade molybdic oxide. W = Withheld proprietary data.   Source: U.S. Geological Survey (USGS)

US Merchant Price of Molybdic Oxide   In Dollars Per Pound

Year	Jan.	Feb.	Mar.	Apr.	May	June	July	Aug.	Sept.	Oct.	Nov.	Dec.	Average
2000	2.86	3.55	3.40	2.55	2.55	2.55	2.55	2.64	2.70	2.70	2.70	2.39	2.74
2001	2.38	2.38	2.38	2.38	2.38	2.38	2.38	2.38	2.38	2.40	2.33	2.33	2.37
2002	2.33	2.33	2.33	2.75	2.99	6.93	5.32	4.75	4.73	4.70	3.82	3.48	3.87
2003	3.63	3.74	4.62	5.20	5.20	5.77	5.86	5.60	5.84	6.25	6.25	6.25	5.35
2004	7.63	8.15	8.93	13.11	14.00	15.03	15.75	16.70	18.27	19.50	22.66	27.50	15.60
2005	33.00	30.15	33.59	34.79	36.41	38.32	32.79	30.00	31.93	32.33	30.33	28.72	32.70
2006	23.70	24.54	23.12	22.93	24.82	26.31	26.01	25.60	26.96	26.02	25.41	25.50	25.08

Source: American Metal Market (AMM)

Nickel

Nickel (symbol Ni) is a hard, malleable, ductile metal that has a silvery tinge that can take on a high polish. Nickel is somewhat ferromagnetic and is a fair conductor of heat and electricity. Nickel is primarily used in the production of stainless steel and other corrosion-resistant alloys. Nickel is used in coins to replace silver, in rechargeable batteries, and in electronic circuitry. Nickel plating techniques, like electro-less coating or single-slurry coating, are employed in such applications as turbine blades, helicopter rotors, extrusion dies, and rolled steel strip.

Nickel futures and options trade at the London Metal Exchange (LME). The nickel futures contract calls for the delivery of 6 metric tons of primary nickel with at least 99.80% purity in the form of full plate, cut cathodes, pellets or briquettes. The contract is priced in terms of US dollars per metric ton.

Prices – Nickel prices rallied sharply in 2006, closing the year at $34,025 per metric ton, up +154% from the 2005 close of $13,372 per metric ton. Nickel prices extended the rally in early 2007 to post a new record high of $44,500 per metric ton. Nickel prices rallied on very strong demand combined with insufficient new mining output.

Supply – World mine production of nickel in 2005 rose +7.9% yr/yr to 1.500 million metric tons. That is more than double the production seen in 1970. The world's largest mine producers of nickel in 2005 were Russia (with 21% of world production), Australia (14%), Canada (13%), Indonesia (9%), and New Caledonia (8%). In 2004 (latest data available) US secondary nickel production fell –0.3% to 83,280 metric tons, down slightly from the record high of 83,960 metric tons in 2002.

Demand – US consumption of nickel in 2004 (latest data available) rose 10.9% to 183,000 metric tons, but still below the 2002 record high of 197,000 metric tons. The primary US nickel consumption use is for stainless and heat-resisting steels, which accounted for 63% of US consumption in 2004. Other consumption uses were nickel alloys (8%), super alloys (8%), electro-plating anodes (7%), copper base alloys (3%), chemicals (3%), alloy steels (2%), and cast irons (2%).

Trade – The US relied on imports for 60% of its nickel consumption in 2006, up from 54% in 2005. US imports of primary and secondary nickel in 2004 rose +13.4% to 154,800 metric tons, up from 2002's 12-year low of 130,110 metric tons. US exports of primary and secondary nickel in 2003 rose 5.0% to 56,300 metric tons, which was still below the record high of 58,050 metric tons posted in 2000.

World Mine Production of Nickel   In Metric Tons (Contained Nickel)

Year	Australia[3]	Botswana	Brazil	Canada	China	Dominican Republic	Greece	Indonesia	New Caledonia	Phillip-pines	Russia	South Africa	World Total
1999	119,226	33,733	41,522	186,236	49,500	39,997	16,050	89,111	110,062	20,689	300,000	36,202	1,160,000
2000	166,500	38,420	45,317	190,793	50,300	39,943	19,535	98,200	128,789	17,388	315,000	36,616	1,290,000
2001	205,000	26,714	45,456	194,058	51,500	39,120	20,830	102,000	117,734	27,359	320,000	36,443	1,340,000
2002	207,800	28,600	44,928	189,297	53,700	38,859	22,670	123,000	99,841	26,532	305,000	38,546	1,350,000
2003	210,000	32,740	45,160	163,244	61,000	45,400	21,410	143,000	112,013	19,537	310,000	40,842	1,390,000
2004[1]	178,100	32,980	45,200	186,546	64,000	47,000	21,700	133,000	118,279	16,973	315,000	39,850	1,390,000
2005[2]	210,000	37,100	46,000	196,000	71,000	47,000	22,100	140,000	122,000	22,000	315,000	41,700	1,500,000

[1] Preliminary.   [2] Estimate.   [3] Content of nickel sulfate and concentrates.   *Source: U.S. Geological Survey (USGS)*

Salient Statistics of Nickel in the United States   In Metric Tons (Contained Nickel)

Year	Net Import Reliance as a % of Apparent Consumption	Production Plant[4]	Production Secondary[5]	Alloy Sheets	Cast Irons	Copper Base Alloys	Electro-plating Anodes	Nickel Alloys	Stainless & Heat Resisting Steels	Super Alloys	Chemicals	Apparent Consumption	Stocks, Dec. 31 At Consumers' Plants	Stocks, Dec. 31 At Producer Plants	Primary & Secondary Nickel Exports	Primary & Secondary Nickel Imports	Avg. Price LME $/Lb.
1998	64	4,290	63,100	9,590	908	7,470	16,400	17,500	93,000	18,600	1,970	186,000	15,960	13,100	43,540	156,500	2.10
1999	63		71,000	8,100	495	10,500	15,400	15,200	102,000	18,900	1,580	190,000	10,050	12,700	38,840	148,480	2.73
2000	58		83,900	7,700	198	9,940	15,700	18,200	108,000	19,400	991	189,000	14,260	12,300	58,050	166,700	3.92
2001	52		101,500	7,590	886	7,190	12,500	17,900	121,000	18,400	1,630	188,000	13,910	12,600	57,050	144,760	2.70
2002	52		83,960	3,920	427	5,280	12,300	14,200	135,000	12,600	1,280	197,000	11,560	6,150	45,920	130,110	3.07
2003[2]	50		83,510	3,730	591	5,200	11,400	14,600	114,000	13,400	2,400	165,000	11,070	8,040	53,630	136,500	4.37
2004[3]	55		83,280	3,770	311	5,920	11,900	15,400	116,000	15,100	6,300	183,000	10,740	6,580	56,300	154,800	6.27

[1] Exclusive of scrap.   [2] Preliminary.   [3] Estimate.   [4] Smelter & refinery.   [5] From purchased scrap (ferrous & nonferrous).   W = Withheld proprietary data.   NA = Not avaliable.   *Source: U.S. Geological Survey (USGS)*

Average Price of Nickel[1] in the United States   In Cents Per Pound

Year	Jan.	Feb.	Mar.	Apr.	May	June	July	Aug.	Sept.	Oct.	Nov.	Dec.	Average
2002	261.00	261.00	261.00	261.00	288.00	320.00	331.00	332.00	322.00	310.00	342.00	351.00	303.33
2003	365.17	406.25	397.38	377.72	395.63	424.56	427.68	454.67	482.62	530.81	574.10	665.26	458.49
2004	720.75	714.31	650.28	615.29	532.52	638.94	705.77	646.11	630.61	679.95	662.30	645.37	653.52
2005	685.93	723.02	763.44	761.75	804.52	779.54	700.08	709.31	684.33	601.56	584.44	644.94	703.57
2006	693.44	705.73	702.46	841.84	982.34	981.11	1,255.21	1,443.11	1,406.17	1,526.68	1,493.07	1,606.51	1,136.47

[1] Plating material, briquettes.   *Source: American Metal Market (AMM)*

Oats

Oats are seeds or grains of a genus of plants that thrive in cool, moist climates. There are about 25 species of oats that grow worldwide in the cooler temperate regions. The oldest known cultivated oats were found inside caves in Switzerland and are believed to be from the Bronze Age. Oats are usually sown in early spring and harvested in mid to late summer, but in southern regions of the northern hemisphere, they may be sown in the fall. Oats are used in many processed foods such as flour, livestock feed, and furfural, a chemical used as a solvent in various refining industries. The oat crop year begins in June and ends in May. Oat futures and options are traded on the Chicago Board of Trade (CBOT) and the Winnipeg Commodity Exchange (WCE).

Prices – Oat prices on the CBOT weekly nearest futures chart started the 2006 year at about $1.85 per bushel, showed weakness through April to post a low of $1.68, rallied into the summer to hit a high of $2.32, sank again to a low of $1.75 in August and then recovered through the remainder of the year to post a high of $2.80 at the end of December.

Regarding cash prices, the average monthly price received by farmers for oats in the US in the first 9 months of the 2006-07 marketing year (i.e., June 2006 to February 2007) rose 13.2% yr/yr to $1.91 per bushel.

Supply – World oat production in 2006-07 was virtually unchanged yr/yr at 23.540 million metric tons, which was a new record low. World annual oat production in the past three decades has dropped very sharply from levels above

50 million metric tons in the early 1970s. The world's largest oat producers are the European Union with 32% of world production in 2006-07, Russia with 21%, Canada with 15%, the US with 6%, and Australia with 4%.

US oat production in the 2006-07 marketing year fell by –18.4% yr/yr to 93.764 million bushels, which was a new record low. US oat production has fallen sharply from levels mostly above 1 billion bushels seen from the early 1900s into the early 1960s. US farmers harvested only 1.576 million acres of oats in 2006-07, which was down –13.5% from the previous year and posted a new record low. That is down from the almost 40 million acres harvested back in the 1950s. The oat yield in 2006-07 was down –5.6% to 59.5 bushels per acre, which was a new record low. Oat stocks in the US as of December 2006 were up 0.6% yr/yr to 96.244 million bushels, which was up only slightly from last year's record low of 95.717 million bushels. The largest US oat-producing states in 2006 were the northern states of Wisconsin (with 16% of US production), Minnesota (12%), Iowa (9%), Pennsylvania (8%), and South Dakota (6%).

Demand – US usage of oats in 2006-07 fell –4.3% yr/yr to a record low of 202.0 million bushels. Regarding US usage of oats in 2006-07, 62% was for feed and residual, 32% for food, alcohol and industrial, 5.4% for seed, and 1.0% for exports.

Trade – US exports of oats fell –3.8% to a mere 2.0 million bushels in 2006-07. US imports of oats in 2006-07 rose +15.4% yr/yr to a 6-year high of 105.0 million bushels.

World Production of Oats   In Thousands of Metric Tons

Year	Argentina	Australia	Belarus	Brazil	Canada	China	EU-25	Norway	Turkey	Ukraine	United States	Russia	World Total
1997-98	517	1,634	822	286	3,485	400	6,665	360	280	1,062	2,428	9,400	31,035
1998-99	383	1,798	501	250	3,958	650	6,147	387	310	778	2,406	4,600	25,691
1999-00	555	1,118	368	250	3,641	600	8,117	356	290	760	2,114	4,400	24,110
2000-01	645	1,050	495	330	3,389	600	8,383	397	314	881	2,165	6,000	25,977
2001-02	645	1,434	530	277	2,691	600	8,091	330	265	1,116	1,707	7,700	27,033
2002-03	500	957	575	390	2,911	600	9,280	279	290	943	1,684	5,700	25,599
2003-04	348	2,018	500	413	3,691	600	8,623	333	285	925	2,096	5,200	26,572
2004-05[1]	508	1,321	770	433	3,683	600	8,755	359	290	1,000	1,679	4,950	25,930
2005-06[2]	350	1,416	600	517	3,432	600	7,386	349	290	800	1,667	4,550	23,546
2006-07[3]	400	1,000	550	475	3,600	600	7,468	349	290	900	1,361	5,000	23,540

[1] Preliminary.   [2] Estimate.   [3] Forecast.   Source: Foreign Agricultural Service, U.S. Department of Agriculture (FAS-USDA)

Official Oats Crop Production Reports in the United States   In Thousands of Bushels

Year	July 1	Aug. 1	Sept. 1	Oct. 1	Dec. 1	Final	Year	July 1	Aug. 1	Sept. 1	Oct. 1	Dec. 1	Final
1995	181,508	186,167	186,167	----	----	162,027	2001	132,150	135,445	----	----	----	117,024
1996	154,968	157,663	----	----	----	153,245	2002	147,584	142,580	----	----	----	116,002
1997	182,672	187,127	----	----	----	167,246	2003	147,895	151,345	----	----	----	144,383
1998	183,201	177,211	----	----	----	165,981	2004	121,860	127,950	----	----	----	115,695
1999	----	162,096	----	----	----	146,218	2005	131,314	127,819	----	----	----	114,878
2000	151,380	152,745	----	----	----	149,545	2006[1]	110,322	107,423	----	----	----	93,764

[1] Preliminary.   Source: National Agricultural Statistics Service, U.S. Department of Agriculture (NASS-USDA)

Oat Stocks in the United States   In Thousands of Bushels

	On Farms				Off Farms				Total Stocks			
Year	Mar. 1	June 1	Sept. 1	Dec. 1	Mar. 1	June 1	Sept. 1	Dec. 1	Mar. 1	June 1	Sept. 1	Dec. 1
1997	56,200	33,100	107,950	83,200	39,362	33,576	48,972	61,051	95,562	66,676	156,922	144,251
1998	58,800	34,500	110,300	81,500	52,418	39,498	51,502	61,835	111,218	73,998	161,802	143,335
1999	61,700	40,700	97,300	79,800	50,850	40,678	51,151	53,872	112,550	81,378	148,451	133,672
2000	53,300	36,000	101,200	86,900	48,500	40,031	49,177	57,237	101,800	76,031	150,377	144,137
2001	55,800	32,050	74,800	58,100	54,128	40,677	41,592	56,117	109,928	72,727	116,392	114,217
2002	40,200	28,650	70,500	52,500	53,158	34,552	41,212	51,284	93,358	63,202	111,712	103,784
2003	35,000	20,600	82,100	64,400	47,879	29,233	49,637	54,900	82,879	49,833	131,737	119,300
2004	45,600	27,500	74,300	60,400	49,414	37,348	41,458	44,513	95,014	64,848	115,758	104,913
2005	43,500	25,350	71,700	60,100	38,946	32,592	41,803	35,617	82,446	57,942	113,503	95,717
2006[1]	42,200	25,190	60,800	53,000	32,673	27,376	39,284	43,244	74,873	52,566	100,084	96,244

[1] Preliminary.   *Source: National Agricultural Statistics Service, U.S. Department of Agriculture (NASS-USDA)*

Supply and Utilizationof Oats in the United States   In Millions of Bushels

	Acreage		Yield Per Acre	Pro- duction	Imports	Total Supply	Feed & Residual	Food, Alcohol & Industrial	Seed	Exports	Total Use	Ending Stocks	Farm Price	Findley Loan Rate	Target Price
	Planted	Harvested													
Year	1,000 acres		(Bushels)			In Millions of Bushels							Dollars Per Bushel		
1997-98	5,068	2,813	59.5	167.2	98.4	332.3	184.6	59.0	12.6	2.1	258.3	74.0	1.60	1.11	NA
1998-99	4,892	2,755	60.2	166.0	108.0	347.7	195.6	57.0	12.0	1.7	266.3	81.4	1.10	1.11	NA
1999-00	4,668	2,445	59.6	145.6	99.0	326.0	180.0	56.8	11.2	1.8	250.0	76.0	1.12	1.13	NA
2000-01	4,473	2,325	64.2	149.5	106.0	332.0	189.0	57.0	11.0	1.7	259.0	73.0	1.10	1.16	NA
2001-02	4,403	1,905	61.4	117.0	96.0	286.3	148.3	59.2	12.8	2.8	223.1	63.2	1.59	1.21	NA
2002-03	4,995	2,058	56.4	116.0	95.1	274.3	149.9	60.2	11.8	2.6	224.5	49.8	1.81	1.35	1.40
2003-04	4,597	2,220	65.0	144.4	89.7	284.0	143.7	62.4	10.5	2.5	219.1	64.9	1.48	1.35	1.40
2004-05	4,085	1,787	64.7	115.7	90.3	270.9	136.3	63.0	11.0	2.7	212.9	57.9	1.48	1.33	1.44
2005-06[1]	4,246	1,823	63.0	114.9	91.0	264.0	135.0	62.9	11.1	2.1	211.0	52.6	1.63		
2006-07[2]	4,168	1,576	59.5	93.8	105.0	251.0	125.0	64.0	11.0	2.0	202.0	49.0	1.60-2.00		

[1] Preliminary.   [2] Forecast.   NA = Not available.   *Source: Economic Research Service, U.S. Department of Agriculture (ERS-USDA)*

Production of Oats in the United States, by States   In Thousands of Bushels

Year	Illinois	Iowa	Michigan	Minnesota	Nebraska	New York	North Dakota	Ohio	Penn- slyvania	South Dakota	Texas	Wisconsin	Total
1997	5,550	16,790	4,880	17,400	5,850	5,850	18,700	6,660	8,990	14,850	6,760	20,160	167,246
1998	3,920	10,915	4,800	19,530	5,320	6,510	25,200	6,500	8,480	20,100	6,890	18,300	165,981
1999	4,260	11,375	4,875	17,700	4,650	4,760	16,830	7,000	7,975	12,800	4,840	18,600	146,218
2000	4,015	12,060	4,800	22,320	1,890	3,900	19,845	6,840	8,265	13,420	4,300	19,040	149,165
2001	3,200	9,100	3,520	12,600	3,660	5,520	14,880	6,205	7,475	7,800	7,200	12,480	117,024
2002	3,285	13,300	4,160	14,840	2,365	4,160	12,600	3,355	7,015	5,400	6,160	15,000	116,002
2003	4,450	10,790	5,250	18,815	6,570	4,410	21,240	3,960	6,490	15,640	6,300	15,410	144,383
2004	2,450	10,080	4,420	13,300	3,400	3,250	14,080	3,150	6,050	13,940	6,400	13,650	115,695
2005	3,160	9,875	4,575	12,710	4,380	4,050	14,160	3,600	6,050	12,960	4,730	13,760	114,878
2006[1]	3,080	8,360	4,030	11,200	2,255	4,958	4,920	4,125	7,040	5,415	3,700	14,490	93,764

[1] Preliminary.   *Source: National Agricultural Statistics Service, U.S. Department of Agriculture (NASS-USDA)*

Average Cash Price of No. 2 Heavy White Oats in Toledo   In Dollars Per Bushel

Year	June	July	Aug.	Sept.	Oct.	Nov.	Dec.	Jan.	Feb.	Mar.	Apr.	May	Average
1997-98	2.12	1.79	1.84	1.80	1.77	NQ	NQ	NQ	NQ	NQ	NQ	NQ	1.86
1998-99	NQ	NQ	NQ	NQ	NQ	NQ	NQ	NQ	NQ	NQ	NQ	NQ	NQ
1999-00	NQ	NQ	NQ	NQ	NQ	NQ	NQ	NQ	NQ	NQ	NQ	NQ	NQ
2000-01	NQ	NQ	NQ	NQ	NQ	NQ	NQ	NQ	NQ	NQ	NQ	NQ	NQ
2001-02	NQ	NQ	NQ	NQ	NQ	NQ	NQ	NQ	NQ	NQ	NQ	NQ	NQ
2002-03	NQ	NQ	NQ	NQ	NQ	NQ	NQ	NQ	NQ	NQ	NQ	NQ	NQ
2003-04	NQ	NQ	NQ	NQ	NQ	NQ	NQ	NQ	NQ	NQ	NQ	NQ	NQ
2004-05	NQ	NQ	NQ	NQ	NQ	NQ	NQ	NQ	NQ	NQ	NQ	NQ	NQ
2005-06	NQ	NQ	NQ	NQ	NQ	NQ	NQ	NQ	NQ	NQ	NQ	NQ	NQ
2006-07[1]	NQ	NQ	NQ	NQ	NQ	NQ	NQ						

[1] Preliminary.   NQ = No quotes.   *Source: Economic Research Service, U.S. Department of Agriculture (ERS-USDA)*

OATS

Oat Futures - Chicago Board of Trade
(weekly close) as of December 29, 2006

Cents per bushel

Volume of Trading in Oats Futures in Chicago   In Contracts

Year	Jan.	Feb.	Mar.	Apr.	May	June	July	Aug.	Sept.	Oct.	Nov.	Dec.	Total
1997	34,238	51,608	39,607	41,988	27,028	29,632	25,473	26,486	21,241	42,630	38,187	19,214	397,332
1998	21,150	51,247	25,551	65,381	23,490	55,376	29,870	42,156	27,131	31,426	51,172	18,924	442,874
1999	23,747	35,706	43,671	44,974	22,399	40,722	35,812	27,928	17,893	16,155	42,029	20,370	371,406
2000	27,073	43,332	29,707	31,653	38,647	50,461	30,885	42,814	21,846	21,476	48,890	15,406	402,190
2001	26,377	38,040	24,903	41,482	20,516	41,926	50,440	22,883	31,252	50,580	53,578	38,877	440,854
2002	41,516	46,435	30,662	51,889	32,386	39,229	35,217	29,647	23,968	32,847	35,412	15,932	415,140
2003	26,149	31,892	27,766	26,022	20,442	24,113	23,230	21,562	26,658	33,621	30,273	27,170	318,898
2004	33,743	34,605	55,216	49,746	38,951	35,356	25,451	31,023	32,322	25,443	33,942	20,650	416,448
2005	26,439	35,921	36,808	35,199	24,696	33,748	28,353	26,134	17,708	27,080	32,687	26,766	351,539
2006	25,667	40,534	30,437	35,799	39,362	42,812	35,751	30,790	25,700	43,724	51,304	25,435	427,315

Source: Chicago Board of Trade (CBT)

Average Open Interest of Oats in Chicago   In Contracts

Year	Jan.	Feb.	Mar.	Apr.	May	June	July	Aug.	Sept.	Oct.	Nov.	Dec.
1997	8,088	9,650	12,649	11,024	9,830	9,395	8,131	8,606	8,618	10,953	11,816	10,964
1998	12,782	15,368	16,553	17,748	17,441	16,437	14,255	15,052	14,771	16,263	18,466	17,048
1999	17,126	17,019	16,677	15,398	13,491	12,705	11,927	11,670	9,802	10,638	12,754	12,360
2000	15,343	17,521	17,719	18,183	176,686	16,178	15,550	15,225	13,176	13,985	14,377	14,119
2001	14,093	15,060	14,873	14,962	14,875	13,695	11,861	11,707	10,059	12,111	14,453	12,142
2002	12,640	13,137	11,833	10,976	9,047	10,381	10,230	10,970	9,881	9,550	9,134	6,008
2003	6,929	6,715	5,945	6,135	5,833	5,640	5,811	5,958	6,261	6,194	6,268	5,122
2004	6,284	6,314	10,018	12,988	11,903	11,339	10,293	9,153	6,669	7,010	7,753	6,724
2005	7,691	8,482	7,346	8,110	7,746	7,686	7,779	6,721	5,847	6,914	7,565	9,385
2006	10,200	11,697	10,960	10,961	13,529	14,128	13,965	11,620	11,178	13,483	14,714	13,818

Source: Chicago Board of Trade (CBT)

Oats (monthly average) through December 2006   Cents per bushel

Cents Per Bushel
----- No. 3 White, Chicago (Jan. 1901 - Dec. 1947)
No. 2 White, Chicago (Jan. 1948 - Nov. 1948)
No. 1 White, Heavy, Chicago (Dec. 1948 - Dec. 1974)
No. 2 White, Heavy, Chicago (Jan. 1975 - Aug. 1999)
- - - No. 2 Milling, Minneapolis (Jan. 1975 to date)

Average Cash Price of No. 2 Heavy White Oats in Minneapolis   In Dollars Per Bushel

Year	June	July	Aug.	Sept.	Oct.	Nov.	Dec.	Jan.	Feb.	Mar.	Apr.	May	Average
1997-98	1.89	1.76	1.80	1.78	1.75	1.65	1.71	1.68	1.59	1.65	1.54	1.58	1.70
1998-99	1.52	1.42	1.21	1.30	1.29	1.32	1.31	1.33	1.26	1.35	1.36	1.39	1.34
1999-00	1.34	1.25	1.20	1.17	1.20	1.20	1.28	1.21	1.19	1.34	1.45	NQ	1.26
2000-01	.73	.72	.69	.68	.70	.72	.70	.70	.75	.77	.80	.82	.73
2001-02	.83	.95	1.08	1.04	1.29	1.41	1.48	1.41	1.47	1.51	1.31	1.29	1.26
2002-03	1.40	1.24	1.23	1.36	1.36	1.33	1.36	1.44	1.28	1.28	1.22	1.08	1.30
2003-04	1.05	NQ	.98	1.01	1.00	.99	1.04	.99	1.14	1.08	1.22	1.08	1.05
2004-05	1.04	.96	.99	1.11	1.01	1.04	1.13	1.18	1.15	1.16	1.13	.99	1.07
2005-06	.99	1.20	1.12	1.09	1.16	1.16	1.37	1.33	1.29	1.23	1.25	1.33	1.21
2006-07[1]	1.38	1.41	1.29	1.36	1.52	1.69	1.76	1.74					1.52

[1] Preliminary.   NQ = No quote.   *Source: Economic Research Service, U.S. Department of Agriculture (ERS-USDA)*

Average Price Received by U.S. Farmers for Oats   In Dollars Per Bushel

Year	June	July	Aug.	Sept.	Oct.	Nov.	Dec.	Jan.	Feb.	Mar.	Apr.	May	Average
1997-98	1.81	1.68	1.57	1.47	1.62	1.66	1.57	1.60	1.60	1.64	1.61	1.53	1.61
1998-99	1.39	1.19	1.02	1.07	1.09	1.10	1.19	1.20	1.20	1.20	1.18	1.31	1.18
1999-00	1.22	1.08	.97	1.08	1.06	1.12	1.18	1.20	1.27	1.28	1.35	1.31	1.18
2000-01	1.24	1.07	.93	.95	1.08	1.22	1.14	1.21	1.28	1.24	1.28	1.28	1.16
2001-02	1.38	1.33	1.25	1.39	1.64	1.79	1.92	1.93	1.91	1.99	1.99	1.99	1.71
2002-03	1.95	1.69	1.67	1.80	1.80	1.91	1.95	2.04	2.11	2.08	1.98	1.95	1.91
2003-04	1.83	1.46	1.39	1.39	1.44	1.29	1.58	1.48	1.58	1.60	1.63	1.70	1.53
2004-05	1.61	1.36	1.32	1.42	1.45	1.51	1.60	1.64	1.67	1.74	1.65	1.64	1.55
2005-06	1.75	1.59	1.49	1.54	1.59	1.64	1.73	1.73	1.82	1.81	1.75	1.85	1.69
2006-07[1]	1.93	1.78	1.67	1.70	1.77	2.02	1.97	2.19	2.19				1.91

[1] Preliminary.   *Source: National Agricultural Statistics Service, U.S. Department of Agriculture (NASS-USDA)*

Olive Oil

Olive oil is derived from the fruit of the olive tree and originated in the Mediterranean area. Olives designated for oil are picked before ripening in the fall. Olive picking is usually done by hand. The olives are then weighed and washed in cold water. The olives, along with their oil-rich pits, are then crushed and kneaded until a homogeneous paste is formed. The paste is spread by hand onto metal plates, which are then stacked and pressed hydraulically to yield a liquid. The liquid is then centrifuged to separate the oil. It takes 1,300 to 2,000 olives to produce 1 quart of olive oil. The best olive oil is still produced from the first pressing, which is usually performed within 24 to 72 hours after harvest and is called *extra virgin* olive oil.

Supply – World production of olive oil (pressed oil) in the marketing year 2005-06 fell –11.9% to 2.662 million metric tons, down further from the 2003-04 record high of 3.178. The world's largest producers of olive oil in 2003-04 were Spain (with 32% of world production), Italy (24%),

Greece (17%), Tunisia (8%), Turkey (5%), and Syria (4%). Production levels in the various countries vary considerable from year-to-year depending on various weather and crop conditions.

Demand – World consumption of olive oil in the 2005-06 marketing year fell –3.1% to 2.847 million metric tons, down from the 2004-05 record high of 2.957. The US is the world's largest consumer of olive oil with 8.1% of world consumption in 2005-06. US consumption of olive oil was 231,100 metric tons in 2005-06, only slightly below last year's record of 235.4.

Trade – World olive oil imports in 2005-06 fell –3.7% to 685.3 metric tons. The US was the world's largest importer in 2005-06 with 250,000 metric tons, representing 36% of world imports. The world's largest exporters are Italy (with 32% of world exports), Tunisia (22%), Spain (13%), and Turkey (9%).

World Production of Olive Oil (Pressed Oil)   In Thousands of Metric Tons

Year	Algeria	Argentina	Greece	Italy	Jordan	Libya	Morocco	Portugal	Spain	Syria	Tunisia	Turkey	World Total
1998-99	54.5	7.0	511.0	427.2	23.5	8.0	71.0	40.3	804.0	129.0	231.0	188.0	2,537.1
1999-00	33.5	11.5	454.0	670.0	7.0	7.0	45.0	58.3	694.1	88.0	225.0	61.0	2,412.4
2000-01	26.5	3.0	467.0	508.0	29.5	4.0	39.5	28.5	1,040.0	183.0	141.0	197.5	2,742.7
2001-02	25.5	10.0	388.3	500.0	16.0	7.0	66.0	36.7	1,468.0	104.0	40.0	71.0	2,791.1
2002-03	15.0	11.0	449.0	620.0	30.0	6.5	48.5	31.9	949.4	184.5	76.0	187.0	2,698.0
2003-04[1]	69.5	13.5	332.0	470.0	21.0	6.5	110.0	38.2	1,566.0	121.5	296.0	80.0	3,178.1
2004-05[2]	33.5	10.0	470.0	755.0	31.0	12.5	54.0	51.4	1,034.0	195.0	139.5	152.5	3,020.5
2005-06[3]	47.5	13.0	458.0	636.0	21.0	9.0	81.0	33.5	849.0	110.0	215.0	122.0	2,661.9

[1] Preliminary.   [2] Estimate.   [3] Forecast.   *Source: The Oil World*

World Imports and Exports of Olive Oil (Pressed Oil)   In Thousands of Metric Tons

Year	Australia	Brazil	Italy	Japan	Spain	United States	World Total	Greece	Italy	Spain	Tunisia	Turkey	World Total
	---------- Imports ----------							---------- Exports ----------					
1998-99	23.7	23.5	150.4	28.1	76.8	169.9	573.5	6.3	141.6	70.9	172.5	99.0	572.9
1999-00	24.2	25.6	105.1	27.2	23.4	189.3	507.1	8.8	176.8	95.6	122.4	25.8	496.9
2000-01	29.5	24.7	110.5	29.6	13.3	212.5	549.1	6.3	194.1	97.9	101.0	77.5	543.8
2001-02	26.4	24.0	50.8	31.2	6.6	218.1	486.0	9.5	199.6	116.9	33.0	37.3	470.8
2002-03	32.0	21.1	70.1	31.4	16.6	220.1	531.7	10.6	198.3	118.5	42.9	60.8	533.7
2003-04[1]	30.5	23.2	178.2	33.1	49.1	244.8	716.6	9.7	201.0	123.3	197.0	55.9	715.4
2004-05[2]	28.9	25.7	154.6	32.8	40.7	248.7	711.9	9.1	218.9	125.2	114.7	88.4	704.7
2005-06[3]	25.3	26.4	123.9	33.0	55.0	250.0	685.3	8.3	220.4	93.0	152.8	63.1	695.0

[1] Preliminary.   [2] Estimate.   [3] Forecast.   *Source: The Oil World*

World Consumption and Ending Stocks of Olive Oil (Pressed Oil)   In Thousands of Metric Tons

Year	Brazil	Morocco	Syria	Tunisia	Turkey	United States	World Total	Greece	Italy	Spain	Syria	Turkey	World Total
	---------- Consumption ----------							---------- Ending Stocks ----------					
1998-99	23.5	62.5	107.8	64.8	74.3	160.9	2,538.0	132.0	120.8	554.0	46.0	50.0	1,033.2
1999-00	25.6	55.7	99.0	63.3	76.3	180.1	2,614.0	143.0	177.5	320.0	36.6	9.9	836.4
2000-01	24.7	49.6	121.6	61.3	79.9	205.5	2,751.0	568.6	16.0	97.2	34.0	50.0	833.3
2001-02	24.0	61.1	111.6	38.4	73.7	211.5	2,746.3	708.9	25.3	86.5	3.0	12.0	893.3
2002-03	21.1	64.2	117.7	31.7	91.6	218.7	2,802.7	534.0	19.0	130.9	4.6	47.0	786.6
2003-04[1]	23.2	69.8	135.0	59.2	61.8	225.3	2,921.2	788.0	35.0	93.5	45.0	10.0	1,044.6
2004-05[2]	25.7	62.4	144.0	59.9	61.3	235.4	2,939.0	934.1	11.0	104.7	10.0	13.0	1,133.3
2005-06[3]	26.4	56.2	130.0	62.2	55.1	231.1	2,846.9	819.5	9.8	39.7	11.0	17.0	938.5

[1] Preliminary.   [2] Estimate.   [3] Forecast.   *Source: The Oil World*

Onions

Onions are the bulbs of plants in the lily family. Onions can be eaten raw, cooked, pickled, used as a flavoring or seasoning, or dehydrated. Onions rank in the top 10 vegetables produced in the US in terms of dollar value. Since 1629, onions have been cultivated in the US, but are believed to be indigenous to Asia.

The two main types of onions produced in the US are yellow and white onions. Yellow varieties comprise approximately 75% of all onions grown for bulb production in the US. Onions that are planted as a winter crop in warm areas are milder in taste and odor than onions planted during the summer in cooler regions.

Prices – Onion prices in 2006 averaged $13.10 per hundred pounds, up +5.6% from $12.40 in 2004. Onion prices were weak in early 2006 reaching a low of $8.04 in

February, rallied to $20.30 in July, but then faded after that to close 2006 at $16.50.

Supply – US production in 2005 fell –11.5% to 7.350 billion pounds from the 2004 record high of 8.307 billion pounds. The farm value of the US production crop in 2005 was $849 million, down from the record high of $929 million in 2003. US farmers harvested 165,280 acres in 2005, down –2.3% from 2004. The yield per acre in 2005 was 445 pounds per acre.

Demand – US per capita consumption of onions in 2005 fell to 22.2 pounds from 23.1 pounds in 2004.

Trade – US exports of fresh onions in 2005 totaled 668 million pounds, and imports were not far behind at 659 million pounds.

Salient Statistics of Onions in the United States

Crop Year	Harvested Acres	Yield Per Acre	Pro-duction 1,000 Cwt.	Price Per Cwt.	Farm Value $1,000	Jan. 1 Pack Frozen	Annual Pack Frozen	Imports Canned	Exports (Fresh)	Imports (Fresh)	Per Capita[3] Utilization -- Lbs., Farm Weight -- All	Fresh
						----------------------- In Millions of Pounds -----------------------						
2001	164,990	419	69,961	11.40	680,350	54.9	142.6	5.0	708.2	632.6	19.5	18.5
2002	162,720	429	69,844	12.10	764,994	29.9	387.1	7.1	637.1	595.8	20.4	19.3
2003	160,090	442	73,636	13.70	929,274	39.5	309.6	10.3	679.0	646.1	21.3	19.5
2004	169,150	491	83,065	9.06	671,626	38.6	218.2	10.5	624.5	689.3	23.1	21.6
2005[1]	165,220	445	73,504	12.40	848,798	39.9		22.9	667.8	659.2	22.2	21.2
2006[2]	162,980	440	71,648	13.10	867,744	48.1					21.8	20.6

[1] Preliminary. [2] Forecast. [3] Includes fresh and processing. *Source: Economic Research Service, U.S. Department of Agiculture (ERS-USDA)*

Production of Onions in the United States   In Thousands of Hundredweight (Cwt.)

Year	Arizona	California	Texas	Total (All)	California	Colorado	Idaho	Michigan	Minne-sota	New Mexico	New York	Oregon (Malheur)	Texas	Total (All)	Grand Total
	-------------------- Spring --------------------				--- Summer ---										
2001	1,290	2,666	4,615	11,136	12,069	4,140	4,992	999	73	----	4,224	7,006	----	56,517	67,653
2002	690	2,708	4,725	9,561	11,562	4,400	6,272	897	78	----	2,829	7,800	----	60,283	69,844
2003	750	3,675	3,520	10,133	14,700	3,696	5,880	1,152	65	----	3,808	7,198	----	63,230	73,363
2004	800	3,586	3,875	12,031	13,200	5,500	8,008	986	----	----	5,200	8,658	----	71,034	83,065
2005	920	3,800	4,650	11,575	12,240	4,180	6,080	754	----	----	3,808	7,360	----	61,929	73,504
2006[1]	490	3,279	4,104	11,128	13,515	3,581	5,076	650	----	----	3,861	6,136	----	60,520	71,648

[1] Preliminary. *Source: Agricultural Statistics Board, U.S. Department of Agiculture (ASB-USDA)*

Cold Storage Stocks of Frozen Onions in the United States, on First of Month   In Thousands of Pounds

Year	Jan.	Feb.	Mar.	Apr.	May	June	July	Aug.	Sept.	Oct.	Nov.	Dec.
2001	40,420	39,722	39,407	36,925	36,503	38,705	38,275	29,993	28,912	26,133	27,726	28,987
2002	29,893	33,646	34,851	35,477	40,789	41,066	40,762	33,370	36,895	36,120	39,796	39,310
2003	39,480	39,764	43,624	37,569	35,625	35,617	36,529	35,590	35,907	33,844	38,693	39,467
2004	38,632	32,515	34,080	36,724	39,364	41,525	37,408	34,845	34,888	35,826	38,098	39,789
2005	39,865	40,428	44,191	48,695	50,579	47,418	45,605	47,231	44,834	40,718	43,751	45,690
2006[1]	48,106	52,207	55,182	54,680	54,276	53,341	45,724	43,707	47,176	47,636	50,175	48,731

[1] Preliminary. *Source: National Agricultural Statistics Service, U.S. Department of Agiculture (NASS-USDA)*

Average Price Received by Growers for Onions in the United States   In Dollars Per Hundred Pounds (Cwt.)

Year	Jan.	Feb.	Mar.	Apr.	May	June	July	Aug.	Sept.	Oct.	Nov.	Dec.	Season Average
2001	11.40	10.60	10.70	12.80	15.50	15.30	15.50	12.30	10.70	9.20	7.41	9.35	11.40
2002	9.48	8.27	6.92	16.20	16.10	15.60	15.10	12.20	10.00	9.61	9.79	11.50	12.10
2003	12.30	14.90	21.80	39.30	32.00	22.10	16.70	13.80	12.20	12.60	13.90	12.70	13.70
2004	18.20	21.30	12.80	20.80	18.10	16.50	16.40	13.40	11.30	9.22	9.01	8.58	9.06
2005	6.29	5.61	6.13	18.20	19.70	17.80	14.00	11.10	13.10	12.90	14.00	12.30	12.40
2006[1]	11.70	8.04	9.89	9.81	13.40	17.10	20.30	15.40	13.60	12.20	12.40	16.50	

[1] Preliminary. *Source: Economic Research Service, U.S. Department of Agiculture (ERS-USDA)*

Oranges and Orange Juice

The orange tree is a semi-tropical, non-deciduous tree, and the fruit is technically a hesperidium, a kind of berry. The three major varieties of oranges include the sweet orange, the sour orange, and the mandarin orange (or tangerine). In the US, only sweet oranges are grown commercially. Those include Hamlin, Jaffa, navel, Pineapple, blood orange, and Valencia. Sour oranges are mainly used in marmalade and in liqueurs such as triple sec and curacao.

Frozen Concentrated Orange Juice (FCOJ) was developed in 1945, which led to oranges becoming the main fruit crop in the US. The world's largest producer of orange juice is Brazil, followed by Florida. Two to four medium-sized oranges will produce about 1 cup of juice, and modern mechanical extractors can remove the juice from 400 to 700 oranges per minute. Before juice extraction, orange oil is recovered from the peel. Approximately 50% of the orange weight is juice, the remainder is peel, pulp, and seeds, which are dried to produce nutritious cattle feed.

The US marketing year for oranges begins December 1 of the first year shown (e.g., the 2005-06 marketing year extends from December 1, 2005 to November 30, 2006). Orange juice futures prices are subject to upward spikes during the US hurricane season (officially June 1 to November 30), and the Florida freeze season (late-November through March).

Frozen concentrated orange juice future and options are traded on the NYCE division of the New York Board of Trade (NYBOT). The NYCE orange juice futures contract calls for the delivery of 15,000 pounds of orange solids and is priced in terms of cents per pound.

Prices – NYCE orange juice futures prices in 2006 rallied sharply to extend the 2004-07 rally to a total of 286% and close 2006 up +61% yr/yr at 201.25 cents per pound. OJ prices in February 2007 posted a new 30-year high of 209.50 cents, which was just slightly below the record high of 220 cents per pound posted in November 1977. Bullish factors in 2006 included (1) lasting hurricane damage to orange groves from the 2004 and 2005 seasons which caused a –10.8% yr/yr decline in the 2006-07 Florida orange crop even without any hurricanes in 2006, (2) citrus canker and greening disease, and (3) urban sprawl which is reducing the size of Florida's orange groves. The Florida OJ crop for three straight years has been less than half the average crop size seen during 1994-2003.

Supply – World production of oranges in the 2005-06 marketing year rose +3.5% yr/yr to 47.048 million metric tons, but still below the record level of 50.755 million metric tons seen in 2003-04. The world's largest producers of oranges are Brazil with 39% of world production, followed by the US (17%), and Mexico (8%). US production of oranges in 2005-06 fell –4.2% yr/yr to 207.450 million boxes from 216.500 million boxes in 2004-05. (1 box equals 90 lbs.) Florida's production in 2005-06 fell –1.3% yr/yr to 147.9 million boxes from 149.8 million boxes in 2004-05.

World Production of Oranges   In Thousands of Metric Tons

Year	Argentina	Australia	Brazil	Egypt	Greece	Italy	Mexico	Morocco	South Africa	Spain	Turkey	United States	World Total
1996-97	841	556	18,972	1,613	946	2,100	3,917	774	895	2,200	890	11,618	48,438
1997-98	921	448	15,912	1,350	987	2,100	3,331	1,131	961	2,744	740	12,495	46,282
1998-99	660	515	18,360	1,442	795	1,422	2,903	900	1,048	2,442	970	8,989	43,961
1999-00	789	624	17,136	1,637	1,040	1,750	3,385	845	1,119	2,828	1,100	11,875	48,286
2000-01	913	437	14,729	1,610	976	1,800	3,885	693	1,119	2,688	1,070	11,139	44,588
2001-02	780	633	18,360	1,696	1,076	1,724	4,020	720	1,263	2,822	1,250	11,290	49,828
2002-03	700	407	15,382	1,734	1,145	1,723	3,734	800	1,148	2,950	1,250	10,527	45,775
2003-04[1]	750	453	19,054	1,740	550	1,835	3,901	705	1,113	3,052	1,250	11,734	50,755
2004-05[2]	770	547	16,565	1,775	764	1,997	4,000	813	1,144	2,691	1,300	8,420	45,469
2005-06[3]	700	450	18,523	1,789	962	2,230	3,800	810	1,210	2,260	1,300	8,101	47,048

[1] Preliminary.   [2] Estimate.   [3] Forecast.   NA = Not available.   Source: Foreign Agricultural Service, U.S. Department of Agriculture (FAS-USDA)

Salient Statistics of Oranges & Orange Juice in the United States

						Florida Crop Processed				Frozen Concentrated Orange Juice - Florida			
	Production[4]			Farm Price $ Per Box	Farm Value Million $	Frozen Concen-trates	Chilled Products	Total Pro-cessed	Yield Per Box Gallons[5]	Carry-in	Pack	Total Supply	Total Season Movement
Year	California	Florida	Total U.S.										
	Million Boxes			Box	Million $	Million Boxes				In Millions of Gallons (42 Deg. Brix)			
1996-97	64.0	226.2	293.0	6.16	1,836.7	153.8	65.7	220.4	1.6	41.2	289.6	342.9	273.9
1997-98	69.0	244.0	315.5	6.13	1,965.4	160.9	74.8	236.6	1.6	69.7	290.2	359.9	263.8
1998-99	36.0	186.0	224.6	7.41	1,687.9	97.2	80.1	175.1	1.6	104.7	216.9	321.6	209.1
1999-00	64.0	233.0	299.8	5.56	1,666.1	134.2	90.1	226.7	1.5	105.2	254.0	359.2	239.7
2000-01	54.5	223.3	280.9	5.88	1,682.8	124.1	89.6	215.9	1.6	112.6	245.2	357.8	226.0
2001-02	51.5	230.0	283.8	6.37	1,846.2	136.0	85.9	223.2	1.6	128.3	253.2	381.5	249.9
2002-03	62.0	203.0	267.0	5.80	1,564.7	102.1	92.5	196.0	1.5	120.2	203.3	323.5	200.1
2003-04[1]	50.5	242.0	294.6	5.88	1,774.5	139.7	93.4	233.6	1.6	124.0	249.7	373.7	213.8
2004-05[2]	64.5	149.8	216.5	6.68	1,475.4	54.3	88.5	143.9	1.6	151.8	86.3	238.1	175.2
2005-06[3]	57.5	147.9	207.5	8.44	1,766.3	51.9	88.7	141.9	1.6				

[1] Preliminary.   [2] Estimate.   [3] Forecast.   [4] Fruit ripened on trees, but destroyed prior to picking not included.   [5] 42 deg. Brix equivalent.
Source: Economic Research Service, U.S. Department of Agriculture (ERS-USDA); Florida Department of Citrus

Frozen Concentrate Orange Juice - New York Board of Trade
(weekly close) as December 29, 2006   Cents per pound

Average Open Interest of Frozen Concentrated Orange Juice Futures in New York   In Contracts

Year	Jan.	Feb.	Mar.	Apr.	May	June	July	Aug.	Sept.	Oct.	Nov.	Dec.
1997	29,171	26,929	26,331	28,955	29,868	33,639	31,799	34,339	36,057	40,365	41,811	46,169
1998	38,885	37,893	36,843	33,146	35,749	32,608	25,503	26,394	28,017	26,506	21,984	24,562
1999	25,917	28,965	28,707	31,199	26,669	28,362	28,087	30,021	28,922	27,498	26,893	25,887
2000	23,727	24,647	19,684	22,475	23,456	27,087	27,386	30,272	30,090	32,328	30,192	30,757
2001	28,852	28,011	28,073	27,794	24,199	24,428	22,591	22,073	17,789	18,026	21,506	19,275
2002	15,716	16,593	18,515	22,328	23,498	26,581	28,137	33,206	27,323	23,758	22,651	23,461
2003	25,080	26,588	22,707	21,466	20,634	23,794	25,467	26,518	27,788	30,767	31,575	36,336
2004	36,079	35,325	32,806	36,112	34,704	42,299	39,970	38,259	39,877	38,990	33,342	36,072
2005	33,821	33,619	30,008	32,523	26,171	28,730	32,221	29,034	23,603	28,602	34,966	35,795
2006	30,485	35,479	36,603	36,617	34,418	29,180	27,169	29,872	29,515	30,852	29,873	28,342

Source: New York Board of Trade (NYBOT)

Volume of Trading of Frozen Concentrated Orange Juice Futures in New York   In Contracts

Year	Jan.	Feb.	Mar.	Apr.	May	June	July	Aug.	Sept.	Oct.	Nov.	Dec.	Total
1997	84,982	89,875	66,340	82,772	62,890	78,690	47,242	118,286	55,081	108,413	100,941	134,349	1,029,861
1998	96,020	81,554	66,235	101,651	70,909	79,319	48,844	85,544	81,187	98,639	29,541	75,171	914,614
1999	64,149	92,868	40,027	92,522	49,180	78,627	48,177	99,531	49,323	71,914	42,532	68,734	797,584
2000	45,680	78,532	33,617	71,024	50,475	80,372	46,548	67,312	38,485	64,831	45,966	89,362	712,204
2001	46,655	66,561	27,994	63,012	38,447	66,773	40,870	64,860	22,246	68,364	23,376	48,338	577,496
2002	31,709	50,898	30,316	58,644	37,283	52,238	45,316	78,111	36,053	71,635	24,111	61,443	577,757
2003	45,945	63,224	23,926	70,846	35,791	64,209	27,056	73,792	40,782	87,055	42,084	78,005	652,715
2004	52,908	86,600	41,941	99,532	45,741	123,815	105,220	118,021	65,655	89,064	56,502	85,438	970,437
2005	54,140	85,349	57,557	87,595	40,785	94,913	61,610	92,195	46,868	117,355	50,098	113,574	902,039
2006	65,978	98,034	82,293	92,312	73,517	87,429	63,429	84,160	50,871	95,955	54,975	74,743	923,696

Source: New York Board of Trade (NYBOT)

ORANGES AND ORANGE JUICE

Cold Storage Stocks of Orange Juice Concentrate[2] in the U.S., on First of Month   In Millions of Pounds

Year	Jan.	Feb.	Mar.	Apr.	May	June	July	Aug.	Sept.	Oct.	Nov.	Dec.
1997	1,069.4	1,522.6	1,677.6	1,752.9	1,993.4	2,176.0	1,977.7	1,761.8	1,571.8	1,287.8	1,140.9	1,214.4
1998	1,503.4	1,945.9	2,029.7	2,025.0	2,487.0	2,627.5	2,457.7	2,249.0	2,025.1	1,803.9	1,470.7	1,540.2
1999	1,791.9	1,999.4	2,204.2	2,191.3	2,485.7	2,115.6	1,969.7	1,823.0	1,618.5	1,443.4	1,182.0	1,102.7
2000	1,330.7	1,540.6	1,632.7	1,857.9	1,812.5	1,965.6	2,037.9	1,843.7	1,457.7	1,346.6	1,169.4	1,202.0
2001	1,382.0	1,610.8	1,825.1	1,735.5	1,872.2	2,061.8	2,035.6	1,913.2	1,691.1	1,537.7	1,398.9	1,406.7
2002	1,571.7	1,721.3	1,770.9	1,794.4	1,886.0	1,982.8	1,934.0	1,870.9	1,680.9	1,543.6	1,409.6	1,471.2
2003	1,673.6	1,851.9	1,833.4	1,856.6	1,936.8	2,102.6	2,021.2	1,848.9	1,672.2	1,529.9	1,335.6	1,428.5
2004	1,585.8	1,613.0	1,646.1	1,790.5	1,987.6	2,128.7	2,075.7	1,953.4	1,823.3	1,644.2	1,516.8	1,458.0
2005	1,468.8	1,553.8	1,578.9	1,578.2	1,652.4	1,668.1	1,548.8	1,501.6	1,397.3	1,243.3	1,139.9	1,027.5
2006[1]	1,044.7	1,065.9	1,076.8	1,005.7	1,087.5	1,157.7	1,104.2	1,002.6	888.8	776.0	714.3	650.3

[1] Preliminary.   [2] Adjusted to 42.0 degrees Brix equivalent (9.896 pounds per gallon).   *Source: Agricultural Statistics Board, U.S. Department of Agriculture (ASB-USDA)*

Producer Price Index of Frozen Orange Juice Concentrate   1982 = 100

Year	Jan.	Feb.	Mar.	Apr.	May	June	July	Aug.	Sept.	Oct.	Nov.	Dec.	Average
1997	106.9	106.9	106.0	107.6	107.7	107.3	105.3	105.8	102.7	101.4	95.0	94.2	103.9
1998	94.9	101.2	104.1	103.2	108.8	109.1	109.5	109.6	109.5	110.2	119.1	121.2	108.4
1999	119.7	118.6	118.0	115.5	113.3	113.2	112.5	111.3	112.4	112.5	113.1	112.4	114.4
2000	110.0	108.9	108.0	107.1	106.9	106.6	105.4	104.8	101.5	100.4	99.8	99.1	104.9
2001	98.9	99.2	98.3	96.8	96.8	97.4	97.3	97.2	97.3	97.3	99.6	102.5	98.2
2002	103.0	102.9	103.1	102.9	102.8	103.2	103.2	103.5	107.4	107.4	109.7	110.2	104.9
2003	110.2	110.2	110.7	110.4	108.5	109.4	109.1	108.9	107.1	106.6	105.1	103.0	108.3
2004	103.4	103.2	102.7	101.6	101.6	101.6	98.9	98.9	98.9	98.9	103.3	103.3	101.4
2005	103.3	103.3	105.0	109.0	109.0	109.0	109.3	109.3	108.1	107.9	108.4	126.4	109.0
2006[1]	138.3	142.1	150.1	160.9	161.0	164.1	172.3	174.8	185.4	185.4	NA	208.7	167.6

[1] Preliminary.   *Source: Bureau of Labor Statistics, U.S. Department of Labor (BLS)*

Average Price of Oranges (Equivalent On-Tree) Received by Growers in the U.S.   In Dollars Per Box

Year	Jan.	Feb.	Mar.	Apr.	May	June	July	Aug.	Sept.	Oct.	Nov.	Dec.	Average
1997	3.59	3.67	4.82	4.68	4.74	4.62	6.48	7.45	7.15	4.48	3.09	3.14	4.83
1998	3.14	3.55	5.05	5.44	5.70	6.05	6.77	5.56	5.64	5.98	5.03	4.82	5.23
1999	4.52	4.99	5.90	5.96	6.48	8.04	8.58	6.66	9.96	9.50	4.70	3.42	6.56
2000	3.35	3.18	3.24	4.20	4.39	4.34	2.45	0.35	0.29	1.43	3.20	2.95	2.78
2001	2.85	3.20	4.93	4.84	4.64	4.47	4.63	5.01	6.20	4.99	2.90	3.20	4.32
2002	3.75	4.05	4.64	4.65	4.47	4.00	4.06	6.61	5.33	5.18	3.11	3.23	4.42
2003	3.00	3.14	4.17	4.43	4.43	4.41	3.91	4.27	2.80	2.78	2.32	2.55	3.52
2004	2.45	3.02	3.68	3.68	3.60	4.13	8.85	8.49	15.85	20.87	5.34	3.27	6.94
2005	3.39	3.69	4.84	4.80	5.11	5.43	6.55	4.90	4.29	4.04	5.90	4.46	4.78
2006[1]	5.16	5.27	5.70	6.27	6.81	8.21	6.86	12.03	14.48	16.28	7.94	7.47	8.54

[1] Preliminary.   *Source: Economic Research Service, U.S. Department of Agriculture (ERS-USDA)*

Palm Oil

Palm oil is an edible vegetable oil produced from the flesh of the fruit of the oil palm tree. The oil palm tree is a tropical palm tree that is a native of the west coast of Africa and is different from the coconut palm tree. The fruit of the oil palm tree is reddish, about the size of a large plum, and grows in large bunches. A single seed, the palm kernel, is contained in each fruit. Oil is extracted from both the pulp of the fruit (becoming palm oil) and the kernel (palm kernel oil). About 1 metric ton of palm kernel oil is obtained for every 10 metric tons of palm oil.

Palm oil is commercially used in soap, ointments, cosmetics, detergents, and machinery lubricants. It is also used worldwide as cooking oil, shortening, and margarine. Palm kernel oil is a lighter oil and is used exclusively for food use. Crude palm oil and crude palm kernel oil are traded on the Kuala Lumpur Commodity Exchange.

Prices – The monthly average wholesale price of palm oil (CIF, bulk, US ports) in 2005 fell by −13.7% yr/yr to 29.43 cents per pound. That was down from the record high of 34.09 cents per pound posted in 2004.

Supply – World production of palm oil in the 2005-06 marketing year rose by +5.5% to 35.160 million metric tons.

World palm oil production has grown by almost 17 times from the production level of 1.922 million metric tons seen back in 1970. Malaysia and Indonesia are the world's two major global producers of palm oil.

Malaysian production in 2005-06 rose +0.4% to 15.260 million metric tons and Malaysian production accounted for 43% of world production. Indonesian production rose +11.4% to 14.980 million metric tons in 2005-06 and Indonesian production also accounted for 43% of world production. Other smaller global producers include Nigeria with 2.3% of world production, Thailand (2.02%), and Columbia with (1.9%).

Demand – US total disappearance of palm oil in 2004-05 (latest data available) rose +39.1% yr/yr to 316.300 metric tons from 227,400 metric tons in 2003-04.

Trade – World palm oil exports in 2005-06 rose by 6.1% to 27.730 million metric tons, which was a new record high. The world's largest exporters are Malaysia with a 49% share of world exports, followed by Indonesia with a 41% share. The world's largest importers are China with an 18% share of world imports, followed by India (10%), Pakistan (6%), the Netherlands (6%), UK (3%), and Germany (3%).

World Production of Palm Oil   In Thousands of Metric Tons

Crop Year	Brazil	Cameroon	Colombia	Costa Rica	Ecuador	Ghana	Indonesia	Ivory Coast	Malaysia	Nigeria	Papua/N Guinea	Thailand	World Total
1996-97	90	161	440	97	200	83	5,078	258	9,000	678	248	438	17,569
1997-98	88	140	439	108	205	107	5,320	270	8,509	688	206	469	17,305
1998-99	91	133	466	117	247	110	6,011	265	9,759	713	257	540	19,501
1999-00	105	136	513	136	228	109	6,855	283	10,492	735	300	533	21,266
2000-01	109	138	561	147	199	108	7,775	211	11,940	763	334	601	23,773
2001-02	115	143	517	131	231	109	9,060	239	11,856	774	338	606	25,021
2002-03	128	142	537	148	265	111	10,370	224	13,180	782	310	630	27,752
2003-04[1]	138	145	614	179	272	110	11,970	249	13,418	789	344	664	29,877
2004-05[2]	155	152	647	190	316	116	13,450	273	15,195	798	330	680	33,328
2005-06[3]	171	159	684	220	346	120	14,980	270	15,260	815	335	715	35,160

[1] Preliminary.   [2] Estimate.   [3] Forecast.   *Source: The Oil World*

World Trade of Palm Oil   In Thousands of Metric Tons

Crop Year	Imports							Exports					
	China	Germany	India	Netherlands	Pakistan	United Kingdom	World Total	Hong Kong	Indonesia	Malaysia	Papua/N Guinea	Singapore	World Total
1996-97	1,851	498	1,300	649	1,020	516	11,751	145	2,419	7,794	203	829	11,974
1997-98	1,490	370	1,684	670	1,210	457	11,971	120	2,459	7,847	207	253	11,795
1998-99	1,433	406	2,762	738	1,053	528	12,977	113	3,219	8,482	248	289	13,246
1999-00	1,474	431	3,482	780	1,086	558	14,759	130	3,898	9,051	292	251	14,628
2000-01	2,147	497	3,856	907	1,191	607	17,356	180	4,617	10,707	334	228	17,340
2001-02	2,600	592	3,233	1,101	1,333	721	18,708	302	6,094	10,758	332	217	18,943
2002-03	3,167	562	4,110	1,132	1,442	776	21,572	209	7,167	12,133	329	253	21,584
2003-04[1]	3,570	646	3,574	1,174	1,405	819	23,420	154	8,706	12,186	336	227	23,459
2004-05[2]	4,319	766	3,342	1,438	1,683	869	25,943	63	9,862	13,585	322	223	26,140
2005-06[3]	4,950	810	2,900	1,525	1,700	910	27,604	27	11,300	13,680	324	232	27,730

[1] Preliminary.   [2] Estimate.   [3] Forecast.   *Source: The Oil World*

PALM OIL

Supply and Distribution of Palm Oil in the United States   In Thousands of Metric Tons

Year Beginning Oct. 1	Stocks Oct. 1	Imports	Total Supply	Consumption Edible Products	Consumption Inedible Products	Consumption Total End Products	Total Disap-pearance	Exports	U.S. Import Value[4]	Malaysia, F.O.B., RBD	Palm Kernal Oil, Malaysia, C.I.F. Rotterdam
				In Millions of Pounds					U.S. $ Per Metric Ton		
1996-97	14.0	146.4	160.4	W	91.8	W	134.8	4.2	432	544	680
1997-98	21.4	128.0	149.4	W	93.8	W	128.8	4.4	464	640	653
1998-99	16.1	128.8	144.9	W	72.4	W	118.6	5.2		514	708
1999-00	21.1	156.6	177.7	W	55.0	W	148.5	3.4		338	533
2000-01	25.7	175.5	201.2	W	36.0	W	167.7	6.0		272	313
2001-02	27.5	218.7	246.2	W	22.6	75.1	215.9	6.2		359	379
2002-03	24.1	189.3	213.4	W	W	76.7	183.2	8.1		428	439
2003-04[1]	22.1	282.5	304.6	51.9	37.5	67.9	227.4	13.1		489	619
2004-05[2]	64.0	345.5	409.5	62.3	W	62.3	316.3	16.8		420	638
2005-06[3]	76.4	460.0	536.4	436.4	W	436.4	430.0	24.4		438	597

[1] Preliminary.   [2] Estimate.   [3] Forecast.   [4] Market value in the foreign country, excluding import duties, ocean freight and marine insurance.
Sources: The Oil World; Economic Research Service, U.S. Department of Agriculture (ERS-USDA)

Average Wholesale Palm Oil Prices, CIF, Bulk, U.S. Ports   In Cents Per Pound

Year	Jan.	Feb.	Mar.	Apr.	May	June	July	Aug.	Sept.	Oct.	Nov.	Dec.	Average
1996	27.08	26.52	26.33	27.52	28.57	25.43	24.78	24.46	27.24	26.13	26.95	27.45	26.54
1997	28.68	29.25	28.00	28.18	28.93	27.25	26.17	25.55	25.37	27.33	27.28	25.05	27.25
1998	29.30	29.59	30.53	32.10	31.11	31.42	32.33	33.14	33.14	33.06	33.30	34.00	31.92
1999	31.06	28.58	25.52	25.52	24.50	21.30	18.15	18.70	21.00	20.00	20.00	20.00	22.86
2000	18.65	17.66	17.73	18.21	18.12	16.52	16.85	16.23	15.90	13.19	13.56	12.75	16.28
2001	18.05	18.05	13.50	13.50	12.50	13.00	15.50	18.00	16.75	15.60	16.85	17.45	15.73
2002	17.75	17.06	17.30	17.75	18.85	21.44	20.50	21.85	32.00	31.75	31.75	31.75	23.31
2003	31.75	31.75	31.35	31.25	31.25	31.75	32.25	32.25	32.25	32.25	32.44	33.75	32.02
2004	34.00	35.38	35.25	36.40	36.50	36.50	36.50	36.50	34.00	30.00	29.00	29.00	34.09
2005	28.20	28.00	28.67	30.00	30.00	30.00	30.00	30.00	30.00	30.00	29.25	29.00	29.43

Source: Economic Research Service, U.S. Department of Agriculture (ERS-USDA)

Palm Oil (monthly average) through December 2005   Cents per pound

Paper

The earliest known paper that is still in existence was made from cotton rags around 150 AD. Around 800 AD, paper made its appearance in Egypt but was not manufactured there until 900 AD. The Moors introduced the use of paper to Europe, and around 1150, the first papermaking mill was established in Spain, followed by England in 1495, and the US in 1690.

During the 17th and 18th centuries, the increased usage of paper created a shortage of cotton rags, which were the only source for papermaking. The solution to this problem lead to the introduction of the ground-wood process of pulp-making in 1840 and the first chemical pulp process 10 years later.

Today, the paper and paperboard industries, including newsprint, are sensitive to the economic cycle. As the economy strengthens, paper use increases, and vice versa.

Prices – The average monthly index price for paperboard in 2006 rose 9.3% yr/yr to 191.9, continuing to recover from the 5-year low of 162.7 posted in 2003. The average monthly producer price index of standard newsprint paper in 2006 rose by +10.0% to 152.4, continuing the upward rebound from the 20-year low of 105.7 posted in 2002.

Supply – US production of paper and paperboard in 2005 fell slightly by –0.8% yr/yr to 81.437 million metric tons. The US is the world's largest producer of paper and paperboard by far, followed by Germany with 21.679 million metric tons and Canada with 19.673 million metric tons.

US production of newsprint fell by –2.4% yr/yr to a record low of 416.6 metric tons per month in 2005. US production of newsprint is second in the world, after Canada, which had production of 657.200 metric tons per month in 2005.

Production of Paper and Paperboard by Selected Countries   In Thousands of Metric Tons

Year	Austria	Canada	Finland	France	Germany	Italy	Nether-lands	Norway	Russia	Spain	Sweden	United Kingdom	United States
2000	4,386	20,921	13,509	10,006	18,182	9,129	3,332	2,300	5,310	4,765	10,786	6,605	86,252
2001	4,250	19,834	12,502	9,625	17,879	8,926	3,174	2,220	5,625	5,131	10,534	6,434	81,249
2002	4,419	20,226	12,789	9,809	18,526	9,317	3,346	2,114	5,978	5,365	10,724	6,452	81,879
2003	4,565	20,120	13,058	9,939	19,310	9,491	3,339	2,186	6,377	5,437	11,062	6,455	80,712
2004	4,852	20,599	14,036	10,255	20,391	9,667	3,459	2,294	6,830	5,526	11,589	6,442	82,084
2005[1]	4,950	19,673	12,391	10,332	21,679	9,999	3,471	2,223	7,024	5,697	11,736	6,235	81,437

[1] Preliminary.   Source: Food and Agriculture Organization of the United Nations (FAO-UN)

Production of Newsprint by Selected Countries (Monthly Average)   In Thousands of Metric Tons

Year	Australia	Brazil	Canada	China	Finland	France	Germany	India	Japan	Rep. of Korea	Russia	Sweden	United States
2000	31.8	22.2	768.5	121.0	116.1	86.6	150.5	48.9	284.9	151.5	141.2	211.5	547.5
2001	32.7	19.4	697.7	127.4	106.5	86.0	170.5	53.0	288.7	136.6	144.3	205.3	480.8
2002	32.3	20.6	671.4	156.0	87.3	82.0	173.5	49.6	299.7	137.9	142.8	202.0	437.4
2003	34.0	13.6	673.3	170.9	78.9	60.0	178.1	58.2	292.9	133.3	151.2	210.7	429.2
2004	35.2	11.1	648.0	248.4	60.2	93.8	185.9	58.1	307.6	145.4	164.8	220.8	424.7
2005[1]		11.1	657.2	283.2	47.9	95.7	226.0	71.8	310.0	135.8	167.3	213.0	414.6
2006[2]		10.9		325.4				84.8	318.5	138.6	169.2	211.5	

[1] Preliminary.   [2] Estimate.   Source: United Nations

Index Price of Paperboard   1982 = 100

Year	Jan.	Feb.	Mar.	Apr.	May	June	July	Aug.	Sept.	Oct.	Nov.	Dec.	Average
2000	163.1	163.6	173.6	176.6	180.4	180.3	180.9	181.2	180.9	180.4	180.2	179.5	176.7
2001	179.4	176.6	175.8	175.2	174.1	172.4	172.3	169.8	169.0	167.1	166.8	167.0	172.1
2002	165.0	164.0	162.6	162.8	161.1	161.1	161.8	165.8	166.7	167.1	167.3	166.6	164.3
2003	166.8	166.5	164.4	163.5	163.6	163.4	162.5	162.5	160.5	159.9	159.6	159.7	162.7
2004	157.8	157.4	157.5	162.2	165.5	170.0	175.2	178.5	179.2	179.4	180.1	179.3	170.2
2005	179.7	180.0	180.1	180.7	180.9	176.6	174.6	168.5	168.5	168.6	174.1	173.9	175.5
2006[1]	175.3	184.0	184.3	184.3	193.7	196.7	196.8	197.2	197.5	197.9	197.3	197.2	191.9

[1] Preliminary.   Source: Bureau of Labor Statistics, U.S. Department of Commerce (BLS) (0914)

Producer Price Index of Standard Newsprint   1982 = 100

Year	Jan.	Feb.	Mar.	Apr.	May	June	July	Aug.	Sept.	Oct.	Nov.	Dec.	Average
2000	117.2	116.8	116.5	118.3	123.1	127.1	127.6	130.7	131.5	139.4	141.2	140.5	127.5
2001	140.6	141.4	143.0	150.9	146.8	148.5	146.6	142.4	134.5	130.1	121.6	117.3	138.6
2002	113.6	106.2	106.5	105.7	98.9	100.5	101.0	101.8	104.7	112.2	109.6	107.9	105.7
2003	106.1	107.4	106.3	110.2	112.6	112.5	111.0	114.3	116.8	118.1	114.6	115.0	112.1
2004	116.5	116.7	118.8	122.4	125.0	126.0	125.6	125.7	125.8	129.5	129.8	132.4	124.5
2005	130.3	131.9	131.6	132.8	133.2	135.9	138.8	141.4	152.2	143.5	144.9	145.6	138.5
2006[1]	148.8	148.0	150.5	149.8	152.0	153.7	154.3	153.3	153.9	153.2	152.3	158.4	152.4

[1] Preliminary.   NA = Not available.   Source: Bureau of Labor Statistics, U.S. Department of Commerce (BLS) (0913-02)

Peanuts and Peanut Oil

Peanuts are the edible seeds of a plant from the pea family. Although called a nut, the peanut is actually a legume. Ancient South American Inca Indians were the first to grind peanuts to make peanut butter. Peanuts originated in Brazil and were later brought to the US via Africa. The first major use of peanuts was as feed for pigs. It wasn't until the Civil War that peanuts were used as human food when both Northern and Southern troops used the peanut as a food source during hard times. In 1903, Dr. George Washington Carver, a talented botanist who is considered the "father of commercial peanuts," introduced peanuts as a rotation crop in cotton-growing areas. Carver discovered over 300 uses for the peanut including shaving cream, leather dye, coffee, ink, cheese, and shampoo.

Peanuts come in many varieties, but there are four basic types grown in the US: Runner, Spanish, Valencia, and Virginia. Over half of Runner peanuts are used to make peanut butter. Spanish peanuts are primarily used to make candies and peanut oil. Valencia peanuts are the sweetest of the four types. Virginia peanuts are mainly roasted and sold in and out of the shell.

Peanut oil is extracted from shelled and crushed peanuts through hydraulic pressing, expelled pressing, or solvent extraction. Crude peanut oil is used as a flavoring agent, salad oil, and cooking oil. Refined, bleached and deodorized peanut oil is used for cooking and in margarines and shortenings. The by-product called press cake is used for cattle feed along with the tops of the plants after the pods are removed. The dry shells can be burned as fuel.

Prices – The average monthly price received by farmers for peanuts (in the shell) in the first 7 months of the 2006-07 marketing year (i.e., Aug 2006-Feb 2007) was unchanged from last year at 17.4 cents per pound. The record high is 34.7 cents posted in 1990-91. The average monthly price of peanut oil in the 2006-07 marketing year (through January 2007) rose +14.9% yr/yr to 51.11 cents per pound. The average monthly price of peanut meal (50% Southeast Mills) fell by –7.3% yr/yr in 2006-07 (through January 2007) to a record low of $98.38 per short ton.

Supply – World peanut production in 2006-07 fell by –4.6% yr/yr to 32.303 million metric tons, down from last year's record high of 33.865. The world's largest peanut producers are China with 45% of world production, India with 18%, US with 5%, and Nigeria also with 5%. US peanut production in the 2006-07 marketing year fell by –30.8% to 3.372 billion pounds, far below the record high of 4.927 billion pounds posted in 1991-92.

US farmers harvested 1.213 million acres of peanuts in 2006-07, down –25.5% yr/yr. That was the lowest level since 1930. US peanut yield in 2006-07 fell –7.0% yr/yr to 2,780 pounds per acre, farther down from the record high of 3,159 pounds seen in 2003-04. The largest peanut producing states in the US are Georgia (with 45% of US production in 2006), Texas (17%), Virginia (15%), Alabama (10%), Florida (9%), and North Carolina (9%). US peanut oil production in 2006 rose +19.3% to 191.804 million pounds, but that was still only about half of the record high level of 358,195 million pounds posted in 1996.

Demand – US disposition of peanuts in 2005-06 rose by +7.5% yr/yr to 4.332 billion pounds. Of that disposition, 60% of the peanuts went for food, 15% for crushing into peanut oil, 13% for seed, loss and residual, and 12% for exports. The most popular type of peanut grown in the US is the Runner peanut with 86% of US production in 2005-06. This was followed by the Virginia peanut with 13% of production and the Spanish peanut far behind with only 2% of production. Peanut butter is a primary use for Runner and Virginia peanuts. It accounts for 55% of Runner peanut usage and 53% of Virginia peanut usage. In a poor third place, only 5% of Spanish peanuts are used for peanut butter. Snack peanuts is also a key usage category and accounts for 40% of Spanish peanut usage, 35% of Virginia peanut usage, and 23% of Runner peanut usage. Candy accounts for 53% of Spanish peanut usage, 22% of Runner peanut usage, and 11% of Virginia peanut usage.

Trade – US exports of peanuts in 2005-06 rose by +4.9% yr/yr to 515 million pounds. US imports of peanuts fell by –45.9% yr/yr in 2005-06 to a 12-year low of 20 million pounds.

World Production of Peanuts (in the Shell)   In Thousands of Metric Tons

Year	Argentina	Burma	China	India	Indonesia	Nigeria	Senegal	South Africa	Sudan	Thailand	United States	Zaire	World Total
1997-98	897	559	9,648	7,580	990	1,250	506	97	370	130	1,605	400	27,561
1998-99	486	540	11,886	7,450	930	1,430	541	138	370	135	1,798	410	29,951
1999-00	600	562	12,639	5,500	1,020	1,450	764	165	370	137	1,737	396	29,417
2000-01	564	634	14,437	5,700	1,040	1,470	1,003	186	370	132	1,481	382	31,426
2001-02	517	731	14,415	7,600	1,033	1,490	903	120	370	107	1,940	368	33,817
2002-03	316	756	14,818	5,400	1,086	1,510	260	60	370	112	1,506	355	30,841
2003-04	420	878	13,420	7,700	1,130	1,510	445	115	370	113	1,880	360	32,808
2004-05	585	715	14,340	7,000	1,150	1,520	573	85	370	130	1,945	364	33,428
2005-06[1]	450	715	14,340	7,200	1,170	1,520	700	93	370	130	2,209	365	33,865
2006-07[2]	500	720	14,610	5,900	1,200	1,520	700	85	370	130	1,576	365[2]	32,303

[1] Preliminary.   [2] Estimate.   *Source: Foreign Agricultural Service, U.S. Department of Agriculture (FAS-USDA)*

Salient Statistics of Peanuts in the United States

Crop Year	Agreage Planted	Acreage Harvested for Nuts	Average Yield Per Acre In Lbs.	Production 1,000 Lbs.	Season Farm Price Cents/Lb.	Farm Value Million Dollars	Exports Unshelled	Exports Shelled	Imports Unshelled	Imports Shelled
	----- 1,000 Acres -----						----- Thousand Pounds (Year Beginning August 1) -----			
1997-98	1,434.0	1,413.8	2,503	3,539,380	28.3	1,002.7	682,000	455,264	141,000	101,792
1998-99	1,521.0	1,467.0	2,702	3,963,440	28.4	1,125.9	562,000	----	155,000	----
1999-00	1,534.5	1,436.0	2,667	3,829,490	25.4	971.6	727,000	----	178,000	----
2000-01	1,536.8	1,336.0	2,444	3,265,505	27.4	896.1	527,000	----	216,000	----
2001-02	1,541.2	1,411.9	3,029	4,276,704	23.4	1,000.5	700,000	----	203,000	----
2002-03	1,353.0	1,291.7	2,571	3,321,040	18.2	599.7	490,000	----	75,000	----
2003-04	1,344.0	1,312.0	3,159	4,144,150	19.3	799.4	516,000	----	39,000	----
2004-05	1,430.0	1,394.0	3,076	4,288,200	18.9	813.6	491,000	----	37,000	----
2005-06[1]	1,657.0	1,629.0	2,989	4,869,860	17.3	843.4				
2006-07[2]	1,242.0	1,213.0	2,780	3,372,150	17.2	602.1				

[1] Preliminary. [2] Estimate. *Source: Economic Research Service, U.S. Department of Agriculture (ERS-USDA)*

Supply and Disposition of Peanuts (Farmer's Stock Basis) & Support Program in the United States

Crop Year	Production	Imports	Stocks Aug. 1	Total	Exports	Crushed fior Oil	Seed, Loss & Residual	Food	Total Disappearance	Support Price	Additional	Quantity Mil. Lbs.	% of Production
	Supply				Disposition					Government Support Program		Amount Put Under Support	
	In Millions of Pounds									Cents per Lb.			
1997-98	3,539	141	795	4,475	682	544	303	2,099	3,627	30.50	6.6	417	11.8
1998-99	3,963	155	848	4,966	562	460	374	2,153	3,574	30.50	8.8	----	----
1999-00	3,829	178	1,392	5,399	727	713	493	2,233	4,166	30.50	8.8	----	----
2000-01	3,266	216	1,233	4,715	527	548	360	2,184	3,618	30.50	6.6	----	----
2001-02	4,277	203	1,097	5,576	700	693	482	2,225	4,100	30.50	6.6	----	----
2002-03	3,321	75	1,476	4,873	490	857	410	2,241	3,998	NA	NA	----	----
2003-04	4,144	39	875	5,058	516	536	429	2,456	3,937	NA	NA	----	----
2004-05[1]	4,288	37	1,121	5,446	491	393	547	2,600	4,031	NA	NA	----	----
2005-06[2]	4,870	20	1,415	6,256	515	662	555	2,600	4,332	NA	NA	----	----

[1] Preliminary. [2] Estimate. *Source: Economic Research Service, U.S. Department of Agriculture (ERS-USDA)*

Production of Peanuts (Harvested for Nuts) in the United States, by States — In Thousands of Pounds

Year	Alabama	Florida	Georgia	New Mexico	North Carolina	Okla homa	South Carolina	Texas	Virgina	Total
1997	372,490	228,060	1,333,830	46,710	329,640	184,800	30,450	822,150	191,250	3,539,380
1998	432,415	233,100	1,511,655	62,040	397,155	159,750	28,175	917,900	221,250	3,963,440
1999	448,050	260,380	1,400,800	61,600	298,840	189,600	25,300	926,800	218,120	3,829,490
2000	271,180	213,710	1,328,400	54,990	338,250	120,600	29,500	698,500	210,375	3,265,505
2001	532,325	250,100	1,711,620	67,044	356,475	197,890	30,600	895,900	234,750	4,276,704
2002	379,800	197,800	1,313,000	54,000	210,000	159,600	19,140	868,000	119,700	3,321,040
2003	508,750	345,000	1,863,000	45,900	320,000	98,000	57,800	810,000	95,700	4,144,150
2004	557,200	364,000	1,817,800	59,500	367,500	102,300	112,200	803,700	104,000	4,288,200
2005	613,250	410,400	2,130,000	66,500	288,000	107,910	168,000	975,000	66,000	4,869,860
2006[1]	331,800	288,000	1,523,750	56,000	289,000	66,000	168,000	555,000	496,000	3,372,150

[1] Preliminary. *Source: Agricultural Statistics Board, U.S. Department of Agriculture (ASB-USDA)*

Supply and Reported Uses of Shelled Peanuts and Products in the United States — In Thousands of Pounds

Crop Year Beginning Aug. 1	Stocks, Aug. 1 Edible	Stocks, Aug. 1 Oil Stock[2]	Production Edible	Production Oil Stock[2]	Candy[3]	Snacks[4]	Sandwich Spread	Butter[5]	Other Products	Total	Shelled Peanuts Crushed[6]	Crude Oil Production	Cake & Meal Production
1997-98	498,954	41,000	1,694,016	290,882	351,017	306,908	----	760,230	35,471	1,453,626	409,249	175,853	228,276
1998-99	580,370	14,091	2,227,037	310,459	380,177	349,806	----	744,706	22,131	1,496,820	345,825	145,254	192,425
1999-00	855,572	16,587	2,157,828	448,875	354,953	394,121	----	772,104	20,227	1,541,405	536,164	228,839	291,491
2000-01	707,672	14,463	1,939,736	337,324	355,610	361,516	----	753,239	19,998	1,490,363	411,558	178,523	230,099
2001-02	680,850	16,648	2,090,776	485,092	349,729	360,916	----	818,927	17,284	1,546,856	521,173	230,791	296,874
2002-03	504,186	24,231	1,983,016	611,627	354,232	344,913	----	828,529	24,379	1,552,053	644,194	285,685	356,888
2003-04	603,529	17,686	2,439,231	390,893	365,983	414,588	----	901,637	15,930	1,698,138	402,958	172,977	226,995
2004-05	621,190	17,686	2,357,314	246,663	389,696	450,781	----	938,514	22,547	1,801,538	295,769	126,249	172,668
2005-06[1]	501,868	15,305	2,411,471	357,600	376,777	454,324	----	974,223	12,092	1,817,416	407,817	181,085	232,868

[1] Preliminary. [2] Includes straight run oil stock peanuts. [3] Includes peanut butter made by manufacturers for own use in candy. [4] Formerly titled Salted Peanuts. [5] Includes peanut butter made by manufacturers for own use in cookies and sandwiches, but excludes peanut butter used in candy. [6] All crushings regardless of grade. *Source: National Agricultural Statistics Service, U.S. Department of Agriculture (NASS-USDA)*

PEANUTS AND PEANUT OIL

Shelled Peanuts (Raw Basis) Used in Primary Products, by Type   In Thousands of Pounds

Year	Virginia Candy[2]	Virginia Snack Peanuts	Virginia Peanut Butter[3]	Virginia Total	Runner Candy[2]	Runner Snack Peanuts	Runner Peanut Butter[3]	Runner Total	Spanish Candy[2]	Spanish Snack Peanuts	Spanish Peanut Butter[3]	Spanish Total
1997-98	48,428	80,309	59,228	182,100	302,791	206,718	676,839	1,206,946	19,798	19,581	24,163	64,580
1998-99	36,178	99,401	57,864	196,935	321,838	234,486	670,705	1,244,748	22,161	15,919	16,137	55,137
1999-00	23,173	100,384	73,926	200,804	315,467	278,440	690,564	1,300,393	16,313	15,297	7,614	40,208
2000-01	19,101	100,650	102,050	225,072	320,304	247,739	643,229	1,227,156	16,205	13,127	7,960	38,135
2001-02	26,640	97,046	106,573	233,356	303,668	250,079	702,454	1,269,776	19,421	13,791	9,900	43,724
2002-03	26,930	75,100	77,018	183,226	312,192	257,259	734,844	1,323,846	15,110	12,555	16,667	44,981
2003-04	23,580	68,257	88,053	181,559	328,560	333,198	805,852	1,481,457	13,843	13,133	7,732	35,122
2004-05	25,466	70,216	112,027	209,411	349,437	367,671	824,876	1,562,692	14,793	12,894	1,611	29,435
2005-06[1]	25,738	81,617	123,402	231,893	335,748	361,176	849,176	1,557,025	15,291	11,531	NA	28,498

[1] Preliminary.   [2] Includes peanut butter made by manufacturers for own use in candy.   [3] Includes peanut butter made by manufacturers for own use in cookies and sandwiches, but excludes peanut butter used in candy.   Source: National Agricultural Statistics Service, U.S. Department of Agriculture (NASS-USDA)

Production, Consumption, Stocks and Foreign Trade of Peanut Oil in the U.S.   In Millions of Pounds

Crop Year Beginning Aug. 1	Production Crude	Production Refined	Consumption In Refining	Consumption In End Products	Stocks Dec. 31 Crude	Stocks Dec. 31 Refined	Imports for Consumption	Exports
1998-99	172.9	118.3	123.7	180.1	47.2	3.8	30.3	4.3
1999-00	262.9	195.9	238.9	260.4	19.7	1.7	9.6	5.8
2000-01	222.1	206.3	258.9	277.3	23.1	1.9	19.5	5.5
2001-02	278.5	179.1	291.9	282.5	8.2	1.7	----	----
2002-03	267.7	166.3	W	277.6	52.9	3.5	----	----
2003-04	180.7	115.8	W	203.8	23.0	1.8	----	----
2004-05	135.7	91.0	W	181.9	40.3	2.4	----	----
2005-06[1]	188.0	119.9	W	152.1	15.4	3.7	----	----
2006-07[2]	184.9	119.1	W	W	35.5	5.6	----	----

[1] Preliminary.   [2] Forecast.   Source: Bureau of the Census, U.S. Department of Commerce

Production of Crude Peanut Oil in the United States   In Millions of Pounds

Year	Jan.	Feb.	Mar.	Apr.	May	June	July	Aug.	Sept.	Oct.	Nov.	Dec.	Total
1997	19.9	16.1	18.8	17.9	13.3	15.9	9.9	12.1	6.1	12.2	11.6	14.0	167.7
1998	16.0	14.5	14.3	13.0	10.8	10.0	9.5	6.3	5.8	6.9	13.6	13.9	134.5
1999	16.2	18.2	15.8	18.2	16.4	20.7	20.8	17.8	16.3	13.5	22.6	22.7	219.2
2000	35.2	32.1	27.4	31.9	30.4	28.0	24.1	28.8	21.5	25.4	16.4	15.2	316.3
2001	17.3	15.7	20.1	15.3	12.4	19.1	16.3	16.7	12.9	17.1	13.8	25.6	202.4
2002	24.8	25.5	32.8	28.5	33.8	24.3	22.6	27.7	27.2	26.5	24.9	20.2	319.0
2003	21.7	16.6	19.4	20.5	20.0	23.2	19.8	17.3	18.3	24.1	15.6	13.2	229.6
2004	12.6	15.7	13.0	14.7	11.8	13.7	10.7	9.8	5.8	10.0	11.9	12.6	142.4
2005	14.4	13.1	9.9	11.3	13.3	14.6	8.9	14.5	11.3	15.3	16.4	17.7	160.8
2006[1]	W	16.5	W	15.6	18.1	15.6	15.7	19.7	16.2	18.0	14.4	10.1	191.8

[1] Preliminary.   Source: Bureau of the Census, U.S. Department of Commerce

Average Price of Peanut Meal 50% Southeast Mills   In Dollars Per Short Ton

Year	Oct.	Nov.	Dec.	Jan.	Feb.	Mar.	Apr.	May	June	July	Aug.	Sept.	Average
1997-98	210.00	210.00	210.00	210.00	210.00	210.00	210.00	210.00	210.00	210.00	207.50	205.00	209.60
1998-99	161.00	100.00	103.75	105.00	102.50	91.25	94.50	93.75	100.00	100.00	105.00	102.50	104.94
1999-00	98.00	103.00	103.00	104.00	104.75	110.00	115.00	115.00	119.60	118.00	118.00	118.00	108.15
2000-01	118.00	118.00	118.00	142.50	120.00	118.00	110.75	112.50	NA	123.50	130.50	126.25	121.64
2001-02	115.00	111.25	100.00	102.50	100.00	105.00	110.00	105.00	NA	130.00	135.00	136.88	113.69
2002-03	NA	130.00	122.50	118.50	114.25	124.00	125.00	135.00	135.00	135.75	130.00	130.00	127.27
2003-04	147.10	161.00	163.25	163.35	168.75	200.40	226.00	237.50	204.00	199.33	143.33	133.00	178.92
2004-05	100.38	99.25	93.50	93.25	99.25	112.00	122.75	137.25	145.25	140.83	132.50	109.00	115.43
2005-06	105.50	102.50	100.88	NA	114.50	113.50	113.17	113.33	107.13	107.50	100.00	98.75	106.98
2006-07[1]	98.50	98.50	98.00	98.50									98.38

[1] Preliminary.   NA = Not available.   Source: Agricultural Marketing Service, U.S. Department of Agriculture (AMS-USDA)

Peanuts (monthly average) through December 2006 — Cents per pound

Cents Per Pound
----- Received by Farmers, U.S. (Sept. 1930 - date)

Average Price Received by Producers for Peanuts (in the Shell) in the U.S.   In Cents Per Pound

Year	Aug.	Sept.	Oct.	Nov.	Dec.	Jan.	Feb.	Mar.	Apr.	May	June	July	Average[1]
1997-98	23.3	27.1	25.4	25.0	30.7	24.7	NQ	NQ	NQ	NQ	NQ	NQ	26.0
1998-99	NQ	26.8	26.3	24.6	27.2	NQ	NQ	NQ	NQ	NQ	NQ	NQ	26.2
1999-00	25.7	27.0	25.4	24.1	21.8	14.9	NQ	NQ	NQ	NQ	NQ	NQ	23.2
2000-01	NQ	27.7	26.5	26.1	27.3	31.4	NQ	NQ	NQ	NQ	NQ	NQ	27.8
2001-02	24.1	24.9	22.8	21.0	19.5	13.5	10.7	NQ	NQ	NQ	NQ	NQ	19.5
2002-03	NQ	17.9	17.9	18.0	17.5	19.1	19.6	22.6	18.4	19.6	17.7	NQ	18.8
2003-04	NQ	18.3	18.5	18.4	19.6	20.6	18.9	18.6	19.8	20.6	20.3	17.4	19.2
2004-05	19.0	19.2	20.1	20.3	18.3	18.9	18.6	18.5	18.0	17.8	17.6	16.0	18.5
2005-06	17.0	17.0	17.4	17.5	17.4	17.3	18.6	17.9	17.4	17.3	17.0	17.0	17.4
2006-07[2]	17.0	17.3	17.2	17.2	17.6	17.8	17.9						17.4

[1] Weighted average by sales.   [2] Preliminarily.   NQ = No quote.   *Source: National Agricultural Statistics Service,*
U.S. Department of Agriculture (NASS-USDA)

Average Price of Domestic Crude Peanut Oil (in Tanks) F.O.B. Southeast Mills   In Cents Per Pound

Year	Oct.	Nov.	Dec.	Jan.	Feb.	Mar.	Apr.	May	June	July	Aug.	Sept.	Average
1997-98	49.63	51.00	51.25	51.60	51.00	51.00	50.00	47.20	45.50	44.00	43.75	43.88	48.32
1998-99	45.40	45.00	44.25	44.00	39.75	34.75	35.20	35.00	37.75	39.00	38.75	38.00	39.74
1999-00	40.40	41.00	35.40	33.00	32.50	31.60	33.00	36.25	36.00	35.63	35.00	34.90	35.39
2000-01	34.63	35.50	36.40	37.25	37.00	35.90	34.00	33.00	33.00	33.00	34.00	34.00	34.81
2001-02	36.25	37.00	37.00	35.00	28.00	27.50	27.00	27.00	30.00	34.00	35.20	36.25	32.52
2002-03	NA	42.00	43.67	45.75	46.00	47.00	50.25	52.75	56.60	58.25	60.00	60.67	51.18
2003-04	61.60	63.25	64.50	65.00	61.67	60.00	60.00	56.50	NA	56.00	53.75	55.00	59.75
2004-05	55.00	55.00	55.67	56.00	55.00	50.00	50.00	53.25	52.50	52.38	52.25	50.06	53.09
2005-06	45.50	45.50	45.00	42.50	42.50	42.50	42.50	42.50	43.75	45.00	47.30	49.25	44.48
2006-07[1]	52.67	52.50	50.00	49.25									51.11

[1] Preliminary.   *Source: Agricultural Marketing Service, U.S. Department of Agriculture (AMS-USDA)*

Pepper

The pepper plant is a perennial climbing shrub that originated in India and Sri Lanka. Pepper is considered the world's most important spice and has been used to flavor foods for over 3,000 years. Pepper was once considered so valuable that it was used to ransom Rome from Attila the Hun. Black pepper alone accounts for nearly 35% of the world's spice trade. Unlike many other popular herbs and spices, pepper can only be cultivated in tropical climates. The pepper plant produces a berry called a peppercorn. Both black and white pepper are obtained from the same plant. The colors of pepper are determined by the maturity of the berry at harvest and by different processing methods.

Black pepper is picked when the berries are still green and immature. The peppercorns are then dried in the sun until they turn black. White pepper is picked when the berries are fully ripe and bright red. The red peppercorns are then soaked, washed to remove the skin of the berry, and dried to produce a white to yellowish-white peppercorn. Black pepper has a slightly hotter flavor and stronger aroma than white pepper. Piperine, an alkaloid of pyridine, is the active ingredient in pepper that makes it hot.

Black pepper oil is obtained from crushed berries using solvent extraction. Black pepper oil is used in the treatment of pain, chills, flu, muscular aches, and in some perfumes. It is also helpful in promoting digestion in the colon.

The world's key pepper varieties are known by their place of origin. Popular types of pepper include Lampong Black and Muntok White from Indonesia, Brazilian Black, and Malabar Black and Tellicherry from India.

Prices – The average monthly price for black pepper in 2006 rose by +33.1% to 101.1 cents per pound, up sharply from the 13-year low of 75.6 cents per pound in 2004. The average monthly price for white pepper in 2006 rose sharply by +29.6% to 150.3 cents per pound, but that was still only 42% of the record 356.5 cents seen in 1998.

Trade – The world's largest exporters of pepper in 2003 (latest data available) were Vietnam (with 74,100 metric tons of exports), Indonesia (51,546 metric tons), Brazil (38,972 metric tons), Malaysia (18,346 metric tons), and India (15,318 metric tons).

US imports of black pepper in 2005 rose +2.4% to a record high of 52,152 metric tons. The primary source of US imports of black pepper was Brazil, which accounted for 27% of US imports, followed by Indonesia with 26%, and India with 7%. Imports from Malaysia have dropped by 90% since 2003.

US imports of white pepper in 2005 fell –0.6% to 7,247 metric tons. The primary source of US imports of white pepper was Indonesia, which accounted for 57% of US imports, followed by Brazil with 6%, Singapore with 4%, and Malaysia with 3%.

World Exports of Pepper (Black and White) and Prices in the United States   In Metric Tons

| | Exports (In Metric Tons) | | | | | | | | New York Spot Prices (Cents Per Pound) | | | | |
| | | | | | | | | | Indonesian | | | Indian | |
Year	Brazil	India	Indo-nesia	Mada-gascar	Malay-sia	Mexico	Sri Lanka	Vietnam	Lampong Black	Muntok White	Brazilian Black	Malabar Black	Telli-cherry[2]
1996	24,178	47,211	36,849	1,570	28,124	4,200	2,612	25,300	114.8	178.9	114.8	114.8	140.0
1997	13,962	35,403	33,386	894	29,000	4,210	3,485	24,713	206.7	304.6	206.7	206.7	225.8
1998	17,249	32,859	38,723	339	18,717	3,365	5,493	15,000	239.5	356.5	239.5	239.5	286.6
1999	19,617	35,635	36,293	619	21,804	4,026	3,754	34,800	254.5	334.9	254.5	254.5	296.3
2000	20,469	19,125	47,502	588	23,684	4,534	4,855	36,400	228.1	227.1	228.1	228.1	282.6
2001	36,975	19,641	53,432	811	25,537	4,658	2,161	57,000	116.2	132.6	116.2	116.2	179.3
2002	38,230	21,066	63,214	880	22,840	4,344	7,915	78,400	92.9	120.6	92.9	92.9	127.8
2003[1]	38,972	15,319	51,546	863	18,346	3,861	6,676	74,100	85.8	139.3	85.8	85.8	128.8
2004[1]									75.6	120.9	75.6	75.6	118.8
2005[1]									76.0	116.0	76.0	76.0	109.9

[1] Preliminary.   [2] Extra bold.   Source: Foreign Agricultural Service, U.S. Department of Agriculture (FAS-USDA)

United States Imports of Unground Pepper from Specified Countries   In Metric Tons

| | Black Pepper | | | | | | | White Pepper | | | | | |
Year	Brazil	India	Indo-nesia	Malay-sia	Singa-pore	Sri Lanka	Total	Brazil	China	Indo-nesia	Malay-sia	Singa-pore	Total
1996	4,267	18,350	17,213	1,084	101	411	41,602	519	54	4,370	150	391	5,765
1997	4,328	23,404	13,610	2,203	678	285	45,319	75	522	3,755	199	750	5,751
1998	5,806	15,540	13,045	422	185	578	36,508	32	108	4,571	195	203	5,393
1999	7,093	24,931	8,429	2,392	525	441	47,591	32	451	5,202	420	342	6,789
2000	7,853	10,981	15,713	4,148	306	516	43,539	15	210	6,345	185	215	7,311
2001	11,699	7,998	19,606	2,957	508	279	48,749	48	7	5,807	120	161	6,365
2002	11,300	7,407	13,638	3,213	110	564	50,155	18	73	6,559	103	219	7,207
2003	13,792	4,950	16,370	1,416	163	504	51,124	198	180	4,567	224	904	6,758
2004	15,606	2,039	13,210	97	25	187	50,925	472	98	4,034	192	422	7,290
2005[1]	13,935	3,828	13,502	144	50	269	52,152	460	73	4,134	192	300	7,248

[1] Preliminary.   Source: Foreign Agricultural Service, U.S. Department of Agriculture (FAS-USDA)

Pepper (monthly average) through November 2006   Cents per pound

Cents Per Pound
----- Brazilian Black, New York (Dec. 1919 - date)

Average Black Pepper in New York (Brazilian)   In Cents Per Pound

Year	Jan.	Feb.	Mar.	Apr.	May	June	July	Aug.	Sept.	Oct.	Nov.	Dec.	Average
1997	138.6	151.8	149.0	161.8	173.4	193.8	229.5	255.0	251.3	264.8	266.3	245.0	206.7
1998	199.4	205.5	243.8	262.8	262.8	247.5	253.0	253.8	246.3	243.0	231.3	225.0	239.5
1999	222.5	225.8	252.5	248.0	252.5	250.0	229.0	249.3	263.8	282.0	297.5	281.0	254.5
2000	260.0	256.3	246.0	260.0	265.0	265.0	263.8	252.5	205.0	167.5	147.5	149.0	228.1
2001	157.5	146.3	144.0	150.0	143.8	123.0	97.3	87.0	90.0	89.3	81.6	85.3	116.2
2002	85.0	80.0	81.4	100.5	101.0	92.0	84.8	86.8	93.5	103.5	106.0	100.8	92.9
2003	93.8	89.0	88.5	85.5	83.8	89.0	90.0	86.6	83.5	81.6	80.0	78.0	85.8
2004	78.0	75.5	75.5	75.4	77.3	78.0	76.8	75.0	75.0	74.2	73.3	73.0	75.6
2005	73.0	73.0	73.8	75.2	75.5	77.0	77.0	77.0	77.6	78.0	77.0	77.4	76.0
2006	78.0	78.0	77.8	78.5	80.0	80.4	89.0	112.7	146.0	152.0	139.5		101.1

Source: Foreign Agricultural Service, U.S. Department of Agriculture (FAS-USDA)

Average White Pepper in New York (Indonesian)[1]   In Cents Per Pound

Year	Jan.	Feb.	Mar.	Apr.	May	June	July	Aug.	Sept.	Oct.	Nov.	Dec.	Average
1997	256.0	264.5	255.0	250.0	241.0	248.8	280.3	324.0	332.5	362.0	433.8	407.5	304.6
1998	348.0	346.3	362.5	390.0	393.0	358.8	354.0	356.3	348.8	340.0	340.0	340.0	356.5
1999	361.3	355.0	365.0	355.0	352.5	335.0	310.0	313.8	325.0	327.0	316.3	303.0	334.9
2000	295.0	293.8	264.0	253.8	246.3	242.0	226.3	227.5	205.0	171.3	150.0	150.0	227.1
2001	159.0	151.3	144.0	133.8	130.0	127.0	122.5	129.6	128.0	125.5	120.0	120.0	132.6
2002	111.3	100.3	95.6	108.8	108.0	105.0	104.5	118.8	130.0	154.0	157.5	153.0	120.6
2003	152.4	148.8	150.0	150.0	142.6	133.0	133.0	138.2	137.5	133.6	127.5	125.0	139.3
2004	118.0	118.0	125.8	130.0	130.0	125.0	127.0	120.5	119.0	113.8	109.5	114.6	120.9
2005	119.0	118.0	118.0	116.4	115.0	115.0	115.0	115.0	115.2	115.0	115.0	115.0	116.0
2006	115.0	117.5	125.0	125.0	125.0	126.2	145.0	160.0	210.0	212.5	192.5		150.3

[1] Muntok White.   *Source: Foreign Agricultural Service, U.S. Department of Agriculture (FAS-USDA)*

Petroleum

Crude oil is petroleum that is acquired directly from the ground. Crude oil was formed millions of years ago from the remains of tiny aquatic plants and animals that lived in ancient seas. Ancient societies such as the Persians, 10th century Sumatrans, and pre-Columbian Indians believed that crude oil had medicinal benefits. Around 4,000 BC in Mesopotamia, bitumen, a tarry crude, was used as caulking for ships, as a setting for jewels and mosaics, and as an adhesive to secure weapon handles. The walls of Babylon and the famed pyramids were held together with bitumen, and Egyptians used it for embalming. During the 19th century in America, an oil find was often met with dismay. Pioneers who dug wells to find water or brine, were disappointed when they struck oil. It wasn't until 1854, with the invention of the kerosene lamp, that the first large-scale demand for petroleum emerged. Crude oil is a relatively abundant commodity. The world has produced approximately 650 billion barrels of oil, but another trillion barrels of proved reserves have yet to be extracted. Crude oil was the world's first trillion-dollar industry and accounts for the single largest product in world trade.

Futures and options on crude oil trade at the New York Mercantile Exchange (Nymex) and at the International Petroleum Exchange in London (IPE). The Nymex trades two main types of crude oil: light sweet crude oil and Brent crude oil. The light sweet futures contract calls for the delivery of 1,000 barrels of crude oil in Cushing, Oklahoma. Light sweet crude is preferred by refiners because of its low sulfur content and relatively high yield of high-value products such as gasoline, diesel fuel, heating oil, and jet fuel. The Brent blend crude is based on a light, sweet North Sea crude oil. Brent blend crude production is approximately 500,000 barrels per day, and is shipped from Sullom Voe in the Shetland Islands.

Prices – NYMEX crude oil prices in the first half of 2006 extended the rally that began in 2001 and posted a record high of $78.40 in July 2006. Oil prices were driven higher by continued strong physical and speculative demand, lagging production, and fears of another active US hurricane season that might close down US oil production in the Gulf of Mexico for the third straight year. However, no hurricanes emerged in 2006 to threaten the Gulf of Mexico, which meant that inventories were far too high going into autumn 2006. Producers were forced to liquidate inventories, thus pushing crude oil and petroleum product prices sharply lower and causing a washout of long speculators. By January 2007, crude oil prices fell as low as $50 per barrel. However, OPEC in late 2006 and early 2007 cut production to address the excessive inventory situation with a 1.2 million barrel per day cut announced for November 1, 2006 (only half of which was actually implemented) and a 500,000 bpd cut for February 1, 2007. Those production cuts succeeded in boosting prices from $50 to the $62 area. Crude oil prices were also boosted in early 2007 by various US refinery snafus, which caused the US refinery-operating rate to remain below the 10-year average. Looking ahead, Saudi Arabia and OPEC appear to be targeting crude oil prices roughly in the $50-65 per barrel area. The crude oil markets remain nervous about possible supply disruptions from hurricanes during the US 2007 season, Nigerian production disruptions due to rebel activity, and any US or global confrontation with Iran over its nuclear research program.

Supply – World crude oil production in 2006 rose +0.2% yr/yr to 73.485 million barrels per day, which was a new record high. The world's largest oil producers are Russia (with 12.6% of world production in 2006), Saudi Arabia (12.5%), the United States (7.0%), Iran (5.5%), China (5.0%), and Mexico (4.5%). US crude oil production in 2006 fell –0.5% yr/yr to 5.152 million barrels per day, which was the lowest level in over 30 years. Alaskan production in 2006 fell –14.2% yr/yr to 741,000 barrels per day, the lowest level since 1977 and only 35% of the peak level of 2.107 million barrels per day seen in 1988.

Demand – US demand for crude oil in 2006 rose +0.3% yr/yr to 15.263 million barrels per day, down from the 2004 record high of 15.475. Most of that demand went for US refinery production into products such as gasoline fuel, diesel fuel, aviation fuel, heating oil, kerosene, asphalt, and lubricants.

Trade – The US is highly dependent on imports of crude oil to meet its energy needs. US imports in 2005 (latest data available) rose +0.6% yr/yr to 10.074 million barrels per day, which was a new record high. US imports of petroleum products in 2006 fell –2.3% to 3.504 million barrels per day, imports of distillate fuel oil rose +11.9% yr/yr to 368,000 barrels per day, and imports of residual fuel oil fell -35.7% yr/yr to 341,000 barrels per day.

World Production of Crude Petroleum   In Thousands of Barrels Per Day

Year	Canada	China	Indo-nesia	Iran	Kuwait	Mexico	Nigeria	Russia	Saudi Arabia	United Kingdom	United States	Vene-zuela	World Total
1997	1,893	3,200	1,520	3,664	2,083	3,023	2,317	5,920	8,562	2,517	6,452	3,315	65,690
1998	1,981	3,198	1,518	3,634	2,085	3,070	2,153	2,854	8,389	2,616	6,252	3,167	66,921
1999	1,907	3,206	1,472	3,557	1,898	2,906	2,130	6,079	7,833	2,684	5,881	2,826	65,848
2000	1,977	3,249	1,423	3,696	2,079	3,012	2,165	6,479	8,404	2,275	5,822	3,155	68,342
2001	2,029	3,300	1,340	3,724	1,998	3,157	2,256	6,917	8,031	2,282	5,801	3,010	67,942
2002	2,171	3,390	1,249	3,444	1,894	3,177	2,118	7,408	7,634	2,292	5,746	2,604	66,784
2003	2,306	3,409	1,155	3,743	2,136	3,371	2,275	8,132	8,775	2,093	5,681	2,335	69,235
2004	2,398	3,485	1,096	4,001	2,376	3,383	2,329	8,805	9,101	1,845	5,419	2,557	72,224
2005	2,369	3,609	1,067	4,139	2,529	3,334	2,627	9,043	9,550	1,649	5,178	2,565	73,653
2006[2]	2,512	3,684	1,022	4,029	2,543	3,281	2,436	9,231	9,190	1,489	5,123	2,512	73,485

Includes lease condensate.   [1] Preliminary.   [2] Estimate.   *Source: Energy Information Administration, U.S. Department of Energy (EIA-DOE)*

Refiner Sales Prices of Residual Fuel Oil   In Cents Per Gallon

Year	Jan.	Feb.	Mar.	Apr.	May	June	July	Aug.	Sept.	Oct.	Nov.	Dec.	Average
2001	64.5	61.9	57.2	57.3	58.2	53.0	50.0	50.4	51.2	44.8	40.5	40.0	51.7
2002	51.8	52.2	53.5	59.4	63.5	61.4	63.2	67.4	67.8	72.7	73.6	73.9	64.0
2003	86.6	97.2	98.1	77.3	74.9	71.9	74.5	75.4	72.0	70.7	76.7	79.3	80.4
2004	84.3	80.6	76.3	75.7	80.7	80.5	78.2	81.8	90.3	91.5	96.6	87.2	83.6
2005	86.9	90.8	98.0	106.6	112.2	111.8	116.8	129.2	138.4	142.7	134.3	134.6	116.9
2006[1]	134.6	137.8	136.0	139.7	143.5	148.1	145.1	145.1	132.4	120.1			138.2

Sulfur 1% or less, excluding taxes.   [1] Preliminary.   *Source: Energy Information Administration, U.S. Department of Energy (EIA-DOE)*

Refiner Sales Prices of No. 2 Fuel Oil   In Cents Per Gallon

Year	Jan.	Feb.	Mar.	Apr.	May	June	July	Aug.	Sept.	Oct.	Nov.	Dec.	Average
2001	90.3	82.5	76.3	79.2	82.7	79.3	72.8	77.0	79.0	68.5	60.6	56.6	75.6
2002	57.6	57.8	64.5	68.3	68.4	66.0	68.9	71.3	78.3	79.6	74.8	80.8	69.4
2003	90.0	108.6	105.3	83.0	75.8	76.9	78.9	83.6	77.3	84.2	84.2	88.6	88.1
2004	97.0	93.0	93.6	95.4	103.0	101.9	109.5	118.8	127.0	147.9	139.4	129.9	113.0
2005	131.4	134.4	153.5	155.9	144.4	159.1	164.7	178.4	199.3	207.1	175.2	172.4	164.7
2006[1]	175.6	171.1	179.1	197.2	201.3	198.4	200.6	206.1	179.7	171.3			188.0

Excluding taxes.   [1] Preliminary.   *Source: Energy Information Administration, U.S. Department of Energy (EIA-DOE)*

Refiner Sales Prices of No. 2 Diesel Fuel   In Cents Per Gallon

Year	Jan.	Feb.	Mar.	Apr.	May	June	July	Aug.	Sept.	Oct.	Nov.	Dec.	Average
2001	90.7	85.8	78.1	82.6	89.8	85.3	75.5	80.8	84.1	71.4	61.6	54.7	78.4
2002	54.6	56.7	66.6	70.9	70.6	68.2	71.0	75.7	83.4	85.7	78.9	82.0	72.4
2003	89.2	107.8	102.5	86.4	79.2	81.0	83.7	88.8	80.7	87.0	86.5	89.2	88.3
2004	96.2	96.8	101.0	107.6	112.1	107.1	115.4	124.4	133.0	153.0	142.2	127.2	118.0
2005	130.6	139.1	158.8	163.8	152.2	167.0	171.5	189.8	212.7	232.3	182.6	175.5	173.0
2006[1]	181.0	180.6	190.1	212.2	218.7	218.7	225.0	234.3	191.3	182.3			203.4

Excluding taxes.   [1] Preliminary.   *Source: Energy Information Administration, U.S. Department of Energy (EIA-DOE)*

Refiner Sales Prices of Kerosine-Type Jet Fuel   In Cents Per Gallon

Year	Jan.	Feb.	Mar.	Apr.	May	June	July	Aug.	Sept.	Oct.	Nov.	Dec.	Average
2001	88.2	86.8	80.5	79.5	83.5	82.6	75.9	77.6	80.7	68.5	61.9	55.3	76.3
2002	57.2	57.1	63.9	69.1	69.6	67.8	71.4	73.8	81.5	84.5	75.1	79.9	71.6
2003	89.8	103.1	102.4	82.3	75.1	76.9	81.3	86.2	80.8	83.7	86.5	90.7	87.1
2004	99.7	100.0	101.4	103.3	114.9	108.5	115.6	126.9	132.6	155.1	145.2	132.8	119.7
2005	131.7	138.3	158.2	165.5	155.8	165.0	171.2	184.7	206.9	233.5	181.4	173.8	172.2
2006[1]	182.4	182.5	186.2	203.2	213.2	213.3	217.4	221.4	194.7	181.6			199.6

Excluding taxes.   [1] Preliminary.   *Source: Energy Information Administration, U.S. Department of Energy (EIA-DOE)*

Refiner Sales Prices of Propane   In Cents Per Gallon

Year	Jan.	Feb.	Mar.	Apr.	May	June	July	Aug.	Sept.	Oct.	Nov.	Dec.	Average
2001	86.4	66.9	60.1	58.6	56.2	48.7	43.6	45.6	46.4	46.1	41.6	38.1	54.1
2002	37.4	36.4	39.7	41.6	40.8	37.9	37.5	41.5	47.1	48.9	49.4	53.3	43.1
2003	60.5	72.7	69.2	53.8	54.3	57.1	55.9	58.6	56.7	59.7	58.7	64.8	60.7
2004	71.7	70.1	61.9	60.4	65.5	66.1	72.2	83.0	80.4	88.6	88.3	83.5	74.3
2005	NA	NA	NA	86.0	82.0	83.0	86.0	93.2	108.2	111.6	103.3	106.8	95.6
2006[1]	104.3	97.4	96.6	102.2	103.2	106.1	110.8	111.3	103.2	100.4			103.6

Consumer Grade, Excluding taxes.   [1] Preliminary.   *Source: Energy Information Administration, U.S. Department of Energy (EIA-DOE)*

Supply and Disposition of Crude Oil in the United States   In Thousands of Barrels Per Day

	-- Field Production --		Imports			Unaccounted for Crude	Stock Withdrawal[3]		Disposition		Ending Stocks		
Yearly Average	Total Domestic	Alaskan	Total	SPR[2]	Other	Oil	SPR[2]	Other	Refinery Inputs	Exports	Total	SPR[2]	Other Primary
	In Thousands of Barrels Per Day										In Millions of Barrels		
1999	5,881	1,050	8,731	8	8,722	191	-11	-107	14,804	118	852	567	284
2000	5,822	970	9,071	8	9,062	155	-73	3	15,067	50	826	541	286
2001	5,801	963	9,328	11	9,318	117	26	73	15,128	20	862	550	312
2002	5,746	984	9,140	16	9,124	110	134	-94	14,947	9	877	599	278
2003	5,681	974	9,665	0	9,665	54	108	-24	15,304	12	907	638	269
2004	5,419	908	10,010	77	10,088	143	102	46	15,475	27	961	676	286
2005	5,178	864	10,074	52	10,126	76	25	104	15,220	32	1,008	685	324
2006[1]	5,152	741	NA	NA	10,095	40	11	-10	15,263	24	1,006	689	318

[1] Preliminary.   [2] Strategic Petroleum Reserve.   [3] A negative number indicates a decrease in stocks and a positive number indicates an increase.
Source: Energy Information Administration, U.S. Department of Energy (EIA-DOE)

PETROLEUM

Crude Petroleum Refinery Operations Ratio[1] in the United States In Percent of Capacity

Year	Jan.	Feb.	Mar.	Apr.	May	June	July	Aug.	Sept.	Oct.	Nov.	Dec.	Average
1997	89.3	87.3	90.7	92.6	97.3	97.7	97.1	98.6	99.7	96.7	95.6	97.2	95.0
1998	93.3	91.3	94.4	96.4	97.1	98.9	99.2	99.8	95.0	89.7	94.7	95.1	95.4
1999	90.4	90.0	90.9	94.6	93.9	93.5	94.9	95.5	94.1	91.1	92.0	90.4	92.7
2000	85.7	86.4	89.8	92.6	94.7	96.2	96.9	95.9	94.3	92.4	92.7	94.0	92.6
2001	90.2	90.5	89.4	94.9	96.4	95.6	93.9	93.3	92.2	92.0	92.2	90.2	92.6
2002	87.7	86.6	87.9	93.0	91.5	93.1	93.5	92.9	90.4	87.5	92.6	91.1	90.7
2003	87.2	87.4	90.5	94.1	95.8	94.7	94.0	95.0	93.1	92.4	93.6	93.0	92.6
2004	89.1	88.8	88.5	92.5	95.6	97.5	96.8	97.1	90.1	90.2	94.4	95.0	93.0
2005	91.3	90.6	90.2	92.6	94.1	96.7	94.0	92.1	83.9	81.6	89.0	89.0	90.4
2006[1]	87.0	86.5	85.7	88.1	91.1	93.0	92.4	93.2	93.0	88.0	88.2		89.7

[1] Based on the ration of the daily average crude runs to stills to the rated capacity of refineries per day.   [2] Preliminary.

Source: Energy Information Administration, U.S. Department of Energy (EIA-DOE)

Crude Oil Refinery Inputs in the United States In Thousands of Barrels Per Day

Year	Jan.	Feb.	Mar.	Apr.	May	June	July	Aug.	Sept.	Oct.	Nov.	Dec.	Average
1997	13,632	13,425	14,047	14,283	15,083	15,139	14,958	15,217	15,297	14,790	14,654	14,898	14,662
1998	14,313	14,034	14,590	14,961	15,104	15,368	15,496	15,660	14,854	14,001	14,769	14,832	14,889
1999	14,442	14,309	14,498	15,094	14,973	14,959	15,237	15,299	15,107	14,589	14,704	14,410	14,804
2000	13,779	14,028	14,613	15,053	15,494	15,643	15,819	15,640	15,407	15,029	15,023	15,232	15,067
2001	14,789	14,813	14,649	15,536	15,763	15,650	15,369	15,259	15,005	15,002	15,001	14,688	15,128
2002	14,487	14,306	14,526	15,325	15,301	15,397	15,430	15,338	14,861	14,303	15,155	14,900	14,947
2003	14,338	14,381	14,933	15,575	15,910	15,620	15,546	15,693	15,446	15,342	15,455	15,345	15,304
2004	14,782	14,706	14,787	15,541	15,992	16,240	16,142	16,142	14,980	14,941	15,664	15,750	15,472
2005	15,254	15,142	15,214	15,494	15,905	16,401	15,850	15,664	13,986	13,646	15,032	15,046	15,220
2006[1]	14,806	14,579	14,580	14,936	15,519	15,838	15,667	15,794	15,737	15,000	15,142	15,512	15,259

[1] Preliminary.   *Source: Energy Information Administration, U.S. Department of Energy (EIA-DOE)*

Production of Major Refined Petroleum Products in Continental United States In Millions of Barrels

Year	Asphalt	Aviation Gasoline	Fuel Oil Distillate	Fuel Oil Residual	Gasoline	Jet Fuel	Kero-sene	Natural Gas Plant Liquids	Lubri-cants	Liquified Gasses Total	Liquified Gasses at L.P.G[2]	Liquified Gasses at L.P.G[3]
1996	167.8	7.3	1,213.6	265.5	2,769	554.5	22.8	669.8	63.3	789.1	546.7	242.5
1997	177.0	7.2	1,238.0	258.3	2,826	567.3	23.9	663.3	65.9	799.4	547.3	252.2
1998	179.7	7.3	1,248.6	278.0	2,865	554.6	28.6	639.9	67.2	771.2	526.3	244.9
1999	184.3	7.5	1,240.8	254.8	2,896	571.3	24.4	675.1	66.8	811.0	564.5	246.5
2000	180.6	6.2	1,189.9	234.3	2,664	536.6	20.4	649.4	60.9	788.0	545.5	242.5
2001	177.3	6.5	1,348.4	262.8	2,913	558.2	26.7	680.3	64.1	810.1	569.1	241.0
2002	179.9	6.4	1,309.8	218.8	2,983	552.3	20.8	686.5	63.3	822.5	576.8	245.7
2003	181.0	5.8	1,355.5	241.8	2,992	543.1	20.4	626.7	60.6	766.1	526.4	239.6
2004	185.6	6.2	1,397.6	238.0	3,013	566.3	23.2	662.7	62.0	797.2	561.3	235.9
2005[1]	186.0	6.1	1,441.4	227.9	3,014	561.5	23.6	623.9	60.8	736.9	527.2	209.8

[1] Preliminary.   [2] Gas processing plants.   [3] Refineries.   *Source: Energy Information Administration, U.S. Department of Energy (EIA-DOE)*

Stocks of Petroleum and Products in the United States on January 1 In Millions of Barrels

Year	Crude Petroleum	Strategic Reserve	Total	Asphalt	Aviation Gasoline	Fuel Oil Distillate	Fuel Oil Residual	Finished Gasoline	Jet Fuel	Kero-sene	Liquified Gases[2]	Lubri-cants	Motor Gasoline Total	Motor Gasoline Finished[3]
1997	849.7	565.8	452.6	20.5	2.3	126.7	45.9	157.0	39.9	7.0	86.2	12.7	202	157
1998	868.1	563.4	451.6	22.1	1.7	138.4	40.5	166.4	44.0	7.3	89.5	12.9	213	166
1999	894.9	571.4	407.1	21.4	1.8	156.1	44.9	171.8	44.7	6.9	115.1	13.2	219	172
2000	851.7	567.2	407.1	16.9	1.6	125.5	35.8	154.1	40.5	4.9	89.3	11.8	196	154
2001	826.2	540.7	415.7	25.0	1.3	118.0	36.2	153.0	44.5	4.1	82.5	12.1	207	153
2002	862.2	550.2	445.6	20.6	1.5	144.5	41.0	161.5	42.0	5.4	120.9	13.8	214	161
2003	876.7	599.1	425.1	21.3	1.4	134.1	31.3	161.9	39.2	5.5	105.7	12.0	199	162
2004	906.3	638.4	413.1	19.3	1.2	136.8	37.8	146.8	38.7	5.6	94.4	10.0		147
2005	961.9	675.6	405.6	22.1	1.3	126.0	42.4	143.1	40.2	4.9	111.0	10.4		143
2006[1]	1,007.8	684.5	403.6	21.0	1.2	136.0	37.3	134.8	41.8	5.1	117.6	9.7		135

[1] Preliminary.   [2] Includes ethane & ethylene at plants and refineries.   [3] Includes oxygenated.   *Source: Energy Information Administration, U.S. Department of Energy (EIA-DOE)*

200

Stocks of Crude Petroleum in the United States, on First of Month   In Millions of Barrels

Year	Jan.	Feb.	Mar.	Apr.	May	June	July	Aug.	Sept.	Oct.	Nov.	Dec.
1997	849.7	865.9	862.1	877.6	883.9	890.5	885.3	873.0	864.2	866.6	879.3	886.9
1998	868.1	884.3	885.7	899.8	914.6	916.1	896.4	902.6	893.5	873.0	897.4	906.2
1999	894.4	896.6	897.4	908.0	902.3	914.8	902.8	906.0	889.1	878.0	875.7	866.2
2000	851.6	852.4	855.2	866.5	873.2	864.1	859.5	852.6	858.7	848.2	842.4	833.9
2001	826.2	836.0	824.2	850.8	873.0	871.7	851.5	856.6	851.6	854.1	858.4	859.5
2002	862.2	874.9	887.4	895.0	891.3	898.3	894.1	882.8	878.5	857.8	881.1	884.0
2003	876.7	873.2	870.3	880.8	891.0	888.6	893.1	897.3	897.8	911.1	925.5	914.8
2004	907.3	912.8	931.2	949.4	961.5	965.8	967.2	960.1	947.6	943.3	957.0	961.0
2005	961.3	968.3	985.6	1,007.0	1,022.5	1,026.5	1,025.6	1,018.5	1,012.1	1,000.8	1,006.9	1,007.4
2006[1]	1,007.7	1,007.3	1,026.4	1,028.5	1,035.5	1,029.3	1,024.0	1,018.8	1,019.0	1,020.4	1,025.1	1,020.8

[1] Preliminary.   Source: Energy Information Administration; U.S. Department of Energy (EIA-DOE)

Production of Crude Petroleum in the United States   In Thousands of Barrels Per Day

Year	Jan.	Feb.	Mar.	Apr.	May	June	July	Aug.	Sept.	Oct.	Nov.	Dec.	Average
1997	6,402	6,514	6,452	6,441	6,474	6,442	6,409	6,347	6,486	6,467	6,459	6,531	6,452
1998	6,541	6,476	6,408	6,483	6,347	6,267	6,194	6,203	5,789	6,143	6,140	6,043	6,252
1999	5,963	5,966	5,883	5,887	5,875	5,760	5,798	5,780	5,804	5,947	5,960	5,959	5,881
2000	5,784	5,852	5,918	5,854	5,847	5,823	5,739	5,789	5,758	5,809	5,833	5,855	5,822
2001	5,799	5,780	5,880	5,863	5,829	5,766	5,749	5,725	5,709	5,746	5,881	5,887	5,801
2002	5,848	5,871	5,883	5,859	5,924	5,915	5,770	5,811	5,411	5,363	5,597	5,699	5,746
2003	5,785	5,791	5,817	5,774	5,733	5,701	5,526	5,595	5,683	5,635	5,560	5,579	5,681
2004	5,570	5,556	5,607	5,527	5,548	5,398	5,458	5,333	5,062	5,156	5,396	5,413	5,419
2005	5,441	5,494	5,601	5,556	5,581	5,460	5,240	5,218	4,204	4,534	4,837	4,984	5,179
2006[1]	5,047	5,048	5,016	5,067	5,100	5,219	5,171	5,155	5,188	5,195	5,254	5,360	5,152

[1] Preliminary.   Source: Energy Information Administration, U.S. Department of Energy (EIA-DOE)

U.S. Foreign Trade of Petroleum and Products   In Thousands of Barrels Per Day

	----- Exports -----		---------- Imports ----------						----- Exports -----		---------- Imports ----------			
Year	Total[2]	Petroleum Products	Crude	Petroleum Products	Distillate Fuel Oil	Residual Fuel Oil	Net Imports[3]	Year	Total[2]	Petroleum Products	Crude	Petroleum Products	Distillate Fuel Oil	Residual Fuel Oil	Net Imports[3]
1987	764	613	4,674	2,004	255	565	5,914	1997	1,003	896	8,225	1,936	228	194	9,158
1988	815	661	5,107	2,295	302	644	6,587	1998	945	835	8,706	2,002	210	275	9,764
1989	859	717	5,843	2,217	306	629	7,202	1999	940	822	8,731	2,122	250	237	9,912
1990	857	748	5,894	2,123	278	504	7,161	2000	1,040	990	9,071	2,389	295	352	10,419
1991	1,001	885	5,782	1,844	205	453	6,626	2001	971	951	9,328	2,543	344	295	10,900
1992	950	861	6,083	1,805	216	375	6,938	2002	984	975	9,140	2,390	267	249	10,546
1993	1,003	904	6,787	1,833	184	373	7,618	2003	1,027	1,014	9,665	2,599	333	327	11,237
1994	942	843	7,063	1,933	203	314	8,054	2004	1,048	1,021	10,088	3,057	325	426	12,097
1995	949	855	7,230	1,605	193	187	7,886	2005	1,165	1,133	10,126	3,588	329	530	12,549
1996	981	871	7,508	1,971	230	248	8,498	2006[1]	1,336	1,312	10,095	3,504	368	341	12,264

[1] Preliminary.   [2] Includes crude oil.   [3] Equals imports minus exports.   Source: Energy Information Administration, U.S. Department of Energy (EIA-DOE)

Domestic First Purchase Price of Crude Petroleum at Wells[1]   In Dollars Per Barrel

Year	Jan.	Feb.	Mar.	Apr.	May	June	July	Aug.	Sept.	Oct.	Nov.	Dec.	Average
1997	21.76	19.38	17.85	16.64	17.24	15.90	15.91	16.21	16.44	17.68	16.84	15.06	17.23
1998	13.48	12.16	11.53	11.64	11.49	10.00	10.46	10.18	11.28	11.32	9.65	8.05	10.87
1999	8.57	8.60	10.76	12.82	13.92	14.39	16.12	17.58	20.03	19.71	21.35	22.55	15.56
2000	23.53	25.48	26.19	23.20	25.58	27.62	26.81	27.91	29.72	29.65	30.36	24.46	26.72
2001	24.58	25.27	23.02	23.41	24.06	23.43	22.94	23.08	22.37	18.73	16.49	15.54	21.84
2002	15.89	16.92	20.04	22.14	23.51	22.59	23.51	24.76	26.08	25.29	23.38	25.29	22.51
2003	28.35	31.85	30.09	25.46	24.96	26.83	27.53	27.94	25.23	26.52	27.21	28.54	27.54
2004	30.35	31.21	32.86	33.23	36.07	34.53	36.54	40.10	40.62	46.28	42.81	38.22	36.90
2005	40.18	42.19	47.56	47.26	44.03	49.83	53.35	58.90	59.64	56.99	53.20	53.24	50.53
2006[2]	57.85	55.69	55.59	62.51	64.31	64.36	67.72	67.21	59.36	53.26			60.79

[1] Buyers posted prices.   [2] Preliminary.   Source: Energy Information Administration, U.S. Department of Energy (EIA-DOE)

Light Crude Oil Futures - New York Mercantile Exchange
(weekly close) as of December 29, 2006

USD per barrel

Volume of Trading of Crude Oil Futures in New York   In Thousands of Contracts

Year	Jan.	Feb.	Mar.	Apr.	May	June	July	Aug.	Sept.	Oct.	Nov.	Dec.	Total
1997	1,949.9	1,973.7	2,086.6	2,033.7	2,134.9	2,098.6	2,221.4	2,053.7	2,027.5	2,574.0	1,770.2	1,847.2	24,771.4
1998	2,468.3	2,208.3	2,902.8	2,451.1	2,603.6	3,079.5	2,375.0	2,066.7	2,617.8	2,592.4	2,552.9	2,577.3	30,495.6
1999	2,533.6	2,326.0	3,767.7	3,166.8	3,037.9	3,306.8	3,471.3	3,354.8	3,388.4	3,571.2	3,465.1	2,470.4	37,860.1
2000	3,139.0	3,076.6	3,380.2	2,578.9	3,001.8	3,232.2	2,749.7	3,149.3	3,712.0	3,418.0	2,824.5	2,620.5	36,882.7
2001	3,035.0	2,855.2	3,448.7	3,312.1	3,468.5	3,572.4	3,170.1	3,315.8	2,773.2	2,912.7	3,210.3	2,454.6	37,530.6
2002	3,481.1	3,150.4	3,790.4	4,315.3	4,317.4	3,428.8	3,465.5	3,882.6	3,938.7	4,397.0	3,477.9	4,034.4	45,679.5
2003	4,552.9	4,039.2	4,150.7	3,354.8	3,329.1	3,533.6	3,401.3	3,732.3	3,825.6	4,247.7	3,623.8	3,646.0	45,436.9
2004	4,117.8	3,887.3	4,495.3	4,326.0	4,250.2	4,633.3	4,062.9	4,987.4	4,710.9	4,793.8	4,510.2	4,108.3	52,883.2
2005	4,352.1	4,032.4	5,720.8	5,404.3	5,044.9	5,326.1	4,629.4	6,091.1	5,251.9	5,022.0	4,487.9	4,287.6	59,650.5
2006	5,481.9	5,593.8	5,936.5	5,284.6	5,860.9	5,133.9	4,500.1	5,408.6	6,066.9	7,492.4	7,554.9	6,738.8	71,053.2

Source: New York Mercantile Exchange (NYMEX)

Average Open Interest of Crude Oil Futures in New York   In Contracts

Year	Jan.	Feb.	Mar.	Apr.	May	June	July	Aug.	Sept.	Oct.	Nov.	Dec.
1997	365,522	384,737	408,751	409,719	401,663	397,245	411,292	424,529	405,389	419,821	404,597	424,333
1998	424,810	445,167	468,438	463,961	450,611	467,998	476,516	486,499	486,047	481,657	487,175	501,591
1999	501,655	524,677	581,072	611,727	594,032	582,058	601,212	584,962	622,257	595,743	564,488	531,567
2000	512,049	519,090	513,359	467,259	453,042	462,476	432,571	416,934	461,298	478,242	479,008	438,118
2001	432,892	437,188	432,627	419,904	442,950	462,321	451,005	461,851	434,967	430,774	435,178	436,332
2002	448,063	454,154	497,405	488,061	512,413	474,087	457,033	454,219	505,530	528,548	482,227	531,078
2003	608,254	640,979	568,526	495,456	478,886	494,078	517,539	542,573	507,191	532,024	550,369	580,586
2004	647,658	656,889	673,520	690,021	722,494	705,104	692,850	705,577	684,819	716,973	705,218	676,250
2005	707,934	745,226	829,222	833,759	799,038	785,384	820,131	901,639	870,641	848,728	832,329	841,290
2006	903,481	927,471	954,158	1,000,436	1,055,652	1,016,206	1,068,699	1,163,972	1,181,796	1,168,730	1,176,647	1,200,038

Source: New York Mercantile Exchange (NYMEX)

Plastics

Plastics are moldable, chemically fabricated materials produced mostly from fossil fuels, such as oil, coal, or natural gas. The word plastic is derived from the Greek plastikos, meaning "to mold," and the Latin plasticus, meaning "capable of molding." Leo Baekeland created the first commercially successful thermosetting synthetic resin in 1909. More than 50 families of plastics have since been produced.

All plastics can be divided into either thermoplastics or thermosetting plastics. The difference is the way in which they respond to heat. Thermoplastics can be repeatedly softened by heat and hardened by cooling. Thermosetting plastics harden permanently after being heated once.

Prices – Plastics prices in 2006 showed the fourth consecutive year of strong to moderate gains following the recessionary lows seen in 2001 and 2002. Specifically, the average monthly producer price index of plastic resins and materials in the US in 2006 rose +3.1% yr/yr to 199.0, rebounding farther above the 7-year low of 130.7 posted in 2002. The average monthly producer price index of thermoplastic resins in the US in 2006 rose +2.9% yr/yr to 201.1, rebounding farther above the 7-year low of 129.1 posted in 2002. The average monthly producer price index of styrene plastic materials (also a thermoplastic) in the US in 2003 (latest available data) rose +21.2% to 115.7 from the 25-year low of 95.5 posted in 2002. The average monthly producer price index of thermosetting resins in the US in

2006 rose by +4.1% yr/yr to a record high of 203.1.

Supply – Total US plastics production in 2005 fell by – 2.9% yr/yr to 110.606 billion pounds, down from the 2004 record high of 113.940 billion pounds. US plastics production has more than doubled in the past two decades. By sector, the thermoplastics sector is by far the largest, with 2005 production falling –2.9% yr/yr to 89.595 billion pounds and accounting for 81% of total US plastic production. Production in the thermosetting plastic sector (polyester unsaturated, phenolic, and epoxy) rose +0.4% yr/yr in 2005 to 8.186 billion pounds and accounted for 7% of total US plastics production. The category of "other plastics" fell by –4.8% to 12.825 billion pounds and accounted for 12% of total US plastics production.

Demand – The breakdown by market for the usage of plastic resins shows that the largest single consumption category is "Packaging" with 25.144 billion pounds of usage in 2005, accounting for 30% of total US consumption. After packaging, the largest categories are "Consumer and Industrial" (21% of US consumption), and "Building and Construction" (19% of US consumption).

Trade – US exports of plastics in 2005 fell –1.1% yr/yr to 9.790 billion pounds, but still not far below the record high of 10.048 billion pounds seen in 2002. US exports accounted for 12% of US supply disappearance in 2004.

Plastics Production by Resin in the United States   In Millions of Pounds

	Thermosets				Thermoplastics											
Year	Polyester Unsaturated	Phenlic	Epoxy	Total Thermosets	Thermo-plastic Polyester	Polyvinyl Chloride	Poly-styrene	Poly-propylene	Nylon	Low Density Polyethylene[1]	High Density Polyethylene	Total Thermo-plastics	Total Selected Plastics	Other Plastics	Total Plastics
1996	1,557	3,476	662	8,129	4,031	13,220	6,065	11,991	1,103	14,145	12,373	64,526	72,655	11,640	84,295
1997	1,621	3,734	654	8,647	4,260	14,084	6,380	13,320	1,222	14,579	12,557	67,872	76,519	12,287	88,806
1998	1,713	3,940	639	9,163	4,423	14,502	6,237	13,825	1,285	14,805	12,924	71,209	78,659	13,026	91,685
1999	2,985	4,388	657	8,030	6,735	14,912	7,075	15,493	1,349	15,807	13,864	78,457	86,487	13,467	99,954
2000	3,149	3,965	669	7,783	7,239	14,364	6,676	15,583	1,395	19,588	16,439	84,553	92,336	13,604	105,940
2001	3,021	3,894	597	7,512	6,972	14,626	6,223	16,135	1,159	18,389	15,195	81,726	89,238	12,720	101,958
2002	3,197	4,076	620	7,893	7,480	15,250	6,768	17,084	1,284	19,515	16,190	86,762	94,655	13,607	108,262
2003	3,152	4,015	587	7,754	7,950	14,938	6,478	17,497	1,306	18,915	15,906	86,071	93,825	12,641	106,466
2004	3,294	4,200	658	8,152	8,632	15,883	6,765	18,523	1,357	20,390	17,519	92,317	100,469	13,471	113,940
2005	3,338	4,246	602	8,186	9,139	15,382	6,356	18,061	1,268	19,827	16,492	89,595	97,781	12,825	110,606

[1] Includes LDPE and LLDPE.   *Source: American Plastics Council (APC)*

Total Resin Sales and Captive Use by Important Markets   In Millions of Pounds (Dry Weight Basis)

Year	Adhesive, Inks & Coatings	Building & Construction	Consumer & Industrial	Electrical & Electronics	Exports	Furniture & Furnishings	Industrial & Machinary	Packaging	Transportation	Other	Total
1996	1,833	15,413	9,662	3,022	7,997	3,468	965	18,691	3,469	8,701	73,221
1997	1,713	11,418	10,357	2,806	8,647	3,099	729	19,135	3,411	8,640	69,955
1998	1,758	12,077	11,031	2,816	8,208	3,293	710	19,396	3,588	9,211	71,994
1999	1,753	13,793	11,645	3,036	8,424	2,885	802	21,210	3,632	10,189	77,123
2000	1,167	14,439	13,495	2,787	9,771	3,572	1,084	23,933	4,389	3,003	77,640
2001	1,143	13,988	13,409	2,501	9,295	3,226	968	25,948	4,207	2,705	77,390
2002	1,165	14,729	17,649	3,037	10,048	3,507	998	24,170	4,738	2,283	82,324
2003	1,170	14,495	17,571	2,862	9,009	3,361	962	24,087	4,732	2,021	80,270
2004	1,196	15,676	18,714	3,096	9,900	3,458	1,042	25,952	4,899	2,168	86,101
2005	1,160	15,483	17,400	2,917	9,790	3,406	1,087	25,144	4,711	2,133	83,231

Source: American Plastics Council (APC)

PLASTICS

Average Producer Price Index of Plastic Resins and Materials (066) in the United States   (1982 = 100)

Year	Jan.	Feb.	Mar.	Apr.	May	June	July	Aug.	Sept.	Oct.	Nov.	Dec.	Average
1997	137.0	137.5	138.7	138.9	139.1	139.6	139.3	137.4	136.0	135.9	134.6	133.9	137.3
1998	134.0	132.2	131.0	130.7	128.8	126.8	125.0	123.7	119.6	118.6	117.1	115.9	125.3
1999	115.9	115.8	117.3	118.6	122.1	123.1	127.9	130.0	133.8	135.6	135.8	134.3	125.8
2000	133.2	135.7	139.4	143.7	147.4	147.8	146.4	146.3	142.4	140.7	138.8	137.3	141.6
2001	137.8	139.3	141.4	141.9	139.9	137.6	135.1	131.3	126.8	128.3	126.6	123.9	134.2
2002	122.0	121.3	123.1	125.4	128.0	130.1	135.3	136.4	136.7	138.2	137.0	135.3	130.7
2003	137.2	141.8	149.6	153.2	152.4	149.2	144.9	143.6	144.9	146.2	145.8	144.0	146.1
2004	146.2	150.4	151.4	154.8	156.5	159.6	161.1	164.9	170.6	175.6	181.4	185.2	163.1
2005	190.3	190.8	192.1	192.3	190.3	186.3	185.0	183.4	188.2	203.9	208.6	205.2	193.0
2006[1]	203.9	200.0	198.9	194.4	195.9	198.5	199.2	202.3	202.4	202.6	197.8	192.4	199.0

[1] Preliminary.   Source: Bureau of Labor Statistics, U.S. Department of Commerce (BLS)

Average Producer Price Index of Thermoplastic Resins (0662) in the United States   (1982 = 100)

Year	Jan.	Feb.	Mar.	Apr.	May	June	July	Aug.	Sept.	Oct.	Nov.	Dec.	Average
1997	136.7	137.3	138.6	138.8	139.0	139.7	139.3	137.0	135.5	135.3	133.8	133.0	137.0
1998	133.0	130.7	129.5	129.2	127.0	124.7	122.5	121.0	116.4	115.3	113.7	112.2	122.9
1999	112.3	112.5	114.4	116.1	120.4	121.6	127.5	129.9	134.5	136.7	137.0	135.2	124.9
2000	133.8	136.0	140.4	145.2	149.3	149.6	147.6	147.4	142.7	140.3	137.9	136.0	142.2
2001	136.3	138.0	140.2	140.8	138.4	135.7	133.1	128.6	123.4	125.7	123.9	120.8	132.1
2002	118.4	117.8	120.3	123.8	126.2	128.6	135.0	135.9	136.2	137.6	136.1	133.8	129.1
2003	136.3	142.2	151.4	155.8	153.6	149.5	144.3	142.8	144.7	146.3	146.2	143.9	146.4
2004	146.7	151.9	152.6	156.4	157.5	160.9	162.3	165.5	171.3	176.6	182.3	186.9	164.2
2005	193.2	193.8	195.3	194.9	192.0	187.0	185.4	183.7	189.3	208.4	213.7	209.4	195.5
2006[1]	207.9	202.8	201.5	195.6	197.6	201.1	201.6	205.1	205.0	204.6	198.7	192.2	201.1

[1] Preliminary.   Source: Bureau of Labor Statistics, U.S. Department of Commerce (BLS)

Average Producer Price Index of Styrene Plastics Materials (0662-06) in the United States   (1982 = 100)

Year	Jan.	Feb.	Mar.	Apr.	May	June	July	Aug.	Sept.	Oct.	Nov.	Dec.	Average
1995	129.0	127.0	132.5	134.7	135.9	137.5	135.1	133.2	132.1	130.1	127.9	126.1	131.8
1996	125.7	123.5	125.0	118.3	120.1	122.7	123.4	123.3	123.6	122.8	122.0	120.9	122.6
1997	120.6	123.1	123.0	121.6	121.6	121.6	122.7	117.7	118.0	116.5	113.5	113.7	119.5
1998	113.3	113.9	115.5	114.9	114.1	112.8	111.3	111.2	107.6	107.9	107.1	106.3	111.3
1999	103.5	102.4	103.5	104.7	103.0	102.3	103.1	101.5	101.4	99.8	99.4	100.5	102.1
2000	103.0	104.3	110.5	113.0	116.2	116.9	118.5	116.5	115.0	114.1	112.1	110.4	112.5
2001	110.5	109.2	107.9	108.0	101.8	99.9	97.6	95.7	87.3	89.4	90.0	85.4	98.6
2002	85.7	85.8	87.9	88.5	90.4	91.7	93.7	100.6	100.5	108.9	108.1	103.9	95.5
2003[1]	102.9	110.2	119.5	127.2	126.7	119.1	118.0	113.3	112.8	113.6	113.7	111.6	115.7
2004[1]	NA	NA	NA	NA	NA	NA	NA	NA	NA	NA	NA	NA	NA

[1] Preliminary.   Source: Bureau of Labor Statistics, U.S. Department of Commerce (BLS)

Average Producer Price Index of Thermosetting Resins (0663) in the United States   (1982 = 100)

Year	Jan.	Feb.	Mar.	Apr.	May	June	July	Aug.	Sept.	Oct.	Nov.	Dec.	Average
1997	142.1	142.3	142.7	143.1	143.2	143.0	142.8	142.9	143.0	143.1	142.9	142.9	142.8
1998	143.6	144.0	143.2	142.9	142.6	142.7	142.5	142.2	141.2	140.9	140.1	140.3	142.2
1999	139.9	138.1	137.7	137.4	136.9	136.5	136.2	136.5	136.5	136.5	136.3	136.2	137.0
2000	136.8	141.1	141.3	142.8	144.9	146.0	147.6	147.8	147.5	149.5	150.3	151.0	145.6
2001	152.1	152.9	154.5	154.4	154.2	154.2	152.3	151.3	150.4	148.2	146.3	146.1	151.4
2002	146.2	144.6	143.8	141.2	144.1	145.5	145.8	147.6	148.4	150.3	150.3	150.6	146.5
2003	150.4	149.7	151.7	152.0	156.8	157.9	157.1	156.4	155.7	155.6	153.8	153.8	154.2
2004	154.0	154.2	155.9	158.3	162.2	164.3	166.4	173.2	179.0	183.0	189.3	189.8	169.1
2005	189.9	190.3	190.5	193.5	195.8	195.8	195.5	194.6	196.1	197.5	199.9	200.2	195.0
2006[1]	200.0	200.8	200.8	201.7	201.6	200.5	202.1	203.6	204.2	207.4	207.7	206.2	203.1

[1] Preliminary.   Source: Bureau of Labor Statistics, U.S. Department of Commerce (BLS)

Platinum-Group Metals

Platinum is a relatively rare, chemically inert metallic element that is more valuable than gold. Platinum is a grayish-white metal that has a high fusing point, is malleable and ductile, and has a high electrical resistance. Chemically, platinum is relatively inert and resists attack by air, water, single acids, and ordinary reagents. Weighing almost twice as much as gold, platinum is the heaviest of the precious metals. Platinum is the most important of the six-metal group, which also includes ruthenium, rhodium, palladium, osmium, and iridium. The word "platinum" is derived from the Spanish word platina meaning silver.

Platinum is one of the world's rarest metals with new mine production totaling only about 5 million troy ounces a year. All the platinum mined to date would fit in the average-size living room. Platinum is mined all over the world with supplies concentrated in South Africa. South Africa accounts for nearly 80% of world supply, followed by Russia, and North America.

Because platinum will never tarnish, lose its rich white luster, or even wear down after many years, it is prized by the jewelry industry. The international jewelry industry is the largest consumer sector for platinum, accounting for 51% of total platinum demand. In Europe and the US, the normal purity of platinum is 95%. Ten tons of ore must be mined and a five-month process is needed to produce one ounce of pure platinum.

The second major consumer sector for platinum is for auto catalysts, with 21% of total platinum demand. Catalysts in autos are used to convert most of vehicle emissions into less harmful carbon dioxide, nitrogen, and water vapor. Platinum is also used in the production of hard disk drive coatings, fiber optic cables, infra-red detectors, fertilizers, explosives, petrol additives, platinum-tipped spark plugs, glassmaking equipment, biodegradable elements for household detergents, dental restorations, and in anti-cancer drugs.

Palladium is very similar to platinum and is part of the same general metals group. Palladium is mined with platinum, but it is somewhat more common because it is also a by-product of nickel mining. The primary use for palladium is in the use of automotive catalysts, with that sector accounting for about 63% of total palladium demand. Other uses for palladium include electronic equipment (21%), dental alloys (12%), and jewelry (4%).

Rhodium, another member of the platinum group, is also used in the automotive industry in pollution control devices. To some extent palladium has replaced rhodium. Iridium is used to process catalysts and it has also found use in some auto catalysts. Iridium and ruthenium are used in the production of polyvinyl chloride. As the prices of these metals change, there is some substitution. Therefore, strength of platinum prices relative to palladium should lead to the substitution of palladium for platinum in catalytic converters.

Platinum futures and options and palladium futures are traded on the New York Mercantile Exchange (NYMEX).

Platinum and palladium futures are traded on the Tokyo Commodity Exchange (TOCOM). The NYMEX platinum futures contract calls for the delivery of 50 troy ounces of platinum (0.9995 fineness) and the contract trades in terms of dollars and cents per troy ounce. The NYMEX palladium futures contract calls for the delivery of 50 troy ounces of palladium (0.9995 fineness) and the contract is priced in terms of dollars and cents per troy ounce.

Prices – NYMEX platinum futures prices started 2006 at about $1,040 per troy ounce, rallied to a high of $1,327 per troy ounce in May, but then drifted lower the rest of the year to end the year at about $1,120. A rally began in early 2007 to near $1050 per troy ounce in February of 2007.

NYMEX palladium futures prices started 2006 at about $285 per troy ounce, rallied to a high of $409.00 per troy ounce in May, but then drifted lower the rest of the year to end the year at about $330. A slight rally began in early 2007 to near $358 per troy ounce in February of 2007.

Supply – World mine production of platinum in 2005, the latest reporting year, rose by +4.3% yr/yr to 217,000 kilograms, which was a record high production level. South Africa is the world's largest producer of platinum by far with 78% of world production in 2005, followed by Russia (13%), Canada (3%) and the US (2%). World mine production of palladium in 2005 rose +0.9% to 222,000 kilograms, which was a record high production level. The world's largest palladium producers are Russia with 44%, South Africa with 38% of world production in 2005, Canada with 7%, and the US with 6%. World production of platinum group metals other than platinum and palladium in 2005 rose by +16.2% yr/yr to a new record high of 75,400 kilograms.

US mine production of platinum in 2005 fell by –3.0% yr/yr to 3,920 kilograms, down farther from the record high of 4,390 kilograms posted in 2002. US mine production of palladium in 2005 fell by –2.9% yr/yr to 13,300 kilograms, down farther from the record high of 14,800 kilograms posted in 2002. US refinery production of scrap platinum and palladium in 2005 fell by –2.8% to 21,570 kilograms, which was still just above the record low of 20,900 kilograms in 2002.

Demand – The total of platinum-group metals sold to consuming industries in the US in 2004, the latest data available, rose +7.1% to 91,434 kilograms. The two main US industries that use platinum are the auto industry, which accounts for more than 74% of US platinum usage, and the jewelry industry, which accounts for about 27% of US platinum usage.

Trade – US imports of refined platinum and palladium in 2005 for consumption rose +14.5% yr/yr to 284,849 kilograms, which was well above the 9-year low of 222,356 kilograms seen in 2002. US exports of refined platinum and palladium fell –6.7% yr/yr to 49,385 kilograms, but still up from the 9-year low of 45,124 kilograms seen in 2003. The US relied on imports for 91% of its platinum and palladium consumption in 2005.

PLATINUM-GROUP METALS

World Mine Production of Platinum   In Kilograms

Year	Australia	Canada	Colombia[3]	Finland	Japan	Russia	Serbia/ Montenegro	South Africa	United States	Zimbabwe	World Total
1997	300	4,813	406	60	693	30,000	10	115,861	2,610	345	155,000
1998	150	5,640	411	500	533	30,000	10	116,483	3,240	2,730	160,000
1999	90	5,663	448	500	737	32,000	5	121,304	2,920	479	164,000
2000	171	6,302	339	441	782	34,000	5	114,459	3,110	505	160,000
2001	174	7,733	674	510	791	27,000	5	130,307	3,610	519	172,000
2002	200	9,202	661	508	762	27,000	5	132,897	4,390	2,306	178,000
2003	225	6,990	828	461	770	28,000	5	148,348	4,170	4,270	195,000
2004[1]	230	7,813	1,209	705	750	28,000	5	159,862	4,040	4,438	208,000
2005[2]	240	6,400	1,082	800	730	30,000	----	168,749	3,920	4,834	217,000

[1] Preliminary.   [2] Estimate.   [3] Placer platinum.   Source: U.S. Geological Survey (USGS)

World Mine Production of Palladium and Other Group Metals   In Kilograms

	Palladium										Other Group Metals		
Year	Australia	Canada	Finland	Japan	Russia	Serbia/ Montenegro	South Africa	United States	Zimbabwe	World Total	Russia	South Africa	World Total
1997	400	7,545	180	1,899	70,000	50	55,675	8,430	245	144,000	13,500	25,068	39,200
1998	800	8,905	150	4,151	70,000	50	56,608	10,600	1,855	153,000	13,500	26,862	41,300
1999	816	8,939	150	5,354	67,000	25	58,164	9,800	342	151,000	13,400	37,011	51,200
2000	812	9,949	----	4,712	71,000	25	55,818	10,300	366	153,000	14,100	36,493	51,400
2001	828	8,972	----	4,805	96,000	25	62,601	12,100	371	187,000	14,500	37,005	52,300
2002	810	12,210	----	5,618	96,000	25	63,758	14,800	1,943	196,000	14,500	39,986	55,700
2003	820	12,808	----	5,500	97,000	20	70,946	14,000	3,449	207,000	15,000	46,856	63,500
2004[1]	830	18,551	----	5,300	97,000	20	78,455	13,700	3,564	220,000	15,000	48,265	64,900
2005[2]	840	15,000	----	5,200	97,400	----	84,908	13,300	3,879	222,000	15,500	58,218	75,400

[1] Preliminary.   [2] Estimate.   Source: U.S. Geological Survey (USGS)

Platinum-Group Metals Sold to Consuming Industries in the United States   In Kilograms

Year	Automotive Platinum	Automotive Other[3]	Chemical Platinum	Chemical Other[3]	Electrical Platinum	Electrical Other[3]	Dental & Medical Platinum	Dental & Medical Other[3]	Jewelry & Decorative Platinum	Jewelry & Decorative Other[3]	Petroleum Platinum	Petroleum Other[3]	All PGM Platinum	All PGM Palladium	All PGM Other[3]	Total
1996	28,550	19,282	2,115	2,457	4,541	17,665	778	6,285	1,493	1,493	3,514	902	44,489	45,157	----	89,646
1997	28,923	20,402	2,239	2,426	4,945	19,997	840	6,376	2,115	1,617	3,390	871	46,184	50,227	----	96,411
1998	29,483	26,528	2,301	2,488	5,194	20,215	902	6,376	2,333	1,617	3,390	809	47,396	61,827	----	109,223
1999	31,100	29,390	2,364	2,519	5,443	21,148	933	6,065	3,110	1,679	3,514	778	50,310	65,248	----	115,558
2000	32,344	31,100	2,457	2,139	5,691	19,282	964	3,732	3,670	1,400	3,639	660	52,808	61,889	----	114,697
2001	33,411	34,832	2,644	715	5,909	17,354	995	3,670	4,043	1,431	4,199	715	55,399	62,293	----	117,692
2002	17,727	19,904	3,110	2,333	2,955	6,531	1,244	6,687	9,641	----	1,400	----	33,433	28,768	----	62,200
2003[1]	27,524	37,476	2,955	2,177	2,644	6,687	778	6,998	9,641	----	1,244	----	37,476	47,894	----	85,370
2004[2]	24,880	44,940	2,799	2,644	2,799	6,376	622	7,309	9,019	----	1,089	----	33,588	57,846	----	91,434

[1] Preliminary.   [2] Estimate.   [3] Includes Palladium, iridium, osmium, rhodium, and ruthenium.   Sources: U.S. Geological Survey (USGS); American Metal Market (AMM)

Salient Statistics of Platinum and Allied Metals[3] in the United States   In Kilograms

Year	Net Import Reliance as a % of Apparent Consumption	Mine Production Platinum	Mine Production Palladium	Refinery Production (Secondary)	Total Refined	Refiner, Importer & Dealer Stocks Platinum	Refiner, Importer & Dealer Stocks Palladium	Refiner, Importer & Dealer Stocks Other[4]	Total	Imports for Consumption Refined	Total	Exports Refined	Total	Apparent Consumption
1997	84	2,610	8,430	NA	NA	14,100	39,300	920	54,320	253,114	258,424	67,656	81,249	----
1998	94	3,240	10,600	NA	NA	13,700	38,800	920	53,420	297,101	303,351	52,716	73,162	----
1999	----	2,920	9,800	23,300	23,300	7,060	28,200	784	36,044	337,973	----	64,165	----	----
2000	83	3,110	10,300	23,780	23,780	5,190	19,000	784	24,974	316,633	----	84,087	----	----
2001	66	3,610	12,100	24,790	24,790	3,680	16,300	784	20,764	267,957	----	67,334	----	----
2002	93	4,390	14,800	20,900	20,900	649	5,870	784	7,303	222,356	----	70,943	----	----
2003	96	4,170	14,000	24,250	24,250	649	1,170	562	2,381	223,653	----	45,124	----	----
2004[1]	91	4,040	13,700	22,180	22,180	649	568	501	1,718	248,705	----	52,904	----	----
2005[2]	91	3,920	13,300	21,570	21,570	261	----	189	450	284,849	----	49,385	----	----

[1] Preliminary.   [2] Estimate.   [3] Includes platinum, palladium, iridium, osmium, rhodium, and ruthenium.   [4] Includes iridium, osmium, rhodium, and ruthenium.   W = Withheld proprietary data.   Source: U.S. Geological Survey (USGS)

Platinum and Palladium (monthly average) through December 2006 · USD per troy ounce

Legend:
Platinum: USD Per Troy Ounce
----- Producer, New York (Jan. 1910 - Dec. 1977)
Merchant, New York (Jan. 1978 - date)

Palladium: USD Per Troy Ounce
- - - Dealer, New York (Jan. 1968 - date)

Average Merchant's Price of Platinum in the United States   In Dollars Per Troy Ounce

Year	Jan.	Feb.	Mar.	Apr.	May	June	July	Aug.	Sept.	Oct.	Nov.	Dec.	Average
1997	360.13	362.35	382.82	371.18	385.20	427.12	409.93	423.48	424.00	428.59	396.68	369.55	395.42
1998	375.30	390.56	396.18	412.82	392.60	357.38	379.34	372.24	361.40	347.27	348.42	352.76	373.85
1999	353.53	361.55	370.80	357.30	354.75	357.75	350.30	352.24	365.62	421.52	436.48	438.00	376.44
2000	432.95	517.02	478.28	493.53	519.57	557.45	558.53	572.76	592.53	576.91	592.73	608.28	541.49
2001	623.43	453.56	566.67	589.63	611.07	588.91	643.88	457.37	453.50	437.43	427.25	450.24	531.93
2002	471.52	470.68	511.95	539.20	533.66	554.70	526.32	545.48	556.05	580.11	588.15	594.89	539.39
2003	629.52	681.79	675.00	624.48	649.43	661.43	682.02	692.48	705.33	732.65	760.08	807.10	691.78
2004	851.28	846.33	900.26	880.14	807.28	807.55	809.60	848.43	847.88	841.43	853.81	850.89	845.41
2005	859.03	865.16	865.89	864.55	866.26	880.36	876.60	901.04	918.10	933.76	962.19	977.25	897.52
2006[1]	1029.52	1044.21	1041.65	1104.32	1263.64	1192.73	1233.68	1236.74	1183.30	1085.32	1187.10	1125.20	1143.95

[1] Preliminary.   *Source: American Metal Market (AMM)*

Average Dealer[2] Price of Palladium in the United States   In Dollars Per Troy Ounce

Year	Jan.	Feb.	Mar.	Apr.	May	June	July	Aug.	Sept.	Oct.	Nov.	Dec.	Average
1997	121.48	134.26	151.13	152.75	167.52	203.62	176.84	210.90	190.17	206.52	209.93	200.70	177.15
1998	222.55	237.25	258.01	310.81	353.58	284.34	307.53	287.48	283.88	277.89	281.82	306.73	284.32
1999	317.28	351.38	351.78	358.83	330.70	339.84	333.17	341.64	358.55	387.05	400.38	420.17	357.50
2000	447.45	607.33	687.72	580.00	574.89	640.80	686.63	759.63	731.15	734.91	778.73	887.33	676.55
2001	1054.10	984.37	792.68	699.15	663.41	619.67	525.90	459.83	444.47	340.52	333.14	405.95	610.27
2002	412.62	377.79	377.15	372.50	360.00	339.20	325.41	327.55	330.50	319.09	289.20	243.57	339.55
2003	258.19	255.68	226.38	164.76	168.90	181.76	174.91	185.76	213.24	204.17	200.17	200.86	202.90
2004	221.00	237.95	272.43	299.52	249.55	231.86	222.95	217.36	213.95	220.43	216.00	193.09	233.01
2005	188.45	184.16	200.55	200.57	191.29	188.36	186.95	188.13	191.24	209.71	246.45	266.00	203.49
2006[1]	275.25	291.89	312.61	355.74	372.59	319.00	320.58	332.57	324.40	315.18	326.70	327.95	322.87

[1] Preliminary.   [2] Based on wholesale quantities, prompt delivery.   *Source: U.S. Geological Survey (USGS)*

PLATINUM-GROUP METALS

Volume of Trading of Platinum Futures in New York   In Contracts

Year	Jan.	Feb.	Mar.	Apr.	May	June	July	Aug.	Sept.	Oct.	Nov.	Dec.	Total
1997	60,515	83,325	86,242	57,719	67,000	72,481	37,836	36,391	62,462	46,188	28,913	58,625	698,597
1998	38,198	35,538	65,871	36,169	36,208	47,464	35,223	27,505	58,302	44,381	42,658	60,752	528,629
1999	37,700	53,698	68,350	36,900	26,507	75,444	57,536	36,115	102,196	30,637	32,176	40,009	597,268
2000	33,226	31,352	35,013	28,057	22,741	47,197	16,527	14,739	36,643	12,122	12,662	30,645	320,924
2001	19,278	12,885	31,617	14,961	15,714	23,245	14,494	12,477	17,040	9,957	11,401	22,890	205,969
2002	12,848	13,807	24,434	11,066	12,294	27,176	14,198	18,583	29,762	11,834	9,878	33,891	219,771
2003	15,545	15,157	38,170	13,472	18,968	30,961	10,852	11,878	37,686	19,275	14,040	42,301	268,305
2004	16,337	15,574	42,249	29,228	13,125	28,495	15,598	18,180	34,076	24,393	18,606	39,834	295,695
2005	15,410	20,253	41,297	16,267	20,135	55,588	25,132	26,604	52,535	21,827	30,447	50,684	376,179
2006	20,604	27,572	42,804	17,215	34,684	45,985	16,220	21,428	44,000	21,182	46,754	34,671	373,119

Source: New York Mercantile Exchange (NYMEX)

Average Open Interest of Platinum Futures in New York   In Contracts

Year	Jan.	Feb.	Mar.	Apr.	May	June	July	Aug.	Sept.	Oct.	Nov.	Dec.
1997	25,890	26,092	22,364	16,568	18,933	18,440	13,280	14,180	13,639	13,466	12,396	13,501
1998	10,791	10,932	13,220	13,559	12,048	11,471	10,607	9,733	11,950	14,601	15,709	13,289
1999	12,311	14,481	16,493	11,471	12,256	12,436	14,703	13,777	15,014	14,892	13,402	12,017
2000	10,858	10,952	9,218	8,484	9,057	10,585	9,566	9,731	9,716	8,106	8,163	8,507
2001	8,449	7,311	6,855	6,715	7,436	5,751	6,210	5,996	5,646	5,395	6,102	6,033
2002	6,587	6,213	7,121	6,823	6,031	6,901	5,516	6,405	6,930	7,211	7,406	8,388
2003	8,694	8,132	8,034	6,322	6,599	6,847	7,450	8,556	8,794	8,489	9,421	9,373
2004	8,210	7,379	8,879	7,698	5,555	5,590	5,376	6,282	6,091	6,092	7,208	7,184
2005	6,800	7,486	8,047	8,132	8,496	10,109	8,497	11,729	12,478	13,024	12,377	11,327
2006	10,625	9,995	8,407	9,486	9,681	8,265	8,575	9,889	9,076	7,276	8,332	8,186

Source: New York Mercantile Exchange (NYMEX)

Palladium Futures - New York Mercantile Exchange USD Per Troy Ounce
(weekly close) as of December 29, 2006

Volume of Trading of Palladium Futures in New York   In Contracts

Year	Jan.	Feb.	Mar.	Apr.	May	June	July	Aug.	Sept.	Oct.	Nov.	Dec.	Total
1997	13,908	43,160	22,796	21,604	36,422	17,647	18,097	18,751	8,331	13,094	13,143	11,763	238,716
1998	11,506	17,786	18,678	14,042	17,942	7,370	4,241	8,737	6,214	4,962	12,839	6,933	131,250
1999	3,092	11,614	4,082	7,097	8,890	3,411	5,053	6,868	5,826	3,722	10,670	5,069	75,394
2000	4,584	13,976	2,803	1,833	7,034	2,622	3,120	5,169	2,523	2,460	3,041	1,601	50,766
2001	2,171	6,090	1,397	1,121	3,325	1,013	1,173	3,221	523	1,255	3,261	1,375	25,925
2002	1,275	3,372	1,538	1,527	6,126	2,166	2,154	8,971	1,452	1,710	8,118	2,644	41,053
2003	4,200	7,266	3,256	3,971	8,420	3,430	4,221	15,645	8,152	7,587	18,323	11,142	95,613
2004	17,093	41,036	20,508	30,214	27,343	11,433	7,606	28,895	10,690	15,036	41,269	16,429	267,552
2005	7,728	43,268	16,979	13,316	46,112	13,594	17,185	49,268	17,747	21,680	50,643	24,403	321,923
2006	28,447	59,279	32,573	23,135	64,863	25,857	13,464	41,123	16,222	14,351	47,797	11,005	378,116

Source: New York Mercantile Exchange (NYMEX)

Average Open Interest of Palladium Futures in New York   In Contracts

Year	Jan.	Feb.	Mar.	Apr.	May	June	July	Aug.	Sept.	Oct.	Nov.	Dec.
1997	8,291	10,946	10,528	9,759	9,947	7,072	5,538	4,973	3,822	4,282	4,291	4,030
1998	4,062	4,873	5,220	5,369	4,371	4,219	4,166	3,488	2,959	3,048	2,938	2,700
1999	2,846	3,234	2,957	3,015	2,796	2,757	2,823	2,496	2,755	3,210	3,301	3,045
2000	3,129	3,101	2,367	2,359	2,628	2,015	2,118	1,974	1,757	1,905	1,859	1,837
2001	1,828	1,666	1,525	1,577	1,613	1,385	1,420	1,318	1,383	1,286	1,477	1,244
2002	1,217	1,208	1,042	1,199	1,554	1,806	2,103	2,298	1,878	1,976	1,977	2,025
2003	2,000	2,039	1,948	1,997	2,315	2,609	2,680	3,605	5,184	5,533	6,096	6,737
2004	9,119	11,878	11,465	11,039	8,828	7,861	8,055	8,688	8,933	9,965	11,192	12,188
2005	12,824	13,821	12,946	13,116	13,345	13,527	13,794	14,465	13,340	13,488	14,676	14,477
2006	14,353	16,632	15,426	17,783	18,002	14,251	14,087	13,166	11,247	11,836	12,511	11,210

Source: New York Mercantile Exchange (NYMEX)

Pork Bellies

Pork bellies are the cut of meat from a hog from which bacon is produced. A hog has two belly slabs, generally weighing 8-18 pounds each, depending on the hog's commercial slaughter weight. Total hog slaughter weights average around 255 pounds, equal to a dressed carcass weight of about 190 pounds. Bellies account for about 12% of a hog's live weight, but represent a larger 14% of the total cutout value of the realized pork products. Pork bellies can be frozen and stored for up to a year before processing. The pork belly futures contract at the Chicago Mercantile Exchange calls for the physical delivery of 40,000 pounds of frozen pork bellies, which have been slaughtered at USDA federally inspected slaughtering plants. Each deliverable belly typically weighs 12-14 pounds each.

There are definite seasonal patterns in pork belly prices. Bellies are storable and the movement into cold storage builds early in the calendar year, peaking about mid-year. Net withdrawals from storage then carry stocks to a low around October. The cycle then starts again. Retail bacon demand also follows a time worn trend, peaking in the summer and tapering off to a low during the winter months. While demand patterns would suggest the highest prices in the summer and the lowest in the winter, just the opposite is not unusual. Such contra-seasonal price moves can be partially attributed to supply logistics, notably the availability of frozen storage stocks deliverable against futures at CME exchange-approved warehouses. When stocks prove either too large or small, the underlying demand variables for bacon can be relegated to the backburner as a market-moving factor. The fact that no contract months are traded between August and the following February adds to the late fall futures price distortion.

Belly prices (cash and futures) are sensitive to the inventory in cold storage and to the weekly net movement in and out of storage, which affords some insight to demand, although a better measure is the weekly quantity of bellies being sliced into bacon. Higher retail prices tend to encourage placing more supply into storage because of lower retail bacon demand. Bacon is not a necessary foodstuff so demand can be buoyed by favorable consumer disposable income. However, dietary standards have changed dramatically in recent years and do not favor the consumption of high fat and salt content food, such as bacon. In addition, alternatives to pork bacon have emerged in recent years such as turkey bacon, which has lower fat and calorie content.

Prices – Pork belly futures prices in 2006 rallied during most of the year and closed the year at 91.77 cents per pound, up +12% yr/yr. Pork belly prices in 2006 were boosted mainly by firm domestic and export demand. Pork belly prices in early 2007 rallied to a new 1-1/2 year high due to the severe weather during winter 2007, which caused low carcass weights and reduced supplies. Pork belly prices in 2006 remained well below the record high of 126 cents per pound that was posted in mid-2004.

Supply – The average monthly level of frozen pork belly storage stocks fell sharply in 2006 to 43.985 million pounds, down –18.6% from 2005. As of December 2006, there were 30.553 million pounds of pork bellies in storage.

Average Retail Price of Bacon, Sliced   In Dollars Per Pound

Year	Jan.	Feb.	Mar.	Apr.	May	June	July	Aug.	Sept.	Oct.	Nov.	Dec.	Average
1997	2.66	2.65	2.66	2.66	2.63	2.69	2.72	2.76	2.75	2.73	2.67	2.61	2.68
1998	2.64	2.62	2.54	2.44	2.44	2.46	2.52	2.51	2.58	2.57	2.62	2.58	2.54
1999	2.52	2.52	2.51	2.45	2.47	2.50	2.50	2.93	2.58	2.57	2.66	2.75	2.58
2000	2.75	2.87	2.93	2.95	3.01	3.13	3.17	3.20	3.21	3.07	3.05	3.03	3.03
2001	2.99	3.07	3.16	3.11	3.26	3.25	3.32	3.47	3.49	3.34	3.30	3.30	3.25
2002	3.27	3.32	3.27	3.26	3.18	3.19	3.23	3.29	3.16	3.24	3.21	3.24	3.24
2003	3.20	3.28	3.22	3.29	3.09	3.14	3.16	3.23	3.22	3.16	3.23	3.18	3.20
2004	3.16	3.19	3.13	3.20	3.33	3.42	3.47	3.62	3.59	3.61	3.44	3.37	3.38
2005	3.37	3.40	3.36	3.33	3.56	3.46	3.48	3.44	3.40	3.33	3.26	3.33	3.39
2006[1]	3.36	3.39	3.36	3.34	3.31	3.40	3.51	3.56	3.55	3.61	3.44	3.46	3.44

[1] Preliminary.   Source: Economic Research Service, U.S. Department of Agriculture (ERS-USDA)

Frozen Pork Bellie Storage Stocks in the United States, on First of Month   In Thousands of Pounds

Year	Jan.	Feb.	Mar.	Apr.	May	June	July	Aug.	Sept.	Oct.	Nov.	Dec.
1997	37,930	38,030	44,277	54,767	54,015	55,274	52,274	33,657	18,346	11,148	14,408	25,365
1998	44,763	55,249	55,368	54,441	58,600	59,462	52,010	31,433	14,786	9,452	16,440	41,711
1999	72,657	82,605	93,323	106,194	109,521	108,257	93,383	69,675	34,814	19,273	22,489	26,170
2000	40,300	43,802	49,983	60,527	63,461	68,292	60,097	50,515	33,005	21,341	20,589	38,674
2001	47,099	50,145	47,154	45,440	43,878	46,029	39,552	24,996	12,754	8,960	28,216	36,297
2002	44,301	50,849	57,569	60,721	63,293	62,269	51,019	29,925	14,250	9,452	10,354	18,059
2003	28,254	35,354	38,278	42,971	48,542	45,870	43,504	32,075	17,900	10,180	21,135	33,073
2004	49,017	63,095	57,123	50,126	48,363	41,366	37,185	23,383	15,230	11,344	15,970	33,955
2005	56,026	63,417	75,321	81,265	89,360	81,694	70,657	50,315	22,149	14,117	15,211	28,613
2006[1]	47,925	54,902	64,638	67,631	69,540	64,857	52,535	37,328	11,962	10,199	15,751	30,553

[1] Preliminary.   Source: National Agricultural Statistics Service, U.S. Department of Agriculture (NASS-USDA)

Weekly Pork Belly Storage Movement

				Net					Net
------------------------- Stocks[1] In Thousands of Pounds -------------------------					------------------------- Stocks[1] In Thousands of Pounds -------------------------				
Week Ending	In	Out	On Hand	Move- ment	Week Ending	In	Out	On Hand	Move- ment
Jan 01, 2005	8,459	-42	44,042	8,417	Jan 07, 2006	2,459	-41	37,310	2,418
Jan 08, 2005	7,156	0	51,197	7,156	Jan 14, 2006	3,519	-57	40,772	3,462
Jan 15, 2005	1,494	-3,754	48,937	-2,260	Jan 21, 2006	2,461	-411	42,822	2,050
Jan 22, 2005	2,176	-4,460	46,653	2,284	Jan 28, 2006	2,506	-319	45,009	2,187
Jan 29, 2005	1,462	-162	49,515	1,300	Feb 04, 2006	1,830	-38	46,801	1,792
Feb 05, 2005	1,032	-40	50,507	992	Feb 11, 2006	1,289	0	48,090	1,289
Feb 12, 2005	2,217	-162	52,648	2,055	Feb 18, 2006	1,108	-9	49,189	1,099
Feb 19, 2005	2,332	-905	53,332	1,427	Feb 25, 2006	1,374	0	50,563	1,374
Feb 26, 2005	2,645	-108	55,868	2,537	Mar 04, 2006	124	-243	5,044	-119
Mar 05, 2005	NA	NA	58,843	2,975	Mar 11, 2006	564	-205	50,803	359
Mar 12, 2005	1,472	-41	60,274	1,431	Mar 18, 2006	1,416	-53	52,166	1,363
Mar 19, 2005	492	-452	60,315	40	Mar 25, 2006	640		57,225	640
Mar 26, 2005	218	-337	60,196	-119	Apr 01, 2006	690	-84	57,831	606
Apr 02, 2005	1,542	-246	61,492	1,296	Apr 08, 2006	257	-140	57,948	117
Apr 09, 2005	1,483	-84	62,891	1,399	Apr 15, 2006	713	-123	58,538	590
Apr 16, 2005	2,119	-81	64,929	2,038	Apr 22, 2006	560	-195	58,903	365
Apr 23, 2005	2,268	-368	66,829	1,900	Apr 29, 2006	134	-242	58,795	-108
Apr 30, 2005	1,391	-294	67,926	1,097	May 06, 2006	21	-165	58,651	-144
May 07, 2005	632	-318	68,241	314	May 13, 2006	2	-908	57,745	-906
May 14, 2005	2,382	-1,666	68,957	716	May 20, 2006	465	-1,020	57,190	-555
May 21, 2005	101	-4,655	64,403	-4,554	May 27, 2006	0	-837	56,353	-837
May 28, 2005	631	-1,841	63,193	-1,210	Jun 03, 2006	0	-872	55,481	-872
Jun 04, 2005	95	-610	63,473	-515	Jun 10, 2006	42	-2,086	53,437	-2,044
Jun 11, 2005	44	-1,088	62,429	-1,044	Jun 17, 2006	0	-2,896	50,541	-2,896
Jun 18, 2005	318	-1,718	61,029	-1,400	Jun 24, 2006	83	-3,028	47,596	-2,945
Jun 25, 2005	86	-1,944	59,171	-1,858	Jul 01, 2006	125	-2,604	45,117	-2,479
Jul 02, 2005	112	-1,096	58,186	-984	Jul 08, 2006	40	-3,202	41,955	-3,162
Jul 09, 2005	42	-1,866	56,314	-1,824	Jul 15, 2006	15	-3,738	38,232	-3,723
Jul 16, 2005	489	-3,227	53,624	-2,738	Jul 22, 2006	2	-4,486	33,748	-4,484
Jul 23, 2005	675	-5,173	49,126	-4,498	Jul 29, 2006	444	-3,202	30,990	-2,758
Jul 30, 2005	462	-6,440	43,148	-5,978	Aug 05, 2006	162	-3,639	27,513	-3,477
Aug 06, 2005	116	-7,415	35,848	-7,299	Aug 12, 2006	85	-4,421	23,177	-4,336
Aug 13, 2005	367	-7,732	28,483	-7,365	Aug 19, 2006	41	-3,760	19,458	-3,719
Aug 20, 2005	1,315	-5,577	24,220	-4,262	Aug 26, 2006	0	-3,612	8,599	-3,612
Aug 27, 2005	181	-3,919	20,483	-3,738	Sep 02, 2006	86	-4,034	4,651	-3,948
Sep 03, 2005	105	-4,945	15,643	-4,840	Sep 09, 2006	8	-1,606	3,053	-1,598
Sep 10, 2005	76	-2,326	13,392	-2,250	Sep 16, 2006	62	-1,249	1,865	-1,187
Sep 17, 2005	30	-1,388	12,034	-1,358	Sep 23, 2006	161	-400	1,626	-239
Sep 24, 2005	55	-1,764	10,326	-1,709	Sep 30, 2006	1,132	-325	2,433	807
Oct 01, 2005	55	-1,400	8,981	-1,345	Oct 07, 2006	795	-230	2,998	565
Oct 08, 2005	56	-677	8,360	-621	Oct 14, 2006	310	-597	2,711	-287
Oct 15, 2005	48	-264	8,263	-97	Oct 21, 2006	898	-292	3,317	-606
Oct 22, 2005	215	-480	7,998	-265	Oct 28, 2006	3,287	-167	6,437	3,120
Oct 29, 2005	1,480	-169	9,309	1,311	Nov 04, 2006	1,848	-215	8,070	1,633
Nov 05, 2005	2,280	0	11,438	2,280	Nov 11, 2006	2,014	0	10,084	2,014
Nov 12, 2005	1,403	-202	12,639	1,201	Nov 18, 2006	1,918	-160	11,842	1,758
Nov 19, 2005	2,087	-162	14,442	1,925	Nov 25, 2006	1,682	-41	13,483	1,641
Nov 26, 2005	3,304	-200	17,668	3,104	Dec 02, 2006	3,604	0	17,087	3,604
Dec 03, 2005	1,989	0	19,656	1,989	Dec 09, 2006	1,517	-41	18,563	1,476
Dec 10, 2005	4,633	-201	24,088	4,432	Dec 16, 2006	1,367	-10	19,920	1,357
Dec 17, 2005	1,919	-342	25,665	1,577	Dec 23, 2006	2,970	0	22,890	2,970
Dec 24, 2005	0	0	0	0	Dec 30, 2006	3,393	-3	26,280	3,390
Dec 31, 2005	4,608	-287	34,892	4,321					

[1] 60 Chicago and Outside Combined Chicago Mercantile Exchange approved warehouses.   *Source: Chicago Mercantile Exchange (CME)*

PORK BELLIES

Pork Belly Futures - Chicago Mercantile Exchange
(weekly close) as of December 29, 2006
Cents Per Pound

Volume of Trading of Pork Belly Futures in Chicago   In Contracts

Year	Jan.	Feb.	Mar.	Apr.	May	June	July	Aug.	Sept.	Oct.	Nov.	Dec.	Total
1997	60,761	53,604	56,750	76,072	62,190	54,043	55,043	36,153	31,154	44,277	31,663	33,609	595,319
1998	41,894	50,105	47,249	61,910	36,058	48,913	41,133	33,832	24,006	30,538	30,093	35,521	481,252
1999	39,925	36,293	33,322	31,558	31,321	45,030	36,513	23,536	16,544	20,392	28,920	24,955	368,309
2000	37,650	38,943	39,061	31,464	40,311	31,229	25,051	17,875	10,711	11,854	11,737	13,690	309,576
2001	15,861	16,200	16,675	18,274	18,708	16,989	20,187	18,823	12,719	12,905	15,984	13,034	196,359
2002	16,495	16,650	14,279	17,758	13,648	15,764	16,773	7,490	6,857	8,107	8,659	9,574	152,054
2003	13,635	13,956	13,137	18,279	18,112	16,993	19,540	9,967	7,909	10,235	8,542	11,024	161,329
2004	11,519	14,738	17,699	18,412	17,366	15,136	16,012	10,518	9,410	5,713	7,643	7,783	151,949
2005	7,736	13,995	10,767	13,713	11,020	15,226	12,869	11,275	5,099	9,370	6,438	6,910	124,418
2006	10,806	12,890	11,682	13,183	10,342	12,616	9,842	9,634	4,885	4,375	4,568	2,741	107,564

Source: Chicago Mercantile Exchange (CME)

Average Open Interest of Pork Belly Futures in Chicago   In Contracts

Year	Jan.	Feb.	Mar.	Apr.	May	June	July	Aug.	Sept.	Oct.	Nov.	Dec.
1997	7,504	7,930	7,260	7,165	8,950	7,203	5,905	4,791	5,242	7,520	8,302	9,009
1998	9,187	9,145	9,082	7,825	6,786	5,406	4,185	3,493	2,933	3,841	4,987	7,085
1999	7,217	6,192	4,623	5,113	6,030	6,639	5,003	2,415	2,320	3,206	4,011	4,868
2000	5,872	6,011	6,320	6,563	5,836	5,306	3,650	1,877	1,860	2,093	2,409	2,610
2001	2,719	2,908	2,935	3,138	2,808	2,354	2,526	2,579	2,695	2,321	2,441	2,451
2002	2,574	2,768	2,879	3,271	3,224	2,821	1,885	986	1,116	1,329	2,020	2,548
2003	2,842	2,805	2,915	3,082	3,383	3,410	2,858	1,632	1,899	1,885	2,075	2,484
2004	2,431	3,213	3,491	3,998	3,880	3,158	2,675	1,473	1,399	1,200	1,491	1,900
2005	2,013	3,010	2,858	2,891	3,743	3,725	2,507	1,599	1,143	1,451	1,323	1,868
2006	2,273	2,407	1,949	2,146	2,049	1,938	1,812	1,006	782	907	1,039	1,069

Source: Chicago Mercantile Exchange (CME)

Pork Bellies (monthly average) through December 2006   Cents per pound

Cents Per Pound
----- 12-14 Lb., Chicago (Jan. 1949 - Sept. 1975)
12-14 Lb., Midwest (Oct. 1975 - date)

Average Price of Pork Bellies (12-14 lbs.), Central U.S.   In Cents Per Pound

Year	Jan.	Feb.	Mar.	Apr.	May	June	July	Aug.	Sept.	Oct.	Nov.	Dec.	Average
1997	72.04	68.42	59.05	80.54	82.58	80.68	86.70	85.43	72.25	57.97	53.77	47.52	70.58
1998	43.00	45.89	42.28	54.65	57.87	63.10	68.46	72.99	57.49	42.05	39.13	36.31	51.94
1999	48.80	50.76	46.51	49.23	53.76	53.41	47.78	67.29	57.87	70.83	67.81	71.37	57.12
2000	80.45	82.40	85.00	93.70	97.85	91.99	90.38	75.64	63.94	57.83	51.97	58.36	77.46
2001	66.61	66.68	78.04	85.80	77.91	91.50	102.42	98.39	81.91	61.30	63.68	69.13	78.61
2002	70.87	70.75	72.55	63.48	58.65	65.90	81.06	67.98	57.05	76.24	75.50	78.92	69.91
2003	78.02	79.54	85.80	84.94	96.58	97.05	102.37	85.65	83.15	84.46	78.53	81.00	86.42
2004	79.78	90.76	103.67	109.15	117.53	113.00	118.22	99.92	92.00	88.90	91.50	87.81	99.35
2005	78.00	82.13	84.20	78.13	87.31	68.73	77.48	94.00	89.67	84.07	78.82	75.00	81.46
2006[1]	75.00	71.83	78.67	78.83	87.00	101.25	94.29	90.67	82.56	75.44	78.64	79.50	82.81

[1] Preliminary.   *Source: Economic Research Service, U.S. Department of Agriculture (ERS-USDA)*

Average Price of Pork Loins (12-14 lbs.)[2] Central, U.S.   In Cents Per Pound

Year	Jan.	Feb.	Mar.	Apr.	May	June	July	Aug.	Sept.	Oct.	Nov.	Dec.	Average
1997	112.50	109.50	106.58	117.16	125.68	116.28	122.53	119.28	112.07	99.68	85.99	79.44	108.89
1998	76.50	103.03	104.56	102.51	130.64	113.13	106.51	105.90	97.23	99.63	79.90	72.49	99.34
1999	105.82	92.35	83.47	99.35	107.44	97.62	105.72	111.55	104.99	98.98	94.64	102.75	100.39
2000	99.29	110.66	110.06	127.48	115.38	132.53	131.73	120.45	119.22	119.90	104.19	114.68	117.13
2001	110.80	114.32	128.53	117.98	130.72	132.33	126.41	121.22	116.21	108.69	97.87	98.50	116.97
2002	106.95	105.73	100.08	94.13	101.71	104.80	108.64	97.85	87.17	93.04	82.60	93.03	97.98
2003	91.83	95.75	92.43	96.90	108.93	126.51	102.50	104.85	111.38	97.71	89.06	93.72	100.96
2004	111.98	117.30	110.00	115.48	140.65	130.30	121.36	116.93	119.22	110.00	102.92	109.50	117.14
2005	116.08	114.83	115.88	115.03	133.45	115.62	115.03	119.82	111.31	103.78	96.72	101.12	113.22
2006[1]	95.00	96.21	101.31	107.25	112.77	124.61	114.95	109.35	99.58	99.27	92.02	101.15	104.46

[1] Preliminary.   *Source: Economic Research Service, U.S. Department of Agriculture (ERS-USDA)*

Potatoes

The potato is a member of the nightshade family. The leaves of the potato plant are poisonous and a potato will begin to turn green if left too long in the light. This green skin contains solanine, a substance that can cause the potato to taste bitter and even cause illness in humans. In Peru, the Inca Indians were the first to cultivate potatoes around 200 BC. The Indians developed potato crops because their staple diet of corn would not grow above an altitude of 3,350 meters. In 1536, after conquering the Incas, the Spanish Conquistadors brought potatoes back to Europe. At first, Europeans did not accept the potato because it was not mentioned in the Bible and was therefore considered an "evil" food. But after Marie Antoinette wore a crown of potato flowers, it finally became a popular food. In 1897, during the Alaskan Klondike gold rush, potatoes were so valued for their vitamin C content that miners traded gold for potatoes. The potato became the first vegetable to be grown in outer space in October 1995.

The potato is a highly nutritious, fat-free, cholesterol-free and sodium-free food, and is an important dietary staple in over 130 countries. A medium-sized potato contains only 100 calories. Potatoes are an excellent source of vitamin C and provide B vitamins as well as potassium, copper, magnesium, and iron. According to the US Department of Agriculture, "a diet of whole milk and potatoes would supply almost all of the food elements necessary for the maintenance of the human body."

Potatoes are one of the largest vegetable crops grown in the US, and are grown in all fifty states. The US ranks about 4th in world potato production. The top three types of potatoes grown extensively in the US are white, red, and Russets (Russets account for about two-thirds the US crop). Potatoes in the US are harvested in all four seasons, but the vast majority of the crop is harvested in fall. Potatoes harvested in the winter, spring and summer are used mainly to supplement fresh supplies of fall-harvested potatoes and are also important to the processing industries. The four principal categories for US potato exports are frozen, potato chips, fresh, and dehydrated. Fries account for approximately 95% of US frozen potato exports.

Prices – The average monthly price received for potatoes by US farmers in 2006 rose +5.1% to a record high of $7.42 per hundred pounds.

Supply – The total potato crop in 2006 rose by +3.2% to an estimated 43.479 billion pounds, but that was still well below the record high of 50.936 billion pounds posted in 2000. The fall crop in 2006 rose by 2.3% to an estimated 39,092 billion pounds, accounting for 90% of the total crop. Stocks of the fall crop (as of Dec 1) were estimated at 25.220 billion pounds. In 2006, the spring crop rose +5.6% to 1.977 billion pounds, the summer crop rose +5.0% to 1.844 billion pounds, and the winter crop fell –8.1% to 450 million pounds.

The largest producing states for the fall 2006 crop were Idaho (with 31.1% of the crop), Washington (22.9%), Wisconsin (7.5%), North Dakota (6.5%), and Colorado (5.8%). For the spring crop, the largest producing states were Florida (with 32.6% of the crop), and California (with 30.6% of the crop).

Farmers harvested 1.119 million acres in 2006, up +2.9% from 2005 but still with the second lowest acreage planting since 1980. The yield per harvested acre in 2006 fell by –0.3% to 38,900 pounds per acre.

Demand – Total utilization of potatoes in 2006 fell – 7.0% yr/yr to 42.393 billion pounds. The breakdown shows that the largest consumption category for potatoes is frozen French fries with 31.6% of total consumption, followed closely by table stock (30.8%), chips and shoestrings (13.1%), and dehydration (10.8%). US per capita consumption of potatoes in 2006 fell by –2.5% to 125.9 pounds, which was a 16-year low and well below the record high of 145.0 pounds per capita seen in 1996.

Trade – US exports of potatoes in 2005 rose sharply by +35.1% to 646.800 million pounds. US exports hit a record high of 693.196 million pounds in 2003. US imports rose +7.4% to 617.700 million pounds. The US record high for imports of 737.223 million pounds was posted in 1998.

Salient Statistics of Potatoes in the United States

Crop Year	Acreage Planted (1,000 Acres)	Acreage Harvested (1,000 Acres)	Yield Per Harvested Acre Cwt.	Total Production (In Thousands of Cwt.)	Seed & Feed (In Thousands of Cwt.)	Shrinkage & Loss (In Thousands of Cwt.)	Sold[2] (In Thousands of Cwt.)	Farm Price $/Cwt.	Production[3] (Million $)	Sales (Million $)	Stocks on Jan. 1 1,000 Cwt.	Domestic Exports (Millions of Lbs.)	Imports (Millions of Lbs.)	Consumption Per Capita Fresh (In Pounds)	Consumption Per Capita Total (In Pounds)
1997	1,384	1,354	345	467,091	5,475	32,183	429,433	5.64	2,623	2,421	246,550	670,270	512,321	48.5	141.4
1998	1,417	1,388	343	475,771	5,766	35,454	434,551	5.56	2,635	2,416	246,230	650,918	737,223	47.0	138.1
1999	1,377	1,332	359	478,216	5,569	35,531	437,116	5.77	2,746	2,522	239,910	599,066	610,538	48.0	136.5
2000	1,384	1,348	381	513,621	5,288	43,688	464,645	5.08	2,591	2,360	275,270	676,577	502,706	47.1	137.9
2001	1,247	1,221	358	437,673	5,387	31,208	401,293	6.99	3,058	2,805	224,680	636,176	487,889	46.6	138.8
2002	1,300	1,266	362	458,171	5,622	30,905	421,644	6.67	3,045	2,812	231,690	693,196	621,475	44.3	132.1
2003	1,273	1,249	367	457,814	5,543	35,294	416,977	5.89	2,686	2,458	233,590	589,756	634,971	47.2	138.7
2004	1,193	1,167	391	456,041	4,796	37,408	413,837	5.66	2,575	2,344	236,700	478,856	575,400	45.8	134.7
2005	1,109	1,087	390	423,926	4,791	28,519	390,616	7.06	2,991	2,758	220,500	646,800	617,700	42.4	125.6
2006[1]	1,137	1,119	389	434,789				7.42	3,226		220,000			42.6	126.2

[1] Preliminary.   [2] For all purposes, including food, seed processing & livestock feed.   [3] Farm weight basis, excluding canned and frozen potatoes.
[4] Calendar Year.   Source: Economic Research Service, U.S. Department of Agriculture (ERS-USDA)

Cold Storage Stocks of All Frozen Potatoes in the United States, on First of Month   In Millions of Pounds

Year	Jan.	Feb.	Mar.	Apr.	May	June	July	Aug.	Sept.	Oct.	Nov.	Dec.
1997	1,098.4	1,111.5	1,180.1	1,177.1	1,195.8	1,213.3	1,271.4	1,214.3	1,130.8	1,270.0	1,354.7	1,313.5
1998	1,163.5	1,147.2	1,235.7	1,278.3	1,225.1	1,282.8	1,316.5	1,234.7	1,204.5	1,266.8	1,341.0	1,290.5
1999	1,151.3	1,219.7	1,272.9	1,278.8	1,236.2	1,255.5	1,234.1	1,142.3	1,169.8	1,235.5	1,307.8	1,254.5
2000	1,165.4	1,140.9	1,270.1	1,283.4	1,239.4	1,250.4	1,186.3	1,180.3	1,185.7	1,291.5	1,351.5	1,285.9
2001	1,189.7	1,228.6	1,254.7	1,220.9	1,280.4	1,270.3	1,355.0	1,282.6	1,197.5	1,323.8	1,338.5	1,297.4
2002	1,239.8	1,274.2	1,271.5	1,271.4	1,222.7	1,182.3	1,223.5	1,106.6	1,040.6	1,141.4	1,252.2	1,214.4
2003	1,131.2	1,173.1	1,211.0	1,217.4	1,150.5	1,106.6	1,181.8	1,130.4	1,070.4	1,151.7	1,248.0	1,232.8
2004	1,120.4	1,167.3	1,207.4	1,192.5	1,158.7	1,185.9	1,128.7	1,117.1	1,127.0	1,178.6	1,274.9	1,219.3
2005	1,074.8	1,168.8	1,152.8	1,093.7	1,174.3	1,178.1	1,190.5	1,154.9	1,121.3	1,180.4	1,200.0	1,122.5
2006[1]	1,051.1	1,076.2	1,147.1	1,159.0	1,175.5	1,105.2	1,108.1	996.4	964.1	1,009.6	1,066.6	1,052.1

[1] Preliminary.   Source: Agricultural Statistics Board, U.S. Department of Agriculture (ASB-USDA)

Potato Crop Production Estimates, Stocks and Disappearance in the United States   In Millions of Cwt.

	Crop Production Estimates			Total Storage Stocks[2]							Fall Crop 1,000 Cwt.			
	Total Crop			Fall Crop			Following Year						Disap-	Average	Value
Year	Oct. 1	Nov. 1	Dec. 1	Oct. 1	Nov. 1	Dec. 1	Jan. 1	Feb. 1	Mar. 1	Apr. 1	May 1	Pro- duction	pearance (Sold)	Dec. 1 Price Stocks $/Cwt.	of Sales $ 1,000
1997	----	459.4	----	----	417.5	278.8	246.6	212.6	175.9	134.2	92.8	413,513	387,089	278,830	5.20	2,011,004
1998	----	471.0	----	----	429.0	280.9	246.2	209.6	173.7	131.2	87.9	423,170	392,922	280,910	5.07	1,994,030
1999	----	481.5	----	----	435.6	275.1	239.9	207.2	169.6	128.4	86.9	420,567	390,210	275,100	5.29	2,064,564
2000	----	509.4	----	----	463.4	310.3	275.3	234.3	197.7	153.5	109.2	467,504	420,279	310,300	4.55	1,910,833
2001	----	441.8	----	----	400.7	258.8	224.7	192.1	158.6	120.0	81.2	393,631	358,812	258,750	6.54	2,348,006
2002	----	459.7	----	----	415.0	264.5	231.5	199.0	165.2	125.8	83.0	413,581	378,796	264,485	5.89	2,232,627
2003	----	459.2	----	----	413.5	267.9	233.6	200.2	166.3	126.1	85.0	410,588	371,755	267,900	5.23	1,943,986
2004	----	450.2	----	----	407.8	271.1	236.7	203.5	168.0	128.9	88.6	410,253	369,781	271,100	5.08	1,877,912
2005	----	421.3	----	----	382.2	253.8	220.5	189.1	155.5	115.7	75.9	382,743	351,083	253,800	6.53	2,290,850
2006[1]	----	434.8	----	----	390.9	252.2	220.0	187.8				391,978		252,200	6.73	

[1] Preliminary.   [2] Held by growers and local dealers in the fall producing areas.   Source: Agricultural Statistics Board, U.S. Department of Agriculture

Production of Potatoes by Seasonal Groups in the United States   In Thousands of Cwt.

	- Winter -	Spring		Summer				Fall								
Year	Total	Cali- fornia	Florida	Total	New Mexico	Virginia	Total	Colo- rado	Idaho	Maine	Minne- sota	North Dakota	Oregon	Washing- ton	Wis- consin	Total
1997	3,431	8,073	7,150	22,299	1,248	1,268	18,171	24,993	140,314	19,080	20,440	22,000	27,319	88,160	30,175	423,190
1998	2,980	6,198	7,358	21,121	962	1,380	18,933	25,360	138,000	18,060	21,170	28,670	26,229	93,225	30,895	432,737
1999	4,070	7,600	8,820	25,327	1,247	1,050	18,972	25,762	133,330	17,813	18,020	26,400	28,020	95,200	34,000	429,847
2000	4,960	7,426	6,343	21,921	1,050	1,292	19,236	27,972	152,320	17,920	21,240	26,950	30,683	105,000	33,800	467,504
2001	4,115	6,045	7,970	21,814	770	1,386	18,209	21,357	120,200	16,430	18,425	26,400	20,730	94,400	31,955	393,631
2002	4,206	7,695	7,883	22,452	736	1,386	17,932	27,885	133,385	16,960	18,810	23,460	24,936	92,340	30,750	413,581
2003	4,027	8,360	8,008	24,433	532	1,550	18,766	23,652	123,180	17,030	22,330	27,440	20,991	93,150	32,800	410,588
2004	4,818	8,313	7,678	22,663	340	1,200	18,307	23,791	131,970	19,065	18,920	26,765	19,775	93,810	30,450	410,253
2005	4,892	6,116	6,527	18,724		1,029	17,567	22,910	118,288	15,455	17,630	20,500	22,023	95,480	2,780	382,743
2006[1]	4,495	6,044	6,441	19,766		1,512	18,444	22,686	121,820	18,270	20,400	25,480	18,533	89,900	29,370	391,978

[1] Preliminary.   Source: Agricultural Statistics Board, U.S. Department of Agriculture (ASB-USDA)

Utilization of Potatoes in the United States   In Thousands of Cwt.

				Sales									Non-Sales		
				For Processing					Other Sales			Used on			
Crop Year	Table Stock	Chips, Shoe- strings	For Dehyd- ration	Frozen French Fries	Other Frozen Products	Canned Potatoes	Other Canned Products[2]	Starch & Flour	Live- stock Feed	Seed	Total Sales	Farms Where Grown	Shrink- age & Loss	Total Non- Sales	Total
1996	131,446	48,305	54,261	145,489	28,972	2,785	2,167	1,956	12,073	24,341	451,795	4,797	41,238	47,459	499,254
1997	131,670	48,130	48,389	131,628	33,397	2,822	2,675	1,311	3,603	25,808	429,433	4,167	32,183	37,658	467,091
1998	125,413	51,471	55,522	142,932	24,964	2,730	1,964	1,585	3,111	24,859	434,551	4,358	35,454	41,220	475,771
1999	134,130	52,916	50,831	140,196	23,593	3,311	2,394	1,310	3,141	25,294	437,116	4,415	35,531	41,100	478,216
2000	139,590	52,405	54,332	146,869	26,723	2,368	2,709	1,966	14,265	23,345	464,572	3,792	43,685	48,972	513,544
2001	122,552	54,080	40,759	126,711	23,598	2,590	1,722	1,015	3,496	24,537	401,060	4,088	31,227	36,613	437,673
2002	131,889	51,640	51,357	124,875	28,951	2,744	2,089	1,050	3,044	24,005	421,644	4,144	30,905	36,527	458,171
2003	133,143	52,790	48,418	126,515	23,870	3,086	1,168	1,379	2,005	24,603	416,977	4,000	35,294	40,837	457,814
2004	130,418	50,068	48,541	131,592	23,003	2,843	984	1,531	1,942	22,915	413,837	3,601	37,408	42,204	456,041
2005[1]	120,372	50,998	42,312	123,298	24,747	2,120	934	1,582	1,999	22,254	390,616	3,604	28,519	33,310	423,926

[1] Preliminary.   [2] Hash, stews and soups.   Source: Agricultural Statistics Board, U.S. Department of Agriculture (ASB-USDA)

POTATOES

Per Capita Utilization of Potatoes in the United States   In Pounds (Farm Weight)

				Processing			
				Chips &			
				Shoe-	Dehy-		
Year	Total	Fresh	Freezing	string	drating	Canning	Total
1997	137.8	47.3	57.8	15.5	15.5	1.7	90.5
1998	137.7	46.9	58.1	14.7	16.5	1.5	90.8
1999	136.2	47.7	58.5	15.9	12.4	1.7	88.5
2000	137.9	47.1	57.5	15.9	15.7	1.7	90.8
2001	138.8	46.6	58.2	17.6	14.8	1.6	92.2
2002	132.1	44.3	55.2	16.5	14.7	1.4	87.8
2003	138.2	46.8	57.2	17.3	15.5	1.4	91.4
2004	134.7	45.8	57.3	16.6	13.8	1.2	88.9
2005[1]	129.1	43.1	54.7	16.4	13.8	1.1	86.0
2006[2]	125.9	42.1	53.0	16.2	13.5	1.1	83.8

[1] Preliminary.   [2] Forecast.   *Source: Agricultural Statistics Board, U.S. Department of Agriculture (ASB-USDA)*

Average Price Received by Farmers for Potatoes in the United States   In Dollars Per Cwt.

Year	Jan.	Feb.	Mar.	Apr.	May	June	July	Aug.	Sept.	Oct.	Nov.	Dec.	Season Average
1997	4.22	4.56	4.64	4.67	5.31	5.67	5.66	6.31	5.08	4.93	5.12	5.36	5.64
1998	5.40	5.94	6.41	6.27	6.45	6.16	5.81	5.46	4.97	4.47	4.86	5.30	5.56
1999	5.50	5.75	6.12	6.50	6.13	6.54	7.35	6.02	5.09	4.86	5.52	5.44	5.77
2000	5.68	5.92	6.26	6.46	6.31	6.14	6.93	5.56	4.49	4.27	4.31	4.48	5.08
2001	4.56	5.26	5.12	5.47	5.24	5.75	6.46	7.61	6.04	5.15	5.96	6.66	6.99
2002	6.90	7.34	8.26	8.00	8.62	9.39	10.40	8.00	6.14	5.44	6.38	6.67	6.67
2003	6.67	6.33	6.87	6.94	6.96	6.68	6.30	5.75	5.24	5.03	5.46	5.77	5.89
2004	5.75	5.87	6.09	6.62	6.47	6.16	6.46	5.77	5.32	4.70	5.02	5.36	5.66
2005	5.59	5.79	6.44	6.20	6.23	6.29	7.63	7.02	5.69	5.37	6.26	6.83	7.06
2006[1]	7.07	6.76	8.21	7.97	8.05	8.60	11.02	7.95	6.35	5.97	6.67	6.90	7.42

[1] Preliminary.   *Source: Agricultural Statistics Board, U.S. Department of Agriculture (ASB-USDA)*

Potatoes Processed[1] in the United States, Eight States — In Thousands of Cwt.

States	Storage Season	to Dec. 1	to Jan. 1	to Feb. 1	to Mar. 1	to Apr. 1	to May 1	to June 1	Entire Season
Idaho and	1998-99	27,510	34,700	42,670	51,210	60,040	68,550	76,410	92,860
Oregon-	1999-00	27,970	34,490	40,790	49,220	57,820	66,080	74,110	88,210
Malheur	2000-01	29,290	35,720	43,470	50,580	58,910	66,760	75,270	93,460
Co	2001-02	20,940	27,330	33,620	40,860	47,710	54,150	61,200	73,390
	2002-03	28,380	34,860	41,200	48,600	56,240	63,840	71,280	85,390
	2003-04	24,310	30,730	36,260	43,640	49,570	56,380	63,770	77,530
	2004-05	24,360	30,840	36,820	44,610	51,000	58,090	65,800	84,600
	2005-06	22,840	29,300	35,970	43,300	50,820	57,830	65,030	77,360
	2006-07	26,130	32,810	40,100					
Maine[2]	1998-99	1,430	1,935	2,530	2,985	3,595	4,180	4,705	5,945
	1999-00	1,270	1,700	2,385	3,070	3,765	4,560	5,150	6,670
	2000-01	1,845	2,475	3,105	3,695	4,225	4,760	5,340	7,015
	2001-02	1,975	2,440	3,110	3,700	4,285	4,775	5,515	7,195
	2002-03	2,230	2,715	3,345	3,905	4,505	5,225	5,905	7,835
	2003-04	1,590	2,085	2,720	3,420	4,095	4,740	5,400	7,270
	2004-05	1,540	1,970	2,600	3,135	3,700	4,340	4,910	6,590
	2005-06	1,365	1,880	2,485	3,090	3,800	4,450	5,130	6,825
	2006-07	1,755	2,360	2,910					
Wash. &	1998-99	33,630	38,890	45,650	53,290	60,930	67,180	74,190	83,730
Oregon-	1999-00	33,320	39,620	45,500	53,350	61,080	67,230	74,840	83,210
Other	2000-01	34,770	40,970	47,720	55,250	62,860	69,850	78,010	91,130
	2001-02	29,320	35,310	40,540	47,910	54,970	61,360	69,400	77,180
	2002-03	33,680	39,490	44,190	51,920	58,710	64,300	71,480	79,110
	2003-04	32,670	38,520	43,610	51,210	58,500	64,160	72,350	79,800
	2004-05	32,305	38,130	43,570	50,730	57,140	63,855	71,355	78,680
	2005-06	30,310	35,895	40,545	48,290	55,320	61,855	69,360	78,550
	2006-07	30,980	37,060	42,190					
Other	1998-99	11,570	14,465	18,030	20,850	24,850	28,190	31,365	39,865
States[3]	1999-00	12,455	15,035	17,950	20,855	24,305	27,220	30,410	36,435
	2000-01	12,665	16,215	18,975	22,095	25,410	28,695	31,765	39,020
	2001-02	13,170	14,925	19,000	22,115	24,655	27,815	30,460	37,740
	2002-03	12,675	15,530	18,735	21,780	24,810	27,405	30,655	38,700
	2003-04	13,835	16,505	19,590	22,685	25,920	29,480	32,845	42,160
	2004-05	12,490	15,000	17,965	20,910	24,150	27,480	30,945	41,175
	2005-06	11,055	14,070	17,005	19,895	22,520	25,270	27,740	35,535
	2006-07	13,465	16,905	20,450					
Total	1998-99	74,140	89,990	108,880	128,335	149,415	168,100	186,670	222,400
	1999-00	75,015	90,845	106,625	126,495	146,970	165,090	184,510	214,525
	2000-01	78,570	95,380	113,270	131,620	151,405	170,065	190,385	230,625
	2001-02	65,405	80,005	96,270	114,585	131,620	148,100	166,575	195,505
	2002-03	76,965	92,595	107,470	126,205	144,265	160,770	179,320	211,035
	2003-04	72,405	87,840	102,180	120,955	138,085	154,760	174,365	206,760
	2004-05	70,695	85,940	100,955	119,385	135,990	153,765	173,010	211,045
	2005-06	65,570	81,145	96,005	114,575	132,460	149,405	167,260	198,270
	2006-07	72,330	89,135	105,650					
Dehydrated[4]	2001-02	----	----	----	----	----	----	----	38,581
	2002-03	15,675	19,660	23,710	27,950	31,915	36,105	40,455	48,940
	2003-04	14,250	18,440	22,050	26,090	30,290	34,630	39,070	47,750
	2004-05	14,525	18,540	21,875	25,970	30,020	33,685	38,505	47,805
	2005-06	11,920	15,655	19,225	22,765	26,605	30,065	34,130	41,625
	2006-07	12,860	17,130	21,270					

[1] Total quantity received and used for processing regardless of the State in which the potatoes were produced. Amount excludes quantities used for potato chips in Maine, Michigan and Wisconsin. [2] Includes Maine grown potatoes only. [3] Colorado, Minnesota, Nevada, North Dakota and Wisconsin. [4] Dehydrated products except starch and flour. Included in above totals. Includes CO, ID, NV, ND, OR, WA, and WI. *Source: National Agricultural Statistics Service, U.S. Department of Agriculture (NASS-USDA)*

Rayon and Other Synthetic Fibers

World Cellulosic Fiber Production   In Thousands of Metric Tons

Year	Brazil	Bulgaria	China	CIS	Czech Republic	India	Indo-nesia	Japan	Mexico	Taiwan	Thailand	United States	World Total
1997	36.4	4.2	450.0	108.7	27.3	242.4	212.9	184.1	14.8	148.4	60.2	208.1	2,314
1998	29.2	13.1	451.5	99.6	26.9	264.4	222.0	164.5	15.5	142.6	45.7	165.5	2,227
1999	34.6	13.5	472.1	88.0	17.6	248.5	195.6	135.5	13.5	143.7	55.3	134.7	2,074
2000	36.2	15.0	552.3	83.7	7.1	297.5	207.0	126.2	14.8	141.5	65.0	158.8	2,215
2001	28.7	12.2	608.6	64.4	7.6	251.9	205.0	107.1	22.6	127.4	65.0	103.0	2,083
2002	34.2	5.6	682.1	72.9	7.3	285.7	214.0	68.1	16.8	114.2	71.1	80.7	2,125
2003	47.2	5.2	800.2	78.8	9.1	283.0	223.0	68.3	14.8	121.5	73.8	75.3	2,269
2004	46.8	5.0	966.1	77.2	9.2	311.5	234.0	67.1	12.2	134.9	79.4	66.8	2,485
2005[1]	40.1	5.0	1,107.0	46.6	9.5	295.4	245.0	66.6	ÑÑ	114.5	79.2	46.8	2,529
2006[2]	46.9	6.0	1,285.0	62.8	9.7	361.9	260.0	96.5	ÑÑ	145.2	110.0	30.0	2,943

[1] Preliminary.   [2] Producing capacity.   *Source: Fiber Economics Bureau, Inc. (FEB)*

World Noncellulosic Fiber Production (Except Olefin)   In Thousands of Metric Tons

Year	Brazil	China	India	Indo-nesia	Japan	Korea	Mexico	Pakistan	Taiwan	Thailand	Turkey	United States[3]	World Total
1997	248.3	3,527.2	1,240.7	956.1	1,433.6	2,403.3	612.7	322.7	2,932.4	575.4	500.7	3,420.0	22,396
1998	268.6	4,406.8	1,361.3	881.5	1,363.6	2,446.0	591.1	427.8	3,111.5	542.6	529.8	3,222.7	23,254
1999	292.6	5,235.1	1,493.3	1,037.8	1,299.7	2,592.8	571.2	478.0	2,927.7	694.2	613.5	3,169.5	24,885
2000	311.1	6,158.4	1,568.4	1,142.7	1,307.9	2,659.0	586.8	503.9	3,122.9	769.5	744.5	3,149.2	26,219
2001	288.8	7,322.9	1,570.2	1,190.6	1,239.5	2,471.9	536.4	528.4	2,977.5	784.5	669.2	2,687.6	26,243
2002	293.1	8,849.4	1,695.3	1,132.8	1,129.1	2,455.7	509.6	581.5	3,091.3	852.6	728.1	2,805.0	28,052
2003	314.2	10,456.0	1,792.0	1,144.2	1,030.3	2,418.0	457.6	646.8	3,060.9	872.5	767.1	2,693.2	29,468
2004	330.9	12,475.0	1,904.2	1,064.5	989.2	2,191.3	473.4	659.3	2,965.0	949.0	849.5	2,823.9	31,511
2005[1]	303.9	14,235.6	1,849.2	1,116.2	955.4	1,707.6	390.9	575.3	2,584.9	953.3	800.4	2,627.0	31,761
2006[2]	429.1	22,645.0	3,023.3	1,456.0	1,213.8	1,911.0	488.5	823.0	3,274.1	1,138.0	1,029.2	2,940.1	44,989

[1] Preliminary.   [2] Producing capacity.   [3] Beginning 1995; data for USA and Canada.   Source: Fiber Economics Bureau, Inc. (FEB)

World Production of Synthetic Fibers   In Thousands of Metric Tons

	Noncellulosic Fiber Production (Except Olefin)							Glass Fiber Production							Cigarette Tow Production
	By Fibers				World Total										
Year	Acrylic & Mod-acrylic	Nylon & Aramid	Polyester	Other Fibers[3]	Yarn & Monofil-aments	Staple, Tow & Fiberfill	Total	Europe	Japan	Other Americas	United States	China	Ex-USSR	Total	
1997	2,706	4,028	15,406	256	12,093	10,303	22,396	610	328	100	1,007	75	27	2,431	582
1998	2,656	3,792	16,539	268	12,959	10,295	23,254	660	300	96	1,018	60	30	2,416	551
1999	2,513	3,800	17,879	294	13,660	10,825	24,485	674	300	96	1,126	60	30	2,538	544
2000	2,634	4,117	19,155	313	14,771	11,448	26,219	728	280	96	1,143	60	28	2,580	570
2001	2,562	3,784	19,563	335	14,968	11,276	26,243	701	273	93	1,016	67	32	2,431	590
2002	2,713	3,941	21,048	350	15,993	12,059	28,052	718	251	96	1,222	90	34	2,661	603
2003	2,698	3,972	22,374	425	16,879	12,589	29,468	724	250	100	1,307	120	37	2,790	595
2004	2,813	4,017	24,208	491	17,990	13,538	31,528	740	250	104	1,363	150	40	2,903	604
2005[1]	2,632	3,924	24,701	504	18,222	13,539	31,761								
2006[2]	3,068	4,851	36,316	754	26,114	18,875	44,989								

[1] Preliminary.   [2] Producing capacity.   [3] Alginate, azion, spandex, saran, etc.   *Source: Fiber Economics Bureau, Inc. (FEB)*

Artificial (Cellulosic) Fiber Distribution in the United States   In Millions of Pounds

	Yarn & Monofilament					Staple & Tow					Glass Fiber Shipments
	Producers' Shipments			Imports	Domestic Consumption	Producers' Shipments			Imports	Domestic Consumption	
Year	Domestic	Exports	Total			Domestic	Exports	Total			
1998	111.2	3.5	114.7	38.1	149.3	184.4	31.4	215.8	47.4	231.8	----
1999	111.0	3.0	114.0	28.2	139.3	168.8	29.9	198.7	47.5	216.3	----
2000	76.7	37.8	114.5	23.2	99.9	162.3	69.3	231.5	37.5	199.7	----
2001	54.3	33.7	88.0	14.5	68.8	117.2	35.5	152.7	33.9	151.2	----
2002	41.2	33.2	74.4	12.7	53.9	91.1	12.6	103.7	56.2	147.4	----
2003	32.5	35.5	68.0	11.7	44.2	86.7	13.1	99.8	44.5	131.2	----
2004	26.7	38.7	65.4	12.2	38.9	77.4	9.9	87.2	63.9	141.3	----
2005	22.6	41.4	64.0	9.3	31.9	40.2	8.1	48.2	91.0	131.2	----
2006[1]	22.4	37.6	60.0	7.7	30.1		8.9	8.9	141.4	141.4	----

[1] Preliminary.   *Source: Fiber Economice Bureau, Inc. (FEB)*

Man-Made Fiber Production in the United States   In Millions of Pounds

| | -- Artificial (Cellulosic) Fibers -- Rayon & Acetate -- | | | Synthetic (Noncellulosic) Fibers | | | | | | | | | | Total Manufactured Fibers | Total Glass Fiber |
| | Filament Yarn & Monofilament | Staple & Tow | Total Cellulosic | Yarn & Monofilament | | | | Staple & Tow | | | | | Total Noncellulosic | | |
Year				Nylon	Polyester	Olefin	Total Yarn	Nylon	Polyester	Acrylic & Mod-acrylic	Olefin	Total Staple			
1997	187	266	453	2,039	1,644	2,058	5,740	797	2,446	461	623	4,327	10,067	10,465	2,408
1998	144	216	360	1,887	1,541	2,212	5,640	799	2,357	346	712	4,214	9,853	10,314	2,490
1999	115	199	314	1,896	1,595	2,278	5,769	787	2,291	316	797	4,192	9,960	10,263	2,570
2000	114	232	345	1,947	1,509	2,406	5,860	733	2,405	339	816	4,293	10,153	10,236	2,738
2001	----	153	153	1,642	1,188	2,181	5,011	606	2,040	310	721	3,676	8,687	----	2,638
2002	----	104	104	1,772	1,218	2,331	5,321	681	2,050	340	749	3,820	9,141	----	2,759
2003	----	100	100	1,762	1,145	2,349	5,255	697	1,886	270	680	3,533	8,788	----	2,789
2004	----	----	----	1,837	1,166	2,383	5,386	680	2,064	240	676	3,660	9,047	----	----
2005[1]	----	----	----	1,806	1,018	2,404	5,436	598	2,019	140	699	3,455	8,635	----	----
2006[2]	----	----	----	1,733	1,914	2,243	4,877	556	1,840	7	629	3,032	7,932	----	----

[1] Preliminary.   [2] Estimate.   Source: Fiber Economics Bureau, Inc. (FEB)

Domestic Distribution of Synethic (Noncellulosic) Fibers in the United States   In Millions of Pounds

| | Yarn & Monofilament | | | | | | | Staple & Tow | | | | | | | |
| | Producers' Shipments - Domestic | | | | | | Domestic Consumption | Producers' Shipments - Domestic | | | | | | | Domestic Consumption |
Year	Nylon	Polyester	Olefin	Total Exports		Total Imports		Nylon	Polyester	Acrylic & Mod-acrylic	Olefin	Total Exports		Total Imports	
1998	1,790	1,426	2,167	5,383	218	5,601	637	6,020	763	2,105	267	596	3,732	340	4,072	777	4,509
1999	1,765	1,463	2,251	5,480	244	5,724	719	6,199	756	2,138	233	726	3,852	338	4,190	788	4,640
2000	1,795	1,353	2,371	5,519	250	5,769	790	6,309	674	2,174	244	757	3,849	327	4,176	727	4,576
2001	1,606	1,189	2,144	4,938	155	5,093	697	5,635	607	1,881	228	673	3,389	308	3,698	757	4,146
2002	1,668	1,113	2,289	5,070	189	5,259	765	5,834	637	1,823	255	723	3,438	353	3,791	875	4,312
2003	1,666	1,051	2,318	5,035	179	5,214	766	5,801	673	1,688	211	635	3,206	246	3,452	829	4,035
2004	1,722	1,061	2,347	5,130	249	5,379	785	5,915	658	1,788	200	641	3,287	296	3,583	766	4,053
2005	1,688	938	2,369	4,995	197	5,192	849	5,845	582	1,765	122	650	3,120	292	3,411	914	4,034
2006[1]	1,589	801	2,198	4,588	211	4,799	819	5,407	492	1,624	----	596	2,713	268	2,981	1,007	3,719

[1] Preliminary.   Source: Fiber Economice Bureau, Inc. (FEB)

Mill Consumption of Fiber & Products and Per Capita Consumption in the U.S.   In Millions of Pounds

| | Cellulosic Fibers | | | | Noncellulosic Fibers | | | Total Manufactured Fibers[2] | Cotton | Wool | Other Fibers[3] | Grand Total | Per Capita[4] Mill Consumption (Lbs.) | | | | |
| | Yarn & Monofilament | Staple & Tow | Net Waste | Total Cellulosic | Noncellulosic | Net Waste | Total Noncellulosic | | | | | | Manmade Fibers[2] | Cotton | Wool | Other Fibers[3] | Total All Fibers |
Year																	
1997	189	257	2.5	448	10,520	103	10,623	11,071	5,448	164	42.8	16,726	45.7	31.9	1.3	2.0	80.9
1998	149	232	1.4	383	10,529	165	10,694	11,077	5,225	126	44.2	16,472	46.4	33.7	1.3	1.8	83.1
1999	139	216	1.6	357	10,839	177	11,016	11,373	4,996	99	40.1	16,509	48.0	34.5	1.2	1.9	85.5
2000	133	200	1.9	335	10,884	190	11,075	11,409	4,754	101	38.2	16,302	48.5	34.9	1.3	2.1	86.8
2001	96	151	2.4	249	9,838	193	10,031	10,281	3,983	87	30.1	14,381	44.5	33.0	1.4	1.6	80.5
2002	85	147	1.8	235	10,050	280	10,329	10,564	3,609	56	28.7	14,257	47.6	34.4	1.3	1.9	85.2
2003	78	131	1.3	210	9,778	266	10,045	10,255	3,115	43	35.4	13,449	48.6	34.5	1.4	2.5	86.9
2004	75	141	1.5	218	10,490	145	10,636	10,854	3,000	45	123.4	14,023	50.6	34.8	1.5	3.4	90.2
2005[1]	64	131	1.7	196	9,991	166	10,157	10,353	2,851	42	141.3	13,387	50.3	37.0	1.4	3.1	91.7

[1] Preliminary.   [2] Excludes Glass Fiber.   [3] Includes silk, linen, jute and sisal & others.   [4] Mill consumption plus inports less exports of semimanufactured and unmanufactured products.   Source: Fiber Economics Bureau, Inc. (FEB)

Producer Price Index of Grey Synthetic Broadwovens   (1982 = 100)

Year	Jan.	Feb.	Mar.	Apr.	May	June	July	Aug.	Sept.	Oct.	Nov.	Dec.	Average
1989	114.3	112.0	112.2	112.2	112.1	113.1	114.7	115.0	115.0	115.8	115.9	115.3	114.0
1990	115.6	115.7	115.6	115.7	115.5	115.6	115.7	115.2	115.3	115.6	115.8	116.1	115.6
1991	115.7	114.7	114.4	114.1	114.3	113.9	114.8	116.4	116.5	116.5	116.8	118.2	115.5
1992	119.0	119.9	120.3	120.9	121.8	122.0	122.6	122.0	121.7	120.8	119.4	119.9	120.9
1993	119.6	119.1	119.1	119.2	117.1	118.4	118.0	118.0	116.9	117.3	115.2	114.5	117.7
1994	113.5	112.8	112.9	113.2	113.2	113.3	113.1	113.3	114.1	111.8	112.9	113.8	113.2
1995	114.8	116.8	116.7	116.3	116.6	117.1	115.4	114.8	116.9	116.4	114.7	116.2	116.1
1996	114.3	114.1	116.9	117.9	116.8	115.7	116.1	117.1	116.9	117.2	116.6	117.0	116.4
1997	117.9	118.3	118.3	117.9	118.4	119.0	118.8	118.5	119.4	118.7	117.6	119.6	118.5
1998[1]	120.1	120.4	119.7	120.2	119.8	119.7	118.0	118.1	116.7	114.2	115.1	115.0	118.1

[1] Preliminary.   Source: Bureau of Labor Statistics, U.S. Department of Commerce (BLS) (0337-03)

Rice

Rice is a grain that is cultivated on every continent except Antarctica and is the primary food for half the people in the world. Rice cultivation probably originated as early as 10,000 BC in Asia. Rice is grown at varying altitudes (sea level to about 3,000 meters), in varying climates (tropical to temperate), and on dry to flooded land. The growth duration of rice plants is 3-6 months, depending on variety and growing conditions. Rice is harvested by hand in developing countries or by combines in industrialized countries. Asian countries produce about 90% of rice grown worldwide. Rough rice futures and options are traded on the Chicago Board of Trade (CBOT).

Prices – Rough rice prices on the CBOT nearest futures chart in early 2006 were about $8.50 per hundred pounds. Prices held fairly steady until April and then rallied the rest of the year to about $10.21 per hundred pounds at the end of the year. Regarding cash prices, the average monthly price of rice received by farmers in the US in the first 7 months of the 2006-07 marketing year (i.e., August through December 2006) rose by +25.8% yr/yr to $9.60 per hundred pounds (cwt.).

Supply – World rice production in the 2006-07 marketing year fell –0.5% to 617.988 million metric tons,

down from the record high of 621.054 million metric tons in 2005-06. The world's largest rice producers were China with 30% of world production in 2006-07, India with 22% of world production, Indonesia with 8%, Bangladesh with 7%, Vietnam with 6%, and Thailand with 5%. US production of rice in 2006-07 fell –13.4% yr/yr to 193.3 million cwt (hundred pounds), continuing the downward slide to fall further from the 2004-05 record high of 232.4 million cwt.

Demand – World utilization of rice in 2006-07 rose +1.0% to a record high of 415.943 million metric tons. US rice consumption in 2006-07 rose +2.9% yr/yr to a 5-year high of 122.8 million cwt (hundred pounds) and only slightly below the record high of 123.3 million cwt posted in 1999-2000.

Trade – World exports of rice in 2006-07 rose +3.8% yr/yr to 29.142 million metric tons, which was a new record high. The world's largest rice exporters are Thailand with 30% of world exports, Vietnam with 17%, India with 15%, the US with 11%, and Pakistan with 10%. US rice imports in 2006-07 rose by +5.3% yr/yr to a new record high of 18.0 million cwt (hundred pounds). US rice exports in 2006-07 fell by –16.2% yr/yr to 97.0 cwt, far below the record of 124.6 million cwt posted in 2002-03.

World Rice Supply and Distribution   In Thousands of Metric Tons

	Imports							Utilization			Ending Stocks		
Year	Brazil	Indonesia	European Union	Iran	Nigeria	Saudi Arabia	Total	China	India	Total	China	India	Total
2001-02	625	3,500	1,138	964	1,906	1,053	25,985	136,500	87,611	411,096	79,156	24,480	136,387
2002-03	1,117	2,750	1,198	900	1,897	938	26,190	135,700	79,860	404,900	63,311	11,000	106,522
2003-04	813	650	1,020	950	1,448	1,150	24,830	132,100	85,630	410,393	43,915	10,800	85,394
2004-05[1]	550	500	1,000	983	1,369	1,500	26,305	130,300	80,743	405,667	38,931	8,500	78,146
2005-06[2]	750	550	1,100	1,200	1,777	1,357	26,407	128,000	85,220	411,673	36,782	11,270	81,839
2006-07[3]	850	1,800	1,100	900	1,600	1,000	27,359	127,800	87,500	415,943	36,582	10,470	79,066

[1] Preliminary.   [2] Estimate.   [3] Forecast.   *Source: Foreign Agricultural Service, U.S. Department of Agriculture (FAS-USDA)*

World Production of Rough Rice   In Thousands of Metric Tons

Year	Bangla-desh	Brazil	Burma	China	India	Indonesia	Japan	Rep. of Korea	Pakistan	Philip-pines	Thailand	Vietnam	World Total
2001-02	36,469	10,393	18,000	177,580	140,024	51,101	11,321	7,407	5,824	13,000	26,514	31,873	593,880
2002-03	37,784	10,368	18,600	174,543	107,741	51,800	11,111	6,687	6,719	13,000	26,058	32,617	562,134
2003-04	39,232	12,807	18,500	160,660	132,808	54,301	9,740	6,151	7,273	14,154	27,289	33,458	584,298
2004-05[1]	38,404	13,229	16,500	179,090	124,707	54,000	10,912	6,737	7,381	14,500	26,303	34,418	595,784
2005-06[2]	43,141	11,579	18,000	180,591	137,699	54,200	11,342	6,435	8,321	15,108	27,576	34,503	621,054
2006-07[3]	43,654	11,324	18,103	182,857	136,514	51,628	10,907	6,324	8,401	15,462	27,652	34,500	617,988

[1] Preliminary.   [2] Estimate.   [3] Forecast.   *Source: Foreign Agricultural Service, U.S. Department of Agriculture (FAS-USDA)*

World Exports of Rice (Milled Basis)   In Thousands of Metric Tons

Year	Argentina	Australia	Burma	China	EU-25	Guyana	India	Pakistan	Thailand	Uruguay	Vietnam	United States	World Total
2001-02	134	247	1,002	1,963	336	209	6,300	1,628	7,245	475	3,245	2,954	26,882
2002-03	175	150	388	2,583	250	193	5,440	1,992	7,552	615	3,795	3,860	28,660
2003-04	294	175	130	880	225	200	3,100	1,868	10,137	725	4,295	3,310	27,354
2004-05[1]	325	80	190	656	175	243	4,687	2,801	7,274	775	5,174	3,496	28,360
2005-06[2]	450	325	75	1,216	160	182	3,800	3,000	7,376	825	4,694	3,689	28,073
2006-07[3]	450	125	150	1,200	150	170	4,300	3,000	8,700	650	4,900	3,262	29,142

[1] Preliminary.   [2] Estimate.   [3] Forecast.   *Source: Foreign Agricultural Service, U.S. Department of Agriculture (FAS-USDA)*

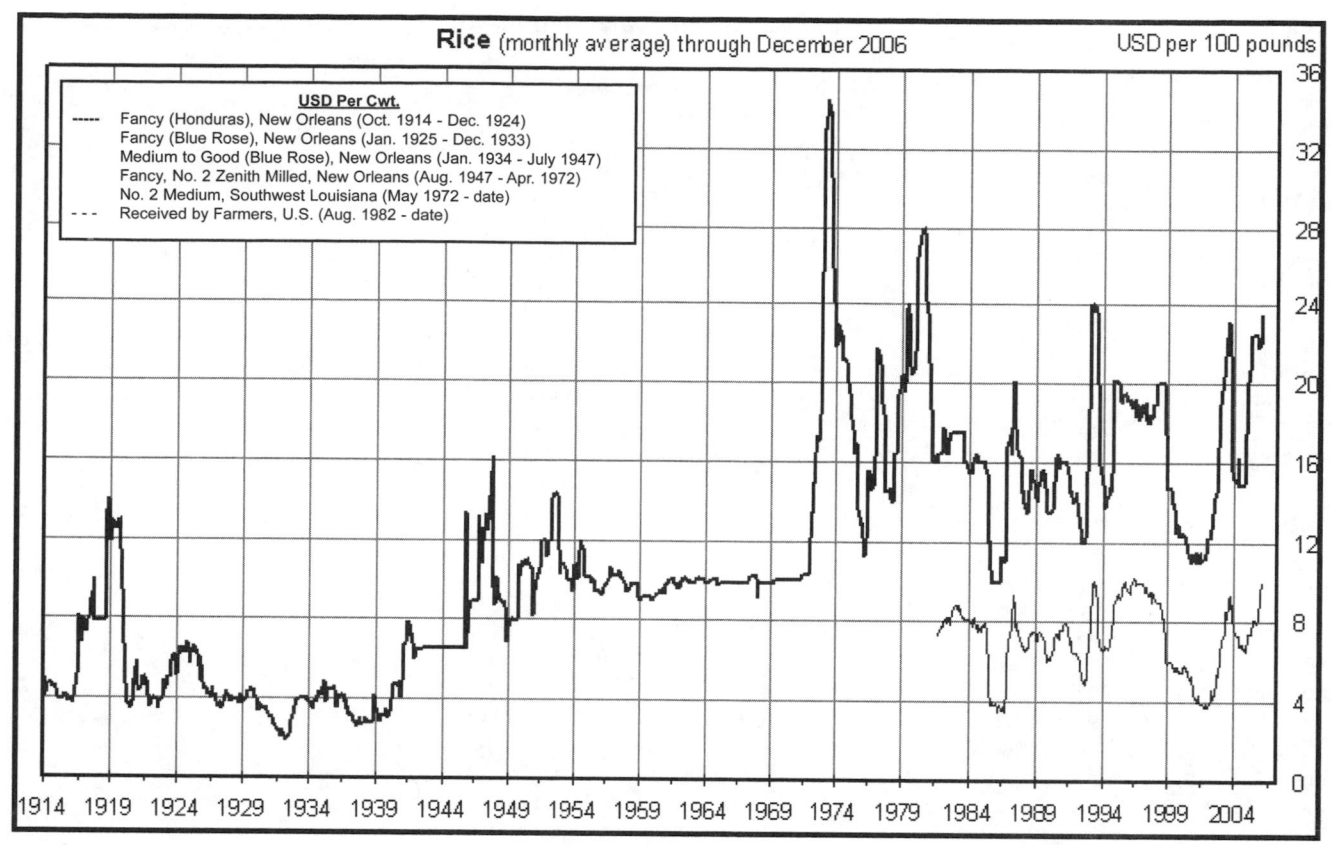

Rice (monthly average) through December 2006 — USD per 100 pounds

Legend: USD Per Cwt.
- Fancy (Honduras), New Orleans (Oct. 1914 - Dec. 1924)
- Fancy (Blue Rose), New Orleans (Jan. 1925 - Dec. 1933)
- Medium to Good (Blue Rose), New Orleans (Jan. 1934 - July 1947)
- Fancy, No. 2 Zenith Milled, New Orleans (Aug. 1947 - Apr. 1972)
- No. 2 Medium, Southwest Louisiana (May 1972 - date)
- Received by Farmers, U.S. (Aug. 1982 - date)

Average Wholesale Price of Rice No. 2 (Medium)[1] Southwest Louisiana In Dollars Per Cwt. Bagged

Year	Aug.	Sept.	Oct.	Nov.	Dec.	Jan.	Feb.	Mar.	Apr.	May	June	July	Average
1997-98	18.25	18.35	18.63	19.00	19.00	19.00	19.00	18.20	18.00	18.13	18.50	18.50	18.55
1998-99	18.35	18.75	19.00	19.00	20.00	20.00	20.00	20.00	20.00	20.00	20.00	20.00	19.59
1999-00	18.60	17.50	14.88	14.70	14.67	14.35	14.00	13.83	13.75	13.40	12.50	12.63	14.57
2000-01	13.00	12.34	12.48	12.41	12.38	12.38	12.25	12.00	11.82	11.53	11.25	11.25	12.09
2001-02	11.06	11.50	11.50	11.50	11.08	11.50	11.50	11.44	11.03	11.13	11.13	11.13	11.29
2002-03	11.13	11.50	12.25	12.25	12.25	12.63	13.50	14.05	14.25	14.44	14.50	14.88	13.13
2003-04	16.75	17.70	19.00	19.75	21.08	21.38	22.25	22.47	22.50	23.25	21.60	21.50	20.77
2004-05	18.60	15.69	15.23	15.13	15.13	16.31	14.88	14.88	14.88	14.88	14.88	14.94	15.45
2005-06	17.00	17.50	18.45	20.13	21.38	22.50	22.50	22.50	22.50	22.50	22.50	22.35	20.98
2006-07[2]	21.94	22.00	22.00	23.50									22.36

[1] U.S. No. 2 -- broken not to exceed 4%.   [2] Preliminary.   *Source: Economic Research Service, U.S. Department of Agriculture (ERS-USDA)*

Average Price Received by Farmers for Rice (Rough) in the United States In Dollars Per Cwt.

Year	Aug.	Sept.	Oct.	Nov.	Dec.	Jan.	Feb.	Mar.	Apr.	May	June	July	Average[2]
1997-98	9.94	9.92	10.00	9.82	9.77	9.57	9.75	9.67	9.40	9.38	9.58	9.58	9.70
1998-99	9.01	9.42	9.31	9.02	9.10	9.09	9.02	8.93	8.49	8.21	8.25	8.26	8.89
1999-00	6.91	6.17	5.91	5.96	6.01	5.98	5.82	5.64	5.75	5.62	5.69	5.59	5.93
2000-01	5.72	5.53	5.57	5.72	5.69	5.86	5.72	5.66	5.68	5.40	5.14	5.32	5.61
2001-02	5.10	4.78	4.36	4.08	4.07	4.30	4.16	3.99	3.94	3.98	3.92	3.81	4.21
2002-03	3.71	3.94	3.69	3.70	4.13	4.66	4.24	4.31	4.61	4.84	5.43	5.31	4.38
2003-04	5.47	6.18	6.44	6.99	7.57	8.57	8.23	8.45	8.65	9.30	9.37	8.79	7.83
2004-05	8.96	8.47	7.60	7.36	7.37	7.39	6.90	6.97	6.98	6.98	6.96	6.82	7.40
2005-06	6.58	6.76	6.99	7.46	7.49	7.80	8.02	8.10	8.19	7.96	8.04	8.16	7.63
2006-07[1]	8.65	8.99	9.46	10.00	9.87	10.20	10.00						9.60

[1] Preliminary.   [2] Weighted average by sales.   *Source: Economic Research Service, U.S. Department of Agriculture (ERS-USDA)*

RICE

Salient Statistics of Rice, Rough & Milled (Rough Equivalent) in the United States   In Millions of Cwt.

Crop Year Beginning Aug. 1	Supply Stocks Aug. 1	Supply Pro-duction	Supply Imports	Supply Total Supply	Disappearance Domestic Food	Disappearance Domestic Brewers	Disappearance Domestic Seed	Disappearance Domestic Total	Resi-dual	Exports	Total Disap-pearance	CCC Stocks July 31	Government Support Program Put Under Price Support	Loan Rate ($ Per Cwt.) Rough Long	Loan Rate ($ Per Cwt.) Rough Medium	All Classes	Milled Long
2001-02	28.5	215.3	13.2	256.9	119.3	4	4.0	123.3	4	94.7	218.0	0	----	6.67	6.09	6.50	10.69
2002-03	39.0	211.0	14.8	264.8	109.7	4	3.7	113.4	4	124.6	238.0	0	----	6.66	6.06	6.50	10.66
2003-04	26.8	199.9	15.0	241.7	110.8	4	4.1	115.0	4	103.1	218.0	0	----	6.64	6.09	6.50	10.65
2004-05	23.7	232.4	13.2	269.2	118.5	4	4.2	122.7	4	108.8	231.5	0	----	6.66	6.04	6.50	10.61
2005-06[1]	37.7	223.2	17.1	278.1	115.8	4	3.5	119.3	4	115.8	235.1	0	----	6.66	6.04	6.50	10.54
2006-07[2]	43.0	193.3	18.0	254.3	118.9	4	4.0	122.8	4	97.0	219.8	0	----	6.64	6.07	6.50	10.52

[1] Preliminary.   [2] Forecast.   [3] Loan rate for each class of rice is the sum of the whole kernels' loan rate weighted by its milling yield (average 56%) and the broken kernels' loan rate weighted by its milling yield (average 12%).   [4] Included in food.
Source: Economic Research Service, U.S. Department of Agriculture (ERS-USDA)

Acreage, Yield, Production and Prices of Rice in the United States

Crop Year	Acreage Harvested (1,000 Acres) Southern States	Acreage Harvested (1,000 Acres) California	Yield Per Harvested Acre (In Lbs.) United States	Yield Per Harvested Acre (In Lbs.) California	Production 1,000 Cwt. United States	Production 1,000 Cwt. Southern States	Production 1,000 Cwt. California	Production 1,000 Cwt. United States	Value of Pro-duction $1,000	Wholesale Prices ($ Per Cwt.) Arkan-sas[2]	Wholesale Prices ($ Per Cwt.) Hous-ton[3]	Milled Rice, Average C.I.F. at Rotterdam U.S. No. 2[4]	Thai "A"[5]	Thai "B"[5]
2001-02	2,843	471	3,314	8,170	6,496	176,780	38,490	215,270	925,055	11.25	12.88	208	----	225
2002-03	2,679	528	3,207	8,140	6,578	167,971	42,989	210,960	979,628	13.39	11.76	221	----	NA
2003-04	2,490	507	2,997	7,700	6,670	160,861	39,036	199,897	1,628,948	21.18	17.60	358	----	NA
2004-05	2,735	590	3,325	8,600	6,942	180,059	50,759	230,818	1,701,822	14.36	17.46	316	----	NA
2005-06	2,838	526	3,364	7,380	6,636	184,399	38,836	223,235	1,741,721	19.03	17.53	293	----	NA
2006-07[1]	2,297	526	2,823	7,600	6,847	153,316	39,976	193,292	1,906,895					

[1] Preliminary.   [2] F.O.B. mills, Arkansas, medium.   [3] Houston, Texas (long grain).   [4] Milled, 4%, container, FAS.   [5] SWR, 100%, bulk.
NA = Not available.   *Source: Economic Research Service, U.S. Department of Agriculture (ERS-USDA)*

U.S. Exports of Milled Rice, by Country of Destination   In Thousands of Metric Tons

Year Beginning October	Canada	Haiti	Iran	Ivory Coast	Jamaica	Mexico	Nether-lands	Peru	Saudi Arabia	South Africa	Switzer-land	United Kingdom	Total
2000-01	182.4	212.3	----	22.2	32.0	516.0	50.8	1.0	156.3	65.9	33.2	104.0	3,058
2001-02	174.5	247.1	----	25.0	28.7	740.4	52.9	11.2	97.0	67.3	18.0	106.0	3,536
2002-03	168.6	324.8	10.3	65.8	60.7	740.6	71.7	23.8	97.6	73.1	26.2	126.4	4,469
2003-04	208.4	242.2	----	32.7	44.5	738.0	30.4	3.5	87.7	.0	10.6	100.2	3,690
2004-05	230.8	299.1	0	32.6	48.2	725.8	44.8	45.7	101.4	.6	18.0	130.9	4,248
2005-06[1]	235.1	343.0	0	25.0	53.5	802.9	38.6	1.7	93.4	.0	12.4	120.3	4,045

[1] Preliminary.   *Source: Economic Research Service, U.S. Department of Agriculture (ERS-USDA)*

U.S. Rice Exports by Export Program   In Thousands of Metric Tons

Fiscal Year	PL 480	Section 416	CCC Credit Pro-grams[2]	CCC African Reliei Exports	EEP[3]	Export Pro-grams[4]	Exports Outside Specified Export Programs	Total U.S. Rice Exports	% Export Programs as a Share of Total Exports
2001	144	30	----	0	0	231	2,828	3,059	8
2002	241	56	----	0	0	356	3,181	3,537	10
2003	263	0	----	0	0	310	4,169	4,478	7
2004	129	0	----	0	0	214	3,484	3,699	6
2005	126	0	----	0	0	150	4,108	4,258	4
2006[1]	53	0	----	0	0	96	3,959	4,055	2

[1] Preliminary.   [2] May not completely reflect exports made under these programs.   [3] Sales not shipments.   [4] adjusted for estimated overlap between CCC export credit and EEP shipments.   *Source: Economice Research Service, U.S. Department of Agriculture (ERS-USDA)*

Production of Rice (Rough) in the United States, by Type and Variety   In Thousands of Cwt.

Year	Long Grain	Medium Grain	Short Grain	Total	Year	Long Grain	Medium Grain	Short Grain	Total
1997	124,485	57,091	1,416	182,992	2002	157,243	52,201	1,516	210,960
1998	139,328	43,404	1,711	184,443	2003	149,011	48,180	2,706	199,897
1999	151,863	50,540	3,624	206,027	2004	170,445	58,689	3,228	232,362
2000	128,756	59,514	2,602	190,872	2005	177,527	42,408	3,300	223,235
2001	167,555	46,105	1,610	215,270	2006[1]	143,674	45,969	3,649	193,292

[1] Preliminary.   *Source: National Agricultural Statistics Service, U.S. Department of Agriculture (NASS-USDA)*

Rubber

Rubber is a natural or synthetic substance characterized by elasticity, water repellence, and electrical resistance. Pre-Columbian Native South Americans discovered many uses for rubber such as containers, balls, shoes, and waterproofing for fabrics such as coats and capes. The Spaniards tried to duplicate these products for many years but were unsuccessful. The first commercial application of rubber began in 1791 when Samuel Peal patented a method of waterproofing cloth by treating it with a solution of rubber and turpentine. In 1839, Charles Goodyear revolutionized the rubber industry with his discovery of a process called vulcanization, which involves combining rubber and sulfur and heating the mixture.

Natural rubber is obtained from latex, a milky white fluid, from the Hevea Brasiliensis tree. The latex is gathered by cutting a chevron shape through the bark of the rubber tree. The latex is collected in a small cup, with approximately 1 fluid ounce per cutting. The cuttings are usually done every other day until the cuttings reach the ground. The tree is then allowed to renew itself before a new tapping is started. The collected latex is strained, diluted with water, and treated with acid to bind the rubber particles together. The rubber is then pressed between rollers to consolidate the rubber into slabs or thin sheets and is air-dried or smoke-dried for shipment.

During World War II, natural rubber supplies from the Far East were cut off, and the rubber shortage accelerated the development of synthetic rubber in the US. Synthetic rubber is produced by chemical reactions, condensation or polymerization, of certain unsaturated hydrocarbons. Synthetic rubber is made of raw material derived from petroleum, coal, oil, natural gas, and acetylene and is almost identical to natural rubber in chemical and physical properties.

Natural rubber and Rubber Index futures are traded on the Osaka Mercantile Exchange (OME). The OME's natural rubber contract is based on the RSS3 ribbed smoked sheet No. 3. The OME's Rubber Index Futures Contract is based on a composite of 8 component grades from 6 rubber markets in the world. Rubber futures are also traded on the Shanghai Futures Exchange (SHFE) and the Tokyo Commodity Exchange (TOCOM).

Prices – The average monthly price for spot crude rubber (No.1 smoked sheets, ribbed, plantation rubber), basis in New York, in 2006 was sharply higher by +38.7% to a record high of 104.91 cents per pound. A 3-decade low of 33.88 cents per pound was seen as recently as 2001 during that recessionary year.

Supply – World production of natural rubber in 2005 rose +1.4% to 8.777 million metric tons. The world's largest producers of natural rubber in 2005 were Thailand with 33.5% of world production, Indonesia (25.9%), Malaysia (12.8%), India (8.8%), Vietnam (5.3%), and China (4.9%).

In 2005, world production of synthetic rubber rose by +0.6% to 12.057 million metric tons. The world's largest producers of synthetic rubber in 2005 were the US with 19.6% of world production, Japan (13.5%), Russia (9.5%), and Germany (7.1%).

US production of synthetic rubber in 2005 rose +1.8% to 2.366 million metric tons from the 14-year low of 2.064 million metric tons posted in 2001. US production of car and truck tires in 2005 fell –4.3% to 223.203 million tires.

Demand – World consumption of natural rubber in 2005 rose by +4.9% to 9.001 million metric tons. The largest consumers of natural rubber in 2005 were the US with 13% of consumption, Japan with 10%, and France, Germany, and the UK with a combined 6%. The world's consumption of natural rubber has tripled since 1970. World consumption of synthetic rubber in 2005 rose by +1.0% to 12.005 million metric tons. The largest consumers of synthetic rubber in 2005 were the US with 16% of consumption, Japan with 10%, and France, Germany, and the UK with a combined 10%. The world's consumption of synthetic rubber has more than doubled since 1970.

US consumption of natural rubber in 2005 rose by +1.3% to 1.159 million metric tons. US consumption of natural rubber has more than doubled since 1970. US consumption of synthetic rubber in 2005 rose +2.5% to 1.955 million metric tons. The US consumption of synthetic rubber has remained about the same as it was in 1970.

Trade – World exports of natural rubber in 2005 rose +2.8% to a record 6.336 million metric tons. The world's largest exporters of natural rubber in 2005 were Thailand with 42% of world exports and Indonesia with 32% of world exports.

US imports of natural rubber in 2005 rose +1.4% to a 5-year high of 1.159 million metric tons. US exports of synthetic rubber in 2005 rose +2.4% to a record high of 1.105 million metric tons.

U.S. Imports of Natural Rubber (Includes Latex & Guayule)   In Thousands of Metric Tons

Year	Jan.	Feb.	Mar.	Apr.	May	June	July	Aug.	Sept.	Oct.	Nov.	Dec.	Total
1997	94.2	92.0	93.9	88.2	93.0	65.1	76.8	90.1	87.5	86.8	87.6	89.0	1,044.2
1998	104.4	76.6	102.8	81.0	98.0	92.9	96.4	100.8	123.2	104.8	84.5	111.4	1,176.8
1999	91.8	90.7	93.4	101.6	84.8	80.0	76.6	112.2	88.7	127.5	83.1	85.9	1,116.3
2000	127.4	88.2	114.1	107.9	114.9	120.1	65.9	96.2	79.2	96.2	92.2	89.3	1,191.6
2001	85.2	69.1	93.9	80.0	74.9	63.8	101.1	109.2	69.9	92.4	69.2	63.4	972.1
2002	104.8	71.2	79.2	90.8	106.1	92.2	108.6	109.7	81.1	94.7	83.0	88.9	1,110.3
2003	104.1	86.2	106.8	99.8	91.4	97.6	94.5	67.4	100.1	70.6	72.3	86.2	1,077.0
2004	116.2	76.6	101.7	96.5	112.6	92.0	87.6	81.7	85.5	120.4	71.0	101.8	1,143.6
2005	99.8	101.9	97.1	115.5	80.9	95.7	84.5	91.7	113.5	92.2	82.7	103.7	1,159.2
2006[1]	113.3	71.8	98.9	80.5	115.6	72.5	724.0	97.3	58.8	83.9			1,819.9

[1] Preliminary.   Source: International Rubber Study Group (IRSG)

RUBBER

World Production[1] of Rubber In Thousands of Metric Tons

				Natural							Synthetic		
Year	China	India	Indo-nesia	Malaysia	Sri Lanka	Thailand	Vietnam	World Total	Ger-many	Japan	United States	Russia	World Total
1996	430.0	540.1	1,527.0	1,082.5	112.5	1,970.4	220.0	6,440	548.1	1,519.9	2,486.0	775.1	9,760
1997	444.0	580.3	1,504.8	971.1	105.8	2,032.7	212.0	6,470	555.1	1,591.5	2,589.0	724.9	10,080
1998	450.0	591.1	1,714.0	885.7	95.7	2,075.9	220.0	6,820	619.0	1,520.1	2,600.0	621.0	9,840
1999	460.0	620.1	1,599.2	768.9	96.6	2,154.6	262.0	6,872	720.1	1,576.7	2,354.0	737.0	10,336
2000	445.0	629.0	1,501.1	927.6	87.6	2,346.4	293.0	6,739	849.2	1,591.7	2,396.8	837.1	10,819
2001	464.0	631.5	1,607.3	882.1	86.2	2,319.6	331.0	7,261	828.4	1,465.5	2,062.1	919.2	10,485
2002	468.0	640.8	1,630.0	889.8	90.5	2,615.1	372.0	7,345	869.2	1,522.0	2,164.4	919.0	10,882
2003	480.0	707.1	1,792.2	985.6	92.0	2,876.0	380.0	7,992	888.0	1,577.4	2,270.1	1,070.0	11,448
2004[1]	486.0	742.6	2,066.2	1,168.7	94.7	2,984.3	415.0	8,645	905.0	1,616.1	2,325.1	1,116.1	11,978
2005[2]	428.0	770.5	2,269.8	1,130.7	94.7	2,910.8	435.5	8,682	842.5	1,626.9	2,365.8	1,147.1	11,965

[1] Including rubber in the form of latex.   [2] Preliminary.   *Source: International Rubber Study Group (IRSG)*

World Consumption of Natural and Synthetic Rubber In Thousands of Metric Tons

			Natural							Synthetic			
Year	Brazil	France	Ger-many	Japan	United Kingdom	United States	World Total	France	Ger-many	Japan	United Kingdom	United States	World Total
1996	160.7	182.2	193.0	714.5	111.0	1,001.7	6,110	436.1	497.0	1,124.5	230.0	2,186.6	9,590
1997	161.0	192.3	214.0	713.0	119.0	1,044.1	6,470	416.2	509.0	1,163.0	235.0	2,322.7	10,010
1998	185.3	223.0	247.0	707.3	139.0	1,157.4	6,580	451.4	582.0	1,115.7	177.0	2,354.4	9,830
1999	184.1	240.0	226.0	734.2	127.0	1,116.3	6,646	434.3	565.0	1,132.9	189.0	2,217.5	10,196
2000	226.6	270.0	250.0	751.8	122.5	1,194.8	7,315	481.5	632.0	1,137.5	188.0	2,189.5	10,764
2001	215.9	282.0	246.0	729.2	98.0	974.1	7,223	464.5	613.0	1,085.1	167.0	1,839.5	10,253
2002	233.4	230.7	247.0	749.0	76.0	1,110.8	7,546	469.3	612.0	1,096.0	210.0	1,895.0	10,723
2003	255.5	300.2	260.3	784.2	90.9	1,078.5	7,967	493.2	615.0	1,110.7	203.9	1,926.4	11,381
2004	281.5	230.1	242.3	814.8	86.3	1,143.6	8,319	420.1	624.5	1,146.3	211.2	1,906.8	11,860
2005[1]	310.9	233.9	260.1	859.4	82.3	1,159.2	8,742	350.7	635.0	1,180.9	206.5	1,954.6	11,917

[1] Preliminary.   *Source: International Rubber Study Group (IRSG)*

World Stocks[1] of Natural & Synthetic Rubber (by Countries) on January 1 In Thousands of Metric Tons

		In Producing Countries							In Consuming Countries (Reported Stocks)				
Year	Total Synthetic	Africa	Indo-nesia	Malaysia	Sri Lanka	Thai-land	Vietnam	Total Natural	Brazil	India	Japan	United States	Total
1997	1,057	20.5	70	190.3	17.6	147.7	28.0	510	13.0	123.4	86.8	79.3	427
1998	1,081	25.5	40	209.5	17.9	159.4	28.0	510	13.0	157.0	87.2	57.2	385
1999	1,116	25.3	30	234.2	18.6	209.5	30.0	750	13.0	194.0	58.0	70.4	406
2000	1,103	28.2	33	236.6	18.6	250.9	32.0	929	34.0	215.1	79.1	46.0	475
2001	1,159	28.9	48	151.1	18.7	188.6	27.0	595	40.0	203.3	95.2	44.6	484
2002	1,139	29.1	26	138.2	19.0	213.0	26.0	566	42.0	225.5	46.9	42.6	429
2003	1,161	27.7	25	135.6	19.0	196.7	19.0	482	42.0	151.7	65.0	42.1	301
2004	1,127	28.0	15	162.6	19.0	202.2	14.0	471	42.0	123.3	73.0	40.6	279
2005	1,040	29.6	18	195.0	19.0	249.4	17.0	559	42.0	122.9	58.1	40.9	264
2006[1]	988	33.1	20	166.2	19.0	258.0	20.0	549	42.0	65.0	47.3	40.9	245

[1] Preliminary.   *Source: International Rubber Study Group (IRSG)*

Net Exports of Natural Rubber from Producing Areas In Thousands of Metric Tons

Year	Cam-bodia	Guat-emala	Indo-nesia	Liberia	Malaysia	Nigeria	Sri Lanka	Thai-land	Vietnam	Other Africa[2]	Other Asia[3]	World Total
1996	31.0	29.2	1,434.3	30.0	709.7	48.8	72.1	1,763.0	194.5	166.7	65.3	4,380
1997	32.0	28.3	1,403.8	67.2	586.8	53.0	61.4	1,837.1	194.2	186.1	58.6	4,580
1998	29.0	24.6	1,641.2	75.0	424.9	46.5	41.4	1,839.4	181.0	181.7	62.8	4,650
1999	42.0	27.7	1,494.6	75.0	435.5	38.0	42.7	1,886.3	218.0	200.4	60.5	4,648
2000	39.0	31.8	1,379.6	73.5	196.4	36.0	32.6	2,166.2	254.0	205.7	62.8	4,977
2001	38.0	33.0	1,496.9	71.7	162.1	30.0	32.0	2,042.1	283.0	212.4	76.5	5,113
2002	40.0	40.1	1,502.2	73.0	430.0	24.0	36.1	2,354.4	325.0	199.8	83.2	5,233
2003	41.0	41.0	1,660.5	71.5	509.7	19.0	35.2	2,573.4	325.0	210.8	94.7	5,687
2004	40.5	52.9	1,875.1	71.3	679.9	24.0	40.3	2,637.1	352.0	222.0	84.3	6,175
2005[1]	41.0	54.0	2,074.5	69.1	659.9	23.0	29.9	2,580.7	371.0	233.0	86.3	6,309

[1] Preliminary.   [2] Includes Cameroon, Cote d'Ivoire, Gabon, Ghana and Zaire.   [3] Includes Myanmar, Papua New Guinea and the Philippines.
Source: International Rubber Study Group (IRSG)

Rubber (monthly average) through December 2006

Cents Per pound
----- Para, New York (1860 - 1907)
Smoked Sheets, New York (Jan. 1908 - date)

Average Spot Crude Rubber Prices (Smoked Sheets[1]) in New York In Cents Per Pound

Year	Jan.	Feb.	Mar.	Apr.	May	June	July	Aug.	Sept.	Oct.	Nov.	Dec.	Average
1999	38.99	38.58	36.34	34.98	35.75	34.64	33.60	33.63	34.45	37.58	42.57	38.88	36.67
2000	38.16	40.36	38.17	37.80	37.76	37.07	36.65	37.90	37.35	37.61	37.02	36.90	37.73
2001	35.98	35.66	34.78	34.50	34.80	35.00	34.80	34.48	33.07	31.98	31.14	30.35	33.88
2002	32.21	34.45	36.50	36.38	36.93	43.53	44.32	45.20	47.90	45.70	44.97	45.39	41.12
2003	47.95	49.25	54.96	52.04	49.32	51.76	51.99	53.71	57.61	65.88	67.63	65.20	55.61
2004	65.63	67.28	68.09	68.84	70.40	69.90	68.10	66.50	66.39	67.30	66.80	63.90	67.43
2005	64.20	66.18	66.80	66.70	68.07	73.75	80.50	82.34	85.51	87.90	83.75	81.99	75.64
2006	93.04	104.01	104.48	105.20	115.03	131.74	124.01	114.94	95.17	94.77	87.95	88.53	104.91

[1] No. 1, ribbed, plantation rubber.   *Source: International Rubber Study Group (IRSG)*

Natural Rubber Prices in London In Euro[1] Per Metric Ton

Year	Jan.	Feb.	Mar.	Apr.	May	June	July	Aug.	Sept.	Oct.	Nov.	Dec.	Average
Buyers' Price RSS 1 (CIF)													
2002	461.8	502.5	522.1	511.9	518.9	NQ	NQ	NQ	NQ	NQ	NQ	NQ	503.4
2003	1,058.7	1,133.6	1,211.6	1,147.2	1,087.4	1,141.2	1,146.1	1,184.2	1,270.0	1,452.5	1,491.0	1,437.5	1,230.1
2004	1,446.8	1,483.2	1,501.2	1,517.6	1,552.1	1,541.0	1,501.3	1,466.1	1,463.6	1,483.7	1,472.7	1,408.8	1,486.5
2005	1,415.4	1,459.1	1,472.7	1,470.5	1,500.7	1,626.0	1,774.7	1,815.2	1,885.2	1,937.8	1,846.4	1,807.5	1,667.6
2006	2,051.1	2,293.1	2,303.3	2,319.2	2,536.0	2,904.3	2,734.0	2,533.9	2,098.2	2,089.4	1,938.9	1,951.7	2,312.8
Buyers' Prices RSS 3 (CIF)													
2002	444.2	486.5	511.3	500.2	515.4	959.9	893.4	932.2	981.1	----	----	----	691.6
2003	930.6	987.3	1,046.6	968.7	905.6	949.7	956.9	1,021.4	1,086.1	1,197.3	1,182.0	1,091.5	1,027.0
2004	1,063.3	1,084.9	1,172.4	1,219.8	1,206.4	1,204.9	1,123.4	1,101.9	1,051.4	1,045.6	1,026.6	973.2	1,106.2
2005	957.2	992.6	1,066.7	1,094.0	1,142.5	1,292.6	1,492.2	1,405.8	1,484.3	1,525.3	1,454.3	1,528.5	1,286.3
2006	1,657.1	1,840.3	1,846.7	1,864.2	2,016.0	2,267.5	2,112.0	1,839.5	1,487.3	1,511.1	1,327.8	1,356.6	1,760.5
Sellers' Prices SMR 20 (CIF)													
2002	428.0	461.3	510.6	500.6	503.5	921.3	864.6	898.5	978.9	----	----	----	674.1
2003	915.0	937.7	942.2	888.2	795.4	800.0	834.4	911.0	1,040.7	1,174.7	1,166.0	1,087.6	957.7
2004	1,030.2	1,072.0	1,104.7	1,118.2	1,094.0	1,042.5	996.8	1,006.9	1,008.1	1,037.3	1,000.2	959.5	1,039.2
2005	950.5	985.8	991.1	1,012.1	1,018.7	1,138.6	1,292.6	1,254.0	1,385.5	1,410.0	1,442.3	1,485.8	1,197.3
2006	1,564.6	1,727.5	1,704.7	1,694.2	1,788.7	1,952.6	1,949.4	1,797.4	1,490.4	1,475.6	13,113.3	1,294.3	2,629.4

[1] Data prior to June 2002 are in British Pound per metric ton.   *Source: International Rubber Study Group (IRSG)*

RUBBER

Consumption of Natural Rubber in the United States   In Thousands of Metric Tons

Year	Jan.	Feb.	Mar.	Apr.	May	June	July	Aug.	Sept.	Oct.	Nov.	Dec.	Total
1997	94.2	92.0	93.9	88.2	93.0	65.1	76.8	90.1	87.5	86.8	87.5	89.0	1,044.1
1998	104.4	76.6	102.7	81.0	98.0	92.9	96.4	91.7	119.1	104.8	78.4	111.4	1,157.4
1999	92.0	92.0	93.0	88.0	88.0	88.0	92.0	92.0	92.0	100.0	100.0	100.0	1,116.3
2000	110.0	110.0	110.0	114.0	114.0	114.0	80.0	80.0	80.0	93.0	93.0	93.0	1,194.8
2001	85.5	69.4	94.1	80.2	75.1	64.1	101.2	109.3	70.0	92.4	69.4	63.4	974.1
2002	104.9	71.3	79.2	90.4	106.3	92.3	108.7	109.7	81.2	94.7	83.1	89.0	1,110.8
2003	104.2	86.3	106.9	100.1	91.2	97.7	94.6	67.5	101.3	69.9	72.5	86.3	1,078.5
2004	116.0	76.5	101.5	96.5	112.5	92.5	87.5	82.0	86.0	120.0	71.0	101.8	1,143.8
2005	99.8	101.9	97.1	115.5	80.9	95.7	84.5	91.7	113.5	92.2	82.7	103.7	1,159.2
2006[1]	113.3	71.8	98.9	80.5	115.6	72.5	72.4	97.3	58.8	83.9			1,038.0

[1] Preliminary.   Source: International Rubber Study Group (IRSG)

Stocks of Natural Rubber in the United States, on First of Month   In Thousands of Metric Tons

Year	Jan.	Feb.	Mar.	Apr.	May	June	July	Aug.	Sept.	Oct.	Nov.	Dec.
1997	79.3	74.2	74.2	76.9	77.5	62.2	55.2	53.6	52.1	51.2	52.4	55.2
1998	57.2	61.2	65.5	63.5	60.9	66.7	53.6	57.9	54.7	58.3	58.9	66.5
1999	70.4	68.0	66.0	64.0	62.0	60.0	58.0	56.0	54.0	52.0	50.0	48.0
2000	46.0	63.4	41.6	45.7	39.6	40.5	46.6	32.5	48.7	47.9	51.1	50.3
2001	46.6	44.3	44.0	43.8	43.6	43.4	43.1	43.0	42.9	42.8	42.8	42.6
2002	42.6	42.5	42.4	42.4	42.8	42.6	42.5	42.4	42.4	42.3	42.3	42.2
2003	42.1	42.0	41.9	41.8	41.5	41.7	41.6	41.5	41.4	40.2	40.9	40.7
2004	40.6	40.8	40.9	40.9	40.9	40.9	40.9	40.9	40.9	40.9	40.9	40.9
2005	40.6	40.6	40.6	40.6	40.6	40.6	40.6	40.6	40.6	40.6	40.6	40.6
2006[1]	40.6	40.6	40.6	40.6	40.6	40.6	40.6	40.6	40.6	40.6	40.6	40.6

[1] Preliminary.   Source: International Rubber Study Group (IRSG)

Stocks of Synthetic Rubber in the United States, on First of Month   In Thousands of Metric Tons

Year	Jan.	Feb.	Mar.	Apr.	May	June	July	Aug.	Sept.	Oct.	Nov.	Dec.
1997	400.5	400.4	408.4	412.7	411.9	403.5	393.1	376.9	378.4	364.4	365.2	377.7
1998	377.7	382.2	375.7	379.5	387.5	402.8	394.6	406.8	394.2	398.7	395.7	396.5
1999	409.3	404.0	404.0	406.0	399.0	420.0	410.0	419.0	413.0	390.0	391.0	389.0
2000	406.0	416.0	413.0	402.0	405.0	416.0	409.0	418.0	400.0	412.0	407.0	419.0
2001	433.0	451.0	467.0	4,559.0	448.0	433.0	426.0	420.0	394.0	400.0	394.0	379.0
2002	392.0	377.0	379.0	393.0	398.0	384.0	385.0	381.0	364.0	375.0	364.0	358.0
2003	390.0	325.0	330.0	325.0	336.0	336.0	332.0	332.0	331.0	328.0	317.0	338.0
2004	343.0	347.0	335.0	315.0	310.0	300.0	300.0	290.0	280.0	280.0	280.0	270.0
2005	260.0	255.0	240.0	240.0	235.0	235.0	240.0	245.0	245.0	245.0	245.0	245.0
2006[1]	248.0	240.0	225.0	215.0	210.0	210.0	210.0	210.0	210.0	210.0	210.0	210.0

[1] Preliminary.   Source: International Rubber Study Group (IRSG)

Production of Synthetic Rubber in the United States   In Thousands of Metric Tons

Year	Jan.	Feb.	Mar.	Apr.	May	June	July	Aug.	Sept.	Oct.	Nov.	Dec.	Total
1997	220.0	200.0	220.0	230.0	220.0	200.0	220.0	220.0	230.0	210.0	210.0	203.0	2,589
1998	230.0	200.0	230.0	220.0	240.0	210.0	220.0	210.0	230.0	210.0	200.0	210.0	2,610
1999	200.0	181.0	209.0	195.0	205.0	190.0	199.0	192.0	180.0	204.0	197.0	202.0	2,354
2000	202.0	202.0	214.0	193.0	216.0	202.0	198.0	187.0	193.0	197.0	194.0	184.0	2,382
2001	203.0	188.6	184.3	172.1	175.5	162.3	166.7	164.7	174.3	178.6	155.1	139.2	2,064
2002	176.1	171.9	192.3	190.6	187.0	184.6	183.5	177.3	175.1	175.0	160.4	176.4	2,150
2003	185.6	180.9	193.6	179.8	182.9	166.3	174.2	172.9	188.4	189.7	192.0	185.6	2,192
2004	208.3	199.0	203.5	193.5	187.1	183.5	183.5	184.1	193.5	198.5	202.1	188.5	2,325
2005	206.9	204.8	209.4	202.7	196.9	188.9	187.3	193.7	182.7	185.8	206.9	199.8	2,366
2006[1]	212.9	213.7	212.9	210.2	195.5	191.8	202.0	202.2	193.5	192.2			2,432

[1] Preliminary.   Source: International Rubber Study Group (IRSG)

Consumption of Synthetic Rubber in the United States   In Thousands of Metric Tons

Year	Jan.	Feb.	Mar.	Apr.	May	June	July	Aug.	Sept.	Oct.	Nov.	Dec.	Total
1997	191.7	181.4	190.0	187.9	192.2	187.7	205.9	208.0	204.2	203.0	181.9	188.8	2,323
1998	196.5	192.5	214.8	194.4	199.8	201.4	192.0	204.5	202.2	200.3	181.2	174.8	2,354
1999	164.0	166.0	195.0	178.0	170.0	186.0	177.0	176.0	191.0	171.0	178.0	161.0	2,218
2000	173.0	185.0	202.0	178.0	194.0	196.0	177.0	189.0	172.0	182.0	168.0	147.0	2,190
2001	170.8	149.6	166.8	153.3	159.8	148.6	156.4	173.0	145.7	162.7	140.8	112.0	1,840
2002	155.5	146.8	153.0	165.8	173.4	160.4	161.5	169.3	154.8	166.7	148.2	139.6	1,895
2003	166.1	156.4	167.7	157.8	162.0	163.0	163.3	152.3	159.0	175.6	147.3	155.9	1,926
2004	170.0	166.2	176.0	156.5	152.2	141.9	158.8	149.2	152.9	155.0	170.0	158.1	1,907
2005	174.7	184.0	180.6	171.5	156.8	147.9	145.2	148.9	153.7	161.2	166.8	163.3	1,955
2006[1]	173.7	182.7	178.0	170.7	140.2	141.5	141.6	142.1	136.5	135.4			1,851

[1] Preliminary.   Source: International Rubber Study Group (IRSG)

U.S. Exports of Synthetic Rubber   In Thousands of Metric Tons

Year	Jan.	Feb.	Mar.	Apr.	May	June	July	Aug.	Sept.	Oct.	Nov.	Dec.	Total
1997	63.1	58.2	57.5	74.2	66.9	61.6	64.1	70.0	65.6	65.6	63.0	58.7	768.5
1998	61.1	60.8	62.8	59.8	66.9	61.8	60.1	64.4	63.7	62.3	59.2	59.2	742.1
1999	57.6	63.3	65.0	70.5	64.7	66.0	61.5	68.2	65.1	79.0	70.2	65.7	796.8
2000	64.3	73.4	83.8	70.2	73.2	72.3	72.4	78.6	78.6	75.2	73.3	70.7	886.0
2001	74.6	67.3	76.4	78.2	75.1	69.6	70.6	71.6	68.1	70.7	62.4	59.4	844.4
2002	67.9	71.6	69.5	74.9	78.5	73.6	74.5	72.8	70.9	73.1	70.8	66.3	864.4
2003	73.1	70.1	80.1	85.2	78.4	75.3	74.4	72.4	73.9	83.7	74.5	79.3	920.4
2004	82.0	87.3	97.0	90.9	96.8	92.6	88.9	91.6	94.8	89.0	87.0	81.6	1,079.5
2005	86.3	89.6	91.8	98.4	98.3	96.9	91.5	100.4	76.4	87.0	101.3	87.5	1,105.4
2006[1]	103.4	97.3	106.7	103.2	109.2	106.8	110.0	112.5	101.3	103.3			1,264.4

[1] Preliminary.   Source: International Rubber Study Group (IRSG)

Production of Tyres (Car and Truck) in the United States   In Thousands of Units

Year	First Quarter	Second Quarter	Third Quarter	Fourth Quarter	Total	Year	First Quarter	Second Quarter	Third Quarter	Fourth Quarter	Total
1989	56,716	56,626	50,086	49,444	212,870	1998	----	----	----	----	270,905
1990	55,915	53,856	51,163	49,729	210,663	1999	----	----	----	----	267,652
1991	51,296	52,796	49,183	51,115	202,391	2000	----	----	----	----	276,765
1992	57,890	57,319	57,554	57,487	230,250	2001	65,367	62,809	62,366	56,106	255,700
1993	61,809	60,752	57,702	57,184	237,447	2002	62,937	64,362	60,524	58,241	246,064
1994	63,586	63,331	57,018	59,442	243,696	2003	62,686	59,311	58,441	55,565	236,003
1995	63,800	63,800	63,800	63,754	255,521	2004	60,272	59,774	58,389	54,824	233,259
1996	64,000	64,000	64,000	63,700	255,723	2005[1]	57,377	58,832	54,920	52,074	223,203
1997	----	----	----	----	263,860	2006[2]	56,787	53,452	49,612		213,135

[1] Preliminary.   [2] Estimate.   Source: International Rubber Study Group IRSG)

U.S. Foreign Trade of Tyres (Car and Truck)   In Thousands of Units

	Imports					Exports				
Year	First Quarter	Second Quarter	Third Quarter	Fourth Quarter	Total	First Quarter	Second Quarter	Third Quarter	Fourth Quarter	Total
1997	13,359	14,487	15,314	16,064	59,434	9,466	11,386	10,456	11,085	42,452
1998	17,046	17,728	18,016	19,346	72,124	12,840	10,678	10,018	10,372	43,923
1999	19,471	22,295	22,194	23,784	87,768	9,874	9,580	10,480	10,537	40,945
2000	24,200	24,698	23,561	22,123	94,019	11,200	10,200	10,200	10,100	44,164
2001	19,563	22,251	22,072	20,956	84,842	10,087	10,362	11,004	10,691	42,144
2002	21,554	25,831	24,868	24,950	97,203	10,438	10,379	10,167	10,380	41,363
2003	26,310	28,557	28,472	27,536	110,875	9,293	2,648	10,263	10,794	32,998
2004	28,996	31,998	30,788	32,707	124,489	10,272	10,902	10,108	10,299	41,581
2005[1]	32,704	36,924	34,391	33,584	137,603	9,808	10,071	10,659	10,570	41,108
2006[2]	34,562	36,863			142,850	10,129	10,617	10,692		41,917

[1] Preliminary.   [2] Estimate.   Source: International Rubber Study Group (IRSG)

Rye

Rye is a cereal grain and a member of the grass family. Hardy varieties of rye have been developed for winter planting. Rye is most widely grown in northern Europe and Asia. In the US, rye is used as an animal feed and as an ingredient in bread and some whiskeys. Bread using rye was developed in northern Europe in the Middle Ages where bakers developed dark, hearty bread consisting of rye, oat and barley flours. Those were crops that grew more readily in the wet and damp climate of northern Europe, as opposed to wheat which fares better in the warmer and drier climates in central Europe. Modern rye bread is made with a mixture of white and rye flours. Coarsely ground rye flour is also used in pumpernickel bread and helps provide the dark color and course texture, along with molasses. The major producing states are North and South Dakota, Oklahoma, and Georgia. The crop year runs from June to May.

Supply – World rye production in 2006-07 fell by –14.8% yr/yr to a new record low of 12.384 million metric tons. The world's largest producers of rye are the European Union with 53% of world production in 2006-07, followed by Russia with 24%, Belarus with 10%, and the Ukraine with 5%. US production of rye accounted for only 1.5% of world production in 2006-07.

US production of rye in 2006 fell –4.6% to 7.193 million bushels. That was far below the production levels above 20 million bushels seen from the late 1800s through the 1960s.

US production of rye fell off in the 1970s, and fell to a record low of 6.971 million bushels in 2001-02.

US acreage harvested with rye in 2006-07 fell –1.8% to 274,000 acres, which was only modestly above the record low of 255,000 acres in 2001-02. US farmers in the late 1800s through the 1960s typically harvested more than 1 million acres of rye, showing how domestic planting of rye has dropped off sharply in the past several decades.

Rye yield in 2005-06 fell –2.6% to 26.3 bushels per acre, which was well below the record high of 33.1 bushels per acre posted in 1984-85. Modern rye production yields are more than double the levels in the teens seen prior to the 1960s when yields started to rise.

Demand – Total US domestic usage of rye in 2005-06 fell –9.9% yr/yr to 12.200 million bushels. The breakdown of domestic usage shows that 27% of rye in 2005-06 was used for food, 25% by industry, 25% as seed, and 24% as feed and residual.

Trade – World exports of rye in the 2006-07 marketing year fell –1.1% yr/yr to a 21-year low of 603,000 metric tons. The largest exporter was the European Union with exports of 400,000 metric tons. World imports of rye fell –13.8% to 537,000 metric tons. US imports of rye in 2006-07 fell –8.6% yr/yr to 127,000 metric tons.

World Production of Rye   In Thousands of Metric Tons

Year	Argentina	Australia	Belarus	Canada	Union	Kazakh-stan	Romania	Russia	Switzer-land	Turkey	Ukraine	United States	World Total
1997-98	62	20	1,788	320	6,021	60	50	7,500	46	235	1,348	207	24,125
1998-99	66	20	1,384	408	6,345	20	45	3,300	20	232	1,140	309	20,074
1999-00	116	20	929	387	11,413	20	50	4,800	20	233	919	280	19,278
2000-01	125	20	1,360	260	10,203	50	50	5,450	20	260	966	213	19,064
2001-02	81	20	1,294	228	11,891	75	50	6,600	20	220	1,822	175	22,568
2002-03	80	20	1,600	134	9,190	50	50	7,150	20	255	1,511	165	20,310
2003-04	37	20	1,200	327	6,907	50	50	4,200	20	240	625	219	13,976
2004-05[1]	89	20	1,400	420	9,966	50	50	2,850	20	240	1,600	210	16,998
2005-06[2]	55	20	1,150	359	7,671	50	50	3,600	20	240	1,050	191	14,543
2006-07[3]	55	20	1,200	300	6,591	50	50	3,000	20	240	600	183	12,384

[1] Preliminary.   [2] Estimate.   [3] Forecast.   Source: Foreign Agricultural Service, U.S. Department of Agriculture (FAS-USDA)

World Imports and Exports of Rye   In Thousands of Metric Tons

	Imports							Exports					
Crop Year	EU-25	Japan	Rep. of Korea	Turkey	Russia	United States	World Total	Belarus	Canada	EU-25	Russia	United States	World Total
1997-98		323	4	----	2	141	676	----	142	487	1	2	651
1998-99	4	391	175	----	306	84	1,470	----	68	939	----	1	1,443
1999-00	368	397	476	183	464	87	2,276	----	87	2,085	----	7	2,387
2000-01	486	337	57	----	193	82	1,224	50	91	1,288	----	10	1,440
2001-02	433	335	121	20	7	126	1,150	30	66	730	4	5	1,129
2002-03	501	414	31	43	----	156	1,433	110	53	748	291	3	1,493
2003-04	76	341	114	43	6	83	822	60	171	626	156	1	1,025
2004-05[1]	6	261	8	59	172	143	788	50	122	575	----	4	855
2005-06[2]	9	279	7	7	49	139	623	50	132	359	----	----	610
2006-07[3]	10	200	10	5	75	127	537	50	150	400	----	3	603

[1] Preliminary.   [2] Estimate.   [3] Forecast.   Source: Foreign Agricultural Service, U.S. Department of Agriculture (FAS-USDA)

Rye (monthly average) through June 2005 — Cents per bushel

Cents Per Bushel
----- No. 2 Minneapolis (July 1909 to Dec. 1997)

Production of Rye in the United States — In Thousands of Bushels

Year	Georgia	Kansas	Michigan	Minnesota	Nebraska	North Dakota	Oklahoma	Pennsylvania	South Carolina	South Dakota	Texas	Wisconsin	Total
1997	1,430	300	450	400	240	513	1,080	400	250	728	330	432	8,132
1998	1,050	375	420	837	288	2,562	1,540	495	400	1,400	400	360	12,161
1999	1,050	300	756	775	405	1,517	1,045	600	500	1,012	450	384	11,038
2000	1,170	[2]	[2]	[2]	[2]	704	1,470	[2]	[2]	546	[2]	[2]	8,386
2001	875	[2]	[2]	[2]	[2]	340	1,150	[2]	[2]	350	[2]	[2]	6,971
2002	560	[2]	[2]	[2]	[2]	210	1,300	[2]	[2]	270	[2]	[2]	6,488
2003	800	[2]	[2]	[2]	[2]	750	1,540	[2]	[2]	672	[2]	[2]	8,634
2004	600	[2]	[2]	[2]	[2]	780	1,620	[2]	[2]	649	[2]	[2]	8,255
2005	810	[2]	[2]	[2]	[2]	[2]	1,400	[2]	[2]	[2]	[2]	[2]	7,537
2006[1]	650	[2]	[2]	[2]	[2]	[2]	1,040	[2]	[2]	[2]	[2]	[2]	7,193

[1] Preliminary. [2] Estimates not published beginning in 2000. Source: Agricultural Statistics Board, U.S. Department of Agriculture (ASB-USDA)

Salient Statistics of Rye in the United States — In Thousands of Bushels

Crop Year Beginning June 1	Supply — Stocks June 1	Supply — Production	Supply — Imports	Supply — Total Supply	Domestic Use — Food	Domestic Use — Industry	Domestic Use — Seed	Domestic Use — Feed & Residual	Domestic Use — Total	Exports	Total Disappearance	Acreage — Planted 1,000 Acres	Acreage — Harvested for Grain 1,000 Acres	Yield Per Harvested Acre Bushels
1997-98	754	8,132	5,562	14,448	3,298	3,000	2,000	5,306	13,604	80	13,684	1,400	316	25.7
1998-99	764	12,161	3,322	16,247	3,639	3,000	3,000	4,392	14,031	33	14,064	1,566	418	29.1
1999-00	2,449	11,038	3,424	16,911	3,300	3,000	3,000	5,736	15,036	286	15,322	1,582	383	28.8
2000-01	1,589	8,386	3,230	13,205	3,300	3,000	3,000	2,307	11,607	390	11,997	1,329	296	28.3
2001-02	1,190	6,971	4,945	13,106	3,300	3,000	3,000	2,970	12,270	193	12,463	1,328	255	27.3
2002-03	568	6,488	6,140	13,196	3,300	3,000	3,000	3,329	12,629	122	12,751	1,355	263	24.8
2003-04	445	8,634	3,286	12,365	3,300	3,000	3,000	2,425	11,725	60	11,785	1,348	319	27.1
2004-05[1]	584	8,255	5,626	14,465	3,300	3,000	3,000	4,237	13,537	145	13,682	1,380	300	27.5
2005-06[2]	783	7,537	4,500	12,820	3,300	3,000	3,000	2,900	12,200	100	12,300	1,433	279	27.0
2006-07[3]		7,193										1,396	274	26.3

[1] Preliminary. [2] Estimate. [3] Forecast Source: Economic Research Service, U.S. Department of Agriculture (ERS-USDA)

Salt

Salt, also known as sodium chloride, is a chemical compound that is an essential element in the diet of humans, animals, and even many plants. Since prehistoric times, salt has been used to preserve foods and was commonly used in the religious rites of the Greeks, Romans, Hebrews, and Christians. Salt, in the form of salt cakes, served as money in ancient Ethiopia and Tibet. As long ago as 1450 BC, Egyptian art shows records of salt production.

The simplest method of obtaining salt is through the evaporation of salt water from areas near oceans or seas. In most regions, rock salt is obtained from underground mining or by wells sunk into deposits. Salt is soluble in water, is slightly soluble in alcohol, but is insoluble in concentrated hydrochloric acid. In its crystalline form, salt is transparent and colorless, shining with an ice-like luster.

Prices – Salt prices in 2005 (vacuum and open pan, FOB mine) rose +1.8% yr/yr to $130.75 per ton, which was a new record high.

Supply – World production of salt in 2005, the last full reporting year, rose +3.9% yr/yr to 238.0 million metric tons. The world's largest salt producers are the US and China, both with 19% of world production in 2005. US salt production in 2005 fell –2.8% yr/yr to 45.200 million metric tons.

Demand – US consumption of salt in 2005 fell –3.9% to 53.600 million metric tons, down from the 2004 record high of 55.800 million metric tons.

Trade – The US relied on imports for 16% of its salt consumption in 2006, down from 21% in 2005. US imports of salt for consumption in 2005 rose +0.8% yr/yr to 12.000 million metric tons, but still below 2003's record high of 12.9 million metric tons. US exports of salt in 2005 fell by –29.4% to 879 million metric tons, with the bulk of those exports (686,000 metric tons) going to Canada.

World Production of All Salt   In Thousands of Metric Tons

Year	Australia	Canada	China	France	Germany	India	Italy	Mexico	Poland	Spain	United Kingdom	United States	World Total
1998	9,033	13,296	22,420	7,000	15,700	11,964	3,600	8,412	4,005	3,500	6,600	41,300	200,000
1999	9,888	12,686	28,124	7,000	15,700	14,453	3,600	8,236	1,623	3,200	5,800	45,000	207,000
2000	8,778	12,164	31,280	7,000	937	14,453	3,600	8,884	1,576	3,200	5,800	45,600	195,000
2001	9,536	13,725	34,105	7,000	14,343	14,503	3,600	8,501	3,476	3,200	5,800	44,800	214,000
2002	9,887	12,736	36,024	7,000	15,632	14,503	3,600	7,802	3,558	3,200	5,800	40,300	212,000
2003	9,800	13,718	32,424	7,000	16,300	15,003	3,600	7,547	4,660	3,200	5,800	43,700	218,000
2004[1]	11,221	14,125	37,101	7,000	18,696	15,003	3,600	8,566	5,142	3,200	5,800	46,500	229,000
2005[2]	12,384	14,500	44,547	7,000	18,700	15,503	3,600	9,242	5,000	3,200	5,800	45,200	238,000

[1] Preliminary.   [2] Estimate.   Source: U.S. Geological Survey (USGS)

Salient Statistics of the Salt Industry in the United States   In Thousands of Metric Tons

Year	Net Import Reliance as a % of Apparent Consumption	Average Value FOB Mine Vacuum & Open Pan $ Per Ton	Production Total	Open & Vacuum Pan	Solar	Rock	Sold or Used Producers Open & Vacuum Pan Brine	Rock Salt	Brine	Total Salt	Value[3] Million $	Imports for Consumption	Exports Total	To Canada	Apparent Consumption
1998	17	114.93	41,200	4,040	3,190	12,900	21,100	4,040	12,700	21,100	40,800	986.0	8,770	731	533	48,800
1999	16	112.49	44,900	4,190	3,580	14,400	22,700	4,190	14,700	22,700	44,400	1,110.0	8,870	892	730	52,400
2000	15	113.95	45,600	4,200	3,810	15,000	22,500	4,190	13,600	22,500	43,300	1,040.0	8,960	642	500	51,600
2001	17	120.02	44,800	4,120	3,310	17,000	20,400	4,090	14,600	20,400	42,200	1,110.0	12,900	1,120	984	54,000
2002	18	120.02	40,300	4,100	3,390	13,500	19,300	4,070	11,400	19,300	37,700	1,010.0	8,160	689	585	45,100
2003	23	124.24	43,700	4,070	3,330	16,300	20,000	4,010	14,100	20,000	41,100	1,130.0	12,900	718	585	53,200
2004[1]	20	128.39	46,500	4,100	3,520	18,300	20,500	4,040	17,400	20,500	45,000	1,270.0	11,900	1,110	971	55,800
2005[2]	21	130.75	45,900	4,170	3,430	17,700	19,900	3,970	18,100	19,800	45,000	1,310.0	12,000	879	686	53,600

[1] Preliminary.   [2] Estimate.   [3] Values are f.o.b. mine or refinery & do not include cost of cooperage or containers.   Source: U.S. Geological Survey

Salt Sold or Used by Producers in the U.S. by Classes & Consumers or Uses In Thousands of Metric Tons

Year	Chemical[2]	Tanning Leather	Textile & Dyeing	Meat Packers	Canning	Baking	Agricultural Distribution	Feed Dealers	Feed Manufacturers	Rubber	Oil	Paper & Pulp	Metal Processing	Water Treatment	Grocery Stores	Water Conditioning Distrib.	Ice Control and/or Stabilization
1998	22,000	93	250	440	275	219	362	1,190	536	68	2,320	115	170	531	807	598	9,490
1999	22,400	103	235	405	225	234	254	1,210	533	72	2,430	112	153	899	831	600	15,300
2000	22,400	82	209	402	220	234	262	1,240	540	71	2,510	106	112	589	823	568	19,700
2001	20,100	87	172	411	213	242	280	1,170	533	61	2,260	100	124	512	824	560	16,800
2002	19,500	79	154	395	230	215	245	1,040	507	61	2,010	93	118	662	781	525	13,300
2003	20,100	71	151	374	231	210	215	1,090	460	67	2,210	88	126	777	802	537	18,500
2004	20,400	56	145	385	225	209	242	1,090	451	69	2,350	86	112	858	794	514	18,000
2005[1]	19,700	55	149	398	211	204	227	1,140	477	65	2,210	81	107	1,140	803	511	21,000

[1] Preliminary.   [2] Chloralkali producers and other chemical.   Source: U.S. Geological Survey (USGS)

Sheep & Lambs

Sheep and lambs are raised for both their wool and meat. In countries that have high wool production, there is also demand for sheep and lamb meat due to the easy availability. Production levels have declined in New Zealand and Australia, but that has been counteracted by a substantial increase in China.

Prices – The average monthly price received by farmers for lambs in the US in 2006 fell by -15.3% to 93.70 cents per pound, but remained above the 10-year low of 67.61 cents seen in 2001. The average monthly price received by US farmers for sheep in 2006 fell by -24.8% to 34.56 cents per pound, but remained above the 12-year low of 29.03 cents in 2002. The average monthly wholesale price of slaughter lambs (choice) at San Angelo, Texas in 2005 fell by -20.9% to 77.31 cents per pound, down from last year's record high of 97.76 cents per pound.

Supply – World sheep and goat numbers in 2004 rose by +2.1% to a new record high of 1.851 billion. The world's largest producers of sheep and goats are China with 18% of world production in 2004, India (10%), Australia (6%), and New Zealand (2%). The number of sheep and lambs on US farms in 2007 (Jan 1) fell –0.7% to 6.185 million head, but up slightly from the 2004 record low of 6.105 million head. The US states with the most sheep and lambs were Texas (with 17% of the US total), California (10%), Wyoming (7%), Colorado (7%), and South Dakota (6%).

World Sheep and Goat Numbers in Specified Countries on January 1   In Thousands of Head

Year	Argentina	Australia	China	India	Kazak-hstan	New Zealand	Romania	Russia	South Africa	Spain	Turkey	United Kingdom	World Total
1995	21,626	121,100	240,528	171,626	25,132	50,135	12,119	34,500	33,385	23,058	43,000	29,484	874,912
1996	17,956	121,200	279,535	173,519	19,600	48,816	11,086	28,336	35,145	21,322	42,400	28,797	897,009
1997	17,295	120,228	236,961	175,976	13,742	47,394	10,317	23,519	35,830	23,981	41,100	28,256	842,179
1998	15,232	117,494	255,055	178,462	10,896	46,970	9,747	20,697	36,821	24,857	39,500	30,027	853,061
1999	13,953	117,091	268,143	180,130	9,556	46,150	9,167	18,213	34,910	24,199	37,300	31,080	897,310
2000	17,550	113,310	298,464	182,800	10,479	43,325	7,776	15,327	35,939	27,415	33,994	35,832	1,777,382
2001	16,887	116,495	290,521	181,700	9,981	45,568	8,195	14,772	35,350	27,230	35,693	36,697	1,772,173
2002	16,400	106,600	297,370	182,800	10,479	39,700	7,776	15,327	35,939	27,415	33,994	35,834	1,776,729
2003[1]	16,650	101,420	316,714	181,886	11,273	39,707	7,945	16,051	32,178	26,650	31,954	35,846	1,812,446
2004[2]	16,650	104,400	340,693	182,500	12,247	39,408	8,086	17,030	31,732	25,505	32,203	35,890	1,851,394

[1] Preliminary.   [2] Forecast.   Source: Foreign Agricultural Service, U.S. Department of Agriculture (FAS-USDA)

Salient Statistics of Sheep & Lambs in the United States (Average Live Weight)   In Thousands of Head

| | -- Inventory, Jan. 1 -- | | | | --- Marketings[3] --- | | ---------- Slaughter ---------- | | | Net Exports | Total Disap-pearance | Pro-duction (Live Weight) Mil. Lbs. | Farm Value ---------- Jan. 1 ---------- | |
Year	Without New Crop Lambs	With New Crop Lambs	Lamb Crop	Total Supply	Sheep	Lambs	Farm	Com-mercial	Total[4]				All Million $	$ Per Head
1998	7,825	7,825	5,013	12,838	977	5,510	57	3,804	3,861	618	5,260	555.7	797.8	102.0
1999	7,215	7,215	4,733	11,948	790	5,208	65	3,701	3,766	393	4,922	533.6	637.6	88.0
2000	7,032	7,032	4,622	11,654	788	4,827	67	3,460	3,527	329	4,554	508.9	668.8	95.0
2001	6,965	6,965	4,495	11,460	711	4,795	68	3,222	3,290	299	4,303	495.6	694.5	100.0
2002	6,685	6,685	4,357	11,042	855	4,794	66	3,286	3,352	266	4,380	485.1	618.1	94.0
2003	6,300	6,321	4,140	10,461	828	4,387	67	2,979	3,046	105	3,804	470.1	656.6	104.0
2004	6,105	6,105	4,096	10,201	695	4,184	65	2,839	2,904			464.0	723.8	119.0
2005[1]	6,135	6,135	4,117	10,252	671	4,206	64	2,698	2,762			475.5	799.3	130.0
2006[2]	6,230	6,230	4,085	10,315									875.5	141.0

[1] Preliminary.   [2] Estimate.   [3] Excludes interfarm sales.   [4] Includes all commercial and farm.   Source: Economic Research Service, U.S. Department of Agriculture (ERS-USDA)

Sheep and Lambs[3] on Farms in the United States on January 1   In Thousands of Head

Year	California	Colorado	Idaho	Iowa	Minnesota	Montana	New Mexico	Ohio	South Dakota	Texas	Utah	Wyoming	Total
1999	810	440	265	260	175	380	275	125	420	1,350	400	630	7,215
2000	800	440	275	265	165	370	290	134	420	1,200	400	570	7,032
2001	840	420	275	270	170	360	255	142	420	1,150	390	530	6,965
2002	800	370	260	250	160	335	230	150	400	1,130	365	480	6,685
2003	730	380	260	255	145	310	175	150	380	1,040	310	460	6,300
2004	680	360	260	250	140	300	160	140	370	1,100	265	430	6,105
2005	670	365	270	245	145	305	145	142	375	1,070	270	450	6,135
2006[1]	650	390	260	235	155	295	155	141	385	1,090	280	450	6,230
2007[2]	610	400	260	235	150	290	130	141	380	1,070	295	460	6,185

[1] Preliminary.   [2] Estimate.   [3] Includes sheep & lambs on feed for market and stock sheep & lambs.   Source: Economic Research Service, U.S. Department of Agriculture (ERS-USDA)

SHEEP & LAMBS

Average Wholesale Price of Slaughter Lambs (Choice) at San Angelo Texas   In Dollars Per Cwt.

Year	Jan.	Feb.	Mar.	Apr.	May	June	July	Aug.	Sept.	Oct.	Nov.	Dec.	Average
1998	74.38	74.31	71.50	63.00	73.00	91.21	82.21	82.05	69.50	67.20	63.33	71.44	73.59
1999	69.31	67.88	68.54	70.50	82.70	81.06	77.29	81.17	77.00	74.81	78.00	83.29	75.96
2000	73.71	76.83	78.17	78.25	89.65	78.30	84.17	82.20	82.00	77.50	76.70	75.33	79.40
2001	81.25	87.00	82.63	83.30	86.07	75.21	69.82	54.47	56.50	57.67	59.00	71.60	72.04
2002	65.85	70.00	64.00	65.15	64.06	68.75	75.83	74.35	73.69	76.20	83.00	86.88	72.31
2003	89.25	90.25	96.25	88.13	95.75	97.25	87.88	85.81	91.44	91.31	91.00	96.17	91.71
2004	99.44	99.94	102.50	92.31	97.50	101.37	97.50	91.12	92.25	91.75	95.58	99.12	96.70
2005	107.25	109.69	101.37	99.37	96.94	99.50	95.00	92.14	91.56	93.00	93.33	94.00	97.76
2006[1]	86.75	76.87	67.47	60.60	68.16	70.94	74.00	84.00	85.30	85.18	85.40	83.00	77.31

[1] Preliminary.   Source: Economic Research Service, U.S. Department of Agriculture (ERS-USDA)

Federally Inspected Slaughter of Sheep & Lambs in the United States   In Thousands of Head

Year	Jan.	Feb.	Mar.	Apr.	May	June	July	Aug.	Sept.	Oct.	Nov.	Dec.	Total
1998	301	300	377	367	270	283	269	263	295	312	290	344	3,671
1999	260	291	411	295	260	259	253	283	294	293	317	341	3,557
2000	271	284	334	330	248	247	229	269	257	266	286	287	3,308
2001	258	236	316	275	227	221	229	258	230	274	273	266	3,065
2002	244	244	311	263	267	216	241	246	259	284	255	262	3,092
2003	227	211	252	280	209	216	225	226	241	251	223	246	2,805
2004	207	199	295	238	175	220	207	219	231	228	228	229	2,676
2005	195	204	268	208	198	210	188	216	219	217	213	219	2,555
2006[1]	210	193	240	236	215	200	191	213	205	223	212	212	2,549

[1] Preliminary.   Source: Economic Research Service, U.S. Department of Agriculture (ERS-USDA)

Cold Storage Holdings of Lamb and Mutton in the U.S., on First of Month   In Thousands of Pounds

Year	Jan.	Feb.	Mar.	Apr.	May	June	July	Aug.	Sept.	Oct.	Nov.	Dec.
1998	13,741	13,920	15,284	16,226	16,306	16,666	16,040	16,188	14,530	12,253	12,558	11,914
1999	11,721	10,452	12,134	12,374	13,146	12,313	12,459	11,975	12,240	9,815	9,210	9,446
2000	8,740	10,394	10,335	11,437	13,345	13,137	13,984	13,557	14,042	12,867	12,195	12,486
2001	13,455	13,833	13,141	13,729	13,551	14,586	15,443	15,744	15,266	13,979	13,238	11,336
2002	11,905	13,110	11,269	10,528	13,172	12,938	13,553	14,215	14,458	11,961	12,004	9,255
2003	7,124	6,232	4,063	3,900	5,016	5,838	5,427	5,929	5,855	6,210	4,485	4,883
2004	3,795	3,671	3,355	3,164	3,251	3,504	3,872	3,376	3,878	4,179	4,166	3,715
2005	3,497	7,549	7,585	7,650	8,739	9,719	9,362	11,756	11,790	10,942	10,137	9,332
2006[1]	9,967	15,730	11,887	10,911	10,345	10,248	9,951	10,360	10,583	10,082	10,216	10,634

[1] Preliminary.   Source: Economic Research Service, U.S. Department of Agriculture (ERS-USDA)

Average Price Received by Farmers for Sheep in the United States   In Dollars Per Cwt.

Year	Jan.	Feb.	Mar.	Apr.	May	June	July	Aug.	Sept.	Oct.	Nov.	Dec.	Average
1998	42.00	39.60	41.00	34.40	30.30	30.20	29.40	28.30	26.80	26.10	26.40	30.10	32.05
1999	32.40	30.20	32.70	31.80	31.50	28.90	32.00	29.80	29.20	26.40	30.20	33.40	30.71
2000	36.80	39.50	38.80	35.00	30.50	30.00	34.20	30.70	30.30	29.50	33.60	36.20	33.76
2001	43.30	47.50	46.60	36.90	36.30	31.70	34.10	32.20	29.90	27.20	27.10	34.00	35.57
2002	36.20	34.30	31.80	26.00	25.30	23.50	25.60	25.60	24.50	25.60	31.30	38.70	29.03
2003	41.30	44.00	40.90	31.10	31.30	29.40	28.60	29.20	32.50	35.00	40.50	45.10	35.74
2004	43.80	40.80	36.70	36.70	36.00	31.30	37.10	37.30	41.20	40.40	41.40	44.60	38.94
2005	53.50	52.40	49.00	45.10	43.70	41.20	41.00	43.00	43.70	43.60	46.20	49.30	45.98
2006[1]	47.70	46.00	39.50	34.90	33.20	28.60	27.40	28.40	31.70	31.10	30.90	35.30	34.56

[1] Preliminary.   Source: Economic Research Service, U.S. Department of Agriculture (ERS-USDA)

Average Price Received by Farmers for Lambs in the United States   In Dollars Per Cwt.

Year	Jan.	Feb.	Mar.	Apr.	May	June	July	Aug.	Sept.	Oct.	Nov.	Dec.	Average
1998	78.40	75.00	70.10	66.00	63.00	88.90	81.30	80.10	71.80	67.60	62.60	64.70	72.46
1999	68.20	67.20	67.40	67.40	82.80	81.30	77.00	80.30	75.30	72.60	76.30	77.60	74.45
2000	70.90	72.00	80.20	82.60	96.40	89.70	87.00	83.60	80.80	76.80	71.50	71.80	80.28
2001	74.10	80.10	84.00	84.30	80.00	71.60	64.30	54.80	52.50	51.40	52.80	61.40	67.61
2002	65.50	67.80	66.70	64.70	64.40	72.90	75.60	75.30	76.30	79.60	84.00	87.20	73.33
2003	92.00	92.40	97.10	93.70	97.60	89.30	89.40	88.60	95.10	96.80	99.70	97.70	94.12
2004	104.00	106.00	103.00	100.00	103.00	105.00	101.00	97.90	100.00	97.70	99.90	101.00	101.54
2005	114.00	114.00	114.00	114.00	114.00	114.00	110.00	109.00	110.00	108.00	107.00	100.00	110.67
2006[1]	96.10	96.80	91.10	86.80	88.90	92.00	93.10	94.80	98.50	98.10	95.00	93.20	93.70

[1] Preliminary.   Source: Economic Research Service, U.S. Department of Agriculture (ERS-USDA)

Silk

Silk is a fine, tough, elastic fiber produced by caterpillars, commonly called silkworms. Silk is one of the oldest known textile fibers. Chinese tradition credits Lady Hsi-Ling-Shih, wife of the Emperor Huang Ti, with the discovery of the silkworm and the invention of the first silk reel. Dating to around 3000 BC, a group of ribbons, threads, and woven fragments was found in China. Also found, along the lower Yangzi River, were 7,000 year-old spinning tools, silk thread, and fabric fragments.

Silk filament was first woven into cloth in Ancient China. The Chinese successfully guarded this secret until 300AD, when Japan, and later India, learned the secret. In 550 AD, two Nestorian monks were sent to China to steal mulberry seeds and silkworm eggs, which they hid in their walking staffs, and then brought them back to Rome. By the 17th century, France was the silk center of the West. Unfortunately, the silkworm did not flourish in the English climate, nor has it ever flourished in the US.

Sericulture is the term for the raising of silkworms. The blind, flightless moth, Bombyx mori, lays more than 500 tiny eggs. After hatching, the tiny worms eat chopped mulberry leaves continuously until they are ready to spin their cocoons. After gathering the complete cocoons, the first step in silk manufacturing is to kill the insects inside the cocoons with heat. The cocoons are then placed in boiling water to loosen the gummy substance, sericin, holding the filament together. The filament is unwound, and then rewound in a process called reeling. Each cocoon's silk filament is between 600 and 900 meters long. Four different types of silk thread may be produced: organzine, crepe, tram, and thrown singles. During the last 30 years, in spite of the use of man-made fibers, world silk production has doubled.

Raw silk is traded on the Kansai Agricultural Commodities Exchange (KANEX) in Japan. Dried cocoons are traded on the Chuba Commodity Exchange (CCE). Raw silk and dried cocoons are traded on the Yokohama Commodity Exchange.

Supply – World production of silk in 2002, the latest reporting year, rose +0.8% to 132,000 metric tons, which was a record high and sharply above the 12-year low of 85,000 posted in 1997. China is the world's largest producer of silk by far with 71% of world production in 2002. Other key producers include India with 11% of world production, Vietnam (9%), and Turkmenistan (3%).

Trade – In 2003, the latest reporting year, the world's largest exporters of silk were China with 62% of world exports, Japan with 2.4%, and Brazil with 1.5%.

In 2003, the world's largest importers of silk were India (with 33% of world imports), Italy (13%), Japan (10%), and South Korea (6%).

World Production of Raw Silk   In Metric Tons

Year	Brazil	China	India	Iran	Japan	North Korea	South Korea	Kyrgy-zstan	Thailand	Turkmen-istan	Uzbek-istan	Viet Nam	World Total
1993	2,450	76,801	14,168	480	4,254	4,600	683	1,000	1,500	500	2,000	550	109,790
1994	2,450	84,001	14,500	600	2,400	4,700	700	1,000	1,600	500	2,000	600	115,796
1995	2,450	80,001	15,000	600	2,400	4,700	700	1,000	1,600	500	2,000	650	112,350
1996	2,000	51,000	16,000	1,000	3,000	5,000	----	1,000	1,000	5,000	2,000	1,000	88,000
1997	2,000	51,000	16,000	1,000	2,000	4,000	----	1,000	1,000	5,000	2,000	1,000	85,000
1998	2,000	68,000	16,000	1,000	1,000	5,000	----	1,000	1,000	5,000	2,000	1,000	102,000
1999	2,000	70,000	16,000	1,000	1,000	5,000	----	1,000	1,000	5,000	1,000	1,000	98,000
2000	2,000	78,000	15,000	1,000	1,000	5,000	----	1,000	1,000	5,000	1,000	3,000	107,000
2001[1]	2,000	94,000	15,000	1,000	1,000	----	----	1,000	2,000	5,000	1,000	10,000	131,000
2002[2]	1,000	94,000	15,000	1,000	1,000	----	----	----	2,000	4,000	1,000	12,000	132,000

[1] Preliminary. [2] Estimate.   *Source: Food and Agricultural Organization of the United Nations (FAO-UN)*

World Trade of Silk by Selected Countries   In Metric Tons

	Imports							Exports					
Year	France	Hong Kong	India	Italy	Japan	South Korea	World Total	Brazil	China	Hong Kong	Japan	North Korea	World Total
1994	1,047	6,165	5,750	9,235	5,772	4,128	44,136	1,739	21,004	6,149	1,265	1,400	41,998
1995	663	4,775	4,276	5,612	4,331	3,513	37,854	966	16,788	5,176	925	1,000	40,633
1996	675	3,978	2,980	4,400	6,098	3,737	37,615	1,071	15,791	4,165	946	1,000	38,587
1997	582	4,320	2,437	5,482	4,229	2,796	45,817	905	14,384	4,501	936	1,000	37,233
1998	592	2,030	2,846	4,088	3,357	1,510	31,908	780	12,250	2,105	612	180	29,611
1999	579	1,258	5,120	4,985	3,792	2,265	35,352	408	16,251	1,153	227	130	35,041
2000	481	866	4,732	5,906	4,020	1,843	32,279	370	17,520	936	239	120	35,033
2001	452	256	6,929	4,506	2,823	1,628	26,876	232	14,485	259	124	90	26,329
2002	706	51	9,266	3,498	2,853	2,108	26,877	331	17,842	128	116	170	30,767
2003[1]	312	88	9,539	3,687	2,852	1,704	28,810	416	17,264	43	684	296	27,935

[1] Preliminary.   *Source: Food and Agricultural Organization of the United Nations (FAO-UN)*

Silver

Silver is a white, lustrous metallic element that conducts heat and electricity better than any other metal. In ancient times, many silver deposits were on or near the earth's surface. Before 2,500 BC, silver mines were worked in Asia Minor. Around 700 BC, ancient Greeks stamped a turtle on their first silver coins. Silver assumed a key role in the US monetary system in 1792 when Congress based the currency on the silver dollar. However, the US discontinued the use of silver in coinage in 1965. Today Mexico is the only country that uses silver in its circulating coinage.

Silver is the most malleable and ductile of all metals, with the exception of gold. Silver melts at about 962 degrees Celsius and boils at about 2212 degrees Celsius. Silver is not very chemically active, although tarnishing occurs when sulfur and sulfides attack silver, forming silver sulfide on the surface of the metal. Because silver is too soft in its pure form, a hardening agent, usually copper, is mixed into the silver. Copper is usually used as the hardening agent because it does not discolor the silver. The term "sterling silver" refers to silver that contains at least 925 parts of silver per thousand (92.5%) to 75 parts of copper (7.5%).

Silver is usually found combined with other elements in minerals and ores. In the US, silver is mined in conjunction with lead, copper, and zinc. In the US, Nevada, Idaho, Alaska, and Arizona are the leading silver-producing states. For industrial purposes, silver is used for photography, electrical appliances, glass, and as an antibacterial agent for the health industry.

Silver futures and options are traded on the Comex division of the New York Mercantile Exchange, the Chicago Board of Trade (CBOT), and the London Metal Exchange (LME). Silver futures are traded on the Tokyo Commodity Exchange (TOCOM). The Nymex silver futures contract calls for the delivery of 5,000 troy ounces of silver (0.999 fineness) and is priced in terms of dollars and cents per troy ounce.

Prices – Nymex silver futures prices rallied sharply in early 2006 to post a new 26-year high of $14.97 per troy ounce, which meant that silver prices more than tripled from the $4 level seen in 2001. The highest month-end price ever posted for cash silver was about $38 per troy ounce back in January 1980. Silver futures prices then fell sharply in June 2006 on a downward correction and a washout of speculators. However, silver futures prices then rallied during the remainder of 2006 on strong demand, finally closing the year at $12.935 per ounce, +14.6% on the year. Demand for silver remained strong in 2006 for jewelry, for industrial purposes (particularly in China where GDP growth was over 10% again), and for investment demand where silver Exchange Traded Funds snapped up physical silver to back their funds. Silver mining has increased but not by enough to satisfy demand tomkeep silver prices from rising.

Supply – World mine production of silver in 2005, the latest reporting year for the series, rose +2.0% yr/yr to a new record high of 20,200 metric tons, continuing to show some improvement after flat production figures in 2000-03. The world's largest silver producers are Peru with 16% of world production in 2005, Mexico (14%), China (12%), Australia (10%), Chili, (7%), and the US (6%). US production of refined silver in 2006 (through November, annualized) fell by -9.5% to 5,115 metric tons, but remained above the 10-year low of 4,442 metric tons seen in 2004.

Demand – US consumption of silver in 2003, the latest reporting year, fell –1.0% yr/yr to 175.3 million troy ounces. The largest consumption of silver is for photographic materials with 35% of total usage, followed by electrical contacts and conductors (23%), jewelry (9%), coinage (7%), and brazing alloys and solders (5%). The world's largest consuming nation of silver for industrial purposes is the US with 20% of world consumption in 2004, followed by Japan (16%), India (10%), and Italy (7%).

Trade – US exports of refined silver in 2005 fell –21.4% yr/yr to 9.709 million troy ounces, which was less that one tenth of the record high of 99.022 million troy ounces seen in 1997. The major destinations for US silver exports are Canada (38%), Switzerland (29%), and the UK (12%). US imports of silver ore and concentrates fell –80.5% yr/yr to 14,000 troy ounces in 2005. US imports of refined silver bullion rose +11.2% yr/yr to 134.387 million troy ounces in 2004. The bulk of those imports came from Mexico (65.908 million troy ounces), Canada (41.474 million troy ounces), and Peru (20.319 million troy ounces).

World Mine Production of Silver   In Thousands of Kilograms In Metric Tons

Year	Australia	Bolivia	Canada[3]	Chile	China	Kazak-hstan	Mexico	Peru	Poland	Russia	Sweden	United States	World Total[2]
1996	1,013	384	1,309	1,047	1,140	468	2,528	1,970	935	400	272	1,570	15,100
1997	1,106	387	1,224	1,091	1,300	690	2,679	2,090	1,038	400	304	2,180	16,500
1998	1,474	404	1,196	1,340	1,300	726	2,686	2,025	1,108	350	299	2,060	17,200
1999	1,720	422	1,174	1,381	1,320	905	2,467	2,231	1,100	375	284	1,950	17,100
2000	2,060	434	1,212	1,242	1,600	927	2,620	2,438	1,148	370	329	1,980	18,100
2001	1,970	411	1,320	1,349	1,910	982	2,760	2,571	1,194	380	306	1,740	18,700
2002	2,077	450	1,408	1,210	2,200	893	2,747	2,870	1,229	400	294	1,350	18,800
2003	1,868	465	1,310	1,313	2,400	827	2,569	2,921	1,237	700	307	1,240	18,800
2004[1]	2,183	407	1,337	1,360	2,450	733	2,569	3,060	1,344	1,277	293	1,250	19,800
2005[2]	2,047	419	1,122	1,400	2,500	832	2,894	3,193	1,300	1,350	267	1,230	20,200

[1] Preliminary.   [2] Estimate.   [3] Shipments.   *Source: U.S. Geological Survey (USGS)*

Silver (monthly average) through December 2006 — Cents per troy ounce

Cents Per Troy Ounce
----- Bullion, London (1833 - 1909)
Handy & Harman, New York (Jan. 1910 - May 1990)
Composite (June 1990 to date)

Average Price of Silver in New York (Handy & Harman)   In Cents Per Troy Ounce (.999 Fine)

Year	Jan.	Feb.	Mar.	Apr.	May	June	July	Aug.	Sept.	Oct.	Nov.	Dec.	Average
1997	483.70	508.76	519.88	476.41	475.80	474.60	435.96	451.36	472.69	501.15	507.30	571.53	489.07
1998	584.58	672.61	617.18	628.86	558.65	526.05	546.82	516.45	502.67	500.18	498.39	476.85	552.68
1999	511.61	554.55	519.85	509.21	529.83	507.73	522.81	529.36	527.86	541.67	519.20	521.95	524.75
2000	523.47	529.65	510.15	510.37	504.30	505.20	501.82	492.76	494.50	488.14	471.93	466.40	499.89
2001	470.19	457.34	439.93	439.25	443.59	436.79	425.45	420.72	441.09	441.87	412.35	437.98	438.88
2002	450.17	444.79	457.00	460.50	473.55	492.13	494.57	456.16	458.93	442.28	453.87	465.78	462.39
2003	485.62	468.11	454.74	453.40	475.29	455.62	486.48	502.90	520.62	503.91	520.64	565.33	491.06
2004	637.13	647.71	729.48	708.57	589.19	588.38	637.55	670.98	641.93	717.55	751.43	712.43	669.36
2005	665.45	709.18	728.50	715.74	705.29	733.64	704.40	702.72	719.33	769.90	786.35	865.88	733.87
2006	918.48	952.13	1,037.52	1,263.71	1,337.84	1,077.41	1,121.24	1,225.39	1,159.93	1,161.55	1,298.45	1,329.83	1,156.96

Source: American Metal Market (AMM)

Average Price of Silver in London (Spot Fix)   In Pence Per Troy Ounce (.999 Fine)

Year	Jan.	Feb.	Mar.	Apr.	May	June	July	Aug.	Sept.	Oct.	Nov.	Dec.	Average
1997	287.63	311.95	323.99	293.08	291.43	289.16	272.73	280.36	295.67	308.69	300.76	348.90	300.36
1998	359.62	416.55	375.76	378.77	339.42	319.05	331.87	317.74	297.40	295.41	298.72	291.77	335.17
1999	312.69	340.46	320.27	315.12	326.80	315.51	328.86	327.98	322.20	326.42	317.53	319.87	322.75
2000	316.08	327.90	320.87	319.61	330.53	331.24	329.35	327.80	340.75	332.24	327.71	317.47	326.94
2001	315.87	312.57	304.50	304.36	310.19	309.54	300.97	277.97	297.93	289.21	286.92	306.25	302.43
2002	315.08	310.55	318.27	316.61	322.58	329.32	316.07	295.93	292.38	282.49	286.93	291.52	306.48
2003	297.21	289.23	287.39	285.06	292.05	272.79	295.53	313.01	320.30	298.01	306.53	320.48	298.13
2004	347.36	339.49	395.67	391.14	327.03	320.36	342.32	368.78	356.35	392.94	402.52	368.43	362.70
2005	354.28	375.57	382.74	377.48	380.46	403.56	402.10	391.55	397.90	436.23	453.10	496.09	404.26
2006	519.94	544.76	594.70	714.36	715.69	584.44	607.69	647.19	615.09	618.97	678.96	677.31	626.59

Source: American Metal Market (AMM)

SILVER

Average Open Interest of Silver Futures in New York (COMEX)   In Contracts

Year	Jan.	Feb.	Mar.	Apr.	May	June	July	Aug.	Sept.	Oct.	Nov.	Dec.
1997	91,385	94,539	90,531	97,434	87,510	90,145	96,777	89,250	79,344	100,464	96,695	93,761
1998	95,717	108,284	91,730	83,045	79,451	91,563	78,353	82,530	74,848	74,451	76,440	78,716
1999	77,946	97,593	82,435	82,824	78,745	78,943	78,151	86,601	77,490	86,577	80,564	70,275
2000	76,187	81,398	75,765	76,213	75,001	76,466	75,199	91,083	73,441	78,222	83,142	73,644
2001	69,408	72,798	74,337	71,589	67,328	67,429	75,019	75,830	65,533	66,530	74,228	66,903
2002	67,442	65,355	67,405	76,158	82,525	100,837	94,731	82,349	80,511	89,094	85,434	78,174
2003	98,561	94,472	84,485	87,445	85,232	80,001	91,544	108,118	110,423	92,216	101,303	103,007
2004	109,860	113,764	117,848	113,172	90,493	87,201	89,062	97,844	85,245	108,762	121,221	107,136
2005	97,744	98,644	101,200	103,562	104,680	124,317	124,521	121,133	117,121	135,335	146,409	136,502
2006	131,767	129,928	132,140	137,121	110,400	110,631	98,733	110,635	102,159	105,167	114,132	105,741

Source: New York Mercantile Exchange (NYMEX), COMEX Division

Volume of Trading of Silver Futures in New York (COMEX)   In Contracts

Year	Jan.	Feb.	Mar.	Apr.	May	June	July	Aug.	Sept.	Oct.	Nov.	Dec.	Total
1997	401,995	530,514	360,871	493,999	280,536	472,306	340,245	425,471	335,400	430,397	488,024	333,762	4,893,520
1998	352,688	550,800	368,127	360,130	310,130	393,971	278,774	367,257	283,475	280,066	319,216	229,982	4,094,616
1999	315,165	550,271	355,559	424,822	274,002	373,662	288,480	422,653	328,907	318,256	344,289	161,434	4,157,500
2000	258,053	425,910	231,336	318,752	216,938	407,455	175,235	370,739	146,007	149,252	303,673	113,667	3,117,017
2001	175,026	302,035	155,658	252,486	204,552	281,846	112,956	267,711	160,329	210,266	266,077	180,256	2,569,198
2002	265,773	271,293	163,898	325,889	243,475	389,798	281,214	296,579	164,537	209,249	292,861	230,998	3,135,564
2003	291,120	409,737	216,660	315,240	251,096	352,729	407,931	442,762	335,508	373,493	464,244	250,835	4,111,355
2004	385,058	544,939	408,447	671,204	278,703	425,501	316,264	427,973	281,737	364,158	541,366	360,775	5,006,125
2005	285,449	513,617	370,338	485,832	392,156	621,647	334,903	600,961	455,033	424,972	652,917	398,526	5,536,351
2006	495,649	624,491	562,330	807,269	513,822	508,746	255,777	452,551	268,393	244,152	424,771	275,112	5,433,063

Source: New York Mercantile Exchange (NYMEX), COMEX division

Mine Production of Recoverable Silver in the United States In Metric Tons

Year	Arizona	California	Colorado	Idaho	Missouri	Montana	Nevada	New Mexico	South Dakota	Washington	Other States	Total
2000	W	8	3	W	W	W	734	W	W	2	1,240	1,980
2001	W	8	3	W	W	W	544	W	W	W	1,180	1,740
2002	W	3	W	W	W	W	424	W	W	W	927	1,350
2003	W	1	W	W	W	W	322	W	W	W	916	1,240
2004	W	1	W	W	W	W	302	W	W	W	943	1,250
2005[1]	W	W	W	W	W	W	276	W	W	W	949	1,230

[1] Preliminary.   W = Withheld proprietary data; included in Other States.   Source: U.S. Geological Survey (USGS)

Consumption of Silver in the United States, by End Use In Millions of Troy Ounces

Year	Brazing Alloy & Solders	Catalysts	Batteries	Mirrors	Electrical Contacts-Conductors	Photo-graphic Materials	Silver-plate	Jewerly	Sterling Ware	Total Net Industrial Con-sumption	Coinage	Total Con-sumption
1994	7.5	4.2	3.6	1.5	19.5	71.0	3.1	3.7	4.2	130.1	8.1	138.2
1995	7.7	4.9	4.1	1.7	20.9	72.9	3.5	4.1	4.4	136.2	7.5	143.7
1996	8.2	5.5	4.5	2.1	22.3	78.3	3.9	4.4	4.8	146.7	5.0	151.7
1997	8.9	5.7	4.8	2.4	26.5	84.6	4.1	4.9	5.1	160.5	5.3	165.8
1998	9.3	5.9	4.9	2.6	28.4	91.0	4.5	5.5	5.7	172.3	5.6	177.9
1999	9.1	5.9	5.0	2.6	29.2	96.0	4.4	5.7	5.8	178.5	10.0	188.5
2000	8.7	6.3	5.2	2.6	50.6	73.9	4.5	6.1	5.6	181.9	13.4	195.3
2001	8.3	6.1	5.3	2.5	34.1	65.8	4.0	4.9	4.6	157.6	12.3	169.9
2002	8.4	NA	NA	NA	37.6	66.2	[2]	[2]	NA	162.9	14.2	177.1
2003[1]	7.9	NA	NA	NA	39.5	61.6	[2]	[2]	NA	162.8	12.5	175.3

[1] Preliminary.   [2] Included in Jewelry.   Source: The Silver Institute

Commodity Exchange, Inc. (COMEX) Warehouse of Stocks of Silver In Thousands of Troy Ounces

Year	Jan. 1	Feb. 1	Mar. 1	Apr. 1	May 1	June 1	July 1	Aug. 1	Sept. 1	Oct. 1	Nov. 1	Dec. 1
1997	204,051	195,450	193,381	191,676	189,498	201,682	184,691	169,079	164,296	138,775	133,470	128,252
1998	110,437	103,778	89,458	86,926	89,715	89,628	85,911	79,136	78,681	73,142	74,260	76,818
1999	75,807	75,108	78,135	79,605	78,819	77,512	73,514	77,592	79,606	79,391	79,155	78,416
2000	75,945	73,948	93,782	104,259	102,589	99,285	102,713	102,291	97,879	99,552	95,749	95,717
2001	93,983	93,195	98,659	96,694	95,745	96,090	98,700	100,494	102,770	101,538	103,982	105,235
2002	104,547	102,395	100,983	102,540	104,526	107,766	105,938	105,563	108,090	107,495	107,440	107,090
2003	107,394	107,610	109,153	108,521	108,168	105,092	107,222	105,406	104,862	106,283	118,238	124,498
2004	124,271	124,181	123,195	122,087	122,687	118,442	118,369	116,253	109,311	107,789	104,624	102,831
2005	103,590	102,390	101,494	103,627	103,995	104,257	104,719	109,467	115,588	116,687	116,257	117,608
2006	119,974	124,793	127,898	125,763	123,627	108,443	102,268	102,086	103,634	105,451	105,313	107,770

Source: New York Mercantile Exchange (NYMEX), COMEX Division

Production[2] of Refined Silver in the United States, from All Sources In Metric Tons

Year	Jan.	Feb.	Mar.	Apr.	May	June	July	Aug.	Sept.	Oct.	Nov.	Dec.	Total
1997	343	262	296	331	250	326	292	344	331	281	340	382	3,778
1998	338	486	426	372	377	374	394	324	463	443	469	447	4,860
1999	424	420	441	356	368	394	404	316	354	371	364	396	4,608
2000	436	1,177	551	399	431	390	361	402	400	469	386	401	5,780
2001	405	343	405	360	360	331	395	380	338	403	442	383	4,545
2002	544	387	465	532	509	398	398	419	473	437	394	485	5,441
2003	483	426	320	412	357	431	430	373	361	809	363	471	5,235
2004	407	418	460	337	361	177	175	351	433	255	390	678	4,442
2005	402	505	515	568	450	558	556	440	356	376	485	439	5,650
2006[1]	506	434	500	444	382	553	490	432	350	388	209		5,115

[1] Preliminary.   [2] Includes U.S. mine production of recoverable silver plus imports of refined silver.   Source: U.S. Geological Survey (USGS)

SILVER

U.S. Exports of Refined Silver to Selected Countries   In Thousands of Troy Ounces

Year	Canada	France	Germany	Hong Kong	Japan	Singapore	South Korea	Switzerland	United Arab Emirates	United Kingdom	Uruguay	Other Countries	World Total
1996	489	[2]	2	646	4,662	3,601	383	2,413	15,850	35,366	624	40	93,346
1997	1,861	[2]	2	797	6,044	[2]	547	5,369	16,750	62,693	402	57	99,022
1998	669	2,205	347	45	585	210	----	604	3,569	62,693	688	38	80,375
1999	2,180	2	1	----	585	37	31	624	4,244	7,716	180	5	19,804
2000	1,906	22	2	----	3,504	1	----	727	----	3,311	109	1	12,217
2001	1,598	----	----	11	1,202	2	----	354	----	20,029	105	10,472	30,960
2002	466	----	1	4	466	10	----	727	----	14,532	----	12,937	28,196
2003	524	3	----	3	17	2	16	630	----	3,086	----	3,083	6,816
2004	7,009	1	3	24	585	166	1	2,321	----	3	108	9,912	12,346
2005[1]	3,729	----	25	3	1	95	18	2,829	----	1,145	563	1,302	9,709

[1] Preliminary.   [2] Included in other countries, if any.   *Source: American Bureau of Metal Statistics, Inc. (ABMS)*

U.S. Imports of Silver From Selected Countries   In Thousands of Troy Ounces

Year	Canada	Mexico	Other Countries	Total	Canada	Chile	Mexico	Peru	Uruguay	Other Countries	Total
1996	256	4,662	----	4,918	35,365	1,874	30,285	12,153	[2]	3,122	82,799
1997	7	4,437	90	4,533	29,385	608	28,774	8,873	----	518	68,158
1998	24	5,851	427	6,301	34,722	813	41,152	9,388	----	3,945	90,020
1999	11	334	2	347	43,403	1,048	33,115	5,433	----	2,521	85,519
2000	46	----	----	46	38,902	225	44,689	2,787	----	35,899	122,502
2001	243	----	----	243	44,046	2,054	41,152	5,498	----	1,771	94,521
2002	149	1,813	----	1,961	48,868	2,331	67,837	6,430	----	6,350	131,815
2003	82	----	----	82	41,795	1,987	62,050	18,261	----	12,223	136,316
2004	71	----	----	71	37,616	2,042	59,156	17,297	----	4,774	120,884
2005[1]	14	----	----	14	41,474	2,514	65,908	20,319	----	4,173	134,387

[1] Preliminary.   [2] Included in other countries, if any.   *Source: American Bureau of Metal Statistics, Inc. (ABMS)*

World Silver Consumption   In Millions of Troy Ounces

	Industrial Uses										Coinage							Grand
Year	Canada	France	Germany	India	Italy	Japan	Mexico	United Kingdom	United States	World Total	Austria	Canada	France	Germany	Mexico	United States	World Total	Total
1995	2.0	30.0	43.6	101.3	49.5	112.7	16.9	31.6	148.7	752.7	.5	.7	1.2	2.4	.6	9.0	24.7	777.4
1996	2.0	26.9	41.0	122.2	51.7	112.1	20.3	33.8	155.0	785.8	.5	.7	.3	4.6	.5	7.1	23.3	809.1
1997	2.2	28.3	42.3	122.9	56.1	119.9	23.3	34.9	166.3	828.2	.4	.6	.3	3.7	.4	6.5	28.5	856.7
1998	2.3	28.4	38.4	114.7	55.9	112.8	21.7	38.6	162.9	801.5	.3	1.1	.3	10.0	.2	7.0	27.8	829.3
1999	2.1	26.6	35.1	121.5	61.8	122.5	21.3	39.3	175.5	840.6	.3	1.4	.3	7.0	.4	10.7	29.2	869.8
2000	2.0	28.8	31.8	131.0	65.1	135.0	16.6	42.7	179.1	871.8	.3	1.0	.4	8.8	.6	13.4	32.1	904.0
2001	2.0	28.7	32.4	154.0	58.2	119.3	15.9	45.9	157.3	836.5	.3	.9	.4	8.1	1.1	12.3	30.5	867.0
2002	2.1	27.1	29.4	122.5	56.0	118.7	17.0	43.1	161.6	807.0	.4	1.0	.5	6.0	1.1	15.3	31.6	838.6
2003	2.2	25.6	29.4	122.5	55.0	115.9	18.7	44.1	160.8	817.5	.4	.3	.5	10.3	1.1	14.5	35.8	853.4
2004[2]	2.1	12.0	30.7	79.2	54.8	125.1	18.6	52.2	164.8	807.0	.5	1.3	.5	10.3	.9	15.5	41.1	836.6

[2] Preliminary.   *Source: The Silver Institute*

Soybean Meal

Soybean meal is produced through processing and separating soybeans into oil and meal components. By weight, soybean meal accounts for about 35% of the weight of raw soybeans (at 13% moisture). If the soybeans are of particularly good quality, then the processor can get more meal weight by including more hulls in the meal while still meeting the 48% protein minimum. Soybean meal can be further processed into soy flour and isolated soy protein, but the bulk of soybean meal is used as animal feed for poultry, hogs and cattle. Soybean meal accounts for about two-thirds of the world's high-protein animal feed, followed by cottonseed and rapeseed meal, which together account for less than 20%. Soybean meal consumption has been moving to record highs in recent years. The soybean meal marketing year begins in October and ends in September. Soybean meal futures and options are traded on the Chicago Board of Trade (CBOT). The CBOT soybean meal futures contract calls for the delivery of 100 tons of soybean meal produced by conditioning ground soybeans and reducing the oil content of the conditioned product and having a minimum of 48.0% protein, minimum of 0.5% fat, maximum of 3.5% fiber, and maximum of 12.0% moisture.

Soybean crush – The term soybean "crush" refers to both the physical processing of soybeans and also to the dollar-value premium received for processing soybeans into their component products of meal and oil. The conventional model says that processing 60 pounds (one bushel) of soybeans produces 11 pounds of soybean oil, 44 pounds of 48% protein soybean meal, 3 pounds of hulls, and 1 pound of waste. The Gross Processing Margin (GPM) or crush equals (0.22 times Soybean Meal Prices in dollars per ton) + (11 times Soybean Oil prices in cents/pound) – Soybean prices in $/bushel. A higher crush value will occur when the price of the meal and oil products are strong relative to soybeans, e.g., because of supply disruptions or because of an increase in demand for the products. When the crush value is high, companies will have a strong incentive to buy raw soybeans and boost the output of the products. That supply increase should eventually bring the crush value back into line with the long-term equilibrium.

Prices – Soybean meal futures prices at the Chicago Board of Trade in 2006 continued near the lower price range seen in late 2005. Prices at the beginning of 2006 were about $175 per ton, moved lower during the first quarter, rallied until June, but then moved lower to a low of $155.80 per ton in September. From there the price moved to a high of $202.80 in November, only to fall again in December to close the year at $191.00 per ton, up about 9% for the year. Regarding cash prices, the average price of soybean meal (48% solvent) in Decatur, Illinois in the first four months of the 2006-07 marketing year (i.e., October 2006 to February 2007) averaged $184.84 per short ton, up by +6.1%yr/yr.

Supply – World soybean meal production in 2006-07 rose +5.6% yr/yr to 152.974 million metric tons, which was a new record high. The world's largest soybean meal producers are the US with 25% of world production in 2006-07, China with 19%, Brazil with 14%, and the European Union with 7%.

US production of soybean meal in 2006-07 rose +2.8% yr/yr to a record high of 42.421 million short tons. US soybean meal stocks in 2006-07 (Oct 1) rose +45.2% yr/yr to a 5-year high of 314,000 short tons.

Demand – World consumption of soybean meal in 2006-07 rose +4.2% to 151.362 million metric tons, which was a new record high. The US accounted for 20% of that consumption and the European Union accounted for 22%. US consumption of soybean meal in 2006-07 rose +2.2% yr/yr to 30.754 million metric tons, which was a new record high.

Trade – World exports of soybean meal in 2006-07 rose +3.3% to 53.078 million metric tons, which was a new record high. Brazil accounted for 22% of world exports in 2004-05 and the US accounted for 15%. World imports of soybean meal in 2006-07 rose +2.8% yr/yr to 51.661 million metric tons, which was a new record high. US exports of soybean meal in 2006-07 rose +7.3% yr/yr to a record high of 8.700 million short tons. US imports of soybean meal in 2006-07 rose 14.5% yr/yr to 165,000 short tons but still below the record high of 285,000 short tons seen in 2003-04.

World Supply and Distribution of Soybean Meal — In Thousands of Metric Tons

Year Beginning Oct. 1	Production Brazil	China	EU	United States	Total	Exports Brazil	United States	Total	Imports EU	Total	Consumption EU	United States	Total	Ending Stocks Brazil	United States	Total
1997-98	15,729	6,717	12,126	34,633	98,034	9,587	8,722	33,260	13,640	34,021	24,562	25,955	98,312	1,298	198	6,182
1998-99	16,651	10,023	12,354	34,285	106,866	9,813	6,979	35,379	16,425	35,668	27,258	27,294	105,805	1,540	300	7,532
1999-00	16,478	11,975	11,213	34,102	106,824	9,950	6,912	35,272	17,806	35,013	28,991	27,269	108,662	1,080	266	5,435
2000-01	17,725	15,050	13,073	35,730	116,126	10,673	7,335	36,553	17,502	36,074	30,375	28,359	116,141	1,253	348	4,941
2001-02	19,407	16,300	13,885	36,552	125,088	11,862	7,271	41,060	19,691	40,488	33,006	29,541	123,711	1,560	218	5,746
2002-03	21,449	21,000	12,825	34,649	130,328	13,657	5,728	42,719	20,382	42,552	33,026	29,096	130,446	1,647	200	5,461
2003-04	22,360	20,190	10,945	32,953	128,542	14,792	4,690	45,604	21,898	45,082	32,480	28,530	128,472	1,801	191	5,009
2004-05	22,658	24,026	11,014	36,936	138,761	14,256	6,659	46,623	21,724	45,767	32,226	30,446	136,962	1,577	156	5,952
2005-06[1]	21,659	27,296	10,470	37,414	144,927	12,895	7,316	51,402	22,609	50,276	32,378	30,097	145,327	936	285	4,426
2006-07[2]	21,629	29,700	10,760	38,484	152,974	11,500	7,893	53,078	22,580	51,661	32,615	30,754	151,362	1,240	272	4,621

[1] Preliminary.   [2] Forecast.   *Source: Foreign Agricultural Service, U.S. Department of Agriculture (FAS-USDA)*

SOYBEAN MEAL

Soybean Meal Futures - Chicago Board of Trade
(weekly close) as of December 29, 2006

USD per ton

Volume of Trading of Soybean Meal Futures in Chicago In Contracts

Year	Jan.	Feb.	Mar.	Apr.	May	June	July	Aug.	Sept.	Oct.	Nov.	Dec.	Total[1]
1997	479,001	481,841	509,515	576,564	581,886	569,760	579,748	452,188	531,299	589,542	561,133	512,471	6,424.9
1998	458,519	454,310	449,806	592,614	499,468	749,765	675,104	536,650	504,088	553,224	521,231	559,067	6,553.8
1999	420,240	509,348	476,104	477,102	390,527	646,806	710,110	597,026	568,859	511,503	572,194	447,078	6,326.9
2000	455,335	537,527	556,010	467,698	566,607	606,190	488,172	469,017	484,617	483,174	690,313	513,328	6,318.0
2001	530,193	431,822	470,608	485,106	584,352	625,089	709,973	630,909	491,398	652,931	659,328	472,063	6,743.8
2002	610,275	398,294	424,684	618,880	567,221	664,687	806,395	673,705	581,155	613,701	657,822	557,688	7,174.5
2003	639,628	551,401	527,723	676,739	599,614	749,844	772,104	692,778	677,194	896,429	700,676	674,315	8,158.4
2004	648,690	767,052	740,696	819,600	795,793	821,580	873,226	638,941	547,282	559,711	703,500	653,172	8,569.2
2005	658,702	857,564	713,368	661,831	571,341	1,024,952	632,797	693,398	602,947	497,895	694,042	715,779	8,324.6
2006	506,851	604,974	575,259	785,627	716,846	976,097	801,549	819,118	807,717	906,098	1,064,227	785,680	9,350.0

[1] In thousands of contracts. *Source: Chicago Board of Trade (CBT)*

Average Open Interest of Soybean Meal Futures in Chicago In Contracts

Year	Jan.	Feb.	Mar.	Apr.	May	June	July	Aug.	Sept.	Oct.	Nov.	Dec.
1997	86,204	97,618	107,763	111,413	113,848	110,780	114,372	108,923	111,447	118,409	125,201	116,760
1998	114,243	122,979	131,390	137,251	136,212	136,216	126,108	139,239	140,904	141,426	134,095	122,788
1999	123,041	130,473	121,435	112,155	104,176	108,134	116,464	121,202	120,462	112,426	117,523	104,246
2000	115,285	124,822	120,157	123,957	123,691	112,425	105,230	94,469	105,240	103,263	120,164	127,529
2001	111,880	108,047	107,253	116,888	119,644	135,046	134,982	129,536	123,644	121,845	145,996	147,576
2002	146,674	137,425	134,880	130,138	132,376	143,956	142,728	132,996	137,799	131,249	137,836	140,902
2003	154,821	168,036	157,670	163,532	163,096	154,985	152,121	146,582	153,505	169,709	170,707	176,191
2004	183,462	186,137	185,647	175,069	162,284	149,584	135,675	134,987	133,045	137,447	152,846	147,307
2005	154,984	165,403	146,326	133,578	129,372	149,882	122,088	109,976	121,833	135,970	140,102	140,959
2006	127,922	132,833	147,837	172,905	181,823	182,940	196,236	230,082	236,351	206,002	216,854	206,762

Source: Chicago Board of Trade (CBT)

Supply and Distribution of Soybean Meal in the United States   In Thousands of Short Tons

Year Beginning Oct. 1	Supply			Distribution			$ Per Ton Decatur 48% Protein Solvent	$ Per Metric Ton		
	For Stocks Oct. 1	Pro-duction	Total Supply	Domestic	Exports	Total		Decatur 44% Protein Solvent	Brazil FOB 45-46% Protein	Rotter-dam CIF
1997-98	210	38,176	38,442	28,894	9,330	38,224	185.28	204	201	197
1998-99	218	37,797	38,114	30,662	7,122	37,784	138.55	153	150	150
1999-00	330	37,591	37,970	30,346	7,331	37,677	167.70	185	182	180
2000-01	293	39,385	39,729	31,643	7,703	39,346	173.60	191	187	188
2001-02	383	40,292	40,818	33,070	7,508	40,578	167.73	180	174	174
2002-03	240	38,194	38,600	32,361	6,019	38,380	181.57	200	163	197
2003-04	220	36,324	36,830	31,449	5,170	36,619	256.05	282	211	273
2004-05[1]	211	40,715	41,073	33,559	7,343	40,902	182.90	202	172	231
2005-06[2]	172	41,242	41,555	33,176	8,064	41,241	174.17	192	176	222
2006-07[3]	314	42,421	42,900	33,900	8,700	42,600	170-185			

[1] Preliminary.   [2] Estimate.   [3] Forecast.   *Source: Economic Research Service, U.S. Department of Agriculture (ERS-USDA)*

U.S. Exports of Soybean Cake & Meal by Country of Destination   In Thousands of Metric Tons

Year	Algeria	Australia	Canada	Dominican Republic	Italy	Japan	Mexico	Nether-lands	Philip-pines	Russia	Spain	Vene-zuela	Total
1997	250.8	136.7	662.9	261.5	295.8	288.1	220.1	508.5	483.2	8.3	345.0	337.1	7,309
1998	263.2	135.7	791.8	221.8	227.7	267.1	198.6	298.2	758.7	----	296.9	447.1	8,230
1999	213.2	167.1	796.7	309.9	60.9	209.6	425.4	231.5	825.5	289.4	77.7	359.6	6,839
2000	202.0	167.7	827.2	357.4	19.0	219.7	264.5	94.6	851.8	90.1	96.5	248.1	6,462
2001	178.8	157.5	1,050.6	364.9	132.8	279.1	419.8	241.1	689.0	102.2	132.4	137.8	7,426
2002	219.2	243.7	1,133.6	358.8	34.4	116.0	506.5	107.4	756.2	112.8	79.7	60.3	6,672
2003	184.7	384.3	1,091.4	317.5	0.4	331.0	762.4	84.3	238.5	60.7	5.6	190.5	5,951
2004	176.2	209.4	1,212.9	156.9	1.1	220.9	944.1	127.6	299.0	18.2	48.4	193.5	5,526
2005	63.0	74.9	1,208.8	264.7	0.5	523.7	1,512.5	46.5	442.3	16.8	26.1	112.5	6,905
2006[1]	18.4	54.5	1,411.0	423.8	1.4	481.4	1,892.2	76.4	520.5	36.6	4.8	27.9	7,967

[1] Preliminary.   *Source: The Oil World*

Production of Soybean Cake & Meal[2] in the United States   In Thousands of Short Tons

Year	Oct.	Nov.	Dec.	Jan.	Feb.	Mar.	Apr.	May	June	July	Aug.	Sept.	Total	Yield in lbs.
1997-98	3,344.0	3,390.6	3,624.2	3,592.1	3,279.2	3,484.0	3,172.5	2,956.7	2,795.2	2,941.5	2,665.6	2,930.7	37,176	47.41
1998-99	3,365.1	3,368.4	3,422.4	3,214.4	3,027.7	3,302.7	3,044.2	3,024.4	2,844.0	3,011.9	3,003.5	3,167.8	37,797	47.25
1999-00	3,573.4	3,400.4	3,413.5	3,332.8	2,998.2	3,123.6	2,906.1	2,882.5	2,845.4	3,118.8	2,906.8	3,089.7	37,591	47.76
2000-01	3,573.9	3,432.8	3,399.4	3,521.6	3,083.0	3,412.5	3,152.3	3,181.0	3,091.6	3,256.6	3,203.6	3,076.8	39,385	48.06
2001-02	3,534.4	3,538.7	3,655.3	3,703.1	3,313.2	3,589.7	3,315.7	3,344.2	3,194.1	3,085.4	3,106.7	2,911.3	40,292	44.27
2002-03	3,499.3	3,424.7	3,526.8	3,358.4	3,048.4	3,360.1	2,994.7	3,072.4	2,873.4	3,064.4	2,966.6	3,023.5	38,213	43.90
2003-04	3,462.1	3,465.9	3,483.7	3,479.3	3,144.9	3,092.4	2,682.4	2,792.4	2,616.2	2,752.2	2,480.2	2,872.6	36,324	
2004-05	3,685.2	3,584.2	3,567.9	3,553.6	3,293.3	3,547.6	3,328.0	3,396.8	3,160.9	3,320.4	3,122.1	3,157.0	40,717	
2005-06	3,700.9	3,562.3	3,518.0	3,589.5	3,215.3	3,504.0	3,212.6	3,474.6	3,250.9	3,507.8	3,351.7	3,354.5	41,242	
2006-07[1]	3,823.5	3,671.9	3,704.7										44,800	

[1] Preliminary.   [2] At oil mills; including millfeed and lecithin.   *Sources: Economic Research Service, U.S. Department of Agriculture (ERS-USDA)*

Stocks (at Oil Mills)[2] of Soybean Cake & Meal in the U.S., on First of Month   In Thousands of Short Tons

Year	Oct.	Nov.	Dec.	Jan.	Feb.	Mar.	Apr.	May	June	July	Aug.	Sept.
1997-98	206.6	218.2	412.2	262.0	269.3	280.7	238.0	210.4	290.2	193.1	205.3	187.2
1998-99	218.1	271.9	352.3	313.9	380.5	436.4	341.0	316.0	447.7	284.2	394.8	279.4
1999-00	330.2	467.6	460.2	436.5	489.8	482.5	350.2	441.2	325.0	260.2	305.8	225.9
2000-01	292.9	317.4	343.8	423.7	333.9	325.8	309.1	313.3	286.9	341.3	338.1	273.9
2001-02	383.3	305.5	302.9	393.7	289.7	272.0	336.5	253.8	212.7	343.3	202.4	256.5
2002-03	240.0	285.2	371.7	337.0	299.1	259.5	335.7	263.5	311.8	271.6	228.4	266.9
2003-04	219.9	317.8	432.4	280.7	328.9	415.8	375.0	338.6	465.5	314.9	344.6	196.3
2004-05	210.7	357.7	286.8	271.3	340.9	310.4	248.0	307.5	349.0	244.8	362.3	238.3
2005-06	171.8	316.1	304.9	338.0	326.6	301.6	286.5	415.4	303.5	266.2	372.6	225.8
2006-07[1]	313.8	388.4	373.6									

[1] Preliminary.   [2] Including millfeed and lecithin.   *Source: Economic Research Service, U.S. Department of Agriculture (ERS-USDA)*

SOYBEAN MEAL

Soybean Meal (monthly average) through December 2006 — USD per ton

Legend (USD Per Ton):
- ----- Chicago (Oct. 1929 - Oct. 1936)
- 41% Protein, Chicago (Nov. 1936 - June 1950)
- 44% Protein, Chicago (July 1950 - Sept. 1965)
- 44% Protein, Decatur (Oct. 1965 - Oct. 1992)
- 48% Protein, Decatur (Nov. 1992 - date)

Average Price of Soybean Meal (44% Solvent) in Decatur Illinois   In Dollars Per Short Ton -- Bulk

Year	Oct.	Nov.	Dec.	Jan.	Feb.	Mar.	Apr.	May	June	July	Aug.	Sept.	Average
1992-93	168.6	170.9	176.4	175.6	167.5	172.4	175.6	181.7	181.3	217.6	206.9	186.5	181.8
1993-94	180.6	195.7	192.5	185.9	184.4	182.0	176.4	191.1	183.0	168.1	165.6	162.5	180.7
1994-95	156.4	150.9	145.4	145.1	149.4	145.7	151.0	148.1	149.1	160.1	157.5	171.8	152.5
1995-96	183.4	194.1	213.6	220.5	216.7	215.7	237.9	232.3	227.9	242.3	251.1	265.5	225.1
1996-97	238.0	242.7	240.9	240.7	253.6	270.4	277.7	296.0	275.9	261.5	261.6	265.7	260.4
1997-98	216.0	231.6	214.9	193.1	182.1	165.3	152.8	150.3	157.8	173.3	135.7	126.9	175.0
1998-99	129.4	139.3	139.6	131.0	124.4	127.2	128.6	127.0	131.7	125.7	135.9	144.1	132.0
1999-00	147.2	148.1	145.4	155.0	163.6	166.6	168.1	180.1	170.2	156.8	151.4	166.9	160.0
2000-01	166.0	173.7	187.9	175.6	158.3	149.1	149.7	155.6	163.1	183.9	170.6	163.5	166.4
2001-02	157.7	157.2	146.6	Disc.	Disc.	Disc.	Disc.	Disc.	Disc.	Disc.	Disc.	Disc.	153.8

Source: Economic Research Service, U.S. Department of Agriculture (ERS-USDA)

Average Price of Soybean Meal (48% Solvent) in Decatur Illinois   In Dollars Per Short Ton -- Bulk

Year	Oct.	Nov.	Dec.	Jan.	Feb.	Mar.	Apr.	May	June	July	Aug.	Sept.	Average
1997-98	229.30	245.30	222.50	202.85	192.75	174.20	162.50	160.00	168.55	183.40	146.25	135.80	185.28
1998-99	135.70	144.45	146.40	138.80	132.30	133.00	134.50	133.20	139.10	132.70	141.70	150.65	138.54
1999-00	153.57	154.70	154.00	163.41	170.85	175.50	177.53	189.34	177.45	163.38	157.48	174.60	167.65
2000-01	171.52	179.95	195.65	183.17	166.08	156.32	158.48	165.14	172.60	184.43	178.46	171.67	173.62
2001-02	165.45	166.10	154.18	158.01	153.11	160.49	161.57	164.28	170.33	187.45	186.25	185.45	167.72
2002-03	168.20	163.20	163.60	167.40	176.80	175.40	182.10	195.40	191.90	187.30	189.70	217.95	181.58
2003-04	225.20	242.00	231.54	252.15	257.39	301.14	311.83	300.69	285.81	284.05	205.34	175.51	256.05
2004-05	155.37	153.90	161.60	167.34	167.95	187.96	193.19	198.68	219.28	215.75	198.43	175.40	182.90
2005-06	166.22	170.32	193.17	183.64	176.73	175.07	174.64	175.77	176.83	168.97	159.76	168.87	174.17
2006-07	177.71	190.67	180.63	190.36									184.84

Source: Economic Research Service, U.S. Department of Agriculture (ERS-USDA)

Soybean Oil

Soybean oil is the natural oil extracted from whole soybeans. Typically, about 19% of a soybean's weight can be extracted as crude soybean oil. The oil content of US soybeans correlates directly with the temperatures and amount of sunshine during the soybean pod-filling stages. Edible products produced with soybean oil include cooking and salad oils, shortening, and margarine. Soybean oil is the most widely used cooking oil in the US. It accounts for 80% of margarine production and for more than 75% of total US consumer vegetable fat and oil consumption. Soy oil is cholesterol-free and high in polyunsaturated fat. Soy oil is also used to produce inedible products such as paints, varnish, resins, and plastics. Of the edible vegetable oils, soy oil is the world's largest at about 32%, followed by palm oil and rapeseed oil. Soybean oil futures and options are traded on the Chicago Board of Trade (CBOT).

Prices – Soybean oil futures prices at the Chicago Board of Trade in 2006 were at 21.80 cents per pound in January. Prices moved higher into mid-year and posted a high of 27.37 cents per pound in July. After a drop to about 24.00 cents per pound in September, prices rallied to end the year at 28.40 cents per pound, a gain of about 30%. Regarding cash prices, for the first four months of 2006-07, the average monthly price of crude domestic soybean oil (in tank cars) in Decatur (F.O.B.) rose +15.4% yr/yr to 27.02 cents per pound.

Supply – World production of soybean oil in 2006-07 rose +4.4% yr/yr to a new record high of 35.823 million metric tons, which was more than five times the level of 6.199 million metric tons seen in 1970-71. The US accounts for 25% of world soybean oil production, while Brazil accounts for 15%, and the European Union accounts for 7%. US production of soybean oil in 2006-07 fell –1.1% yr/yr to 20.165 billion pounds, down slightly from the 2005-06 record high of 20.393 billion pounds.

Demand – World consumption of soybean oil in 2006-07 rose +6.6% yr/yr to a record high of 35.938 million metric tons. The US accounted for 24% of world consumption, while Brazil accounted for 9%, the European Union for 9%, and India for 9%. US consumption of soybean oil in 2006-07 rose +6.1% yr/yr to 19.050 billion pounds, which was a new record high.

Trade – World exports of soybean oil in 2004-05 rose +8.5% yr/yr to 9.753 million metric tons, which was a record high. US exports of soybean oil in 2006-07 rose +30.1% yr/yr to 1.500 billion pounds, but that was still well below the record of 3.079 billion pounds seen in 1997-98.

World Supply and Demand of Soybean Oil   In Thousands of Metric Tons

Year Beginning Oct. 1	Production Brazil	Production EU-25	Production United States	Production Total	Exports Brazil	Exports United States	Exports Total	Imports India	Imports Total	Consumption Brazil	Consumption EU-25	Consumption India	Consumption United States	Consumption Total	Stocks[3] United States	Stocks[3] Total
1997-98	3,728	2,746	8,229	22,510	1,184	1,397	6,549	236	6,225	2,724	1,706	1,095	6,922	22,162	627	2,721
1998-99	3,960	2,753	8,202	24,470	1,441	1,076	7,576	833	7,236	2,783	1,694	1,805	7,101	24,404	689	2,447
1999-00	3,943	2,504	8,085	24,491	1,137	624	6,317	790	6,082	2,899	1,639	1,582	7,283	23,959	904	2,744
2000-01	4,333	2,961	8,355	26,753	1,533	636	7,173	1,400	7,005	2,952	2,123	2,024	7,401	26,404	1,255	2,925
2001-02	4,700	3,165	8,572	28,872	1,775	1,143	8,131	1,479	7,751	2,949	2,263	2,300	7,635	28,324	1,070	3,093
2002-03	5,205	2,922	8,360	30,542	2,394	1,027	8,714	1,197	8,306	2,920	2,281	1,900	7,748	30,191	676	3,036
2003-04	5,588	2,500	7,748	30,049	2,718	425	8,786	906	8,301	2,954	2,086	1,885	7,650	29,984	488	2,616
2004-05	5,550	2,505	8,781	32,448	2,414	600	9,259	2,026	8,954	3,089	2,148	2,628	7,910	31,739	771	3,020
2005-06[1]	5,325	2,380	9,250	34,321	2,466	523	9,721	1,684	9,033	3,200	2,840	2,882	8,144	33,701	1,370	2,952
2006-07[2]	5,300	2,450	9,147	35,823	2,025	681	9,950	1,850	9,820	3,275	3,139	3,050	8,641	35,938	1,208	2,707

[1] Preliminary.   [2] Forecast.   [3] End of season.   *Source: Foreign Agricultural Service, U.S. Department of Agriculture (FAS-USDA)*

Supply and Distribution of Soybean Oil in the United States   In Millions of Pounds

Year Beginning Oct. 1	Production	Imports	Stocks Oct. 1	Exports	Total Domestic	Food Shortening	Food Margarine	Food Cooking & Salad Oils	Food Other Edible	Total Food	Non-Food Paint & Varnish	Non-Food Resins & Plastics	Total Non-Food	Total Disappearance
1997-98	18,143	60	1,520	3,079	15,262	4,688	1,623	6,188	78	12,576	49	128	490	18,341
1998-99	18,078	83	1,382	2,372	15,651	4,842	1,589	6,191	120	12,743	37	117	576	18,023
1999-00	17,825	83	1,520	1,376	16,057	7,153	1,481	7,075	132	15,841	65	96	586	17,433
2000-01	18,420	73	1,995	1,401	16,210	7,908	1,465	7,361	125	16,859	60	86	535	17,611
2001-02	18,898	46	2,767	2,519	16,833	8,234	1,298	7,373	125	17,030	60	85	519	19,352
2002-03	18,430	46	2,359	2,261	17,085	8,566	1,212	7,886	119	17,783	64	88	520	19,346
2003-04	17,080	306	1,489	936	16,864	8,304	1,138	7,933	NA	17,375	71	100	623	17,800
2004-05	19,360	26	1,076	1,324	17,439	7,938	1,227	7,790	NA	16,955	81	81	747	18,763
2005-06[1]	20,393	35	1,699	1,153	17,955	7,779	850	8,700	NA	17,329	117	85	1,866	19,108
2006-07[2]	20,165	55	3,019	1,500	19,050						66	82	2,735	20,550

[1] Preliminary.   [2] Forecast.   *Source: Economic Research Service, U.S. Department of Agriculture (ERS-USDA)*

SOYBEAN OIL

Stocks of Crude Soybean Oil in the United States, at End of Month   In Millions of Pounds

Crop Year	Oct.	Nov.	Dec.	Jan.	Feb.	Mar.	Apr.	May	June	July	Aug.	Sept.
2001-02	2,553.4	2,606.0	2,658.1	2,815.7	2,686.6	2,741.9	2,661.2	2,757.5	2,529.3	2,350.9	2,338.2	2,176.7
2002-03	2,097.1	2,114.3	2,197.2	2,186.9	2,062.5	2,028.7	1,916.0	1,843.0	1,706.4	1,595.1	1,458.4	1,282.4
2003-04	1,236.8	1,329.7	1,390.1	1,737.3	1,797.5	1,675.7	1,452.3	1,410.3	1,296.4	1,198.0	1,001.8	887.7
2004-05	1,019.5	1,013.1	1,111.1	1,348.2	1,425.3	1,588.7	1,560.0	1,658.1	1,622.4	1,715.6	1,525.2	1,505.9
2005-06	1,641.0	1,706.5	2,029.6	2,247.4	2,392.2	2,433.1	2,454.7	2,576.8	2,605.3	2,762.9	2,740.2	2,703.5
2006-07[1]	2,680.0	2,719.5	2,680.7									

[1] Preliminary.   *Source: Bureau of the Census, U.S. Department of Commerce*

Stocks of Refined Soybean Oil in the United States, at End of Month   In Millions of Pounds

Crop Year	Oct.	Nov.	Dec.	Jan.	Feb.	Mar.	Apr.	May	June	July	Aug.	Sept.
2001-02	171.4	181.4	210.0	222.9	209.8	210.8	195.6	185.7	206.5	178.7	183.5	183.2
2002-03	197.1	212.0	202.3	209.8	209.5	215.9	204.1	210.8	222.1	199.1	196.0	208.3
2003-04	175.0	200.8	189.9	208.3	190.5	180.2	191.9	241.2	217.7	214.0	178.8	187.8
2004-05	235.8	178.4	200.3	212.6	222.0	222.7	243.4	236.6	216.2	273.8	200.7	193.6
2005-06	254.1	178.9	199.4	251.3	281.2	285.0	300.8	308.2	313.9	343.2	320.9	315.3
2006-07[1]	334.7	355.6	384.8									

[1] Preliminary.   *Source: Bureau of the Census, U.S. Department of Commerce*

U.S. Exports of Soybean Oil[1], by Country of Destination   In Metric Tons

Year Beginning Oct. 1	Canada	Ecuador	Ethiopia	Haiti	India	Mexico	Morocco	Pakistan	Panama	Peru	Turkey	Venezuela	Total
1997-98	26,711	10,897	4,175	14,191	38,610	102,950	30,493	0	13,591	49,426	2,452	654	1,396,755
1998-99	11,316	4,858	2,933	44,957	71,685	99,112	43,346	0	1,369	62,085	8,497	1,464	1,075,699
1999-00	22,715	0	13,627	25,214	23,413	118,079	14,091	0	299	66,686	15,680	414	623,651
2000-01	54,909	9,849	5,224	5,793	54,062	72,456	0	62,999	4,558	60,606	0	577	635,493
2001-02	87,047	0	2,225	9,452	88,529	161,760	39,439	59,999	12,616	37,677	85,199	635	1,142,755
2002-03	124,667	0	11,997	1,997	42,727	188,993	26,517	38,215	2,241	20,349	26,500	311	1,026,638
2003-04	96,450	10	3,665	1,298	14,561	97,099	15,518	17	2,834	25,097	0	169	424,554
2004-05	68,162	0	1,529	4,375	29,385	162,913	6,579	15,506	7,247	15,459	21	6,063	600,399
2005-06[2]	76,309	2	3,270	3,975	23,031	108,515	21,951	12,000	1,546	19,588	4,032	38	523,120

[1] Crude & Refined oil combined as such.   [2] Preliminary.   *Source: Economic Research Service, U.S. Department of Agriculture (ERS-USDA)*

Production of Crude Soybean Oil in the United States   In Millions of Pounds

Year	Oct.	Nov.	Dec.	Jan.	Feb.	Mar.	Apr.	May	June	July	Aug.	Sept.	Total
1998-99	1,598.4	1,598.0	1,610.6	1,527.5	1,438.6	1,586.9	1,452.7	1,450.3	1,383.1	1,451.2	1,452.4	1,528.4	18,078
1999-00	1,687.1	1,596.6	1,599.2	1,579.8	1,417.2	1,481.8	1,367.9	1,396.0	1,359.6	1,485.5	1,388.0	1,466.0	17,825
2000-01	1,672.7	1,590.8	1,579.0	1,642.3	1,435.7	1,602.4	1,485.2	1,478.7	1,448.8	1,525.6	1,506.1	1,452.5	18,420
2001-02	1,680.1	1,629.0	1,696.4	1,706.7	1,543.7	1,661.9	1,550.6	1,574.0	1,506.1	1,461.2	1,474.8	1,413.8	18,898
2002-03	1,692.6	1,631.5	1,696.0	1,612.8	1,473.6	1,633.3	1,447.5	1,491.7	1,391.0	1,482.4	1,440.4	1,445.2	18,438
2003-04	1,630.8	1,610.6	1,604.6	1,618.3	1,462.4	1,461.4	1,260.3	1,314.6	1,236.0	1,304.0	1,185.9	1,391.7	17,081
2004-05	1,759.6	1,688.0	1,682.3	1,680.2	1,564.1	1,686.4	1,579.6	1,620.1	1,497.3	1,586.7	1,484.4	1,531.1	19,360
2005-06	1,828.6	1,756.7	1,717.3	1,765.2	1,594.8	1,746.5	1,586.3	1,709.3	1,608.7	1,737.6	1,657.7	1,684.1	20,393
2006-07[1]	1,833.0	1,725.0	1,755.3										21,253

[1] Preliminary.   *Source: Economic Research Service, U.S. Department of Agriculture (ERS-USDA)*

Production of Refined Soybean Oil in the United States   In Millions of Pounds

Year	Oct.	Nov.	Dec.	Jan.	Feb.	Mar.	Apr.	May	June	July	Aug.	Sept.	Total
1998-99	1,200.6	1,108.8	1,042.2	1,016.7	976.7	1,138.2	1,073.2	1,087.7	1,060.7	1,058.6	1,122.6	1,116.2	13,002
1999-00	1,201.1	1,195.2	1,150.4	1,056.9	1,045.1	1,173.7	1,109.6	1,141.4	1,063.8	1,080.2	1,176.0	1,177.7	13,571
2000-01	1,260.3	1,159.7	1,093.4	1,107.5	1,166.8	1,211.3	1,170.0	1,234.1	1,204.6	1,222.8	1,317.4	1,201.2	14,349
2001-02	1,383.2	1,363.5	1,266.9	1,231.8	1,183.9	1,330.0	1,270.5	1,297.9	1,287.7	1,272.8	1,308.4	1,362.4	15,559
2002-03	1,451.2	1,367.2	1,262.2	1,224.5	1,181.0	1,308.2	1,238.6	1,378.8	1,316.1	1,293.8	1,290.5	1,334.8	15,647
2003-04	1,393.0	1,350.9	1,226.6	1,205.6	1,196.0	1,330.6	1,210.3	1,267.4	1,195.9	1,246.8	1,268.8	1,306.3	15,198
2004-05	1,377.6	1,331.1	1,243.2	1,243.4	1,188.1	1,321.6	1,324.5	1,287.4	1,253.6	1,295.9	1,324.1	1,324.7	15,515
2005-06	1,389.3	1,307.4	1,245.2	1,273.9	1,132.9	1,409.3	1,326.6	1,361.5	1,352.9	1,329.1	1,399.7	1,400.0	15,928
2006-07[1]	1,477.9	1,309.3	1,316.4										16,414

[1] Preliminary.   *Source: Bureau of the Census, U.S. Department of Commerce*

Coconut Oil and Corn Oil (monthly average) through December 2006   Cents per pound

Coconut Oil: Cents Per Pound
----- Crude, New Orleans (Sept. 1918 - date)

Corn Oil: Cents Per Pound
- - - F.O.B. Decatur (July 1924 - June 1985)
Crude, Wet, Milling, Chicago (July 1985 - date)

Consumption of Soybean Oil in End Products in the United States   In Millions of Pounds

Year	Jan.	Feb.	Mar.	Apr.	May	June	July	Aug.	Sept.	Oct.	Nov.	Dec.	Total
1997	1,086.0	979.7	1,104.9	1,060.4	1,034.1	995.2	991.4	1,126.1	1,067.8	1,128.5	1,100.0	1,087.8	12,762
1998	1,045.8	1,020.2	1,129.7	1,066.5	1,101.6	1,070.1	1,062.2	1,123.4	1,122.0	1,231.5	1,150.2	1,057.0	13,180
1999	1,031.5	979.0	1,156.1	1,087.7	1,091.9	1,079.5	1,082.9	1,185.0	1,185.7	1,183.0	1,199.3	1,135.6	13,397
2000	1,096.6	1,050.5	1,217.9	1,158.9	1,183.6	1,102.9	1,121.1	1,226.4	1,163.6	1,306.1	1,139.7	1,079.6	13,847
2001	1,065.9	1,151.7	1,308.8	1,202.4	1,224.2	1,261.6	1,307.6	1,557.5	1,411.0	1,687.3	1,624.0	1,485.8	16,288
2002	1,461.5	1,395.3	1,568.0	1,505.1	1,549.7	1,492.4	1,490.5	1,545.5	1,543.7	1,710.2	1,587.2	1,458.8	18,308
2003	1,418.1	1,347.4	1,490.0	1,494.9	1,552.6	1,493.1	1,509.5	1,483.5	1,577.7	1,660.7	1,544.2	1,451.4	18,023
2004	1,388.1	1,417.6	1,555.2	1,468.0	1,506.7	1,421.1	1,429.2	1,473.6	1,483.2	1,558.3	1,533.7	1,368.9	17,604
2005	1,365.4	1,609.2	1,609.2	1,587.2	1,589.5	1,496.2	1,523.3	1,570.4	1,527.2	1,589.6	1,546.9	1,416.2	18,430
2006[1]	1,505.2	1,368.8	1,661.4	1,561.1	1,634.9	1,653.2	1,575.5	1,746.2	1,727.9	1,775.6	1,638.6	1,575.6	19,424

[1] Preliminary.   *Source: Bureau of the Census, U.S. Department of Commerce*

U.S. Exports of Soybean Oil (Crude and Refined)   In Millions of Pounds

Year	Jan.	Feb.	Mar.	Apr.	May	June	July	Aug.	Sept.	Oct.	Nov.	Dec.	Total
1997	190.7	239.2	301.1	84.9	28.9	44.9	144.1	212.9	152.1	217.2	424.0	199.7	2,240
1998	449.4	387.6	268.6	191.1	148.1	204.7	161.8	316.0	108.9	189.6	343.5	376.7	3,146
1999	246.1	231.1	130.8	230.8	91.3	135.0	111.7	91.2	196.2	209.1	114.9	157.6	1,946
2000	103.0	146.1	161.3	91.5	48.3	109.8	105.8	57.0	69.0	43.9	115.2	261.6	1,313
2001	130.4	184.5	142.4	105.8	51.2	109.9	89.1	96.3	70.6	233.9	138.6	164.8	1,518
2002	249.9	446.7	233.3	233.3	87.3	345.4	180.8	95.3	109.8	113.5	194.9	210.2	2,501
2003	277.5	319.1	273.9	211.6	109.5	966.5	234.5	116.0	105.9	152.5	111.3	133.2	3,011
2004	71.2	62.8	73.5	38.8	44.0	39.3	53.9	68.8	86.8	59.9	184.5	239.5	1,023
2005	77.0	217.2	74.6	74.8	71.9	68.5	52.4	137.3	65.9	76.3	154.1	107.8	1,178
2006[1]	71.3	67.2	178.1	96.6	53.4	82.3	89.3	65.3	111.6	165.5	119.7	275.9	1,376

[1] Preliminary.   *Source: Economic Research Service, U.S. Department of Agriculture (ERS-USDA)*

SOYBEAN OIL

Soybean Oil (monthly average) through December 2006   Cents per pound

Cents Per Pound
---- Crude, New York (Jan. 1911 - Sept. 1929)
Crude, Decatur (Oct. 1929 - date)

Stocks of Soybean Oil (Crude & Refined) at Factories and Warehouses in the U.S.   In Millions of Pounds

Year	Oct. 1	Nov. 1	Dec. 1	Jan. 1	Feb. 1	Mar. 1	Apr. 1	May 1	June 1	July 1	Aug. 1	Sept. 1
1997-98	1,520.2	1,525.6	1,525.5	1,679.6	1,787.9	1,711.2	1,762.6	1,857.6	1,857.0	1,712.6	1,779.1	1,453.2
1998-99	1,382.4	1,416.8	1,406.5	1,312.9	1,505.6	1,607.6	1,716.2	1,640.5	1,767.3	1,647.4	1,671.2	1,630.8
1999-00	1,519.6	1,616.4	1,663.6	1,791.1	2,013.7	2,099.8	2,092.7	2,099.2	1,991.9	2,028.3	2,120.4	2,018.1
2000-01	1,995.3	2,060.8	2,167.5	2,298.0	2,379.7	2,474.0	2,504.0	2,505.8	2,656.1	2,776.7	2,895.5	2,869.9
2001-02	2,877.2	2,724.9	2,787.4	2,868.1	3,038.5	2,896.4	2,952.7	2,856.8	2,943.2	2,735.9	2,529.7	2,521.7
2002-03	2,358.6	2,280.1	2,326.1	2,398.0	2,395.7	2,271.9	2,244.6	2,120.2	2,053.9	1,928.5	1,794.2	1,654.4
2003-04	1,490.6	1,411.8	1,530.4	1,579.9	1,945.6	1,988.0	1,855.9	1,644.1	1,651.6	1,514.0	1,412.0	1,180.6
2004-05	1,075.6	1,255.3	1,191.5	1,311.4	1,560.9	1,647.3	1,811.4	1,803.3	1,894.7	1,838.6	1,989.4	1,725.9
2005-06	1,699.0	1,883.5	1,851.8	2,190.5	2,498.7	2,673.4	2,718.1	2,755.4	2,885.0	2,919.2	3,106.1	3,061.2
2006-07[1]	3,018.9	3,014.7	3,075.1									

[1] Preliminary.   Source: Economic Research Service, U.S. Department of Agriculture (ERS-USDA)

Average Price of Crude Domestic Soybean Oil (in Tank Cars) F.O.B. Decatur   In Cents Per Pound

Year	Oct.	Nov.	Dec.	Jan.	Feb.	Mar.	Apr.	May	June	July	Aug.	Sept.	Average
1997-98	24.31	25.73	25.08	25.09	26.51	27.09	28.10	28.28	25.83	24.88	23.99	25.13	25.84
1998-99	25.20	25.20	24.00	22.90	20.00	19.50	18.80	17.85	16.50	15.30	16.50	16.80	19.88
1999-00	16.08	15.63	15.30	15.63	15.09	16.21	17.52	16.75	15.65	14.70	14.34	14.24	15.60
2000-01	13.50	13.37	13.12	12.53	12.38	13.90	13.53	13.53	14.21	16.49	17.08	15.46	14.09
2001-02	14.38	15.23	15.10	14.82	14.15	14.75	15.31	15.98	17.69	19.12	20.61	20.32	16.46
2002-03	20.75	23.00	22.60	21.50	21.20	21.56	22.40	23.17	22.90	21.80	20.40	23.20	22.04
2003-04	27.40	27.76	29.54	30.34	33.05	34.66	34.19	32.68	30.07	28.05	25.98	25.87	29.97
2004-05	23.23	22.95	21.79	20.46	20.70	23.60	23.09	23.38	24.70	25.46	23.59	23.19	23.01
2005-06	24.26	22.52	21.00	21.63	22.21	23.21	22.98	24.76	24.20	25.86	24.80	23.54	23.41
2006-07[1]	24.80	27.64	27.63	28.00									27.02

[1] Preliminary.   Source: Economic Research Service, U.S. Department of Agriculture (ERS-USDA)

Soybean Oil Futures - Chicago Board of Trade
(weekly close) as of December 29, 2006 — Cents per pound

Volume of Trading of Soybean Oil Futures in Chicago   In Contracts

Year	Jan.	Feb.	Mar.	Apr.	May	June	July	Aug.	Sept.	Oct.	Nov.	Dec.	Total[1]
1997	473,290	381,921	503,998	445,848	389,741	439,626	442,846	375,122	417,970	413,722	489,541	511,369	5,285.0
1998	443,562	556,982	497,887	673,091	624,518	648,098	629,642	491,155	558,032	383,844	450,073	540,379	6,498.3
1999	367,303	555,097	520,622	463,236	350,850	489,184	516,205	552,198	523,376	395,243	497,090	433,491	5,663.9
2000	424,232	451,677	483,212	438,526	451,162	533,376	422,418	456,195	436,841	378,419	507,044	386,801	5,369.9
2001	327,570	458,445	416,718	443,454	403,110	541,194	751,299	612,349	447,390	550,995	579,460	502,341	6,034.3
2002	474,824	497,396	468,878	496,990	526,918	588,386	701,455	648,853	529,442	549,942	705,373	628,026	6,816.5
2003	522,939	540,645	473,694	618,483	520,043	740,549	761,460	594,687	636,469	733,405	656,464	618,502	7,417.3
2004	521,293	722,580	736,173	760,153	631,157	642,917	657,542	549,538	565,439	552,890	654,338	599,294	7,593.3
2005	475,115	799,873	579,599	636,304	565,511	852,259	548,334	637,067	594,781	607,054	672,849	707,384	7,676.1
2006	531,908	611,192	597,607	866,397	688,613	1,024,453	801,198	816,745	728,998	939,319	1,003,283	878,811	9,488.5

[1] In thousands of contracts.   Source: *Chicago Board of Trade (CBT)*

Average Open Interest of Soybean Oil Futures in Chicago   In Contracts

Year	Jan.	Feb.	Mar.	Apr.	May	June	July	Aug.	Sept.	Oct.	Nov.	Dec.
1997	89,112	89,348	102,388	101,191	101,544	104,433	105,346	95,282	94,521	107,471	119,877	106,406
1998	105,798	121,657	142,100	160,004	159,248	139,934	117,487	112,177	115,879	115,260	110,386	104,738
1999	115,407	131,875	136,967	133,404	131,993	147,749	157,999	147,280	146,239	155,768	163,439	144,798
2000	131,948	135,196	143,699	155,114	134,093	140,582	134,392	135,506	136,590	135,584	142,712	134,873
2001	134,677	133,497	123,770	128,360	142,877	151,713	162,395	166,318	159,467	164,521	167,803	154,589
2002	149,103	158,157	149,913	136,198	128,707	129,480	135,762	143,144	146,759	139,626	169,978	155,871
2003	143,607	140,272	131,323	142,123	147,584	143,218	147,610	157,066	141,596	161,556	183,747	191,176
2004	198,361	212,204	186,745	159,478	141,772	136,887	135,649	142,574	132,936	147,046	154,316	151,800
2005	159,229	174,091	161,971	145,808	135,515	155,962	147,542	132,351	139,489	165,634	175,229	186,760
2006	171,317	183,717	192,643	204,132	244,580	241,962	276,251	269,208	259,464	256,153	279,091	273,375

Source: *Chicago Board of Trade (CBT)*

Soybeans

Soybean is the common name for the annual leguminous plant and its seed. The soybean is a member of the oilseed family and is not considered a grain. The soybean seeds are contained in pods and are nearly spherical in shape. The seeds are usually light yellow in color. The seeds contain 20% oil and 40% protein. Soybeans were an ancient food crop in China, Japan, and Korea and were only introduced to the US in the early 1800s. Today, soybeans are the second largest crop produced in the US behind corn. Soybean production in the US is concentrated in the Midwest and the lower Mississippi Valley. Soybean crops in the US are planted in May or June and are harvested in autumn. Soybean plants usually reach maturity 100-150 days after planting depending on growing conditions.

Soybeans are used to produce a wide variety of food products. The key value of soybeans lies in the relatively high protein content, which makes it an excellent source of protein without many of the negative factors of animal meat. Popular soy-based food products include whole soybeans (roasted for snacks or used in sauces, stews and soups), soy oil for cooking and baking, soy flour, protein concentrates, isolated soy protein (which contains up to 92% protein), soy milk and baby formula (as an alternative to dairy products), soy yogurt, soy cheese, soy nut butter, soy sprouts, tofu and tofu products (soybean curd), soy sauce (which is produced by a fermentation process), and meat alternatives (hamburgers, breakfast sausage, etc).

The primary market for soybean futures is at the Chicago Board of Trade. The CBOT's soybean contract calls for the delivery of 5,000 bushels of No. 2 yellow soybeans (at contract par), No. 1 yellow soybeans (at 6 cents per bushel above the contract price), or No. 3 yellow soybeans (at a 6 cents under the contract price). Soybean futures are also traded at exchanges in Brazil, Argentina, China, and Tokyo.

Prices – Soybean futures prices traded sideways to lower in the high-$5 per bushel area in the first 9 months of 2006 due to favorable growing conditions in the US and a record 2006-07 soybean crop of 3.188 billion bushels. Soybean prices fell to a 1-1/2 year low in August 2006 as the record size of the crop became clear. The USDA projected a record US carry-over for soybeans in 2006-07 of 575 million bushels. However, soybean prices then rallied sharply starting in September due to the rally in corn prices. Soybeans finally ended 2006 at $6.835 per bushel, up +13.5% yr/yr. The 80% rally in corn prices was sparked by strong demand from ethanol producers and a sharp drawdown in 2006-07 corn inventories. Soybean prices followed corn higher starting in September, rallying from the $5.50 area to as high as $7.91 by February 2007. The soybean market recognized that US farmers would be slashing their soybean planting in spring 2007 in order to plant more corn and take advantage of the surge in corn prices. As of March 2007, the industry consensus was that US farmers would have to plant 10-12 million more acres of corn in spring 2007 in order to satisfy strong corn demand. Most of those acres would be taken away from soybean planting, meaning that the US soybean crop in 2007-08 is likely to fall 10-15% because of fewer planted acres. Soybean prices also boosted in early 2007 due to heavy rains in key parts of the Brazilian soybean growing areas, which ruined some crops and increased soybean rust problems.

Supply – World soybean production during the 2006-07 marketing year (Sep-Aug) rose by +5.3% yr/yr to 229.398 million metric tons, which was a new record high. World soybean production has more than doubled from the 81 million metric ton level seen in 1980. The world's largest soybean producers were the US with 38% of world production in 2006-07, Brazil (25%), Argentina (19%), China (7%), and India (3%). China's soybean production has roughly doubled since 1980. Brazil's production has risen by almost 4 times since 1980.

US soybean production in 2006-07 rose by +5.3% yr/yr to 3.204 billion bushels which is a new record high. U.S. farmers harvested 74.602 million acres of soybeans in 2006-07, which is also a new record high. The average yield of 42.7 bushels per acre in 2006-07, however, was down -0.7% from the 2005-06 record high of 43.0. US ending stocks for the 2006-07 marketing year (September 1), rose sharply by +75.7% to 449 million bushels from 256 million bushels in 2005-06 and thus recovered further from the 3-decade low of 112 million bushels seen in 2003-04.

Demand – Total US distribution in 2006-07 rose +6.1% to 3.047 billion bushels. The distribution tables for US soybeans for the 2006-07 marketing year show that 58% of US soybean usage went for crushing into soybean oil and meal, 36% for exports, and 6% for seed and residual. The quantity of soybeans that went for crushing rose +2.4% yr/yr in 2006-07 to 1.780 billion bushels. The world soybean crush rose +5.3% yr/yr in 2006-07 to 194.125 million metric tons, which was a new record high and was more than double the level seen in 1980.

Trade – World exports of soybeans in 2006-07 rose +8.5% yr/yr to 69.508 million metric tons, which was a new record high. The world's largest soybean exporters are the US with 43% of world exports in 2006-07, Brazil with 38% of world exports, and Argentina with 11% of world exports. US soybean exports in 2006-07 rose +16.1% yr/yr to 29.937 million metric tons, which was a new record high. Brazil's soybean exports have more than quadrupled in the past decade and in 2006-07 were virtually unchanged from the record high of 25.911 million metric tons posted in 2005-06. The world's largest importers of soybeans in 2006-07 were China with 46% of world imports, the European Union with 21%, Japan with 6%, and Mexico with 6%. China's imports in 2006-07 rose +11.2% yr/yr to a record high of 31.500 million metric tons from negligible levels prior to 1994.

World Production of Soybeans   In Thousands of Metric Tons

Crop Year[4]	Argen-tina	Bolivia	Brazil	Canada	China	India	Indo-nesia	Mexico	Para-guay	Thai-land	United States	Russia	World Total
1997-98	19,500	1,120	32,500	2,738	14,728	5,350	1,306	189	2,988	338	73,176	280	157,992
1998-99	20,000	970	31,300	2,737	15,152	6,000	1,300	143	2,980	335	74,598	297	159,828
1999-00	21,200	1,200	34,700	2,776	14,290	5,200	1,300	123	2,911	330	72,224	334	160,409
2000-01	27,800	1,150	39,500	2,703	15,400	5,250	1,020	103	3,502	312	75,055	342	175,771
2001-02	30,000	1,245	43,500	1,635	15,410	5,400	870	66	3,547	270	78,672	350	184,832
2002-03	35,500	1,650	52,000	2,336	16,510	4,000	780	89	4,500	250	75,010	423	196,774
2003-04	33,000	1,850	51,000	2,263	15,394	6,800	820	125	3,911	220	66,778	393	186,512
2004-05[1]	39,000	2,027	53,000	3,042	17,400	5,850	825	132	4,050	240	85,013	555	215,724
2005-06[2]	40,500	2,060	55,000	3,161	16,350	6,300	832	145	4,000	230	83,368	689	217,894
2006-07[3]	44,000	2,150	57,000	3,500	16,200	7,300	845	160	4,700	230	86,770	900	229,398

[1] Preliminary.   [2] Estimate.   [3] Forecast.   [4] Spilt year includes Northern Hemisphere crops harvested in the late months of the first year shown combined with Southern Hemisphere crops harvested in the early months of the following year.   *Sources: Oil World; Foreign Agricultural Service, U.S. Department of Agriculture (FAS-USDA)*

World Crushings and Ending Stocks of Soybeans   In Thousands of Metric Tons

Year	Argen-tina	Brazil	China	EU-25	India	Japan	Mexico	Taiwan	United States	World Total	Brazil	United States	World Total
				Crushings								Ending Stocks	
1997-98	12,886	19,946	8,450	15,278	4,770	3,720	3,600	2,043	43,464	123,256	7,894	5,438	27,287
1998-99	17,507	21,174	12,607	15,344	5,400	3,700	3,950	1,874	43,262	134,675	8,086	9,484	29,341
1999-00	17,074	21,084	15,070	13,994	4,400	3,750	4,100	2,098	42,927	135,144	9,418	7,897	30,901
2000-01	17,300	22,742	18,900	16,598	4,525	3,775	4,450	2,128	44,625	146,543	9,448	6,743	34,244
2001-02	20,859	24,693	20,250	17,636	4,629	3,885	4,610	2,187	46,259	158,024	12,593	5,663	36,161
2002-03	23,526	27,168	26,540	16,325	3,420	4,217	4,335	2,135	43,948	165,510	16,636	4,853	43,665
2003-04	25,021	29,323	25,439	13,909	5,534	3,536	3,889	2,046	41,632	163,713	15,507	3,059	38,804
2004-05[1]	27,313	29,252	30,362	13,995	5,030	3,149	3,729	2,013	46,160	175,683	16,750	6,960	48,453
2005-06[2]	31,886	28,050	34,500	13,310	5,435	2,820	3,783	2,180	47,320	184,292	15,270	12,229	52,327
2006-07[3]	35,000	27,900	37,500	13,670	6,335	2,925	3,900	2,270	48,444	194,125	16,101	16,200	57,499

[1] Preliminary.   [2] Estimate.   [3] Forecast.   *Sources: Oil World; Foreign Agricultural Service, U.S. Department of Agriculture (FAS-USDA)*

World Imports and Exports of Soybeans   In Thousands of Metric Tons

Year	China	EU-25	Japan	Rep. of Korea	Mexico	Taiwan	World Total	Argen-tina	Brazil	Canada	Paraguay	United States	World Total
			Imports							Exports			
1997-98	2,940	15,137	4,873	1,349	3,502	2,387	38,171	3,171	8,760	769	2,293	23,760	39,627
1998-99	3,850	14,859	4,807	1,400	3,766	2,124	39,340	3,403	8,931	876	2,299	21,898	38,268
1999-00	10,100	14,129	4,907	1,606	4,039	2,408	46,194	4,127	11,101	949	2,025	26,537	45,625
2000-01	13,245	17,525	4,767	1,389	4,381	2,330	53,157	7,414	15,469	747	2,509	27,103	53,871
2001-02	10,385	18,539	5,023	1,434	4,510	2,578	54,515	6,004	14,504	502	2,285	28,948	52,941
2002-03	21,417	16,872	5,087	1,516	4,230	2,351	63,109	8,714	19,629	726	2,806	28,423	61,074
2003-04	16,933	14,638	4,688	1,368	3,797	2,217	54,059	6,741	20,417	897	2,776	24,128	55,988
2004-05[1]	25,802	14,544	4,295	1,240	3,640	2,256	63,706	9,568	20,137	1,093	2,888	29,860	64,635
2005-06[2]	28,317	13,934	3,957	1,190	3,667	2,498	63,996	7,249	25,911	1,326	2,400	25,778	64,068
2006-07[3]	31,500	14,138	4,100	1,275	3,775	2,550	69,126	7,250	25,900	1,550	3,300	29,937	69,508

[1] Preliminary.   [2] Estimate.   [3] Forecast.   *Sources: Oil World; Foreign Agricultural Service, U.S. Department of Agriculture (FAS-USDA)*

Supply and Distribution of Soybeans in the United States   In Millions of Bushels

Crop Year Beginning Sept. 1	Farms	Mills, Elevators[3]	Total	Pro-duction	Total Supply	Crushings	Exports	Seed, Feed & Residual	Total Distri-bution
	Stocks, Sept. 1 — Supply					Distribution			
1997-98	43.6	88.2	131.8	2,688.8	2,825.6	1,597.0	874.0	155.0	2,626.0
1998-99	84.3	115.5	199.8	2,741.0	2,945.0	1,590.0	805.0	202.0	2,597.0
1999-00	145.0	203.5	348.5	2,653.8	3,006.0	1,578.0	973.0	165.0	2,716.0
2000-01	112.5	177.7	290.2	2,757.8	3,052.0	1,640.0	996.0	168.0	2,804.0
2001-02	83.5	164.2	247.7	2,890.7	3,141.0	1,700.0	1,064.0	169.0	2,933.0
2002-03	62.7	145.3	208.0	2,756.1	2,969.0	1,615.0	1,044.0	131.0	2,791.0
2003-04	58.0	120.3	178.3	2,453.7	2,638.0	1,530.0	887.0	109.0	2,525.0
2004-05	29.4	83.0	112.4	3,123.7	3,242.0	1,696.0	1,097.0	193.0	2,986.0
2005-06[1]	99.7	156.0	255.7	3,063.2	3,322.0	1,739.0	947.0	187.0	2,873.0
2006-07[2]	176.3	273.0	449.3	3,188.2	3,642.0	1,780.0	1,100.0	167.0	3,047.0

[1] Preliminary.   [2] Estimate.   [3] Also warehouses.   *Source: Economic Research Service, U.S. Department of Agriculture (ERS-USDA)*

SOYBEANS

Salient Statistics & Official Crop Production Reports of Soybeans in the U.S.   In Millions of Bushels

Year	Planted ---- 1,000 Acres ----	Acreage Harvested	Yield Per Acre (Bu.)	Farm Price ($ / Bu.)	Farm Value (Million Dollars)	Yield of Oil	Yield of Meal	Crop Production Reports In Thousands of Bushels Aug. 1	Sept. 1	Oct. 1	Nov. 1	Dec. 1	Final
1997-98	70,005	69,110	38.9	6.47	17,396	11.25	47.41	2,744,451	2,745,891	2,721,843	2,736,115	----	2,688,750
1998-99	72,025	70,441	38.9	4.93	13,513	11.30	47.25	2,824,744	2,908,604	2,768,919	2,762,609	----	2,741,014
1999-00	73,730	72,446	36.6	4.63	12,287	11.34	47.76	2,869,519	2,778,392	2,696,272	2,672,972	----	2,653,758
2000-01	74,266	72,408	38.1	4.54	12,548	11.24	48.06	2,988,669	2,899,571	2,822,821	2,777,036	----	2,757,810
2001-02	74,075	72,975	39.6	4.38	12,606	11.14	44.27	2,867,474	2,833,511	2,907,042	2,922,914	----	2,890,682
2002-03	73,963	72,497	38.0	5.64	15,253	11.39	43.90	2,628,387	2,655,819	2,653,798	2,689,691	----	2,756,147
2003-04	73,404	72,476	33.9	7.95	18,014	11.20	44.32	2,862,039	2,642,644	2,468,390	2,451,759	----	2,453,665
2004-05	75,208	73,958	42.2	5.90	17,895	11.33	44.26	2,876,627	2,835,989	3,106,861	3,150,441	----	3,123,686
2005-06[1]	72,032	71,251	43.0	5.63	17,269			2,791,133	2,856,449	2,967,075	3,043,116	----	3,063,237
2006-07[2]	75,522	74,602	42.7	6.04	19,694			2,927,634	3,092,970	3,188,576	3,203,908	----	3,188,247

[1] Preliminary.   [2] Forecast.   Source: National Agricultural Statistics Service, U.S. Department of Agriculture (NASS-USDA)

Stocks of Soybeans in the United States   In Thousands of Bushels

Year	On Farms Mar. 1	Jun. 1	Sept. 1	Dec. 1	Off Farms[1] Mar. 1	Jun. 1	Sept. 1	Dec. 1	Total Stocks Mar. 1	Jun. 1	Sept. 1	Dec. 1
1997	514,000	216,000	43,600	1,048,000	541,754	283,890	88,233	951,417	1,055,754	499,890	131,833	1,999,417
1998	637,000	318,000	84,300	1,187,000	565,922	275,654	115,499	999,440	1,202,922	593,654	199,799	2,186,440
1999	815,000	458,000	145,000	1,150,000	642,338	390,573	203,482	1,032,666	1,457,338	848,573	348,482	2,182,666
2000	730,000	370,000	112,500	1,217,000	665,986	404,425	177,662	1,022,791	1,395,986	774,425	290,162	2,239,791
2001	780,000	365,000	83,500	1,240,000	623,908	343,180	164,247	1,035,713	1,403,908	708,180	247,747	2,275,713
2002	687,000	301,200	62,700	1,170,000	648,987	383,721	145,320	943,641	1,335,987	684,921	208,020	2,113,641
2003	636,500	272,500	58,000	820,000	565,528	329,862	120,329	868,653	1,201,028	602,362	178,329	1,688,653
2004	355,900	110,000	29,400	1,300,000	549,947	300,604	83,014	1,004,640	905,847	410,604	112,414	2,304,640
2005	795,000	356,100	99,700	1,345,000	586,364	343,174	156,038	1,157,098	1,381,364	699,274	255,738	2,502,098
2006[1]	872,000	495,500	176,300	1,461,000	797,206	495,199	273,026	1,236,498	1,669,206	990,699	449,326	2,697,498

[1] Includes stocks at mills, elevators, warehouses, terminals and processors.   NA = Not avaliable.   Source: National Agricultural Statistics Service, U.S. Department of Agriculture (NASS-USDA)

Commercial Stocks of Soybeans in the United States, on First of Month   In Millions of Bushels

Year	Jan.	Feb.	Mar.	Apr.	May	June	July	Aug.	Sept.	Oct.	Nov.	Dec.
1997	32.6	28.8	22.9	26.0	29.2	24.7	14.3	12.8	6.3	4.5	50.2	49.4
1998	35.3	31.2	22.9	18.4	14.5	14.2	10.2	9.7	8.7	18.6	43.5	40.6
1999	39.1	31.5	29.0	28.7	25.0	18.9	16.1	17.3	14.1	19.5	46.9	42.3
2000	34.1	28.3	30.0	23.9	23.8	20.6	17.0	12.3	8.6	15.5	38.2	37.9
2001	34.5	28.8	25.2	22.5	16.3	15.0	12.9	13.4	11.9	9.6	34.7	38.2
2002	29.6	27.0	22.2	21.0	18.4	15.4	14.4	10.2	4.6	8.4	26.9	28.4
2003	25.9	13.2	13.9	12.8	9.7	9.4	11.7	7.6	4.5	7.0	33.0	36.7
2004	35.5	26.2	26.0	19.4	15.7	13.5	8.0	5.9	4.4	10.8	31.1	32.9
2005	26.5	21.5	19.5	16.0	14.8	12.1	11.5	8.8	5.4	17.0	36.7	36.1
2006	36.8	30.2	26.1	25.7	17.6	20.5	14.6	14.5	14.5	19.0	40.1	43.7

Source: Livestock Division, U.S. Department of Agriculture (LD-USDA)

Stocks of Soybeans at Mills in the United States, on First of Month   In Millions of Bushels

Year	Sept.	Oct.	Nov.	Dec.	Jan.	Feb.	Mar.	Apr.	May	June	July	Aug.
1995-96	52.8	54.2	125.6	129.1	120.0	123.3	121.9	110.6	104.2	92.5	70.4	57.4
1996-97	40.7	23.4	101.1	117.4	106.0	112.6	122.2	104.9	89.2	78.2	64.0	43.6
1997-98	28.3	37.0	126.4	124.3	110.3	98.7	93.4	72.0	56.9	41.0	42.5	44.1
1998-99	32.8	66.5	175.0	154.3	131.0	109.6	102.5	93.7	80.5	56.9	55.5	48.1
1999-00	41.7	70.8	162.9	144.7	144.2	140.3	137.8	129.6	98.7	78.7	78.4	52.1
2000-01	52.1	56.8	179.4	166.8	137.8	143.3	127.0	120.6	94.9	86.1	79.3	69.0
2001-02	69.0	41.3	152.8	137.1	121.4	129.6	128.2	112.9	104.2	88.2	67.9	65.4
2002-03	46.4	36.3	114.5	113.5	106.0	109.2	102.9	91.5	91.6	76.0	64.9	55.6
2003-04	35.3	31.9	129.9	121.0	121.7	125.6	124.5	134.3	114.8	91.2	76.0	61.4
2004-05[1]	37.0	74.8	114.1	113.1	100.3	85.6	88.1	88.8	70.9	59.2	66.1	51.7

[1] Preliminary.   Source: Economic Research Service, U.S. Department of Agriculture (ERS-USDA)

Production of Soybeans for Beans in the United States, by State   In Millions of Bushels

Crop Year	Arkansas	Illinois	Indiana	Iowa	Kentucky	Michigan	Minnesota	Mississippi	Missouri	Nebraska	Ohio	Tennessee	Total
1997-98	109.8	427.9	230.6	478.4	42.1	71.6	255.5	64.2	174.6	143.8	191.0	40.8	2,688.8
1998-99	85.0	464.2	231.0	496.8	36.0	73.7	285.6	48.0	170.0	165.0	193.2	35.1	2,741.0
1999-00	92.4	443.1	216.5	478.4	24.4	77.6	289.8	44.7	147.1	180.6	162.0	22.8	2,653.8
2000-01	80.3	459.8	252.1	464.6	45.2	73.1	293.2	34.8	175.0	173.9	186.5	28.8	2,757.8
2001-02	91.2	477.9	273.9	480.5	48.8	63.9	266.4	37.0	186.2	223.0	187.8	35.4	2,890.7
2002-03	96.5	453.7	239.5	499.2	42.6	78.5	308.9	43.8	170.0	176.3	151.0	34.7	2,756.1
2003-04	111.3	379.6	204.1	342.9	53.9	54.7	238.4	55.8	146.0	182.3	164.8	47.0	2,453.7
2004-05	122.9	495.0	284.3	497.4	57.2	75.2	232.7	61.5	223.2	218.5	207.7	48.4	3,123.7
2005-06	102.0	439.4	263.6	525.0	53.3	76.6	306.0	58.0	181.7	235.3	201.6	41.8	3,063.2
2006-07[1]	110.2	502.5	289.7	502.5	61.2	85.1	311.8	42.6	206.0	255.0	212.5	42.9	3,188.2

[1] Preliminary.   Source: Agricultural Statistics Board, U.S. Department of Agriculture (ASB-USDA)

United States Exports of Soybeans   In Millions of Bushels

Year	Sept.	Oct.	Nov.	Dec.	Jan.	Feb.	Mar.	Apr.	May	June	July	Aug.	Total
1997-98	42.6	174.3	150.4	121.2	91.1	94.8	56.9	36.7	27.3	24.7	27.9	26.6	874.3
1998-99	27.9	135.6	106.3	90.4	84.3	66.8	72.4	52.5	37.8	36.4	36.7	57.5	804.7
1999-00	69.4	122.8	104.5	109.1	104.0	103.1	109.7	50.6	45.6	46.0	50.3	58.4	973.4
2000-01	51.4	141.4	123.0	106.6	103.3	126.5	135.2	52.8	39.8	39.5	33.1	43.4	995.9
2001-02	31.7	158.9	158.0	133.2	157.2	132.0	63.8	46.0	45.6	43.2	56.0	38.0	1,063.7
2002-03	30.9	136.7	152.8	114.7	159.3	151.5	92.1	66.4	35.9	31.9	37.9	34.3	1,044.4
2003-04	34.0	165.3	186.4	143.2	109.3	82.6	69.9	28.7	19.1	20.2	14.8	10.8	884.2
2004-05	47.2	177.7	181.0	155.0	121.9	123.2	96.4	65.2	49.6	35.2	20.0	30.3	1,102.7
2005-06	32.3	143.1	140.1	83.1	111.8	111.3	95.6	43.4	46.5	39.0	47.6	51.0	944.8
2006-07[1]	64.8	178.0	131.0										1,495.2

[1] Preliminary.   Source: Economic Research Service, U.S. Department of Agriculture (ERS-USDA)

Spread Between Value of Products and Soybean Price in the United States   In Cents Per Bushel

Year	Sept.	Oct.	Nov.	Dec.	Jan.	Feb.	Mar.	Apr.	May	June	July	Aug.	Average
1995-96	68	82	58	64	53	48	53	67	44	50	52	47	57
1996-97	84	92	105	92	74	74	62	54	82	67	94	123	83
1997-98	177	96	108	87	57	51	35	33	33	29	53	43	67
1998-99	53	53	38	40	33	30	35	37	34	36	47	45	40
1999-00	48	61	64	58	75	61	70	70	80	81	69	62	66
2000-01	81	76	77	89	85	59	65	72	67	81	96	92	78
2001-02	102	108	106	83	86	65	65	65	57	63	64	89	79
2002-03	77	73	52	60	53	52	61	53	62	59	72	74	62
2003-04	117	88	94	81	84	81	96	96	85	97	150	127	99
2004-05[1]	132	95	70	66	75	76	67	78	69	75	73	82	79

Source: Economic Research Service, U.S. Department of Agriculture (ERS-USDA)

Soybean Crushed (Factory Consumption) in the United States   In Millions of Bushels

Year	Sept.	Oct.	Nov.	Dec.	Jan.	Feb.	Mar.	Apr.	May	June	July	Aug.	Total
1997-98	110.8	142.2	142.8	153.1	151.8	138.3	147.0	134.0	123.9	117.5	123.8	111.9	1,597
1998-99	123.9	142.4	143.0	144.6	136.4	127.6	140.0	128.4	128.0	121.2	127.3	126.9	1,590
1999-00	133.8	150.2	142.8	143.0	139.2	125.4	130.4	121.5	121.0	117.9	130.2	122.2	1,578
2000-01	128.9	149.1	143.1	142.3	146.7	128.9	141.8	131.1	132.7	128.0	133.6	133.5	1,640
2001-02	128.2	150.2	149.1	153.4	155.1	139.0	149.8	139.2	140.6	134.6	129.8	130.6	1,700
2002-03	122.3	149.5	145.7	150.2	142.7	129.2	142.8	127.0	129.8	121.4	129.3	125.1	1,615
2003-04	127.6	146.2	145.6	145.8	146.0	131.4	129.6	112.5	117.5	109.4	115.3	103.0	1,530
2004-05	121.0	155.3	151.1	150.0	148.6	137.6	148.5	139.4	142.8	132.0	139.5	130.3	1,696
2005-06	133.2	157.7	151.5	148.4	152.4	136.3	149.5	135.5	146.2	137.4	148.5	142.1	1,739
2006-07[1]	142.4	161.7	155.1	156.2									1,846

One Bushel = 60 Pounds.   [1] Preliminary.   Source: Economic Research Service, U.S. Department of Agriculture (ERS-USDA)

SOYBEANS

Soybean Futures - Chicago Board of Trade
(weekly close) as of December 29, 2006

Cents per bushel

Volume of Trading of Soybean Futures in Chicago   In Thousands of Contracts

Year	Jan.	Feb.	Mar.	Apr.	May	June	July	Aug.	Sept.	Oct.	Nov.	Dec.	Total
1997	1,119.8	1,254.2	1,405.9	1,585.5	1,391.1	1,355.6	1,217.4	835.0	852.3	1,505.8	1,010.7	1,006.6	14,540
1998	875.7	971.2	935.9	1,116.2	973.6	1,378.8	1,286.3	884.5	864.4	1,264.6	867.0	1,012.9	12,431
1999	871.1	1,025.3	1,440.1	963.5	823.6	1,149.5	1,502.5	1,669.8	903.0	1,158.6	839.4	872.3	12,482
2000	1,071.9	1,099.3	1,191.6	1,079.1	1,321.6	1,302.0	883.4	801.4	860.9	1,188.8	932.5	895.3	12,628
2001	935.0	947.4	843.1	916.3	909.5	1,155.6	1,508.1	1,122.0	648.7	1,356.1	964.7	844.1	12,150
2002	1,078.8	899.9	1,065.7	1,238.6	1,048.3	1,311.8	1,762.2	1,346.4	1,002.9	1,486.1	1,070.9	1,163.5	14,475
2003	1,267.3	1,222.9	997.1	1,588.9	1,368.2	1,723.4	1,385.7	1,193.5	1,308.5	2,416.3	1,535.4	1,538.5	17,546
2004	1,509.7	1,879.6	1,957.2	2,036.2	1,593.2	1,601.7	1,551.3	1,107.6	1,052.8	1,635.3	1,395.3	1,526.1	18,846
2005	1,398.6	2,085.8	1,959.9	1,656.5	1,454.6	2,577.3	1,675.4	1,487.2	1,069.1	1,765.0	1,241.5	1,845.1	20,216
2006	1,503.4	1,889.1	1,501.2	1,916.6	1,682.6	2,443.2	1,798.2	1,638.5	1,420.2	2,884.7	2,017.4	1,952.6	22,648

Source: Chicago Board of Trade

Average Open Interest of Soybean Futures in Chicago   In Contracts

Year	Jan.	Feb.	Mar.	Apr.	May	June	July	Aug.	Sept.	Oct.	Nov.	Dec.
1997	157,728	176,242	189,352	188,617	186,792	159,720	141,658	133,732	150,606	172,098	148,760	150,201
1998	135,340	142,778	147,900	152,732	143,994	149,563	133,532	140,236	158,627	163,759	143,814	146,463
1999	152,757	166,003	162,690	166,565	164,777	163,663	157,433	134,105	146,087	174,583	164,306	153,693
2000	149,468	172,494	174,465	195,189	193,500	167,678	140,894	126,952	149,074	183,734	168,023	177,324
2001	160,730	164,017	148,190	156,781	137,227	153,190	181,194	165,630	167,677	195,366	175,522	173,116
2002	156,898	169,242	169,882	164,388	156,548	188,692	220,758	201,494	201,808	210,033	208,099	213,868
2003	201,536	217,680	226,421	251,314	230,325	222,185	190,206	190,533	232,030	265,088	241,320	252,874
2004	258,708	267,482	263,737	262,919	222,310	199,108	172,194	171,791	190,006	242,654	228,700	241,972
2005	244,197	266,745	295,324	268,081	252,582	313,724	278,738	256,853	249,030	285,070	275,308	290,370
2006	315,640	359,379	354,211	374,507	375,124	371,155	336,000	348,321	361,643	384,069	394,259	414,374

Source: Chicago Board of Trade (CBT)

Average Cash Price of No. 1 Yellow Soybeans at Illinois Processor   In Cents Per Bushel

Year	Sept.	Oct.	Nov.	Dec.	Jan.	Feb.	Mar.	Apr.	May	June	July	Aug.	Average
1995-96	632	656	686	717	737	730	726	791	808	778	795	816	739
1996-97	820	711	704	708	737	769	833	854	878	837	769	741	780
1997-98	703	684	727	699	679	680	662	649	649	640	642	556	664
1998-99	533	536	572	558	532	490	475	480	468	462	425	465	500
1999-00	485	470	464	460	473	500	513	529	542	510	474	463	490
2000-01	484	468	483	506	477	457	451	441	457	474	517	510	477
2001-02	469	430	441	438	437	440	464	471	492	519	575	567	479
2002-03	579	541	575	566	570	590	580	611	640	635	601	589	590
2003-04	639	729	763	772	823	872	975	992	958	890	809	641	822
2004-05[1]	562	519	534	545	539	544	628	622	644	701	703	639	598

[1] Preliminary.   Source: Economic Research Service, U.S. Department of Agriculture (ERS-USDA)

Average Price Received by Farmers for Soybeans in the United States   In Dollars Per Bushel

Year	Sept.	Oct.	Nov.	Dec.	Jan.	Feb.	Mar.	Apr.	May	June	July	Aug.	Average
1997-98	6.72	6.50	6.85	6.71	6.69	6.57	6.40	6.26	6.26	6.16	6.14	5.43	6.47
1998-99	5.25	5.18	5.40	5.37	5.32	4.80	4.61	4.63	4.51	4.44	4.20	4.39	4.93
1999-00	4.57	4.48	4.45	4.43	4.62	4.79	4.91	5.00	5.19	4.93	4.53	4.45	4.63
2000-01	4.59	4.45	4.55	4.78	4.68	4.46	4.39	4.22	4.33	4.46	4.79	4.85	4.54
2001-02	4.53	4.09	4.16	4.20	4.22	4.22	4.38	4.47	4.64	4.88	5.35	5.53	4.38
2002-03	5.39	5.20	5.46	5.46	5.51	5.55	5.59	5.82	6.07	6.09	5.82	5.68	5.64
2003-04	6.06	6.60	7.05	7.17	7.35	8.28	9.28	9.62	9.56	9.08	8.46	6.83	7.95
2004-05	5.83	5.56	5.36	5.45	5.57	5.42	5.95	6.03	6.21	6.58	6.65	6.15	5.90
2005-06	5.77	5.67	5.62	5.78	5.87	5.67	5.57	5.52	5.68	5.61	5.61	5.23	5.63
2006-07[1]	5.24	5.52	6.07	6.18	6.38	6.83							6.04

[1] Preliminary.   Source: Economic Research Service, U.S. Department of Agriculture (ERS-USDA)

Stock Index Futures, U.S.

A stock index simply represents a basket of underlying stocks. Indices can be either price-weighted or capitalization-weighted. In a price-weighted index, such as the Dow Jones Industrials Average, the price of each of the stocks are simply added up and then divided by a divisor, meaning that stocks with higher prices have a higher weighting in the index value. In a capitalization-weighted index, such as the Standard and Poor's 500 index, the weighting of each stock corresponds to the size of the company as determined by its capitalization (i.e., the total dollar value of its stock). Stock indices cover a variety of different sectors. For example, the Dow Jones Industrials Average contains 30 blue-chip stocks that represent the industrial sector. The S&P 500 index includes 500 of the largest blue-chip US companies. The NYSE index includes all the stocks that trade at the New York Stock Exchange. The Nasdaq 100 includes the largest 100 companies that trade on the Nasdaq Exchange. The most popular US stock index futures contract is the S&P 500 at the Chicago Mercantile Exchange (CME).

Prices – The S&P 500 index in 2006 extended the bull market that began in October 2002 and rallied to a new 6-year high, closing +13.6% on the year. The stock market rally continued into early 2007 when the S&P 500 posted another new 6-year high of 1461.57, which represented an overall rally of +90.2% from the bear market low of 768.63 posted in October 2002. The S&P 500 index corrected downward by 6% in March 2007 but was still only moderately below the 6-year high posted in February 2007.

The US stock market in 2006 extended its rally as US earnings growth remained very strong. Annual earnings growth in 2006 for the S&P 500 companies was very strong at +16.5% yr/yr, extending the string of double-digit earnings

growth to four consecutive years (2006 +16.5%, 2005 +13.7%, 2004 +20.2%, 2003 +18.4%), according to Thomson Financial. The double-digit earnings growth seen in 2003-06 was an extraordinary performance for earnings growth and was far in excess of the 25-year average for S&P 500 earnings growth of +8.6%.

The strong earnings performance allowed US stock market valuations to remain relatively attractive despite the rally in stock prices. The S&P 500 forward price/earnings ratio (based on forward-looking earnings) remained near 16 during 2006, which was below the 3-year average of 16.6 and the 10-year average of 19.8.

The US stock market was driven higher in 2006, not only by strong earnings performance, but also by a very active mergers and acquisitions market. Private equity funds, as well as public companies, were active buyers of companies in the public market, thus supporting valuation levels and reducing the supply of stock available to public investors. The US stock market took in stride the rally in crude oil prices to a record high of $78.40 in July 2006, and then benefited as crude oil prices fell back in the latter half of 2006. The stock market also saw underlying support from the US interest rate picture as the Federal Reserve in mid-2006 halted its rate hike regime with the federal funds rate at 5.25%. US long-term interest rates then fell substantially in the latter half of 2006, thus keeping US interest rates at historically low levels. The stock market in March 2007 stumbled, however, and showed a downward correction of about 6% on spillover effects from a global stock market correction and on the deceleration in US earnings to the +6% growth area after four consecutive years of double-digit growth.

Dow Jones Industrial Average (30 Stocks)

Year	Jan.	Feb.	Mar.	Apr.	May	June	July	Aug.	Sept.	Oct.	Nov.	Dec.	Average
1997	6,707.0	6,917.5	6,901.1	6,657.5	7,242.4	7,599.6	7,990.7	7,948.4	7,866.6	7,875.8	7,677.4	7,909.8	7,441.1
1998	7,808.4	8,323.6	8,709.5	9,037.4	9,080.1	8,873.0	9,097.1	8,478.5	7,909.8	8,164.3	9,005.8	9,018.7	8,625.5
1999	9,345.9	9,323.0	9,753.6	10,443.5	10,853.9	10,704.0	11,052.2	10,935.5	10,714.0	10,396.9	10,809.8	11,246.4	10,464.9
2000	11,281.3	10,541.9	10,483.4	10,944.4	10,580.3	10,582.9	10,663.0	11,014.5	10,967.9	10,441.0	10,666.1	10,652.4	10,734.9
2001	10,682.7	10,774.6	10,081.3	10,234.5	11,005.0	10,767.2	10,444.5	10,314.7	9,042.6	9,220.8	9,721.8	9,979.9	10,189.1
2002	9,923.8	9,891.1	10,501.0	10,165.2	10,080.5	9,492.4	8,616.5	8,685.5	8,160.2	8,048.1	8,625.7	8,526.7	9,226.4
2003	8,474.4	7,916.2	7,977.7	8,332.1	8,623.4	9,098.1	9,154.5	9,284.8	9,492.5	9,683.6	9,762.2	10,124.7	8,993.7
2004	10,540.1	10,601.5	10,323.7	10,419.9	10,083.8	10,364.9	10,152.1	10,032.8	10,204.6	10,001.6	10,411.8	10,673.4	10,317.5
2005	10,539.5	10,723.8	10,682.1	10,283.2	10,377.2	10,486.6	10,545.4	10,554.3	10,532.5	10,324.3	10,695.3	10,827.8	10,547.7
2006	10,872.5	10,971.2	11,144.5	11,234.7	11,333.9	10,998.0	11,032.5	11,257.4	11,533.6	11,963.1	12,185.2	12,377.6	11,408.7

Average.   Source: New York Stock Exchange (NYSE)

Dow Jones Transportation Average (20 Stocks)

Year	Jan.	Feb.	Mar.	Apr.	May	June	July	Aug.	Sept.	Oct.	Nov.	Dec.	Average
1997	2,295.0	2,341.4	2,427.8	2,464.0	2,635.1	2,711.4	2,858.0	2,925.8	3,086.0	3,239.9	3,155.7	3,233.5	2,781.1
1998	3,275.8	3,456.8	3,521.5	3,586.5	3,401.9	3,373.2	3,459.3	3,021.1	2,763.0	2,647.8	2,953.4	3,027.6	3,207.3
1999	3,172.0	3,188.3	3,296.4	3,477.7	3,628.2	3,396.1	3,423.7	3,207.0	3,006.2	2,928.7	2,988.7	2,902.1	3,217.9
2000	2,812.2	2,483.4	2,534.5	2,823.9	2,813.2	2,717.2	2,822.3	2,835.6	2,641.5	2,491.0	2,792.3	2,822.9	2,715.8
2001	3,029.9	3,010.2	2,792.5	2,776.6	2,908.2	2,770.4	2,887.3	2,852.1	2,344.8	2,217.3	2,404.6	2,603.0	2,716.4
2002	2,735.3	2,719.1	2,942.9	2,776.0	2,734.8	2,702.2	2,432.1	2,318.5	2,216.0	2,216.6	2,321.6	2,331.7	2,537.2
2003	2,297.3	2,102.5	2,094.6	2,278.7	2,429.9	2,459.6	2,554.5	2,617.3	2,744.7	2,841.3	2,920.0	2,969.3	2,525.8
2004	3,021.0	2,889.4	2,838.3	2,941.1	2,877.1	3,069.0	3,099.8	3,065.8	3,205.1	3,372.6	3,589.4	3,750.0	3,143.2
2005	3,587.0	3,614.5	3,779.4	3,527.8	3,548.8	3,542.1	3,663.1	3,726.1	3,637.0	3,673.1	4,051.7	4,152.1	3,708.6
2006	4,224.5	4,362.5	4,519.5	4,679.6	4,761.4	4,663.1	4,636.1	4,291.1	4,363.3	4,654.7	4,761.6	4,660.0	4,548.1

Average.   Source: New York Stock Exchange (NYSE)

Dow Jones 30 Industrials - Logarithmic Scale
(monthly close) through December 2006

Index Value

Dow Jones Industrial Average (30 Stocks)

Year	Jan.	Feb.	Mar.	Apr.	May	June	July	Aug.	Sept.	Oct.	Nov.	Dec.	Average
1997	6,707.0	6,917.5	6,901.1	6,657.5	7,242.4	7,599.6	7,990.7	7,948.4	7,866.6	7,875.8	7,677.4	7,909.8	7,441.1
1998	7,808.4	8,323.6	8,709.5	9,037.4	9,080.1	8,873.0	9,097.1	8,478.5	7,909.8	8,164.3	9,005.8	9,018.7	8,625.5
1999	9,345.9	9,323.0	9,753.6	10,443.5	10,853.9	10,704.0	11,052.2	10,935.5	10,714.0	10,396.9	10,809.8	11,246.4	10,464.9
2000	11,281.3	10,541.9	10,483.4	10,944.4	10,580.3	10,582.9	10,663.0	11,014.5	10,967.9	10,441.0	10,666.1	10,652.4	10,734.9
2001	10,682.7	10,774.6	10,081.3	10,234.5	11,005.0	10,767.2	10,444.5	10,314.7	9,042.6	9,220.8	9,721.8	9,979.9	10,189.1
2002	9,923.8	9,891.1	10,501.0	10,165.2	10,080.5	9,492.4	8,616.5	8,685.5	8,160.2	8,048.1	8,625.7	8,526.7	9,226.4
2003	8,474.4	7,916.2	7,977.7	8,332.1	8,623.4	9,098.1	9,154.5	9,284.8	9,492.5	9,683.6	9,762.2	10,124.7	8,993.7
2004	10,540.1	10,601.5	10,323.7	10,419.9	10,083.8	10,364.9	10,152.1	10,032.8	10,204.6	10,001.6	10,411.8	10,673.4	10,317.5
2005	10,539.5	10,723.8	10,682.1	10,283.2	10,377.2	10,486.6	10,545.4	10,554.3	10,532.5	10,324.3	10,695.3	10,827.8	10,547.7
2006	10,872.5	10,971.2	11,144.5	11,234.7	11,333.9	10,998.0	11,032.5	11,257.4	11,533.6	11,963.1	12,185.2	12,377.6	11,408.7

Average.   Source: New York Stock Exchange (NYSE)

Standard & Poor's 500 Composite Price Index

Year	Jan.	Feb.	Mar.	Apr.	May	June	July	Aug.	Sept.	Oct.	Nov.	Dec.	Average
1997	766.1	798.4	792.2	763.9	833.1	876.3	925.3	927.7	937.0	951.2	938.9	962.4	872.7
1998	963.4	1,023.7	1,076.8	1,112.2	1,108.4	1,108.4	1,156.6	1,074.6	1,020.7	1,032.5	1,144.5	1,190.0	1,084.3
1999	1,248.7	1,246.6	1,281.7	1,334.8	1,332.1	1,322.6	1,381.0	1,327.5	1,318.2	1,300.0	1,391.0	1,428.7	1,326.1
2000	1,425.6	1,388.9	1,442.2	1,461.4	1,418.5	1,462.0	1,473.0	1,485.5	1,468.0	1,390.1	1,375.0	1,330.9	1,426.8
2001	1,335.6	1,305.8	1,185.9	1,189.8	1,270.4	1,238.8	1,204.5	1,178.5	1,047.6	1,076.6	1,129.7	1,144.9	1,192.3
2002	1,140.2	1,100.7	1,153.8	1,112.0	1,079.3	1,014.1	903.6	912.6	867.8	854.6	909.9	899.2	995.6
2003	895.8	837.6	846.6	890.0	936.0	988.0	992.5	989.5	1,019.4	1,038.7	1,049.9	1,080.6	963.7
2004	1,132.5	1,143.4	1,124.0	1,133.1	1,102.8	1,132.8	1,105.9	1,088.9	1,117.7	1,118.1	1,168.9	1,199.2	1,130.6
2005	1,181.4	1,199.6	1,194.9	1,164.4	1,178.3	1,202.3	1,222.2	1,224.3	1,225.9	1,192.0	1,237.3	1,262.1	1,207.1
2006	1,278.7	1,276.7	1,293.7	1,302.2	1,290.0	1,253.1	1,260.2	1,287.2	1,317.8	1,363.3	1,388.6	1,416.4	1,310.7

Average.   Source: Index and Option Market (IOM), division of the Chicago Mercantile Exchange (CME)

STOCK INDEX FUTURES, U.S.

Composite Index of Leading Indicators   (1992 = 100)

Year	Jan.	Feb.	Mar.	Apr.	May	June	July	Aug.	Sept.	Oct.	Nov.	Dec.	Average
1997	102.8	103.3	103.4	103.3	103.6	103.6	103.9	104.0	104.3	104.4	104.7	104.6	103.8
1998	104.8	105.2	105.4	105.4	105.4	105.2	105.6	105.6	105.6	105.7	106.2	106.4	105.5
1999	104.5	104.7	104.8	104.7	105.0	105.3	105.6	105.5	105.4	105.5	105.7	110.3	105.6
2000	110.7	110.3	110.5	110.5	110.5	110.4	109.8	109.9	109.9	109.5	109.2	108.8	110.0
2001	108.9	109.0	108.7	108.6	109.3	109.5	109.8	109.7	109.1	109.2	110.1	110.5	109.4
2002	111.0	111.0	111.0	110.8	111.4	111.2	111.0	110.9	110.4	110.4	111.0	111.1	110.9
2003	111.0	110.6	110.4	110.5	111.6	112.0	112.8	113.2	113.3	113.9	114.2	114.3	112.3
2004	114.7	114.8	115.7	115.8	116.3	134.5	135.0	135.1	135.2	135.2	136.0	136.1	127.0
2005	135.8	136.3	135.4	135.5	135.6	137.1	136.9	137.0	135.8	136.9	138.2	138.5	136.6
2006[1]	139.1	138.4	138.9	138.6	137.9	138.2	137.8	137.4	138.0	138.1	138.2		138.2

[1] Preliminary.   Source: The Conference Board (TCB) Copyrighted.

Consumer Confidence, The Conference Board   (1985 = 100)

Year	Jan.	Feb.	Mar.	Apr.	May	June	July	Aug.	Sept.	Oct.	Nov.	Dec.	Average
1997	118.7	118.9	118.5	118.5	127.9	129.9	126.3	127.6	130.2	123.4	128.1	136.2	125.4
1998	128.3	137.4	133.8	137.2	136.3	138.2	137.2	133.1	126.4	119.3	126.4	126.7	131.7
1999	128.9	133.1	134.0	135.5	137.7	139.0	136.2	136.0	134.2	130.5	137.0	141.7	135.3
2000	144.7	140.8	137.1	137.7	144.7	139.2	143.0	140.8	142.5	135.8	132.6	128.6	139.0
2001	115.7	109.3	116.9	109.9	116.1	118.9	116.3	114.0	97.0	85.3	84.9	94.6	106.6
2002	97.8	95.0	110.7	108.5	110.3	106.3	97.4	94.5	93.7	79.6	84.9	80.7	96.6
2003	78.8	64.8	61.4	81.0	83.6	83.5	77.0	81.7	77.0	81.7	92.5	94.8	79.8
2004	97.7	88.5	88.5	93.0	93.1	102.8	105.7	98.7	96.7	92.9	92.6	102.7	96.1
2005	105.1	104.4	103.0	97.5	103.1	106.2	103.6	105.5	87.5	85.2	98.3	103.8	100.3
2006[1]	106.8	102.7	107.5	109.8	104.7	105.4	107.0	100.2	105.9	105.1	105.3		105.5

[1] Preliminary.   Source: The Conference Board (TCB) Copyrighted.

Capacity Utilization Rates (Total Industry)   In Percent

Year	Jan.	Feb.	Mar.	Apr.	May	June	July	Aug.	Sept.	Oct.	Nov.	Dec.	Average
1997	83.3	83.9	84.1	83.6	83.6	83.5	83.5	84.0	84.3	84.3	84.6	84.4	83.9
1998	84.2	83.7	83.3	83.1	83.1	82.2	81.5	82.8	82.3	82.5	82.1	81.9	82.7
1999	82.0	82.0	81.8	81.7	82.0	81.7	81.9	82.0	81.3	82.1	82.2	82.6	81.9
2000	82.5	82.5	82.5	82.7	82.7	82.5	82.0	81.4	81.5	80.9	80.7	80.1	81.8
2001	79.2	78.4	77.9	77.6	76.9	76.3	75.9	75.4	75.0	74.5	74.0	73.9	76.3
2002	74.3	74.1	74.7	74.9	75.2	75.8	75.6	75.6	75.6	75.3	75.5	75.2	75.2
2003	75.5	75.6	75.4	74.9	74.9	75.1	75.4	75.5	76.0	76.1	76.8	76.9	75.7
2004	77.2	77.8	77.6	78.1	78.8	78.4	78.8	79.0	78.7	79.2	79.3	79.7	78.6
2005	79.6	80.0	79.9	79.9	80.2	80.6	80.5	80.7	79.2	80.0	80.7	81.3	80.2
2006[1]	81.1	81.1	81.4	81.9	81.7	82.3	82.4	82.4	82.0	81.7	81.5	81.8	81.8

[1] Preliminary.   Source: Bureau of Economic Analysis, U.S. Department of Commerce (BEA)

Manufacturers New Orders, Durable Goods   In Billions of Constant Dollars

Year	Jan.	Feb.	Mar.	Apr.	May	June	July	Aug.	Sept.	Oct.	Nov.	Dec.	Average
1997	171.73	174.80	170.02	173.13	177.05	176.93	175.82	181.08	181.15	181.33	189.71	181.44	177.03
1998	184.33	183.87	184.17	187.35	181.58	182.22	186.22	190.39	193.18	189.33	190.21	197.11	194.42
1999	211.18	203.31	209.39	204.68	206.78	207.27	216.02	218.02	214.83	212.77	215.34	229.47	209.76
2000	225.14	221.12	230.44	217.17	232.76	254.20	220.74	227.27	232.41	217.30	221.14	220.90	220.55
2001	197.36	205.41	209.56	198.11	201.86	196.99	196.53	194.41	174.92	199.09	187.14	188.34	195.44
2002	190.08	194.99	191.78	192.65	193.48	184.76	200.59	198.62	189.66	192.67	190.66	190.01	192.80
2003	194.21	192.26	194.57	190.00	189.13	194.23	197.39	197.18	201.29	208.82	203.42	206.56	197.41
2004	201.03	208.36	219.67	212.63	209.43	211.13	214.32	212.78	214.36	211.53	215.33	218.24	194.74
2005	215.03	214.09	210.62	213.77	216.61	219.48	206.67	216.05	212.28	212.43	217.31	219.01	206.56
2006[1]	201.93	208.63	220.58	209.61	209.37	215.00	208.03	345.12	346.15	207.48	210.37		234.75

[1] Preliminary.   Source: Bureau of Economic Analysis, U.S. Department of Commerce (BEA)

Corporate Profits After Tax -- Quarterly   In Billions of Dollars

Year	First Quarter	Second Quarter	Third Quarter	Fourth Quarter	Average	Year	First Quarter	Second Quarter	Third Quarter	Fourth Quarter	Average
1995	446.4	467.4	494.2	504.1	478.0	2001	556.2	565.2	516.9	614.4	563.2
1996	504.0	518.4	526.2	544.3	523.2	2002	654.5	675.8	698.5	746.0	693.7
1997	599.1	619.4	641.5	629.6	622.4	2003	727.6	783.3	822.2	865.6	799.7
1998	562.9	547.6	554.2	548.6	553.3	2004	889.4	887.3	858.2	926.4	890.3
1999	593.2	592.9	582.1	602.5	592.7	2005	919.0	950.1	887.5	968.9	931.4
2000	551.8	560.5	551.5	547.2	552.8	2006[1]	1,112.1	1,115.7	1,162.7		1,130.2

[1] Preliminary.   Source: Bureau of Economic Analysis, U.S. Department of Commerce (BEA)

Change in Manufacturing and Trade Inventories   In Billions of Dollars

Year	Jan.	Feb.	Mar.	Apr.	May	June	July	Aug.	Sept.	Oct.	Nov.	Dec.	Average
1997	107.0	103.4	76.3	56.2	25.2	76.8	20.9	19.1	91.5	55.2	43.1	28.2	47.1
1998	27.8	86.1	85.7	38.5	5.5	11.4	-91.6	47.9	67.6	36.3	51.0		34.0
1999	10.4	36.8	66.7	31.2	44.4	61.6	67.2	42.5	58.0	50.4	121.1	70.9	50.6
2000	69.5	59.5	17.5	38.8	82.8	129.5	8.7	87.4	10.1	77.7	26.4	5.8	63.7
2001	1.7	-40.5	-73.0	-36.6	-38.9	-105.1	-68.2	-34.2	-75.3	-200.6	-139.2	-78.7	-65.2
2002	-0.9	-31.5	-47.8	-20.1	33.6	27.8	78.5	3.5	-106.8	18.5	33.0	-86.0	17.6
2003	-118.4	-60.3	-18.3	0.1	111.8	89.5	24.1	-39.4	78.7	54.4	57.5	45.7	17.6
2004	16.6	108.5	107.0	101.2	88.6	153.5	139.9	373.6	-12.2	54.3	166.0	29.5	110.5
2005	130.5	84.6	60.3	40.0	218.4	-5.7	-66.0	57.9	272.9	81.3	78.8	305.6	54.5
2006[1]	104.8	13.5	-120.2	104.9	173.9	138.9	104.8	104.0	49.1	26.8	59.1		69.1

[1] Preliminary.   *Source: Bureau of Economic Analysis, U.S. Department of Commerce (BEA)*

Productivity: Index of Output per Hour, All Persons, Nonfarm Business -- Quarterly   (1992 = 100)

Year	First Quarter	Second Quarter	Third Quarter	Fourth Quarter	Average	Year	First Quarter	Second Quarter	Third Quarter	Fourth Quarter	Average
1995	101.7	101.9	102.0	102.9	102.1	2001	116.7	118.3	118.8	120.6	118.6
1996	103.9	104.9	105.2	105.4	104.9	2002	122.7	122.9	124.2	124.1	123.5
1997	105.1	106.3	107.2	107.7	106.6	2003	125.2	126.9	130.1	129.9	128.0
1998	108.5	108.8	110.1	110.6	109.5	2004	130.6	132.1	132.2	132.3	131.8
1999	111.6	111.7	112.5	114.5	112.6	2005	133.6	134.1	135.4	135.2	134.6
2000	113.9	115.9	115.6	116.7	115.5	2006[1]	136.3	136.7	136.6	137.1	136.7

[1] Preliminary.   *Source: Bureau of Economic Analysis, U.S. Department of Commerce (BEA)*

Civilian Unemployment Rate

Year	Jan.	Feb.	Mar.	Apr.	May	June	July	Aug.	Sept.	Oct.	Nov.	Dec.	Average
1997	5.4	5.3	5.2	4.9	4.8	5.0	4.9	4.9	4.9	4.8	4.6	4.7	5.0
1998	4.6	4.6	4.7	4.3	4.4	4.5	4.5	4.5	4.5	4.5	4.4	4.3	4.5
1999	4.3	4.4	4.2	4.3	4.2	4.3	4.3	4.2	4.2	4.1	4.1	4.1	4.2
2000	4.0	4.1	4.1	3.9	4.1	4.0	4.0	4.1	3.9	3.9	4.0	4.0	4.0
2001	4.2	4.2	4.3	4.5	4.4	4.5	4.5	4.9	4.9	5.4	5.7	5.8	4.8
2002	5.6	5.5	5.7	6.0	5.8	5.9	5.9	5.7	5.6	5.7	6.0	6.0	5.8
2003	5.7	5.8	5.8	6.0	6.1	6.4	6.2	6.1	6.1	6.0	5.9	5.7	6.0
2004	5.6	5.6	5.7	5.6	5.6	5.6	5.5	5.4	5.4	5.5	5.4	5.4	5.5
2005	5.2	5.4	5.1	5.1	5.1	5.0	5.0	4.9	5.1	4.9	5.0	4.9	5.1
2006[1]	4.7	4.8	4.7	4.7	4.6	4.6	4.8	4.7	4.6	4.4	4.5	4.5	4.6

[1] Preliminary.   *Source: Bureau of Economic Analysis, U.S. Department of Commerce (BEA)*

S&P 500 Index - Logarithmic Scale
(monthly close) through December 2006

STOCK INDEX FUTURES, U.S.

Dow Jones 30 Industrials Index (weekly close) as of December 29, 2006

S&P 500 Index (weekly close) as of December 29, 2006

NASDAQ 100 Index (weekly close) as of December 29, 2006

Value Line 'A' Index (weekly close) as of December 29, 2006

Volume of Trading of S&P 500 Stock Index Futures in Chicago   In Thousands of Contracts

Year	Jan.	Feb.	Mar.	Apr.	May	June	July	Aug.	Sept.	Oct.	Nov.	Dec.	Total
1997	3,371	2,857	4,163	3,608	3,203	3,955	2,617	2,848	3,556	3,136	1,994	2,982	38,290
1998	2,270	1,878	3,018	2,237	2,253	3,524	2,139	3,019	3,802	2,598	1,831	2,835	31,404
1999	1,994	2,145	3,018	1,960	2,007	2,768	1,756	2,200	3,017	2,150	1,675	2,322	27,013
2000	1,911	1,917	2,956	1,651	1,685	2,226	1,079	1,358	2,149	1,681	1,636	2,212	22,461
2001	1,552	1,631	2,781	1,624	1,653	2,154	1,320	1,598	2,571	1,798	1,692	2,124	22,498
2002	1,459	1,677	2,251	1,473	1,585	2,721	2,206	1,615	2,943	1,931	1,374	2,465	23,700
2003	1,443	1,343	2,900	1,257	1,416	2,782	1,223	1,079	2,412	1,118	921	2,281	20,175
2004	945	839	2,487	880	938	2,136	837	965	2,076	866	1,105	2,101	16,176
2005	764	874	2,330	916	892	2,090	618	979	2,090	902	880	2,041	15,377
2006	711	773	2,199	607	1,122	2,322	726	891	1,883	686	936	1,989	14,845

Source: Index and Option Market (IOM), division of the Chicago Mercantile Exchange (CME)

Average Open Interest of S&P 500 Stock Index Futures in Chicago   In Contracts

Year	Jan.	Feb.	Mar.	Apr.	May	June	July	Aug.	Sept.	Oct.	Nov.	Dec.
1997	393,086	396,528	417,542	377,100	392,034	417,006	372,274	392,812	423,449	391,922	402,044	417,717
1998	394,410	408,851	417,721	365,746	371,732	412,739	370,410	385,820	434,838	405,395	421,928	435,907
1999	399,093	406,516	410,164	381,402	391,035	400,503	372,455	385,809	408,176	394,316	408,751	416,425
2000	369,295	374,365	400,089	379,651	383,677	409,448	380,118	391,867	416,600	413,912	447,245	498,049
2001	488,284	495,621	517,666	498,594	490,148	505,063	485,839	501,281	556,737	529,730	550,201	551,175
2002	495,352	519,023	542,358	513,048	542,839	592,888	594,727	621,558	644,806	607,848	631,224	647,022
2003	596,064	619,738	658,749	622,917	643,030	691,003	611,564	611,578	631,509	582,111	589,392	633,997
2004	612,911	614,843	624,209	595,593	587,717	604,154	586,760	597,581	632,050	636,566	686,531	714,420
2005	678,739	686,413	719,141	681,149	697,818	700,618	656,266	653,430	669,849	642,704	657,097	681,868
2006	655,483	668,113	682,218	653,044	664,790	670,449	625,142	634,579	634,817	609,410	640,481	679,221

Source: Index and Option Market (IOM), division of the Chicago Mercantile Exchange (CME)

Volume of Trading of S&P 400 Midcap Stock Index Futures in Chicago   In Contracts

Year	Jan.	Feb.	Mar.	Apr.	May	June	July	Aug.	Sept.	Oct.	Nov.	Dec.	Total
1997	13,698	14,968	33,860	16,993	15,463	33,287	12,162	14,923	39,164	18,063	10,776	43,242	266,599
1998	13,622	12,896	42,781	15,623	17,023	38,656	15,345	19,967	44,913	23,591	16,713	48,870	310,000
1999	18,752	20,938	43,395	27,664	16,574	42,709	17,790	18,188	39,723	18,341	19,974	42,073	326,121
2000	16,918	15,298	45,942	23,892	19,863	42,514	12,140	12,515	42,658	21,701	25,334	59,265	338,040
2001	21,527	19,884	58,286	18,061	19,258	50,331	22,029	23,805	50,706	23,741	19,591	51,641	378,860
2002	22,322	22,814	43,819	23,019	22,484	51,775	30,607	23,075	52,375	25,593	21,262	48,105	387,250
2003	18,827	18,392	44,454	15,841	15,194	40,603	15,153	12,082	43,112	15,253	13,109	50,797	302,817
2004	13,647	10,361	46,214	13,921	13,078	45,940	12,602	13,582	36,701	7,923	9,824	36,971	260,764
2005	6,486	5,736	36,685	5,130	7,235	39,025	4,603	7,699	42,503	5,736	4,988	39,232	205,058
2006	5,668	3,739	34,668	3,671	4,619	31,924	2,656	3,311	23,289	3,718	6,409	29,596	153,268

Source: Index and Option Market (IOM), division of the Chicago Mercantile Exchange (CME)

Average Open Interest of S&P 400 Midcap Stock Index Futures in Chicago   In Contracts

Year	Jan.	Feb.	Mar.	Apr.	May	June	July	Aug.	Sept.	Oct.	Nov.	Dec.
1997	11,215	11,825	11,258	9,721	10,807	10,877	11,292	12,346	13,505	11,595	11,874	13,329
1998	12,688	13,319	14,363	14,130	13,352	13,940	12,964	13,589	14,893	16,645	16,768	17,569
1999	16,191	16,309	14,573	12,154	12,705	14,422	14,263	13,496	13,182	12,699	13,933	14,902
2000	12,810	13,119	13,965	12,495	13,355	14,040	12,957	13,162	15,026	16,143	16,510	17,479
2001	15,246	15,461	17,235	16,953	15,623	16,606	16,334	16,132	16,718	15,109	15,307	15,337
2002	13,691	14,109	14,954	14,340	16,402	16,611	15,121	16,213	17,006	14,695	15,394	16,432
2003	13,793	13,498	14,530	13,120	13,353	13,986	13,123	13,029	13,726	14,014	15,465	17,446
2004	15,911	15,988	16,554	15,870	15,819	17,148	13,939	13,600	14,213	13,339	14,046	14,755
2005	13,078	13,313	14,861	11,812	11,832	13,811	12,380	12,420	14,477	12,890	12,955	13,822
2006	12,168	11,940	12,409	10,999	10,892	10,447	9,307	9,687	9,194	8,442	9,884	9,794

Source: Index and Option Market (IOM), division of the Chicago Mercantile Exchange (CME)

STOCK INDEX FUTURES, U.S.

Volume of Trading of NASDAQ 100 Index Futures in Chicago   In Contracts

Year	Jan.	Feb.	Mar.	Apr.	May	June	July	Aug.	Sept.	Oct.	Nov.	Dec.	Total
2000	349,813	366,408	575,942	503,064	460,085	432,062	296,944	310,549	445,334	490,863	400,412	464,454	5,095,930
2001	422,811	416,445	650,488	498,026	487,334	542,305	369,731	369,845	474,133	516,469	391,042	434,690	5,573,319
2002	380,076	367,561	436,495	378,294	443,579	529,496	454,630	334,242	466,898	367,750	315,925	428,341	4,903,287
2003	360,307	301,454	487,916	301,395	330,640	519,597	350,514	251,058	488,363	322,898	259,960	447,119	4,421,221
2004	271,404	268,590	591,556	321,242	297,320	427,805	286,693	245,050	433,251	286,048	226,853	356,171	4,011,983
2005	254,437	198,956	375,435	217,304	170,882	281,483	125,500	159,789	289,113	200,952	155,141	253,066	2,682,058
2006	186,649	162,841	295,163	113,885	169,399	305,557	132,661	149,906	256,605	136,433	140,407	220,364	2,269,870

Source: Index and Option Market (IOM), division of the Chicago Mercantile Exchange (CME)

Average Open Interest of NASDAQ 100 Index Futures in Chicago   In Contracts

Year	Jan.	Feb.	Mar.	Apr.	May	June	July	Aug.	Sept.	Oct.	Nov.	Dec.
2000	27,242	34,555	37,795	36,512	37,578	35,314	29,974	32,922	34,754	35,559	44,022	48,757
2001	46,582	49,495	59,916	56,328	49,337	54,394	50,854	55,234	61,665	51,977	61,196	67,769
2002	49,992	52,883	52,617	51,157	65,219	73,151	60,625	67,760	84,317	72,229	77,451	76,660
2003	71,219	79,905	87,252	71,636	77,717	88,914	80,002	83,940	91,685	75,191	85,651	86,480
2004	73,805	74,892	89,874	81,220	80,905	83,282	69,818	71,711	84,355	74,161	83,675	87,172
2005	72,299	81,327	78,387	56,668	57,116	56,836	49,357	53,270	61,369	60,918	59,754	63,712
2006	61,254	62,994	69,322	60,603	65,224	65,908	54,289	57,585	54,235	53,832	68,347	61,397

Source: Index and Option Market (IOM), division of the Chicago Mercantile Exchange (CME)

Volume of Trading of Dow Jones Industrials Index Futures in Chicago   In Contracts

Year	Jan.	Feb.	Mar.	Apr.	May	June	July	Aug.	Sept.	Oct.	Nov.	Dec.	Total
2000	322,046	340,377	472,179	321,026	284,005	270,374	215,234	211,612	277,620	319,636	267,051	268,010	3,569,170
2001	275,814	310,088	594,326	411,767	377,620	389,919	320,335	410,927	573,479	520,885	375,793	329,898	4,890,851
2002	409,009	472,893	538,804	467,571	456,210	616,754	811,518	539,507	639,154	699,005	427,235	407,665	6,485,325
2003	452,579	426,198	559,372	428,972	410,967	473,432	368,277	286,508	367,845	218,394	157,726	266,032	4,416,302
2004	224,713	207,423	362,668	203,745	208,229	246,564	183,469	149,931	230,829	169,627	152,412	237,528	2,577,138
2005	149,353	107,824	226,113	157,010	124,999	192,165	96,885	121,793	188,541	133,636	108,737	180,349	1,787,405
2006	119,593	111,738	220,880	106,325	152,340	272,494	108,053	97,964	237,988	121,736	111,993	258,743	1,919,847

Source: Chicago Board of Trade (CBT)

Average Open Interest of Dow Jones Industrials Index Futures in Chicago   In Contracts

Year	Jan.	Feb.	Mar.	Apr.	May	June	July	Aug.	Sept.	Oct.	Nov.	Dec.
2000	13,713	16,331	20,443	18,157	19,253	17,394	14,367	15,748	14,840	15,087	19,113	20,966
2001	21,830	23,423	28,340	32,497	33,767	29,357	26,792	33,015	35,451	31,997	30,598	27,018
2002	23,862	35,588	37,582	28,714	32,810	34,482	32,412	32,272	34,665	31,923	34,045	31,892
2003	27,032	30,429	34,371	31,160	34,936	36,352	36,773	43,974	41,747	34,066	37,835	39,727
2004	34,656	44,306	50,172	44,494	45,304	46,641	42,790	42,042	45,940	41,250	43,662	53,469
2005	47,754	48,665	48,423	40,068	41,367	36,909	29,042	30,921	37,232	36,378	37,588	43,819
2006	39,641	39,943	43,595	43,351	45,756	53,833	56,451	58,799	60,497	61,996	63,061	69,927

Source: Chicago Board of Trade (CBT)

Volume of Trading of E-mini NASDAQ 100 Index Futures in Chicago   In Thousands of Contracts

Year	Jan.	Feb.	Mar.	Apr.	May	June	July	Aug.	Sept.	Oct.	Nov.	Dec.	Total
2000	304	382	604	628	745	762	756	883	1,508	1,589	1,446	1,512	11,118
2001	1,845	1,942	2,603	2,873	2,908	2,969	2,529	2,568	2,387	3,935	3,151	2,595	32,304
2002	3,719	3,649	3,652	4,227	4,625	4,713	5,789	4,225	4,337	6,252	4,812	4,490	54,491
2003	5,200	4,620	5,749	5,132	5,075	6,323	6,369	4,816	7,095	6,601	5,254	5,655	67,889
2004	6,157	5,640	8,011	6,387	6,749	5,646	7,139	6,123	6,476	7,322	5,844	5,675	77,169
2005	7,174	6,149	7,336	7,256	5,735	6,233	4,895	5,171	5,624	6,583	5,288	5,008	72,453
2006	6,628	5,803	7,479	5,459	7,386	8,258	6,741	6,315	7,074	6,769	6,333	5,696	79,940

Source: Index and Option Market (IOM), division of the Chicago Mercantile Exchange (CME)

Average Open Interest of E-mini NASDAQ 100 Index Futures in Chicago   In Contracts

Year	Jan.	Feb.	Mar.	Apr.	May	June	July	Aug.	Sept.	Oct.	Nov.	Dec.
2000	8,582	9,250	11,117	15,625	23,465	26,095	23,863	31,506	30,956	33,123	58,709	54,420
2001	45,370	65,061	79,962	78,094	90,822	95,236	90,803	131,259	132,349	75,686	115,350	124,023
2002	78,070	94,150	98,159	100,849	153,348	176,394	130,337	171,043	162,133	110,952	154,104	155,987
2003	169,160	227,905	258,023	196,739	240,759	257,390	262,564	316,032	287,936	214,659	279,379	244,333
2004	205,078	251,011	251,486	257,573	304,034	261,067	213,080	256,749	299,794	279,170	374,750	384,492
2005	339,077	419,715	382,805	310,664	331,447	290,759	270,134	325,508	307,007	365,277	382,667	371,388
2006	351,240	361,807	345,533	309,746	381,178	427,387	386,930	421,179	437,975	457,275	498,584	433,456

Source: Chicago Board of Trade (CBT)

Volume of Trading of E-mini S&P 500 Index Futures in Chicago   In Thousands of Contracts

Year	Jan.	Feb.	Mar.	Apr.	May	June	July	Aug.	Sept.	Oct.	Nov.	Dec.	Total
2000	1,306	1,388	1,489	1,462	1,676	1,550	1,403	1,439	1,683	2,109	1,843	1,673	19,021
2001	2,226	2,231	3,191	3,067	2,931	2,905	2,925	3,478	3,601	5,255	4,021	3,289	39,119
2002	4,933	5,337	5,609	7,165	7,564	9,772	14,277	11,200	11,765	17,175	11,054	9,892	115,742
2003	13,584	12,631	15,820	13,520	12,846	15,040	14,854	10,860	15,354	14,558	11,002	11,108	161,177
2004	13,087	11,355	18,033	14,993	15,889	12,428	14,361	12,921	12,755	14,636	13,705	13,039	167,203
2005	15,447	12,561	18,478	20,182	16,591	17,371	14,400	17,759	18,786	22,929	16,088	16,503	207,096
2006	18,716	16,095	21,357	18,174	24,750	30,359	21,629	19,107	21,986	22,377	23,616	19,760	257,927

Source: Index and Option Market (IOM), division of the Chicago Mercantile Exchange (CME)

Average Open Interest of E-mini S&P 500 Index Futures in Chicago   In Contracts

Year	Jan.	Feb.	Mar.	Apr.	May	June	July	Aug.	Sept.	Oct.	Nov.	Dec.
2000	17,180	25,282	29,645	28,738	38,257	39,918	33,696	45,619	42,442	49,468	66,143	63,052
2001	55,514	68,516	79,934	91,866	110,788	91,638	97,093	126,197	152,253	134,662	224,754	178,681
2002	86,278	120,099	139,965	156,392	225,593	246,288	291,654	349,037	319,341	312,885	418,964	385,220
2003	265,170	356,616	490,037	567,591	741,790	718,511	399,502	492,470	513,398	460,938	467,668	525,310
2004	510,518	576,446	643,118	545,385	579,876	645,794	603,841	697,956	693,529	708,359	979,884	969,343
2005	827,306	901,656	1,013,623	943,262	1,014,855	986,841	932,564	1,060,846	1,110,079	1,042,151	1,166,371	1,211,347
2006	1,149,157	1,194,630	1,334,134	1,211,254	1,402,451	1,525,312	1,371,240	1,512,306	1,582,373	1,549,539	1,754,351	1,810,914

Source: Index and Option Market (IOM), division of the Chicago Mercantile Exchange (CME)

Volume of Trading of NYSE Composite Stock Index Futures[1] in New York   In Contracts

Year	Jan.	Feb.	Mar.	Apr.	May	June	July	Aug.	Sept.	Oct.	Nov.	Dec.	Total
2000	15,324	16,603	21,235	14,394	10,637	11,210	4,307	5,574	5,085	6,145	5,170	9,974	125,658
2001	5,490	4,307	19,300	6,594	4,091	10,353	23,855	32,182	23,399	22,276	19,231	34,661	205,739
2002	20,273	21,056	26,949	27,801	24,166	22,325	21,873	14,561	13,193	10,821	5,897	7,564	216,479
2003	3,917	5,622	9,210	7,718	2,794	4,366	628	553	1,940	408	726	3,282	41,164
2004	3,427	1,127	2,532	159	56	1,705	76	412	1,766	46	915	2,457	14,678
2005	610	2,469	5,022	3,272	50	900	44	22	802	73	31	752	14,047
2006	35	26	746	10	50	751	15	6	740	0	4	830	3,213

[1] Data thru Feb 2003 are Old Index ($500), Mar 2003 thru Sep 2003 are Old ($500) and New Index ($50).   *Source: New York Futures Exchange (NYFE)*

Average Open Interest of NYSE Composite Stock Index Futures[1] in New York   In Contracts

Year	Jan.	Feb.	Mar.	Apr.	May	June	July	Aug.	Sept.	Oct.	Nov.	Dec.
2000	3,653	3,715	3,747	3,285	2,533	2,597	2,452	2,793	2,463	1,690	1,943	2,406
2001	2,387	2,648	3,510	3,694	2,929	2,408	5,271	5,802	5,451	6,448	6,884	6,617
2002	4,341	4,215	5,147	4,141	3,605	3,178	5,157	5,772	3,649	1,567	2,209	2,065
2003	1,255	1,496	1,898	1,670	1,391	1,294	936	1,009	1,106	533	604	752
2004	1,180	1,230	999	733	758	734	696	717	703	656	837	739
2005	1,108	668	711	659	340	344	300	296	313	298	300	309
2006	302	299	300	299	301	315	314	311	298	280	282	280

[1] Data thru Feb 2003 are Old Index ($500), Mar 2003 thru Sep 2003 are Old ($500) and New Index ($50).   *Source: New York Futures Exchange (NYFE)*

Volume of Trading of Mini-Value Line Stock Index Futures in Kansas City   In Contracts

Year	Jan.	Feb.	Mar.	Apr.	May	June	July	Aug.	Sept.	Oct.	Nov.	Dec.	Total
2000	1,397	1,097	1,468	1,054	1,280	811	698	642	1,003	1,328	1,526	1,460	13,764
2001	1,248	1,470	2,441	1,650	902	1,325	1,183	1,071	1,982	1,591	1,104	1,387	17,354
2002	1,513	1,237	1,598	1,283	1,794	1,511	1,878	1,113	974	1,472	1,467	1,530	17,370
2003	376	181	721	264	90	88	46	153	80	94	94	204	2,391
2004	130	134	159	175	63	215	77	33	126	76	67	174	1,429
2005	84	68	45	6	247	584	437	320	408	532	2,109	2,266	7,106
2006	1,155	1,686	3,716	1,895	76	15	0	0	0	0	0	0	8,543

Source: Kansas City Board of Trade (KCBT)

Average Open Interest of Mini-Value Line Stock Index Futures in Kansas City   In Contracts

Year	Jan.	Feb.	Mar.	Apr.	May	June	July	Aug.	Sept.	Oct.	Nov.	Dec.
2000	273	284	246	135	155	148	155	216	179	182	181	185
2001	233	333	377	233	275	285	283	268	222	125	249	368
2002	299	348	367	372	359	229	142	161	100	127	300	417
2003	376	328	169	89	45	33	26	33	48	36	40	46
2004	47	64	49	48	47	56	61	56	40	15	22	32
2005	32	33	18	10	17	49	71	59	68	104	166	185
2006	175	231	139	100	81	38	3	3	3	0	0	0

Source: Kansas City Board of Trade (KCBT)

Stock Index Futures, Worldwide

World stocks – World stock markets in 2006 put in a fourth consecutive year of strong gains following the 2000-02 bear market. Many world stock market indexes in 2006 rallied to new record highs. The MSCI World Index, a benchmark for large companies based in 23 developed countries, rallied by +20.7% in 2006, staging the fourth consecutive year of double-digit percentage gains (2003 +33.8%, 2004 +15.2%, 2005 +10.0%, 2006 +20.7%).

The MSCI World Index showed a fairly steady rally all during 2006. The main bullish factor was strong earnings growth driven by continued strong global economic growth. World GDP growth was very strong at +5.1% in 2006, according to the IMF, maintaining the growth levels of +4.9% seen in 2005 and +5.3% in 2004. The US economy slowed to the low-2% area in the latter half of 2006, but faster GDP growth in Japan and Europe offset slower US growth. The Chinese economy continued to be a key driver of global economic growth, putting in another year of growth near 10%. That helped drive the Chinese stock market sharply higher by +130%. India was also a major contributor to the global economy with 8% growth and India's stock market rallied by +47%.

Crude oil prices were a negative factor for the global stock markets in the first half of 2006 as crude oil prices surged to a record high of $78.40 in July 2006. However, even high crude oil prices were not enough to derail the global economic expansion and crude oil prices then fell back in the latter half of 2006. G7 central banks generally raised short-term interest rates in 2006 to address rising inflation pressures and to lift interest rates back to more normalized levels. However, global long-term interest rates remained generally low in 2006 as bond investors were satisfied with central bank efforts to keep inflation under control.

Small-Capitalization Stocks – World small-cap stocks showed a double-digit rally in 2006 but trailed large-cap stocks for the first time in four years. The MSCI World Small-Cap Index, which tracks companies with market caps between $200 million and $1.5 billion, rallied +15.8% in 2006, putting in its fourth consecutive double-digit annual gain (2003 +55.5%, 2004 +22.6%, 2005 +14.2%, 2006 +15.8%). However, MSCI World Small-Cap Index in 2006 lagged the large-cap MSCI World Index gain of +20.7% points by 4.9 percentage points. That broke the string of 3 years of out-performance by small-cap stocks.

World Industry Groups – The Morgan Stanley Industry Sectors in 2006 performed as follows in terms of ranking: Utilities +31.5%, Telecom +27.8%, Materials +26.2%, Financials +20.9%, Consumer Discretionary +19.35, Consumer Staples +18.0%, Industrials +16.8%, Energy +15.8%, Health Care +9.0%, and Info Technology +8.6%. The Energy sector lagged in 2006 and fell to the number 8 position after taking the number 1 position in stock market performance in 2004 and 2005. Oil stocks were hurt by the decline in crude oil prices in the latter half of 2006.

Emerging markets – Emerging stock markets did very well again in 2006 as the bull market encouraged investors to reach for riskier and potentially more rewarding stocks. The stronger world economy put the emerging countries on a more solid footing, particularly emerging countries that export oil or commodities, or that produce cheap-labor products that are becoming more attractive in the global marketplace as trade barriers fall. The MSCI Emerging Markets Free Index, which tracks companies based in 26 emerging countries, rallied +29.2%, beating the MSCI World Index gain of +20.7% by 8.5 percentage points.

G7 – All of the G7 stock markets saw double-digit gains except for Japan. Of the G7 countries, the ranked stock market gains are as follows: German DAX index +22.0%, France CAC40 +17.5%, Italy MIB +16.0%, Canada Toronto Composite +14.5%, US S&P 500 +13.6%, UK FTSE 100 +10.7%, and the Japan Nikkei 225 +6.9%.

North America – In North America, Mexico's stock market beat both the US and Canadian stock markets for the third straight year. The Mexican Bolsa index closed 2006 up +48.6%, beating the S&P 500 gain in the US of +13.6% and the Toronto Exchange Composite index gain of +14.5%.

Latin America – Latin America stock markets generally closed sharply higher again in 2006: Peru's Lima General Index +168.3%, Venezuela's Stock Market Index +156.1%, Costa Rica's Stock Market Index +77.1%, Chile's Stock Market Select Index +37.1%, Argentina's Merval Index +35.5%, Brazil's Bovespa Index +32.9%, Ecuador's Guayaqui Bolsa Index +29.7%, Columbia's General Index +17.3%, and Jamaica's Stock Exchange Index –3.7%.

Europe – European stocks in 2006 put in another strong year with double-digit percentage gains. The Dow Jones Stoxx 50 index closed +10.7% in 2006, after gains of +20.7% in 2005, +4.3% in 2004 and +10.5% in 2003. European stocks were again helped by the European Central Bank's accommodative monetary policy and the improving Eurozone economy. The five big European powers all saw double-digit gains: Spain +31.8%, Germany +22.0%, France +17.5%, Italy +16.0%, UK +10.7%.

Asia – Asia saw strong stock market gains in 2006 for the fourth consecutive year, as Asia continued to be boosted by torrid economic demand from China. The Morgan Stanley Far East Index showed a gain of +8.9% in 2006, adding to the gains of +24.2% seen in 2005, +16.7% in 2004, and +36.3% in 2003. Japan's Nikkei index closed only moderately higher by +6.9% in 2006, following 2005's sharp gain of +40.2%. South Korea's stock market rose only +4.0% following 2005's stellar gain of +54.0% gain. China's Shanghai Composite Index soared by +130.4% as the Chinese stock market entered into a bubble zone. The ranked closes for the Asian stock markets are as follows: China's Shanghai Composite index +130.4%, Indonesia's Jakarta Composite Index +56.3%, India's Mumbai Sensex 30 index +46.7%, Philippines' Composite index +42.3%, Hong Kong Hang Seng +34.2, Singapore's Straights Times index +27.2%, Malaysia's Kuala Lumpur Composite index +21.8%, New Zealand's Exchange 50 index +20.3%, Australia's All-Ordinaries index +19.9%, Taiwan's TAIEX index of +19.5%, Pakistan's 100 Index +5.1%, and Thailand's Stock Exchange index –4.7%.

Comparison of International Stock Price Indexes   (1990 = 100)

Year	Jan.	Feb.	Mar.	Apr.	May	June	July	Aug.	Sept.	Oct.	Nov.	Dec.	Average
United States													
2000	419.2	410.7	450.5	436.6	427.0	437.2	430.1	456.2	431.8	429.7	395.3	396.9	426.8
2001	410.6	372.7	348.8	375.6	377.5	368.0	364.1	340.7	312.9	318.6	342.5	345.1	356.4
2002	339.7	332.7	344.9	323.7	320.8	297.5	274.0	275.4	245.1	266.2	281.4	264.5	297.2
2003	257.2	252.8	255.0	275.6	289.6	292.9	297.7	303.0	299.4	315.8	318.1	334.2	290.9
2004	340.0	344.2	338.5	332.8	336.9	342.9	331.2	331.9	335.0	339.7	352.8	364.3	340.9
2005	355.1	361.8	354.9	347.7	358.2	358.1	371.0	366.8	369.4	362.8	375.6	375.2	363.1
2006[1]	384.8	385.0	389.2	394.0	381.8	381.8	383.8	391.9	401.5	414.2	421.0		393.5
Canada													
2000	247.9	266.8	276.6	273.2	270.4	298.0	304.2	328.8	303.3	281.8	257.8	261.1	280.8
2001	272.5	236.1	222.4	232.3	238.6	226.1	224.8	216.3	199.9	201.3	217.1	224.7	226.0
2002	223.6	223.2	229.5	224.0	223.8	208.9	193.1	193.3	180.7	182.7	192.1	193.3	205.7
2003	192.0	191.6	185.4	192.5	200.5	204.1	212.2	219.5	216.9	227.2	229.7	240.3	209.3
2004	249.1	256.9	251.0	241.0	246.0	249.8	247.2	244.9	253.4	259.3	264.0	270.3	252.7
2005	269.0	282.6	281.0	273.9	280.8	289.5	304.7	311.9	321.9	303.5	316.4	329.5	297.1
2006[1]	349.2	341.7	354.0	356.7	343.3	339.4	345.8	352.9	343.8	360.8	372.8		350.9
France													
2000	311.4	340.6	345.9	353.2	353.6	354.7	360.0	364.5	344.8	352.0	326.2	326.1	344.4
2001	330.0	295.3	285.0	310.3	300.1	287.5	279.8	258.0	224.4	238.9	246.3	254.5	275.8
2002	245.5	245.6	257.9	245.5	235.2	214.5	187.9	185.2	152.8	173.3	183.0	168.6	207.9
2003	161.6	151.5	144.1	162.5	164.6	169.7	176.6	182.2	172.5	185.6	188.4	195.8	171.3
2004	200.2	205.0	199.5	202.2	201.9	205.4	200.7	197.8	200.3	204.0	206.5	210.2	202.8
2005	215.3	221.6	223.8	215.2	226.7	232.7	244.9	242.1	253.1	244.1	251.3	259.4	235.9
2006[1]	272.2	275.1	287.3	285.5	271.3	273.2	275.6	284.2	288.9	294.3	293.1		281.9
Germany													
2000	404.2	452.0	449.3	438.4	420.4	407.9	425.1	426.7	401.9	418.5	376.8	380.4	416.8
2001	401.8	367.1	344.7	370.4	362.0	358.2	346.5	306.8	254.7	269.6	295.0	305.1	331.8
2002	302.0	297.9	319.1	298.1	284.9	259.1	218.8	219.5	163.7	186.4	196.3	171.0	243.1
2003	162.5	150.6	143.3	173.9	176.4	190.4	206.2	206.0	192.6	216.2	221.5	234.4	189.5
2004	240.0	237.6	228.0	235.6	231.9	239.6	230.3	223.8	230.2	234.1	243.9	251.6	235.6
2005	251.6	257.2	257.1	247.4	263.7	271.2	288.9	285.6	298.2	291.4	307.1	319.8	278.3
2006[1]	335.5	342.7	353.0	355.3	336.6	336.0	335.9	346.4	355.0	370.6	373.0		349.1
Italy													
2000	276.8	330.7	308.7	303.1	307.1	309.0	308.5	320.5	307.2	318.8	316.3	298.3	308.8
2001	303.3	276.4	267.4	278.1	266.1	254.1	249.1	237.9	197.7	208.7	220.9	223.1	248.6
2002	223.6	220.8	233.9	227.6	214.5	196.7	182.7	183.2	157.1	170.0	185.9	170.0	197.2
2003	162.6	166.3	157.2	173.3	180.5	181.1	181.6	184.4	181.5	189.0	196.3	195.6	179.1
2004	201.3	203.3	199.4	204.9	200.5	206.5	202.1	199.1	206.4	212.2	218.6	229.6	207.0
2005	234.9	237.8	241.0	230.5	237.0	241.1	251.9	249.5	261.7	242.9	252.5	261.4	245.2
2006[1]	271.8	282.9	286.3	285.5	269.9	271.5	274.1	283.7	287.2	296.4	304.2		283.0
Japan													
2000	67.8	69.2	70.6	62.4	56.7	60.4	54.6	58.5	54.6	50.4	50.8	47.8	58.7
2001	48.0	44.7	45.1	48.3	46.0	45.0	41.1	37.2	33.9	36.0	37.1	36.6	41.6
2002	34.7	36.7	38.2	39.9	40.8	36.8	34.3	33.4	32.6	30.0	32.0	29.8	34.9
2003	28.9	29.0	27.7	27.2	29.2	31.5	33.2	35.9	35.5	35.5	35.0	37.0	32.1
2004	37.4	38.3	40.6	40.8	39.0	41.1	39.3	38.4	37.5	37.4	37.8	39.9	39.0
2005	39.5	40.7	40.5	38.2	39.1	40.2	41.3	43.1	47.1	47.2	51.6	55.9	43.7
2006[1]	57.8	56.2	59.2	58.6	53.7	53.8	53.6	56.0	55.9	56.9	56.5		56.2
United Kingdom													
2000	274.9	276.2	287.3	277.3	278.7	279.9	282.9	296.3	279.8	284.4	272.1	275.6	280.5
2001	279.9	264.9	250.5	265.0	259.7	252.0	246.1	239.3	216.2	222.9	232.2	233.1	246.8
2002	230.6	227.9	236.2	232.1	228.7	209.1	189.4	189.0	166.4	179.1	185.0	174.9	204.0
2003	159.1	162.5	160.3	174.7	181.9	182.1	189.0	190.7	187.3	196.3	198.3	203.9	182.2
2004	202.0	207.2	202.9	206.7	203.4	205.9	202.5	204.5	209.8	212.2	216.6	222.7	208.0
2005	225.5	230.5	227.0	221.4	229.4	236.5	244.3	245.6	253.6	246.1	253.2	263.0	239.7
2006[1]	270.5	273.1	281.6	284.0	269.4	274.1	277.5	277.8	281.8	290.1	288.2		278.9

[1] Preliminary.   Not Seasonally Adjusted.   *Source: Economic and Statistics Administration, U.S. Department of Commerce (ESA)*

FT-SE 100 Stock Index (weekly close) as of December 29, 2006

Deutscher Aktienindex (DAX) (weekly close) as of December 29, 2006

Toronto 300 Stock Index (weekly close) as of December 29, 2006

Index Value

CAC-40 Stock Index (weekly close) as of December 29, 2006

Index Value

Hang Seng Stock Index (weekly close) as of December 29, 2006

Index Value

Nikkei 225 Stock Index (weekly close) as of December 29, 2006

Index Value

Sugar

The white crystalline substance called "sugar" is the organic chemical compound sucrose, one of several related compounds all known as sugars. These include glucose, dextrose, fructose, and lactose. All sugars are members of the larger group of compounds called carbohydrates and are characterized by a sweet taste. Sucrose is considered a double sugar because it is composed of one molecule of glucose and one molecule of fructose. While sucrose is common in many plants, it occurs in the highest concentration in sugarcane (Saccharum officinarum) and sugar beets (Beta vulgaris). Sugarcane is about 7 to 18 percent sugar by weight while sugar beets are 8 to 22 percent.

Sugarcane is a member of the grass family and is a perennial. Sugarcane is cultivated in tropical and subtropical regions around the world roughly between the Tropics of Cancer and Capricorn. It grows best in hot, wet climates where there is heavy rainfall followed by a dry season. The largest cane producers are Florida, Louisiana, Texas, and Hawaii. On a commercial basis, sugarcane is not grown from seeds but from cuttings or pieces of the stalk.

Sugar beets, which are produced in temperate or colder climates, are annuals grown from seeds. Sugar beets do best with moderate temperatures and evenly distributed rainfall. The beets are planted in the spring and harvested in the fall. The sugar is contained in the root of the beet, but the sugars from beets and cane are identical. Sugar beet production takes place mostly in Europe, the US, China, and Japan. The largest sugar beet producing states are Minnesota, Idaho, North Dakota, and Michigan. Sugar beets are refined to yield white sugar and very little raw sugar is produced.

Sugar beets and sugarcane are produced in over 100 countries around the world. Of all the sugar produced, about 25 percent is processed from sugar beets and the remaining 75% is from sugar cane. The trend has been that production of sugar from cane is increasing relative to that produced from beets. The significance of this in that sugarcane is a perennial plant while the sugar beet is an annual, and due to the longer production cycle, sugarcane production and the sugar processed from that cane, may not be quite as responsive to changes in price.

Sugar futures are traded on the Bolsa de Mercadorias & Futuros (BM&F), Kansai Commodities Exchange (KANEX), the Tokyo Grain Exchange (TGE), the London International Financial Futures and Options Exchange (LIFFE), and the CSCE Division of the New York Board of Trade (NYBOT). Options are traded on the BM&F, the TGE, the LIFFE and the NYBOT.

Raw sugar is traded on the CSCE Division of the New York Board of Trade while white sugar is traded on the London International Financial Futures Exchange (LIFFE). The most actively traded contract is the No. 11 (World) sugar contract at the CSCE. The No. 11 contract calls for the delivery of 112,000 pounds (50 long tons) of raw cane centrifugal sugar from any of 28 foreign countries of origin and the United States. The CSCE also trades the No. 14 sugar contract (Domestic), which calls for the delivery of raw centrifugal cane sugar in the United States. Futures on white sugar are traded on the London International Financial Futures Exchange and call for the delivery of 50 metric tons of white beet sugar, cane crystal sugar, or refined sugar of any origin from the crop current at the time of delivery.

Prices – World sugar prices on the CSCE No.11 sugar nearest-futures chart in early 2006 extended the rally that started in 2004 and posted a 24-year high of 19.73 cents per pound in February 2006. Sugar prices more than tripled over the course of the 2004-06 rally from the 5.27 cents in February 2004 to 19.73 cents two years later in February 2006. However, sugar prices then plunged by 51% from the February 2006 high to a 1-year low of 9.70 cents by September 2006, finally consolidating through the remainder of the year to close 2006 at 11.75 cents, -20% yr/yr. Sugar prices in early 2006 extended the rally due to heavy bullish commodity speculation, strong demand, and restricted sugar supplies after three straight years of sugar deficits in 2003-04, 2004-05, and 2005-06. However, sugar prices then plunged starting in February 2006 after production started rising and speculators were washed out of their huge long positions. High sugar prices did their job in causing producers to rev up production and produce a small surplus for 2006-07. Brazil, which is already the world's largest sugar producer, has plenty of land available to boost sugar production further if prices are high enough.

Supply – World production of centrifugal (raw) sugar in the 2006-07 marketing year (Oct 1 to Sep 30) rose +7.2% to 155.166 million metric tons. That is a new record high. The world's largest sugar producers are Brazil with 20% of world production in 2006-07, India with 216%, and the European Union with 11%. US centrifugal sugar production in 2006-07 rose +5.0% to 7.727 million metric tons. World ending stocks in 2005-06 rose +14.7% to 33.193 million metric tons, up following declines in the past three years. The stocks/consumption ratio rose to 22.7% in 2006-07, relieving the tightest situation since 1994-95. US production in 2006-07 of cane sugar rose +21.9% to 3.603 million short tons, and beet sugar production rose +14.6% yr/yr to 5.092 million short tons.

Demand – World domestic consumption of centrifugal (raw) sugar in 2006-07 rose by +2.3% yr/yr to 146.037 million metric tons. US domestic disappearance (consumption) of sugar in 2006-07 rose by +1.3% yr/yr to 10.615 million short tons. The latest available figures show US per capita sugar consumption at 63.4 pounds per year in 2005-06, which is only about two-thirds of the levels seen in the early 1970s.

Exports – World exports of centrifugal sugar in 2006-07 fell –5.9% yr/yr to 45.698 million metric tons, which was down from the record high of 50,691 million metric tons posted in 2005-06. The world's largest sugar exporter is Brazil, where exports in 2006-07 rose +14.4% to 19.550 million metric tons and accounted for 41% of world exports. The next largest exporters are Thailand with 9% of world exports, Australia with 8%, and India with 4%. US sugar imports in 2006-07 fell –36.0% yr/yr to 2.203 million short tons, down from last year's 22-year high of 3,443. US sugar exports in 2006-07 fell –1.5% yr/yr to 200,000 short tons.

World Production, Supply & Stocks/Consumption Ratio of Sugar   In 1000's of Metric Tons (Raw Value)

Marketing Year	Beginning Stocks	Production	Imports	Total Supply	Exports	Domestic Consumption	Ending Stocks	Stocks/ Consumption Percentage
1997-98	29,683	125,505	34,450	189,638	37,683	123,475	28,480	23.1
1998-99	28,480	130,894	37,244	196,618	37,658	125,415	33,545	26.7
1999-00	33,545	136,264	36,753	206,562	41,700	127,581	37,281	29.2
2000-01	37,281	130,867	40,414	208,562	38,441	130,123	39,998	30.7
2001-02	39,998	134,432	39,707	214,137	42,358	134,959	36,820	27.3
2002-03	36,820	148,516	41,557	226,893	47,440	138,947	40,506	29.2
2003-04	40,506	142,362	41,997	224,865	46,813	139,600	38,452	27.5
2004-05[1]	38,452	140,726	45,002	224,180	47,663	142,789	33,728	23.6
2005-06[2]	33,728	144,709	44,022	222,459	50,691	142,823	28,945	20.3
2006-07[3]	28,945	155,166	42,817	226,928	47,698	146,037	33,193	22.7

[1] Preliminary.   [2] Forecast.   Source: Foreign Agricultural Service, U.S. Department of Agriculture (FAS-USDA)

World Production of Sugar (Centrifugal Sugar-Raw Value)   In Thousands of Metric Tons

Year	Aus- tralia	Brazil	China	Cuba	EU-25	India	Indo- nesia	Mexico	Pakistan	Thailand	United States	Ukraine	World Total
1997-98	5,567	15,700	8,631	3,200	19,305	14,592	2,190	5,486	3,805	4,245	7,276	2,032	125,505
1998-99	4,997	18,300	8,969	3,760	17,818	17,436	1,492	4,982	3,791	5,386	7,597	2,000	130,894
1999-00	5,448	20,100	7,525	4,060	19,498	20,219	1,690	4,979	2,595	5,721	8,203	1,720	136,264
2000-01	4,162	17,100	6,849	3,500	18,519	20,480	1,800	5,220	2,648	5,107	7,956	1,687	130,867
2001-02	4,662	20,400	8,305	3,700	16,153	20,475	1,725	5,169	3,453	6,397	7,167	1,790	134,432
2002-03	5,461	23,810	11,380	2,250	18,675	22,140	1,755	5,229	3,944	7,286	7,644	1,550	148,516
2003-04	5,178	26,400	10,734	2,550	17,132	15,150	1,730	5,330	4,047	7,010	7,847	1,580	142,362
2004-05[1]	5,388	28,175	9,826	1,300	21,648	14,170	2,050	6,149	3,115	5,187	7,146	1,900	140,726
2005-06[2]	5,297	26,850	9,446	1,200	21,847	21,070	2,100	5,604	2,615	4,835	6,713	1,850	144,709
2006-07[3]	4,950	30,850	11,150	1,500	16,836	25,100	2,500	5,650	3,720	6,250	7,727	1,900	155,166

[1] Preliminary.   [2] Estimate.   Source: Foreign Agricultural Service, U.S. Department of Agriculture (FAS-USDA)

World Stocks of Centrifugal Sugar at Beginning of Marketing Year   In Thousands of Metric Tons (Raw Value)

Year	Aus- tralia	Brazil	China	Cuba	EU-25	India	Indonesia	Iran	Mexico	Philip- pines	Russia	United States	World Total
1997-98	253	560	2,515	568	2,871	5,850	520	365	991	183	1,105	1,523	28,480
1998-99	183	1,010	2,548	488	2,870	7,374	908	405	941	454	2,650	1,487	33,545
1999-00	518	710	1,851	438	3,493	10,710	1,330	207	1,063	330	3,000	2,013	37,281
2000-01	634	860	1,004	302	3,420	11,985	1,415	207	1,548	322	3,100	1,978	39,998
2001-02	507	210	869	312	2,717	11,670	1,385	167	1,172	239	2,130	1,386	36,820
2002-03	662	270	2,021	212	3,581	12,430	1,340	267	1,194	277	1,050	1,515	40,506
2003-04	543	1,030	2,323	307	4,699	9,070	1,170	292	1,237	405	440	1,721	38,452
2004-05[1]	343	585	1,757	217	5,339	5,165	1,120	197	2,045	239	580	1,208	33,728
2005-06[2]	312	-285	1,118	162	3,697	4,735	1,170	102	1,515	253	470	1,598	28,945
2006-07[3]	281	215	1,658	312	4,458	6,785	1,370	155	1,495	265	400	1,696	33,193

[1] Preliminary.   [2] Estimate.   Source: Foreign Agricultural Service, U.S. Department of Agriculture (FAS-USDA)

Centrifugal Sugar (Raw Value) Imported into Selected Countries   In Thousands of Metric Tons

Year	Algeria	Canada	China	EU-25	Iran	Japan	Rep. of Korea	Malaysia	Morocco	Nigeria	Russia	United States	World Total
1997-98	925	1,056	420	1,829	921	970	1,592	1,424	1,065	660	4,210	1,962	34,450
1998-99	940	1,129	543	1,867	1,702	1,085	1,542	1,403	1,188	700	5,400	1,655	37,244
1999-00	900	1,207	687	1,786	1,949	960	1,650	1,514	1,256	825	5,170	1,484	36,753
2000-01	975	1,211	1,083	1,839	1,591	1,000	1,486	1,574	1,325	714	5,650	1,443	40,414
2001-02	1,015	1,235	1,375	2,025	1,600	1,010	1,407	1,590	1,385	775	4,850	1,393	39,707
2002-03	1,094	1,329	842	2,150	1,600	955	1,483	1,590	1,406	1,000	4,000	1,569	41,557
2003-04	1,040	1,323	1,235	1,900	1,500	610	1,364	1,682	1,484	1,150	3,670	1,591	41,997
2004-05[1]	1,130	1,245	1,360	2,549	1,450	595	1,328	1,652	1,459	1,150	4,300	1,905	45,002
2005-06[2]	1,275	1,451	1,300	2,280	1,800	675	1,350	1,669	1,414	1,200	2,900	3,123	44,022
2006-07[3]	1,270	1,335	1,100	2,850	1,800	650	1,350	1,680	1,515	1,400	3,400	2,001	42,817

[1] Preliminary.   [2] Estimate.   Source: Foreign Agricultural Service, U.S. Department of Agriculture (FAS-USDA)

Sugar (monthly average) through December 2006 — Cents per pound

Cents Per Pound
- - - - - "Fair Refining", Duty Paid, New York (1846 - 1888)
Raw (96%), Duty Paid, New York (1889 - 1900)
Spot Raw (cif) New York (Jan. 1901 - Jan. 1961)
No. 8 World Raw, New York (Feb. 1961 - Dec. 1970)
No. 11 World Raw, New York (Jan. 1971 - date)
- - - Refined Beet, Midwest (Jan. 1975 - date)

Centrifugal Sugar (Raw Value) Exported From Selected Countries   In Thousands of Metric Tons

Year	Aus-tralia	Brazil	Colombia	Cuba	Dominican Republic	EU-25	India	Guate-mala	Mau-ritius	South Africa	Swazi-land	Thai-land	Total
1997-98	4,554	7,200	1,020	2,426	270	6,361	1,361	21	560	1,160	267	2,839	37,683
1998-99	4,076	8,750	960	3,120	191	5,329	1,086	10	649	1,355	283	3,352	37,658
1999-00	4,123	11,300	959	3,400	185	6,138	1,140	25	426	1,410	284	4,147	41,700
2000-01	3,056	7,700	965	2,980	185	6,607	1,190	1,360	555	1,580	287	3,394	38,441
2001-02	3,594	11,600	1,085	3,070	185	4,793	1,310	1,130	628	1,235	208	4,157	42,358
2002-03	4,114	14,000	1,306	1,800	185	5,600	1,335	1,410	542	1,296	278	5,280	47,440
2003-04	4,157	15,240	1,200	1,827	185	4,900	1,335	250	587	1,070	285	4,860	46,813
2004-05[1]	4,447	18,020	1,231	825	185	6,028	1,497	40	577	1,010	298	3,115	47,663
2005-06[2]	4,187	17,090	890	805	253	8,665	1,242	1,150	550	1,230	320	2,800	50,691
2006-07[3]	3,840	19,550	860	800	200	1,501	1,423	2,000	557	1,210	358	4,300	47,698

[1] Preliminary.   [2] Estimate.   Source: Foreign Agricultural Service, U.S. Department of Agriculture (FAS-USDA)

Average Wholesale Price of Refined Beet Sugar[1]--Midwest Market   In Cents Per Pound

Year	Jan.	Feb.	Mar.	Apr.	May	June	July	Aug.	Sept.	Oct.	Nov.	Dec.	Average
1997	29.00	29.00	28.13	28.00	28.00	27.50	27.00	26.65	26.38	24.90	25.00	25.50	27.09
1998	25.50	25.50	25.50	25.50	26.00	26.00	26.00	26.00	26.50	26.90	27.00	27.00	26.12
1999	27.20	27.13	27.00	27.00	27.00	27.00	27.00	27.00	27.00	26.00	26.00	25.20	26.71
2000	23.38	22.25	21.50	21.00	19.75	19.00	19.00	19.00	20.70	21.25	21.00	21.80	20.80
2001	23.13	22.75	22.00	20.50	21.38	21.90	22.50	22.50	24.63	25.75	26.20	26.50	23.31
2002	26.75	26.00	25.95	24.63	24.50	24.00	24.00	25.40	26.25	26.75	27.40	27.88	25.79
2003	27.80	26.50	27.13	27.63	28.00	28.00	27.63	25.50	24.00	24.70	23.94	23.63	26.21
2004	23.70	23.50	23.50	23.50	23.50	23.50	23.50	23.50	23.50	23.50	23.38	23.20	23.48
2005	23.50	23.50	23.25	23.80	24.75	25.88	26.00	26.75	40.10	40.00	40.00	36.90	29.54
2006[1]	34.50	36.50	37.10	36.38	35.00	35.00	35.00	34.50	31.20	28.75	27.19	26.10	33.10

[1] These are f.o.b. basis prices in bulk, not delivered prices.   [2] Preliminary.   Source: Economic Research Service, U.S. Department of Agriculture (ERS)

Average Price of World Raw Sugar[1]   In Cents Per Pound

Year	Jan.	Feb.	Mar.	Apr.	May	June	July	Aug.	Sept.	Oct.	Nov.	Dec.	Average
1997	11.13	11.06	11.17	11.50	11.54	12.02	12.13	12.54	12.65	12.86	13.19	12.90	12.06
1998	11.71	11.06	10.66	10.27	10.17	9.33	9.70	9.50	8.21	8.24	8.73	8.59	9.68
1999	8.40	7.05	6.11	5.44	5.83	6.67	6.11	6.39	6.98	6.90	6.54	6.00	6.54
2000	5.64	5.51	5.54	6.48	7.33	8.72	10.18	11.14	10.35	10.96	10.02	10.23	8.51
2001	10.63	10.26	9.64	9.27	9.96	9.80	9.48	8.77	8.60	7.15	7.80	8.02	9.12
2002	7.96	6.81	7.27	7.12	7.33	7.07	8.02	7.86	8.54	8.84	8.87	8.81	7.88
2003	8.56	9.14	8.50	7.92	7.41	6.85	7.18	7.30	6.70	6.74	6.83	6.95	7.51
2004	6.42	7.01	8.23	8.21	8.08	8.41	9.19	8.99	9.10	9.84	9.65	10.19	8.61
2005	10.33	10.51	10.57	10.19	10.23	10.45	10.89	11.09	11.59	12.40	12.86	15.09	11.35
2006[2]	17.27	18.93	18.01	18.21	17.83	16.19	16.61	13.58	12.42	12.09	12.38	12.47	15.50

[1] Contract No. 11, f.o.b. stowed Caribbean port, including Brazil, bulk spot price.   [2] Preliminary.   *Source: Economic Research Service, U.S. Department of Agriculture (ERS-USDA)*

Average Price of Raw Sugar in New York (C.I.F., Duty/Free Paid, Contract #12/#14)   In Cents Per Pound

Year	Jan.	Feb.	Mar.	Apr.	May	June	July	Aug.	Sept.	Oct.	Nov.	Dec.	Average
1997	21.88	22.07	21.81	21.79	21.70	21.62	22.04	22.21	22.30	22.27	21.90	21.93	21.96
1998	21.85	21.79	21.74	22.14	22.31	22.42	22.66	22.19	21.92	21.67	21.83	22.19	22.06
1999	22.41	22.38	22.55	22.57	22.65	22.61	22.61	21.24	20.10	19.50	17.45	17.87	21.16
2000	17.70	17.24	18.46	19.43	19.12	19.31	17.64	18.12	18.97	21.15	21.39	20.56	19.09
2001	20.81	21.18	21.40	21.51	21.19	21.04	20.64	21.10	20.87	20.90	21.19	21.43	21.11
2002	21.03	20.69	19.92	19.73	19.52	19.93	20.86	20.91	21.65	21.94	22.22	22.03	20.87
2003	21.62	21.91	22.14	21.87	21.80	21.62	21.32	21.26	21.34	20.92	20.91	20.37	21.42
2004	20.54	20.57	20.86	20.88	20.69	20.03	20.14	20.10	20.47	20.31	20.40	20.55	20.46
2005	20.57	20.36	20.54	21.21	21.96	21.89	21.94	20.49	21.10	21.71	21.83	21.74	21.28
2006[1]	23.61	24.05	23.10	23.56	23.48	23.32	22.44	21.38	21.27	20.22	19.66	19.59	22.14

[1] Preliminary.   *Source: Economic Research Service, U.S. Department of Agriculture (ERS-USDA)*

Supply and Utilization of Sugar (Cane and Beet) in the United States   In 1,000's of Short Tons (Raw Value)

													Utilization				
		--- Supply ---										Net		- Domestic Disappearance -			
				----- Offshore Receipts -----							Changes	Refining	In Poly-		Per
	---- Production ----				Terri-		Beginning	Total	Total		in Invisible	Loss Ad-	hydric		Capita
Year	Cane	Beet	Total	Foreign	tories	Total	Stocks	Supply	Use	Exports	Stocks	justment	Alcohol[4]	Total	Pounds
1998-99	3,945	4,421	8,366	1,823	0	1,823	1,679	11,868	10,238	230	-67	0	24	9,873	64.9
1999-00	4,076	4,974	9,050	1,636	0	1,636	1,639	12,325	10,090	124	-126	0	32	9,993	66.3
2000-01	4,089	4,680	8,769	1,590	0	1,590	2,216	12,575	10,396	141	113	0	33	10,000	65.5
2001-02	3,985	3,915	7,900	1,535	0	1,535	2,180	11,615	10,087	137	-24	0	33	9,785	64.5
2002-03	3,964	4,462	8,426	1,730	0	1,730	1,528	11,684	10,014	142	161	0	24	9,504	63.3
2003-04	3,957	4,692	8,649	1,750	0	1,750	1,670	12,070	10,172	288	23	0	41	9,678	61.0
2004-05[1]	3,265	4,611	7,876	2,100	0	2,100	1,897	11,873	10,542	259	94	0	48	10,019	61.7
2005-06[2]	2,955	4,444	7,399	3,443	0	3,443	1,332	12,174	10,476	203	-67	0	51	10,184	63.4
2006-07[3]	3,603	5,092	8,695	2,203	0	2,203	1,698	12,596	10,615	200	0	0	40	10,250	NA

[1] Preliminary.   [2] Estimate.   [3] Forecast.   [4] Includes feed use.   Source: Economic Research Service, U.S. Department of Agriculture (ERS-USDA)

Sugar Cane for Sugar & Seed and Production of Cane Sugar and Molasses in the United States

		Yield of	----- Production -----					------ Farm Value ------		----- Sugar Production -------					
	Acreage	Cane Per				Sugar	Farm	of Cane	of Cane Used for	---- Raw Value ----					
	Harvested	Harvested	for	for		Yield Per	Price	Used for	Sugar	Total	Per Ton	Refined Basis	--- Molasses Made ---		
	1,000	Acre	Sugar	Seed	Total	Acre	$ Per	Sugar	& Seed	1,000	of Cane	1,000	Edible	Total[3]
Year	Acres	Net Tons	----------- 1,000 Tons -----------			Short Tons	Ton	----- 1,000 Dollars -----		Tons	in Lbs.	Tons	---- 1,000 Gallons ----	
1998	947.1	36.6	32,743	1,964	34,707	----	27.3	893,049	944,562	----	----	----	----	----
1999	993.3	35.5	33,577	1,722	35,299	----	25.6	859,175	901,900	----	----	----	----	----
2000	1,023.3	35.0	34,291	1,823	36,114	----	26.1	895,917	941,791	----	----	----	----	----
2001	1,027.8	33.7	32,775	1,812	34,587	----	29.0	951,813	1,003,046	----	----	----	----	----
2002	1,023.2	34.7	33,903	1,650	35,553	----	28.4	961,896	1,007,142	----	----	----	----	----
2003	992.3	34.1	31,942	1,916	33,858	----	29.5	943,646	998,269	----	----	----	----	----
2004	938.2	30.9	27,243	1,770	29,013	----	28.3	771,734	821,118	----	----	----	----	----
2005[1]	921.9	28.9	24,728	1,878	26,606	----	28.4	701,920	754,529	----	----	----	----	----
2006[2]	908.8	32.7	28,123	1,633	29,756	----				----	----	----	----	----

[1] Preliminary.   [2] Estimate.   [3] Excludes edible molasses.   *Source: Economic Research Service, U.S. Department of Agriculture (ERS-USDA)*

SUGAR

U.S. Sugar Beets, Beet Sugar, Pulp & Molasses Produced from Beets and Raw Sugar Spot Prices

Year of Harvest	Acreage Planted	Acreage Harvested	Yield Per Harvested Acre Ton	Pro-duction 1,000 Tons	Sugar Yield Per Acre Sh. Tons	Price[3] Dollars	Farm Value $1,000	Sugar Production - Equiv-alent Raw Value[4]	Refined Basis	World[5] Refined #5	#11 World	CSCE N.Y. Duty Paid	Wholesale List Price HFCS (42%) Midwest
	---- 1,000 Acres ----							-- 1,000 Short Tons --		------- In Cents Per Pound ------			
1997	1,459	1,428	20.9	29,886	3.00	38.80	1,160,029	----	----	14.33	12.06	21.96	10.70
1998	1,498	1,451	22.4	32,499	----	36.40	1,181,494	----	----	11.59	9.68	22.06	10.58
1999	1,561	1,527	21.9	33,420	----	37.20	1,242,895	----	----	9.10	6.54	21.16	11.71
2000	1,564	1,373	23.7	32,541	----	34.20	1,113,030	----	----	9.97	8.51	19.09	11.32
2001	1,371	1,243	20.7	25,764	----	39.80	1,025,306	----	----	11.29	9.12	21.11	11.90
2002	1,427	1,361	20.4	27,707	----	39.60	1,097,329	----	----	10.35	7.88	20.87	13.05
2003	1,365	1,348	22.7	30,583	----	41.40	1,270,026	----	----	9.74	7.51	21.42	13.24
2004	1,346	1,307	23.0	30,021	----	36.90	1,109,272	----	----	10.87	8.61	20.46	13.20
2005[1]	1,300	1,243	22.2	27,537	----	43.50	1,193,151	----	----	13.19	11.35	21.28	13.58
2006[2]	1,367	1,304	25.9	33,765						19.01	15.50	22.14	17.03

[1] Preliminary. [2] Estimate. [3] Includes support payments, but excludes Government sugar beet payments. [4] Refined sugar multiplied by factor of 1.07. [5] F.O.B. Europe. *Source: Economic Research Service, U.S. Department of Agriculture (ERS-USDA)*

Sugar Deliveries and Stocks in the United States   In Thousands of Short Tons (Raw Value)

Year	Quota Allocation	Actual Imports	Cane Sugar Refineries	Beet Sugar Factories	Importers of Direct Con-sumption Sugar	Mainland Cane Sugar Mills[3]	Total Deliveries	Total Domestic Con-sumption	Cane Sugar Re-fineries[4]	Beet Sugar Factories	CCC	Refiners' Raw	Mainland Cane Mills	Total
1997	1,791.3	1,733.3	5,553	3,997	27	----	9,578	9,755	196	1,520	0	323	1,156	3,195
1998	1,289.7	1,254.2	5,349	4,313	24	----	9,686	9,854	212	1,535	0	322	1,308	3,377
1999	----	----	5,419	4,536	41	----	9,996	10,167	255	1,499	0	332	1,335	3,421
2000	----	----	5,508	4,433	36	----	9,977	10,091	208	1,554	0	356	1,737	3,855
2001	----	----	5,172	4,680	58	----	9,911	10,075	262	1,500	767	274	1,533	4,337
2002	----	----	5,407	4,291	109	----	9,808	9,994	288	1,472	634	351	1,781	4,525
2003	----	----	5,232	4,219	60	----	9,511	9,713	298	1,300	246	299	1,289	3,432
2004	----	----	4,989	4,668	64	----	9,722	9,901	326	1,817	0	286	1,659	4,088
2005[1]	----	----	5,136	4,710	197	----	10,043	10,212	368	1,753	28	245	1,635	4,029
2006[2]									328	1,429	0	217	1,382	3,357

[1] Preliminary. [2] Estimate. [3] Sugar for direct consumption only. [4] Refined. *Source: Economic Research Service, U.S. Department of Agriculture (ERS-USDA)*

Sugar, Refined--Deliveries to End User in the United States   In Thousands of Short Tons

Year	Bakery & Cereal Products	Beverages	Confec-tionery[2]	Hotels, Restaurant & Insti-tutions	Ice Cream & Dairy Products	Canned, Bottled & Frozen Foods	All Other Food Uses	Retail Grocers[3]	Whole-sale Grocers[4]	Non-food Uses	Non-industrial Uses	Industrial Uses	Total Deliveries
1996	1,993	196	1,335	80	445	318	849	1,263	2,241	66	3,759	5,202	8,962
1997	2,161	158	1,350	78	436	308	793	1,281	2,283	66	3,828	5,272	9,100
1998	2,301	165	1,336	79	438	331	907	1,230	2,223	76	3,761	5,556	9,317
1999	2,312	179	1,361	72	499	346	862	1,263	2,257	71	3,804	5,630	9,434
2000	2,264	168	1,328	71	499	330	817	1,242	2,241	85	3,893	5,491	9,383
2001	2,273	158	1,316	59	484	310	800	1,255	2,250	74	3,927	5,414	9,341
2002	2,069	189	1,221	53	530	297	727	1,322	2,374	99	4,122	5,132	9,253
2003	2,108	214	1,130	52	548	303	632	2,387	1,279	99	4,039	5,034	9,073
2004	2,180	242	1,125	76	603	315	697	2,398	1,267	91	3,956	5,254	9,210
2005[1]	2,353	239	1,153	110	590	344	609	2,411	1,270	132	4,046	5,419	9,466

[1] Preliminary. [2] And related products. [3] Chain stores, supermarkets. [4] Jobbers, sugar dealers. *Source: Economic Research Service, U.S. Department of Agriculture (ERS-USDA)*

Deliveries[1] of All Sugar by Primary Distributors in the U.S., by Quarters   In Thousands of Short Tons

Year	First Quarter	Second Quarter	Third Quarter	Fourth Quarter	Total	Year	First Quarter	Second Quarter	Third Quarter	Fourth Quarter	Total
1995	2,105	2,311	2,542	2,379	8,801	2001	2,370	2,486	2,580	2,474	9,911
1996	2,191	2,355	2,519	2,430	8,964	2002	2,227	2,439	2,645	2,497	9,808
1997	2,143	2,401	2,591	2,443	9,100	2003	2,183	2,360	2,464	2,504	9,511
1998	2,233	2,428	2,565	2,458	9,213	2004	2,286	2,368	2,520	2,547	9,722
1999	2,208	2,553	2,655	2,580	9,996	2005	2,335	2,471	2,666	2,571	10,037
2000	2,318	2,484	2,611	2,564	9,977	2006[2]	2,436	2,487	2,690		10,150

Raw Value. [1] Includes for domestic consumption and for export. [2] Preliminary. *Source: Economic Research Service, U.S. Department of Agriculture (ERS-USDA)*

Sugar #11 Futures - New York Board of Trade
(weekly close) as of December 29, 2006

Cents per pound

Volume of Trading of World Sugar No. 11 Futures in New York   In Thousands of Contracts

Year	Jan.	Feb.	Mar.	Apr.	May	June	July	Aug.	Sept.	Oct.	Nov.	Dec.	Total
1997	436.9	493.2	268.3	618.2	308.6	575.3	400.2	427.1	580.6	440.2	323.3	413.2	5,285.0
1998	601.4	688.0	431.8	551.6	364.2	687.0	294.4	370.2	527.3	304.0	358.1	346.2	5,524.1
1999	683.9	543.5	452.5	688.2	361.9	762.3	346.5	408.3	657.6	344.4	405.5	256.8	5,911.3
2000	422.5	609.8	501.1	617.6	523.9	717.7	376.8	420.6	622.4	507.6	371.8	242.0	5,933.9
2001	410.5	545.5	380.6	567.9	427.0	515.6	356.5	419.1	447.3	348.9	414.0	317.4	5,150.3
2002	568.8	629.5	417.3	693.6	412.2	610.3	529.5	381.0	756.0	402.8	432.1	340.6	6,173.8
2003	566.0	797.6	443.8	729.5	489.2	719.8	535.9	545.9	760.2	475.3	403.1	674.4	7,140.7
2004	513.6	1,018.7	1,181.1	993.7	617.3	1,100.6	614.6	679.5	1,248.7	626.5	539.5	632.7	9,766.6
2005	981.5	1,279.3	957.1	1,258.6	657.6	1,366.8	779.2	1,198.3	1,803.5	915.8	816.6	992.8	13,007.1
2006	1,444.2	1,601.2	1,092.2	1,467.4	1,147.7	1,459.1	825.0	1,278.6	1,746.7	1,095.7	918.7	1,024.0	15,100.6

Source: New York Board of Trade (NYBOT)

Average Open Interest of World Sugar No. 11 Futures in New York   In Contracts

Year	Jan.	Feb.	Mar.	Apr.	May	June	July	Aug.	Sept.	Oct.	Nov.	Dec.
1997	155,156	147,198	143,623	166,143	150,480	175,139	165,884	197,331	187,477	158,065	200,486	201,922
1998	206,100	212,072	183,472	182,770	171,555	186,978	149,536	152,754	155,076	138,762	139,896	148,983
1999	165,717	176,465	168,624	188,324	196,864	177,266	142,416	151,621	189,606	161,760	167,549	175,125
2000	191,464	199,031	193,554	187,810	201,756	200,973	172,361	171,808	160,809	154,101	148,035	145,760
2001	157,478	158,192	158,448	167,555	131,640	126,426	112,483	128,181	139,915	146,058	163,358	170,710
2002	184,096	205,138	194,541	187,415	157,738	158,276	149,202	170,667	202,144	207,456	207,598	217,904
2003	244,036	265,758	220,971	192,497	170,867	184,257	180,898	196,857	195,200	185,917	200,605	207,995
2004	246,347	269,863	268,250	275,423	267,362	282,842	300,961	309,436	292,917	322,079	304,462	332,803
2005	375,713	391,006	357,056	352,521	355,922	366,568	404,141	473,757	468,737	464,829	478,097	523,820
2006	526,575	501,074	462,871	474,241	490,201	453,021	457,301	479,420	493,931	447,817	503,364	563,844

Source: New York Board of Trade (NYBOT)

Sulfur

Sulfur (symbol S) is an odorless, tasteless, light yellow, nonmetallic element. As early as 2000 BC, Egyptians used sulfur compounds to bleach fabric. The Chinese used sulfur as an essential component when they developed gunpowder in the 13th century.

Sulfur is widely found in both its free and combined states. Free sulfur is found mixed with gypsum and pumice stone in volcanic regions. Sulfur dioxide is an air pollutant released from the combustion of fossil fuels. The most important use of sulfur is the production of sulfur compounds. Sulfur is used in skin ointments, matches, dyes, gunpowder, and phosphoric acid.

Supply – World production of sulfur (all forms) in 2005 was unchanged yr/yr at 66.000 million metric tons, which is the record high. The world's largest producers of sulfur are the US with 14.3% of world production, Canada (13.6%),

China (12%), and Russia (11%). US production of sulfur fell by −6.3% yr/yr in 2005 to 9.460 million metric tons, but is still above the 3-decade low of 9.270 million metric tons seen in 2002.

Demand – US consumption of sulfur in all forms fell by −3.9% in 2005 to 12.300 million metric tons, but is still above the 17-year low of 10.900 million metric tons seen in 2001. US consumption of elemental sulfur fell −3.5% in 2005 to 10.900 million metric tons. US consumption of sulfuric acid rose +4.2% yr/yr in 2005 to 9.680 million metric tons.

Trade – US exports of recovered sulfur in 2005 fell −27.9% yr/yr to 684,000 metric tons, and is now only slightly above the 11-year low of 675,000 metric tons seen in 2001. US imports of recovered sulfur in 2005 fell by −1.1% yr/yr to 2.820 million metric tons, down a little more from the 2003 record high of 2.870 million metric tons.

World Production of Sulfur (All Forms)   In Thousands of Metric Tons

Year	Canada	China	France	Germany	Iraq	Japan	Mexico	Poland	Russia	Saudi Arabia	Spain	United States	World Total
1998	9,694	6,170	1,110	1,180	450	3,428	1,387	1,675	4,651	2,050	993	11,700	57,400
1999	9,815	5,770	1,100	2,358	----	3,462	1,334	1,524	5,265	1,940	955	11,500	58,500
2000	9,452	5,560	1,150	2,401	----	3,456	1,325	1,831	5,790	2,101	708	10,500	59,300
2001	9,444	5,510	1,100	3,421	----	3,743	1,450	1,352	6,130	2,350	668	9,470	61,400
2002	8,925	5,980	1,020	3,592	----	3,191	1,465	1,220	6,500	2,360	685	9,270	62,600
2003	9,028	6,500	1,010	3,376	----	3,232	1,591	1,240	6,720	2,180	706	9,600	64,200
2004[1]	9,510	7,150	961	2,506	----	3,158	1,825	1,230	6,920	2,230	634	10,100	66,000
2005[2]	8,973	7,710	945	2,520	----	3,260	1,717	1,220	6,950	2,300	616	9,460	66,000

[1] Preliminary. [2] Estimate. *Source: U.S. Geological Survey (USGS)*

Salient Statistics of Sulfur in the United States   In Thousands of Metric Tons (Sulfur Content)

	------- Production of -------											Apparent Con- sumption (All Forms)	Sales Value of Shipments F.O.B. Mine/Plant $ Per Metric Ton		
	Elemental Sulfur				By- product Sulfuric Acid	Other Sulfuric Acid Com- pounds	Pro- duction (All Forms)	Imports Sulfuric Acid[4]	Exports Sulfuric Acid[4]	Producer Stocks Dec. 31[5]					
	Native - Sulfur[3] -	----- Recovered -----													
Year	Frasch	Petroleum & Coke	Natural Gas	Total	Acid	pounds	Forms)	Acid[4]	Acid[4]	Dec. 31[5]	Forms)	Frasch	Recovered	Average
1998	1,800	6,060	2,160	8,220	1,610	----	11,700	2,040	155	283	14,200	W	W	29.14
1999	1,780	6,210	2,010	8,220	1,320	----	11,500	1,370	155	451	13,800	W	W	37.81
2000	900	6,360	2,020	8,380	1,030	----	10,500	1,420	191	208	12,700	----	----	24.73
2001	----	6,480	2,000	8,490	982	----	9,470	1,410	210	232	10,900	----	----	10.01
2002	----	6,750	1,760	8,500	772	----	9,270	1,060	147	181	11,400	----	----	11.84
2003	----	6,970	1,950	8,920	683	----	9,600	908	205	206	11,900	----	----	28.70
2004[1]	----	7,390	1,990	9,380	739	----	10,100	2,400	204	185	12,800	----	----	32.62
2005[2]	----	6,940	1,810	8,750	711	----	9,460	2,680	338	160	12,300	----	----	30.92

[1] Preliminary. [2] Estimate. [3] Or sulfur ore; Withheld included in natural gas. [4] Basis 100% H2SO4, sulfur equivalent. [5] Frasch & recovered.
[6] Data 1996 to date includes Frasch.   W = Withheld proprietary data.   *Source: U.S. Geological Survey (USGS)*

Sulfur Consumption & Foreign Trade of the United States   In Thousands of Metric Tons (Sulfur Content)

	---------- Consumption ----------			---------- Sulfuric Acid Sold or Used, by End Use[2] ----------						----------------------- Foreign Trade -----------------------				
	Native Sulfur Frasch	Re- covered Sulfur	Total Elemental Form	Total Sulfuric Acid	Pulpmills & Paper Product	Inorganic Chem- icals[3]	Synthetic Rubber & Plastic	Pho- sphatic Fertilizers	Petro- leum Refining[4]	---------- Exports ----------		---------- Imports ----------		
Year										Frasch	Re- covered	Value 1,000 $	Frasch	Re- covered	Value 1,000 $
1998	W	11,900	11,900	10,600	134	174	69	7,590	632	----	889	35,400	----	2,270	58,400
1999	W	11,700	11,700	10,400	138	174	68	7,770	508	----	685	35,800	----	2,580	51,600
2000	W	11,100	11,100	9,620	136	152	68	7,110	497	----	762	53,700	----	2,330	39,400
2001	W	9,520	9,520	9,530	194	158	68	6,840	591	----	675	48,800	----	1,730	22,100
2002	W	10,400	10,400	8,380	122	27	66	6,660	90	----	687	40,000	----	2,560	26,800
2003	W	10,900	10,900	10,100	225	71	82	6,660	140	----	840	54,400	----	2,870	70,600
2004	W	11,300	11,300	9,290	272	154	70	6,870	248	----	949	63,300	----	2,850	76,800
2005[1]	W	10,900	10,900	9,680	267	312	64	7,000	188	----	684	55,200	----	2,820	70,500

[1] Preliminary.   [2] Sulfur equivalent.   [3] Including inorganic pigments, paints & allied products, and other inorganic chemicals & products.
[4] Including other petroleum and coal products.   W = Withheld proprietary data.   NA = Not available.   *Source: U.S. Geological Survey (USGS)*

Sunflowerseed, Meal and Oil

Sunflowers are native to South and North America, but are now grown almost worldwide. Sunflower-seed oil accounts for approximately 14% of the world production of seed oils. Sunflower varieties that are commercially grown contain from 39% to 49% oil in the seed. Sunflower crops produce about 50 bushels of seed per acre on average, which yields approximately 50 gallons of oil.

Sunflower-seed oil accounts for around 80% of the value of the sunflower crop. Refined sunflower-seed oil is edible and used primarily as a salad and cooking oil and in margarine. Crude sunflower-seed oil is used industrially for making soaps, candles, varnishes, and detergents. Sunflower-seed oil contains 93% of the energy of US No. 2 diesel fuel and is being explored as a potential alternate fuel source in diesel engines. Sunflower meal is used in livestock feed and when fed to poultry, increases the yield of eggs. Sunflower seeds are also used for birdfeed and as a snack for humans.

Prices – The average monthly price received by US farmers for sunflower seeds in the first six months of the 2006-07 marketing year (i.e., September through February 2007) was $13.05 per hundred pounds. The price was up 8.6% but was still below the record high of $14.21 seen in the 2004-05 marketing year.

Supply – World sunflower-seed production in the 2005-06 marketing year (latest data available) rose +12.5% yr/yr to a record high of 29.660 million metric tons. The world's largest sunflower-seed producers are the former USSR with 39% of world production, Argentina with 13%, China with 6%, and France and India both with 5%. The US produced 1.700 million metric tons, up 82.8% from 2004-05, and that accounted for 5.7% of world production in 2005-06.

US production of sunflower seeds in 2006-07 fell by –46.7% yr/yr to 972,000 metric tons, which was far below the record production level of 3.309 million metric tons posted in 1979-80. US farmers harvested 1.864 million acres of sunflowers in 2006-07, down from the 6-year high of 2.610 million acres posted in 2005-06.

Demand – Total US disappearance of sunflower seeds in 2006-07 fell –20.8% yr/yr to 1.264 million metric tons, of which 50% went to crushing for oil and meal, 38% went to non-oil and seed use, and 12% went to exports.

Trade – World sunflower-seed exports in 2005-06 rose +12.9% yr/yr to 1.754 million metric tons. The world's largest exporters are the former USSR which accounted for 35% of world exports in 2005-06 and the US which accounted for 11% of world exports.

World Production of Sunflowerseed   In Thousands of Metric Tons

Crop Year	Argen-tina	Bulgaria	China	France	Hungary	India	Romania	South Africa	Spain	Turkey	United States	Ex-USSR	World Total
1996-97	5,450	527	1,333	1,996	905	1,250	1,096	560	1,178	670	1,614	5,316	24,410
1997-98	5,630	438	1,176	1,995	540	890	869	585	1,373	672	1,668	5,442	23,452
1998-99	7,180	524	1,465	1,713	718	944	1,073	1,109	1,097	850	2,392	5,762	27,405
1999-00	5,760	606	1,765	1,868	793	694	1,301	531	579	820	1,969	7,396	26,718
2000-01	2,970	425	1,954	1,833	484	646	721	638	848	630	1,608	7,824	23,099
2001-02	3,730	405	1,478	1,584	632	726	824	929	871	530	1,551	5,467	21,230
2002-03	3,350	645	1,946	1,497	777	1,060	1,003	643	757	830	1,112	7,851	23,872
2003-04	2,990	789	1,820	1,530	992	1,160	1,506	648	763	560	1,209	10,210	26,960
2004-05[1]	3,750	1,030	1,750	1,462	1,186	1,450	1,240	620	785	640	930	8,773	26,376
2005-06[2]	3,820	850	1,850	1,518	1,102	1,500	1,220	557	361	800	1,700	11,526	29,660

[1] Preliminary.   [2] Forecast.   *Source: Economic Research Service, U.S. Department of Agriculture (ERS-USDA)*

World Imports and Exports of Sunflowerseed   In Thousands of Metric Tons

Crop Year	France	Germany	Nether-lands	Spain	Turkey	World Total	Argen-tina	France	Hungary	Ex-USSR	United States	Uraguay	World Total
	---Imports---						---Exports---						
1996-97	338	406	496	296	532	3,343	65	78	212	2,422	117	91	3,310
1997-98	208	278	439	312	554	3,049	504	64	104	1,744	265	60	3,049
1998-99	395	364	477	576	766	4,015	940	29	152	1,977	291	106	4,080
1999-00	128	124	576	443	486	2,772	265	27	23	1,295	168	28	2,620
2000-01	174	193	413	368	322	2,460	94	11	6	1,865	153	21	2,462
2001-02	45	73	189	200	164	1,312	342	24	16	186	176	130	1,309
2002-03	74	79	210	232	287	1,844	232	3	20	577	122	223	1,940
2003-04	305	89	215	244	630	2,763	45	25	15	1,374	136	127	2,730
2004-05[1]	41	82	78	254	518	1,586	99	21	71	167	116	134	1,554
2005-06[2]	31	70	100	395	330	1,751	55	7	30	604	190	52	1,754

[1] Preliminary.   [2] Forecast.   *Source: Economic Research Service, U.S. Department of Agriculture (ERS-USDA)*

SUNFLOWERSEED, MEAL AND OIL

Sunflowerseed Statistics in the United States   In Thousands of Metric Tons

Crop Year Beginning Sept. 1	Harvested Acres 1,000	Harvested Yield Per Cwt.	Farm Price $ Per Metric Ton	Value of Production Million $	Supply Stocks, Sept. 1	Supply Production	Supply Imports	Supply Total	Disappearance Crush	Disappearance Exports	Disappearance Non-oil Use & Seed	Disappearance Total
1999-00	3,441	12.62	166	326.9	231	1,969	41	2,241	1,139	205	666	2,010
2000-01	2,647	13.39	151	244.2	231	1,608	66	1,905	923	201	625	1,749
2001-02	2,555	13.38	212	326.0	156	1,551	76	1,783	760	235	679	1,674
2002-03	2,167	11.31	266	294.6	109	1,112	98	1,319	319	166	635	1,120
2003-04	2,197	12.13	267	316.2	199	1,209	90	1,498	627	170	538	1,335
2004-05	1,711	11.98	302	272.7	163	930	44	1,137	276	141	630	1,047
2005-06[1]	2,610	15.40	267	487.7	90	1,823	39	1,952	566	178	852	1,596
2006-07[2]	1,864	11.34	309	301.9	356	972	66	1,394	626	156	482	1,264

[1] Preliminary.   [2] Forecast.   Source: Economic Research Service, U.S. Department of Agriculture (ERS-USDA)

World Production of Sunflowerseed Oil and Meal   In Thousands of Metric Tons

Year	Sunflowerseed Oil Argentina	France	Spain	Turkey	Ex-USSR	World Total	Sunflowerseed Meal Argentina	France	Spain	Turkey	United States	Ex-USSR	World Total
1998-99	2,356	591	612	628	1,469	9,303	2,426	759	711	701	624	1,479	11,011
1999-00	2,143	614	527	520	2,220	9,544	2,111	749	613	583	555	2,205	10,970
2000-01	1,463	645	503	400	2,383	8,660	1,441	797	585	449	464	2,320	9,962
2001-02	1,308	471	444	299	2,083	7,408	1,268	604	516	336	364	2,104	8,541
2002-03	1,368	487	454	404	2,929	8,662	1,342	599	527	454	173	2,853	9,789
2003-04	1,204	565	459	510	3,401	9,602	1,184	734	534	572	305	3,392	10,982
2004-05[1]	1,507	416	459	473	3,294	9,399	1,509	504	533	531	138	3,435	10,776
2005-06[2]	1,528	429	406	456	4,301	10,540	1,519	538	472	512	331	4,257	11,816

[1] Preliminary.   [2] Forecast.   Source: Economic Research Service, U.S. Department of Agriculture (ERS-USDA)

Sunflower Oil Statistics in the United States   In Thousands of Metric Tons

Crop Year Beginning Oct. 1	Supply Stocks, Oct. 1	Supply Production	Supply Imports	Supply Total	Disappearance Exports	Disappearance Domestic	Disappearance Total	Minneapolis, Crude $ Per Metric Ton
1999-00	55	474	2	531	286	174	460	368
2000-01	71	396	4	471	247	162	409	350
2001-02	62	305	16	383	205	168	373	513
2002-03	10	138	28	176	51	113	164	730
2003-04	12	270	12	294	107	169	276	737
2004-05	18	120	34	172	57	105	162	860
2005-06[1]	10	247	26	283	95	163	258	
2006-07[2]	25	272	11	308	70	211	281	

[1] Preliminary.   [2] Forecast.   Source: Economic Research Service, U.S. Department of Agriculture (ERS-USDA)

Sunflower Meal Statistics in the United States   In Thousands of Metric Tons

Crop Year Beginning Oct. 1	Supply Stocks, Oct. 1	Supply Production	Supply Imports	Supply Total	Disappearance Exports	Disappearance Domestic	Disappearance Total	28% Protein $ Per Metric Ton
1999-00	5	549	----	554	21	528	554	83
2000-01	5	458	----	463	8	450	463	100
2001-02	5	358	26	389	26	358	389	96
2002-03	5	172	63	240	3	232	240	116
2003-04	5	308	20	333	12	316	333	122
2004-05	5	136	----	141	3	133	141	105
2005-06[1]	5	278	5	288	6	277	288	
2006-07[2]	5	308	----	313	5	303	313	

[1] Preliminary.   [2] Forecast.   Source: Economic Research Service, U.S. Department of Agriculture (ERS-USDA)

Average Price Received by Farmers for Sunflower[2] in the United States   In Dollars Per Hundred Pounds

Year	Sept.	Oct.	Nov.	Dec.	Jan.	Feb.	Mar.	Apr.	May	June	July	Aug.	Average
2001-02	8.64	8.19	9.10	9.71	9.52	10.00	10.20	10.50	10.50	11.80	13.80	12.90	10.41
2002-03	13.10	12.00	12.00	12.30	12.10	12.50	12.50	12.30	12.20	12.00	11.60	10.90	12.13
2003-04	10.40	11.40	11.50	11.70	12.10	12.80	13.10	13.50	13.70	13.50	13.30	13.60	12.55
2004-05	12.90	12.40	12.80	13.40	13.70	15.00	15.00	15.10	15.40	15.20	15.20	14.40	14.21
2005-06	13.20	12.80	12.20	12.20	11.40	11.20	11.40	11.90	11.80	11.70	11.90	12.50	12.02
2006-07[1]	11.70	12.10	12.50	13.60	13.80	14.60							13.05

[1] Preliminary.   [2] KS, MN, ND and SD average.   Source: Economic Research Service, U.S. Department of Agriculture (ERS-USDA)

Tall Oil

Tall oil is a product of the paper and pulping industry. Crude tall oil is the major byproduct of the kraft or sulfate processing of pinewood. Crude tall oil starts as tall oil soap which is separated from recovered black liquor in the kraft pulping process. The tall oil soap is acidified to yield crude tall oil. The resulting tall oil is then fractionated to produce fatty acids, rosin, and pitch. Crude tall oil contains 40-50 percent fatty acids such as oleic and linoleic acids; 5-10 percent sterols, alcohols, and other neutral components. The demand is for the tall oil rosin and fatty acids which are used to produce adhesives, coatings, and ink resins. The products find use in lubricants, soaps, linoleum, flotation and waterproofing agents, paints, varnishes, and drying oils.

Since tall oil and its production are derived from the paper and pulping industry, the amount of tall oil produced is related in part to the pulp industry and in part to the U.S. economy.

Consumption of Tall Oil in Inedible Products in the United States — In Millions of Pounds

Year	Jan.	Feb.	Mar.	Apr.	May	June	July	Aug.	Sept.	Oct.	Nov.	Dec.	Total
1998	86.7	114.4	113.2	120.0	108.0	101.8	117.2	114.8	120.3	111.6	119.0	121.0	1,348
1999	99.4	115.1	111.0	114.0	99.9	109.2	119.1	113.0	103.9	108.4	106.4	102.2	1,302
2000	91.7	88.1	106.4	97.5	90.9	98.8	91.8	106.6	94.9	93.7	89.4	96.2	1,146
2001	97.7	96.4	104.4	101.6	105.1	100.7	99.9	98.3	102.4	81.4	87.7	74.4	1,150
2002	93.4	132.9	115.0	121.3	109.3	121.6	128.5	130.2	121.5	141.9	115.5	118.6	1,450
2003	136.1	119.9	136.9	126.3	121.7	121.9	119.3	111.6	131.4	124.1	104.9	120.1	1,474
2004	126.8	109.4	136.1	123.7	135.7	160.5	166.9	140.8	125.3	124.6	129.4	110.7	1,590
2005	134.9	115.4	124.5	97.3	144.4	128.3	125.0	127.5	115.6	137.0	120.3	118.2	1,488
2006[1]	120.4	112.1	135.8	120.2	153.2	131.0	140.6	144.3	134.3	129.6	134.8	133.1	1,590

[1] Preliminary.   *Source: Bureau of the Census, U.S. Department of Commerce*

Production of Crude Tall Oil in the United States — In Millions of Pounds

Year	Oct.	Nov.	Dec.	Jan.	Feb.	Mar.	Apr.	May	June	July	Aug.	Sept.	Total
1998-99	118.4	113.4	119.3	118.0	115.2	134.6	121.0	103.8	100.7	103.2	103.5	113.6	1,364.8
1999-00	93.8	101.6	107.8	101.3	104.6	115.2	95.4	91.8	99.5	94.5	97.0	86.5	1,202.6
2000-01	92.3	91.6	81.4	94.9	83.7	103.7	99.7	99.9	95.1	94.1	105.4	93.0	1,134.8
2001-02	99.1	100.7	86.5	101.8	93.7	105.5	104.2	96.0	88.5	94.7	103.6	91.4	1,165.6
2002-03	102.5	87.3	101.8	108.7	89.8	111.5	108.3	99.6	91.8	109.2	100.8	97.1	1,208.6
2003-04	102.1	87.9	109.0	113.7	96.1	112.1	102.8	106.8	99.2	94.4	108.9	104.1	1,236.9
2004-05	88.1	93.7	99.6	110.0	97.9	109.4	107.3	109.8	101.5	101.0	101.0	98.9	1,218.1
2005-06	95.5	92.1	100.3	103.9	103.4	108.1	110.4	117.6	101.4	104.6	109.7	99.7	1,246.8
2006-07[1]	104.8	103.7	109.5										1,271.9

[1] Preliminary.   *Source: Bureau of the Census, U.S. Department of Commerce*

Stocks of Crude Tall Oil in the United States, on First of Month — In Millions of Pounds

Year	Oct.	Nov.	Dec.	Jan.	Feb.	Mar.	Apr.	May	June	July	Aug.	Sept.
1998-99	268.7	219.8	200.3	197.5	164.8	156.9	163.3	177.5	183.0	180.7	183.6	152.7
1999-00	146.8	130.9	135.3	121.5	131.8	153.5	136.6	138.5	154.6	130.5	136.7	117.1
2000-01	110.5	102.4	105.4	117.0	118.9	118.2	134.4	139.6	171.7	132.0	160.5	145.4
2001-02	132.7	125.6	142.1	127.9	135.8	155.2	165.6	177.4	190.7	175.4	161.8	155.1
2002-03	160.2	154.1	155.7	160.5	176.0	167.4	156.3	173.4	163.7	180.3	199.3	209.5
2003-04	210.7	207.3	203.0	210.2	209.6	216.3	205.3	207.1	194.1	190.5	196.1	162.2
2004-05	174.1	140.3	124.4	95.0	109.9	108.8	134.0	132.1	130.5	126.3	122.0	121.8
2005-06	107.5	97.3	83.4	81.5	102.8	118.7	82.6	88.3	94.7	93.9	82.0	92.7
2006-07[1]	73.9	61.7	72.1	75.6								

[1] Preliminary.   *Source: Bureau of the Census, U.S. Department of Commerce*

Stocks of Refined Tall Oil in the United States, on First of Month — In Millions of Pounds

Year	Oct.	Nov.	Dec.	Jan.	Feb.	Mar.	Apr.	May	June	July	Aug.	Sept.
1998-99	15.1	14.9	17.0	12.5	14.8	9.9	7.2	7.6	7.2	7.3	6.3	7.0
1999-00	7.5	7.0	8.5	9.1	9.8	11.0	9.8	13.7	10.4	7.8	11.9	8.2
2000-01	9.6	9.0	9.9	10.2	10.7	12.5	11.8	13.9	12.6	19.5	13.4	21.6
2001-02	22.4	17.2	17.1	19.9	20.7	20.9	21.5	22.7	20.9	18.6	18.4	16.0
2002-03	13.3	16.5	18.7	20.1	20.1	18.6	20.4	19.7	15.8	14.5	13.5	13.9
2003-04	13.1	20.1	19.6	19.9	19.2	13.7	14.3	12.7	16.3	14.2	16.6	17.7
2004-05	14.8	16.6	16.9	17.0	15.2	20.4	16.0	18.2	16.9	17.2	14.5	17.5
2005-06	18.7	28.1	26.9	32.9	28.5	W	6.1	5.3	6.6	4.5	5.9	6.9
2006-07[1]	7.7	7.5	5.3	5.4								

[1] Preliminary.   *Source: Bureau of the Census, U.S. Department of Commerce*

Tallow and Greases

Tallow and grease are derived from processing (rendering) the fat of cattle. Tallow is used to produce both edible and inedible products. Edible tallow products include margarine, cooking oil, and baking products. Inedible tallow products include soap, candles, and lubricants. Production of tallow and greases is directly related to the number of cattle produced. Those countries that are the leading cattle producers are also the largest producers of tallow. The American Fats and Oils Association provides specifications for a variety of different types of tallow and grease, including edible tallow, lard (edible), top white tallow, all beef packer tallow, extra fancy tallow, fancy tallow, bleachable fancy tallow, prime tallow, choice white grease, and yellow grease. The specifications include such characteristics as the melting point, color, density, moisture content, insoluble impurities, and others.

Prices – The monthly average price of tallow (inedible, No. 1 Packers-Prime, delivered Chicago) in 2006 fell –3.3% yr/yr to 16.89 cents per pound. That was further below the record high of 21.60 cents posted in 1979. The wholesale price of edible tallow in 2006 fell –1.9% yr/yr to 18.63 cents per pound from 18.99 cents in 2005, and remained well below the record high of 30.25 cents per pound posted in 1981.

Supply – World production of tallow and greases (edible and inedible) in 2005, the latest available reporting year,

fell by –0.6% yr/yr to 8.200 million metric tons, down from the record high of 8.251 million metric tons posted in 2004. The world's largest producer of tallow and greases by far is the US with 44% of world production, followed by Brazil with 7%, Australia with 6%, and Canada with 4%.

U.S. production of edible tallow in 2005 fell –4.2% yr/yr to 1.741 billion pounds, down from the 2002 record high of 1.974. US production of inedible tallow and greases in 2006 rose by +4.1% yr/yr to 6.460 billion pounds, which was well below the record high of 7.156 billion pounds posted in 2002.

Demand – US consumption of inedible tallow and greases in 2006 rose +5.4% yr/yr to 2.589 billion pounds, of which virtually all went to animal feed. US consumption of edible tallow in 2005 fell –12.5% yr/yr to 1.449 billion pounds, down from the 2004 record high of 1.656. US per capita consumption of edible tallow fell –15.0% to 3.4 pounds per person per year, down from the 2000 and 2004 record high of 4.0.

Trade – US exports of inedible tallow and grease in 2006 rose 25.2% yr/yr to 346.0 million pounds, and accounted for 4.7% of total US supply. US exports of edible tallow in 2004 rose +13.7% yr/yr to 290 million pounds, and accounted for 16.4% of US supply.

World Production of Tallow and Greases (Edible and Inedible)   In Thousands of Metric Tons

Year	Argentina	Australia	Brazil	Canada	France	Germany	Rep. of Korea	Netherlands	New Zealand	Russia	United Kingdom	United States	World Total
1996	142	438	314	228	165	139	14	161	162	232	163	3,581	7,417
1997	159	461	368	244	165	136	17	191	187	215	166	3,510	7,591
1998	146	462	379	256	160	135	19	203	154	202	173	3,679	7,806
1999	160	471	394	285	160	140	18	178	167	186	158	3,979	8,171
2000	161	503	430	293	151	132	17	171	170	178	148	3,948	8,202
2001	144	507	446	296	140	126	15	151	173	172	115	3,503	7,694
2002	147	469	468	305	154	124	14	143	162	179	123	3,826	8,076
2003	154	456	487	289	164	121	15	141	174	182	120	3,707	8,036
2004[1]	178	486	508	343	166	124	14	133	192	179	123	3,714	8,251
2005[2]	184	493	533	351	162	121	15	125	168	173	125	3,604	8,200

[1] Preliminary.   [2] Forecast.   Source: Foreign Agricultural Service, U.S. Department of Agriculture (FAS-USDA)

Salient Statistics of Tallow and Greases (Inedible) in the United States   In Millions of Pounds

Year	Supply Production	Supply Stocks, Jan. 1	Supply Total	Exports	Consumption Soap	Consumption Feed	Consumption Total	Wholesale Prices, Cents/Lb. Edible, (Loose) Chicago	Wholesale Prices, Cents/Lb. Inedible, No. 1 Chicago
1997	6,249	266	6,515	775	245	2,401	2,646	23.5	20.8
1998	6,644	339	6,983	1,041	228	2,533	2,761	19.1	17.5
1999	7,079	437	7,516	877	229	2,847	3,076	15.1	13.0
2000	7,035	405	7,440	791	146	2,727	2,849	11.7	10.0
2001	6,870	347	7,217	616	107	2,834	2,843	13.7	12.0
2002	7,156	327	7,482	384	W	2,886	2,886	14.8	13.5
2003	6,246	240	6,486	307	W	2,434	2,434	20.3	18.3
2004	6,173	282	6,455	336	W	2,536	2,536	19.8	18.0
2005[1]	6,204	281	6,485	276	W	2,456	2,456	19.0	17.5
2006[2]	6,460	309	6,769	346	W	2,589	2,589	18.6	16.9

[1] Preliminary.   [2] Estimate.   Sources: Economic Research Service, U.S. Department of Agriculture (ERS-USDA); Bureau of the Census, U.S. Department of Commerce

Tallow (monthly average) through December 2006 — Cents per pound

Cents Per Pound
----- Inedible Prime, Chicago (Jan. 1910 - Dec. 1948)
Bleachable, Chicago (Jan. 1949 - date)

Supply and Disappearance of Edible Tallow in the United States   In Millions of Pounds, Rendered Basis

| Year | Supply | | | Disappearance | | | | | |
	Stocks Jan. 1	Production	Total	Domestic	Exports	Total	Diret Use	Baking or Frying Fats	Per Capita (Lbs.)
1996	43	1,520	1,568	1,317	218	1,535	602	320	2.2
1997	33	1,416	1,455	1,223	185	1,408	585	312	2.1
1998	47	1,537	1,586	1,301	246	1,547	868	259	3.1
1999	39	1,729	1,775	1,425	317	1,742	998	262	3.6
2000	33	1,825	1,866	1,581	248	1,829	1,125	283	4.0
2001	37	1,792	1,859	1,455	364	1,819	869	W	3.0
2002	40	1,974	2,023	1,487	511	1,998	974	W	3.4
2003	25	1,966	1,996	1,552	420	1,972	1,108	W	3.8
2004[1]	24	1,818	1,842	1,656	255	1,820	1,163	W	4.0
2005[2]	22	1,741	1,764	1,449	290	1,739	1,030	W	3.4

[1] Preliminary.   [2] Forecast.   *Sources: Economic Research Service, U.S. Department of Agriculture (ERS-USDA); Bureau of the Census, U.S. Department of Commerce*

Wholesale Price of Tallow, Inedible, No. 1 Packers (Prime), Delivered, Chicago   In Cents Per Pound

Year	Jan.	Feb.	Mar.	Apr.	May	June	July	Aug.	Sept.	Oct.	Nov.	Dec.	Average
1997	23.40	22.88	19.35	17.39	18.09	19.64	19.65	20.10	20.88	22.13	22.88	22.60	20.75
1998	18.20	16.88	17.58	17.70	20.35	19.63	17.31	17.57	16.69	16.98	16.90	16.70	17.71
1999	16.30	12.53	11.18	11.38	10.40	11.49	11.50	11.69	14.38	16.37	14.95	13.88	13.00
2000	11.89	10.14	10.67	10.21	11.60	10.74	9.19	9.48	10.07	10.05	9.35	11.23	10.39
2001	12.17	9.46	9.62	10.26	10.19	12.35	15.44	16.83	13.75	11.24	10.60	12.34	12.02
2002	10.00	10.54	12.64	11.06	11.59	15.47	14.80	14.00	14.23	13.98	15.91	18.08	13.53
2003	17.13	15.65	16.60	16.54	16.48	17.30	16.08	15.85	18.70	22.78	23.37	23.08	18.30
2004	23.23	16.72	17.80	21.05	18.01	18.08	19.55	16.92	17.20	14.33	15.61	16.97	17.96
2005	16.20	16.03	18.73	20.95	19.38	18.23	15.11	15.31	17.54	17.40	17.96	16.67	17.46
2006[1]	17.52	17.05	14.98	13.47	14.77	15.27	17.05	17.35	15.59	17.71	20.42	21.46	16.89

[1] Preliminary.   *Sources: Economic Research Service, U.S. Department of Agriculture (ERS-USDA)*

Tea

Tea is the common name for a family of mostly woody flowering plants. The tea family contains about 600 species placed in 28 genera and they are distributed throughout the tropical and subtropical areas, with most species occurring in eastern Asia and South America. The tea plant is native to Southeast Asia. There are more than 3,000 varieties of tea, each with its own distinct character, and each is generally named for the area in which it is grown. Tea may have been consumed in China as long ago as 2700 BC and certainly since 1000 BC. In 2737 BC, the Chinese Emperor Shen Nung, according to Chinese mythology, was a scholar and herbalist. While his servant boiled drinking water, a leaf from the wild tea tree he was sitting under dropped into the water and Shen Nung decided to try the brew. Today, half the world's population drinks tea. Tea is the world's most popular beverage next to water.

Tea is a healthful drink and contains antioxidants, fluoride, niacin, folic acid, and as much vitamin C as a lemon. The average 5 oz. cup of brewed tea contains approximately 40 to 60 milligrams of caffeine (compared to 80 to 115 mg in brewed coffee). Decaffeinated tea has been available since the 1980s. Herbal tea contains no true tea leaves but is actually brewed from a collection of herbs and spices.

Tea grows mainly between the tropic of Cancer and the tropic of Capricorn, requiring 40 to 50 inches of rain per year and a temperature ideally between 50 to 86 degrees Fahrenheit. In order to rejuvenate the bush and keep it at a convenient height for the pickers to access, the bushes must be pruned every four to five years. A tea bush can produce tea for 50 to 70 years, but after 50 years, the yield is reduced.

The two key factors in determining different varieties of tea are the production process (sorting, withering, rolling, fermentation, and drying methods) and the growing conditions (geographical region, growing altitude, and soil type). Black tea, often referred to as fully fermented tea, is produced by allowing picked tea leaves to wither and ferment for up to 24 hours. After fermenting, the leaves are fired, which stops oxidation. Green tea, or unfermented tea, is produced by immediately and completely drying the leaves and omitting the oxidization process, thus allowing the tea to remain green in color.

Supply – World production of tea in 2004, the latest full reporting year for the series, rose +4.2% to 3.342 million metric tons, which was a record high. The world's largest producers of tea in 2004 were India (with 26.0% of world production), China (26%), Sri Lanka (9), Kenya (9%), Turkey (6%), and Indonesia (5%).

Trade – US tea imports in 2006 rose +6.3% to 195,872 metric tons, which was a new record high. World tea imports in 2003, the latest data available, fell –8.6% to 1.320 million metric tons. The world's largest tea importers in 2003 were Russia (with 13% of total world imports), the United Kingdom (12%), Pakistan (8%), and the US (7%). The world's largest exporters in 2003 were Kenya (with 21% of world exports), China (19%), India (13%), Sri Lanka (12%), Indonesia (6%), Vietnam (4%), and Argentina (4%).

World Tea Production, in Major Producing Countries — In Thousands of Metric Tons

Year	Argentina	Bangladesh	China	India	Indonesia	Iran	Japan	Kenya	Malawi	Sri Lanka	Turkey	Ex-USSR[2]	World Total
1998	57.0	51.0	688.0	870.0	166.0	60.0	83.0	294.0	40.0	280.0	178.0	52.0	3,040
1999	56.0	56.0	697.0	870.0	161.0	80.0	88.0	249.0	48.0	284.0	178.0	65.0	3,078
2000	53.0	46.0	704.0	835.0	162.0	50.0	85.0	236.0	45.0	306.0	139.0	27.0	2,947
2001	63.0	52.0	722.0	848.0	163.0	51.0	85.0	217.0	37.0	295.0	143.0	25.0	2,980
2002	63.0	52.0	760.0	826.0	163.0	51.0	85.0	287.0	38.0	310.0	150.0	23.0	3,100
2003	64.0	60.0	800.0	885.0	159.0	52.0	92.0	290.0	45.0	303.0	131.0	26.0	3,207
2004[1]	64.0	56.0	855.0	851.0	165.0	52.0	101.0	295.0	50.0	308.0	202.0	26.0	3,342

[1] Preliminary. [2] Mostly Georgia and Azerbaijan. *Sources: Foreign Agricultural Service, U.S. Department of Agriculture (FAS-USDA); Food and Agriculture Organization of the United Nations (FAO-UN)*

World Tea Exports from Producing Countries — In Metric Tons

Year	Argentina	Bangladesh	Brazil	China	India	Indonesia	Kenya	Malawi	P. New Guinea	Sri Lanka	Vietnam	Zimbabwe	World Total
1997	56,806	21,740	3,404	205,381	191,472	66,843	199,224	39,824	6,500	267,726	32,901	13,057	1,315,534
1998	58,987	25,049	3,208	219,325	201,798	67,219	263,685	40,518	6,600	270,938	33,000	11,076	1,415,223
1999	52,144	21,494	2,914	202,681	177,507	97,847	245,716	30,000	8,200	268,330	37,300	15,722	1,372,179
2000	50,000	11,000	3,714	230,696	200,868	105,581	217,282	69,600	8,500	287,005	55,600	16,916	1,489,215
2001	58,110	6,400	4,082	252,204	177,603	99,797	207,244	32,200	8,800	293,524	67,900	6,162	1,446,657
2002[1]	57,643	3,964	3,979	254,875	181,617	100,185	88,311	36,631	5,200	290,500	77,000	18,855	1,375,260
2003[2]	59,062	7,348	4,209	262,663	174,246	88,176	293,751	37,945	6,600	161,773	59,800	13,355	1,383,544

[1] Preliminary. [2] Estimate. *Source: Food and Agriculture Organization of the United Nations (FAO-UN)*

Imports of Tea in the United States — In Metric Tons

Year	Jan.	Feb.	Mar.	Apr.	May	June	July	Aug.	Sept.	Oct.	Nov.	Dec.	Total
2001	14,596	11,917	15,237	16,772	15,802	16,426	16,041	14,415	11,917	14,072	14,548	11,150	172,893
2002	14,785	14,237	16,029	17,326	18,747	15,158	15,189	11,977	9,777	14,384	12,148	12,073	171,829
2003	15,051	13,519	15,651	17,810	18,863	15,089	15,290	13,778	11,240	16,417	11,439	13,054	177,201
2004	15,089	14,716	18,355	19,279	18,813	18,782	16,511	14,116	14,530	13,851	14,876	14,698	193,615
2005	16,728	13,977	17,877	20,502	16,696	18,445	15,714	14,146	12,775	14,376	11,276	11,750	184,261
2006[1]	15,645	14,556	17,307	18,997	22,024	20,080	15,693	16,377	14,560	11,869	15,392	13,372	195,872

[1] Preliminary. *Source: Foreign Agricultural Service, U.S. Department of Agriculture (FAS-USDA)*

Tin

Tin (symbol Sn) is a silvery-white, lustrous gray metallic element. Tin is soft, pliable and has a highly crystalline structure. When a tin bar is bent or broken, a crackling sound called a "tin cry" is produced due to the breaking of the tin crystals. People have been using tin for at least 5,500 years. Tin has been found in the tombs of ancient Egyptians. In ancient times, tin and lead were considered different forms of the same metal. Tin was exported to Europe in large quantities from Cornwall, England, during the Roman period, from approximately 2100 BC to 1500 BC. Cornwall was one of the world's leading sources of tin for much of its known history and into the late 1800s

The principal ore of tin is the mineral cassiterite, which is found in Malaya, Bolivia, Indonesia, Thailand, and Nigeria. About 80% of the world's tin deposits occur in unconsolidated placer deposits in riverbeds and valleys, or on the sea floor, with only about 20% occurring as primary hard-rock lodes. Tin deposits are generally small and are almost always found closely allied to the granite from which it originates. Tin is also recovered as a by-product of mining tungsten, tantalum, and lead. After extraction, tin ore is ground and washed to remove impurities, roasted to oxidize the sulfides of iron and copper, washed a second time, and then reduced by carbon in a reverberatory furnace. Electrolysis may also be used to purify tin.

Pure tin, rarely used by itself, was used as currency in the form of tin blocks and was considered legal tender for taxes in Phuket, Thailand, until 1932. Tin is used in the manufacture of coatings for steel containers used to preserve food and beverages. Tin is also used in solder alloys, electroplating, ceramics, and in plastic. The world's major tin research and development laboratory, ITRI Ltd, is funded by companies that produce and consume tin. The focus of the research efforts have been on possible new uses for tin that would take advantage of tin's relative non-toxicity to replace other metals in various products. Some of the replacements could be lead-free solders, antimony-free flame-retardant chemicals, and lead-free shotgun pellets. No tin is currently mined in the U.S.

Tin futures and options trade on the London Metal Exchange (LME). Tin has traded on the LME since 1877 and the standard tin contract began in 1912. The futures contract calls for the delivery of 5 metric tons of tin ingots of at least 99.85% purity. The contract trades in terms of US dollars per metric ton.

Prices – The average monthly price of tin (straights) in New York in 2006 rose by +18.5% yr/yr to a 21-year high of $5.68 per pound. The 2006 price of $5.68 is double the 3-decade low of $2.83 per pound seen as recently as 2002. The average monthly price of ex-dock tin in New York in 2006 rose by +16.4% yr/yr to $4.17 per pound, and that is more than double the 3-decade low of $1.99 per pound posted in 2002.

Supply – World mine production of tin in 2005 (latest data available) rose by +6.9% yr/yr to a record high of 280,000 metric tons. The world's largest mine producers of tin are China with 41% of world production in 2005, Indonesia with 29%, and Peru with 15%. World smelter production of tin fell –7.9% in 2005 to 280,000 metric tons, which was mildly below the record high of 304,000 metric tons produced in 2004. The world's largest producers of smelted tin are China with 41% of world production in 2005, Indonesia with 27%, and Bolivia with 6%. The US does not mine tin, and therefore supply consists only of scrap and imports. US tin recovery in 2005 fell –0.4% to 7,670 metric tons, which was a new record low.

Demand – US consumption of tin (pig) in 2006 (through November) fell –9.4% to an annualized 42,278 metric tons, which is a 12-year low. The breakdown of US consumption of tin by finished products in 2005 shows that the largest consuming industry of tin is solder (with 34% of consumption), followed by chemicals (23%), tin plate (20%), and bronze and brass (8%).

Trade – The US relied on imports for 79% of its tin consumption in 2006. US imports of unwrought tin metal in 2004 rose +28.3% to 47,600 metric tons, up from the 2003 7-year low of 37,100 metric tons. The largest sources of US imports in 2004 were China (5,310 metric tons), Bolivia (with 5,060 metric tons of imports), Indonesia (4,660 metric tons), and Brazil (4,330 metric tons). US exports of tin in 2004 fell –1.1% yr/yr to 3,650 metric tons.

World Mine Production of Tin   In Metric Tons (Contained Tin)

Year	Australia	Bolivia	Brazil	China	Indo-nesia	Malaysia	Nigeria	Peru	Portugal	Russia	Thailand	United Kingdom	World Total
1996	8,828	14,802	19,617	69,600	52,304	5,174	139	27,004	4,637	8,000	1,300	2,103	220,000
1997	10,169	12,898	19,065	67,500	55,175	5,065	150	27,952	2,667	7,500	746	2,396	217,000
1998	10,204	11,308	14,238	70,100	53,959	5,754	200	49,574	3,100	4,500	1,656	376	231,000
1999	10,011	12,417	13,202	80,100	47,754	7,339	3,300	59,191	2,200	2,500	2,712	----	246,000
2000	9,146	12,464	13,773	99,400	51,629	6,307	2,760	70,901	1,200	2,500	1,930	----	277,000
2001	9,602	12,298	14,200	95,000	61,862	4,972	2,870	69,696	1,200	2,000	1,950	----	281,000
2002	6,268	15,242	14,200	62,000	88,142	4,215	2,800	38,815	1,000	1,300	1,130	----	241,000
2003	3,819	16,755	12,217	102,000	71,694	3,359	3,700	40,202	200	2,000	817	----	263,000
2004[1]	800	16,800	12,200	110,000	65,772	3,000	3,000	41,613	500	2,500	567	----	262,000
2005[2]		17,000	12,300	115,000	80,000	2,000		42,000	500	3,000	650	----	280,000

[1] Preliminary.   [2] Estimate.   *Source: U.S. Geological Survey (USGS)*

TIN

World Smelter Production of Primary Tin In Metric Tons

Year	Australia	Bolivia	Brazil	China	Indo-nesia	Japan	Malaysia	Mexico	Russia	South Africa	Spain	Thailand	World Total
1996	460	16,733	18,361	71,500	39,000	524	38,051	1,234	9,000	----	150	10,981	211,000
1997	605	16,853	17,525	67,700	52,658	507	34,822	1,188	6,700	----	150	11,986	241,000
1998	655	11,102	14,900	79,300	53,401	500	27,201	1,078	3,000	----	100	15,353	247,000
1999	600	11,166	12,787	90,800	49,105	568	28,913	1,262	4,500	----	50	17,306	267,000
2000	775	9,353	13,825	112,000	46,432	593	26,228	1,204	4,800	----	----	17,076	288,000
2001	1,171	11,292	13,800	105,000	53,470	668	30,417	1,789	4,569	----	----	22,387	300,000
2002	611	10,976	11,675	82,000	67,455	659	30,887	1,756	4,615	----	----	17,548	280,000
2003	597	10,976	10,761	98,000	65,000	662	18,250	1,769	5,500	----	----	15,763	280,000
2004	478	11,000	11,000	115,000	65,000	707	30,000	1,775	5,500	----	----	15,500	304,000
2005[1]	800	17,000	12,300	115,000	80,000								280,000

[1] Preliminary. Source: U.S. Geological Survey (USGS)

United States Foreign Trade of Tin In Metric Tons

Year	Exports (Metal)	Concentrates[2] (Ore) Total All Ore	Concentrates[2] (Ore) Bolivia	Concentrates[2] (Ore) Peru	Imports for Consumption — Unwrought Tin Metal Total All Metal	Bolivia	Brazil	China	Indo-nesia	Malaysia	Singa-pore	Thailand	United Kingdom
1995	2,790	-----	-----	-----	33,200	6,630	8,070	5,610	7,230	3,810	40	-----	97
1996	3,670	-----	-----	-----	30,200	6,290	9,460	2,760	7,550	965	120	-----	243
1997	4,660	57	-----	-----	40,600	6,680	8,610	4,710	7,610	1,640	120	600	20
1998	5,020	-----	-----	-----	44,000	5,160	4,710	9,870	7,880	1,870	822	540	790
1999	6,770	-----	-----	-----	47,500	3,850	4,700	13,900	7,930	944	60	20	60
2000	6,640	-----	-----	-----	44,900	6,330	5,860	10,200	5,320	214	20	-----	514
2001	4,350	-----	-----	-----	37,500	6,040	5,510	6,360	3,880	674	145	-----	118
2002	2,940	-----	-----	-----	42,200	6,150	4,840	7,600	3,340	122	-----	-----	2
2003	3,690	-----	-----	-----	37,100	5,720	3,000	4,340	3,070	490	-----	-----	143
2004[1]	3,650	-----	-----	-----	47,600	5,060	4,330	5,310	4,660	6,600	-----	500	97

[1] Preliminary. [2] Tin content. Source: U.S. Geological Survey (USGS)

Consumption (Total) of Tin (Pig) in the United States In Metric Tons

Year	Jan.	Feb.	Mar.	Apr.	May	June	July	Aug.	Sept.	Oct.	Nov.	Dec.	Total
1997	4,953	4,025	4,023	4,067	3,999	4,079	3,936	3,912	4,050	4,098	3,964	4,250	44,350
1998	4,410	4,493	4,445	4,508	4,388	4,483	4,273	4,300	4,404	4,402	4,348	4,268	52,720
1999	4,660	4,667	4,790	4,790	4,760	4,700	4,254	4,396	4,340	4,316	4,275	4,227	55,100
2000	4,362	4,466	4,430	4,377	4,466	4,470	4,398	4,476	4,397	4,460	4,244	4,157	47,040
2001	4,252	4,185	4,095	4,141	4,148	4,128	4,055	4,163	4,153	4,197	4,129	3,974	49,620
2002	3,965	3,866	3,868	3,819	4,087	3,887	3,887	3,842	3,835	3,966	3,822	3,811	46,655
2003	3,814	3,808	3,851	3,891	3,701	3,814	3,841	3,850	3,803	3,816	3,764	3,887	45,840
2004	3,851	3,632	3,887	3,837	3,874	4,001	3,844	3,871	3,850	3,870	3,947	3,772	46,236
2005	4,097	3,990	4,027	3,874	3,825	3,918	3,806	3,900	3,824	3,833	3,849	3,699	46,642
2006[1]	3,877	3,694	3,508	3,439	3,447	3,580	3,475	3,420	3,456	3,442	3,417		42,278

[1] Preliminary. Source: U.S. Geological Survey (USGS)

Tin Stocks (Pig-Industrial) in the United States, on First of Month In Metric Tons

Year	Jan.	Feb.	Mar.	Apr.	May	June	July	Aug.	Sept.	Oct.	Nov.	Dec.
1997	4,670	5,100	5,610	5,600	5,070	5,270	5,180	5,650	5,590	5,420	5,290	5,590
1998	6,100	5,570	5,390	5,840	6,170	5,940	5,830	5,580	6,660	6,270	5,880	5,710
1999	5,620	8,120	7,770	7,760	7,760	7,510	7,750	7,560	7,870	7,790	8,390	8,800
2000	8,300	8,330	7,960	7,580	7,810	7,930	8,090	8,240	7,820	8,210	7,200	7,970
2001	8,140	8,330	8,360	8,460	8,270	8,640	8,760	8,760	8,920	9,030	7,630	7,470
2002	7,700	7,320	7,020	6,990	6,870	6,600	6,540	6,590	6,670	7,130	6,880	6,950
2003	7,280	6,980	6,690	6,640	6,390	6,400	6,380	6,420	6,250	6,180	6,190	6,340
2004	6,520	6,010	6,130	6,280	5,850	6,000	5,900	6,290	6,110	6,030	5,900	6,410
2005	6,140	5,260	5,570	5,420	5,770	5,400	5,670	5,830	5,540	5,350	5,330	5,410
2006[1]	5,400	5,380	5,330	5,350	5,400	5,380	5,420	5,400	5,740	5,650	5,650	5,640

[1] Preliminary. Source: U.S. Geological Survey (USGS)

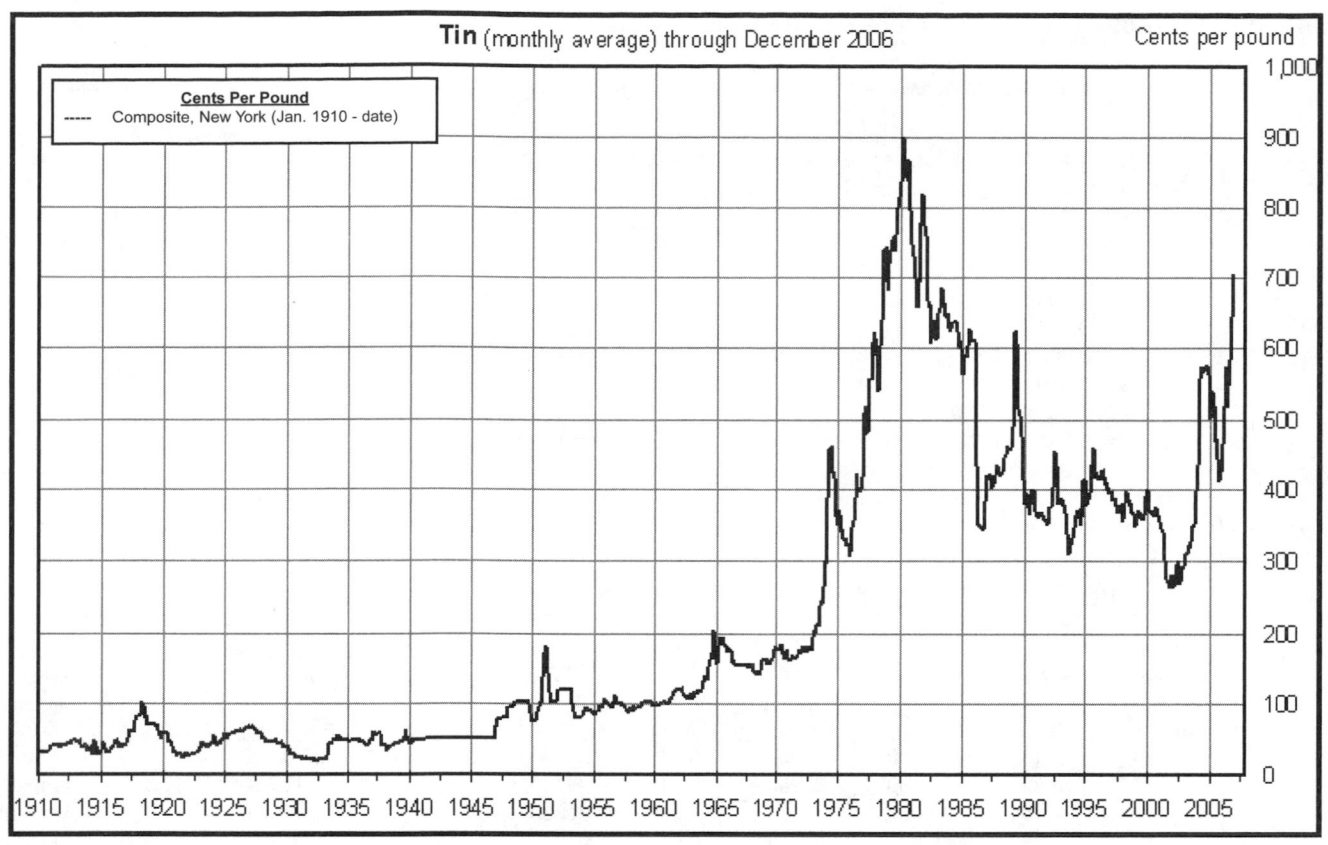

Tin (monthly average) through December 2006   Cents per pound

Cents Per Pound
----- Composite, New York (Jan. 1910 - date)

Average Price of Ex-Dock Tin in New York[1]   In Cents Per Pound

Year	Jan.	Feb.	Mar.	Apr.	May	June	July	Aug.	Sept.	Oct.	Nov.	Dec.	Average
1997	281.91	281.34	281.51	274.36	274.23	267.31	261.03	259.85	262.56	266.77	268.33	262.61	270.15
1998	249.39	252.65	262.36	271.65	279.50	284.27	268.87	270.98	260.79	259.17	261.82	251.75	264.43
1999	244.46	251.04	255.13	256.97	269.42	253.64	251.09	251.32	256.38	260.70	278.24	274.51	258.73
2000	283.63	271.70	263.42	259.59	259.70	260.16	257.77	255.92	262.54	254.56	253.64	252.19	261.24
2001	249.32	246.91	243.14	238.33	238.53	231.14	210.17	188.42	179.53	181.38	194.77	195.90	216.46
2002	189.23	183.23	187.65	195.36	201.95	208.01	211.51	188.36	193.79	206.67	205.94	206.63	199.15
2003	212.68	217.98	219.58	217.90	225.40	223.69	225.81	229.58	233.59	248.22	252.93	285.40	232.73
2004	305.34	313.55	357.66	418.57	449.29	438.72	439.24	437.68	438.91	436.80	439.24	414.16	407.43
2005	376.37	393.05	408.41	395.40	394.68	367.81	347.78	347.96	331.01	313.73	300.96	323.43	358.38
2006	338.27	373.87	378.76	420.35	420.53	376.76	400.64	404.26	428.83	461.66	475.57	524.69	417.02

Source: American Metal Market (AMM)

Average Price of Tin (Straights) in New York   In Cents Per Pound

Year	Jan.	Feb.	Mar.	Apr.	May	June	July	Aug.	Sept.	Oct.	Nov.	Dec.	Average
1997	396.18	395.50	395.64	386.52	386.58	377.83	369.97	369.01	372.45	377.39	378.00	371.35	381.37
1998	356.97	359.76	370.96	381.99	392.16	397.36	377.72	380.02	368.89	366.87	370.49	357.69	373.41
1999	348.77	356.50	361.11	363.01	372.62	359.05	359.96	357.35	366.06	370.68	392.04	288.77	357.99
2000	400.90	384.13	372.50	368.42	370.13	370.81	366.49	364.65	375.25	363.54	362.94	360.68	371.70
2001	356.37	352.87	348.19	341.59	340.61	329.68	302.57	276.55	263.17	264.88	281.23	279.46	311.43
2002	271.59	263.91	270.54	280.98	288.74	296.02	299.39	269.30	277.60	293.79	292.40	292.95	283.10
2003	304.44	312.32	314.52	312.26	321.92	319.67	322.10	327.16	332.21	350.90	356.46	396.46	330.87
2004	422.33	433.50	485.99	557.29	575.39	570.99	565.68	568.14	572.72	573.79	577.07	550.97	537.82
2005	500.93	519.61	539.30	522.71	522.18	492.64	467.71	466.67	444.80	426.36	411.23	440.30	479.54
2006	464.54	509.45	519.31	574.53	575.57	517.52	548.29	552.06	583.57	623.07	644.19	705.62	568.14

Source: U.S. Geological Survey (USGS)

Tin Plate Production & Tin Recovered in the United States In Metric Tons

Year	----- Tin Content of Tinplate Produced ----- ------- Tinplate (All Forms) ------- Tinplate Waste ---- Gross Weight ----		Tin Content (Tonne)	Tin Per Tonne of Plate (Kilograms)	--------------------------------- Tin Recovered from Scrap by Form of Recovery --------------------------------- Tin Metal	Bronze & Brass	Solder	Type Metal	Babbitt	Anti-monial Lead	Chemical Com-pounds	Misc.[2]	Grand Total
1996	181,100	1,551,000	9,617	6.2	W	11,400	W	37	34	171	W	W	11,600
1997	157,000	2,010,000	9,300	4.6	W	12,200	W	W	W	149	W	W	12,300
1998	W	1,700,000	8,900	5.2	NA	NA	NA	NA	NA	NA	NA	NA	NA
1999	W	1,750,000	9,080	5.2	NA	NA	NA	NA	NA	NA	NA	NA	NA
2000	119,000	1,320,000	8,800	6.7	NA	NA	NA	NA	NA	NA	NA	NA	NA
2001	97,800	2,000,000	7,800	3.9	NA	NA	NA	NA	NA	NA	NA	NA	NA
2002	45,900	2,450,000	7,750	3.2	NA	NA	NA	NA	NA	NA	NA	NA	NA
2003	W	2,500,000	7,750	3.1	NA	NA	NA	NA	NA	NA	NA	NA	NA
2004	W	2,550,000	7,700	3.0	NA	NA	NA	NA	NA	NA	NA	NA	NA
2005[1]	W	2,270,000	7,670	3.4	NA	NA	NA	NA	NA	NA	NA	NA	NA

[1] Preliminary. [2] Includes foil, terne metal, cable lead, and items indicated by symbol W. W = Withheld Proprietary data.
Source: U.S. Geological Survey (USGS)

Consumption of Primary and Secondary Tin in the United States In Metric Tons

Year	Net Import Reliance as a % of Apparent Consumption	Industry Stocks Jan. 1[2]	--------------------------- Net Receipts --------------------------- Primary	Secondary	Scrap	Total	Available Supply	Stocks Dec. 31 (Total Available Less Total Processed)	Total Processed	Consumed in Manu-facturing Products
1995	84	8,480	39,400	5,020	6,240	50,600	59,100	13,000	46,100	46,000
1996	83	9,300	39,200	2,750	6,140	48,100	57,300	12,500	44,900	44,700
1997	85	9,180	39,000	2,360	6,010	47,300	56,500	11,900	44,600	44,400
1998	85	9,280	39,900	2,490	6,240	48,600	57,900	12,000	45,800	45,700
1999	85	9,290	40,500	2,790	6,360	49,700	58,900	11,900	47,000	46,900
2000	86	8,910	41,400	2,990	6,050	50,400	59,300	12,200	47,100	47,000
2001	88	8,830	34,500	2,180	4,770	41,400	50,200	8,220	42,000	41,900
2002	79	8,500	34,200	1,610	4,230	40,100	48,600	8,550	40,000	39,800
2003	91	8,220	32,400	1,380	3,440	37,300	45,500	7,770	37,700	37,400
2004[1]	88	7,310	37,200	1,840	4,350	43,400	50,700	11,300	39,500	39,000

[1] Preliminary. [2] Includes tin in transit in the U.S. Source: U.S. Geological Survey (USGS)

Consumption of Tin in the United States, by Finished Products In Metric Tons (Contained Tin)

Year	Tinplate[2]	Solder	Babbitt	Bronze & Brass	Tinning	Chem-icals[3]	Tin Powder	Bar Tin & Anodes	White Metal	Other	------------- Total ------------- Total	Primary	Secondary
1995	9,670	17,700	871	2,830	1,110	7,060	W	1,200	965	4,550	46,000	35,200	10,800
1996	9,340	15,600	851	2,760	2,050	7,520	573	1,150	1,340	3,230	44,700	36,500	8,180
1997	9,350	15,900	909	3,160	1,210	8,170	W	684	754	3,980	44,400	36,200	8,250
1998	8,900	16,900	1,020	3,610	1,100	8,180	W	704	778	4,260	45,700	37,100	8,620
1999	9,150	18,700	1,610	3,410	905	8,220	W	721	943	3,220	46,900	38,000	8,890
2000	8,800	18,800	1,660	3,360	1,200	8,040	W	714	1,260	3,210	47,000	38,100	8,940
2001	7,800	17,000	770	3,430	1,070	7,590	W	570	1,390	2,230	41,900	34,200	7,630
2002	7,750	13,800	1,310	3,040	679	8,400	W	617	1,320	2,920	39,800	34,000	5,830
2003	7,790	10,600	2,570	2,600	833	8,720	W	852	1,220	2,180	37,400	32,900	4,510
2004[1]	7,700	13,300	724	3,070	798	9,120	W	680	937	2,630	39,000	33,300	5,670

[1] Preliminary. [2] Includes small quantity of secondary pig tin and tin acquired in chemicals. [3] Including tin oxide. W = Withheld proprietary data.
Source: U.S. Geological Survey (USGS)

Titanium

Titanium (symbol Ti) is a silver-white, metallic element used primarily to make light, strong alloys. It ranks ninth in abundance among the elements in the crust of the earth but is never found in the pure state. It occurs as an oxide in various minerals. It was first discovered in 1791 by Rev. William Gregor and was first isolated as a basic element in 1910. Titanium was named after the mythological Greek god Titan for its strength.

Titanium is extremely brittle when cold, but is malleable and ductile at a low red heat, and thus easily fabricated. Due to its strength, low weight, and resistance to corrosion, titanium is used in metallic alloys and as a substitute for aluminum. It is used extensively in the aerospace industry, in desalination plants, construction, medical implants, paints, pigments, and lacquers.

Prices – The price of the mineral ilmenite, a primary source of titanium, traded in the range of $75-85 per metric ton in 2005 versus $72-90 in 2004. The price of titanium metal sponge traded in the range of $3.46-12.22 per pound in 2005 versus $3.55-6.44 in 2004. The price of titanium dioxide pigments (Anatase) traded in the range of $.95-$1.00 cents per pound in 2005 versus 90-95 cents per pound in 2004.

Supply – World production of titanium ilmenite concentrates in 2005 rose +3.5% to 5.840 million metric tons, to post a new record high. The world's largest producers of titanium ilmenite concentrates are Australia with 36% of world production in 2005, China with 15%, Norway with 15%, the Ukraine with 12%, and India with 9%.

World production of titanium rutile concentrates in 2005 rose +4.2% yr/yr to 369,000 metric tons, which was well below the record high of 545,000 metric tons seen in 1994. The world's largest producers are Australia with 48% of world production in 2005, followed by South Africa with 30% and the Ukraine with 16%.

Demand – US consumption of titanium dioxide pigment in 2005 fell by –3.4% yr/yr to 1.130 million metric tons, down from 2004's record high of 1.170 million metric tons. US consumption of ilmenite in 2005 fell –12.8% to 1.290 million metric tons, from 2004's 8-year high of 1.480 million metric tons. US consumption of rutile in 2005 fell –4.7% yr/yr to a 7-year low of 424,000 metric tons.

Trade – US imports of titanium dioxide pigment in 2005 rose +29.2% to a new record high of 341,000 metric tons. US imports of ilmenite in 2005 rose +17.3% yr/yr to 822,000 metric tons. US imports of rutile in 2005 rose +1.7% yr/yr to 366,000 metric tons.

Average Prices of Titanium in the United States

Year	Ilmenite F.O.B. Australian Ports	Slag, 85% TiO2 F.O.B. Richards Bay, South Africa	Rutile Large Lots Bulk, F.O.B. U.S. East Coast	Rutile Bagged F.O.B. Australian Ports	Average Price of Grade A Titanium Sponge, F.O.B. Shipping Point	Titanium Metal Sponge	Titanium Dioxide Pigments, F.O.B. U.S. Plants	
	------ Dollars Per Metric Ton ------					------ Dollars Per Pound ------		
1996	82-92	353	525-600	700-800	----	4.25-4.50	1.06-1.08	1.08-1.10
1997	68-81	391	500-550	650-710	----	4.25-4.50	1.01-1.03	1.04-1.06
1998	72-77	386	470-530	570-620	----	4.25-4.50	.96-.98	.97-.99
1999	90-103	406	435-510	500-530	----	3.70-4.80	.92-.94	.99-1.02
2000	83-105	425	470-500	480-570	----	3.95	.92-.94	.99-1.02
2001	90-110	419	450-500	475-565	----	3.58	.92-.94	1.00-1.09
2002	85-100	445	430-470	400-540	----	3.64	.85-.95	.85-.95
2003	80-100	401	415-445	430-540	----	2.72-3.95	.85-.95	.85-.90
2004[1]	72-90	----	430-480	550-650	----	3.55-6.44	.90-.95	.90-.95
2005[2]	75-85	----	460-480	550-650	----	3.46-12.22	.95-1.00	.95-1.00

[1] Preliminary. [2] Estimate. NA = Not available. *Source: U.S. Geological Survey (USGS)*

Salient Statistics of Titanium in the United States   In Metric Tons

Year	Titanium Dioxide Pigment Production	Imports[3]	Apparent Consumption	Ilmenite Imports[3]	Ilmenite Consumption	Titanium Slag Imports[3]	Titanium Slag Consumption	Rutile[4] Imports[3]	Rutile Consumption	Exports Ores & Concentrates	Exports Scrap	Exports Dioxide & Pigments	Exports Ingots, Billets, Etc.
1996	1,230,000	167,000	1,070,000	939,000	1,400,000	421,000	----	324,000	398,000	15,500	3,410	292,000	3,130
1997	1,340,000	194,000	1,130,000	952,000	1,520,000	430,000	----	336,000	489,000	23,800	5,500	362,000	3,860
1998	1,330,000	200,000	1,140,000	1,010,000	1,300,000	626,000	----	387,000	421,000	59,700	7,010	356,000	3,780
1999	1,350,000	225,000	1,160,000	1,070,000	1,280,000	678,000	----	344,000	494,000	9,380	8,130	344,000	3,390
2000	1,400,000	218,000	1,150,000	918,000	1,250,000	533,000	----	438,000	537,000	18,900	5,060	423,000	2,980
2001	1,330,000	209,000	1,100,000	1,060,000	1,180,000	594,000	----	325,000	483,000	7,800	7,500	349,000	3,260
2002	1,410,000	231,000	1,110,000	840,000	1,300,000	445,000	----	390,000	487,000	3,810	6,000	485,000	3,460
2003	1,420,000	240,000	1,070,000	804,000	1,300,000	409,000	----	427,000	489,000	10,300	5,320	518,000	3,960
2004[1]	1,540,000	264,000	1,170,000	701,000	1,480,000	457,000	----	360,000	445,000	8,690	9,760	576,000	4,990
2005[2]	1,310,000	341,000	1,130,000	822,000	1,290,000	667,000	----	366,000	424,000	20,900	20,600	486,000	6,350

[1] Preliminary. [2] Estimate. [3] For consumption. [4] Natural and synthetic. W = Withheld proprietary data. *Source: U.S. Geological Survey (USGS)*

TITANIUM

World Production of Titanium Illmenite Concentrates — In Thousands of Metric Tons

Year	Australia[2]	Brazil	China	Egypt	India	Malaysia	Norway	Ukraine	United States	Vietnam	World Total	-- Titaniferous Slag[3] -- Canada	South Africa
1996	2,061	98	165	124	330	245	747	500	W	50	4,380	825	1,000
1997	2,265	97	170	125	332	168	750	500	W	50	4,470	850	1,100
1998	2,433	103	175	125	378	125	590	507	W	80	4,560	950	1,100
1999	2,008	96	180	130	378	128	600	537	W	91	4,150	950	1,168
2000	2,173	123	250	125	380	125	750	436	400	174	4,940	910	1,090
2001	2,047	165	300	125	430	130	750	485	500	180	5,110	1,010	1,025
2002	1,956	177	750	125	460	106	750	512	400	180	5,420	900	973
2003	2,063	170	800	125	500	95	840	421	500	180	5,690	873	1,010
2004	1,966	133	840	125	520	61	860	370	500	200	5,640	863	1,020
2005[1]	2,089	135	900	125	550	70	860	700	500	180	5,840	860	1,020

[1] Preliminary.   [2] Includes leucoxene.   [3] Approximately 10% of total production is ilmenite. Beginning in 1988, 25% of Norway's ilmenite production was used to produce slag containing 75% TiO2.   W = Withheld proprietary data.   *Source: U.S. Geological Survey (USGS)*

World Production of Titanium Rutile Concentrates — In Metric Tons

Year	Australia	Brazil	India	Sierre Leone	South Africa	Sri Lanka	Thailand	Ukraine	World Total
1996	180,000	2,018	15,000	----	115,000	3,532	----	50,000	366,000
1997	233,000	1,742	14,000	----	123,000	2,970	----	50,000	425,000
1998	238,000	1,800	16,000	----	130,000	1,930	----	50,000	438,000
1999	179,000	4,300	16,000	----	100,000	----	----	49,000	348,000
2000	208,000	3,162	17,000	----	100,000	----	----	58,600	387,000
2001	206,000	1,791	19,000	----	90,000	----	----	60,000	377,000
2002	218,000	1,878	18,000	----	138,000	----	----	70,000	446,000
2003	173,000	2,337	18,000	----	108,000	----	----	60,000	361,000
2004	162,000	3,000	19,000	----	110,000	----	----	60,000	354,000
2005[1]	177,000	3,000	19,000	----	110,000	----	----	60,000	369,000

[1] Preliminary.   NA = Not available.   *Source: U.S. Geological Survey (USGS)*

World Production of Titanium Sponge Metal & U.S. Consumption of Titanium Concentrates

| | Production of Titanium (In Metric Tons) Sponge Metal[2] | | | | | -- U.S. Consumption of Titanium Concentrates, by Products (In Metric Tons) -- Ilmenite (TiO$_2$ Content) | | | | Rutile (TiO$_2$ Content) | | | |
Year	China	Japan	Russia	United Kingdom	United States	Total	Pigments	Misc.	Total	Welding Rod Coatings	Pigments	Misc.	Total
1996	2,000	21,100	18,000	----	W	51,000	1,010,000	[3]	1,010,000	W	341,000	24,200	365,000
1997	2,000	24,100	20,000	----	W	58,000	1,410,000	[3]	1,410,000	W	406,000	27,600	434,000
1998	----	----	----	----	----	----	1,290,000	14,000	1,300,000	W	384,000	37,300	421,000
1999	----	----	----	----	----	----	1,270,000	13,400	1,280,000	----	469,000	25,800	494,000
2000	----	----	----	----	----	----	1,240,000	13,900	1,250,000	----	513,000	24,100	537,000
2001	----	----	----	----	----	----	1,160,000	15,400	1,180,000	----	455,000	28,500	483,000
2002	----	----	----	----	----	----	1,280,000	16,000	1,300,000	----	464,000	22,900	487,000
2003	----	----	----	----	----	----	1,280,000	16,700	1,300,000	----	466,000	22,500	489,000
2004	----	----	----	----	----	----	1,460,000	19,300	1,480,000	----	418,000	26,700	445,000
2005[1]	----	----	----	----	----	----	1,260,000	34,000	1,290,000	----	394,000	30,000	424,000

[1] Preliminary.   [2] Unconsolidated metal in various forms.   [3] Included in Pigments.   NA = Not available.   W = Withheld proprietary data.
Source: U.S. Geological Survey (USGS)

Average Price of Titanium[1] in United States — In Dollars Per Pound

Year	Jan.	Feb.	Mar.	Apr.	May	June	July	Aug.	Sept.	Oct.	Nov.	Dec.	Average
2001	5.25	5.79	6.95	6.95	6.95	7.11	7.25	7.64	7.75	7.75	7.73	7.25	7.03
2002	7.25	6.78	6.13	6.13	6.13	6.13	5.58	5.38	5.38	5.38	5.28	4.90	5.87
2003	4.90	4.90	4.90	4.90	4.90	4.90	4.90	4.90	4.90	4.90	4.90	4.90	4.90
2004	4.90	4.90	5.60	5.75	7.61	7.75	7.89	8.50	8.64	9.25	9.25	9.92	7.50
2005	10.60	11.25	11.25	15.44	17.25	20.25	20.25	20.33	22.00	22.00	22.00	22.13	17.90
2006	24.75	24.75	25.53	26.10	27.50	27.58	27.75	27.75	27.75	27.75	27.75	27.75	26.89

[1] Ingot, 6A1 - 4V   *Source: American Metal Market (AMM)*

Tobacco

Tobacco is a member of the nightshade family. It is commercially grown for its leaves and stems, which are rolled into cigars, shredded for use in cigarettes and pipes, processed for chewing, or ground into snuff. Christopher Columbus introduced tobacco cultivation and use to Spain after observing natives from the Americas smoking loosely rolled tobacco-stuffed tobacco leaves.

Tobacco is cured, or dried, after harvesting and then aged to improve its flavor. The four common methods of curing are: air cured, fire cured, sun cured, and flue cured. Flue curing is the fastest method of curing and requires only about a week compared with up to 10 weeks for other methods. Cured tobacco is tied into small bundles of about 20 leaves and aged one to three years.

Virginia tobacco is by far the most popular type used in pipe tobacco since it is the mildest of all blending tobaccos. Approximately 60% of the US tobacco crop is Virginia-type tobacco. Burley tobacco is the next most popular tobacco. It is air-cured, burns slowly and provides a relatively cool smoke. Other tobacco varieties include Perique, Kentucky, Oriental, and Latakia.

Prices – US tobacco farm prices in 2006 rose +1.8% to 167.2 cents per pound from 164.2 cents per pound in 2005. That is, however, far below the record high of 196.7 cents per pound posted in 2003.

Supply – World production of tobacco in 2004 (latest data available) rose by +6.7% yr/yr to 6.651 million metric tons, rebounding upward from the 18-year low of 6.232 million metric tons seen in 2003. The world's largest producers of tobacco are China with 36% of world production, followed at a distance by Brazil (with 13% of world production), India (10%), and the US (6%). US production in 2004 rose by +5.4% yr/yr to 397,347 metric tons, where it was down by more than half from the 2-decade high of 810,154 metric tons posted in 1997.

Tobacco in the US is primarily grown in the Mid-Atlantic States, which account for the vast majority of US production. Specifically, the largest tobacco producing states in the US are North Carolina (with 46% of US production in 2004), Kentucky (26%), Tennessee (7%), South Carolina (7%), Virginia (6%), and Georgia (4%).

Flue-cured tobacco (type 11-14) is the most popular tobacco type grown in the US and US production in 2006 rose sharply by +17.2% yr/yr to 446.510 million pounds. The second most popular type is burley tobacco (type 31), which saw US production in 2006 rise +6.7% to 217.085 million pounds.

Total US production of tobacco in 2006 rose +12.7% yr/yr to 727 million pounds, which is less than half of the 2-decade high of 1.787 billion pounds posted in 1997. US farmers have sharply reduced the planting acreage for tobacco. In 2006, harvested tobacco acreage rose by +14.1% yr/yr to 338.950 acres which is up from the 2005 record low of 297,080 but still far below the 24-year high of 836,230 posted just 9 years ago in 1997. Yields have been fairly constant and have averaged about 2,100 pounds per acre for the past 10 years. The farm value of the US tobacco crop in 2006 rose by +14.7% yr/yr to $1.215 billion.

US marketings of flue-cured tobacco (Types 11-14) in the 2006-07 marketing year rose by +18.5% yr/yr to 453.8 million pounds. US marketings of burley tobacco (Type 31) in the 2006-07 marketing year rose by +6.9% yr/yr to 217.4 million pounds.

US production of cigarettes in 2006 rose by +1.5% to 496.4 billion cigarettes, which was down sharply from the record high of 754.5 million posted in 1996. US production of cigars rose by +8.2% yr/yr to 3.977 billion in 2006. US production of chewing tobacco in 2006 fell by −3.1% to 38.0 million pounds, which was a record low.

Demand – US per capita consumption of tobacco products in 2006 was unchanged at 3.69 pounds per person but there appears to be a shift from cigarettes to cigars. The 3.69 pounds per capita consumption of tobacco in 2006 is less than half the record high of 9.68 pounds per person that occurred at the beginning of the series in 1970. Per capita cigarette consumption in 2006 fell −1.5% yr/yr to 1,691 cigarettes per person, which was a record low. Per capita consumption of cigars in 2006 rose +1.9% yr/yr to a record high of 47.80 cigars per person. Per capita consumption of loose smoking tobacco in 2006 fell −6.3% yr/yr to 0.15 pounds.

Trade – US tobacco exports in 2004 (latest data available) rose +3.5% yr/yr to 354.0 million pounds, rebounding further from the record low of 325.8 million pounds seen in 2002. Meanwhile, US tobacco imports in 2004 fell −10.9% yr/yr to 561.7 million pounds from the 11-year high of 630.1 million pounds see in 2003. The US exported 11.3 billion cigarettes and 180 million cigars in 2006.

World Production of Leaf Tobacco   In Metric Tons

Year	Brazil	Canada	China	Greece	India	Indo-nesia	Italy	Japan	Pakistan	Turkey	United States	Zim-babwe	World Total
1995	398,000	79,287	2,404,700	131,875	587,100	171,400	124,492	78,212	80,917	204,900	575,380	209,042	6,452,451
1996	439,000	65,320	3,234,000	131,000	562,750	177,000	130,590	66,031	80,760	229,400	688,258	207,767	7,467,560
1997	576,600	71,110	3,234,000	132,450	623,700	17,500	140,634	68,504	86,279	310,850	810,154	192,144	7,882,078
1998	447,000	69,300	2,365,000	132,200	633,200	148,980	132,030	63,959	92,728	260,750	671,257	223,977	7,214,471
1999	595,000	64,864	2,469,300	129,700	648,600	156,882	130,762	64,727	103,430	250,484	586,355	198,967	7,263,347
2000	589,000	48,271	2,552,000	126,700	661,600	185,121	129,937	60,803	104,096	250,495	453,600	245,214	7,240,343
2001	542,400	53,112	2,349,627	126,000	585,600	172,200	131,761	60,565	82,854	207,261	449,510	207,253	6,769,761
2002	674,000	49,015	2,447,000	123,000	650,000	170,000	125,811	58,174	92,880	151,722	398,707	169,844	6,620,190
2003[1]	636,700	42,683	2,257,000	124,000	660,000	169,000	122,235	50,662	86,411	163,482	376,935	84,022	6,231,737
2004[2]	890,500	39,870	2,369,100	114,000	665,000	169,000	121,000	50,662	95,600	153,750	397,347	70,022	6,651,111

[1] Preliminary.   [2] Estimate.   *Source: Foreign Agricultural Service, U.S. Department of Agriculture (FAS-USDA)*

TOBACCO

Production and Consumption of Tobacco Products in the United States

Year	Cigarettes - Billions -	Cigars[3] - Millions -	Plug	Chewing Tobacco Twist	Loose-leaf	Total	Smoking Tobacco	Snuff[4]	Cigarettes Number	Cigars[3]	Consumption[5] of Per Capita[6] Cigarettes	Cigars[3]	Smoking Tobacco	Chewing Tobacco	Total Products
				In Millions of Pounds							In Pounds				
1997	722.8	2,324	3.5	1.0	53.7	58.1	11.4	64.3	2,422	37.3	4.10	.61	.11	.60	4.85
1998	679.7	2,751	3.1	1.0	49.2	53.3	11.7	65.5	2,275	37.1	3.60	.61	.12	.53	4.32
1999	611.5	2,938	2.8	0.9	47.2	50.9	14.7	67.0	2,101	38.5	3.50	.63	.13	.51	4.23
2000	594.1	2,825	2.5	0.8	46.0	49.4	13.6	69.5	2,049	38.0	3.40	.62	.13	.48	4.10
2001	562.8	3,741	2.4	0.8	43.9	47.0	12.8	70.9	2,051	41.2	3.50	.68	.15	.47	4.30
2002	532.0	3,819	2.0	0.7	40.2	43.0	15.5	72.7	1,982	41.8	3.40	.68	.16	.43	4.16
2003	499.4	4,017	1.7	0.7	37.9	40.3	17.8	73.8	1,890	44.5	3.20	.73	.16	.40	3.97
2004	493.5	4,407	1.7	0.7	37.0	39.3	16.1	79.3	1,814	47.9	3.10	.79	.15	.37	3.87
2005[1]	489.0	3,674	1.4	0.6	37.2	39.2	17.4	86.7	1,716	46.9	2.90	.77	.16	.36	3.69
2006[2]	496.4	3,977	1.3	0.5	36.1	38.0	16.5	81.8	1,691	47.8	2.90	.78	.15	.37	3.69

[1] Preliminary. [2] Estimate. [3] Large cigars and cigarillos. [4] Includes loose-leaf. [5] Consumption of tax-paid tobacco products. Unstemmed processing weight. [6] 18 years and older. NA = Not available. *Source: Economic Research Service, U.S. Department of Agriculture (ERS)*

Production of Tobacco in the United States, by States   In Thousands of Pounds

Year	Florida	Georgia	Indiana	Kentucky	Maryland	North Carolina	Ohio	Pennsylvania	South Carolina	Tennessee	Virginia	Wisconsin	Total
1997	19,053	89,225	18,690	497,928	12,000	731,199	22,230	17,020	126,360	114,292	117,576	5,690	1,787,399
1998	17,102	90,200	17,000	443,628	9,100	551,730	17,934	15,720	92,250	111,100	95,898	4,230	1,479,867
1999	15,312	64,020	11,700	408,492	9,100	448,980	17,052	11,170	78,000	122,601	88,855	2,818	1,292,692
2000	11,475	68,820	7,980	283,065	8,265	406,500	13,200	10,170	81,260	95,958	56,613	2,255	1,052,999
2001	11,700	64,206	9,450	254,653	3,300	386,920	11,956	6,166	78,400	86,893	63,415	3,619	991,223
2002	11,960	53,000	7,800	222,991	1,800	347,920	9,625	6,815	59,475	71,331	64,407	3,817	871,122
2003	11,000	59,400	8,190	225,042	1,595	299,995	8,745	7,880	63,000	65,632	38,818	4,255	802,560
2004	9,800	46,690	8,610	235,003	1,870	350,560	10,976	8,100	63,450	65,381	67,285	3,541	881,875
2005	5,500	27,760	----	174,260	----	278,900	6,732	10,700	39,900	51,670	40,351	----	645,015
2006[1]	2,860	30,090	----	186,700	----	330,410	7,000	16,240	48,300	49,135	46,645	----	726,724

[1] Preliminary. *Source: Agricultural Statistics Board, U.S. Department of Agriculture (ASB-USDA)*

Salient Statistics of Tobacco in the United States

Year	Acres Harvested 1,000 Acres	Yield Per Acre Pounds	Production Million Pounds	Farm Price Cents/Lb.	Farm Value Million $	Tobacco (July - June) Exports[2]	Imports[3]	U.S. Exports of Cigarettes Millions	Cigars & Cheroots	All Smoking Tobacco	Smoking Tobacco[4]	Stocks of Tobacco[5] Various Types All Tobacco	Fire Cured[6]	Cigar Filler[7]	Maryland
						- Million Pounds -		Millions		In Millions of Pounds					
1997	836.2	2,137	1,787	180.2	3,217	450.1	565.8	217,000	86	487	118.2	2,031	83.3	13.2	15.0
1998	717.7	2,061	1,480	182.8	2,701	461.9	529.6	201,300	93	467	142.5	2,250	84.8	13.0	18.7
1999	647.2	1,997	1,293	182.8	2,356	394.7	480.2	151,400	84	423	151.1	2,301	86.7	11.4	20.6
2000	472.4	2,229	1,053	191.0	2,002	351.4	457.8	148,300	113	397	136.1	2,388	87.8	9.5	16.0
2001	432.3	2,293	991	195.7	1,940	386.7	568.0	133,900	124	411	118.2	1,893	93.8	12.1	13.4
2002	427.3	2,039	871	193.6	1,687	325.8	549.7	127,400	123	338	144.0	1,738	99.5	12.3	9.7
2003	411.2	1,952	803	196.7	1,576	342.1	630.1	121,500	155	343	121.2	1,584	100.5	10.7	8.2
2004	408.1	2,161	882	198.4	1,750	354.0	561.7	118,700	171	361	45.4	1,529	101.5	9.7	7.2
2005	297.1	2,171	645	164.2	1,059			113,300	301			1,455		9.9	5.0
2006[1]	339.0	2,144	727	167.2	1,215			111,317	180			1,167		10.8	0.8

[1] Preliminary. [2] Domestic. [3] For consumption. [4] In bulk. [5] Flue-cured and cigar wrapper, year beginning July 1; for all other types, October 1. [6] Kentucky-Tennessee types 22-23. [7] Types 41-46. *Source: Economic Research Service, U.S. Department of Agriculture (ERS-USDA)*

Tobacco Production in the United States, by Types   In Thousands of Pounds (Farm-Sale Weight)

Year	11-14	21	22	23	31	32	35-36	37	41	41-61	51	54	55	61
1997	1,047,438	1,968	27,952	12,342	648,633	18,240	8,196	119	10,780	22,511	3,637	4,194	1,496	2,404
1998	812,797	2,340	25,922	11,573	582,336	15,370	9,663	122	9,450	19,744	3,633	3,270	960	2,431
1999	656,752	2,672	24,773	10,630	555,185	14,350	11,640	155	5,920	16,535	4,169	2,252	566	3,628
2000	598,915	2,548	34,167	14,920	362,788	13,395	15,896	165	5,040	10,205	1,070	1,825	430	1,840
2001	579,091	2,202	30,720	12,377	334,066	5,346	13,949	154	4,120	13,318	3,822	3,042	577	1,757
2002	514,385	1,471	23,292	10,145	293,537	4,205	10,570	116	4,410	13,401	4,021	3,151	666	1,153
2003	456,690	839	23,504	10,165	281,698	4,195	11,230	84	5,280	14,155	3,386	3,472	783	1,234
2004	521,535	1,345	24,800	11,006	292,172	5,830	11,798	124	4,140	13,265	3,767	2,744	797	1,915
2005	380,850	----	----	----	203,383	3,000	----	----	2,860	8,621	4,117	----	----	----
2006[1]	446,510	----	----	----	217,085	2,090	----	----	2,600	8,569	4,519	----	----	----

[1] Preliminary. *Source: Agricultural Statistics Board, U.S. Department of Agriculture (ASB-USDA)*

U.S. Exports of Unmanufactured Tobacco   In Millions of Pounds (Declared Weight)

Year	Australia	Belgium-Luxem.	Denmark	France	Germany	Italy	Japan	Nether-lands	Sweden	Switzer-land	Thailand	United Kingdom	Total
1997	4.2	38.9	15.5	7.0	72.2	18.3	80.5	30.2	5.2	11.4	21.6	18.2	487.4
1998	5.0	25.2	14.8	6.6	84.6	13.6	85.3	43.9	2.6	10.3	14.2	15.6	466.3
1999	3.2	18.3	14.9	5.6	71.9	15.1	60.3	64.5	3.9	16.1	6.8	9.0	417.5
2000	3.6	23.2	15.7	5.5	86.1	15.8	63.6	19.7	3.5	9.5	7.3	7.3	402.4
2001	3.4	49.7	12.2	11.5	94.8	6.2	51.6	21.6	3.6	14.4	7.7	1.6	409.7
2002	4.5	29.4	13.6	10.3	59.5	8.6	49.6	10.3	1.2	27.3	12.6	6.0	338.0
2003	6.3	61.7	13.5	8.8	55.8	7.6	42.4	9.8	1.6	34.8	3.6	4.8	343.3
2004	3.6	27.4	10.2	15.8	53.5	6.6	34.6	15.8	.6	9.4	8.5	4.0	361.0
2005	2.9	12.7	8.4	10.6	55.3	5.8	34.6	25.4	.7	15.6	4.1	3.2	339.0
2006[1]	3.3	7.9	6.3	4.3	43.4	1.5	2.6	24.1		27.4	3.0	.6	260.3

[1] Preliminary.   Source: Economic Research Service, U.S. Department of Agriculture (ERS-USDA)

U.S. Salient Statistics for Flue-Cured Tobacco (Types 11-14) in the United States   In Millions of Pounds

Crop Year	Acres Harvested 1,000	Yield Per Acre Pounds	Mar-ketings	Stocks July 1	Total Supply	Exports	Domestic Disap-pearance	Total Disap-pearance	Farm Price Cents/Lb.	Placed Under Gov't Loan Million Lb.	Price Support Level Cents/Lb.	Loan Stocks Nov. 30	Loan Stocks Uncom-mitted
1997-98	458.3	2,285	1,014	1,117	2,130	336	541	877	172.0	195.5	162.1	145.3	.0
1998-99	368.8	2,204	815	1,253	2,068	341	492	834	175.5	82.4	162.8	311.5	182.7
1999-00	303.8	2,162	654	2,162	2,816	262	437	699	173.7	136.4	163.2	318.3	144.9
2000-01	250.0	2,396	564	1,189	1,754	238	479	717	179.3	27.4	164.0	256.9	135.9
2001-02	238.1	2,432	544	1,036	1,581	276	389	665	185.7	15.0	166.0	93.2	65.0
2002-03	245.6	2,094	565	916	1,481	220	423	643	182.5	24.8	165.6	17.8	12.8
2003-04	233.4	1,957	508	838	1,345	216	307	522	185.1	59.8	166.3	70.6	68.7
2004-05	228.4	2,283	499	823	1,322	189	338	526	184.5	94.9	169.0	108.2	128.5
2005-06[1]	174.5	2,182	383	796	1,179	258	317	575	147.4	NA	NA	79.0	NA
2006-07[2]	213.1	2,095	454	604	1,058	270	248	518	NA	NA	NA	NA	NA

[1] Preliminary.   [2] Estimate.   NA = Not available.   Source: Economic Research Service, U.S. Department of Agriculture (ERS-USDA)

Salient Statistics for Burley Tobacco (Type 31) in the United States   In Millions of Pounds

Crop Year	Acres Harvested 1,000	Yield Per Acre Pounds	Mar-ketings	Stocks Oct. 1	Total Supply	Exports	Domestic Disap-pearance	Total Disap-pearance	Farm Price Cents/Lb.	Gross Sales[3]	Price Support Level Cents/Lb.	Loan Stocks Nov. 30	Loan Stocks Uncom-mitted
1997-98	335.3	1,934	628	751	1,379	168	379	548	188.5	337.9	176.0	105.6	38.5
1998-99	307.1	1,896	590	832	1,422	169	349	520	190.3	431.6	177.8	183.8	142.2
1999-00	303.6	1,829	551	901	1,453	139	273	413	182.9	356.6	178.9	226.6	186.7
2000-01	193.8	1,957	315	1,040	1,355	142	524	666	196.3	169.7	180.5	420.7	336.5
2001-02	167.6	2,033	344	689	1,033	140	245	385	197.3	258.5	182.6	119.3	74.8
2002-03	157.7	1,861	300	648	948	149	221	370	197.4	217.7	183.5	124.2	46.1
2003-04	152.3	1,850	272	578	1,850	174	136	310	197.7	197.3	184.9	91.7	26.5
2004-05	153.2	1,908	280	540	820	228	100	328	199.4	202.3	187.3	115.1	8.5
2005-06[1]	100.2	2,031	203	493	696	208	84	293	156.4	NA	NA	78.7	NA
2006-07[2]	103.6	2,095	217	403	621	190	56	246	NA	NA	NA	NA	NA

[1] Preliminary.   [2] Estimate.   [3] Before Christmas holidays.   NA = Not available.   Source: Economic Research Service, U.S. Department of Agriculture

Exports of Tobacco from the United States (Quantity and Value)   In Metric Tons

Year	Unmanufactured Flue-Cured	Unmanufactured Value 1,000 USD	Unmanufactured Burley	Unmanufactured Value 1,000 USD	Unmanufactured Total	Unmanufactured Value 1,000 USD	Manu-factured	Value 1,000 USD
1996	112,797	786,473	52,202	380,012	222,316	1,390,311	83,383	5,238,340
1997	116,457	832,381	56,803	454,849	221,510	1,553,314	85,734	4,956,392
1998	110,435	776,640	50,167	409,773	211,930	1,458,877	NA	4,517,500
1999	86,838	611,054	49,398	404,564	191,975	1,311,643	NA	3,232,862
2000	84,980	606,145	36,649	306,883	179,892	1,204,085	NA	4,012,711
2001	89,930	660,924	42,464	361,567	186,302	1,268,839	NA	2,734,377
2002	73,125	532,713	40,170	334,621	153,427	1,049,709	NA	1,950,188
2003	70,669	519,732	41,876	346,504	155,722	1,038,073	NA	1,843,922
2004[1]	67,183	490,547	58,764	373,001	163,693	1,044,440	NA	1,566,223
2005[2]	62,477	418,225	61,096	408,626	152,197	983,213	NA	1,298,291

[1] Preliminary.   [2] Forecast.   NA = Not available.   Source: Foreign Agricultural Service, U.S. Department of Agriculture (FAS USDA)

Tung Oil

Tung oil is a yellow drying oil produced from the seed of the tung tree. The seeds or nuts of the tung tree are harvested and pressed to yield tung oil. Tung oil is used mostly as an industrial lubricant and drying agent, and is the most powerful drying agent known. It is also used in paints and varnishes, soaps, inks, and electrical insulators. Tung oil is poisonous, containing glycerol esters of unsaturated fats. The oil is also used as a substitute for linseed oil in paints, varnishes, and linoleum, and as a waterproofing agent.

Prices – The price of tung oil in 2005 rose by +15.1% yr/yr to 98.33 cents per pound, recovering further from the 16-year low of 43.77 cents per pound seen in 2002.

Demand – US consumption of tung oil has fallen sharply over the past decade. In 2006 US consumption fell by –7.1% yr/yr to 1.766 million pounds. The 2006 consumption level was only 8% of 1996's 16-year high of 21.645 million pounds.

Trade – World imports of tung oil in 2005 fell –10.0% yr/yr to 22,511 metric tons. US imports of tung oil in 2005 fell sharply by –37.3% to 1,866 metric tons. The world's largest importers of tung oil are South Korea with 17% of world imports, Taiwan with 13%, the Netherlands with 11%, Japan with 9%, and the US with 8%. The world's largest exporter of tung oil by far is China with 16,563 metric tons of exports in 2005, accounting for 71% of total world exports.

World Tung Oil Trade — In Metric Tons

Year	Germany	Hong Kong	Japan	Nether- lands	South Korea	Taiwan	United States	World Total	Argen- tina	China	Hong Kong	Para- guay	World Total
				Imports							Exports		
1999	1,002	470	2,455	2,488	3,560	6,699	5,822	31,528	1,425	24,172	560	2,303	30,890
2000	885	416	2,225	2,156	4,900	4,346	3,554	28,273	1,870	24,213	494	2,799	30,649
2001	582	36	1,647	1,904	3,390	2,113	4,429	23,594	1,061	17,615	108	1,974	21,991
2002	325	702	1,930	1,793	6,968	5,185	4,166	29,760	916	23,334	589	4,390	30,351
2003	303	306	2,023	1,687	6,396	3,974	4,287	27,489	2,299	19,509	323	2,479	25,951
2004[1]	100	207	1,900	1,778	5,486	3,529	2,975	25,006	1,299	18,850	240	3,626	25,501
2005[2]	43	190	2,067	2,376	3,769	2,938	1,866	22,511	1,035	16,563	186	4,306	23,465

[1] Preliminary. [2] Estimate. Source: The Oil World

Consumption of Tung Oil in Inedible Products in the United States — In Thousands of Pounds

Year	Jan.	Feb.	Mar.	Apr.	May	June	July	Aug.	Sept.	Oct.	Nov.	Dec.	Total
2000	1,065	1,083	1,064	1,193	1,159	1,176	1,107	1,224	733	711	700	648	11,863
2001	1,044	842	533	366	281	431	253	430	399	411	243	235	5,468
2002	427	476	583	410	471	454	428	877	695	978	862	886	7,547
2003	685	276	508	317	322	233	270	349	406	269	376	228	4,239
2004	428	400	350	402	264	324	338	310	186	186	101	109	3,398
2005	128	110	144	151	371	127	161	189	92	171	146	110	1,900
2006[1]	174	175	138	103	128	193	198	114	198	134	136	75	1,766

[1] Preliminary. Source: Bureau of the Census, U.S. Department of Commerce

Stocks of Tung Oil at Factories & Warehouses in the U.S., on First of Month — In Thousands of Pounds

Year	Jan.	Feb.	Mar.	Apr.	May	June	July	Aug.	Sept.	Oct.	Nov.	Dec.
2000	691	910	611	2,555	2,254	1,982	1,658	1,381	1,262	1,217	1,011	827
2001	685	2,438	2,181	2,131	1,881	1,727	1,578	1,168	1,046	714	W	W
2002	W	W	W	W	1,341	1,206	885	516	483	551	560	478
2003	490	W	858	763	722	790	398	W	W	W	W	W
2004	W	W	W	519	229	209	226	137	91	161	121	117
2005	90	128	107	182	130	141	134	122	114	93	116	70
2006[1]	109	99	98	124	81	116	128	85	128	125	76	98

[1] Preliminary. W = Withheld proprietary data. Source: Bureau of the Census, U.S. Department of Commerce

Average Price of Tung Oil (Imported, Drums) F.O.B. in New York — In Cents Per Pound

Year	Jan.	Feb.	Mar.	Apr.	May	June	July	Aug.	Sept.	Oct.	Nov.	Dec.	Average
1999	100.00	100.00	100.00	100.00	100.00	74.00	74.00	74.00	74.00	74.00	74.00	74.00	84.83
2000	59.00	59.00	59.00	59.00	59.00	59.00	59.00	59.00	59.00	59.00	59.00	59.00	59.00
2001	60.50	62.00	62.00	62.00	62.00	62.00	62.00	62.00	62.00	62.00	60.50	60.50	61.63
2002	60.50	44.50	44.50	42.00	40.00	40.00	40.00	40.00	40.00	43.75	45.00	45.00	43.77
2003	45.00	45.00	52.80	84.75	85.00	85.00	85.00	85.00	85.00	85.00	85.00	85.00	75.63
2004	85.00	85.00	85.00	85.00	85.00	85.00	85.00	85.00	85.00	85.00	85.00	90.00	85.42
2005[1]	92.50	95.00	97.50	97.50	97.50	97.50	97.50	102.50	105.00	105.00	97.50	95.00	98.33

[1] Preliminary. Source: Economic Research Service, U.S. Department of Agriculture (ERS-USDA)

Tungsten

Tungsten (symbol W) is a grayish-white, lustrous, metallic element. The atomic symbol for tungsten is W because of its former name of Wolfram. Tungsten has the highest melting point of any metal at about 3410 degrees Celsius and boils at about 5660 degrees Celsius. In 1781, the Swedish chemist Carl Wilhelm Scheele discovered tungsten.

Tungsten is never found in nature but is instead found in the minerals wolframite, scheelite, huebnertite, and ferberite. Tungsten has excellent corrosion resistance qualities and is resistant to most mineral acids. Tungsten is used as filaments in incandescent lamps, electron and television tubes, alloys of steel, spark plugs, electrical contact points, cutting tools, and in the chemical and tanning industries.

Prices – The average monthly price of tungsten at US ports in 2006 rose sharply by +24.2% yr/yr to a record high of $265.68 per short ton.

Supply – World concentrate production of tungsten in 2005 rose by +1.0% yr/yr to 70,100 metric tons. That was another new record high.

The world's largest producer of tungsten by far is China with 67,000 metric tons of production in 2005, which was 87% of total world production. Russia is the next largest producer with 6.3% with only a miniscule amount of 4,400 metric tons.

Trade – The US in 2005 relied on imports for 70% of its tungsten consumption. US imports for consumption in 2004 fell by –10.0% yr/yr to 2,080 metric tons, which was a 12-year low. US exports in 2005 were negligible at 52 metric tons.

World Concentrate Production of Tungsten In Metric Tons (Contained Tungsten[3])

Year	Austria	Bolivia	Brazil	Burma	Canada	China	Mongolia	North Korea	Portugal	Russia	Rwanda	Thailand	World Total
1998	1,423	497	----	178	----	30,000	35	500	831	3,000	109	35	37,000
1999	1,610	334	13	87	----	31,100	27	500	434	3,500	41	30	37,700
2000	1,600	382	18	74	----	37,000	52	500	743	3,500	108	30	44,000
2001	1,237	533	22	48	----	38,500	63	500	698	3,500	142	53	45,300
2002	1,377	399	24	83	2,295	55,100	35	600	693	5,300	153	31	66,100
2003	1,381	441	30	93	3,636	55,500	40	600	715	5,450	78	208	68,200
2004[1]	1,335	401	262	106	----	60,000	77	600	746	5,500	120	180	69,400
2005[2]	1,350	522	250	100	700	61,000	78	600	815	4,400	120	150	70,100

[1] Preliminary. [2] Estimate. [3] Conversion Factors: WO3 to W, multiply by 0.7931; 60% WO3 to W, multiply by 0.4758.
Source: U.S. Geological Survey (USGS)

Salient Statistics of Tungsten in the United States In Metric Tons (Contained Tungsten)

Year	Net Import Reliance as a % of Apparent Consumption	Total Consumption	Tool	Steel Stainless & Heat Assisting	Alloy Steel[3]	Super-alloys	Cutting & Wear Resistant Materials	Products Made from Metal Powder	Miscellaneous	Chemical and Ceramic	Exports	Imports for Consumption	Stocks at End of Year — Concentrates — Consumers	Producers
1998	78	3,210	[4]	532	219	333	6,640	1,270	532	97	10	4,750	603	W
1999	81	2,100	W	486	189	306	5,910	1,860	----	93	26	2,870	376	W
2000	68	W	W	408	W	498	5,960	W	----	89	70	2,370	W	W
2001	59	W	W	389	W	599	5,650	W	----	80	220	2,680	W	W
2002	70	W	W	313	W	426	4,820	W	----	133	94	4,090	W	W
2003	69	W	W	312	W	W	5,210	W	----	129	20	4,690	W	W
2004[1]	73	W	W	259	W	W	6,020	W	----	130	43	2,310	W	W
2005[2]	70	W	W	280	W	W	6,020	W	----	130	52	2,080	W	W

[1] Preliminary. [2] Estimate. [3] Other than tool. [4] Included with stainless & heat assisting. W = Withheld proprietary data; included with Miscellaneous. *Source: U.S. Geological Survey*

Average Price of Tungsten at U.S. Ports (Including Duty) In Dollars Per Short Ton

Year	Jan.	Feb.	Mar.	Apr.	May	June	July	Aug.	Sept.	Oct.	Nov.	Dec.	Average
1999	49.50	49.50	49.50	49.50	48.57	48.75	49.16	50.88	51.50	54.44	54.75	54.75	52.00
2000	53.75	53.75	53.75	53.29	50.50	50.50	51.88	53.50	69.00	74.00	76.00	78.92	64.67
2001	83.50	86.00	90.00	93.00	96.15	96.50	93.88	92.88	91.00	89.89	83.84	79.57	87.72
2002	----	70.00	70.00	70.00	70.00	68.13	57.88	59.88	60.25	60.25	60.25	60.25	64.26
2003	60.25	61.55	63.00	63.00	63.00	63.00	63.00	63.00	63.00	63.00	63.00	63.00	62.65
2004	63.00	63.00	66.83	89.77	92.50	92.50	88.95	86.09	87.00	89.86	92.00	93.83	83.78
2005	97.08	109.32	134.13	178.21	272.26	277.61	275.25	237.28	232.50	244.05	255.00	255.00	213.97
2006	255.00	265.66	282.50	275.00	266.36	265.00	265.00	265.00	266.13	267.50	262.00	253.00	265.68

U.S. Spot Quotations, 65% WO3, Basis C.I.F. *Source: U.S. Geological Survey (USGS)*

Turkeys

During the past three decades, the turkey industry has experienced tremendous growth in the US. Turkey production has more than tripled since 1970, with a current value of over $7 billion. Turkey was not a popular dish in Europe until a roast turkey was eaten on June 27, 1570, at the wedding feast of Charles XI of France and Elizabeth of Austria. The King was so impressed with the birds that the turkey subsequently became a popular dish at banquets held by French nobility.

The most popular turkey product continues to be the whole bird, with heavy demand at Thanksgiving and Christmas. The primary breeders maintain and develop the quality stock, concentrating on growth and conformation in males and fecundity in females, as well as characteristics important to general health and welfare. Turkey producers include large companies that produce turkeys all year round, and relatively small companies and farmers who produce turkeys primarily for the seasonal Thanksgiving market.

Prices – The average monthly price received by farmers for turkeys in the US in 2006 rose by +6.9% yr/yr to a record high of 48.1 cents per pound. The monthly average retail price of turkeys (whole frozen) in the US in 2006 rose +1.8% yr/yr to a record high of 110.8 cents per pound. Turkey prices have nearly tripled from the low 40-cent area seen in

the early 1970s.

Supply – World production of turkeys in 2007 is forecasted to rise by +1.1% yr/yr to 4.882 million metric tons, mildly below the record high of 5.018 posted in 2002. World production of turkeys has grown by more than two and one-half times since 1980 when production was a mere 2.090 million metric tons. The US is the largest producer of turkeys in the world by far with 2.565 million metric tons of production in 2006 which is 53% of world production. The value of US turkey production in the US in 2005 was $3.233 billion.

Demand – World consumption of turkeys in 2007 is forecasted to rise by +0.1% to 4.716 million metric tons, which will be mildly below the record high of 4.788 million metric tons posted in 2002. Forecasted US turkey consumption of 2.281 million metric tons in 2007 will account for 48% of world consumption.

US per capita consumption of turkeys in 2007 is forecasted to fall by –0.6% yr/yr to 16.8 pounds per person per year. US per capital consumption of turkeys has been in the range of 17-18 pounds since 1990, but has now dropped slightly below that level. The USDA is projecting that per capita consumption will continue to drop.

Production and Consumption of Turkey Meat, by Selected Countries — In Thousands of Metric Tons (RTC)

	Production							Consumption						
Year	Brazil	Canada	European Union	Mexico	Russia	United States	World Total	Brazil	Canada	European Union	Mexico	Russia	United States	World Total
1998	107	139	1,700	11	9	2,366	4,571	87	139	1,526	127	156	2,214	4,519
1999	115	139	2,100	12	8	2,372	4,839	89	136	1,890	136	169	2,224	4,807
2000	137	152	2,019	12	7	2,419	4,844	93	137	1,818	146	170	2,223	4,753
2001	165	149	2,098	13	7	2,490	4,934	96	135	1,931	157	171	2,269	4,827
2002	182	147	2,102	13	9	2,557	5,018	92	142	1,910	153	174	2,316	4,835
2003	200	148	2,025	14	12	2,529	4,936	88	136	1,912	171	126	2,301	4,786
2004	240	145	2,038	13	15	2,441	4,901	104	141	1,931	156	92	2,272	4,750
2005	275	155	1,917	14	17	2,464	4,851	114	143	1,832	199	124	2,247	4,711
2006[1]	290	160	1,810	14	19	2,529	4,831	137	144	1,770	204	115	2,282	4,710
2007[2]	320	164	1,790	15	21	2,565	4,882	160	147	1,755	215	122	2,281	4,716

[1] Preliminary. [2] Forecast. *Source: Foreign Agricultural Service, U.S. Department of Agriculture (FAS-USDA)*

Salient Statistics of Turkeys in the United States

			Liveweight		Value of Production		Ready-to-Cook Basis							Wholesale Ready-to-Cook
	Poults Placed[3]	Number Raised[4]	Produced	Price	of Production	Production	Beginning Stocks	Exports	Consumption Total	Per Capita	Costs Feed	Costs Total	Production Costs	3-Region Pro-Weighted Average Price[5]
Year	---- In Thousands ----		Mil. Lbs.	Cents/Lb.	Million $	----------- In Millions of Pounds -----------				Lbs.	-- Liveweight Basis --			
1996	325,375	302,713	7,222.8	43.3	3,124.5	5,401	271	438	4,907	18.2	31.60	45.30	72.90	66.80
1997	305,612	301,251	7,225.1	39.9	2,884.4	5,412	328	606	4,720	17.3	28.20	41.90	68.70	63.80
1998	297,798	285,204	7,050.9	38.0	2,683.5	5,215	415	446	4,880	17.7	22.96	36.66	62.12	62.15
1999	297,387	270,494	6,886.4	40.8	2,806.6	5,231	304	378	4,905	17.6	19.00	32.70	57.17	67.81
2000	298,094	269,969	6,942.8	40.7	2,828.5	5,334	254	445	4,903	17.4	19.98	33.68	58.40	68.06
2001	301,721	272,059	7,154.8	39.0	2,796.8	5,489	241	487	5,004	17.5	20.55	34.25	59.11	63.63
2002	296,877	275,477	7,494.9	36.5	2,732.5	5,638	241	439	5,108	17.7	20.85	34.55	59.48	61.09
2003	289,542	274,048	7,487.3	36.1	2,699.7	5,576	333	484	5,074	17.4	22.59	36.29	61.66	60.41
2004[1]	277,717	263,207	7,278.4	42.0	3,054.3	5,372	354	443	5,003	17.1				
2005[2]	293,683	256,270	7,206.6	44.9	3,232.6	5,502	288	510	5,034	16.7				

[1] Preliminary. [2] Estimate. [3] Poults placed for slaughter by hatcheries. [4] Turkeys place August 1-July 31. [5] Regions include central, eastern and western. Central region receives twice the weight of the other regions in calculating the average. *Source: Economic Research Service, U.S. Department of Agriculture (ERS-USDA)*

Turkey-Feed Price Ratio in the United States   In Pounds[2]

Year	Jan.	Feb.	Mar.	Apr.	May	June	July	Aug.	Sept.	Oct.	Nov.	Dec.	Average
1997	5.4	5.1	5.0	5.1	5.3	5.6	6.0	5.9	6.1	6.2	6.2	5.8	5.7
1998	5.4	5.2	5.4	5.7	5.8	6.1	6.5	7.6	8.1	8.3	8.2	7.5	6.7
1999	6.5	7.1	7.5	7.8	8.2	8.7	9.7	9.5	9.6	10.0	9.9	9.2	8.6
2000	7.6	7.2	7.6	7.9	7.8	8.5	9.5	10.0	10.1	10.0	9.8	8.1	8.7
2001	7.3	7.5	7.7	8.0	8.1	8.3	7.9	7.8	8.3	9.6	9.6	8.1	8.2
2002	7.2	7.2	6.8	6.8	7.3	7.3	6.9	6.3	6.0	6.1	6.5	6.4	6.7
2003	5.7	5.7	5.9	5.9	5.7	5.8	5.9	5.7	6.0	6.3	6.3	5.7	5.9
2004	5.1	4.6	4.5	4.5	4.8	5.2	5.8	7.0	7.9	8.4	8.7	8.2	6.2
2005	6.9	6.9	6.6	6.7	6.9	7.0	7.3	8.0	9.0	9.5	10.0	9.5	7.9
2006[1]	7.0	6.9	6.9	7.4	7.2	7.7	7.8	8.6	9.5	9.8	9.5	6.0	7.9

[1] Preliminary.   [2] Pounds of feed equal in value to one pound of turkey, liveweight.   Source: Economic Research Service, U.S. Department of Agriculture (ERS-USDA)

Average Price Received by Farmers for Turkeys in the United States (Liveweight)   In Cents Per Pound

Year	Jan.	Feb.	Mar.	Apr.	May	June	July	Aug.	Sept.	Oct.	Nov.	Dec.	Average
1997	38.6	36.4	37.8	39.7	41.3	41.6	41.1	41.0	41.1	41.0	41.9	38.7	40.0
1998	35.5	34.0	34.6	35.7	35.5	35.9	37.5	38.6	40.2	42.7	43.8	40.3	37.9
1999	34.8	35.7	37.0	38.7	39.4	41.3	42.0	43.0	44.3	45.3	45.3	42.2	40.8
2000	36.4	35.7	38.2	40.0	40.8	41.8	42.2	43.2	44.8	46.1	47.1	40.5	41.4
2001	36.6	36.3	37.1	37.6	38.2	38.3	38.5	38.7	40.5	44.2	44.5	38.7	39.1
2002	34.1	34.1	32.9	32.9	35.8	37.2	38.6	38.2	37.2	37.2	39.8	38.7	36.4
2003	34.6	34.5	35.1	35.6	34.9	34.9	33.6	32.7	36.2	39.1	41.2	38.2	35.9
2004	34.9	35.0	36.6	38.4	40.1	41.7	43.3	45.1	46.2	48.1	48.7	45.9	42.0
2005	39.3	38.0	38.1	38.8	40.7	42.1	44.6	46.5	50.3	52.5	54.5	53.9	44.9
2006[1]	40.8	39.6	40.3	42.9	43.7	45.8	46.4	49.1	54.1	63.4	67.1	43.4	48.1

[1] Preliminary.   Source: Economic Research Service, U.S. Department of Agriculture (ERS-USDA)

Average Wholesale Price of Turkeys[1] (Hens, 8-16 Lbs.) in New York   In Cents Per Pound

Year	Jan.	Feb.	Mar.	Apr.	May	June	July	Aug.	Sept.	Oct.	Nov.	Dec.	Average
1997	59.71	57.84	59.30	62.93	66.64	68.60	68.59	68.20	67.89	67.33	70.07	62.18	64.94
1998	55.65	54.04	55.49	55.49	58.68	58.14	58.68	63.17	65.65	71.52	72.95	69.00	61.54
1999	57.67	58.84	61.69	63.02	65.55	68.89	71.62	73.57	76.28	79.30	78.99	72.39	68.98
2000	61.58	61.84	65.35	67.38	69.18	70.36	71.55	73.61	76.53	78.74	79.58	70.31	70.50
2001	61.50	61.18	62.38	63.45	65.65	66.00	66.10	66.38	68.81	72.86	73.48	67.71	66.29
2002	60.86	60.03	59.00	59.52	63.52	65.68	66.52	66.56	67.15	67.75	69.79	66.96	64.45
2003	61.04	61.13	61.24	61.43	60.36	60.12	58.18	57.74	61.52	66.08	69.33	66.85	62.09
2004	62.13	61.61	62.62	64.52	66.41	68.95	71.21	73.32	74.69	76.89	78.29	76.05	69.72
2005	67.63	65.34	64.68	65.86	67.69	69.50	72.56	75.98	80.90	82.40	85.75	82.60	73.41
2006[2]	68.29	65.84	67.67	69.75	71.27	72.95	74.95	78.70	84.40	95.83	99.51	74.20	76.95

[1] Ready-to-cook.   [2] Preliminary.   Source: Economic Research Service, U.S. Department of Agriculture (ERS-USDA)

Certified Federally Inspected Turkey Slaughter in the U.S. (RTC Weights)   In Millions of Pounds

Year	Jan.	Feb.	Mar.	Apr.	May	June	July	Aug.	Sept.	Oct.	Nov.	Dec.	Total
1997	439.7	389.5	399.6	448.8	465.8	481.4	488.8	453.0	457.6	510.0	450.6	457.9	5,443
1998	430.5	407.7	437.8	444.0	419.1	454.2	456.0	409.9	425.3	470.5	459.5	428.2	5,243
1999	408.9	361.0	428.8	435.8	438.6	452.4	434.7	464.3	451.3	468.7	487.6	425.4	5,257
2000	396.9	412.4	466.2	413.5	489.2	479.4	422.8	481.6	423.0	494.7	478.2	396.5	5,354
2001	458.3	405.9	458.7	425.1	485.1	460.7	465.1	481.7	409.2	536.2	477.7	413.2	5,477
2002	477.2	442.1	447.8	487.2	496.7	448.0	474.7	475.9	439.4	519.0	488.2	457.9	5,654
2003	473.6	427.1	464.6	471.1	475.8	478.0	483.9	449.3	453.6	522.8	450.3	436.1	5,586
2004	435.5	389.0	466.6	445.2	445.1	462.8	455.4	462.2	451.2	461.5	479.6	434.4	5,389
2005	439.0	396.3	459.4	439.7	456.3	485.8	427.5	483.7	450.6	479.1	478.2	434.4	5,430
2006[1]	443.0	412.4	487.9	430.3	492.8	504.4	453.5	493.6	456.5	535.8	499.7	423.5	5,633

[1] Preliminary.   Source: Economic Research Service, U.S. Department of Agriculture (ERS-USDA)

TURKEYS

Per Capita Consumption of Turkeys in the United States   In Pounds

Year	First Quarter	Second Quarter	Third Quarter	Fourth Quarter	Total	Year	First Quarter	Second Quarter	Third Quarter	Fourth Quarter	Total
1996	3.7	3.9	4.6	6.2	18.5	2002	3.5	3.9	4.4	5.9	17.7
1997	3.5	4.0	4.2	6.0	17.6	2003	3.6	3.9	4.6	5.3	17.4
1998	3.9	3.9	4.2	6.0	18.1	2004	3.6	4.0	4.5	5.0	17.1
1999	3.8	3.8	4.4	5.8	18.0	2005	3.6	3.9	4.2	5.1	16.7
2000	3.7	4.2	4.4	5.5	17.8	2006[1]	3.5	3.9	4.3	5.2	16.9
2001	3.9	3.8	4.3	5.6	17.5	2007[2]	3.6	3.9	4.3	5.0	16.8

[1] Preliminary.   [2] Estimate.   Source: Economic Research Service, U.S. Department of Agriculture (ERS-USDA)

Storage Stocks of Turkeys (Frozen) in the United States on First of Month   In Millions of Pounds

Year	Jan.	Feb.	Mar.	Apr.	May	June	July	Aug.	Sept.	Oct.	Nov.	Dec.
1997	328.0	401.0	446.4	496.5	543.3	611.8	667.9	714.3	742.0	770.7	736.6	438.6
1998	415.1	497.6	512.7	527.0	579.7	614.1	656.5	701.8	706.8	699.5	658.7	310.4
1999	304.3	363.8	375.6	374.9	455.4	494.3	556.1	599.0	580.3	596.4	494.5	252.3
2000	254.3	319.4	353.9	391.4	416.9	480.3	506.8	524.0	524.9	528.1	473.9	261.1
2001	241.3	291.4	333.5	355.8	392.6	456.0	506.7	534.2	545.3	542.0	497.9	260.0
2002	240.5	327.1	413.2	457.6	515.2	578.2	644.1	706.2	685.6	672.4	624.9	334.3
2003	333.0	451.9	492.7	549.3	573.5	658.8	718.2	722.5	706.5	647.5	582.7	350.7
2004	354.0	420.5	471.7	504.6	548.8	571.1	597.6	599.6	600.2	527.4	472.3	294.9
2005	288.4	332.9	379.4	414.2	440.1	465.9	506.3	518.9	523.1	477.8	417.6	194.7
2006[1]	206.2	260.5	317.9	380.4	423.7	466.6	507.5	512.2	500.3	463.9	404.2	214.5

[1] Preliminary.   Source: Economic Research Service, U.S. Department of Agriculture (ERS-USDA)

Average Retail Price of Turkeys (Whole frozen) in the United States   In Cents Per Pound

Year	Jan.	Feb.	Mar.	Apr.	May	June	July	Aug.	Sept.	Oct.	Nov.	Dec.	Average
1997	106.3	106.7	104.7	103.2	104.5	107.8	107.4	109.2	108.9	106.2	97.6	98.2	105.1
1998	103.4	100.1	99.6	97.2	95.7	99.1	100.8	102.4	105.2	102.5	93.4	95.4	99.6
1999	96.9	100.1	98.4	93.6	97.5	100.5	103.1	101.5	101.8	102.5	96.4	97.6	99.2
2000	101.3	102.5	101.5	99.7	102.9	106.5	109.5	104.5	104.4	106.7	98.1	99.4	103.1
2001	108.8	112.5	112.7	109.7	109.4	110.9	111.0	113.5	116.2	114.6	98.0	99.5	109.7
2002	102.2	105.1	106.6	104.0	102.5	107.3	108.0	106.8	106.6	111.7	103.8	98.8	105.3
2003	106.6	105.8	105.5	100.1	106.0	110.6	113.4	116.2	116.7	111.2	100.6	105.4	108.2
2004	108.4	109.4	113.4	108.4	109.0	111.7	112.9	114.2	108.8	112.3	99.6	100.3	109.0
2005	105.8	106.3	106.1	105.8	106.9	108.0	116.5	116.6	112.1	113.7	102.3	106.6	108.9
2006[1]	106.9	119.7	120.9	111.1	108.4	112.8	113.0	110.6	115.1	114.9	97.3	99.1	110.8

[1] Preliminary.   Source: Economic Research Service, U.S. Department of Agriculture (ERS-USDA)

Average Retail-to-Consumer Price Spread of Turkeys (Whole) in the United States   In Cents Per Pound

Year	Jan.	Feb.	Mar.	Apr.	May	June	July	Aug.	Sept.	Oct.	Nov.	Dec.	Average
1997	38.3	40.7	37.5	32.0	29.6	32.0	32.0	34.5	34.3	31.9	20.0	26.9	32.5
1998	38.8	37.2	35.2	31.2	29.4	30.7	29.6	29.0	29.3	21.3	10.3	19.0	28.4
1999	29.9	32.7	28.6	21.3	22.5	22.6	23.2	29.1	18.5	17.6	12.0	19.6	23.1
2000	32.1	33.9	29.1	25.9	27.6	29.5	30.9	23.7	21.1	21.7	13.4	23.1	26.0
2001	39.5	43.3	42.5	39.1	37.7	38.7	38.6	40.5	41.0	35.6	18.7	27.0	36.9
2002	34.2	37.9	40.7	38.3	32.9	35.9	35.9	34.9	35.4	40.2	29.8	24.6	35.1
2003	38.4	37.6	36.8	31.2	38.1	42.9	47.1	50.0	47.2	37.8	25.1	33.2	38.8
2004	39.4	40.4	42.5	35.0	33.5	33.9	33.3	32.5	25.7	26.9	14.0	18.0	31.3
2005	31.3	33.4	33.3	31.5	30.9	29.4	25.6	22.4	24.1	22.9	8.7	16.8	25.9
2006[1]	29.4	44.5	44.8	32.8	28.6	30.8	29.6	22.9	21.5	9.3	-11.3	15.9	24.9

[1] Preliminary.   Source: Economic Research Service, U.S. Department of Agriculture (ERS-USDA)

Uranium

Uranium (symbol U) is a chemically reactive, radioactive, steel-gray, metallic element and is the main fuel used in nuclear reactors. Uranium is the heaviest of all the natural elements. Traces of uranium have been found in archeological artifacts dating back to 79 AD. Uranium was discovered in pitchblende by German chemist Martin Heinrich Klaproth in 1789. Klaproth named it uranium after the recently discovered planet Uranus. French physicist Antoine Henri Becquerel discovered the radioactive properties of uranium in 1896 when he produced an image on a photographic plate covered with a light-absorbing substance. Following Becquerel's experiments, investigations of radioactivity led to the discovery of radium and to new concepts of atomic organization.

The principal use for uranium is fuel in nuclear power plants. Demand for uranium concentrates is directly linked to the level of electricity generated by nuclear power plants. Uranium ores are widely distributed throughout the world and are primarily found in Canada, DRC (formerly Zaire), and the US. Uranium is obtained from primary mine production and secondary sources. Two Canadian companies are the primary producers of uranium from deposits in the Athabasca Basin of northern Saskatchewan. Specifically, the companies Cameco accounted for 19% of global mine production in 2000 and Cogema Resources accounted for 15% of world production. Secondary sources of uranium include excess inventories from utilities and other fuel cycle participants, used reactor fuel, and dismantled Russian nuclear weapons.

Prices – The average price of delivered uranium in 2002 (the latest data available) rose by +2.1% yr/yr to $10.36 per pound from $10.15 in 2001. The 2001 price of $10.15 was a record low for the data series that goes back to 1981. The price of delivered uranium in 2002 of $10.36 was roughly one-third of the price of $30 per pound and above seen in the 1980s through 1986 when the price started falling.

Supply – World production of uranium oxide (U308) concentrate in 2003 (the latest data available) rose +7.3% yr/yr to a 13-year high of 56,552 short tons from last 2002's 52,709 short tons. The world's largest uranium producers in 2003 were Canada with 17,050 short tons of production in 2003 (30% of world production), the US with 10,200 short tons of production (18% of world production), and Australia with 9,326 short tons of production (16% of world production). US production in 2003 was the highest since 1983.

US uranium production in 2003 rose +64.4% yr/yr to a 20-year high of 10,200 short tons, up sharply from the record low of 1,315 short tons in 2001. US production had reached a peak of 21,850 short tons in 1980 and production had since fallen steadily to the record low in 2001, which was only 6% of the record level of production.

Trade – US imports of uranium in 2003 (latest data available) rose +0.7% yr/yr to a record high of 53.044 million pounds. The US is being forced to import more uranium as domestic production steadily declines. US exports of uranium fell −14.3% yr/yr to 13.187 million pounds, which was still well above the 7-year low of 8.510 million pounds posted in 1999.

World Production of Uranium Oxide (U₃O₈) Concentrate   In Short Tons (Uranium Content)

Year	Australia	Canada	China	Czech Rep. & Slovakia	France	Gabon	Germany	Namibia	Niger	South Africa	United States	Ex-USSR	World Total
1994	3,050	11,950	----	----	1,700	750	----	2,500	3,800	2,250	1,950	----	41,750
1995	4,900	13,600	----	----	1,250	800	----	2,600	3,750	1,850	3,050	----	43,050
1996	6,450	15,250	----	----	1,200	750	----	3,150	4,300	2,200	3,150	----	46,650
1997	7,150	15,650	----	----	940	600	----	3,770	4,500	1,065	2,900	----	46,550
1998	6,350	14,200	----	----	660	950	----	3,590	4,850	1,250	2,435	----	44,110
1999	7,875	10,680	----	----	450	380	----	3,495	3,790	1,195	2,325	----	39,640
2000	9,830	13,875	655	795	525	----	45	2,430	3,270	1,305	1,890	655	43,475
2001	10,035	16,270	650	595	195	----	----	2,910	3,795	1,135	1,315	1,050	47,395
2002[1]	10,857	17,153	W	0	----	W	W	1,082	W	764	6,206	W	52,709
2003[2]	9,326	17,050	W	W	----	0	0	1,034	0	1,438	10,200	W	56,552

[1] Preliminary. [2] Estimate. *Source: American Bureau of Metal Statistics, Inc. (ABMS)*

Commercial and U.S. Government Stocks of Uranium, End of Year   In Millions of Pounds U₃O₈ Equivalent

Year	Utility — Natural Uranium	Utility — Enriched Uranium[1]	Domestic Supplier — Natural Uranium	Domestic Supplier — Enriched Uranium[1]	Total Commercial Stocks	DOE Owned & USEC Held — Natural Uranium	DOE Owned & USEC Held — Enriched Uranium[1]
1996	42.2	23.9	13.0	1.0	80.0	83.2	25.3
1997	47.1	18.8	10.3	30.1	106.2	53.2	----
1998	42.1	23.7	35.0	35.7	136.5	24.5	----
1999	44.8	13.5	29.5	39.4	127.1	53.1	----
2000	36.0	18.9	12.6	43.8	111.3	53.1	----
2001	34.4	21.2	9.2	39.0	103.8	53.1	----
2002	31.0	22.4	15.0	32.9	102.1	51.8	----
2003	22.7	23.0	[2]	39.9	85.2	W	W
2004	27.3	29.1	[2]	38.0	94.3	W	W
2005	45.4	19.4	[2]	29.0	93.8	W	W

[1] Includes amount reported as UF₆ at enrichment suppliers. [2] Included in Enriched beginning 2003. DOE = Department of Energy
USEC = U.S. Energy Commission *Source: Energy Information Administration, U.S. Department of Energy (EIA-DOE)*

URANIUM

Reported Average Price Settlements for Purchases by U.S. Utilities and Domestic Suppliers — In $/Pound

Year of Delivery	Contract Price	Market Price[1]	Price & Cost Floor	Total	Contract & Market	Year of Delivery	Contract Price	Market Price[1]	Price & Cost Floor	Total	Contract & Market
	---- Averages of Reported Prices ----						---- Averages of Reported Prices ----				
1995	10.58	10.19	17.86	12.05	10.79	2000	12.31	9.11	----	11.04	----
1996	13.40	13.66	16.13	14.91	13.72	2001	11.72	8.04	----	10.15	----
1997	13.33	11.20	14.52	12.11	13.13	2002	10.73	9.79	----	10.36	----
1998	12.53	9.33	13.50	10.31	12.37	2003	----	----	----	10.81	----
1999	12.72	9.52	14.75	11.16	12.57	2004	----	----	----	12.61	----

[1] No floor.   Note: Price excludes uranium delivered *under litigation settlements. Price is given in year-of-delivery dollars.*
Source: Energy Information Administration, U.S. Department of Energy (EIA-DOE)

Uranium Industry Statistics in the United States — In Millions of Pounds U_3O_8

Year	Production Mine	Production Concentrate rate	Concentrate Shipments	Exploration	Mining	Milling	Processing	Total	Deliveries to U.S. Utilities[1]	Average Price Delivered Uranium $/Lb. U_3O_8	Imports	Avg. Price Delivered Uranium Imports $/Lb. U_3O_8	Exports
1996	4.7	6.300	6.000	27	333	155	175	1,118	47.3	14.12	45.4	13.15	11.5
1997	4.7	5.600	5.800	30	413	175	175	1,097	42.0	12.88	43.0	11.81	17.0
1998	4.8	4.700	4.900	30	518	160	203	1,120	42.7	12.14	43.7	11.19	15.1
1999	4.5	4.600	5.500	7	310	201	132	848	47.9	11.63	47.6	10.55	8.5
2000	3.1	4.000	3.200	1	157	106	137	627	51.8	11.04	44.9	9.84	13.6
2001	2.6	2.600	2.200	0	81	42	122	423	55.4	10.15	46.7	9.51	11.7
2002	2.4	2.300	3.800	W	W	104	100	426	52.7	10.36	52.7	10.05	15.4
2003	2.2	2.000	1.600	W	W	W	W	321			53.0	10.59	13.2
2004	2.5	2.300	2.300	18	108	W	W	420					
2005	3.0	2.700	2.700	78	147	142	145	638					

[1] From suppliers under domestic purchases.   *Source: Energy Information Administration, U.S. Department of Energy (EIA-DOE)*

Month-End Uranium (U_3O_8) Transaction Values[1] — In Dollars Per Pound

Year	Jan.	Feb.	Mar.	Apr.	May	June	July	Aug.	Sept.	Oct.	Nov.	Dec.	Average
1997	15.33	15.08	14.85	14.75	14.43	10.95	10.68	10.45	10.55	10.48	10.43	10.53	12.37
1998	10.63	10.63	10.60	10.05	10.00	9.80	9.80	9.73	9.55	9.35	9.25	9.05	9.87
1999	9.03	9.08	9.20	9.20	9.53	9.48	9.48	9.40	9.35	9.23	9.18	9.13	9.27
2000	9.03	8.70	8.55	8.50	8.40	8.18	8.13	7.98	7.88	7.40	7.15	6.80	8.06
2001	6.78	6.83	6.83	7.25	7.38	7.45	7.83	7.95	9.00	9.47	9.44	9.50	7.97
2002	9.58	9.72	9.90	9.76	9.90	9.90	9.88	9.85	9.79	9.85	9.86	9.97	9.83
2003	10.20	10.10	10.10	10.16	10.84	10.90	10.90	11.13	11.47	12.32	13.18	13.98	11.27
2004	14.85	15.47	16.50	17.52	17.75	17.86	17.90	17.90	18.60	20.80	20.20	20.50	17.99
2005	20.55	21.18	21.20	21.20	21.20	21.20	21.20	21.20	21.20	21.20	21.20	21.20	21.14
2006	21.20	21.20	21.20	21.20	21.20	21.20	21.20	21.20	21.20	21.20	21.20	21.20	21.20

[1] Transaction value is a weighed average price of recent natural uranium sales transactions, based on prices paid on transactions closed within the previous three-month period for which delivery is scheduled within one year of the transaction date; at least 10 transactions involving a sum total of at least 2 million pounds of U_3O_8 equivalent.   *Source: American Metal Market (AMM)*

Uranium (U_3O_8) Transaction Values (monthly average) through December 2006 — USD per pound

Vanadium

Vanadium (symbol V) is a silvery-white, soft, ductile, metallic element. Discovered in 1801, but mistaken for chromium, vanadium was rediscovered in 1830 by Swedish chemist Nils Sefstrom, who named the element in honor of the Scandinavian goddess Vanadis.

Never found in the pure state, vanadium is found in about 65 different minerals such as carnotite, roscoelite, vanadinite, and patronite, as well as in phosphate rock, certain iron ores, some crude oils, and meteorites. Vanadium is one of the hardest of all metals. It melts at about 1890 degrees Celsius and boils at about 3380 degrees Celsius.

Vanadium has good structural strength and is used as an alloying agent with iron, steel, and titanium. It is used in aerospace applications, transmission gears, photography, as a reducing agent, and as a drying agent in various paints.

Prices – The price of vanadium in 2005 rose very sharply by +231% to a record high of $17.50 per pound.

Supply – Virtually all (99%) of vanadium is produced from ores, concentrates, and slag, with the remainder coming from petroleum residues, ash, and spent catalysts. World production from ore, concentrates and slag rose 13.2% to 58,200 metric tons. World production of all vanadium in 2005 rose 13.3% yr/yr to a record high of 58,800 metric tons.

The world's largest producer of vanadium from ores, concentrates and slag is South Africa with 25,000 metric tons of production in 2005, and that was 43% of world production. The two other major producers are China with 29% of world production and Russia with 26% of world production. Production in Russia and South Africa has been relatively stable in recent years, while China's production grew sharply in the late 1990s. China's production level of 17,000 metric tons in 2005 is a new record high and is more than triple the levels seen in the early 1990s. Japan is the only significant producer of vanadium from petroleum residues, ash, and spent catalysts with 560 metric tons of production in 2005.

Trade – The US exports very little vanadium.

US imports of vanadium were mainly in the form of ore, slag and residues with 3,370 metric tons of imports in 2005, down sharply by –63.4% yr/yr. Other key import categories of vanadium were ferro-vanadium (11,900 metric tons, +294% yr/yr), vanadium pent-oxide, anhydride (1,370 metric tons, +32 yr/yr), and oxides & hydroxides (186 metric tons, +55% yr/yr).

World Production of Vanadium   In Metric Tons (Contained Vanadium)

| | ------- From Ores, Concentrates and Slag ------- | | | | | | From Petroleum Residues | | | |
| | | | | | | | ------- Ash, Spent Catalysts ------- | | | |
Year	Australia	China[3]	Kazak-hstan	Russia	South Africa	Total[4]	Japan[5]	United States[6]	Total	World Total
2000	1,520	12,000	1,000	7,500	18,021	40,000	245	----	245	40,300
2001	2,660	12,000	1,000	7,500	18,184	41,300	245	----	245	41,600
2002	3,060	13,200	1,000	8,000	20,500	45,800	245	----	245	46,000
2003	160	13,200	1,000	5,800	27,172	47,300	560	----	560	47,900
2004[1]	150	16,000	1,000	10,900	23,302	51,400	560	----	560	51,900
2005[2]	100	17,000	1,000	15,100	25,000	58,200	560	----	560	58,800

[1] Preliminary.   [2] Estimate.   [3] In vanadiferous slag product.   [4] Excludes U.S. production.   [5] In vanadium pentoxide product.
[6] In vanadium pentoxide and ferrovanadium products.   *Source: U.S. Geological Survey(USGS)*

Salient Statistics of Vanadium in the United States   In Metric Tons (Contained Vanadium)

| | Con-sumer & Producer Stocks, Dec. 31 | ------- Vanadium Consumption by Uses in the U.S. ------- | | | | | | | | | ------- Exports ------- | | | | ------- Imports ------- | | | |
| | | | | High Strength, & Heat | | | | | | | Vanadium | | | | Ores, Vanadium | | | |
Year		Tool Steel	Cast Irons	Low Alloy	Stainless & Heat Re-sisting	Super-alloys	Carbon	Full Alloy	Total	Average $ Per Lb. V₂O₅	Pent-oxide, Anhydride	Oxides & Hydr-oxides	Ferro-Vana-dium	Slag, Re-sidues	Pent-oxide, Anhydride	Oxides & Hydr-oxides	Ferro-Vana-dium
2000	303	225	W	944	W	17	1,090	773	3,510	1.82	653	100	172	1,890	902	21	2,510
2001	251	146	W	797	W	18	1,030	689	3,210	1.37	670	385	70	1,670	600	57	2,550
2002	221	270	W	900	38	12	731	748	3,080	1.34	453	443	142	1,870	406	66	2,520
2003	250	143	W	938	70	13	1,030	808	3,240	2.21	185	284	397	2,220	474	74	1,360
2004[1]	305	239	W	1,160	60	17	1,300	1,060	4,050	5.28	240	584	285	9,200	1,040	120	3,020
2005[2]	275	402	W	974	60	36	1,170	1,010	3,910	17.50	254	899	504	3,370	1,370	186	11,900

[1] Preliminary.   [2] Estimate.   W = Withheld proprietary data.   *Source: U.S. Geological Survey (USGS)*

Average Price of Vanadium Pentoxide in United States   In Dollars Per Pound

Year	Jan.	Feb.	Mar.	Apr.	May	June	July	Aug.	Sept.	Oct.	Nov.	Dec.	Average
2001	1.43	1.41	1.38	1.41	1.44	1.46	1.46	1.45	3.52	3.90	2.08	1.30	1.85
2002	1.23	1.11	1.26	1.24	1.55	1.75	1.75	1.45	1.45	1.45	1.45	1.52	1.43
2003	1.55	1.55	1.55	1.55	1.55	1.55	1.55	1.55	1.55	1.55	1.95	2.10	1.63
2004	2.50	3.43	3.74	5.25	5.25	5.25	5.26	4.64	4.40	5.15	7.00	8.63	5.04
2005	9.65	10.24	13.75	15.00	20.36	26.16	19.96	11.63	11.10	13.74	13.75	11.00	14.70
2006	8.73	9.11	8.78	7.92	8.15	8.08	7.40	7.07	7.85	7.70	7.27	6.70	7.90

Source: American Metal Market (AMM)

Vegetables

Vegetables are the edible products of herbaceous plants, which are plants with soft stems. Vegetables are grouped according to the edible part of each plant including leaves (e.g., lettuce), stalks (celery), roots (carrot), tubers (potato), bulbs (onion), fruits (tomato), seeds (pea), and flowers (broccoli). Each of these groups contributes to the human diet in its own way. Fleshy roots are high in energy value and good sources of the vitamin B group, seeds are relatively high in carbohydrates and proteins, while leaves, stalks, and fruits are excellent sources of minerals, vitamins, water, and roughage. Vegetables are an important food for the maintenance of health and prevention of disease. Higher intakes of vegetables have been shown to lower the risks of cancer and coronary heart disease.

Vegetables are best consumed fresh in their raw state in order to derive the maximum benefits from their nutrients. While canned and frozen vegetables are often thought to be inferior to fresh vegetables, they are sometimes nutritionally superior to fresh produce because they are usually processed immediately after harvest when nutrient content is at its peak. When cooking vegetables, aluminum utensils should not be used, because aluminum is a soft metal that is affected by food acids and alkalis. Scientific evidence shows that tiny particles of aluminum from foods cooked in aluminum utensils enter the stomach and can injure the sensitive lining of the stomach.

Prices – The monthly average index of fresh vegetable prices received by growers in the US in 2006 rose by +4.5% to a record level of 160.5 from last year's level of 143.5.

Demand – The leading vegetable in terms of US per capita consumption in 2006 was the potato with 125.8 pounds of consumption. Runner-up vegetables were tomatoes (84.0 pounds), sweet lettuce (32.4 pounds), corn (26.4 pounds), and onions (21.8 pounds). Total US per capita vegetable consumption in 2006 was down –0.1% at 443.3 pounds. That is up about 25% higher than the 356.2 pounds consumed in 1980.

Index of Prices Received by Growers for Commercial Vegetables[1] in the United States

Year	Jan.	Feb.	Mar.	Apr.	May	June	July	Aug.	Sept.	Oct.	Nov.	Dec.	Average
2001	121	147	138	137	144	120	125	145	134	103	109	171	133
2002	158	192	272	120	115	109	115	121	119	105	110	104	137
2003	112	113	123	129	138	152	119	138	144	143	180	159	138
2004	128	143	115	132	112	110	105	132	134	159	163	120	129
2005	95	122	167	184	133	126	111	115	128	129	142	210	139
2006[1]	132	125	150	149	123	132	140	147	161	128	119	150	138

Not seasonally adjusted. 1990-92=100. [1] Includes fresh and processing vegetables. [2] Preliminary. *Source: National Agricultural Statistics Service, U.S. Department of Agriculture (NASS-USDA)*

Index of Prices Received by Growers for Fresh Vegetables (0113-02) in the United States

Year	Jan.	Feb.	Mar.	Apr.	May	June	July	Aug.	Sept.	Oct.	Nov.	Dec.	Average
2001	147.0	168.6	178.7	145.6	144.9	129.4	109.7	127.2	132.3	112.3	105.9	121.0	135.2
2002	146.1	188.7	242.5	101.7	107.2	123.2	127.1	125.4	116.7	126.9	127.4	119.0	137.7
2003	147.8	127.5	153.0	167.7	165.0	138.8	133.3	136.6	164.7	156.9	148.4	184.7	152.0
2004	143.8	125.9	140.3	133.1	132.9	101.0	102.8	128.3	141.9	200.0	211.1	143.7	142.1
2005	122.0	152.8	168.5	174.7	144.2	160.0	126.8	132.3	153.3	144.0	163.1	200.8	153.5
2006[1]	207.6	138.8	137.6	174.4	147.9	128.7	134.1	179.5	193.1	166.7	138.8	178.3	160.5

Not seasonally adjusted. 1990-92=100. [1] Preliminary. *Source: National Agricultural Statistics Service, U.S. Department of Agriculture (NASS)*

Producer Price Index of Canned[1] Processed Vegetables (0244) in the United States   1982 = 100

Year	Jan.	Feb.	Mar.	Apr.	May	June	July	Aug.	Sept.	Oct.	Nov.	Dec.	Average
2001	121.4	121.4	121.3	121.3	121.4	121.9	124.1	124.9	125.3	126.5	128.0	128.1	123.8
2002	128.3	128.2	128.0	128.2	128.3	128.0	127.7	129.4	128.7	129.5	129.1	129.1	128.5
2003	128.8	129.0	128.9	129.3	129.4	129.3	129.4	129.1	130.0	130.7	131.1	131.3	129.7
2004	131.5	131.7	131.9	131.9	131.7	132.8	133.0	133.3	133.4	134.6	135.4	135.5	133.1
2005	135.7	135.9	136.1	136.3	137.6	137.6	137.7	137.7	137.5	137.7	137.6	138.0	137.1
2006[1]	138.0	136.8	137.1	137.3	138.8	140.2	140.0	140.5	141.4	141.0	141.7	142.2	139.6

Not seasonally adjusted. [1] Includes canned vegetables and juices, including hominy and mushrooms. [2] Preliminary. *Source: Bureau of Labor Statistics, U.S. Department of Labor (BLS)*

Producer Price Index of Frozen Processed Vegetables (0245) in the United States   1982 = 100

Year	Jan.	Feb.	Mar.	Apr.	May	June	July	Aug.	Sept.	Oct.	Nov.	Dec.	
2001	127.6	128.5	127.7	128.7	128.4	127.7	128.9	128.8	128.8	130.0	129.2	129.1	128.6
2002	130.0	131.1	130.1	131.2	130.7	129.7	131.4	131.3	131.5	132.2	131.9	132.6	131.1
2003	133.4	134.1	133.3	134.0	134.1	133.9	134.9	134.2	134.2	135.2	135.1	135.0	134.3
2004	135.1	136.0	135.3	135.3	134.3	134.7	135.4	135.8	136.8	138.1	137.2	137.0	135.9
2005	137.3	137.3	137.4	137.5	137.5	137.4	137.2	136.8	136.6	136.7	136.1	136.4	137.0
2006[1]	137.3	137.7	138.7	138.6	138.8	139.5	139.4	139.3	139.9	142.0	143.1	143.0	139.8

Not seasonally adjusted. [1] Preliminary. *Source: Bureau of Labor Statistics, U.S. Department of Labor (BLS)*

Per Capita Use of Selected Commercially Produced Fresh and Processing Vegetables in the U.S.
In Pounds, farm weight basis

Crop	1996	1997	1998	1999	2000	2001	2002	2003	2004	2005[10]	2006[11]
Asparagus, All	0.9	1.0	1.0	1.2	1.3	1.2	1.2	1.3	1.4	1.5	1.5
Fresh	0.6	0.7	0.7	0.9	1.0	0.9	1.0	1.0	1.1	1.2	1.2
Canning	0.2	0.2	0.2	0.2	0.2	0.2	0.2	0.2	0.2	0.2	0.2
Freezing	0.1	0.1	0.1	0.1	0.1	0.1	0.1	0.1	0.1	0.1	0.1
Snap beans, All	7.2	6.7	7.4	7.6	7.9	7.8	7.2	7.5	7.6	7.6	7.6
Fresh	1.5	1.3	1.6	1.9	2.0	2.2	2.1	2.0	1.9	1.8	1.9
Canning	3.8	3.6	3.8	3.7	4.0	3.8	3.4	3.7	3.7	4.0	3.8
Freezing	1.9	1.8	2.0	2.0	1.8	1.9	1.8	1.9	1.9	1.8	1.9
Broccoli, All [1]	7.0	7.3	7.1	8.3	8.1	7.4	7.5	8.1	8.5	8.4	8.5
Fresh	4.5	5.0	5.0	6.2	5.9	5.4	5.4	5.5	5.9	5.6	5.7
Freezing	2.5	2.3	2.1	2.1	2.3	2.0	2.1	2.6	2.7	2.7	2.8
Cabbage, All	9.3	10.4	9.8	8.8	10.3	10.1	9.5	8.7	9.4	9.3	9.3
Fresh	8.3	9.0	8.4	7.6	8.9	8.8	8.3	7.6	8.3	8.1	8.1
Canning (kraut)	1.0	1.4	1.4	1.2	1.4	1.3	1.2	1.1	1.1	1.2	1.1
Carrots, All [2]	16.9	18.2	13.7	13.1	13.0	12.7	11.5	12.0	11.9	11.5	11.7
Fresh	12.4	14.1	9.5	9.3	9.2	9.4	8.4	8.8	8.8	8.7	8.7
Canning	1.7	1.5	1.4	1.4	1.1	1.9	1.2	1.6	1.8	1.5	1.6
Freezing	2.8	2.6	2.8	2.4	2.7	1.5	1.9	1.5	1.3	1.4	1.5
Cauliflower, All [1]	2.2	2.2	2.2	2.3	2.3	2.0	1.7	1.9	1.9	1.9	1.9
Fresh	1.7	1.8	1.5	1.8	1.7	1.5	1.4	1.6	1.6	1.5	1.5
Freezing	0.5	0.4	0.8	0.5	0.6	0.5	0.3	0.4	0.4	0.4	0.4
Celery	7.0	6.5	6.5	6.5	6.3	6.4	6.3	6.3	6.2	6.1	6.1
Sweet Corn, All [3]	29.1	27.5	28.4	28.3	27.1	27.2	26.1	26.8	26.5	26.7	26.4
Fresh	8.3	8.3	9.3	9.1	9.0	9.2	9.0	9.5	9.2	8.9	9.0
Canning	10.4	9.1	9.2	9.1	9.0	8.7	7.8	8.3	8.2	9.0	8.5
Freezing	10.4	10.1	9.8	10.1	9.0	9.3	9.3	9.0	9.1	8.7	8.9
Cucumbers, All	10.0	11.6	10.5	10.9	11.2	10.0	11.9	10.5	11.3	10.3	10.7
Fresh	5.9	6.4	6.5	6.7	6.4	6.3	6.5	6.1	6.5	6.5	6.4
Pickling	4.1	5.2	4.0	4.2	4.9	3.7	5.4	4.4	4.9	3.8	4.4
Melons	28.9	28.2	27.3	29.0	27.2	28.1	27.3	26.5	25.2	25.9	26.5
Watermelon	16.6	15.5	14.3	15.2	13.8	15.0	14.0	13.5	13.0	13.8	14.2
Cantaloupe	10.3	10.5	10.6	11.4	11.1	11.2	11.1	10.8	10.0	10.1	10.2
Honeydew	2.0	2.2	2.3	2.5	2.3	2.0	2.2	2.2	2.2	2.0	2.1
Lettuce, All	27.4	30.5	28.9	32.5	31.8	31.0	32.1	33.3	32.6	32.1	32.4
Head lettuce	21.6	23.9	22.3	24.9	23.5	23.0	22.5	22.2	21.3	20.3	20.4
Romaine & Leaf	5.8	6.6	6.6	7.6	8.4	8.0	9.6	11.1	11.4	11.7	12.1
Onions, All	19.1	19.7	19.5	20.8	20.4	19.5	20.4	21.3	23.1	22.2	21.8
Fresh	18.3	18.8	18.4	18.5	18.9	18.5	19.3	19.5	21.6	21.2	20.6
Dehydrating	0.8	0.9	1.1	2.3	1.6	1.0	1.1	1.8	1.5	1.0	1.3
Green Peas, All [4]	3.4	3.5	3.3	3.4	3.7	3.3	2.8	3.2	2.9	2.7	2.8
Canning	1.5	1.5	1.4	1.4	1.5	1.4	1.1	1.3	1.2	1.0	1.2
Freezing	1.9	2.0	1.9	2.0	2.1	2.0	1.7	1.9	1.7	1.7	1.6
Peppers, All	11.7	10.9	11.1	11.4	12.1	12.1	12.6	12.5	13.1	12.6	13.1
Bell Peppers, All	7.1	6.4	6.4	6.7	7.0	6.9	6.8	6.9	7.0	6.6	6.9
Chile Peppers, All	4.6	4.5	4.7	4.7	5.2	5.2	5.8	5.6	6.1	6.0	6.2
Tomatoes, All	90.8	89.9	92.5	90.3	89.1	84.7	89.6	89.3	90.6	94.2	94.0
Fresh	17.4	17.3	18.5	19.1	19.0	19.2	20.3	19.5	20.1	20.6	20.7
Canning	73.4	72.6	74.0	71.2	70.1	65.5	69.3	69.8	70.5	73.6	73.3
Other, Fresh [5]	8.8	9.2	10.0	10.5	17.7	16.6	17.2	17.7	18.7	19.4	19.5
Other, Canning [6]	2.2	2.3	2.1	2.5	2.6	2.8	2.4	2.5	2.9	3.0	3.1
Other, Freezing [7]	3.1	3.0	2.9	3.2	3.2	3.2	4.3	3.9	3.9	4.0	4.4
Subtotal, All [8]	285.0	288.6	284.2	290.5	295.3	286.2	291.7	293.1	297.8	299.2	301.3
Fresh	158.1	163.5	158.6	166.1	172.0	170.3	171.4	171.5	174.7	174.2	175.2
Canning	102.9	101.9	102.2	99.6	100.0	94.4	97.8	98.6	100.7	103.3	103.3
Freezing	23.2	22.3	22.3	22.5	21.8	20.4	21.5	21.1	21.0	20.7	21.5
Potatoes, All	145.0	137.8	137.7	136.2	137.9	138.8	132.1	138.2	134.7	129.1	125.8
Fresh	49.9	47.3	46.9	47.7	47.1	46.6	44.3	46.8	45.8	43.1	42.1
Processing	95.1	90.5	90.8	88.5	90.8	92.2	87.8	91.4	88.9	86.0	83.7
Sweet Potatoes	4.3	4.3	3.8	3.7	4.2	4.4	3.8	4.7	4.6	4.5	4.6
Mushrooms	3.9	4.0	3.9	4.1	4.1	3.9	4.1	4.1	4.1	4.0	4.1
Dry Peas & Lentils [9]	0.5	0.9	0.8	0.6	0.8	0.8	0.8	0.6	0.7	0.7	0.7
Dry Edible Beans	7.5	7.4	7.3	7.8	7.6	6.9	6.7	6.6	6.0	6.3	6.8
Total, All Items	446.2	442.9	437.7	442.9	449.9	441.0	439.2	447.3	448.0	443.8	443.3

[1] All production for processing broccoli and cauliflower is for freezing.   [2] Industry allocation suggests that 27 percent of processing carrot production is for canning and 73 percent is for freezing.   [3] On-cob basis.   [4] In-shell basis.   [5] Includes artichokes, brussels sprouts, eggplant, endive/escarole, garlic, radishes, and spinach.   [6] Includes beets, chile peppers (1980-94, all uses), and spinach.   [7] Includes green lima beans, spinach, and miscellaneous freezing vegetables.   [8] Fresh, canning, and freezing data do not add to the total because onions for dehydrating are included in the total.
[9] Preliminary.   [10] Forecast.   Source: Economic Research Service, U.S. Department of Agriculture (ERS-USDA)

VEGETABLES

Average Price Received by Growers for Broccoli in the United States   In Dollars Per Cwt.

Year	Jan.	Feb.	Mar.	Apr.	May	June	July	Aug.	Sept.	Oct.	Nov.	Dec.	Season Average
1999	27.70	20.10	23.20	20.20	18.60	23.10	18.70	27.40	29.30	23.00	21.60	39.20	24.10
2000	22.60	20.10	27.40	23.20	44.30	30.00	31.50	25.20	27.70	34.10	56.00	34.10	31.20
2001	22.70	32.30	24.70	26.90	25.50	27.00	23.60	27.10	22.90	24.20	22.20	20.00	26.50
2002	55.30	44.40	33.80	24.00	20.80	28.40	27.00	29.60	40.60	24.00	37.10	35.00	31.40
2003	25.20	40.90	28.10	27.10	29.70	24.60	27.00	29.80	49.10	38.90	48.00	40.00	32.70
2004	33.60	28.50	21.60	24.00	27.20	28.70	24.20	29.70	57.00	43.90	44.20	45.40	33.20
2005	22.60	33.30	42.60	39.80	22.40	39.70	22.40	30.50	27.70	22.40	20.90	34.10	28.50
2006[1]	32.50	23.80	27.60	32.40	29.00	51.10	26.20	56.90	39.40	24.60	27.60	53.10	28.50

[1] Preliminary.   *Source: National Agricultural Statistics Service, U.S. Department of Agriculture (NASS-USDA)*

Average Price Received by Growers for Carrots in the United States   In Dollars Per Cwt.

Year	Jan.	Feb.	Mar.	Apr.	May	June	July	Aug.	Sept.	Oct.	Nov.	Dec.	Season Average
1999	16.10	19.60	21.50	26.50	25.40	22.80	17.20	13.30	10.10	10.50	11.30	11.50	16.80
2000	22.60	20.10	27.40	23.20	44.30	30.00	31.50	25.20	27.70	34.10	56.00	34.10	31.20
2001	22.70	32.30	24.70	26.90	25.50	27.00	23.60	27.10	22.90	24.20	22.20	20.00	26.50
2002	55.30	44.40	33.80	24.00	20.80	28.40	27.00	29.60	40.60	24.00	37.10	35.00	31.40
2003	25.20	40.90	28.10	27.10	29.70	24.60	27.00	29.80	49.10	38.90	48.00	40.00	32.70
2004	24.50	24.90	24.60	24.20	24.90	22.50	20.20	18.00	16.70	16.40	17.20	18.00	20.20
2005	20.30	21.00	21.00	21.10	21.20	21.30	21.80	21.40	20.00	21.40	23.10	22.00	20.90
2006[1]	21.40	21.50	21.50	21.50	20.80	21.40	21.50	23.00	19.30	19.60	20.20	19.10	28.50

[1] Preliminary.   *Source: National Agricultural Statistics Service, U.S. Department of Agriculture (NASS-USDA)*

Average Price Received by Growers for Cauliflower in the United States   In Dollars Per Cwt.

Year	Jan.	Feb.	Mar.	Apr.	May	June	July	Aug.	Sept.	Oct.	Nov.	Dec.	Season Average
1999	29.40	31.10	42.80	46.40	23.40	25.50	19.60	25.40	21.70	22.30	35.10	55.50	29.70
2000	22.60	20.10	27.40	23.20	44.30	30.00	31.50	25.20	27.70	34.10	56.00	34.10	31.20
2001	22.70	32.30	24.70	26.90	25.50	27.00	23.60	27.10	22.90	24.20	22.20	20.00	26.50
2002	55.30	44.40	33.80	24.00	20.80	28.40	27.00	29.60	40.60	24.00	37.10	35.00	31.40
2003	25.20	40.90	28.10	27.10	29.70	24.60	27.00	29.80	49.10	38.90	48.00	40.00	32.70
2004	27.30	42.20	24.20	23.50	28.80	46.20	27.60	26.30	31.10	32.20	43.80	54.40	30.80
2005	27.70	38.20	50.60	36.70	29.70	38.10	25.60	31.50	28.50	19.70	25.50	43.90	30.30
2006[1]	33.10	26.40	35.80	44.40	27.10	27.90	24.00	28.40	47.10	20.90	34.40	41.60	28.50

[1] Preliminary.   *Source: National Agricultural Statistics Service, U.S. Department of Agriculture (NASS-USDA)*

Average Price Received by Growers for Celery in the United States   In Dollars Per Cwt.

Year	Jan.	Feb.	Mar.	Apr.	May	June	July	Aug.	Sept.	Oct.	Nov.	Dec.	Season Average
1999	9.51	8.47	8.35	10.20	12.80	18.30	14.00	10.30	10.60	9.14	12.80	17.20	12.00
2000	22.60	20.10	27.40	23.20	44.30	30.00	31.50	25.20	27.70	34.10	56.00	34.10	31.20
2001	22.70	32.30	24.70	26.90	25.50	27.00	23.60	27.10	22.90	24.20	22.20	20.00	26.50
2002	55.30	44.40	33.80	24.00	20.80	28.40	27.00	29.60	40.60	24.00	37.10	35.00	31.40
2003	25.20	40.90	28.10	27.10	29.70	24.60	27.00	29.80	49.10	38.90	48.00	40.00	32.70
2004	20.80	24.40	13.90	15.60	15.00	13.80	12.00	10.00	11.90	15.10	18.10	13.40	14.80
2005	12.90	22.90	28.40	20.80	15.50	9.62	10.00	10.80	12.80	12.20	13.10	10.70	14.30
2006[1]	9.64	10.80	14.90	16.60	12.70	17.80	20.90	23.40	27.60	27.20	22.00	20.20	28.50

[1] Preliminary.   *Source: National Agricultural Statistics Service, U.S. Department of Agriculture (NASS-USDA)*

Average Price Received by Growers for Sweet Corn in the United States   In Dollars Per Cwt.

Year	Jan.	Feb.	Mar.	Apr.	May	June	July	Aug.	Sept.	Oct.	Nov.	Dec.	Season Average
1999	19.60	23.30	21.80	18.90	18.50	15.00	17.30	16.60	17.30	16.50	28.40	40.70	16.90
2000	31.50	25.10	19.30	18.70	14.40	18.00	22.00	20.70	20.10	24.00	16.80	33.00	18.50
2001	32.70	34.00	26.10	18.10	24.60	18.60	19.80	19.20	19.00	23.80	24.80	22.60	19.50
2002	24.80	23.50	26.30	19.40	20.80	18.80	27.90	21.80	22.50	25.80	15.50	18.30	19.20
2003	29.00	24.00	18.90	14.90	16.60	23.20	21.30	20.10	19.70	23.70	30.70	22.60	19.30
2004	30.80	20.70	20.20	17.60	18.10	22.80	21.80	22.90	24.10	33.50	46.70	36.80	20.80
2005	21.30	28.60	26.10	21.50	18.10	22.60	22.20	20.30	24.70	25.50	37.30	21.20	22.10
2006[1]	36.50	35.00	33.70	27.20	16.20	23.00	23.50	19.70	22.70	21.70	19.80	14.40	22.10

[1] Preliminary.   *Source: National Agricultural Statistics Service, U.S. Department of Agriculture (NASS-USDA)*

Average Price Received by Growers for Head Lettuce in the United States   In Dollars Per Cwt.

Year	Jan.	Feb.	Mar.	Apr.	May	June	July	Aug.	Sept.	Oct.	Nov.	Dec.	Season Average
1997	14.90	9.58	13.50	15.70	10.40	14.90	17.10	22.80	22.30	34.80	22.20	25.10	17.50
1998	19.00	10.90	12.50	27.20	14.30	11.80	15.50	16.40	14.00	21.00	10.80	12.50	16.20
1999	10.30	15.50	16.30	20.20	14.00	11.40	12.70	12.00	13.10	13.10	10.70	16.20	13.30
2000	14.60	9.28	14.10	22.80	23.60	13.50	15.00	19.20	29.40	16.20	19.90	12.00	17.30
2001	13.60	22.80	15.10	21.60	18.80	12.10	16.40	26.90	26.20	11.50	10.90	10.00	17.90
2002	26.20	44.10	86.40	14.10	10.20	10.60	11.30	14.60	14.30	13.50	11.90	30.00	21.10
2003	12.10	11.80	9.64	12.50	21.20	32.20	11.90	21.50	23.90	26.30	31.70	21.30	18.10
2004	15.40	19.80	10.40	14.80	10.50	13.30	10.70	17.10	15.20	24.10	14.90	15.70	16.90
2005	11.50	11.70	27.90	30.10	13.90	17.30	11.00	13.50	12.70	12.40	9.81	16.60	15.60
2006[1]	10.50	12.00	19.10	22.30	33.70	11.80	12.20	20.70	16.30	11.80	12.70	22.40	15.60

[1] Preliminary.   Source: National Agricultural Statistics Service, U.S. Department of Agriculture (NASS-USDA)

Average Price Received by Growers for Tomatoes in the United States   In Dollars Per Cwt.

Year	Jan.	Feb.	Mar.	Apr.	May	June	July	Aug.	Sept.	Oct.	Nov.	Dec.	Season Average
1997	32.10	45.90	57.40	24.90	32.20	30.30	29.20	27.60	25.90	26.50	43.60	40.80	31.70
1998	26.40	44.00	34.00	37.20	36.50	29.00	40.90	25.10	28.40	43.00	42.10	42.20	35.20
1999	33.50	23.40	22.30	23.70	21.00	29.00	23.10	25.00	26.50	21.30	26.00	28.90	25.80
2000	21.40	21.10	33.00	34.80	23.10	21.80	24.60	33.90	29.50	42.60	47.80	37.60	30.70
2001	43.80	29.10	56.40	19.00	37.80	28.50	27.40	27.60	23.50	28.60	28.50	25.00	30.00
2002	40.50	26.60	38.50	34.30	29.60	33.00	28.50	25.80	23.70	27.60	40.10	38.00	31.60
2003	47.20	31.70	53.30	30.00	23.70	45.70	37.60	41.00	35.70	30.10	30.50	29.10	37.40
2004	34.50	36.30	42.20	44.20	32.20	21.70	23.40	37.80	38.20	67.90	89.00	47.10	37.50
2005	15.40	40.90	40.70	65.10	49.40	40.00	28.00	26.10	46.10	37.30	36.50	96.80	41.50
2006[1]	79.20	46.50	31.50	46.90	31.10	32.00	27.00	36.10	88.20	52.30	28.40	24.80	41.50

[1] Preliminary.   Source: National Agricultural Statistics Service, U.S. Department of Agriculture (NASS-USDA)

Frozen Vegetables: January 1 and July 1 Cold Storage Holdings in the U.S.   In Thousands of Pounds

Crop	2002 July 1	2003 Jan. 1	2004 July 1	2004 Jan. 1	2004 July 1	2005 Jan. 1	2005 July 1	2006 Jan. 1	2006 July 1	2007[1] Jan. 1
Asparagus	10,954	6,988	10,977	7,368	14,064	9,280	13,943	9,029	11,929	6,178
Limas, Fordhook	7,323	13,068	4,646	5,984	1,960	8,450	3,502	7,687	2,368	6,543
Limas, Baby	30,017	45,544	20,570	46,383	21,716	48,955	27,360	40,867	21,851	41,849
Green Beans, Reg. Cut	48,312	167,669	55,559	126,175	51,147	151,229	76,655	171,319	24,377	183,610
Green Beans, Fr. Style	7,398	19,726	7,272	23,166	6,596	22,925	8,157	22,341	8,388	27,433
Broccoli, Spears	56,679	49,326	53,689	30,185	50,314	35,882	45,581	35,814	32,699	27,628
Broccoli, Chopped & Cut	66,486	67,727	81,782	47,135	58,843	57,607	62,382	62,561	61,769	46,855
Brussels sprouts	10,645	20,220	11,053	18,961	11,588	23,519	16,028	21,660	10,243	21,650
Carrots, Diced	47,110	99,188	36,340	98,398	49,485	117,745	63,871	128,877	64,540	117,159
Carrots, Other	91,705	143,368	90,741	154,404	75,288	140,440	93,702	150,317	97,528	127,449
Cauliflower	25,589	35,635	16,083	28,146	12,518	37,123	19,916	43,836	18,694	38,196
Corn, Cut	137,242	402,164	176,505	494,490	227,404	502,025	234,965	464,177	188,556	475,671
Corn, Cob	85,566	262,338	108,477	288,957	109,612	242,271	78,525	263,818	71,738	281,694
Mixed vegetables	45,248	41,396	42,360	43,537	56,156	46,892	49,493	55,236	50,856	51,925
Okra	35,964	46,616	35,847	37,596	33,111	33,875	28,097	31,734	26,363	31,507
Onion Rings	8,619	9,636	7,772	6,915	8,426	6,587	6,181	4,757	7,532	7,533
Onions, Other	32,143	29,844	28,757	31,717	28,862	33,278	39,424	43,349	38,192	37,386
Blackeye Peas	5,896	6,323	5,340	3,292	3,004	2,693	1,878	2,348	4,080	4,784
Green Peas	198,452	171,161	162,836	180,850	206,413	230,326	227,162	214,851	222,513	230,351
Peas and Carrots Mixed	6,746	6,597	7,897	6,581	5,674	5,641	5,416	5,227	5,422	4,946
Spinach	106,198	56,193	104,522	46,492	83,287	34,724	87,983	42,464	107,607	52,674
Squash, Dummer/Zucchini	36,878	44,617	33,549	43,614	31,326	45,724	39,164	61,518	50,704	64,255
Southern greens	26,478	22,986	20,243	18,749	16,330	17,328	18,905	13,750	17,546	14,826
Other Vegetables	24,187	313,421	265,556	329,499	248,416	363,579	267,205	353,315	238,391	323,249
Total	1,369,523	2,081,751	1,388,373	2,118,594	1,411,540	2,218,098	1,515,495	2,250,852	1,413,886	2,225,351
Potatoes, French Fries	937,933	877,292	900,194	869,521	864,111	838,438	947,971	848,595	877,400	758,254
Potatoes, Other Frozen	285,605	253,920	281,594	250,897	263,341	236,381	242,493	202,504	230,710	196,566
Potatoes, Total	1,223,538	1,131,212	1,181,788	1,120,418	1,127,452	1,074,819	1,190,464	1,051,099	1,108,110	954,820
Grand total	2,593,061	3,212,963	2,570,161	3,239,012	2,538,992	3,292,917	2,705,959	3,301,951	2,521,996	3,180,171

[1] Preliminary.   Source: National Agricultural Statistics Service, U.S. Department of Agriculture (NASS-USDA)

Wheat

Wheat is a cereal grass, but before cultivation it was a wild grass. It has been grown in temperate regions and cultivated for food since prehistoric times. Wheat is believed to have originated in southwestern Asia. Archeological research indicates that wheat was grown as a crop in the Nile Valley about 5,000 BC. Wheat is not native to the US and was first grown here in 1602 near the Massachusetts coast. The common types of wheat grown in the US are spring and winter wheat. Wheat planted in the spring for summer or autumn harvest is mostly red wheat. Wheat planted in the fall or winter for spring harvest is mostly white wheat. Winter wheat accounts for nearly three-fourths of total US production. Wheat is used mainly as a human food and supplies about 20% of the food calories for the world's population. The primary use for wheat is flour, but it is also used for brewing and distilling, and for making oil, gluten, straw for livestock bedding, livestock feed, hay or silage, newsprint, and other products.

Wheat futures and options are traded on the Mercado a Termino de Buenos Aires (MAT), Sydney Futures Exchange (SFE), London International Financial Futures and Options Exchange (LIFFE), Marche a Terme International de France (MATIF), Budapest Commodity Exchange (BCE), the Chicago Board of Trade (CBOT), the Kansas City Board of Trade (KCBT), the Minneapolis Grain Exchange (MGE), the Mid America Commodity Exchange (MidAm) and the Winnipeg Commodity Exchange (WCE). The Chicago Board of Trade's wheat futures contract calls for the delivery of soft red wheat (No. 1 and 2), hard red winter wheat (No. 1 and 2), dark northern spring wheat (No. 1 and 2), No.1 northern spring at 3 cents/bushel premium, or No. 2 northern spring at par.

Prices – Wheat prices on the CBOT nearest futures chart rallied sharply in the first half of 2006 by a total of 90% from a low of $2.925 per bushel in December 2005 to a 10-year high of $5.57 per bushel in October 2006. Wheat prices then fell back through the remainder of 2006 on long liquidation pressure, finally closing 2006 at $5.01 per bushel, up +48% yr/yr. The rally in wheat prices in 2006 was due to very poor wheat crops in key world growing areas. The US wheat crop in 2006-07 was hurt by hot and dry weather in the southern Plains and fell –14.2% yr/yr to 1.806 billion bushels. That was the second smallest crop in the US in the past 25 years and caused the US wheat carry-over in 2006-07 to fall sharply by –17.3% to 472 million bushels, which was the tightest inventory level in 10 years. However, growing conditions were also poor in Europe where heat caused significant damage to the wheat crop. The situation was even worse in Australia where a severe drought slashed wheat production by about one-third. The end result was a sharp –18% decline in the global carry-over of wheat in 2006-07 to 120.8 metric tons.

Supply – World wheat production in the 2006-07 marketing year fell –4.4% to 593.108 million metric tons

from the record high of 628.585 million metric tons seen in 2004-05. The world's largest wheat producers are the European Union with 20% of world production in 2006-07, China (18%), India (12%), the US (8%), Russia (7%), and Canada (5%). China's wheat production in 2006-07 rose +17.5% yr/yr to 103.5 million metric tons, but still well below its record high of 123.289 million metric tons in 1997-98. Australia's wheat production fell –58.0% yr/yr to 10.500 million metric tons in 2006-07, which was well below its record high of 26.132 million metric tons in 2003-04. The world land area harvested with wheat in 2006-07 fell –2.9% yr/yr to 212.0 million hectares (1 hectare equals 10,000 square meters or 2.471 acres), but remaining above 209.9 million hectares in 2003-04, which was the smallest wheat harvest area since 1970-71. World wheat yield in 2006-07 was unchanged at 2.80 metric tons per hectare, remaining below the record high of 2.90 metric tons per hectare seen in 2004-05.

US wheat production in 2006-07 fell –13.9% yr/yr to 1.812 billion bushels, which was well below the record US wheat crop of 2.785 billion bushels seen in 1981-82. The US winter wheat crop in 2006 fell –13.4% yr/yr to 1.298 billion bushels, which was well below the record winter wheat crop of 2.097 billion bushels seen in 1981. US production of durum wheat in 2006 fell –47.1% yr/yr to 53.475 million bushels. US production of other spring wheat fell –8.7% yr/yr to 460.480 million bushels. The largest US producing states of winter wheat are Kansas with 22% of US production in 2006, Montana with 6%, Washington with 9%, and Oklahoma with 6%. US farmers planted 57.344 million acres of wheat in 2006, which was up +0.2% yr/yr and was the second smallest wheat acreage since 1972. US wheat yield in 2006-07 was 38.7 bushels per acre, which was well below the record yield of 44.2 bushels per acre seen in 2003-04. Ending stocks for US wheat for 2006-07 are projected by the USDA at 472.2 million bushels, down –17.3% yr/yr from 571.2 million bushels in 2005-06.

Demand – World wheat utilization in 2006-07 fell –1.4% yr/yr to 615.2 million metric tons, down from the 2005-06 record high of 623.8. US consumption of wheat in 2006-07 rose +0.4% yr/yr to 1.151 billion bushels, which was well below the record high of 1.381 billion bushels seen in 1998-99. The consumption breakdown shows that 84% of US wheat consumption in 2006-07 went for food, 13% for feed and residuals, and 7% for seed.

Trade – World trade in wheat in 2006-07 fell –1.6% yr/yr to 111.9 million metric tons from the record of 113.7 million metric tons seen in 2005-06. US exports of wheat in 2006-07 fell –13.3% yr/yr to 875,000 million bushels from 1.009 billion bushels in 2005-06 and remained well below the record of 1.771 billion bushels of exports seen in 1981-82. US imports of wheat in 2006-07 rose sharply by +40.8% to 115.8 million bushels and showed a further recovery from the 16-year low of 63.0 million bushels seen in 2003-04.

World Production of Wheat   In Thousands of Metric Tons

Year	Argentina	Australia	Canada	China	EU-25	India	Iran	Pakistan	Kazak-hstan	Russia	Turkey	United States	World Total
1997-98	15,740	19,224	24,280	123,289	94,181	69,350	10,000	8,950	16,651	44,200	16,000	67,534	609,959
1998-99	13,300	21,465	24,082	109,726	103,085	66,350	12,000	4,700	18,694	27,000	18,000	69,327	589,960
1999-00	16,400	24,757	26,941	113,880	114,741	70,780	8,500	11,200	17,858	31,000	16,500	62,475	585,817
2000-01	16,230	22,108	26,519	99,640	124,197	76,369	8,000	9,100	21,079	34,450	18,000	60,641	581,500
2001-02	15,500	24,299	20,568	93,873	113,553	69,680	9,500	12,700	19,024	46,900	15,500	53,001	581,138
2002-03	12,300	10,132	16,198	90,290	124,829	71,810	12,450	12,600	18,227	50,550	16,800	43,705	567,643
2003-04	14,500	26,132	23,552	86,490	106,878	65,100	13,500	11,000	19,183	34,100	16,800	63,814	554,595
2004-05[1]	16,000	22,600	25,860	91,950	136,778	72,150	14,000	9,950	19,500	45,400	18,500	58,738	628,585
2005-06[2]	14,500	25,000	26,775	97,450	122,665	68,640	14,500	11,000	21,500	47,700	18,000	57,280	620,607
2006-07[3]	14,200	10,500	27,300	103,500	117,052	69,350	14,000	13,500	21,700	43,500	18,000	49,316	593,108

[1] Preliminary.   [2] Estimate.   [3] Forecast.   Source: Foreign Agricultural Service, U.S. Department of Agriculture (FAS-USDA)

World Supply and Demand of Wheat   In Millions of Metric Tons/Hectares

Crop Year	Area Harvested	Yield	Pro-duction	World Trade	Utilization Total	Ending Stocks	Stocks as a % of Utilization
1997-98	228.4	2.70	610.0	104.5	577.3	197.1	34.1
1998-99	225.1	2.60	590.0	102.0	579.0	208.1	35.9
1999-00	215.4	2.70	585.8	112.7	585.0	208.9	35.7
2000-01	217.6	2.70	581.5	104.1	583.9	206.5	35.4
2001-02	214.7	2.70	581.1	110.8	585.0	202.7	34.6
2002-03	214.6	2.60	567.6	110.1	603.8	166.6	27.6
2003-04	209.9	2.60	554.6	104.5	588.5	132.7	22.5
2004-05[1]	218.9	2.90	628.8	113.1	610.1	151.4	24.8
2005-06[2]	218.3	2.80	619.7	113.7	623.8	147.4	23.6
2006-07[3]	212.0	2.80	588.6	111.9	615.2	120.7	19.6

[1] Preliminary.   [2] Estimate.   [3] Forecast.   Source: Foreign Agricultural Service, U.S. Department of Agriculture (FAS-USDA)

Salient Statistics of Wheat in the United States

Crop Year	Planting Intentions	Acreage Harvested Winter	Spring	All	Average - All Yield Per Acre in Bushels	Value of Production $1,000	Foreign Trade[5] Domestic Exports[2]	Imports[3]	Per Capita[4] Consumption Flour	Cereal
		1,000 Acres					In Millions of Bushels		In Pounds	
1997-98	70,412	41,340	21,500	62,840	39.5	8,286,741	1,040.4	94.9	147.0	3.9
1998-99	65,821	40,126	18,876	59,002	43.2	6,780,623	1,045.7	103.0	143.0	3.9
1999-00	62,664	35,436	18,337	53,773	42.7	5,593,989	1,086.5	94.5	144.0	3.8
2000-01	62,549	35,002	18,061	53,063	42.0	5,782,107	1,062.0	89.8	146.0	3.8
2001-02	59,597	31,295	17,338	48,633	40.2	5,440,217	962.3	107.6	141.0	3.8
2002-03	60,318	29,742	16,166	45,824	35.0	5,637,416	850.2	77.4	137.0	3.7
2003-04	62,141	36,753	16,310	53,063	44.2	7,929,039	1,158.3	63.0	137.0	3.7
2004-05	59,674	34,462	15,537	49,999	43.2	7,283,324	1,065.9	70.6	134.0	3.7
2005-06	57,229	33,794	16,325	50,119	42.0	7,171,441	1,009.3	81.7	----	----
2006-07[1]	57,344	31,117	16,769	46,810	38.7	7,721,028	875.0	115.0	----	----

[1] Preliminary.   [2] Includes flour milled from imported wheat.   [3] Total wheat, flour & other products.   [4] Civilian only.   [5] Year beginning June.
Source: Economic Research Service, U.S. Department of Agriculture (ERS-USDA)

Supply and Distribution of Wheat in the United States   In Millions of Bushels

Crop Year Beginning June 1	Supply Stocks, June 1 On Farms	Mills, Elevators[3]	Total Stocks	Production	Imports[4]	Total Supply	Domestic Disappearance Food	Seed	Feed & Res-idual[5]	Total	Exports[4]	Total Disappear-ance
1997-98	154.6	289.0	443.6	2,481.5	94.9	3,020.0	914.1	92.5	250.5	1,257.1	1,040.4	2,297.5
1998-99	224.2	498.3	722.5	2,547.3	103.0	3,372.8	909.7	80.4	390.7	1,381.1	1,045.7	2,426.9
1999-00	277.7	668.2	945.9	2,299.0	94.5	3,336.0	921.0	91.7	279.3	1,299.7	1,086.5	2,386.2
2000-01	226.8	723.0	949.7	2,232.5	89.8	3,267.7	949.6	79.5	300.4	1,329.5	1,062.0	2,391.6
2001-02	197.3	678.9	876.2	1,957.0	107.6	2,931.2	926.4	83.4	182.0	1,191.8	962.3	2,154.1
2002-03	216.8	560.3	777.1	1,605.9	77.4	2,460.4	918.6	84.4	115.7	1,118.7	850.2	1,968.9
2003-04	132.1	359.3	491.4	2,344.8	63.0	2,899.2	911.9	79.7	202.9	1,194.4	1,158.3	2,352.8
2004-05	131.9	414.6	546.4	2,158.2	70.6	2,775.3	909.6	77.6	182.1	1,169.2	1,065.9	2,235.2
2005-06[1]	161.3	378.8	540.1	2,104.7	81.7	2,726.5	915.2	77.7	153.2	1,146.1	1,009.3	2,155.3
2006-07[2]	111.0	460.2	571.2	1,812.0	115.0	2,498.2	925.0	81.0	145.0	1,151.0	875.0	2,026.0

[1] Preliminary.   [2] Estimate.   [3] Also warehouses and all off-farm storage not otherwise designated, including flour mills.   [4] Imports & exports are for wheat, including flour & other products in terms of wheat.   [5] Mostly feed use.   Source: Economic Research Service, U.S. Department of Agriculture

WHEAT

Stocks, Production and Exports of Wheat in the United States, by Class   In Millions of Bushels

Year Beginning June 1	Hard Spring Stocks June 1	Hard Spring Pro-duction	Hard Spring Exports[3]	Durum[2] Stocks June 1	Durum[2] Pro-duction	Durum[2] Exports[3]	Hard Winter Stocks June 1	Hard Winter Pro-duction	Hard Winter Exports[3]	Soft Red Winter Stocks June 1	Soft Red Winter Pro-duction	Soft Red Winter Exports[3]	White Stocks June 1	White Pro-duction	White Exports[3]
1997-98	166	491	240	31	88	57	143	1,098	358	45	472	180	59	332	205
1998-99	220	486	247	26	138	40	307	1,180	453	80	443	105	90	301	198
1999-00	233	448	230	55	99	44	435	1,051	486	136	454	170	87	247	160
2000-01	218	502	230	50	110	50	458	846	403	133	471	176	91	303	203
2001-02	210	476	216	45	84	50	411	767	349	135	400	199	75	232	147
2002-03	230	351	259	33	80	32	363	620	309	78	321	105	73	233	148
2003-04	145	500	272	28	97	44	188	1,071	512	55	380	140	75	297	192
2004-05	157	525	314	26	90	31	227	856	388	64	380	122	72	306	207
2005-06	159	467	282	38	101	47	193	930	430	88	309	76	63	298	175
2006-07[1]	132	432	250	40	53	30	215	682	265	106	390	130	78	254	200

[1] Preliminary.   [2] Includes Red Durum.   [3] Includes four made from U.S. wheat & shipments to territories.   Source: Economic Research Service, U.S. Department of Agriculture (ERS-USDA)

Seeded Acreage, Yield and Production of all Wheat in the United States

Year	Seeded Acreage – 1,000 Acres Winter	Seeded Acreage Other Spring	Seeded Acreage Durum	Seeded Acreage All	Yield Per Harvested Acre (Bushels) Winter	Yield Other Spring	Yield Durum	Yield All	Production (1,000,000 Bushels) Winter	Production Other Spring	Production Durum	Production All
1997	47,985	19,117	3,310	70,412	44.6	29.9	27.6	39.5	1,845.5	548.2	87.8	2,481.5
1998	46,449	15,567	3,805	65,821	46.9	34.9	37.0	43.2	1,880.7	528.5	138.1	2,547.3
1999	43,331	15,348	4,035	62,714	47.8	34.1	27.8	42.7	1,696.6	503.1	99.3	2,299.0
2000	43,393	15,299	3,937	62,629	44.7	38.4	30.7	42.0	1,562.7	556.6	109.8	2,232.5
2001	41,078	15,609	2,910	59,597	43.5	35.2	30.0	40.2	1,361.5	512.0	83.6	1,957.0
2002	41,766	15,639	2,913	60,318	38.2	29.1	29.5	35.0	1,137.0	388.9	80.0	1,605.9
2003	45,384	13,842	2,915	62,141	46.7	39.5	33.7	44.2	1,716.7	531.4	96.6	2,344.8
2004	43,350	13,763	2,561	59,674	43.5	43.2	38.0	43.2	1,499.4	568.9	89.9	2,158.2
2005	40,433	14,036	2,760	57,229	44.4	37.1	37.2	42.0	1,499.1	504.5	101.1	2,104.7
2006[1]	40,575	14,899	1,870	57,344	41.7	33.2	29.5	38.7	1,298.1	460.5	53.5	1,812.0

[1] Preliminary.   Source: Economic Research Service, U.S. Department of Agriculture (ERS-USDA)

Production of Winter Wheat in the United States, by State   In Thousands of Bushels

Year	Colorado	Idaho	Illinois	Kansas	Missouri	Montana	Neb-raska	Ohio	Okla-homa	Oregon	Texas	Wash-ington	Total
1997	86,400	68,800	66,490	501,400	58,320	55,100	70,300	68,670	169,600	53,790	118,900	141,900	1,845,528
1998	99,450	63,140	57,600	494,900	57,500	48,750	82,800	74,240	198,900	52,930	136,500	136,500	1,880,733
1999	103,200	53,960	60,600	432,400	44,160	36,860	81,600	72,100	150,500	29,610	122,400	96,860	1,696,580
2000	68,150	65,700	52,440	347,800	49,400	44,550	59,400	79,920	142,800	45,260	66,000	131,400	1,562,733
2001	66,000	51,830	43,920	328,000	41,040	19,140	59,200	60,300	122,100	28,000	108,800	106,750	1,361,479
2002	36,300	48,510	30,870	270,600	33,440	21,840	50,160	50,220	103,600	29,820	78,300	104,400	1,137,001
2003	77,000	57,600	52,650	480,000	53,070	67,340	83,720	68,000	179,400	47,940	96,600	117,000	1,716,721
2004	45,900	63,000	53,100	314,500	48,360	66,830	61,050	55,180	164,500	47,580	108,500	117,250	1,499,434
2005	52,800	66,430	36,600	380,000	29,160	94,500	68,640	58,930	128,000	47,580	96,000	120,600	1,499,129
2006[1]	39,900	54,670	60,970	291,200	49,140	82,560	61,200	65,280	81,600	38,690	33,600	118,800	1,298,081

[1] Preliminary.   Source: Crop Reporting Board, U.S. Department of Agriculture (CRB-USDA)

Official Winter Wheat Crop Production Reports in the United States   In Thousands of Bushels

Crop Year	May 1	June 1	July 1	August 1	September 1	Current December	Final
1997-98	1,561,470	1,603,580	1,780,554	1,855,474	-----	-----	1,845,528
1998-99	1,706,784	1,743,294	1,898,719	1,914,359	-----	-----	1,880,733
1999-00	1,614,799	1,611,559	1,673,222	1,688,582	-----	-----	1,696,580
2000-01	1,648,805	1,621,966	1,588,376	1,594,321	-----	-----	1,561,723
2001-02	1,341,381	1,321,126	1,366,192	1,385,048	-----	-----	1,361,479
2002-03	1,300,726	1,237,671	1,178,320	1,158,710	-----	-----	1,137,001
2003-04	1,563,314	1,626,376	1,715,912	1,712,150	-----	-----	1,716,721
2004-05	1,550,395	1,530,742	1,469,735	1,489,408	-----	-----	1,499,434
2005-06	1,590,862	1,545,971	1,525,302	1,520,848	-----	-----	1,499,129
2006-07[1]	1,322,831	1,263,766	1,280,005	1,283,134	-----	-----	1,298,081

[1] Preliminary.   Source: Crop Reporting Board, U.S. Department of Agriculture (CRB-USDA)

Production of All Spring Wheat in the United States, by State   In Thousands of Bushels

| | | | Durum Wheat | | | | | | Other Spring Wheat | | | | | |
Year	Arizona	California	Mon-tana	North Dakota	South Dakota	Total Durum	Idaho	Minne-sota	Mon-tana	North Dakota	Oregon	South Dakota	Wash-ington	Total Other
1997	8,010	13,680	7,540	57,860	513	87,783	45,030	75,200	118,900	210,000	6,600	63,000	23,220	548,155
1998	15,120	15,750	12,040	94,400	624	138,119	39,270	78,720	108,000	211,200	4,560	59,200	20,925	528,469
1999	7,275	8,925	9,450	72,000	1,512	99,322	50,560	78,000	108,000	168,000	5,049	59,850	27,280	503,108
2000	8,075	9,700	13,160	78,300	468	109,805	42,750	95,550	77,500	233,600	8,280	60,040	33,480	556,632
2001	7,917	8,505	11,880	54,600	576	83,556	33,320	79,200	65,550	234,600	4,650	64,350	25,830	512,008
2002	8,928	9,000	12,995	48,750	147	79,960	29,900	61,200	75,900	165,200	4,680	24,000	25,370	388,917
2003	11,500	11,500	14,490	58,410	621	96,637	27,060	104,400	60,500	252,800	5,600	56,280	22,345	531,402
2004	9,603	9,000	17,985	52,800	450	89,893	38,710	88,550	88,350	243,950	8,400	71,910	26,250	568,918
2005	7,900	6,555	16,380	68,250	260	101,105	32,400	70,930	81,600	224,400	5,980	67,600	18,700	504,456
2006[1]	7,400	6,435	6,715	31,500	90	53,475	34,310	77,550	63,800	212,350	5,750	42,600	21,250	460,480

[1] Preliminary.   Source: Crop Reporting Board, U.S. Department of Agriculture (CRB-USDA)

Grindings of Wheat by Mills in the United States   In Millions of Bushels (60 Pounds Each)

Year	July	Aug.	Sept.	Oct.	Nov.	Dec.	Jan.	Feb.	Mar.	Apr.	May	June	Total
1997-98	76.4	75.8	78.4	82.7	75.3	74.8	-----	215.5	-----	-----	216.6	-----	895.5
1998-99	-----	224.7	-----	-----	238.6	-----	-----	213.5	-----	-----	228.0	-----	904.9
1999-00	-----	234.0	-----	-----	242.2	-----	-----	225.6	-----	-----	226.8	-----	928.7
2000-01	-----	244.7	-----	-----	247.7	-----	-----	223.8	-----	-----	221.3	-----	937.5
2001-02	-----	230.2	-----	-----	238.7	-----	-----	217.0	-----	-----	217.6	-----	903.6
2002-03	-----	230.3	-----	-----	224.4	-----	-----	215.8	-----	-----	217.4	-----	888.0
2003-04	-----	231.8	-----	-----	224.2	-----	-----	210.9	-----	-----	212.3	-----	879.1
2004-05	-----	224.8	-----	-----	222.1	-----	-----	214.9	-----	-----	216.5	-----	878.3
2005-06	-----	229.3	-----	-----	223.4	-----	-----	215.9	-----	-----	214.6	-----	883.2
2006-07[1]	-----	228.8	-----	-----	224.7	-----	-----	-----	-----	-----	-----	-----	907.1

[1] Preliminary.   Source: Bureau of the Census, U.S. Department of Commerce

Wheat Stocks in the United States   In Millions of Bushels

| | On Farms | | | | Off Farms | | | | Total Stocks | | | |
Year	Mar. 1	June 1	Sept. 1	Dec. 1	Mar. 1	June 1	Sept. 1	Dec. 1	Mar. 1	June 1	Sept. 1	Dec. 1
1997	320.8	154.6	794.4	604.0	501.1	289.0	1,282.0	1,015.2	821.8	443.6	2,076.3	1,619.2
1998	399.9	224.2	885.7	680.2	766.6	498.3	1,499.6	1,215.5	1,166.6	722.5	2,385.3	1,895.7
1999	471.2	277.7	888.1	647.4	979.2	668.2	1,557.0	1,236.3	1,450.4	945.9	2,445.0	1,883.7
2000	424.7	226.8	808.4	623.4	991.8	723.0	1,544.3	1,182.7	1,416.5	949.7	2,352.7	1,806.1
2001	384.8	197.3	696.9	517.9	953.6	678.9	1,459.0	1,105.6	1,338.4	876.2	2,155.8	1,623.5
2002	338.5	216.8	580.2	384.8	871.3	560.3	1,170.8	935.1	1,209.8	777.1	1,751.0	1,319.9
2003	236.3	132.1	687.3	491.9	670.3	359.3	1,351.7	1,028.4	906.6	491.4	2,039.0	1,520.3
2004	257.9	131.9	790.6	531.0	762.7	414.6	1,147.8	899.3	1,020.6	546.4	1,938.4	1,430.3
2005	304.7	161.3	721.4	513.0	679.7	378.8	1,201.9	916.4	984.4	540.1	1,923.3	1,429.4
2006[1]	256.0	111.0	572.0	403.3	716.2	460.2	1,178.5	911.4	972.2	571.2	1,750.5	1,314.6

[1] Preliminary.   Source: National Agricultural Statistics Service, U.S. Department of Agriculture (NASS-USDA)

Wheat Supply and Distribution in Canada, Australia and Argentina   In Millions of Metric Tons

| | Canada (Year Beginning Aug. 1) | | | | | Australia (Year Beginning Oct. 1) | | | | | Argentina (Year Beginning Dec. 1) | | | | |
| | Supply | | | Disappearance | | Supply | | | Disappearance | | Supply | | | Disappearance | |
Crop Year	Stocks Aug. 1	New Crop	Total Supply	Domestic	Exports[3]	Stocks Oct. 1	New Crop	Total Supply	Domestic	Exports[3]	Stocks Dec. 1	New Crop	Total Supply	Domestic	Exports[3]
1997-98	9.0	24.3	33.3	7.3	20.1	2.4	19.2	21.6	4.0	15.3	1.0	15.7	16.7	4.8	11.2
1998-99	6.0	24.1	30.1	8.1	14.7	2.3	21.5	23.8	4.5	16.5	.8	13.3	14.1	4.9	8.6
1999-00	7.4	26.9	34.4	8.1	19.2	2.8	24.8	27.6	5.2	17.8	.7	16.4	17.1	4.9	11.6
2000-01	7.3	26.5	33.8	7.0	17.3	4.6	22.1	26.7	5.3	15.9	.6	16.2	16.8	5.0	11.3
2001-02	9.7	20.6	30.2	7.6	16.3	5.5	24.3	29.8	5.4	16.4	.6	15.5	16.1	4.9	10.1
2002-03	6.7	16.2	22.9	8.2	9.4	8.0	10.1	18.2	6.2	9.1	1.1	12.3	13.4	5.2	6.8
2003-04	5.7	23.6	29.3	7.6	15.8	3.1	26.1	29.3	6.0	18.0	1.5	14.5	16.0	5.2	9.4
2004-05	6.1	25.9	31.9	9.4	14.9	5.4	22.6	28.0	6.2	14.7	1.4	16.0	17.4	5.0	11.8
2005-06[1]	7.9	26.8	34.7	9.2	16.1	7.1	24.5	31.6	6.4	16.0	.6	14.5	15.1	5.0	9.6
2006-07[2]	9.7	27.3	37.0	10.2	20.5	9.3	10.5	19.8	6.9	10.5	.5	14.2	14.7	4.9	9.5

[1] Preliminary.   [2] Forecast.   [3] Including flour.   Source: Foreign Agricultural Service, U.S. Department of Agriculture (FAS-USDA)

WHEAT

Quarterly Supply and Disappearance of Wheat in the United States — In Millions of Bushels

Crop Year Beginning June 1	Beginning Stocks	Production	Imports[3]	Total Supply	Food	Seed	Feed & Residual[6]	Total	Exports[3]	Disap-pearance	Gov't Owned[4]	Privately Owned[5]	Total Stocks
1996-7	376.0	2,277.4	92.3	2,745.7	890.7	102.3	307.6	1,300.6	1,001.5	2,302.1	93.0	350.6	443.6
June-Aug.	376.0	2,277.4	14.9	2,668.3	223.7	8.7	377.5	610.0	334.1	944.1	109.5	1,614.7	1,724.2
Sept.-Nov.	1,724.2	-----	20.7	1,744.9	233.8	59.9	-76.0	217.8	308.3	526.1	96.1	1,122.7	1,218.8
Dec.-Feb.	1,218.8	-----	27.1	1,245.9	212.7	1.8	30.3	244.7	179.3	424.1	95.3	726.5	821.8
Mar.-May	821.8	-----	29.7	851.6	220.5	31.8	-24.2	228.1	179.8	407.9	93.0	350.6	443.6
1997-8	443.6	2,481.5	94.9	3,020.0	914.1	92.5	250.5	1,257.1	1,040.4	2,297.5	94.2	628.3	722.5
June-Aug.	443.6	2,481.5	22.7	2,947.8	227.9	3.1	352.2	583.2	288.2	871.4	93.2	1,983.1	2,076.3
Sept.-Nov.	2,076.3	-----	22.8	2,099.1	238.7	58.6	-113.4	183.9	296.0	479.9	93.1	1,526.1	1,619.2
Dec.-Feb.	1,619.2	-----	23.8	1,643.0	219.2	2.1	.3	221.6	254.9	476.4	93.0	1,073.6	1,166.6
Mar.-May	1,166.6	-----	25.7	1,192.2	228.3	28.7	11.4	268.4	201.3	469.8	94.2	628.3	722.5
1998-9	722.5	2,547.3	103.0	3,372.8	909.7	80.5	542.1	1,532.4	1,042.2	2,574.6	127.9	818.0	945.9
June-Aug.	722.5	2,547.3	24.4	3,294.2	225.7	1.0	424.9	651.6	257.3	908.9	99.8	2,285.5	2,385.3
Sept.-Nov.	2,385.3	-----	23.9	2,409.2	240.7	54.9	73.8	369.5	291.8	661.2	126.6	1,769.1	1,895.7
Dec.-Feb.	1,895.7	-----	27.7	1,923.4	213.2	1.4	11.6	226.2	246.8	473.0	124.2	1,326.2	1,450.4
Mar.-May	1,450.4	-----	27.0	1,477.4	230.1	23.2	31.8	285.1	246.3	531.5	127.9	818.0	945.9
1999-00	945.9	2,299.0	94.5	3,339.4	924.7	91.6	283.8	1,300.1	1,089.5	2,389.6	103.9	845.8	949.7
June-Aug.	945.9	2,299.0	30.6	3,275.5	230.5	6.4	270.0	506.9	323.6	830.5	132.2	2,312.8	2,445.0
Sept.-Nov.	2,445.0	-----	19.5	2,464.5	241.1	54.6	-8.0	287.7	291.3	579.0	115.0	1,770.6	1,885.6
Dec.-Feb.	1,885.6	-----	19.4	1,905.1	220.9	2.3	30.7	253.9	235.9	489.8	108.7	1,306.6	1,416.5
Mar.-May	1,415.3	-----	25.0	1,440.3	232.2	28.4	-8.8	251.8	238.8	490.6	103.9	845.8	949.7
2000-1	949.7	2,228.2	89.8	3,267.7	949.6	79.5	300.4	1,329.5	1,062.0	2,391.6	97.0	779.2	876.2
June-Aug.	949.7	2,228.2	20.4	3,198.3	238.8	1.1	317.9	557.8	287.8	845.6	108.9	2,243.8	2,352.7
Sept.-Nov.	2,352.7	-----	25.1	2,377.8	253.0	49.8	-24.5	278.4	293.3	571.6	102.9	1,703.2	1,806.1
Dec.-Feb.	1,806.1	-----	21.4	1,827.5	228.2	3.5	11.4	243.1	246.1	489.1	104.4	1,234.0	1,338.4
Mar.-May	1,338.4	-----	22.9	1,361.3	229.7	25.2	-4.5	250.3	234.8	485.1	97.0	779.2	876.2
2001-2	876.2	1,947.5	107.6	2,931.2	926.4	83.4	182.0	1,191.8	962.3	2,154.1	99.0	678.1	777.1
June-Aug.	876.2	1,947.5	25.7	2,849.3	233.8	3.5	237.9	475.2	218.3	693.5	97.7	2,058.1	2,155.8
Sept.-Nov.	2,155.8	-----	29.0	2,184.9	245.1	51.6	-23.1	273.6	287.8	561.4	96.9	1,526.6	1,623.5
Dec.-Feb.	1,623.5	-----	27.6	1,651.0	221.1	2.0	-6.6	216.5	224.7	441.2	96.9	1,112.9	1,209.8
Mar.-May	1,209.8	-----	25.2	1,235.0	226.4	26.3	-26.2	226.4	231.5	457.9	99.0	678.1	777.1
2002-03	777.1	1,605.9	77.4	2,460.4	918.6	84.4	115.7	1,118.7	850.2	1,968.9	66.4	425.0	491.4
June-Aug.	777.1	1,605.9	26.7	2,409.6	233.2	2.7	184.5	420.4	240.2	660.7	91.4	1,657.6	1,749.0
Sept.-Nov.	1,749.0	-----	23.1	1,772.1	237.8	54.6	-74.7	217.7	234.5	454.2	80.9	1,239.0	1,319.9
Dec.-Feb.	1,319.9	-----	12.7	1,332.6	218.9	3.1	14.1	236.1	189.8	425.9	74.1	832.5	906.6
Mar.-May	906.6	-----	14.9	921.6	228.4	23.9	-8.2	244.5	185.7	430.2	66.4	425.0	491.4
2003-04	491.4	2,344.8	63.1	2,899.3	911.9	79.6	202.9	1,194.4	1,158.1	2,352.5	60.9	485.5	546.4
June-Aug.	491.4	2,344.8	15.7	2,851.9	230.5	2.1	315.3	547.9	264.9	812.8	60.3	1,978.7	2,039.0
Sept.-Nov.	2,039.0	-----	17.8	2,056.7	239.6	53.3	-61.9	231.0	305.4	536.4	60.4	1,459.6	1,520.3
Dec.-Feb.	1,520.3	-----	12.9	1,533.2	215.9	2.2	3.1	221.2	291.4	512.6	60.0	960.6	1,020.6
Mar.-May	1,020.6	-----	16.7	1,037.3	225.9	22.0	-53.6	194.3	296.4	490.7	60.9	485.5	546.4
2004-05	546.4	2,158.2	70.6	2,775.2	904.6	78.9	188.9	1,172.4	1,062.9	2,235.3	54.0	486.1	540.1
June-Aug.	546.4	2,158.2	17.4	2,722.1	227.5	4.1	265.2	496.8	286.8	783.6	61.9	1,876.5	1,938.4
Sept.-Nov.	1,938.4	-----	18.7	1,957.1	235.6	48.2	-57.0	226.8	300.0	526.8	61.7	1,369.0	1,430.3
Dec.-Feb.	1,430.3	-----	17.8	1,448.1	216.3	2.4	7.7	226.4	237.4	463.8	55.9	928.5	984.4
Mar.-May	984.4	-----	16.7	1,001.1	225.2	24.2	-27.0	222.4	238.7	461.1	54.5	485.6	540.1
2005-06[1]	2,105.0	2,104.7	81.0	4,290.7	914.0	78.0	154.0	1,146.0	1,009.0	2,155.0			571.0
June-Aug.	540.1	2,104.7	19.0	2,663.0	231.0	2.0	263.0	496.0	244.0	740.0	48.3	1,875.0	1,923.0
Sept.-Nov.	1,923.0	-----	20.0	1,944.0	238.0	51.0	-61.0	228.0	286.0	514.0	44.1	1,385.4	1,429.0
Dec.-Feb.	1,429.0	-----	20.0	1,450.0	219.0	1.0	1.0	221.0	257.0	478.0			972.0
Mar.-May	972.0	-----	22.0	995.0	226.0	24.0	-49.0	201.0	222.0	423.0			571.0
2006-07[2]	571.0	1,812.0	112.0	2,495.0	954.0	114.0	332.0	1,400.0	852.0	2,252.0			
June-Aug.	571.0	1,812.0	26.0	2,410.0	233.0	2.0	211.0	446.0	214.0	660.0			1,751.0
Sept.-Nov.	1,743.0	-----	30.0	1,780.0	244.0	55.0	-45.0	254.0	212.0	466.0			1,315.0

[1] Preliminary.   [2] Forecast.   [3] Imports & exports include flour and other products expressed in wheat equivalent.   [4] Uncommitted, Government only.
[5] Includes total loans.   [6] Includes alcoholic beverages.   Source: Economic Research Service, U.S. Department of Agriculture (ERS-USDA)

Wheat Government Loan Program Data in the United States   Loan Rates (Cents Per Bushel)

Crop Year Beginning June 1	National Average[3]	Target Rate[4]	Corn Belt (Soft Red Winter)	Central & Southern Plains (Hard Winter)	Northern Plains (Spring & Durum)	Pacific Northwest (White)	Placed Under Loan	% of Production	Acquired by CCC Under Program	Total Stocks	Total CCC Stocks	CCC Loans	Farmer-Owned Reserve	"Free"
										In Millions of Bushels				
1998-99	258	NA	253	257	258	271	363	14.2	0	946	128	140	0	818
1999-00	258	NA	253	257	258	271	154	6.7	0	950	104	62	0	846
2000-01	258	NA	253	257	258	271	181	8.1	0	876	97	42	0	779
2001-02	258	NA	NA	NA	NA	NA	197	9.9	0	777	99	78	0	678
2002-03	280	386	NA	NA	NA	NA	120	7.5	2	491	66	51	0	425
2003-04	280	386	NA	NA	NA	NA	186	7.9	2	546	61	45	0	485
2004-05[1]	275	392	NA	NA	NA	NA				540	54	NA	0	486
2005-06[2]	275		NA	NA	NA	NA				571	43	NA	0	528

[1] Preliminary.   [2] Estimate.   [3] The national average loan rate at the farm as a percentage of the parity-priced wheat at the beginning of the marketing year.   [4] 1996-97 through 2001-02 marketing years, target prices not applicable.   NA = Not avaliable.   *Source: Agricultural Marketing Service, U.S. Department of Agriculture (AMS-USDA)*

Exports of Wheat (Only)[2] from the United States   In Thousands of Bushels

Year	June	July	Aug.	Sept.	Oct.	Nov.	Dec.	Jan.	Feb.	Mar.	Apr.	May	Total
1998-99	67,372	86,605	96,664	90,507	109,168	81,913	96,486	73,017	63,794	65,522	86,066	85,057	1,002,171
1999-00	90,594	110,814	107,168	91,438	96,154	89,211	84,460	71,763	64,198	68,836	73,815	87,789	1,036,240
2000-01	88,581	82,739	104,944	113,785	82,716	86,034	94,705	60,743	85,797	71,502	83,157	68,908	1,023,611
2001-02	59,190	64,911	89,582	86,941	94,598	99,800	81,369	72,114	63,446	78,070	84,211	58,449	932,681
2002-03	63,219	78,013	92,345	73,606	78,866	75,678	69,485	62,769	48,618	65,990	55,764	59,438	823,791
2003-04	54,665	88,042	115,869	125,312	101,168	76,222	79,811	109,607	94,480	96,685	102,588	91,917	1,136,366
2004-05	80,599	97,962	103,222	119,965	92,634	83,947	81,718	77,349	73,131	76,612	81,885	75,575	1,044,599
2005-06	64,553	90,760	83,173	102,761	103,423	77,164	91,531	84,659	71,175	74,420	69,050	72,209	984,878
2006-07[1]	63,115	67,846	78,225	76,431	70,752	60,595							833,928

[1] Preliminary.   [2] Grains.   *Source: Economic Research Service, U.S. Department of Agriculture (ERS-USDA)*

United States Wheat and Wheat Flour Imports and Exports   In Thousands of Bushels

Crop Year Beginning June 1	Wheat — Suitable for Milling	Wheat — Unfit for Human Consumption	Grain	Flour & Products[2]	Total	P.L. 480	Foreign Donations Sec. 416	Aid[3]	Total Concessional	CCC Export Credit	Export Exhancement Programs	Total U.S. Wheat Exports
			Wheat Equivalent				In Thousands of Metric Tons					
1997-98	73,245	----	73,245	21,556	94,801	1,453	0	NA	1,727	5,460	0	25,791
1998-99	79,766	----	79,768	23,219	102,987	556	4,682	NA	5,334	3,621	0	28,806
1999-00	72,408	----	72,407	22,104	94,512	674	2,635	NA	3,436	3,691	0	27,838
2000-01	66,313	----	66,313	23,511	89,824	1,294	1,638	NA	3,109	4,026	0	25,275
2001-02	82,615	----	82,615	24,935	107,551	1,093	875	NA	2,035	4,614	0	25,411
2002-03	52,889	----	49,741	27,633	77,374	1,475	213	NA	2,081	3,633	0	24,395
2003-04	37,156	----	37,156	25,871	63,026	1,211	20	NA	1,628	3,739	0	31,179
2004-05[1]	44,525	----	44,525	26,452	70,597	1,867	12	NA	2,139	2,554	0	26,406

[1] Preliminary.   [2] Includes macaroni, semolina & similar products.   [3] Shipment mostly under the Commodity Import Program, financed with foreign aid funds.   NA = Not available.   *Source: Economic Research Service, U.S. Department of Agriculture (ERS-USDA)*

Comparative Average Cash Wheat Prices   In Dollars Per Bushel

Crop Year Beginning June 1	Received by U.S. Farmers	No. 2 Soft Red Winter, Chicago	No. 1 Hard Red Ordinary Protein, Kansas City	No. 2 Soft Red Winter, St. Louis	No. 1 Dark Northern Spring 14%	No. 1 Hard Amber Durum	No. 1 Soft White, Portland, Oregon	No. 2 Western White Pacific Northwest	No. 2 Soft White, Toledo	Australian Standard Wheat	Canada Vancouver No. 1 CWRS 13 1/2%	No. 1 Argentina F.O.B. B.A.	U.S. Gulf No. 2 Hard Winter	Rotterdam C.I.F. U.S. No. 2 Hard Winter
1999-00	2.48	2.19	2.87	2.39	3.65	4.22	3.02	2.72	1.94	143	152	114	112	NA
2000-01	2.62	2.39	3.30	2.39	3.62	4.59	2.99	2.72	2.98	145	149	118	114	163
2001-02	2.78	2.69	3.25	2.80	3.61	4.99	3.56	3.67	2.67	157	149	121	125	161
2002-03	3.56	3.40	4.22	3.50	4.47	4.25	3.95	4.58	3.34	185	194	158	160	189
2003-04	3.40	3.66	4.03	3.76	4.39	5.31	3.95	4.24	3.59	182	188	161	156	204
2004-05	3.40	3.01	3.99	3.37	4.66	NQ	3.93	4.04	3.10	177	204	127	151	213
2005-06	3.42	3.13	4.45	3.20	4.98	NQ	3.57	4.35	3.15	182	209	137	168	224
2006-07[1]	4.20-4.30	3.84	5.34	3.93	5.33	NQ	4.47	5.37	3.69				205	

[1] Preliminary.   [2] Calendar year.   NA = Not available.   *Source: Economic Research Service, U.S. Department of Agriculture (ERS-USDA)*

WHEAT

Wheat (monthly average) through December 2006 — Cents per bushel

Cents Per Bushel
----- Cash, Chicago (1862 - 1900)
No. 2 Red, Chicago (Jan. 1901 - Mar. 1982)
No. 2 Soft, Red, St. Louis (Apr. 1982 - date)

Average Price of No. 2 Soft Red Winter (30 Days) Wheat in Chicago   In Dollars Per Bushel

Year	June	July	Aug.	Sept.	Oct.	Nov.	Dec.	Jan.	Feb.	Mar.	Apr.	May	Average
1997-98	3.38	3.30	3.52	3.49	3.51	3.44	3.31	3.27	3.26	3.25	2.91	2.87	3.29
1998-99	2.72	2.51	2.39	2.32	2.56	2.58	2.49	2.46	2.28	2.63	2.31	2.24	2.46
1999-00	2.20	1.94	2.09	2.12	1.98	1.96	2.12	2.34	2.38	2.34	2.30	2.45	2.19
2000-01	2.41	2.14	2.08	2.13	2.36	2.42	2.47	2.57	2.49	2.56	2.52	2.51	2.39
2001-02	2.40	2.56	2.57	2.57	2.68	2.75	2.83	2.96	2.74	2.76	2.75	2.73	2.69
2002-03	2.81	3.19	3.42	3.92	3.89	3.85	3.53	3.32	3.44	3.14	3.08	3.25	3.40
2003-04	3.11	3.23	3.63	3.46	3.42	3.87	3.92	3.90	3.84	3.85	3.92	3.73	3.66
2004-05	3.46	3.26	2.92	2.97	2.82	2.79	2.88	2.93	2.95	3.28	2.92	2.96	3.01
2005-06	3.09	3.22	3.04	2.93	2.99	2.83	2.98	3.11	3.34	3.29	3.21	3.54	3.13
2006-07[1]	3.26	3.43	3.20	3.39	4.40	4.35	4.49	4.19					3.84

[1] Preliminary.   *Source: Economic Research Service, U.S. Department of Agriculture (ERS-USDA)*

Average Price[1] Received by Farmers for Wheat in the United States   In Dollars Per Bushel

Year	June	July	Aug.	Sept.	Oct.	Nov.	Dec.	Jan.	Feb.	Mar.	Apr.	May	Average
1997-98	3.52	3.23	3.56	3.67	3.55	3.50	3.45	3.33	3.27	3.32	3.15	3.06	3.38
1998-99	2.77	2.56	2.39	2.41	2.79	2.97	2.87	2.80	2.74	2.65	2.62	2.53	2.68
1999-00	2.50	2.22	2.53	2.58	2.57	2.66	2.52	2.51	2.54	2.59	2.57	2.59	2.53
2000-01	2.50	2.32	2.41	2.44	2.68	2.83	2.87	2.85	2.83	2.87	2.86	2.98	2.70
2001-02	2.74	2.70	2.73	2.85	2.87	2.87	2.88	2.87	2.83	2.87	2.83	2.81	2.82
2002-03	2.92	3.21	3.63	4.21	4.38	4.25	4.06	3.89	3.70	3.55	3.37	3.33	3.71
2003-04	3.08	2.95	3.35	3.39	3.44	3.61	3.68	3.68	3.77	3.83	3.88	3.82	3.54
2004-05	3.55	3.37	3.27	3.36	3.43	3.46	3.40	3.43	3.36	3.42	3.35	3.31	3.39
2005-06	3.23	3.20	3.24	3.36	3.43	3.45	3.53	3.52	3.66	3.79	3.81	4.09	3.53
2006-07[2]	4.01	3.89	3.91	4.06	4.59	4.59	4.51	4.54	4.66				4.31

[1] Includes an allowance for unredeemed loans and purchases.   [2] Preliminary.   *Source: Economic Research Service, U.S. Department of Agriculture*

Average Price of No. 1 Hard Red Winter (Ordinary Protein) Wheat in Kansas City   In Dollars Per Bushel

Year	June	July	Aug.	Sept.	Oct.	Nov.	Dec.	Jan.	Feb.	Mar.	Apr.	May	Average
1997-98	4.08	3.57	3.84	3.86	3.88	3.87	3.72	3.61	3.64	3.61	3.39	3.41	3.71
1998-99	3.16	3.02	2.74	2.81	3.30	3.42	3.31	3.27	3.05	3.02	2.94	2.89	3.08
1999-00	2.93	2.68	2.85	2.92	2.80	2.89	2.81	2.90	2.94	2.91	2.84	2.95	2.87
2000-01	3.07	2.97	2.89	3.13	3.41	3.45	3.47	3.54	3.35	3.45	3.41	3.49	3.30
2001-02	3.32	3.20	3.15	3.18	3.28	3.37	3.26	3.29	3.25	3.23	3.24	3.21	3.25
2002-03	3.55	3.92	4.29	5.04	5.10	4.76	4.40	4.06	4.08	3.80	3.79	3.87	4.22
2003-04	3.63	3.34	3.87	3.74	3.79	4.21	4.31	4.32	4.25	4.30	4.35	4.28	4.03
2004-05	4.13	3.97	3.73	4.01	3.95	4.22	4.22	4.14	4.00	4.00	3.76	3.80	3.99
2005-06	3.87	3.83	3.96	4.30	4.57	4.53	4.52	4.46	4.72	4.62	4.86	5.21	4.45
2006-07[1]	5.25	5.27	5.00	5.16	5.62	5.61	5.49	5.29					5.34

[1] Preliminary.   Source: Economic Research Service, U.S. Department of Agriculture (ERS-USDA)

Average Price of No. 1 Dark Northern Spring (14% Protein) Wheat in Minneapolis   In Dollars Per Bushel

Year	June	July	Aug.	Sept.	Oct.	Nov.	Dec.	Jan.	Feb.	Mar.	Apr.	May	Average
1997-98	4.44	4.36	4.49	4.36	4.35	4.42	4.27	4.12	4.15	4.26	4.29	4.24	4.31
1998-99	4.01	3.89	3.58	3.53	4.03	4.15	3.97	3.92	3.78	3.79	3.65	3.61	3.83
1999-00	3.73	3.68	3.58	3.55	3.70	3.78	3.64	3.37	3.59	3.65	3.69	3.80	3.65
2000-01	3.78	3.50	3.29	3.17	3.69	3.77	3.52	3.79	3.68	3.63	3.73	3.88	3.62
2001-02	3.81	3.72	3.54	3.52	3.71	3.69	3.59	3.55	3.51	3.51	3.55	3.59	3.61
2002-03	3.64	4.03	4.37	5.24	5.20	4.99	4.47	4.34	4.52	4.36	4.22	4.20	4.47
2003-04	4.12	4.00	4.15	4.03	4.31	4.59	4.43	4.44	4.64	4.63	4.69	4.69	4.39
2004-05	4.56	4.31	4.12	4.68	4.87	5.14	4.93	5.01	4.13	4.79	4.69	4.69	4.66
2005-06	5.03	4.71	4.83	4.80	5.11	5.11	5.28	4.87	4.90	4.83	4.94	5.31	4.98
2006-07[1]	5.59	5.65	4.94	4.86	5.36	5.55	5.44	5.27					5.33

[1] Preliminary.   Source: Economic Research Service, U.S. Department of Agriculture (ERS-USDA)

Average Farm Prices of Winter Wheat in the United States   In Dollars Per Bushel

Year	June	July	Aug.	Sept.	Oct.	Nov.	Dec.	Jan.	Feb.	Mar.	Apr.	May	Average
1999-00	2.32	2.12	2.35	2.46	2.47	2.42	2.27	2.32	2.37	2.37	2.32	2.44	2.35
2000-01	2.43	2.23	2.31	2.37	2.63	2.70	2.76	2.77	2.74	2.85	2.77	2.94	2.63
2001-02	2.68	2.67	2.71	2.81	2.82	2.82	2.78	2.81	2.75	2.81	2.75	2.73	2.76
2002-03	2.90	3.19	3.63	4.15	4.32	4.18	3.87	3.66	3.52	3.30	3.19	3.19	3.59
2003-04	2.94	2.89	3.28	3.31	3.37	3.56	3.62	3.66	3.67	3.76	3.79	3.72	3.46
2004-05	3.46	3.31	3.19	3.26	3.34	3.39	3.34	3.28	3.27	3.32	3.27	3.23	3.31
2005-06	3.15	3.15	3.16	3.28	3.34	3.27	3.45	3.45	3.59	3.82	3.76	4.06	3.46
2006-07[1]	3.99	3.82	3.77	4.03	4.63	4.68	4.51	4.53	4.62				4.29

[1] Preliminary.   Source: National Agricultural Statistics Service, U.S. Department of Agriculture (NASS-USDA)

Average Farm Prices of Durum Wheat in the United States   In Dollars Per Bushel

Year	June	July	Aug.	Sept.	Oct.	Nov.	Dec.	Jan.	Feb.	Mar.	Apr.	May	Average
1999-00	2.93	2.89	2.76	2.29	2.30	2.64	2.96	2.90	2.88	2.63	2.89	3.02	2.76
2000-01	2.71	2.90	2.33	2.32	2.42	2.97	3.03	2.94	2.60	2.40	2.52	2.53	2.64
2001-02	3.37	2.74	2.38	3.02	2.91	3.04	3.41	3.44	3.49	3.33	3.33	3.41	3.16
2002-03	3.41	3.44	3.54	4.18	4.43	4.52	4.26	4.23	4.28	4.14	3.93	3.99	4.03
2003-04	3.99	3.85	3.78	3.95	3.89	3.95	3.95	3.96	4.08	4.14	4.19	4.21	4.00
2004-05	4.35	4.09	3.86	3.89	3.87	3.79	3.67	3.64	3.72	3.70	3.63	3.67	3.82
2005-06	3.67	3.72	3.35	3.38	3.39	3.28	3.37	3.29	3.34	3.39	3.40	3.94	3.46
2006-07[1]	3.81	3.83	4.09	4.07	4.55	4.63	4.74	4.70	4.97				4.38

[1] Preliminary.   Source: National Agricultural Statistics Service, U.S. Department of Agriculture (NASS-USDA)

Average Farm Prices of Other Spring Wheat in the United States   In Dollars Per Bushel

Year	June	July	Aug.	Sept.	Oct.	Nov.	Dec.	Jan.	Feb.	Mar.	Apr.	May	Average
1999-00	3.01	2.93	2.86	2.86	2.79	2.94	2.87	2.82	2.82	2.85	2.89	2.92	2.88
2000-01	2.90	2.74	2.59	2.59	2.80	2.97	2.98	2.96	2.99	2.99	3.05	3.13	2.89
2001-02	3.03	2.78	2.84	2.87	2.96	2.91	2.96	2.88	2.86	2.90	2.91	2.91	2.90
2002-03	2.98	3.31	3.66	4.30	4.45	4.26	4.15	4.03	3.82	3.72	3.48	3.55	3.81
2003-04	3.45	3.31	3.42	3.42	3.53	3.68	3.72	3.67	3.84	3.90	3.94	4.01	3.66
2004-05	3.83	3.55	3.38	3.48	3.50	3.57	3.48	3.61	3.49	3.51	3.39	3.37	3.51
2005-06	3.51	3.45	3.43	3.51	3.61	3.71	3.68	3.70	3.83	3.85	3.94	4.18	3.70
2006-07[1]	4.18	4.41	4.11	4.11	4.48	4.48	4.48	4.52	4.67				4.38

[1] Preliminary.   Source: National Agricultural Statistics Service, U.S. Department of Agriculture (NASS-USDA)

WHEAT

Wheat Futures - Chicago Board of Trade
(weekly close) as December 29, 2006

Cents per bushel

Volume of Trading of Wheat Futures in Chicago   In Thousands of Contracts

Year	Jan.	Feb.	Mar.	Apr.	May	June	July	Aug.	Sept.	Oct.	Nov.	Dec.	Total
1997	312.7	373.4	368.5	567.1	422.9	469.2	471.0	493.2	401.3	406.0	432.6	340.7	5,058.6
1998	363.5	473.1	452.2	514.6	432.2	601.1	401.5	490.2	475.8	543.7	539.5	394.2	5,681.6
1999	426.5	597.4	710.4	559.2	444.7	674.6	523.5	665.9	536.0	437.7	613.6	380.4	6,570.0
2000	467.1	691.1	522.4	490.7	627.7	759.4	461.1	572.9	388.2	466.3	596.6	364.1	6,407.5
2001	551.8	595.3	536.1	580.0	537.8	720.4	695.3	600.3	385.9	629.5	614.7	354.3	6,801.5
2002	603.0	593.1	501.1	563.1	419.3	689.8	586.4	651.6	682.9	609.4	594.4	378.8	6,872.9
2003	438.0	526.0	411.0	496.8	638.6	661.8	585.1	689.6	536.5	778.9	739.8	465.4	6,967.4
2004	656.9	771.7	783.1	786.2	606.1	786.5	501.7	747.4	520.9	478.7	913.7	402.3	7,955.2
2005	613.0	1,053.6	827.8	937.5	694.7	1,088.0	690.3	1,024.8	660.0	717.4	1,164.5	642.4	10,114.1
2006	889.2	1,421.3	1,059.6	1,300.0	1,511.6	1,617.1	1,067.4	1,659.9	1,365.9	1,938.1	1,613.7	781.2	16,224.9

Source: Chicago Board of Trade (CBT)

Average Open Interest of Wheat Futures in Chicago   In Contracts

Year	Jan.	Feb.	Mar.	Apr.	May	June	July	Aug.	Sept.	Oct.	Nov.	Dec.
1997	63,388	71,304	76,747	85,516	84,721	83,675	92,815	105,320	104,587	108,480	101,089	90,386
1998	96,870	99,103	97,585	114,193	115,199	116,008	121,794	127,240	125,747	131,322	130,186	116,249
1999	119,096	131,961	118,503	117,905	111,541	117,075	120,365	129,748	128,403	135,884	140,798	124,063
2000	127,419	135,316	123,980	128,462	130,938	133,527	139,194	144,953	141,803	150,592	153,287	134,997
2001	145,802	146,927	137,377	138,876	134,051	151,951	142,399	143,574	136,514	126,772	113,456	104,975
2002	118,192	118,484	112,469	112,870	96,050	98,047	118,041	131,303	129,913	114,544	101,354	82,934
2003	92,679	99,882	95,464	99,500	97,750	96,230	92,484	119,817	110,703	109,449	125,335	120,376
2004	130,101	137,459	141,239	155,383	127,086	135,322	154,623	166,422	154,431	156,290	172,064	182,402
2005	201,297	223,108	218,153	208,149	207,407	223,014	239,219	256,533	276,741	297,319	301,838	298,523
2006	320,974	380,405	389,284	385,698	466,013	491,343	473,749	459,650	455,755	476,906	435,059	426,976

Source: Chicago Board of Trade (CBT)

Commercial Stocks of Domestic Wheat[1] in the United States, on First of Month   In Millions of Bushels

Year	July	Aug.	Sept.	Oct.	Nov.	Dec.	Jan.	Feb.	Mar.	Apr.	May	June
1997-98	80.1	186.3	235.2	268.1	258.1	231.4	196.8	178.1	170.6	158.0	146.4	145.7
1998-99	209.8	265.0	314.9	325.6	307.3	291.3	272.9	265.7	256.8	251.5	236.7	218.3
1999-00	248.6	294.9	335.8	354.0	334.6	301.5	277.4	273.7	267.8	266.3	247.6	240.3
2000-01	285.5	310.3	335.3	335.5	306.2	286.6	263.7	251.7	243.2	243.7	224.5	221.0
2001-02	271.0	296.6	318.7	321.9	291.9	251.8	224.5	224.6	217.2	195.6	177.3	176.0
2002-03	193.9	207.7	237.2	241.0	237.7	218.8	195.1	179.7	158.3	133.1	107.2	93.8
2003-04	133.3	171.9	212.0	226.3	220.7	198.1	145.0	126.3	113.1	94.0	89.6	85.4
2004-05	118.3	147.6	174.3	173.5	161.6	137.8	129.8	122.5	113.4	103.8	92.2	88.8
2005-06	127.5	138.6	159.9	163.5	158.5	147.8	137.9	130.9	128.8	122.9	116.7	126.2
2006-07	154.3	172.5	190.3	170.9	166.8	159.5						

[1] Domestic wheat in storage in public and private elevators in 39 markets and wheat afloat in vessels or barges at lake and seaboard ports, the first Saturday of the month.   *Source: Livestock Division, U.S. Department of Agriculture (LD-USDA)*

Stocks of Wheat Flour Held by Mills in the United States   In Thousands of Sacks -- 100 Pounds

Year	Jan. 1	April 1	July 1	Oct. 1	Year	Jan. 1	April 1	July 1	Oct. 1
1995	7,060	6,496	6,312	6,582	2001	5,241	5,506	5,178	5,393
1996	6,869	6,927	6,400	6,350	2002	5,377	5,164	4,632	4,184
1997	6,671	6,040	5,820	6,330	2003	4,265	4,707	4,622	4,554
1998	6,343	6,245	6,210	7,345	2004	4,764	4,666	4,700	4,868
1999	7,544	5,920	5,697	4,265	2005	5,085	4,268	4,637	4,781
2000	5,099	5,217	5,062	5,244	2006[1]	5,211	5,563	5,237	5,272

[1] Preliminary.   *Source: Bureau of the Census, U.S. Department of Commerce*

Average Producer Price Index of Wheat Flour (Spring[2])   June 1983 = 100

Year	Jan.	Feb.	Mar.	Apr.	May	June	July	Aug.	Sept.	Oct.	Nov.	Dec.	Average
1997	119.4	119.3	116.6	121.8	120.8	117.4	112.1	113.5	115.1	112.6	111.5	111.1	115.9
1998	106.8	108.1	111.5	110.1	109.9	106.4	105.5	101.8	100.9	106.6	107.8	104.8	106.7
1999	104.8	102.7	105.0	100.5	102.2	102.7	100.7	103.5	101.4	99.8	101.4	96.8	101.8
2000	99.9	99.9	100.2	99.4	100.1	101.7	100.2	100.4	101.2	105.2	103.6	104.4	101.4
2001	104.7	105.1	106.2	105.7	106.9	108.2	107.9	106.8	107.4	110.0	109.5	108.8	107.3
2002	109.6	109.6	110.6	106.5	108.2	108.8	112.6	115.5	120.9	123.0	119.3	116.6	113.4
2003	119.4	121.6	120.2	120.3	122.6	121.6	119.2	122.2	120.4	117.2	121.1	122.4	120.7
2004	123.5	125.1	123.9	124.0	127.6	126.4	125.2	121.0	128.5	127.2	130.2	128.5	125.9
2005	128.5	130.4	130.8	127.6	129.6	130.8	130.3	129.7	130.6	131.4	133.6	131.8	130.4
2006[1]	130.2	134.2	132.8	139.4	142.2	144.2	148.5	141.6	144.2	151.9	151.8	148.3	142.4

[1] Preliminary.   [2] Standard patent.   *Source: Bureau of Labor Statistics, U.S. Department of Commerce (BLS) (0212-0301)*

World Wheat Flour Production (Monthly Average)   In Thousands of Metric Tons

Year	Australia	France	Germany	Hungary	India	Japan	Kazakhstan	Rep. of Korea	Mexico	Poland	Russia	Turkey	United Kingdom
1997	129.7	NA	404.8	77.7	412.5	388.1	127.3	145.9	216.0	175.3	361.9	159.1	369.0
1998	146.8	NA	407.5	69.5	302.1	382.0	128.5	143.5	213.2	172.1	872.7	152.7	377.0
1999	154.8	NA	423.6	69.1	196.6	386.5	104.9	152.8	204.8	125.0	899.1	156.6	NA
2000	NA	NA	405.5	73.5	202.5	383.0	120.8	155.9	206.0	125.4	864.0	162.0	374.0
2001	NA	NA	403.1	72.4	197.2	387.2	116.5	142.8	221.1	126.8	866.6	145.2	374.0
2002	NA	NA	415.3	67.6	211.6	389.4	143.4	151.2	218.1	135.2	794.3	139.6	368.0
2003	NA	NA	424.4	70.7	234.1	391.0	137.3	149.3	218.6	143.1	821.3	159.8	364.0
2004	NA	NA	427.3	67.6	239.9	390.1	138.5	157.5	217.6	135.2	799.5	178.4	369.0
2005[1]	NA	NA	415.7	72.3	209.2	384.7	182.2	152.8	219.3	128.6	439.4	191.5	354.5
2006[2]	NA	NA	427.4	63.2	186.7	377.7	189.6	150.0	219.8	145.6	451.4	175.3	NA

[1] Preliminary.   [2] Estimate.   NA = Not available.   *Source: United Nations (UN)*

WHEAT

Production of Wheat Flour in the United States   In Millions of Sacks (100 Pounds Each)

Year	July	Aug.	Sept.	Oct.	Nov.	Dec.	Jan.	Feb.	Mar.	Apr.	May	June	Total
1998-99	-----	100.2	-----	-----	106.5	-----	-----	96.1	-----	-----	103.5	-----	406.3
1999-00	-----	104.2	-----	-----	108.2	-----	-----	101.1	-----	-----	101.6	-----	415.2
2000-01	-----	108.8	-----	-----	109.7	-----	-----	99.4	-----	-----	97.2	-----	415.1
2001-02	-----	102.1	-----	-----	105.8	-----	-----	96.0	-----	-----	96.3	-----	400.2
2002-03	-----	102.1	-----	-----	100.3	-----	-----	95.9	-----	-----	96.8	-----	395.0
2003-04	-----	103.1	-----	-----	100.5	-----	-----	95.7	-----	-----	95.8	-----	395.1
2004-05	-----	100.9	-----	-----	99.7	-----	-----	95.9	-----	-----	96.2	-----	392.7
2005-06	-----	102.5	-----	-----	100.3	-----	-----	97.3	-----	-----	96.4	-----	396.4
2006-07[1]	-----	102.9	-----	-----	100.8	-----	-----					-----	407.5

[1] Preliminary.   Source: Bureau of the Census, U.S. Department of Commerce

United States Wheat Flour Exports (Grain Equivalent[2])   In Thousands of Bushels

Year	June	July	Aug.	Sept.	Oct.	Nov.	Dec.	Jan.	Feb.	Mar.	Apr.	May	Total
1998-99	1,971	1,740	2,027	2,914	3,812	2,354	6,838	2,551	3,341	4,126	3,105	1,948	36,728
1999-00	4,160	3,638	2,586	6,503	4,576	2,332	3,023	2,924	6,108	2,615	3,193	1,286	42,944
2000-01	3,620	3,805	1,623	3,174	4,165	2,332	2,741	2,236	2,365	2,200	3,868	2,163	34,292
2001-02	1,412	661	1,990	1,005	3,226	2,534	2,479	2,207	3,294	2,301	2,802	2,759	26,670
2002-03	1,474	1,547	753	1,373	2,437	2,854	4,645	1,049	884	1,146	1,083	541	19,786
2003-04	824	1,074	3,444	1,087	765	1,295	1,673	1,789	1,342	1,020	732	1,386	16,431
2004-05	742	1,220	885	770	834	1,005	1,347	955	617	756	722	781	10,634
2005-06	859	686	839	720	840	871	734	572	620	937	1,188	966	9,832
2006-07[1]	720	488	780	610	532	754							7,768

[1] Preliminary.   [2] Includes meal, groats and durum.   Source: Economic Research Service, U.S. Department of Agriculture (ERS-USDA)

Supply and Distribution of Wheat Flour in the United States

Year	Wheat Ground - 1,000 Bu. -	Millfeed Production - 1,000 Tons -	Flour Production[2]	Flour & Product Imports	Total Supply	Exports — Flour	Products	Domestic Disappear-ance	Total Population July 1 - Millions -	Per Capita Disappear-ance - Pounds -
			In 1,000 Cwt.							
1998	902,532	7,301	403,880	9,830	413,625	12,574	1,353	394,817	276.0	145.9
1999	917,797	7,040	411,968	9,295	416,354	21,297	1,633	393,377	279.3	142.6
2000	944,868	7,374	421,270	9,666	430,936	16,005	1,693	413,238	282.4	146.3
2001	914,036	7,273	404,521	10,130	414,651	10,507	1,695	402,449	285.4	141.0
2002	889,412	6,893	394,700	11,287	405,987	9,226	2,683	394,077	288.2	136.7
2003	889,188	7,029	396,215	11,241	407,456	5,768	3,953	397,734	291.1	136.6
2004	876,047	6,764	393,925	10,718	404,643	5,152	4,662	394,829	293.9	134.3
2005	884,101	6,826	394,973	11,247	404,376	3,614	4,727	396,035	296.8	133.5
2006[1]	884,056	6,823	397,360							

[1] Preliminary.   [2] Commercial production of wheat flour, whole wheat, industrial and durum flour and farina reported by Bureau of Census.
Source: Economic Research Service, U.S. Department of Agriculture (ERS-USDA)

Wheat and Flour -- Price Relationships at Milling Centers in the United States   In Dollars

Crop Year (June-May)	At Kansas City					At Minneapolis				
	Cost of Wheat to Produce 100 lb. Flour[1]	Bakery Flour 100 lb. Flour[2]	By-Products Obtained 100 lb. Flour[3]	Total Products — Actual	Over Cost of Wheat	Cost of Wheat to Produce 100 lb. Flour[1]	Bakery Flour 100 lb. Flour[2]	By-Products Obtained 100 lb. Flour[3]	Total Products — Actual	Over Cost of Wheat
1997-98	9.03	9.99	1.43	11.41	2.38	9.83	10.62	1.34	11.96	2.12
1998-99	7.91	9.06	1.08	10.15	2.23	8.76	9.80	1.02	10.82	2.06
1999-00	7.74	8.86	.98	9.84	2.10	8.29	9.30	.95	10.24	1.95
2000-01	7.95	9.36	1.06	10.42	2.48	8.24	9.28	.97	10.24	2.01
2001-02	7.64	8.98	1.14	10.11	2.48	8.20	9.11	1.10	10.21	2.01
2002-03	9.66	11.04	1.16	12.20	2.54	9.80	11.03	1.15	12.17	2.38
2003-04	9.43	10.58	1.36	11.95	2.52	9.98	10.67	1.15	11.82	1.84
2004-05	9.33	10.88	.95	11.83	2.50	10.62	11.31	.94	12.25	1.62
2005-06	9.67	11.45	.83	12.28	2.61	11.24	12.14	.86	13.00	1.76
June-Aug.	9.07	10.80	.66	11.46	2.39	11.07	11.58	.88	12.46	1.39
Sept.-Nov.	10.28	12.10	1.00	13.10	2.82	11.42	12.70	.85	13.55	2.13
Dec.-Feb.										

[1] Based on 73% extraction rate, cost of 2.28 bushels: At Kansas City, No. 1 hard winter 13% protein; and at Minneapolis, No. 1 dark northern spring, 14% protein.   [2] quoted as mid-month bakers' standard patent at Kansas City and spring standard patent at Minneapolis, bulk basis.   [3] Assumed 50-50 millfeed distribution between bran and shorts or middlings, bulk basis.   Source: Agricultural Marketing Service, U.S. Department of Agriculture (AMS-USDA)

Wool

Wool is light, warm, absorbs moisture, and is resistant to fire. Wool is also used for insulation in houses, for carpets and furnishing, and for bedding. Sheep are sheared once a year and produce about 4.3 kg of "greasy" wool per year.

Greasy wool is wool that has not been washed or cleaned. Wool fineness is determined by fiber diameter, which is measured in microns (one millionth of a meter). Fine wool is softer, lightweight, and produces fine clothing. Merino sheep produce the finest wool.

Wool futures and options are traded on the Sydney Futures Exchange (SFE), where there are futures and options contracts on greasy wool, and futures on fine wool and broad wool. All three futures contracts call for the delivery of merino combing wool. Wool yarn futures are traded on the Chubu Commodity Exchange (CCE), the Osaka Mercantile Exchange (OME) and the Tokyo Commodity Exchange (TOCOM).

Prices – Average monthly wool prices at US mills in 2006 fell –3.2% yr/yr to $1.80 per pound, down further from the 8-year high of $2.41 posted in 2003. Wool prices in 2006 were still about 65% higher than the 3-decade low of $1.09 posted in 2000. The value of US wool production in 2005 was $26.272 million, up 72% from the record low of $15.311 million in 2001.

Supply – World production of wool has been falling in the past decade due to the increased use of polyester fabrics.

Wool production in 2002, the latest reporting year for the data series, fell –1.4% yr/yr to a new record low of 1.292 million metric tons. The world's largest producers of degreased wool in 2002 were Australia with 31% of world production, followed by New Zealand (15%), and China (12%).

US wool production of 10,000 metric tons in 2002 accounted for only 0.8% of world production. US production of wool goods rose +18.1% yr/yr in 2005 (6 months annualized) to 23.4 million yards, up from the record low of 19.8 million yards in 2004. However, that was only 11% of the 2-decade high in wool goods production seen in 1998. The US sheep herd in 2005 was virtually unchanged at the record low of 5.072 million sheep.

Demand – US consumption of apparel wool has dropped sharply, along with production, and fell –13.5% yr/yr to a record low of 13.333 million pounds in 2006. The breakdown of US mill consumption in 2003, the latest data available, showed that wool usage for carpets was 6.017 million pounds, which was a new record low. Wool usage for apparel production was 43.869 million pounds, up +21.8%, up from the 2002 record low of 36.015 million pounds.

Trade – US exports of domestic wool in 2004 fell –4.5% yr/yr to 14.023 million pounds. US imports in 2005 rose +0.3% to 6.220 million pounds.

World Production of Wool   In Metric Tons--Degreased

Year	Argentina	Australia	China	Kazak-hstan	New Zealand	Pakistan	Romania	Russia	South Africa	United Kingdom	United States	Uruguay	Total
1994	48,000	570,000	130,000	55,000	214,000	31,000	17,000	73,000	40,000	47,000	16,000	50,000	1,693,000
1995	44,000	475,000	141,000	35,000	214,000	32,000	16,000	56,000	35,000	48,000	15,000	46,000	1,512,000
1996	39,000	457,000	152,000	25,000	199,000	32,000	16,000	46,000	37,000	46,000	13,000	43,000	1,459,000
1997	36,000	472,000	130,000	21,000	228,000	34,000	13,000	36,000	34,000	46,000	13,000	46,000	1,440,000
1998	34,000	452,000	141,000	15,000	219,000	23,000	12,000	29,000	32,000	48,000	12,000	42,000	1,388,000
1999	36,000	437,000	144,000	13,000	220,000	23,000	13,000	24,000	34,000	47,000	11,000	34,000	1,369,000
2000	32,000	452,000	146,000	14,000	202,000	23,000	11,000	20,000	32,000	45,000	11,000	32,000	1,356,000
2001[1]	32,000	416,000	149,000	14,000	199,000	24,000	10,000	20,000	32,000	39,000	10,000	32,000	1,310,000
2002[2]	31,000	395,000	152,000	14,000	199,000	24,000	12,000	20,000	32,000	42,000	10,000	27,000	1,292,000

[1] Preliminary.   [2] Estimate.   Source: Food and Agriculture Organization of the United Nations (FAO-UN)

Production of Wool Goods[2] in the United States   In Millions of Yards

Year	First Quarter	Second Quarter	Third Quarter	Fourth Quarter	Total	Year	First Quarter	Second Quarter	Third Quarter	Fourth Quarter	Total
1997	42.7	49.7	42.3	40.5	175.2	2002	7.4	8.6	6.2	5.5	27.7
1998	38.8	37.5	29.6	26.3	132.2	2003	6.5	6.4	5.2	4.9	23.0
1999	25.0	20.9	17.4	14.6	77.9	2004	5.5	5.9	4.2	4.2	19.8
2000	17.9	18.0	13.4	17.4	66.7	2005	4.9	6.9	4.2	4.3	20.3
2001	20.8	12.4	11.0	9.0	53.2	2006[1]	4.1	3.9	2.8	W	14.5

[1] Preliminary.   [2] Woolen and worsted woven goods, except woven felts.   Source: Bureau of the Census, U.S. Department of Commerce

Consumption of Apparel Wool[2] in the United States   In Millions of Pounds--Clean Basis

Year	First Quarter	Second Quarter	Third Quarter	Fourth Quarter	Total	Year	First Quarter	Second Quarter	Third Quarter	Fourth Quarter	Total
1997	33.1	33.8	30.6	32.8	130.4	2002	11.0	10.5	6.5	W	36.0
1998	29.3	29.6	21.9	17.5	98.4	2003	W	W	W	W	W
1999	17.3	16.8	15.8	13.6	63.5	2004	W	W	W	W	W
2000	17.4	16.1	14.6	13.9	63.0	2005	2.3	5.2	3.9	4.0	15.4
2001	17.0	13.5	11.6	10.9	53.0	2006[1]	3.7	3.8	2.8	3.0	13.3

[1] Preliminary.   [2] Woolen and worsted woven goods, except woven felts.   Source: Bureau of the Census, U.S. Department of Commerce

WOOL

Salient Statistics of Wool in the United States

Year	Sheep & Lambs Shorn[4] -1,000's-	Weight Per Fleece -In Lbs.-	Shorn Wool Production -1,000 Lbs.-	Price Per Lb.	Value of Production 1,000 $	Payment Support	Payment Rate	Total Wool Production	Domestic Production	Exports Domestic Wool	Dutiable Imports for Consumption[3] 48's & Finer	Total New Supply[2]	Duty Free Imports (Not Finer than 46's)	Apparel	Carpet
						--Cents Per Lb.--								Mill Consumption	
1997	7,032	7.70	53,889	84.0	45,172	----	----	53,578	28,630	4,732	51,484	100,003	24,295	130,386	13,576
1998	6,428	7.70	49,255	60.0	29,415	----	----	49,255	30,321	1,700	45,760	94,814	23,121	98,373	16,331
1999	6,150	7.60	46,549	38.0	17,860	----	20.0	46,549	24,800	3,694	21,251	63,955	20,723	63,535	13,950
2000	6,100	7.60	46,400	33.0	15,377	----	40.0	46,446	24,500	6,629	23,874	62,785	20,003	62,041	15,205
2001	5,700	7.60	43,000	36.0	15,311	----	----	43,016	22,712	6,154	15,843	52,128	19,727	52,969	13,310
2002	5,476	7.50	41,322	53.0	21,876	100	18.0	41,322	21,818	8,461	10,526	38,042	14,159	36,015	6,891
2003	5,074	7.50	38,229	73.0	28,126	100	20.0	38,299	20,222	14,678	4,986	26,279	15,749	43,869	6,017
2004	5,073	7.40	37,622	80.0	29,921	100	21.0	37,622	19,864	14,023	6,201	28,500	16,455		
2005[1]	5,072	7.30	37,232	71.0	26,272	100					6,220		12,180		

[1] Preliminary.   [2] Production minus exports plus imports; stocks not taken into consideration.   [3] Apparel wool includes all dutiable wool; carpet wool includes all duty-free wool.   [4] Includes sheep shorn at commercial feeding yards.   *Source: Economic Research Service, U.S. Department of Agriculture (ERS-USDA)*

Shorn Wool Prices

Year	U.S. Farm Price Shorn Wool Greasy Basis[1] -Cents/Lb.-	Grade 70's Type 61	Grade 64's Type 63	Grade 64/70's Type 62	Grade 60/62's Type 64A	Grade 58's-56's 433-34	Market Indicator[3] -Cents/Kg.-	64's Staple 2 3/4" & up	60's Staple 3" & up	58's Staple 3 1/4" & up	56's Staple 3 1/4" & up	54's Staple 3 1/2" & up
1997	84.0	3.56	2.57	2.90	2.06	1.95	615	2.38	1.78	1.64	1.43	1.14
1998	60.0	2.60	1.84	1.92	1.64	1.60	663	1.62	1.31	1.21	1.06	.94
1999	38.0	2.53	1.48	1.66	1.36	1.33	524	1.10	.85	.74	.66	.59
2000	33.0	2.80	1.50	1.69	1.37	1.30	764	1.08	.75	.65	.57	.53
2001	36.0	2.42	1.66	1.69	1.60	1.54	841	1.21	.91	.77	.66	.65
2002	53.0	2.87	2.68	2.70	2.63	2.55	1,051	1.90	1.41	1.40	1.19	1.02
2003	73.0	3.23	3.14	3.16	3.02	2.81	821	2.41	1.73	1.79	1.48	1.24
2004	80.0	3.21	2.75	2.89	2.49	2.33		2.35	1.59	1.74	1.50	1.25
2005	71.0	2.99	2.57	2.65	2.42	2.23		1.86	1.46	1.39	1.41	1.03

[1] Annual weighted average.   [2] F.O.B. Australian Wool Corporation South Carolina warehouse in bond.   [3] Index of prices of all wool sold in Australia for the crop year July-June.   [4] Wool principally produced in Texas and the Rocky Mountain States.   *Source: Economic Research Service, U.S. Department of Agriculture (ERS-USDA)*

Average Wool Prices[1] --Australian-- 64's, Type 62, Duty Paid--U.S. Mills   In Cents Per Pound

Year	Jan.	Feb.	Mar.	Apr.	May	June	July	Aug.	Sept.	Oct.	Nov.	Dec.	Average
1997	234	261	254	261	279	287	NA	270	262	250	245	240	258
1998	218	225	247	205	214	179	NA	144	144	140	156	147	184
1999	158	150	157	156	150	149	152	148	139	139	143	137	148
2000	154	146	144	156	156	154	155	151	149	146	140	148	150
2001	160	168	164	158	164	166	167	172	169	159	166	183	166
2002	218	243	250	251	249	259	255	254	268	312	322	328	267
2003	344	346	326	333	296	326	316	308	306	292	285	290	314
2004	304	294	288	281	261	275	277	263	255	255	270	271	275
2005	273	271	268	242	265	266	270	259	252	244	233	236	257
2006	243	256	259	251	258	254	260	260	258	260	308	315	265

[1] Raw, clean basis.   NA = Not available.   *Source: Economic Research Service, U.S. Department of Agriculture (ERS-USDA)*

Average Wool Prices --Domestic[1]-- Graded Territory, 64's, Staple 2 3/4 & Up--U.S. Mills   In Cents Per Pound

Year	Jan.	Feb.	Mar.	Apr.	May	June	July	Aug.	Sept.	Oct.	Nov.	Dec.	Average
1997	190	190	208	228	248	255	255	255	255	255	260	260	238
1998	236	195	195	188	177	170	170	150	115	115	115	115	162
1999	115	115	115	110	117	122	116	110	105	100	110	95	111
2000	95	95	101	110	125	125	125	120	107	105	105	97	109
2001	95	100	108	129	137	125	127	122	126	130	122	127	121
2002	134	150	170	181	189	200	200	200	198	204	223	233	190
2003	236	260	258	250	223	234	239	243	243	243	232	233	241
2004	233	239	240	240	235	229	233	236	240	236	230	230	235
2005	215	207	200	185	185	185	179	186	195	181	168	140	186
2006	NQ	NQ	162	183	173	171	165	165	165	NQ	212	220	180

[1] Raw, shorn, clean basis.   *Source: Economic Research Service, U.S. Department of Agriculture (ERS-USDA)*

Wool (monthly average) through December 2006 — Cents per pound

Cents Per Pound
----- Fine Scoured Fleece, Ohio (1851 - 1902)
Fine Combing, Scoured (64's), Boston (1903 - 1909)
Fine Combing, Scoured (64's), Boston (Jan. 1910 - date)
- - - Tops (Jan. 1924 - date)

Wool: Mill Consumption, by Grades in the U.S., Scoured Basis   In Millions of Pounds

| | Apparel Class[1] | | | | | | | |
| | Woolen System | | | Worsted System | | | | |
Year	60's & Finer	Coarser Than 60's	Total	60's & Finer	Coarser Than 60's	Total	All Total	Carpet Wool[2]
1996	42,141	27,575	69,716	46,057	13,752	59,809	129,525	12,311
1997	49,038	21,303	70,341	48,153	11,892	60,045	130,386	13,576
1998	31,258	15,079	46,337	42,243	9,793	52,036	98,373	16,331
1999	18,379	10,772	29,151	27,429	6,955	34,384	63,535	13,950
2000	18,503	13,432	31,935	NA	NA	30,106	62,041	15,205
2001	16,062	9,849	25,911	NA	NA	27,058	52,969	13,310
2002	9,627	8,482	18,109	NA	NA	17,906	36,015	6,891
2003	6,681	5,309	11,990	NA	NA	31,879	43,869	6,017
2004[3]	NA	NA	NA	NA	NA	NA	NA	NA
2005[4]	NA	NA	NA	NA	NA	NA	NA	NA

[1] Domestic & duty-paid foreign.   [2] Duty-free foreign.   [3] Preliminary.   [4] Estimate.   Source: Economic Research Service, U.S. Department of Agriculture (ERS-USDA)

United States Imports[2] of Unmanufactured Wool (Clean Yield)   In Millions of Pounds

Year	Jan.	Feb.	Mar.	Apr.	May	June	July	Aug.	Sept.	Oct.	Nov.	Dec.	Total
1997	5.1	5.8	5.8	6.6	5.8	4.2	4.9	4.2	4.8	8.5	7.3	8.6	71.5
1998	8.8	5.4	5.4	7.2	5.9	5.5	5.7	4.4	3.3	7.3	4.9	4.3	68.0
1999	6.2	3.6	3.9	7.9	3.5	3.0	3.7	3.1	2.6	3.8	2.8	2.5	46.3
2000	4.9	3.8	3.8	4.6	5.1	2.7	3.2	3.7	4.3	3.2	3.5	2.4	45.0
2001	4.9	4.3	4.3	1.5	2.9	2.8	4.0	1.9	2.0	2.8	1.3	1.3	34.1
2002	1.9	1.8	2.6	2.4	2.3	1.5	1.6	1.2	1.9	2.4	2.1	3.1	24.6
2003	2.5	2.8	2.3	2.2	2.1	1.8	1.2	1.1	0.8	1.6	1.1	1.2	20.8
2004	1.3	1.5	2.1	1.8	1.4	2.8	1.6	1.9	2.7	2.4	1.9	1.2	22.7
2005	2.3	1.1	2.0	1.5	1.5	2.0	1.5	1.4	1.0	1.7	1.5	1.0	18.4
2006[1]	1.9	1.0	1.8	1.5	1.3	1.6	0.9	1.5	1.2	1.5	1.6	1.6	17.3

[1] Preliminary.   [2] For consumption.   Source: Economic Research Service, U.S. Department of Agriculture (ERS-USDA)

Zinc

Zinc (symbol Zn) is a bluish-while metallic element that is the 24th most abundant element in the earth's crust. Zinc is never found in its pure state but rather in zinc oxide, zinc silicate, zinc carbonate, zinc sulfide, and in minerals such as zincite, hemimorphite, smithsonite, franklinite, and sphalerite. Zinc is utilized as a protective coating for other metals, such as iron and steel, in a process known as galvanizing. Zinc is used as an alloy with copper to make brass and also as an alloy with aluminum and magnesium. There are, however, a number of substitutes for zinc in chemicals, electronics, and pigments. For example, with aluminum, steel and plastics can substitute for galvanized sheets. Aluminum alloys can also replace brass. Zinc is used as the negative electrode in dry cell (flashlight) batteries and also in the zinc-mercuric-oxide battery cell, which is the round, flat battery typically used in watches, cameras, and other electronic devices. Zinc is also used in medicine as an antiseptic ointment.

Zinc futures and options are traded on the London Metals Exchange (LME). The LME zinc futures contract calls for the delivery of 25 metric tons of at least 99.995% purity zinc ingots (slabs and plates). The contract trades in terms of US dollars per metric ton. Zinc first started trading on the LME in 1915.

Prices – Zinc prices in 2006 rose to a record high monthly average of 158.44 cents per pound, up sharply by +136.4% from 2005. Prices in January of 2007 were even higher at about 184 cents per pound.

Supply – World smelter production of zinc in 2005 rose +2.9% to 10.700 million metric tons, which was a new record high. The world's largest producer of zinc is China with 26% of world smelter production, followed by Canada with 8%, Japan with 6%, and Australia and Spain each with 5%. US smelter production accounted for only 2.9% of world production in 2005. Australia's production rose rapidly in the 1999-2002 period but the 2005 level of 507,800 metric tons was below the record high of 571,500 metric tons seen in 2002. China's production of 2.800 million metric tons in 2005 was more than five times its production level of 550,000

metric tons seen in 1990. US zinc smelter production in 2005 of 309,000 metric tons was less than half of its production of 796,300 metric tons seen in 1970.

US mine production of recoverable zinc in 2006 fell – 1.5% yr/yr to an annualized (through November) level of 710,836 metric tons. US production in 2005 of slab zinc on a primary basis rose by +1.1% to 191,000 metric tons, while secondary production rose +0.9% yr/yr to 118,000 metric tons.

Demand – US consumption of slab zinc in 2005 fell by –19.1% yr/yr to 939,000 metric tons, which was an 15-year low. US consumption of all classes of zinc fell by –16.4% yr/yr in 2005 to 1.170 million metric tons, which was a 14-year low. US consumption of slab zinc by fabricators in 2006 (through November) fell by –1.3% yr/yr to an annualized 400,036 metric tons, which was a new record low.

The breakdown of consumption by industries for 2005 showed that 49% of slab zinc consumption was by galvanizers, 17% for brass products, and the rest for other miscellaneous industries. The consumption breakdown by grades showed that 65% was for special high grade, 14% prime western, 13% high grade, and 8% re-melt and other. Within that grade breakdown, prime Western consumption has fallen by nearly half in the past 3 years.

Trade – The US in 2006 relied on imports for 63% of its consumption of zinc, up sharply from the 35% average seen in the 1990s. US imports for consumption of slab zinc fell by –17.7% yr/yr to 668,000 metric tons in 2005, while imports of zinc ore fell by –32.5% yr/yr to 156,000 metric tons. The dollar value of US zinc imports in 2005 rose by +4.8% yr/yr to a 5-year high of $1.198 billion. The breakdown of imports in 2005 shows that most zinc is imported for blocks, pigs and slabs (668,000 metric tons); followed by ores (156,000 metric tons); dust, powder and flakes (23,400 metric tons); dross, ashes and fume (15,800 metric tons); waste and scrap (9,580 metric tons); and sheets, plates and other (3,630 metric tons).

Salient Statistics of Zinc in the United States — In Metric Tons

Year	Slab Zinc Production Primary	Slab Zinc Production Secondary	Mine Production (Recovered)	Imports for Consumption Slab Zinc	Imports for Consumption Ore (Zinc Content)	Exports Slab Zinc	Exports Ore (Zinc Content)	Consumption Slab Zinc	Consumption Consumed as Ore	Consumption All Classes[3]	Net Import Reliance as a % of Consumption	High-Grade, Price -Cents/Lb.-
1996	226,000	140,000	586,000	827,000	15,100	1,970	425,000	1,210,000	1,400	1,450,000	33	51.11
1997	226,000	141,000	605,000	876,000	49,600	3,630	461,000	1,260,000	----	1,500,000	35	64.56
1998	234,000	134,000	722,000	879,000	46,300	2,330	552,000	1,290,000	----	1,590,000	35	51.43
1999	241,000	131,000	808,000	1,060,000	74,600	1,880	531,000	1,430,000	----	1,700,000	30	53.48
2000	228,000	143,000	805,000	915,000	52,800	2,770	523,000	1,330,000	----	1,630,000	60	55.61
2001	203,000	108,000	799,000	813,000	84,000	1,180	696,000	1,150,000	----	1,420,000	60	43.96
2002	182,000	113,000	701,000	874,000	122,000	1,160	822,000	1,170,000	----	1,420,000	60	38.64
2003	187,000	116,000	738,000	758,000	164,000	1,680	841,000	1,080,000	----	1,340,000	57	40.63
2004[1]	189,000	117,000	715,000	812,000	231,000	3,300	745,000	1,160,000	----	1,400,000	56	52.47
2005[2]	191,000	118,000	720,000	668,000	156,000	785	786,000	939,000	----	1,170,000	52	67.11

[1] Preliminary. [2] Estimate. [3] Based on apparent consumption of slab zinc plus zinc content of ores and concentrates and secondary materials used to make zinc dust and chemicals. *Source: U.S. Geological Survey (USGS)*

World Smelter Production of Zinc[3]   In Thousands of Metric Tons

Year	Australia	Belgium	Canada	China	France	Germany	Italy	Japan	Kazak-hstan	Mexico	Spain	United States	World Total
1996	331.0	234.4	715.6	324.3	327.0	269.0	642.3	190.0	221.7	163.1	360.8	366.0	7,610
1997	317.0	243.6	703.8	346.1	251.7	227.7	650.2	189.0	231.4	171.0	364.2	367.0	7,920
1998	322.0	205.0	745.1	321.0	334.0	231.6	652.7	240.7	230.3	175.0	360.0	368.0	8,170
1999	348.5	232.4	776.9	1,700.0	333.1	333.0	152.8	683.6	249.3	218.9	393.0	371.0	8,550
2000	494.5	251.7	779.9	1,980.0	350.0	327.5	170.3	698.8	262.2	235.1	386.3	371.0	9,020
2001	558.5	259.3	661.2	2,040.0	347.0	358.3	177.8	684.1	277.1	303.8	418.0	311.0	9,320
2002	571.5	260.0	793.4	2,100.0	350.0	378.6	176.0	673.9	286.3	302.1	488.0	295.0	9,720
2003	557.5	244.0	761.2	2,320.0	253.0	388.1	123.0	686.1	279.0	320.4	519.0	303.0	9,900
2004[1]	477.5	263.0	804.2	2,720.0	260.0	382.0	130.0	667.2	316.5	325.2	525.0	306.0	10,400
2005[2]	507.8	257.0	805.0	2,800.0	268.0	380.0	121.0	675.2	356.9	360.0	546.0	309.0	10,700

[1] Preliminary.   [2] Estimate.   [3] Secondary metal included.   Source: U.S. Geological Survey (USGS)

Consumption (Reported) of Slab Zinc in the United States, by Industries and Grades   In Metric Tons

		By Industries					By Grades			
Year	Total	Gal-vanizers	Brass Products	Zinc-Base Alloy[3]	Zinc Oxide	Other	Special High Grade	High Grade	Remelt and Other	Prime Western
1996	788,000	398,000	87,400	142,000	[4]	161,000	385,000	111,000	54,000	238,000
1997	672,000	347,000	76,800	107,000	[4]	141,000	319,000	88,700	57,200	207,000
1998	647,000	320,000	60,300	122,000	[4]	145,000	331,000	72,800	51,700	192,000
1999	614,000	308,000	78,200	105,000	[4]	124,000	317,000	58,400	55,400	184,000
2000	640,000	293,000	82,800	123,000	[4]	NA	332,000	60,600	41,500	206,000
2001	543,000	281,000	74,400	91,200	[4]	NA	294,000	54,000	30,300	165,000
2002	496,000	265,000	86,800	103,000	[4]	NA	294,000	61,400	28,000	113,000
2003	506,000	264,000	87,400	113,000	[4]	NA	310,000	60,000	27,600	109,000
2004[1]	510,000	248,000	96,700	W	[4]	NA	321,000	58,800	33,600	96,200
2005[2]	486,000	238,000	83,900	W	[4]	NA	316,000	62,100	40,300	68,000

[1] Preliminary.   [2] Estimated.   [3] Die casters.   [4] Included in other.   Source: U.S. Geological Survey (USGS)

United States Foreign Trade of Zinc   In Metric Tons

		Imports for Consumption						Zinc Ore & Manufactures Exported						
								Blocks, Pigs, Anodes, etc.		Wrought & Alloys				
Year	Ores[1]	Blocks, Pigs, Slabs	Sheets, Plates, Other	Waste & Scrap	Dross, Ashes, Fume	Dust, Powder & Flakes	Total Value $1,000	Un-wrought	Un-wrought Alloys	Sheets, Plates & Strips	Angles, Bars, Rods, etc.	Waste & Scrap	Dust (Blue Powder)	Zinc Ore & Con-centrates
1996	15,100	827,000	16,900	31,900	14,500	10,300	1,001,800	----	----	----	----	45,500	11,100	425,000
1997	49,600	876,000	19,200	29,600	----	11,700	1,340,390	----	----	----	----	46,100	9,980	461,000
1998	46,300	879,000	16,900	29,200	----	17,600	1,098,690	----	----	----	----	35,000	5,530	552,000
1999	74,600	966,000	22,600	26,600	20,000	21,300	1,133,890	----	----	----	----	28,200	5,050	531,000
2000	52,800	915,000	9,380	36,500	15,500	26,700	1,272,750	----	----	----	----	36,100	4,830	523,000
2001	84,000	813,000	7,240	39,300	12,000	26,700	937,110	----	----	----	----	44,000	4,690	696,000
2002	122,000	874,000	1,640	31,200	15,500	30,900	887,785	----	----	----	----	47,700	5,660	822,000
2003	164,000	758,000	1,790	10,300	14,100	27,400	839,705	----	----	----	----	50,200	6,550	841,000
2004[2]	231,000	812,000	2,500	10,800	16,100	24,800	1,142,733	----	----	----	----	53,900	7,640	745,000
2005[3]	156,000	668,000	3,630	9,580	15,800	23,400	1,198,040	----	----	----	----	56,000	9,310	786,000

[1] Zinc content.   [2] Preliminary.   [3] Estimate.   NA = Not available.   Source: U.S. Geological Survey (USGS)

Mine Production of Recoverable Zinc in the United States   In Thousands of Metric Tons

Year	Jan.	Feb.	Mar.	Apr.	May	June	July	Aug.	Sept.	Oct.	Nov.	Dec.	Total
1997	46.2	45.7	45.8	47.9	49.7	45.3	45.9	49.8	53.0	47.6	44.2	48.4	574.0
1998	50.1	48.3	56.5	56.2	56.7	55.0	59.5	57.2	60.1	55.7	62.0	61.9	722.0
1999	61.4	57.6	63.0	67.0	61.7	62.8	68.2	72.1	60.8	67.8	61.2	65.9	808.0
2000	64.4	56.6	68.5	64.5	70.2	65.3	68.1	71.4	59.6	62.3	63.5	67.2	814.0
2001	68.4	60.5	62.2	65.2	66.9	66.1	66.7	67.6	60.9	67.1	54.0	55.4	799.0
2002	61.3	60.4	67.8	55.2	63.4	63.8	66.0	67.2	54.4	68.3	61.3	65.5	754.6
2003	65.2	60.2	62.7	54.0	65.2	64.0	64.5	59.6	63.3	58.6	61.0	60.5	738.8
2004	60.4	55.3	57.9	58.5	56.1	59.0	60.8	62.0	61.6	61.6	56.8	56.5	706.5
2005	53.6	56.0	64.1	56.7	53.3	64.6	64.5	68.9	61.8	64.4	51.2	62.3	721.4
2006[1]	58.1	51.4	61.5	54.2	54.3	59.8	64.7	62.3	65.8	66.3	53.2		710.8

[1] Preliminary.   Source: U.S. Geological Survey (USGS)

ZINC

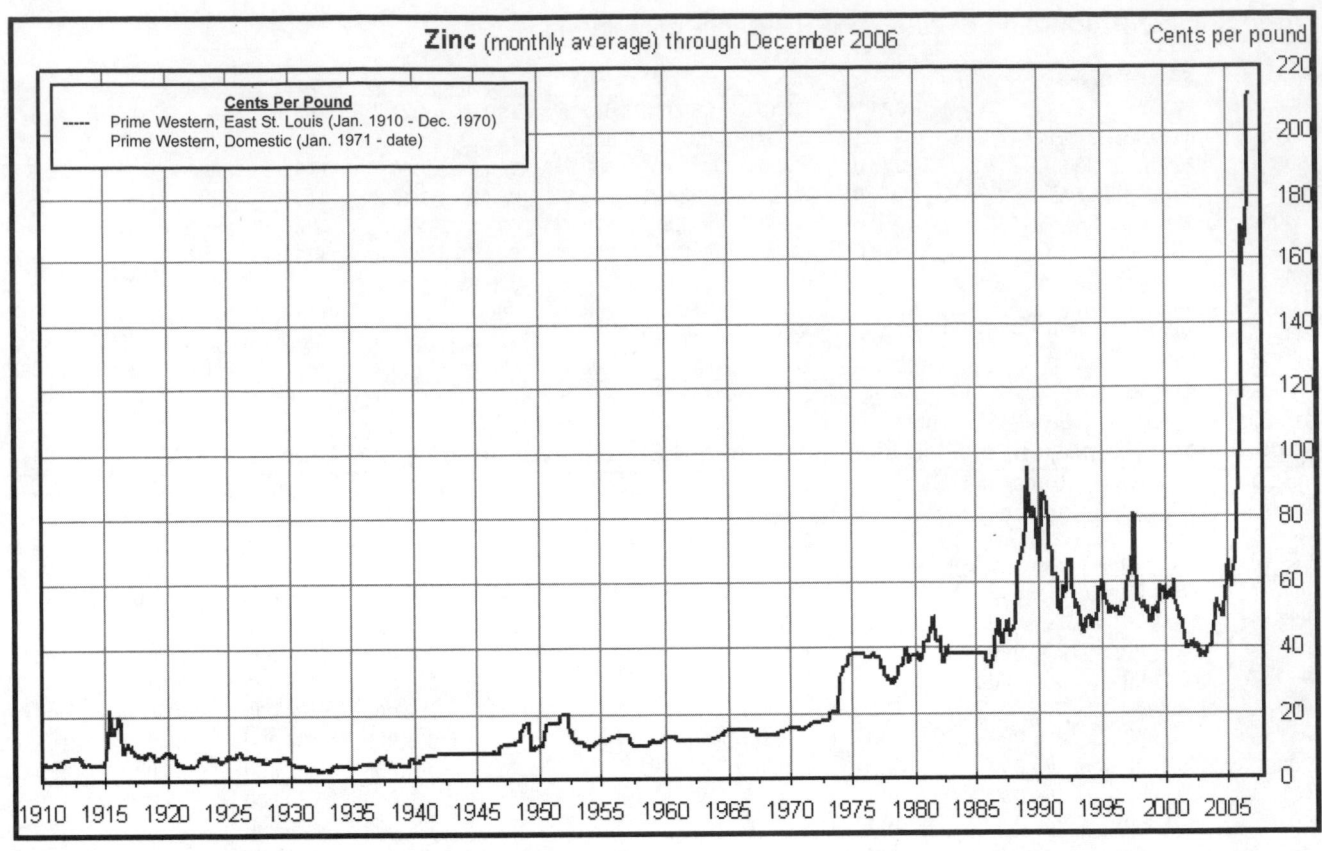

Zinc (monthly average) through December 2006   Cents per pound

Cents Per Pound
- - - Prime Western, East St. Louis (Jan. 1910 - Dec. 1970)
Prime Western, Domestic (Jan. 1971 - date)

Consumption of Slab Zinc by Fabricators in the United States   In Thousands of Metric Tons

Year	Jan.	Feb.	Mar.	Apr.	May	June	July	Aug.	Sept.	Oct.	Nov.	Dec.	Average
1997	47.2	43.1	48.6	50.1	48.1	45.3	45.1	45.5	50.9	49.6	44.3	46.2	588.0
1998	46.3	45.2	47.4	44.8	45.4	49.0	46.0	45.0	45.9	45.9	40.5	43.9	647.0
1999	40.5	45.4	43.8	40.3	42.5	47.1	37.8	40.1	42.0	42.8	41.1	39.7	614.0
2000	41.8	44.6	47.7	45.6	44.4	49.1	42.0	43.3	42.6	47.5	43.8	40.2	640.0
2001	45.4	43.5	44.1	42.7	43.6	38.2	30.6	39.2	37.7	35.7	32.1	27.3	543.0
2002	31.2	31.3	30.4	33.1	34.9	34.4	34.3	35.8	36.1	36.1	32.7	33.3	403.6
2003	33.1	33.1	34.4	35.2	34.7	38.2	34.2	35.5	36.8	36.8	35.3	36.4	423.7
2004	35.1	36.2	36.6	36.7	35.9	37.0	33.7	33.6	33.8	34.6	34.3	33.4	420.9
2005	33.6	33.9	34.1	33.5	33.8	34.1	31.3	33.7	34.8	34.7	33.8	34.1	405.4
2006[1]	34.8	34.5	34.8	34.0	33.1	34.2	32.4	33.4	31.4	32.8	31.3		400.0

[1] Preliminary.   Source: U.S. Geological Survey (USGS)

Average Price of Zinc, Prime Western Slab (Delivered U.S. Basis)   In Cents Per Pound

Year	Jan.	Feb.	Mar.	Apr.	May	June	July	Aug.	Sept.	Oct.	Nov.	Dec.	Total
1997	55.64	59.82	63.28	62.62	65.65	67.78	75.29	80.89	78.96	62.55	57.83	54.45	65.40
1998	55.43	51.86	51.98	54.31	52.77	50.78	52.23	51.64	50.29	47.63	48.74	48.44	51.23
1999	47.29	51.11	51.68	51.07	52.20	50.35	53.73	56.28	59.12	57.07	56.91	58.75	53.84
2000	58.44	54.67	55.60	56.14	57.44	55.67	56.52	58.04	60.53	54.67	53.07	53.00	56.15
2001	51.82	51.29	50.55	48.95	47.54	45.56	43.62	42.53	41.14	39.53	39.99	39.25	45.15
2002	40.98	39.97	42.15	41.66	39.97	39.70	41.01	38.91	39.26	39.08	36.99	38.52	39.64
2003	38.88	38.46	38.48	36.99	37.86	38.57	40.30	39.77	39.84	43.44	44.11	47.60	40.36
2004	49.61	53.31	54.63	51.89	51.88	51.53	49.85	49.31	49.37	53.36	54.61	58.32	52.31
2005	61.10	64.57	66.59	63.55	60.70	61.97	58.26	62.76	67.73	72.10	77.60	87.45	67.03
2006	100.02	106.57	116.10	147.28	170.57	158.11	163.89	164.23	166.56	185.80	210.32	211.82	158.44

Source: American Metal Market (AMM)

CRB Yearbook CD

Table of Contents

CRB Yearbooks CD Copyright © Commodity Research Bureau All rights reserved.

QuickSearch is a trademark of dataDisc, Inc.
Segments of this manual reprinted with permission by dataDisc, Inc.

Factual information contained in the CRB Yearbooks CD has been obtained from sources believed to be reliable but are not necessarily inclusive and are not guaranteed in any way and should not be construed as a representation by us.

Chapter 1: Installation

Installing QuickSearch

To run QuickSearch, you will need:
- A computer with a 120 Mhz or faster processor, running any current Windows or Macintosh operating system
- At least 32 MB of total RAM installed on your computer; for best performance, we recommend at least 64 MB
- A CD-ROM drive

To Install:
1) Place the disc in the CD-ROM drive. If installation does not start automatically proceed to step 2.
2) Click Start; Select Run
3) Type D:\Autoplay, where D is the letter representing your CD-ROM drive. Press the enter key and follow the instructions.

Chapter 2: Searching and Browsing

Selecting Text to Search

Searches can be conducted across all the text in a *QuickSearch* document (full-text), restricted to a specific field (fielded search), or restricted to a selected table of contents section.

Everywhere in text - searches the full text of the *QuickSearch* document (except for user-defined notes and bookmarks). Choose **Everywhere in text** in the Search dialog box to specify a full-text search.

Fielded Search - searches a specific field and ignores all text outside of that field. To specify a fielded search:

1) Click **Selected field** under **Select where to search.**
2) Select a field from the list of available fields.

Current Table of Contents section - restricts a re-search only to a Table of Contents (TOC) section.

1) Click the TOC section in the TOC window.
2) Click the Search button on the toolbar <u>OR</u> select Search/<u>S</u>earch from the main menu.
3) Click *Current Table of Contents section* under *Select where to search*.

Note: Search results will represent the selected TOC Section and its sublevels.

Types of Searches

Search for Phrase
Type an exact phrase you wish to find, e.g. "Business is the key." Use quotation marks around the search text to distinguish a *phrase search* from a *word search* or choose *Search for phrase* in the **Search/More>>** dialog box. The QuickSearch default setting is a phrase search.

Search for Words
Two types of word searches may be conducted - single words or words in proximity as determined by **Search Operators**. To conduct a word search, choose *Search for word(s)* in the **Search/More>>** dialog box.

1) **Single Word** - Enter any single word, e.g. BUSINESS, to find all occurrences in the document.

2) **Words in Proximity** - Enter any series of words that you wish to find near each other (e.g. BUSINESS INCREASE). Before conducting a *proximity search*, define a search range/proximity in the **Search/ More>>** dialog box. The default setting is 4 words. A typical sentence has 10 words, a typical paragraph has 25 words, and a typical page has 500 words.

Refine Last Search

The **Refine last search** feature can be used to modify your most recent search. (See the Advanced Searching section of this chapter.)

Search Operators

Boolean, wildcard and phrase search operators are available by selecting **MORE>>** in the **Search** dialog box. Double-click on any operator to add it to the Search command line *or* type the operator in the **Type the text to find** box.

To see example of each operator:
- Click the **Search** button and then the **More>>** button.
  OR
- Select **Search/Search** from the main menu and **More>>**.
- Click once on the operator you wish to view.

The following operators are available for a word search:

AND (&) - BUSINESS AND INCREASE - Returns all occurrences of BUSINESS and INCREASE in the specified search range that are near each other. "Near" is defined using the Word Proximity setting in the **Search/ More>>** dialog box.

OR (|) - BUSINESS OR INCREASE - Returns all occurrences of the words in the specified search range without regard to proximity.

NOT (~) - BUSINESS NOT INCREASE - Returns all occurrences of the word BUSINESS that are not near the word INCREASE in the specified search range. "Near" is defined using the Word Proximity setting in the **Search/ More>>** dialog box.

Wildcard (*) - Use the asterisk (*) at the end of any part of a word to represent any character or combination of characters. For example, BUSI* may return hits such as *business, businesses, busing,* and *Businowski.* The wildcard operator cannot be used in a phrase search.

Basic Searching

1) Click the Search button on the Reader toolbar OR select Search/Search from the main menu.

2) In the **Search** dialog box, select where to search choosing one of the following:
- Everywhere in text
- Selected field*
- Current Table of Contents

*Note: Click a field or a TOC entry before choosing Selected field or Current Table of Contents section.

3) Type the search text (word, words within proximity or phrase) in the *Type the text to find* box or double click on any entry in the **Word Wheel** to select it as search text.

4) Click **Search** in the dialog box. "Hits" will be highlighted in the text and displayed in context in a separate **Hit List** window. The number of hits also will be displayed on the status bar at the bottom of the screen.

Advanced Searching

Search for Words

1) Begin a search by completing steps 1-3 of a Basic Search.

2) Select **More>>** to expand the Search dialog box and change to a *Search for Word(s)* and/or select other **Search Operators** which alter the nature of the search to be conducted. A *Search for Phrase* is conducted unless you select another type of search.

3) Specify the **Word Proximity** in the **Search/ More>>** dialog box, if you are conducting an AND or NOT search. The default proximity is 4 words.

4) Click **Search** in the dialog box. "Hits" will be highlighted in the text and displayed in context in a separate **Hit List** window. The number of hits also will be displayed on the status bar at the bottom of the screen.

Refine Last Search

To refine the last research:

1) Begin a search by completing steps 1-3 of a Basic Search. Click the **More>>** button on the **Search** dialog box to access all search parameters.

2) Click the **Refine last search** box in the lower left corner of the **Search** dialog box.

3) Select the **Boolean** operator to be applied to the refined search (just to the right of the *Refine last search* check box).

4) Preview the format for the refined search in the *Refined Search box* at the bottom of the **Search** dialog box.

5) Type the **[New text to Find]** word(s) in the *Type the text to find* box at the top of the **Search** dialog box.

6) Click **Search**.

Example:

Your first search in the Constitution was for the word "House." If you want to narrow the search results to include only hits of "House" which are not near "senate," you can return to the **Search** dialog box, select **Refine last search**, select the *NOT* operator, specify the word proximity, type "Senate" in the *Type the text to* find box at the top of the **Search** dialog box and click the **Search** button. The **Hit List** will display only hits of "House" which were not located near "Senate" ("near" depends on the proximity that you specified). The final search command would look as follows:

(House) ~ (Senate)

This search could be further refined by selecting **Refine last search** and repeating the steps above.

Example:

If you want to find only occurrences of "House *NOT* Senate" which are near "Representative," return to the Search dialog box, select **Refine last search**, select the *AND* operator, specify the word proximity, type "Representatives" in the *Type the text to find* box at the top of the **Search** dialog box and click on the **Search** button. The **Hit List** would display only hits of "House" which were near "Representatives" but not located near "Senate" ("near" depends on the proximity that you specified). The final search command would look as follows:

[(House) ~ (Senate)] & (Representatives)

Search Results

Browsing Search Results

Hit List

After conducting a search, each occurrence of the e search text in the document will be displayed in context in a separate **Hit List** window. Double click on any entry in the **Hit List** to move to the corresponding section of text.

Highlighted Hits in the Text

After conducting a search, each occurrence of the search text is highlighted in the text of the document.

1)   Click the **First/Previous/Next/Last (Hit)** buttons to move between highlighted hits in the text.
2)   The number of the current hit being viewed and the total number of hits are displayed in the Status bar at the bottom of the screen.

Removing the Hit List

1)   Click the **Clear** button on the toolbar **OR** select **Search/Clear Search** from the main menu to remove the current **Hit List** window and the highlighting from the hits in the text.
2)   Turn off the **Hit List** for future searches by selecting **Edit/Preferences** to open the **Document Preferences** dialog box. Click the **Reader** tab to open **Reader Preferences.** Deselect *Show Hit List?*.

Reader Preferences

Select **Edit/Preferences** from the main menu to open the **Document Preference** dialog box. The box includes three tabs: **Reader, Author,** and **Stopper Word List.**

Reader Preferences include:

CD-ROM Drive Letter

Every CD-ROM player is assigned a drive letter. (It is usually the last drive letter after your other drives.)

Default Word Search Proximity

Set the default proximity (the number of words between selected words) to be applied in multiple word (non-phrase) searches.

Show Hit List?

Click **Show Hit List***?* to open a **Hit List** automatically after conducting a Search. The Hit List shows "hits" - items found - when you do a search. Browse hits by clicking the **Next/Previous Hit** buttons on the toolbar or selecting **Search/Search** from the main menu. All hits will be highlighted in the text even if a **Hit List** is not activated.

TOC Window Color

Click the **TOC Window Color** button to open a dialog box containing table of Contest background color options. Select from a present color chart, or create a custom color and select it. Click **OK.**

SAVE YOUR DOCUMENT after you select preferences!

Table of Contents Browsing

Hyperlinks

The Table of Contents (TOC) provides a convenient method for accessing any section of the *QuickSearch* document. Each TOC entry is hyper-linked to the corresponding section of text; just click on an entry and *QuickSearch* automatically will move the corresponding section to the text window.

Multiple Levels

QuickSearch TOC's may include up to 32 levels. If there are sublevels in a TOC section, a "+" will appear in front of the TOC entry. To open the next level, click on the "+".

Automatic Tracing

As you move through a *QuickSearch* document (scroll, Next Hit, Previous Hit, etc.) the Table of Contents will "track" your location in the document automatically. A box outline indicates the current TOC section.

Chapter 3: Viewing Images

A *QuickSearch* document may contain *hyperlinked* or *embedded* images. Different methods are used for finding and viewing each type of image

Finding Images

Finding Hyperlinked Images

You can find hyperlinked images in a *QuickSearch* document by using any of the following options:
- **List** of images
- **Next/Previous Image** buttons or menu selections
- **Search** feature
- **Special formatting**/camera icon

Image List - Open a comprehensive list of hyperlinked images in the document.
1) Click the **Image List** button on the Toolbar *OR* select **Search/Image List** from the main menu.
2) Double click on an image title in the **Image List** to open the image.

Browsing Images - You can browse through images using the **Next/Previous Image** buttons or menu selections.
1) Select Nest/Previous Image buttons OR Search/First (Nest, Previous, Last) Image from the main menu.
2) The **Next and Previous Image** buttons or menu selections move the reader sequentially through images in the document.
3) The **First** and **Last Image** menu selections move only to the first or last image in the document.

Searching for Words in Hyperlinked Image Titles - As each hyper-linked image file is added to a *QuickSearch* document, it is given an *Image Title*. The Image Title appears with an optional camera icon at the point you have chosen in the text window. The Image Title is indexed with other text and may be found using a word or phrase search (see Chapter 1 - *Searching & Browsing*).

Look for Special Formatting/Camera Icon – Hyperlinked images can be found by looking for words that have special formatting (the default is double-underlined text). Double click on the specially formatted text to open the image. A camera icon may precede the specially formatted image title. The image can also be opened by clicking on the camera icon.

Finding Embedded Images

Embedded images appear in the text at the point you have chosen. They may be found by:
- Scrolling through text
- Conducting a search for words/phrases that appear near the image.

Scrolling for an Embedded Image
Use the vertical scroll bar to scan text and locate embedded images.

Searching for an Embedded Image*
Search for text that has been placed near an image and marked as hidden.

*Note: **Titles of embedded images will** NOT **appear on an Image List.** The Image List feature is only for hyperlinked images.

Zooming Hyper-linked Images

Marquee Image Zooming*

Marquee Image Zooming allows you to select a portion of a **hyper-linked image** and enlarge it to the size of the image window. *QuickSearch* allows you to zoom to a single pixel.
*Note: Marquee Image Zooming **is available ONLY for hyper-linked images.**

1) Click a **hyperlinked image title** or camera icon to open the image window.
2) Click on and hold the **left mouse** button and drag a box around the image area you want to enlarge.
3) When the area is defined, release the mouse button. The area selected will fill the **Image Window**.
4) Steps 2 and 3 may be repeated to continuing zooming.
5) To return the image to its original size, click once on the image with the **left mouse** button.

Image Panning

Image Panning allows you to use the horizontal/vertical scroll bars* to move around a **hyperlinked** image that has been enlarged by Marquee zooming.
Click an arrow on the scroll bar *OR* click and drag the horizontal or vertical scroll bar button to move the image across the screen.
*Note: **Scroll bars do not appear on-screen until an image has been zoomed.**

Scale to Gray

Some 1 bit (black & white) hyperlinked images can be sharpened by using the **Scale to Gray** feature. **Scale to Gray** will fill in missing pixels to improve the quality of an image. This feature is particularly useful for viewing scanned document images.

To use Scale to Gray:
1) Open a hyperlinked image
2) Select **View/Scale to Gray** from the main menu
3) **Scale to Gray** will remain active until it is deselected.

Chapter 4: Printing

The **Print** feature will print **text** and **images** in the following forms:
- Highlighted lines or blocks of text
- Selected Tables of Contents section(s)
- Search results ("hit" lists)
- Embedded images
- Hyper-linked images
- Zoomed portions of Hyper-linked images

Print Hints

Highlighted text, images and TOC sections will print in order as they are found in the document.

The printed size of Zoomed and Hyper-linked images may vary between portrait and landscape page orientation settings (found via **File/Print Setup**).

You can print *multiple* TOC sections by:
- Using the **Shift** key to select a series of *adjacent* TOCs.
- Using the **CTRL** key to individually select *specific* TOCs.
- Using the **Shift** and **CTRL** keys alternately to select specific TOC groupings.

Printing specifications can be set from the Windows Print Manager utility.

Make **Print Setup** modifications *before* you **Print**.

Printing Text or Images

To Print portions of a document:
1) Highlight lines and/or block(s) of text.
2) Click the **Print** button on the toolbar.
OR
Select the **File/Print** from the main menu.
OR
Press **CTRL+P**.

To Print a Single TOC section:
1) Click the TOC heading in the **Table of Contents** window.
2) Click the **Print** button on the toolbar.
OR
Select the **File/Print TOC selection(s)** from the main menu.
OR
Click the **right mouse** button and select **Print TOC selection(s).**
OR
Press **CTRL+P**.
*Note: All the sublevels in the TOC section will be printed.

To Print Multiple TOC sections:
1) Click the first TOC section you want to print from the **Table of Contents** window.
2) Press and hold the **CTRL** key while you click the order TOC sections you want to print. They do not have to be adjacent.
3) When you have finished selecting TOCs, click the **Print** button on the toolbar.
OR
Select **File/Print TOC selection(s)** from the main menu.
OR
Click the **right mouse** button and select **Print TOC selection(s).**
OR
Press **CTRL+P**.

To Print adjacent TOC sections:
1) Click the *first* TOC section you want to print from the **Table of Contents** window.
2) Press and hold the **Shift** key, and click the last TOC section in the series (all TOC sections between the first and last will be selected automatically).
3) Click the **Print** button on the toolbar.
OR
Select **File/Print TOC selection** from the main menu.
OR
Click the **right mouse** button and select **Print TOC selection(s).**
OR
Press **CTRL+P**.

*Note: **Multiple TOC Selection functions (highlighting using the** Shift **and/or** CTRL **keys) can be used in combination to select specific TOC groupings.**

To Print Embedded Images:
1) Highlight (double click) the embedded image(s) you want ant to print.
2) Click the **Print** button on the Toolbar.
OR
Select **File/Print** from the main menu.
OR
Press **CTRL+P**.

To Print a Hyperlinked Image:
You can print a **Hyperlinked Image** or a zoomed portion of a Hyperlinked Image.
1) Open the image by double clicking the **Image title** and/or the **camera icon.**
OR
Click the **Image List** button on the toolbar and double click the **Image title** from the list.
2) Click the **Print** button on the Toolbar.
OR
Select **File/Print** from the main menu.
OR
Press **CTRL+P**.

Print Setup

The Print Setup option allows you to select printer type, page orientation, paper size, paper source, and printer properties (paper, graphics, fonts, device options). Make these selections **before** you print.

To change the Print Setup:
1) Select **File/Print Setup** from the main menu.
2) In the **Print Setup** dialog box, click the down arrow in the **Name** pull down menu, select a printer type and enter it in the **Name** window (or click **Network** to access Network printer options).
3) To select new printer properties select **Properties** and make modifications.
4) Select **Landscape** or **Portrait.**
5) Select **OK** to exit.

Page Layout

You can adjust the top, bottom, left, and right margins of a printed page as follows:
1) Select **File/Page Layout** from the main menu.
2) In the **Page Parameters** dialog box, set margins (in inches) and click **OK.**

Chapter 5: User Annotations

The reader may customize a *QuickSearch* document by adding "margin" Bookmarks and Notes.

Annotate functions enable the reader to make customized **Bookmarks** in the text and make private, unsearchable comments about a document with **Notes**. The **Bookmark** feature enables the reader to "save his place," while the **Notes** feature allows the reader to "write in the margins" of the text.

Using Bookmarks

To add a Bookmark to a document:
1) Highlight a portion of text or place the cursor where you would like to add the Bookmark.
2) Click on the **Bookmark** icon on the Reader toolbar *OR* select **Annotate/Bookmark** from the main menu or select **Insert Bookmark** from the **right mouse** button menu. If text has been highlighted, it is shown in the **Edit Bookmark/Name** text box. If not, enter a name for the bookmark in the text box.
3) Click **Add** to place the selected text in the **Current Bookmarks** list.
4) Click **Go to** to scroll text to the point where the bookmark appears.
5) Click **Close** to close the Bookmark dialog box.

To go to a Bookmark:
1) Click on the **Bookmark** button on the toolbar *OR* select **Insert Bookmark** from the **right mouse** button menu to open the list of Current Bookmarks.
2) Highlight the bookmark you want to move to in the text.
3) Click **Go to.** The selected text will move to the top of the text window.

To edit a Bookmark:
1) Click on the **Bookmark** icon on the toolbar *OR* select **Annotate/Bookmark** from the main menu *OR* select **Insert Bookmark** from the **right mouse** button menu to open the dialog box containing current bookmarks.
2) In the **Current Bookmarks** list, click on the bookmark you wish to edit. It will appear in the **Edit Bookmark/Name** window.
3) Make changes and click **Add**.

To remove a Bookmark:
1) Click the **Bookmark** icon on the Reader toolbar or select **Insert Bookmark** from the **right mouse** button menu to open the dialog box containing current bookmarks.
2) In the **Current Bookmarks** list, click on the bookmark you wish to remove. It will appear in the **Edit Bookmark/Name** text box.
3) Click **Remove.**

Using Notes

To add a Note to a document:
1) Place the cursor in the text window where you want the note to appear.
2) Click on the **Notepad** button *OR* select **Annotate/Notes/Insert** from the main menu *OR* select **Insert Note** from the **right mouse** button menu to open the **Notepad** dialog box.
3) Type in the note and click **Save**; a Notepad icon appears in the left margin next to the specified line of text.

To View a Note:
1) Double click the **Notepad** icon in the left margin.
2) The **Notepad** dialog box displays the note.

To Edit a Note:
1) Double click the icon of the note you want to edit.
2) Make changes to text.
3) Click **Save.**

To Remove a Note:
1) Place the cursor on the **Notepad** icon and select **Annotate/Note/Delete** from the main menu *OR* select **Delete Note** from the **right mouse** button menu.
2) A dialog box will ask you to confirm the note deletion.
3) Click **Yes.** The icon will disappear after scrolling in the document.